CW01395015

Praise for *Family Law: Text, Cases, and Materials*

'*Family Law: Text, Cases, and Materials* is a fantastic core text offering a thorough explanation and exploration of the essential areas covered in most family law courses. It offers a perceptive analysis of controversial issues including appropriate contextual material to enable students to really engage with both law and policy.'

Professor Thérèse Callus, Professor of Law, University of Reading

'Engaging and appropriately pitched for my undergraduate students. Its clear and accessible contents has something to offer students of all abilities.'

Professor Sara Fovargue, Professor of Law, University of Sheffield

'*Family Law: Text, Cases, and Materials* draws extensively on a broad range of sources from statutes and case law to academic commentary and official reports. The authors deftly and seamlessly integrate these sources alongside their own, often critical and challenging, views in such a way that encourages students to look beyond the mere black letter of the law and consider the effects that these legal provisions have on families in society.'

Dr Philip Bremner, Lecturer, University of Sussex

'A first-rate text with analysis by experts in the field, which usefully highlights the intersection between family law and other areas of law.'

Dr Andy Hayward, Associate Professor, Durham University

'This book provides an approachable, comprehensive review of the law. Using extracts from key materials, the authors analyse the effectiveness of the law and its underlying messages, putting the law in a critical context that is thought-provoking and accessible.'

Polly Morgan, Associate Professor of Law, University of East Anglia

'An invaluable resource for students who want to delve in-depth into family law.'

Rachel Heah, Lecturer, Lancaster University

'The authors provide an expert narrative weaving together up-to-date cases and materials … It is no surprise that this book remains a favourite for students learning about family law in England and Wales.'

Lesley-Anne Barnes Macfarlane, Senior Lecturer, University of Glasgow

FAMILY LAW

Text, Cases, and Materials

FIFTH EDITION

Rob George, Sharon Thompson,
and Joanna Miles

OXFORD
UNIVERSITY PRESS

OXFORD
UNIVERSITY PRESS

Great Clarendon Street, Oxford, OX2 6DP,
United Kingdom

Oxford University Press is a department of the University of Oxford.
It furthers the University's objective of excellence in research, scholarship,
and education by publishing worldwide. Oxford is a registered trade mark of
Oxford University Press in the UK and in certain other countries

Second edition 2011
Third edition 2015
Fourth edition 2019

Published in the United States of America by Oxford University Press
198 Madison Avenue, New York, NY 10016, United States of America

British Library Cataloguing in Publication Data
Data available

Library of Congress Control Number: 2023936132

ISBN 978–0–19–286568–7

Printed in the UK by
Ashford Colour Press Ltd, Gosport, Hampshire

PREFACE TO THE FIFTH EDITION

It has been a busy few years for family law. Major statutory reforms (long overdue) have been enacted in relation to divorce, and a new statutory regime introduced in relation to protection from domestic abuse. Meanwhile, the courts continue to find new and ever more complex cases to consider, with close to 150 new decisions cited in this edition. For all this activity, though, resourcing of the system—for the courts themselves, for litigants in terms of legal aid, for Cafcass, and perhaps most pressingly for local authority children's services departments—is a major concern. These remain ever more challenging times in family justice.

As in the previous editions, we have endeavoured to provide readers with a thorough understanding of the law relating to families and to do so in a way that stimulates critical reflection on the law. We ask how and why the law has developed as it has, what policies it claims to be pursuing, whether it balances the rights and interests of individuals, families, and the wider public appropriately, and how it operates in practice. As in the previous editions, the material in the book is fully integrated with the online resources. The online resources can be found at www.oup.com/he/familytcm5e.

The online resources provide a wealth of useful information, not least of which are our regular updates on changes to the law since the manuscript of the book was completed. It also contains questions, supplementary text and materials, and suggestions for further reading. Some of these augment the topics covered in the book, while others provide information for interested readers on material which is less central to family law and not covered systematically in the book. A guide to using this book and the online materials is found in the online resources.

This edition sees another change to the authorial team, with the addition of Sharon Thompson. She has come on board now in anticipation of the fact that this is Joanna's last edition (as she has now changed career into horticulture after over a quarter-century in the law!). So in this edition, Joanna was responsible for chapters 4, 5, and 7, while Sharon took on chapters 2, 3, and 6, and Rob continues to be responsible for the chapters relating to children (8–13). As previously, we co-wrote chapter 1.

We are grateful to the team at OUP, and especially to Emily Cunningham and Sarah Jacobs, who were patient and helpful in the development of this new edition. We are also grateful to our colleagues and students who have helped us in our thinking about family law. Particular thanks are due to Stephen Gilmore and Aleisha Ebrahimi for comments on chapters 4 and 11, and to Caitlin Levins for research assistance on a point in chapter 5. We have endeavoured to state the law as it was on 1 December 2022, though we have been able to include some updates in early 2023.

RG
ST
JM

NEW TO THIS EDITION

- Revisions to chapter 2 in recognition of the advent of mixed-sex civil partnership
- Consideration of the Law Commission's proposed reform of weddings law, particularly in relation to what are currently non-qualifying ceremonies
- A thoroughly reworked chapter on divorce, following the implementation of the Divorce, Dissolution and Separation Act 2020
- New content in chapter 4 (domestic abuse) to deal with new concepts and remedies created by the Domestic Abuse Act 2021
- A revised analysis of *Gillick* competence and children's autonomy rights in light of recent case law
- Discussion of the Law Commissions' 2023 proposals for reforming surrogacy law
- Detailed consideration of the latest developments in relation to contact and domestic abuse
- Updated case law, including *HM Attorney-General v Akhter and Khan* [2020], *Guest v Guest* [2022], *Brack v Brack* [2018], *Bell v Tavistock and Portman NHS Trust* [2021], *R (McConnell) v The Registrar General for England and Wales* [2020], *Re H-N (Domestic Abuse: Finding of Fact Hearings)* [2021], *Re H-W (Care Proceedings)* [2022], and *Re A, B and C (Adoption: Notification of Fathers and Relatives)* [2020]

PREFACE TO THE FIRST EDITION

This book has two principal aims: to provide readers with a thorough understanding of the law relating to the family and to do so in a way that stimulates critical reflection on that law: how and why has the law developed as it has, what policies is it seeking to pursue, does it achieve the right balance between the rights and interests of individual family members and wider public interests, how does it operate in practice?

As part of the *Text, Cases, and Materials* series, alongside our own description of and commentary on the law, the book includes a large number of extracts from primary sources, both statute and case law, and from official data, academic commentaries, qualitative research findings, and policy and reform papers. Several of these extracts are edited for use in the book. Deletions are indicated by . . . and textual insertions and editorial amendments made by us are contained in square brackets. We have generally removed all original footnotes and references from the extracts; where an original footnote is retained, we have indicated this in the footnote. The occasional footnotes attached to extracts are otherwise our own.

Inevitably, it has not been possible to cover all of the issues relating to families in England and Wales today that we might have wished to include. In particular, we do not discuss public funding for family proceedings, criminal offences against children and reasonable chastisement, international child abduction, inter-country adoption, the law relating to the elderly and other vulnerable adults, the law of succession, immigration law, private international law, European law relating to the family, or housing law. We have been able to give only brief attention to the laws of taxation and social security, formalities for marriage and civil partnership, wardship, and disputes regarding the child's name and relocation. We have, however, included material on some of these topics in the online resources.

There are a number of people to whom we are immensely grateful, for reading draft chapters, advising on specific issues, or both: Stuart Bridge, John Eekelaar, Jonathan Herring, Matthew Jolley, Mavis Maclean, Judith Masson, Jo McCaffrey, Clare McGlynn, Howard Miles, Cheryl Morris, Rebecca Probert, Daniel Robinson, Nick Wikeley, and the anonymous reviewers for Oxford University Press. We have also benefited greatly from the research assistance of Gemma Nicholls, Anna Shadboldt, Phil Harris, and Andrew Brown. Any errors and omissions are, of course, our own. We also thank all the students whom we have taught family law and the wider family law community: we have learnt a lot from them all, and still have more to learn. Thanks are also due to Angela Griffin, our original commissioning editor at OUP, and to Melanie Jackson and the rest of the team who have seen us through the project and accommodated our various needs.

Sonia Harris-Short is responsible for chapters on the law relating to children: chapters 8–13. Joanna Miles is responsible for chapters covering issues relating to adults and financial and property disputes: chapters 2–7. We co-wrote chapter 1. This book has been written as a teaching and learning aid for undergraduate family law courses. The information and commentary contained in this book do not, and are not intended to, constitute legal advice to any person in relation to a specific case or matter. We have endeavoured to state the law as it was at 1 October 2006. Updates on developments in areas of law addressed in the book will be posted in the online resources.

SHS
JM

ACKNOWLEDGEMENTS

We are grateful to all authors and publishers of copyright material used in this book and in particular to the following for permission to reprint from the sources indicated:

Extracts from Law Commission Reports, Legal Services Commission Reports, DHSS, Cafcass, and ONS publications are Crown copyright material. Crown copyright material is reproduced with the permission of the Controller, HMSO (under the terms of the Click Use licence). Parliamentary material is reproduced with the permission of the Controller of HMSO on behalf of Parliament. This book contains public sector information licensed under the Open Government Licence v3.0 (http://www.nationalarchives.gov.uk/doc/open-government-licence/open-government-licence.htm).

Department for Education: J. Selwyn, S. Meakings, and D. Wijedasa, *Beyond the Adoption Order: Challenges, Interventions and Adoption Disruption* (London: Department for Education, 2014), 77–79, 273–4. © University of Bristol 2014. Open Government Licence v3.0.

Ashgate Publishing and the authors for extracts from F. Kaganas, 'Contact, Conflict and Risk', in S. Day Sclater and C. Piper (eds), *Undercurrents of Divorce* (Aldershot: Ashgate, 1999), 99, 105–10; and B. Neale and C. Smart, 'In Whose Best Interests? Theorising Family Life Following Parental Separation or Divorce', in S. Day Sclater and C. Piper (eds), *Undercurrents of Divorce* (Aldershot: Ashgate, 1999).

Bloomsbury Publishing Plc for extracts from Family Court Reports [FCR].

Susan Boyd for extracts from S. Boyd, 'From gender specificity to gender neutrality? Ideologies in Canadian child custody law', in C. Smart and S. Sevenhuijsen (eds), *Child Custody and the Politics of Gender* (London: Routledge, 1998).

Council of Europe & European Court of Human Rights for extract from *Neulinger and Shuruk v Switzerland* (App No 41615/07, ECHR) (2010). © Council of Europe/European Court of Human Rights.

Baroness Ruth Deech for extract from R. Deech, 'The Unmarried Father and Human Rights', (1992) 4 Journal of Child Law 3.

Domestic Abuse Commissioner for extract from *Reluctance—Resistance—Refusal: A Child Centric Approach to Domestic Abuse in Private Family Law Proceedings (London: DAC, 2023).* © 2023 Domestic Abuse Commissioner.

Gingerbread for extract from 'Government plans for child maintenance: Gingerbread briefing (2011)', briefing paper on child support reforms.

Hart Publishing, an imprint of Bloomsbury Publishing Plc, for extracts from M. Maclean and J. Eekelaar, *The Parental Obligation: A Study of Parenthood Across Households* (Oxford: Hart Publishing, 1997) and N. Wikeley, *Child Support: Law and Policy* (Oxford: Hart Publishing, 2006). © Nick Wikeley, 2006, *Child Support: Law and Policy*, Hart Publishing, an imprint of Bloomsbury Publishing Plc.

The Incorporated Council of Law Reporting for extracts from Appeal Cases [AC], Family Division Law Reports [Fam], and Weekly Law Reports [WLR]. Courtesy of the Incorporated Council of Law Reporting.

Robert Mnookin for extract from R. Mnookin, 'Child-custody adjudication: Judicial functions in the face of indeterminacy', (1975) 39 Law & Contemporary Problems 266.

Nuffield Foundation for extract from E. J. Trinder, D. Braybrook, C. Bryson, L. Coleman, C. Houlston, and M. Sefton, *Finding Fault? Divorce Law and Practice in England and Wales.* (London: Nuffield Foundation, 2017).

Oxford University Press for extract from C. Fenton-Glynn, Children and the European Court of Human Rights (Oxford, OUP, 2021). By Permission of Oxford University Press.

Oxford University Press Journals for extracts from International of Law, Policy and the Family and Current Legal Problems: I. Ellman, S. McKay, J. Miles, and C. Bryson, 'Child Support Judgments: Comparing Public Policy to the Public's Policy' (2014) International Journal of Law, Policy and the Family 28; T. Campbell, 'The Rights of the Minor: As Person, As Child, As Juvenile, As Future Adult', (1992) 6 International Journal of Law and the Family 1; M. Freeman, 'Taking Children's Rights More Seriously', (1992) 6 International Journal of Law and the Family 52; E. Jackson et al, 'Financial Support on Divorce: The Right Mixture of Rules and Discretion?', (1993) 7 *International Journal of Law and the Family* 230; and H. Reece, 'The Paramountcy Principle: Consensus or Construct?', (1996) 49 Current Legal Problems 267. By permission of Oxford University Press.

Reed Elsevier (UK) Ltd trading as LexisNexis for extracts from All England Law Reports [All ER], Family Court Reports [FCR], Family Law Reports [FLR], A. Barlow and J. Smithson, 'Legal Assumptions, Cohabitants' Talk and the Rocky Road to Reform' 2010. 22 Child and Family Law Quarterly 328; J. Miles, 'Charman v Charman (No 4): Making Sense of Need, Compensation and Equal Sharing after Miller/McFarlane', (2008) 20 Child and Family Law Quarterly 378; J. Eekelaar, 'Family Law: Keeping Us "On Message"', (1999) 11 Child and Family Law Quarterly 387; L. Smith, 'Clashing Symbols? Reconciling Support for Fathers and Fatherless Families after the Human Fertilisation and Embryology Act 2008', (2010) 22 Child and Family Law Quarterly 46.

Springer for extract from L. Flynn and A. Lawson, 'Gender, sexuality and the doctrine of detrimental reliance', (1995) 3 *Feminist Legal Studies* 105. Permission conveyed through Copyright Clearance Center, Inc.

Sweet & Maxwell Ltd for extract from Law Quarterly Review and Journal of Social Welfare and Family Law: J. Eekelaar, 'Do parents have a duty to consult?', (1998) 114 Law Quarterly Review 337. Reproduced by permission of Thomson Reuters (Professional) UK Limited.

Taylor & Francis Group for extracts from Journal of Social Welfare and Family Law: M. Harding and A. Newnham, 'Section 8 Orders on the Public-Private Divide' (2017) 39 Journal of Social Welfare and Family Law 83; L. Fox-Harding, 'The Children Act 1989 in Context: Four Perspectives in Child Care Law and Policy (1)', (1991) 13 Journal of Social Welfare and Family Law 179. Rights managed by Taylor & Francis Group.

Taylor & Francis Group for extract from J. Eekelaar and R. George (eds), *Routledge Handbook of Family Law and Policy*. (Abingdon: Routledge, 2021); C. Gibson, Dissolving Wedlock (London: Routledge, 1994); M. Freeman (ed), Divorce: Where Next (Aldershot: Dartmouth, 1996a); and J. Pahl, *Private Violence and Public Policy: The Needs of Battered Women and the Response of Public Services* (London: Routledge & Kegan Paul, 1985). Reproduced by permission of Taylor & Francis Group.

Every effort has been made to trace and contact copyright holders but this has not been possible in every case. If notified, the publisher will undertake to rectify any errors or omissions at the earliest opportunity.

OUTLINE TABLE OF CONTENTS

1 Introduction to Family Law 1

2 Family Relationships Between Adults 30

3 Ending Relationships: Divorce, Dissolution, and Separation 130

4 Protection from Domestic Abuse 180

5 Financial Provision for Children 278

6 Financial Remedies on Divorce 349

7 Property and Finances When Non-Formalized Relationships End 446

8 Fundamental Principles in the Law Relating to Children 526

9 Becoming a Legal Parent and the Consequences of Legal Parenthood 601

10 Parental Responsibility 673

11 Private Disputes over Children 721

12 Child Protection 813

13 Adoption 901

Bibliography 973

Index 1023

TABLE OF CONTENTS

Table of Cases xxviii
Table of Statutes xlix
Table of Statutory Instruments lxiii
Table of International Instruments lxv
Abbreviations lxvi

1 INTRODUCTION TO FAMILY LAW 1

1.1 Families and Family Law in England and Wales today 1
1.1.1 What Is 'Family'? 1
1.1.2 What Is Family Law? 2
1.2 Themes and Issues in Contemporary Family Law 3
1.2.1 The Importance of Rights 3
1.2.1.a Welfare versus rights 3
1.2.1.b Contemporary rights in family law: the European Convention on Human Rights 4
1.2.1.c A Resistance to rights? 9
1.2.2 Rules versus Discretion 10
1.2.3 Women's and Men's Perspectives on Family Law 12
1.2.3.a Feminist perspectives 12
1.2.3.b Men and the family 15
1.2.4 Gender Identity 16
1.2.5 Sexual Orientation 18
1.2.6 Cultural Diversity 19
1.2.7 State Intervention versus Private Ordering 21
1.2.7.a The role of the family court 22
1.2.7.b Non-court dispute resolution 25
1.2.7.c Is private ordering in family disputes a 'good' thing? 27
1.3 Concluding Thoughts 29

2 FAMILY RELATIONSHIPS BETWEEN ADULTS 30

2.1 Introduction 31
2.2 Family Relationships in England and Wales 32
2.2.1 Formalized Relationships: Marriage and Civil Partnership 32
2.2.2 Non-Formalized Relationships: Cohabitation 34
2.2.3 Other Relationships Within and Between Households 35

2.3 Gender Identity, Sexual Orientation, and Gender Roles 35
2.3.1 Determining Gender 36
2.3.2 Same-Sex Relationships: The Road to Same-Sex Marriage 38
2.3.2.a Judicial developments 38
2.3.2.b The creation of civil partnership 41
2.3.2.c The arrival of same-sex marriage in English law 43
2.3.3 The Extension of Civil Partnerships to Mixed-Sex Couples 46
2.3.4 Ideological Implications of Relationship Formalization? 50
2.3.4.a Same-sex marriage: a mixed blessing? 51
2.3.4.b Exercising the choice: marriage or civil partnership? 53
2.3.4.c Fighting for the choice: mixed-sex civil partnership 55
2.3.4.d Transformation or stagnation? 57
2.4 Status-Based Relationships: Marriage and Civil Partnership 59
2.4.1 The Nature of Marriage and Civil Partnership 59
2.4.2 The Significance of Status 61
2.4.3 A Right to Marry, or Not to Marry? 63
2.5 Creating a Valid Marriage or Civil Partnership 66
2.5.1 The Law of Nullity: Void and Voidable Marriages, and Non-Qualifying Ceremonies 66
2.5.2 The Practical Importance of the Law of Nullity 68
2.5.3 Formal Requirements for Creating Marriage and Civil Partnership 68
2.5.3.a Marriage formalities 69
2.5.3.b Civil partnership formalities 70
2.5.3.c Consequences of failing to comply with formalities 70
2.5.3.d Reform? 70
2.6 Grounds on Which a Marriage or Civil Partnership Is Void 72
2.6.1 Void Grounds: Incapacity to Marry or Form a Civil Partnership 72
2.6.1.a Prohibited degrees of relationship and associated formalities 72
2.6.1.b The age of the parties and related formalities 75
2.6.1.c Monogamy 76
2.6.1.d Polygamy 77
2.6.2 Void Grounds, Non-Qualifying Ceremonies, and Presumptions: Disregard of Formal Requirements 77
2.6.2.a Void marriages and civil partnerships 77
2.6.2.b Non-qualifying ceremonies (formerly known as non-marriages) 78
2.6.2.c Rescuing doubtful marriages via the presumption of marriage 87
2.7 Grounds on Which a Marriage or Civil Partnership Is Voidable 88
2.7.1 Lack of Valid Consent 89
2.7.1.a Duress 91
2.7.1.b Mistake 96
2.7.1.c Unsoundness of mind 97
2.7.1.d 'Or otherwise' 100
2.7.2 Mental Disorder Rendering Person 'Unfit' for Marriage or Civil Partnership 100

2.7.3 The Respondent Was Pregnant by Another at the Time of the Ceremony 100
2.7.4 Grounds Relating to Gender Recognition 101
2.7.5 A Ground Unique to Marriage: Venereal Disease 102
2.7.6 Grounds Unique to Mixed-Sex Marriage: Failure to Consummate 103
2.7.6.a Consummation 104
2.7.6.b Incapacity 105
2.7.6.c Wilful refusal 105
2.7.6.d Why consummation? Different conceptions of 'marriage' 106
2.7.6.e Opening the door to other types of formalized relationship? 109
2.8 Non-Formalized Relationships: Cohabitants and Other 'Family' 111
2.8.1 Identifying 'Family' 112
2.8.1.a A panoply of tests 112
2.8.1.b Sharing a household 113
2.8.1.c The functional approach in action 114
2.8.2 Cohabitants 118
2.8.2.a The legal definitions 118
2.8.2.b Some policy questions 120
2.8.2.c Human rights issues 123
2.8.3 The Platonic, Non-Conjugal Family 124
2.8.3.a The Burden sisters' case 125
2.8.3.b Taking functionalism to its logical conclusion 128
2.9 Conclusion 129

3 ENDING RELATIONSHIPS: DIVORCE, DISSOLUTION, AND SEPARATION 130

3.1 Introduction 131
3.2 The Normalization of Divorce 132
3.2.1 Divorces in England and Wales 133
3.2.2 Who Divorces? 135
3.3 The Nature, Function, and Limits of Divorce Law 136
3.3.1 Fault or 'No Fault'? 136
3.3.2 'Easier' or 'Harder' Divorce and Supporting the Institution of Marriage 137
3.3.3 Can Divorce Law Affect Marital and Divorcing Behaviour? 138
3.3.4 A Legal or Non-Legal Approach? 139
3.3.5 Regulation or Regularization? 139
3.4 A Brief History of Divorce Law to 1969 140
3.5 The Matrimonial Causes Act 1973: As It Was Before 2022 142
3.5.1 The Former Substantive Law 142
3.5.2 The Former Procedure for Divorce 143
3.5.3 Defects of the Former Law 147
3.5.3.a The law was confusing and misleading 148

3.5.3.b The law was discriminatory and unjust 150
3.5.3.c The law distorted parties' bargaining positions 152
3.5.3.d The law provoked unnecessary hostility and bitterness 152
3.5.3.e The law did nothing to save the marriage 154
3.5.3.f The law could make things worse for the children 155

3.6 The Route to Reform 157
3.6.1 The Family Law Act 1996 Scheme 157
3.6.2 *Owens v Owens* [2018] UKSC 41 162
3.6.3 Proposals for Reform 164

3.7 The Matrimonial Causes Act 1973: The Present Law 165

3.8 Bars and Other Restrictions on Divorce 167
3.8.1 Financial Protection for Certain Respondents 167
3.8.2 Time Bars on Divorce 168
3.8.3 Special Protection for Parties to Some Religious Marriages 169
3.8.4 The Role of the King's Proctor 169

3.9 Judicial Separation 170

3.10 Evaluation of the Current Law 170
3.10.1 Should Conduct Have Any Relevance? 172
3.10.2 Do We Have Divorce by Mutual Consent? 176
3.10.3 Do We Have Divorce on Unilateral Demand? 177
3.10.4 Do We Have 'Regularized' Divorce Law? 178

3.11 Conclusion 178

4 PROTECTION FROM DOMESTIC ABUSE 180

4.1 Introduction 181

4.2 Background Issues: Domestic Abuse and Key Policy Questions 182
4.2.1 Defining 'Domestic Abuse' 182
4.2.2 Evidence about Domestic Abuse 184
4.2.2.a The prevalence of domestic abuse 184
4.2.2.b The gender dimension 187
4.2.2.c Causes and risk factors 187
4.2.2.d Why not just leave? 189
4.2.2.e The justice gap 189
4.2.3 Feminist Perspectives on Domestic Abuse Law, Policy, and Practice 190
4.2.4 The Human Rights Dimension 195
4.2.4.a Article 2 196
4.2.4.b Article 3 197
4.2.4.c Article 14 197
4.2.4.d Article 8 198

4.3 The Criminal Law and Domestic Abuse 200
4.3.1 The Criminal Law 200
4.3.2 The Criminal Justice System 201

4.4 The Civil Law and Domestic Abuse: Introduction 204
4.5 The Family Law Act 1996, Part 4 207
4.5.1 The Range of Relationships Covered 208
4.5.2 Non-Molestation Orders 213
4.5.2.a Molestation 213
4.5.2.b The court's discretion 216
4.5.2.c Duration of orders 217
4.5.3 Occupation Orders 219
4.5.3.a 'Entitlement to occupy' in the occupation order scheme 221
4.5.3.b Section 33: entitled applicants—associated persons 222
4.5.3.c Section 35: non-entitled former spouse or civil partner; entitled respondent 224
4.5.3.d Section 36: non-entitled current or former cohabitant; entitled respondent 226
4.5.3.e Sections 37 and 38: current and former spouses, civil partners, and cohabitants, where neither party is entitled to occupy 228
4.5.3.f Ancillary orders under s 40 229
4.5.3.g The balance of harm test and questions 230
4.6 Domestic Abuse Protection Orders under the DAA 2021, Part 3 240
4.6.1 The Range of Relationships Covered 240
4.6.2 What the DAPO Can Do 241
4.6.2.a Restrictions designed to protect from 'domestic abuse' 242
4.6.2.b Regulation of occupation 243
4.6.2.c Other positive requirements 244
4.6.3 Substantive Basis for Making a DAPO 244
4.6.3.a Preconditions for making a DAPO 244
4.6.3.b Relevant factors and constraints 245
4.6.4 Duration of Protection 246
4.7 Applications, Undertakings, and Enforcement of FLA 1996 and Private DAA 2021 Orders 247
4.7.1 Orders on Application by the Victim 247
4.7.2 'Without Notice' Orders 248
4.7.3 Undertakings: FLA 1996 Only 249
4.7.4 Enforcement of Orders under the FLA 1996 and DAA 2021 250
4.7.4.a Occupation orders under the FLA 1996 251
4.7.4.b Non-molestation orders and DAPOs 254
4.8 Orders Made Without Application by the Victim 260
4.8.1 Orders Made of the Court's Own Motion 261
4.8.2 Applications Made by Police and Other Third Parties 262
4.8.2.a Third party applications for DAPOs 262
4.8.2.b Police use of DAPNs 263
4.8.3 Pros and Cons of Third Party Action 263
4.8.3.a Victim protection versus victim autonomy? 263
4.8.3.b Symbol of public seriousness or risk of downgrading? 266

4.9 The Future: Which Order, Which Route? 268
4.9.1 Reasons to Use the FLA 1996 268
4.9.2 Reasons to Use the DAA 2021 269
4.10 Forced Marriage Protection Orders 270
4.10.1 Which Marriages are Affected? 271
4.10.2 Forced Marriage Protection Orders 271
4.10.2.a What is a 'forced' marriage? 271
4.10.2.b Content of the order 272
4.10.2.c The court's discretion 274
4.10.2.d When—and on whose application—an order may be made 275
4.10.2.e Enforcement of FMPOs, and free-standing criminal offences 276
4.10.3 Use of FMPOs 276
4.11 Conclusion 276

5 FINANCIAL PROVISION FOR CHILDREN 278

5.1 Introduction 279
5.2 A Brief History of Financial Provision for Children 281
5.3 Overview of the Current Law 284
5.3.1 The Parties' Relationships 284
5.3.2 CMS or Court? 284
5.4 Child Support: The Current Law 285
5.4.1 The Relevant Parties 285
5.4.1.a The 'qualifying child' 285
5.4.1.b The 'non-resident parent' 286
5.4.1.c The 'person with care' 286
5.4.1.d The 'relevant other child' 287
5.4.2 General Principles 287
5.4.3 Application to CMS 288
5.4.3.a Encouraging private agreement 288
5.4.3.b Application to CMS where agreement fails 288
5.4.4 The Maintenance Calculation 289
5.4.4.a Basing the calculation on gross historic earned income 289
5.4.4.b The basic rate 290
5.4.4.c The reduced rate 291
5.4.4.d The flat rate 291
5.4.4.e The nil rate 291
5.4.4.f 'Shared care' 291
5.4.4.g Apportionment 293
5.4.4.h Set-off 293

5.4.5 Variations 293
5.4.5.a The cases for a variation 294
5.4.5.b The discretion 296
5.4.6 Termination of the Calculation 297
5.4.7 Enforcement of Child Maintenance 297
5.4.7.a 'Enforcement' via reliance on tax and benefit records 297
5.4.7.b Enforcement by CMS 298
5.4.7.c No enforcement of CMS calculations by person with care 299
5.5 Court-Based Provision: The Current Law 303
5.5.1 Lump Sum and Property-Related Orders 303
5.5.2 Periodical Payments 303
5.5.2.a Where CMS has jurisdiction 303
5.5.2.b Where CMS has no jurisdiction 306
5.5.3 The Statutory Schemes 307
5.5.3.a The orders available 308
5.5.3.b Who can be made liable for whom? 308
5.5.3.c Who can apply? 308
5.5.3.d The child's age and the duration of orders 310
5.5.4 The Grounds for Orders and the Courts' Discretion 311
5.5.5 Principles from the Case Law 312
5.5.5.a Unwanted births and births to unmarried parents 313
5.5.5.b The basic objective: meeting the child's needs 313
5.5.5.c Indirect benefit for others 314
5.5.5.d Property orders 315
5.5.5.e Periodical payments 316
5.5.6 Enforcement of Court Orders 319
5.6 'Family-Based Arrangements' and Other Private Ordering 320
5.6.1 Private Ordering of Maintenance 320
5.6.2 Private Ordering of Other Financial Issues for Children 322
5.7 Policy Questions Relating to Financial Provision for Children 323
5.7.1 Children's Rights or Parents' Responsibilities? 323
5.7.2 Public and Private 327
5.7.2.a Protecting the private sphere 327
5.7.2.b A limited form of privacy? 328
5.7.2.c Whose privacy? The dangers of private ordering 329
5.7.3 Legal and Social Parenthood 334
5.7.3.a Who should pay for whom? 335
5.7.3.b The relationship between the child's living arrangements and child support 337
5.7.4 The Policy Choices Behind the Formula 342
5.7.5 Rules or Discretion? 345
5.8 Conclusion 347

6 FINANCIAL REMEDIES ON DIVORCE 349

6.1 Introduction 350

6.2 The Social Context: The Family Economy 350

6.3 A Brief History of Financial Remedies on Divorce 353

6.4 The Current Law: The Toolbox of Orders and Resources Available 356

6.4.1 The Resources Available to the Court 356

6.4.2 Financial Provision Orders 357

6.4.2.a Periodical payments 357

6.4.2.b Lump sums 358

6.4.3 Property Adjustment Orders and Orders for Sale 358

6.4.3.a Orders relating to owner-occupied homes 358

6.4.3.b Orders relating to rented homes 359

6.4.4 Pension Orders 360

6.4.5 When May Orders be Made? 361

6.4.6 Enforcement 361

6.5 The Current Law: The Principles Governing the Grant of Remedies 361

6.5.1 Introduction: The Statutory Discretion and the Case Law Principles 362

6.5.2 First Consideration: The Welfare of Minor Children 366

6.5.3 Meeting the Parties' Material Needs 366

6.5.3.a What is 'need'? 367

6.5.3.b Housing first 369

6.5.3.c The source of available resources 369

6.5.3.d The source of the parties' needs 370

6.5.3.e The needs and resources of second families 373

6.5.3.f Criticism of the law relating to needs 375

6.5.3.g Contribution-based awards in non-sharing, non-needs cases? 375

6.5.4 Compensation: Relationship-Generated Economic Disadvantage 376

6.5.4.a Compensation: a distinct principle? 377

6.5.4.b Compensation: need in disguise? 379

6.5.4.c Compensating for what? 380

6.5.5 Entitlement: Equal Sharing 382

6.5.5.a Does the equal sharing principle provide a starting point? 385

6.5.5.b To what property does equal sharing apply? 386

6.5.5.c When will there be good reason to divide matrimonial property unequally? 393

6.5.5.d The indeterminacy of the equal sharing principle 398

6.5.5.e What is the relationship of equal sharing to the other principles? 399

6.5.6 The Parties' Conduct 402

6.5.6.a Financial misconduct and anti-avoidance powers 405

6.5.6.b Litigation misconduct 406

6.5.6.c Delayed or late applications 406

6.5.6.d Nullity cases: criminal offences relating to the marriage or civil partnership 407

6.5.6.e 'Positive' conduct 408

6.6 Achieving Finality on Divorce 408
6.6.1 Ending Ongoing Financial Ties Between the Parties 408
6.6.1.a The statutory provisions 409
6.6.1.b The courts' approach 410
6.6.2 The Clean Break in Practice 411
6.6.3 Applications to Vary, Set Aside, and for Leave to Appeal Final Orders 413
6.6.3.a Orders that may be varied 413
6.6.3.b Other orders 413
6.7 Private Ordering: Marital Agreements 416
6.7.1 Consent Orders 417
6.7.2 Separation and Maintenance Agreements 421
6.7.3 Post-Nuptial Agreements 425
6.7.4 Pre-Nuptial Agreements 426
6.7.4.a The public policy objection removed 426
6.7.4.b The *Hyman* principle: the treatment of agreements in the matrimonial court 427
6.7.5 Criticism of the Current Law 435
6.8 Reform 439
6.8.1 Reform of the Substantive Law 439
6.8.2 Reform of the Law Relating to Agreements 442
6.9 Conclusion 445

7 PROPERTY AND FINANCES WHEN NON-FORMALIZED RELATIONSHIPS END 446

7.1 Introduction 447
7.2 Ascertaining Ownership of the Shared Home and Other Land 450
7.2.1 Transfers and Express Trusts: Formal Requirements 451
7.2.2 Implied Trusts of Land and Proprietary Estoppel: Introduction 453
7.2.3 Implied Trusts of Land: The Presumptions of Resulting Trust and Advancement 454
7.2.3.a The presumption of resulting trust 454
7.2.3.b The presumption of advancement 455
7.2.4 Implied Trusts of Land: 'Common Intention' Constructive Trusts 456
7.2.4.a When should the common intention constructive trust be deployed? 456
7.2.4.b Common intention constructive trusts: the basics 459
7.2.4.c Cases where the legal title is in the parties' joint names 464
7.2.4.d Cases where the legal title is in the sole name of one party 470
7.2.5 Proprietary Estoppel 476
7.2.5.a Finding an assurance, representation, or promise 477
7.2.5.b Detrimental reliance 478
7.2.5.c Remedying the unconscionability of repudiation 478
7.2.6 Criticisms of the Current Law Relating to Ownership of Land 480
7.2.6.a The *Stack/Jones* starting point 481

7.2.6.b The problem of intention 484
7.2.6.c The problem of detrimental reliance 488
7.2.6.d The position of the homemaker and other non-financial contributors 490
7.2.6.e The problems of uncertainty, destabilization, and democratic legitimacy 491
7.3 Occupation and Sale of the Owned Family Home 495
7.3.1 Rights to Occupy the Family Home 495
7.3.1.a The general law 495
7.3.1.b The case of children 496
7.3.2 Decision-Making about Sale and Other Transactions Relating to the Family Home 497
7.3.2.a Disputes involving legal and beneficial owners 497
7.3.2.b The position of non-owners 497
7.3.3 Resolving Disputes about the Future of the Family Home 497
7.3.3.a Disputes between beneficial co-owners 498
7.3.3.b Occupation remedies for non-entitled claimants 502
7.3.4 The Case of Rented Homes 503
7.4 Ownership and Use of Other Property 503
7.4.1 Creating and Transferring Ownership: The Basics 504
7.4.2 Income and Bank Accounts 506
7.4.3 Use-Rights Over the Contents of the Family Home 508
7.5 Private Ordering for Relationship Breakdown 509
7.5.1 The Law 509
7.5.2 The Reality? 511
7.6 Reform for Cohabitants 512
7.6.1 A Stock-Take of the Current Position 513
7.6.2 Does Civil Partnership Solve the Problem? 515
7.6.3 Functional, Remedial, 'Family Law' Reform? 515
7.6.3.a The parameters of the reform debate 516
7.6.3.b The Law Commission's recommended approach 521
7.6.3.c Reception of the Commission's scheme 522
7.6.4 But Does Functionalism Require Bolder Reform? 524
7.7 Conclusion 525

8 FUNDAMENTAL PRINCIPLES IN THE LAW RELATING TO CHILDREN 526

8.1 Introduction 527
8.2 The Welfare Principle 528
8.2.1 The Paramountcy of the Child's Welfare 528
8.2.1.a The meaning of 'paramount' 529
8.2.1.b The meaning of 'welfare' 529
8.2.1.c When will the welfare principle apply? 534

8.2.2 Criticisms of the Welfare Principle 537
8.2.2.a Indeterminacy 537
8.2.2.b Lack of transparency and irrelevant considerations 539
8.2.2.c Why should the child's welfare be paramount? 542
8.3 Alternatives to the Welfare Principle 545
8.3.1 Re-Conceptualizing the Welfare Principle 545
8.4 The ECHR and Child-Related Disputes 549
8.4.1 Establishing a 'Right' under Article 8(1) 549
8.4.2 Establishing a Breach of Article 8(1) 550
8.4.3 Justifying a Breach under Article 8(2) 551
8.4.4 The Relationship Between the Welfare Principle and Article 8 551
8.4.4.a The domestic courts' approach 552
8.4.4.b The Strasbourg Court's approach 554
8.5 Children's Rights 558
8.5.1 Are Children's Rights Important? 559
8.5.2 The Theoretical Foundations of Children's Rights 561
8.5.2.a The will or power theory of rights 561
8.5.2.b The interest theory of rights 563
8.5.2.c Children's rights and paternalism 564
8.5.3 The Development of Children's Rights in English Law 566
8.5.4 Children's Rights and the ECHR 567
8.5.5 The UN Convention on the Rights of the Child (UNCRC) 568
8.5.6 Children's Rights in the Domestic Courts 570
8.5.6.a Children's welfare-based rights to care and protection 570
8.5.6.b Children's autonomy rights 571
8.6 The Court, the State, and Private Family Life 583
8.6.1 The Children Act's 'No Order' Principle 584
8.6.2 The State and Parental Decision-Making 589
8.6.2.a When will the court intervene? 592
8.6.2.b The role of the parents' views 595
8.7 The Inherent Jurisdiction of the High Court 598
8.8 Conclusion 600

9 BECOMING A LEGAL PARENT AND THE CONSEQUENCES OF LEGAL PARENTHOOD 601

9.1 Introduction 602
9.2 Concepts of Parenthood and Possible Approaches to Determining Legal Parenthood 603
9.2.1 What is a 'Parent'? 603
9.2.2 The Importance of Legal Parenthood 605
9.2.3 Policy Arguments about Legal Parenthood 606

9.3 Determining Parenthood in the Context of Natural Reproduction 610
9.3.1 Establishing Maternity 610
9.3.2 Establishing Paternity 612
9.3.2.a Fathers in a formalized relationship with the mother: the presumption of legitimacy 613
9.3.2.b Unmarried fathers and prima facie evidence based on registration of the birth 613
9.3.3 Court Proceedings to Determine the Parentage of a Child 615
9.3.3.a Rebutting the presumptions and the advent of DNA testing 617
9.3.3.b Directing tests under the FLRA 1969, s 20 618
9.3.3.c Consent requirements for the taking of samples 626
9.3.3.d Telling the child the 'truth' about parentage 629
9.4 Determining Parenthood in the Context of Assisted Reproduction 630
9.4.1 The Brave New World of Assisted Reproduction 630
9.4.2 Access to Treatment: Is Parenthood a Right or a Privilege? 631
9.4.2.a The right to reproductive freedom under Article 8 ECHR 633
9.4.2.b Legitimate restrictions on the right to reproductive freedom: Article 8(2) 634
9.4.2.c The right to reproductive freedom under Article 12 ECHR 638
9.4.3 Determining Parenthood under the HFEA 2008 638
9.4.3.a Mothers: s 33 640
9.4.3.b Fathers and second female parents: ss 34–40 640
9.4.3.c Reflections on the parenthood provisions in the HFEA 2008 647
9.4.4 The Child's Right to Know Their Genetic Parentage 650
9.4.4.a Why is the right to know important? 650
9.4.4.b The right to know in the HFEA 1990 653
9.5 Surrogacy 657
9.5.1 Early Attitudes to Surrogacy 658
9.5.2 Surrogacy Arrangements Act 1985 659
9.5.3 Determining Parentage in Surrogacy Arrangements: The HFEA 2008 660
9.5.3.a The child's legal parents 660
9.5.3.b Parental orders 660
9.5.3.c Revoking parental orders 666
9.5.4 Disputes when Surrogacy Agreements Break Down 666
9.5.5 Reform of Surrogacy Law 669
9.6 Adoption 672
9.7 Conclusion 672

10 PARENTAL RESPONSIBILITY 673

10.1 Introduction 674
10.2 What is Parental Responsibility? 675

10.2.1 From Rights to Responsibility 675
10.2.1.a The parent–child relationship 675
10.2.1.b The parent–state relationship 677
10.2.2 Defining Parental Responsibility 679
10.3 How is Parental Responsibility Obtained? 682
10.3.1 Mothers 682
10.3.2 Fathers and Second Female Parents under ss 42 and 43 of the HFEA 2008 683
10.3.2.a Fathers and second female parents who are married to, or are in a civil partnership with, the mother 683
10.3.2.b Unmarried fathers and second female parents 683
10.3.3 Lesbian Mothers and Known Fathers/Donors 689
10.3.4 Step-Parents 692
10.3.5 Holders of a Child Arrangements Order 693
10.3.5.a Orders that the child live with a person 693
10.3.5.b Orders that the child spend time or otherwise have contact with a person 694
10.3.5.c Limitations on parental responsibility arising from a child arrangements order 694
10.3.6 Special Guardians 695
10.3.7 Guardians 695
10.3.8 Adoption 695
10.3.9 Local Authorities 696
10.4 Who Should Have Parental Responsibility? 696
10.4.1 The Arguments for Further Reform 696
10.4.2 Arguments Against Conferring Equal Status on Unmarried Fathers 697
10.4.3 Reviewing the Current Position 702
10.5 Exercising Parental Responsibility 705
10.5.1 A Duty to Consult or a Right of Unilateral Action? 705
10.5.2 Limitations on the Exercise of Parental Responsibility 711
10.5.2.a The *Gillick*-competent child 712
10.5.2.b The state 712
10.6 Terminating Parental Responsibility 714
10.6.1 Mothers, Fathers Who Are in a Formalized Relationship, and Second Female Parents under HFEA 2008, s 42 714
10.6.2 Unmarried Fathers, Second Female Parents under HFEA 2008, s 43, and Step-Parents 716
10.6.2.a Unmarried fathers 716
10.6.2.b Second female parents under HFEA 2008, s 43 718
10.6.2.c Step-parents 718
10.6.3 Guardians, Special Guardians, and Others 718
10.7 Caring for Children Without Parental Responsibility 718
10.8 Conclusion 719

11 PRIVATE DISPUTES OVER CHILDREN 721

11.1 Introduction 722
11.2 Private Law Orders under the Children Act 1989 723
11.3 Procedural Matters Germane to All Section 8 Orders 724
11.3.1 When May a Section 8 Order Be Made? 724
11.3.2 Who May Apply for a Section 8 Order? 724
11.3.2.a Entitled applicants 724
11.3.2.b Applicants requiring leave 725
11.3.2.c Principles to be applied on an application for leave 726
11.3.2.d Prohibited applicants 727
11.3.2.e Restricted applicants under section 91(14) 728
11.3.3 The Participation of Children in Private Law Disputes 729
11.3.3.a Section 7 reports 730
11.3.3.b Giving evidence as a witness 731
11.3.3.c Children as parties to proceedings 731
11.3.3.d Judges meeting children 733
11.4 General Principles Applicable to All Section 8 Orders 735
11.5 Child Arrangements Orders: Introduction 737
11.6 Child Arrangements Orders: 'Live With' Orders 738
11.6.1 The Historic Approaches to 'Live With' Orders 738
11.6.2 The Current Approach to 'Live With' Orders 742
11.6.3 Shared Living Arrangements 745
11.6.3.a Development of the courts' approach 746
11.6.3.b Policy debates about shared care arrangements 752
11.6.4 Particular Issues Applicable to 'Live With' Orders 754
11.6.4.a Gay and lesbian parents 754
11.6.4.b Racial, religious, and cultural factors 755
11.6.5 'Natural Parents' versus Others 758
11.6.5.a Factors favouring a 'presumption' 759
11.6.5.b Factors opposing a 'presumption' 761
11.6.6 The Effects of a 'Live With' Order 764
11.6.6.a Conferring certain rights, etc 764
11.6.6.b Imposing certain restrictions 764
11.7 Child Arrangements Orders: 'Spending Time' and 'Having Contact' Orders 766
11.7.1 Overview of 'Spending Time' and 'Having Contact' Orders 766
11.7.2 A Presumption in Favour of Orders to Spend Time or Have Contact 767
11.7.2.a The statutory presumption 767
11.7.2.b The courts' approach 768
11.7.3 Contact and Domestic Abuse 779
11.7.3.a Historic approaches 779
11.7.3.b The shift in *Re L* (2000) 780

11.7.3.c The current approach 782
11.7.3.d Criticisms of the current approach 786
11.7.4 Enforcing Orders to Spend Time or Have Contact 793
11.7.4.a Committal proceedings 794
11.7.4.b Enforcement measures under the CA 1989 795
11.7.4.c Transferring residence 796
11.7.5 Taking Contact out of the Courts 798
11.8 Specific Issue and Prohibited Steps Orders 800
11.8.1 General Principles 800
11.8.2 Relocation Disputes 801
11.8.2.a The legal approach to relocation cases 801
11.8.2.b 'Unilateral relocation' 805
11.8.2.c Relocation cases in practice 806
11.8.3 Changing a Child's Name 809
11.9 Conclusion 811

12 CHILD PROTECTION 813

12.1 Introduction 813
12.2 Principles of State Intervention into Family Life 816
12.2.1 Competing Approaches and the Children Act 1989 816
12.2.2 The Human Rights Dimension 819
12.2.3 The Problem of Resources 821
12.3 State Support for Children and Families in England under Part III 821
12.3.1 The General Duty to Children in Need: Section 17 823
12.3.2 Providing Accommodation for a Child in England 825
12.3.2.a The duty to accommodate: s 20(1) 825
12.3.2.b The power to accommodate: voluntary accommodation under s 20(4) 827
12.3.2.c The courts' approach to s 20 accommodation 828
12.3.2.d Voluntary accommodation for older children 831
12.3.3 Local Authority Duties with Respect to Looked After Children 832
12.3.4 Part III: A Success? 835
12.4 The Child Protection System: Investigating Allegations of Child Abuse 835
12.4.1 Section 47 Investigation 835
12.4.2 Section 37 Investigation 838
12.5 Care and Supervision Proceedings under Part IV 839
12.5.1 Who May Apply for a Care or Supervision Order? 839
12.5.2 When May a Care or Supervision Order be Made? 839
12.5.3 The Threshold Criteria 841
12.5.3.a Is suffering or likely to suffer significant harm 842
12.5.3.b 'Is attributable to the care given to the child not being what it would be reasonable to expect a parent to give to him' 855
12.5.3.c Standard of proof for establishing the threshold criteria 860

12.5.4 The Welfare Stage 862
12.5.4.a 'Ascertainable wishes and feelings of the child' 862
12.5.4.b 'Any harm which he has suffered or is at risk of suffering' 864
12.5.4.c 'The range of powers available to the court' 867
12.5.5 The Care Plan 869
12.5.5.a The role of the court 870
12.5.5.b Changes to the care plan 876
12.5.6 Effect of a Care Order 877
12.5.6.a Accommodating the child 877
12.5.6.b Exercising parental responsibility 878
12.5.7 Contact with a Child in Care 881
12.5.8 Supervision Orders 884
12.5.8.a Effect of a supervision order 884
12.5.8.b When is a supervision order appropriate? 886
12.5.9 Leaving Care 887
12.5.9.a Varying and discharging care orders 887
12.5.9.b Leaving care at age 18 887
12.6 Emergency Protection under Part V 888
12.6.1 Police Protection Powers 888
12.6.2 Emergency Protection Orders 890
12.7 Interim Care and Supervision Orders 894
12.8 Conclusion 899

13 ADOPTION 901

13.1 Introduction 902
13.2 What is Adoption? 903
13.3 The Changing Face of Adoption 906
13.3.1 Looked After Children: Does Adoption Offer the Best Solution? 908
13.3.2 Adopting Children Out of Care: New Challenges 911
13.3.2.a Post-adoption support 911
13.3.2.b Open adoption 911
13.4 ACA 2002: The Core Principles 912
13.4.1 The Welfare Principle 912
13.4.2 Parental Consent 915
13.4.2.a Adoption with parental consent 915
13.4.2.b Dispensing with parental consent 919
13.4.3 Rights, Welfare, Reform, and the Fundamental Principles of Adoption 923
13.5 The Adoption Process 927
13.5.1 Placing the Child for Adoption 927
13.5.1.a Placing the child with the birth parent's consent 927
13.5.1.b Placing the child without consent: placement orders 927

13.5.1.c Consequences of the child being placed or being authorized to be placed for adoption 930
13.5.1.d Contact with a child who is placed or authorized to be placed for adoption 930
13.5.1.e Restrictions on removing a child who is placed for adoption 931
13.5.1.f Revoking the placement order 931
13.5.2 The Adoption Application 932
13.5.2.a Residence conditions 933
13.5.2.b The requirement to give notice 933
13.5.3 The Final Hearing: Conditions on Making the Adoption Order 934
13.5.3.a Age restrictions 934
13.5.3.b Applications by one person 934
13.5.3.c Consent and leave to defend the adoption proceedings 936
13.5.3.d Welfare 941
13.6 In the Best Interests of the Child? Controversial Issues 941
13.6.1 Birth Family versus The 'Perfect' Adoptive Couple 941
13.6.2 Trans-Racial Adoption 944
13.6.3 Step-Parent Adoption 950
13.6.4 Adoption by a Sole Natural Parent 954
13.7 Open Adoption 955
13.7.1 The Right to Information 956
13.7.2 The Child's Right to Know? 957
13.7.3 Post-Adoption Contact 958
13.7.3.a The empirical evidence on post-adoption contact 958
13.7.3.b Post-adoption contact in the courts 961
13.7.3.c Should there be stronger intervention by the courts? 965
13.8 Alternatives to Adoption: Special Guardianship 967
13.9 Conclusion 971

Bibliography 973
Index 1023

TABLE OF CASES

A (A Child), Re [2014] EWCA Civ 1577 . . . 313, 314
A (A Child: Findings of Fact), Re [2022] EWCA Civ 1652 . . . 786
A (A Child) (Joint Residence: Parental Responsibility), Re [2008] EWCA Civ 867 . . . 749
A (A Child) (Order: Restriction on Applications), Re [2009] EWCA Civ 1548 . . . 728
A (A Minor) (Custody), Re [1991] FCR 569 . . . 739
A (A Minor) (Paternity: Refusal of Blood Test), Re [1994] 2 FLR 463 . . . 629
A (A Minor) (Residence Order), Re [1998] 2 FCR 633 . . . 741
A (A Minor) (Residence Order: Leave to Apply), Re [1993] 1 FLR 425 . . . 726
A (Abduction: Contempt), Re [2008] EWCA Civ 1138 . . . 795
A (Application for Leave), Re [1998] 1 FLR 1 . . . 729
A (Care: Discharge Application by Child), Re [1995] 1 FLR 599 . . . 887
A (Care Proceedings: Burden of Proof), Re [2018] EWCA Civ 1718 . . . 861–2
A (Child of the Family), Re [1998] 1 FLR 347 . . . 725
A (Children), Re [2001] EWCA Civ 1795 . . . 751
A (Children), Re [2009] EWCA Civ 1141 . . . 771, 796
A (Children) (Conjoined Twins: Surgical Separation), Re [2001] Fam 147 . . . 536, 591, 596–7
A (Fact-Finding: Judge Meeting Child), Re [2012] EWCA Civ 185 . . . 863
A (Father: Knowledge of Child's Birth), Re [2011] EWCA Civ 273 . . . 918
A (Implacable Hostility: Contact), Re [2015] EWCA Civ 910 . . . 768, 771
A (Intractable Contact Dispute), Re [2013] EWCA Civ 1104 . . . 770, 790
A (Minors: Residence Order), Re [1992] Fam 182 . . . 535
A (Non-Molestation Proceedings by a Child), Re [2009] NI Fam 22 . . . 213, 248
A (Placement Order: Imposition of Conditions on Adoption), Re [2013] EWCA Civ 1611 . . . 930
A (Sexual Abuse: Disclosure), Re [2012] UKSC 60 . . . 6
A (Supervision Order: Extension), Re [1995] 1 WLR 482 . . . 886
A (Suspended Residence Order), Re [2010] 1 FLR 1679 . . . 796
A (Withdrawal of Treatment: Legal Representation), Re [2022] EWCA Civ 1221 . . . 570
A v A [2004] EWHC 2818 . . . 398
A v A (Financial Provision for Child) [1995] 1 FCR 309 . . . 311, 313, 314, 315–16, 319
A v A (Minors) (Shared Residence Order) [1994] 1 FLR 669 . . . 746, 748
A v A (Shared Residence) [2004] EWHC 142 . . . 710–11
A v B (Financial Relief: Agreements) [2005] EWHC 314 . . . 424
A v B (No 2) [2018] EWFC 45 . . . 407
A v B and C (Contact: Alternative Families) [2012] EWCA Civ 285 . . . 692, 778
A v C [1985] FLR 445 . . . 667
A v C (Surrogacy: Parental Order) [2016] EWFC 42 . . . 664
A v Croatia (App No 55164/08, ECHR) . . . 198
A v East Sussex County Council [2010] EWCA Civ 743 . . . 889
A v L [2011] EWHC 3150 . . . 409
A v M [2005] EWHC 1721 . . . 316
A v M and Walsall Metropolitan Borough Council [1993] 2 FLR 244 . . . 896
A v N (Committal: Refusal of Contact) [1997] 2 FCR 475 . . . 794, 795
A v P (Surrogacy: Parental Order: Death of Applicant) [2011] EWHC 1738 . . . 664
A v SM and HB [2012] EWHC 435 . . . 275
A and B (Children: Restrictions on Parental Responsibility: Extremism and Radicalisation in Private Law), Re [2016] EWFC 40 . . . 784
A and B (Recission of Order: Change of Circumstances), Re [2021] EWFC 76 . . . 727
A and S (Children) v Lancashire County Council [2012] EWHC 1689 . . . 835, 873, 931
A and W, Re [1992] 2 FLR 154 . . . 726
A, B and C (Adoption: Notification of Fathers and Relatives), Re [2020] EWCA Civ 41 . . . 916–18
A Chief Constable, AA v YK and 5 others [2010] EWHC 2438 . . . 270, 273, 274
A County Council v M [2021] EWFC 35 . . . 727, 918
A Father v A Mother [2020] EWFC B57 . . . 688, 689
A Local Authority v GC [2008] EWHC 2555 . . . 916
A Local Authority v X [2013] EWHC 3274 . . . 92
A Local Authority v Y, Z and others [2006] 2 FLR 41 . . . 968

A Mother v Derby CC [2021] EWCA Civ 1867 . . . 599
A Ward of Court, Re [2017] EWHC 1022 . . . 598
AB (Medical Treatment: Care Proceedings), Re [2018] EWFC 3 . . . 591, 713, 879
AB v CD (Jurisdiction: Global Maintenance Orders) [2017] EWHC 3164 . . . 306
AB v CD (Surrogacy) [2018] EWHC 1590 . . . 665, 668
AB v CD, The Tavistock and Portman NHS Foundation Trust and others [2021] EWHC 741 . . . 581–2, 712
AB v HT and others [2018] EWCOP 2 . . . 272
Abbey National Bank v Stringer [2006] EWCA Civ 338 . . . 457
Abbott v Abbott [2007] UKPC 53 . . . 472, 473, 476, 490
AC v DC (Financial Remedies: Effect of s 37 Avoidance Orders) [2012] EWHC 2032 . . . 405
AC v DC (No 2) [2012] EWHC 2420 . . . 391
Adekunle v Ritchie [2007] EW Misc 5 . . . 457, 470
Adoption Application (Payment for Adoption), Re [1987] Fam 81 . . . 664
Agar-Ellis, In re (1883) 24 Ch D 317 . . . 566
Agarwala v Agarwala [2013] EWCA Civ 1763 . . . 476
Ahmed v Mustafa [2014] EWCA Civ 277 . . . 406
AI v MT [2013] EWHC 100 . . . 27
Airey v Ireland (No 1) (App No 6289/73, ECHR) (1979-80) 2 EHRR 305 . . . 6, 23
Akhter v Khan [2018] EWFC 54 . . . 78, 84
Akhter v Khan [2020] EWCA Civ 122 . . . 78, 84, 85
AL v AL [2011] EWHC 3150 . . . 367
Al Nashif v Bulgaria (App No 50963/99, ECHR) (2003) . . . 7, 549
Alireza v Radwan [2017] EWCA Civ 1545 . . . 357, 375
Al-M (Non Molestation Application), Re [2020] EWHC 3305 . . . 215–16, 217
A-M v A-M (Divorce: Jurisdiction: Validity of Marriage) [2001] 2 FLR 6 . . . 78, 82, 87
Amin v Amin [2020] EWHC 2675 . . . 476
Ampthill Peerage Case [1977] AC 547 . . . 610
AMS v Child Support Officer [1998] 1 FLR 955 . . . 303
An Application by the Northern Ireland Human Rights Commission, Re [2018] UKSC 27 . . . 5
An NHS Trust v X [2021] EWHC 65 . . . 579–80
Anaghara v Anaghara [2020] EWHC 3091 . . . 479
Anayo v Germany (App No 20578/07, ECHR) (2010) . . . 7, 550
Ansari v Ansari [2008] EWCA Civ 1456 . . . 405
Aquilar Quila and others v Secretary of State for the Home Department [2010] EWCA Civ 1482 . . . 63
AR (A Child: Relocation), Re [2010] EWHC 1346 . . . 805
AR v AR [2011] EWHC 2717 . . . 393
ARB v IVF Hammersmith [2018] EWCA Civ 2803 . . . 643
Arbili v Arbili [2015] EWCA Civ 542 . . . 370
Arthur JS Hall and Co (A Firm) v Simons et al [2002] 1 AC 615 . . . 420
AS v Norway (App No 60371/17, ECHR) (2019) . . . 557
Ashburn Anstalt v Arnold [1989] Ch 1 . . . 92
Ashingdane v United Kingdom (App No 8225/78, ECHR) (1985 . . . 5
Ashley v Blackman [1988] Fam 85 . . . 371
Aspden v Elvy [2012] EWHC 1387 . . . 473, 474, 476
Assad v Kurter [2013] EWHC 3852 . . . 80, 87
Atkinson v Atkinson [1988] Fam 93 . . . 374
AX and BX (Adoption: Revocation), Re [2021] EWHC 1121 . . . 905
AZ v FM (Capitalisation of Child Maintenance) [2021] EWFC 2 . . . 306
Azizi v Aghaty [2016] EWHC 110 . . . 408

B (A Child), Re [2009] UKSC 5 . . . 743, 761, 762–3
B (A Child) (Care Proceedings: Joinder), Re [2012] EWCA Civ 737 . . . 726
B (A Child: Inherited Property), Re [2022] EWFC 7 . . . 528
B (A Child: Post-Adoption Contact), Re [2019] EWCA Civ 29 . . . 964, 965
B (A Minor) (Adoption by Parent), Re [1975] Fam 127 . . . 950
B (A Minor) (Adoption: Natural Parent), Re [2001] UKHL 70 . . . 552, 715, 935, 954
B (Adoption: Jurisdiction to Set Aside), Re [1995] Fam 239 . . . 904, 905, 906
B (Care Proceedings: Appeal), Re [2013] UKSC 33 . . . 10, 552, 760, 841, 842, 843, 844, 846, 855, 868, 915, 923–4, 925, 926, 927, 938, 939, 943, 952
B (Care Proceedings: Interim Care Orders), Re [2009] EWCA Civ 1254 . . . 895
B (Care Proceedings: Joinder), Re [2012] EWCA Civ 737 . . . 714
B (Children) (Care Proceedings: Standard of Proof), Re [2008] UKHL 35 . . . 843, 845–6, 848–9, 852, 860–1, 866
B (Children: Uncertain Perpetrator), Re [2019] EWCA Civ 575 . . . 859
B (Contact: Child Support), Re [2006] EWCA Civ 1574 . . . 339
B (Foreign Surrogacy), Re [2016] EWFC 77 . . . 664
B (Habitual Residence: Inherent Jurisdiction), Re [2016] UKSC 4 . . . 766
B (Interim Care Order: Directions), Re [2002] 1 FLR 545 . . . 898
B (Medical Treatment), Re [2008] EWHC 1996 . . . 591

B (Minors) (Termination of Contact: Paramount Consideration), Re [1993] Fam 301 . . . 881, 882–3
B (Prohibited Steps Order), Re [2007] EWCA Civ 1055 . . . 802
B (Psychiatric Therapy for Parents), Re [1999] 1 FLR 701 . . . 898
B (Refusal to Grant Interim Care Order), Re [2012] EWCA Civ 1275 . . . 895
B (Role of Biological Father), Re [2007] EWHC 1952 . . . 589
B (Transfer of Foster Placement), Re [2013] 1 FLR 633 . . . 871
B (Transfer of Residence to Grandmother), Re [2012] EWCA Civ 858 . . . 760
B (Welfare: Child Arrangements Order), Re [2017] EWHC 488 . . . 763
B v B [2007] EWHC 789 . . . 308
B v B [2008] EWCA Civ 543 . . . 365, 385, 388
B v B [2012] EWHC 314 . . . 370
B v B (Financial Provision: Welfare of Child and Conduct) [2002] 1 FLR 555 . . . 369, 405
B v B (Lump Sums on Deferred Realisation of Shares) [2015] EWHC 210 . . . 358
B v B (Mesher Order) [2002] EWHC 3106 . . . 369, 377, 378, 410
B v B (Occupation Order) [1999] 2 FCR 251 . . . 231, 233, 236
B v B (Residence Order: Restricting Applications) [1997] 1 FLR 139 . . . 728
B v I [2010] 1 FLR 1721 . . . 90
B v S [2009] EWCA Civ 548 . . . 794
B v United Kingdom (App No 36536/02, ECHR) (2006) . . . 73, 74
B v United Kingdom (App No 39067/97, ECHR) (1999) . . . 701, 717
B and C (Change of Names: Parental Responsibility: Evidence), Re [2017] EWHC 3250 . . . 715, 810, 811
B and G (Care Proceedings), Re [2015] EWFC 3 . . . 855
B and G (Minors) (Custody), Re [1985] FLR 134 . . . 756
B and P v United Kingdom (App Nos 36337/97 and 35974/97, ECHR) (2001) . . . 66
Babiarz v Poland (App No 1955/10, ECHR) (2017) . . . 131
Bagum v Hafiz [2015] EWCA Civ 801 . . . 499
Balfour v Balfour [1919] 2 KB 571 . . . 421
Bank of Scotland v Brogan [2012] NICh 21 . . . 473, 476
Banks v Banks [1999] 1 FLR 726 . . . 216
Barder v Calouri [1988] AC 20 . . . 414–15, 416
Barnes v Phillips [2015] EWCA Civ 1056 . . . 462, 464, 470
Barnet London Borough Council v AL [2017] EWHC 125 . . . 591
Baxter v Baxter [1948] AC 274 . . . 105, 106
BB v CC (Residence Order) [2018] EWFC B78 . . . 766, 806
BD v FD [2016] EWHC 594 . . . 367
BD v FD (Maintenance) [2014] EWHC 4443 . . . 361
Beds Police Constabulary v RU [2013] EWHC 2350 . . . 276
Bell v Tavistock and Portman NHS Trust [2021] EWCA Civ 1363 . . . 574–5, 582
Bellinger v Bellinger [2001] EWCA Civ 1140 . . . 59
Bellinger v Bellinger [2003] UKHL 21 . . . 17, 106
Bennet v Bennet (1879) 10 Ch D 474 . . . 455
Bennett v Bennett [1952] 1 KB 249 . . . 421
Bennett v Bennett [1969] 1 WLR 430 . . . 100
Bevacqua v Bulgaria (App No 71127/01, ECHR) (2008) . . . 198
Bezeliansky v Bezelianskaya [2017] EWCA Civ 76 . . . 413
Bhaji v Chauhan, Queen's Proctor Intervening (Divorce: Marriages Used for Immigration Purposes) [2003] 2 FLR 485 . . . 146, 170
Bibi v United Kingdom (App No 19628/92, ECHR) (1992) . . . 77
Birch v Birch [2017] UKSC 53 . . . 413
Birmingham City Council v H (A Minor) [1994] 2 AC 212 . . . 536
B-J (A Child) (Non-Molestation Order: Power of Arrest), Re [2001] Fam 415 . . . 217–18, 252
BN v MA [2013] EWHC 4250 . . . 426, 429
Bokor-Ingram v Bokor-Ingram [2009] EWCA Civ 412 . . . 414
B-P (Children: Adoption or Fostering), Re [2018] EWCA Civ 2042 . . . 818, 910
B(R) v Children's Aid Society of Metropolitan Toronto [1995] 1 SCR 315 . . . 585
BR v VT [2015] EWHC 2727 . . 238
Brack v Brack [2018] EWCA Civ 2862 . . . 434, 435
Brewster, Re [2017] UKSC 8 . . . 124
Briers v Briers [2017] EWCA Civ 15 . . . 407
Brodie v Brodie [1917] P 271 . . . 106
Brookes v Secretary of State for Work and Pensions and C-MEC [2010] EWCA Civ 420 . . . 298
B-S (Children) (Adoption: Application of Threshold Criteria), Re [2013] EWCA Civ 1146 . . . 10, 876, 925–6, 927, 937, 938–40, 943
B-T v B-T (Divorce: Procedure) [1990] 2 FLR 1 . . . 417
BT v CU [2021] EWFC 87 . . . 416
Buchberger v Austria (App No 32899/96, ECHR) (2003) . . . 555
Buckland v Buckland (orse Camilleri) [1968] P 296 . . . 92, 93, 101
Bull v Hall [2013] UKSC 73 . . . 60

Burden and Burden v United Kingdom (App No 13378/05, ECHR) (2008) . . . 31, 110, 125, 126–7
Burgess v Burgess [1996] 2 FLR 34 . . . 385
Burns v Burns [1984] Ch 317 . . . 473, 490, 491, 523
Burrows v United Kingdom (App No 27558/95, ECHR) (1996) . . . 337

C, Re; Application by Mr and Mrs X under s 30 of the Human Fertilisation and Embryology Act 1990 [2002] EWHC 157 . . . 664
C (A Child), Re [2007] EWCA Civ 866 . . . 796
C (A Minor) (Adoption Order: Condition), Re [1986] 1 FLR 315 (CA) . . . 961
C (A Minor) (Adoption Order: Conditions), Re [1989] AC 1 (HL) . . . 961
C (A Minor) (Care: Child's Wishes), Re [1993] 1 FLR 832 . . . 862
C (A Minor) (Interim Care Order: Residential Assessment), Re [1997] AC 489 . . . 896, 897–8
C (A Minor) (Leave to Seek Section 8 Orders), Re [1994] 1 FLR 26 . . . 727
C (Adoption: Notice), Re [1999] 1 FLR 384 . . . 726
C (Child in Care: Choice of Forename), Re [2016] EWCA Civ 374 . . . 591, 592, 714, 811, 879, 880
C (Direct Contact: Suspension), Re [2011] EWCA Civ 521 . . . 770, 772–3
C (Financial Provision), Re [2007] 2 FLR 13 . . . 318
C (Interim Care Order), Re [2011] EWCA Civ 918 . . . 895
C (Interim Separation), Re [2019] EWCA Civ 1988 . . . 895
C (Internal Relocation), Re [2015] EWCA Civ 1305 . . . 801, 802, 804–5
C (Minors), Re [1992] 2 All ER 86 . . . 688
C (Minors) (Change of Surname), Re [1997] 3 FCR 310 . . . 707, 708, 709, 710
C (Older Children: Relocation), Re [2015] EWCA Civ 1298 . . . 730, 801
C ('Parental Alienation': Instruction of Expert), Re [2023] EWHC 345 . . . 791
C (Residence Orders: Permission to Appeal), Re [2018] EWHC 557 . . . 798
C (Surrogacy: Consent), Re [2023] EWCA Civ 16 . . . 663
C (Welfare of Child: Immunisation), Re [2003] EWHC 1376 . . . 710
C v C [1942] NZLR 356 . . . 96–7
C v C [1997] 2 FLR 26 . . . 411
C v C [2001] EWCA Civ 1625 . . . 215, 216
C v C [2007] EWHC 2033 . . . 390
C v C [2018] EWHC 3186 . . . 392
C v C (Custody of Child) [1991] FCR 254 . . . 754, 755
C v C (No 2) [1992] FCR 206 . . . 754
C v C (Non-Molestation Order: Jurisdiction) [1998] 1 FLR 554 . . . 215
C v D (Parental Responsibility) [2018] EWHC 3312 . . . 717
C v F (Disabled Child: Maintenance Orders) [1999] 1 FCR 39 . . . 305, 310
C v Secretary of State for Work and Pensions [2002] EWCA Civ 1854 . . . 291
C v XYZ County Council [2007] EWCA Civ 1206 . . . 550, 916, 918
C and A (Children: Acquisition and Discharge of Parental Responsibility by an Unmarried Father), Re [2023] EWHC 516 . . . 684
C and B (Children) (Care Order: Future Harm), Re [2000] 2 FCR 614 . . . 867, 868
C and V (Contact and Parental Responsibility), Re [1998] 1 FLR 392 . . . 687, 688
CA v DR [2021] EWFC 21 . . . 318
Cackett (orse Trice) v Cackett [1950] P 253 . . . 105
Cambra v Jones and Jones [2014] EWHC 913 . . . 731
Camm v Camm (1983) 4 FLR 577 . . . 423, 424
Campbell v Corley (1856) 4 WR 675 . . . 78
Campbell v Griffin [2001] EWCA Civ 990 . . . 478
Campbell v MGN Ltd [2004] UKHL 47 . . . 568
Capehorn v Harris [2015] EWCA Civ 955 . . . 462
Carlton v Goodman [2002] EWCA Civ 545 . . . 451, 452, 455
CB v KB [2019] EWHC 78 . . . 317
CF v KM [2010] EWHC 1754 . . . 305
CH v CT [2018] EWHC 1310 . . . 795
CH v WH [2017] EWHC 2379 . . . 359
Chadwick v Chadwick [1985] FLR 606 . . . 374
Chalmers v Johns [1999] 2 FCR 110 . . . 224, 231, 234, 239, 503
Chan v Leung [2002] EWCA Civ 1075 . . . 500
Chandler v Kerley [1978] 1 WLR 693 . . . 496, 510
Chapman v Jaume [2012] EWCA Civ 476 . . . 455
Charman v Charman [2006] EWHC 1879 . . . 366, 395, 398, 404
Charman v Charman [2007] EWCA Civ 503 . . . 356, 357, 376, 385, 388, 393, 394, 395, 397, 400, 401, 440
Chaudhry v Chaudhry [1987] 1 FLR 347 . . . 269
Chechi v Bashir [1999] 2 FLR 489 . . . 216, 258
Chief Adjudication Officer v Bath [2000] 1 FLR 8 . . . 31, 87
Chief Constable of the Hertfordshire Police v Van Colle; Smith v Chief Constable of Sussex Police [2008] UKHL 50 . . . 197
Chiva v Chiva [2014] EWCA Civ 1558 . . . 410
Chopra v Bindra [2009] EWCA Civ 203 . . . 453
Clark v Clark [1999] 2 FLR 498 . . . 405, 406
Clarke v Meadus [2010] EWHC 3117 . . . 451
Clarke (otherwise Talbott) v Clarke [1943] 2 All ER 540 . . . 105
Clibbery v Allan [2002] EWCA Civ 45 . . . 6

Cole, Re [1964] Ch 175 . . . 505
Commissioner of Police of the Metropolis v DSD [2018] UKSC 11 . . . 197
Constantinides v Constantinides [2013] EWHC 3688 . . . 361
Cook v Cook [1988] 1 FLR 521 . . . 415
Cooke v Head [1972] 1 WLR 518 . . . 489
Coombes v Smith [1986] 1 WLR 808 . . . 478, 489, 496
Cooper-Hohn v Cooper-Hohn [2014] EWHC 4122 . . . 394
Corbett v Corbett (otherwise Ashley) [1971] P 83 . . . 17, 18, 36, 37, 42, 46, 105
Cornick v Cornick [1994] 2 FLR 530 . . . 414, 415
Cossey v United Kingdom (App No 10843/84, ECHR) (1993) . . . 37, 38, 45
Courten v United Kingdom (App No 4479/06, ECHR) (2008) . . . 123
Coventry City Council v C [2012] EWHC 2190 . . . 828
Coventry City Council v O (Adoption) [2011] EWCA Civ 729 . . . 932, 933
Cowan v Cowan [2001] EWCA Civ 679 . . . 387
Cox v Jones [2004] EWHC 1486 . . . 475
CPS v Piper [2012] EWHC 3570 . . . 473, 476
CR v CR [2007] EWHC 3334 . . . 376, 380, 401
Crake v Supplementary Benefits Commission [1982] 1 All ER 498 . . . 119, 209
Critchell v Critchell [2015] EWCA Civ 436 . . . 415
Crossley v Crossley [2007] EWCA Civ 1491 . . . 427
Crozier v Crozier [1994] Fam 114 . . . 328
Culliford v Thorpe [2018] EWHC 426 . . . 476, 479
Curley v Parkes [2004] EWCA Civ 1515 . . . 455
Curran v Collins [2015] EWCA Civ 404 . . . 462, 471, 472, 473, 475

D (A Child) (Care Order: Evidence), Re [2010] EWCA Civ 1000 . . . 855
D (A Minor) (Care or Supervision Order), Re [1993] 2 FLR 423 . . . 886
D (A Minor) (Wardship: Sterilisation), Re [1976] Fam 185 . . . 592, 598
D (Care: Natural Parent Presumption), Re [1999] 1 FLR 134 . . . 759
D (Children) (Non-Accidental Injury), Re [2009] EWCA Civ 472 . . . 859
D (Contact and Parental Responsibility: Lesbian Mothers and Known Father) (No 2), Re [2006] EWHC 2 . . . 690, 691, 703, 712
D (Contact: Reasons for Refusal), Re [1997] 2 FLR 48 . . . 770, 790
D (Contact: Supervisor's Fees), Re [2016] EWCA Civ 89 . . . 767
D (Domestic Violence: Court Orders), Re [2014] EWHC 2355 . . . 715
D (International Recognition), Re [2016] EWCA Civ 12 . . . 570
D (Intractable Contact Dispute: Publicity), Re [2004] EWHC 727 . . . 6, 799
D (Paternity), Re [2006] EWHC 3545 . . . 627, 628
D (Prohibited Steps Order), Re [1996] 2 FLR 273 . . . 766, 800
D (Residence Order: Deprivation of Liberty), Re [2019] UKSC 42 . . . 679, 680
D (Withdrawal of Parental Responsibility), Re [2014] EWCA Civ 315 . . . 716, 717
D v D (County Court Jurisdiction: Injunctions) [1993] 2 FLR 802 . . . 838
D v D (Nullity: Statutory Bar) [1979] Fam 70 . . . 89, 105
D v D (Shared Residence Order) [2000] EWCA Civ 3009 . . . 746, 747–8, 752
D v East Berkshire Community Health NHS Trust [2003] EWCA Civ 1151 . . . 819
D v East Berkshire Community Health NHS Trust [2005] UKHL 23 . . . 820
D and H (Care: Termination of Contact) [1997] 1 FLR 841 . . . 884
D O'H (Children), Re [2011] EWCA Civ 1343 . . . 876
da Silva Mouta v Portugal (App No 33290/96, ECHR) (1999) . . . 19, 550, 755
Damnjonovic v Serbia (App No 5222/07, ECHR) (2009) . . . 798
Darke v Strout [2003] EWCA Civ 176 . . . 321
Darnton v Darnton [2006] EWCA Civ 1081 . . . 144
Davies v Davies [2016] EWCA Civ 463 . . . 477
Davis v Johnson [1979] AC 264 . . 230
Dawson v Wearmouth [1999] UKHL 18, [1999] 2 AC 308, [1998] Fam 75 . . . 589, 708, 765, 800, 810
Day v Day [1980] Fam 29 . . . 146
DB v DLJ (Challenge to Arbitral Award) [2016] EWHC 324 . . . 27, 416, 418
DB v PB (Pre-Nuptial Agreement: Jurisdiction) [2016] EWHC 3431 . . . 280
D-E v A-G, falsely calling herself D-E (1845) 1 Rob Eccl 279 . . . 104
DE (Care Order: Change of Care Plan), Re [2014] EWFC 6 . . . 714, 876
DE v AB [2011] EWHC 3792 . . . 312, 313
De Lasala v De Lasala [1980] AC 546 . . . 417
Delaney v Delaney [1991] FCR 161 . . . 368, 370, 373–4
Demetriou v DPP [2012] EWHC 2443 . . . 201
Dickson v Rennie [2014] EWHC 4306 . . . 303, 305
Dickson v United Kingdom (App No 44362/04, ECHR) (2007) . . . 634, 635, 636–7
Dinch v Dinch [1987] 1 WLR 252 . . . 420
Dixon v Marchant [2008] EWCA Civ 11 . . . 415
DL v A Local Authority [2012] EWCA Civ 253 . . . 265

DL, ML v London Borough of Newham [2011] EWHC 1127 . . . 931
DN v HN [2014] EWHC 3435 . . . 422
Dobson v Griffey [2018] EWHC 1117 . . . 448–9, 462, 474, 476, 487, 491, 514
Dodsworth v Dodsworth (1973) 228 EG 1115 . . . 479
Dolan v Corby [2011] EWCA Civ 1664 . . . 224, 239
Dorney-Kingdom v Dorney-Kingdom [2000] 3 FCR 20 . . . 306
Down Lisburn Health and Social Services Trust v H [2006] UKHL 36 . . . 962
Draper v United Kingdom (App No 8186/78, ECHR) (1980) . . . 59, 65
Dredge v Dredge (otherwise Harrison) [1947] 1 All ER 29 . . . 105
D-S (Contact with Children in Care: Covid-19), Re [2020] EWCA Civ 1031 . . . 882
Dudgeon v UK (1981) 4 EHRR 149 . . . 41
Dukali v Lamrani [2012] EWHC 1748 . . . 83
Durham v Durham (1885) 10 PD 80 . . . 62
Duxbury v Duxbury [1990] 2 All ER 77 . . . 400, 409
DW v CMEC [2010] UKUT 196 (ACC) . . . 295
Dyer v Dyer (1788) 2 Cox Eq Cas 92 . . . 455
Dyson Holdings Ltd v Fox [1976] QB 503 . . . 115

E (A Child: Burial Arrangements), Re [2019] EWHC 3639 . . . 606
E (A Minor) (Wardship: Medical Treatment), Re [1992] 2 FCR 219 . . . 576, 578
E (Adoption by One Person), Re [2021] EWFC 45 . . . 113
E (Children in Care: Contact), Re [1994] 1 FCR 584 . . . 881, 884
E (Minors: Blood Transfusion), Re [2021] EWCA Civ 1888 . . . 580
E (Residence: Imposition of Conditions), Re [1997] EWCA Civ 3084 . . . 766, 802
E (SA) (A Minor) (Wardship), Re [1984] 1 WLR 156 . . . 598, 599
E (Wardship Order: Child in Voluntary Accommodation), Re [2012] EWCA Civ 1773 . . . 834
E v C (Calculation of Child Maintenance) [1996] 1 FLR 472 . . . 316
E v L [2021] EWFC 60 (Fam) . . . 385
Edgar v Edgar [1980] 1 WLR 1410 . . . 323, 422–3, 424, 425, 427, 429, 511
Egeneonu v Egeneonu (Adjournment of Committal Application) [2017] EWHC 2451 . . . 795
EH v Greenwich London Borough Council; Re A (Children) (Non-Accidental Injury) [2010] EWCA Civ 344 . . . 821
EJ (as attorney for DMM) v SD [2017] EWCOP 32 . . . 97
El Gamal v Al Maktoum [2011] EWHC 3763 . . . 81
Elliott v Elliott [2001] 1 FCR 477 . . . 369
Ely v Robson [2016] EWCA Civ 774 . . . 510
E-R (Child Arrangements) (No 2), Re [2017] EWHC 2382 . . . 766
E-R (Child Arrangements), Re [2015] EWCA Civ 405 . . . 742, 763, 764
Erlam v Rahman [2016] EWHC 111 . . . 457
Evans v Amicus Healthcare Ltd [2004] EWCA Civ 727 . . . 633, 634–5
Evans v Evans [1989] 1 FLR 351 . . . 404
Evans v Evans [2013] EWHC 506 . . . 394
Evans v United Kingdom (App No 6339/05, ECHR) (2007) . . . 633, 634, 635
Eves v Eves [1975] 1 WLR 1338 . . . 471, 473, 475, 489

F, Re; F v Lambeth London Borough Council [2002] 1 FLR 217 . . . 871, 900
F (A Child), Re [2009] EWCA Civ 313 . . . 742–3
F (A Child) (Placement Order), Re [2008] EWCA Civ 439 . . . 932
F (A Minor) (Blood Tests: Parental Rights), Re [1993] Fam 314 . . . 623, 624, 628
F (Assessment of Birth Family), Re [2021] EWFC 31 . . . 918
F (Children: Contact, Name, Parental Responsibility), Re [2014] EWFC 42 . . . 811
F (Internal Relocation), Re [2010] EWCA Civ 1428 . . . 802
F (International Relocation Cases), Re [2015] EWCA Civ 882 . . . 533, 803–4
F (Paternity Jurisdiction), Re [2007] EWCA Civ 873 . . 629
F (Placement Order: Proportionality), Re [2018] EWCA Civ 2761 . . . 926, 929
F (Shared Residence Order), Re [2003] EWCA Civ 592 . . . 748, 749
F v Child Support Agency [1999] 2 FLR 244 . . . 629
F v F (2008) 38 FL 183 . . . 406
F v F (Clean Break: Balance of Fairness) [2003] 1 FLR 847 . . . 397
F v G (Child: Financial Provision) [2004] EWHC 1848 . . . 319
F v M [2021] EWFC 4 . . . 784, 785
F v Switzerland (App No 11329/85, ECHR) (1987) . . . 131, 168, 169
F and G (Discharge of Special Guardianship Order), Re [2021] EWCA Civ 622 . . . 887
F and M (Thai Surrogacy: Enduring Family Relationship), Re [2016] EWHC 1594 . . . 113, 663
FB v PS [2015] EWHC 2797 . . . 386
FF v KF [2017] EWHC 1093 . . . 371
Fisher v Fisher [1989] 1 FLR 432 . . . 373
Fisher-Aziz v Aziz [2010] EWCA Civ 673 . . . 369

Fitzpatrick v Sterling Housing Association Ltd [1998] Ch 304 (CA) . . . 115–16
Fitzpatrick v Sterling Housing Association Ltd [2001] 1 AC 27 (HL) . . . 31, 39, 51, 116–17, 118, 124–5
Flavell v Flavell [1997] 1 FLR 353 . . . 409, 410, 411
Fleming v Fleming [2003] EWCA Civ 1841 . . . 409, 410
Ford v Ford (1987) 17 Fam Law 232 . . . 106
Foster v Foster [2003] EWCA Civ 565 . . . 384
Fowler v Barron [2008] EWCA Civ 377 . . . 466, 467, 468–9, 473, 482, 488, 489, 490
Frasik v Poland (App No 22933/02, ECHR) (2010) . . . 65
Fretté v France (App No 36515/97, ECHR) (2003) . . . 7, 549
FS v RS and another [2020] EWFC 63 . . . 309
Furniss v Furniss (1982) 3 FLR 46 . . . 368

G (A Child) (Order: Restriction on Applications), Re [2008] EWCA Civ 1468 . . . 728
G (A Minor) (Blood Test), Re [1994] 1 FLR 495 . . . 628
G (A Minor) (Interim Care Order: Residential Assessment), Re [2005] UKHL 68 . . . 898–9
G (A Minor) (Parental Responsibility Order), Re [1994] 1 FLR 504 . . . 686, 687
G (Care: Challenge to Local Authority's Decision), Re [2003] EWHC 551 . . . 820, 837, 878
G (Care Orders), Re [2010] EWCA Civ 1271 . . . 875
G (Care Proceedings: Threshold Conditions), Re [2001] EWCA Civ 968 . . . 842, 845
G (Care Proceedings: Welfare Evaluation), Re [2013] EWCA Civ 965 . . . 864, 867, 926
G (Children), Re [2005] EWCA Civ 1283 . . . 589
G (Children: Fair Hearing), Re [2019] EWCA Civ 126 . . . 895
G (Children) (Residence: Same-Sex Partner), Re [2006] UKHL 43 . . . 602, 604–5, 755, 758, 761–2, 763
G (Declaration of Parentage: Removal of Person Identified as Mother from Birth Certificate) (No 1), Re [2018] EWHC 3379 . . . 570, 610, 615, 758
G (Declaration of Parentage: Removal of Person Identified as Mother from Birth Certificate) (No 2), Re [2018] EWHC 3361 . . . 610, 615, 758
G (Discharge of Care Orders: Injunction Under Human Rights Act), Re [2019] EWCA Civ 1779 . . . 876
G (Education: Religious Upbringing), Re [2012] EWCA Civ 1233 . . . 21, 531, 532, 756–7, 800
G (Financial Provision: Liberty to Restore Application for Lump Sum), Re [2004] EWHC 88 . . . 371
G (Minors) (Interim Care Order), Re [1993] 2 FCR 557 . . . 896
G (Parental Responsibility: Education), Re [1995] 2 FCR 53 . . . 707
G (Parental Responsibility Order), Re [2006] EWCA Civ 745 . . . 689
G (Residence: Same-Sex Partner), Re [2006] EWCA Civ 372 . . . 755
G (Shared Residence: Biological Mother of Donor Egg Children), Re [2014] EWCA Civ 336 . . . 755, 758
G (Sperm Donor: Contact Order), Re; Re Z (Sperm Donor: Contact Order) [2013] EWHC 134 . . . 778
G v F (Non-Molestation Order: Jurisdiction) [2000] Fam 186 . . . 209–10
G v G [2012] EWHC 167 . . . 367, 411
G v G (Financial Provision: Equal Division) [2002] EWHC 1339 . . . 393
G v G (Occupation Order) [2000] 3 FCR 53 . . . 223, 232, 235
G v G (Parental Order: Revocation) [2012] EWHC 1979 . . . 666
G v M (1885) 10 App Cas 171 . . . 105
G v N County Council [2009] 1 FLR 774 . . . 878
G v W [2022] EWHC 1101 . . . 305
Gallarotti v Sebastianelli [2012] EWCA Civ 865 . . . 457, 458, 470, 476
Galloway v Goldstein [2012] EWHC 60 . . . 83
Gammans v Ekins [1950] 2 KB 328 . . . 115
Gandhi v Patel [2002] 1 FLR 603 . . . 82
Garcia v Garcia [1992] Fam 83 . . . 167
Gard litigation *see* Yates v Great Ormond Street Hospital [2017]
Geary v Rankine [2012] EWCA Civ 555 . . . 462, 472, 474
Gereis v Yagoub [1997] 1 FLR 854 . . . 82, 88
Ghaidan v Godin-Mendoza [2004] UKHL 30 . . . 9, 39–41, 43, 44
Gillick v West Norfolk and Wisbech Area Health Authority [1986] AC 112 . . . 567, 571–83, 591, 674, 675–6, 712
Gissing v Gissing [1971] AC 886 . . . 455, 459, 461, 463
Glaser v United Kingdom (App No 32346/96, ECHR) (2000) . . . 6, 551, 769, 798
Gloucestershire County Council v P [2000] Fam 1 . . . 726
Gnahoré v France (App No 40031/98) (2000) . . . 555
Gohil v Gohil [2015] UKSC 61 . . . 357, 414, 416
Goodman v Gallant [1986] Fam 106 . . . 451
Goodwin v United Kingdom (App No 28957/95, ECHR) (2002) . . . 9, 17, 36, 106
Goodyear v Goodyear (Deceased) [2022] EWFC 96 . . . 415
Görgülü v Germany (App No 74969/01, ECHR) (2004) . . . 555, 760

Gow v Grant [2012] UKSC 29 . . . 490, 522–3
GR v CMEC (CSM) [2011] UKUT 101 . . . 287
Graham-York v York [2015] EWCA Civ 72 . . . 464, 470, 475, 476, 492
Grant v Edwards [1986] Ch 638 . . . 471, 475, 478, 488, 489
Greasley v Cooke [1980] 1 WLR 1306 . . . 478, 479, 495
Green v Adams (No 2) [2017] EWFC 52 . . . 295, 345–6
Green v Secretary of State for Work and Pensions and Adams [2018] UKUT 377 . . . 296
Grey v Grey [2009] EWCA Civ 1424 . . . 374
Grey v Grey (No 3) [2010] EWHC 1055 . . . 374
Griffiths v Dawson & Co [1993] 2 FLR 315 . . . 167
Griffiths v Griffiths [2022] EWHC 113 . . . 767
Grigson v Grigson [1974] 1 WLR 228 . . . 168
Grimes (otherwise Edwards) v Grimes [1948] P 323 . . . 105
Gross v French (1976) 238 EG 39 . . . 455
Grubb v Grubb [2009] EWCA Civ 976 . . . 224, 238
GS v L [2011] EWHC 1759 . . . 430
Guerroudj v Rymarczyk [2015] EWCA Civ 743 . . . 503
Guest v Guest [2022] UKSC 27 . . . 477, 479–80, 494–5
Gull v Gull [2007] EWCA Civ 900 . . . 216
Gully v Dix [2004] EWCA Civ 139 . . . 114, 503
Gunn-Russo v Nugent Care Society and Secretary of State for Health [2001] EWHC 566 . . . 957
GW v RW (Financial Provision: Departure from Equality) [2003] EWHC 611, [2003] 2 FLR 108 . . . 316–17, 321, 362, 367, 384

H, Re [2001] 1 FCR 350 . . . 895
H (A Child), Re [2014] EWCA Civ 271 . . . 777
H (A Child: Surrogacy Breakdown), Re [2016] EWFC 80 . . . 667
H (A Child: Surrogacy Breakdown), Re [2017] EWCA Civ 1798 . . . 663, 668
H (A Minor) (Blood Tests: Parental Rights), Re [1997] Fam 89 . . . 535, 624–5, 627, 628, 650, 651, 958
H (A Minor) (Contact), Re [1994] 2 FCR 419 . . . 770, 777
H (A Minor: Custody), Re [1990] 1 FLR 51 . . . 739
H (A Minor) (Section 37 Direction), Re [1993] 2 FLR 541 . . . 839, 845
H (A Minor) (Shared Residence), Re [1994] 1 FLR 717 . . . 746
H (Care and Adoption: Assessment of Wider Family), Re [2019] EWFC 10 . . . 918
H (Care Proceedings: Children's Guardian), Re [2002] 1 FCR 251 . . . 885
H (Children), Re [2009] EWCA Civ 245 . . . 748
H (Children), Re [2009] EWCA Civ 902 . . . 751
H (Children) (Contact Order) (No 2), Re [2001] 3 FCR 385 . . . 769
H (Children) (Termination of Contact), Re [2005] EWCA Civ 318 . . . 882
H (Minors) (Local Authority: Parental Rights) (No 3), Re [1991] Fam 151 . . . 685, 686
H (Minors) (Sexual Abuse: Standard of Proof), Re [1996] AC 563 . . . 231, 845, 846–8, 849, 850, 852, 854, 856, 860, 864, 865
H (Parental Responsibility: Maintenance), Re [1996] 1 FLR 867 . . . 339
H (Parental Responsibility: Vaccination), Re [2020] EWCA Civ 664 . . . 599, 710, 713, 879, 880
H (Prohibited Steps Order), Re [1995] 1 WLR 667 . . . 800
H (Residence Order: Child's Application for Leave), Re [1994] 1 FLR 26 . . . 727
H (Residence Order: Child's Application for Leave), Re [2000] 1 FLR 780 . . . 727
H (Respondent Under 18: Power of Arrest), Re [2001] 1 FCR 370 . . . 253
H v C [2009] EWHC 1527 . . . 319
H v H [2007] EWHC 459 . . . 392
H v H [2008] EWHC 935 . . . 390
H v H [2014] EWCA Civ 1523 . . . 378, 380
H v H (Financial Provision: Conduct) [1994] 2 FLR 801 . . . 405
H v H (Financial Relief: Attempted Murder as Conduct) [2005] EWHC 2911 . . . 404
H v R (No 1) [2020] EWFC 74 . . . 615–16
H v R (No 2) [2021] EWHC 1943 . . . 616
H v S (Surrogacy Agreement) [2015] EWFC 36 . . . 667
H v United Kingdom (App No 32185/20, ECHR) (2022) . . . 668
H and A, Re [2002] 1 FLR 1145 . . . 627
H and A (Children) (Paternity: Blood Test), Re [2002] EWCA Civ 383 . . . 617
Haase v Germany (App No 11057/02, ECHR) (2005) . . . 551, 820, 893
Hadjuova v Slovakia (App No 2660/03, ECHR) (2010) . . . 198
Hale v Tanner [2000] EWCA Civ 5570, [2000] 1 WLR 2377 . . . 253–4
Haley v Haley [2020] EWCA Civ 1369 . . . 416
Halpern et al v Attorney General of Canada et al (2003) 169 OAR 172 . . . 43
Hamilton v Hamilton [2013] EWCA Civ 13 . . . 358, 419
Hammerton v UK (App No 6287/10, ECHR) (2016) . . . 253
Hammond v Mitchell [1991] 1 WLR 1127 . . . 475, 485
Hannaford v Selby (1976) 239 EG 811 . . . 496, 502

Haroutunian v Jennings (1980) 1 FCR 62 . . . 314
Harris v Manahan [1997] 1 FLR 205 . . . 419
Harrogate BC v Simpson (1985) 17 HLR 205 . . . 38, 115
Hart v Hart [2017] EWCA Civ 1306 . . . 356, 365, 389, 390, 406
Harvey v Harvey [1982] Fam 83 . . . 359
Hashem v Shayif [2008] EWHC 2380 . . . 357, 408
Hayatleh v Modfy [2017] EWCA Civ 70 . . . 87
H-B (Contact), Re [2015] EWCA Civ 389 . . . 676, 677
HC v FW [2017] EWHC 3162 . . . 373
Helby v Rafferty [1979] 1 WLR 13 . . . 115, 120
Henry v Henry [2010] UKPC 3 . . . 478
Her Royal Highness Haya Bint Al Hussein v His Highness Mohammed Bin Rashid Al Maktoum [2021] EWFC 94 . . . 306, 314
HG (Specific Issue Order: Sterilisation), Re [1993] 1 FLR 587 . . . 800
HH; PH v Deputy Prosecutor of the Italian Republic, Genoa [2012] UKSC 25 . . . 569
Hill v Hill [1997] 1 FLR 730 (FD) . . . 415
Hill v Hill [1998] 1 FLR 198 (CA) . . . 407, 415
Hipgrave v Jones [2004] EWHC 2901 . . . 215
Hirani v Hirani (1983) 4 FLR 232 . . . 95
H-N (Domestic Abuse: Findings of Fact Hearings), Re [2021] EWCA Civ 448 . . . 784–5, 788
Hoffman v Austria (A/255-C, ECHR) (1994) . . . 551
Hokkanen v Finland (App No 19823/92, ECHR) (1994) . . . 769, 798
Holman v Howes [2007] EWCA Civ 877 . . . 469, 500
Holmes-Moorhouse v London Borough of Richmond upon Thames [2009] UKHL 7 . . . 360, 751, 752
Hopkins v Hopkins [2015] EWHC 812 . . . 429, 434
Horner v Horner [1982] Fam 90 . . . 213, 215
Horrocks v Foray [1976] 1 WLR 230 . . . 496, 509
Horton v Horton [1947] 2 All ER 871 . . . 105
Hudson v Hathaway [2022] EWCA Civ 1648 . . . 462
Hudson v Leigh [2009] EWHC 1306 . . . 79, 80–1, 84
Human Fertilisation and Embryology Act 2008 (Case G), Re [2016] EWHC 729 . . . 641
Humberside County Council v B [1993] 1 FLR 257 . . . 231, 862, 864
Huntingford v Hobbs [1993] 1 FLR 736 . . . 455
Hussain v Hussain [2021] EWHC 1954 . . . 475, 476
H-W (Care Proceedings), Re [2022] UKSC 17 . . . 831, 841, 867, 868–9
Hyde v Hyde (1866) LR 1 P&D 130 . . . 66
Hyman v Hyman [1929] AC 601 . . . 416, 418, 421, 422, 424, 426, 436, 510
Hypo-Mortgage Services Ltd v Robinson [1997] 2 FLR 71 . . . 496
I (Children: Child Assessment Order), Re [2020] EWCA Civ 281 . . . 836, 837
Ismailova v Russia (App No 37614/02, ECHR) (2007) . . . 756
IX v IY [2018] EWHC 3053 . . . 362
J (A Child) (Care Proceedings: Fair Trial), Re [2006] EWCA Civ 545 . . . 821
J (A Minor) (Contact), Re [1994] 1 FLR 729 . . . 770
J (Adoption: Appeal), Re [2018] EWFC 8 . . . 905
J (Care Proceedings: Possible Perpetrators), Re [2013] UKSC 9 . . . 846, 849, 850, 851–3, 854, 856, 861
J (Child's Religious Upbringing and Circumcision), Re [2000] 1 FCR 307 . . . 21
J (Contact Orders: Procedure), Re [2018] EWCA Civ 115 . . . 768
J (Income Support: Cohabitation), Re [1995] 1 FLR 660 . . . 119
J (Leave to Issue Application for Residence Order), Re [2002] EWCA Civ 1364 . . . 726
J (Minors) (Care: Care Plan), Re [1994] 1 FLR 253 . . . 870, 873
J (Specific Issue Order: Leave to Apply), Re [1995] 1 FLR 669 . . . 800
J v C [1970] AC 668 . . . 529, 544, 546, 547
J v C (Child: Financial Provision) [1998] 3 FCR 79 . . . 311, 313, 314
J v C (Void Marriage: Status of Children) [2006] EWCA Civ 551 . . . 683
J v J [1991] 2 FLR 385 . . . 746
J and K v L [2021] EWFC B104 . . . 309, 310
Jäggi v Switzerland (App No 58757/00, ECHR) (2006) . . . 620
James v Thomas [2007] EWCA Civ 1212 . . . 463, 473, 474, 475–6, 487, 490
Jennings v Human Fertilisation and Embryology Authority [2022] EWHC 1619 . . . 647
Jennings v Rice [2002] EWCA Civ 159 . . . 478, 479
JL v SL (No 2) (Financial Remedies: Rehearing: Non-Matrimonial Property) [2015] EWHC 360 . . . 386
JM (A Child) (Medical Treatment), Re [2015] EWHC 2832 . . . 594, 714
JM v CZ [2014] EWHC 1125 . . . 210, 248, 249
JM v KK [2021] EWFC 54 . . . 368
Johansen v Norway (1997) (App No 17383/90, ECHR) (1997) . . . 552, 554–5, 556, 557, 914, 921, 922, 952
Johnson v Walton [1990] 1 FLR 350 . . . 215
Johnston v Ireland (App No 9697/82, ECHR) (1986) . . . 123, 131
Jones (Alleged Contempt of Court), Re [2013] EWHC 2579 . . . 795
Jones v Jones [1976] Fam 8 . . . 371, 402

Jones v Jones [2011] EWCA Civ 41 . . . 365, 388, 389, 392
Jones v Kernott [2011] UKSC 53 . . . 455, 456, 457, 458, 459–60, 462, 463, 464, 465, 466, 469, 471, 472, 473, 476, 480, 481
Jones v Maynard [1951] Ch 572 . . . 508
Jones v Padavattan [1969] 1 WLR 328 . . . 509
Joram Developments Ltd v Sharratt [1979] 1 WLR 928 . . . 115
JP v LP [2014] EWHC 595 (Fam) . . . 664
JP v NP (Financial Remedies: Costs) [2014] EWHC 1101 . . . 361
JS (Disposal of Body), Re [2016] EWHC 2859 . . . 711, 727

K, Re [2005] EWHC 2956 . . . 21, 855
K, Re [2007] EWHC 393 . . . 870, 884
K (A Child), Re [2008] EWCA Civ 526 . . . 748
K (A Minor) (Ward: Care and Control), Re [1990] 1 WLR 431 . . . 759
K (Application to Remove from Jurisdiction), Re [1998] 2 FLR 1006 . . . 800
K (Care Proceedings: Joinder of Father), Re [1999] 2 FLR 408 . . . 839
K (Contact: Condition Ousting Parent from Family Home), Re [2011] EWCA Civ 1075 . . . 766
K (Forced Marriage: Passport Order), Re [2020] EWCA Civ 190 . . . 266, 274–5
K (Private Placement for Adoption), Re [1991] FCR 142 . . . 760, 941, 942
K (Residence Order: Securing Contact), Re [1999] 1 FLR 583 . . . 21
K (Threshold Findings), Re [2018] EWCA Civ 2044 . . . 841
K v K [2005] EWHC 2886 . . . 374
K v K (Ancillary Relief: Prenuptial Agreement) [2003] 1 FLR 120 . . . 427
K v K (Conduct) [1990] 2 FLR 225 . . . 405
K v K (Fact-Finding) [2022] EWCA Civ 468 . . . 26, 784, 786, 799
K v K (Financial Relief: Widow's Pension) [1997] 1 FLR 35 . . . 168
K v K (Financial Remedy Order Prior to Decree Nisi) [2016] EWFC 23 . . . 361
K v K (International Relocation: Shared Care Arrangement) [2011] EWCA Civ 793 . . . 802–3, 804
K v K (Minors: Property Transfer) [1992] 1 WLR 530 . . . 314
K v L [2010] EWCA Civ 125 . . . 403
K v L [2011] EWCA Civ 550 . . . 365, 388, 389, 391
K and T v Finland (App No 25702/94, ECHR) (2001) . . . 892
K, W and H (Minors) (Medical Treatment), Re [1993] 1 FLR 854 . . . 581
KA v Finland (App No 27751/95, ECHR) (2003) . . . 551
KA v MA (Pre-Nuptial Agreement: Needs) [2018] EWHC 499 . . . 427, 430, 431–2, 434, 438
Kaleta v Poland (App No 11375/02, ECHR) (2009) . . . 798
Karner v Austria (App No 40016/98, ECHR) (2004) . . . 39, 43
Kaur v Dhaliwal [2014] EWHC 1991 . . . 120
Kaur v Singh [1972] 1 WLR 105 . . . 106
Kautzor v Germany (App No 23338/09, ECHR) (2012) . . . 622
KC and NNC v City of Westminster Social and Community Services Department and anor [2008] EWCA Civ 198 . . . 92, 109
KD (A Minor) (Ward: Termination of Access) Re [1988] 1 AC 806 . . . 552, 758, 759, 760, 924
Kehoe v UK (App No 2010/06, ECHR) (2008) . . . 301
Kelly (orse Hyams) v Kelly (1932) 49 TLR 99 . . . 90
Kemmis v Kemmis [1988] 1 WLR 1307 . . . 405
Kent County Council v C [1993] FLR 308 . . . 884
Kernott v Jones [2010] EWCA Civ 578 . . . 462, 466, 469
Khan v United Kingdom (App No 11579/85, ECHR) (1986) . . . 76
Kiely v Kiely [1988] 1 FLR 248 . . . 313
Kingston upon Thames BC v Prince [1999] 1 FLR 593 . . . 496
KM v CV [2020] EWFC B22 . . . 360
Kopf v Austria (App No 1598/06, ECHR) (2012) . . . 772
Kosmopoulou v Greece (App No 60457/00, ECHR) (2004) . . . 549, 772
Kotke v Saffarini [2005] EWCA Civ 221 . . . 113, 120
KP (Abduction: Judge Meeting Child: Conduct of Interview), Re [2014] EWCA Civ 554 . . . 735, 863
Kremen v Agrest (No 11) [2012] EWHC 45 . . . 427
Kroon v Netherlands (App No 18535/91, ECHR) (1994) . . . 621–2
Kurt v Austria (App No 62903/15, ECHR) (2021) . . . 194, 195, 197
Kyte v Kyte [1988] Fam 145 . . . 404, 405

L, Re [2009] EWCA Civ 1239 . . . 624
L (A Child), Re; Re Oddin [2016] EWCA Civ 173 . . . 795
L (A Child) (Contact: Domestic Violence), Re [2001] Fam 260 . . . 738, 768, 771, 775–6, 780–1, 798–9
L (A Child: Step-Parent Adoption), Re [2021] EWCA Civ 801 . . . 951, 961
L (A Minor) (Care Proceedings: Wardship), Re [1991] 1 FLR 29 . . . 942–3
L (Adoption: Contacting Natural Father) [2007] EWHC 1771 . . . 916

L (Adoption: Identification of Possible Father) [2020] EWCA Civ 577 . . . 918
L (Care: Assessment: Fair Trial), Re [2002] EWHC 1379 . . . 820
L (Care Order: Prison Mother and Baby Unit), Re [2013] EWCA Civ 489 . . . 895
L (Care: Threshold Criteria), Re [2007] 1 FLR 2050 . . . 590, 842–3
L (Children), Re [2012] EWCA Civ 721 . . . 231, 238–9
L (Children) (Care Proceedings), Re [2006] EWCA Civ 1282 . . . 845
L (Injunction and Committal: Guardian ad Litem), Re (1997) 17 FL 91 . . . 241
L (Interim Care Order: Power of Court), Re [1996] 2 FLR 742 . . . 895
L (Minors) (Access Order: Enforcement), Re [1989] 2 FLR 359 . . . 794
L (Relocation: Second Appeal), Re [2017] EWCA Civ 2121 . . . 748, 785, 805
L (Sexual Abuse: Standard of Proof), Re [1996] 1 FLR 116 . . . 882
L (Surrogacy: Parental Order), Re [2010] EWHC 3146 . . . 662
L v Human Fertilisation and Embryology Authority [2008] EWHC 2149 . . . 646
L v L [2006] EWHC 956 . . . 359, 414, 417, 420
L v L [2008] EWHC 3328 . . . 390
L v L (Anticipatory Child Arrangements Order) [2017] EWHC 1212 . . . 724
L v P (Paternity Test: Child's Objections) [2011] EWHC 3399 . . . 620
L and M (Children: Private Law), Re [2014] EWHC 939 . . . 796
L-A (Care: Chronic Neglect), Re [2009] EWCA Civ 822 . . . 895
Lambert v Lambert [2002] EWCA Civ 1685 . . . 393
Lancashire County Council v B [2000] 2 AC 147 . . . 849, 850–1, 855, 856, 857–8, 859, 865
Langford v Secretary of State for Defence [2019] EWCA Civ 1721 . . . 120, 123
Langley v Liverpool City Council [2005] EWCA Civ 1173 . . . 889–90
Laskar v Laskar [2008] EWCA Civ 347 . . . 457, 458
Lauder v Lauder [2007] EWHC 1227 . . . 376, 379
Lawrence v Gallagher [2012] EWCA Civ 394 . . . 362
Layton v Martin [1986] 2 FLR 227 . . . 478
LC (Children) (Abduction: Habitual Residence: State of Mind of Child), Re [2014] UKSC 1 . . . 536, 730, 731
Le Foe v Le Foe and Woolwich plc [2001] 2 FLR 970 . . . 405, 406, 473
Leadbeater v Leadbeater [1985] FLR 789 . . . 378
Lebbink v Netherlands (App No 45582/99, ECHR) (2004) . . . 7, 550
Ledger-Beadell v Peach and Ledger-Beadell [2006] EWHC 2940 . . . 457
Leeds Teaching Hospital NHS Trust v A and others [2003] EWHC 259 . . . 641, 642
Leicester City Council v AB [2018] EWHC 1960 . . . 830, 855
Leicestershire County Council v G [1994] 2 FLR 329 . . . 886
LG (Re-Opening of Fact-Finding), Re [2017] EWHC 2626 . . . 782
Liden v Burton [2016] EWCA Civ 275 . . . 478
Lindo v Belisari (1795) 1 Hag Con 216 . . . 59
Lindop v Agus [2009] EWHC 1795 . . . 120
Lissimore v Downing [2003] 2 FLR 308 . . . 478, 479
Livesey v Jenkins [1985] AC 424 . . . 359, 414, 416, 417
Livingstone-Stallard v Livingstone-Stallard [1974] Fam 47 . . . 162
Lloyds Bank v Rosset [1991] 1 AC 107 . . . 471, 472, 473, 485, 486, 489
Logan v United Kingdom (App No 24875/94, ECHR) (1996) . . . 340
Lomas v Parle [2003] EWCA Civ 1804 . . . 253, 254
Lord Chancellor v Farooqi [2018] EWHC 3638 . . . 473
Loving v Virginia 388 US 1 (1967) . . . 45, 64
Luckwell v Limata [2014] EWHC 502 . . . 435
LW (Contact Order: Committal), Re [2010] EWCA Civ 1253 . . . 795

M (A Child) (Parental Responsibility Order), Re [2013] EWCA Civ 969 . . . 686, 728
M (A Minor) (Care Orders: Threshold Conditions), Re [1994] 2 AC 424 . . . 844–5
M (A Minor) (Contempt of Court: Committal of Court's Own Motion), Re [1999] Fam 263 . . . 794
M (Care: Challenging Decisions by Local Authority), Re [2001] 2 FLR 1300 . . . 5, 837, 871
M (Care Proceedings: Judicial Review), Re [2003] EWHC 850 . . . 838
M (Children) (Contact), Re [2012] EWHC 1948 . . . 797, 798
M (Children) (Placement Order), Re [2007] EWCA Civ 1084 . . . 931, 932, 933
M (Contact: Long-Term Best Interests), Re [2005] EWCA Civ 1090 . . . 769
M (Contact: Parental Responsibility), Re [2001] 2 FLR 342 . . . 689
M (Fact-Finding Hearing: Burden of Proof), Re [2012] EWCA Civ 1580 . . . 860

M (Family Proceedings: Affidavits), Re [1995] 2 FLR 100 . . . 730
M (Minors) (Care Proceedings: Child's Wishes), Re [1994] 1 FLR 749 . . . 863
M (Minors) (Interim Care Order: Directions), Re [1996] 3 FCR 137 . . . 897
M (Ultra-Orthodox Judaism: Transgender), Re [2017] EWCA Civ 2164 . . . 21, 532–3, 755, 771
M v B (Ancillary Proceedings: Lump Sum) [1998] 1 FCR 213 . . . 369
M v C and Calderdale Metropolitan Borough Council [1994] Fam 1 . . . 724
M v D [2021] EWHC 1351 . . . 209
M v H (Private Law: Vaccination) [2020] EWFC 93 . . . 710
M v M [2004] EWHC 688 . . . 377
M v M (Child: Access) [1973] 2 All ER 81 . . . 768
M v M (Children) [2009] EWHC 3172 . . . 839
M v M (Parental Responsibility) [1999] 2 FLR 737 . . . 689
M v M (Pre-Nuptial Agreement) [2002] 1 FLR 654 . . . 427
M v M (Third Party Subpoena: Financial Conduct) [2006] 2 FCR 555 . . . 405
M v W (Non-Molestation Order: Duration) [2000] 1 FLR 107 . . . 217
M and B (Children) (Care Proceedings: Family Life), Re [2010] EWCA Civ . . . 821
M and R (Minors) (Sexual Abuse: Expert Evidence), Re [1996] 4 All ER 239 . . . 864–5
MA (Care Threshold), Re [2009] EWCA Civ 853 . . . 843
MA v JA [2012] EWHC 2219 . . . 84, 87
MA v RS (Contact: Parenting Roles) [2011] EWHC 2455 . . . 691
Mabon v Mabon [2005] EWCA Civ 634 . . . 583, 732–3
McCartney v Mills McCartney [2008] EWHC 401 . . . 366
MacDougall v SW (Sperm Donor: Parental Responsibility or Contact) [2022] EWFC 50 . . . 778
Macey v Macey (1982) 3 FLR 7 . . . 374
McFarlane v McFarlane (No 2) [2009] EWHC 891 . . . 378, 380
McFarlane; Parlour [2004] EWCA Civ 872 . . . 410
McKenzie v McKenzie [2003] 2 P&CR DG6 . . . 455
McLaughlin, Re [2018] UKSC 48 . . . 123
MacLeod v MacLeod [2008] UKPC 64 . . . 421, 424, 425, 426, 427
McMichael v United Kingdom (A/308, ECHR) (1995) . . . 701
Mahmood v Mahmood 1993 SLT 589 . . . 95
Mahmud v Mahmud 1994 SLT 599 . . . 92
Majrowski v Guy's and St Thomas' NHS Trust [2005] EWCA Civ 251 . . . 216
MAK and RK v United Kingdom (App Nos 45901/05 and 40146/06, ECHR) (2010) . . . 820
Mandet v France (App No 30955/12, ECHR) (2016) . . . 620
Manjra v Shaikh [2020] EWHC 1805 . . . 217
Mansfield v Mansfield [2011] EWCA Civ 1056 . . . 370
MAP v MFP (Financial Remedies: Add-Back) [2015] EWHC 627 . . . 406
MAP v RAP [2013] EWHC 4784 . . . 414
Marckx v Belgium (A/31, ECHR) (1979–80) . . . 7, 549, 550, 551
Marr v Collie [2017] UKPC 17 . . . 454, 458, 459, 476, 477, 481, 492
Martin v Martin [1978] Fam 12 . . . 359
Martin-Dye v Martin-Dye [2006] EWCA Civ 681 . . . 360
Maskell v Maskell [2001] EWCA Civ 858 . . . 415
Maskell v Maskell [2003] 1 FLR 1138 . . . 360
MBC v AM (DOLS Order for Children Under 16) [2021] EWHC 2472 . . . 598
M-D (A Child), Re [2014] EWCA Civ 1363 . . . 729
Mehta v Mehta [1945] 2 All ER 689 . . . 97
Mendal v Mendal [2007] EWCA Civ 437 . . . 407
Mercier v Mercier [1903] 2 Ch 98 . . . 455
Merritt v Merritt [1970] 1 WLR 1211 . . . 421
Mesher v Mesher [1980] 1 All ER 126 . . . 359
Metropolitan Properties Co Ltd v Cronan (1982) 44 P&CR 1 . . . 496
Michael v Chief Constable of South Wales [2015] UKSC 2 . . . 197
Middleton v Middleton [1998] 2 FLR 821 . . . 415
Midland Bank v Cooke [1995] 4 All ER 562 . . . 462
Midland Bank v Green (No 3) [1979] Ch 496 . . . 62
Midland Bank v Green (No 3) [1982] Ch 529 . . . 62
Mikulić v Croatia (App No 53176/99, ECHR) (2002) . . . 619, 620, 622
Militante v Ogunwomoju [1993] 2 FCR 355 . . . 97
Miller v Miller; McFarlane v McFarlane [2006] UKHL 24 . . . 349, 355, 357, 363, 364, 365, 366, 367, 371, 375, 376, 377, 380, 381, 383, 384–5, 386–8, 390, 392, 393–4, 395, 396, 397, 399, 401, 403, 408, 409, 410, 428, 438, 440, 464, 492, 517, 522
Miller Smith v Miller Smith [2009] EWCA Civ 1297 . . . 350
Mills v Mills [2018] UKSC 38 . . . 373
Minister for Home Affairs v Fourie, Case 60/04 Constitutional Court of South Africa . . . 64
Minkin v Landsberg [2015] EWCA Civ 1152 . . . 420, 421
M-J (A Child) (Adoption Order or Special Guardianship Order) [2007] EWCA Civ 56 . . . 969
M-M (Schedule 1 Provision), Re [2014] EWCA Civ 276 . . . 316

Montalto v Popat [2020] EWHC 810 . . . 503
Montreuil v Andreewitch [2020] EWHC 2068 . . . 505
Morgan v Hill [2006] EWCA Civ 1602 . . . 314, 315, 323
Morgan v Morgan [1959] P 92 . . . 106
Morris v Morris [2008] EWCA Civ 257 . . . 474, 490
Moss v Moss [1897] P 263 . . . 96, 97, 101
Mossop v Mossop [1989] Fam 77 . . . 455
MS v RS and BT (Paternity Testing) [2020] EWFC 30 . . . 613, 620–1
Ms L, Re; Re Ms M (Declaration of Parentage) [2022] EWFC 38 . . . 616
Muema v Muema [2013] EWHC 3864 . . . 405
Muñoz Díaz v Spain (App No 49151/07, ECHR) (2009) . . . 68, 71
Murphy v Murphy [2009] EWCA Civ 1258 . . . 377
Murphy v Murphy [2014] EWHC 2263 . . . 409, 410, 411
Mutch v Mutch [2016] EWCA Civ 370 . . . 409
MW v United Kingdom (App No 11313/02, ECHR) (2009) . . . 123
Myerson v Myerson [2009] EWCA Civ 282 . . . 397, 416
MZ v FZ [2022] EWHC 295 . . . 696, 715

N (A Child), Re [2007] EWCA Civ 1053 . . . 667, 668, 742
N (A Child), Re [2009] EWHC 11 . . . 310, 318
N (A Child) (Religion: Jehovah's Witness), Re [2011] EWHC 3737 . . . 758, 796
N (A Minor) (Access: Penal Notice), Re [1992] 1 FLR 134 . . . 793, 794
N (Abduction), Re [2020] EWFC 35 . . . 599
N (Children) (Adoption: Jurisdiction), Re [2015] EWCA Civ 1112 . . . 828, 829, 831
N (Surrogacy: Enduring Family Relationship: Child's Home), Re [2019] EWFC 21 . . . 663, 664
N v C [2013] EWHC 399 . . . 307, 309, 314
N v D [2008] 1 FLR 1629 . . . 312, 314, 319
N v F [2011] EWHC 586 . . . 370, 388, 389
N v N (Divorce: Ante-Nuptial Agreement) [1999] 2 FCR 583 . . . 169
N v N (Financial Provision: Sale of Company) [2001] 2 FLR 69 . . . 397, 398
NA v MA [2006] EWHC 2900 . . . 425, 427
Nasim v Nasim [2015] EWHC 2620 . . . 415
Neulinger and Shuruk v Switzerland (App No 41615/07, ECHR) (2010) . . . 555, 556, 557, 915, 922, 923
Newlon Housing Trust v Al-Sulaimen [1999] 1 AC 313 . . . 405
Niboyet v Niboyet (1878) 4 PD 1 . . . 59
Nightingale v Nightingale [2014] EWHC 77 . . . 406
Norris v Hudson [2005] EWHC 2934 . . . 500
North v North [2007] EWCA Civ 760 . . . 370, 373
North Yorkshire CC v SA [2003] EWCA Civ 839 . . . 859
Northamptonshire CC v S [1993] 1 FLR 554 . . . 867
Nottinghamshire County Council v P [1994] Fam 18 . . . 837, 839, 840–1
NS v MI [2006] EWHC 1646 . . . 91, 92
NS-H v Kingston upon Hull City Council [2008] EWCA Civ 493 . . . 932
Nutting v Southern Housing Group Ltd [2004] EWHC 2982 . . . 120
Nwogbe v Nwogbe [2000] 2 FLR 744 . . . 254, 359
NY (Abduction: Inherent Jurisdiction), Re [2019] UKSC 49 . . . 598, 599

O (A Child), Re [2009] EWCA Civ 1266 . . . 749
O (A Child) (Supervision Order: Future Harm), Re [2001] EWCA Civ 16 . . . 887
O (A Minor) (Care Order: Education: Procedure), Re [1992] 2 FLR 7 . . . 843
O (A Minor) (Contact: Indirect Contact), Re [1996] 1 FCR 317 . . . 769
O (A Minor) (Custody or Adoption), Re [1992] 1 FCR 378 . . . 760, 941
O (Adoption: Withholding Agreement), Re [1999] 2 FCR 262 . . . 943
O (Non-Accidental Injury), Re [2003] UKHL 18 . . . 850, 851
O v O (Jurisdiction: Jewish Divorce) [2000] 2 FLR 147 . . . 169
O v P [2014] EWHC 2225 . . . 311
O and N (Minors) (Care: Preliminary Hearing), Re [2003] UKHL 18 . . . 849, 865–6
Oberman v Collins [2020] EWHC 3533 . . . 473, 476
O'Donaghue v United Kingdom (App No 34848/07, ECHR) (2011) . . . 65, 70
Official Solicitor v Yemoh [2010] EWHC 3727 . . . 77
Oliari v Italy (App No 18766/11 and 36030/11, ECHR) (2015) . . . 43
O'Neill v Holland [2020] EWCA Civ 1583 . . . 459, 462, 475
Opuz v Turkey (App No 33401/02, ECHR) (2009) . . . 195, 196, 197–8, 199, 200
Orlandi v Italy (App No 26431/12 et al, ECHR) (2018) . . . 43 43
Osborne v Arnold [2022] EWHC 1983 . . . 615
Owens v Owens [2017] EWCA Civ 182 . . . 149, 162, 164, 166, 177
Owens v Owens [2018] UKSC 41 . . . 143, 157, 162–4
Oxfordshire County Council v B [1998] 3 FCR 521 . . . 867, 887

Oxfordshire County Council v X [2010] EWCA Civ 581 . . . 964
Oxley v Hiscock [2005] Fam 211 . . . 460

P, Re [2008] UKHL 38 . . . 123
P (A Child) (Adoption Order: Leave to Oppose Making of Adoption Order), Re [2007] EWCA Civ 616 . . . 937–8
P (A Child) (Adoption: Step-Parent), Re [2014] EWCA Civ 1174 . . . 693, 951–3
P (A Child: Financial Provision), Re [2003] EWCA Civ 837 . . . 309, 311, 314, 315, 317–19
P (A Child) (Residence Order: Child's Welfare), Re [2000] Fam 15 . . . 728
P (A Minor) (Contact), Re [1994] 2 FLR 374 . . . 779
P (A Minor) (Parental Responsibility Order), Re [1994] 1 FLR 578 . . . 688
P (Care Proceedings: Father's Application to be Joined as Party), Re [2001] 1 FLR 781 . . . 839
P (Children) (Adoption: Parental Consent), Re [2008] EWCA Civ 535 . . . 920, 921–2, 923, 925, 928, 953, 962–4
P (Children Act 1989, ss 22 and 26: Local Authority Compliance), Re [2000] 2 FLR 910 . . . 878
P (Emergency Protection Order), Re [1996] 1 FLR 482 . . . 892
P (Forced Marriage), Re [2011] EWHC 3467 . . . 92
P (Parental Responsibility), Re [1997] 2 FLR 722 . . . 686, 689
P (Parental Responsibility), Re [1998] 2 FLR 96 . . . 689
P (Terminating Parental Responsibility), Re [1995] 1 FLR 1048 . . . 716, 717
P v P (Variation of Post-Nuptial Settlement) [2015] EWCA Civ 447 . . . 358
P v R (Forced Marriage: Annulment: Procedure) [2003] 1 FLR 661 . . . 95
P and N (Section 19(14): Application for Permission to Apply: Appeal), Re [2019] EWHC 421 . . . 729
P, C and S v United Kingdom (App No 56547/00, ECHR) (2002) . . . 892
Palau-Martinez v France (App No 64927/01, ECHR) (2004) . . . 755
Pankhania v Chandegra [2012] EWCA Civ 1438 . . . 451
Paradiso and Campanelli v Italy (App No 25358/12) (2017) . . . 7, 549
Parker v Parker [2003] EWHC 1846 . . . 496
Parkes v Legal Aid Board [1997] 1 WLR 1547 . . . 500
Parlour v Parlour [2004] EWCA Civ 872 . . . 377
Parr v Parr [2013] EWHC 4105 . . . 357
Parrott v Parkin [2007] EWHC 210 . . . 505
Parry v United Kingdom (App No 42971/05, ECHR) (2006) . . . 101
Parveen v Hussain [2022] EWCA Civ 1434 . . . 170
Pascoe v Turner [1979] 1 WLR 431 . . . 479, 489
Paul v Constance [1977] 1 WLR 527 . . . 507
Pawndeep Singh v Entry Clearance Office, New Delhi [2004] EWCA Civ 1075 . . . 20
Payne v Payne [2001] EWCA Civ 166 . . . 552, 802, 803, 804, 805, 807
P-B (Contact: Committal), Re [2009] EWCA Civ 143 . . . 884
Peacock v Peacock [1984] 1 All ER 1069 . . . 370
Pearson v Franklin [1994] 1 WLR 370 . . . 800
Pettitt v Pettitt [1970] AC 777 . . . 455, 463, 485, 489
PF v CF [2016] EWHC 3117 . . . 231, 238
PG v TW (No 1) (Child: Financial Provision: Legal Funding) [2012] EWHC 1892 . . . 308, 314
Phillips v Peace [1996] 2 FCR 237 . . . 295, 303, 313, 345
Phillips v Peace [2004] EWHC 3180 . . . 308, 314
Pierce v Society of Sisters 268 US 510 (1925) . . . 843
Pippa Knight, Re [2021] EWCA Civ 362 . . . 528
PK v BC (Financial Remedies: Schedule 1) [2012] EWHC 1382 . . . 309
PK v Mr and Mrs K [2015] EWHC 2316 . . . 906
PM v United Kingdom (App No 6638/03, ECHR) (2006) . . . 123
Poel v Poel [1970] 1 WLR 1469 . . . 803
Potter v Potter (1975) 5 Fam Law 161 . . . 105
Pounds v Pounds [1994] 1 WLR 1535, [1994] 1 FLR 775 . . . 144, 361, 424–5
Pounds v Pounds [1999] 2 FLR 176 . . . 417–18
Premium Jet AG v Sutton [2017] EWHC 186 . . . 469
Prest v Petrodel Resources Ltd and others [2013] UKSC 34 . . . 357
Prokopovich v Russia (App No 58255/00, ECHR) (2006) . . . 496
P-S (Care Orders), Re [2018] EWCA Civ 1407 . . . 877
P-S (Care Proceedings: Right to Give Evidence), Re [2013] EWCA Civ 223 . . . 862, 863

Q (Adoption), Re [2012] EWCA Civ 1610 . . . 943
Q (Children: Interim Care Order: Jurisdiction), Re [2019] EWHC 512 . . . 896
Q v Q [2008] EWHC 1874 . . . 476
Q v Q (Ancillary Relief: Periodical Payments) [2005] EWHC 402 . . . 376
Qayyum v Hameed [2009] EWCA Civ 352 . . . 451
Quaintance v Tandan [2012] EWHC 4416 . . . 469
Queen, The v Jackson [1891] 1 QB 671 . . . 191–2

R (A Child) (Residence Order), Re [2009] EWCA Civ 358 . . . 759
R (A Minor) (Blood Transfusion), Re [1993] 2 FLR 757 . . . 592, 713, 800
R (A Minor) (Contact: Biological Father), Re [1993] 2 FLR 762 . . . 619
R (A Minor) (Residence: Religion), Re [1993] 2 FLR 163 . . . 756
R (A Minor) (Wardship: Consent to Treatment), Re [1992] Fam 11 . . . 577–9, 580, 581
R (Adoption: Contact), Re [2005] EWCA Civ 1128 . . . 962, 964, 965
R (Adoption: Judicial Approach), Re [2014] EWCA Civ 1625 . . . 926
R (Care Proceedings: Child's Right to Give Oral Evidence), Re [2015] EWCA Civ 167 . . . 863
R (Children), Re [2005] EWCA Civ 542 . . . 748
R (Children: Peremptory Return), Re [2011] EWCA Civ 558 . . . 806
R (Internal Relocation: Appeal), Re [2016] EWCA Civ 1016 . . . 806
R (No Order for Contact: Appeal), Re [2014] EWCA Civ 1664 . . . 770, 772
R (Parental Responsibility), Re [2011] EWHC 1535 . . . 777
R v B and Capita Trustees [2017] EWHC 33 . . . 402
R v Bham [1966] 1 QB 159 . . . 77
R v Briscoe [2010] EWCA Crim 373 . . . 258
R v Debnath [2005] EWCA Crim 3472 . . . 215
R v E and F (Female Parents: Known Father) [2010] EWHC 417 . . . 691
R v East Sussex County Council, *ex parte* W [1998] 2 FLR 1082 . . . 837
R v Ethical Committee of St Mary's Hospital (Manchester), *ex parte* H [1988] 1 FLR 512 . . . 633
R v Franks [2010] EWCA Crim 1030 . . . 258
R v Herrington [2017] EWCA Crim 889 . . . 266
R v HFEA, *ex parte* Blood [1999] Fam 151 . . . 646
R v Nicholson [2006] EWCA Crim 1518 . . . 255
R v Nottingham County Court, *ex parte* Byers [1985] 1 WLR 403 . . . 146
R v O'Neill [2016] EWCA Civ 92 . . . 216
R v R [1992] 1 AC 599 . . . 107, 192, 384
R v R [2011] EWHC 3093 . . . 365, 367
R v R [2013] EWHC 4244 . . . 405
R v R (Family Court: Procedural Fairness) [2014] EWFC 48 . . . 217, 248
R v Richards [2010] EWCA Crim 835 . . . 255
R v Secretary of State for the Home Department, *ex parte* Craven [2001] EWHC Admin 850 . . . 217
R v Secretary of State for Social Security, *ex parte* Biggin [1995] 1 FLR 851 . . . 293
R v Secretary of State for Social Security, *ex parte* W [1999] 2 FLR 604 . . . 614
R v Tameside Metropolitan BC, *ex parte* J [2000] 1 FCR 173 . . . 834
R v Thayaparan [2019] EWCA Crim 247 . . . 473, 476
R (A) v London Borough of Croydon [2009] UKSC 8 . . . 824
R (AB) v Secretary of State for Justice [2021] UKSC 28 . . . 570
R (Axon) v Secretary of State for Health [2006] QB 539 . . . 575
R (Baiai) v Secretary of State for Home Department [2008] UKHL 53 . . . 8, 64, 65, 70, 90
R (CD) v Isle of Anglesey County Council [2004] EWHC 1635 . . . 833
R (Crown Prosecution Service) v Registrar General of Births, Deaths and Marriages [2002] EWCA Civ 1661 . . . 63, 65
R (DA) v Secretary of State for Work and Pensions [2019] UKSC 21 . . . 569
R (Elan-Cane) v Secretary of State for the Home Department [2021] UKSC 56 . . . 16, 17
R (G) v Barnet London Borough Council [2003] UKHL 57 . . . 821, 824, 826–7
R (G) v London Borough of Southwark [2009] UKHL 26 . . . 826, 831
R (G) v Nottingham City Council [2008] EWHC 152 . . . 828, 829, 830
R (G) v Nottingham City Council [2008] EWHC 400 . . . 828
R (Gudanaviciene) v Director of Legal Aid Casework [2014] EWCA Civ 1622 . . . 23, 24
R (H) v Kingston upon Hull City Council [2013] EWHC 388 . . . 895
R (H) v Secretary of State for Health and Social Care [2019] EWHC 2095 . . . 668
R (H) v Wandsworth London Borough Council [2007] EWHC 1082 . . . 826
R (Hodkin and another) v Registrar General of Births, Deaths and Marriages [2013] UKSC 77 . . . 69
R (Kehoe) v Secretary of State for Work and Pensions [2005] UKHL 48 . . . 282, 299, 300, 325, 328, 329
R (M) v London Borough of Hammersmith and Fulham [2008] UKHL 14 . . . 826, 831
R (McConnell) v The Registrar General for England and Wales [2020] EWCA Civ 559 . . . 610, 611, 612
R (Mellor) v Secretary of State for the Home Department [2001] EWCA Civ 472 . . . 9
R (Plumb) v Secretary of State for Work and Pensions [2002] EWHC 1125 . . . 338
R (Rights of Women) v Secretary of State for Justice [2016] EWCA Civ 91 . . . 23, 24
R (Rose) v Secretary of State for Health [2002] EWHC 1593 . . . 650–1
R (S) v Swindon Borough Council [2001] EWHC 334 . . . 838

R (SC) v Secretary of State for Work and Pensions [2021] UKSC 26 . . . 569, 570
R (SG) v Secretary of State for Work and Pensions [2015] UKSC 16 . . . 535, 558, 569
R (Steinfeld and Keidan) v Secretary of State for International Development [2018] UKSC 32 . . . 16, 47, 59
R (TG) v Lambeth London Borough Council [2011] EWCA Civ 526 . . . 826
R (TT) v Registrar General for England and Wales [2019] EWHC 2384 . . . 610, 611
R (VC) v Newcastle City Council and Secretary of State for the Home Department [2011] EWHC 2673 . . . 824
R (Waxman) v CPS [2012] EWHC 133 . . . 198
R (Williamson) v Secretary of State for Education and Employment [2005] UKHL 15 . . . 594
R and H v United Kingdom (App No 35348/06, ECHR) (2011) . . . 556
Radmacher v Granatino [2010] UKSC 42, [2009] EWCA Civ 649 . . . 371, 379, 417, 422, 424, 425, 426–7, 428, 429–30, 432–3, 435, 436–7, 438, 439, 443, 444, 511
Rampal v Rampal (No 2) [2001] EWCA Civ 989, [2002] Fam 85 . . . 407, 408
Ramsay-Fairfax (orse Scott-Gibson) v Ramsay-Fairfax [1956] P 115 . . . 106
Raqeeb v Barts NHS Foundation Trust [2019] EWHC 2530 . . . 598
Ratcliffe v Secretary of State for Defence [2009] EWCA Civ 39 . . . 123
RC v JC [2020] EWHC 466 . . . 382, 401
Regina v R [1992] 1 AC 599 . . . 107, 192, 384
Reiterbund v Reiterbund [1974] 1 WLR 788 (HC) . . . 138
RH (A Minor) (Parental Responsibility), Re [1998] 2 FCR 89 . . . 686, 689
RH v SV [2020] EWFC B23 . . . 360
Richards v Richards [1984] 1 AC 174 . . . 230
Richardson v Richardson [2011] EWHC 79 . . . 415
Richardson v Richardson (No 2) [1994] 2 FLR 1051 (HC) . . . 366, 424
Richardson v Richardson (No 2) [1996] 2 FLR 617 (CA) . . . 417
Riley v Riley [1986] 2 FLR 429 . . . 747
RK and AK v United Kingdom (App No 38000/05, ECHR) (2008) . . . 820
Roberts v Roberts [1970] P 1 . . . 366, 373
Robertson v Robertson [2016] EWHC 613 . . . 366, 391, 395
Robinson v Murray [2005] EWCA Civ 935 . . . 253
Robson v Robson [2010] EWCA Civ 1171 . . . 365, 370, 385, 409
Rodriguez v Ministry of Housing of the Government of Gibraltar [2009] UKPC 52 . . . 41, 123
Rose v Rose [2002] EWCA Civ 208 . . . 416, 421
Ross v Collins [1964] 1 WLR 425 . . . 116, 124
Rowe v Prance [1999] 2 FLR 787 . . . 505–6
Rowland v Blades [2021] EWHC 426 . . . 457, 469
Roxar v Jaladoust [2017] EWHC 977 . . . 409
Roy v Roy [1996] 1 FLR 541 . . . 452
Rozanski v Poland (App No 55339/00, ECHR) (2006) . . . 622
RP v RP [2006] EWHC 3409 . . . 365, 376, 400
Rubin v Dweck [2012] BPIR 854 . . . 473, 476
Rubin v Rubin [2014] EWHC 611 . . . 361

S, Re; Re W (Section 20 Accommodation) [2023] EWCA Civ 1 . . . 589, 830, 831, 869
S (A Child), Re [2018] EWCA Civ 2512 . . . 876
S (A Child) (Adoption Order or Special Guardianship Order), Re [2007] EWCA Civ 54 . . . 920, 968–70
S (A Child) (Identification: Restrictions on Publication), Re [2003] EWCA Civ 963 . . . 568
S (A Child) (Identification: Restrictions on Publication), Re [2004] UKHL 47 . . . 535
S (A Minor) (Adoption: Blood Transfusion), Re [1995] 2 FCR 177 . . . 904
S (A Minor) (Custody), Re [1991] FCR 155 . . . 739
S (A Minor) (Parental Responsibility), Re [1995] 3 FCR 225 . . . 674, 687
S (Abduction: Hague and European Conventions), Re [1997] 1 FLR 958 (CA), aff'd [1998] 1 FLR 122 (HL) . . . 719
S (An Infant), Re [1958] 1 WLR 391 . . . 739
S (Care or Supervision Order), Re [1996] 1 FLR 753 . . . 885, 886
S (Children) (Restrictions on Applications), Re [2006] EWCA Civ 1190 . . . 729
S (Children) (Termination of Contact), Re [2004] EWCA Civ 1397 . . . 882
S (Contact: Application by Sibling), Re [1999] 1 Fam 283 . . . 726, 727, 777, 962
S (Contact: Children's Views), Re [2002] EWHC 540 . . . 730
S (Discharge of Care Order), Re [1995] 2 FLR 639 . . . 887
S (Minors) (Care Order: Implementation of Care Plan), Re [2002] UKHL 10 . . . 871–3, 874–5, 876
S (Parental Alienation: Cult), Re [2020] EWCA Civ 568 . . . 771, 790
S (Relocation: Interests of Siblings), Re [2011] EWCA Civ 454 . . . 536
S (Transfer of Residence), Re [2010] 1 FLR 1785 . . . 796
S (Unmarried Parents: Financial Provision), Re [2006] EWCA Civ 479 . . . 314
S v B [2004] EWHC 2089 . . . 359
S v F (Occupation Order) [2000] 3 FCR 365 . . . 226
S v J [2016] EWHC 559 . . . 469

S v J (Beneficial Ownership) [2016] EWHC 586 . . . 498
S v McC and M; W v W [1972] AC 24 . . . 617, 623, 624, 625, 627
S v P (Settlement by Collaborative Law Process) [2008] 2 FLR 2040 . . . 416
S v S [2006] EWHC 2793 . . . 404, 405
S v S [2008] EWHC 519 . . . 367
S v S (Ancillary Relief: Consent Order) [2002] EWHC 223 . . . 415
S v S (Financial Remedies: Arbitral Award) [2014] EWHC 7 . . . 27, 418
S v S (otherwise C) [1954] 3 All ER 736 . . . 105
S v V (Children: Leave to Remove) [2018] EWFC 28 . . . 805
S and D (Child Case: Powers of Court), Re [1995] 1 FCR 626 . . . 870
S and G v Italy (App Nos 39221/98 and 41963/98, ECHR) (2000) . . . 881
SA (Vulnerable Adult with Capacity: Marriage), Re [2005] EWHC 2942 . . . 66, 91, 96
SA v PA [2014] EWHC 392 . . . 376, 379, 380
Sahin v Germany; Sommerfeld v Germany (App No 30943/96, ECHR) (2003) . . . 6, 555
Salgueiro De Silva Mouta v Portugal (App No 33290/96, ECHR) (2001) . . . 7
Sandwell MBC v RG and others [2013] EWHC 2373 . . . 88, 99
Santos v Santos [1972] Fam 247 . . . 113, 114, 144
Saucedo Gomez v Spain (App No 37784/97, ECHR) (1999) . . . 112, 123
S-B (Non-Accidental Injury) [2009] UKSC 17 . . . 553, 850, 851, 855, 859, 867
SC (A Minor) (Leave to Seek Residence Order), Re [1994] 1 FLR 96 . . . 727
Scatliffe v Scatliffe [2016] UKPC 36 . . . 388
Schalk and Kopf v Austria (App No 30141/04, ECHR) (2010) . . . 7, 43, 106, 112
Schuller v Schuller [1990] 2 FLR 193 . . . 370
Scott (falsely called Sebright) v Sebright (1886) LR 12 PD 21 . . . 94–5
Seabrook v Sullivan [2014] EWHC 4110 . . . 500
Seaton v Seaton [1986] 2 FLR 398 . . . 373
Secretary of State for Work and Pensions v M [2006] UKHL 11 . . . 43
Sefton Holdings Ltd v Cairns (1987) 20 HLR . . . 124
Şerife Yiğit v Turkey (App No 3976/05, ECHR) (2009) . . . 68, 71
SH v Austria (App No 57813/00) (2007) . . . 638
SH v KH 2006 SC 129 . . . 91
Shackell v United Kingdom (App No 45851/99, ECHR) (2000) . . . 123, 126, 127
Sharland v Sharland [2015] UKSC 60 . . . 357, 414, 416
Sharp v Sharp [2017] EWCA Civ 408 . . . 396–7, 433
Sharpe (A Bankrupt), Re [1980] 1 WLR 219 . . . 455
Sheffield City Council v E and another [2004] EWHC 2808, [2005] Fam 326 . . . 62, 63, 97, 98–9
Sheffield City Council v Wall [2010] EWCA Civ 922 . . . 115
Siddiqui v Siddiqui [2020] EWFC 63 . . . 309
Siddiqui v Siddiqui [2021] EWCA Civ 1572 . . . 307, 309
Simister v Simister (No 1) [1987] 1 FLR 194 . . . 424
Simpson v United Kingdom (App No 11716/85, ECHR) (1986) . . . 38
Sims v Dacorum BC [2014] UKSC 63 . . . 503
Singh v Heer [2016] EWCA Civ 424 . . . 451
Singh v Kaur (1981) 11 Fam Law 152 . . . 94, 95
Singh v Singh [1971] P 226 . . . 94, 105
Singla v Browne [2007] EWHC 405 . . . 451
S (J) (A Minor) (Care or Supervision Order), Re [1993] 2 FCR 193 . . . 886
SK (Proposed Plaintiff) (An Adult by Way of her Litigation Friend), Re [2004] EWHC 3202 . . . 91
SL v CMEC (CSM) [2010] AACR 24 . . . 297
Slade v Slade [2009] EWCA Civ 748 . . . 254
Sledmore v Dalby (1996) 72 P&CR 196 . . . 479
Smith v Lancashire Teaching Hospitals NHS Foundation Trust [2017] EWCA Civ 1916 . . . 123
Smith v McInerney [1994] 2 FLR 1077 . . . 328, 424
Smith v Secretary of State for Work and Pensions [2006] UKHL 35 . . . 280, 295, 569
Smith v Smith [2000] 3 FCR 374 . . . 424
Smith v Smith (Smith and others Intervening) [1992] Fam 69 . . . 414, 415
Soar v Foster (1858) 4 K&J 152 . . . 455
Söderbäck v Sweden (App No 113/1997/897/1109, ECHR) (1998) . . . 951, 952
Sorrell v Sorrell [2005] EWHC 1717 . . . 394
South Glamorgan County Council v W and B [1993] 1 FLR 574 . . . 836, 891
Southwark London Borough Council v B [1998] 2 FLR 1095 . . . 845
Southwell v Blackburn [2014] EWCA Civ 1347 . . . 477, 478, 518
Sporer v Austria (App No 35637/03, ECHR) (2011) . . . 701
SR v HR [2018] EWHC 606 . . . 358, 413
SRJ v DWJ (Financial Provision) [1999] 3 FCR 153, [1999] 2 FLR 176 . . . 370, 377, 378, 379
SS v NS [2014] EWHC 4183 . . . 372, 409, 411
S-T (formerly J) v J [1998] Fam 103 . . . 67, 407

Stack v Dowden [2005] EWCA Civ 857 . . . 454, 499
Stack v Dowden [2007] UKHL 17 . . . 451, 452, 455, 456, 457, 458, 459, 460–3, 464–9, 470, 471, 472, 473, 476, 480, 481, 482, 486, 488, 490, 491, 492, 499
Steinfeld and Keidan v Secretary of State for Education [2017] EWCA Civ 81 . . . 55
Stevens v Stevens [1979] 1 WLR 885 . . . 149
Stoeckert v Geddes (No 2) [2004] UKPC 54 . . . 508
Strand Lobben v Norway (App No 37283/13, ECHR) (2019) . . . 556, 557
Stübing v Germany (App No 43547/08, ECHR) (2012) . . . 75
Sulaiman v Juffali [2002] 1 FLR 479 . . . 169
Sullivan v Sullivan, falsely called Oldacre (1818) 2 Hag Con 238 . . . 100
Suter v Suter [1987] Fam 111 . . . 366, 374
Sutton v Mischon de Reya and another [2003] EWHC 3166, [2004] 3 FCR 142 . . . 510
Swift v Secretary of State for Justice [2013] EWCA Civ 193 . . . 124
SY v SY (orse W) [1963] P 37 . . . 105
Szechter v Szechter (orse Karsov) [1971] P 286 . . . 93, 95

T (A Child), Re [2005] EWCA Civ 1397 . . . 758
T (A Child), Re [2017] EWCA Civ 1889 . . . 215
T (A Child) (Care Order), Re [2009] EWCA Civ 121 . . . 867
T (A Child) (DNA Tests: Paternity), Re [2001] 3 FCR 577 . . . 625, 626, 627
T (A Child: Murdered Parent), Re [2011] EWHC 1185 . . . 217, 223
T (A Minor) (Care or Supervision Order), Re [1994] 1 FLR 103 . . . 886
T (A Minor) (Wardship: Medical Treatment), Re [1997] 1 WLR 242 . . . 595
T (Abuse: Standard of Proof), Re [2004] EWCA Civ 558 . . . 861
T (Accommodation by Local Authority), Re [1995] 1 FLR 159 . . . 825
T (Children: Placement Order), Re [2008] EWCA Civ 248 . . . 928
T (Judicial Review: Local Authority Decisions Concerning Child in Need), Re [2003] EWHC 2515 . . . 833
T (Minors) (Custody: Religious Upbringing), Re (1981) 2 FLR 239 . . . 756, 757
T (Non-Accidental Injury), Re [2009] EWCA Civ 1208 . . . 867
T (Non-Molestation Order), Re [2017] EWCA Civ 1889 . . . 216
T (Placement Order), Re [2018] EWCA Civ 650 . . . 821, 868, 870, 877
T (Residential Parenting Assessment), Re [2011] EWCA Civ 812 . . . 899
T (Secure Accommodation of Child), Re [2021] UKSC 35 . . . 599
T (Suspension of Contact: Section 91(14) CA 1989), Re [2015] EWCA Civ 719 . . . 728
T v B [2010] EWHC 1444 . . . 284, 308
T v R (Maintenance after Remarriage: Agreement) [2016] EWFC 26 . . . 421, 422
T v T [2010] EWCA Civ 1366 . . . 682
T v T (Agreement not Embodied in Consent Order) [2013] EWHC B3 . . . 421, 424
T v Wakefield Metropolitan District Council [2008] EWCA Civ 199 . . . 885
T and M v OCC and C [2010] EWHC 964 . . . 113
Tanner v Tanner [1975] 1 WLR 1346 . . . 496, 510
Tavli v Turkey (App No 11449/02, ECHR) (2006) . . . 622
Tavoulareas v Tavoulareas [1998] 2 FLR 418 . . . 314
Taylor v Taylor [2017] EWHC 1080 . . . 452
Tchenguiz v Imerman [2010] EWCA Civ 908 . . . 357
Tee v Hillman [1999] 2 FLR 613 . . . 350
Thakkar v Thakkar [2016] EWHC 2488 . . . 168
Thomas v Thomas [1995] 2 FLR 668 . . . 357
Thompson v Hurst [2012] EWCA Civ 1752 . . . 462, 475, 476
Thompson v Park [1944] KB 408 . . . 496
Thomson v Humphrey [2009] EWHC 3576 . . . 474
Thorner v Major [2009] UKHL 18 . . . 477, 478
Thwaite v Thwaite (1981) 2 FLR 280 . . . 413
TJ v CV [2007] EWHC 1952 . . . 691
TL v Coventry City Council [2007] EWCA Civ 1383 . . . 933
TL v ML and others (Ancillary Relief: Claim Against Assets of Extended Family) [2005] EWHC 2860 . . . 357
Tommey v Tommey [1983] Fam 15 . . . 414
TP and KM v United Kingdom (App No 28945/95, ECHR) (2001) . . . 6, 819
Traharne v Limb [2022] EWFC 27 . . . 430
Treharne v Secretary of State for Work and Pensions [2008] EWHC 3222 . . . 325
T-S (Children: Care Proceedings), Re [2019] EWCA Civ 742 . . . 880
TT (Children: Discharge of Care Order), Re [2021] EWCA Civ 742 . . . 887

U (A Child) (Serious Injury: Standard of Proof), Re [2004] EWCA Civ 567 . . . 860

UD v DN [2021] EWCA Civ 1947 . . . 310, 314
UL v BK (Freezing Orders: Safeguards: Standard Examples) [2013] EWHC 1735 . . . 405

V (A Minor) (Adoption: Consent), Re [1987] Fam 57 . . . 961
V (A Minor) (Care or Supervision Order), Re [1996] 2 FCR 555 . . . 885, 886
V (Care: Pre-Birth Actions), Re [2004] EWCA Civ 1575 . . . 821
V (Long-term Fostering or Adoption), Re [2013] EWCA Civ 913 . . . 910
V v C [2004] EWHC 1739 . . . 410
V v M (Child Arrangements Order: International Relocation) [2020] EWHC 488 . . . 805
V v V [2011] EWHC 3230 . . . 430, 434
V v V (Child Maintenance) [2001] 2 FLR 799 . . . 304, 306
V v W [2020] EWFC B25 . . . 500, 501–2
Valier v Valier (otherwise Davis) (1925) 133 LT 830 . . . 97
Vallianatos v Greece (App Nos 29381/09 and 32684/09, ECHR) (2013) . . . 7, 9, 43, 112, 120
Van Kück v Germany (App No 35968/97, ECHR) (2003) . . . 6
Vaughan v Vaughan [1973] 1 WLR 1159 . . . 214–15
Vaughan v Vaughan [2007] EWCA Civ 1085 . . . 380
Vaughan v Vaughan (No 2) [2010] EWCA Civ 349 . . . 370, 373
VB v JP [2008] EWHC 112 . . . 365, 377, 379, 401
Venema v Netherlands (App No 35731/97, ECHR) (2003) . . . 551
Versteegh v Versteegh [2018] EWCA Civ 1050 . . . 390, 427, 430, 432, 433
Vervaeke (formerly Messina) v Smith and others [1983] 1 AC 145 . . . 31, 90–1, 93, 111, 138
Vicary v Vicary [1992] 2 FLR 271 . . . 414
Villiers v Villiers [2022] EWCA Civ 772 . . . 355
VK v Croatia (App No 38380/08, ECHR) (2012) . . . 131
Volodina v Russia (App No 41261/17, ECHR) (2019) . . . 197
VV v VV [2022] EWFC 41 . . . 385
VV v VV [2022] EWFC 46 . . . 406

W (A Child) (Adoption: Leave to Oppose), Re [2010] EWCA Civ 1535 . . . 938
W (A Child) (Illegitimate Child: Change of Surname), Re [2001] Fam 1 . . . 800, 810–11
W (A Child: Leave to Oppose Adoption), Re [2020] EWCA Civ 16 . . . 940
W (A Child) (Parental Contact: Prohibition), Re [2000] Fam 130 . . . 884
W (A Minor) (Contact), Re [1994] 2 FLR 441 . . . 771
W (A Minor) (Medical Treatment: Court's Jurisdiction), Re [1993] Fam 64 . . . 579, 580, 581
W (Care Proceedings: Court's Function), Re [2013] EWCA Civ 1227 . . . 868, 877
W (Care Proceedings: Leave to Apply), Re [2004] EWHC 3342 . . . 881
W (Children), Re [2009] EWCA Civ 59 . . . 814
W (Children) (Abuse: Oral Evidence), Re [2010] UKSC 12 . . . 731, 863
W (Children) (Change of Name), Re [2013] EWCA Civ 1488 . . . 811
W (Children: Domestic Violence), Re [2012] EWCA Civ 528 . . . 782
W (Contact: Application by Grandparent), Re [1997] 1 FLR 793 . . . 727
W (Direct Contact), Re [2012] EWCA Civ 999 . . . 676, 710, 769, 770
W (Parental Agreement with Local Authority), Re [2014] EWCA Civ 1065 . . . 828
W (Parental Responsibility Order: Inter-Relationship with Direct Contact), Re [2013] EWCA Civ 335 . . . 686
W (Secure Accommodation Order), Re [2016] EWCA Civ 804 . . . 831, 832
W (Shared Residence Order), Re [2009] EWCA Civ 370 . . . 748, 749
W v Ealing London Borough Council [1993] 2 FLR 788 . . . 689
W v H (Divorce: Financial remedies) [2020] EWFC B10 . . . 360
W v Norfolk County Council [2009] EWCA Civ 59 . . . 905
W v United Kingdom (App No 9749/82, ECHR) (1988) . . . 5, 7, 551
W v W [2009] EWHC 3076 . . . 380
W v W (Joinder of Trusts of Land Act and Children Act Applications) [2003] EWCA Civ 924 . . . 499, 500
W v W (Physical Inter-Sex) [2001] Fam 111 . . . 17
W and X (Surrogacy), Re [2022] EWFC 120 . . . 661
W (orse K) v W [1967] 1 WLR 1554 . . . 105
W (RJ) v W (SJ) [1972] Fam 152 . . . 308
W Sussex CC & the Chief Constable of Sussex Police v F, M, N, P and T [2018] EWHC 1702 . . . 273
WA v Executors of the Estate of HA and others [2015] EWHC 2233 . . . 386, 415
Wachtel v Wachtel [1973] Fam 72 . . . 356, 387, 402

Waggott v Waggott [2018] EWCA Civ 727 . . . 365, 377, 381–2, 392, 400, 411
Walkden v Walkden [2009] EWCA Civ 627 . . . 416
Wall v Munday [2018] EWHC 879 . . . 469
Walsh v Singh [2009] EWHC 3219 . . . 474
Warrender v Warrender (1835) 6 ER 1239, 2 Cl & F 488 . . . 83
Watson v Lucas [1980] 1 WLR 1493 . . . 120
Watson (Decd), Re [1999] 3 FCR 595 . . . 119–20
Wayling v Jones [1995] 2 FLR 1029 . . . 475, 478, 488, 489
WC v HC [2022] EWFC 22 . . . 430
WD v HD [2015] EWHC 1547 . . . 411
Webster v Webster [2008] EWHC 31 . . . 473
Wells v Wells [2002] EWCA Civ 476 . . . 397
Whiston v Whiston [1995] Fam 198 . . . 407, 408
White v White [2001] 1 AC 596 . . . 364, 370, 382–3, 384, 385, 386, 391, 393, 415, 428, 438, 440
Whitehouse-Piper v Stokes [2008] EWCA Civ 1049 . . . 361
Whiting v Whiting [1988] 1 WLR 565 . . . 373
Whitlock v Moree [2017] UKPC 44 . . . 507
Whittington Hospital NHS Trust v XX [2020] UKSC 14 . . . 657, 663, 664, 665
Wilkinson v Kitzinger [2006] EWHC 2022 . . . 42, 106
Williams v Lindley [2005] EWCA Civ 103 . . . 415
Williams v London Borough of Hackney [2018] UKSC 37 . . . 712, 822, 827, 828, 829–30, 831
Williams v Williams [1985] FLR 509 . . . 779
Williamson v Sheikh [2008] EWCA Civ 990 . . . 461
Wilson v Wilson [1973] 1 WLR 555 . . . 168
Windeler v Whitehall [1990] 2 FLR 505 . . . 506–7
WM v HM [2017] EWFC 25 . . . 389, 394
Wodzicki v Wodzicki [2017] EWCA Civ 95 . . . 457, 471
Work v Gray [2017] EWCA Civ 270 . . . 394, 395, 399
W-P (Children), Re [2019] EWCA Civ 1120 . . . 968
Wright v Wright [2015] EWCA Civ 201 . . . 410
WS v HS (Sale of Matrimonial Home) [2018] EWFC 11 . . . 358
WSCC v M, F and others [2010] EWHC 1914 . . . 887
WW v HW (Pre-Nuptial Agreement: Needs: Conduct) [2015] EWHC 1844 . . . 429, 435
Wyatt (A Child) (Medical Treatment: Parents' Consent), Re [2004] EWHC 2247 . . . 597
Wyatt v Vince [2015] UKSC 14 . . . 361, 372, 373, 375, 406, 407
Wyatt v Vince [2016] EWHC 1368 . . . 375

X (A Child: Foreign Surrogacy), Re [2018] EWFC 15 . . . 106, 664
X (Foreign Surrogacy: Death of Intended Parent), Re [2022] EWFC 34 . . . 664
X (Surrogacy: Death of Applicant), Re [2020] EWFC 39 . . . 664
X (Surrogacy: Time Limit), Re [2014] EWHC 3135 . . . 664
X v Federal Republic of Germany (App No 6167/73, ECHR) (1974) . . . 68
X v Latvia (App No 27853/09, ECHR GC) (2013) . . . 556
X v Netherlands 24 DR 176 . . . 638
X v X (Application for a Financial Remedies Order) [2016] EWHC 1995 . . . 394
X v X (Y and Z Intervening) [2002] 1 FLR 508 . . . 424
X v Y (Parental Order: Adult) [2022] EWFC 26 . . . 664
X and Y (Foreign Surrogacy), Re [2008] EWHC 3030 . . . 663, 665
X and Y v A Local Authority (Adoption: Procedure) [2009] EWHC 47 . . . 961, 962
X and Y v United Kingdom (App No 7229/75, ECHR) (1978) . . . 638
X Council v B (Emergency Protection Orders) [2004] EWHC 2015 . . . 893–4
X, Y and Z v United Kingdom (App No 21830/93, ECHR) (1997) . . . 7, 550
XW v XH [2017] EWFC 76 . . . 389, 394, 397
XW v XH (Financial Remedies: Business Assets) [2019] EWCA Civ 2262 . . . 395, 397
Xydhias v Xydhias [1999] 1 FLR 683 . . . 417, 421, 422

Y (Care Proceedings: Proportionality Assessment), Re [2014] EWCA Civ 1553 . . . 885
Y (Children in Care: Change of Nationality), Re [2020] EWCA Civ 1038 . . . 879, 880
Y (Children) (Occupation Order), Re [2000] 2 FCR 470 . . . 235
Y (Children) (Occupation Order), Re [2000] 2 FCR 481 . . . 237
Y (Removal from Jurisdiction: Failure to Consider Family Segmentation), Re [2014] EWCA Civ 1287 . . . 536
Y v Bulgaria (App No 9077/18, ECHR) (2022) . . . 197, 198
Y v Y (Financial Remedy: Marriage Contract) [2014] EWHC 2920 . . . 430
Y v Z [2017] EWFC 60 . . . 666
Yates v Great Ormond Street Hospital [2017] EWCA Civ 410 . . . 577, 593
Yates v Yates [2012] EWCA Civ 532 . . . 373
YC v United Kingdom (App No 4547/10, ECHR) (2012) . . . 553, 556, 868, 915, 922–3

Yeoman's Row Management Ltd v Cobbe [2008] UKHL 55 . . . 477, 478
York CC v C [2013] EWCA Civ 478 . . . 99
Young v Bristol Aeroplane Co Ltd [1944] KB 718 . . . 92
Young v Young [1993] 4 SCR 3 . . . 567
Young v Young [1998] 2 FLR 1131 . . . 406
Young v Young [2012] EWHC 138, [2013] EWHC 34 . . . 406
Yousef v Netherlands (App No 33711/96, ECHR) (2002) . . . 555

Z (A Child: Human Fertilisation and Embryology Act: Parental Order), Re [2015] EWFC 73 . . . 662
Z (A Minor) (Freedom of Publication), Re [1997] Fam 1 . . . 535, 800
Z (Egyptian Fostering: UK Adoption), Re [2016] EWHC 2963 . . . 570
Z (Embryo Adoption: Declaration of Non-Parentage), Re [2018] EWFC 68 . . . 684
Z (Interim Care Order) [2021] EWCA Civ 1755 . . . 731
Z (Surrogacy), Re [2022] EWFC 18 . . . 657
Z v United Kingdom (App No 29392/95, ECHR) (2001) . . . 5, 819
Z v Z (No 2) [2011] EWHC 2878 . . . 430, 433, 434
Z and Y (Leave to Withdraw Application for a Parental Order), Re [2019] EWFC 43 . . . 666
ZH (Tanzania) v Secretary of State for the Home Department [2011] UKSC 4 . . . 535, 554, 569

TABLE OF STATUTES

ENGLAND AND WALES

Administration of Estates Act 1925 . . . 447
Adoption Act 1926 . . . 906
Adoption Act 1976 . . . 692, 957, 962
s 6 . . . 913
s 15(3) . . . 934, 935
s 15(3)(a) . . . 935
s 15(3)(b) . . . 935
s 16 . . . 681
s 72 . . . 681
Adoption and Children Act 2002 . . . 529, 549, 553, 609, 663, 665, 684, 692, 873, 880, 901, 902, 908, 912–27, 930, 947, 951, 961, 962, 965, 967, 972
s 1 . . . 528, 662, 913, 921, 922, 923, 937, 952, 962, 963, 965, 969, 970
s 1(1) . . . 528, 927
s 1(1)–(2) . . . 912
s 1(2) . . . 528, 922, 932, 941
s 1(4) . . . 530, 913, 920, 921, 922, 961
s 1(4)(c) . . . 913, 922
s 1(4)(f) . . . 913, 922, 930, 961, 963, 970
s 1(5) . . . 947, 948, 949
s 1(6) . . . 925, 963
s 1(7) . . . 927, 932, 937, 963
s 1(8)(b) . . . 913
ss 18–29 . . . 927
s 18(3) . . . 930
s 19 . . . 834, 916, 931
s 19(1) . . . 927
s 19(3) . . . 927
s 20 . . . 915, 937
s 20(1) . . . 927
s 20(2) . . . 927
s 20(3) . . . 927
s 20(4)(a) . . . 927
s 20(4)(b) . . . 927
s 21 . . . 834, 927
s 21(1) . . . 927
s 21(2) . . . 927–8
s 21(4) . . . 931
s 22 . . . 928
s 24 . . . 880, 931, 932
s 24(1)–(2) . . . 931
s 24(2) . . . 963
s 24(2)–(3) . . . 931
s 24(5) . . . 932
s 25(1)–(2) . . . 930
s 25(3)–(4) . . . 930
s 25(4) . . . 963
s 26 . . . 930, 961, 963, 965
s 26(1) . . . 930
s 26(2)–(4) . . . 930
s 26(5) . . . 961, 963
s 27 . . . 963
s 27(1) . . . 930
s 27(2) . . . 930
s 27(4) . . . 930, 965
s 29(1) . . . 930
s 30(1) . . . 931
s 32(1) . . . 931
s 32(2) . . . 931
s 32(5) . . . 931
s 34(1) . . . 931
s 35(1) . . . 931
s 35(2) . . . 931
s 35(5) . . . 931
s 36 . . . 933
ss 36–37 . . . 933
s 38(5) . . . 933
s 39(3) . . . 933
s 40 . . . 933
s 42(2) . . . 933
s 42(3) . . . 933
s 42(4) . . . 933
s 42(5)–(6) . . . 933
s 42(6) . . . 933
s 42(7) . . . 933
s 44(2) . . . 933
s 44(3) . . . 933
s 44(4) . . . 933
s 44(5) . . . 933
s 46 . . . 616, 672, 903, 961
s 46(1) . . . 695, 903, 951
s 46(2) . . . 695, 903
s 46(2)(a) . . . 951
s 46(2)(b) . . . 887
s 46(3)(b) . . . 692
s 46(5) . . . 961
s 46(6) . . . 961, 963, 965
s 47 . . . 936, 937, 940

s 47(1) . . . 936
s 47(2) . . . 936
s 47(2)(b) . . . 915, 937
s 47(3) . . . 936, 937
s 47(4) . . . 936
s 47(4)(b)(i) . . . 939
s 47(4)(c) . . . 936
s 47(5) . . . 936, 937, 938, 939, 963
s 47(6) . . . 936
s 47(7) . . . 936, 937
s 50 . . . 934
s 51 . . . 934
s 51(2) . . . 692, 693
s 51(3)–(3A) . . . 934
s 51(4) . . . 934
s 51A . . . 961, 964, 965
s 51A(2)(b) . . . 962
s 51A(5) . . . 961
s 51A(8) . . . 961
s 51B . . . 965
s 52 . . . 915, 919, 927, 940, 952, 953
s 52(1) . . . 920, 921
s 52(1)(a) . . . 920
s 52(1)(b) . . . 553, 920, 921, 922, 925, 953
s 52(3) . . . 916
s 52(5) . . . 915
s 52(6) . . . 681, 916
s 55 . . . 904
s 56 . . . 956, 957
ss 56–65 . . . 956
s 57 . . . 957
s 57(5) . . . 957
s 58 . . . 957
s 60(2) . . . 956
s 60(2)(b) . . . 956
s 60(3) . . . 956
s 60(4) . . . 956
s 61(2) . . . 957
s 61(3) . . . 957
s 61(5) . . . 957
s 62(2) . . . 957
s 62(3) . . . 957
s 62(4) . . . 957
s 62(6)(a) . . . 957
s 62(6)(b) . . . 957
s 62(7) . . . 957
s 67 . . . 616, 672, 903
s 67(1) . . . 615, 616, 693, 695, 903, 951
s 67(2) . . . 616
s 67(2)(b) . . . 904
s 67(3) . . . 616, 903
s 67(3)(a) . . . 951
s 74 . . . 73, 75, 903
s 111 . . . 684
s 116 . . . 825
s 144 . . . 693
s 144(4)–(7) . . . 113
Anti-Social Behaviour, Crime and Policing Act
4 . . . 201201
s 121 . . . 271
Arbitration Act 1996 . . . 27

Births and Death Registration Act 1953
s 2 . . . 613
s 10 . . . 614, 684
s 10A . . . 684
British Nationality Act 1981 . . . 606
s 1(5) . . . 879

Child Abduction Act 1984 . . . 711, 801, 805
s 1 . . . 765, 805
s 2 . . . 828
Child Abduction and Custody Act 1985 . . . 801
Child Maintenance and Other Payments Act
2008 . . . 282, 325, 330
Child Support Act 1991 . . . 278, 283, 284, 285, 286, 287, 300, 301, 303, 306, 309, 310, 313, 326, 329, 335, 336, 337, 345, 447, 502, 513, 615
s 1 . . . 287, 326, 678
s 1(1) . . . 287, 606
s 1(2) . . . 287
s 1(3) . . . 287
s 2 . . . 287, 296, 298
s 3 . . . 286
s 3(2) . . . 286
s 3(3) . . . 286
s 3(3)(c) . . . 287
s 3(4) . . . 286
s 3(5) . . . 286
s 4 . . . 288, 299
s 4(1) . . . 299
s 4(2) . . . 299
s 4(2)(b) . . . 299
s 4(2A) . . . 288, 320
s 4(3) . . . 300
s 4(10) . . . 307, 316, 320
s 4(10)(aa) . . . 316, 321
s 7 . . . 309, 310
s 8 . . . 285, 299, 303
s 8(2) . . . 307
s 8(3) . . . 306
s 8(3A) . . . 304, 306
s 8(5) . . . 304
s 8(6) . . . 304, 305, 317
s 8(7) . . . 305
s 8(8) . . . 305, 310

s 8(9) . . . 305
s 8(10) . . . 307
s 8(11) . . . 320
s 9(1) . . . 321
s 9(2) . . . 321
s 9(2A) . . . 288, 320
s 9(3) . . . 321
s 9(4) . . . 321
s 10(1) . . . 321
s 10(2) . . . 321
s 14A . . . 298
s 16 . . . 294
s 26 . . . 286
ss 28A–28G . . . 293
s 28E(1) . . . 296
s 28E(2) . . . 296
s 28E(3) . . . 296
s 28E(4) . . . 296
s 28F(1) . . . 296
s 28F(2) . . . 296
ss 29–41A . . . 297
s 41A . . . 298
s 41C . . . 293
ss 41D–41E . . . 298
s 43 . . . 298
s 43A . . . 298
s 44 . . . 285, 307
s 54 . . . 286, 681
s 55 . . . 285
s 55(1) . . . 291
s 55(2) . . . 286
s 55(3) . . . 286
Sch 1, para 2 . . . 290
Sch 1, para 2(3) . . . 290
Sch 1, para 3 . . . 291
Sch 1, para 4 . . . 291
Sch 1, para 5 . . . 291
Sch 1, para 5A . . . 293
Sch 1, para 6 . . . 293
Sch 1, para 7 . . . 292
Sch 1, para 8 . . . 293
Sch 1, para 10 . . . 289
Sch 1, para 10(3) . . . 290
Sch 1, para 10C . . . 287
Sch 1, para 10C(4) . . . 291
Sch 1, para 10C(5) . . . 291
Sch 1, para 16(1) . . . 297
Sch 4A . . . 293
Sch 4B . . . 293
Sch 4B, para 2 . . . 294
Sch 4B, para 4 . . . 295
Child Support Act 1995
s 18(6) . . . 321
Children (Abolition of Defence of Reasonable Punishment) (Wales) Act 2020 . . . 680, 843
Children Act 1975 . . . 709
Children Act 1989 . . . 234, 235, 310, 311, 339, 448, 526, 529, 530, 534, 535, 543, 549, 552, 553, 554, 557, 583, 584, 586, 587, 589, 591, 592, 594, 595, 598, 599, 600, 624, 668, 673, 675, 676, 677, 680, 682, 692, 700, 701, 705, 708, 709, 713, 715, 716, 723–4, 728, 737, 795, 801, 810, 814, 816–19, 822, 824, 841, 865, 871, 872, 876, 880, 881, 882, 883, 887, 889, 898, 913, 924, 942, 947, 950, 951, 954, 955, 967
Pt II . . . 724
Pt III . . . 813, 816, 818, 821–35, 845, 899, 933
Pt IV . . . 244, 530, 727, 816, 822, 824, 831, 832, 835, 839, 840, 841, 857, 921
Pt V . . . 832, 835, 838, 888, 921
s 1 . . . 311, 528, 534, 535, 552, 571, 686, 736, 737, 758, 802, 803, 860, 864, 865, 882, 922
s 1(1) . . . 528, 589, 735, 752, 769, 922, 924
s 1(2) . . . 735, 875
s 1(2A) . . . 530, 736, 742, 767, 768, 769, 773, 779, 783, 784, 790, 793
s 1(2B) . . . 530, 746, 767, 769
s 1(3) . . . 529–30, 717, 730, 735, 736, 810, 862, 864, 912, 913, 922, 961, 969
s 1(3)–(4) . . . 767
s 1(3)(a) . . . 533, 730
s 1(3)(c) . . . 743
s 1(3)(e) . . . 864
s 1(3)(g) . . . 924, 925
s 1(4) . . . 530, 717, 862
s 1(5) . . . 584, 586, 588, 589, 711, 712, 717, 735, 818, 869, 925
s 1(6) . . . 530, 767, 784
s 2 . . . 707
s 2(1) . . . 682, 683
s 2(2) . . . 683
s 2(5) . . . 682
s 2(6) . . . 682
s 2(7) . . . 706, 707, 708, 709, 711
s 2(8) . . . 706
s 3 . . . 326, 676
s 3(1) . . . 589, 675, 679, 680, 681, 682
s 3(5) . . . 684, 718–19, 827, 830
s 4 . . . 614, 683, 684, 685, 694, 716, 719, 764
s 4(1) . . . 683–4
s 4(1C) . . . 684
s 4(2) . . . 684
s 4(2A) . . . 716
s 4(3) . . . 716
s 4(4) . . . 716
s 4A . . . 692, 693, 718, 951
s 4A(1) . . . 692
s 4ZA . . . 683, 694, 716, 764

s 4ZA(4)–(5) . . . 718
s 5 . . . 309
s 5(3) . . . 681, 695
s 5(4) . . . 695
s 5(6) . . . 695
s 6 . . . 695
s 7 . . . 730
s 8 . . . 309, 338, 577, 594, 663, 668, 711, 714, 723, 724–37, 778, 840, 867, 930, 952, 961, 963
s 8(1) . . . 723
s 8(2) . . . 735, 737
s 8(3)–(4) . . . 724, 839
s 9(1) . . . 714, 727, 800, 811
s 9(2) . . . 727, 840
s 9(3) . . . 726
s 9(5)(a) . . . 727, 800, 840
s 9(5)(b) . . . 800
s 9(6) . . . 737
s 9(6A)–(6B) . . . 737
s 10 . . . 535, 693, 714, 841
s 10(1) . . . 724, 737
s 10(2) . . . 724
s 10(4) . . . 309, 681, 724, 725
s 10(5) . . . 724–5
s 10(5A) . . . 725
s 10(5B) . . . 725
s 10(5C) . . . 725
s 10(8) . . . 727
s 10(9) . . . 726, 727, 729, 778, 932, 961
s 11(4) . . . 749
s 11(5) . . . 737
s 11(6) . . . 737
s 11(7) . . . 765, 766, 767, 841
s 11(7)(c) . . . 737
s 11(7)(d) . . . 766
s 11A–11G . . . 771
s 11A(5) . . . 783
s 11H(2) . . . 796
s 11H(6) . . . 796
s 11J(2)–(4) . . . 796
s 11L . . . 796
s 11M . . . 796
s 11O . . . 796
s 12(1) . . . 685, 694, 764
s 12(1A) . . . 685, 694, 755
s 12(2) . . . 681, 693, 694, 695, 718, 764
s 12(2A) . . . 694, 695, 749, 755
s 12(3) . . . 681, 695
s 12(4) . . . 716
s 13 . . . 680, 706, 708, 765, 801, 809, 811
s 13(1) . . . 682, 707, 708, 765
s 13(2) . . . 765, 801
s 13(3) . . . 765
s 13(4) . . . 765
s 14A . . . 309, 724
ss 14A–14AF . . . 967
s 14A(3) . . . 968
s 14A(5) . . . 968
s 14A(6) . . . 968
s 14B(1)(a) . . . 968
s 14B(1)(b) . . . 968
s 14C(1)(a) . . . 695, 718, 968
s 14C(1)(b) . . . 695, 706, 968
s 14C(2) . . . 706
s 14C(3) . . . 706, 968
s 14C(4) . . . 968
s 15 . . . 724
s 16 . . . 724
s 16(4A) . . . 796
s 17 . . . 823–5, 826
s 17(1) . . . 823, 827
s 17(2) . . . 824
s 17(4A) . . . 825
s 17(6) . . . 824, 825
s 17(10) . . . 824
s 17(11) . . . 824
s 19(12) . . . 887
s 20 . . . 764, 825, 826, 828–31, 832, 855, 869
s 20(1) . . . 825–7, 829, 831
s 20(1)–(5) . . . 829
s 20(3) . . . 825, 831
s 20(4) . . . 825, 827–8, 829
s 20(5) . . . 825, 831
s 20(6) . . . 825
s 20(7) . . . 682, 827, 828, 829, 830
s 20(7)–(11) . . . 829
s 20(8) . . . 682, 827, 828, 830
s 20(9) . . . 764, 827
s 20(11) . . . 831
s 22 . . . 830, 832, 833
s 22(1) . . . 832
s 22(3) . . . 832, 833, 880
s 22(3)(a) . . . 832
s 22(3A) . . . 832, 833
s 22(4) . . . 833, 880
s 22(5) . . . 833, 880
s 22(5)(c) . . . 833
s 22C . . . 929
s 22C(2) . . . 834, 877
s 22C(2)–(4) . . . 827, 834
s 22C(3) . . . 826
s 22C(5) . . . 877
s 22C(5)–(9) . . . 834

s 22C(6) . . . 834
s 22C(6)(a) . . . 834
s 22C(8)–(9) . . . 834
s 22C(8)(b) . . . 833
s 22C(9A)–(9B) . . . 834
s 22C(9A)–(9C) . . . 929
s 22C(10)(a) . . . 834
s 22D . . . 877
s 23A . . . 887
s 23B . . . 887
s 23C . . . 887
s 23CA . . . 887
s 23E . . . 887
s 23ZA . . . 835
s 23ZB . . . 835
s 24 . . . 887
s 24A . . . 887
s 24B . . . 887
s 25 . . . 599, 832
s 25(1) . . . 832
ss 25A–25C . . . 835
s 26(2)(d) . . . 681
s 26(2)(f) . . . 873
s 26(2)(k) . . . 873
s 26(2A) . . . 873
s 31 . . . 552, 584, 590, 592, 712, 727, 800, 840, 841, 851, 857, 864, 865, 881, 886, 887, 888, 895, 928
s 31(1) . . . 839, 877
s 31(1)(a) . . . 839
s 31(1)(b) . . . 839
s 31(2) . . . 231, 553, 841, 842, 844, 845, 855, 858, 860, 879, 899, 924
s 31(2)(a) . . . 845, 846, 847, 849
s 31(2)(b) . . . 857
s 31(2)(b)(i) . . . 857, 858
s 31(3) . . . 877
s 31(3A) . . . 870, 877, 880
s 31(9) . . . 839, 842
s 31(10) . . . 843
s 31(11) . . . 696, 895
s 31A . . . 869, 880
s 31A(1) . . . 869
s 32(1)(a) . . . 888
s 33 . . . 877, 879
s 33(3) . . . 696, 713
s 33(3)(a) . . . 591, 834, 878
s 33(3)(b) . . . 696, 878, 879, 880
s 33(4) . . . 878
s 33(6) . . . 680, 878
s 33(7) . . . 708, 878
s 33(8) . . . 880
s 34 . . . 881, 882, 884, 896, 930
s 34(1) . . . 764, 881, 882, 883, 884
s 34(1)(a) . . . 681
s 34(1)(c) . . . 764
s 34(4) . . . 882
s 34(5) . . . 881
s 34(6) . . . 882
s 34(11) . . . 881
s 35(1) . . . 885
s 37 . . . 838–9
s 37(1) . . . 838
s 37(3) . . . 839
s 37(4) . . . 839
s 38 . . . 727, 800, 874, 895, 896, 898, 899
s 38(1) . . . 894
s 38(2) . . . 895
s 38(4) . . . 896
s 38(6) . . . 896, 897, 898, 899
s 38(7) . . . 898
s 38A . . . 266, 896
s 39 . . . 871, 880, 887
s 39(1)–(2) . . . 887
s 39(1)(a) . . . 682
s 39(3) . . . 887
s 39(3A) . . . 887
s 39(3B) . . . 887
s 39(4) . . . 887
s 39(5) . . . 887
s 41 . . . 862
s 41(6) . . . 862
s 43 . . . 836, 893
s 43(1) . . . 836
s 43(4) . . . 836
s 43(5) . . . 836
s 43(6) . . . 836
s 43(8) . . . 836
s 44 . . . 889, 890
s 44(1) . . . 891
s 44(3) . . . 891
s 44(4) . . . 891
s 44(4)(b)(i) . . . 894
s 44(4)(c) . . . 696
s 44(5) . . . 894
s 44(5)(a) . . . 891
s 44(5)(b) . . . 891
s 44(6) . . . 894
s 44(6)(a) . . . 891
s 44(6)(b) . . . 891
s 44(7) . . . 891
s 44(10) . . . 891
s 44(10)(a) . . . 894
s 44(11)(a) . . . 894

s 44(12) . . . 891
s 44(13) . . . 891, 894
s 44A . . . 266
s 44A(2)(a) . . . 891
s 44A(2)(b) . . . 891
s 44A(5) . . . 891
s 44B . . . 891
s 45(1) . . . 890, 891
s 45(4)–(6) . . . 892
s 45(5) . . . 890
s 45(8)–(11) . . . 892
s 45(10) . . . 892
s 46 . . . 263, 829, 888, 890
s 46(3)(e) . . . 888
s 46(3)(f) . . . 888
s 46(6) . . . 888
s 46(7) . . . 888
s 46(9) . . . 888
s 46(10) . . . 888
s 47 . . . 835–8
s 47(3)(a) . . . 837
s 47(6) . . . 836
s 91(1) . . . 764, 877, 887
s 91(5A) . . . 877, 887
s 91(12) . . . 877
s 91(14) . . . 728–9, 788
s 91A . . . 788
s 91A(2) . . . 728
s 91A(4) . . . 729
s 100 . . . 834, 879, 880
s 100(2) . . . 800, 839, 870
s 100(2)(a) . . . 598
s 100(3) . . . 598
s 100(4) . . . 713
s 100(4)(a) . . . 713
s 100(4)(b) . . . 592, 713, 880
s 105 . . . 284, 311
s 105(1) . . . 725, 824
Sch 1 . . . 280, 285, 303, 307, 308, 309, 310, 311, 312, 315, 317, 344, 447, 448, 497, 498, 499–500, 501, 502, 503, 508, 511, 513, 514, 523, 606, 724
Sch 1, para 1 . . . 307, 308
Sch 1, para 2 . . . 309
Sch 1, para 2(4) . . . 307
Sch 1, para 3 . . . 310
Sch 1, para 3(3) . . . 310
Sch 1, para 3(4) . . . 311
Sch 1, para 4 . . . 311, 315
Sch 1, para 4(1) . . . 313
Sch 1, para 4(1)(b) . . . 315
Sch 1, para 4(1)(c) . . . 315
Sch 1, para 5 . . . 311
Sch 1, para 5(2) . . . 303
Sch 1, para 6(4) . . . 310
Sch 1, para 10 . . . 323
Sch 1, para 16(2) . . . 308, 309
Sch 2, Pt I . . . 824
Sch 2, Pt I, para 1 . . . 824
Sch 2, Pt I, para 3 . . . 824
Sch 2, Pt I, para 4 . . . 824
Sch 2, Pt I, para 5 . . . 824
Sch 2, Pt I, para 8 . . . 824
Sch 2, Pt II, para 15 . . . 881, 930
Sch 2, Pt II, para 15(1) . . . 835
Sch 2, Pt II, para 17(1)–(2) . . . 835
Sch 2, Pt II, para 19(1) . . . 880
Sch 2, Pt II, para 19B . . . 887
Sch 2, Pt II, para 19C . . . 887
Sch 3, Pt I . . . 885
Sch 3, Pt I, para 1 . . . 885
Sch 3, Pt I, para 2 . . . 885
Sch 3, Pt I, para 3(1) . . . 885
Sch 3, Pt I, para 3(1)(a) . . . 885
Sch 3, Pt I, para 3(1)(b) . . . 885
Sch 3, Pt I, para 3(1)(c) . . . 885
Sch 3, Pt I, para 3(3) . . . 885
Sch 3, Pt I, paras 4–5 . . . 885
Sch 3, Pt I, para 4(4) . . . 885
Sch 3, Pt I, para 5(5) . . . 885
Sch 3, Pt I, para 8 . . . 885
Sch 3, Pt II . . . 885
Sch 3, Pt II, para 6(1) . . . 885
Sch 3, Pt II, para 6(3) . . . 885
Sch 3, Pt II, para 8(2) . . . 885
Children Act 2004 . . . 833
Children and Adoption Act 2006 (CAA 2006) . . . 795, 796
Children and Families Act 2014 . . . 530, 722, 723, 736, 738, 767, 790, 799, 815, 834, 870, 877, 901, 911, 929, 961
s 2 . . . 929
s 3 . . . 948
s 10(1) . . . 26
ss 13–15 . . . 815
s 13(6) . . . 730
s 18 . . . 157
Children (Leaving Care) Act 2000 . . . 887
Children and Social Work Act 2017 . . . 833
s 1 . . . 832
s 1(1) . . . 832–3
s 9 . . . 913, 930
Children and Young Persons Act 1933
s 1 . . . 496, 590, 680

Children and Young Persons Act 2008 . . . 833
Civil Partnership Act 2004 . . . 16, 33, 41, 42, 46, 47, 50, 70, 127, 131, 170, 280, 285, 349, 405, 447, 492, 498, 508, 510, 692, 755
s 1 . . . 60
s 1(1) . . . 47
s 2(5) . . . 61
s 3 . . . 47
s 3(1)(a) . . . 47
s 3(1)(b) . . . 76
s 3(1)(c) . . . 75
s 3(1)(d) . . . 73
s 4 . . . 75
s 6 . . . 61
ss 6–6A . . . 70
ss 31–33 . . . 70
ss 37–48 . . . 165
s 37(3) . . . 89
s 39 . . . 106
s 41 . . . 168
s 44 . . . 142, 165
s 44(2) . . . 144
s 46 . . . 170
s 48(2)–(5) . . . 167
s 49 . . . 72
s 49(a) . . . 76
s 49(b) . . . 77, 78
s 49(c) . . . 77, 78
s 50 . . . 88
s 50(1)(a) . . . 90
s 50(1)(b) . . . 100
s 50(1)(c) . . . 100
s 50(1)(d) . . . 101
s 50(1)(e) . . . 101
s 51 . . . 89
s 51(1) . . . 89
s 51(2)–(4) . . . 90, 100, 101
s 51(5) . . . 101
s 51(6) . . . 101
ss 56–57 . . . 168, 170
s 57 . . . 63
s 72 . . . 284
s 80 . . . 70, 76
ss 212–218 . . . 42
Sch 1, Pt 1 . . . 74
Sch 1, Pt 2 . . . 75
Sch 2, Pt 1 . . . 76
Sch 5 . . . 303, 307
Sch 5, Pt 1 . . . 308
Sch 5, Pt 2 . . . 308
Sch 5, Pt 2, para 2(d)–(f) . . . 308
Sch 5, Pt 3 . . . 308
Sch 5, Pt 5, para 20 . . . 311
Sch 5, Pt 5, para 22 . . . 311
Sch 5, Pt 9 . . . 307
Sch 5, Pt 9, para 39(1) . . . 311
Sch 5, Pt 10, para 49 . . . 310
Sch 5, Pt 11, para 55 . . . 309
Sch 5, Pt 14, para 80(2) . . . 308
Sch 6 . . . 307, 308
Sch 6, para 1 . . . 311
Sch 6, para 2(2) . . . 303
Sch 6, para 6 . . . 311
Sch 6, para 27 . . . 310
Sch 6, para 27(6) . . . 310
Sch 6, para 29 . . . 307, 311
Sch 6, para 39 . . . 309
Sch 8, para 13(3) . . . 41
Sch 20 . . . 42
Civil Partnerships, Marriages and Deaths (Registration etc.) Act 2019 . . . 16, 31, 47, 55
Contempt of Court Act 1981
s 14 . . . 253
Crime and Security Act 2010 . . . 180, 262, 263, 267, 268
ss 24–29 . . . 262
Criminal Justice Act 2003
s 189 . . . 256
s 190 . . . 256
Criminal Law Act 1977
s 2(2)(a) . . . 62

Divorce, Dissolution and Separation Act 2020 . . . 130, 132, 135, 137, 144, 157, 165, 167, 168, 170, 171, 172, 177, 178, 179
Divorce Reform Act 1969 . . . 33, 134, 140, 142, 144, 354, 402
Divorce (Religious Marriages) Act 2002 . . . 169
Divorce (Scotland) Act 1976 . . . 147
Domestic Abuse Act 2021 . . . 180, 183, 200, 204, 208, 240, 241, 242, 243, 246, 247–60, 261, 262, 263, 267, 268, 269, 448, 497, 498, 500, 502, 503, 509, 514, 728, 779
Pt 3 . . . 240–7
s 1 . . . 183, 205, 242, 263, 782
s 1(1) . . . 782
s 1(2) . . . 248, 782
s 1(3) . . . 182, 782
s 1(4) . . . 182, 782
s 1(5) . . . 182, 248, 782
s 2 . . . 182, 189, 205, 207, 221, 240, 241, 263
s 2(1) . . . 240
s 2(1)(e) . . . 241
s 2(1)(f) . . . 241
s 2(1)(g) . . . 241

s 2(2) . . . 240
s 2(3) . . . 240
s 3 . . . 231, 248, 779, 792
s 22(1)–(4) . . . 263
s 24 . . . 263
s 24(4) . . . 263
s 25(1) . . . 263
s 27 . . . 205
s 27(1) . . . 248
s 28(2) . . . 206
s 28(2)(a) . . . 247
s 28(2)(b) . . . 206
s 28(2)(b)–(d) . . . 262
s 28(3) . . . 263
s 28(5) . . . 206
s 28(5)–(6) . . . 262
s 28(6) . . . 206
s 29 . . . 206, 263
s 31 . . . 206, 261
s 31(3)–(6) . . . 261
s 32 . . . 205, 263
s 32(1) . . . 244
s 32(2) . . . 244
s 32(3) . . . 244
s 32(5) . . . 205, 241
s 33 . . . 205
s 33(1) . . . 245
s 33(1)(c) . . . 245
s 33(2) . . . 245
s 33(2)(b) . . . 263
s 33(3) . . . 262, 274
s 34 . . . 248
s 34(2) . . . 263
s 35 . . . 205, 241–2
s 35(1) . . . 241, 242, 245, 246
s 35(2) . . . 241
s 35(3) . . . 241, 242
s 35(4) . . . 242
s 35(5) . . . 242, 243
s 35(6) . . . 242, 244
s 36(1) . . . 206, 245
s 36(2)–(7) . . . 244
s 37 . . . 244
s 38 . . . 206
s 38(3) . . . 246
s 38(4) . . . 246
s 38(5) . . . 246
s 39 . . . 206
ss 39–40 . . . 254
s 39(3) . . . 258
s 39(4) . . . 258
s 40 . . . 206
s 40(4) . . . 262
s 41 . . . 244
s 41(2) . . . 242
s 41(3) . . . 242
s 43 . . . 254
s 44(3) . . . 262
s 44(8) . . . 246
s 44(9) . . . 246
s 44(10) . . . 247
s 44(11) . . . 247
s 44(12) . . . 247
s 44(13) . . . 247
s 48(1)–(2) . . . 261
s 65 . . . 258, 788
s 67 . . . 788

Domestic Abuse (Scotland) Act 2018
s 2 . . . 182

Domestic Proceedings and Magistrates' Courts Act 1978 . . . 204, 285, 307, 308
s 1(b) . . . 311
s 2(3) . . . 303
s 3 . . . 311
s 5 . . . 310
s 5(4) . . . 310
s 20(12) . . . 309
s 25 . . . 307
s 25(1) . . . 311
Sch 6 . . . 307

Domestic Violence, Crime and Victims Act 2004 . . . 204, 255
Explanatory Notes . . . 210, 255
s 5 . . . 590

Domestic Violence and Matrimonial Proceedings Act 1976 . . . 204

Education Act 1996
s 7 . . . 590, 680, 681
s 576 . . . 681

Equality Act 2010 . . . 70, 755
s 199 . . . 455

Family Law Act 1986
Pt III . . . 615, 616
s 44 . . . 169
s 55 . . . 615
s 55A . . . 615, 641
s 55A(1) . . . 615, 616
s 56 . . . 615
s 57 . . . 615
s 58(1) . . . 615, 617
s 58(2) . . . 615

Family Law Act 1996 . . . 150, 157–62, 168, 180, 201, 204, 207, 208, 210, 211, 216, 219, 221, 231, 235, 240, 241, 242, 243, 245, 246, 247–60, 261, 262, 268–9, 276, 358, 359, 403, 448, 497, 498, 500, 502, 503, 508, 511, 514, 516, 766
Pt II . . . 157, 173
Pt IV . . . 207–39, 237, 252, 534, 800
Pt 4A . . . 271
s 30 . . . 220, 221, 222, 224, 269
s 30(1) . . . 221
s 30(2) . . . 221–2
s 30(7) . . . 222
s 30(8) . . . 222
s 30(9) . . . 222
s 33 . . . 205, 206, 219, 220, 221, 222–4, 226, 227, 229, 230, 233, 239, 269, 500, 503
ss 33–38 . . . 205, 206
s 33(1) . . . 222, 247
s 33(1)(a)(i) . . . 221
s 33(2) . . . 208
s 33(2A) . . . 208
s 33(3) . . . 205, 222–3, 243
s 33(3)(c) . . . 223, 225
s 33(3)(d) . . . 225
s 33(3)(f) . . . 225
s 33(3)(g) . . . 223, 225
s 33(4) . . . 222
s 33(6) . . . 205, 223, 224, 228, 239
s 33(7) . . . 205, 223, 224, 233
s 33(10) . . . 223
s 35 . . . 206, 219, 220, 221, 224–6, 227, 228, 229, 230, 269
ss 35–36 . . . 219
ss 35–38 . . . 221
s 35(1) . . . 224
s 35(2) . . . 247
s 35(3) . . . 205, 224
s 35(4) . . . 205, 225
s 35(5) . . . 225, 226
s 35(6) . . . 205, 225
s 35(6)(a)–(e) . . . 226
s 35(7) . . . 226
s 35(8) . . . 205, 226
s 35(10) . . . 225
s 35(11)–(12) . . . 224, 502
s 36 . . . 206, 219, 220, 221, 224, 226–8, 229, 230, 502, 503
s 36(1) . . . 226
s 36(2) . . . 247
s 36(6) . . . 205, 227
s 36(7) . . . 205, 227
s 36(8) . . . 205, 227
s 36(10) . . . 227
s 36(11)–(12) . . . 502
s 37 . . . 206, 219, 220, 221, 228, 230, 269
ss 37–38 . . . 219
s 37(1) . . . 228
s 37(2) . . . 247
s 37(3) . . . 205, 228
s 37(5) . . . 228
s 38 . . . 206, 219, 220, 221, 228, 230, 502, 503
s 38(1) . . . 228
s 38(2) . . . 247
s 38(3) . . . 228
s 38(4) . . . 228
s 38(6) . . . 228
s 40 . . . 229–30, 243, 254, 507
s 40(1) . . . 229
s 40(2) . . . 229
s 40(3) . . . 229
s 42 . . . 205, 206, 220
s 42(1) . . . 213
s 42(2) . . . 206
s 42(2)(a) . . . 247
s 42(2)(b) . . . 261
s 42(4) . . . 208
s 42(4A) . . . 261
s 42(4ZA) . . . 208
s 42(5) . . . 205, 213, 216, 218
s 42(6) . . . 213
s 42(7) . . . 206, 213, 218
s 42A . . . 206, 255, 256, 257, 258
s 42A(1) . . . 255
s 42A(2) . . . 255
s 42A(3) . . . 255, 258
s 42A(4) . . . 255, 258
s 42A(5) . . . 255
s 43(2) . . . 248
s 44 . . . 208
s 45(1) . . . 248
s 45(2) . . . 248
s 45(3) . . . 248
s 46(2) . . . 251
s 46(3) . . . 251
s 46(3A) . . . 250
s 47 . . . 206
s 47(2) . . . 251, 252
s 47(3) . . . 251
s 47(4) . . . 252
s 47(6) . . . 251
s 47(7) . . . 251
s 47(8) . . . 206, 254
s 47(9) . . . 251
s 60 . . . 262
s 62 . . . 112, 210

s 62(1) . . . 209
s 62(2) . . . 212
s 62(3) . . . 205, 207, 208, 210, 500
s 62(3)(a) . . . 208, 210
s 62(3)(aa) . . . 208, 210
s 62(3)(b) . . . 208, 209, 210, 241
s 62(3)(c) . . . 124, 208, 210, 221, 241
s 62(3)(d) . . . 208, 210
s 62(3)(d)–(g) . . . 210
s 62(3)(e) . . . 208, 210
s 62(3)(ea) . . . 113, 208, 210
s 62(3)(eza) . . . 208, 210
s 62(3)(f) . . . 208, 210
s 62(3)(g) . . . 208, 221, 241
s 62(4) . . . 208
s 63 . . . 212, 213, 261, 509
s 63(1) . . . 207, 208–9, 230–1
s 63(2) . . . 206
ss 63A–63S . . . 271
s 63A(1) . . . 271, 275
s 63A(2) . . . 274
s 63A(3) . . . 274
s 63A(4) . . . 271
s 63A(5) . . . 272
s 63A(6) . . . 272
s 63B(1) . . . 273
s 63B(2) . . . 273
s 63B(3) . . . 273
s 63C(1) . . . 275
s 63C(1)(b) . . . 275
s 63C(2) . . . 275
s 63C(4) . . . 275
s 63C(6) . . . 275
s 63CA . . . 276
s 63D . . . 276
s 63F . . . 273
s 63R . . . 271
s 63S . . . 271
s 64A . . . 275
Sch 7 . . . 360, 498, 503, 514
Sch 7, para 5 . . . 360, 503
Sch 7, para 10 . . . 503
Sch 7, para 14(1) . . . 360, 503
Family Law Reform Act 1969
s 8 . . . 579
s 20 . . . 535, 618–26, 627
ss 20–25 . . . 618
s 20(1) . . . 618, 623, 627
s 21 . . . 627
s 21(1) . . . 626
s 21(2) . . . 627
s 21(3) . . . 627, 628
s 23 . . . 628
s 26 . . . 613, 617
Family Law Reform Act 1987 . . . 615, 688
s 1 . . . 622
s 1(3)(a) . . . 683
s 1(3)(b) . . . 683
s 1(4) . . . 613, 683
s 4(1) . . . 685
Fatal Accidents Act 1976 . . . 113, 124

Gender Recognition Act 2004 . . . 16, 18, 36, 101, 102
ss 2–3 . . . 18
s 3(6A)–(6C) . . . 101
s 4(2) . . . 101
s 11A . . . 101
s 12 . . . 611
Guardianship of Infants Act 1886
s 5 . . . 566
Guardianship of Infants Act 1925 . . . 738
s 1 . . . 529

Homeless Persons Act 1977 . . . 204
Housing Act 1980
s 50(3) . . . 38
Housing Act 1996 . . . 826
s 190 . . . 236
s 193 . . . 236
Human Fertilisation and Embryology Act 1990 . . . 609, 630, 631, 633, 634, 635, 639, 642, 649, 653–7, 662, 667
s 13(5) . . . 635, 636, 637, 645
s 27(1) . . . 640
s 28 . . . 642
s 28(2) . . . 641, 642
ss 31–35 . . . 654
ss 31–31ZE . . . 654
s 31(1)–(2) . . . 654
s 31ZA . . . 654
s 31ZA(3)(b) . . . 654
s 31ZB . . . 75, 654
s 31ZB(3)(c) . . . 654
s 31ZC . . . 654
s 31ZD . . . 654
s 31ZE(3)(c) . . . 654
s 31ZF . . . 654
Sch 3 . . . 633, 635, 647
Sch 3, para 2(2) . . . 646
Sch 3, para 2(2A) . . . 646
Sch 3, para 4A . . . 635
Sch 3, para 8(1) . . . 646

Human Fertilisation and Embryology Act 2008 . . . 284, 601, 606, 609, 610, 615, 635, 637, 638–50, 654, 660–6, 761
Pt 2 . . . 639
s 33 . . . 647, 660
s 33(1) . . . 640
s 34 . . . 640
ss 34–40 . . . 640–7
s 34(1) . . . 639
s 35 . . . 639, 641–3, 644, 647, 660, 668
s 35(1) . . . 639, 641, 642
s 35(1)(b) . . . 639
s 36 . . . 643, 644, 647, 660
ss 36–37 . . . 639
ss 36–38 . . . 643–5
s 36(a) . . . 639
s 36(b) . . . 644
s 36(d) . . . 639
s 37 . . . 644, 660
s 37(1) . . . 643–4
s 37(1)(e) . . . 645
s 37(2) . . . 644
s 38(2) . . . 641
s 39 . . . 639, 646
ss 39–40 . . . 646
s 39(3) . . . 646
s 40 . . . 639, 647
s 40(1) . . . 639
s 40(2) . . . 639
s 41 . . . 639, 647
s 41(2) . . . 639, 646
s 42 . . . 101, 639, 644, 646, 647, 673, 683–9, 714–15
ss 42–47 . . . 645–6
s 42(1) . . . 639, 645, 778
s 43 . . . 646, 647, 673, 683–9, 715, 716–18, 764
ss 43–44 . . . 639
s 43(1) . . . 645
s 44(1) . . . 646
s 44(2) . . . 646
s 45(1) . . . 646, 778
s 46 . . . 639, 646, 647
s 46(1) . . . 639
s 46(2) . . . 639
s 47 . . . 647
s 48(1) . . . 645, 646, 647
s 54 . . . 113, 605, 660, 661, 662–6, 669, 693, 715
ss 54–55 . . . 657
s 54(1) . . . 661
s 54(1)(a) . . . 662
s 54(1)(b) . . . 662
s 54(2) . . . 661, 662, 663
s 54(2)–(8) . . . 663
s 54(2)(a) . . . 661
s 54(3) . . . 661, 664
s 54(4) . . . 661, 663, 664
s 54(4)(a) . . . 662
s 54(4)(b) . . . 666
s 54(5) . . . 661
s 54(6) . . . 661, 662, 663, 669
s 54(7) . . . 661, 663
s 54(8) . . . 662, 664
s 54A . . . 660, 661, 662–6, 715
s 55(1) . . . 661
Human Rights Act 1998 . . . 3, 4, 9, 10, 39, 46, 112, 527, 549, 551, 552, 553, 567, 568, 580, 625–6, 633, 716, 769, 813, 820, 867, 871, 876, 877, 931
s 3 . . . 41, 252, 552, 642
s 4 . . . 552, 662
s 6 . . . 298
s 6(1) . . . 878
s 7 . . . 819, 871, 872, 873
s 8 . . . 871, 872

Immigration Act 1988
s 2 . . . 77
Inheritance (Provision for Family and Dependants) Act 1975 . . . 114, 357, 447, 512, 525
s 1(1)(a) . . . 82
s 1(1A) . . . 120
s 1(3) . . . 241
s 15 . . . 410
s 25(4) . . . 82

Land Registration Act 2002
s 27 . . . 451
s 40 . . . 497
s 44(1) . . . 452
Sch 3, para 2 . . . 496
Law of Property Act 1925
s 1(6) . . . 496
s 34(2) . . . 451
s 52 . . . 451
s 53(1)(b) . . . 451
s 53(2) . . . 451
Law Reform (Husband and Wife) Act 1962 . . . 62
Law Reform (Miscellaneous Provisions) Act 1970
s 2(1) . . . 455, 498
Legal Aid, Sentencing and Punishment of Offenders Act 2012 . . . 23, 24, 26, 722, 800
s 10 . . . 23
Sch 1, paras 11–12 . . . 23, 181
Sch 1, para 13 . . . 23

Legitimacy Act 1976
s 1(1) . . . 683
s 2 . . . 683
s 3 . . . 683
s 10 . . . 683
s A1(2) . . . 613

Marriage Acts . . . 82
Marriage Act 1836 . . . 60, 69
Marriage Act 1949 . . . 77, 78, 81, 82, 83, 84
Pt II . . . 69
s 1 . . . 74
s 2 . . . 75
s 3 . . . 75, 76
s 3(1A)(a) . . . 682
s 3(1A)(b) . . . 682
s 16(1A)–(2B) . . . 75
s 24 . . . 78
s 25 . . . 77, 78
s 26(1)(a) . . . 69
s 26(1)(c) . . . 69
s 26(1)(d) . . . 69
s 26A . . . 70
s 26B . . . 70
ss 27B–27C . . . 75
s 30 . . . 78
s 35 . . . 69, 82
ss 41–44 . . . 69, 82
ss 46A–46B . . . 69
s 47 . . . 69
s 48 . . . 78
s 49 . . . 77, 78
ss 75–77 . . . 70
Sch 1 . . . 74, 606
Marriage and Civil Partnership (Minimum Age) Act 2022 . . . 76, 271
s 1 . . . 72
s 1(2) . . . 75
s 1(3) . . . 76
Marriage (Enabling Act) 1960 . . . 72
Marriage (Prohibited Degrees of Relationship) Act 1986 . . . 72
Marriage (Registrar-General's Licence) Act 1970
s 3 . . . 75
Marriage (Same Sex Couples) Act 2013 . . . 16, 19, 31, 33, 36, 70, 133, 142, 661, 755
s 1(3) . . . 69
s 1(4) . . . 69
s 2 . . . 69
s 8 . . . 70
s 9 . . . 36
s 11(1) . . . 59
s 11(6) . . . 69
Sch 3 . . . 59
Sch 3, para 2 . . . 118
Sch 4 . . . 59
Married Women's Property Act 1882
s 17 . . . 498
Matrimonial Causes Act 1857 . . . 140
Matrimonial Causes Act 1937 . . . 140
Matrimonial Causes Act 1963 . . . 133
Matrimonial Causes Act 1973 . . . 77, 90, 92, 142–56, 157, 165–7, 168, 170, 178, 226, 280, 285, 316, 349, 356, 361, 405, 422, 424, 427, 446, 447, 448, 491, 492, 500, 508, 510, 513, 514, 516, 520, 521
Pt I . . . 131
Pt II . . . 303, 307, 356
s 1 . . . 63, 165, 166, 404
s 1(1) . . . 142, 165
s 1(2) . . . 142–3, 165
s 1(3) . . . 144, 146, 165
s 1(3)(a) . . . 166
s 1(4) . . . 144, 149, 165
s 1(5) . . . 165–6
s 2(6) . . . 113
s 3 . . . 168
s 4 . . . 170
s 8 . . . 106
s 9(2) . . . 168, 169
s 10 . . . 166, 167, 168, 171
s 10(2)–(4) . . . 167
s 10A . . . 169
s 11 . . . 72, 82
s 11(a) . . . 84
s 11(a)(i) . . . 73
s 11(a)(ii) . . . 75
s 11(b) . . . 76
s 11(c) . . . 77
s 11(d) . . . 77
s 12(1) . . . 88
s 12(1)(a) . . . 103
s 12(1)(b) . . . 103
s 12(1)(c) . . . 90
s 12(1)(d) . . . 100
s 12(1)(e) . . . 102
s 12(1)(f) . . . 100
s 12(1)(g) . . . 101
s 12(1)(h) . . . 101
s 12(2) . . . 88, 103
s 12A . . . 72, 88
s 13 . . . 89, 105
s 13(1) . . . 89, 106
s 13(2) . . . 90, 100
s 13(2)–(5) . . . 101, 103
s 13(2A) . . . 101

s 13(4) . . . 90, 92, 100
s 13(5) . . . 90, 100
s 15 . . . 106
s 16 . . . 89
ss 17–18 . . . 168, 170
s 17(1)(a) . . . 170
s 18 . . . 63
s 18(1) . . . 170
s 21A . . . 360
s 22 . . . 361, 421
s 22ZA . . . 421
ss 22ZA–22ZB . . . 361
s 23 . . . 308, 357, 423
s 23(1) . . . 407
s 23(1)(a) . . . 306
s 23(1)(b) . . . 357
s 23(1)(c) . . . 358
s 23(1)(d)–(f) . . . 308
s 23(5) . . . 361
s 24 . . . 308, 360
ss 24–24A . . . 358
s 24(1) . . . 407
s 24(1)(a) . . . 498
s 24(1)(c) . . . 357
s 24(3) . . . 361
s 24A . . . 308, 358
ss 24B–24D . . . 360
s 25 . . . 365, 369, 375, 385, 403, 410, 417, 418, 423, 424
s 25(1) . . . 311, 362, 366
s 25(2) . . . 362–3, 366, 434
s 25(2)(a) . . . 356, 369, 378, 409
s 25(2)(c) . . . 367
s 25(2)(f) . . . 375, 382, 393, 402
s 25(3)–(4) . . . 311
s 25A . . . 362, 409, 410, 417
s 25A(1) . . . 363
s 25A(2) . . . 409, 411
s 25A(3) . . . 409
ss 25B–25D . . . 360
s 27 . . . 307, 421
s 27(1) . . . 311
s 27(3A) . . . 311
s 27(6) . . . 310
s 27(6A) . . . 309
s 27(6B) . . . 309
s 28(1) . . . 409
s 28(1)(a) . . . 374
s 28(1)(b) . . . 409
s 28(1A) . . . 409
s 28(3) . . . 357, 361, 374, 409
s 29 . . . 310
s 29(4) . . . 310
s 31 . . . 357, 374, 409, 413
s 31(2)(d) . . . 358
s 31(7) . . . 363, 409
s 31(7B) . . . 410
s 33A . . . 417, 418
s 33A(1) . . . 418
s 34 . . . 421, 422, 425
s 34(1) . . . 422
s 35 . . . 323, 422, 424
s 35(1) . . . 422
s 35(2)(a) . . . 422
s 35(2)(b) . . . 422
s 35(6) . . . 422
s 36 . . . 422
s 37 . . . 405
s 37(6) . . . 405
s 49 . . . 148
s 52 . . . 284, 308
s 52(1) . . . 363
Matrimonial and Family Proceedings Act 1984 . . . 356
Pt 4B . . . 258
ss 31Q–31T . . . 788
Matrimonial Homes Act 1967 . . . 204
Matrimonial Proceedings and Property Act 1970
s 5(1) . . . 355
s 20 . . . 63, 427
Mental Capacity Act 2005 . . . 97, 580

Offences Against the Person Act 1861
s 57 . . . 76

Perjury Act 1911
s 3 . . . 70, 76
s 4 . . . 613, 614
Places of Worship Registration Act 1855 . . . 69, 82
Police and Criminal Evidence Act 1984 . . . 202
Presumption of Death Act 2013
s 1 . . . 76
s 2 . . . 76
s 3(2) . . . 76
s 6(2) . . . 76
Protection from Eviction Act 1977
s 3A(2)–(3) . . . 496
Protection from Harassment Act 1997 (PHA 1997) . . . 201, 204, 210, 241, 261, 268
s 5A . . . 201, 261

Rent Act 1977 . . . 40, 41, 116, 120
Sch 1, para 2(2) . . . 39, 41
Sch 1, para 3(1) . . . 39, 115

Sentencing Act 2020
ss 359–364 . . . 201, 261
Serious Crime Act 5 . . . 201201
s 76 . . . 201, 216
s 77(1) . . . 785
Sexual Offences Act 2003
ss 5–13 . . . 75
ss 25–29 . . . 75
s 27(4) . . . 75
ss 30–37 . . . 99
s 43 . . . 99
ss 64–65 . . . 75, 606
Social Security Contributions and Benefits Act 1992
s 137(1) . . . 506
Social Services and Well-Being (Wales) Act 2014 . . . 813, 816, 821, 827
s 21 . . . 823
s 76 . . . 825
s 76(6) . . . 764, 827
Stalking Protection Act 2019 . . . 201
Surrogacy Arrangements Act 1985 . . . 657, 659–60, 665
s 1A . . . 659
s 2(1) . . . 659
s 2(2) . . . 660
s 2A . . . 660
s 3 . . . 660

Trustee Act 1925
s 34(2) . . . 451
Trusts of Land and Appointment of Trustees Act 1996 . . . 358, 480, 497, 498–9, 500, 501, 513
s 6 . . . 499
s 10 . . . 497
s 11 . . . 497
s 12 . . . 495
s 13 . . . 499
s 14 . . . 498
s 15(1) . . . 499
s 15(1)(a) . . . 499
s 15(1)(b) . . . 499
s 15(1)(c) . . . 499
s 15(2) . . . 499
s 15(3) . . . 499

Welfare Reform Act 2009 . . . 280, 614

Youth Justice and Criminal Evidence Act 1999
Pt II, Ch I . . . 202

AUSTRALIA

Domestic Relationships Act 1994 (ACT) . . . 124, 525
Property (Relationships) Act 1984 (NSW) . . . 124, 525
Relationships Act 2003 (Tas) . . . 525
s 5 . . . 124

BELGIUM

Civil Law
s 146 . . . 91

GERMANY

Civil Code
§1377 . . . 389

IRELAND

Civil Partnership and Certain Rights and Obligations of Cohabitants Act 2010 . . . 512

SCOTLAND

Family Law (Scotland) Act 1985 . . . 363, 371
Family Law (Scotland) Act 2006 . . . 512, 522
Gender Recognition Reform (Scotland) Act 2022 . . . 18

SWEDEN

Marriage Code
Ch 5 . . . 160

UNITED STATES

Ariz Rev Stat Ann Sect 25-901-906 (Arizona) . . . 174
Covenant Marriage Act of 2001 (Arkanas) . . . 174
La Rev Stat Ann Sect 9:272-5, 307-9 (Louisiana) . . . 174

TABLE OF STATUTORY INSTRUMENTS

Adopted Children and Adoption Contact Registers Regulations 2005, SI 2005/924
reg 8 . . . 956
Adoption Agencies Regulations 2005, SI 2005/389
reg 45(2)(d) . . . 930
Care Planning, Placement and Case Review (England) (Amendment) Regulations 2021, SI 2021/161 . . . 600
r 4 . . . 599
Care Planning, Placement and Case Review (England) Regulations, SI 2010/959
Pt 4 . . . 834
reg 5 . . . 870
reg 14 . . . 878
reg 18 . . . 877
reg 28 . . . 835
reg 33 . . . 835
reg 35 . . . 873
reg 39 . . . 828
reg 41 . . . 828
reg 43 . . . 828
reg 45 . . . 873
Child Maintenance (Written Agreements) Order 1993, SI 1993/620 . . . 304
Child Support (Collection and Enforcement) Regulations 1992, SI 1992/1989
Pt IIA . . . 298
Child Support Fees Regulations 2014, SI 2014/612 . . . 288, 289
Pt 4 . . . 298
reg 4 . . . 289
reg 4(3) . . . 289
Child Support Information Regulations 2008, SI 2008/2551 . . . 298
reg 9A . . . 289
Child Support (Maintenance Arrangements and Jurisdiction) Regulations 1992, SI 1992/2645
reg 2 . . . 320
reg 3 . . . 321
reg 4 . . . 321
Child Support Maintenance Calculation Regulations 2012, SI 2012/2677 (CSMCR) . . . 285
regs 14–16 . . . 294
regs 19–22 . . . 289
reg 23 . . . 289
regs 34–42 . . . 289
reg 43 . . . 291
reg 44 . . . 291
reg 45 . . . 291
regs 46–47 . . . 292
reg 47 . . . 293
regs 47–75 . . . 293
reg 48 . . . 293
reg 49 . . . 289
reg 50 . . . 291
reg 51 . . . 287
reg 53 . . . 287
reg 60 . . . 297
reg 63 . . . 294
regs 63–68 . . . 294
reg 64 . . . 294
reg 65 . . . 294
reg 66 . . . 294
reg 67 . . . 294
reg 68 . . . 294
reg 69 . . . 295
regs 69–71 . . . 295
reg 69A . . . 295
reg 69A(4) . . . 296
reg 70 . . . 295
reg 71 . . . 295
regs 72–75 . . . 297
reg 76 . . . 285
reg 77 . . . 287
reg 78 . . . 287
Child Support (Management of Payments and Arrears) Regulations 2009, SI 2009/3151
reg 5 . . . 293
reg 6 . . . 293
Child Support (Miscellaneous Amendments) Regulations 2018, SI 2018/1279 . . . 295
Child Support (Variations) Regulations 2000, SI 2001/156
regs 18–20 . . . 295
Child Support (Voluntary Payments) Regulations 2000, SI 2000/3177 . . . 289
Civil Legal Aid (Procedure) (Amendment) (No. 2) Regulations, SI 2017/1237 . . . 23
Civil Legal Aid (Procedure) Regulations 2012, SI 2012/3098
reg 33 . . . 23, 181
reg 34 . . . 23
Sch 1 . . . 23
Sch 1, para 8 . . . 250
Civil Partnership (Opposite-Sex Couples) Regulations 2019, SI 2019/1458 . . . 16, 613

Disclosure of Adoption Information (Post-Commencement Adoptions) Regulations 2005, SI 2005/888
reg 4 . . . 957
reg 4(4) . . . 957
reg 11 . . . 957
Education (Student Support) Regulations 2011, SI 2011/1986
Sch 4 . . . 327
Family Law Act 1996 (Forced Marriage) (Relevant Third Party) Order 2009, SI 2009/2023 . . . 275
Family Procedure (Amendment No. 3) Rules 2016, SI 2016/1013 . . . 955
Family Procedure Rules 2010, SI 2010/2955 (FPR 2010)
r 2.3 . . . 350
r 2.61D-E . . . 416
r 3.3 . . . 26
r 3.8 . . . 26
PD 3A . . . 799
PD 3A, paras 17–21 . . . 26
r 4.1(6) . . . 413
r 7.20(2) . . . 146
r 9.2A . . . 732
r 9.2A(6) . . . 732
r 9.9A . . . 413
r 9.10 . . . 309
r 9.13 . . . 359
r 9.15 . . . 416
r 9.26 . . . 417, 418
PD 9A . . . 413
r 12.3(1) . . . 727, 839
r 12.8 . . . 839
r 12.14(3) . . . 862
PD 12C . . . 839
PD 12J . . . 782, 784, 785, 786, 787, 788, 789
PD 12J, para 3 . . . 782
PD 12J, para 7 . . . 783, 784
PD 12J, para 36 . . . 783
PD 12J, para 37 . . . 783
PD 12J, para 38 . . . 783
PD 12J, para 39 . . . 784
r 14.2 . . . 955
r 14.3(1) . . . 937
r 16 . . . 731
r 16.3 . . . 862
r 16.4 . . . 731
r 16.6(3) . . . 583
r 16.20 . . . 862
r 16.21 . . . 862
r 16.33(4) . . . 730
PD 16A . . . 731–2
Pt 28 . . . 406, 416
Human Fertilisation and Embryology Authority (Disclosure of Donor Information) Regulations 2004, SI 2004/1511
reg 2(2)(f)–(h) . . . 656
Human Fertilisation and Embryology (Mitochondrial Donation) Regulations 2015, SI 2015/572 . . . 650
Human Fertilisation and Embryology (Parental Orders) Regulations 2010, SI 2010/985 . . . 662
Immigration Rules
r 278 . . . 77
Justices' Clerks and Assistants Rules 2014, SI 2014/603 . . . 146
Land Registration Rules 2003, SI 2003/1417
r 95(2)(a) . . . 452
Marriage Act 1949 (Remedial) Order 2006, SI 2007/348 . . . 73
Marriage of Same Sex Couples (Conversion of Civil Partnership) Regulations 2014, SI 2014/3181 . . . 70
Marriages and Civil Partnerships (Approved Premises) (Amendment) Regulations 2011, SI 2011/2661 . . . 70
Marriages and Civil Partnerships (Approved Premises) (Amendment) Regulations 2022, SI 2022/295 . . . 69
Non-contentious Probate Rules 1987, SI 1987/2024
r 22 . . . 606

TABLE OF INTERNATIONAL INSTRUMENTS

Charter of Fundamental Rights of the European Union 2000
- Art 9 . . . 63
- Art 23 . . . 570
- Art 24(2) . . . 555

Council of Europe Convention on preventing and combating violence against women and domestic violence (Istanbul Convention) . . . 197

European Convention on Human Rights . . . 4–9, 39, 43, 64, 70, 71, 99, 124, 131, 169, 197, 202, 273, 549–57, 558, 567, 569, 580, 619, 664, 755, 756, 893, 902, 914, 915, 918, 922
- Art 1 . . . 558
- Art 2 . . . 5, 195, 196–7, 198, 200, 217, 246, 570
- Art 2(1) . . . 196
- Art 3 . . . 4–5, 195, 197, 198, 200, 217, 246, 266, 274, 275, 567, 570, 819
- Art 5 . . . 196, 567, 680
- Art 6 . . . 5–6, 8, 23, 249, 253, 298, 299, 300, 301, 302, 726, 728, 821, 871, 872, 873, 899, 931
- Art 6(1) . . . 5, 701, 873
- Art 8 . . . 5, 6–8, 9, 17, 38, 39, 41, 42, 47, 64, 65, 68, 84, 91, 112, 120, 123, 124, 196, 198–200, 217, 246, 265, 266, 270, 274, 280, 298, 325, 337, 340, 496, 526, 545, 549–57, 567, 569, 581, 598, 619, 621, 622, 625, 626, 633–4, 635, 636, 637, 638, 664, 669, 701, 726, 732, 760, 769, 772, 798, 819, 820, 821, 843, 851, 852, 868, 871, 872, 873, 876, 877, 878, 879, 880, 881, 892, 899, 914, 915, 916, 921, 923, 924, 931, 952, 953, 955, 969
- Art 8(1) . . . 6, 8, 549–51, 663, 664, 867
- Art 8(2) . . . 6, 8, 10, 551, 552, 626, 634–8, 867, 869, 872, 876, 914, 922
- Art 9 . . . 65, 70, 76, 756
- Art 10 . . . 65, 215, 217
- Art 11 . . . 65
- Art 12 . . . 8–9, 17, 39, 42, 63, 64, 65, 66, 68, 70, 71, 73, 76, 84, 106, 126, 127, 131, 168, 270, 638
- Art 14 . . . 8, 9, 19, 38, 39, 40, 42, 47, 68, 70, 71, 76, 112, 123, 125, 127, 195, 197–8, 701
- Art 17 . . . 199
- Protocol 1, Art 1 . . . 123, 125, 298
- Protocol 7, Art 5 . . . 455

Hague Convention on the Civil Aspects of International Child Abduction 1980 . . . 711, 801, 805

Hague Convention on Inter-country Adoption 1993 . . . 947

Hague Convention on Jurisdiction, Applicable Law, Recognition, Enforcement and Co-operation in Respect of Parental Responsibility and Measures for the Protection of Children 1996 . . . 684

International Covenant on Civil and Political Rights 1966
- Art 23 . . . 63, 843

UN Convention on Consent to Marriage, Minimum Age for Marriage and Registration of Marriage . . . 87
- Art 1 . . . 89

UN Convention on the Elimination of All Forms of Discrimination Against Women
- Art 1 . . . 197
- General Recommendation No. 21 . . . 89

UN Convention on the Rights of the Child 1989 . . . 10, 280, 325, 526, 535, 553, 554, 558, 568–70, 571, 619, 697, 741, 768, 843, 914, 918, 923, 924, 947
- Art 2 . . . 568–9
- Art 3 . . . 84, 535, 564, 569
- Art 3(1) . . . 535
- Art 5 . . . 596, 916
- Art 6 . . . 569, 570, 596, 598
- Art 7 . . . 570, 618, 619, 697, 760, 919
- Art 8 . . . 570, 618, 619, 697, 919
- Art 9 . . . 697, 741
- Art 9(3) . . . 768
- Art 11 . . . 570
- Art 12 . . . 569, 570, 729, 732, 733, 863
- Art 12(1) . . . 729
- Art 12(2) . . . 729
- Art 16 . . . 496
- Art 18 . . . 280, 697
- Art 19 . . . 89, 570, 819
- Art 20 . . . 570, 949
- Art 21 . . . 913, 924
- Art 23 . . . 598
- Art 24 . . . 598
- Art 26 . . . 280
- Art 27 . . . 280
- Art 27(4) . . . 280
- Art 35 . . . 89

UN Declaration on the Rights of the Child 1959 . . . 741
- Principle 6 . . . 739

Universal Declaration of Human Rights
- Art 16 . . . 89

ABBREVIATIONS

AA 1976	Adoption Act 1976
ACA 2002	Adoption and Children Act 2002
ADR	alternative dispute resolution
AID	artificial insemination by donor
BAAF	British Association for Adoption and Fostering
BME	black and minority ethnic
BSA	British Social Attitudes
CA 1989	Children Act 1989
CA 2004	Children Act 2004
CAA 2006	Children and Adoption Act 2006
Cafcass	Children and Family Court Advisory and Support Service
CAO	child arrangements order
CFA 2014	Children and Families Act 2014
CMEC	Child Maintenance and Enforcement Commission
CMOPA 2008	Child Maintenance and Other Payments Act 2008
CMS	Child Maintenance Service
CPA 2004	Civil Partnership Act 2004
CPA 2019	Civil Partnerships, Marriages and Deaths (Registration etc.) Act 2019
CPAG	Child Poverty Action Group
CPC	child protection conference
CPS	Crown Prosecution Service
CQC	Care Quality Commission
CSA	Child Support Agency
CSA 1991	Child Support Act 1991
CSA 2010	Crime and Security Act 2010
CSEW	Crime Survey for England and Wales
CSMCR 2012	Child Support Maintenance Calculation Regulations 2012
DAA 2021	Domestic Abuse Act 2021
DAPN	domestic abuse protection notice
DAPO	domestic abuse protection order
DCA	Department for Constitutional Affairs
DCLG	Department for Communities and Local Government
DCMS	Department for Culture, Media and Sport
DCSF	Department for Children, Schools and Families
DDSA 2020	Divorce, Dissolution and Separation Act 2020
DFE	Department for Education
DFES	Department for Education and Skills
DH/DOH	Department of Health
DHSS	Department of Health and Social Security
DPMCA 1978	Domestic Proceedings and Magistrates' Courts Act 1978
DSS	Department of Social Security
DTI	Department of Trade and Industry
DVCVA 2004	Domestic Violence, Crime and Victims Act 2004

DVPN	domestic violence protection notice
DVPO	domestic violence protection order
DWP	Department for Work and Pensions
ECHR	European Convention on Human Rights
EEA	European Economic Area
EPO	emergency protection order
FLA 1986	Family Law Act 1986
FLA 1996	Family Law Act 1996
FLRA 1969	Family Law Reform Act 1969
FLRA 1987	Family Law Reform Act 1987
FMU	Forced Marriage Unit
FPR 2010	Family Procedure Rules 2010, SI 2010/2955
GRA 2004	Gender Recognition Act 2004
HFEA	Human Fertilisation and Embryology Authority
HFEA 1990	Human Fertilisation and Embryology Act 1990
HFEA 2008	Human Fertilisation and Embryology Act 2008
HMCPSI	His Majesty's Crown Prosecution Service Inspectorate
HMCTS	His Majesty's Courts and Tribunals Service
HMIC	His Majesty's Inspectorate of Constabulary
HMICFRS	His Majesty's Inspectorate of Constabulary, Fire and Rescue Services
HMRC	His Majesty's Revenue and Customs
HO	Home Office
HRA 1998	Human Rights Act 1998
ICCPR	International Covenant on Civil and Political Rights
IDVA	Independent Domestic Violence Advocate
IFS	Institute for Fiscal Studies
IRO	independent reviewing officer
IVF	in vitro fertilization
LA	local authority
LASPO	Legal Aid, Sentencing and Punishment of Offenders Act 2012
Law Com	Law Commission
LCD	Lord Chancellor's Department
LPA 1925	Law of Property Act 1925
LRA 2002	Land Registration Act 2002
MA 1949	Marriage Act 1949
MCA 1973	Matrimonial Causes Act 1973
MIAM	Mediation Information and Assessment Meeting
MOJ	Ministry of Justice
M(SSC)A 2013	Marriage (Same Sex Couples) Act 2013
NatCen	National Centre for Social Research
NMO	non-molestation order
NRP	non-resident parent
NSPCC	National Society for the Prevention of Cruelty to Children
OECD	Organisation for Economic Cooperation and Development
ONS	Office for National Statistics
PHA 1997	Protection from Harassment Act 1997
PR	parental responsibility
PRA	parental responsibility agreement

PRO	parental responsibility order
PSO	prohibited steps order
PWC	parent with care
SAA 1985	Surrogacy Arrangements Act 1985
Scot Law Com	Scottish Law Commission
SGO	special guardianship order
SIO	specific issue order
SSWB(W)A 2014	Social Services and Well-Being (Wales) Act 2014
TOLATA 1996	Trusts of Land and Appointment of Trustees Act 1996
UNCRC	United Nations Convention on the Rights of the Child 1989

1

INTRODUCTION TO FAMILY LAW

The purpose of this chapter is to introduce you to:

- the idea of family law
- some key themes and debates which feature in several areas of family law and are dealt with in later chapters of the book
- this book and its companion online resources

We hope that you will find it helpful.

1.1 FAMILIES AND FAMILY LAW IN ENGLAND AND WALES TODAY

1.1.1 WHAT IS 'FAMILY'?

This apparently simple question is actually a complex one to which people might offer different answers in different contexts. To many, 'family' implies a group linked by blood relationship and by marriage, and commonly by a shared home. The world of advertising would have us believe that we all live, or at least grew up, in nuclear families: households composed of two parents and their children. However, the reality of domestic life for many people diverges from that traditional image, as census data show.[1]

In 2001, the census showed that just over half (51 per cent) of the usually resident adult population was married;[2] by 2011, the proportion had fallen to 47 per cent,[3] while the 2021 census showed the proportion of the population in a marriage or civil partnership down to 44.6 per cent.[4] This is a continuation of a trend seen since the 1970s: the popularity of marriage declining and divorce becoming much more common.[5] Increasing numbers of couples live together without getting married and just over half of children are now born to parents who are not married to each other.[6] There were nearly 14.5 million dependent children in the UK in 2021: of those, 64 per cent were living in married couple families,

[1] ONS (2013). We provide more detailed statistical information in later chapters.
[2] ONS (2003). [3] ONS (2013). [4] ONS (2022f).
[5] For discussion of this trend with possible reasons for it, see ONS (2012a); Garrison (2014).
[6] ONS (2022c), table 1.

14 per cent in cohabiting couple families, and 22 per cent in lone parent families.[7] Some children are adopted, fostered, or otherwise 'parented' by people other than their biological parents. Same-sex couples are gaining social acceptance and have more or less identical legal recognition to that of mixed-sex couples: they can marry, register a civil partnership (which bestows rights and responsibilities akin to those of spouses), adopt children together, or become parents using assisted reproduction. Some households, particularly in certain minority ethnic communities, comprise 'extended' families of more than two generations and/or adult siblings.[8] Many people, particularly in early and late adult life, share households with friends in platonic relationships. Increasing numbers of young people remain in their parents' homes into adulthood. Many individuals live alone, but are nevertheless members of families by virtue of blood and other ties; some couples physically live apart and yet still regard themselves as being 'together'. In one way or another, all of these groups may consider themselves 'family'.

Whether, to what extent, and how the law recognizes this diversity in family life is of central importance for family lawyers. The supportive and protective functions of 'family law' are reserved to those the law accepts as 'family'. For those whom the law rejects, denied legal recognition of their family status, solutions must be found elsewhere. For example, those who have not formalized their relationships by marriage or civil partnership cannot access the specialist financial remedies applicable on divorce to spouses and civil partners; the general law of contract, trusts, and property must be relied upon to determine financial and property disputes between such individuals on relationship breakdown. A key issue for contemporary family law is therefore to decide which social 'families' to admit to 'family law', how to regulate their relationships, and whether to confer more extensive rights and duties on some categories of family than others, for example by privileging marriage.

1.1.2 WHAT IS FAMILY LAW?

Defining 'family law' is also surprisingly complicated.[9] In jurisdictions with codified laws, we might expect to find a code containing the Family Law of that country. Identifying a corpus of family law for England and Wales is less straightforward. Much of the law that regulates family life here is specifically devised for families, but to some extent aspects of the general law are relevant too.

The shape and focus of family law has also changed substantially over the decades: family law textbooks written in the 1950s looked very different from ours.[10] At that point in the social and legal history of the English family, marriage—then meaning only mixed-sex marriage, of course—was almost universal, cohabitation almost unheard of, and divorce rare by comparison with today's standards. It was therefore more natural to focus on law governing the ongoing relationship between the spouses (and not much else). Much has changed since then. The law relating to children has dramatically expanded, such that the parent–child relationship now takes centre stage, regarded by some commentators as the central relationship of family law. And rather than the functioning family, it is the pathology of family breakdown that has come to preoccupy the discipline. Divorce and its financial

7 ONS (2022b), table 4.
8 ONS (2022f), 5.
9 Brown (2019a).
10 Probert (2004a), 903–5.

consequences, domestic abuse, disputes over the upbringing of children, and protection of children from abuse within the home now constitute the core of family law.

In recognition of the breadth of contemporary 'family' and 'family law', this book examines the law relating to a wide range of 'families', not just those based on marriage, and addresses issues relevant to the ongoing family, as well as those arising on relationship breakdown.

1.2 THEMES AND ISSUES IN CONTEMPORARY FAMILY LAW

You will find that studying family law involves quite a lot of 'black letter' law, particularly in areas which are regulated closely by statute. However, our understanding and evaluation of the law is considerably enriched by thinking about various theoretical and policy implications of the social issues with which family law is concerned. Indeed, an important feature of contemporary family law scholarship is the identification of broad trends in the way in which law has been used to regulate the family in many western jurisdictions.[11] Throughout this book, you will encounter inter-related themes, issues, and perspectives on family law. We introduce the most important of these in this section to set the scene for the specific debates in the following chapters.

1.2.1 THE IMPORTANCE OF RIGHTS

1.2.1.a Welfare versus rights

Family law has oscillated between rights-based and welfare-based approaches to the family. To what extent, if at all, should family law be based on the notion that individual family members have rights and duties that they exercise against each other and against the state? (And, insofar as they are relevant, what rights should those be?) Or should family law, and family dispute resolution, be based on welfare-based criteria, seeking to achieve the 'best' outcome for the parties in their particular circumstances? The rights–welfare spectrum relates closely to a similar tension between law based on rules and law based on discretion, which we discuss next. A lawmaker who wishes to enforce rights and duties may naturally adopt a rule-based approach. But a lawmaker concerned to achieve the best outcome in all the circumstances of the individual case may prefer to rely on discretion, affording decision-makers flexibility to produce optimal outcomes.

As Stephen Parker has related,[12] historically, both rights-based and welfare-based approaches have been evident in legal regulation of the family. One or other predominates at particular points in time, but neither is ever completely absent. Put at its most basic, from an approach initially dominated by rights (principally those of the husband and the father), the twentieth century witnessed a clear shift towards a welfare-orientated approach (exemplified by the best interests principle in relation to children and the redistribution of property and finance on divorce), with a recent re-emphasis on rights both within and as a challenge to the welfare approach, particularly following the Human Rights Act 1998.

[11] See, e.g., Dewar (2003). [12] Parker (1992), 321–5 on which the following draws.

In general terms, a rights-based approach reflects the view that the state should not seek to bring about certain consequences, such as maximization of social welfare, but simply protect individuals' rights to pursue their own vision of the 'good life'. Pre-twentieth century rights-based family law consisted of a fairly rigid system of rules prescribing fixed roles for each family member that were ostensibly applied without regard to the implications for the individuals concerned. A utility-based model, by contrast, involves identifying a social goal and balancing individual interests to attain it. Broad discretion is conferred on judges to conduct this interest-balancing exercise guided only by vaguely defined 'goals and standards'. However, as Parker explains, growing dissatisfaction with the broad discretionary nature of a welfare-orientated approach led to a renewed focus on a more rule-orientated, rights-based approach. Clearly, the rights of contemporary family law are rather different in substance from those of the nineteenth century, not least in being (on their face) gender neutral. But the result has been an uneasy tension as family law tries to accommodate both welfare and rights.

1.2.1.b Contemporary rights in family law: the European Convention on Human Rights

The Human Rights Act 1998 (HRA 1998) has intensified this ideological 'struggle' between rights and utility in family law. The HRA 1998 gave effect to the European Convention on Human Rights (ECHR) in domestic law. The HRA 1998 has implications for statutory interpretation, the development of case law, and the exercise of judicial discretion. Consequently, sound knowledge of the HRA, the ECHR, and the Strasbourg jurisprudence is essential. In this section, we introduce the key ECHR Articles likely to be encountered by family lawyers.[13]

ONLINE RESOURCES

Readers requiring information on the operation of the HRA 1998 will find further guidance and materials in the online resources at www.oup.com/he/familytcm5e.

Article 3

In some areas of family law—child protection and domestic abuse—the most basic human rights may be at stake.

Article 3

No one shall be subjected to torture or to inhuman or degrading treatment or punishment.

13 For analysis of the case law of the European Court of Human Rights, see Fenton-Glynn (2021).

Article 3 subjects the state to a negative obligation: it must not perpetrate abuse itself or through its agents.[14] Like other Convention rights, Article 3 has also been held to impose positive obligations on the state, requiring the state to take reasonable steps to protect adults and children from abuse perpetrated by others.[15] In extreme cases, Article 2—the right to life—may also be implicated; it too imposes positive obligations on the state. The state's obligations towards children who are suffering or at risk of suffering harm are particularly far-reaching.

Article 6

Article 6—along with Article 8[16]—creates procedural rights for those involved in family law disputes, whether between the state and family members (e.g. child protection and adoption) or between private individuals (e.g. disputes between parents about arrangements for children).

Article 6(1)

In the determination of his civil rights and obligations or of any criminal charge against him, everyone is entitled to a fair and public hearing within a reasonable time by an independent and impartial tribunal established by law. Judgment shall be pronounced publicly but the press and public may be excluded from all or part of the trial in the interests of morals, public order or national security in a democratic society, where the interests of juveniles or the protection of the private life of the parties so require, or to the extent strictly necessary in the opinion of the court in special circumstances where publicity would prejudice the interests of justice. . . .

Procedural rights are as important as substantive rights (i.e. the right to a particular outcome), bringing both instrumental and non-instrumental advantages. Conferring procedural rights on individuals likely to be affected by the outcome of a decision-making process may improve the accuracy and quality of that decision. But procedural rights also perform a dignity-protecting function: they acknowledge affected individuals' entitlement to participate in decisions affecting them, rather than simply subjecting them arbitrarily to the closed decision-making of a third party. Whether doing so makes any practical difference to the outcome does not matter for these purposes—what matters is that the affected individual is heard.

Ascertaining what 'fairness' requires under Article 6 involves weighing the applicant's demands against the exigencies of the particular procedure involved and the rights of other parties to those proceedings,[17] in a manner similar to the proportionality exercise conducted under Article 8 (below). Articles 6 and 8 have been found to apply both to court-based and out-of-court decision-making, and may support various rights, for example: to participate in decision-making affecting the applicant;[18] to be legally represented before

[14] On the potential scope of this obligation, see Lord Kerr's minority judgment in *Re An Application by the Northern Ireland Human Rights Commission* [2018] UKSC 27, [214]–[262] (on abortion law in Northern Ireland).

[15] *Z v United Kingdom* (App No 29392/95, ECHR) (2001).

[16] *W v United Kingdom* (App No 9749/82, ECHR) (1988).

[17] *Ashingdane v United Kingdom* (App No 8225/78, ECHR) (1985).

[18] *Re M (Care: Challenging Decisions by Local Authority)* [2001] 2 FLR 1300.

decision-making forums;[19] to legal aid;[20] to adequate notice of proceedings (rather than 'without notice' proceedings, conducted without notifying the respondent);[21] to be given access to key evidence;[22] and to be given access to a court or other forum to enforce legal rights.[23] Articles 6 and 8 also offer protection regarding the effect of delay on the resolution of cases,[24] and the privacy or otherwise of legal proceedings and judgments in family cases.[25]

Article 8

Article 8 is a key provision for family lawyers, carrying potential significance for almost any sort of family law dispute. Any case under Article 8 will have three stages: demonstrating that the right applies; showing that the state has interfered with the right; determining whether that interference can be justified by the state.

Article 8

1. Everyone has the right to respect for his private and family life, his home and his correspondence.
2. There shall be no interference by a public authority with the exercise of this right except such as is in accordance with the law and is necessary in a democratic society in the interests of national security, public safety or the economic well-being of the country, for the prevention of disorder or crime, for the protection of health or morals, or for the protection of the rights and freedoms of others.

To establish a case under Article 8, the applicant must first show that the complaint falls within the scope of Article 8(1). The right to respect for private life and the right to respect for family life arise most commonly in family law cases; the right to respect for the home may also be relevant, for example, in relation to rights to succeed to a tenancy or to occupy property.

The right to respect for private life has been particularly important for those who have traditionally struggled to establish 'family life' rights, such as same-sex couples and transgender people, or where no family ties currently exist. The scope of private life protection, while not unlimited,[26] is potentially extremely broad, covering 'physical and psychological integrity', 'physical and social identity', 'gender identification, name and sexual orientation and sexual life', 'personal development', 'personal autonomy', and 'the right to establish and develop relationships with other human beings and the outside world'.[27] It has been invoked in various situations.

[19] E.g. on children's rights to participate in legal proceedings: *Sahin v Germany* (App No 30943/96, ECHR) (2001).

[20] *Airey v Ireland (No 1)* (App No 6289/73, ECHR) (1979).

[21] E.g. in domestic abuse or child protection proceedings: see 4.7.2 and 12.6.2.

[22] E.g. in relation to child protection: *TP and KM v United Kingdom* (App No 28945/95, ECHR) (2001); *Re A (Sexual Abuse: Disclosure)* [2012] UKSC 60.

[23] See, e.g., 5.4.7 on parents' rights to enforce child support.

[24] E.g. in relation to child-related disputes: *Glaser v United Kingdom* (App No 32346/96, ECHR) (2000); *Re D (Intractable Contact Dispute: Publicity)* [2004] EWHC 727; see chapter 11.

[25] In relation to disputes about children's upbringing: *B and P v United Kingdom* (App Nos 36337/97 and 35974/97, ECHR) (2001); and in relation to disputes between adults: *Clibbery v Allan* [2002] EWCA Civ 45.

[26] Scherpe (2007), (2021).

[27] *Van Kück v Germany* (App No 35968/97, ECHR) (2003), [69].

The right to respect for family life is the most frequently invoked provision of the Convention in domestic family law proceedings, in both private law and child protection cases. Establishing the existence of family life is not always straightforward. A well-established line of authority makes it clear that Article 8 affords respect only to existing family relationships: it does not safeguard the 'mere desire' to found a family or create new familial relationships.[28] Moreover, until recently the European Court of Human Rights has clearly favoured the traditional married unit, where 'family life' between the various individuals, including children of the marriage, is established automatically by the simple fact of the marital tie.[29] Establishing family life where the adult parties are unmarried has been more difficult.[30] However, the Court has been increasingly willing to embrace de facto family life,[31] including relationships between both mixed-sex and same-sex cohabiting couples (regardless of whether they have children),[32] and the relationships between transgender, gay, and lesbian parents and their children.[33]

Once the applicant has established the existence of one of the relevant interests protected by Article 8 (whether private life or family life, etc.), it must then be determined whether the state has, prima facie, interfered with the right. This raises the question of what the right 'to respect' for private and family life entails. Article 8 imposes a range of specific obligations on the state. Many of those are negative: for example, prohibiting the state from removing children from their parents. Others are positive, requiring the state to act in a particular way. As noted earlier, sometimes Article 8 imposes procedural obligations: for example, requiring that parents be given the opportunity to be consulted about decisions made by the state in relation to their children.[34] We shall come across many examples of Article 8 obligations throughout the book. Some examples of situations in which Article 8 might plausibly be invoked—we shall see later whether successfully or not—include:

- to achieve the legal recognition of transgender people's preferred gender;
- to protect the competing interests in cases of domestic abuse: for example, the victim's right to physical and psychological integrity, versus the alleged perpetrator's right to remain undisturbed in his own home;
- to recognize the parental status of unmarried fathers;
- to protect the competing interests of parties to disputes relating to the upbringing of a child following parental separation;
- to protect the mutual family life interests of parents and children where it is proposed to take a child into state care, and to protect their ongoing relationship once a care order has been made;
- to protect parents' and children's interests when adoption is proposed.

[28] *Fretté v France* (App No 36515/97, ECHR) (2003), [32]; *Paradiso and Campanelli v Italy* (App No 25358/12) (2017), [141]. Art 8 may protect a potential relationship between a father and a child once the child is born even if there is no existing relationship between them (*Anayo v Germany* (App No 20578/07, ECHR) (2010)), but that can be seen as being about the recognition of a family relationship rather than the creation of one.

[29] *Al Nashif v Bulgaria* (App No 50963/99, ECHR) (2003).

[30] *Marckx v Belgium* (A/31, ECHR) (1979).

[31] *Lebbink v Netherlands* (App No 45582/99, ECHR) (2004).

[32] *Schalk & Kopf v Austria* (App No 30141/04, ECHR) (2010), [90]–[95]; *Vallianatos v Greece* (App Nos 29381/09 and 32684/09, ECHR) (2013), [73]. See chapter 2.

[33] *X, Y and Z v United Kingdom* (App No 21830/93, ECHR) (1997); *Salgueiro De Silva Mouta v Portugal* (App No 33290/96, ECHR) (2001).

[34] *W v United Kingdom* (App No 9749/82, ECHR) (1988).

Article 8 is a 'qualified' right, which means that even if the state is prima facie obliged to respect the right in a particular way, it may be justifiable for it to do otherwise. In many Article 8 cases, individuals will be asserting competing rights, and a decision clearly has to be made about how best to balance them. Protecting one person's rights often entails encroaching on the rights of the other; for example, protecting one parent's right to spend time with his child against the wishes of the parent with whom the child mainly lives will necessarily interfere with the latter parent's right to respect for family life.

Once it has been demonstrated that the applicant has a right under Article 8(1) which has been interfered with in some way by the state, the burden then shifts to the state to justify its action. Article 8(2) sets out three basic criteria that must be met in order for the interference to be justified, it must: (i) be 'in accordance with the law'; (ii) pursue one of the legitimate aims specified in the list in Article 8(2); and (iii) be 'necessary in a democratic society'. In practice, the first two requirements of Article 8(2) are usually easily satisfied. Often, the state will have acted in accordance with domestic law to protect the rights and interests of a child, unquestionably a 'legitimate aim'.

The most difficult test to satisfy is showing that the interference with the applicant's rights was 'necessary in a democratic society'. This test comprises several requirements: the interference must correspond with a pressing social need, be based on relevant and sufficient reasons, and be proportionate to the aim being pursued. The key concept here is *proportionality*, the tool used to resolve conflicts between competing parties' rights, or between rights and other 'legitimate aims'. The concept of proportionality is also relevant to several other provisions, including Articles 6 and 14. The proportionality test requires the decision-maker to carry out a balancing exercise, weighing the various rights and interests in order to determine whether the degree of interference with the applicant's rights is no more extensive than is required to meet the needs of the stated aim. But applying the proportionality test is not a mechanical, value-neutral exercise: it is impossible to determine the proper relationship between competing rights and interests without ascribing each of them relative weight—the question is a normative rather than factual one: 'which right ought to prevail?'; or 'how extensive ought the state's obligation to be?'

Article 12

By contrast with the breadth of Article 8, Article 12 has a very specific focus.

Article 12

Men and women of marriageable age have the right to marry and to found a family, according to the national laws governing the exercise of this right.

The rights protected under Article 12 are expressed in unqualified terms and, although subject to 'national law', at least as regards the right to marry, it is impermissible to read into Article 12 the same limitations as set down in Article 8(2).[35] The position as regards the

[35] *R (Baiai) v Secretary of State for Home Department* [2008] UKHL 53, [15].

right to found a family is more uncertain.[36] Although the European Court has generally interpreted Article 12 cautiously and conservatively, evolving social conditions and trends may prompt change. As we shall see in chapter 2, European Court decisions concerning the right of transgender persons to marry[37] and recognizing same-sex couples as having family life under Article 8[38] may signal a shift away from the traditional concept of marriage as a mixed-sex, biological-sex-based relationship, to one based more broadly on gender and social function. Article 12 has also become potentially important in the field of reproduction as individuals seek to take advantage of new reproductive technologies. The controversial issue of whether Article 12 offers a legal basis for an individual right to become a parent, whether through natural conception or assisted reproduction, is discussed in chapter 9.

Article 14

Article 14 is the Convention's non-discrimination clause. As we shall see in chapter 2, it has been used with notable success in the English courts since the HRA came into force to advance the legal rights of same-sex couples.

Article 14

The enjoyment of the rights and freedoms set forth in this Convention shall be secured without discrimination on any ground such as sex, race, colour, language, religion, political or other opinion, national or social origin, association with a national minority, property, birth or other status.

The principle of non-discrimination has been described by Baroness Hale as 'essential to democracy'—guaranteeing that power is not exercised arbitrarily, everyone is valued equally, and, where distinctions are drawn between different groups, such distinctions have a rational basis.[39]

Article 14 is not a free-standing anti-discrimination provision: it guards against discrimination only in the exercise of other Convention rights. Any claim under Article 14 must therefore begin by demonstrating that the factual circumstances of the case fall within the scope of one of the other rights. However, this does not require the applicant to demonstrate that that other right has itself been breached. Article 14 also demands that if the state chooses to grant rights beyond those required by the Convention, it must not do so in a discriminatory way: it must grant that right equally unless the difference in treatment can be justified.[40]

1.2.1.c A Resistance to rights?

The return to a rights-based approach to the family, prompted by the HRA 1998, gives previously excluded groups such as transgender people and same-sex couples additional tools with which to argue for change, providing them with rights that they can assert against the

[36] Ibid, and see *R (Mellor) v Secretary of State for the Home Department* [2001] EWCA Civ 472, [28]–[29]. For further discussion, see 9.4.2.c.

[37] *Goodwin v United Kingdom* (App No 28957/95, ECHR) (2002).

[38] *Vallianatos v Greece* (App Nos 29381/09 and 32684/09, ECHR) (2013).

[39] *Ghaidan v Godin-Mendoza* [2004] UKHL 30, [131]–[132]. [40] Ibid, [135].

state in order to demand legal recognition. However, the rights-based discourse has not met with unanimous support from family lawyers. Some family lawyers, including some family judges, have resisted the (re)introduction and potential predominance of rights-based reasoning. The continuing ambivalence about the rights of individual family members has meant that the impact of the HRA 1998 on the balance between welfare and rights in family law has varied considerably depending on the nature of the dispute.[41]

There are various reasons for this resistance.[42] For some conservative groups, the perceived alliance between strong liberal values and human rights discourse breeds concern that, by emphasizing individualism, equality, and non-discrimination, rights-based reasoning will undermine the traditional family unit and the values it protects.[43] Other commentators are concerned that the individualistic focus of rights-based reasoning is inappropriate when dealing with the interdependence of contemporary family life.[44] Scepticism about rights-based reasoning is particularly strong in cases relating to children, where there are concerns that focusing on rights will lead to children's interests being marginalized.[45] Those concerns are understandable. It is only fairly recently that the notion of parents holding autonomous 'proprietary' rights over their children has given way to a welfare-based discourse that strives to put children's interests at the heart of the decision-making process.[46] For many family lawyers, the principle that children's interests should be paramount in decisions concerning their future welfare and upbringing is sacrosanct; to revert to reasoning dominated by the individual rights of parents would be a retrograde step.

Despite these concerns, rights-based arguments have found a natural home in family law disputes. A rights-based, more rule-orientated approach can lead to (arguably) more 'just' outcomes.[47] The discourse of rights demands that the individual needs and interests of all family members are identified and weighed. Clear articulation of the parties' individual needs and interests may bring more predictability, transparency, and accountability in family law decision-making. It can also address concerns that welfare-based approaches allow legitimate rights and interests to be obscured by children's interests.[48]

One of the most controversial issues in carrying out the balancing exercise demanded by Article 8(2) is the weight to be accorded to children's interests, in particular whether they are to be the *paramount* consideration such that any interference with an adult's rights will automatically be deemed 'necessary in a democratic society' if undertaken with the aim of protecting a child's rights and interests. This is an important issue, explored in chapter 8. It exemplifies, more clearly than any other area of family law, the ideological struggle between welfare and rights.

1.2.2 RULES VERSUS DISCRETION

The legislature has adopted two principal modes of law-making in relation to the family: (i) the imposition of rules; and (ii) the creation of judicial (or executive) discretion (though judges sometimes term this an 'evaluation' or 'value judgement'[49]). Some legislation

[41] On ECHR rights in relation to children, see 8.4; for children's rights specifically, including the UN Convention on the Rights of the Child 1989, see 8.5.

[42] Harris-Short (2005), on which the following draws.

[43] E.g. Hafen and Hafen (1995–6).

[44] E.g. Herring (1999a), 232–5; Diduck (2011b).

[45] O'Neill (1992).

[46] Parker (1992), 321–5.

[47] Dewar (1998a), 473.

[48] See 8.2.2.b.

[49] E.g. *Re B (Care Proceedings: Appeal)* [2013] UKSC 33, [44], [57], and [199]; *Re B-S (Adoption: Application of Threshold Criteria)* [2013] EWCA Civ 1146, [72].

creates prescriptive, exhaustive rules to govern particular disputes; child support law is the classic example of this approach. Here, the courts' (or other decision-makers') function is confined to determining the meaning of statutory language and applying it to the facts of the case, though this is not a straightforward or value-neutral task. Other legislation confers wide discretion on the family courts: the statute may set down broad principles, or just indicate relevant factors for the courts to consider, giving no close indication of the 'right' outcome for any particular case. Many areas of family law, such as decisions about future arrangements for children's living arrangements and financial provision on divorce, are heavily discretionary. Here, the courts' role is very different: interpretation of the legislation is less difficult and less important to the determination of individual cases. Instead the emphasis is on the courts' assessment of the individual circumstances of each case, and on their judgement of what will be a 'fair' outcome, or one which best promotes the welfare of particular family members, guided only rather loosely by general statutory principles.[50]

There are various pros and cons to rules and discretion. Does discretion create inconsistency and so unfairness? Are rules equally capable of yielding unjust outcomes? Does discretion render the system unpredictable and so impede private negotiation? Are rules preferable insofar as they can be used by the state to try to affect our behaviour? A strong reason in favour of discretion in family law is that family life is so variable that it would be impossible to lay down sufficiently nuanced rules in advance. Discretion thus maximizes 'individualized justice', achieving the fairest outcome in each individual case.[51] However, rules also have advantages. As Carl Schneider has observed, rules have 'democratic legitimacy': they are publicly accessible and readily susceptible to public debate. They also further one of the most fundamental principles of justice: that like cases should be treated alike. It is suggested that where the rules to be applied are clear and democratically sanctioned, even losing parties should feel that they have been treated fairly rather than abandoned to the vagaries of individual judges' personal prejudices and preferences.[52] Yet, as Schneider also points out, this confidence in the capacity of rules to guard against a sense of injustice in family disputes may be naïve. Rather than passively accept defeat, the losing party is very likely to contend that the rules are wrong or have been unfairly applied to the circumstances of their case. Falling back on the individualized justice afforded by discretion, our disaffected litigant is likely to call for a more careful examination of the individual circumstances of their case to ensure justice is done.

A particular concern of opponents of discretion is that it hampers negotiated settlements.[53] It is often said that parties 'bargain in the shadow of the law',[54] that they negotiate in light of what they anticipate a court would order. This can sometimes be difficult, given the highly discretionary—and so unpredictable—nature of family law.[55] By contrast, rules appear to provide clear guidance about how a court is likely to resolve the dispute, helping parties to negotiate settlements out of court, but also performing the important normative

[50] This has implications for the proper handling of case law in the family field, discussed in the online resources. Cf 6.8.1.

[51] Dewar (1997), 311–14.

[52] Schneider (1992), 74–7.

[53] There have long been calls for 'templates' to help parties understand the general patterns of how families make arrangements after separation, most recently renewed by McFarlane (2022a).

[54] Mnookin and Kornhauser (1979).

[55] On the other hand, it has been suggested that this very uncertainty provides the parties with an incentive to settle so as to avoid the unpredictability of court: Harris (2008).

function of telling disputants how society believes the dispute ought to be resolved.[56] As we shall see in various chapters, this normative function of family law has become particularly important and controversial in the context of divorce and post-separation parenting, as the state has sought to re-inject some sense of 'family values' and 'responsibility' in the wake of the removal of 'fault' from family law.

We are not faced, then, simply with a choice between rules and discretion, but more fundamentally with a dilemma regarding the proper purposes of family law: to modify behaviour in line with some moral code (better effected by rules), or to resolve practical problems by reference to more (apparently) value-neutral principles. Dewar has observed that there has been a shift in several jurisdictions (particularly in areas such as child support and spousal maintenance) away from discretion (and welfare), partly as a result of attempts to re-invigorate the moral messages conveyed by the law with a view to delivering more 'just' and 'principled' outcomes.[57] But the promotion of some rights—such as the right to autonomy—raises concerns that other rights-based gains (e.g. to equal treatment) may be lost.[58]

1.2.3 WOMEN'S AND MEN'S PERSPECTIVES ON FAMILY LAW

The interests of some groups and individuals have at various times been neglected by family law. Commentators from various schools of thought and proponents of reform have sought to draw attention to these omissions. Feminism has long been the most dominant of these discourses, highlighting the historical oppression of women by the law in general and family law in particular. By contrast, recent years have witnessed a burgeoning fathers' rights movement and the growth of masculine studies, seeking to encourage equivalent examination of men's position(s) within the family.

1.2.3.a Feminist perspectives

There is a wealth of literature bringing a variety of feminist perspectives to family law. Feminist scholars do not speak with one voice, with very different approaches to family law issues evident. For example, views differ sharply on whether women have legitimate claims to ongoing financial support following divorce, and on whether perceived judicial bias towards women in disputes about children's living arrangements should be supported as recognizing and valuing women's care-giving role, or resisted as further entrenching traditional stereotypes portraying women's 'natural' and appropriate role as resting within the private realm of the family. However, despite the diversity, feminist writers share some core concerns.

The 'difference' of gender

The first such concern is the issue of gender itself and whether gender does and/or should make a difference. For 'liberal feminists', gender is unproblematic: all that is required to secure true equality is the removal of legal and structural barriers to women's full participation in the public sphere.[59] For 'difference' or 'cultural feminists', however, gender is crucial: they focus on 'the perception that women and men have differing modes of reasoning

[56] Mnookin and Kornhauser (1979).
[57] Dewar (1997), 313–16; Dewar (1998a), 473–4.
[58] Diduck (2011b). See further, 1.2.7.
[59] Barnett (1998), 17–18.

and different socially-constructed roles which are explanatory of women's inferiority and exclusion from the gendered, male, world'.[60] The work of Carol Gilligan, an educational psychologist, is most closely associated with the 'difference' school of feminist thinking. Based on her research into the moral development of boys and girls, she suggests that men and women think differently and approach moral problems in different ways.[61] Although controversial, Gilligan's work has a potentially important application to many legal issues. She describes the 'ethic of care', which she identifies with feminine thinking, as an approach which sees moral problems within a web of complex relationships to be resolved through dialogue and communication. This supports a model of family justice based on negotiation, mediation, and other forms of non-court dispute resolution rather than the adversarial, rights-based approach of traditional adjudication—the latter more readily fitting with the 'ethic of justice' that Gilligan associates with male thinking.[62] Gilligan's work on the importance of resolving disputes by situating them within the context of the realities of people's lives has also been advanced as the most appropriate model for resolving disputes about children's living arrangements, in preference to abstract, rights-based reasoning.[63]

Gender also matters for the radical feminist school. Gender is here understood as the manifestation of power disparities between men and women as created and sustained by the law. As Barnett explains, 'from this perception, woman's role is determined by her socially constructed gender, which ensures her inequality and subordination in relation to law and society which is characterised by male dominance'.[64] The insights of radical feminists have made an important contribution to our understanding of men's violence against women, particularly within the domestic sphere.

The public/private divide

A second core concern of feminist writers is the world's division into 'public' and 'private' spheres, and the role of that division in securing what O'Donovan terms 'the universal oppression of women'.[65] It is argued that whereas men have been identified with the rational, economically productive world of work and politics, women have been identified with the emotionally driven world of the family where work is undertaken for love not money.[66] This has led to an economic and power imbalance between the sexes which, in turn, has secured men's dominance over women in all spheres of life. Moreover, it is argued that the exclusion of women from the public sphere of government, politics, and work, and the reluctance of public bodies to intervene in what is regarded as the quintessentially private realm of family life, have rendered women invisible to the law and allowed dominance, inequality, violence, and abuse to continue unchecked. The law's historically muted response to the problem of domestic abuse provides a strong example of legislators' reluctance to intervene in the 'private affairs' of family members. It is sobering to remember that it was only in 1991 that rape within marriage was criminalized. As Barnett argues, 'that which law does not explicitly proscribe infers implicit acceptance'. In the now seminal phrase, 'the personal is political'.[67]

[60] Ibid. [61] Graycar and Morgan (2002), 194–5. [62] See also Barlow et al (2017); Hunter et al (2018).
[63] See, e.g., Neale and Smart (1999). [64] Barnett (1998), 18. [65] O'Donovan (1985), 15.
[66] Ibid, 8–9. [67] Barnett (1998), 65–6.

Women as mothers

The confinement of women within the private sphere of domestic life is closely related to feminism's third core concern: women's traditional mothering role and its implications for achieving women's equality. Whether the reproductive and maternal role of women should be a cause for celebration or concern, it has relevance to several areas of family law, from financial provision on divorce to disputes about children's living arrangements. The close association between the enduring inequalities faced by women and their child-bearing and child-rearing responsibilities has been the subject of much comment by both radical and liberal feminists.

For radical feminists, women's mothering role can be deeply problematic. Katherine O'Donovan argues that women's confinement in the private sphere as a result of their reproductive and child-rearing role has secured their subordination to men, who, she contends, are able to maintain this dominance and authority by distancing themselves from the domestic work of raising a family. She argues that women's continuing subordination is rooted in both biology and culture: law and society have constructed male and female roles on the basis of an interpretation of biology that dictates that 'biological differences should determine the social order'. Thus the answer for a radical feminist is to free women from mothering: 'to abolish current methods of biological reproduction through the substitution of artificial methods and the socialisation of child care'.[68]

Liberal feminists have similar concerns about how traditional assumptions about the 'natural', biologically determined role of women within the family have limited women's opportunities in the public world of work, although their solutions to this problem are less drastic. Clare McGlynn's analysis of the 'ideology of motherhood' underpinning judicial decision-making in family law within the European Union is instructive for domestic lawyers, particularly regarding disputes about children's living arrangements and the perceived bias operating against fathers in such cases. According to McGlynn, the 'ideology of motherhood' reflects a deep-rooted belief that 'all women need to be mothers, that all mothers need their children and that all children need their mothers'.[69] This belief permeates the law such that motherhood is simply accepted as the natural, appropriate, and inevitable role for all women. From here, child-care is readily understood as the primary responsibility of women, underpinned by a welfare discourse that identifies the physical and emotional needs of all young children with their mothers. To protect this core relationship, the mother–child relationship is thus privileged by the law to the detriment of women's equality in the wider public sphere. However, as McGlynn points out, this privileging of motherhood is not just damaging for women but also for men, denying fathers an active caring role within the family. The answer for McGlynn is not to negate the importance of the mothering role, but to reject the privileging of motherhood over fatherhood. It is, she argues, 'parenting' not 'mothering' which should be valued, opening up an egalitarian vision of life in which both men and women are free to participate as equal partners in the private and the public spheres.[70]

However, the world of gender neutrality to which liberal feminist scholars such as McGlynn would aspire is not shared by all feminists. Indeed, in a world which remains deeply gendered, entrenching 'formal equality' within the law based on a gender-blind vision of life may be a cause of further oppression for many women. As noted previously, for some feminists, gender does make a difference and the key to achieving equality is not to

[68] O'Donovan (1985), 15–16. [69] McGlynn (2001), 326, citing Anne Oakley. [70] Ibid, 326–30.

ignore and suppress those differences but to ensure the law attributes equal value and respect to female experiences. On family law issues bearing upon the mother–child relationship, cultural/difference feminists would thus be more receptive to approaches that sought to support and uphold the mothering work of women and the (perhaps unique?) mother–child bond, seeing it not as a source of oppression but as a source of empowerment and strength.

1.2.3.b Men and the family

Much less developed than feminist jurisprudence is a growing body of work focusing on men's engagement with the law. Many men are increasingly disenchanted with what they perceive as the bias towards women in family law, particularly the law relating to children. This disenchantment has coincided with an important 'repositioning' of fatherhood in contemporary political, legal, and cultural thought. Recent years have seen the strong emergence of what Richard Collier terms the idea of the 'new democratic family'.[71] Central to this model of the family is a vision of fatherhood which is active, engaged, and emotionally involved. Thus we see a move away from the dominant normative construction of the father as detached economic provider, towards a more 'progressive' idea of the father as 'hands-on' parent. This revisioning of fatherhood was strongly promoted by the Labour governments of 1997–2010, which introduced initiatives aimed at encouraging and supporting fathers, particularly economically and socially vulnerable men, to engage actively in family life.[72] However, as Collier explains, this emerging image of the 'new', 'hands-on father' is not unproblematic. The 'new father' is just one of several conflicting popular images of fatherhood in contemporary discourse.[73] There remains, for example, strong political and cultural allegiance to the concept of the father as the 'guarantor of social and familial order'. Firmly rooted in appeals to traditional notions of masculinity, the father is here perceived as strong and authoritarian, the disciplinarian within the family charged with ensuring correct behaviour. He is expected to provide a positive role model for his children, particularly his sons, by fulfilling his primary role as economic provider. Yet, strongly contradicting these overwhelmingly positive images of fatherhood is continuing distrust of men in family life. Thus the negative perception of at least some men as irresponsible and feckless, the 'deadbeat dad' who is superfluous to the family, remains entrenched in popular discourse. Still further away from any positive conception of the father is the legal, political, and cultural acceptance of the dangerous family man—a man who subjects his family to violence and other abuse.

Moreover, there are questions about the extent to which the rhetoric surrounding the emergence of the new 'hands-on' father is rooted in the actual practices of family life. Indeed, as Richard Collier argues, there would appear to be a serious disjuncture between the rhetoric and the reality of 'new fatherhood'.[74] Rather than a revolution in the traditional gendered division of labour in the UK, the empirical evidence strongly suggests that women continue to take on the bulk of the domestic labour whilst men remain principally committed to paid employment outside the home.[75] Despite various recent initiatives, the

[71] Collier (2003), 245. [72] Ibid, 245–7, 249–51. See also Gillies (2009), 52.

[73] Collier (2003), 257–9 on which the following draws. See also Collier (2014).

[74] Collier (2003), 255–6.

[75] While the proportion of men staying home to care for children has risen in the last couple of decades, child-care remains strongly gendered. Only 2.2 per cent of men with dependent children (compared to 14.9 per cent of women) were 'economically inactive' because they were caring for children, and only 5.6 per cent of men with dependent children (compared to 46.6 per cent of women) were working part-time: ONS (2022e). See also 5.1.

evidence suggests that rather than embracing the opportunity for change, men (and some women) remain resistant to sociopolitical pressure—or feel economically unable—to cede their traditional roles.

This debate signals some important dangers for family law. The recent focus on fatherhood and the rhetoric surrounding the 'new', 'hands-on' father has led to what Collier describes as a 'devaluing and systematic negation of the social importance of mothers and mothering'.[76] This devaluing of motherhood is particularly problematic given that it appears to be occurring against a 'mythical' understanding of contemporary fatherhood. Family law decision-making based on unfounded assumptions about contemporary equality between the sexes risks betraying the investment made by women in their parenting role, and ultimately the welfare of the child. The extent to which the role of fathers has changed, and whether such changes demand a different approach by the law to parent–child relationships, will be an important question throughout the child law chapters.

1.2.4 GENDER IDENTITY

Gender is important in various parts of family law. Terminology here can be confusing: although the law talks in terms of 'opposite-sex' and 'same-sex' relationships,[77] it is clear that what actually matters most of the time legally is not 'sex' in a narrow, biologically determined sense, but a person's legally recognized 'gender'.[78] Until 2013, marriage could be contracted only by parties of different legal genders, while civil partnership was available only to parties of the same gender until 2019.[79] An individual's legal gender may also determine whether and how they can become a child's parent and/or gain parental responsibility. It is important to emphasize that the issue here is one of legal gender (i.e. whether the person is male or female), not sexual orientation (i.e. the gender of people to whom one is sexually attracted).

Legal gender is generally uncontroversial. However, matters are less straightforward for people who identify as transgender (or 'trans'), non-binary, or inter-sex,[80] and here the Supreme Court has noted that '[t]he choice of language in the discussion of gender identification often signifies allegiance to a particular point of view'.[81] The government's 'tentative estimate' is that there are between 200,000 and 500,000 trans people in the UK, but only 6,010 had obtained a Gender Recognition Certificate by 2021.[82] The problems that such

[76] Collier (2003), 266.

[77] E.g. Marriage (Same Sex Couples) Act 2013. We have adopted the term 'mixed-sex' in our own writing, as opposed to 'opposite-sex'—though, in keeping with our general approach, when we extract or quote from other documents we retain the original language of the source.

[78] E.g. GRA 2004.

[79] This position breached human rights law: *R (Steinfeld and Keidan) v Secretary of State for International Development* [2018] UKSC 32. The Civil Partnerships, Marriages and Deaths (Registration etc.) Act 2019 required the Civil Partnership Act 2004 to be extended to mixed-sex couples, which was done by the Civil Partnership (Opposite-Sex Couples) Regulations 2019: see chapter 2.

[80] See generally Scherpe (2015). Some sources, including the European Court of Human Rights, now refer to non-trans people as 'cisgender'. On challenges for trans people in the UK, see Women and Equalities Committee (2016); compare Government Equalities Office (2016). On social attitudes towards trans people, see Albakri et al (2019), 12.

[81] *R (Elan-Cane) v Secretary of State for the Home Department* [2021] UKSC 56, [2].

[82] Government Equalities Office (2022a), table GRP-1. Up to 1 per cent of people at birth cannot be decisively labelled male or female on biological criteria (by reference to their reproductive anatomy): Chau and Herring (2004), 204.

people encounter under a law which seeks to place everyone into one of two boxes—male or female—raise interesting questions, not least, why does the law insist on categorizing us in that way? While trans people often self-identify as either male or female and so might accept this 'binary' male/female taxonomy, inter-sex, non-binary, and gender-fluid individuals (in particular) may regard themselves as belonging to a 'third' gender or reject the concept of (fixed) gender entirely.[83]

In medical terms, sex is determined by various factors, the first immutable, the others more or less susceptible to medical intervention: chromosomes (XY for male, XX for female); gonads and other internal sex organs; genitalia; and secondary sexual characteristics generated by hormones, such as body hair and body shape. Gender is connected to biological sex and much of the development associated with gender happens in the womb,[84] but it is also influenced by upbringing, lifestyle, and self-perception (which might have a neurological as well as psychological aspect).[85] Usually, these factors are congruent: biological sex is obvious from birth, and legal gender follows from it. However, for inter-sex, non-binary, and trans people, matters are more complex.

In inter-sex cases, the individual's physiology is ambiguous, featuring both male and female characteristics. A judgement is simply made about which legal gender to ascribe to the individual concerned.[86] In transgender cases, by contrast, the chromosomes, gonads, and genitalia all usually unambiguously denote one biological sex, yet the individuals self-identify as of the other gender or as non-binary. This phenomenon is commonly understood to be a psychiatric condition, diagnosed as 'gender dysphoria', though recent research suggests that it may have a biological cause during foetal development.[87] Following assessment at a gender identity clinic, medical treatment available to deal with this condition now involves hormonal treatment to alter secondary sexual characteristics; living in society as the other gender, with psychiatric therapy and support; and ultimately, and if clinically appropriate and desired by the individual, surgery to remove unwanted gonads and genitalia, and construct genitalia and bodily features of the other sex.[88]

English law—following *Corbett v Corbett*[89]—for a long time declined to recognize transgender individuals in their preferred gender, even after they had undertaken extensive surgery, insisting that gender must be determined for legal purposes exclusively by reference to the chromosomal, gonadal, and genital evidence. English law came under repeated challenge before the European Court of Human Rights, applicants complaining of breaches of Articles 8 and 12. After several decisions in which the matter was essentially left to the state's margin of appreciation, finally in *Goodwin v UK* the Court held that English law was in breach of both Articles.[90] The English courts being unable to remedy the breach through human rights-compliant interpretation of the relevant statutes,[91] Parliament enacted the

[83] See generally Scherpe, Dutta, and Helms (2018) and Garland and Travis (2018). Many countries allow individuals in certain circumstances to have their gender officially recorded as 'non-binary', 'inter-sex', 'other', or 'X'; the Austrian Constitutional Court ruled in 2018 that Art 8 ECHR guarantees official recognition of gender identities other than 'male' and 'female': Verfassungsgerichtshof, G 77/2018–19, 15 June 2018. While many UK organizations accept 'Mx' as a person's gender, there is no universal position and, e.g., UK passports cannot be issued without the holder being specified as male or female: the Supreme Court dismissed a challenge to this policy in *R (Elan-Cane) v Secretary of State for the Home Department* [2021] UKSC 56.

[84] NHS (2016). [85] *Bellinger v Bellinger* [2003] UKHL 21, [5].

[86] E.g. *W v W (Physical Inter-Sex)* [2001] Fam 111. For a children's rights perspective, see Mills and Thompson (2020).

[87] NHS (2016). [88] Ibid. [89] [1971] P 83. [90] (App No 28957/95, ECHR) (2002).

[91] *Bellinger v Bellinger* [2003] UKHL 21.

Gender Recognition Act 2004 (GRA 2004). The Act provides a procedure whereby individuals can obtain full legal recognition in their preferred gender, confirmed by a certificate. Notably, there is no requirement that individuals undergo gender confirmation surgery before recognition can be granted. But a formal diagnosis of 'gender dysphoria' must be made,[92] which causes 'significant offence and distress' to many individuals involved.[93] The Women and Equalities Committee said that this approach 'pathologises trans identities' and 'runs contrary to the dignity and personal autonomy of applicants', and consequently recommended reform.[94] However, after consulting on the issue in 2018,[95] in 2020 the UK government decided to enact only small procedural reforms, such as reducing the application fee from £140 to £5.[96] If an individual does not use the gender recognition procedure, the *Corbett* position stands, and they remain classed in their birth-assigned gender (corresponding with their biological sex) for all legal purposes.

We explore in chapters 2 and 9 the key areas of family law where legal gender matters. However, as family law becomes increasingly gender-neutral—for example, marriage and civil partnership are available to all couples, regardless of gender pattern, and legal parentage can be acquired by same-sex couples by various means—the question increasingly arises whether we need to retain the concepts of sex and gender in law at all.[97]

1.2.5 SEXUAL ORIENTATION

For centuries, individuals with non-heterosexual orientation were outlaws. Anal intercourse, even if consensual, was a serious criminal offence, subject to the death penalty until 1861. The offence of gross indecency—introduced in 1885—was aimed explicitly at gay behaviour. Lesbianism, by contrast, inhabited the shadows: the suggestion in 1921 that lesbian acts be brought within the scope of the offence of 'gross indecency' was dismissed on the basis that criminalization would 'tell the whole world there is such an offence, . . . bring it to the notice of women who have never heard of it, never dreamed of it. I think this is a very great mischief.'[98] Needless to say, quasi-conjugal relationships between same-sex couples received no legal recognition.

However, over the last 60 years English law's approach towards gay and lesbian individuals, their sexual relationships, their place in civil society, and their relationships has been transformed. Kees Waaldijk has suggested that most countries follow a series of standard legislative steps towards recognition of same-sex relationships: first, homosexual acts are decriminalized and any distinctions between mixed-sex and same-sex sexual relations, such as the age of consent, are removed from criminal law; secondly, the civil law prohibits any discrimination against homosexuals in employment and the provision of goods and services; thirdly, family law is extended to embrace same-sex relationships in various ways, ending finally with acceptance of same-sex marriage.[99] In the UK, as in most western countries, lesbian, gay, and bisexual people have now clearly 'arrived' in family law, prompting

[92] GRA 2004, ss 2–3. [93] As reported to the Women and Equalities Committee (2016), paras 36–41.
[94] Ibid, paras 44–5. [95] Government Equalities Office (2018c).
[96] For a helpful summary of the consultation and government response, see Fairbairn, Pyper and Balogun (2022). By contrast, the Scottish Parliament passed the Gender Recognition Reform (Scotland) Act 2022 in December 2022, introducing wide-ranging (but as yet unimplemented) reforms in Scotland.
[97] For versions of this argument, see Polikoff (2008) and Herring (2014).
[98] Lord Birkenhead, quoted in Playdon (2004), 136. [99] Waaldijk (2003).

questions about the proper regulation of same-sex—and mixed-sex—relationships, some of which draw on lessons learned from the feminist project.

Just as feminism is not a single school of thought, nor are advocates for gay and lesbian rights a homogenous group, and some criticize the way in which the new liberalism has been achieved and the potential implications of reform. The principal motive for reform has been equality. As we noted previously, Article 14 ECHR has been used successfully on several occasions in Strasbourg and domestically to further the cause of gay and lesbian law reform, even though sexual orientation is not expressly enumerated as one of the prohibited grounds of discrimination.[100] The concept of equality is not, however, straightforward. The argument that same-sex couples should be treated in the same way as mixed-sex couples is conceptually simple, carries political and legal weight, and is readily accepted by the general population. As Craig Lind argued presciently in 2004,[101] it was inevitable in today's political climate that this version of equality would take us inexorably towards the 'full equality' symbolically enshrined in same-sex marriage.[102] However, equality is complex, and does not necessarily require that everyone be treated the same. Sometimes it demands that different people be treated differently. The crucial question for family lawyers thus remains whether 'admission to marriage and other forms of heterosexual family regulation enhance the "real" equality of lesbians and gay men'.[103]

The main concern here is the potentially 'normalizing' effects of formal equality arguments and their suppression of the diversity of gay and lesbian life.[104] As Edwin Cameron asks: 'on whose terms—and on what basis—is recognition to be gained? Are our relationships to be recognised only if they are in all respects, save for the gender of our partners, indistinguishable from traditional heterosexual marriages?'[105] The dilemma is a very real one for political activists. It is through emphasizing the 'sameness' of homosexuality that the greatest legal and political mileage has been made. So, Cameron asks, is assimilation to the heterosexual norm and rejection of the rich diversity and difference of same-sex relationships to be the inevitable price of equality?[106]

1.2.6 CULTURAL DIVERSITY

The cultural and religious diversity of the population of England and Wales raises important issues for family law. The 2021 census revealed that nearly 11 million people or 18.3 per cent of the usual resident population of England and Wales are from a minority ethnic community.[107] There is considerable diversity within the minority ethnic population, which includes those of Indian, Pakistani, Bangladeshi, Black Caribbean, Black African, Chinese, and mixed-race origin, as well as a significant number of European migrants. Religious identity is also an increasingly important consideration. The census data from 2021 showed that 27.5 million people (46 per cent of the total population in 2021) identified as Christian; the next largest religious groups were Muslims (3.9 million), Hindus (1.0 million), Sikhs (524,000), Jews (271,000), and Buddhists (273,000).[108] Over a third of people (22.2 million) identified as having no religion.[109]

[100] See *da Silva Mouta v Portugal* (App No 33290/96, ECHR) (1999). [101] Lind (2004), 115–19.
[102] Marriage (Same Sex Couples) Act 2013. [103] Lind (2004), 119.
[104] See further Norrie (2000); Harding (2014). [105] Cameron (2001), v. [106] See 2.3.3.
[107] ONS (2022h), 5. [108] ONS (2022g) 3. [109] Ibid.

Given this diversity, religious and cultural factors play an important role in family disputes. The family sits at the heart of most cultural and religious communities. It is through the family that cultural and religious practices and beliefs are transmitted and preserved for the next generation. Cultural and/or religious practices are therefore often particularly strongly entrenched within the protected, private realm of family life. Traditions surrounding core family practices such as marriage and child-rearing are particularly resistant to change and, within immigrant communities, are often strongly defended when felt to be under threat from the assimilating pressures of the majority population. As John Eekelaar observes: '[i]t is natural that adults should be deeply concerned about the cultural context in which their children grow up. They tend to see it as part of their own interests.'[110] Respect for cultural identity is also a key part of liberalism's respect for individual liberty and choice, respect that extends to both adults and children.

The difficult question facing multicultural societies is to what extent minority practices and beliefs, whether rooted in religion or culture, should be accommodated within the law when in conflict with the normative standards of the majority population. An overly prohibitive approach can lead to charges of cultural imperialism, even racism. An overly tolerant approach can constitute an affront to the mores of the majority population, who may then complain that their own traditions and values are being undermined and eroded. The application of different principles and standards to different ethnic and religious groups also generates concern that vulnerable individuals within those communities are being denied equal treatment and protection under the law. The suggestion in 2008 (at least as reported in the media) by Dr Rowan Williams, then Archbishop of Canterbury, that some form of legal pluralism was 'unavoidable' in the UK and that Islamic courts should be able to apply Sharia Law to a range of family disputes caused a popular outcry.[111] It was condemned by David Cameron, then Leader of the Opposition, as 'dangerous' and 'illiberal'.[112] But religious bodies already play an important role in family law, both formally and informally.[113]

The potential for difficulty arises in several areas of family law, and the cultural norms and practices at stake are hugely significant to the communities in question.[114] There is no clear policy in English law determining how cases involving sensitive cultural or religious issues should be dealt with. It has been said that the starting point of the law is 'a tolerant indulgence to cultural and religious diversity and an essentially agnostic view of religious beliefs'.[115] Minority practices with respect to marriage have attracted considerable attention. The first wave of immigration following the Second World War raised the difficult question of whether polygamous marriages and child marriages entered into abroad should be recognized by English law.[116] In the context of divorce, women from various communities have looked to English law to help address difficulties in obtaining a divorce in accordance with their personal religious law.[117] Intra-cultural and religious disputes concerning marriage and divorce require the English courts to navigate a difficult path between according appropriate respect to the cultural and religious mores of the community, whilst seeking to do justice between the parties in accordance with the norms of English law.[118]

[110] Eekelaar (2004), 178. [111] See <http://news.bbc.co.uk/1/hi/uk/7239409.stm>.
[112] See <http://news.bbc.co.uk/1/hi/uk_politics/7264740.stm>.
[113] Douglas et al (2012); Sandberg and Thompson (2016); Eekelaar (2017), 173–8.
[114] Murphy (2000), 650–1.
[115] *Pawndeep Singh v Entry Clearance Office, New Delhi* [2004] EWCA Civ 1075, [67].
[116] See Shah (2003). [117] See 3.5.6. [118] See, e.g., Probert and Saleem (2018).

This task is made particularly difficult when differing interpretations of the cultural/religious norms and practices at the heart of the dispute are advanced by the opposing parties. Clearly, Parliament and the courts must be responsive to the potential difficulties caused, especially for women, by traditional family practices. However, there are no simple answers. Measures intended to protect vulnerable individuals within minority ethnic communities, such as refusing to recognize polygamous or child marriages to protect basic human rights and promote gender equality, can have the opposite effect, leaving vulnerable groups unprotected and driving prohibited practices underground.[119] Prakash Shah suggests that a more effective response is to afford official recognition to these diverse cultural and religious practices, bringing them within the law's protective scope.[120]

Cultural and religious conflict can also arise in various contexts relating to children. In the private law arena, disputes between parents of different religious and/or ethnic backgrounds over the upbringing of their children are increasingly common.[121] The weight to be accorded to cultural and religious identity in the context of adoption has also been controversial.[122] Less well recognized, but equally important, is the potential impact of different child-rearing practices within minority communities on the outcome of disputes about children's living arrangements after parental separation. In contrast to the model of the nuclear family which predominates in the West, the extended family has a much more central role in many Asian and African cultures, as is reflected in the typical household size amongst ethnic minority communities in Great Britain.[123] Care must be taken that parents, particularly mothers, from these communities are not unfairly prejudiced in disputes about where children should live because they fail to comply with the patterns of child-care predominating in western nuclear families.[124] Members of the extended family should not be overlooked as full-time carers for children because of the much less significant role played by equivalent relations within western families. Similar considerations apply in the child protection context. On the one hand, social workers and the courts must be alert to the dangers of cultural imperialism in misinterpreting culturally rooted child-rearing practices as harmful or abusive.[125] On the other hand, social workers and the courts must be equally alert to the danger of the 'culture' argument being manipulated by parents with the result that vulnerable children are left in dangerous situations.[126]

1.2.7 STATE INTERVENTION VERSUS PRIVATE ORDERING

One of the most fundamental debates in family law is about how far the state should intervene in family life, rather than leaving people to make their own arrangements. The extent to which the law can exert moral force in contemporary family life is closely tied to its willingness to intervene in family decision-making. The more emphasis placed upon the privacy of the family unit, the more difficult it is for the state to enforce normative standards and interests. The problem is particularly acute in the context of family breakdown. If the state

[119] Shah (2003), 399. [120] Ibid.

[121] See, e.g., *Re J (Child's Religious Upbringing and Circumcision)* [2000] 1 FCR 307; *Re G (Education: Religious Upbringing)* [2012] EWCA Civ 1233; *Re M (Ultra-Orthodox Judaism: Transgender)* [2017] EWCA Civ 2164: see 8.2.1.

[122] See 13.6.2. [123] ONS (2014b).

[124] See *Re K (Residence Order: Securing Contact)* [1999] 1 FLR 583.

[125] See *Re K* [2005] EWHC 2956. [126] Eekelaar (2004), 190.

is neutral about how such disputes should be resolved, families can be left to settle their own problems. By contrast, if the state is committed to promoting, for example, a particular model for the division of family assets on divorce, it may be expected to try to enforce its view of the 'right' or 'preferable' outcome through the law. However, state intervention in family life has always been controversial.

The privacy of the family unit is fiercely protected within liberal western thought. Intervention in this protected realm by outside agencies has typically been perceived as harmful and undesirable. However, as Andrew Bainham explains, the private realm is not 'naturally preconstituted'.[127] Its boundaries are constructed by the state to serve the state's interests. Whilst the concept of family privacy is an important constraint on state intervention, it is not an inherent good. Consequently, where the privacy accorded to the family unit serves the wider public interest, the state will happily adhere to a 'hands-off' approach; but when the family fails to serve that wider public interest, the state will intervene. Bainham illustrates this point with the example of child-rearing. Child-rearing can be understood as a private matter subject to state intervention only when certain norms are breached. However, child-rearing may more accurately be understood as an inherently public matter which, whilst typically delegated to parents, remains subject to the state's overriding control and scrutiny.[128]

Whichever conceptualization is preferred, the public interest in regulating the family is such that state intervention into the private realm will sometimes be justified. This will most often be the case when the family is in crisis, for example where children are abused within the family home. The state may also have an interest in enforcing financial obligations between family members. The difficulty lies in deciding when the privacy of the family should be protected and when the public interest—social, economic, or moral—is sufficiently strong to merit intervention.

Debates concerning the location of the public/private boundary, the proper role of the state, and the practical limits of governance have become particularly acute in light of criticisms of the family justice system and increasingly determined efforts by successive governments to move family disputes out of the courts. It is through the law and the courts that governments have traditionally sought to regulate families, particularly at the point of breakdown. However, in recent years, government seems to have lost faith in the family courts as an effective mode of family governance. More fundamentally, such has been the dramatic withdrawal of 'law' from family dispute resolution, that serious questions are now raised about whether the state has abandoned its normative and regulatory aims within this sphere.

1.2.7.a The role of the family court

More flexible and informal than other parts of the legal system, the family justice system prides itself on its conciliatory approach to family disputes. Relatively few families therefore find themselves in the family court.[129] Current policy initiatives are nevertheless strongly focused on diverting more family members away from court and into other dispute resolution mechanisms.

[127] Bainham (1990), 206–7. [128] Ibid.

[129] In a survey of 2,489 separated parents, around a quarter had used the family court. Of those, around 75 per cent had used the court for private law children issues; 5 per cent for public law children issues; 15 per cent for financial issues; 15 per cent for 'other' issues, including domestic abuse remedies; and 1 per cent for adoption proceedings: Dabhi, Anand, and Tu (2022), 5.3. (Percentages total more than 100 because some people use the court for multiple reasons.)

One means by which this policy is manifested is through the 2012 reforms to legal aid which imposed significant reductions to legal aid for family disputes. Opponents of the cuts argue that the provision of public funding to those who are unable to afford the costs of private legal advice and representation is essential to secure access to justice, whether obtained via lawyer-led negotiation and settlement of a dispute or, far less commonly, by resort to contested litigation and adjudication of the issues.[130] Matrimonial matters were within the scope of the original legal aid scheme, part of the welfare state, from its inception in the late 1940s. However, the 2010–15 Coalition government made radical reforms to legal aid,[131] including the removal of entire areas of private law family disputes from the scope of public funding for legal advice and legal representation, in particular those concerning arrangements for children, financial remedies following relationship breakdown, and financial provision for children.[132] The principal justification offered was the need to reduce financial spending, but the relevant consultation papers suggested an ideological motivation as well.[133] Family court cases were regarded as having lower priority for funding, since they 'result[ed] from a litigant's own decisions in their personal life',[134] and consequently litigation was 'unnecessary'.[135] By contrast, those who managed to settle their cases by agreement out of court were regarded as 'able and willing to take responsibility'[136] for their own affairs: by implication, litigation is 'irresponsible'.

Despite strong opposition and warnings by opponents about the effects the reforms would have on vulnerable adults and children,[137] the Legal Aid, Sentencing and Punishment of Offenders Act 2012 (LASPO) was enacted. LASPO removed public funding for lawyers' services for all private law disputes, other than: (i) for victims of 'domestic violence', provided that they can evidence that abuse in one of the prescribed ways;[138] and (ii) where a child who is the subject of the proceedings is at risk of 'harm' from another party.[139] Funding is also (in theory) available on the basis of 'exceptional case funding' (ECF), where necessary to protect the applicant's rights under Article 6 ECHR.[140] Very few cases were initially granted ECF;[141] however, following judicial review of the government's previous guidance,[142] numbers have increased (though the total is still a tiny drop in the ocean of family litigation).[143]

One important effect of LASPO was a significant drop in the number of family court cases starting at all, particularly private law cases: in 2014 and 2015, there were about 45,000 applications per year in private law children matters, compared with an average of 56,000 over the previous three years.[144] This effect was predicted—indeed, desired—by the government, and was intended to support an increasingly clear policy aim of moving private family law away from court-based solutions towards 'private ordering', with settlement promoted

[130] E.g. George (2012a), ch 1; (2021). [131] MOJ (2010). [132] See chapters 5–7, and 11.

[133] Eekelaar (2011); George (2012a), ch 1. [134] MOJ (2010), para 4.19.

[135] Ibid, paras 2.11, 4.209, 5.6, and 5.14. [136] Ibid, para 4.157.

[137] E.g. Eekelaar (2011); Williams (2011); George (2011a).

[138] LASPO, Sch 1, paras 11–12; SI 2012/3098, r 33 and Sch 1, as amended by SI 2017/1237. The original Regulations setting out the requirements for satisfying the domestic abuse 'gateway' were found to be unlawfully narrow in *R (Rights of Women) v Secretary of State for Justice* [2016] EWCA Civ 91.

[139] LASPO, Sch 1, para 13; SI 2012/3098, r 34.

[140] LASPO, s 10: see *Airey v Ireland* (App No 6289/73) (1979–80) 2 EHRR 305; Miles (2011c), (2011d).

[141] In 2013–14, only nine family cases were given ECF, from 819 applications: MOJ (2022c), table 8.2.

[142] *R (Gudanaviciene) v Director of Legal Aid Casework* [2014] EWCA Civ 1622.

[143] Since 2015–16, an average of 152 family law cases have been granted ECF per year: MOJ (2022c), table 8.2.

[144] MOJ (2022a), table 2.

out of court. However, numbers of applications have since risen again, with over 55,000 in 2020 and 2021.[145] This follows successful challenges to the government's approach to both the domestic abuse and ECF routes to legal aid,[146] but largely reflects increasing numbers of litigants in person,[147] and a rejection by families of government-promoted alternatives to court.[148]

The difficulties for the courts arising from litigants in person are significant.[149] Without a lawyer, cases are much slower to process, and hearings frequently have to be adjourned.[150] The closure of face-to-face services during the Covid-19 pandemic only served to exacerbate these problems, while further impairing the courts' already limited capacity to support litigants in person.[151] These difficulties coincide with a sustained period of immense pressure on the family justice system in general.[152] Alongside the legal aid reforms, the family court has seen cuts to its budget, pressures to modernize and make the system more 'transparent',[153] huge budgetary and other challenges facing local authority children's services departments,[154] and a massive increase in the number of child protection and other cases.[155] The effect is a system facing 'acute difficulties', euphemistically (and understatedly) described by the new President of the Family Division in November 2018 as a 'workload challenge'.[156] While the position might justifiably be perceived as a 'crisis',[157] it was apparent that the problems had become chronic: under-resourcing and increasing backlogs of cases were part of 'a continuing open-ended situation',[158] with no apparent sign of improvement. Then came the pandemic.[159]

The family court during and after the Covid-19 pandemic

The pressures on the family court, as with most areas of society, increased dramatically in March 2020 with the onset of the pandemic. Maclean and George liken the courts' response in the initial weeks to the five stages of grief: denial, anger, bargaining, depression, and finally acceptance.[160] Courts moved to entirely remote working, with telephone and video hearings becoming the 'new normal', even for the most complex of cases. While research highlighted some positive aspects of the new working conditions (though more for professional court users than for the individuals whom the system is designed to help), it was also clear that a huge amount was lost. Delays—which were already bad—worsened markedly in all aspects of the family justice system, including the courts.[161] However, there were also

[145] Ibid.

[146] *R (Gudanaviciene) v Director of Legal Aid Casework* [2014] EWCA Civ 1622; *R (Rights of Women) v Secretary of State for Justice* [2016] EWCA Civ 91.

[147] In 2022, at least one party was unrepresented in more than 70 per cent of private law cases: MOJ (2022b), table 11.

[148] Hunter (2017).

[149] See generally Mant (2022); Trinder et al (2014). We discuss this further in the online resources.

[150] Mant (2020), 422. [151] Mant (2022), 9. [152] McFarlane (2018); Justice (2022).

[153] Doughty, Reed, and Magrath (2018); McFarlane (2021b). [154] E.g. Trowler (2018).

[155] See, especially, 12.1. [156] McFarlane (2018), 13.

[157] E.g. Munby (2016); Ryan and Tunnard (2018). [158] McFarlane (2018), 2.

[159] The major report on the family courts and access to justice by human rights organization Justice (2022), para 1.2, notes that the LASPO cuts have combined with 'limited resources within the court system' and the pandemic to create 'a system at breaking point'.

[160] Maclean and George (2021). For parents' and professionals' perspectives in the family justice system during the Covid-19 pandemic, see also Ryan et al (2021).

[161] E.g. the mean time taken for public law children cases increased from a low of 27.0 weeks in 2016 to 33.3 weeks in 2019, but was 46.1 weeks by the end of 2021; private law children cases increased from a mean of 22.3 weeks in 2016 to 27.6 weeks in 2019 and then to 43 weeks at the end of 2021: MOJ (2022a), tables 8 and 9.

concerns about the actual court experience, with significant disparities between those with resources to be able to afford multiple devices and high-speed internet and those who could not, for example.[162]

While the research evidence suggested that the actual decisions that *judges* were making were largely unchanged as a result of the move to remote hearings, George argues that this is only a small part of the story.[163] Not only do most families make arrangements entirely away from the court, but the actual family court process is designed to promote settlement at every stage—the consequence is that '[a]djudication [i.e. a decision being imposed by a judge] is a rare event' and one that legal professionals try to avoid.[164] However, one of the functions of the family court is as a place to negotiate, where judges can give parties a more informal 'steer', and lawyers can use the pressure of the moment and 'the borrowed authority of the judge . . . as a tool for reaching informed settlements'.[165] During the pandemic, however, data suggested that more cases were ending with a court-imposed outcome—insofar as the system is premised on *agreements* being the best outcome, an increase in judicial decisions is a mark of failure. Moreover, as George puts it, '[i]n this context, how parties *feel* about their cases is a significant part of how the outcome should be measured', because the parties have to live with the decisions that are taken about their family life.[166] It is arguable, therefore, that the remote family court loses something of importance, even inasmuch as it was able to continue to function, because as Sir Andrew McFarlane P has put it, 'there is more to a Family Court hearing than simply transacting business'[167]—particularly if the 'business' of the court is thought to be judges imposing decisions.

1.2.7.b Non-court dispute resolution

There are numerous alternative means of resolving family disputes, collectively known as non-court dispute resolution.[168] As noted, government has been actively encouraging those with private family law disputes to avoid the courts and resolve their disputes using other mechanisms. We consider two approaches here.

Mediation

The most high-profile non-court dispute resolution option is mediation. While mediation might include a therapeutic element designed to enable the parties to adjust to the future, for example to help them to cooperate in joint parenting after separation, it does not aim to reunite couples. Family mediation involves an impartial third party, the mediator, assisting the couple to reach agreement about the future arrangements for their property, finances, and children. The mediator's role is purely facilitative: they have no power to impose a settlement. As Walker explains, 'it is seen as a more sensible way of settling family disputes and as a civilised and civilising procedure, a process which returns to, or keeps control in, the couple'.[169]

Interest in mediation as an alternative to lawyer-based dispute settlement on relationship breakdown first peaked in the 1990s, when it became a key component of subsequently abandoned divorce law reforms.[170] Many commentators were concerned that those debates were based on polarized (and rather distorted) depictions of what mediation and lawyers/the

[162] Maclean and George (2021), 231.
[163] George (2022b) and (2023), on which this section is based.
[164] Maclean and Eekelaar (2009), 120.
[165] George (2023).
[166] Ibid.
[167] McFarlane (2021a), 3.
[168] Previously known as 'alternative dispute resolution' or ADR.
[169] Walker (2000), 401–2.
[170] LCD (1993), para 7.11.

legal system were each supposed to offer.[171] Mediation was said to have been 'dangerously idealised'[172] as offering cheap conflict-free divorce, while law and lawyers were pilloried for fanning the flames of conflict and viewed as inevitably inducing contested litigation.

Research has never supported either stereotype,[173] yet despite the lack of clear evidence of its claimed benefits, mediation returned to the spotlight as a central feature of the Family Justice Review 2011[174] and as a privileged area for receipt of public funding following the LASPO legal aid reforms. Mediation now sits—theoretically, at least—at the centre of the private law family justice system.[175] Since 2014, applicants in private law children or finance proceedings have been required to attend a Mediation Information and Assessment Meeting (MIAM) before applying to the court.[176] That application must contain either the mediator's confirmation of attendance, or a claim by the applicant (or certification from the mediator) that the case falls within one of the prescribed exceptions: for example, there is evidence of domestic abuse, or the mediator is satisfied that the case is unsuitable for mediation for some other reason.[177] Family courts are now also required to consider, at every stage, whether non-court dispute resolution is appropriate for the parties.[178]

However, the intended increase in mediation clients has never materialized. Despite the public funding changes prioritizing mediation, the number of mediation assessments, mediation starts, and mediation agreements all dropped dramatically following LASPO and have continued to decline, reversing what had been a rising trend.[179] This drop is generally attributed to the fact that many couples had previously attended mediation on the suggestion of their solicitors, reflecting family lawyers' settlement-oriented approach.[180] As fewer people can now afford solicitors, this natural conduit of clients into mediation has dried up, and 'family mediation is a brand to which many consumers remain indifferent' when informal agreement is not possible.[181] Various measures were put in place to try to rebuild mediation numbers,[182] but again without success. Hunter has suggested that the lack of public appetite for mediation in this context means that '[r]ather than more of the same attempts to induce demand for family mediation, it is time to learn from the past and think much more openly and creatively about how to meet the demand for post-separation assistance that actually exists'.[183] A House of Lords Select Committee in 2022 recommended that MIAMs be abolished and be replaced with an opportunity for people to access 'a source of clear, impartial information on separation and, if necessary, general legal advice which can direct them to non-court or court-based resolution as appropriate'.[184]

[171] E.g. Maclean and Eekelaar (2016); Eekelaar, Maclean, and Beinart (2000), ch 1; Walker (1996); Eekelaar (1995).

[172] Brown and Day Sclater (1999), 158.

[173] Maclean and Eekelaar (2016).

[174] Norgrove (2011), paras 4.94 et seq.

[175] Maclean and Eekelaar (2016).

[176] Children and Families Act 2014 (CFA 2014), s 10(1).

[177] Family Procedure Rules 2010 (FPR 2010), r 3.8; Practice Direction 3A (2018), paras 17–21. However, this requirement 'is honoured more in the breach than the observance': McFarlane (2022a). See also *K v K (Fact-Finding)* [2022] EWCA Civ 468.

[178] FPR 2010, r 3.3.

[179] MOJ (2022c).

[180] E.g. Davis, Cretney, and Collins (1994); Eekelaar, Maclean, and Beinart (2000); Eekelaar (1995); Maclean and Eekelaar (2009).

[181] Hunter (2017), 200.

[182] MOJ (2014b).

[183] Hunter (2017), 200. See also Barlow (2017); Blakey (2022).

[184] House of Lords Select Committee (2022), para 140. This approach appears to have the support of Sir Andrew McFarlane (2022a).

Arbitration

Another form of non-court dispute resolution, currently much less commonly used, is arbitration. In arbitration, the parties attend some form of hearing in front of an independent third party, the arbitrator, who determines the dispute, much as a judge does in court. Outside family law, arbitration is well recognized and widely used, governed by the Arbitration Act 1996, but arbitration has had a slow start in family disputes.

The Institute of Family Law Arbitrators, a non-profit organization to accredit suitable arbitrators and provide guidelines on family arbitration, was established in 2012, and a number of applications for consent orders following arbitration were approved by the courts.[185] Practice guidance was issued by the President of the Family Division in 2015,[186] with more specific guidance in relation to arbitration in children matters following in 2018.[187] The guidance stresses that any arbitration must be based on English law, and children matters must follow the guidance given in relation to private law children disputes in Practice Direction 12B. In both contexts, the guidance approves remarks by the President in *S v S (Financial Remedies: Arbitral Award)* that 'where the parties are putting the matter before the court by consent, . . . it can only be in the rarest of cases that it will be appropriate for the judge to do other than approve the order'.[188] Opportunities to challenge the arbitral award are also limited.[189] Because one of the features of arbitration is that it is private, there are no records kept of how many family disputes are resolved in this way, but the numbers do not appear to be high.

1.2.7.c Is private ordering in family disputes a 'good' thing?

A reduction in the number of families going to court and consequently (one might assume) an increase in those resolving their disputes either entirely privately or through a form of non-court dispute resolution, might be viewed as a positive thing: this approach promotes autonomy and reduces the state's involvement in people's lives. However, such claims are not uncontested: questions arise about whether issues are really *resolved* or whether the status quo merely becomes *fixed* with no meaningful opportunity to challenge it.[190]

At a fundamental level, the non-interventionist policy associated with private ordering sends out a strong message about the value placed on the rights and interests at stake in family disputes. For this reason, this approach towards the family has been subjected to cogent criticism, particularly by feminists, on the basis that it reinforces the status quo and legitimizes 'structural inequalities between the sexes'.[191] It is argued, for example, that the state's formerly non-interventionist policy in areas such as domestic abuse left vulnerable family members unprotected. Private ordering on family breakdown runs a similar risk.

[185] See, e.g., *AI v MT* [2013] EWHC 100, following religious arbitration before a Beth Din; *S v S (Financial Remedies: Arbitral Award)* [2014] EWHC 7.

[186] Practice Guidance (2015).

[187] Practice Guidance (2018). Not all private children matters are currently within the scope of arbitration, with international matters in particular excluded at present.

[188] [2014] EWHC 7, [21], approved in Practice Guidance (2015), para 12 and Practice Guidance (2018), para 14. For guidance on when the court may interfere, see *DB v DLJ (Challenge to Arbitral Award)* [2016] EWHC 324, *Haley v Haley* [2020] EWCA Civ 1369, and 6.7.1.

[189] Practice Guidance (2015), paras 15–18; Practice Guidance (2018), paras 18–22.

[190] E.g. George (2012a), ch 1. [191] Bainham (1990), 207.

If parties' agreements on matters such as finances or children are not subjected to outside scrutiny and control, power rather than principle may dictate the outcome of negotiations.[192]

Specific concerns arise concerning mediation. While some separating couples do make fair and sensible arrangements about finances and children by themselves, in other cases there is a considerable power imbalance between the parties: one party may flatly refuse to negotiate or mediate, and/or they may not understand their legal rights. How, if at all, can mediation be used where one party has abused the other, and what safeguards can help identify such cases and ensure that the funding available for lawyers' services in such cases is accessed instead?[193] Since children might not participate directly or at all in the process, can mediation ensure that their interests are given adequate attention?[194] The extent to which 'autonomy' is promoted in a dispute resolution process unable to address these basic inequalities of power is questionable. Moreover, it is not just power imbalances between the parties that are problematic. There is a danger that mediation simply replaces one set of professionals (lawyers and judges) with another (mediators), who may be unable to maintain a neutral, orchestrating role and avoid interposing their view of the 'right' outcome.[195] Does mediation thus simply become a form of informal adjudication without the safeguards of formal legal process?[196]

It might be said that, to be acceptable, a private agreement must be negotiated on a relatively level playing field by parties who understand the rules of the game they are playing. There are therefore important benefits for parties who are trying to resolve their family disputes out of court, whether via mediation or not, being able to rely on the partisan help and advice of a lawyer.[197] For example, there is nothing inherently wrong in a party to a divorce seeking to uphold their rights to proper financial support. A 'bad' privately mediated agreement could leave that individual in a vulnerable position (potentially at a cost to the state). As Eekelaar puts it, the government's 'diminished concept of what constitutes justice in regard to family matters' has the effect of 'depriv[ing] legal rights of all effect' in the family context.[198] These concerns are echoed by George who observes that the effect of cutting access to legal advice and family courts may be 'to withdraw justice from the family, and leave the weak at the mercy of the powerful'.[199]

The nature of the 'autonomy' being promoted in arbitration is open to rather different criticism. Ferguson has observed that there is a difference between the parties negotiating an outcome (e.g. with a pre-nuptial or separation agreement or through mediation) and the parties agreeing to be bound by an outcome selected by someone else.[200] The autonomy involved in the former might be considered more deserving of the law's respect than the latter: agreeing to an outcome arguably involves greater expression of autonomy than agreeing to a process by which someone else will determine an outcome. Ferguson suggests that the autonomy argument 'operates here as a smokescreen for ideological reform in which law withdraws from intimate family life'.[201] Arbitration can be seen as a way for the wealthy to 'buy' a quicker tribunal (and a more controllable one, since the parties choose the arbitrator) to resolve their disputes than is available for those left to use the court system.

[192] George (2012a), ch 1; Hunter et al (2018).
[193] See, e.g., Greatbatch and Dingwall (1999); Hunter (2011); Choudhry and Herring (2017).
[194] See, e.g., Diduck (2003), 118–19; Pearce (2013); Ewing et al (2015).
[195] Dingwall (1988); Maclean and Eekelaar (2016).
[196] Stylianou (1998). See also Blakey (2022).
[197] Eekelaar, Maclean, and Beinart (2000).
[198] Eekelaar (2011), 313.
[199] George (2012a), 21.
[200] Ferguson (2015a), (2013a).
[201] Ibid.

Consequently, while there are potential benefits to be had from encouraging at least some family disputes to be resolved out of court, there are concerns about denying people the *possibility* of going to court. If the normative and protective function of family law is to be taken seriously, there is a strong argument that legal intervention is needed in some family disputes.

1.3 CONCLUDING THOUGHTS

Family law is an intellectually stimulating and challenging subject, but it also matters beyond the lecture room. Family law affects real people and their lives on a daily basis. Family life can be full of love and happiness, a rich and rewarding experience—but it can also be a cause of great pain and sadness. Families often turn to the law for help. Getting the law right is therefore important. We hope you enjoy studying it as much as we do.

ONLINE RESOURCES

You will find materials supplementing the discussion in this chapter in the online resources, which we hope you will find useful. In addition to the topics addressed here, you will find sections on:

- ***The sources of family law***: statute law; case law; international and European law; non-legal sources.
- ***The family justice system***: including the family courts; resolving family disputes out of court; some current challenges facing the family justice system and changes made in response to them.

Also available in the online resources are:

- ***A guide to using this textbook and the online resources.***
- ***Supporting materials for each chapter***: questions, suggestions for further reading, and supplementary materials for each chapter, including updates on developments in family law since this book was published.

The online resources are found at **www.oup.com/he/familytcm5e.**

2

FAMILY RELATIONSHIPS BETWEEN ADULTS

CENTRAL ISSUES

1. Whilst retaining a binary concept of gender, English family law is increasingly blind to gender pattern in adult relationships. Once outlaws, same-sex couples can now marry. Once in legal limbo, trans people can have their preferred gender formally acknowledged and form relationships in that gender. And where civil partnership was once only available to same-sex couples, the introduction of mixed-sex civil partnership in 2019 now gives all unrelated couples—but only such couples—the same options to formalize their relationships.
2. Many legal consequences flow automatically from two status-based relationships: marriage and civil partnership. The law of nullity—which sets out the grounds on which a marriage or civil partnership is void or voidable—identifies who has the right to acquire each status, and tells us something about the law's conception of each status.
3. For many faiths, marriage is the basis for family life. English marriage law currently gives a privileged position to Anglican rites in the formation of (mixed-sex) marriage. Only monogamous marriages can be created in England and Wales. But the law has had to deal with questions raised by the marriage traditions of other faiths practised in England and Wales.
4. English law increasingly recognizes relationships that have not been formalized in marriage or civil partnership, but tends still to focus on couples. Relationships between platonic companions, adult relatives who share a home, and individuals in relationships across different households receive less attention. Should law move 'beyond conjugality' and recognize the wider range of relationships that are important to people's domestic lives and identities?

2.1 INTRODUCTION

A man and a woman go through a civil marriage ceremony to give the woman the status necessary to acquire a British passport; after the ceremony, they go their separate ways.[1] Another couple go through a Sikh marriage ceremony and live together as husband and wife for nearly 40 years.[2] A same-sex couple cohabit for over 20 years until the death of one partner, who had been nursed by the other for several years following an accident.[3] Two unmarried elderly sisters live together for their entire life, for the last 30 years in the house built by their brother on land inherited from their parents.[4] Which of these relationships is recognized in English law, on what basis, and with what consequences?

This chapter seeks to answer the first two parts of that question in relation to these and other examples. There are many situations in which legal recognition of relationships between two or more adults is relevant, only some of which are addressed in this book: for example, determining rights to inherit on intestacy, calculating welfare benefits entitlements, accessing remedies against domestic abuse and financial remedies on relationship breakdown, protection of the shared home in the event of insolvency, enjoyment of tax exemptions, and eligibility to apply to adopt a child together.

Identifying which relationships are recognized for such legal purposes, and how, used to be relatively easy. Family law focused on (mixed-sex) marriage and the legal consequences that flow automatically from it. Little recognition was afforded to unmarried mixed-sex couples, none to same-sex couples, and blood relatives appeared only on the periphery. Transgender people were not recognized in their preferred gender and so, if heterosexual, were unable to marry their chosen partner. Those excluded from law's concept of family sought admission to it for the dignity, status, and legitimacy that flows from legal recognition, and for access to the accompanying rights and responsibilities.

Status-based family law has rapidly expanded in response to these claims. Since 2005, same-sex couples have been able to formalize their relationships by registering a civil partnership, a status which confers almost all of the legal consequences of marriage, and following implementation of the Marriage (Same Sex Couples) Act 2013 (M(SSC)A 2013) in 2014 they have been able to marry. This created a new discrimination against mixed-sex couples who at that time could not register a civil partnership. However, this was subsequently reformed under the Civil Partnerships, Marriages and Deaths (Registration etc.) Act 2019 (CPA 2019), so that both mixed- and same-sex couples can now register as civil partners. Trans people can obtain legal recognition of their preferred gender and formalize relationships with their partners, whether by marriage or civil partnership. Identifying these status-based relationships is largely straightforward: legal recognition flows from the fact of marriage or civil partnership, proved (and, in the case of civil partnership, created) by registration.

Increasing recognition has also been granted to relationships not formalized in marriage or civil partnership. Cohabitants, mixed-sex and same-sex, have acquired more legal recognition, albeit far less extensive than that of spouses and civil partners. Identifying

[1] *Vervaeke v Smith* [1983] 1 AC 145, see 2.7.1.

[2] *Chief Adjudication Officer v Bath* [2000] 1 FLR 8, see 2.6.2.

[3] *Fitzpatrick v Sterling Housing Association Ltd* [2001] 1 AC 27, see 2.8.1.

[4] *Burden and Burden v United Kingdom* (App No 13378/05, ECHR) (2008), see 2.8.3.

'non-formalized' relationships is less straightforward than ascertaining whether parties are married. The law recognizes these relationships where they *function* like a family or, more specifically, like spouses. This 'functional' approach to identifying relationships involves a close factual inquiry into the parties' everyday lives.

However, recognition of such relationships prompts further questions. Commentators have asked whether marriage is an unnecessary legal concept.[5] They are not advocating the abolition of marriage, but asking why we attach certain legal rights and duties to some relationships, traditionally marriage, and not others. The fact that parties happen to be spouses or civil partners may not be a sufficient or even necessary reason for particular legal consequences to arise, either at all or from that type of relationship alone. The next candidates for legal recognition tend to be couples who cohabit in a relationship akin to marriage or civil partnership. But what about individuals who share a home, who may or may not be blood relations, and do not have an intimate (sexual) relationship? Why focus on couples or pairs, and not on wider networks? And what about those individuals who identify as neither male nor female?[6]

The basic question is what characteristics of relationships *should* be relevant to determining the scope of legal recognition in each context. The answer depends on what we think is the purpose or function of each law and so which relationships ought therefore to be included. But there may be other objectives at stake: should the law actively promote marriage by attaching certain privileges exclusively to it, and continue to impose special rules on entry into marriage, to preserve a particular understanding of what marriage itself entails? Or should a more neutral stance be taken on relationship form, and attention focus instead on families' practical situations, regardless of status? We consider some of the evidence relevant to debates on these questions in the last section of the chapter (2.8). First, we examine demographic data about families in England and Wales today.

2.2 FAMILY RELATIONSHIPS IN ENGLAND AND WALES

The transformation of family law reflects substantial change in patterns of relationship formation in recent decades. But, as Rebecca Probert has observed, it is possible amidst the undoubted change to overlook the continuity: most couples are married and stay married.[7]

2.2.1 FORMALIZED RELATIONSHIPS: MARRIAGE AND CIVIL PARTNERSHIP

Most families are based on formalized relationships: in 2021, of the 19 million families in the UK ('family' here consisting of couples, with or without dependent children, or lone parents living with a child), around two-thirds—12.7 million—were spouses or civil partners.[8] But, reflecting a worldwide trend,[9] the number of marriages contracted each year has declined markedly since the all-time high in the 1970s and fell by 50 per cent between 1972 and 2019.[10] In 2019, the mixed-sex marriage rate in England and Wales (i.e. the number marrying per thousand unmarried people in the population aged over 16) was at its lowest

[5] E.g. Clive (1980); Hoggett (1980). [6] Cooper et al (2022). [7] Probert (2012a), 74–5.
[8] ONS (2022b), 2. [9] OECD (2018). [10] ONS (2022j), 2. Wilson and Smallwood (2007).

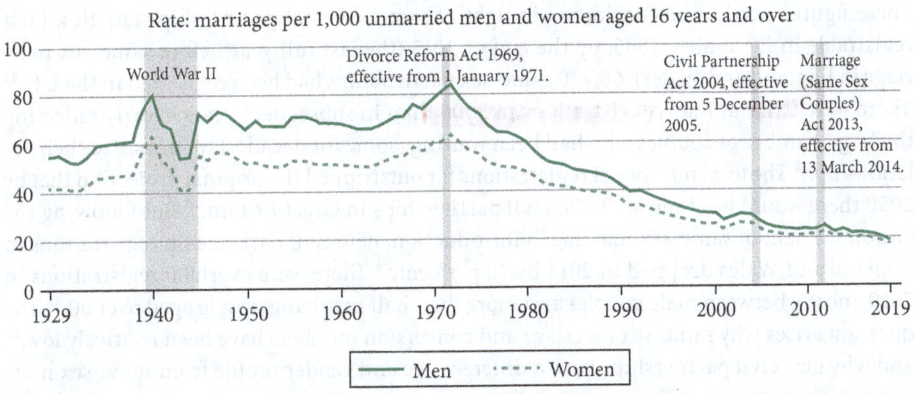

Figure 2.1 Marriage rates for mixed-sex couples: England and Wales, 1929–2019
Source: Reproduced from the Office for National Statistics, by Crown copyright © 2022; ONS (2022j).

since calculations began in 1862, and the number of marriages contracted in England and Wales was nearly the lowest since 1893 (when, of course, the population was much smaller).[11] Figure 2.1 shows the marriage rates for mixed-sex couples in England and Wales from 1929 to 2019. Obtaining an accurate picture of the married population is complicated by the fact that the data exclude the large number of marriages apparently contracted abroad by UK residents—so the decline in marriage may not be as 'precipitous' as the data suggest.[12] As many as 10 per cent of marriages between UK residents may now be occurring abroad, as 'wedding package holidays' become popular.[13]

The average age at marriage for mixed-sex couples has significantly increased since the 1970s, the mean age at *first* marriage for both sexes now being over 30.[14] So those who do marry are now doing so later, in most cases following a period of cohabitation.[15]

While the marriage rate and overall number of marriages have dropped, the number of *remarriages* stayed fairly constant from the 1970s, having risen after divorce law was liberalized in 1969, but is now also declining. However, remarriages (for one or both parties) constitute a large proportion of total marriages—just under a third of all marriages contracted in England and Wales in 2019.[16]

Marriage practices vary between ethnic groups. Census data looking at family types by reference to the country of birth of the 'family reference person' show that families based on marriage are most common (and cohabitation least common) where that person is of Middle Eastern or Asian origin.[17]

The data discussed so far concern mixed-sex marriage. Same-sex marriage has been possible since late March 2014, and the process for converting a same-sex civil partnership to a marriage has been available since December 2014. In 2019, 6,728 same-sex marriages took place, compared with 213,122 marriages between mixed-sex couples that year.[18] Since same-sex marriage was introduced, most marriages have involved female couples (57.4 per cent in 2019)[19] and the mean age at marriage in 2019 was around 38 for men and 34 for women.[20]

[11] ONS (2022j), 2–3. [12] Probert (2012a), 83.
[13] Government Actuary's Department (2005); ONS (2017c). [14] ONS (2022j), 3.
[15] Beaujouan and Ní Bhrolcháin (2011), 8–10. [16] ONS (2022j), 8.
[17] ONS (2014b), 11–12. [18] ONS (2022j), 2. [19] Ibid. [20] Ibid, 5.

These figures need to be considered in light of same-sex civil partnership statistics. First registrable in December 2005, by the end of 2013 (the last full year before same-sex marriage in England and Wales), 66,730 same-sex partnerships had been registered in the UK.[21] There were twice as many registrations in 2006 than in subsequent years, clearly reflecting the large number of couples who had been waiting (some for decades) to formalize their relationship.[22] The total number of registrations far outstripped the original projection that by 2050 there would be at most 42,500 civil partnerships in Great Britain.[23] But following the announcement of same-sex marriage's introduction, new civil partnership registrations in England and Wales dropped in 2014 by 70 per cent.[24] There were over 900 registrations in 2019, mostly between male couples and more than half involving people aged over 50.[25] The question arises why same-sex marriage and conversion numbers have been relatively low,[26] and why new civil partnerships have a different age and gender profile from same-sex marriage. We explore possible reasons at 2.3.3.

The first mixed-sex civil partnerships in England and Wales were registered on New Year's Eve, 2019. Data are available up to the end of 2020, the first full year, which saw 7,566 mixed-sex registrations compared with only 785 same-sex registrations (the lowest since civil partnerships were introduced in 2005).[27] However, it is important to view these data with caution. The number of civil partnership registrations is likely to have been affected by the Covid-19 pandemic. Furthermore, the much larger proportion of mixed-sex registrations compared with same-sex registrations can be attributed to a backlog of couples wishing to formalize their relationships without having to marry.

2.2.2 NON-FORMALIZED RELATIONSHIPS: COHABITATION

It is harder to measure the incidence of cohabitation and cohabitants' characteristics since such relationships are unregistered, but various surveys and the census give a good sense of their prevalence. As marriage rates are falling, cohabitation is increasing, particularly amongst younger cohorts, and is the fastest growing family type. There were 3.6 million cohabiting couple families in the UK in 2021 (up from just over 2 million in the 2001 census).[28] Numbers of cohabitants are predicted to rise, with more older people cohabiting as young couples age without formalizing their relationships, and those divorcing choosing to cohabit instead of marrying their new partners.[29]

Amongst mixed-sex couples, cohabitation is commonly used as a prelude to marriage, which the rising age at first marriage indicates is being postponed. Increasing numbers of couples may not marry at all, despite evidence of widespread intentions to do so.[30] Older cohabitants are more likely to be divorced and to cohabit instead of marrying. Research suggests that by their tenth anniversary, half of cohabiting couples have married each other, while four in ten have separated—leaving just 10 per cent cohabiting long term.[31] But the

[21] ONS (2015a). [22] Ross et al (2011). [23] DTI (2004), 33–6. [24] ONS (2016b).

[25] ONS (2021e), 2. There were 671 same-sex civil partnerships in 2020, but these data are not indicative of overall trends, as far fewer registrations could take place because of the Covid-19 pandemic.

[26] In 2019, the number of conversions decreased by 28 per cent from 2018: ONS (2022j), 9.

[27] ONS (2021e), 2. [28] ONS (2022b), 2.

[29] ONS (2010a) and ONS (2014c), fig. 8 and associated text.

[30] See Coast (2009); de Waal (2008), discussed at 2.8.2. [31] Beaujouan and Ní Bhrolcháin (2011).

average duration of cohabiting relationships is increasing. The median duration in the early 2000s was three years.[32] The British Social Attitudes survey in 2006 found a mean duration of 4.6 years for past cohabitations; relationships ongoing at the date of the survey had lasted on average 6.9 years, 8.5 where the couple had children.[33] So while cohabiting relationships are on average shorter than marriages, they are not universally characterized by a lack of commitment.[34]

Another significant change is the boom in births outside marriage and a liberalization of attitudes to having children outside marriage.[35] More than half of births now occur outside marriage, and over a third of births are registered by parents who are living together.[36] Data from the Millennium Cohort Study of children born in 2000 indicate that cohabitants' relationships may be less stable than marriage. By the time the child was aged 7, 87 per cent of originally married parents were still together compared to 69 per cent of originally cohabiting parents, of which 20 per cent had married, the remainder still cohabiting.[37]

We discuss some of the policy questions raised by this growth in cohabitation and its relative instability as a family form in 2.8, in light of further empirical data about the characteristics of individuals who do and do not marry.

2.2.3 OTHER RELATIONSHIPS WITHIN AND BETWEEN HOUSEHOLDS

Not everyone lives in couple-based families. Nearly three in ten UK households—8.2 million in total—contain an individual living alone.[38] Just 791,000 households consist of two or more unrelated adults not living as a couple (e.g. as flat-sharers or companions),[39] and 280,000 (1 per cent of all households) comprise multiple families under the same roof (e.g. elderly parents living with their adult children and their families or unrelated families living together).[40] Meanwhile, it is estimated that nearly 10 per cent of British adults 'live apart together': couples who share an intimate relationship, without living in the same household.[41]

2.3 GENDER IDENTITY, SEXUAL ORIENTATION, AND GENDER ROLES

Historically, many 'family' relationships were not legally recognized because they failed to fit the law's family template: a (mixed-sex) married couple with children, or as Katherine O'Donovan once called it, the advertisers' 'cornflakes family'.[42] However, human rights arguments have been used to extend the legal conception of family to non-traditional family forms. We examine two issues here in order to set the scene for the current law discussed later in this chapter: gender identity and the treatment of transgender and non-binary people in law; and relationships between same-sex couples. How the law has dealt with these issues reveals some important features of the law's (traditional) view of what marriage, in particular,

32 Ibid, 13 and fn 41. 33 Barlow et al (2008). 34 Lewis et al (1999); Smart and Stevens (2000).
35 NatCen (2016). 36 ONS (2022d), table 2. 37 Calderwood (2010), table 3.9.
38 ONS (2022b), table 7. 39 Ibid. 40 Ibid.
41 Duncan et al (2013); Haskey and Lewis (2006). 42 O'Donovan (1993), 30.

is all about. We then consider how legal relationship forms may, or may be perceived to, rest on particular gendered norms about the roles of men and women in conjugal relationships, and how those norms might influence some people's behaviour in relationship formation.[43]

2.3.1 DETERMINING GENDER

The recognition of adult relationships is one area in which the legally recognized gender of each person matters, though less so than formerly. As noted at 1.2.4, although the law refers to 'opposite-sex' (we prefer 'mixed-sex') and 'same-sex' relationships,[44] the key criterion is in fact not 'sex' in a narrow, biologically determined sense, but a person's legally recognized 'gender'.[45]

Until recently, only couples of different legal gender could marry and only couples of the same legal gender could register a civil partnership. The arrival of same-sex marriage and mixed-sex civil partnership in England and Wales changed that, of course. However, we still need to know for some legal purposes whether a marriage or civil partnership involves a same-sex couple.[46] So it remains necessary that each of us has a legally determined gender. That question is not straightforward for individuals who do not identify with the gender assigned to them at birth—transgender ('trans') people,[47] even less so for those who identify as non-binary (a category not presently accommodated in law at all).[48]

As we noted at 1.2.4, the GRA 2004 provides a procedure for trans people to have their preferred gender recognized for all purposes, including marriage and civil partnership law, following adverse rulings by the European Court of Human Rights regarding the UK's previous refusal to recognize preferred gender.[49] The common law position—whereby legal gender is determined on purely biological criteria—established in *Corbett v Corbett*, continues to apply if a gender recognition certificate is not obtained under the 2004 Act procedure. Recent data indicate that, owing to the intrusive and burdensome nature of the process, a high proportion of trans people have not obtained a certificate,[50] and so those individuals' legal gender for the purposes of relationship recognition laws remains governed by the common law, which of course also dictates the legal gender of individuals who identify in non-binary terms. *Corbett* concerned the validity of a marriage contracted between a man and April Ashley, who was born a biological male but self-identified as female and had undergone gender confirmation surgery. At the time, a marriage would be void if not contracted between 'a man and a woman'.[51] What is most striking about Ormrod J's decision that April Ashley was legally a man is the exclusive, question-begging nature of the reasoning, a feature that we shall encounter elsewhere in this chapter: he sets up the issue in such a way that his answer is unavoidable. His view about the 'essential role of a woman in marriage' is also noteworthy:[52]

---

43 Fenton-Glynn (2022). 44 E.g. Marriage (Same Sex Couples) Act 2013.

45 E.g. Gender Recognition Act 2004 (GRA 2004).

46 E.g. availability of marriage solemnized by a religious body, availability of particular grounds of nullity: see 2.5.3. Gender is relevant to civil partnership because only same-sex civil partners can convert a civil partnership to a marriage (made clear by the Marriage (Same Sex Couples) Act 2013, s 9).

47 Cf inter-sex people—discussed at 1.2.4. 48 See Cooper et al (2022).

49 *Goodwin v United Kingdom* (App No 28957/95, ECHR) (2002).

50 Government Equalities Office (2018a), 10–11. 51 See Gilmore (2011).

52 Diduck and Kaganas (2012), 53–5.

Corbett v Corbett (otherwise Ashley) [1971] P 83 (Fam Div), 105–6

ORMROD J:

. . . [S]ex is clearly an essential determinant of the relationship called marriage because it is and always has been recognised as the union of man and woman. It is the institution on which the family is built, and in which the capacity for natural hetero-sexual intercourse is an essential element. It has, of course, many other characteristics, of which companionship and mutual support is an important one, but the characteristics which distinguish it from all other relationships can only be met by two persons of opposite sex. . . .

Since marriage is essentially a relationship between man and woman, the validity of the marriage . . . depends, in my judgment, upon whether the respondent is or is not a woman. . . . The question then becomes, what is meant by the word "woman" in the context of a marriage, for I am not concerned to determine the "legal sex" of the respondent at large. Having regard to the essentially hetero-sexual character of the relationship which is called marriage, the criteria must, in my judgment, be biological, for even the most extreme degree of transsexualism in a male or the most severe hormonal imbalance which can exist in a person with male chromosomes, male gonads and male genitalia cannot reproduce a person who is naturally capable of performing the essential role of a woman in marriage. In other words, the law should adopt in the first place . . . the chromosomal, gonadal and genital tests, and if all three are congruent, determine the sex for the purpose of marriage accordingly, and ignore any operative intervention.

Ormrod J's words stand in stark contrast to the language used by Judge Martens in his dissenting judgment in *Cossey v United Kingdom*, one of the early—unsuccessful—challenges to English law's refusal to recognize the preferred gender of transgender persons.

Cossey v United Kingdom (App No 10843/84, ECHR) (1993)

JUDGE MARTENS (dissenting):

4.5.1 . . . [It] is arbitrary and unreasonable in this context to ignore successful gender reassignment surgery and to retain the criterion of biological sex.

4.5.2 This is all the more so because Mr Justice Ormrod's arguments are clearly unacceptable. Marriage is far more than sexual union, and the capacity for sexual intercourse is, therefore, not "essential" for marriage. Persons who are not or are no longer capable of procreating or having sexual intercourse may also want to and do marry. That is because marriage is far more than a union which legitimates sexual intercourse and aims at procreating: it is a legal institution which creates a fixed legal relationship between both the partners and third parties . . .; it is a societal bond, in that married people (as one learned writer put it) "represent to the world that theirs is a relationship based on strong human emotions, exclusive commitment to each other and permanence"; it is, moreover, a species of togetherness in which intellectual, spiritual and emotional bonds are at least as essential as the physical one.

In one sense, transgender people seeking recognition of their preferred gender in order to marry posed less of a 'threat' to traditional marriage than claims for same-sex marriage: the trans person living in their preferred gender in a mixed-sex couple did not challenge the mixed-sex model of marriage, they merely questioned how legal gender would be determined for these purposes. By contrast, recognition of same-sex marriage would prove far more controversial—though Judge Martens's remarks in *Cossey v United Kingdom* might apply whatever the parties' legal genders.

2.3.2 SAME-SEX RELATIONSHIPS: THE ROAD TO SAME-SEX MARRIAGE

One might assume that by 'same-sex' we mean gay or lesbian. But where the law is concerned about parties' respective legal genders, that is all that it is concerned about; the parties' sexual orientation is legally irrelevant.[53] However, in reality, of course, relationship recognition is most pressing for those in couple-relationships, which usually have a sexual aspect. For many of those couples, achieving the right to marry has been the ultimate goal. Now that English law permits marriage by couples whatever their gender pattern,[54] we focus here on that most recent development, providing only a brief overview of the history leading up to that point.[55]

2.3.2.a Judicial developments

In 1985, a Court of Appeal judge had no hesitation in saying:

> I am . . . firmly of the view that it would be surprising in the extreme to learn that public opinion is such today that it would recognise a homosexual union as being akin to a state of living as husband and wife. The ordinary man and woman . . . would in my opinion not think even remotely of there being a true resemblance between those two very different states of affairs.[56]

That judge was right, insofar as the British Social Attitudes survey of 1983 indicated that only 17 per cent of the British public were completely accepting of same-sex relationships; contrast the figure in 2016: 64 per cent.[57] And so, a woman was denied the right to succeed to the tenancy that had been held in the name of her deceased lesbian partner, on the basis that they could not be regarded—in the terms of the governing statute—as having lived together 'as husband and wife',[58] as mixed-sex cohabitants would be. The European Commission on Human Rights found no violation of Article 14 in conjunction with Article 8: it was legitimate for the state to protect 'the family' (including mixed-sex cohabitants)—which Ms Simpson and her partner were not.[59]

53 Green (2011).

54 Though there are differences for same-sex marriages, particularly regarding their solemnization by religious bodies: see 2.5.3; this will potentially matter both for some trans people without a certificate for their preferred gender and for non-binary individuals.

55 See Cretney (2006a) for a fuller history.

56 Watkins LJ, *Harrogate BC v Simpson* (1985) 17 HLR 205, 209.

57 Swales and Attar Taylor (2017), 4.

58 Housing Act 1980, s 50(3).

59 *Simpson v United Kingdom* (App No 11716/85, ECHR) (1986), [7].

Yet 15 years later, while the House of Lords was still not prepared to regard a same-sex couple's relationship as akin to husband and wife (a finding that would have conferred stronger legal protection), it was prepared to find that they were members of each other's 'family', thereby acquiring some protection under different tenancy succession legislation:[60]

Fitzpatrick v Sterling Housing Association Ltd [2001] 1 AC 27, 44, 51

LORD NICHOLLS:

I am in no doubt that this question should be answered affirmatively. A man and woman living together in a stable and permanent sexual relationship are capable of being members of a family for this purpose. Once this is accepted, there can be no rational or other basis on which the like conclusion can be withheld from a similarly stable and permanent sexual relationship between two men or between two women. . . .

LORD CLYDE:

The concept of the family has undergone significant development during recent years, both in the United Kingdom and overseas. Whether that is a matter for concern or congratulation is of no relevance to the present case, but it is properly part of the judicial function to endeavour to reflect an understanding of such changes in the reality of social life.

Lord Slynn observed in *Fitzpatrick* that the exclusion of same-sex couples from the tenancy succession legislation's more beneficial, quasi-spousal category might be found incompatible with the European Convention on Human Rights (ECHR) once the Human Rights Act 1998 (HRA 1998) came into force.[61] The House of Lords reached that conclusion in 2004, when it was successfully argued that the survivor's rights under Article 14 in conjunction with Article 8's right to respect for the home were violated by denying him the security of tenure enjoyed by a mixed-sex partner on the tenant's death. The argument focused on whether the undoubted difference in treatment of same-sex and mixed-sex unmarried couples in this context could be justified. Baroness Hale explained eloquently why it could not:

Ghaidan v Godin-Mendoza [2004] UKHL 30

BARONESS HALE:

138. We are not here concerned with a difference in treatment between married and unmarried couples. The European Court of Human Rights accepts that the protection of the 'traditional family' is in principle a legitimate aim: see *Karner v Austria* [(App No 40016/98)] . . . para 40. The traditional family is constituted by marriage. The Convention itself, in article 12,

[60] Rent Act 1977, Sch 1, paras 2(2) and 3(1); for commentary, see Sandland (2000); Diduck (2001); and further discussion at 2.8.1.

[61] [2001] 1 AC 27, 34.

singles out the married family for special protection by guaranteeing to everyone the right to marry and found a family. Had [the Rent Act, the tenancy succession legislation] stopped at protecting the surviving spouse, it might have been easier to say that a homosexual couple were not in an analogous situation. But it did not. It extended the protection to survivors of a relationship which was not marriage but was sufficiently like marriage to qualify for the same protection. It has therefore to be asked whether opposite and same-sex survivors are in an analogous situation for this purpose.

139. There are several modern statutes which extend a particular benefit or a particular burden, granted to or imposed upon the parties to a marriage, to people who are or were living together 'as husband and wife'[62] . . . Working out whether a particular couple are or were in such a relationship is not always easy. . . . What matters most is the essential quality of the relationship, its marriage-like intimacy, stability, and social and financial inter-dependence. Homosexual relationships can have exactly the same qualities of intimacy, stability and inter-dependence that heterosexual relationships do.

140. It has not been suggested to us that the nature of the sexual intimacies each enjoys is a relevant difference. Nor can the possibility of holding oneself out as a legally married couple be a relevant difference here . . . [not least given the inability of same-sex couples to marry at this stage].

141. The relevant difference which has been urged upon us is that a heterosexual couple may have children together whereas a homosexual couple cannot. But this too cannot be a relevant difference in determining whether a relationship can be considered marriage-like for the purpose of the Rent Act. First, the capacity to bear or beget children has never been a prerequisite of a valid marriage in English law . . .[63] Secondly, however, the presence of children is a relevant factor in deciding whether a relationship is marriage-like but if the couple are bringing up children together, it is unlikely to matter whether or not they are the biological children of both parties. Both married and unmarried couples, both homosexual and heterosexual, may bring up children together . . .[64] Thirdly, however, there is absolutely no reason to think that the protection given by the Rent Act to the surviving partner's home was given for the sake of the couple's children . . . It is the longstanding social and economic interdependence, which may or may not be the product of having brought up children together, that qualifies for the protection of the Act. . . .

142. Homosexual couples can have exactly the same sort of interdependent couple relationship as heterosexuals can. Sexual 'orientation' defines the sort of person with whom one wishes to have sexual relations. It requires another person to express itself. Some people, whether heterosexual or homosexual, may be satisfied with casual or transient relationships. But most human beings eventually want more than that. They want love. And with love they often want not only the warmth but also the sense of belonging to one another which is the essence of being a couple. And many couples also come to want the stability and permanence which go with sharing a home and a life together, with or without the children who for many people go to make a family. In this, people of homosexual orientation are no different from people of heterosexual orientation.

143. It follows that a homosexual couple whose relationship is marriage-like in the same ways that an unmarried heterosexual couple's relationship is marriage-like are indeed in an analogous situation. Any difference in treatment is based upon their sexual orientation. It requires an objective justification if it is to comply with article 14. Whatever the scope for a 'discretionary area of judgment' in these cases may be, there has to be a legitimate aim

[62] See 2.8.2. [63] Cf 2.7.6 on the consummation requirement.

[64] See chapters 9 and 13 for details about the various ways in which same-sex couples can now become legal parents together.

before a difference in treatment can be justified. But what could be the legitimate aim of singling out heterosexual couples for more favourable treatment than homosexual couples? It cannot be the *protection* of the traditional family. The traditional family is not protected by granting it a benefit which is denied to people who cannot or will not become a traditional family. What is really meant by the 'protection' of the traditional family is the *encouragement* of people to form traditional families and the *discouragement* of people from forming others. . . . Once [the Act] went beyond marriage to unmarried relationships, the aim would have to be encouraging one sort of unmarried relationship and discouraging another. . . . But, . . . it is difficult to see how heterosexuals will be encouraged to form and maintain such marriage-like relationships by the knowledge that the equivalent benefit is being denied to homosexuals. The distinction between heterosexual and homosexual couples might be aimed at discouraging homosexual relationships generally. But that cannot now be regarded as a legitimate aim. It is inconsistent with the right to respect for private life accorded to 'everyone', including homosexuals, by art 8 since *Dudgeon v UK* (1981) 4 EHRR 149. If it is not legitimate to discourage homosexual relationships, it cannot be legitimate to discourage stable, committed, marriage-like homosexual relationships of the sort which qualify the survivor to succeed to the home. Society wants its intimate relationships, particularly but not only if there are children involved, to be stable, responsible and secure. It is the transient, irresponsible and insecure relationships which cause us so much concern.[65]

144. I have used the term 'marriage-like' to describe the sort of relationship which meets the statutory test of living together 'as husband and wife'. Once upon a time it might have been difficult to apply those words to a same-sex relationship because both in law and in reality the roles of the husband and wife were so different and those differences were defined by their genders. That is no longer the case. The law now differentiates between husband and wife in only a very few and unimportant respects. Husbands and wives decide for themselves who will go out to work and who will do the homework and child care. Mostly each does some of each. The roles are inter-changeable. There is thus no difficulty in applying the term 'marriage-like' to same-sex relationships.

And so the House of Lords interpreted the Rent Act provision under s 3 of the HRA 1998 to include same-sex couples, ensuring compatibility with Convention rights.

2.3.2.b The creation of civil partnership

The same year marked the enactment of the Civil Partnership Act 2004 (CPA 2004), which for the first time permitted same-sex couples to formalize their relationships and thereby acquire the vast majority of the rights and duties of marriage, but without the label 'marriage'. The Act reinforced *Ghaidan v Godin-Mendoza* by amending legislation dealing with cohabitants to ensure that it covered same-sex as well as mixed-sex couples, by requiring same-sex couples to demonstrate that they live together 'as if they were civil partners'.[66] But although the institutions of marriage and civil partnership, and their non-formal analogues, were kept semantically distinct, they were intended to operate socially and legally in the same way[67] in order to achieve equality for same-sex couples.[68]

[65] See also *Rodriguez v Ministry of Housing of the Government of Gibraltar* [2009] UKPC 52.

[66] See, e.g., CPA 2004, Sch 8, para 13(3), amending Rent Act 1977, Sch 1, para 2(2).

[67] There are some exceptions in the conditions for creating valid marriage and civil partnership: see 2.6 and 2.7.

[68] Women and Equality Unit (2003a), paras 1.1–1.2.

Hansard, *Official Report*—Civil Partnership Bill Debates, Hansard HC Deb, vol 426, col 776, 9 November 2004: Report Stage

Deputy Minister for Women and Equality (Jacqui Smith):

We introduced [the Bill] with a specific purpose, which is to provide legal recognition for unrelated same-sex couples who do not currently have the option, which is available to opposite-sex couples, to marry. We seek to create a parallel but different legal relationship that mirrors as fully as possible the rights and responsibilities enjoyed by those who can marry, and that uses civil marriage as a template for the processes, rights and responsibilities that go with civil partnership. We are doing this for reasons of equality and social justice . . . We had some discussion about this in Committee, and our view was that, unless there was an objective justification for a difference in the approaches taken to civil marriage and civil partnership, no difference should exist. There are very few areas in which any difference does exist. The whole point, however, is that civil partnership is not civil marriage, for a variety of reasons, such as the traditions and history—religious and otherwise—that accompany marriage. It is not marriage, but it is, in many ways—dare I say it?—akin to marriage. We make no apology for that.

The introduction of civil partnership attracted vocal opposition, notably from those who were unconvinced by the government's denials that civil partnership was essentially 'gay marriage' or, more pejoratively, 'a parody of marriage for homosexual couples'.[69] The CPA 2004 reinforced the policy position that it was not a 'gay marriage' Act by providing that those who had contracted a same-sex marriage abroad in a jurisdiction that permitted same-sex marriage would not be recognized as spouses in English law—instead, they would be treated as civil partners.[70] The attempt of Susan Wilkinson and Celia Kitzinger, who had married in Canada, to obtain a declaration that that was incompatible with their rights under Articles 8, 12, and 14 ECHR failed.[71] They had argued that to offer same-sex couples the 'consolation prize' of civil partnership rather than the 'gold standard' of marriage was offensive and demeaning, breaching basic principles of equality. In finding justification under Article 14 for the undoubted difference in treatment in relation to the right to marry, the President's approach to marriage entailed the sort of exclusive reasoning seen in *Corbett v Corbett*:

Wilkinson v Kitzinger [2006] EWHC 2022

SIR MARK POTTER P:

120. If marriage . . . is[,] by longstanding definition and acceptance, a formal relationship between a man and a woman, primarily (though not exclusively) with the aim of producing and rearing children as I have described it, and if that is the institution contemplated and safeguarded by Article 12, then to accord a same-sex relationship the title and status of marriage would be to fly in the face of the Convention as well as to fail to recognise physical reality.

[69] Hansard HL Deb, vol 660, col 405, 22 April 2004, Baroness O'Cathain.

[70] CPA 2004, ss 212–18, Sch 20.

[71] *Wilkinson v Kitzinger* [2006] EWHC 2022; for commentary see Bamforth (2007a); Harding (2007); Auchmuty (2008); Monaghan and Harding (2010).

To this, one might respond with the words of one Canadian court: 'Stating that marriage is heterosexual because it has always been heterosexual is merely an explanation for the opposite-sex requirement of marriage; it is not an objective that is capable of justifying [different treatment].'[72] The President's reasoning was criticized for adopting a 'heteronormative' approach, presupposing traditional gender roles at odds with many contemporary mixed-sex relationships.[73] It sits awkwardly alongside Baroness Hale's judgment in *Ghaidan*, particularly as she made clear that procreation is not (as a plain matter of English law) a necessary correlative of marriage—but many same-sex couples do raise children.[74] Nor is it obvious how the practice of marriage in its traditional form is promoted by excluding from its ambit same-sex couples who wish to lead a similar life.[75] However, English law was already well ahead of what the ECHR required by way of legal recognition for same-sex couples, so it was doubtful that pursuing the matter in Strasbourg would advance matters.[76]

2.3.2.c The arrival of same-sex marriage in English law

With relatively little forewarning (the issue having not appeared as a manifesto commitment of either coalition party), in 2012 the Coalition Government conducted a consultation exercise on same-sex marriage—or 'equal marriage', as it called it.[77] It elicited the largest response of any consultation process in UK history, attracting over 228,000 individual responses (over half of which supported the proposal to allow same-sex couples to marry in a civil ceremony) and 19 petitions against the proposal (between them collecting half a million signatures). The government's consultation response summarized the key arguments for and against the basic proposition.

HM Government, *Equal Marriage: The Government's Response* (2012)

3.4 Within the 53% of people and organisations[78] who agreed with allowing same-sex couples to have a civil marriage some expressed views on the nature and importance of marriage. This included their belief that it is right to allow same-sex couples to express their love and happiness in the same way as opposite sex couples, and to allow them to have access to marriage which is socially and legally seen as a strong bond between the couple.

3.5 Respondents acknowledged that the introduction of civil partnerships was a significant step forward in society. A few respondents, who agreed with the proposals, nevertheless felt that there are too many differences, both practically and symbolically, between marriage and civil partnerships. For example, respondents commented that "civil partnerships can be seen as a second class form of registration" and that the difference means that "same-sex relationships are demeaned by dismissing them as 'only civil partners' and 'not really married'". Stonewall[79] commented in their response that "by insisting marriages and civil

[72] *Halpern et al v Attorney General of Canada et al* (2003) 169 OAR 172.

[73] Harding (2007); Auchmuty (2008).

[74] Cf 2.7.6; see also Strasser (2020), 48–9.

[75] See also *Secretary of State for Work and Pensions v M* [2006] UKHL 11, [113].

[76] An attempt to do so was held inadmissible: Ferguson et al (2011); DCMS (2014), 20. For the key ECHR case law, see *Karner v Austria* (App No 40016/98, ECHR) (2004); *Schalk and Kopf v Austria* (App No 30141/04, ECHR) (2010); *Vallianatos v Greece* (App Nos 29381/09 and 32684/09, ECHR) (2013); *Oliari v Italy* (App Nos 18766/11 and 36030/11, ECHR) (2015); *Orlandi v Italy* (App Nos 26431/12 et al, ECHR) (2018).

[77] Government Equalities Office (2012).

[78] Excluding the petitions.

[79] The gay, lesbian, and bisexual campaign group.

partnerships be kept separate, organisations and individuals perpetuate the notion, even if inadvertently, that relationships between same-sex couples are not as valid as those between heterosexual couples." . . .

3.7 In a similar vein, most respondents who agreed with the proposals saw allowing same-sex couples to have a marriage ceremony as a matter of equality, and/or human rights. . . .

3.8 In addition to the equality benefits of the proposals, a number of those who agreed with them felt that allowing same-sex couples to marry would be good for society as a whole, and would reflect the position of society and social views regarding same-sex couples. . . .

3.9 However, others disagreed with these views and did not believe that same-sex couples should be able to get married. Most of these responses commented that this was because it did not fit in with the current legal definition of marriage, as being between a man and a woman. Of those who indicated they were against the proposals, most said that this was because the true meaning of marriage could not include same-sex couples. The Catholic Bishops Conference of England and Wales quoted the definition included in the Catechism:

> "The matrimonial covenant, by which a man and a woman establish between themselves a partnership of the whole of life, is by its very nature ordered to the good of the spouses and the procreation and education of offspring" . . .[80]

3.14 Many also felt that allowing same-sex couples to marry would be bad for society as a whole. They believed it would, for example, have wider negative consequences or send out the wrong message to children. Respondents raised concerns that the role and place of marriage in society would be taken too lightly, or that it would "bring about more instability to marriages in this country". They saw marriage between a man and a woman as of fundamental benefit to society, In contrast, some responses, including that of the Evangelical Alliance, felt that allowing same-sex couples to get married would have a negative impact on all people's marriages, and therefore society, as the institution would be "diluted."

Many of the objections put against same-sex marriage in the consultation exercise have been put elsewhere. In the following extract, Mark Strasser—writing from a US perspective—challenges the argument that recognizing same-sex marriage would threaten 'traditional marriage'.[81] Much of what he says resonates with Baroness Hale's speech in *Ghaidan v Godin-Mendoza*, see 2.3.2.a.

M. Strasser, 'Family, Same-Sex Unions and the Law', in J. Eekelaar and R. George (eds), *Routledge Handbook of Family Law and Policy*, 2nd edn (Abingdon: Routledge, 2020), 50–3

Sometimes, the alleged harm of same-sex marriage is that it undermines the purpose of marriage, namely, 'the need to provide a biological father and mother committed to each other, hopefully for life, for the purpose of rearing healthy children'. But this is incorrect, at least in part, because there is no single purpose for marriage. Individuals who will not or cannot procreate are not (and should not be) precluded from marrying on that account, which suggests that the state recognizes that marriage serves a variety of purposes, only one of which is that

[80] The Church of England and Muslim Council of Britain made similar points.
[81] See also Norrie (2014).

it provides a setting in which children might thrive. But same-sex couples fulfil many of the purposes of marriage, including providing a place where the young can be nurtured, and this provides a strong policy reason why they should have their relationships recognized. In cases in which the relationship must be dissolved, the state has interests implicated in ensuring an orderly dissolution of the relationship, including an equitable distribution of property, the provision of support in appropriate cases, and visitation and custody awards where children are involved. But the state's interests in assuring an orderly breakdown of long-term relationships are implicated whether the couple is composed of individuals of the same sex or different sexes.

But does giving same-sex couples the right to have civil partnership not provide all the protection that is necessary to advance the state's purposes? This is where it is necessary to turn to arguments based on equality and equal respect:

When the US Supreme Court struck down Virginia's interracial marriage ban in *Loving v Virginia*, the Court reasoned that the prohibition was 'designed to maintain White Supremacy' and as such was 'invidious racial discrimination' that had no legitimate independent purpose. The Court would presumably also have rejected a 'separate but equal' status as stigmatizing and hence unconstitutional. One must wonder what legitimate, independent purpose is served by refusing to permit same-sex couples to marry. The point here is not to undermine the desirability of same-sex couples having a legal status for their relationships even if it is a civil partnership rather than a marriage, because even a separate status would afford many of the emotional, religious, and tangible benefits afforded by marriage. Those are important and are not to be taken lightly. Nevertheless, by creating a separate status, the state sends additional messages, for example, that it does not want the institution of marriage to be tainted by permitting those with a same-sex orientation to have access to it. Yet, that is presumably exactly the kind of message that the state should not be sending insofar as it wishes to promote respect for all persons. By the same token, when the state makes marriage a restricted institution only open to certain individuals even though those denied access would both benefit from and serve the purposes of the institution, the state sends additional messages, for example, that marriage itself is simply yet another pawn to be used in the culture wars. But sending such a message does more to demean the institution in the eyes of many than permitting same-sex couples and their families to enter the fold ever could.

Perhaps it would be thought that recognizing same-sex marriage somehow sends a message of disapproval to those who oppose such unions. But it is of course true that individuals who oppose same-sex unions are not being told that they cannot marry. So, too, individuals who believe that it is important for individuals to marry within their faith are not somehow being denigrated when the state permits individuals of different faiths or no faiths to marry. The recognition of same-sex marriages does not imply that different-sex marriages are not valuable, just as the recognition of interracial, interreligious or intergenerational marriages does not imply that intra-racial, intra-religious or intra-generational marriages are not valuable.

The government promoted the Marriage (Same Sex Couples) Bill[82] in simple terms, echoing the view of marriage expressed by Judge Martens in *Cossey* (extracted at 2.3.1) in relation to transgender individuals' right to marry:

[82] For analysis of the parliamentary and associated debates, see Eekelaar (2014); Harding (2014), (2015).

Hansard, *Official Report*—Marriage (Same Sex Couples) Bill Debates, Hansard HC Deb, vol 558, col 125, 5 February 2013: 2nd Reading

The Minister for Women and Equalities (Maria Miller):

Mr Speaker, you and I know that every marriage is different – indeed, any husband or wife of a member of this House has a distinct set of challenges to face every day – but what marriage offers us all is a lifelong partner to share our journey, a loving stable relationship to strengthen us and mutual support throughout our lives. I believe that that should be embraced by more couples. The depth of feeling, love and commitment between same-sex couples is no different from that depth of feeling between opposite-sex couples. The Bill enables society to recognise that commitment in the same way, too, through marriage. Parliament should value people equally in the law, and enabling same-sex couples to marry removes the current differentiation and distinction.

The Bill inevitably attracted opposition in Parliament. A major focus of the debates was the need to secure the position of religious bodies, particularly the Church of England, which do not wish to solemnize marriages between same-sex couples, whilst providing a mechanism to enable those religious bodies that do wish to solemnize such marriages to do so. But others fundamentally objected to the Bill, taking the position of the Coalition for Marriage, which had gathered one of the main petitions on the proposition: 'I support the legal definition of marriage which is the voluntary union for life of one man and one woman to the exclusion of all others. I oppose any attempt to redefine it.' This position again shares much with that of Ormrod J in *Corbett* (extracted at 2.3.1), refusing to accept the possibility of an alternative view of who might marry whom.

Hansard, *Official Report*—Marriage (Same Sex Couples) Bill Debates, Hansard HL Deb, vol 745, col 942, 3 June 2013: 2nd Reading

Lord Dear:

[W]e find ourselves in a world where an ill considered Bill seeks to overturn centuries of tradition, heedless of public opinion and the views of religious leaders and blind to the laws of unintended consequences. It seeks to alter totally the concept of marriage as we have always known it, it seeks to divide a nation with an argument that hides behind the concept of equality when in reality it is about sameness, and it stands on its head all considerations of electoral mandate.

The opposition failed, and so in 2014 the first same-sex marriages were formalized—and a new discrimination created: for while mixed-sex couples could simply marry or not marry, same-sex couples had a choice between marriage, civil partnership, or neither. This triggered a campaign to extend civil partnership to mixed-sex couples, as discussed in the next section.

2.3.3 THE EXTENSION OF CIVIL PARTNERSHIPS TO MIXED-SEX COUPLES

In June 2018, Rebecca Steinfeld and Charles Keidan obtained a declaration of incompatibility under the HRA 1998 from the Supreme Court in relation to the CPA 2004's restriction to same-sex couples. The different range of choice open to same-sex and mixed-sex couples following the introduction of same-sex marriage was held to constitute unjustifiable discrimination under Article 14 ECHR in conjunction with Article 8.[83] By the time the case reached the court, the government had almost conceded the point, arguing only about whether further delay in rectifying the acknowledged discrimination could be justified while it gathered data and decided what to do. Answer: no, it could not.

In principle, there were two plausible ways of curing the discrimination: (i) leave existing civil partnerships alone, but close the institution to all *new* entrants, with the result that the institution would in time wither away and die when the last civil partnership ended by dissolution or the death of one partner; or (ii) extend civil partnership to mixed-sex couples.[84] While there was no clear human rights mandate in either direction,[85] and the Supreme Court decision left the choice to Parliament, the government announced plans to pursue the second option, following strong evidence of public support for 'equal civil partnership'[86] and facing parliamentary pressure.[87] This was then overtaken by the CPA 2019 which amended the CPA 2004 to allow mixed-sex civil partnerships through very simple statutory drafting.[88]

At present, only same-sex civil partners are able to convert to marriage; there is no equivalent provision for mixed-sex civil partners. This conversion facility was created when same-sex marriage was introduced, in order to allow couples who had been denied access to marriage the opportunity simply to 'upgrade' their existing relationship to marriage at minimal (administrative) cost. However, given there is currently no provision for conversion from marriage to civil partnership in England and Wales, this raises the question of whether married mixed-sex couples who had been denied access to a relationship form that they would have preferred to adopt should now have the option to change their relationship to one of civil partnership.

The government has considered introducing this option, which would permit two types of conversion: same-sex civil partnership to marriage and mixed-sex marriage to civil partnership.[89] However, John Haskey has suggested that any extension in conversion rights permitted by the government will be carefully limited:

J. Haskey, 'Perspectives on Civil Partnerships and Marriages in England and Wales: Aspects, Attitudes and Assessments', (2021) *Family Law* 816, 824–5

> The government is evidently wary of what might be termed a proliferation of conversion rights, and has had a history of guardedly arguing against extending them, adopting a cautionary approach in the light of developments, most particularly when a new form of civil partnership or marriage has been legislated, creating new possible conversions. One can sympathise with the government's reluctance when faced with the potential complexity and far-reaching ramifications. In 2012, when consulting about same sex marriage, the

[83] *R (Steinfeld and Keidan) v Secretary of State for International Development* [2018] UKSC 32.

[84] See Scherpe (2017) for a comparative law overview.

[85] Cf Fenwick and Hayward (2018).

[86] Populus (2018); Fraser (2018), reporting research by Barlow.

[87] See Hayward (2019), 284.

[88] Specifically, by deleting 'of the same sex' from s 1(1) of the Civil Partnership Act 2004; and deleting '(a) they are not of the same sex,' in the grounds for eligibility (and so of grounds making a purported civil partnership void) set out in s 3.

[89] Government Equalities Office (2022b).

> government accepted the need for conversions from same-sex civil partnerships to marriage but said there was 'no justification or requirement' for the reverse conversion. In the most recent consultation in July 2019, with regard to conversions in general, the government's long term stated view was: 'We do not want to encourage concepts of 'trading up' or swapping one relationship for another. We are also keen to minimise administrative complexity and scope for confusion about the status of relationships or the rights of couples'. Also: 'this could involve creating conversion rights which may never be used.'

It is not clear that these are strong arguments in themselves, or that they outweigh the disadvantages that a lack of conversion rights would impose on some couples. Haskey summarizes the reasons in support of *four* potential conversion options (mixed- and same-sex marriage to civil partnership, and mixed- and same-sex civil partnership to marriage) as follows:

> [T]his argument of lack of opportunity should be regarded as only one of several considerations . . . [and] does not necessarily mean that only the conversion from opposite sex marriage to opposite sex civil partnership ought to be permitted. Other arguments might be deployed for enactment of one, other, or both of the remaining two conversions, possibly based on grounds of equality or discrimination. Another argument might be that the four conversion options would encourage all couples periodically to review the meaning and legal nature of their relationship – both of which could change over time. Indeed, as mentioned above, some same sex couples regard civil partnerships as a stepping stone to marriage. Nor does the argument of 'having had the opportunity' necessarily hold sway with the public if there is strong demand for the other two conversions, although the likely actual numbers would be more decisive. Although a final decision has yet to be taken, it looks unlikely that the remaining two conversions will find their way onto the statute book, but the consultation results, the government's response, and organised pressure, might prove otherwise.
>
> Nevertheless, despite the reasoned argument by the government, it might usefully be recalled that it only takes one couple – such as Steinfeld and Keidan – with widespread support and a strong rallying argument, citing the banner of equality, successfully to ensure additional rights are created and legally recognised.

Indeed, there are several plausible scenarios in which the possibility of conversion would be important. For instance, a mixed-sex couple in a civil partnership may undergo a religious conversion or have some other personal reason for now wishing to be married to one another. Or, a mixed-sex couple in a civil partnership may wish to move overseas to a jurisdiction that will not recognize the partnership but would recognize a marriage. Under the present law, these couples could not convert their relationship.

Although some have argued that the advent of mixed-sex civil partnership over-complicates the array of legally recognized relationship forms,[90] it offers various technical and practical advantages. For example, it has ameliorated the previously anomalous position of trans people in same-sex civil partnerships, who had been required to dissolve their partnership or convert to a marriage following legal recognition of their preferred gender.

[90] Norrie (2015); see also concerns of Scherpe (2017), extracted at 2.3.4.d, 53.

The reform has also eased international recognition of equivalent relationships (e.g. from the Netherlands and New Zealand). It has removed the 'outing' effect of civil partnership, as declaration of that relationship status no longer indicates that the relationship is same-sex. Finally, the reform retains an option entirely free of religious connotations for same-sex couples who, for religious reasons (or otherwise[91]), do not want to marry.[92]

While the technical, practical, and symbolic implications of this reform are clearly beneficial, it is important not to overstate the extent to which it has addressed issues of law and policy affecting unmarried cohabitants. When Steinfeld and Keidan obtained a declaration of incompatibility in the Supreme Court, they stated they had fought 'for 3.3 million cohabitants in England and Wales'.[93] However, several commentators have signalled caution at this assertion:

A. Hayward, 'The Steinfeld Effect: Equal Civil Partnerships and the Construction of the Cohabitant', (2019) 31 *Child and Family Law Quarterly* 283, 300

> It needs to be understood that equal civil partnerships are not a panacea capable of directly tackling all forms of relationship-generated disadvantage. It is clear that they will offer a desired option for formalisation for a significant minority of cohabiting couples, but it is statistically more likely that the majority will not formalise their relationship.

As Anne Barlow has noted, couples opting for mixed-sex civil partnership are likely to be 'Ideologues'; so-called because they 'reject (legal) marriage on ideological grounds'.[94] But as we discuss in 2.8.2, this does not represent the majority of cohabiting couples.

A. Barlow, 'Modern Marriage Myths: The Dichotomy Between Expectations of Legal Rationality and Lived Law', in R. Akhtar, P. Nash, and R. Probert (eds), *Cohabitation and Religious Marriage: Status, Similarities and Solutions* (Bristol: BUP, 2020), 49–50

> In terms of the wider group of cohabitants, it is suggested that equal civil partnership will only be attractive to a relatively small group, again not resolving the problem for the vast majority. Drawing on our two samples of opposite-sex cohabitants interviewed in 2006–7, the Ideologues will undoubtedly embrace civil partnership. Indeed the couple who challenged the current law in the courts, Rebecca Steinfeld and Charles Keiden, expressed the views of many of our ideological couples about wanting to avoid the patriarchal nature of marriage. However, only 10 per cent of our national sample . . . were put in this Ideologue group . . .

Therefore, Barlow concluded that mixed-sex civil partnership is 'a remedy for the few not the many'.[95] Failing to account for this could be detrimental to the case for further reform:

[91] See 2.3.4.c. [92] See Gaffney-Rhys (2014), (2017); Draghici (2017); Hayward (2017).

[93] <http://equalcivilpartnerships.org.uk/category/latest-news/page/3/> cited in Miles and Probert (2019), 303.

[94] Barlow (2020), 49. [95] Ibid, 50. See also Barlow (2022).

J. Miles and R. Probert, 'Civil Partnership: Ties That (also) Bind?', (2019) 31 *Child and Family Law Quarterly* 303, 318–19

[I]t would be deeply unfortunate if the choice of equal civil partnership – and an associated, exclusive rhetoric of formalisation, autonomy and choice that neglects the real-life situation of many cohabitants, especially those in 'uneven' relationships – had the effect of distracting reform attention from the pressing issues that will continue to affect cohabitants, different-sex and same-sex.

Aside from these predominantly practical effects, the primary motivations for mixed-sex civil partnership appear to have been underpinned by wider ideological debates generated by English law's shifting parameters around relationship formalization. This is considered further in the next section.

2.3.4 IDEOLOGICAL IMPLICATIONS OF RELATIONSHIP FORMALIZATION?

Both the advent of same-sex marriage and the extension of civil partnership have prompted fundamental debate about the ideological role and desirability of each institution, especially given (in some quarters) concerns about (in other quarters, promotion of) gendered, 'heteronormative' ideals that are particularly associated with marriage. For some, marriage is an icon, and as such an important prize to be won, even if civil partnership or some other institution affords identical rights and duties. But for others, marriage is a patriarchal monolith to be avoided in favour of more diverse, egalitarian ways of living, or simply an irrelevance in contemporary society. Curiously, these debates appear at times to give conservative religious organizations and other 'traditionalists' common cause with some feminist and radical queer commentators, insofar as these distinct groups (with very different motivations) oppose gay marriage and/or mixed-sex civil partnership.[96] They can also be conducted rather bluntly, as Daniel Monk has observed:

D. Monk, 'Judging the Act: Civil Partnership Disputes in the Courtroom and the Media', in N. Barker and D. Monk (eds), *From Civil Partnership to Same-Sex Marriage: Interdisciplinary Reflections* (Abingdon: Routledge, 2015), 183–4

Arguments both for and against the CPA, and gay marriage more generally, frequently make broad claims about their effects. For example, within 'progressive' circles, supporters claim that the legislation will 'modernise' the institution of marriage (for the better), while detractors claim that the institution will 'normalise' gays and lesbians (for the worse). These causal arguments are often crude. On both sides ideological aspirations are too often expressed as empirical predictions.

With that caveat in mind, we shall survey some of the key arguments.

[96] For discussion of the various viewpoints, see Crompton (2004); Eskridge (2001); Norrie (2000); Finnis (1993); Bamforth (2001), (2007b); Auchmuty (2008).

2.3.4.a Same-sex marriage: a mixed blessing?

Some pro-gay rights commentators view same-sex marriage with ambivalence. Does legal recognition come only at the cost of being required to behave in a way that conforms to heterosexual models of relationship? Couples who fear that might prefer the distinctiveness of civil partnership, if they chose to register their relationship with the state at all.

A. Diduck, 'A Family by Any Other Name . . . or Starbucks™ Comes to England', (2001) 28 *Journal of Law and Society* 290, 292–4

Boyd and other . . . scholars have previously brought to our attention the deradicalizing potential of widening the net of traditional families . . . and I wish to argue that important lessons can be learned from their insights. Boyd, for example, says that each time a case to redefine spouse or family is brought forward, a challenge to heteronormativity is made, but often the way that legal arguments have to be formulated and, I would add, the way the decision is ultimately framed means that the potentially disruptive gay/lesbian subject is absorbed back into familiar roles and his or her disruptive potential is displaced. We can see evidence of this in the *Fitzpatrick* case. In arguing first for legal recognition as a spouse, and alternatively as family, Fitzpatrick was forced to submit that his relationship with Mr Thompson was 'akin to marriage', and the way the court framed its decision seems to suggest that it agreed.

Diduck finds traditional equality arguments problematic because applicants must demonstrate that they are treated differently from analogous individuals. The claim's success hangs on gay and lesbian applicants showing that their relationships are the same as heterosexual ones: this 'retains the pitfall of instantiating in law characteristics, relationships, and subjectivities already dominant'.[97] Craig Lind argues that this creates new demarcations: homosexuality per se no longer bars admission to 'family', but those whose relationships fail to make the grade in other respects—for example, because not monogamous, or because not perceived as being sufficiently committed—remain excluded:[98]

C. Lind, 'Sexuality and Same-Sex Relationships in Law', in B. Brooks-Gordon et al (eds), *Sexuality Repositioned* (Oxford: Hart Publishing, 2004), 126

[A]lternative ways of living domestic lives are being marginalised by the . . . process of normalisation. People who are unsuited to these lifestyles remain outsiders in society. And the question we must ask ourselves is whether or not we have really progressed when we have managed to enlarge the group of the privileged and retain our prejudices in relation to others.

Diduck has also raised concerns about the tendency of relationship formalization to entail the privatization of care.[99] This theme is picked up by Nicola Barker, noting the language of

[97] Diduck (2001), 304.
[98] See further Eskridge (2001); Halley (2001); Norrie (2000).
[99] Diduck (2005).

'commitment' and 'mutual support' used by Prime Minister David Cameron to advocate for gay marriage:

N. Barker, 'After the Wedding, What Next? Conservatism and Conjugality', in N. Barker and D. Monk (eds), *From Civil Partnership to Same-Sex Marriage: Interdisciplinary Reflections* (Abingdon: Routledge, 2015), 222–3

> These terms are not particularly surprising in that they are frequently used when politicians discuss marriage in general, but they are not empty rhetoric. Behind them is a troubling economic policy: the privatisation of care and dependency. This refers to the burdens and costs of social reproduction (for example raising a child) being borne almost exclusively by the family unit as the state retracts welfare provision and support services. For example, as Susan Boyd . . . has argued, an expectation that childcare will be done in the home for free by mothers is linked to both childcare work being underpaid and the absence of publicly funded daycare. It can also refer to an expectation of mutual support between partners, which results in the reduction or withdrawal of state support such as unemployment benefits based on a partner's income. . . .
>
> In this sense, marriage and civil partnership play a key role in supporting the politics of state austerity and the rolling back of the welfare state. This is motivated not only by immediate financial concerns but also by an ideology that reifies the small state. The state recognises same-sex relationships in order to encourage lesbians and gay men to take on these care burdens and financial (inter)dependencies as part of the process of welfare retrenchment. . . .

But others take a different view of the arrival of same-sex marriage, either regarding normalization as unproblematic or rejecting the view that the concept of family will remain fixed. The 'conservative approach', outlined by Lind in this extract, rejects the notion that marriage is institutionally unacceptable and embraces normalization:

C. Lind, 'Sexuality and Same-Sex Relationships in Law', in B. Brooks-Gordon et al (eds), *Sexuality Repositioned* (Oxford: Hart Publishing, 2004), 122–4, 126

> For some . . ., what distinguishes people with same-sex desire from those with different-sex desire is only their desire. In all other respects lesbians and gay men are 'normal'. Furthermore, their identity is perceived as immutable. And inequality arising out of an immutable, unchosen, characteristic, it is argued, is unjust. The argument goes on to assert that society could easily remedy that inequality by extending the privileges of the majority to the minority. Sexuality should be an irrelevant consideration in legal regulation; in the regulation of family relationships, for example, lesbians and gay men should be able to attract exactly the same legal regulation as different-sex couples. Society would, in effect, acknowledge the 'normality' of lesbians and gay men by adapting its significant institutions to provide for them. Even amongst those who acknowledge the constructed nature of sexuality there are those who take the view that a socially responsible sexuality is a constrained sexuality . . . Fitting same-sex desire into the normal patterns of life is an acceptable way of controlling it so that it becomes socially responsible rather than socially obnoxious. Normalisation of sexuality should occur . . .

Recent research amongst younger generations of same-sex couples who had formed civil partnerships suggests that most such couples do indeed just want to be normal—or 'ordinary'—rather than to be at the vanguard of a radical movement experimenting with alternative forms of relationship.[100]

B. Heaphy, C. Smart, and A. Einarsdottir, *Same-Sex Marriages: New Generations, New Relationships* (Basingstoke: Palgrave Macmillan, 2013), 5

Indeed, notable findings from our research include the common belief among younger same-sex partners that gender and sexual inequalities in relationships have largely been overcome, and that *couple-centred* life remains the obvious and natural answer to life-political questions about how to live and relate. These beliefs partly influenced many partners' claims to have 'ordinary' marriages,[101] which in turn were grounded in a conviction that contemporary heterosexual and same-sex relationships were much the same. This is linked to a conviction that heterosexual and same-sex relationships are now equal in the eyes of the law, and are generally accepted as on a par with each other in day-to-day life. It is also linked to the strong sense that active commitments are more important than gender and sexuality in the making of 'good' relationships and marriages. Such beliefs and claims were thought to be evidenced by real changes that had taken place with respect to sexuality in law and in everyday life, which enabled younger same-sex couples to live their lives relatively free from the constraints encountered by previous generations. While previous generations of feminist and lesbian and gay liberationists linked the cultural privileging of the couple and marriage to constraining power, the tendency among our younger same-sex partners was to link their personal privileging of the couple and marriage to the historically increased quanta of power that sexual minorities have over their ordinary lives. At the same time, their beliefs that their relationships were more similar to, rather than different from, their heterosexual generational peers were grounded in a conviction that the latter tended to be less 'traditional' and more equal relationships than was the case for their parents' generation. This implied that gender was nowadays relatively insignificant in shaping heterosexual relationships and marriages. This is the imagined social world that many younger same-sex partners invoke in telling their stories of their 'ordinary' relationships.

Heaphy et al emphasize that the 'ideals of ordinariness . . . cannot simply be equated with the "normalisation" or "assimilation" of these relationships' of the sort that would trouble Diduck. Rather, the claim to be ordinary is viewed as a claim to be part of the common 'mass of people (heterosexual and non-heterosexual) in "the middle" who must work at creating "mature" and "responsible" relationships'.[102]

2.3.4.b Exercising the choice: marriage or civil partnership?

Notably, the couples in the Heaphy et al study had grown up and spent all or most of their adult lives in a time when the advances in gay rights and relationship recognition (all bar same-sex marriage) had already been made. It seems likely that members of older cohorts, who had

[100] Cf Mitchell et al (2009).
[101] This term was being used in relation to civil partnership; see also Peel (2015).
[102] Heaphy et al (2013), 170.

fought both those battles and those of feminism from the 1970s onwards, might take a very different view, rejecting what they view as the (undesirably) normalizing heteronormativity of marriage.[103] This may explain the existence of the remaining customer-base for civil partnership registrations since the advent of same-sex marriage and, in particular, the higher average age of those new civil partners. Indeed, it is also notable that there have been far fewer conversions of civil partnership to marriage than might have been expected.[104] After all, 87 per cent of respondents to the government's consultation exercise on 'equal marriage' had answered 'yes' to the question: 'if you are in a civil partnership would you wish to take advantage of this policy and convert your civil partnership into a marriage?'[105] So why has there not been a flood of conversions? What does civil partnership mean to people? Views clearly vary. One qualitative study amongst existing civil partners and same-sex spouses offers some insight:

A. Jowett and E. Peel, '"A Question of Equality and Choice": Same-Sex Couples' Attitudes Towards Civil Partnership After the Introduction of Same-Sex Marriage', (2017) 8 *Psychology and Sexuality* 69, 77–8

Within our data, there were conflicting views on civil partnership that divided our respondents in roughly equal numbers. It appeared that non-heterosexuals are more likely to advocate the discontinuation of civil partnership if they view them as a stepping stone to true equality. Respondents who held this view were also more likely to have converted their civil partnership to a marriage, planned to do so or had chosen to get married once it became possible. Meanwhile, those who endorse extending civil partnership to different-sex couples tend to view marriage as a heteronormative, patriarchal and/or religious institution, and view civil partnership as a modern alternative. Respondents expressing these views more often chose not to convert their civil partnerships to a marriage or, in some cases, had formed a civil partnership despite marriage being an option . . . Others meanwhile were more ambivalent both about the name of the legal contract and whether civil partnership were extended or discontinued.

However, there was one thing that respondents broadly agreed upon. Formal equality (treating everyone exactly the same in law) was a principle that, on the whole, underpinned the arguments on all sides . . . Some felt that civil partnership should be abolished because formal equality had been achieved in the form of marriage equality. Others believed that civil partnership should be extended to different-sex couples to bring about formal equality. . . . The principle of formal equality is what Billig refers to as a taken-for-granted cultural 'commonplace'. However, this construction of equality as treating everyone the same can obscure structural oppression of particular groups. For instance, the principle of formal equality can be used as a basis to argue that equality measures represent reverse discrimination, which . . . often constitutes a form of mundane heterosexism. As several respondents note, the campaign for 'equal civil partnerships' may fail to acknowledge heterosexual privilege, and the social context in which civil partnership was created. Different-sex couples are not denied access to civil partnership because heterosexuals are oppressed but rather as an unintended consequence of the historic oppression of lesbians and gay men.

[103] See Auchmuty (2015); Fenwick and Hayward (2018), 116–17.

[104] See 2.2.1; Hayward (2017), 534.

[105] HM Government (2012), Question 9.

2.3.4.c Fighting for the choice: mixed-sex civil partnership

So who were those mixed-sex couples who campaigned for 'equal civil partnership' and why did they want it? The stance of the 'poster couple' of the campaign has been described thus:

Steinfeld and Keidan v Secretary of State for Education [2017] EWCA Civ 81

ARDEN LJ:

5. The appellants, Rebecca Steinfeld and Charles Keidan, are a young couple in a committed long-term relationship. They wish to formalise their relationship, but they have deep-rooted and genuine ideological objections to marriage based upon what they consider to be its historically patriarchal nature.[106] They consider that the status of civil partnership would reflect their values and give due recognition to the equal nature of their relationship. Ms Steinfeld and Mr Keidan in good faith consider that marriage does not reflect the way in which they understand their commitment to each other or wish their relationship to be seen. . . .

Steinfeld and Keidan, who have two children, are far from alone. Responses to government consultation exercises on the matter[107] and various empirical research projects reveal an appetite for civil partnership amongst mixed-sex couples who want the legal consequences of marriage without what they regard as the negative connotations of that institution.

A. Barlow and J. Smithson, 'Legal Assumptions, Cohabitants' Talk and the Rocky Road to Reform', (2010) 22 *Child and Family Law Quarterly* 328, 336–7

Both of our qualitative studies confirmed that Ideologues [those in long-term, committed relationships in which one or both partners have an ideological objection to marriage] who were choosing not to marry for very clear reasons are capable of adopting a legally rational approach, other than in relation to marriage itself. Participants in this group had almost all made wills, made declarations of ownership in respect of the family home, and drawn up next of kin documents in each other's favour. The one legal step they were not generally prepared to take was that of getting married, however advantageous this might prove to be in terms of issues like pensions and inheritance tax. Many expressed their frustration that there was no mechanism other than marriage – often objected to for its patriarchal baggage – through which they could achieve parity with married couples. The symbolism and values associated with the language of marriage was a problem for some:

> 'The "marriage" word is what's value-laden with all the concepts that we dislike. That's what I object to. If they called it something like "civil contract and joint responsibilities," then fine.' (Peter, long term cohabitant, no children)

[106] See generally 2.4.2, the law of consummation, discussed at 2.7.6, and the laws that currently permit only the spouses' fathers to be named on the marriage certificate, not their mothers: cf changes that might follow under the Civil Partnerships, Marriages and Deaths (Registration etc.) Act 2019.

[107] Notably DCMS (2014), para 2.19.

> Whereas the term 'civil partnership' was much more positively viewed, as Hannah summed up –
>
> > 'I think just the language of civil partnership is quite interesting. The "civil" clearly is making a statement about it being you know, not religious; being secular. And "partnership" is clearly about . . . For me it communicates something about equality, um in terms of two equal people making that . . . Progressing to that point where they want to register their partnership. Whereas marriage comes with so many things in terms of society's expectations or belief about it that, you know, it's very difficult to separate out the legal stuff and the religious stuff from the kind of, um . . . The way our society operates around traditional male-female relationships.' (Hannah, long term cohabitant)

Given the strong views expressed against marriage despite knowledge of the consequences in terms of foregone legal protections, it seems likely that a policy that tried to encourage marriage would have little impact on this group.

> Yet the legal and psychological needs of this very committed and legally rational group would easily be met by the extension of a marriage-like civil partnership to different-sex couples along the lines of the Dutch model. The couples here were not looking for any lesser commitment than marriage – indeed a number considered themselves far more committed to each other than the average married couple – but the patriarchal and quasi-religious tenets embedded within even civil marriage was not something this group were prepared to sign up to, whatever the cost. To view this form of partnership as 'marriage-like' would be to misunderstand the nature and motivations for this style of cohabitation relationship and exposes a weakness in family policy if it fails to provide legal safeguards for what seem to be the 'strong and stable' families it stated it wants to support.

There is clearly a constituency for whom civil partnership would confer its own 'intrinsic value', distinct from marriage. But there are arguments the other way. It should not be assumed that civil partnership offers an idyll of perfect equality and harmony for its constituents.[108] Same-sex couples in Rosemary Auchmuty's small-scale qualitative study of civil partnership dissolution were clearly disappointed that civil partnership had apparently not offered them a better way of doing relationships—Auchmuty concludes that 'not only are same-sex couples not immune to the problems suffered by opposite-sex couples but . . . destructive . . . dynamics might actually be built into our legal model of marriage'.[109] Other commentators, reflecting on the mixed-sex experience, have observed that 'equal access to civil partnerships cannot be presented as a panacea . . . excising fully the ills flowing from the more value-laden institution of marriage, given structural inequalities in society influencing the nature of personal relationships':[110] for example, the typically gendered division of paid and unpaid work driven by labour market factors such as the gender pay gap and lack of affordable child-care.[111] More prosaically, some have expressed concern that mixed-sex civil partnership might be 'mis-sold' as something different from marriage when, in terms

[108] Bendall (2019). [109] Auchmuty (2015), 213. [110] Fenwick and Hayward (2018), 98–9.
[111] See data discussed at 6.2.

of the intensity of its legal consequences, it is largely identical.[112] In that sense, it would be wrong to view civil partnership as a stepping stone to marriage: civil partnership would itself confer all the same rights and obligations that marriage would confer. And, of course, as seen in 2.3.3, it would do nothing for those couples who cannot persuade their partners to formalize their relationship or for adults within the prohibited degrees who want more legal recognition for their non-conjugal relationship.[113]

2.3.4.d Transformation or stagnation?

What of the argument that the inception of same-sex marriage has the potential to transform the institution of marriage? As Ferguson has argued, Steinfeld and Keidan's position seems to attach no weight to the fact that marriage is clearly capable of profound change, as evidenced by the creation of same-sex marriage.[114] While Heaphy's younger cohorts of couples may reject the role of radical relationship innovators, the wider recognition of same-sex couples, culminating in their right to marry, may mean that these couples unwittingly have a transformative, modernizing effect on marriage, for mixed-sex as well as same-sex couples:

C. Lind, 'Sexuality and Same-Sex Relationships in Law', in B. Brooks-Gordon et al (eds), *Sexuality Repositioned* (Oxford: Hart Publishing, 2004), 126

> Giving same-sex couples access to ordinary family regulation will, it is argued, go some way (if not all the way) towards addressing the concerns of feminists and others about the patriarchal nature of family regulation. Recognising same-sex relationships will force an internal transformation in the basic tenets of all relationships . . . Although the desire to be married is regarded as a conservative phenomenon . . . the desire to compel the state to recognise same-sex marriage is radical. It brings into public discourse a different way of being married. Same-sex couples will be bound to behave differently from the norm of marriage . . . This is particularly true in relation to gendered roles and other unquestioned behavioural patterns in different sex family lives . . . For this reason same-sex relationships destabilise the ideal of marriage. Same-sex couples introduce a reflective element into expectations of behaviour in relationships. As a result of this characteristic they will, it is argued, reveal different ways of being married. In particular, they will undermine gendered power in relationships. A more equitable family ethic will emerge. Same-sex families will, in effect, live the feminist ambition for a family life characterised by real equality. In doing so they will, in effect, foster its achievement beyond their own families. Ideologically suspect relationships will benefit from the disruption to the norm that normalisation of abnormal relationships will cause.
>
> The transformative potential is not limited to 'leadership by example', however. The fact that there is a debate surrounding same-sex marriages will create (indeed, has created) a discourse around the nature of marriage, adult relationships and state regulation. It has increased the scope and variety of relationships that are socially recognised and the mechanisms that the state is prepared to use to regulate them. It has, in effect, led to a tangible increase in the diversity of recognised family forms in society. This, it is argued, is a radical departure from the married/single binary which has been the dominant feature of modern family life. . . .

[112] See, e.g., Hansard HC Deb vol 635, col 1141, 2 February 2018, Michelle Donelan MP; Hayward (2019), 300.
[113] See 2.8. [114] Ferguson (2016), 355.

Barker similarly sees transformative potential:

N. Barker, 'After the Wedding: What Next? Conservatism and Conjugality', in N. Barker and D. Monk (eds), *From Civil Partnership to Same-Sex Marriage: Interdisciplinary Reflections* (Abingdon: Routledge, 2015), 226

> [It] will take the continuing engagement of those who have fought for social justice in the form of same-sex marriage to prevent same-sex marriage from reinforcing the existing inequalities and injustices within the institution of marriage, including the economic vulnerabilities of carers and those reliant on state benefits, and the stigmatisation of non-normative sexualities, whether these are homosexual or heterosexual.

But is this transformative potential for marriage endangered now that civil partnership has been opened up to mixed-sex couples?

J. Scherpe, 'The Past, Present and Future of Registered Partnerships', in J. Scherpe and A. Hayward (eds), *The Future of Registered Partnerships* (Cambridge: Intersentia, 2017), 586

> [P]roviding a scheme identical to marriage for all those who would like the rights and duties of that legal regime but reject the (actual or perceived) ideology behind it carries the risk of 'abandoning' marriage – in the sense that those most likely to demand and work for modernisation of marriage would have no incentive to do so as an ideology-free alternative (which may well develop its own particular ideology in time) would be available for them. A stagnant marriage law would be detrimental to any society. Marriage as an institution has changed considerably over the last decades and even the law few years, reflecting and accommodating societal changes. The fact that in many jurisdictions . . . marriage has been opened up to same-sex couples will undoubtedly have significant impact on the perception of marriage as a gendered/patriarchal institution. The societal perception of marriage will continue to change, and ensuring that modern marriage law fits modern societies will therefore certainly be on the legislative agendas sooner or later. For this, particularly the voices of those who reject the 'old' ideology need to be heard.

These voices must be uncovered through additional research. For as Hayward has noted:

A. Hayward, 'Mixed-Sex Civil Partnerships and Relationality: A Perspective From Law', (2021) 10 *Families, Relationships and Societies* 205, 210

> [L]aw can only go so far in encouraging or facilitating the behaviour of individuals in an interpersonal relationship. What now needs to occur is a more holistic analysis of the lived experiences and decision-making processes of mixed-sex civil partners.

We leave the final word to Lady Hale, speaking extra-judicially before the Supreme Court hearing in *Steinfeld and Keidan*:

Lady Hale, Keynote Speech, Resolution National Conference, Bristol (2018)

> It is all very puzzling. Why do people have conscientious objections to marriage these days, when its patriarchal features have virtually disappeared from the law? It is a perfectly serviceable method of giving legal status, rights and responsibilities to couples. On the other hand, why were so many same sex couples so keen to marry, when they too had a perfectly serviceable method of giving legal status, rights and responsibilities in civil partnership? It shows that, in both directions, for and against, marriage has a social and psychological significance which has nothing to do with its legal consequences.

2.4 STATUS-BASED RELATIONSHIPS: MARRIAGE AND CIVIL PARTNERSHIP

English law recognizes two formalized relationships: marriage and civil partnership. Both are status-based relationships recognized simply by virtue of the parties completing state-prescribed formalities; the legal existence or validity of such a relationship does not generally depend upon the parties subsequently behaving in a particular way, so, for example, they need not cohabit.[115] As we shall see, there are some differences in the law governing the formation and validity of, and exit from, marriage by mixed-sex couples, marriage by same-sex couples, and civil partnership (available to both mixed- and same-sex couples). But the legal effect of all marriages and civil partnerships are otherwise essentially identical,[116] and so we discuss them in parallel throughout this chapter and the rest of the book, noting and exploring differences as we encounter them. We begin by examining the essential legal nature of such relationships and the right to form them, before turning to the conditions that must be satisfied in order to create them.

2.4.1 THE NATURE OF MARRIAGE AND CIVIL PARTNERSHIP

Marriage has long been considered multifaceted: at once a religious institution, a contract between the parties, and a legal status from which particular rights and responsibilities flow, both between the parties themselves, and vis-à-vis the spouses and third parties, including the state.[117] As such, marriage is difficult to categorize juristically:

[115] *Draper v United Kingdom* (App No 8186/78, ECHR) (1980), [60].
[116] M(SSC)A 2013, s 11(1), subject to Schs 3 and 4.
[117] *Lindo v Belisari* (1795) 1 Hag Con 216, 230; *Niboyet v Niboyet* (1878) 4 PD 1, 11; *Bellinger v Bellinger* [2001] EWCA Civ 1140, [99] and [128].

K. O'Donovan, *Family Law Matters* (London: Pluto Press, 1993), 43–4

As a contract, so presented in legal discourse throughout the history of the common law, it cannot stand. Its terms are not negotiated by the parties, but prescribed by law. It is not a contract freely entered into by any adult but is open only to certain persons under specified conditions according to law. Termination of marriage can occur only as denoted by law, and not by the partners. Within the legal married state, the law's prescriptions allocate roles ascriptively, according to gender, and not according to the wishes of the parties. Legal marriage requires the sacrifice of personal autonomy but not on equal terms for the parties. An ascriptive quality, gender, is incorporated in the legal institution [notably, the marital rape exemption, see 4.2.3]. This differentiation of partners produces inequality.

Where the notion of marriage as free contract is rejected, writers tend to use the word 'institution' instead, and this may be an appropriate word. When one enters an institution one does so on terms set by that body, one is bound by rules to which one consents on entry. However, the membership may collectively agree a change of rules. It is not easy to apply this analysis to marriage. It is the law, not the partners, which lays down the rules, not only of entry, but also of membership. Collective agreement on the alteration of the rules by the partners is not possible. We are up against something not easily analysed in institutional terms. Marriage has contractual and institutional elements, but it is also *sui generis*, a law unto itself.

As for its religious aspect, much of current marriage law has origins in ecclesiastical law. But it is questionable whether the contours of contemporary, secular marriage law should continue to be shaped by Christian doctrine in a multi-cultural, multi-faith society in which it has been possible to contract a civil marriage since 1836.[118] Indeed, several changes in marriage law over the years—of which the introduction of same-sex marriage is only the most recent—have taken the institution of marriage as recognized by law progressively further away from its ecclesiastical roots.[119]

The nature of civil partnership attracted attention during parliamentary debates. Section 1 of the CPA 2004 describes civil partnership as a 'relationship'. Some thought it ought to be described as a 'contract'. The government disagreed:[120]

Hansard, *Official Report*—Civil Partnership Bill Debates, Hansard HL Deb, vol 662, cols 1361–2, 24 June 2004: Report Stage

Minister of State for the Criminal Justice System and Law Reform (Baroness Scotland of Asthal):

The noble Lord wishes to describe civil partnership as a contract. However, civil partnership is not governed by the law of contract and there is no room for individual variation of the statutory rules governing eligibility, or governing formation or dissolution of a civil partnership, nor of those setting out its consequences.

118 Marriage Act 1836.

119 Note also the introduction and gradual liberalization of divorce (chapter 3), and the narrowing of the prohibited degrees of relationship, discussed at 2.6.1. Contrast the implicit view of the Church of England (2013) that introduction of same-sex marriage would uniquely have that effect, despite its opposition to the earlier developments having been cast in similar terms: Woodhead (2014).

120 See also *Bull v Hall* [2013] UKSC 73, [26] and [36].

The change of status from single person to civil partner affects a couple's relationship with each other. After the formation of their civil partnership they would have an entirely new legal relationship with each other. Forming a civil partnership also affects their status; in other words, their position as an individual in relation to everyone else. Each would now be a civil partner. This change of status is permanent in that on the ending of a civil partnership, civil partners do not revert to being single people. They will be marked by having been in a civil partnership in that they will be former civil partners or a surviving civil partner. Civil partnership is a new statutory relationship that provides same-sex couples with legal recognition of their life together as a couple.

While marriage and civil partnership combine contract and status, save for one recent change which we discuss at 2.5.3, it is clear that civil partnership has no religious aspect in law. Adopting the rules that apply to civil marriages, no religious service may be used while the registrar is officiating at the signing of the civil partnership document (the act which creates a civil partnership).[121] The original decision to create the separate institution of civil partnership rather than simply permit same-sex marriage was influenced by the fact that many regard marriage as a religious sacrament incapable of accommodating same-sex unions. Indeed, special rules now govern whether and when a same-sex marriage may be solemnized by a religious body. But once created, however created, they all have the same effect in law.

One key contemporary debate is the extent to which spouses and civil partners can devise their own terms for the relationship by agreement. Since marriage arises from the parties' mutual consent, should they be similarly free to divorce simply because both wish to do so? Should they be free to agree their property and financial arrangements on separation?[122] Though the law formally continues to require application to court to terminate the legal status, if one party decides to divorce, the law will authorize this. However, despite increased weight attaching to marital agreements, the law retains the power to intervene in parties' financial settlements: as O'Donovan observes, having joined the club, members cannot simply change the rules as it suits them.

2.4.2 THE SIGNIFICANCE OF STATUS

Historically, marriage had a profound and unequal effect on the legal status of the individuals concerned:

W. Blackstone, *Commentaries on the Laws of England*, vol 1 (1765, Facsimile edn: Chicago: University of Chicago Press, 1979), 430

By marriage, the husband and wife are one person in law: that is, the very being or legal existence of the woman is suspended during the marriage, or at least is incorporated and consolidated into that of her husband: under whose wing, protection, and *cover*, she performs every thing . . . Under this principle, of an union of person in husband and wife, depend almost all the legal rights, duties, and disabilities, that either of them acquire by the marriage.

[121] CPA 2004, ss 2(5) and 6.

[122] See 3.7 and 6.7.

The common law doctrine of unity fused husband and wife's legal personalities into one person, and, as Lord Denning once pithily put it, that person was the husband.[123] This fiction generated surprising consequences. For example, spouses were unable to sue each other in tort.[124] Nor (still) can they be guilty of conspiring with each other.[125] That dubious benefit aside, lack of distinctive legal personality caused wives substantial disabilities. Notably, until the late nineteenth century, they could not own property at law (and so could not sue anyone in tort or contract), and were subject to their husbands' powers of physical control.[126] True, wives had the quid pro quo of husbands' common law duty to maintain and house them. But, as John Stuart Mill put it in his essay on *The Subjection of Women*: 'If married life were all that it might be expected to be, looking to the laws alone, society would be a hell upon earth.'[127] But over the course of the late nineteenth century and throughout the twentieth century, wives' legal disabilities and husbands' rights of control were gradually removed. Marriage has, at least in theory, developed from legally condoned patriarchy to a 'partnership of equals':

Sheffield City Council v E and another [2004] EWHC 2808

MUNBY J:

111. . . . [I]n *Durham v Durham* (1885) . . . Sir James Hannen P described the contract of marriage in these terms:

> "It is an engagement between a man and woman to live together, and love one another as husband and wife, to the exclusion of all others. This is expanded in the promises of the marriage ceremony by words having reference to the natural relations which spring from that engagement, such as protection on the part of the man, and submission on the part of the woman." . . .

116. It seems to me that . . . these observations about the husband's duty to protect and maintain and the wife's duty of submission have now to be read with very considerable caution. Indeed, I doubt that they any longer have any place in our contemporaneous understanding of marriage, . . . as a civil institution whose duties and obligations are regulated by the secular courts of an increasingly secular society. For, although we live in a multi-cultural society of many faiths, it must not be forgotten that as a secular judge my concern . . . is with marriage as a civil contract, not as a religious vow . . .

131. Today both spouses are the joint, co-equal heads of the family. Each has an obligation to comfort and support the other. It is not for the husband alone to provide the matrimonial home or to decide where the family is to live. Husband and wife both contribute. And where they are to live is, like other domestic matters of common concern, something

[123] *Midland Bank v Green (No 3)* [1982] Ch 529, 538.

[124] Until the Law Reform (Husband and Wife) Act 1962.

[125] This exemption is now justified on the basis of marital sanctity and confidentiality, rather than marital unity: Criminal Law Act 1977, s 2(2)(a); *Midland Bank v Green (No 3)* [1979] Ch 496, 521. The Law Commission has recommended its abolition: Law Com (2009), para 5.16.

[126] In relation to the latter, see 4.2.3. The history of spouses' rights regarding property and husbands' economic duties towards their wives are explored in a supplement to chapter 6 in the online resources.

[127] (1869), 465.

to be settled by agreement, not determined unilaterally by the husband. Insofar as the concept of consortium—the sharing of a common home and a common domestic life, and the right to enjoy each other's society, comfort and assistance—still has any useful role to play, the rights of husband and wife must surely now be regarded as exactly reciprocal.

The notion that spouses owe each other legal duties to comfort, support, and cohabit is problematic. No such duties are specifically enforceable,[128] but until 2022 divorce could be obtained on the basis of desertion, separation, or behaviour such that the petitioner cannot reasonably be expected to live with the respondent.[129]

Civil partnership has nothing like the history and ideological baggage of (mixed-sex) marriage.[130] It is a creature of modern statute largely replicating existing matrimonial legislation, the exemption from criminal liability for conspiracy included. The common law doctrines of unity and consortium presumably have no application to civil partnership[131] or to same-sex marriage. However, as Munby J observed in the *Sheffield* case, it is doubtful whether those doctrines have any modern significance for mixed-sex spouses: although never formally abolished, they have been compromised substantially by legislation.[132]

We examine particular rights and duties arising from marriage and civil partnership throughout the book.[133] It will be clear that, while their status is less distinctive than it was historically, spouses and civil partners still enjoy a special position in English law, particularly compared with cohabitants whose de facto relationships—discussed at 2.8.2—attract rather fewer, less intensive legal consequences.

2.4.3 A RIGHT TO MARRY, OR NOT TO MARRY?

Marriage and civil partnership are vehicles for the acquisition of distinctive rights and duties, many of which cannot be created by private contract. Whether one has the right to form a marriage or civil partnership is therefore a vital question. It has been said that English law has always recognized the right to marry,[134] but the right is enshrined in Article 12 ECHR and other international conventions.[135]

[128] The action for restitution of conjugal rights was abolished in 1970: Matrimonial Proceedings and Property Act 1970, s 20: see Cretney (2003a), ch 4; Douglas (2018a), ch 3.

[129] See 3.5.

[130] Though see the concerns of commentators such as Diduck (2005), discussed at 2.3.4.

[131] Harper et al (2005), 42. Note the contrast between s 18 MCA 1973 and s 57 CPA 2004: there is no reference in the latter to a duty to cohabit: Douglas (2018a), 95.

[132] Bridge (2001), 15.

[133] For exhaustive analysis, see Lowe et al (2021), ch 3.

[134] *R (On the Application of the Crown Prosecution Service) v Registrar General of Births, Deaths and Marriages* [2002] EWCA Civ 1661, [20]; *Aquilar Quila and others v Secretary of State for the Home Department* [2010] EWCA Civ 1482.

[135] E.g. International Covenant on Civil and Political Rights (1966), Art 23; Charter of Fundamental Rights of the EU (2000), Art 9.

European Convention on Human Rights (1953), Article 12

Men and women of marriageable age have the right to marry and to found a family, according to the national laws governing the exercise of this right.

The importance and universal recognition of this right was described by Baroness Hale in a case concerning procedural restrictions placed on marriages by non-EEA (European Economic Area) nationals in an effort to prevent sham marriages contracted purely for immigration purposes:

R (On the Application of Baiai and others) v Secretary of State for the Home Department and others [2008] UKHL 53

BARONESS HALE:

44. . . . As Chief Justice Warren . . . said [in *Loving et ux. v Virginia*, 388 US 1 (1967), landmark US Supreme Court decision quashing bans on mixed-race marriages] "Marriage is one of the 'basic civil rights of man', fundamental to our very existence and survival". Even in South Africa, where marriage is not constitutionally protected because of fears that this might entrench a particular model of marriage within a multi-cultural society, "the provision of the constitutional text would clearly prohibit any arbitrary state interference with the right to marry or to establish and raise a family. The text enshrines the values of human dignity, equality and freedom" (see *Minister for Home Affairs v Fourie*, Case 60/04 Constitutional Court of South Africa, para 47, Sachs J). Denying to members of minority groups the right to establish formal, legal relationships with the partners of their choice is one way of setting them apart from society, denying that they are "free and equal in dignity and rights."

45. Even in these days, when many in British society believe that there is little social difference between marrying and living together, marriage still has deep significance for many people, quite apart from the legal recognition, status, rights and obligations which it brings. "Marriage law . . . goes well beyond its earlier purpose in the common law of legitimising sexual relations and securing succession of legitimate heirs to family property. And it is much more than a piece of paper." (Sachs J, para 70). It brings legal, social and psychological benefits to the couple when they marry, while they are married and when it ends.

Article 12 expressly preserves states' entitlement to govern the exercise of the right. Although not required by the ECHR to do so, Parliament has now exercised that right to confer on all individuals the right to marry regardless of the other person's legal gender. But however a state defines marriage, the state's freedom then to govern the exercise of the right to marry, so defined, is not unlimited. In this extract, Lord Bingham responds to the suggestion that the right to marry in Article 12 is absolute:[136]

[136] Art 12 is inapplicable in this sense to civil partnership; however, analogous restrictions on access to civil partnership might breach Art 8.

R (On the Application of Baiai and others) v Secretary of State for the Home Department and others [2008] UKHL 53

LORD BINGHAM:

13. If by "absolute" is meant that anyone within the jurisdiction is free to marry any other person irrespective of age, gender, consanguinity, affinity or any existing marriage, then plainly the right protected by article 12 is not absolute. But equally plainly . . . it is a strong right. . . . In contrast with articles 8, 9, 10 and 11 of the Convention, it contains no second paragraph permitting interferences with or limitations of the right in question which are prescribed by law and necessary in a democratic society for one or other of a number of specified purposes. The right is subject only to national laws governing its exercise.

14. The Strasbourg case law reveals a restrictive approach towards national laws. Thus it has been accepted that national laws may lay down rules of substance based on generally recognised considerations of public interest, of which rules concerning capacity, consent, prohibited degrees of consanguinity and prevention of bigamy are examples. . . . But from early days the right to marry has been described as "fundamental", it has been made clear that the scope afforded to national law is not unlimited and it has been emphasised that national laws governing the exercise of the right to marry must never injure or impair the substance of the right and must not deprive a person or category of person of full legal capacity of the right to marry or substantially interfere with their exercise of the right. . . .

16. The Strasbourg jurisprudence requires the right to marry to be treated as a strong right which may be regulated by national law both as to procedure and substance but may not be subjected to conditions which impair the essence of the right.

In *Baiai*, it was held that it was legitimate to seek to prevent sham marriages for immigration purposes by imposing restrictions on the right to marry, but that such restrictions must be proportionate and non-discriminatory in their operation; the scheme in question failed that test.[137] Other notable cases involving the UK have involved marriage by prisoners. The adverse finding in *Draper v United Kingdom*[138] prompted reform to allow marriages in prisons. Such restrictions must also have a clear basis in law: so a general statutory discretion not to issue marriage licences to remand prisoners could not lawfully be exercised on the basis that a particular marriage would frustrate an impending trial, the defendant's intended wife then no longer being compellable as a witness.[139]

Domestic rules regarding capacity to marry and the formalities required to create a marriage must also be compatible with Article 12. For example, Article 12 was invoked, without substantial analysis or adjudication, to permit the then Prince of Wales to contract a civil marriage; it had previously been understood that members of the Royal Family were able to marry in England and Wales only in an Anglican ceremony.[140] But Article 12 is relevant to the wider population too, and on examining the law of nullity we shall see how current English law fares under Article 12.

[137] See also *O'Donaghue v United Kingdom* (App No 34848/07, ECHR) (2011).

[138] (App No 8186/78, ECHR) (1980).

[139] *R (On the Application of the Crown Prosecution Service) v Registrar General of Births, Deaths and Marriages* [2002] EWCA Civ 1661; *Frasik v Poland* (App No 22933/02, ECHR) (2010).

[140] See (2005) FL 345; for comment, Probert (2005).

Case law has also considered what is in effect the right *not* to marry, implicit in Article 12. A marriage to which one or both parties is not consenting is voidable, but the courts have developed their inherent jurisdiction to intervene where it is feared either that an impending marriage would be forced,[141] or that one party may lack the mental capacity to consent to marriage or be unable to make a fully informed, genuine choice to enter a particular marriage.[142] The marriage in the latter type of case might often be valid, since English law takes a narrow view of what must be understood and consented to for a marriage to be valid. But the 'serious emotional and psychological harm' that might nevertheless be suffered has been held to justify the grant of protective orders designed to 'ensure that any marriage really is what [the individual] wants'.[143]

2.5 CREATING A VALID MARRIAGE OR CIVIL PARTNERSHIP

The law does little to provide *positive* definitions of marriage and civil partnership. The most famous, if 'positively misleading',[144] definition of marriage comes from the nineteenth century: 'I conceive that marriage, as understood in Christendom, may . . . be defined as the voluntary union for life of one man and one woman to the exclusion of all others.'[145]

This statement was not accurate even when it was first made, not least because marriage can be terminated by divorce, so may not endure for the parties' joint lives. But, rightly or wrongly, it is nevertheless frequently cited as a starting point for discussion of marriage, in particular in attempts to resist same-sex marriage. We discover rather more about the law's conception of marriage and civil partnership from the *negative* law of nullity. That law performs a dual function. First, it prescribes those characteristics or conditions that are so fundamental to the law's understanding of marriage and civil partnership that if one or more of them is absent or not satisfied, the relationship cannot or may not be regarded as valid. And it provides a mechanism whereby an apparent marriage or civil partnership that fails to satisfy any of those criteria can be unravelled.

2.5.1 THE LAW OF NULLITY: VOID AND VOIDABLE MARRIAGES, AND NON-QUALIFYING CEREMONIES

It is important to appreciate the distinction between nullity and divorce (or, in the case of civil partnership, dissolution). Divorce entails the termination of what had been a valid marriage. Nullity is concerned with the validity of a purported marriage from its inception. However, the distinction is not clear-cut, as the law of nullity distinguishes between void and voidable marriages and civil partnerships:

141 See now statutory remedies discussed at 4.10.

142 See *Re SA (Vulnerable Adult with Capacity: Marriage)* [2005] EWHC 2942.

143 Ibid, [126] per Munby J. See generally 2.7.1.

144 Probert (2007a), 323.

145 *Hyde v Hyde* (1866) LR 1 P&D 130, 133, per Lord Penzance.

Law Commission, *Report on Nullity of Marriage*, Law Com No 33 (London: HMSO, 1970)

3. . . . [T]he present distinction between valid, void and voidable marriages correspond[s] to factual differences in the situations of the parties which call for different relief from the courts. The difference between the three types of marriage may be summarised thus:

(a) A valid marriage is one which is in no sense defective and is, therefore, binding on the parties (and on everyone else); it can only be terminated by death or by a decree of divorce, which decree acknowledges the existence of a valid marriage and then proceeds to put an end to it.

(b) A void marriage is not really a marriage at all, in that it never came into existence because of a fundamental defect; the marriage is said to be void *ab initio*; no decree of nullity is necessary to make it void and parties can take the risk of treating the marriage as void without obtaining a decree. But either of the spouses or any person having a sufficient interest in obtaining a decree of nullity may petition for a decree at any time, whether during the lifetime of the spouses or after their death. In effect, the decree is a declaration that there is not and never has been a marriage.

(c) A voidable marriage is a valid marriage unless and until it is annulled; it can be annulled only at the instance of one of the spouses during the lifetime of both, so that if no decree of nullity is pronounced during the lifetime of both spouses, the marriage becomes unimpeachable as soon as one of the spouses dies.

4. In many Civil Law countries marriages which we would regard as void are treated as voidable in the sense that a marriage once formally celebrated cannot be disregarded until it has been set aside. This seems to be based on the importance which those countries place on official records. The English view, however, is that registration of a marriage merely records the celebration of marriage and affords no guarantee of its validity. To require legal proceedings to be instituted before parties could regard themselves as free from a marriage which was palpably invalid because, for example, one party was already married to another or was under the age of 16, would, in our view, add needlessly to the expense to the parties and to the public.

Although no court proceedings are needed to 'end' a void marriage, they may still be desirable: to provide the certainty of a court order definitively stating the legal position; and to invoke the court's jurisdiction to make financial orders between the parties.[146] It may seem surprising that a void marriage should attract any legal consequences. However, to give one example, an innocent party to what is later discovered to have been a bigamous marriage might have compromised their position assuming the marriage to be valid such that their need for financial relief is identical to that of a party to a valid marriage. Whether a remedy is awarded depends on the court's discretion; where the applicant is responsible for the relationship's invalidity, no remedy may be forthcoming.[147]

The last, rather curious category is the 'non-qualifying ceremony' (formerly known as 'non-marriage', as discussed at 2.6.2.b). These cases involve purported marriages that depart

[146] *S-T (formerly J) v J* [1998] Fam 103.

[147] See 6.5.6.

so far from what constitutes a marriage under English law, usually because no attempt has been made to comply with the required formalities, that they cannot be regarded even as a void marriage and so *no* legal consequences flow from them. This is a particularly grave conclusion when one or both parties honestly believed the marriage to be valid. As we shall see in 2.7.1.a, it seems that the courts have sometimes stretched the boundaries of what constitutes a non-qualifying ceremony in forced marriage cases in order to achieve just outcomes, but on a questionable legal basis. Conversely, case law has at times been surprisingly generous in categorizing as 'void' what would hitherto have been classed as a non-qualifying ceremony.

2.5.2 THE PRACTICAL IMPORTANCE OF THE LAW OF NULLITY

If the significance of the law of nullity were measured by reference to the number of nullity decrees granted, we would conclude that it was relatively unimportant. In 2021, just 234 decrees of nullity were granted, compared with 113,505 divorce decrees.[148] This in part reflects the limited scope of the grounds for nullity and the breadth of the bases on which divorce may be obtained. However, much more significant is the law of nullity's role in delineating the scope of the right to marry or form a civil partnership, and the unknown numbers of individuals who might thereby be prevented from formalizing their relationship. Restricting access to these institutions to certain *types* of relationships tells us something about the law's view of the social function of marriage and civil partnership. The most interesting questions, then, are why have *these* entry requirements been imposed; and why are the grounds on which a marriage or civil partnership may be voidable not relegated to the law of divorce?

2.5.3 FORMAL REQUIREMENTS FOR CREATING MARRIAGE AND CIVIL PARTNERSHIP

Before we examine the grounds for nullity, we must outline the formal requirements for creating a marriage or civil partnership. Since marriage and civil partnership transform the parties' legal status, both between themselves and as against the world, public formalities must self-evidently be performed, not least to ensure that the parties are free to marry and consent to do so, and to establish clearly who enjoys the legal status of spouse or civil partner.[149] Requiring parties to jump through specific procedural hoops, rather than permitting them to create marriages by whatever method they privately choose, is compatible with Article 12.[150] Specifically, a state does not violate Article 8, 12, or 14 in refusing to recognize religious marriages and requiring parties who wish to have a religious ceremony additionally to complete further formalities to create a civil law marriage.[151]

English law relating to formalities for marriage suffers from 'bewildering' complexity, entirely the product of history,[152] and the introduction of same-sex marriage—to which yet more rules apply—has further complicated matters. Separate rules govern the creation of

[148] ONS (2022i), tables 2a and 2b.
[149] Law Com (1973), Annex, para 4.
[150] *X v Federal Republic of Germany* (App No 6167/73, ECHR) (1974).
[151] *Şerife Yiğit v Turkey* (App No 3976/05, ECHR) (2009); *Muñoz Díaz v Spain* (App No 49151/07, ECHR) (2009).
[152] Law Com (1973), Annex, para 6.

civil partnership. The formal requirements for marriage and civil partnership can broadly be divided into three categories:

(i) the preliminary procedures—giving public notice of intention to marry or register a civil partnership in order to allow interested parties to lodge objections (e.g. on the ground that the parties lack the capacity to marry);

(ii) rules that must be satisfied and procedures that must be completed to create the marriage or civil partnership—regarding the time and location of the ceremony, the identity of the celebrant, the presence of witnesses, and (for marriage) the exchange of particular words or (for civil partnership) the signing of the civil partnership document; and

(iii) bureaucratic registration requirements, recording and so proving the existence of the marriage or civil partnership—in the case of marriage, this is a separate stage; in the case of civil partnership, the act of registration both creates and records the legal status.

2.5.3.a Marriage formalities

In the case of marriage, different rules govern stages (i) and (ii), depending on the location and/or religious format, if any, of the intended ceremony, and, if it is a marriage between a same-sex couple, on whether the solemnizing authority has the power to marry them at all. The registration requirement (iii) is universal.

For marriages conducted in a civil ceremony, the situation is straightforward: whether the ceremony is conducted in a register office or other premises approved for the solemnization of marriage (e.g. stately homes, hotels, and other venues),[153] any couple—mixed- or same-sex—may be married in a civil ceremony. The option of civil marriage was created in 1836.[154] Previously, marriage could *only* be solemnized in a religious ceremony in an Anglican church, though Jews and Quakers were also permitted to use their own marriage practices. Since 1992, civil ceremonies have outnumbered religious ceremonies, in 2011 accounting for 70 per cent of all marriages.[155]

The Church of England still enjoys a privileged position as the one religious body that can use its own forms of preliminary procedure and whose own buildings, ceremony, and celebrants (clergy) are qualified to create and register marriages without any further state sanction.[156] However, the Church will only—and under the current state of the legislation can only—conduct marriages for mixed-sex couples.[157] Jews and Quakers[158] may still use their own marriage practices, but must complete the preliminaries applicable to civil marriage.[159] Adherents to other Christian denominations and other religions[160] may straightforwardly marry mixed-sex couples in their own religious premises following completion of the civil preliminaries, provided further requirements regarding the registration of the building and presence of an authorized person are satisfied.[161] Any faith group that wishes to conduct same-sex marriages must specifically 'opt in' to do so, a procedure that requires

[153] Marriage Act 1949 (MA 1949), ss 46A–B; Law Com (2015), fig. 5. Pursuant to the Marriages and Civil Partnerships (Approved Premises) (Amendment) Regulations 2022, civil weddings and partnerships can take place outdoors provided the location is attached to approved premises.

[154] Marriage Act 1836.

[155] Law Com (2015), 2–3 and fig. 1, citing ONS data.

[156] MA 1949, Part II.

[157] See M(SSC)A 2013, ss 1(3)(4), 2, 11(6).

[158] MA 1949, s 47.

[159] Ibid, s 26(1)(c)(d).

[160] See *R (Hodkin and another) v Registrar General of Births, Deaths and Marriages* [2013] UKSC 77.

[161] MA 1949, ss 26(1)(a), 35, 41–4; Places of Worship Registration Act 1855.

the written consent of the relevant governing authority.[162] This mechanism is not available to the Church of England.[163]

Same-sex couples who have a civil partnership but wish to marry have since December 2014 been able to convert their civil partnership to a marriage, using either a simple one-stage process at a register office or a two-stage process in which the conversion is completed at another venue, enabling the couple to hold a ceremony to celebrate the occasion either at approved premises or at religious premises that have been registered for marriage of same-sex couples using the opt-in procedure.[164]

2.5.3.b Civil partnership formalities

Civil partnership was originally an entirely non-religious institution: the original CPA 2004, like the rules for civil marriages, barred the use of religious premises as a venue for creating a civil partnership and required that the registration be conducted by a civil registrar, not a religious celebrant. This scheme frustrated faith groups such as Liberal Jews and Quakers who wanted to be able to host registration ceremonies. The Equality Act 2010 accordingly removed the bar on use of religious premises, leaving the matter instead to the decision of each faith group, just as the M(SSC)A 2013 leaves the matter of same-sex marriage to individual faith groups to decide.[165] However, the registration process must still be conducted by a registrar, not by the religious celebrant.

2.5.3.c Consequences of failing to comply with formalities

Failure to comply with the prescribed form does not necessarily render the marriage or civil partnership void. Some defects may result in nullity—see 2.6.2. Other breaches do not affect validity, though someone—usually the registrar or equivalent person—may be guilty of a criminal offence.[166] Conversely, if failure to comply with the formal requirements is sufficiently fundamental, the resulting union may be regarded as a non-qualifying ceremony—see 2.6.2.b.

2.5.3.d Reform?

Rationalization and simplification of the law in this area is long overdue. It may in time be required in order to avoid a challenge under Article 14 ECHR in conjunction with Articles 12 and 9, barring discrimination in the exercise of the right to marry on grounds of religion. It is not obvious that the special status of the Church of England regarding mixed-sex marriage, and the relatively disadvantageous positions of other faiths and denominations, should be maintained.[167] However, ECHR case law suggests that the universal availability

[162] MA 1949, ss 26A, 26B. [163] The situation of the Church in Wales is dealt with by M(SSC)A 2013, s 8.

[164] Marriage of Same Sex Couples (Conversion of Civil Partnership) Regulations 2014, SI 2014/3181. Cf 2.3.3.

[165] CPA 2014, ss 6–6A. Marriages and Civil Partnerships (Approved Premises) (Amendment) Regulations 2011, SI 2011/2661.

[166] MA 1949, ss 75–7; CPA 2004, ss 31–3. Parties may be guilty of perjury if they make false declarations: Perjury Act 1911, s 3; CPA 2004, s 80. See generally Probert (2018a).

[167] Cf the concession made by the UK government in *O'Donaghue v United Kingdom* (App No 34848/07, ECHR) (2011), [110] that excluding Anglican marriages from special immigration rules (considered in *R (Baiai) v Secretary of State for the Home Department* [2008] UKHL 53) violated the Convention. See also MOJ (2014a).

of civil marriage to members of all faiths or none prevents any violation of Article 14 in conjunction with Article 12.[168] The ECHR aside, the Law Commission has concluded that comprehensive reform is needed:[169]

Law Commission, *Celebrating Marriage: A New Weddings Law*, Law Com No 408 (London: TSO, 2022)

1.4 The problems with the law can be attributed to its antiquity. The fundamental structure of the law and its rules date from the 18th and 19th centuries, when virtually everyone lived, married and died within a single community, and most people shared the same faith and beliefs. In short, many of the rules were devised to reflect a way of life that bears little resemblance to life today.

1.5 Weddings law in England and Wales restricts how couples are permitted to celebrate their weddings, for historical reasons rather than current policy reasons. Complexity and inconsistency mean that different couples are bound by different rules. Because of unnecessary restrictions, many couples cannot have a legally recognised wedding in a place that is meaningful to them. Many couples also cannot have a ceremony which contains the vows, rituals and music that best reflect their beliefs and preferences. Unnecessary regulation and bureaucracy contribute to some couples having to spend more on the legal aspects of their wedding than other couples.

1.6 To comply with their religious and cultural traditions, or to marry in a way that is meaningful to them, some couples celebrate in a way that the law does not recognize at all. Some of these couples will have two or more ceremonies: one which complies with the law, and one or more which honours their beliefs or values. However, other couples will only have one ceremony, either not realising that the ceremony they have had is not legally recognised, or intentionally choosing to comply with the requirements of their beliefs, culture or values rather than the law.

1.7 To address the significant problems with the law, we recommend comprehensive reform: an entirely new scheme to govern weddings law. Our recommendations will change the law from the foundations up, transforming the law from a system based on the building in which a ceremony takes place to an officiant-based scheme.

In July 2022, the Commission published its final report on weddings law. If introduced, the Commission's recommendations would mean sweeping reform, including: simplified civil preliminaries; changes to giving notice (e.g. couples could register their intention to marry online); facilitating couples' choice on where to marry (provided it were deemed by the officiant to be safe and dignified); removal of restrictions on the inclusion of religious aspects (e.g. texts or songs) in civil ceremonies; removal of requirements for prescribed words in the marriage ceremony; and, amendments to the law on appropriate officiants.[170] By changing the requirements for a valid marriage, this would also impact the types of ceremonies that are currently non-qualifying. This is discussed further at 2.6.2.b.

[168] *Muñoz Díaz v Spain* (App No 49151/07, ECHR) (2009) [79]–[81]. Cf *Şerife Yiğit v Turkey* (App No 3976/05, ECHR) (2009); and see Probert and Saleem (2018), 19; Barton and Probert (2018), 1546.

[169] Reform proposals: General Register Office (2003); Probert (2002a), (2004b), (2018c); Barton (2002); Eekelaar (2013); Pywell and Probert (2018a); Hopkins et al (2021); Sandberg (2021); Probert et al (2022).

[170] The government's response to the Law Commission's report was expected in early 2023 but is still forthcoming: Hansard HL Deb, vol 825, col 1668, 29 November 2022, Lord Bellamy.

Table 2.1 Grounds on which marriage or civil partnership void

Marriage: MCA 1973, s 11	Civil Partnership: CPA 2004, s 49
Parties within the prohibited degrees	Parties within the prohibited degrees
Both parties not over 18	Both parties not over 18[171]
Either party already a spouse or civil partner	Either party already a spouse or civil partner
Rules regarding polygamy breached	[no equivalent ground]
Certain formalities disregarded	Certain formalities disregarded

2.6 GROUNDS ON WHICH A MARRIAGE OR CIVIL PARTNERSHIP IS VOID

The grounds on which marriage and civil partnership are void, summarized in Table 2.1, are identified in the MCA 1973, s 11[172] and CPA 2004, s 49. They fall into two categories: (i) the first addresses the parties' 'capacity' to marry or 'eligibility' to form a civil partnership; (ii) the last concerns the failure to observe specified formalities.

2.6.1 VOID GROUNDS: INCAPACITY TO MARRY OR FORM A CIVIL PARTNERSHIP

With the exception of minimum age, the rules relating to capacity do not wholly bar individuals from becoming a spouse or civil partner. The issue is whether the given *couple* have the capacity to marry *each other*.

2.6.1.a Prohibited degrees of relationship and associated formalities

The law of marriage has always barred unions between certain relatives. Over the centuries, the range of prohibited relationships has gradually narrowed[173] and the degree of prohibition on one remaining category (step-relations) relaxed. The latest relaxation, removing all restrictions on marriages between parents- and children-in-law, was prompted by a decision of the European Court of Human Rights. B and L, both divorced, were father- and daughter-in-law. They had been cohabiting for some time, along with B's grandson (L's son), and wished to marry, but were barred from doing so under the law then in force until both B's first wife (the mother of B's son) and B's son (L's first husband) had both died (a quite unpredictable eventuality), or unless they invoked a costly and cumbersome procedure, with 'no discernible rules or precedent', to obtain a personal Act of Parliament permitting their

[171] Amended by the Marriage and Civil Partnership (Minimum Age) Act 2022, s 1.

[172] See also s 12A for marriages converted from civil partnership.

[173] E.g. Marriage (Enabling Act) 1960; Marriage (Prohibited Degrees of Relationship) Act 1986. See Cretney (2003a), ch 2.

marriage. The majority of a group appointed by the Archbishop of Canterbury had earlier concluded that this bar could not be justified.[174] The restrictions were held to breach B and L's right to marry under Article 12.

B v United Kingdom (App No 36536/02, ECHR) (2006)

36. Article 12 expressly provides for regulation of marriage by national law and given the sensitive moral choices concerned and the importance to be attached to the protection of children and the fostering of secure family environments, this Court must not rush to substitute its own judgment in place of the authorities who are best placed to assess and respond to the needs of society. . . . [A] large number of Contracting States have a similar bar in their law, reflecting apparently similar concerns about allowing marriages of this degree of affinity.

37. The Court must however examine the facts of the case in the context pertaining in the United Kingdom. It observes that this bar on marriage is aimed at protecting the integrity of the family (preventing sexual rivalry between parents and children) and preventing harm to children who may be affected by the changing relationships of the adults around them. These are, without doubt, legitimate aims.

38. Nonetheless, the bar on marriage does not prevent the relationships occurring . . . There are no incest, or other criminal law, provisions to prevent extra-marital relationships between parents-in-law and children-in-law being established notwithstanding that children may live in these homes. It cannot, therefore, be said that in the present case the ban on the applicants' marriage prevents any alleged confusion or emotional insecurity to the second applicant's son . . .

The Court was also unimpressed that the private Act of Parliament route had enabled some parties in the applicants' position to marry. In response to the government's argument that the bar should be retained because this procedure ensured that exceptions were made only in cases where no harm would arise, it commented:

40. . . . that there is no indication of any detailed investigation into family circumstances in the Parliamentary procedure and that in any event a cumbersome and expensive vetting process of this kind would not appear to offer a practically accessible or effective mechanism for individuals to vindicate their rights. [The Court] would also view with reservation a system that would require a person of full age in possession of his or her mental faculties to submit to a potentially intrusive investigation to ascertain whether it is suitable for them to marry . . .

The in-law restrictions were subsequently repealed.[175]

The current law—identical in effect for marriage and civil partnership—is most clearly set out in the CPA 2004.[176] Different rules apply to: (i) consanguineous and some adoptive[177]

[174] Archbishop of Canterbury's Group (1984).

[175] Marriage Act 1949 (Remedial) Order 2006, SI 2007/348.

[176] CPA 2004, s 3(1)(d), (2); MCA 1973, s 11(a)(i).

[177] Adoption and Children Act 2002 (ACA 2002), s 74: adopted persons remain members of their birth family for the purposes of these rules; within their adopted family they are barred only from parent/child unions.

relationships, where marriage or civil partnership is absolutely barred; and (ii) step-relationships, where it is permitted in certain cases:[178]

Civil Partnership Act 2004, Sch 1, Part 1: Prohibited Degrees of Relationship

Absolute prohibitions

1 (1) Two people are within prohibited degrees of relationship if one falls within the list below in relation to the other.

Adoptive child
Adoptive parent
Child
Former adoptive child
Former adoptive parent
Grandparent
Grandchild
Parent
Parent's sibling
Sibling
Sibling's child

(2) In the list "sibling" means a brother, sister, half-brother or half-sister.

Qualified prohibitions

2 (1) Two people are within prohibited degrees of relationship if one of them falls within the list below in relation to the other, unless—

(a) both of them have reached 21 at the time when they register as civil partners of each other, and

(b) the younger has not at any time before reaching 18 been a child of the family in relation to the other.

Child of former civil partner
Child of former spouse
Former civil partner of grandparent
Former civil partner of parent
Former spouse of grandparent
Former spouse of parent
Grandchild of former civil partner
Grandchild of former spouse

(2) "Child of the family", in relation to another person, means a person who—

(a) has lived in the same household as that other person, and

(b) has been treated by that other person as a child of his family.

[178] Following *B v United Kingdom* (App No 36536/02, ECHR) (2006), para 3 was not commenced. For marriage, see MA 1949, s 1 and Sch 1, as amended.

Where parties falling within the qualified prohibitions wish to marry or become civil partners, additional formal preliminaries apply, though it seems that failure to comply would not void the union.[179]

The rules prohibiting marriage between relations were based originally on biblical grounds.[180] Latterly, the prohibitions were justified by reference to the genetic health of any offspring of such unions.[181] It is curious that identical restrictions apply to civil partnerships and same-sex marriages, since same-sex couples cannot (yet[182]) procreate with the genetic material of both partners. Moreover, genetic problems can arise between unrelated persons and between cousins, who may marry in English law, and the prohibitions extend to adoptive and step-relations. So the rules are better rationalized on social grounds: the undesirability of relatives forming conjugal relationships disrupting other family relationships. The special limits imposed on marriages between step-relations reflect concerns about abuse of power by older family members; barring such marriages may deter people from pursuing these relationships at all. The criminalization of sexual activity between family members now largely corresponds with the remaining prohibited degrees.[183] One curious exception relates to adoptive relationships, where marriage between adoptive parent and child is absolutely barred, even though sexual activity between them, once both are adult, is apparently permitted.[184] However, the law fails to pursue the social rationale to its logical limit. For example, why are adopted relatives (aside from parent and child) excluded from the prohibitions?[185] Why can people marry former *cohabiting* partners of their parents without restriction? While step-grandparents and child are barred from marrying before both are 21 where the younger has at *any* time when under 18 been treated as a child of the step-grandparent's family in the same household, the criminal law seems not to ban sexual activity between them once the child is over 16 and they no longer share a household.[186] Given these inconsistencies, the prohibited degrees may yet be subject to further reform.[187]

2.6.1.b The age of the parties and related formalities

Until 1929, the minimum age for marriage was 12 for a girl and 14 for a boy.[188] The basic rule now is that no person under the age of 18 may enter into marriage or civil partnership.[189] In the case of marriages between step-relations, the prohibited degrees rules raise the age limit to 21. The basic age rule corresponds with the criminal law of sexual offences against children[190] so it may be surmised that it is designed to protect younger children

[179] MA 1949, ss 16(1A)–(2B), 27B–C; Marriage (Registrar-General's Licence) Act 1970, s 3; CPA 2004, Sch 1, Part 2.

[180] Canon law has biblical origins: Leviticus chs 18 and 20; Deuteronomy 27; 1 Corinthians 5.

[181] Law Com (1970), paras 51–3; Archbishop of Canterbury's Group (1984); cf Human Fertilisation and Embryology Act 1990, s 31ZB.

[182] Except in the case of mitochondrial donation, which it is contemplated would only be used in case of medical need, not simply as a means of permitting two women to be genetically related to the child: see 9.4.3.

[183] Sexual Offences Act 2003, ss 64–5, and where one party is under 18, ss 25–9; cf *Stübing v Germany* (App No 43547/08, ECHR) (2012).

[184] ACA 2002, s 74.

[185] Law Com (1970), para 50; consensual sexual activity between adult adoptive relations is not criminal.

[186] Sexual Offences Act 2003, s 27(4). [187] See Gaffney-Rhys (2005), 957; cf Cretney (2006b).

[188] The Marriage and Civil Partnership (Minimum Age) Act 2022, s 1(2) raised the minimum age from 16 to 18.

[189] MCA 1973, s 11(a)(ii); MA 1949, ss 2 and 3; CPA 2004, ss 3(1)(c) and 4.

[190] Sexual Offences Act 2003, principally ss 5–13.

from undesirable sexual activity. The existence of an age limit also reflects the seriousness of marriage and civil partnership and the obligations inherent in them, and the need for a mature consent.[191]

The age limits selected by English law may not be compatible with the marriage practices of some minority religions observed in the UK. An application to Strasbourg challenging this as incompatible with Articles 9, 12, and 14 ECHR was declared inadmissible, the age limits falling with the state's freedom to regulate marriage.[192]

The Law Commission considered but rejected the argument that marriages of children should be merely voidable (valid unless annulled at the instance of one of the parties); or ratifiable (void unless affirmed by the parties after majority is attained).[193] Under-age marriages are therefore void, and so vulnerable to challenge by third parties, even many years after the child in question has reached majority and is happily married, and even if both parties were ignorant that either of them was under 18 at the time of marriage, or under 16 if the parties were married before February 2023, when the minimum age was raised.[194]

2.6.1.c Monogamy

Under English law, marriage and civil partnership are monogamous and mutually exclusive states: one may only have one spouse or civil partner at any one time and one cannot simultaneously be a spouse and a civil partner.[195] A marriage or civil partnership contracted where either party is already a spouse or civil partner is automatically void, regardless of the parties' knowledge, and remains void even if the other spouse or civil partner subsequently dies or that union is dissolved. The statutory offence of bigamy is confined to marriage,[196] but parties who knowingly give false information regarding their status in this regard for the purpose of procuring a marriage or civil partnership commit an offence.[197]

Cases may arise where one party's original spouse or partner has been missing for some time, and is honestly and reasonably presumed to be dead. A second union will nevertheless be void if it transpires that the 'deceased' was alive at the time of the ceremony. However, a declaration that the missing party is presumed to be dead will dissolve the marriage or civil partnership.[198] The presumption arises if the missing party is continuously absent for seven years and the applicant has no reason to believe that they have been alive during that time.[199] The declaration made, the 'survivor' may then validly form a new marriage or civil partnership, even if the 'deceased' later appears and the declaration is varied or revoked.[200]

[191] For international human rights instruments in this field and comparative examples, see Gaffney-Rhys (2009).

[192] *Khan v United Kingdom* (App No 11579/85, ECHR) (1986).

[193] Law Com (1970), paras 16–20.

[194] Before the Marriage and Civil Partnership (Minimum Age) Act 2022 came into effect, mature minors (those ages 16 or 17) could validly marry or become civil partners provided they had the consent of a parent with parental responsibility and/or of another statutorily defined 'appropriate person': MA 1949, s 3; CPA 2004, Sch 2, Part 1. Since February 2023, this is no longer possible, pursuant to s 1(3) of the 2022 Act.

[195] MCA 1973, s 11(b); CPA 2004, ss 3(1)(b), 49(a).

[196] Offences Against the Person Act 1861, s 57.

[197] Perjury Act 1911, s 3; CPA 2004, s 80.

[198] Presumption of Death Act 2013, ss 1 and 3(2).

[199] Ibid, s 2.

[200] Ibid, s 6(2).

2.6.1.d Polygamy

Rules about polygamous unions apply only to marriage, and in practice only to mixed-sex marriage. Since no jurisdiction permits polygamous civil partnership or same-sex marriage, the issue does not arise there. Polygamy has required attention from English law as a result of migration from jurisdictions where polygamy is lawfully practised.[201] English law does not itself permit the creation of polygamous marriages, so any purportedly polygamous marriage created by a ceremony conducted in England and Wales will at best be void,[202] and may be treated as a non-qualifying ceremony. To create a valid marriage through a ceremony conducted, for example, in a mosque, that ceremony must comply with the formal requirements set out in the MA 1949 for non-Anglican religious marriages, and will create a monogamous marriage.[203]

But does English law recognize polygamous marriages contracted abroad by those domiciled in England and Wales?[204] Here, actually and potentially polygamous marriages must be distinguished. If a man takes more than one wife, both marriages are actually polygamous. A marriage is only *potentially* polygamous when a husband takes his first wife under a law permitting him to take another. In 1972, Parliament had adopted a policy of cultural assimilation: any actually or merely potentially polygamous marriage contracted by someone domiciled in England and Wales would be void. As Sebastian Poulter observed:

> the provision was framed so widely that it was liable to bar, for example, Muslims from the Indian subcontinent who had acquired a domicile of choice here, from returning to their countries of origin to enter into a first marriage through an Islamic wedding. This restricted them in their choice of ceremony since an Islamic form of marriage cannot validly be contracted in England.[205]

After unsatisfactory judicial attempts to mitigate the resulting harshness, the Law Commission recommendation for reform was adopted.[206] So now a *potentially* polygamous marriage contracted abroad by someone domiciled in England and Wales is valid.[207] If a second marriage is then celebrated abroad by either party, the first marriage will not be invalidated: validity is determined at the start of marriage. But if either party to that second marriage is domiciled in England and Wales, that second—actually polygamous—marriage will be void.[208]

2.6.2 VOID GROUNDS, NON-QUALIFYING CEREMONIES, AND PRESUMPTIONS: DISREGARD OF FORMAL REQUIREMENTS

2.6.2.a Void marriages and civil partnerships

The MCA 1973 and MA 1949 collectively provide that a marriage will be void where the parties knowingly and wilfully intermarry under the provisions of the Marriage Act in disregard of certain requirements for the formation of marriage specified in the 1949 Act.[209] The

[201] See 1.2.6. On associated immigration rules, see Immigration Act 1988, s 2; Immigration Rules, r 278; *Bibi v United Kingdom* (App No 19628/92, ECHR) (1992).

[202] *R v Bham* [1966] 1 QB 159. [203] See 2.5.3.

[204] Recognition of marriages contracted abroad by those domiciled abroad is an issue of private international law: see Collins (2012), ch 17; *Official Solicitor v Yemoh* [2010] EWHC 3727.

[205] Poulter (1998), 50–1. [206] Law Com (1985a). [207] MCA 1973, s 11(d).

[208] Ibid. For detailed exploration of English legal responses to polygamy, see Naqvi (2023).

[209] MCA 1973, s 11(c) and MA 1949, s 49; see also s 25 for Anglican marriages; cf CPA 2004, s 49(b)(c).

rules about which formal defects invalidate particular types of marriage are as labyrinthine as the laws relating to the formalities themselves. The MA 1949 is silent about the effect of failing to comply with some formalities: in the absence of provision expressly voiding a marriage for that reason, it will be upheld as valid despite the formal defect.[210] We considered the effect of breach of the requirements regarding, for example, step-relations earlier, so turn now to the general formality requirements.

Some formal requirements are mandatory—their non-observance will render the marriage or civil partnership void, though only if both parties are guilty of 'knowing and wilful disregard'[211] of the fact that they are failing to comply with that requirement. As to which defects will have that effect, broadly speaking, a marriage or civil partnership is void where the parties knew at the time that the ceremony or registration was conducted: without completion of the key preliminary requirements; in a place other than that specified in the original notice; after expiry of the period of time following completion of the preliminaries during which the marriage or partnership may be celebrated; or without an appropriate celebrant/authorized person being present.[212]

Other requirements are directory—their non-observance may involve a criminal offence by the registrar or other responsible person, but will not invalidate the union, even if the parties knew that they had failed to comply with them. For example, breaches of the rules regarding the time of the ceremony, public access to it, the presence of witnesses, use of the prescribed words, and failure to register are not invalidating.[213]

2.6.2.b Non-qualifying ceremonies (formerly known as non-marriages)

Some departures from the mandatory formalities are so substantial that the courts have held there to be no marriage at all, not even a void one.[214] Since the parties have not purported to marry 'under the provisions of' the Marriage Act,[215] this category of relationship was previously known as 'non-marriage'. Yet, given that in many of these cases the parties were married in the eyes of their faith, the Court of Appeal in *Akhter v Khan* (discussed further later in this section) has consigned the term 'non-marriage' to history,[216] endorsing the lower court's view in *Akhter* that it is 'inapt', 'pejorative', and 'instinctively inappropriate'.[217] Thus, in the following discussion, we use the term 'non-qualifying ceremony', though some extracts use the previous terminology of 'non-marriage', and we refer to the parties as 'husband' and 'wife' even though as a matter of English law they lack that status.

Law Commission, *Celebrating Marriage: A New Weddings Law*, Law Com No 408 (London: TSO, 2022)

1.37 Some couples marry in a way that is not legally recognised. These ceremonies, called non-qualifying ceremonies, are a particular concern where the couple having them do so

[210] *Campbell v Corley* (1856) 4 WR 675. [211] For civil partnerships: 'know': CPA 2004, s 49(b).
[212] MA 1949, ss 25, 30, and 49; CPA 2004, s 49(b)(c).
[213] Law Com (1973), Annex, para 120; see also MA 1949, ss 24 and 48.
[214] Though the parties may be validly married according to their religion: see generally Probert and Saleem (2018).
[215] See *AM v AM* [2001] 2 FLR 6, [56]. [216] [2020] EWCA Civ 122, [7].
[217] *Akhter v Khan* [2018] EWFC 54, [8]–[9].

without realising their lack of legal status, or where the law has placed a barrier to the couple having a legal wedding that is meaningful to them, with the couple prioritising a ceremony that is significant to them rather than one that complies with the law. Although many couples have ceremonies conducted by Humanist celebrants and independent celebrants, which are not legally recognised, the evidence suggests that those couples do so knowingly, and will usually have a separate legal wedding in addition. Other couples do not, and only have their meaningful, often religious, ceremony.

There are important legal repercussions for those couples who do not have a separate legal wedding in addition to their non-qualifying ceremony:[218]

9.2 Whether a ceremony results in a valid or void marriage or is non-qualifying has significant consequences. A valid marriage brings a range of legal rights and responsibilities. If a marriage is void, a court has the same powers to reallocate assets between the couple as upon divorce; in other contexts, however, a void marriage does not have the same consequences as a valid marriage. If the ceremony is nonqualifying, the couple are simply treated as cohabitants; in such cases a court has no power to reallocate assets between the couple on separation and couples have fewer rights overall than if they had a void marriage.

Hudson v Leigh offers an illustration of a non-qualifying ceremony. The parties wished to marry. The wife, a devout Christian, wanted to marry in a religious ceremony, but the husband, a wealthy 'atheist Jew', did not. They compromised. They would have a Christian ceremony (in South Africa) that would satisfy the wife that they were 'married in the eyes of God', but it was agreed by them and the celebrant that the service would not create a legal marriage. Specific passages from the normal wedding service were accordingly omitted, in particular the question whether anyone present knows any lawful impediment to their marriage and any reference to the parties as 'lawful' husband or wife, or to their being 'lawfully' married. The service proceeded as planned. The parties then returned to London where, it had been understood, they would marry in a civil ceremony. Unfortunately, their relationship broke down between fixtures, and the wife began divorce proceedings.

But could they divorce? Not if there were no valid marriage to begin with. Nor would the wife be entitled to a decree of nullity and the right to apply for financial orders consequent upon that decree unless there was a void marriage. The wife argued that the South African ceremony had created a lawful marriage, or at least a void marriage, contending that cases suggesting the existence of a third category of non-qualifying ceremony were wrongly decided. The husband argued that the ceremony amounted only to a non-qualifying ceremony, and that the wife therefore had no right to apply for financial orders. The husband won. The South African ceremony was certainly defective as a result of South African

[218] See Miles (2020).

marriage formalities law so was at least void.[219] But the judge went further, holding there was no marriage at all:

Hudson v Leigh [2009] EWHC 1306

BODEY J:

69. I would find it unrealistic and illogical to conclude that there is no such concept as a ceremony or event which, whilst having marriage-like characteristics, fails in law to effect a marriage. Such is the ingenuity of human beings that we will always be able to come up with some sort of ritual or happening which one party claims created a marriage, but which the other says fell short of doing so. Rare though this will be, the law has to be able to determine the issue without being constrained (except of course where statute so requires) to go down the nullity route . . . Rebecca Probert [(2002a) suggests that] the 'marriage within a play' example (such as in Romeo and Juliet) . . . is a 'non-marriage' . . . because it in no way ever purports to be a real marriage, a feature which she suggests is linked to, but distinct from, the issue of the parties' intentions. The concept of 'non-marriage' should she argues: ". . . also apply to alternative, self-devised rituals, should anyone wish to argue the legal validity of, for example hand-fasting or a broomstick wedding" (these being old rites here and on the continent, thought by some in days gone by to create married status).[220]

70. It is inherently difficult to come up with examples (of a questionable ceremony, ritual or event) which do not appear fanciful; but take a nervous and eccentric couple who wished to have a full dress-rehearsal of their wedding ceremony, so as to be sure that everything would go alright on the day. Assume that the vicar was present and that he used the full wording of the marriage service. Assume wedding-outfits, bridesmaids, flowers, music, an Order of Ceremony and the presence of many of the intended guests, but with its being known that the occasion was not the real thing. What if that the relationship were then to break down prior to the actual wedding day?

71. . . . [I]t was but a rehearsal and was neither arranged to, nor intended to, nor was it purporting to achieve any legal outcome at all (even though in principle the parties' underlying wish and purpose was to be married). . . . I distinguish the possible example of where the minister is intending to celebrate a marriage in the normal way, but where the parties are participating for a (perhaps) drunken bet, or dare: that is a very different matter and would call for quite different considerations should it arise . . .

Bodey J then set out key factors for determining the status of a purported marriage:

78. . . . [I]t is not in my view either necessary or prudent to attempt in the abstract a definition or test of the circumstances in which a given event having marital characteristics should be held not to be a marriage. Questionable ceremonies should I think be addressed on a case by case basis, taking account of the various factors and features mentioned above including particularly, but not exhaustively: (a) whether the ceremony or event set out and purported

[219] The formal validity of the marriage was governed by South African law, as the law of the place where the ceremony had occurred. On applicable law in case of a foreign marriage, see *Assad v Kurter* [2013] EWHC 3852.

[220] See Probert (2009b) on the falsity of these beliefs.

to be a lawful marriage; (b) whether it bore all or enough of the hallmarks of marriage; (c) whether the three key participants (most especially the officiating official) believed, intended and understood the ceremony as giving rise to the status of lawful marriage [under English law[221]]; and (d) the reasonable perceptions, understandings and beliefs of those in attendance [though these cannot be decisive in converting an occasion which all three participants fundamentally meant not to be effective into a marriage in law]. In most if not all reasonably foreseeable situations, a review of these and similar considerations should enable a decision to be satisfactorily reached.

He accordingly made a declaration that there never was a marriage.

It may be felt that no injustice was done to the wife in that case, who was apparently deliberately trying not to create a marriage in the South African ceremony. The same might not always be said about the apparently growing number of ceremonies conducted in England and Wales in which parties marry in accordance with their own religious rites but who (entirely innocently) fail to comply with the formal requirements necessary to create a marriage recognized in English law.[222] Many of these marriages may be solemnized on religious premises; these can be authorized as registered premises for civil marriages, but it appears that—particularly in the case of mosques—relatively few have been.[223] Some of these marriages take place on private premises. Unlike actors in a stage play or couples rehearsing, these couples may honestly believe that they are validly married in the eyes of the state as well as their god—and women may be left especially vulnerable. Indeed, it may seem perverse that these 'innocent' departures from what the law requires condemn parties to a 'non-qualifying ceremony', while those who 'knowingly and wilfully disregard' mandatory Marriage Act requirements (without going completely 'off-piste') end up with a void marriage.[224] The issue appears to be particularly acute within the Muslim community.[225]

Law Commission, *Celebrating Marriage: A New Weddings Law*, Law Com No 408 (London: TSO, 2022)

1.37 Although not exclusively arising in the Islamic community, research suggests Islamic couples who have a nikah ceremony might be especially likely to be among those who do not have an additional, legal wedding ceremony. While the reasons why such couples have only a religious-only marriage are complex, and include situations where one of the couple is pressured by the other to have a non-legally recognised wedding, the result is that they lack the protection of legal marriage. As a result, individuals, disproportionately women and the children of these relationships, may suffer serious financial difficulties when the relationship ends or when their partner dies.

221 *El Gamal v Al Maktoum* [2011] EWHC 3763, [81].
222 See Talwar (2010); Gaffney-Rhys (2013), 58.
223 Law Com (2015), fig. 10; see 2.5.3.
224 Probert and Saleem (2018), 22–3.
225 See Douglas et al (2012); Bano (2012); Parveen (2020); Uddin (2018); HO (2018), 17–18, cf Probert's (2018a) compelling critique of this review's proposed solution.

There are many examples in the case law. In *Gandhi v Patel*,[226] the parties had a lavish Hindu wedding conducted by a Brahmin priest in an Indian restaurant in London, but did not observe any formal requirements of English law; they could only have created a valid marriage by marrying 'again' in a register office or other approved or registered premises.[227] Unbeknownst to the wife, the husband was already married, so any marriage would in any event have been void for that reason. But would the restaurant marriage even count as a void marriage, given the informal circumstances of its creation? The issue arose when the husband died having made no financial provision for the wife in his will. She sought to apply to court under its powers to redistribute property from the deceased's estate amongst certain family members. To be eligible to make that application, she had to prove at least a void marriage,[228] a claim which the beneficiaries of the husband's estate rejected. The judge decided that the ceremony created only a non-qualifying ceremony, relying on dicta in another case, *A-M v A-M*, concerning the celebration of a wedding under Islamic rites in a private flat:

A-M v A-M (Divorce: Jurisdiction: Validity of Marriage) [2001] 2 FLR 6 (Fam Div)

HUGHES J:

58. . . . A marriage which purports to be conducted under [the Marriage Acts] may nevertheless be void for want of formality . . . But unless a marriage purports to be of the kind contemplated by the Marriage Acts, it is not . . . a marriage for the purposes of s 11. . . . No doubt it is possible to envisage cases where the question whether a particular ceremony or other event does or does not purport to be a marriage of the kind contemplated by the Marriage Acts is a fine one. *Gereis v Yagoub* [1997] 1 FLR 854 was one such, where [the judge] concluded that but for the absence of notice to the superintendent registrar and the lack of registration of the building the ceremony would have been one valid in English law; the decision may have been a merciful one. It is clear, however, that the present ceremony did not begin to purport to be a marriage according to the Marriage Acts, with or without fatal defects. It was not conducted under the rites for the Church of England, nor was there ever any question of an application for, still less a grant of, a superintendent registrar's certificate, and it was conducted in a flat which was clearly none of the places which were authorised for marriage. The ceremony was consciously an Islamic one rather than such as is contemplated by the Marriage Acts . . . [N]obody purported to conduct or take part in a Marriage Act 1949 ceremony, and the fact that no one applied their mind to how English law would view what they did does not alter that conclusion . . . [T]he . . . ceremony is neither a valid marriage in English law nor one in respect of which jurisdiction exists to grant a decree of nullity.

The courts have struggled to provide a coherent account of which formal requirements are so essential to creating a Marriage Act-style marriage that their omission plunges couples into the legal black hole of a ceremony that is non-qualifying. Whilst at first sight appealing, the notion that the parties' intentions should be relevant is problematic. Upsetting parties' intentions and beliefs about their marriage's validity may appear harsh:

[226] [2001] 2 FLR 603.
[227] Which could include a temple: MA 1949, ss 35, 41–4; Places of Worship Registration Act 1855.
[228] Inheritance (Provision for Family and Dependants) Act 1975, ss 1(1)(a) and 25(4).

the parties in *Dukali v Lamrani*, following in the footsteps of many others before them, celebrated their marriage in a notarized ceremony in the Moroccan Consulate. They had given no notice of intention to marry, the notary was not an authorized person, and the Consulate was not an appropriate venue:[229] it was a non-qualifying ceremony.[230] However, Rebecca Probert has cogently argued that parties' intentions (and those of the celebrant and witnesses) should neither rescue something from being a non-qualifying ceremony because of its egregious lack of formalities, nor cause a non-qualifying ceremony to emerge from a ceremony that is formally valid.[231] If party intentions were relevant, even determinative, why would we bother having formal requirements at all? And can we even ascertain the parties' intentions sufficiently reliably to determine such an important issue of legal status?

R. Probert, 'The Evolving Concept of Non-Marriage', (2013) 25 *Child and Family Law Quarterly* 318, 333–4

From a pragmatic point of view, the difficulties of placing weight on the intention of the parties alone are obvious. After all, it will be rare for a case to come to court where the parties are in agreement about their intentions. If they have discovered some flaw in their ceremony and wish to remedy it, it would be simpler, quicker, and cheaper to go through a new ceremony of marriage rather than to litigate over the status of the first. If they have separated, then at least one of them may wish to deny that there was ever any intention to marry. And if one has died, then, despite sympathy for the survivor, claims based solely on intention should be regarded with caution.

And it is not, after all, a simple conflict between intention and form. Couples manifest their intention to enter into a legally binding marriage by going through a ceremony in a prescribed form. As Lord Brougham put it in *Warrender v Warrender*, each nation lays down its own forms and solemnities, 'compliance with which shall be deemed the only criterion of the intention to enter into the contract' . . .

Moreover, given that many of the disputed ceremonies involve religious weddings, ascertaining whether there was an intention to enter into a legally binding ceremony of marriage may be difficult. . . . [Their conduct following the ceremony, e.g. in starting to live together and to commence a sexual relationship] may, of course, simply indicate that they regarded the religious ceremony as sufficient to legitimate their subsequent relationship, regardless of its legal standing. For those with strong religious convictions, a ceremony that is valid in the eyes of their god may well be more important in this sense than one that is legally valid. In short, intention alone is an unsatisfactory criterion by which to assess the validity of a marriage.

Instead, she argues, the answer to what will yield a non-qualifying ceremony can be discerned by careful reading of the MA 1949. Thus, total non-compliance with formalities (as in *Dukali*) will clearly result in a non-qualifying ceremony; but, she argues, provided the parties have either given the required notice or married in an authorized location, their

[229] Being neither an approved premises for civil marriages (which this was not), nor a registered place of worship for a religious marriage.

[230] [2012] EWHC 1748.

[231] Cf *Galloway v Goldstein* [2012] EWHC 60.

marriage will be valid, notwithstanding innocent[232] breaches of the other formal requirements.[233] If we are dissatisfied with that, the answer lies not in undermining formality law by allowing party intention to influence the outcome unpredictably, but instead in reforming our formality law to make it easier, in particular, for adherents to minority faiths to create valid marriages through their own religious ceremonies.[234]

The need for such reform is underscored by the confusion and criticism arising from *Akhter v Khan*. The first instance judge, Williams J, had, rather surprisingly, found a void marriage between a couple who had gone through a purely religious marriage ceremony. As in *Hudson v Leigh*, both parties knew the ceremony was legally ineffective, and had agreed that it would be followed by a (legally effective) civil ceremony. The subsequent ceremony never happened, despite the wife's frequent attempts to pursue the matter with the husband. Classifying the marriage as void benefited the wife, for it enabled her to seek financial remedies following the parties' 18-year long, four-child relationship.[235]

Williams J modified the *Hudson v Leigh* test to include reference to 'whether the parties had agreed that the necessary legal formalities would be undertaken' and 'whether the failure to complete all the legal formalities was a joint decision or due to the failure of one party to complete them'.[236] In other words, he focused on the parties' initial agreement to have a civil ceremony following their religious-only wedding, and that it was the *husband's* choice—not the wife's—not to adhere to that agreement. The decision caused consternation in many legal circles, appearing to depart from consistent case law that would clearly have classed this as a non-qualifying ceremony.[237] Indeed, given the parties' full legal awareness of what they were (and were not) doing, this was not one of those very 'hard' cases in which one might feel compelled to rescue a party or parties who, in good faith, had honestly believed that they were validly married. The decision was appealed by the Attorney General and duly overturned by the Court of Appeal, restoring orthodoxy to this area of law.[238] The court rejected both the judge's interpretation of the key statutes (the MA 1949, to which the MCA 1973, s 11(a) refers), deciding it was too great a leap to convert a ceremony that all parties knew was not legally effective into a void marriage on the basis that a *further* ceremony was intended.[239]

Reform requires a 'nuanced response': 'it cannot simply be assumed that religious-only marriages are a problem that needs to be eliminated either by universal recognition or a blanket ban'.[240] For neither solution would recognize the autonomy of couples who do not want the legal consequences of civil marriage.[241] As Rajnaara Akhtar notes, young British Muslims sometimes wish to contract a religious-only marriage while deliberately *not* intending also to have a civil marriage:[242]

[232] Cf 'knowing and wilful disregard', which will result in a void marriage.

[233] Probert (2013); e.g. *MA v JA* [2012] EWHC 2219.

[234] See 2.5.3.

[235] Williams J deployed human rights law—notably Arts 8 and 12 ECHR, with reference to Art 3 of the United Nations Convention on the Rights of the Child (UNCRC)—in an inventive manner to support what he described as a 'slightly more flexible' interpretation of the MCA 1973 provision: [2018] EWFC 54, [92]–[96].

[236] Ibid, [94](b).

[237] Nash (2020).

[238] *Akhter v Khan* [2020] EWCA Civ 122.

[239] The court also rejected Williams J's human rights arguments (see n 264).

[240] Probert and Saleem (2018), 2. See also Barton and Probert (2018).

[241] Naqvi (2020); Sandberg and Thompson (2017).

[242] See also Parveen (2020).

R. Akhtar, 'Religious-Only Marriages and Cohabitation: Deciphering Differences', in R. Akhtar, P. Nash, and R. Probert (eds), *Cohabitation and Religious Marriage: Status, Similarities and Solutions* (Bristol: BUP, 2020), 73–4

The motivations for entering a religious-only marriage are not uniform and depend very much on the individual circumstances of the couple. While case law such as *Akhter v Khan* speaks to marriages which are long established and where one party is denying the other a formal legally recognized marriage, the landscape is often far more complex and reflective of many interwoven factors . . . [S]ignificantly, there has been a particular cultural shift among young Muslims and their relationship norms, which is being revealed in research findings. Young people in general are more cautious about making marital commitments early, however, those youth who are religiously observant will not enter an intimate relationship without a religious marriage in place. Young Muslims appear to be adapting new relationship norms as they navigate religious laws, community norms, wider peer group behaviours, and the law.

In many other cases, couples simply want the freedom to get married legally in a way that is meaningful to them:

R. Probert, R. Akhtar, and S. Blake, *When is a Wedding Not a Marriage? Exploring Non-Legally Binding Ceremonies* (London: Nuffield, 2022), 134

Perhaps one of the most important findings is how the non-legally binding ceremonies in our study reflected the beliefs and values of the individuals involved. Many held very strong religious beliefs and would not have regarded themselves as married without a ceremony conducted in line with the norms of their faith group. These individuals were drawn from a range of different faiths: Christian, Muslim, Hindu, Pagan, Buddhist, Zoroastrian, Sikh, Jewish, and Bahá'í. Others chose a Humanist ceremony because this aligned with their beliefs and values, or had a ceremony led by an independent celebrant, a friend, or a member of the family. These latter types of ceremony did not follow a standard script or prescribed rites but were highly personalised. That said, it was striking how often they included rituals that were designed to emphasise not only the commitment that the couple were making to each other but also the new bonds being forged between families. At least some of these rituals were religious in origin, suggesting that there is no sharp dividing line between 'religious' and 'non-religious' ceremonies but rather a spectrum of practices.

In other words, for the vast majority of the couples in our sample the non-legally binding ceremony was a vitally important part of the process of getting married. Many of those whose legal wedding preceded or followed their non-legally binding ceremony would have preferred to have had a single ceremony that was both legally recognised and conducted in a manner (and at a location) that was meaningful to them. That this was not an option for them is a reflection of the limitations of the current law.

In any case, it is unsatisfactory that the status of marriages—even void marriages attracting significant legal consequences—should turn on party intention regarding any ceremony (particularly one that they never undertook), rather than more objectively ascertainable facts about what was and was not done. Comprehensive statutory reform is needed. Russell Sandberg has suggested that this could be achieved by reforming the validity requirements of marriage, as well as broader reform of the rights of unmarried cohabitants: (see 7.6).[243]

R. Sandberg, *Religion and Marriage Law: The Need for Reform* (Bristol: BUP, 2021), 145–6

> It is difficult to dispute that the law on marriage in England and Wales is antiquated and is in need of reform . . . Legal redress should be provided to those in unregistered religious marriages where the failure to comply with registration requirements is unwitting or is not truly voluntary on the part of one of the parties. Education and awareness raising has an important part to play here but this would be aided considerably if the legal framework were accessible and principled. And, ultimately, there is a role for law here in terms of providing backstops whereby some redress can be given to those who unwittingly or involuntarily enter into unregistered religious marriages. Reform of the law of validity to make some unregistered religious marriages void could provide such a backstop and there is a limited role for some criminal offences. However, the most important backstop that could be provided would be by providing some limited cohabitation rights of the type that exist in neighbouring jurisdictions.

In 2022, the Law Commission published its final report on weddings law. It recommended extensive reform (see 2.5.3.d) and made specific recommendations addressing the problem of non-qualifying ceremonies:[244]

Law Commission, *Celebrating Marriage: A New Weddings Law*, Law Com No 408 (London: TSO, 2022)

> 1.9 Our recommendations will give couples, as well as religious groups and (if enabled by Government to conduct weddings) non-religious belief groups, the freedom to decide where and how their weddings will take place.
>
> (1) They will be allowed to choose the location where their weddings will take place, without unnecessary restrictions and costs. This approach will allow all types of wedding – both civil and belief ceremonies – to take place outdoors, including in forests and fields, and in a wide variety of buildings, including in private homes and on military sites.
> (2) They will be allowed to choose the form their wedding ceremonies will take. This will allow the variety of ceremonies that people use to mark their weddings, including religious ceremonies, to be recognised as the legal ceremony at which the couple is married, eliminating the need for a couple to have, and pay for, more than one ceremony.
>
> Our recommendations also clarify the consequences when a couple has not complied with the required formalities. Importantly, they will ensure that fewer weddings conducted according to religious rites result in a marriage that the law does not recognise at all.

[243] See also Naqvi (2020), who has argued that cohabitation reform could address some of the issues surrounding religious-only marriages that are not civilly registered, if parties were able to opt out of legal recognition.

[244] Cummings (2021).

At the time of writing, the government has not responded to these proposals.[245] Time will tell whether this much-needed reform will be introduced.

2.6.2.c Rescuing doubtful marriages via the presumption of marriage

The courts have sometimes avoided a finding of a non-qualifying ceremony or void marriage via the rebuttable presumption of marriage.[246] This presumption has two forms: (i) it may be presumed, without *positive* evidence of *any* ceremony, that the parties are validly married where they have cohabited for such a period of time and in such circumstances that they are reputed to be married; or (ii) where there is evidence of *a* ceremony having taken place that was in theory *capable* of creating a marriage valid under the applicable law and the parties subsequently lived together as husband and wife, it will be presumed that that ceremony complied with the formal requirements and that the parties are validly married.[247] While we have come to this issue last in our discussion of the law, as a presumption of validity absent evidence *against* the marriage, it should logically be the starting point—and will be the ending point where, perhaps unusually, there is no rebutting evidence.

But there is confusion in the case law. In *Chief Adjudication Officer v Bath*,[248] the parties went through a Sikh wedding ceremony that may not have fulfilled English law's formal requirements; there was no marriage certificate. Nevertheless, the couple lived as husband and wife for nearly 40 years, during which time the man paid his tax and national insurance contributions on the basis that he was married. The woman later applied for a widow's pension, but her application was refused because there was no evidence of a valid marriage. The Court of Appeal upheld the marriage: it could not be proved on the facts that the marriage was void as formally defective. However, it was suggested that, alternatively, the presumption of marriage saved the marriage. This reasoning has been cogently criticized by Rebecca Probert, insofar as it appears to suggest that the presumption can save marriages that are patently formally defective. It is logical to presume that a valid marriage occurred when, despite the lack of any positive evidence of a ceremony, the parties have behaved as if one has taken place, or when there is no evidence proving that the ceremony that did occur was formally defective. But it would be improper to presume a valid marriage where the only known ceremony was plainly invalid (whether making it void or a non-qualifying ceremony) and there is no evidence that a further (presumptively valid) ceremony might have occurred.[249]

By contrast, it was conceivable in *A-M v A-M (Divorce: Jurisdiction: Validity of Marriage)*[250] that the parties, domiciled abroad, might have contracted an Islamic marriage by proxy (under the applicable foreign law), the wife having granted power of attorney to her husband for this purpose. Here, the presumption could *logically* be applied. However, Probert queries whether the English courts *should* presume that a marriage has been contracted in these circumstances. In that case, it was advantageous to the wife to presume a marriage. But in other circumstances, the assertion of a marriage by proxy—a procedure readily open to abuse—might be undesirable in policy terms, not least since the UK is a signatory to the UN Convention on Consent to Marriage, which requires that consent be given in person.[251]

245 This was anticipated in early 2023: Hansard HL Deb, vol 825, col 1668, 29 November 2022, Lord Bellamy.
246 E.g. *Hayatleh v Modfy* [2017] EWCA Civ 70; cf *Assad v Kurter* [2013] EWHC 3852.
247 *Halsbury's Laws of England* vol 72, paras 7–8; see Probert (2018b) for detailed analysis.
248 [2000] 1 FLR 8.
249 Probert (2002a), 412–13; e.g. *MA v JA* [2012] EWHC 2219, [83].
250 [2001] 2 FLR 6.
251 Probert (2002a), 416.

Probert concludes that the courts are using the presumption of marriage in an unprincipled manner in order to achieve fair outcomes (if only in some cases) for parties to non-Christian faiths who seem to be particularly susceptible to a finding of a non-qualifying ceremony for want of proper formalities.[252] Again, the better solution lies in statutory reform of marriage formalities, as discussed at 2.5.3.d and 2.6.2.b.

2.7 GROUNDS ON WHICH A MARRIAGE OR CIVIL PARTNERSHIP IS VOIDABLE

The voidable grounds for mixed-sex and same-sex marriage and for civil partnership are mostly shared (see Table 2.2), and it will be assumed in the following discussion that principles from the case law relating to marriage apply to civil partnership.[253] However, some sex-related grounds—concerning failure to consummate and venereal disease—do not apply to civil partnership, and failure to consummate does not apply to same-sex marriage. Why this should be is intriguing in two senses: why they should apply only to (mixed-sex) marriage, and why they should apply to any marriage at all.

Nearly all of the grounds on which marriage and civil partnership can be avoided may be regarded as in some way related to a defect in the parties' consent,[254] either in the sense that no consent was given, or that the apparent consent was vitiated by the presence or absence of some factor or condition with or without which the consent could not—in the eyes of the law—be fully effective. Since all voidable grounds can be raised only by a party to the relationship, the spouses essentially have discretion to determine what matters to them.[255]

Table 2.2 Grounds on which marriage and civil partnership voidable

Marriage: MCA 1973, s 12(1)	Civil Partnership: CPA 2004, s 50
Lack of valid consent by either party	Lack of valid consent by either party
Either party suffering from mental disorder rendering 'unfit' for marriage	Either party suffering from mental disorder rendering 'unfit' for civil partnership
Respondent pregnant by a third party at time of marriage	Respondent pregnant by a third party at time of civil partnership
Grounds relating to gender recognition	Grounds relating to gender recognition
Respondent had venereal disease at time of marriage	[no equivalent ground]
Grounds relating to non-consummation —***mixed-sex marriage only***—no equivalent for same-sex marriage: s 12(2)	[no equivalent ground]

[252] Cf the Coptic Orthodox Christians in *Gereis v Yagoub* [1997] 1 FLR 854.
[253] See also s 12A for marriages converted from same-sex civil partnership.
[254] Law Com (1970), para 24(b).
[255] *Sandwell MBC v RG and others* [2013] EWHC 2373.

Statutory bars prevent decrees of nullity in some circumstances.[256] Several of the voidable grounds are subject to specific bars, which we examine in this section. But a general, estoppel-type bar applies to all grounds:[257]

Matrimonial Causes Act 1973, s 13(1)

> The court shall not . . . grant a decree of nullity on the ground that a marriage is voidable if the respondent satisfies the court—
>
> (a) that the petitioner, with knowledge that it was open to him to have the marriage avoided, so conducted himself in relation to the respondent as to lead the respondent reasonably to believe that he would not seek to do so; and
>
> (b) that it would be unjust to the respondent to grant the decree.

e.g if husband said "I won't seek to annul" ∴ he can't later annul

This provision, which replaced the old defence of approbation, was considered in *D v D (Nullity: Statutory Bar)*.[258] The court noted differences between the old defence and s 13: the matter need no longer be considered from the perspective of public policy, but simply in terms of what is required to do justice between the parties. The test's second limb may make it hard to invoke: given the jurisdiction to make financial orders on nullity decrees, and the ready availability of divorce, the bar may rarely be imposed.

Since a voidable marriage or civil partnership is valid unless and until annulled on the application of one of the parties during their joint lives, we might ask why these grounds should exist at all, rather than simply leaving dissatisfied parties to divorce. However, the concept of the voidable marriage is important for faith groups, since to annul a marriage because of some impediment present from the outset is doctrinally distinct from dissolving a valid marriage.[259] The category of voidable marriage has therefore been retained—and extended to civil partnership (notwithstanding the wholly secular nature of that institution). Annulment of voidable unions takes effect prospectively: the existence of the marriage or civil partnership prior to the decree is unaffected.[260]

2.7.1 LACK OF VALID CONSENT

Consent lies at the heart of both marriage and civil partnership. The need for consent—and the right not to be married without it—is recognized by several international human rights instruments.[261] The issue has arisen recently in relation to forced marriage and parties with limited mental capacity, often in cases concerned to prevent such marriages going ahead at all, rather than in subsequent nullity proceedings. It may seem odd that so important an issue as lack of consent should not render a marriage void—indeed, that was the position at common law. However, such a marriage could subsequently be ratified by the

[256] MCA 1973, s 13; CPA 2004, s 51. [257] CPA 2004, s 51(1).
[258] [1979] Fam 70. [259] Law Com (1970), Part III. [260] MCA 1973, s 16; CPA 2004, s 37(3).
[261] Universal Declaration of Human Rights, Art 16; UN Convention on the Elimination of All Forms of Discrimination Against Women, General Recommendation No 21; UNCRC, Arts 19 and 35; UN Convention on Consent to Marriage, Minimum Age for Marriage and Registration of Marriage, Art 1.

non-consenting party, and the need for close factual investigation of alleged lack of consent makes it better suited to the voidable category. So the MCA 1973 made that change, on the Law Commission's recommendation.[262]

The MCA 1973 and the CPA 2004 provide that marriage or civil partnership will be voidable wherever one party did not 'validly consent' to it, enumerating situations in which that might be so: 'duress, mistake, unsoundness of mind, or otherwise'.[263] Lack of consent may be relied on by either party, not only the party whose consent it is claimed was lacking. Proceedings on this ground must ordinarily be initiated within three years of the marriage or civil partnership.[264]

Before examining the bases on which consent might be vitiated or absent, we must identify what it is that must be consented to. *Vervaeke v Smith* is instructive on this point and on English law's attitude towards the institution of marriage. The petitioner, a Belgian sex worker, had married an Englishman in order to acquire British nationality and so avoid deportation.[265] The couple parted immediately after the ceremony, never intending to live as husband and wife and never doing so. The issue of the marriage's validity arose years later when the petitioner sought to inherit from her second 'husband'. She could only succeed (at that time) if the first marriage were void[266] for want of consent. She failed in the English courts, but subsequently obtained a decree of nullity in Belgium that she then sought to have recognized in England. In the course of considering—and refusing—that application, the House of Lords approved remarks of Ormrod J:

Vervaeke (formerly Messina) v Smith and others [1983] 1 AC 145, 151–3

> "Where a man and a woman consent to marry one another in a formal ceremony, conducted in accordance with the formalities required by law, knowing that it is a marriage ceremony, it is immaterial that they do not intend to live together as man and wife. . . . [I]f the parties exchange consents to marry with due formality, intending to acquire the status of married persons, it is immaterial that they intend the marriage to take effect in some limited way or that one or both of them may have been mistaken about or unaware of some of the incidents of the status which they have created. To hold otherwise would impair the effect of the whole system of law regulating marriages in this country, and gravely diminish the value of the system of registration of marriages upon which so much depends in a modern community. Lord Merrivale in *Kelly (orse. Hyams) v. Kelly* . . . said: 'In a country like ours, where the marriage status is of very great consequence and where the enforcement of the marriage laws is a matter of great public concern, it would be intolerable if the marriage of law could be played with by people who thought fit to go to a register office and subsequently, after some change of mind, to affirm that it was not a marriage because they did not so regard it.' . . ."

[262] Law Com (1970), paras 11–15; cf McClean and Hayes (2011), 79–80.

[263] MCA 1973, s 12(1)(c); CPA 2004, s 50(1)(a).

[264] MCA 1973, s 13(2)(4)(5); CPA 2004, s 51(2)–(4). Cf *B v I* [2010] 1 FLR 1721, a decision under the inherent jurisdiction addressed later in relation to duress.

[265] Cf the rules designed to prevent such marriages considered in *R (On the Application of Baiai and others) v Secretary of State for the Home Department* [2008] UKHL 53 and various criminal offences connected with 'sham marriages' under immigration legislation.

[266] Would the English courts' reasoning apply equally now that the marriage is merely voidable? Cf Bradney (1984) on duress cases.

Interestingly, Lord Hailsham went on to contrast the approaches of English and Belgian law, the latter having granted a decree of nullity where the former would not. As the Belgian court had put it in this case:

> According to section 146 Civil Law, there is no marriage when there is no consent. The consent being an essential condition and element of the marriage, the lack of consent has as consequence the absolute invalidity of that marriage. As the parties . . . delusively indulged in a marriage ceremony without in fact really consenting to a marriage, they behaved against public policy. The disturbance of public order, the protection of what belongs to the essence of a real marriage and of human dignity, exact that such a sham-marriage be declared invalid.

While English law reaches the opposite result, declaring the marriage valid, it is striking that its reasons for doing so are very similar to Belgian law's reasons for reaching the opposite conclusion: upholding the seriousness of the institution of marriage as a matter of public policy.[267]

2.7.1.a Duress

The law on duress has received considerable attention in cases involving forced marriages.[268] It is important to appreciate the difference between forced and arranged marriages:[269]

Re SK (Proposed Plaintiff) (An Adult by Way of her Litigation Friend) [2004] EWHC 3202

SINGER J:

> 7. . . . [T]here is a spectrum of forced marriage from physical force or fear of injury or death in their most literal form, through to the undue imposition of emotional pressure which is at the other end of the forced marriage range, and . . . a grey area then separates unacceptable forced marriage from marriages arranged traditionally which are in no way to be condemned, but rather supported as a conventional concept in many societies. Social expectations can of themselves impose emotional pressure and the grey area . . . is where one may slip into the other: arranged may become forced but forced is always different from arranged.

Statutory civil remedies and criminal offences now exist to protect potential and actual victims of forced marriages.[270] The courts have also developed the inherent jurisdiction to protect suspected victims[271] and generally to ensure that vulnerable individuals are able to give full and genuine consent to any marriage proposed for them, beyond what the law of nullity requires by way of consent for the marriage to be valid.[272] Prevention is better than cure.[273]

267 See also *SH v KH* 2006 SC 129 in Scots law.
268 For information on forced marriage protection orders, see 4.10.
269 See generally Mody (2015).
270 See 4.10.
271 *Re SK (Proposed Plaintiff) (An Adult by Way of her Litigation Friend)* [2004] EWHC 3202.
272 *Re SA (Vulnerable Adult with Capacity: Marriage)* [2005] EWHC 2942.
273 *NS v MI* [2006] EWHC 1646, [7].

Our principal concern here, however, is with the diagnosis and cure: to determine when a marriage or civil partnership may be annulled owing to duress. Forced marriages are voidable under the MCA 1973; arranged marriages, to which both parties consent, are not. One difficulty in this scheme has been encountered (and simply sidestepped) in cases involving the recognition of forced marriages contracted abroad. The victims brought their proceedings too late in terms of the MCA 1973: as noted previously, nullity petitions based on lack of consent must be brought within three years of the ceremony. That period cannot be extended, say, because the victim of a forced marriage was prevented by family circumstances (which may be tantamount to false imprisonment) from seeking assistance and bringing proceedings.[274] The courts have sought to 'avoid' the time bar by granting declarations under the inherent jurisdiction that the ceremony created no marriage capable of recognition in English law—that is, treating the case as one of a non-qualifying ceremony.[275] Whilst the outcome may appear just, releasing victims of forced marriages without incurring the stigma (in their community's eyes) of a divorce, it must be doubted whether these cases are rightly decided under the law as it stands,[276] and the court's jurisdiction to make financial orders is not available following a finding of a non-qualifying ceremony, to the potential detriment of the victim 'spouse'.

That problem aside, the chief difficulty lies in navigating Singer J's 'grey area' between forced and arranged marriages. The courts have shown considerable sensitivity towards minority cultural practices.[277] It is clear that the duress may come from the other party to the marriage or from third parties. However, the law is uncertain because competing lines of authority espouse different tests, one subjective, the other objective. Since there are Court of Appeal decisions on both sides, that court and those below it remain free to apply either test until the Supreme Court resolves the issue.[278] However, the subjective test is generally preferred, some judges and commentators considering that it already represents the law.[279] When assessing cases decided before 1971 espousing an objective test, it may be important to bear in mind that lack of consent then rendered a marriage void, rather than voidable, and so a stricter test may have been considered desirable.[280] But whichever test were applied to these facts, the reported cases would arguably have been decided the same way.

The objective test

In *Buckland v Buckland,* the husband, a member of the armed forces serving in Malta, found himself in an awkward position. Falsely alleged to be the father of a young girl's child, he was told by his senior officers and lawyer that his only escape from prosecution and

[274] Cf s 13(4): extension in case of mental disorder only.

[275] E.g. *KC and NNC v City of Westminster Social and Community Services Department and another* [2008] EWCA Civ 198; *Re P (Forced Marriage)* [2011] EWHC 3467; for criticism, see Probert (2008a) and (2013), 330–2.

[276] Cf *A Local Authority v X* [2013] EWHC 3274, where the court required that a decree of nullity be sought: the marriage being void on grounds of age as well as voidable for non-consent, there was no bar to be avoided by granting a declaration instead.

[277] *NS v MI* [2006] EWHC 1646, [37]; see also Scottish cases, e.g. *Mahmud v Mahmud* 1994 SLT 599; for criticism, see Bradney (1984), (1994); Lim (1996).

[278] *Young v Bristol Aeroplane Co Ltd* [1944] KB 718; *Ashburn Anstalt v Arnold* [1989] Ch 1, 21.

[279] *NS v MI* [2006] EWHC 1646; Masson, Bailey-Harris, and Probert (2008), 71–2.

[280] Bradney (1984), 279. When void, no time bar would have applied to forced marriages.

imprisonment for under-age sex would be to marry the girl. The judge set out a three-stage test in declaring the marriage void (as it would have been then):

Buckland v Buckland (orse Camilleri) [1968] P 296 (Probate Div), 301

SCARMAN J:

[I]n a case where it is alleged that the petitioner's consent to marriage has been vitiated by fear, it must be shown, first, that fear of sufficient degree to vitiate consent was present; and, secondly, that the fear was reasonably entertained. . . . [A] third proposition may be stated to the effect that, even if the fear is reasonably entertained, it will not vitiate consent, unless it arises from some external circumstance for which the petitioner is not himself responsible.

The conclusion which I have reached, on the facts in the present case, is that the petitioner agreed to marry the girl because he was afraid, and that his fear was brought about by an unjust charge preferred against him . . . The fear which originated in this way was greatly strengthened by the advice given to the petitioner by his own solicitor and by his superior officer. I am satisfied that when he presented himself in the church for the marriage ceremony, he believed himself to be in an inescapable dilemma—marriage or prison: and, fearing prison, he chose marriage . . .

Accordingly, in my judgment, he is entitled to a declaration that the marriage ceremony was null and void.

The test was elaborated in *Szechter v Szechter*.[281] A Polish Jewish woman in very poor health married an academic at Warsaw University (who had divorced his wife, with her full consent, to facilitate the plan) in order to enable the woman to escape totalitarian Poland, where she had been imprisoned for offences against the regime. She had served several months of imprisonment and lengthy interrogation before trial, during which time she faced various grave threats, causing her already fragile health to fail. The court considered *Buckland* on the way to annulling the marriage.[282] As McClean and Hayes have observed, however, given *Vervaeke v Smith*, it seems odd to say that the woman did not consent to marry in this case where she did so precisely in order to acquire the status necessary to flee:[283]

Szechter v Szechter (orse Karsov) [1971] P 286 (Probate Div), 297–8

SIR JOCELYN SIMON P:

[T]he instant case seems to me to be stronger than . . . *Buckland v. Buckland*. It is, in my view, insufficient to invalidate an otherwise good marriage that a party has entered into it in order to escape from a disagreeable situation, such as penury or social degradation. In order for the impediment of duress to violate an otherwise valid marriage, it must, in my judgment, be proved that the will of one of the parties thereto has been overborne by genuine and reasonably held fear caused by threat of immediate danger (for which the party is not himself responsible) to life, limb or liberty, so that the constraint destroys the reality of consent to ordinary wedlock.

[281] [1971] P 286.
[282] Polish law was formally determinative, but the position under English law was also considered.
[283] McClean and Hayes (2011), 88.

Two Court of Appeal cases approved this line of authority. Both involved arranged marriages which were held to be valid; indeed, it is questionable whether either case would have succeeded under the subjective test. In *Singh v Singh*,[284] a young woman married under parental pressure—not under a threat to life, limb, or liberty, but rather out of a sense of reluctant duty to her parents and religion. In *Singh v Kaur*,[285] it was the husband who gave in to family pressure. Aged 21 and having always lived at home, he was threatened that if he did not marry, he would lose his job in the family business, and have no income or transport:

Singh v Kaur (1981) 11 Fam Law 152 (CA)

ORMROD LJ:

[O]ne can see that, through our English eyes, he is in a sad position but, at the same time, he has to make up his mind, as an adult, whether to go through with the marriage or whether to withstand the pressure put upon him by his family. It is quite clear that this court cannot possibly . . . hold that this marriage is invalid by reason of duress unless it can be shown that there were threats to his life, limb and liberty. Quite clearly, the evidence falls far, far short of that. There was no threat of that kind and . . . it would be a very serious matter if this court were, even if it could in law, to water down Sir Jocelyn Simon's test . . . because there are many of these arranged marriages, not only in the Sikh community in this country but in other communities, and not only Asiatic communities. There are other European communities who adopt this custom, and it would be a most serious thing for this court to introduce any less rigorous burden of proof in these matters than that which the court decided was right in the case of *Singh v Singh* . . .

The subjective test

The alternative, subjective test requires no particular type of threat, but simply focuses on the state of mind of the party in question, which is not measured against any objective standard of steadfastness. The test originates in *Scott v Sebright*: the young bride was blackmailed by a rogue who had borrowed her fortune to pay his debts, and threatened her with bankruptcy, scandalmongering within the drawing rooms of polite London society, and (immediately before the ceremony) death, should she not marry him. That last threat would clearly have satisfied the objective test, but the court did not express itself so narrowly:

Scott (falsely called Sebright) v Sebright (1886) LR 12 PD 21 (Probate Div), 23–4, 31

BUTT J:

The Courts of law have always refused to recognize as binding contracts to which the consent of either party has been obtained by fraud or duress, and the validity of a contract of marriage must be tested and determined in precisely the same manner as that of any other contract. True it is that in contracts of marriage there is an interest involved above and beyond that of the

[284] [1971] P 226. [285] (1981) 11 Fam Law 152.

immediate parties. Public policy requires that marriages should not be lightly set aside, and there is in some cases the strongest temptation to the parties more immediately interested to act in collusion in obtaining a dissolution of the marriage tie. These reasons necessitate great care and circumspection on the part of the tribunal, but they in no wise alter the principle or the grounds on which this, like any other contract, may be avoided. It has sometimes been said that in order to avoid a contract entered into through fear, the fear must be such as would impel a person of ordinary courage and resolution to yield to it. I do not think that is an accurate statement of the law. Whenever from natural weakness of intellect or from fear—whether reasonably entertained or not—either party is actually in a state of mental incompetence to resist pressure improperly brought to bear, there is no more consent than in the case of a person of stronger intellect and more robust courage yielding to a more serious danger. The difficulty consists not in any uncertainty of the law on the subject, but in its application to the facts of each individual case. . . .

Here, however, the facts clearly pointed to the conclusion that no true consent had been given.

Having received only passing reference in *Singh v Kaur*,[286] the subjective test found support from the Court of Appeal in *Hirani v Hirani*.[287] A young Hindu woman was threatened with eviction from the family home should she not submit to an arranged marriage, precipitated by her parents' abhorrence of her dating a Muslim. Ormrod LJ delivered the short judgment, curiously overlooking the previous Court of Appeal cases endorsing an objective test to which he had been a party. He adopted a limited reading of *Szechter v Szechter*, at odds with his reading of the case in *Singh v Kaur*. Like the judge in *Scott*, he drew an analogy with contract law to conclude that:[288]

Hirani v Hirani (1983) 4 FLR 232 (CA), 234

ORMROD LJ:

The crucial question in these cases, particularly where a marriage is involved, is whether the threats, pressure, or whatever it is, is such as to destroy the reality of consent and overbears the will of the individual. It seems to me that this case, on the facts, is a classic case of a young girl, wholly dependent on her parents, being forced into a marriage with a man she has never seen and whom her parents have never seen in order to prevent her (reasonably, from her parents' point of view) continuing in an association with a Muslim which they would regard with abhorrence. But it is as clear a case as one could want of the overbearing of the will of the petitioner and thus invalidating or vitiating her consent.

Hirani was applied in *P v R (Forced Marriage: Annulment: Procedure)*,[289] the facts of which would readily satisfy the objective test. A British Pakistani family took their daughter to

[286] Ibid. [287] (1983) 4 FLR 232. [288] Note *Mahmood v Mahmood* 1993 SLT 589, 591.
[289] [2003] 1 FLR 661.

Pakistan for a relative's funeral. During the visit, the parents arranged a marriage which the daughter was forced to go through with under threat of violence in circumstances where she was unable to escape owing to illness, close supervision, and lack of funds and knowledge of the local area. Her apparent assent during the ceremony was caused by her mother standing behind her and pushing her head to create the appearance of a nod. The marriage was patently voidable for want of consent.

2.7.1.b Mistake

Mistakes only vitiate consent to marriage (or civil partnership) where they relate either to the identity (not merely the attributes) of the other party, or to the nature of the ceremony. Such mistakes may be spontaneous or induced by the fraud of the other party or a third party. Other mistakes will not vitiate consent, though the courts have a protective jurisdiction to prevent marriages involving vulnerable individuals going ahead under such misapprehensions.[290]

Mistake as to identity

C v C [1942] NZLR 356 (High Court, New Zealand), 358–9

CALLAN J:

The topic was carefully considered . . . in . . . *Moss v Moss* . . .: "But when in English law fraud is spoken of as a ground for avoiding a marriage, this does not include such fraud as induces a consent, but is limited to such fraud as procures the appearance without the reality of consent" . . . "Error about the family or fortune of the individual, though produced by disingenuous representations, does not at all affect the validity of the marriage." . . . [T]his is a case of real consent although induced by fraud, and not a case of no consent or absence of consent. The petitioner truly consented to marry the human being to whom she was married by the Registrar. It is true that he was married under the name of Michael Miller, the Australian boxer, whereas in truth he is Samuel Henry Coley, a New Zealander, not a boxer at all, and a person of very different fortune of the person he represented himself to be, of no fortune at all really. But I am also satisfied that Michael Miller, as a human being, meant really nothing to this lady. What she was interested in was the man before her, the man who, after this very rapid courtship, proposed marriage to her, and she accepted that human being because she believed, on his fraudulent representations, that his position as to fortune and his prospects were ample for starting her in a good way in the married state . . . The point was that she was willing to marry this man whom she believed to be able to support her, and the identity of Michael Miller in the matter was merely accidental. It is possible to conceive a case . . . where this principle can be applied successfully. Suppose A. proposes marriage to B. by correspondence, never having seen B. before, but really on what A. knows about B.'s family circumstances and so on, or perhaps A. has not seen B. for very many years, and

[290] *Re SA (Vulnerable Adult with Capacity: Marriage)* [2005] EWHC 2942: concern that a marriage arranged for a deaf and dumb young Pakistani woman should only proceed with her full and genuine consent to the specific marriage proposed.

that proposal is accepted, and then on the day of the marriage C. fraudulently impersonates B., and gets away with it, because A. does not know the present personal appearance of B. There would be, I should think, a case of no true consent. But that is not this case.

However, the line between mistakes as to identity and attributes may not be certain. In *Militante v Ogunwomoju*,[291] the court voided a marriage involving an illegal immigrant who had assumed the identity of someone living legally in the UK. *Moss v Moss* was cited, but the refined arguments of *C v C* were not considered in the very short judgment. One commentator notes that it is not known whether the petitioner 'thought she was marrying another man, or simply [as in *C v C*] that she thought the man had a different name'.[292]

Mistake as to the nature of the ceremony

In these cases, a language barrier often creates the confusion. For example, in *Valier v Valier (otherwise Davis)*,[293] the Conte Jerome Valier, an Italian resident of France who had fallen on hard times, was working in a garage and was 'not quick on the uptake' when spoken to in English. He went through a marriage ceremony with May Winifred Davis, aspiring actress, at St Giles', London register office. Not realizing that he had thus been married, he later married the Marchesa Balbi in Italy. His London marriage was annulled on the ground that he had no idea when he attended the register office and signed a document, which he never subsequently saw or read, that he was contracting a marriage. In Italy, engaged couples must sign a document at the town hall and wait three weeks before obtaining a licence to marry, the marriage then being solemnized at the town hall and thereafter in church. He mistakenly thought that he was merely performing this preliminary. The marriage was annulled.[294]

2.7.1.c Unsoundness of mind

Ability to give valid consent to marriage or civil partnership requires mental capacity to do so. The appropriate test for determining capacity was analysed in a case concerning a woman referred to as 'E'. E had spina bifida and hydrocephalus, and was alleged to have a mental age of 13 and to be vulnerable to exploitation. She had formed a relationship with an older man, S, who had several convictions for serious sex offences. E's local authority, SCC, applied under the inherent jurisdiction for injunctive relief to prevent their planned marriage. Munby J had to identify the appropriate test for capacity to marry so that the expert witnesses charged with assessing E's capacity could be properly instructed. The starting point is that adults are presumed to have capacity; it is for those who assert that an individual lacks capacity to prove that. No one, including the court, can consent to marriage on behalf of someone lacking capacity to marry; and the court cannot interfere with the decision of someone who does have capacity just because it thinks the decision unwise.[295]

291 [1993] 2 FCR 355. 292 Douglas (1994a). 293 (1925) 133 LT 830.
294 See also *Mehta v Mehta* [1945] 2 All ER 689.
295 *Sheffield City Council v E* [2004] EWHC 2808, [18]–[23], [101]. There is no distinction between that common law test, which continues to be applied, and the statutory test under the Mental Capacity Act 2005: *EJ (as attorney for DMM) v SD* [2017] EWCOP 32, which concerned P's capacity to marry, particularly given that marriage would automatically revoke his will.

Capacity is assessed on an issue-by-issue basis, rather than as a general matter. The test is whether the individual understands the nature and quality of the relevant transaction. In the case of marriage, what does that involve?

Sheffield City Council v E and another [2004] EWHC 2808

MUNBY J:

68. . . . The law . . . can be summed up in four propositions:

i) It is not enough that someone appreciates that he or she is taking part in a marriage ceremony or understands its words.

ii) He or she must understand the nature of the marriage contract.

iii) This means that he or she must be mentally capable of understanding the duties and responsibilities that normally attach to marriage.

iv) That said, the contract of marriage is in essence a simple one, which does not require a high degree of intelligence to comprehend. The contract of marriage can readily be understood by anyone of normal intelligence.

So, what are the duties that normally attach to marriage?

132. . . . Marriage, whether civil or religious, is a contract, formally entered into. It confers on the parties the status of husband and wife, the essence of the contract being an agreement between a man and a woman to live together, and to love one another as husband and wife, to the exclusion of all others. It creates a relationship of mutual and reciprocal obligations, typically involving the sharing of a common home and a common domestic life and the right to enjoy each other's society, comfort and assistance.[296]

Importantly—given the undesirability of E's intended spouse—Munby J held that the test is also a general one: did E have the capacity to marry *generally*, not to decide to marry S, *specifically*. So the test was one of capacity to enter this type of transaction (marriage), not a test of the wisdom of the specific marriage contemplated:[297]

85. . . . [T]he *nature of the contract of marriage* is necessarily something shared in common by all marriages. It is not something that differs as between different marriages or depending upon whether A marries B or C. The implications for A of choosing to marry B rather than C may be immense. B may be a loving pauper and C a wife-beating millionaire. But this has nothing to do with the nature of the contract of marriage into which A has chosen to enter. Whether A marries B or marries C, the contract is the same, its nature is the same, and its legal consequences are the same. The emotional, social, financial and other implications for A may be very different but the nature of the contract is precisely the same in both cases.

[296] We considered the general validity of this point at 2.4.2.

[297] Cf the theoretical scope for a court considering the marriage of a minor to withhold consent on best interest grounds: see Probert (2009a), 249.

This decision has been criticized, not least in the light of a more recent decision that whether an individual has capacity to decide to *live with* someone is to be addressed in the context of the particular context and proposed partner.[298] It has been noted that the decisions on capacity to marry on which Munby J relies predate more sophisticated case law dealing with capacity in relation to medical treatment, and that it is somewhat unreal to deal with marriage as an abstract proposition rather than to consider capacity to marriage in the context of the social reality of the particular marriage.[299] At one point, Munby J opined that:

> 144. There are many people in our society who may be of limited or borderline capacity but whose lives are immensely enriched by marriage. We must be careful not to set the test of capacity to marry too high, lest it operate as an unfair, unnecessary and indeed discriminatory bar against the mentally disabled.

That remark encapsulates what some feminist scholars consider entails a failure to protect the vulnerable in this area, potentially breaching the state's positive obligations under the ECHR.[300] The following extract comes from an imagined Court of Appeal decision overturning Munby J's decision:

J. Herring, N. Barker, and M. Fox, '*Sheffield County Council v E*', in R. Hunter et al (eds), *Feminist Judgments: From Theory to Practice* (Oxford: Hart Publishing, 2010), 355

BARKER AND FOX LLJ

21. . . . [A]lthough there are certain (largely unarticulated) social norms and ideals associated with marriage, it is impossible to capture the range of relationships that may be encompassed within the legal framework of marriage in an abstract definition. Marriage should not be universalised. Nor should it be idealised. In contrast to commonly held romantic notions of what marriage is, we must recognise that legal marriages . . . "need not be loving, sexual, stable, faithful, long-lasting, or contented". All too often they are unpleasant, abusive and violent. In this context, it is appropriate that E should, at a minimum, be aware of the fact that sometimes marriage is not pleasant and have the capacity to weigh the potential benefits *and* risks inherent in a marriage to S.

22. On this basis, we reject Munby J's view that marriage is a universal and simple contract. Once it is recognised that marriage no longer has (or should have) what Professor O'Donovan referred to . . . as a sacred, magical status, and that there is no universal fixed essence of marriage, it can be seen that the analogy with medical treatment is appropriate. Just as there are different types of medical treatment, there are varieties of marriage. Just as the level of risk involved in medical treatment depends on the type of treatment and who administers it, the level of risk within marriage depends on the spouses and other circumstances.

[298] *York CC v C* [2013] EWCA Civ 478. [299] Herring, Barker, and Fox (2010); Herring (2013).

[300] On that point, see Herring, Barker, and Fox (2010), 359. Cf *Sandwell MBC v RG and others* [2013] EWHC 2373 (COP) in which Holman J declined to declare that it was in the incapacitated party's best interests to initiate nullity proceedings, given the benefit he derived from being married. Cf protection afforded by criminal law in the Sexual Offences Act 2003: ss 30–7, to which s 43's marriage exemption does not apply.

2.7.1.d 'Or otherwise'

One other situation that might vitiate an apparent consent involves intoxication. Probably only extreme intoxication temporarily depriving the individual of *capacity* to consent will suffice; mere loss of inhibition through drink, which causes the individual to provide a consent that they would not have given when sober, will not:

Sullivan v Sullivan, falsely called Oldacre (1818) 2 Hag Con 238 (Consistory Court), 246, 248

SIR WILLIAM SCOTT:

Suppose three or four persons were to combine to [procure a marriage] by intoxicating another, and marrying him in that perverted state of mind, this Court would not hesitate to annul a marriage on clear proof of such a cause connected with such an effect. Not many other cases occur to me in which the co-operation of other persons to produce a marriage can be so considered, if the party was not in a state of disability, natural or artificial, which created a want of reason or volition amounting to an incapacity to consent . . . [But i]f he is capable of consent, and has consented, the law does not ask how the consent has been induced.

2.7.2 MENTAL DISORDER RENDERING PERSON 'UNFIT' FOR MARRIAGE OR CIVIL PARTNERSHIP

This ground[301] may be relied upon by either party, and must ordinarily be invoked within three years of the ceremony.[302] It must be distinguished from mental incapacity vitiating consent. Here, the individual is competent to consent, but the nature of their disorder is such that they are nevertheless 'unfit' for marriage or civil partnership at the time of the ceremony. This is more difficult territory than the consent ground, as it appears to require an evaluation of the individual's behaviour and an understanding of what it is for which they must be 'fit'. In *Bennett v Bennett*, Ormrod J posed the question as follows: 'Is this person capable of living in a married state, and of carrying out the ordinary duties and obligations of marriage?'—but did not elaborate.[303] In *Bennett*, the wife was occasionally violent and periodically hospitalized with neurosis. The court remarked that she might be a person to whom it would be difficult to be married and would need an understanding husband. But her mental illness was not so extreme as to make her unfit. Indeed, Ormrod J's experience of the divorce courts suggested to him that there were many people of normal mental state who might be thought considerably less fit for marriage than this wife.[304] It remains to be decided what qualities are necessary to render someone fit for civil partnership.

2.7.3 THE RESPONDENT WAS PREGNANT BY ANOTHER AT THE TIME OF THE CEREMONY

This ground[305] may only be relied upon by the other party, must ordinarily be invoked within three years of the ceremony, and that party must have been ignorant that the respondent was

[301] MCA 1973, s 12(1)(d); CPA 2004, s 50(1)(b). [302] MCA 1973, s 13(2)(4)(5); CPA 2004, s 51(2)–(4). [303] [1969] 1 WLR 430, 434. [304] Ibid. [305] MCA 1973, s 12(1)(f); CPA 2004, s 50(1)(c).

pregnant by another at the time of the ceremony.[306] The ground was introduced in 1937, the courts having declined to regard such mistakes as sufficiently fundamental to a vitiate husband's consent to marriage—pregnancy is an 'attribute' only, and not an issue going to the wife's identity.[307] It has been suggested that the ground is justified on two bases: that the husband only married the wife because he believed the child to be his own (bearing in mind that he will be presumed to be the father[308]); and/or that the husband believed the wife to be chaste.[309] The latter is rightly regarded as inappropriate to modern conditions. The lack of equivalent ground upon which it can be complained that a male partner is fathering children elsewhere suggests that the concern is not (male) sexual fidelity or chastity. It may be better to leave female infidelity resulting in pregnancy, in extreme cases, to the law relating to duress (as in *Buckland*) or to the divorce courts.

The ground applies to civil partnership and same-sex marriage, even though it is (currently) biologically impossible for one female to be pregnant *other than* by someone who is not her (female) civil partner. Where the parties have together embarked on a course of assisted reproduction, necessarily using donor sperm, the non-pregnant party ought not to be allowed to complain.[310] The requirement that she be ignorant of her partner's pregnancy at the time of the civil partnership registration goes some way to ensure justice, and the general, estoppel-type bar to nullity practically eliminates the possibility of annulment in such cases.

2.7.4 GROUNDS RELATING TO GENDER RECOGNITION

The GRA 2004 (discussed further at 1.2.4 and 2.3.1) added two voidable grounds relating to trans people.

The first ground provides that if one party was unaware at the time of the ceremony that the other person had previously obtained legal recognition of their preferred gender under the GRA 2004, the marriage or civil partnership will be voidable on the application of the first party (ordinarily only within three years of the ceremony), who may not wish to continue in the relationship given this discovery, even though the marriage or civil partnership is not void.[311]

The second ground caters for trans people who are spouses or civil partners when they apply for legal gender recognition. Where the parties are married before one of them obtains legal gender recognition, that marriage can continue as such following recognition if both parties consent.[312] But in cases where the other spouse does not consent, the marriage or civil partnership is voidable,[313] and either party has six months from the issue of the interim gender recognition certificate in which to apply for a decree of nullity.[314] By requiring spousal consent for the marriage to continue, these voidable grounds are the subject of

[306] MCA 1973, s 13(2)–(5); CPA 2004, s 51(2)–(4), (6).

[307] *Moss v Moss* [1897] P 263.

[308] See 9.3.2.

[309] Hayes and Williams (1999), 503–4. The authors question why this particular 'attribute' mistake should have been selected; why not the belated discovery that one's spouse is a convicted rapist?

[310] See 9.4.3 on Human Fertilisation and Embryology Act 2008, s 42.

[311] See MCA 1973, ss 12(1)(h) and 13(2)–(5); CPA 2004, ss 50(1)(e) and 51(2)–(4), (6).

[312] GRA 2004, ss 3(6A)–(6C), 4(2), 11A. Cf the previous situation, *Parry v United Kingdom* (App No 42971/05, ECHR) (2006). For criticism, see Renz (2015).

[313] MCA 1973, s 12(1)(g); CPA 2004, s 50(1)(d).

[314] MCA 1973, s 13(2A); CPA 2004, s 51(5).

considerable controversy. In response to the government's consultation on reform of the GRA 2004, 84.9 per cent of respondents disagreed with the current law.[315] Some of the dominant arguments surrounding this issue are summarized here:[316]

C. Fairbairn, D. Pyper, and B. Balogun, *Gender Recognition Act Reform: Consultation and Outcome*, House of Commons Library Research Briefing No 09079 (London: TSO, 2022), 25–6

In the consultation paper, the Government said it was aware that, among many trans people, the need for spousal consent was a particular cause for concern. The Government said it understood the primary concerns to be:

- Requiring spousal consent extends the ability to make decisions over a trans person's gender identity to someone else, beyond the power given to the GRP [Gender Recognition Panel];
- If spousal consent is not forthcoming, this can substantially delay the legal gender recognition process whilst the dissolution of the marriage takes place. This can be particularly time-consuming if the dissolution is difficult, perhaps because it involves complicated financial or child contact arrangements. Complicated dissolution arrangements can also be costly;
- Withholding consent might potentially be used by an abusive spouse to perpetrate domestic abuse. It can give the spouse an additional means of control; and
- Spousal consent may not be possible, for example if the spouse cannot be contacted or lacks mental capacity.

The government responded by setting out its rationale for retaining the voidable grounds relating to gender recognition as follows:

On the other hand, it could be argued that as marriage is an agreement between two individuals, it is appropriate that both spouses should have an equal say in the future of that contract in the event of a fundamental change like a change in the gender of one of the parties to it. This was the principal rationale behind introducing the spousal consent provisions in the same-sex marriage legislation.

Since reform of divorce law in England and Wales now essentially means *all* marriages require the consent of both parties in order to continue—as we shall see in chapter 3 (3.10.3)—it remains to be seen whether the option for annulment *in addition to* divorce in these circumstances will be susceptible to further challenge.

2.7.5 A GROUND UNIQUE TO MARRIAGE: VENEREAL DISEASE

A marriage, but not a civil partnership, may be annulled on the ground that the respondent had communicable venereal disease at the time of the marriage.[317] Civil partners aggrieved in similar circumstances must seek dissolution instead. It is not clear what 'venereal disease' covers, and in particular whether only serious infections such as HIV are included, or all

[315] Government Equalities Office (2020), 65. [316] See also Sharpe (2012).
[317] MCA 1973, s 12(1)(e).

sexually transmitted diseases, including minor, relatively common, and readily treatable conditions such as chlamydia. It is significant that the ground was introduced in the pre-antibiotic age. This ground may be relied on ordinarily only within the first three years of marriage, and only if the petitioner was ignorant of the problem at the date of the marriage.[318] Given the reasons offered by government for not adopting this ground for civil partnership and its abolition in some other jurisdictions, its retention for marriage must be questioned:

Hansard, *Official Report*—Civil Partnership Bill Debates, HC Standing Committee D, col 162, 26 October 2004

Mrs McGuire [Parliamentary Under-Secretary of State]:

[T]he Government's intention in drafting the Bill was that civil partners would be treated in the same way as spouses except where there was justification for a difference in treatment. This was one matter on which we felt that there was justification for difference. It is a medical fact that men and women may carry certain sexually transmitted infections for many years without knowing it, and we do not believe that it is appropriate in present-day circumstances to include that as a ground for nullifying a civil partnership. The deliberate transmission of a sexually transmitted infection might well be considered as a basis for dissolution, [using the 'behaviour' fact—see 3.5.3].

I suggest that were we starting now to create marriage law, it would be highly questionable whether we would include such a provision in that law. It is a provision from a bygone age when, perhaps, we were less informed about sexually transmitted diseases. The Government have clearly stated in their national strategy for sexual health and HIV that we need to destigmatise the whole issue of sexually transmitted infections if we are to tackle the increasing infection rate . . . Suggesting that sexually transmitted diseases should be treated differently from any other communicable diseases in that regard is counterproductive to that aim.

2.7.6 GROUNDS UNIQUE TO MIXED-SEX MARRIAGE: FAILURE TO CONSUMMATE

A mixed-sex marriage may be annulled where not consummated owing either to the wilful refusal of the respondent or to incapacity of either party.[319] The disapplication of these grounds for same-sex marriages[320] might suggest that same-sex marriage, like civil partnership, is to be regarded as sexless. However, the difference can be explained more prosaically. As we shall see at 2.7.6.a, consummation is defined—very specifically—in terms of penile penetration of the vagina. Self-evidently, such a concept cannot apply to same-sex relationships. But it is questionable whether the ground should exist even for mixed-sex marriages. Indeed, close examination of the definition of consummation undermines many *assumptions* about what the ground might be about, and so why its retention might be justified. The government clearly has no appetite for what is a long overdue fundamental review of these aspects of marriage law, but the retention of non-consummation leaves us with interesting questions about what these grounds say about the nature of (mixed-sex) marriage, an issue that we explore in the following sections.

318 Ibid, s 13(2)–(5). 319 Ibid, s 12(1)(a) and (b). 320 Ibid, s 12(2).

Neither non-consummation ground is subject to the three-year limitation period applying to most of the other voidable grounds, and so may be raised at any time until consummation occurs. Until the introduction of the special gender recognition ground, wilful refusal to consummate was the only ground clearly related to problems postdating the marriage, rather than facts present at the time of the ceremony; it has been noted that the statute does not expressly confine incapacity to cases where the condition existed at the time of the ceremony, leaving open the possibility of a nullity decree on grounds of supervening incapacity.[321] Despite suggestions that this ground should be demoted to the law of divorce, it remains part of nullity law.[322]

It is necessary to examine three issues: the meaning of 'consummation'; and then the two ways in which non-consummation may warrant a nullity decree: incapacity and wilful refusal to consummate.

2.7.6.a Consummation

Both grounds rely on the concept of consummation:

D-E v A-G, falsely calling herself D-E (1845) 1 Rob Eccl 279 (Consistory Court), 298

DR LUSHINGTON:

Sexual intercourse, in the proper meaning of the term, is ordinary and complete intercourse; it does not mean partial and imperfect intercourse: yet I cannot go the length of saying that every degree of imperfection would deprive it of its essential character. There must be degrees difficult to deal with; but if so imperfect as scarcely to be natural, I should not hesitate to say that, legally speaking, it is no intercourse at all. I can never think that the true interest of society would be advanced by retaining within the marriage bonds parties driven to such disgusting practices. Certainly it would not tend to the prevention of adulterous intercourse, one of the greatest evils to be avoided . . . If there be a reasonable probability that the lady can be made capable of vera copula—of the natural sort of coitus, *though without power of conception*—I cannot pronounce this marriage void. If, on the contrary, she is not and cannot be made capable of more than an incipient, imperfect, and unnatural coitus, I would pronounce the marriage void.[323] [Emphasis added]

The cases have been preoccupied, then, not with the question of fertility, but with what 'ordinary and complete intercourse' entails. No other form of sexual activity counts. The case law makes for extraordinary reading. Often, the issue is whether the wife has a sufficiently accommodating vaginal cavity which can be penetrated, and whether the husband is capable of sufficient penile penetration of it. The 'impervious cul-de-sac' of the wife in *D-E v A-G* was deemed insufficiently deep, at 2½ inches, to permit consummation. As medical science advanced, so too did the courts' willingness to accept artificially created (or extended) vaginas,

[321] Masson, Bailey-Harris, and Probert (2008), 2-027.

[322] Cf Royal Commission on Marriage and Divorce (1956), paras 88–9, 283; Law Com (1970), para 27.

[323] Now only voidable.

though only when created in a biological female.[324] As for the husband's contribution, ejaculation in the vagina, at least, is not required, but an erection of some endurance is: the efforts of the husband whose erection 'collapsed' immediately upon penetration could not 'without a violation of language be described as ordinary and complete intercourse'.[325] The courts have been divided on the acceptability of *coitus interruptus* for these purposes,[326] but no less authority than the House of Lords has condoned the use of condoms, further underlining the fact that procreation need not be intended or anticipated as a possible by-product of the exercise.[327] This point is driven home by *Clarke (otherwise Talbott) v Clarke*,[328] in which *despite* the wife's conceiving a child by a rogue, persistent sperm, the marriage was nevertheless unconsummated for want of actual intercourse. Whether any sexual satisfaction is obtained is irrelevant to the legal perfection of the intercourse,[329] and intercourse need only occur once for the marriage to be consummated. The parties' sexual compatibility is therefore not the issue; that is a matter for the divorce courts. Pre-marital intercourse between the parties does not preclude a finding of non-consummation if the act is not repeated after marriage.[330]

2.7.6.b Incapacity

The incapacity to consummate may be physical. If it is curable by non-dangerous surgery, a refusal to undergo treatment might amount to wilful refusal.[331] Alternatively, the incapacity may be psychological. In *Clarke*,[332] the wife had an invincible repugnance to sexual intercourse, described in the language of 1940s psychology as 'frigidity'. Care must be taken to differentiate incapacity from wilful refusal, since while a spouse may plead their own incapacity, wilful refusal may only be relied on by the other party. In *Singh v Singh*, the claim of invincible repugnance was rejected on the evidence: mere lack of desire to consummate did not suffice, and might instead amount to wilful refusal.[333] However, psychological incapacity can be specific to one person, so the aversion need not relate to sexual relations per se.[334]

2.7.6.c Wilful refusal

Not any refusal to have intercourse suffices. Since consummation need occur only once, refusal to repeat the exercise will not render the marriage voidable. 'Wilful refusal' was described in *Horton v Horton* as a 'settled and definite decision reached without just excuse', viewed in light of the whole history of the marriage.[335] Here, consummation had been delayed by the war, and an unsuccessful attempt subsequently made. The court acknowledged that in such 'false start' cases, one or both parties would frequently be reluctant and hesitant to try again, and in light of the wife's evident anxiety to resolve the problem, she could not be said to be wilfully refusing. Nor, according to *Potter v Potter*, is natural loss of ardour to be equated with wilful refusal.[336] The parties in *Ford v Ford* were frustrated by

[324] *S v S (otherwise C)* [1954] 3 All ER 736; *SY v SY (orse W)* [1963] P 37; cf *Corbett v Corbett* [1971] P 83. The courts should review their approach to consummation where there is a gender recognition certificate, otherwise the marriages of trans women remain vulnerable to voidability on this ground, unless the estoppel bar applies: MCA 1973, s 13.

[325] *W (orse K) v W* [1967] 1 WLR 1554.

[326] *Cackett (orse Trice) v Cackett* [1950] P 253; cf *Grimes (otherwise Edwards) v Grimes* [1948] P 323.

[327] *Baxter v Baxter* [1948] AC 274. [328] [1943] 2 All ER 540. [329] *SY v SY (orse W)* [1963] P 37.

[330] *Dredge v Dredge (otherwise Harrison)* [1947] 1 All ER 29.

[331] *D v D (Nullity: Statutory Bar)* [1979] Fam 70. [332] [1943] 2 All ER 540. [333] [1971] P 226.

[334] *G v M* (1885) 10 App Cas 171. [335] [1947] 2 All ER 871. [336] (1975) 5 Fam Law 161.

the husband's imprisonment in an institution with no facilities for conjugal visits and rules specifically prohibiting intercourse during visits. Whilst other prisoners and their spouses were apparently content to take their chances, the husband's disinclination to do so did not constitute wilful refusal.[337] The concept of wilful refusal has acquired a special meaning in the context of marriages between parties whose faith demands that a religious ceremony be performed, as well as a civil marriage ceremony, before intercourse is permitted. In *Kaur v Singh*, the husband's refusal to perform his obligation to arrange such a ceremony was interpreted as a wilful refusal to consummate.[338]

2.7.6.d Why consummation? Different conceptions of 'marriage'

Consummation has always been regarded as integral to the traditional definition of marriage, that is, in its mixed-sex form. Lord Denning once remarked, 'No one can call a marriage a real marriage when it has not been consummated.'[339] So important is consummation that express pre-marital agreements not to have sex have been struck down as being void on grounds of public policy, though the courts' views seem to depend upon the parties' age or situation. As the court observed in *Morgan v Morgan*,[340] while agreements between young couples never to cohabit and have sexual relations have been struck down on grounds of public policy,[341] an agreement between an elderly or infirm couple who wish to marry purely for companionship is a different matter. It would be unjust for one to be permitted subsequently to have the marriage annulled for incapacity to consummate when it had never been intended that it should be consummated.[342]

Further evidence of the seriousness of marriage—and the consummation requirement—is provided by the intervention in *Morgan* of the then Queen's—now King's—Proctor,[343] a Crown officer statutorily empowered to intervene in matrimonial and civil partnership proceedings to represent the public interest in the interpretation of the legislation, and to guard against fabrication of evidence by the parties. The court in *Morgan* observed that it 'must always treat nullity cases as of national importance irrespective of the wishes of the parties'.[344] However, the importance of consummation is easily overstated: its location amongst the voidable grounds necessarily confers substantial privacy in the matter, letting the parties decide whether they want a purely companionate marriage; and the estoppel bar may then prevent nullity actions from succeeding in such cases: see s 13(1), discussed earlier at 2.7.

And yet, even if a matter for the parties, it is still there as a matter identified by the state as sufficiently grave to warrant nullity proceedings. So what does it signify? Surprisingly perhaps, consummation clearly has nothing to do with procreation.[345] Yet procreation has extraordinary persistence even in some judicial accounts of marriage, forming a key plank, for example, in *Wilkinson v Kitzinger*,[346] even though the European Court has removed it from its conceptualization of the relationship protected by Article 12.[347] The concept of consummation may also seem perplexing given its one-off nature, again an aspect which

[337] (1987) 17 Fam Law 232. [338] [1972] 1 WLR 105.
[339] *Ramsay-Fairfax (orse Scott-Gibson) v Ramsay-Fairfax* [1956] P 115, 133. [340] [1959] P 92, 101.
[341] *Brodie v Brodie* [1917] P 271.
[342] See also the platonic marriage in *Re X (A Child: Foreign Surrogacy)* [2018] EWFC 15.
[343] MCA 1973, ss 8 and 15; CPA 2004, s 39. [344] [1959] P 92, 96.
[345] *Baxter v Baxter* [1948] AC 274.
[346] [2006] EWHC 2022, discussed at 2.3.2; see also *Bellinger v Bellinger* [2003] UKHL 21, [46]–[47] and [64].
[347] *Goodwin v United Kingdom* (App No 28957/95, ECHR) (2002); *Schalk and Kopf v Austria* (App No 30141/04, ECHR) (2010).

substantially detracts from any procreative purpose. An historical view may throw light on the matter: until 1991, husbands were permitted to have sexual intercourse with their wives regardless of whether they were then consenting, the original act of consummation (itself consensual) entitling the husband to sexual relations thereafter.[348]

Consummation and the (now historical) marital rape exemption—and what they imply about the (traditional) institution of marriage—have inevitably attracted academic comment, in particular from law and gender scholars:[349]

K. O'Donovan, *Family Law Matters* (London: Pluto Press, 1993), 46–8

> The marriage contract establishes the possession of the wife's body by her husband, but she has no corresponding right. After consummation further heterosexual acts are assumed to take place in accordance with male desire. It is evident that the law approves heterosexuality in marriage but withholds its constitutive power from other relationships not legally approved.
>
> The requirement of consummation places primacy on penetrative sex, an act constitutive of masculinity. . . . Reported cases reveal bizarre knowledge against which questions were asked about 'how long, and how wide, and how far, and whether, and what'. Determination of the standard, the norm, against which to measure the answers created a 'knowledge' of male sexuality and a discourse of normal masculinity. Law's insistence on consummation as the final performative act constituting marriage marginalises other sexual practices. The missionary position, in which the woman lies under the man and facing him in readiness for coition, has been privileged in this discourse . . .
>
> . . . The story of marriage as an institution in which the sexes are united and opposed relates to the uncovering of the sexual contract. Not only is a particular form of marriage constituted, with a delineation of social roles and hierarchy, but marriage has much to say about the meaning of masculinity and femininity. Marriage establishes 'orderly access by men to women's bodies' according to Pateman. This law of male sex-right embodies women as sexual beings. Although personal autonomy over sexuality has largely been won by women today, elements of the history of marriage remain. The story helps to understand what it is to be masculine or feminine in modern civil society. No matter how much we try to avoid replicating patriarchal marital relations, these are reproduced in the institution of marriage . . .

Mixed-sex marriage (at least) also has a religious aspect, again evidenced by consummation:

> The sacred character of marriage as an institution calls on a past, understood and shared tradition, and on an eternal future, a perpetuity. Marriage is an emblem of continuity, of reproduction of the race . . . Not only are sexual needs to be met but marriage is the place for the veneration of motherhood, for deference to patriarchy, for the continuance of tradition, learned yet known anew by each generation and in each generative act.
>
> Through marriage the couple become one flesh, one body. In legal terms, this biblical notion takes form in the constitution of the couple as a unit headed by the husband. . . . The 'consummation most devoutly to be wished for' is the final performative act of consecration of the marriage. . . .

[348] See now *R v R* [1992] 1 AC 599, discussed at 4.2.3. While the point is unclear, some sources indicate or assume that consummation did have to be consensual: see O'Donovan (1993), 46–7.

[349] E.g. Collier (1995), ch 4; O'Donovan (1993), 66–8.

It is 'doubtful that any intelligible secular principle can be wrought from the "one-flesh" dogma'.[350] However, despite this patriarchal reading of marriage (which repels couples like Steinfeld and Keidan), as we have seen, those historically excluded from marriage (trans persons, same-sex couples) sought access to the institution and were finally admitted. Those individuals clearly identified something in marriage that they wanted to obtain, without necessarily endorsing its traditional form. As we saw at 2.4.2, there are many benefits that flow from marriage—from the legal and social recognition of the relationship—which have nothing to do with the parties' genders or whether they have any sort of sexual relationship. This opening up of marriage, taking it definitively away from its traditional roots, makes the retention of non-consummation as a ground of nullity even more peculiar. Thus, some commentators have argued for it to be excised from the law:

A. Maine, 'Queer(y)ing Consummation: An Empirical Reflection on the Marriage (Same Sex Couples) Act 2013 and the Role of Consummation', (2021) 33 *Child and Family Law Quarterly* 143, 160–1

[R]emoving consummation from the law entirely (much as adultery has been removed by the advent of notification-based divorce) would also serve the equality objective, while avoiding the practical problems inherent in defining same-sex consummation. While this would preclude any express, symbolic validation of same-sex intercourse, not doing so can be justified on the basis that the state has no interest in any spouses' consensual sexual activities, especially non-procreative activities. Moreover, given the religious foundation of different-sex consummation, there can clearly be no logical counterpart for same sex relationships, and so a further argument for the abolition of consummation is that a religiously grounded notion has no place in contemporary secular law in any event. So this . . . option appears to be the more practicable, easier solution, that would simply bring the sexual hierarchy implicit in the current law of consummation to an end.

Whilst of limited practical significance (in terms of numbers of nullity petitions that might have been brought on the basis of non-consummation), simply removing consummation from different-sex marriage would provide equality both in relationship recognition and in access to financial remedies in matrimonial proceedings. It would thereby, and more importantly, have symbolic significance, disestablishing heteronormativity in the law.

As well as this symbolic significance, removing the consummation requirement would create space for the prioritization of other values in relationships, such as care and dependency:

G. Black, 'Adult Relationships and the Ongoing Legal Significance of Sexual Intimacy', in J. Sherpe and S. Gilmore (eds), *Family Matters: Essays in Honour of John Eekelaar* (Cambridge: Intersentia, 2022), 399

If we remove sex from legal equations, we can start to place the focus on the important functions carried out by families through an assumption of responsibility, such as support, care and economic interdependence. These can arise in any relationship: between siblings,

350 Green (2011), 15.

between non-sexual couples, between parent and child. By continuing to give credence to the presence or absence of sex, we are continuing to promote the sexual family – relationships which are given privileged legal status by virtue of the conjugal relationship which is, or is assumed to be, at their heart. Is sex really the best reason for giving certain relationships property protection, tax breaks and pension rights, for ascribing legal parental status, and for limiting the number of parents to two?

The admission of non-traditional partnerships into marriage may have a transformative effect on our view of the institution and its functions. But minority cultures in England and Wales also take a very different view of the function of marriage. This is highlighted in a case concerning the marriage of a severely mentally disabled young Muslim man, IC (who patently lacked capacity to marry as a matter of English law), which was not recognized by the English court:

KC and NNC v City of Westminster Social and Community Services Department
[2008] EWCA Civ 198

WALL LJ:

44. The appeal throws up a profound difference in culture and thinking between domestic English notions of welfare and those embraced by Islam. This is a clash which . . . this court cannot side-step or ignore. To the Bangladeshi mind, . . . the marriage of IC is perceived as a means of protecting him, and of ensuring that he is properly cared for within the family when his parents are no longer in a position to do so.

45. To the mind of the English lawyer, by contrast, such a marriage is perceived as exploitative and indeed abusive. Under English law, a person in the position of IC is precluded from marriage for the simple reason that he lacks the capacity to marry. . . . Furthermore, as IC is incapable of giving his consent to any form of sexual activity, NK [the wife] would commit a criminal offence in English law by attempting . . . any form of sexual contact with him.

46. To the mind of the English lawyer, the marriage is also exploitative of NK, although the evidence is that she entered into it with a full knowledge of IC's disability. The English lawyer inevitably poses the theoretical question: what young woman of marriageable age, given a free choice, would ally herself for life in marriage to a man who she will have to care for as if for a child; with whom, on the evidence, she will be unable to hold a rational conversation, let alone any form of normal social intercourse; by whom she cannot have children, and indeed with whom any form of sexual contact will, under English law . . . constitute a criminal offence?[351]

2.7.6.e Opening the door to other types of formalized relationship?

The curiosity of consummation and its omission from civil partnership law (in particular) have invited questions about why the legal privileges of marriage and civil partnership attach only to particular relationships. The government struggled to articulate during the passage of the Civil Partnership Bill why no sexual relationship should be required between the

[351] Probert (2008a), 403–4.

parties, even though the prohibited degrees would bar civil partnership between blood relatives.[352] The Church of England's observations on civil partnership are thought-provoking, both about the (lack of) analogy with marriage, and what that implied about who should be eligible to acquire the legal status associated with marriage and civil partnership. This debate would be reopened by the Burden sisters,[353] whose case we consider later in this chapter (at 2.8.3.a), and arose again during the passage of the same-sex marriage legislation, and the creation of mixed-sex civil partnership.[354]

Church of England, *Response to Civil Partnership Consultation* (2003)

12. . . . [T]here is an ambiguity at the heart of the Government's proposals about the nature of the proposed partnerships and about what precisely the couple are promising to be to each other. This is reflected in the shifting language in the document between 'gay, lesbian and bisexual' couples in some places and 'same sex partnerships' (potentially a wider category) in others. In a matter of this kind clarity is crucial.

13. The extremely close parallel between the new arrangements and the legal framework for marriage is likely to deter some people who might otherwise register—for example those who choose to share a home with others for a substantial period and may wish to benefit from the new partnership provisions in relation to successor tenancy rights but are not homosexual. Conversely, gay and lesbian couples will receive less protection than they might expect from a legal framework so akin to marriage—. . . no equivalent to a nullity process should a sexual relationship be wilfully refused . . .

14. . . . Is the primary aim to remedy injustice and create some new legal rights and safeguards for those who are not married but who may wish to share important parts of their lives with each other, whether or not within a sexual relationship? If so, the logical approach would be to remove the prohibited degrees of relationship, thereby enabling, say, two brothers or two sisters to access the new set of rights. Indeed, if this is the primary aim it could be argued that they should not be confined to same-sex couples.

15. If, on the other hand, the Government's primary aim is to confer rights on gay and lesbian people in long-term, committed relationships, the logic would be for the legal framework to acknowledge the sexual nature of the relationship.

Several attempts were made to amend the Civil Partnership Bill to allow registration of non-conjugal relationships between blood relatives.[355] Although unsuccessful, the debates increased awareness that marriage itself is a legal concept, as well as an important social, cultural, and religious institution.

But why do particular legal rights and duties attach to marriage and civil partnership at all, and only to those institutions and not other relationships? If the legal consequences are justified simply on the basis that the parties have elected to form a legal union, why cannot any two people do so? The fact that the law only permits certain pairings to become spouses and civil partners suggests that there is more to it than party autonomy. So what is the

[352] See, e.g., the exchange between Baroness Scotland and Lord Tebbit, Hansard HL Deb, vol 666, col 1479, 17 November 2004.

[353] *Burden and Burden v United Kingdom* (App No 13378/05, ECHR) (2008).

[354] E.g. Gillett (2018).

[355] See Glennon (2005); Stychin (2006); e.g. Hansard HL Deb, vol 660, cols 405 et seq, 22 April 2004, Baroness O'Cathain.

justification for confining marriage and civil partnership to presumptively sexual/intimate relationships between legal strangers? Nothing in law prevents *unrelated* platonic pairs from forming a marriage or civil partnership. But the cultural aura of romantic love surrounding both institutions, and implied by the prohibited degrees, inevitably inhibits this. Should there be some mechanism whereby related or unrelated individuals could register their relationships in order to acquire a legal status akin to marriage, or to nominate particular individuals to benefit in specific legal contexts? In the absence of any registration option, such relationships can only be recognized on a non-formalized basis. It is to those relationships that we now turn.

2.8 NON-FORMALIZED RELATIONSHIPS: COHABITANTS AND OTHER 'FAMILY'

Everyone has 'family' relationships outside marriage or civil partnership. In matters relating to children, the nature of the parents' relationship is now largely irrelevant. But in the law dealing with the relationship between the adults, relationships other than marriage and civil partnership are only recognized in relatively limited circumstances and with limited consequences. This is even the case for blood relatives, who are undoubtedly 'family' but whose relationships rarely attract specific legal consequences. In the absence of family law provision when such relationships break down, parties are left to use the general law (of property, contract, trusts, etc.) to ascertain their legal position as regards financial and property matters. As we shall see in chapter 7, that law is not often suited to family disputes.

Where they are recognized, there is no uniformly defined set of 'second-tier', non-formalized relationships. Various formulae are used in different areas of the law to describe family relationships to which rights and duties attach. The most commonly recognized non-formalized family type is 'cohabitation': the relationship of couples who live together in circumstances akin to marriage and civil partnership. Ironically, in order to gain legal recognition, such couples have to work rather harder than spouses and civil partners to get it, even though the rewards are usually less generous. Spouses and civil partners are recognized simply by virtue of their legal status. Even parties to void marriages and civil partnerships achieve quite substantial recognition and potential protection. This basic recognition flows regardless of how the parties actually live their lives, as *Vervaeke v Smith*[356] illustrates: the parties' relationship in that case was non-existent in social and functional terms, yet they had the status of spouses, and so held the passport to a wide range of legal rights and duties. By contrast, those seeking recognition as cohabitants must demonstrate that their relationship actually functions in the way that we imagine many marriages in fact do, but legally need not.

However, although spouses are not subjected to such scrutiny as a precondition of legal recognition, many legal remedies depend on the exercise of the courts' discretion, and the judge examines all the circumstances before making any order. If, as in *Vervaeke v Smith*, a marriage is in fact just an empty legal shell, a remedy is likely to be unnecessary or inappropriate, and none is likely to be granted. Moreover, although formalized and non-formalized relationships are still treated differently in many respects, there has been some convergence. Many of the traditional rights and duties of husband and wife have been eroded and divorce

[356] See 2.7.1.

is easier, making status per se less significant as a source of automatic rights and duties, while non-formalized relationships are increasingly recognized in some areas. The logical conclusion of these developments might be that marriage and civil partnership should no longer have automatic legal implications: as Eric Clive put it, that marriage is unnecessary as a legal concept.[357] Instead, the law should adopt an entirely functionalist or 'de facto' model, providing rights, duties, and remedies for parties to relationships that in fact need them, for example because of the parties' economic interdependence, not purely because of their legal ('de jure') form.[358]

England and Wales are currently a long way from adopting a thoroughgoing functional approach. Lisa Glennon argues that the inception of civil partnership—and now recognition of same-sex marriage—re-emphasizes formal conceptions of family.[359] The marriage/civil partnership passport remains important to many areas of law. This may seem ironic at a time when marriage rates are at an historical low and cohabitation the fastest growing family type.[360] However, any move to reduce the legal significance of marriage would face stiff political opposition; and marriage (and civil partnership) have been rewarded with a (rather modest) tax allowance.[361] Increasing the legal consequences automatically attaching to non-formalized relationships would also be opposed by those who wish to preserve personal autonomy outside marriage.[362] Nevertheless, recent years have seen growing recognition of non-formalized family relationships, which we address here.

2.8.1 IDENTIFYING 'FAMILY'

2.8.1.a A panoply of tests

The term 'family' itself appears infrequently in domestic legislation, mainly appearing in statutes governing tenancy succession. The HRA 1998 requires English courts to consider the scope of 'family life' for the purposes of Article 8. Same-sex couples and mixed-sex couples, with[363] or without children[364] are now regarded by the Strasbourg Court as having 'family life', even if they are not actually cohabiting, provided the relationship is stable.[365] As we saw in 2.3.2, before the European Court reached that position, both domestic case law interpreting 'family' under tenancy succession legislation and recently enacted legislation had already accommodated a wide range of non-traditional family forms.[366] But there remain limits to what English courts regard as constituting 'family' for these purposes, and little legislation extends beyond 'cohabitants' to confer rights on other forms of relationship.

The parliamentary draftsman has produced a panoply of terms, many of which are undefined and have yet to receive judicial attention. The concept of 'associated person' governs eligibility to access remedies regarding domestic abuse, forced marriage, and occupation of the home.[367] It covers a broad range of relationships, exhaustively listed by the legislation,

[357] (1980). [358] See also Bailey-Harris (1996); Probert and Barlow (2000); Dewar (2003).
[359] (2008). [360] Auchmuty (2008); see data at 2.2.
[361] See <www.gov.uk/marriage-allowance>; for criticism, see Probert (2012a).
[362] See, e.g., discussion in Law Com (2006), Part 5; Deech (2009b).
[363] *Saucedo Gomez v Spain* (App No 37784/97, ECHR) (1999).
[364] *Schalk and Kopf v Austria* (App No 30141/04, ECHR) (2010).
[365] *Vallianatos v Greece* (App Nos 29381/09 and 32684/09 ECHR) (2013), [73].
[366] Though the 'home' rather than 'family' aspect of Art 8, in conjunction with Art 14 ECHR, was key to many of these cases.
[367] Family Law Act 1996 (FLA 1996), s 62: see chapter 4.

including spouses, civil partners, cohabitants, relatives, and platonic home-sharers. It also covers 'intimate personal relationships . . . of significant duration': this does not require cohabitation by the parties, or a blood or formalized relationship, but its scope is unclear.[368] It will be interesting to see whether 'intimate' is held to encompass non-sexual relationships, such as between carers and their dependants. 'Partners [living] in an enduring family relationship' are eligible to adopt[369] and to acquire parenthood via surrogacy;[370] certain blood relations are specifically excluded from the scope of this expression, but the terms are otherwise undefined. However, *Re E (Adoption by One Person)*[371] has affirmed that 'living as partners in an enduring family relationship' can include two people who are no longer in a loving relationship with each other and who were never married or civil partners.

2.8.1.b Sharing a household

Some statutes, either expressly or as a result of judicial interpretation, require the parties to share a 'household'. Merely living under the same roof does not mean that you share a household: the latter requires a degree of domestic interaction. But you may be a member of a household despite periodical absence from it. *Kotke v Saffarini* concerned a compensation claim under the Fatal Accidents Act 1976. The applicant had to show that she had been living with the deceased in the same household as (if) husband and wife for two years immediately before his death. But what is a 'household' for these purposes?

Kotke v Saffarini [2005] EWCA Civ 221

POTTER LJ:

28. . . . Use of [the word 'household'] embodies a concept somewhat elusive of definition, combining as it does both the physical connotation of a place i.e. a particular house or home and personal connotations of association i.e. the family or household resident within it. Both aspects are covered by the various dictionary definitions available. . . .

29. In the context of matrimonial law . . . ([MCA 1973, s 2(6):] "For the purposes of this Act a husband and wife shall be treated as living apart unless they are living with each other in the same household") it has been said:

> "First, it does not use the word 'house', which relates to something physical, but 'household', which has an abstract meaning. Secondly, that the words 'living with each other in the same household' should be construed as a single phrase . . . On the contrary, use is again made of words with a well settled matrimonial meaning—'living together', a phrase which is simply the antithesis of living apart, and 'household', a word which essentially refers to people held together by a particular kind of tie, even if temporarily separated . . ." (per Sachs LJ in *Santos v Santos*). . . .

[368] FLA 1996, s 62(3)(ea). [369] ACA 2002, s 144(4)–(7): see chapters 9 and 13.
[370] Human Fertilisation and Embryology Act 2008, s 54.
[371] [2021] EWFC 45. Cf interpretation of 'cohabitant' whereby parties to such relationships need not cohabit: *T and M v OCC and C* [2010] EWHC 964; see also *Re F and M* [2016] EWHC 1594, discussed at 9.5.3.

Potter LJ next considered a case decided under the Inheritance (Provision for Family and Dependants) Act 1975, *Gully v Dix*,[372] where a similar issue arose:

> 31. . . . [T]he issue . . . was whether Mrs Gully, who, without marrying the deceased, had co-habited with him for many years, but had left the deceased and lived apart from him for the last three months of his life, was yet able to demonstrate that she was living in the same household as the deceased during the whole of the period of two years immediately before the date of his death. The judgment of Ward LJ . . . referred . . . to the observations of Sachs LJ in *Santos v Santos* quoted above and stated:
>
> > "24. In my judgment, similar considerations must apply to the meaning to be given to the statute with which we are presently concerned. Thus the claimant may still have been living with the deceased in the same household as the deceased at the moment of his death even if they had been living separately at that moment in time. The relevant word is 'household' not 'house', and 'household' bears the meaning given to it by Sachs LJ. Thus they will be in the same household if they are tied by their relationship. The tie of that relationship may be made manifest by various elements, not simply their living under the same roof, but the public and private acknowledgment of their mutual society, and the mutual protection and support that binds them together. In former days one would possibly say one should look at the whole *consortium vitae*." . . .
>
> 41. . . . It is clear from the authorities that in principle a person may be a member of household A, albeit he has a second house or home elsewhere at B to which he departs temporarily from time to time. . . .

Two years before his death, the deceased had owned a house in Doncaster where he slept several nights a week and kept most of his belongings, from which he commuted to work in London, and which he retained as his official address. The applicant lived in Sheffield. The deceased stayed with her there and shared shopping expenses at weekends, 'living out of an overnight bag'. They discussed buying a house together, but the deceased's negative equity problem delayed their plans. Were they sharing a household at this point? The applicant subsequently became pregnant, and was left with a young baby when the deceased died, having only recently moved in. But this was not enough:

> 59. . . . We consider the judge was correct in drawing a distinction between wanting and intending to live in the same household, planning to do so, and actually doing so. . . . [The] relationship of these parties [as described in the text above] did not cross the statutory threshold into the final stage. . . . [The] situation only changed after the pregnancy when . . . the deceased's centre of gravity began to move and they really began to make plans. The mere sharing of the shopping expenses when the claimant and the deceased were together [in Sheffield] was evidence of a sharing relationship, but one which fell short of the establishment of a joint household.

2.8.1.c The functional approach in action

Most of the tests for identifying non-formalized relationships turn on 'functional' criteria. The case law interpreting the 'family' concept in the tenancy succession legislation shows a clear evolution as courts' perception of the 'ordinary meaning' and the 'ordinary man's

[372] [2004] EWCA Civ 139.

view' of family changed. A decision in the 1950s refused to characterize a mixed-sex cohabiting couple as 'family': only a marital, parental, or quasi-parental relationship would suffice.[373] By the 1970s, the courts accepted that an 'ordinary person' would regard such a relationship as familial, provided it was sufficiently permanent.[374] But in the 1980s, a similar relationship between a same-sex couple was denied 'family' status.[375]

The issue arose again in relation to a same-sex relationship in *Fitzpatrick*. Mr Fitzpatrick's case could not have had stronger factual merits. The deceased, Mr Thompson, and the appellant had lived together in a 'close, loving and faithful' relationship in Mr Thompson's rented flat for ten years when the deceased was rendered tetraplegic after an accident. Mr Fitzpatrick personally provided the constant care which Mr Thompson needed until his death eight years later. Could Mr Fitzpatrick succeed to the tenancy? The relevant statutory provision offered him two arguments, one of which was to show that he had been a 'member of [Mr Thompson's] family'.[376] Crucially, 'family' was undefined, leaving the matter to judicial interpretation. Ward LJ in the Court of Appeal provided a nice account of the functional approach:

Fitzpatrick v Sterling Housing Association Ltd [1998] Ch 304 (CA), 336–9

WARD LJ (dissenting):

Since the inception of the Rent Acts in or before 1920, the home of members of the tenant's family has been preserved for them. As the decided cases show, the meaning of family has been progressively extended. The movement has been away from the confines of relationships by blood and by marriage to the reality of family life, and from de jure to de facto relationships. . . . The trend in the cases, as I see them, is to shift the focus, or the emphasis, from structure and components to function and appearance—what a family does rather than what it is, or, putting it another way, a family is what a family does. I see this as a functionalist approach to construction as opposed to a formalist approach. Thus whether the *Joram Developments Ltd. v. Sharratt* [1979] 1 WLR 928 test is satisfied, i.e. whether there is "at least a broadly recognisable de facto familial nexus." or a conjugal nexus, depends on how closely the alternative family or couple resemble the traditional family or husband and wife in function if not in precise form . . .

A family unit is a social organisation which functions through linking its members closely together. The functions may be procreative, sexual, sociable, economic, emotional. The list is not exhaustive. Not all families function in the same way.

. . . Whilst there clearly is no right of self-determination it cannot be immaterial to have regard to the view the parties have of their own relationship. If the officious commuter on the Clapham omnibus had paid a visit to the deceased's household, asked all the relevant questions about their relationship and asked the deceased finally, "What is Mr. Fitzpatrick to you? Is he one of the family?." it seems to me to be inconceivable that the deceased would not have testily suppressed him by replying, "Of course he is." I doubt whether the ordinary man would be surprised by the answer . . . I am quite certain that he would not treat the answer

[373] *Gammans v Ekins* [1950] 2 KB 328; see Probert (2004c); cf *Sheffield City Council v Wall* [2010] EWCA Civ 922.
[374] *Dyson Holdings Ltd v Fox* [1976] QB 503; cf *Helby v Rafferty* [1979] 1 WLR 13.
[375] *Harrogate BC v Simpson* (1985) 17 HLR 205.
[376] Rent Act 1977, Sch 1, para 3(1).

as an abuse of the English language. Indeed I am satisfied that the ordinary man is liberated enough to accept in 1997. . . ., looking broadly at the plaintiff's life and comparing it with the other rich patterns of family life he knows, that the bond between the plaintiff and the deceased was de facto familial.

Ward LJ was dissenting. When the case reached the House of Lords, as we saw at 2.3.2, the majority were persuaded that the relationship was familial. Lord Slynn's judgment reflects the functional character of the majority's reasoning, focused on the purpose of the housing legislation:

Fitzpatrick v Sterling Housing Association Ltd [2001] 1 AC 27, 34–40, 48–9, 51

LORD SLYNN:

[I have found this question] difficult largely because of preconceptions of a family as being a married couple and, if they have children, their children; difficult also because of the result in some of the earlier cases when applying the law to the facts. It is, however, obvious that the word "family" is used in a number of different senses, some wider, some narrower. "Do you have any family?" usually means "Do you have children?" "We're having a family gathering" may include often distant relatives and even very close friends. "The family of nations", "the Christian family" are very wide. This is no new phenomenon. Roman law, as I understand it, included in the familia all members of the social unit though other rights might be limited to spouses or heirs . . .

Given . . . that the word ["family"] is to be applied flexibly, and does not cover only legally binding relationships, it is necessary to ask what are its characteristics in this legislation and to answer that question to ask further what was Parliament's purpose. It seems to me that the intention in 1920 was that not just the legal wife but also the other members of the family unit occupying the property on the death of the tenant with him should qualify for the succession . . .

The hall marks of the relationship were essentially that there should be a degree of mutual interdependence, of the sharing of lives, of caring and love, of commitment and support. In respect of legal relationships these are presumed, though evidently are not always present as the family law and criminal courts know only too well. In de facto relationships these are capable, if proved, of creating membership of the tenant's family. If, as I consider, this was the purpose of the legislation, the question is then who . . . today . . . are capable in law of being members of the tenant's family. It is not who would have been so considered in 1920. . . .

In particular if the [amendment which introduced a specific provision for cohabitants] had not been made I would have had no hesitation in holding today when, it appears, one-third of younger people live together unmarried, that where there is a stable, loving and caring relationship which is not intended to be merely temporary and where the couple live together broadly as they would if they were married, that each can be a member of the other's family for the purpose of the 1977 Act.

If, as I think, in the light of all the authorities this is the proper interpretation of the Act of 1920 I hold that as a matter of law a same-sex partner of a deceased tenant can establish the necessary familial link. They are capable of being in Russell LJ's words in *Ross v Collins* . . .: "A broadly recognisable de facto familial nexus." It is then a question of fact as to whether he or she does establish the necessary link . . .

It seems to be suggested that the result which I have so far indicated would be cataclysmic. In relation to this Act it is plainly not so. The onus on one person claiming that he or she was a member of the same-sex original tenant's family will involve that person establishing rather than merely asserting the necessary indicia of the relationship. A transient superficial relationship will not do even if it is intimate. Mere cohabitation by friends as a matter of convenience will not do . . . Far from being cataclysmic it is . . . in accordance with contemporary notions of social justice.

In the following extract, Jenni Millbank describes the feminist roots of the functional approach, comparing it with normative alternatives:

J. Millbank, 'The Role of "Functional Family" in Same-Sex Family Recognition Trends', (2008) 20 *Child and Family Law Quarterly* 155, 156

Functional family approaches accord with a core objective of feminist legal scholarship and law reform projects – to centre 'lived lives' rather than legal doctrine or formal legal categories. Not coincidentally, therefore, many of the proponents of functional family approaches in relationship law are feminist and progressive scholars who embrace the idea of dynamic change in law to reflect changing social practices. By positing law's role as reflecting and assisting actual families' experiences and needs, rather than as encouraging or mandating a particular family form, functional family approaches run directly counter to normative approaches to law such as the so-called 'channelling' purpose of family law. The 'channelling function' has been expressed as one which 'supports social institutions which are thought to serve desirable ends', such as marriage, by 'channelling' people towards them. In this competing view, law's role is to tell people, both individually and collectively, how they should form families (and, to a greater or less extent, to provide inducements for those who listen to these messages, and impose punitive consequences on those who do not). Not coincidentally, proponents of the normative or channelling approach to family law are often conservative scholars and religious organisations, who wish to maintain established legal traditions and use them to (attempt to) stem or reverse changing social practices.

However, the functional approach, as applied by the judges, has been criticized by some commentators for its tendency to make legal recognition contingent upon compliance with one particular model of 'family' relations to the exclusion of others.[377] Conversely, Probert has argued that we should be wary of too quickly assuming the functional equivalence of certain relationships: some family forms might function more effectively and there may consequently be a case for privileging them in law; we need to examine the evidence.[378] Thus, Kathy Griffiths has suggested that instead of replacing a status-based approach to relationship recognition (i.e. recognizing relationships formalized through marriage or civil partnership) with one based upon function, it is better to view both approaches as intersecting and operating in tandem:

377 See Diduck (2001) at 2.3.4; Leckey (2013). 378 Probert (2009c), 322.

K. Griffiths, 'From "Form" to Function and Back Again: A New Conceptual Basis for Developing Frameworks for the Legal Recognition of Adult Relationships', (2019) 31 *Child and Family Law Quarterly* 227, 248

> [B]oth frameworks of recognition need to be used alongside each other because they offer different benefits. Same-sex marriage and opposite-sex civil partnerships are developments in relationship recognition that can be celebrated because of the benefits offered by formalised relationships. But the concern is that these developments should not be the last word on the development of relationship recognition in England and Wales . . . Varying reasons lay behind people's relationship practices and different relationships will require different responses from the law. Offering different options to formalise relationships alongside the safety net of function-based recognition for those who do not formalise, with an opt-out provision for legally aware couples who wish to avoid recognition, provides a framework that has something for everyone.

As we shall see at 7.6.3 and in the following section, this view is particularly apposite in the context of unmarried cohabitants.

2.8.2 COHABITANTS

The functional family most frequently recognized in law is cohabitation, mixed-sex, and same-sex.[379] The law has not always been as accommodating of unmarried couples as it is today.[380] But since the 1970s, both courts and Parliament have become increasingly aware of the needs of the growing number of cohabitants. Reform of this area is discussed further at 7.6.

2.8.2.a The legal definitions

Many statutory provisions refer to couples who 'live together as if they were husband and wife',[381] or 'as if they were civil partners', expressly drawing an analogy between them and marriage/civil partnership in a way some commentators find restrictive. In some contexts, parties must have lived together in this manner for a minimum period before acquiring the relevant legal protection; this may need investigation, since cohabiting relationships do not always have firm start and end dates, unlike marriage and civil partnership. Cohabitation is not defined uniformly throughout the law. Given the range of formulae now used to describe non-formalized relationships, it may not be immediately obvious to any couple what all their legal rights and duties are.

As we shall see in later chapters, the courts' willingness to accept a given relationship as cohabitation may be conditioned by the context and the remedy sought. Here, we outline the test commonly used throughout family law to ascertain whether a couple are 'living together as husband and wife'. The test is borrowed from social security law, which treats cohabitants in the same way as spouses for certain purposes. Like *Fitzpatrick*'s approach to defining 'family', it focuses on how the couple functions as a unit.

379 See 2.3.2.
380 See Probert (2004c) and (2012b) for a discussion of the varied history of cohabitants in law.
381 Now to be read as referring equally to same-sex spouses: M(SSC)A 2013, Sch 3, para 2.

Crake v Supplementary Benefits Commission [1982] 1 All ER 498, 502–3, 505

WOOLF J:

. . . [For the purposes of the social security rule] it is not sufficient, to establish that a man and woman are living together as husband and wife, to show that they are living in the same household. . . . [I]n each case it is necessary to . . . ascertain, in so far as this is possible, the manner in which and why they are living together in the same household; and if there is an explanation which indicates that they are not there because they are living together as man and wife, then . . . they are not two persons living together as husband and wife.

It is impossible to categorise all the explanations which would result in [the rule] being inapplicable but it seems to me that if the reason for someone living in the same household as another person is to look after that person because they are ill or incapable for some other reason of managing their affairs, then that in ordinary parlance is not what one would describe as living together as husband and wife. . . .

Quite clearly if that were not the position, housekeepers performing no other functions, other than those of housekeepers, could be regarded as falling within this paragraph. A couple who live together because of some blood relationship could be treated as falling within this paragraph. In my view it was not the intention of Parliament that they should. What Parliament had in mind was . . . that where a couple live together as husband and wife, they shall not be in any different position whether they are married or not . . .

Woolf J then adopted the 'six signposts' that have become a standard set of criteria for identifying a cohabiting relationship:

[They] are admirable signposts to help a tribunal . . . to come to a decision whether in fact the parties should be regarded as being within the words 'living together as husband and wife'. They are: whether they are members of the same household; then there is a reference to stability; then there is a question of financial support; then there is the question of sexual relationship; the question of children; and public acknowledgment . . .

It has been said that it is most important to evaluate the parties' 'general relationship', in light of six signposts, rather than just ticking off those boxes, but that had the parties never had a sexual relationship, it might be difficult to classify them as cohabitants.[382]

Despite the diversity of couple-relationships, there are limits to what will be recognized:

Re Watson (Decd) [1999] 3 FCR 595 (Ch Div), 601

NEUBERGER J:

[O]ne must beware of indulging in too much over-analysis. Anyone who reads newspapers or law reports does not need to be told that marriages, like, perhaps even more than, other human relationships, can vary from each other in multifarious ways. However, in my judgment, when considering whether two people are living together as husband and wife, it

[382] *Re J (Income Support: Cohabitation)* [1995] 1 FLR 660, 665–6.

> would be wrong to conclude that they do so simply because their relationship is one which a husband and wife could have. If the test were as wide as that, then, bearing in mind the enormous variety of relationships that can exist between husband and wife, virtually every relationship between a man and a woman living in the same household would fall within s 1(1A). It seems to me that, when considering the question, the court should ask itself whether, in the opinion of a reasonable person with normal perceptions, it could be said that the two people in question were living together as husband and wife; but, when considering that question, one should not ignore the multifarious nature of marital relationships.

The Court of Appeal has approved the suggestion that the parties must have made a 'lifetime commitment to permanence' and the relationship must be 'openly and unequivocally displayed to the outside world' for the parties to be regarded as 'living together as husband and wife' (or as civil partners) in the context of tenancy succession.[383] But the fact that one party remains formally married to someone else may not automatically prevent cohabitants from being found to constitute a family.[384]

Couples who 'live apart together', perhaps *unable* to reside permanently together in one location owing to the constraints of their respective employments and so who maintain separate homes (as in *Kotke v Saffarini*[385]), will not be regarded as cohabiting. They may be economically interdependent to some extent, and be as intimate and committed as many cohabitants. Yet lack of a shared household precludes their legal recognition in many domestic contexts, even though they may now be regarded as having 'family life' under Article 8 ECHR if the relationship is sufficiently stable.[386] But it is clear both that there is huge variation in the types of relationship that fall into this category, particularly in the degree of interdependence and support between them, and that the views of parties to such relationships on the question of legal recognition also vary considerably.[387]

2.8.2.b Some policy questions

The legal regulation of cohabitants—couples who (given the ready availability of divorce) are generally free to marry or form civil partnerships—is a hotly contested area of family policy. These debates have particularly focused on whether cohabitants should have access to financial remedies on relationship breakdown, a topic we address in chapter 7.

As we noted at 2.2, the cohabiting population is heterogeneous: people cohabit at different life stages for different reasons. Cohabitation is increasingly used as a prelude or alternative to marriage, and is lasting longer. Social attitudes towards relationships are becoming more liberal, especially amongst younger cohorts of the population.[388] Two-thirds of people consider that there is little social difference between marriage and cohabitation, and only one in four think spouses make better parents than cohabitants.[389] But the important *legal* differences between marriage and cohabitation are not fully appreciated. While some deliberately do not formalize their relationship in order to avoid the legal consequences of doing

[383] *Nutting v Southern Housing Group Ltd* [2004] EWHC 2982; *Helby v Rafferty* [1979] 1 WLR 13; see also *Lindop v Agus* [2009] EWHC 1795. Cf Monk (2015): this may be difficult for some older same-sex couples.

[384] *Watson v Lucas* [1980] 1 WLR 1493: applying the 'member of the tenant's family' Rent Act test. See also *Langford v. Secretary of State for Defence* [2019] EWCA Civ 1721.

[385] [2005] EWCA Civ 221, see extract; cf *Kaur v Dhaliwal* [2014] EWHC 1991.

[386] *Vallianatos v Greece* (App Nos 29381/09 and 32684/09, ECHR) (2013), [73].

[387] Duncan et al (2012).

[388] Swales and Attar Taylor (2017).

[389] Duncan and Phillips (2008).

so, the British Social Attitudes (BSA) survey in 2000[390] made startling revelations about the so-called 'common law marriage myth'—the erroneous belief that couples who live together have the same legal status as spouses:[391]

A. Barlow, 'Regulation of Cohabitation, Changing Family Policies and Social Attitudes: A Discussion of Britain within Europe', (2004) 26 *Law and Policy* 57, 72–3

That people see cohabitation or marriage as personal lifestyle choices was underlined by their surprising lack of awareness about the different legal consequences of these relationships. Fifty-six percent of the BSA national survey believed that cohabiting for a period of time gave rise to a common-law marriage giving them the same legal rights as married couples. Among cohabitants, this false belief rose to 59 percent and the in-depth sample found that the source of this was most often family and friends although the media and official social security application forms had also informed a significant number of views. None of the interviewees had sought legal advice specifically in relation to their position as cohabitants . . . When you add to this the finding by another research team, that 41 percent of their sample of 173 engaged couples (73 percent of whom were cohabiting) thought that marriage would not change the legal nature of their relationship (Hibbs, Barton and Beswick 2001), a disturbing picture of legal misperceptions emerges. What is more worrying still to policymakers, is that consciously at least, in most cases people's perceptions of the legal consequences had no impact on their decision to cohabit or marry.

Such misconceptions about the law are concerning if they mean that individuals are organizing their lives oblivious of the legal implications. Moreover, public ignorance of the law will impair attempts by government to encourage marriage by withholding key legal rights from other relationships.[392]

How should the law respond? Many—particularly those keen to promote marriage—consider that, rather than change the law to match people's beliefs, we should better educate the public about the law in the hope that they will then take 'legally rational' decisions.[393] A government-funded campaign accordingly sought to dispel the 'common law marriage myth'. The campaign to some extent improved legal knowledge (at least amongst those who accessed the information) and a later survey indicates that most people do believe marriage offers greater financial security than cohabitation.[394] But for many reasons the campaign did little to change most couples' behaviour, whether by prompting them to marry or to take other steps to secure their legal position, for example by drafting wills or 'living together' agreements.[395] When the BSA survey was repeated in 2018, it found that the common law marriage myth is still very much alive, with almost half of the public believing the myth. Worryingly, the view is more prevalent amongst members of households that have children—55 per cent of those individuals believe in the myth, compared with 41 per cent of those without children.[396]

390 Barlow et al (2001).

391 Probert (2009b), (2011b), (2012b) demonstrates the lack of historical foundation for this belief.

392 Barlow and Duncan (2000).

393 Cf Reece (2015).

394 See also Barlow et al (2008): 2006 BSA findings.

395 Barlow and Smithson (2010).

396 Albakri et al (2019), 12.

However, while non-marital relationships are now increasingly common and socially acceptable, marriage is not regarded as irrelevant: only a small minority—9 per cent of all BSA respondents, 19 per cent of cohabitants—think that marriage is 'just a piece of paper'.[397] Surveys find that a large majority of young people aspire to marry.[398] This will please commentators and policy-makers who wish actively to encourage marriage, considering that marriage ensures a more stable, committed relationship than cohabitation.[399] However, the empirical basis for such views is doubtful. Cohabiting relationships are more susceptible to breakdown than marriages. But it is important to compare like with like: for example, many cohabiting relationships involve young couples, and youth is known to be a predictor of relationship instability, married or not; meanwhile, many long-term cohabitations are indistinguishable from marriages. While spouses may generally report higher levels of commitment, it is hard to disentangle cause and effect, as the following extract—which focuses on the impact of relationship form for children—explains.[400] While the process of making the promises entailed in marriage may have some stabilizing effect,[401] overall, marriage may be the product of pre-existing commitment, rather than a creator of commitment:[402]

British Academy Working Group, *Social Science and Family Policies* (London: British Academy, 2009), 48–50

But is marriage the cause or consequence of that commitment? . . .

[One] consideration involves the major factors involved in 'selection effects', meaning the fact that those who marry before they have children are likely to be rather different sorts of people from those who have children while cohabiting. The factors predisposing childbirth outside marriage include being economically worse off, lower educational attainments, less religious commitment, the experience of sex before 16, having a widowed mother, black ethnicity, having been a teenage parent, and having a low income. . . . Accordingly, it is quite possible that the disadvantages experienced by children born to those who are unmarried but living together have more to do with the characteristics of the people concerned than with whether or not they are legally married . . . Bearing in mind these findings, a thought experiment can be carried out. If legal steps were taken to ensure that more people in the high risk group married, what would happen to marriage stability? The evidence suggests that probably it would lessen and that the differences between the married and the cohabiting would diminish. . . . [I]t cannot be claimed that we have adequate evidence on the pros and cons of marriage versus non-marital cohabitation. . . . Also, the scientific findings make it very clear that any conclusions on the benefits of marriage must be based on considerations that include differences between people who do, and who do not, choose to marry. In other words, people choose whether or not to marry, and the differences in child outcomes between groups of married and cohabiting couples with children may reflect the sorts of people who choose to marry, rather than the effects of the marital situation as such. That is not to say that marriage does not engender commitment. But we cannot ascribe all the differences between the married and non-married to the degree of commitment between partners (either as a cause or consequence of marriage).

397 Barlow et al (2008). 398 De Waal (2008); Coast (2009).
399 E.g. Centre for Social Justice (2009).
400 See also Goodman and Greaves (2010); Crawford et al (2012).
401 Probert (2009c), 325, (2012a), 78–9.
402 De Waal (2008); see also Garrison (2020); Fahey (2020), 106–8.

2.8.2.c Human rights issues

Strasbourg case law currently offers limited support for equal treatment of cohabitants with spouses and civil partners under Article 14 ECHR. The Court has endorsed the UK's maintenance of 'bright-line rules', excluding cohabitants from various legal protections, to pursue the legitimate aim of promoting marriage (and now civil partnership), family life based on the parties' having undertaken public, legally binding commitments towards each other.[403] The issue has often arisen in the context of welfare benefits or taxation, in relation to which the Court has consistently held that spouses' distinctive legal status means that spouses and cohabitants are not in analogous situations, so the different treatment requires no justification. Strasbourg case law involving other states has considered eligibility for financial remedies on separation and death. A cohabiting couple with children have 'family life' under Article 8, but the state has no positive duty under that Article to provide access to such remedies.[404] Nor is there discrimination under Article 14 in conjunction with Article 8: in *Saucedo Gomez v Spain*, the Commission seemed prepared to accept that cohabitants and spouses might be regarded as analogous in that context, but held that states could justifiably distinguish marriage from cohabitation to promote the traditional concept of family.[405]

English courts have sometimes declined to find any discrimination, at least where the couple in question could have formalized their relationship in law.[406] However, particularly perhaps where the discrimination impacts *children*, a different view may be taken. The House of Lords in *Re P*[407] found Northern Irish adoption law incompatible with Article 14 in conjunction with Article 8 in refusing to permit unmarried couples to be considered as potential adopters: in this context, where the child's best interests are paramount, the law could not rationally exclude an entire class of potential adopters simply because of their marital status. Children were again critical in *Re McLaughlin*, where the Supreme Court held that denying surviving cohabitants access to widowed parents' allowance breached Article 14 in conjunction with both Article 8 and Article 1 of Protocol 1.[408] The House in *Re P* acknowledged that in some areas of law maintaining a bright-line rule distinguishing married from unmarried couples could be lawful, certainly where the parties are free to marry (so have some choice about their legal status).[409] But even in childless cases, the issues must be considered in context,[410] and the ultimate question is functional: whether the grant of the legal benefit in question is rationally based on parties' marital status, or on some other concern equally applicable to cohabitants. Where cohabitants *are* recognized, the inclusion in

[403] E.g. *Courten v United Kingdom* (App No 4479/06, ECHR) (2008); *MW v United Kingdom* (App No 11313/02, ECHR) (2009); *Shackell v United Kingdom* (App No 45851/99, ECHR) (2000)—cf *Re McLaughlin* [2018] UKSC 48. One exception concerned taxation of unmarried fathers' child maintenance payments: *PM v United Kingdom* (App No 6638/03, ECHR) (2006).

[404] *Johnston v Ireland* (A-112, ECHR) (1987).

[405] (App No 37784/97, ECHR) (1999).

[406] E.g. *Ratcliffe v Secretary of State for Defence* [2009] EWCA Civ 39; cf *Rodriguez v Minister of Housing of the Government of Gibraltar* [2009] UKPC 52. In *Langford v Secretary of State for Defence* [2019] EWCA Civ 1721, it was held that the restriction of survivors' benefits under an armed forces pension scheme was unlawful discrimination. The appellant in this case had been in a 'substantial and exclusive' cohabiting relationship with the deceased and had been unable to marry because she was in a moribund marriage to another man.

[407] [2008] UKHL 38.

[408] [2018] UKSC 48, not following Strasbourg decisions at n 398 as failing adequately to address the impact on the children.

[409] [2008] UKHL 38, at [13]–[16] and [108]–[110].

[410] *Smith v Lancashire Teaching Hospitals NHS Foundation Trust* [2017] EWCA Civ 1916, [88]–[90]; *Re McLaughlin* [2018] UKSC 38, [26]–[27] on the closely related 'analogous situation' issue.

eligibility criteria of a minimum duration requirement is unlikely to violate the Convention: such a requirement, if arbitrary, 'is a simple way of demonstrating a real relationship of constancy and permanence' that merits protection which the state is entitled to impose.[411]

2.8.3 THE PLATONIC, NON-CONJUGAL FAMILY

Another set of families that has attracted recent attention, particularly during the Civil Partnership Bill debates,[412] is platonic relationships, often between legal strangers (i.e. those not already related by blood or formalized relationship). Few laws expressly apply, or have been interpreted as applying, to platonic home-sharers and friends, or even blood relationships. Surprisingly, even blood relations such as adult siblings and elderly parents with their adult children are rarely regarded by the ECHR has having 'family life' for the purposes of Article 8.[413] Relationships with a sexual aspect are readily classified as quasi-conjugal and so fall within the scope of laws applying to cohabitants. But the absence of sexual intimacy probably excludes platonic relationships from laws applicable to 'cohabitants'. Just as marriage (in particular) is based on sex, so too, it seems, must its analogues, however central a platonic friendship may be to the lives of those concerned.[414] Platonic home-sharers who are not blood or adoptive relatives have even been excluded from judicial interpretations of the ambit of 'family' in the tenancy succession statutes, however long-standing and close the relationship.[415] But they do fall within some of the more broadly framed concepts used by family law statutes. For example, the mere sharing of a household in a non-commercial context makes parties 'associated persons' for the purposes of domestic abuse legislation.[416] By contrast, some jurisdictions have brought non-sexual, caring domestic relationships within the scope of family law more generally,[417] in the case of Tasmania, including where the parties are related by family,[418] creating opportunities both to register the relationship and to be recognized on a de facto basis.

One reason for English law's reluctance to extend beyond conjugal and quasi-conjugal couples, especially to parties not related by blood, might be the perceived difficulties of defining family beyond those examples and so of drawing a clear line (assuming that such relationships cannot be formalized in law). However, some would say that the line drawn by the *present* law is unsustainable:

Fitzpatrick v Sterling Housing Association Ltd [2001] 1 AC 27, 64, 67

LORD HUTTON (dissenting):

A further difficulty which confronts the argument on behalf of [Mr Fitzpatrick] is that if it is correct and if the underlying purpose of the legislation is to provide a secure home for a person who shares his or her life with the tenant in a relationship of mutual affection,

[411] *Swift v Secretary of State for Justice* [2013] EWCA Civ 193: no breach in the context of the Fatal Accidents Act 1976 requirement of two years' cohabitation. Cf *Re Brewster* [2017] UKSC 8: no need for minimum duration *and* a registration requirement to access a survivor pension.

[412] Glennon (2005). [413] Draghici (2018). [414] See Westwood (2013).

[415] *Ross v Collins* [1964] 1 WLR 425, 432; *Sefton Holdings Ltd v Cairns* (1987) 20 HLR 124.

[416] FLA 1996, s 62(3)(c): see chapter 4.

[417] See Australian states' experience, e.g. Property (Relationships) Act 1984 (NSW), as amended; Domestic Relationships Act 1994 (ACT).

[418] Relationships Act 2003 (Tas), s 5.

commitment and support, it is difficult to see why two elderly spinsters who live together for mutual support and companionship in old age without any sexual element in their relationship and who give each other devoted care should not qualify as members of the same family. I do not consider that the absence of a sexual relationship distinguishes such a case from the present one. The sexual relationship between a couple is a very important and enriching part of their life together, but I am unable to accept that there is such a distinction between an elderly homosexual couple who once had an active sexual relationship and two elderly spinsters who never had a sexual relationship that the homosexual couple should be regarded as members of each other's family and the spinsters should not. If the courts depart from the requirement of . . . [a broadly recognisable familial nexus, which the dissenting judges in *Fitzpatrick* take to require a heterosexual, (and so) marriage-like relationship] it is difficult to discern what criterion would include one person residing with the tenant and exclude another.

English law's exclusion of such relationships from various legal rights and duties raises difficult and interesting questions. It can be argued that if the law's purpose is to assist those in practical need, the presence or absence of a sexual or blood relationship should be irrelevant to legal recognition. For example, in the context of financial and property rights and remedies, the existence of economic interdependence, or dependence, might be felt the more obvious criterion for identifying relationships eligible for legal recognition.[419] The restrictions on access to marriage and civil partnership, particularly the rules regarding prohibited degrees, combined with the absence of legal protection for non-formalized relationships, leave some parties with no mechanism for acquiring the legal protection they might be thought to need or deserve. While parties can protect themselves to some extent through contract, declarations of trust, and wills, that will not solve all of their problems, particularly where the complaint involves an issue of public law such as taxation.

2.8.3.a The Burden sisters' case

These issues hit the headlines when the Burden sisters unsuccessfully challenged English tax law before the European Court of Human Rights.[420] The unmarried Burden sisters had lived together all their lives, for the last 30 years in a jointly owned house worth £875,000, built by their brother on land inherited from their parents. When one died, the survivor would have to pay inheritance tax on the deceased sister's share of the house.[421] Spouses or civil partners in the same position would be exempt from inheritance tax. And that was the basis of the sisters' complaint: why should they not be able to enjoy a similar exemption, having lived interdependently for decades? Being related within the prohibited degrees, they could not arrange their affairs to avoid the liability by forming a civil partnership. The case provoked debate on why only spouses and civil partners should be able to enjoy the exemption—and why marriage and civil partnership are open only to pairs unrelated by family within the prohibited degrees.

The sisters formulated their complaint as a breach of Article 14 taken in conjunction with Article 1 of Protocol 1 to the ECHR (the right to peaceful enjoyment of possessions), marshalling an impressive range of arguments. They argued that their position is analogous to spouses or civil partners, having 'chosen to live together in a loving, committed and

[419] Bailey-Harris (1998), 85.

[420] *Burden and Burden v United Kingdom* (App No 13378/05, ECHR) (2008).

[421] Despite suggestions that this would mean selling the house, this appears unlikely to be necessary: see Auchmuty (2009).

stable relationship for several decades, sharing their only home, to the exclusion of other partners'.[422] The fact that their relationship was not sexual could not be relevant, as civil partnership law has no sexual aspect. They argued that they should not be prejudiced by the fact that their relationship arose initially by accident of birth and entailed no legally enforceable financial obligations expressly elected by them by formalizing their relationships: being unable in law to form a civil partnership, their decision to live together should itself be regarded as an equivalent exercise of self-determination to assume responsibility for each other.[423] If the purpose of the tax exemption, as described by the government, were to promote stable and committed relationships, that purpose applied equally to adult siblings who live together in such circumstances, so denying them the same exemption served no legitimate aim.[424] They argued that English law should reach beyond conjugality by introducing a statutory scheme conferring certain fiscal benefits on pairs of siblings or other close relations who had lived together for a minimum period and not married or formed civil partnerships with third parties. In response to the suggestion that extending such a tax exemption would deprive the public purse of revenue, they argued that this would potentially be offset by gains in other areas: for example, people would be encouraged to care for disabled and elderly relations and so avoid the need for state-funded care.[425]

Their case failed both at first instance and on appeal. The court of first instance reached no decision on whether the sisters' position was analogous to that of spouses and civil partners, who are exempt from inheritance tax. Instead, it found that the difference in treatment could in any event be justified within the state's margin of appreciation. Two dissenting judges noted that while the state might have been able to justify its position by reference to Article 12 had the tax exemption been confined to spouses, the position changed once it was extended to civil partners: 'once the legislature decides that a permanent union of two persons could or should enjoy tax privileges, it must be able to justify why such a possibility has been offered to some unions while continuing to be denied to others'.[426] This meant that it was important to examine the point left undecided by the majority. While earlier case law had compared the treatment of spouses with cohabitants—that is, people who were free to acquire the privileged legal status but had not done so[427]—the sisters' position was quite different, being barred by their blood relationship from formalizing their relationship and so acquiring the tax exemption.[428]

By contrast, the majority of the Grand Chamber considered that the sisters fell at the first hurdle: their position was not analogous to that of spouses and civil partners. The majority's reasoning here is generally regarded as somewhat weak. They took what may be called a formalistic (and somewhat circular) approach, failing to engage with arguments about the functional similarity between the sisters and spouses in relation to the issue of inheritance tax and possible loss of a shared home:

Burden and Burden v United Kingdom (App No 13378/05, ECHR) (2008)

> 62. . . . [T]he relationship between siblings is qualitatively of a different nature to that between married couples and homosexual civil partners . . . The very essence of the connection between siblings is consanguinity, whereas one of the defining characteristics of a marriage

422 Judgment of first instance ECtHR, [50].

423 Cf the government's argument, [46] and [48].

424 Judgment of first instance ECtHR, [51]. Cf the government's argument, [47].

425 Ibid, [52].

426 Dissenting judgment of Judges Bonello and Garlicki, [2].

427 E.g. *Shackell v United Kingdom* (App No 45851/99, ECHR) (2000).

428 Judges Bonello and Garlicki, [3].

or [civil partnership] is that it is forbidden to close family members . . . The fact that the applicants have chosen to live together all their adult lives, as do many married and Civil Partnership Act couples, does not alter this essential difference between the two types of relationship.

63. Moreover, the Grand Chamber notes that it has already held that marriage confers a special status on those who enter into it. The exercise of the right to marry is protected by Article 12 of the Convention and gives rise to social, personal and legal consequences . . .

65. As with marriage, the Grand Chamber considers that the legal consequences of civil partnership . . ., which couples expressly and deliberately decide to incur, set these types of relationship apart from other forms of co-habitation. Rather than the length or the supportive nature of the relationship, what is determinative is the existence of a public undertaking, carrying with it a body of rights and obligations of a contractual nature. Just as there can be no analogy between married and Civil Partnership Act couples, on the one hand, and heterosexual or homosexual couples who choose to live together but not to become husband and wife or civil partners, on the other hand (see *Shackell v UK*), the absence of such a legally binding agreement between the applicants renders their relationship of co-habitation, despite its long duration, fundamentally different to that of a married or civil partnership couple.

The weaknesses of the majority reasoning were recognized by two other judges who, while also dismissing the appeal for reasons similar to those of the first instance court, were expressly critical of the majority's approach to whether the sisters were in an analogous position to spouses and civil partners:

JUDGE BJÖRGVINSSON:

The reasoning of the majority . . . is in my view flawed by the fact that it is based on comparison of factors of a different nature and which are not comparable from a logical point of view. It is to a large extent based on reference to the specific legal framework which is applicable to married couples and civil partnership couples but which does not, under the present legislation, apply to the applicants as cohabiting sisters. However, although in the strict sense the complaint only relates to a difference in treatment as concerns inheritance tax, in the wider context it relates, in essence, to the facts that different rules apply and that consanguinity between the applicants prevents them from entering into a legally binding agreement similar to marriage or civil partnership, which would make the legal framework applicable to them, including the relevant provisions of the law on inheritance tax.

I believe that in these circumstances any comparison of the relationship between the applicants, on the one hand, and the relationship between married couples and civil partnership couples, on the other, should be made without specific reference to the different legal framework applicable, and should focus only on the substantive or material differences in the nature of the relationship as such. Despite important differences, mainly as concerns the sexual nature of the relationship between married couples and civil partner couples, when it comes to the decision to live together, closeness of the personal attachment and for most practical purposes of daily life and financial matters, the relationship between the applicants in this case has, in general and for the alleged purposes of the relevant inheritance tax exemptions in particular, more in common with the relationship between married or civil partnership couples, than there are differences between them. Despite this fact, the law prohibits them from entering into an agreement similar to marriage or civil partnership and thus take advantage of the applicable rules, including the inheritance tax rules. That being so, I am not convinced that the relationship between the applicants as cohabiting sisters cannot be compared with married or civil partner couples for the purposes of Article 14 of the Convention. On the contrary there is in this case a difference in treatment of persons in situations which are, as a matter of fact, to a large extent similar and analogous.

One interesting question to ponder is: what if there had been a third Burden sister? In that case, given the monogamy model of English law, any analogy with marriage or civil partnership (so understood) would have been unavailable. Yet it is an obvious example that merits an answer.

2.8.3.b Taking functionalism to its logical conclusion

Many writers have argued that family law should be completely realigned to focus not on the form of the family type or its conjugal nature (i.e. a focus on sexual relationships), but on the fact of care-giving within relationships, on the basis that care is a far more valuable phenomenon for the state to recognize, promote, and protect.[429] In the following extract, Alison Diduck outlines how a purely functional approach can be taken to determining the proper reach of legal regulation. It is worth considering how this approach might be applied to a situation such as the Burdens' (including the hypothetical third sister):

A. Diduck, 'Shifting Familiarity', (2005) 58 *Current Legal Problems* 235, 249

In 2001, the Law Commission of Canada . . . observed the growing diversity in family life and it concluded that recognising and supporting the great variety of caring personal adult relationships is 'an important state objective'. It identified certain basic principles and values that the state must attend to when it devises a principled and comprehensive approach to the needs of all in relationships. It concluded that the state must value equality and autonomy, personal security, privacy, freedom of conscience and religion and coherence and efficiency. It further concluded that the distinction between conjugal and non-conjugal is inconsistent with the value of equality, since conjugality 'is not an accurate marker of the qualitative attributes of personal adult relationships that are relevant to practical legislative [and policy] objectives'. It said that 'the state's role should be neutral regarding the roles that people assume in their personal relationships'.

Instead, then, of simply arguing that some relationships currently excluded should be included in legal recognition, it proposed that we start from scratch and 'look at the way governments have relied upon relational status in allocating rights and responsibilities', and try to design a legislative regime that accomplishes its goals by relying less on whether people are living in certain kinds of relationships. Sometimes some characteristics of the relationship will be important, other times they would not be, but conjugality would never be important.

On the one hand this approach runs the risk of even broader familialisation,[430] yet on the other, it eschews the word family completely in these contexts, and focuses on the variety of personal and caring relationships in which people live. Instead of being concerned about families, then, it is concerned about the individual rights and responsibilities that accrue from different relationships and about how the law can help distribute them among people more equitably. For me the change in language is important. It allows us to think outside the 'family' box.

[429] Notably Herring e.g. (2014).

[430] See concerns of Diduck and Barker at 2.3.4 that (apparently liberal) designation of relationships as 'family' is a way to privatize particular *obligations*, particularly in times of state austerity.

2.9 CONCLUSION

As we have discussed in this chapter, the law's definition and adjudication of family relationships is ever shifting:

Lady Hale, 'What Do We Mean by a Family?', Family Justice Council Bridget Lindley Memorial Lecture, (2021) 20

> So it is that our concept of what constitutes a family recognized by the law has changed dramatically in recent decades. The old concepts of affinity – marriage – and consanguinity – blood relationship – are no longer sufficient to define what we mean by a family. And the driving force behind these changes is human need: most people want to form enduring intimate relationships if they can; most people want to have children if they can. The law is now prepared to recognize – even to facilitate – a much greater variety of ways in which to fulfil those human needs than it did in the past.

Whether individuals have the legal status of spouse or civil partner—and whether they are legally permitted to acquire that status—still makes a considerable difference to their treatment in many areas of the law. Other family relationships between adults are acknowledged in some areas, but not in others. Extending legal rights and duties beyond marriage is often politically controversial, many fearing that such developments undermine the institution of marriage. We shall consider in later chapters what practical impact continued difference of treatment has on the individuals involved, and whether it can be justified.

ONLINE RESOURCES

Questions, suggestions for further reading, and updates on developments in this area of family law since this book was published may be found in the online resources at **www.oup.com/he/familytcm5e.**

3

ENDING RELATIONSHIPS: DIVORCE, DISSOLUTION, AND SEPARATION

CENTRAL ISSUES

1. The law of divorce has always been controversial owing to its implications for the institution of marriage and the family. Attempts to reform the law trigger heated debate between those who wish to retain state control over exit from marriage and those who wish to promote party autonomy.
2. Divorce used to be clearly fault-based, available only if the respondent had committed a 'matrimonial offence'. Since 1969, divorce has been available on the basis that the marriage has irretrievably broken down. Until the Divorce, Dissolution and Separation Act 2020 came into effect, the ground of irretrievable breakdown could only be satisfied by proving one of five 'facts', based upon conduct or separation. However, since the Act's implementation in April 2022, a statement of irretrievable breakdown is all that is required. This removal of any substantive legal requirement means the other spouse can no longer challenge the breakdown of their relationship in court.
3. The law of civil partnership dissolution is largely identical to the law of divorce, save that the legal end of a civil partnership is termed 'dissolution' instead of divorce.
4. In 2022, the introduction of truly no-fault divorce, as well as the new option for parties to apply jointly, is compatible with the emphasis in current family policy on 'divorcing responsibly' and resolving disputes on family breakdown by agreement.
5. Divorce and dissolution have—even long before 2022, in uncontested cases—become a largely administrative process. The traditional paper-based application process for divorce has been overtaken by online applications, and amendments to online divorce in 2022 mean that the vast majority of divorces will now be completed online.
6. The almost complete withdrawal of the law from the process of divorce and dissolution raises interesting questions about the nature, function, and limits of divorce law.

3.1 INTRODUCTION

Thousands of families are touched by divorce every year. That sad fact attracts a range of responses. Some see divorce as the death of family, symptomatic of moral decay, a cause of social dislocation, economic cost to society, and damage to children. From this perspective, divorce and separation must therefore be curtailed and marriage promoted as the functional and ideological 'gold standard'. Others, however, are more sanguine, seeing divorce as a common stage in contemporary family life beyond which family continues, albeit reconfigured across two households. On this view, the issue is how law can enable families to adjust and maintain good relationships after relationship breakdown, particularly where the couple have children.[1] These concerns apply equally to couples who cohabit and become parents without marrying. Issues surrounding parenting and property arrangements on separation are as pressing for them as they are for divorcing spouses. But while all separating couples share many practical problems, spouses and civil partners may wish (and need) to end their relationship not only in fact but also in law. Simply separating does not extinguish the legal status of marriage or civil partnership. The legal rights and duties attaching to the status continue, and, while they may cohabit with another, the parties are unable to marry or form a civil partnership with anyone else. Releasing the parties from their legal status is the job of the law of divorce, the principal focus of this chapter.

There is a human right to marry, but the European Convention on Human Rights (ECHR) does not recognize a right to divorce.[2] Nevertheless, all European states now permit divorce and Article 12 ECHR entitles divorcees to remarry without unreasonable restrictions.[3] However, each state is free to determine the basis on which divorce is granted and there is considerable variety across Europe.[4] Divorce in England and Wales is governed by Part I of the Matrimonial Causes Act 1973 (MCA 1973) and equivalent provisions of the Civil Partnership Act 2004 (CPA 2004). Unless clear from the context, references here to 'divorce' and associated terminology include civil partnership dissolution.[5]

Like its law of nullity,[6] a society's divorce law (or its absence) reveals something about that society's understanding of the nature and significance of marriage, and about the boundaries between public and private, between community interest and individual interest. It involves basic questions about the role of the state and the law in regulating adults' private lives and the nature that that regulation should take. If the law makes no provision for divorce, then marriage is a lifelong status. If divorce is permitted, on what basis? Is marriage a status terminable only if one party commits some 'offence' regarded by the state as sufficiently grave to excuse the innocent party from continued participation in the marriage? Is it a contract dissoluble by mutual consent, its terms (to that extent) implicitly agreed by the parties, rather than the state? Or can marriage last only for so long as both parties assent to its continuation, allowing one party to end it unilaterally? Even if divorce in England and

[1] Hasson (2006). Lewis (2001a), 162 observes that it is difficult to prove the cause and effect relationship between divorce and outcomes for children, since it is hard to disentangle the impact of divorce (specifically) on children's outcomes from other factors affecting families before, during, or after separation.

[2] *Johnston v Ireland* (App No 9697/82, ECHR) (1986); *Babiarz v Poland* (App No 1955/10, ECHR) (2017).

[3] *F v Switzerland* (App No 11329/85, ECHR) (1987), [32]: three-year ban on remarriage by a serial divorcee and adulterer was unreasonable; *VK v Croatia* (App No 38380/08, ECHR) (2012).

[4] Boele-Woelki et al (2004).

[5] Cf Auchmuty (2015) on experience of civil partnership dissolution.

[6] See 2.6 and 2.7.

Wales is now freely available in this sense,[7] should the law seek to influence parties' behaviour surrounding divorce in other ways, for example by imposing waiting periods?[8]

These questions must be considered in light of substantial changes to the legal requirements of divorce in 2022, as well as the divorce process more generally. As we shall see later in this chapter at 3.7, under the Divorce, Dissolution and Separation Act 2020 (DDSA 2020), spouses can now divorce simply because they consider that the marriage has broken down irretrievably. This means their decision to divorce no longer needs to be based upon legally approved reasons; parties may divorce simply because they no longer wish to be married. These changes signal a withdrawal of the law from the field of divorce; a shift that must be contextualized within broader debates considered throughout this chapter about the nature and normalization of divorce.[9]

3.2 THE NORMALIZATION OF DIVORCE

Most marriages in England and Wales still end by death, but the number and proportion of marriages ending by divorce increased dramatically during the last century. This overall trend is matched across much of the developed world, although differences in laws and social, cultural, and religious factors are reflected in countries' divorce rates.[10] In one sense at least, changes in the substantive and procedural law governing divorce contributed to this increase: it is now legally possible for many of those who wish to divorce to do so when previously they could not. But this does not itself mean that more marriages now fail: before the law permitted divorce, many couples in unhappy marriages physically separated.[11] Some formed new relationships that, without a divorce from the earlier marriage, could not be formalized by marriage. A restrictive divorce law may therefore not have kept unhappy couples together, but simply prevented them from terminating their legal relationship.[12]

The huge social changes of the twentieth century were also major contributing factors to increasing divorce, especially those regarding women's position in the home and their increased participation in the labour market, birth control, liberalized sexual morality, declining levels of religious adherence, and the transformation of home and family from a unit of production to a haven from the outside world. These changes affected people's expectations of marriage, now principally regarded as a source of companionship through life.[13] Moreover, greater longevity has exposed more marriages to the test of time: in 1820, the same proportion of marriages ended by death within 15 years of marriage as ended by divorce in 1980.[14] However, the relationship between social behaviour and law reform is complex. Commentators and researchers have disagreed about whether and to what extent reforms liberalizing divorce either responded to social demand or increased the divorce rate amongst couples who would otherwise have stayed together. But the better view seems to be that reforms have probably had only a modest and short-term impact on divorce rates.[15] Increasingly accessible divorce may have helped it to become more normalized, but this does not mean that divorce is the experience of the majority who marry.[16]

[7] See 3.10.3. [8] See 3.10.4. [9] See 3.3 and 3.10. [10] Fahey (2020).
[11] Ibid; Eekelaar (2017), 19. [12] Law Com (1988a), paras 2.15–2.16.
[13] Rheinstein (1972), 273–6; Phillips (1991), ch 9. [14] Walker (1991).
[15] Fahey (2020), 103; Trinder et al (2017), 11.2–11.3. [16] Probert (2022).

3.2.1 DIVORCES IN ENGLAND AND WALES

In the early 1900s, around 500 divorces were granted each year in England and Wales. Thereafter, the numbers rose after each reform enlarging the grounds on which divorce could be obtained.[17] After 1923, there were about 2,500 divorces annually, from 1937, around 7–8,000. Social upheaval during and following the Second World War unsurprisingly generated an exceptional 60,300 divorces in 1947, but otherwise around 25–30,000 divorces were granted per year post-war until the 1960s.[18] This increase was partly attributable to the availability of public funding for legal services, ('legal aid') from 1948 until the mid-1970s, which made divorce accessible to those who had previously been unable to afford it. During the 1960s, the number of divorces doubled independently of any major substantive legal change.[19] Following reform in 1969 the number of divorces each year spiked, quickly exceeding 100,000 per year and peaking at 165,018 in 1993. But—when compared with data from the 1990s—numbers have, on the whole, declined markedly since the early 2000s. In 2019, 108,421 divorces were granted in England and Wales (107,599 between mixed-sex couples and 822 between same-sex couples).[20] Since 2019, numbers have fluctuated between 103,592 divorces in 2020 and 113,505 divorces in 2021, but these figures are skewed by the Covid-19 pandemic, which caused disruption to family court activities, as well as divorce applications.[21] Only 1.4 per cent of all divorces are among same-sex couples, because same-sex divorce was not possible until 2015.[22] It was anticipated that the *numbers* of divorces would drop over the coming decades as fewer people marry. Those who do marry increasingly do so later in life, reducing the number of youthful marriages, which are more prone to divorce.[23] Indeed, more recent marriage cohorts, who married in 2005 and 2015, are showing reduced levels of divorce as the data depicted in Figure 3.3 show.

Another useful measure is the divorce *rate*: how many people each year divorce per 1,000 members of the married population: see Figure 3.2 (like Figure 3.1, showing figures for mixed-sex couples only). This statistic is unaffected by changes in the overall population or the number of marriages and so more accurately indicates the frequency of divorce in the relevant population. In England and Wales, the divorce rate in 1961, before the 1969 reforms, was 2.1 per 1,000 of the married population.[24] By 1971, it had already climbed to 6.0; it then rose over the years, peaking at 14.1 in 2004, and then dropping to 7.5 in 2018 (the lowest rate since 1973).[25] While Figure 3.2 indicates an increase in the divorce rate to 9.3 since 2018, this can be attributed to processing delays being addressed, as well as the pandemic. Overall, this suggests that the current married population are more likely to stay married. Indeed, while the divorce rate and numbers of divorces have generally declined, so too has the marriage rate, and with the average age at first marriage rising, those who do marry are more likely to stay together.[26] Nevertheless, around 41 per cent of married couples are estimated to divorce by their 25th wedding anniversary.[27] The number

[17] See 3.4; Haskey (2018b). [18] Stone (1990).

[19] The Matrimonial Causes Act 1963 amended the laws of condonation and collusion: Cretney (2003a), 349–51; there was also some liberalization in the case law during the 1960s: ibid, 352–3.

[20] These figures are 18 per cent higher than the number of divorces in 2018, but the ONS has explained this increase as resulting in part from divorce centres processing a backlog of casework. ONS (2020h), 2.

[21] ONS (2022i), 2.

[22] Same-sex marriage was introduced in 2014 under the Marriage (Same Sex Couples) Act 2013 (see chapter 2) and the parties must be married for at least one year before they can apply for divorce.

[23] ONS (2022b), table 1. [24] Law Com (1988a), Appendix A. [25] ONS (2020h), 2.

[26] See 2.2.1; Beaujouan and Ní Bhrolcháin (2011), 14–15. [27] ONS (2022j), 4.

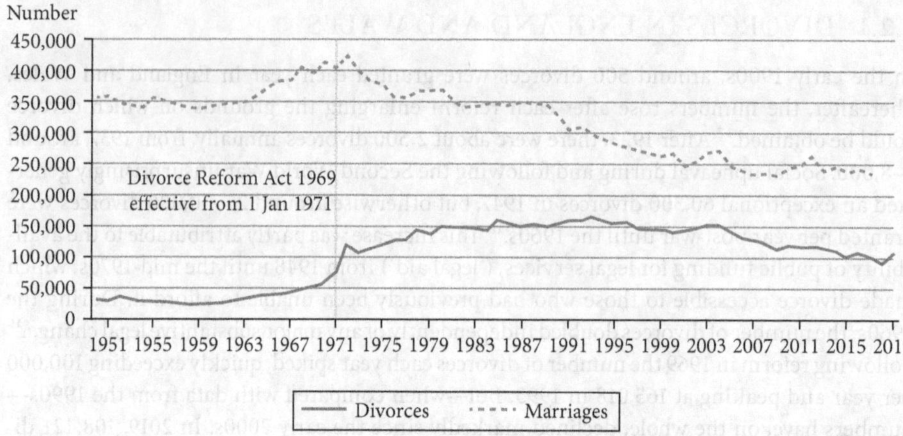

Notes:
1. Marriage statistics are only available up to the 2017 data year.
2. The Divorce Reform act 1969, which came into effect on 1 January 1971, made it easier for couples to divorce upon separation and is associated with the increase in the number of divorces during the 1970s.

Figure 3.1 Number of marriages and divorces of opposite-sex couples, England and Wales, 1950 to 2019: ONS 2020

Source: Reproduced from ONS (2020h), by Crown copyright ©.

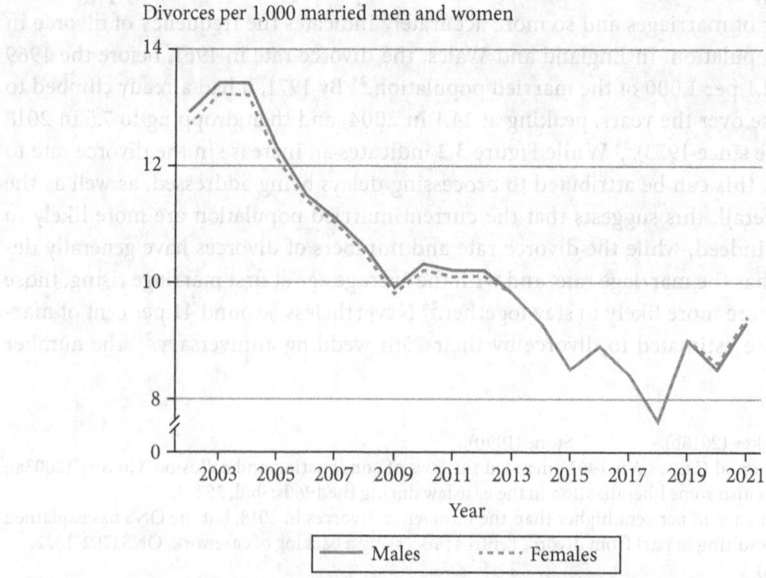

Figure 3.2 Divorce rates for males and females per 1,000 of the married population aged 16 years and over, England and Wales, 2002 to 2021

Source: Reproduced from ONS (2022j), by Crown copyright ©.

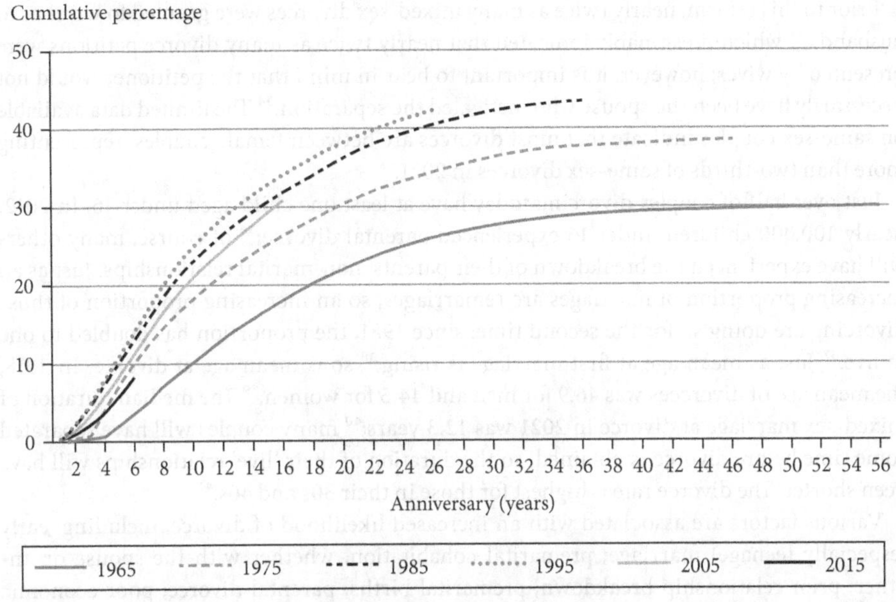

Figure 3.3 Cumulative percentage of marriages ending in divorce by year of marriage and by year of anniversary, England and Wales, 1965 to 2015

Source: Reproduced from ONS (2022j), by Crown copyright ©.

of same-sex civil partnership dissolutions remains relatively low, even dropping slightly in 2020.[28] As mixed-sex couples have only been able to enter civil partnerships since December 2019, it is too early for there to be meaningful statistics about dissolution.

Divorce statistics tell us nothing about marital breakdown that does not culminate in divorce.[29] Nor, of course, can they tell us about the breakdown of cohabiting relationships. Owing to the informal nature of these relationships, gathering data about them is challenging, but survey evidence indicates that their breakdown rate is higher than that of spouses.[30]

3.2.2 WHO DIVORCES?

As we shall see in 3.7, the new law of divorce is likely to influence the question of who divorces. It is too early to tell what impact the DDSA 2020 will have upon who instigates divorce, given that it was brought into effect in April 2022. Early data suggest the immediate effect of the Act's implementation has been a spike in divorce rates,[31] but research on patterns of divorce show this is a predictable consequence of any liberalization of divorce law.[32] This spike could also be attributed to a 'backlog effect', with spouses applying when they would previously have had to wait for a five-year period of separation to expire because the other party would not consent to the divorce (see 3.5.1). However, several years of data are needed to glean a reliable understanding of the new law's effect.

[28] ONS (2021e), 2; numbers dropped by 27 per cent from 916 in 2019 to 671 in 2020. However, as for divorce, these data are likely to have been affected by the pandemic.
[29] See Fahey (2020). [30] See discussion at 2.8.2. [31] MOJ (2022b), table 12b.
[32] Haskey (2022), 42.

Prior to this reform, nearly twice as many mixed-sex divorces were granted to wives as to husbands,[33] which presumably indicated that nearly twice as many divorce petitions were presented by wives; however, it is important to bear in mind that the petitioner would not necessarily have been the spouse who instigated the separation.[34] The limited data available on same-sex couples indicate that most divorces are between female couples, representing more than two-thirds of same-sex divorces in 2021.[35]

Just over half of couples divorcing today have at least one child aged under 16. In 2012, nearly 100,000 children under 16 experienced parental divorce;[36] of course, many others will have experienced the breakdown of their parents' non-marital relationships. Just as an increasing proportion of marriages are remarriages, so an increasing proportion of those divorcing are doing so for the second time: since 1981, the proportion has doubled to one in five.[37] Just as mean age at first marriage is rising,[38] so is mean age at divorce. In 2018, the mean age of divorcees was 46.9 for men and 44.5 for women.[39] The median duration of mixed-sex marriage at divorce in 2021 was 12.3 years;[40] many couples will have separated some time before divorce is obtained, so the duration of their 'live' relationships will have been shorter. The divorce rate is highest for those in their 30s and 40s.[41]

Various factors are associated with an increased likelihood of divorce, including: early (especially teenage) marriage; premarital cohabitation, whether with the spouse or another; prior relationship breakdown; premarital births; parental divorce; poor economic circumstances (also associated with young marriage); and poor psychological and physical well-being.[42] Similar characteristics are associated with separation by unmarried couples.

3.3 THE NATURE, FUNCTION, AND LIMITS OF DIVORCE LAW

Before examining the historical development of divorce law in more detail at 3.4, we sketch some inter-related themes which have been debated since judicial divorce was introduced in 1857. It is striking how timeless many of the political concerns about marriage and divorce seem to be, despite massive social and legal change. A law of divorce can assume various shapes, depending on the chosen degree, nature, and purpose of state intervention and the state's view of marriage. How can and should the law be used in relation to divorce?

3.3.1 FAULT OR 'NO FAULT'?

The legal system characteristically dispenses justice, adjudicating on right and wrong. Divorce law could do the same, providing 'justice' for a wronged party and enforcing responsibility for wrongdoing. A fault-based divorce law identifies various 'matrimonial offences',

33 In 2019, the wife was the applicant in 62 per cent of mixed-sex divorces: ONS (2020h), 6.

34 Davis and Murch (1988), 64–6. 35 ONS (2022j), 2.

36 ONS (2014a), 8; the numbers were slightly lower in 2013 (nearly 95,000), the last year in which these data were collected.

37 Ibid. 38 See 2.2.1. 39 ONS (2019b), 7. 40 ONS (2022j), 5.

41 ONS (2019b), fig. 4.

42 Clarke and Berrington (1999); Kiernan and Mueller (1998); Coleman and Glenn (2010); Beaujouan and Ní Bhrolcháin (2011).

commission of which render the 'guilty' spouse vulnerable to the penalty of being divorced on the other's application. Alternatively (and strictly not 'fault'-based), the grounds for divorce could reflect some conduct on the part of one spouse that justifies the other's request to divorce. This to some extent reflects a contractual view of marriage,[43] the guilty party's breach excusing the other from continued performance of the contract and entitling that party to some form of compensation. But, undermining the contract analogy, the couple do not decide what constitutes a breach: that is determined for them by the law of divorce (though it is for the innocent party, once a breach has occurred, to decide whether to instigate divorce). A fault/conduct-based law also performs an exhortatory function, establishing a moral/behavioural code for marriage. However, a primary driver of the DDSA 2020 was the problem with administering fault/conduct-based divorce.[44]

3.3.2 'EASIER' OR 'HARDER' DIVORCE AND SUPPORTING THE INSTITUTION OF MARRIAGE

A perennial theme is whether the law makes divorce too easy or too hard, and whether any reform would make divorce easier or harder. This is linked to the degree of support that the law appears to offer the institution of marriage: easy divorce is said to undermine it, hard divorce to support it. These political debates continue despite Otto Kahn-Freund's observation over 50 years ago that 'it is a hopeless quest to promote the stability of marriage by making divorce "difficult" and . . . the problem is far more complex and more profound than the crude question whether divorce should be a little more or a little less "easy".'[45] Davis and Murch expand on this theme:

G. Davis and M. Murch, *Grounds for Divorce* (Oxford: Clarendon Press, 1998), 148

It is tempting to view this debate in light of a liberal/conservative battleground, with the liberals seeking 'easier' divorce through shorter time periods or the abandonment of fault, whilst the conservatives struggle to maintain some disincentive to ill-considered termination of marriage through longer time periods or the maintenance of fault. But 'fault' and time constraints, whilst they may each be thought to make divorce more difficult, make it more difficult *in different ways*—and for different people. In other words, there are arguments for and against delay; there are also arguments for and against fault; but they are not the *same* arguments and they should not be lumped together under the heading of 'easier' or 'more difficult' divorce.

As Davis and Murch have explained, divorce is a difficult process for different, complex reasons, which are not coterminous. For example, a law that allows a spouse to obtain a divorce in under six months because of the other's adultery would be rendered considerably 'harder' if fault were replaced by a uniform one-year separation requirement. On the other hand, such a reform would make divorce 'easier' for a spouse who has to be separated for two years before divorce is permitted. But that same reform would be 'harder'

[43] See discussion at 2.4.1.
[44] See 3.5.3, and compare Rowthorn (1999) and Ellman (1997).
[45] Kahn-Freund (1967), 181.

for those individuals if it required them to use the one-year period to resolve all issues regarding their children and finances. All of this overlooks the emotional pain of divorce, even for those who ostensibly desire it, which the law can do little to alleviate.[46] Divorce in that sense is never 'easy'.

It is often said that the law of divorce should seek to support the institution of marriage, but again what this implies for the ease or difficulty of divorce is ambiguous. A restrictive divorce law, for example requiring proof of grave fault by the respondent, could be said to support marriage by emphasizing the seriousness of matrimonial obligations and requiring people to remain married, however dissatisfied they may be, unless one partner commits a relevant offence. But the same law could be said to undermine marriage by insisting that marriages of poor quality be upheld, even if the parties have long since separated. By contrast, an 'easy' divorce law that released those who were dissatisfied with their marriages could be said to support the institution by reserving marriage and its legal consequences for 'good quality' relationships.[47] Might such a law encourage people to adopt a 'throwaway' approach to marriage and give up too soon? But is the law the, or even a, principal determinant of people's behaviour in this arena? And, if it is, how might it best seek to influence them?

M. Richards, 'Private Worlds and Public Intentions – the Role of the State at Divorce', in A. Bainham and D. Pearl (eds), *Frontiers of Family Law* (London: Wiley, 1995), 17

Those who argue for harder divorce seem to have an exaggerated view of the power of the law to control people's domestic living arrangements. Their model seems to be that of a sluice gate which stands between the married and the divorced. The wider this sluice is opened, the more of the married that will become divorced. Such a view suggests that it is only the difficulty of getting out that keeps people married.

3.3.3 CAN DIVORCE LAW AFFECT MARITAL AND DIVORCING BEHAVIOUR?

Martin Richards's words bring us to our next theme. Commentators disagree on whether divorce law should simply provide a mechanism for individuals to terminate their marriage, or whether it can or should go further, seeking to influence relationship behaviour. We have noted the arguments about whether liberal divorce causes more marriages to fail. But other questions arise. Can and should divorce law be based on fault or (more broadly) conduct to deter whatever (bad) behaviour gives grounds for divorce? Does divorce law affect parties' willingness to invest in their marriages, easier divorce reducing parties' reliance on marriage? If divorce is hard, might some be dissuaded from marrying at all? If so, would that be a good or bad thing? Can the law rescue couples from divorce by helping them to save saveable marriages? It has been said that the notion that divorce law can save individual marriages (as opposed to the institution more generally) is one that 'conventional wisdom has long firmly rejected'.[48] Nevertheless, the idea that something should be done to 'save saveable marriages'

46 See Law Com (1990), paras 3.46–3.47; LCD (1993), 6.51–6.53.

47 Cf *Reiterbund v Reiterbund* [1974] 1 WLR 788; *Vervaeke v Smith* [1983] 1 AC 145; Smart (2000), 371.

48 Cretney (1996a), 45.

has persistent political appeal.[49] The law might also encourage parties to divorce in a particular manner—or at least make it easier for them to do so in a way that limits any bitterness and hostility. Government publications in recent decades have emphasized 'responsibility' on divorce and in dealing with the consequences of relationship breakdown.[50] The concern here is not with responsibility to respect the lifelong commitment of marriage or a guilty party's duty to accept responsibility (blame) for its breakdown. Rather, the new concept of responsibility requires *both* parties to 'divorce responsibly';[51] in particular, 'responsible' couples resolve their differences by way of mediation rather than via lawyers and the courts. However, whether law can steer parties' behaviour in this manner is questionable. Evidence that such attempts would fail caused major divorce reforms to be abandoned,[52] and legal aid reforms in 2013 prompted mediation numbers to plummet rather than rise as hoped.[53]

3.3.4 A LEGAL OR NON-LEGAL APPROACH?

While terminating spousal status is inevitably a legal process, the legal system need not have a monopoly over resolving the practical issues that arise on divorce (regarding children and financial settlements) or over determining whether the spouses' relationship has ended. Non-legal disciplines may have roles here: education and information provision, therapeutic intervention such as marriage counselling and social work, and mediation[54] may be able to perform some of those functions that the state is keen to pursue but which the *legal system* cannot fulfil. In particular, the legal system may be unable to save marriages or to help parties to cope psychologically with divorce. But the law could provide a framework for the delivery and funding of such services when divorce is sought, or earlier. Whether the legal system can help couples to cooperate in resolving the practical consequences is hotly contested by lawyers and mediators.[55] Non-legal approaches to relationship support and breakdown have become increasingly prominent. However, the current substantive law of divorce, experienced by most couples as a fault-based process, sits somewhat uneasily alongside the outlook of non-legal disciplines and the forward-looking focus of the law governing financial remedies and arrangements for children on divorce.

3.3.5 REGULATION OR REGULARIZATION?

Divorce law can have more or less substantial roles, described by John Eekelaar as 'regulation' and 'regularization'. Regularization:

> accepts, fatalistically, that separation and divorce will occur whatever the legal process does. It wishes to ensure that that process does not add to its harms, and leaves it largely to the people involved to settle the consequences. The legal process is therefore largely confined to ensuring that cases are processed efficiently and formalities attended to properly.[56]

[49] E.g. LCD (1993), (1995). See Hasson (2006).
[50] LCD (1993), (1995); HO (1998); MOJ (2010), (2019a).
[51] Reece (2003). [52] See 3.6.1. [53] See 1.2.7.
[54] Not to be confused with counselling and reconciliation: see 1.2.7. [55] Ibid.
[56] Eekelaar (1991b), 142.

A divorce law aligned with these tenets of regularization suggests a relatively straightforward, and entails a low-cost administrative rather than judicial, process, which could be instigated by both parties, or even by one of them. Divorce would thus be the product of a private decision. There might be disputes about *consequences* of divorce, for example regarding children or finances, in which the state might assert an interest to protect vulnerable family members or the public purse. But judicial determination of these ancillary issues would not detract from the essentially private, administrative nature of the underlying divorce.

By contrast, 'regulation' implies some more substantial role for the law, imposing restrictions on divorce that reflect the seriousness of that step and, by implication, the importance of marriage to the welfare of the parties, any children of the marriage, and society at large. The precise *nature* of that role and those restrictions would depend upon the state's view of marriage and its interest in it. But it would be more paternalistic, interventionist, and directive than mere 'regularization'. As we shall see in this chapter, the role of divorce law in England and Wales has been characterized both by regulation and regularization throughout history.

3.4 A BRIEF HISTORY OF DIVORCE LAW TO 1969

Until 1857, divorce by way of court order terminating marriage did not exist.[57] The ecclesiastical courts issued decrees of nullity and various remedies short of divorce. A valid marriage could only be ended by Private Act of Parliament, a complex route open only to the wealthy.[58] Following a Royal Commission, the ecclesiastical courts' jurisdiction was replaced by a new civil court with the power to dissolve marriages. Under the Matrimonial Causes Act 1857, divorce could be obtained by the husband on the ground of his wife's adultery, and by the wife on the ground that her husband had been guilty of incestuous adultery, bigamy with adultery, rape (of someone other than the wife[59]), sodomy, bestiality, or adultery coupled either with desertion for two years or with cruelty. The gender inequality persisted until 1923, when wives were permitted to petition on grounds of adultery alone.[60] Adultery was effectively the sole ground for divorce until 1937:

Law Commission, *Facing the Future: A Discussion Paper on the Ground for Divorce*, Law Com No 170 (London: HMSO, 1988a)

2.1 Before the Divorce Reform Act 1969, a divorce could only be obtained [under the Matrimonial Causes Act 1937] by proving that the respondent had committed a matrimonial offence (the only material offences were adultery, cruelty and desertion for three years). A petitioner who was himself guilty of such an offence, or had somehow contributed to the offence of the other, or had condoned it, might be refused relief.[61] No divorce could be

[57] For the long history, see Stone (1990) and Cretney (2003a), Part II; for analysis of divorce data over time: Haskey (2018b).

[58] Probert (2011a).

[59] At that time, husbands could not be guilty of raping their wives: see 4.2.3.

[60] Probert (1999); Russell (2018).

[61] The law barred divorce (absolutely or on a discretionary basis) where the petitioner had colluded with the respondent in drafting the petition, condoned or connived in the respondent's offence, or had also committed a matrimonial offence: see Cretney (2003a), 176–7.

granted within three years of marriage, unless special leave was given on the ground that the petitioner would suffer exceptional hardship or that the respondent was guilty of exceptional depravity.

2.2 Since the 1950s there had been increasing disillusionment with the operation of the fault-based law.[62] It was clear that there was no real barrier to consensual divorce where both parties wanted it and one was prepared to commit, or perhaps appear to commit, a matrimonial offence to supply the necessary ground [though technically collusion was an absolute bar to divorce until 1963]. On the other hand, where parties were not prepared to resort to such expedients, there was often no remedy, even though the marriage had irretrievably broken down. It was argued by the proponents of reform that the court was in no position to allocate blame; that in many cases both parties were at fault, and that matrimonial offences were often merely symptomatic of the breakdown of the marriage rather than the cause. However, the majority of the Royal Commission on Marriage and Divorce (the Morton Commission of 1956) affirmed the matrimonial offence as the sole basis of divorce because they saw this as the only means to ensure the stability of the institution of marriage. Three attempts, in Private Members' Bills, to introduce a provision allowing for divorce after long periods of separation were unsuccessful. Finally, the publication in 1966 of the report of the Archbishop of Canterbury's Group [Mortimer Commission], entitled *Putting Asunder—A Divorce Law for Contemporary Society*, paved the way for reform. The report found the existing law concentrated exclusively on making findings of past delinquencies, whilst ignoring the current viability of the marriage. It therefore recommended that the matrimonial offence be abolished and be replaced by the principle of breakdown as the sole ground for divorce. It was envisaged that the court would determine whether the marriage had broken down after considering all the evidence.

2.3 The Lord Chancellor referred *Putting Asunder* to the Law Commission, whose response was published later in the same year, entitled Reform of the Grounds of Divorce—the Field of Choice. The Commission agreed with the Archbishop's Group's criticisms of the existing law. In particular, it found that the need to prove a matrimonial offence caused unnecessary bitterness and distress to the parties and their children. The law did not accord with social reality, in that many spouses who could not obtain a divorce simply left the "empty shells" of their marriages and set up "stable illicit unions" with new partners.[63] The Commission also agreed that where both parties wanted to end the marriage, divorce was easily available if they were prepared to commit or appear to commit a matrimonial offence. The Commission considered the objectives for a good divorce law to be:

(i) To buttress, rather than to undermine, the stability of marriage; and
(ii) When, regrettably, a marriage has irretrievably broken down, to enable the empty legal shell to be destroyed with the maximum fairness, and the minimum bitterness, distress and humiliation. . . .

2.4 Thus, both bodies agreed that the fault principle was unsatisfactory and that the law should be reformed to allow marriages which had irretrievably broken down to be dissolved in a humane fashion. The difficulty, of course, was how to identify those marriages which had irretrievably broken down. The Law Commission did not favour the solution advocated by the Archbishop's Group. First, it considered the proposed inquest impracticable partly because breakdown was not a justiciable issue. Secondly, it was concerned that such an inquest into the conduct of the parties in order to determine breakdown would cause unnecessary bitterness and humiliation and prevent the marital ties being dissolved with decency and

[62] See Law Com (1966), paras 19 et seq. [63] Ibid, paras 33 et seq.

dignity. After consultations between the various interested bodies, a compromise solution was reached whereby breakdown would become the sole ground for divorce, but would be inferred from the existence of one of a number of facts rather than by judicial inquest. This solution was enacted in the Divorce Reform Act 1969.

As well as summarising key points in the evolution of divorce law in the last century, in this extract the Law Commission also revisits its assertion of what 'good' divorce law looks like. These objectives for divorce—to buttress the stability of marriage, to maximize fairness, and to minimize bitterness—were pursued by the Divorce Reform Act 1969, which was later absorbed into the MCA 1973. The MCA 1973 is where the present law (set out at 3.7) is found, yet now looks quite different from when it was first enacted. It is that original iteration of the MCA 1973 that we explore next.

3.5 THE MATRIMONIAL CAUSES ACT 1973: AS IT WAS BEFORE 2022

The present law of divorce is found in the MCA 1973, and so understanding how this Act has changed is vital in order to appreciate the significance of its reform. After all, bar amendments introduced by the Marriage (Same Sex Couples) Act 2013 to facilitate divorce between same-sex couples, the substantive divorce law under the MCA 1973 remained virtually the same for more than 50 years. We first look briefly, in this section, at the MCA 1973 as it was when it was introduced and (at 3.6) why it was reformed, before turning at 3.7 and 3.8 to the substantive law under which a divorce must now be obtained.

3.5.1 THE FORMER SUBSTANTIVE LAW

A divorce petition (i.e. application for divorce) under the former law could be initiated by only one of the parties—the petitioner. Thus the law required one spouse (the petitioner) to divorce the other (the respondent), even where both parties wanted to end the marriage. The MCA introduced one ground for divorce: that the marriage has irretrievably broken down. This is still the sole ground for divorce today. Yet while irretrievable breakdown is not now fault- or conduct-based, under the former substantive law the petitioner could not simply assert that their marriage had irretrievably broken down, however clear that may have been. It was also necessary to prove one of five 'facts'.[64]

Matrimonial Causes Act 1973, s 1

(1) . . . [A] petition for divorce may be presented to the court by either party to a marriage on the ground that the marriage has broken down irretrievably.

(2) The court hearing a petition for divorce shall not hold the marriage to have broken down irretrievably unless the petitioner satisfies the court of one or more of the following facts, that is to say—

[64] CPA 2004, s 44.

(a) that the respondent has committed adultery and the petitioner finds it intolerable to live with the respondent;
(b) that the respondent has behaved in such a way that the petitioner cannot reasonably be expected to live with the respondent;
(c) that the respondent has deserted the petitioner for a continuous period of at least two years immediately preceding the presentation of the petition;
(d) that the parties to the marriage have lived apart for a continuous period of at least two years immediately preceding the presentation of the petition (hereafter in this Act referred, to as "two years' separation") and the respondent consents to a decree being granted;
(e) that the parties to the marriage have lived apart for a continuous period of at least five years immediately preceding the presentation of the petition (hereafter in this Act referred to as "five years' separation").

Three of the five facts under the former law—adultery, desertion, and behaviour by the respondent—*appeared* to be principally fault-based. However, as we shall see, the behaviour fact could apply in situations that clearly involved no fault by the respondent, and none of the facts relied on needed to have caused the marriage's demise. So in that sense, even a spouse who had committed adultery might not always have been regarded as being at fault, and the spouse applying for divorce need not have had 'clean hands'.[65] And so it is more accurate to describe these first three facts as 'conduct-based',[66] though it is clear that many—indeed most—divorcing couples experienced the current law as if it were fault-based, as we shall see when looking at the criticisms of these facts (at 3.5.3).[67] The other two facts—based on separation, for two years if the respondent consented to the divorce, for five years without that consent—were very clearly no-fault facts (and for ease we shall refer to them as such). The only difference of *substance* between divorce and civil partnership dissolution was that civil partnership could not be dissolved on the basis of 'adultery', though sexual infidelity by a civil partner would readily have satisfied the 'behaviour' fact.[68]

3.5.2 THE FORMER PROCEDURE FOR DIVORCE

As well as understanding the *substantive* legal basis on which divorce could be obtained, it is essential also to appreciate how the former divorce *procedure* worked, because this provides important context for understanding many of the criticisms of that law. Once the petition was served, the respondent had to decide whether they wished to defend it. This was a key stage in divorces under the original MCA 1973 law, as the procedure—and so the experience of divorce -would (after 1977) be very different depending on whether the petition was contested (defended) or uncontested. Pre-1977, however, all cases notionally went to 'trial'.

From 1857 (until 2022), statute required divorce judges to perform an inquisitorial function.[69] When reform was being considered during the 1960s, the Archbishop's Group desired a thorough judicial investigation into the end of couples' relationships. For practical reasons,

[65] Contrast the old discretionary bars to divorce: Cretney (2003a), 188–95.
[66] *Owens v Owens* [2018] UKSC 41, [48].
[67] See Trinder et al (2017).
[68] Cf 2.7.6 on the omission of consummation from the nullity grounds for civil partnership and same-sex marriage.
[69] See generally Booth Committee (1985), paras 2.13 et seq and Eekelaar (1994a).

that approach was rejected.[70] However, although not required to conduct a wide-ranging inquiry into the various causes of the claimed irretrievable breakdown, the judges still had a limited inquisitorial role:[71]

Matrimonial Causes Act 1973, s 1

(3) On a petition for divorce it shall be the duty of the court to inquire, so far as it reasonably can, into the facts[72] alleged by the petitioner and into any facts alleged by the respondent.
(4) If the court is satisfied on the evidence of any [of the five facts set out in s 1(2)], then, unless it is satisfied on all the evidence that the marriage has not broken down irretrievably, it shall, subject to section 5 [now removed by the DDSA 2020], grant a decree of divorce.

Even pre-1969 when the concept of the matrimonial offence still prevailed, the reality of divorce trials, which were heard in the High Court, had long since failed to live up to the image projected by the substantive law.

C. Gibson, *Dissolving Wedlock* (London: Routledge, 1994), 175–80

It is not known whether the guardianship of High Court divorce judges made couples more decorous within their marital relationships. But it is clear that the vast majority of divorces were undefended petitions which were speedily processed by Special Divorce Commissioners masquerading as High Court judges.[73] Undefended cases, as Mr Harvey QC explained in a caustic exposition of the post-war divorce procedure, 'works almost on the slot machine principle'. . . . Sir Hartley Shawcross, the Attorney-General, recalled to the House of Commons in 1951: 'One used to handle these undefended cases at the rate of about one in two minutes . . . it did not impress me at the time that there was any real principle operating in practice in the administration of our divorce laws'.

When the Divorce Reform Act 1969 (later the MCA 1973) came into force, that inquiry ostensibly remained the function of the senior judiciary, and appellate decisions emphasized the importance of judges making factual findings even in undefended cases, rather than merely rubber-stamping the petition.[74] However, the distance between substance and procedure would soon become greater with the introduction of what, until 2011, was called the 'special procedure' for *uncontested* divorces.[75]

[By] 1977 the divorce process had been changed into a private arrangement validated within an administrative setting. This most radical transformation in the approach to, and meaning of, divorce took place without serious Parliamentary debate. The new process was essentially

[70] Law Com (1966), paras 60 et seq. [71] CPA 2004, s 44(2).
[72] *Darnton v Darnton* [2006] EWCA Civ 1081, [8]–[9].
[73] County court judges had been designated as High Court judges for the purposes of granting divorces locally to help process the otherwise unmanageable numbers of cases.
[74] E.g. *Santos v Santos* [1972] Fam 247, 263–4.
[75] See Black et al (2015), ch 9; *Pounds v Pounds* [1994] 1 FLR 775, 778.

> the outcome of a cost-saving exercise rather than a purposeful Parliamentary rethinking of what the legislative, administrative and social needs of a modern divorce policy should be.
>
> When introduced in 1973 the new arrangements were properly termed 'special procedure', for availability was restricted to petitioners without dependent children who sought divorce on the fact of two years' . . . separation. Two further extensions have meant that since April 1977 all undefended divorces are dealt with by special procedure. And this, in fact, is the general everyday procedure used by 99.9 per cent of all petitioners. The parties are not required to appear before a judge unless . . . there are ancillary matters to be resolved. The district judge examines the papers in his office for both conformity to administrative requirements and assurance that the petition and its supporting affidavit evidence meets the substantive requirements for divorce. When satisfied on these two counts the district judge certifies his approval. This is the crucial decision, for with this certificate to hand the divorce judge must pronounce the decree nisi [provisional decree of divorce].

As Gibson goes on to explain, the extension of what had been a 'special' procedure to all undefended cases, regardless of the fact relied on, effected a 'fundamental change . . . to the administration and regulation of divorce':

> The Bishop of Durham could write to *The Times* (4 April 1977):
>
>> I am disturbed at the implications of divorce by post, and even more disturbed by the apparently casual manner in which such a fundamental change has been made . . . To avoid public action tilts the concept of marriage breakdown dangerously in the direction of divorce by consent, and in doing so widens the gulf between Christian and purely contractual understandings of marriage. I believe it would be an immeasurable loss if those who, from both sides, wish to widen this gulf were given encouragement to do so by a piece of administrative convenience.
>
> But executive endorsement of special procedure was not governed by a radical belief that divorce should now be seen as an essentially administrative process that no longer required a court hearing. Rather, at a time of economic crisis, causing the Treasury to insist on major cuts in public spending and the government to announce that there was to be little or no increase in expenditure on legal aid for the next five years, the Lord Chancellor concluded that there was only one area within civil legal aid where sizeable savings could justifiably be made. This was the field of divorce . . .
>
> When Lord Chancellor Elwyn-Jones announced in 1976 the extension of the special procedure to all undefended divorces he also declared that legal aid would no longer be available in such proceedings. The rationale behind this change was that as determination of the undefended petition would not now require a court hearing there was no longer need for a lawyer's attendance at court. However, legal aid would still be available where the need for a hearing arose for which legal representation was necessary. This covered contested petitions and such matters as disputes over ancillary questions involving maintenance, property or arrangements for children. Ancillary proceedings were, in the words of the Lord Chancellor, 'the areas of real contest between the parties to divorce proceedings today, not the question whether the petitioner should get a decree' . . .
>
> The divorce process has been radically transformed from a public judicial inquest titularly undertaken by High Court judges to a private administrative ratification of the spouses' decision to divorce.

Defended cases continued to involve a trial—but these were increasingly rare. Indeed, given the near-universal application of the procedure (because the vast majority of cases were *uncontested*), the label 'special' was a 'complete misnomer',[76] and it was dropped from the rules.[77] It was said that the objectives of this procedure for undefended divorces were 'simplicity, speed and economy', so that, whilst the essentials of the petition must be satisfactory and its contents proved, 'there should be no room for over-meticulousness and over-technicality in approach'; substance should be preferred over form.[78] It was also said that 'the judge's duty pursuant to s 1(3) . . . to enquire, so far as he reasonably can, into the facts alleged by the petitioner is . . . emasculated almost into invisibility'.[79] The rule change meant that the s 1(3) duty was ordinarily performed by court officers who checked the paperwork,[80] rather than by a judge,[81] and the work was parcelled out to a limited number of Regional Divorce Centres for bulk-processing, rather than in local courts, rendering the procedure even less 'special' and more administrative than ever. The judge in most cases just formally granted the decrees on the back of the officials' assessment of the forms. This made the reality of undefended divorce very different from what the 'law on the books' might suggest about how divorce law was intended to operate, as the findings from a major empirical study of divorce practice underlined (see further section 4 of that report):

L. Trinder et al, *Finding Fault? Divorce Law and Practice in England and Wales*
(London: Nuffield Foundation, 2017), 13 and 71

We found from our case file study, observations and interviews that scrutiny is thorough, but it is primarily an administrative process, not a judicial inquiry into the truth. Indeed, scrutiny is generally no longer done by judges but by legally-trained legal advisers employed by HMCTS. In the four minutes or so available for each file, scrutiny is focused on ensuring the paperwork is completed correctly and that the petitioner has described circumstances that meet the requirements of one of the five 'Facts'. Scrutiny in practice does not (cannot, in reality) include whether that Fact alleged is true. In none of the 592 cases in our file or observation samples did the court raise questions about whether the petition was true. Only 1% of file sample cases failed to make progress on substantive legal grounds, but because the unrepresented petitioner could not understand the law, not because of doubts about the contents of the petition. . . .

In practice, the petitioner's allegations are taken at face value in undefended cases. This is so even where the respondent denies or rebuts the allegations, as occurred in 37% of behaviour petitions in our file study, without formally defending the case. All rebuttals are ignored if the case is undefended. . . .

It is not clear, however, that that is what Parliament had in mind when formulating section 1(3), even with the let-out clause requiring courts "to inquire, so far as it reasonably can." Nor does what is in effect the rewriting of section 1(3) so that the respondent's allegations are investigated *in defended cases only* appear to meet what Parliament would appear to have intended. The statute makes no distinction between defended and undefended cases. [Emphasis in original]

[76] *Day v Day* [1980] Fam 29, 32, per Ormrod LJ.
[77] See Family Procedure Rules 2010 (FPR 2010), r 7.20(2).
[78] *R v Nottingham County Court, ex parte Byers* [1985] 1 WLR 403, 406.
[79] *Bhaji v Chauhan* [2003] 2 FLR 485, 487.
[80] The petition itself may now be submitted online: <www.gov.uk/divorce/file-for-divorce>. For criticism, see Herring (2012).
[81] The Justices' Clerks and Assistants Rules 2014, SI 2014/603.

Indeed, Stephen Cretney had earlier suggested that 'in relation to divorce, procedural change has over the years often had more impact than changes in the substantive law', and certainly affected public perceptions of the law.[82] As Trinder et al's findings showed, the 'special' procedure for undefended divorce necessarily radically reduced the courts' ability to make any effective inquiry in these divorces and so reduced the influence of the substantive law.[83] Of course, the substantive law was not *irrelevant* to undefended cases, as the evidence submitted had to fulfil the substantive requirements. However, only in *defended* cases did the judge have room to operate as envisaged by the case law. In undefended cases, divorce was therefore far more easily obtained than the face of the legislation and case law suggested it could (or should) be.

Thus, English law had reached an apparently 'hypocritical compromise',[84] whereby the law on the face of the statute promised state control over divorce whilst the law in practice deprived the state of any real possibility of control in most cases, and where the reality for many couples was, in effect, divorce by mutual consent—or even on unilateral demand.

3.5.3 DEFECTS OF THE FORMER LAW

Before the passage of the MCA 1973, divorce was only available on the basis of adultery, cruelty, incurable insanity, and desertion. The introduction of a sole ground of irretrievable breakdown—and its supporting facts—was significant, because, while those old grounds were echoed in the first three 'facts' listed in s 1, the new law allowed a petitioner to establish the new sole ground by proving they had been separated for a specified period of time (depending upon whether the respondent consented to the divorce petition). But the MCA 1973 as originally enacted had not broken entirely with the regulatory aspects of divorce law that had characterized the old law, precisely because it required marital breakdown to be framed in terms deemed acceptable by law. If the parties did not wish to be married any longer, they had to separate and wait; if they could not separate or did not wish to wait, one spouse would need to draft a petition based on the respondent's conduct. These limitations are perhaps unsurprising given that this law was drafted in the 1960s, at a time when divorce on demand would have been unthinkable.[85] But in the decades that followed, it became increasingly apparent that the substantive law of the original MCA 1973 was often exacerbating an already difficult situation for families, while the process of proving irretrievable breakdown did not match the realities of relationship breakdown. This was exemplified by 'false' narratives on divorce petitions identified by research, as well as the small number of cases where a divorce petition was challenged by the respondent in court. As Miles et al noted, the 'Act itself was irretrievably broken'.[86]

Indeed, the defects of this system were catalogued many times: by the Law Commission,[87] the government,[88] and academic researchers.[89] The criticisms reported by the Law

[82] Cretney (2003a), 165. The different procedures under the Divorce (Scotland) Act 1976 are probably a cause of most Scottish divorces' reliance on separation rather than fault-based facts: Law Com (1990), para 3.17; Trinder et al (2017), 151–2.

[83] See also Booth Committee (1985), para 2.8.

[84] Antokolskaia (2020), 94.

[85] Indeed, for the Morton Commission, even divorce by mutual consent was anathema: Royal Commission on Marriage and Divorce (1956).

[86] Miles et al (2022), 15.

[87] Most fully, Law Com (1988a), Part III.

[88] LCD (1993), (1995).

[89] E.g. Davis and Murch (1988); Eekelaar (1991b); Gibson (1994); Trinder et al (2017); Trinder and Sefton (2018).

Commission in its 1990 report echoed findings 30 years later in the research of Trinder et al. Extracts from Trinder et al's findings are interpolated in the following extended passage from the Law Commission report. These criticisms were six-fold, that the law was: (i) confusing and misleading; (ii) discriminatory and unjust; (iii) distorted the parties' bargaining positions; (iv) provoked unnecessary hostility and bitterness; (v) did nothing to save the marriage; and (vi) could make things worse for children.

3.5.3.a The law was confusing and misleading

Law Commission, *The Ground for Divorce*, Law Com No 192 (London: HMSO, 1990)

2.8 There is a considerable gap between theory and practice, which can only lead to confusion and lack of respect for the law. Indeed, some would call it downright dishonest. There are several aspects to this. First, the law tells couples that the only ground for divorce is irretrievable breakdown, which apparently does not involve fault. But next it provides that this can only be shown by one of five "facts", three of which apparently do involve fault. There are several recent examples of divorces being refused despite the fact that it was clear to all concerned that the marriage had indeed irretrievably broken down. The hardship and pain involved for both parties can be very great.

2.9 Secondly, the fact which is alleged in order to prove the breakdown need not have any connection with the real reason why the marriage broke down. The parties may, for example, have separated because they have both formed different associations, but agree to present a petition based on the behaviour of one of them, because neither wishes their partner to be publicly named [see MCA 1973, s 49]. The sex, class and other difference in the use of the facts make it quite clear that these are chosen for a variety of reasons which need have nothing to do with the reality of the case. This is a major source of confusion, especially for respondents who do not agree with the fact alleged. As has long been said, "whatever the client's reason for wanting divorce, the lawyer's function is to discover grounds."

2.10 The behaviour fact is particularly confusing. It is often referred to as "unreasonable behaviour", which suggests blameworthiness or outright cruelty on the part of the respondent; but this has been called a "linguistic trap", because the behaviour itself need be neither unreasonable nor blameworthy: rather, its effect on the petitioner must be such that it is unreasonable to expect him or her to go on living with the respondent. . . .

2.11 Finally, and above all, the present law pretends that the court is conducting an inquiry into the facts of the matter, when in the vast majority of cases it can do no such thing [owing to the procedure for undefended divorce]. This is not the fault of the court, nor is it probably any more of a problem under the present law and procedure than it was under the old. It may be more difficult to evaluate the effect of the respondent's behaviour from the papers than from the petitioner's account in the witness box, but it has always been difficult to get at the truth in an undefended case. Moreover, the system still allows, even encourages, the parties to lie, or at least to exaggerate, in order to get what they want. The bogus adultery cases of the past may have all but disappeared, but their modern equivalents are the "flimsy" behaviour petition or the pretence that the parties have been living apart for a full two years. In that "wider field which includes considerations of truth, the sacredness of oaths, and the integrity of professional practice", the present law is just as objectionable as the old.

As the Law Commission asserted, in addition to the 'linguistic trap' of the behaviour fact, parties' experience of the law was doubtless all the more confusing given that the law did *not* require that the 'fact' relied on be a cause of the irretrievable breakdown. Quite simply, once the fact was proved, the court had to find the ground made out unless satisfied that the marriage had *not* irretrievably broken down.[90]

L. Trinder et al, *Finding Fault? Divorce Law and Practice in England and Wales* (London: Nuffield Foundation, 2017), 36

> Given the complexity of the law, and the inclusion of the three fault Facts, it is not surprising that lay people can and do assume that there should be a causal relationship established between the reason for the breakdown and the Fact relied upon. This misunderstanding has consequences. . . . [S]ome petitioners with a literalist orientation [wrongly assuming that the Fact cited must be the cause of the breakdown] will seek to establish their version of events, at considerable emotional and financial cost, on the basis that that is their understanding of what the law means. Similarly, some respondents will be angered by particulars that do not reflect their view of why the relationship broke down. In both cases, the misunderstanding of the law and what the law requires has the potential to increase conflict.

The 'special' procedure for uncontested cases (see 3.5.2) also meant that the petitioner's account of the respondent's behaviour went largely unchecked. As Liz Trinder found:

L. Trinder, 'Telling Tales? Establishing Irretrievable Breakdown under the Matrimonial Causes Act 1973', in J. Miles, D. Monk, and R. Probert (eds), *Fifty Years of the Divorce Reform Act* (Oxford: Hart Publishing 2022), 184

> [T]he few minutes of scrutiny time per case were focused on checking that the identities of the parties were correctly established and the minimum ingredients of one of the five facts had been described, not whether the particulars were true, or even plausible.

In other words, while the petitioner was required to produce an account of the respondent's behaviour to fit the legal requirements for divorce, this process was largely administrative and lacking in scrutiny. It is therefore unsurprising that Trinder found that in cases where the respondent did not defend the divorce, the court was only too willing to accept 'boilerplate accounts of marriage breakdown' which could have been generated at random by computer software.[91] Members of the judiciary criticized this process as lacking 'intellectual honesty'.[92] This also created a disconnect between undefended divorces, which were seemingly no more than an administrative process, and defended divorces, which did require scrutiny.

[90] MCA 1973, s 1(4); *Stevens v Stevens* [1979] 1 WLR 885. See further Trinder and Sefton (2018), 7.3 and 7.5 in relation to defended divorces.

[91] Trinder (2022), 195.

[92] *Owens v Owens* [2017] EWCA Civ 182, [94].

L. Trinder et al, *Finding Fault? Divorce Law and Practice in England and Wales* (London: Nuffield Foundation, 2017), 36, 54

The other area of lay misunderstanding relates to the scrutiny process. In practice, the inevitable logistical constraints of processing many tens of thousands of petitions each year and philosophical shifts away from fault mean that the scrutiny process is not able to test the truth of allegations. . . . The public are largely unaware of this, and not unfairly assume that real judicial inquiry into the ending of the marriage will be undertaken. Again, this public misperception, based on the gap between the law in the books and the law in action, does have consequences, including increased anxiety amongst those who worry (probably needlessly) that their reasons will not pass what they imagine to be the judicial scrutiny. . . .

The theory underpinning the use of fault as a basis for divorce is that petitions are an accurate account of who or what was responsible for the breakdown of the marriage . . . What the law in fact requires, as well as the practice, are different. Rather than accurate accounts of the primary reason for the breakdown of the marriage, petitions are probably best read as narratives produced to achieve a divorce. Even if the parties were to agree on what had caused the breakdown, and our opinion poll suggested that will not often be the case, then the reason for the breakdown is just one of the potential factors that will shape the petition. Other factors, including circumstantial factors such as the need for speed, the desire to reduce conflict and understanding of how the law works in practice can be equally, if not more, important.

The elaborate and expensive charades of the hotel divorce are no longer necessary to secure a divorce. They have instead been replaced by a far more prosaic gaming of the system where behaviour has become the Fact of choice available in (almost) any circumstance and where the petition is produced using tried and tested generic formulas designed to do the job. Yet if the petition is not a broadly accurate reflection of the reasons for the marriage breakdown, it is open to question what purpose fault is serving and what value the parties or the state accrue from what can be the ritualistic production of particulars.

3.5.3.b The law was discriminatory and unjust

Law Commission, *The Ground for Divorce*, Law Com No 192 (London: HMSO, 1990)

2.12 83% of respondents to our public opinion survey thought it a good feature of the present law that couples who do not want to put the blame on either of them do not have to do so, but these couples have to have lived apart for at least two years. This can be extremely difficult to achieve without either substantial resources of one's own, or the co-operation of the other spouse at the outset, or an ouster order from the court.[93] . . . The law does recognise that it is possible to live apart by conducting two separate households under the same roof. In practice, this is impossible in most ordinary houses or flats, especially where there are children: it inevitably requires the couple to co-operate in a most unnatural and artificial

[93] See 4.5.3 on occupation orders under the FLA 1996.

lifestyle. It is unjust and discriminatory of the law to provide for a civilised "no-fault" ground for divorce which, in practice, is denied to a large section of the population. A young mother with children living in a council house is obliged to rely upon fault whether or not she wants to do so and irrespective of the damage it may do.

2.13 The fault-based facts can also be intrinsically unjust. "Justice" in this context has traditionally been taken to mean the accurate allocation of blameworthiness for the breakdown of the marriage. Desertion is the only fact which stills attempts to do this . . . Desertion, however, is hardly ever used, because its place has been taken by the two separation facts. A finding of adultery or behaviour certainly need not mean that the respondent is any more to blame than the petitioner for the breakdown of the marriage. . . .

2.14 This inherent potential for injustice is compounded by the practical problems of defending or bringing a cross-petition of one's own. It is extremely difficult to resist or counter allegations of behaviour. Defending them requires time, money and emotional energy far beyond the resources of most respondents. Even if the parties are prepared to go through with this, what would be the point? If the marriage is capable of being saved, a long-fought defended divorce, in which every incident or characteristic that might amount to behaviour is dragged up and examined in detail, is not going to do this. It can only serve to make matters worse and to consume resources which are often desperately needed elsewhere, particularly if there are children. . . . Small wonder, then, that lawyers advise their clients not to defend and that their clients feel unjustly treated.

L. Trinder et al, *Finding Fault? Divorce Law and Practice in England and Wales* (London: Nuffield Foundation, 2017), 15–16

Petitions may be produced jointly between the parties and with 'allegations' that both can accept, more or less. In other cases, the drafting is not a collaborative process and the respondent will disagree with some, or all, of the allegations. That does matter, since the petitioner's account in undefended cases will be taken as true, even where the respondent rebuts the allegations without taking the procedural steps necessary to mount a formal defence. On the face of it, the court's automatic endorsement of the allegations of one of the parties appears to be procedurally unfair, a point not lost on respondents:

> 'The petition doesn't need to be true, it doesn't need to be fair, it doesn't need to be just, it doesn't need to be anything that stands up to rigour. In which case, it serves no purpose other than in my case to cause upset and I would much prefer that she actually be forced to substantiate the claims rather than just wildly vomit bile onto a page and click submit . . .' (Interviewee WK22)

There are options available to the respondent to try to shape or challenge the petition, but none are available in all circumstances, or without financial or emotional costs. Defending the divorce is prohibitively expensive, legally challenging and unlikely to work, even after the *Owens* case. Family lawyers therefore encourage respondent clients to 'suck it up', focusing on the petition as 'a means to an end', while recognizing that the allegations are unfair.[94]

[94] See further Trinder et al (2017) section 8, and Trinder and Sefton (2018), 7.4 in relation to defended divorces.

3.5.3.c The law distorted parties' bargaining positions

Law Commission, *The Ground for Divorce*, Law Com No 192 (London: HMSO, 1990)

2.15 Not only can the law be unjust in itself, it can also lead to unfair distortions in the relative bargaining power of the parties. When a marriage breaks down there are a great many practical questions to be decided: with whom are the children to live, how much are they going to see the other parent, who is to have the house, and what are they all going to live on? Respondents to [the Law Commission's earlier discussion paper] told us that the battles which used to be fought through the grounds for divorce are now more likely to be fought through the so-called ancillary issues which in practice matter so much more to many people. The policy of the law is to encourage the parties to try and resolve these by agreement if they can, whether through negotiation between solicitors or with the help of a mediation or conciliation service. Questions of the future care of children, distribution of family assets, and financial provision are all governed by their own legal criteria. It is not unjust for negotiations to be affected by the relative merits of the parties' cases on these matters. Yet negotiations may also be distorted by whichever of the parties is in a stronger position in relation to the divorce itself. The strength of that position will depend upon a combination of how anxious or reluctant that party is to be divorced and how easy or difficult he or she will find it to prove or disprove one of the five facts. That might not matter if these represented a coherent set of principles, reflecting the real reasons why the marriage broke down; but as we have already seen, they do not. The potentially arbitrary results can put one party at an unfair disadvantage.

3.5.3.d The law provoked unnecessary hostility and bitterness

The requirement that the petitioner had to prove a 'fact' meant parties could not divorce immediately by mutual consent. As a result, Trinder et al's research showed that parties who were seeking a faster divorce—and who also had access to a solicitor to explain the law to them—were more likely to rely upon the conduct-based ground of behaviour.

L. Trinder et al, *Finding Fault? Divorce Law and Practice in England and Wales* (London: Nuffield Foundation, 2017), 41

[T]he qualitative data from lawyers and parties going through the process points towards the parties being steered by solicitors towards the behaviour Fact to secure a faster divorce, whilst the unrepresented may either be unaware of the availability of behaviour [in particular, not appreciating how low the threshold is[95]] or be unwilling to use it.

One issue with this is that it appeared to contradict the Law Commission's objectives of divorce law, as set out at 3.4. Relying upon conduct-based facts—often perceived as fault-based by the respondents whose conduct was being cited—would not minimize bitterness and humiliation in the way separation/no-fault facts would.

[95] See Trinder et al (2017), section 5.

Law Commission, *The Ground for Divorce*, Law Com No 192 (London: HMSO, 1990)

2.16 A law which is arbitrary or unjust can exacerbate the feelings of bitterness, distress and humiliation so often experienced at the time of separation and divorce. Even if the couple have agreed that their marriage cannot be saved, it must make matters between them worse if the system encourages one to make allegations against the other. The incidents relied on have to be set out in the petition. Sometimes they are exaggerated, one-sided or even untrue. Allegations of behaviour or adultery can provoke resentment or hostility in a respondent who is unable to put his own side of the story on the record. We are not so naive as to believe that bitterness and hostility could ever be banished from the divorce process. It is not concerned with cold commercial bargains but with the most intimate of human relations. The more we expect of marriage the greater the anger and grief when marriage ends. But there is every reason to believe that the present law adds needlessly to the human misery involved. . . .

The hope that the separation facts would be the most popular proved unfounded, statistics showing that in 2018 behaviour accounted for nearly half of divorces between mixed-sex couples and three-quarters of divorces between same-sex couples.[96] Trinder et al's findings substantiated the Law Commission's assertion, while revealing the impact this had on parties' experience of divorce:

L. Trinder et al, *Finding Fault? Divorce Law and Practice in England and Wales* (London: Nuffield Foundation, 2017), 15

In our national survey, 62% of petitioners and 78% of respondents said using fault had made the process more bitter, 21% of fault-respondents said fault had made it harder to sort out arrangements for children, and 31% of fault-respondents thought fault made sorting out finances harder. . . .

Lawyers and other advice agencies place great emphasis on trying to reduce harm, such as keeping behaviour particulars short and mild and trying to agree draft petitions . . . in advance of filing. Those harm-minimisation strategies depend upon awareness and receptivity from both sides, including where parties are unrepresented. But even with positive intentions on both sides, there is an elevated risk of conflict. . . . Respondent interviewees . . . reported that there was something inherently upsetting about seeing a series of allegations about them laid out in a legal document and described how that could undermine trust. That was particularly so where particulars had not been agreed, but was even the case where the respondent understood that the petition was intended just as a means to an end.

Conflict will occur on separation whether the divorce law includes fault or not. However, the current divorce law appears to introduce an entirely unnecessary additional source of conflict. It is only in relation to the divorce itself that the law allows the parties to focus on conduct. The law does not allow fault or conduct to influence arrangements for children or money other than in extreme circumstances. Once triggered, however, conflict and an undermining of trust can be very difficult to resolve.[97]

[96] ONS (2019b), 8.

[97] Even to the point of creating defended divorces, where 'indignant' respondents would not 'suck it up', but wanted to 'put the record straight': Trinder and Sefton (2018), 41. See further Trinder et al (2017), section 7, and Trinder and Sefton (2018), 7.2 in relation to defended divorces.

3.5.3.e The law did nothing to save the marriage

Law Commission, *The Ground for Divorce*, Law Com No 192 (London: HMSO, 1990)

2.17 None of this is any help with the law's other objective, of supporting those marriages which have a chance of survival. The law cannot prevent people from separating or forming new relationships, although it may make it difficult for people to get a divorce. The law can also make it difficult for estranged couples to become reconciled. The present law does make it difficult for some couples—in practice a very small proportion—to be divorced, but it does so in an arbitrary way depending upon which facts may be proved. It also makes it extremely difficult for couples to become reconciled. A spouse who wishes to be divorced is obliged either to make allegations against the other or to live apart for a lengthy period. If the petitioner brings proceedings based on behaviour, possibly without prior warning, and sometimes while they are still living together, the antagonism caused may destroy any lingering chance of saving the marriage. The alternative of two or five years' separation may encourage them to part in order to be able to obtain a divorce, when their difficulties might have been resolved if they had stayed together. From the very beginning, attention has to be focussed on how to prove the ground for divorce. The reality of what it will be like to live apart, to break up the common home, to finance two households where before there was only one, and to have or to lose that day-to-day responsibility for the children which was previously shared, at least to some extent: none of this has to be contemplated in any detail until the decree nisi [provisional decree] is obtained. If it had, there might be some petitioners who would think again.

2.18 . . . A defended suit is not going to [preserve the marriage], and if a case is, or becomes, undefended, there is little opportunity to explore the possibility of saving the marriage. An undefended divorce can be obtained in a matter of weeks. If both parties are contemplating divorce, the system gives them every incentive to obtain a "quickie" decree based on behaviour or separation [sic, presumably adultery was meant, rather than separation], and to think out the practical consequences later

This last point about defended divorces merits further consideration. Under the former substantive law, as little as 0.015 per cent of all divorce applications were defended.[98] Even if a respondent did not agree with the particulars of a divorce petition, challenging this in court could be an expensive and largely pointless process, as many respondents would want to get divorced, just not like the way the case had been put: disagreeing with the statement of case on a divorce petition is a separate issue from disagreeing that the marriage is over. For this reason, when a case was defended, the judge was forced to conduct an inquiry into whether the conduct alleged on the petition was sufficient to prove adultery, behaviour, or desertion. This left judges with an unenviable task, for as Miles has noted:

J. Miles, 'Judging Matrimonial Behaviour', in J. Miles, D. Monk, and R. Probert (eds), *Fifty Years of the Divorce Reform Act* (Oxford: Hart Publishing, 2022), 177

They . . . trod a careful line ensuring that the 'facts' prescribed by [Parliament] were not interpreted in such a way as to render them nugatory, given Parliament's clear intention not to allow divorce on grounds of mere incompatibility.

[98] Trinder and Sefton (2018), 59.

As we shall see in 3.6.2, it was one of these defended divorce cases that ultimately became one of the catalysts for reform.

3.5.3.f The law could make things worse for the children

Law Commission, *The Ground for Divorce*, Law Com No 192 (London: HMSO, 1990)

2.19 The present system can also make things worse for the children. The children themselves would usually prefer their parents to stay together. But the law cannot force parents to live amicably or prevent them from separating. It is not known whether children suffer more from their parents' separation or from living in a household in conflict where they may be blamed for the couple's inability to part. It is probably impossible to generalise, as there are so many variables which may affect the outcome, including the age and personality of the particular child. But it is known that the children who suffer least from their parents' break-up are usually those who are able to retain a good relationship with them both. Children who suffer most are those whose parents remain in conflict.

2.20 These issues have to be faced by the parents themselves, as they agonise over what to do for the best. However regrettably, there is nothing the law can do to ensure that they stay together, even supposing that this would indeed be better for their children. On the other hand, the present law can, for all the reasons given earlier, make the conflict worse. . . . It is often said that couples undergoing marital breakdown are too wrapped up in their own problems to understand their children's needs. There are also couples who, while recognising that their own relationship is at an end, are anxious to do their best for their children. The present system does little to help them to do so.

L. Trinder et al, *Finding Fault? Divorce Law and Practice in England and Wales* (London: Nuffield Foundation, 2017), 15

Interviewees – petitioners and respondents – gave examples of how the use of fault, mainly behaviour, had had a negative impact on contact arrangements, including fuelling litigation over children. Some described threats to show the petition to children.[99]

Law Commission, *The Ground for Divorce*, Law Com No 192 (London: HMSO, 1990)

Conclusion

2.21 These defects alone would amount to a formidable case for reform. The response to [the consultation paper] very largely endorsed its conclusion that "Above all, the present law fails to recognise that divorce is not a final product but part of a massive transition for the parties and their children."

[99] See further Trinder et al (2017), section 9, and Trinder and Sefton (2018), 7.6.

And so, while the case for reform was not universally accepted,[100] the Law Commission concluded that the most suitable role for the law on divorce lay in adjudicating not on the breakdown of the marriage itself, but instead on the practical issues—arrangements for children, financial remedies—that inevitably flow from divorce where agreement cannot be reached. The original MCA 1973 law did nothing to help the parties come to terms with the life-changes associated with divorce, may have done much to stoke up bitterness and hostility that might otherwise not have arisen, and was at odds with the forward-looking 'settlement orientation' of the rest of family law. As Trinder and Sefton showed compellingly in their study of contested divorce, the prevalence of that attitude amongst family justice professionals *in practice* meant that the system did all it could to discourage defences:

L. Trinder and M. Sefton, *No Contest: Defended Divorce in England and Wales* (London: Nuffield Foundation, 2018), 7–8

> The very active promotion of settlement at each stage, with lawyers and judges working in concert, reflects the dominant family justice perspective that agreed outcomes are less costly and damaging, that trying to apportion blame is a fruitless and inherently non-justiciable task and that defence is futile where one party has decided that the marriage is over.

But this practice came at the expense of creating a disjunction between the law on the books and the law as experienced by the parties.

Divorcing couples, lawyers, and government expressed concern that, for many of those relying on the undefended, conduct-based route, divorce was too quick and 'easy' and so might encourage precipitate divorce where a marriage could be saved.[101] Over a third of divorces were finalized within six months, with nearly two-thirds completing within a calendar year.[102] Those relying on conduct-based facts need not have waited the two or more years before petitioning that separation-fact petitioners face, and even then Trinder et al found evidence that conduct-based petitions were issued far more promptly than separation petitions.[103] In one sense, this appears to undermine suggestions that divorce was made 'harder' by requiring that it be based on fault/conduct. Given the ease with which fault could be alleged and the briskness of the procedure for undefended divorces, the 'quickie' divorce might have seemed rather attractive, certainly facilitating divorce on the basis (in effect) of mutual consent, and even enabling divorce on the basis of unilateral demand where the respondent felt little choice but to accede to the petitioner's wish to divorce.

But the fact that divorce may be readily available does not necessarily encourage irresponsible behaviour; divorce is rarely entered into lightly.[104] Moreover, it was said that where it was clear that a marriage had irretrievably broken down, petitioners forced to rely on the five-year separation fact were made to wait too long for their divorce and so for access to the full powers of the court to make financial orders.[105] Indeed, participants in Trinder et al's public attitude survey overwhelmingly considered five years too long.[106]

[100] E.g. Deech (1990). [101] Davis and Murch (1988), 66–70. See also 3.3.2.
[102] MOJ (2022a), table 14. [103] (2017), 131.
[104] Davis and Murch (1988); Walker (1991); Trinder et al (2017), 134–5.
[105] Law Com (1988a), para 3.12. [106] Trinder et al (2017), 162.

3.6 THE ROUTE TO REFORM

The problems identified by the Law Commission in 3.5.3 revealed deeply rooted problems with divorce law. But achieving reform was to prove difficult. While the evidence base provided by Trinder et al's research certainly galvanized the case for reform and helped drive the legislation passed in 2020, other important events help explain both why reform eventually happened and why it took so long. In this section, we explore some of the milestones leading to the DDSA 2020, including the abortive attempt at reform via the Family Law Act 1996 (FLA 1996) and the Supreme Court case of *Owens v Owens* in 2018.[107] These events highlight some of the themes considered earlier in this chapter, such as the problem with administering fault/conduct-based divorce (at 3.3.1), and the question of whether the role of divorce is or should be one of regularization or regulation (at 3.3.5).

3.6.1 THE FAMILY LAW ACT 1996 SCHEME

The (unimplemented) divorce law contained in Part II of the FLA 1996 was an important precursor to the law today because, whilst rather more complex than the current law, it adopted the essential no-fault approach now found in the MCA 1973, as reformed by the DDSA 2020.

The FLA 1996 scheme was based on recommendations made by the Law Commission, subsequently revised by the government and further amended during its passage through Parliament.[108] The scheme received considerable support when originally proposed and would have revolutionized English divorce law. For reasons which we explore briefly here, the legislation was repealed without implementation.[109]

Under the FLA 1996, irretrievable breakdown would have remained the sole ground for divorce and the bar on divorce in the first year of marriage would still have applied, but there the similarity to the current law would have ended. The 'facts' would have been abolished, non-adversarial terminology adopted, and joint applications for divorce made possible. Separation prior to divorce would not have been required. Instead, the ground for divorce would have been established by a statement, made by the applicant(s) following the mandatory 'period of reflection and consideration', that the marriage had irretrievably broken down. During that period, parties would have been expected to consider whether their marriage could be saved and, if not, to resolve issues relating to the future care of their children and their property. The clock would only have started to run three months after the applicant(s) had attended a mandatory information meeting. Mediation came to be seen as a key way for parties to negotiate these issues on divorce. Divorce under this scheme would have taken much longer for parties previously relied on the quick conduct-based facts.[110]

A key feature of the FLA scheme was that the 'period of reflection and consideration' was not intended to operate neutrally, like a mere period of separation. Instead, a new role for the state on divorce and new obligations for divorcing spouses were envisaged.[111] As Carol Smart has described, the radical nature of the proposed change generated fierce debate between two groups: those who advocated the retention of fault to provide clear, public 'rules of conduct' for marriage, the cornerstone of family and society; and those who viewed family

[107] [2018] UKSC 41. [108] Law Com (1988a), (1990); LCD (1993), (1995).
[109] Albeit only after nearly 20 years, by the Children and Families Act 2014, s 18.
[110] LCD (1995), para 2.7. [111] See generally Reece (2003).

in more fluid terms, where moral questions are negotiable matters for the parties themselves. The FLA 1996, a victory for the second group, would have transformed the state's role with regard to marriage and divorce but also made new demands on divorcing couples:

C. Smart, 'Divorce in England 1950–2000: A Moral Tale?', in S. Katz, J. Eekelaar, and M. Maclean (eds), *Cross Currents: Family Law and Policy in the US and England* (Oxford: OUP, 2000), 376–7

As with the debates some decades earlier, the main point of contention in the 1990s was over the best method(s) for the state to deploy in order to facilitate/ensure supportive, stable, and responsible family relationships . . . The core elements of the Bill, namely the information meetings, the period of reflection, and the preference for mediation over litigation, all constituted a prime example of the practice of governance as opposed to government. The theme of the legislation was based on the idea that people need knowledge about divorce and the financial problems it brings, the difficulties it creates for children, and the need to plan such things as resuming work and pension provision. The period of reflection was proposed as a form of 'time out' in which emotions could settle down in order to allow the divorcing couple to become more rational and more competent citizens, equipped either to manage the transition to divorce, or to change their minds and stay married. Mediation was intended as a way of helping to plan and to resolve any outstanding differences and problems mutually. The modern citizen envisaged by the Family Law Bill was the fact-gathering, rational, caring parent who would make decisions on the basis of knowledge. This citizen could be compared (unfavourably) with the divorced spouse of the former fault-based system who was encouraged to look backwards and cherish resentments and blame, who seized upon children as weapons in the battle, and who—in their emotional haze—failed to make proper provision either for themselves or for their former partners and children. The aim of governance would be to produce the former citizen. The aim of government in the latter scenario would be to adjudicate on who should be rewarded and who punished, while admonishing the most guilty for their failure.

Even amongst those who favour no-fault divorce, the FLA scheme was not universally supported. It was criticized for being unrealistic in hoping that couples would 'spend time reflecting on whether their marriage can be saved, and, if not to face up to the consequences of their actions and make arrangements to meet their responsibilities'.[112]

S. Cretney, 'Divorce Reform: Humbug and Hypocrisy or a Smooth Transition?', in M. Freeman (ed), *Divorce: Where Next* (Aldershot: Dartmouth, 1996a), 52–3

This is a very laudable aspiration. But how is this 'requirement' to be enforced? May not some of those concerned prefer to spend their time in the far more pleasurable activity of conceiving—necessarily illegitimate—babies? May not some spend the time seeking means of exploiting their emotional or financial advantage, or brooding on grievances and perhaps using the available legal procedures as a way of seeking satisfaction for the wrongs they

[112] LCD (1995), para 4.16.

> have suffered? The way in which the Law Commission's proposals were presented seemed almost reminiscent of those earnest Victorian reformers who invented the so-called 'separate system'—prisoners deprived of all corrupting influences would be driven to reflect in their solitude on the evil of their ways and thereby be well prepared to receive the sympathy, advice and religious consolation provided for those truly humbled by their experience. It was, of course, all very well-intentioned; and yet succeeded in inflicting scarcely imaginable cruelty on hundreds of helpless human beings. We would all hope that the parties will indeed give anxious consideration to whether the marriage has broken down irretrievably and to the consequential arrangements. We must all hope that mediation and counselling will be successful in this respect. But the evidence for believing that these expectations will be fulfilled is not overwhelmingly convincing.

Cretney also accused the FLA scheme of hypocrisy: that the emphasis on reflection and consideration concealed what in fact amounted to divorce on unilateral demand:

> It is true that the government's proposals will end the sometimes damaging ritual of filing a petition alleging—perhaps unjustly—that the other spouse has committed adultery or been guilty of behaviour such as to make it unreasonable for the spouses to go on living together. But a man who has behaved cruelly and unreasonably will still be able to insist on divorce against the wishes of his wife; and the wife's anger, grief and bitterness may reasonably not be assuaged by assurances that the new law promotes consideration and reflection—and that since her case is a simple one she is not to receive any public help to pay a lawyer who will defend her interests. There seems to be a serious risk that countless people will find themselves uncomprehendingly ensnared in a monstrous and costly legal/social work/counselling nightmare. The Law Commission . . . identifies the 'incoherence' of the law and the confusion thereby caused to people caught up in the divorce process as one of the law's most significant weaknesses; and the Commission rightly attributes these defects to the compromise nature of the 1969 divorce reforms. But there is a serious risk that the incoherence and confusion will be perpetuated and even increased. We shall still have to pretend that the ground for divorce is the breakdown of the marriage; whereas the reality is that it is the wish of one party to divorce the other. The information and mediation sessions merely conceal that simple truth and, in so doing, they make matters worse.

The scheme could also be criticized for being patronizing and unduly restricting access to divorce for at least some couples. Many couples (especially, perhaps, those without children) may have separated and resolved all arrangements for the future long before initiating divorce proceedings.[113] How might such couples feel if then required to reflect and consider for a further year? Or even if just required to *wait* (without any instruction about how to spend the time)?

Might such a system encourage people to set that clock ticking early—perhaps enticing them into a divorcing mindset precipitately—to ensure that the option of immediate divorce would be there once the decision was reached? Should there be an alternative track for immediate divorce by mutual consent—or even unilaterally—for parties who have been separated for a defined period and/or who had no minor children?[114] For example, immediate

[113] See Trinder et al (2017), 9.3, 9.5, and 147.

[114] For criticism of allowing children to affect the duration of any period, see LCD (1995), paras 4.17–4.18.

divorce is available in Sweden if both parties want it and they have no minor children. If only one party wishes to divorce or if the parties have children, they must ordinarily wait for a six-month period of reflection (during which they need not separate)—a period of time rather longer than some undefended English divorces under the old law.[115] But if they have been separated for two years and—importantly—provided the financial matters have been settled, a divorce may be granted immediately.[116] John Eekelaar has observed that were childless marriages left effectively unregulated at divorce, there would be little to distinguish them from childless cohabitation; 'marriage will [to that extent] have become, in Clive's (1980) phrase, an "unnecessary legal concept"'.[117]

On the other hand, many couples are reported to regret having got divorced—though that might not mean that they would not still *want* a divorce, in the circumstances. The law might therefore be justified in imposing some waiting period on all cases. To deny immediate divorce to those who genuinely wish to have it may be a modest price to pay for a system that does not risk propelling those experiencing emotional stress towards a divorce that they may later regret.

The fate of the FLA 1996 divorce scheme is instructive about policy priorities in the family justice arena. Importantly, the scheme was not dropped because of concerns about its no-fault philosophy.[118] Its abandonment followed pilot projects designed to explore the best format for the initial information meetings. The pilots (necessarily conducted in the context of the pre-DDSA 2020 law) had been devised simply to test formats for information delivery, but the government subsequently evaluated the results by reference to the likelihood, following receipt of the information, of parties electing to use mediation rather than seeking legal advice in relation to their divorce.[119] This reflected the way in which the Law Commission's original scheme had changed in emphasis as it developed in the hands of successive governments and in Parliament.[120] The Law Commission had conceived of the period for reflection and consideration principally as a way of proving irretrievable marital breakdown. Parties might well use mediation and other non-legal services during that period, but use of mediation was not central to the scheme at that stage. When the Conservative Government took over the project, divorce reform become inextricably linked with concerns to save marriages and to promote mediation in preference to legal services, and so the information meetings were inserted into the scheme. It then became clear under the Labour Government that these meetings would not be neutral conduits for the delivery of factual information. 'Information' here had a persuasive function, aimed at steering parties towards attempts to save their marriage or, if that were impossible, towards behaving 'responsibly' in relation to their divorce; and 'responsibility' was synonymous with use of mediation.[121]

Given these ambitions, the Labour Government was 'disappointed'[122] by the results of the pilot projects. Only a small minority of couples were diverted to marriage counselling; counselling had limited success in preventing divorce, but did help individuals cope with the transition through divorce and improve the quality of their post-divorce relationship. The failure of the meetings to save more marriages was perhaps unsurprising: only one spouse had to attend and that individual was often too far down the psychological road to divorce for the meeting to affect the decision to end the marriage. Nor were the meetings particularly successful in diverting couples into mediation: only 10 per cent of individuals

[115] Trinder et al (2017), 27. [116] Swedish Marriage Code, ch 5. [117] Eekelaar (1991b), 171.
[118] Trinder et al (2017), 30. [119] Newcastle Centre for Family Studies (2001b), 21.
[120] See Eekelaar, Maclean, and Beinart (2000), ch 1. [121] See Reece (2003), Eekelaar (1999).
[122] LCD (1999).

attending the meetings went to mediation with their spouses within two years of the meeting, while 73 per cent went to lawyers in that time.[123] Interim results had found 39 per cent reporting that having attended the information meeting they were now *more likely* to seek legal advice.[124] This was not the ringing public endorsement of mediation for which the government had hoped, particularly bearing in mind that all those who participated in the pilot projects were volunteers, who might therefore have been expected to be more amenable to new options.

The pilot projects reported many positive findings—an overwhelming majority (90 per cent) of those who had attended meetings were glad to have done so; the information meetings succeeded in 'increasing knowledge and empowering citizens to take informed decisions'.[125] Yet despite these good outcomes, the FLA 1996 divorce scheme was abandoned.[126] The government's disappointment that parties still wished to use lawyers rather than mediators and so failed to match the image of 'responsible' divorce attracted strong criticism from John Eekelaar, worried by the implications of the government's position for the rule of law:

J. Eekelaar, 'Family Law: Keeping Us "On Message"', (1999) 11 *Child and Family Law Quarterly* 387, 395–6

I do not wish to argue against the importance of people being under duties and having responsibilities. Indeed, to the extent that any individual has rights, others (individually or collectively) will have responsibilities to respect those rights. It is also the case that an individual's rights and duties are not exhausted by their statement in the law. This is obvious in the case of moral rights and duties. It is also true in relation to an individual's socially constructed rights and duties: so, while, for example, the law may not require an able, adult, child to give any assistance to his or her indigent parent, there may well be a socially accepted obligation to provide it. But in the examples discussed here, we have an apparent tension between what the state proclaims in its law and how it wants people actually to behave. The legal framework of marriage and divorce has, under the influence of liberal individualism, become a neutral edifice within which parties have worked out their lives according to a wide variety of beliefs and customs. Now the state is actively intervening, through institutions of its creation or to which individuals will be strongly steered, in an attempt to bring about certain forms of behaviour which are not legally required, and may not even be consistent with widely accepted social norms.

Eekelaar went on to note that the FLA 1996 allowed grants to be made for research into marital breakdown, its causes, and prevention methods, and funding for marriage counselling. He raised no objection to this expenditure, accepting that it might be thought right, even a matter of duty, for the state to seek through various means to promote 'good' behaviour. But are there limits to the appropriateness of such state intervention?

Perhaps we would not feel uncomfortable if the state were to do this to modify behaviour to make people more racially tolerant, for example, or to discourage domestic violence. One might not even feel too uncomfortable with a scheme which attempts to motivate people

[123] Newcastle Centre for Family Studies (2001a). [124] LCD (1999). [125] Walker (2000), 410.
[126] LCD (2001).

> to earn their income rather than rely on welfare benefits. Is it different when we are dealing with marriage and divorcing behaviour? It may be. The legal provisions themselves [i.e. the FLA 1996, and the substantive law governing children and property division on divorce] have largely moved away from a prescriptive role to a position of neutrality, although they do provide a range of options which are available to protect the vital interests of those who are harmed in their personal lives. This has emerged from gradual acceptance that the way people organise their personal lives evolves in response to changing moral, social and economic factors which are not easily controlled by governments. There can, I think, be no objection to the government playing a part, although by no means the sole part, in influencing those factors. We may, however, become uncomfortable when the government intervenes at key points in the institutional processes of marriage and divorce and attempts to impose its own vision of how people should be behaving at those times. At best, it risks being made to appear foolish and ineffectual. Worse, it can appear heavy handed, domineering and insensitive in an area of behaviour to which all citizens have a strong claim to privacy, provided that they do not threaten the clear interests of other individuals. But my main objection is *where it utilises the institutions of law itself to obstruct individuals from access to the rights conferred on them by law.* This could be deeply corrupting of the law itself. We should not forget that both marriage and divorce are *rights* and that post-divorce settlements *do* reflect legal entitlements (however imperfectly expressed in the discretionary system). Disenchantment with some of the excesses of the legal process should never obscure these facts. The role of the legal profession has perhaps never been more important in helping people to negotiate their way through some of the hazards which changing behaviour patterns and an increasingly complex material world visit on them.

Eekelaar's concerns have only been increased by subsequent policy developments in relation to the public funding of legal services and mediation in family cases, discussed at 1.2.7. These build on the notion that responsible action is synonymous with mediation and—by implication—inconsistent with hiring the services of lawyers instead, even as a means of achieving out-of-court settlement.

3.6.2 *OWENS V OWENS* [2018] UKSC 41

Another notable point along the path to divorce reform—following shortly after the publication of Liz Trinder's important research—was *Owens v Owens*, a case that garnered significant public attention.[127]

When Mrs Owens petitioned for divorce, she sought to establish irretrievable breakdown by relying on the 'behaviour' fact—in other words, that Mr Owens had behaved in such a way that she could not be expected to live with him.[128] Had Mr Owens *not* challenged this petition, the petition would likely have gone through the special procedure without any prospect of challenge from the court.[129] But because Mr Owens decided to take the statistically unusual decision of defending the divorce petition, the court had to decide whether or not his behaviour was such that Mrs Owens could not reasonably be expected to live with him.

At first instance, HHJ Tolson found that Mr Owens's behaviour did not meet the threshold.[130] Then, though there was some disagreement over HHJ Tolson's *application* of

[127] Burton (2020). [128] See 3.5.1.

[129] This was confirmed in *Owens v Owens* [2017] EWCA Civ 182, [93]. For detail on the 'special' procedure, see 3.5.2.

[130] Applying *Livingstone-Stallard v Livingstone-Stallard* [1974] Fam 47.

the law to the facts, both the Court of Appeal and the Supreme Court refused Mrs Owens' appeal, finding that the judge had asked himself the correct questions under the then-law.

Owens v Owens [2018] UKSC 41

LADY HALE:

46. I have found this a very troubling case. It is not for us to change the law laid down by Parliament - our role is only to interpret and apply the law that Parliament has given us.

Lady Hale was not the only member of the Supreme Court to express discomfort, especially when it came to assessing Mr Owens's behaviour in the marriage:

LORD WILSON:

42. There is no denying that the appeal of Mrs Owens generates uneasy feelings: an uneasy feeling that the procedure now conventionally adopted for the almost summary despatch of a defended suit for divorce was inapt for a case which was said to depend on a remorseless course of authoritarian conduct and which was acknowledged to appear unconvincing if analysed only in terms of a few individual incidents; an uneasy feeling about the judge's finding that the three incidents which he analysed were isolated in circumstances in which he had not received oral evidence of so many other pleaded incidents; and an uneasy feeling about his finding that Mrs Owens had significantly exaggerated her entire case in circumstances in which Mr Owens had not disputed much of what she said.

43. But uneasy feelings are of no consequence in this court, nor indeed in any other appellate court.

Practically, without Mr Owens's consent to the divorce, Mrs Owens would have to wait five years until she could legally end her marriage using the last, separation-based fact.

Following *Owens*, calls for reform came loudly from the media,[131] adding to the chorus of voices—including senior members of the judiciary—who had been appealing for statutory reform for years. Shortly after the FLA 1996's tenth anniversary, Sir Nicholas Wall—the then President of the Family Division—founded his arguments for no-fault divorce on support for the institution of marriage:

I do believe strongly in the institution of marriage as the best way to bring up children and that's one of the reasons why I would like to end the quick and easy divorces based on the fault system. I think that it actually undermines marriage.[132]

While (as we shall see at 3.10.1) some would have wanted fault to be reinstated in divorce law, for Sir Nicholas, fault simply promoted conflict thus making it more difficult to maintain good relations post-divorce. Following the Court of Appeal's trenchant criticism of the

[131] See, e.g., *The Times* Family Matters campaign: <www.thetimes.co.uk/article/urgent-call-for-new-divorce-laws-as-judges-demand-overhaul-of-corrosive-system-8k0ncg7gt>.

[132] Verkaik (2006).

current law in *Owens*,[133] Lord Wilson in the Supreme Court concluded his speech in *Owens* by quietly observing that 'Parliament may wish to consider whether to replace a law which denies to Mrs Owens any present entitlement to a divorce . . .'[134]

3.6.3 PROPOSALS FOR REFORM

Within months of the *Owens* judgment, press coverage calling for reform, and in the wake of Liz Trinder's compelling research findings[135] and a Private Members' Bill proposed by another past President of the Family Division, Baroness Butler-Sloss,[136] the government published its consultation paper seeking views on proposed fundamental reform for a system of divorce based on notification followed by a waiting period:

MOJ, *Reducing Family Conflict: Reform of the Legal Requirements for Divorce* (London: MOJ, 2018), 5–6

Marriage is a solemn commitment, and the process of divorce should reflect the seriousness of the decision to end a marriage. The Government believes that the law should not exacerbate conflict and stress at what is already a difficult time. The Government accepts the principle that it is not in the interests of children, families and society to require people to justify their decision to divorce to the court. . . .

The Government therefore proposes to reform the legal requirements of the divorce process so that it is consistent with the approach taken in other areas of family law, and to shift the focus from blame and recrimination to support adults better to focus on making arrangements for their own futures and their children's. The reformed law should have two objectives: to make sure that the decision to divorce continues to be a considered one, and that spouses have an opportunity to change course; and to make sure that divorcing couples are not put through legal requirements which do not serve their or society's interests and which can lead to conflict and accordingly poor outcomes for children.

To deliver these two objectives, this consultation proposes adjusting what the law requires to bring a legal end to a marriage that has broken down irretrievably. This adjustment includes removing the ability to allege "fault". We propose to move way from an approach that requires justification to the court of the reason for the irretrievable breakdown of the marriage to a process that requires notification to the court of irretrievable breakdown. We also propose to remove the ability of a spouse, as a general rule, to contest a divorce . . . The Government reasons that if one spouse has concluded that the marriage is over, then the legal process should respect that decision and should not place impediments in the way of a spouse who wants to bring the marriage to a legal end. Importantly, this change would also prevent the legal process from being used to exercise coercive control by one spouse over the other spouse who may be a victim of domestic abuse.

Starting with these key principles, this consultation seeks views on the detail of how best to change the law in a way that will help to reduce family conflict and strengthen family responsibility. The consultation also seeks views on the length of the divorce process and period for couples to reflect on the decision to divorce and to make arrangements for the future where divorce is inevitable. We seek views, too, on whether provision should be made for a couple to petition jointly for divorce, reflecting the reality that for many couples this may be a shared and considered decision.

[133] Notably from Munby P: [2017] EWCA Civ 182, [82]–[98].
[134] [2018] UKSC 41, [45].
[135] Trinder et al (2017); Trinder and Sefton (2018).
[136] Divorce (etc.) Law Review Bill [HL] 2017–19.

In February 2019, the Justice Secretary announced his intention to introduce divorce reform in the next parliamentary session, following overwhelming support for the no-fault proposals outlined in the consultation paper. The resulting Bill provided for the five 'facts' to be replaced with a notification process that would itself evidence that the ground—irretrievable breakdown—was made out. The Bill progressed swiftly through Parliament and was enacted in the summer of 2020. The DDSA 2020 amends the MCA 1973. It shares common philosophical ground with the FLA scheme, but—as we examine at 3.7—pursues that philosophy in a far more simple manner.

3.7 THE MATRIMONIAL CAUSES ACT 1973: THE PRESENT LAW

As noted previously, the present law of divorce is still to be found in the MCA 1973, but now as amended by the DDSA 2020, which modernizes the terminology as well as changing the substantive law.[137]

Section 1 of the MCA 1973 sets out the sole ground for divorce, which is still irretrievable breakdown of the marriage.[138] However, the route to establishing irretrievable breakdown is now different.

Matrimonial Causes Act 1973

1. Divorce on breakdown of marriage.

(1) Subject to section 3, either or both parties to a marriage may apply to the court for an order (a "divorce order") which dissolves the marriage on the ground that the marriage has broken down irretrievably.

(2) An application under subsection (1) must be accompanied by a statement by the applicant or applicants that the marriage has broken down irretrievably.

(3) The court dealing with an application under subsection (1) must—

(a) take the statement to be conclusive evidence that the marriage has broken down irretrievably, and

(b) make a divorce order.

(4) A divorce order—

(a) is, in the first instance, a conditional order, and

(b) may not be made final before the end of the period of 6 weeks from the making of the conditional order.

(5) The court may not make a conditional order unless—

(a) in the case of an application that is to proceed as an application by one party to the marriage only, that party has confirmed to the court that they wish the application to continue, or

[137] The corresponding law of civil partnership dissolution—modelled on divorce law—can be found in ss 37–48 of the CPA 2004.

[138] CPA 2004, s 44.

(b) In the case of an application that is to proceed as an application by both parties to the marriage, those parties have confirmed to the court that they wish the application to continue; and a party may not give confirmation for the purposes of this subsection before the end of the period of 20 weeks from the start of proceedings.

There are several notable ways in which this amended s 1 is different from the MCA 1973 as originally enacted. First, either or both parties may apply, thereby facilitating joint applications for the first time. Secondly, a statement of irretrievable breakdown is 'conclusive evidence' that the marriage has broken down irretrievably, and the requirement for one of five 'facts' to establish breakdown is removed.[139] The inquisitorial function performed by judges under the former law has now been swept away, meaning the question of whether the parties' marriage has broken down is decided purely by the parties themselves—not by the law.

As well as removing the five 'facts', the notification procedure streamlines the divorce and dissolution process for marriage and civil partnership breakdown. The previous law used the terminology 'petitioner', 'respondent', and 'petition' in the context of divorce, and 'applicant', 'respondent', and 'application' in the context of civil partnership dissolution. Now the current law uses the latter terminology for both divorce and dissolution.

The party initiating the divorce must first decide if they wish to apply solely or to try to obtain their spouse's agreement to a joint application. Sole applications might be made if the applicant feels their spouse will not cooperate with the divorce. The new option for parties to apply jointly requires each spouse to confirm their wish to divorce separately, although if one of the parties fails to respond as the divorce proceeds, the other can still proceed with the divorce as a sole applicant. As a result, if one of the parties objects to the divorce—as in *Owens*—there is little that can be done to stop the process, unless there are legal or procedural grounds on which to object (see 3.8.1). As Figure 3.4 shows, divorce proceeds in two main stages: the conditional order and final order.[140]

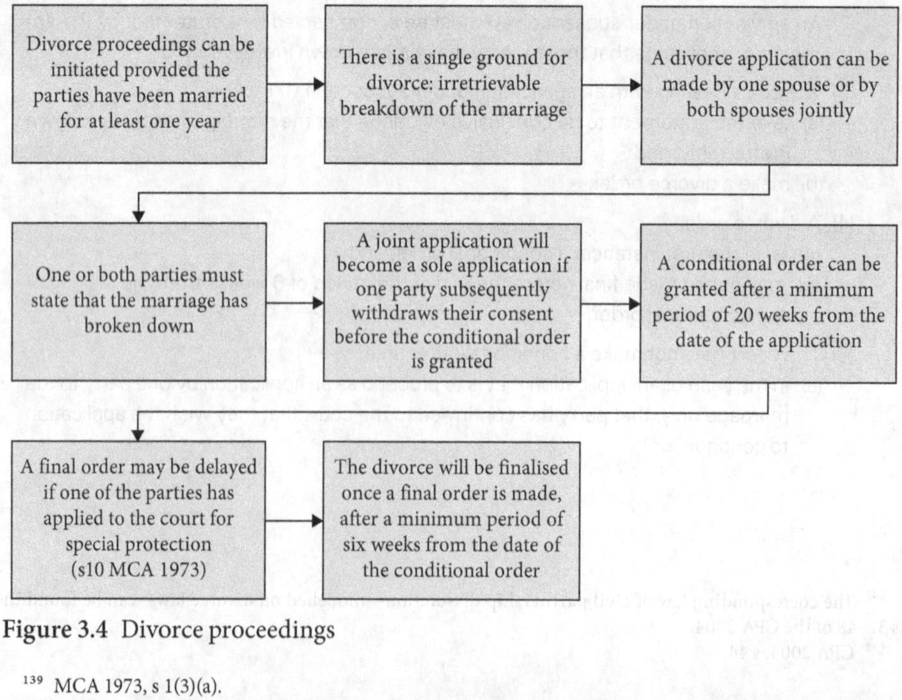

Figure 3.4 Divorce proceedings

[139] MCA 1973, s 1(3)(a).

[140] Known respectively as the decree nisi and decree absolute under the former substantive law.

The entire process takes a minimum of 26 weeks (six months), with a gap of 20 weeks between the initial application and the conditional order, and six weeks between the conditional order and final order. This timetable was one of the more controversial aspects of the DDSA 2020 as it went through Parliament, in particular related to the time from which the first 20 weeks start to run. 'The start of the proceedings' is understood to be the date of the application, not (in sole applicant cases) the date on which the respondent receives formal notice (service) of that application. Concern was expressed that this will unfairly deny some respondents the benefit of having the full 26-week period that the law otherwise appears to require prior to the final order if they do not receive notice until (much) later.[141] Conversely, the problem in such cases is frequently that the respondent is deliberately evading service, as a means to frustrate the applicant's attempts to secure a divorce.[142]

This timetable might make the process of divorce easier—in that the applicant no longer needs to prove that the marriage has broken down irretrievably—but it does not necessarily make it quicker. Petitions relying upon conduct under the old law could take as little as four months to be processed compared with the six months now mandated under the new scheme. On the other hand, for those parties who would previously have petitioned on the basis of no-fault separation facts under the old law, a wait of more than two years is no longer required. Now, parties are not compelled to craft a narrative of fault to suit the law's requirements and speed up the process as they were under the old law.[143] Nevertheless, the two-stage process and waiting periods are still important, for as well as ensuring cooling-off periods for the parties, there are protections built into the process for financially vulnerable parties, as we discuss at 3.8.

3.8 BARS AND OTHER RESTRICTIONS ON DIVORCE

There are several bars and restrictions on divorce under the MCA 1973. In practice, the principal function of most of these bars is to give one party bargaining power: to hold up the divorce (and so the opportunity to remarry) pending a desirable settlement of ancillary matters, particularly financial issues. Divorce is rarely delayed substantially, let alone barred outright, by a bar or restriction being invoked.

3.8.1 FINANCIAL PROTECTION FOR CERTAIN RESPONDENTS

Respondents are entitled to apply under s 10 to have their financial position post-divorce considered by the court once a conditional order has been made, and before the divorce is finalized.[144] Under the original MCA 1973, it was said that in cases involving middle-aged clients, the respondent's solicitor (unless instructed otherwise) may be negligent if they do not file a s 10 application to enable a proper investigation of the financial circumstances, particularly regarding pension rights, to be made prior to grant of the final order.[145] If loss of potential pension rights associated with ongoing marital status—principally a widow's pension—could put the respondent in financial difficulty, the divorce should be delayed until suitable financial remedies have been explored.[146]

141 MOJ (2019a), 32. 142 Ibid. 143 See 3.5.3.d.

144 MCA 1973, s 10(2)–(4); CPA 2004, s 48(2)–(5). It may be used to seek compensation for arrears accrued under past financial obligations: *Garcia v Garcia* [1992] Fam 83.

145 *Griffiths v Dawson & Co* [1993] 2 FLR 315. 146 See 6.4.4.

Under the old law, financial protection pursuant to s 10 was only available to respondents in separation-based cases against whom no (conduct-based) 'fact' had been found. However, under the MCA 1973 as amended by the DDSA 2020, this special protection is now available to *all* respondents in sole applications and, in joint applications, to a spouse who has withdrawn from the joint application since it was made.

Where such an application has been made, the court may not ordinarily grant the final order unless satisfied in all the circumstances either that: (i) no financial provision ought to be made by the applicant; or (ii) the financial provision that has been made[147] is reasonable and fair or the best that can be made in the circumstances. The low standard of 'the best [financial provision] that can be made in the circumstances' recognizes that where resources are limited financial hardship may be unavoidable, yet divorce should still be permitted.[148] Even if *not* satisfied that the best possible provision has been made (or that no provision should be made), the court may still finalize the divorce if: (i) it is desirable to do so in the circumstances without delay; and (ii) the applicant has made satisfactory undertakings to make provision that is approved—in fairly firm and achievable outline[149]—by the court. Courts are wary of allowing cases to proceed with mere undertakings if, having obtained the desired divorce, the applicant might fail to cooperate further in financial remedy proceedings.[150]

As a result, while s 10 purports to offer special protection to financially vulnerable parties, it does not necessarily protect the respondent from financial hardship. Nor was it used often in practice under the old law. It is too soon to ascertain whether this will change under the new law, but it is possible that s 10 will gain new prominence given that it will now be available to a much wider range of respondents.[151]

3.8.2 TIME BARS ON DIVORCE

It is not possible to petition for divorce or apply for dissolution of a civil partnership during the first year of the union.[152] This may be viewed as an attempt to encourage spouses to make a go of a new union. Whether this provision does—or ever could—save saveable marriages is doubtful; indeed, they were not introduced with any great hopes that they would.[153]

The remedy of judicial separation (addressed at 3.9) provides relief, including access to financial remedies, where necessary during that first year.[154] Nullity proceedings can also be brought immediately where grounds to do so apply.[155] Occupation and non-molestation orders under the FLA 1996 can provide protection from domestic abuse.[156]

This bar delays divorce and so delays remarriage. To that extent, it might be argued that it breaches the right to marry under Article 12 ECHR. In *F v Switzerland*,[157] it was briefly

[147] Not merely proposed: *Wilson v Wilson* [1973] 1 WLR 555.

[148] *K v K (Financial Relief: Widow's Pension)* [1997] 1 FLR 35.

[149] *Grigson v Grigson* [1974] 1 WLR 228.

[150] Cf *Thakkar v Thakkar* [2016] EWHC 2488, on the court's power to permit respondent to apply for decree absolute: s 9(2).

[151] However, see Salter who advises caution on using s 10 where not appropriate to do so: <https://financialremediesjournal.com/content/mca-1973-s-10-2-ndash-4-a-new-lease-of-life.747b9e83536e40d28539249ded712cd5.htm>.

[152] MCA 1973, s 3; CPA 2004, s 41.

[153] See Law Com (1966), paras 29–32. For research on impact of these provisions, see Trinder et al (2017), 9.4.

[154] MCA 1973, ss 17–18; CPA 2004, ss 56–7.

[155] See 2.5–2.7.

[156] See chapter 4.

[157] (App No 11329/85, ECHR) (1987).

asserted that this sort of rule does not violate the Convention. Although the Court offered no reasoning, it may be inferred that since the rule operates during a marriage, and as a condition of divorce, it can be distinguished from the bar on remarriage arising after divorce that was successfully challenged in that case. Since the Convention does not confer a right to divorce, it cannot restrict the terms on which divorce may be granted, so a time bar of this sort is legitimate. But once a divorce has been granted—as in *F*—the state must not disproportionately restrict the right to remarry.

3.8.3 SPECIAL PROTECTION FOR PARTIES TO SOME RELIGIOUS MARRIAGES

Some marriages cannot, in a sense, be wholly dissolved by civil divorce. Although the state recognizes the divorce for all purposes, the religious law under which a marriage was (also) contracted may not recognize civil divorce, and further procedures may have to be completed before the parties will be free to remarry in accordance with their religious rites.[158] Conversely, religious divorces obtained in England and Wales will not dissolve marriage for civil law purposes; there must be a civil divorce.[159] This perhaps contrasts oddly with the recognition of certain religious marriage ceremonies as being competent to create a marriage for civil law purposes.[160]

Difficulty arises where only one spouse wishes to remarry under religious law but cannot do so without the other's cooperation. For example, under Jewish law the parties are only divorced if the husband gives and the wife accepts a formal document issued under the auspices of a rabbinic court called a 'Get'. If the husband is content to remarry outside the faith, he has no incentive to fulfil this procedure. That leaves the wife effectively unable to remarry within her faith and any children she might have will be illegitimate under Jewish law.

Following a series of cases[161] highlighting the problem faced by some Jewish wives, a provision designed expressly to deal with the problem—s 10A—was introduced.[162] This empowers the court, if it is just and reasonable to do so, to withhold the final order until both parties have taken any steps required to dissolve the marriage under their religious law. In many cases (assuming that the intransigent party wants a civil divorce), the threat of invoking s 10A may produce the desired result. Evidently, no equivalent issue arises for civil partners.

3.8.4 THE ROLE OF THE KING'S PROCTOR

The delay between the conditional and final orders also provides an opportunity for intervention by the King's Proctor, the Crown officer charged with representing the public interest in the law and practice of divorce against manipulation by private individuals who

[158] See Morris (2005); Schuz (1996), writing before the reform discussed in the text; see also Douglas et al (2012) for research into the practices of religious tribunals.

[159] Family Law Act 1986, s 44; *Sulaiman v Juffali* [2002] 1 FLR 479.

[160] Schuz (1996); see 2.5.3, particularly in relation to Jewish and Quaker marriages, which proceed entirely under their own rites without any additional civil requirements save registration.

[161] E.g. *N v N (Divorce: Ante-Nuptial Agreement)* [1999] 2 FCR 583; *O v O (Jurisdiction: Jewish Divorce)* [2000] 2 FLR 147, in which s 9(2) was used to delay granting a decree absolute to the respondent husband.

[162] Divorce (Religious Marriages) Act 2002: it currently applies only to Jewish marriages, though a 2018 review recommended its extension to Islamic marriages: HO (2018), 18.

wish to evade the substantive law and effectively divorce on their own terms.[163] This role carried greater weight under the former substantive law, when one of the five facts needed to be proven to support the claim of irretrievable breakdown. The then Queen's Proctor may have been called upon where it had been alleged that false accusations had been made on the divorce petition. Now that divorce is obtained simply on the basis of the prescribed statements of breakdown being made within the set procedure, opportunities for use of the proctorial intervention are considerably more limited. However, the King's Proctor can still intervene when there is suspected abuse of process.[164]

3.9 JUDICIAL SEPARATION

One or both parties, perhaps for religious reasons, may not wish to divorce but nevertheless wish to separate.[165] Other individuals may require early protection where they find themselves in an impossible, perhaps abusive, relationship before they can apply for divorce. A judicial separation order cannot require either party to leave the matrimonial home (an occupation order would be required for that[166]), but on making the decree the court can make financial orders, as it can on divorce and annulment.[167] The decree releases spouses from the duty to cohabit without effecting any change of status, save in relation to inheritance on intestacy.[168]

The law of judicial separation reflects aspects of the law of divorce, and so was reformed in 2020 to align with the new law. In order to obtain a decree of judicial separation, it is therefore now necessary for either or both parties to apply to the court for a judicial separation order. When making this application, the party or parties also need to include a statement that they seek to be judicially separated from their partner.[169] Judicial separation cannot simply be converted into a divorce. Should the parties wish subsequently to divorce, it is necessary to issue a separate application accompanied instead with a statement that the marriage has broken down irretrievably.[170] Comparatively small numbers of judicial separation orders are now made each year—in 2021, there were just 260 applications and 89 final judicial separation orders, dwarfed by the 113,842 final orders of divorce.[171]

3.10 EVALUATION OF THE CURRENT LAW

Given the many criticisms of the original iteration of the MCA's divorce law and procedure[172]—including the apparent 'ease' of divorce, and the claimed effects of divorce on children and society, it is worth evaluating how far the DDSA 2020 has addressed, or perhaps exacerbated, such long-standing concerns. One way of taking stock is to consider

[163] The King's Proctor may also intervene in nullity and judicial separation cases.

[164] E.g. sham divorce petitions used to make false claims for immigration purposes: *Bhaji v Chauhan, Queen's Proctor Intervening (Divorce: Marriages Used for Immigration Purposes)* [2003] 2 FLR 485 (Fam Div) or to intervene in matters relating to validity of transnational divorces: *Parveen v Hussain* [2022] EWCA Civ 1434.

[165] Under the old law, this may have risked a finding of desertion (3.5.1).

[166] See 4.5.3. [167] See 6.4.5.

[168] MCA 1973, ss 17–18; CPA 2004, ss 56–7; Law Com (1990), paras 4.2–4.11; Cretney (2003a), 149 et seq.

[169] MCA 1973, s 17(1)(a). [170] Ibid, s 4; CPA 2004, s 46. [171] MOJ (2022b), table 12.

[172] See Hasson (2006), 285–90.

whether the new law has fulfilled the government's stated policy objectives. Just as the Law Commission had outlined its objectives for a 'good' divorce law in the 1960s, the Ministry of Justice outlined four intended effects of the 2020 reform.

Ministry of Justice, *Reducing Family Conflict – Reform of the Legal Requirements for Divorce: Impact Assessment* (London: MOJ, 2019), 1

1. To ensure that the decision to divorce or dissolve a civil partnership is a considered one
2. To minimise the adversarial nature of the legal process, to reduce conflict and to support better outcomes by maximising the opportunity for the parties to agree arrangements for the future
3. To make the legal process fair, transparent, and easier to navigate
4. To reduce the opportunities for an abuser to misuse the legal process for divorce to perpetrate further abuse

Such objectives are relatively uncontroversial. Removing acrimony where possible, ensuring the decision to divorce is not taken lightly, and that the process is fair and protected from abuse are all broadly the same as those offered by the Law Commission. And it is easy to see how the DDSA reform facilitates this better than previous law. The six-month timetable enables a cooling-off period so that, by the date of the final order, the divorce is more likely to be a considered decision confirmed by at least one of the parties. The new option for joint applications increases the likelihood of cooperative divorces, so increasing potential for agreements about arrangements for children and finances. Parties given the option to apply together can avoid the sometimes fraught decision of who will divorce whom, which can affect power dynamics and create or increase tensions between the parties. The process is undoubtedly more transparent than the original MCA 1973 scheme. While undefended divorces were previously administrative processes operating under a guise of judicial scrutiny, the straightforward and administrative nature of the new law is laid bare. The disjunction between the law on the books and the law as experienced by the parties is no more. The process is also made easier for many through the expansion of the online divorce service. Since 2020, the online divorce hub has been extended to solicitors, thus enabling a fully online process from the initial application to the final order. Finally, the DDSA 2020 has largely consigned defended divorces to history as the grounds for challenge (essentially now only jurisdictional) are so narrowed. This again aligns with the Ministry of Justice's policy objectives, by removing from the abuser a tool of control that could be used to draw out the process. As we have seen, when divorce needs to be delayed for other reasons—such as the financial vulnerability of the respondent—the s 10 safety net remains, and indeed now applies in principle to all but fully joint divorces, rather than to only a subset of cases.

As well as evaluating the DDSA 2020 from the perspective of policy and practice, it is also useful to return to the themes discussed at 3.3, to consider what this reform means for the nature of divorce (and so of marriage). Now that truly no-fault divorce has been introduced, is a party's conduct in relation to the breakdown of the marriage irrelevant? Furthermore, is it now correct to characterize our divorce process—in joint application cases at least—as one based on mutual consent? Or, can we even describe our present law of divorce as one available on unilateral demand? And is the role of our present law now one of regularization? We consider these questions in the next sections.

3.10.1 SHOULD CONDUCT HAVE ANY RELEVANCE?

One of the arguments put forward by opponents of the DDSA 2020 was that introducing a purely no-fault divorce process removed an important outlet for petitioners who felt wronged, because under the old system they could put the bad behaviour of their spouse on record.[173] This concern has in turn led to speculation that this may spill into financial remedies proceedings,[174] where conduct is currently only relevant when it would be inequitable for the court to disregard it.[175] These concerns may be unfounded: as Trinder et al's research found, public awareness of the role of fault in the divorce process was low, and so it is unlikely that there will be a throng of people seeking an alternative outlet to recording their former partner's conduct on a divorce petition.[176] Nevertheless, it is important to note that, although this debate has re-emerged in the context of the new law, it is not new.

The Morton Commission of 1956 considered that the role of divorce law was to give relief where wrong had been done.[177] There is still popular support for fault: 84 per cent of respondents to a public opinion survey for the Law Commission conducted in the late 1980s supported divorce for fault, though not as the sole basis for divorce.[178] Thirty years on, Trinder et al found 71 per cent support for the retention of fault amongst public survey respondents, but noted that many of those individuals would probably not have a good understanding of how fault currently operates in the law, notably the very low threshold for 'behaviour' petitions, lack of causation requirement between fact and ground, and lack of judicial scrutiny. Indeed, they also found majority public support for the proposition that 'in many cases it's unfair to blame just one spouse for the marriage breakdown'.[179] But jurisdictions worldwide have been retreating from fault. It has been said that the legal concept of marriage which requires spouses to be subservient to a particular view of moral duty has been replaced by a concern for the quality of individual relationships and the psychological well-being of the individuals involved.[180]

Some commentators and legislators seek to resist this trend, considering that fault should remain a central feature of divorce law and family justice more generally. Ruth Deech makes the case for fault in these terms:

R. Deech, 'Divorce Law – A Disaster?', (2009a) Gresham Lectures 2009–10

> It seem[s] to me to be clear that [the lack of morality in public life] is because over the last forty years or so we have abandoned, in terms of approbation/disapprobation, law and categorisation, any pressure to conform to basic, long unchallenged tenets of private morality. At the time I applauded the liberalising laws of the 1960s and still think that on balance they did more good than harm – the legalisation of abortion and homosexuality, the ending of the criminalisation of suicide, [ending] the stigmatising of illegitimacy, and the liberalising of contraception and divorce. Yet the effect, when taken all together a few decades on, is to live in a society where there are no constraints on private morality, no judgmentalism, no

[173] Even though, as we have seen, a spouse's adultery or behaviour need not have caused the irretrievable breakdown.

[174] Edwards and Calver (2022). [175] See 6.5.6. [176] Edwards and Calver (2022).

[177] Royal Commission on Marriage and Divorce (1956), para 69(xii).

[178] Law Com (1990), 183. [179] (2017), section 10.

[180] Ellman (2000), 344; this is not to say that people no longer feel a sense of obligation and commitment within their intimate relationships: see Lewis (2001b).

finger wagging or name calling, only acceptance of anything that anyone does, short of the criminal law, in the name of the pursuit, if not of individual happiness, then at least individual choice. . . . So individual happiness is pitted against, and prevails over the good of one's family and others.

Contemporary debate about fault was first stimulated by the divorce reforms in Part II of the Family Law Act 1996, which as we saw at 3.6.1 was never brought into force. It would have removed fault entirely from English divorce law. Concerns were expressed during the passage of the Act about what opponents saw as the removal of individual responsibility from marriage. As Lord Stallard put it, 'No fault, to me, means no responsibility, no commitment and no security.'[181] Economist Robert Rowthorn later offered the following analysis:

R. Rowthorn, 'Marriage and Trust: Some Lessons from Economics', (1999) 23 *Cambridge Journal of Economics* 661, 662–3

[M]arriage should be seen as an institution for creating trust between individuals in the sphere of family life, and . . . legal and social policy should be fashioned so as to allow this function to be effectively performed. Many of the legal and social reforms which have been implemented in modern times have undermined the ability of marriage to perform its basic role as a trust-creating institution. To get married is no longer such a major commitment and no longer offers the degree of security which it once did, since divorce is now relatively easy and the responsibilities and rights of the married and the unmarried are increasingly similar. These developments are often presented as an advance in human freedom since they allow individuals to exit unilaterally from unhappy relationships at minimum cost to themselves and with minimum delay. However, this is a one-sided view, since it ignores the benefits and freedoms associated with trust and security. The fact that individuals can now exit easily, and unilaterally, from a relationship makes it difficult for couples to make credible commitments to each other. They can promise anything they want, but many of these promises are no longer legally enforceable, and many are undermined by social policies which reward those who break their promises. By eroding the ability of couples to make credible commitments to each other, modern reforms have deprived them of an important facility which, for all its defects, the old system provided.

. . . The marriage contract has been diluted to the point that it is now much less binding than the average business deal. While employment law has increased job security and protection for workers, legal security in the family has been weakened and in many Western countries the marriage contract can now be terminated at will virtually without penalty. Marriage is now one of the few contracts where the law and government policy frequently protect the defaulting party at the expense of his or her partner.

The debate about fault and no-fault divorce has been particularly strong in the United States, where no-fault divorce was introduced during the 1970s. Many states permit divorce on unilateral demand after six months' separation, often alongside traditional fault-based grounds.[182] A guilty party can therefore divorce fairly easily. In reaction to this, rather than

[181] Hansard HL Deb, vol 569, col 1651, 29 February 1996. [182] See Ellman (2000).

advocate a wholesale return to fault-based divorce, some commentators devised a special class of marriage—with more restrictive grounds for divorce—that couples can select at the outset: 'covenant marriage'. The concern is principally to secure the position of the spouse who is unwilling to divorce, so covenant marriage adopts a private contract view of marriage, rather than a public interest model that seeks to uphold marriage by keeping parties together in the absence of fault, even where *both* wish to part. Under covenant marriage, an innocent party can instigate divorce immediately on fault-based grounds, but divorce is also available on no-fault grounds less generous than the US norm; for example, Louisiana's covenant marriage law permits unilateral divorce following a more onerous two years of separation. Three states have enacted covenant marriage laws, but the take-up has been very low.[183] The principal architect of the Louisiana covenant marriage statute makes the case for this form of marriage:

E. Spaht, 'Louisiana's Covenant Marriage Law: Recapturing the Meaning of Marriage for the Sake of the Children', in A. Dnes and R. Rowthorn (eds), *The Law and Economics of Marriage and Divorce* (Cambridge: CUP, 2002), 110–11

Restoration of "moral discourse" to divorce law . . . troubles most critics of the covenant marriage law more than any other aspect of the legislation. The "moral discourse" consists of society's collective condemnation of certain conduct within the marital relationship. Returning to objective moral judgments about a spouse's conduct threatens the notion that morality cannot be legislated. Congress and legislatures do it every day. Only when the morals to be legislated have the potential of impeding the affected person's "liberty" to leave his or her family when he or she so chooses and be considered legally "a single person" do we hear objections. In matters of breach of contract, no one has objected to assigning *blame* for failure to perform a contract, requiring that contracts be performed in good faith, and assessing damages based upon whether the party breached the contract in good faith or bad faith. If principles of contract law involve moral judgments in the context of a relationship between strangers,[184] why should the law hesitate to make a moral judgment about spouses who have been married for thirty years and have three children?

Another argument against the restoration of fault to divorce law is the assertion that fault cannot be proven, thus, those who desire divorce will be relegated to perjury, allegedly a widespread practice prior to no-fault divorce. Fault in the nature of adultery or physical abuse sufficient for an immediate divorce [under covenant marriage law] may be proven by mere preponderance of the evidence (more likely than not), and that evidence need only be circumstantial, not direct. Surely, it is no more difficult to prove adultery by a spouse than to prove which driver's fault, and the degree of that fault expressed in a percentage, caused a car accident. As a response to the expressed concern about widespread perjury, the answer is that the judiciary and attorneys bear responsibility. Even though perjury should surely be condemned, the fraud upon the court did at least require *cooperation of both spouses* and precluded the current practice [under no-fault divorce] of legalized desertion by one spouse.

[183] Louisiana (La Rev Stat Ann Sect 9:272–5, 307–9), Arizona (Ariz Rev Stat Ann Sect 25-901-906), Arkansas (Covenant Marriage Act of 2001); Bills have been introduced in several other states, but not been passed.

[184] By contrast with many other legal systems, English contract law has no general good faith doctrine.

Arguments about fault in divorce law are hotly contested. Some view fault-based divorce as a tool for influencing behaviour: to deter divorce and to deter bad behaviour during marriage (i.e. whatever behaviour would give the other spouse grounds for divorce).[185] It is also argued that the knowledge that divorce may only occur if each party misbehaves (or consents to divorce, where divorce is also available on the basis of mutual consent) would encourage spouses to 'invest' in the marriage for their mutual benefit (e.g. by one spouse reducing paid employment in order to raise the children), assured that their investments are protected for so long as the other party has no grounds for divorce.[186]

But others question whether deterrence of bad behaviour is properly or realistically the role of divorce law, rather than criminal or tort law. If conduct is not sufficiently grave to warrant the intervention of criminal or tort law, or cannot be defined sufficiently clearly for those purposes, that may suggest that it is not something that should be adjudicated on even by the divorce courts.[187] And, while proponents of fault contest the validity of these objections,[188] the Law Commission and others (most recently Trinder et al) have identified an array of practical reasons to reject fault.[189] Ascribing guilt and innocence in intimate relationships is often far from straightforward, and the legal system is ill-equipped to identify the causes of a marriage's demise. If done properly (assuming even that it could be), it would be extremely costly, for both the parties and the family justice system.[190]

Even if fault is properly a matter for family law, it may be also doubted whether spouses invest in marriage because the law places barriers in the way of divorce: most couples are affected by 'optimism bias'—few spouses enter marriage thinking that theirs might be one of the many marriages that will end badly—and most people have no detailed knowledge of family law.[191] Many also question whether law is a sufficiently sophisticated mechanism for influencing conduct within marriage and encouraging commitment; social norms may be more potent.[192]

Moreover, the strength of the 'sanction' of divorce as a deterrent to bad behaviour will only be as strong as the guilty party's desire not to be divorced and that party's unwillingness to satisfy the terms that the innocent party may demand as a condition for agreeing to divorce.[193] Proponents of fault say that a guilty party who *wants* divorce can be punished under fault-based law by the innocent party withholding divorce. But critics have argued that this course of action may rarely be in the interests of the innocent party, who might be rather better protected by the courts' powers to make financial orders that arise on divorce.[194] And the spouse wishing to leave may simply do so, without bothering about a divorce at all.[195]

In making the case for covenant marriage, Spaht argues that, logically, the revival of fault should extend to the determination of child arrangements and financial remedies. If fault-based divorce law is to achieve its aims, it may indeed be logical to ensure that a finding of fault is

[185] E.g. Royal Commission on Marriage and Divorce (1956), para 69(xxxvii).
[186] E.g. Rowthorn (1999). [187] Ellman (1997), 226. [188] Rowthorn (1999), 684–5.
[189] See 3.5.3 and Law Com (1990), paras 3.6–3.9, 3.40; O'Donovan (1993), 110–15; Scott (2002), 50–1.
[190] Trinder (2017), 146. [191] Herring, Probert, and Gilmore (2015), 199.
[192] Contrast Deech (1990); Schuz (1993); Eekelaar (2000). [193] Ellman (1997), 226.
[194] Eekelaar (2017), 118–22. One response to this would be to open up wider remedies outside the divorce context.
[195] See Fahey (2020) on the prevalence of marital separation in jurisdictions with restrictive divorce laws.

reflected in decisions about those issues: the children would live with the 'innocent' party, who could claim financial recompense from the 'guilty' party for lost expectations on divorce.[196] But adopting fault as the key criterion for these decisions would entail a major reversal in policy, prioritizing 'justice' between the spouses over the welfare and rights of individual children. This proposal has therefore been criticized by Carol Smart for returning children to the status of 'trophies in the adversarial system'.[197] Moreover, John Eekelaar and others have argued that financial settlements on divorce can promote 'responsibility' on divorce and protect parties' investments in marriage via mechanisms other than fault.[198] Indeed, simply adjudicating fault—even without that having direct implications for the children and finances—can only be damaging to the parties' future relations as joint parents of their children.

Finally, there is another psychological angle to consider. Some commentators have cautioned against attempts to 'sanitize' divorce by removing any opportunity for parties to express their sense of grievance. From a psychological perspective, the emotional conflict accompanying divorce is neither trivial nor pathological, but a normal part of the process of bereavement experienced on divorce.[199] It may be desirable for the divorce process to contain that conflict, rather than simply try to deny or reduce it,[200] and to recognize that current norms associated with 'good' divorce, such as the importance of joint parenting following separation, may themselves fuel conflict.[201] The question is whether the *legal* forum, whether via the grounds for divorce or otherwise, provides the environment in which emotional consequences of divorce can most be satisfactorily addressed. Trinder's team found 'no evidence to support the lightning conductor argument that fault can be a mechanism to work through conflict quickly'.[202] But providing at least some facility for divorce on grounds of fault (perhaps alongside no-fault options) might send a valuable signal that fault *is* sometimes unequivocally present on one side, for example in cases of domestic abuse: 'To deny the existence of fault . . . would reinforce the feeling of many victims that the abuse is in some way *their* fault.'[203] The question then is whether sending that signal for the benefit of those cases comes at too great a cost for all the others in which fault is relied on with counter-productive results.

3.10.2 DO WE HAVE DIVORCE BY MUTUAL CONSENT?

The Law Commission has found substantial support for divorce on the basis of mutual consent: 90 per cent of survey respondents in the late 1980s thought that divorce should be available on this basis.[204] Long gone are the days when the public interest demanded that parties be prevented from reaching agreements regarding divorce. It is no exaggeration to say that many of the divorces under the original MCA 1973 scheme were effectively obtained on this 'ground' thanks to the procedure for uncontested divorces, albeit that the petition

[196] Rowthorn (1999), 671; Dnes (1998), 345 argues instead that, rather than find fault in a traditional sense, a party who unilaterally seeks divorce without good cause should be regarded as being 'in breach', and so treated as the guilty party. Determining whether 'good cause' exists might, however, reintroduce traditional fault arguments.

[197] Smart (2000), 380.

[198] Eekelaar (2017), 118–22; Ellman (1997); see 6.5.6 on the marginal relevance of fault in English law of financial remedies on divorce.

[199] Day Sclater (1999), 180.

[200] Brown and Day Sclater (1999), 158; Walker (1991), 236.

[201] Collier (1999), 262.

[202] Trinder et al (2017), 103.

[203] Herring, Probert, and Gilmore (2015), 213.

[204] Law Com (1990), 183.

would have been framed in terms of one of the conduct-based facts or two years' separation.[205] If so, adopting mutual consent as an immediate ground for divorce could be viewed simply as 'a technical fix aimed at improving the functioning of the judicial system rather than... a fundamental change in family policy'.[206] Mutual consent is not a ground under the DDSA 2020, for as we saw at 3.7, the sole ground is irretrievable breakdown of the marriage. But the DDSA's introduction of joint applications and removal of conduct-based facts would suggest that England and Wales now *effectively* has divorce by mutual consent when parties apply together. Statistically, however, early data show most divorces are initiated by sole applications.[207] Thus, it is perhaps more accurate *not* to characterize divorce law as based upon mutual consent, but as based upon unilateral demand, as discussed in the following section.

3.10.3 DO WE HAVE DIVORCE ON UNILATERAL DEMAND?

If divorce should be available where a marriage has irretrievably broken down, the corollary might be to accept that divorce should be available not only where the parties agree on that course, but wherever *one* party desires it. Many consider that the question whether a marriage has irretrievably broken down is simply not justiciable, even putting to one side the formidable resources question.[208] The wish to make the notion of lifelong obligation meaningful by subjecting the dissolution of marriage 'to an authority that is independent of the will of the parties... a real exercise of judgment by the Court, acting on the community's behalf'[209] may simply be unrealizable. And so, on this view, consent of both parties to divorce ought not to be a necessary precondition: the consent of both parties ought to be necessary for marriage to *continue* and if one party wishes to divorce, that is surely the best evidence available that the marriage is over. This appears to describe conceptually the present law under the DDSA 2020. If a spouse withdraws their consent to the *marriage*, the law permits them to divorce. Yet even when a divorce application was initiated jointly, if one spouse subsequently withdraws their consent to the *divorce*, this will not stop the divorce from being finalized.

Like any other no-fault option, divorce on unilateral demand entails a very different understanding of marriage and of the nature and extent of the public interest in divorce from a fault-based law. The state is removed from adjudication on the end of the marriage, and can only protect the unwilling party via decisions relating to arrangements for children and finances.[210] Unlike divorce by mutual consent, no-fault unilateral divorce is criticized for undermining each spouse's ability to rely upon the marriage contract, and so damaging the quality of their partnership.[211] Conversely, it might be argued that the institution is made stronger by removing any risk of one spouse being trapped in any unwanted marriage.

Though we now *appear* to have divorce on unilateral demand under the DDSA 2020, this does not mean the law simply permits immediate divorce when one party decides to leave the marriage. Indeed, there is still an important role for the law in regulating divorce, and so caution should be exercised before concluding that divorce is an unrestricted, private—or 'regularized'—process, as we explore next.

205 See *Owens v Owens* [2017] EWCA Civ 182, [94].
206 Ellman (2000), 341. This was true as early as 1966: Law Com (1966), para 79.
207 MOJ (2022b). 208 Law Com (1988a), paras 4.6–4.7.
209 Mortimer Commission (1966), para 48.
210 Law Com (1988a), para 4.14. Even if the divorce itself were not granted on the basis of fault, ancillary decisions still could be: see Ellman (1997), 218; Dnes (1998).
211 Rowthorn (1999); see also Scott (2002).

3.10.4 DO WE HAVE 'REGULARIZED' DIVORCE LAW?

In these days of mass divorce, it has been suggested that the focus has shifted from delivering substantive justice to aggrieved parties to considerations related to 'consumer choice, efficiency and pragmatism'.[212] On a spectrum of regulation—whereby the law is inherently interventionist—to regularization—whereby divorce is the product of private decision (see 3.3.5)—the DDSA 2020 appears to have aligned divorce law more closely with the latter.

However, while the state no longer has an adjudicative role over divorce, and the new law generally does not restrict the *substantive* grounds on which a divorce may be obtained beyond the technical requirement of irretrievable breakdown of the marriage, it would be inaccurate to characterize the current no-fault system as being purely regularized. For the process retains some shades of regulation, with—as outlined in 3.8—restrictions relating to waiting periods, timing, and safety nets to ensure special protection for financially vulnerable parties where necessary. Therefore, the new law could be seen as slowing down and influencing the decision-making *process*, either to guard against precipitate divorces, or to encourage those determined to divorce to do so in a particular way. This suggests the state may not be prepared to give up all attempts to regulate divorcing behaviour. The 'consumers' of divorce are not left entirely free to divorce as and when they wish to. Such regulation seems sensible in light of Schuz's observation: 'Would it not be ironic if a consumer were allowed to "back out" of an agreement to purchase life assurance or a timeshare after a "cooling-off" period, but would be bound with immediate effect to an agreement to divorce?'[213]

3.11 CONCLUSION

More than three decades ago, Davis and Murch concluded that 'we have . . . moved to a position where the *state*'s interest in the breakdown of marriage has receded almost to vanishing point . . . in favour of an increased emphasis on private agreement'.[214] And in 2009, Deech observed that 'conceptually and procedurally, it is far more difficult to terminate those other pillars of a stable life, employment and a tenancy, than marriage'.[215] The grant of divorce may ultimately rest with a judge, but that judge is essentially discharging an administrative responsibility rather than adjudicating in any substantial sense. From this perspective, the reform introduced by the DDSA 2020 is characterized by continuity as much as change. It simply codified an administrative exercise that already existed in most cases, while injecting simplicity and transparency into the process. Yet this reform is also significant on several fronts. As we have seen, removing fault from the process has many benefits. As well as making the process easier to navigate, the timing of one's divorce is no longer dependent upon whether the applicant is able or willing to make allegations about the behaviour of the other spouse on the divorce petition. Now, when a marriage has—in the view of just one spouse—broken down irretrievably, the divorce will take a minimum of six months to be finalized—no matter the reason for this breakdown. The days of judges adjudicating on behavioural expectations of matrimony are well and truly over.[216]

Ascertaining the impact of the DDSA 2020 will take time. At the time of writing, statistics suggest far fewer couples are taking up the option to apply for divorce jointly, a key feature of the newly reformed MCA 1973. This could be because coordinating an application with one's separated spouse is more onerous than submitting a sole application.[217] Or it could be because

212 O'Donovan (1993), 112. 213 Schuz (1993), 581. 214 Davis and Murch (1988), 13.
215 Deech (2009a). 216 Miles (2022). 217 MOJ (2022b).

the historic narrative of one spouse divorcing the other remains embedded in social understandings of divorce. Or it could simply be because it will take time for the divorcing public to become aware of the novelty of joint applications. As Haskey has suggested, tracking the proportion of joint applications compared with sole applications will be important going forward. For if joint applications signify agreement between the parties regarding their divorce, the prevalence of joint applications may well be a measure of the DDSA's ultimate success.[218] Most prosaically, however, it is likely that a good part of the explanation for the currently low level of joint applications is the fact that there are a number of unilateral cases that were being held up under the old law—for example, by the absence of any conduct argument and so the need to wait for the relevant period of separation to expire—which are now able to proceed. As has always been the case after every divorce reform during the previous century, there will almost certainly be a rise in the number of divorces in the first year or so after the new law comes into force while these cases work their way through the system. So it will take a few years before any reliable patterns of use of the new law really emerge.

In any event, divorce law in England and Wales now sits more coherently alongside the rest of contemporary family law and the dominant ethos of family law practice. Couples are now positively encouraged to make their own arrangements for children and child support, and enabled to place more reliance on pre-nuptial and other financial agreements on divorce.[219] Since April 2022, they are now also permitted to decide for themselves when their marriage is over, with the law simply and quietly enabling that conclusion to be given dignified effect. Though opponents of this reform had concerns that an easier process would undermine the institution of marriage, this reform could be seen as supporting marriage more than the former law.[220] As Alex Chalk MP noted when the DDSA 2020 was debated in the House of Commons: 'When consent disappears [in marriage], so, too, does its legitimacy.'[221] However, this does not mean that the withdrawal of law from the adjudication of irretrievable breakdown has made divorce a lawless process. Indeed, when looking to the future of divorce law, it is important to heed Eekelaar's words:

J. Eekelaar, 'Afterword', in J. Miles, D. Monk, and R. Probert (eds), *Fifty Years of the Divorce Reform Act* (Oxford: Hart Publishing, 2022), 287

Power has moved to the parties, but power imbalances (mainly but not only economic) between them remain and attention should be sharply focused on what institutional provision, including advice and support, should be available to ensure relationship breakdown does not impact unfairly on either party, or the children. The legal process still has an important part to play in this.

ONLINE RESOURCES

Questions, suggestions for further reading, and updates on developments in this area of family law since this book was published may be found in the online resources at **www.oup.com/he/familytcm5e**.

218 Haskey (2022), 49. 219 See chapters 5, 6, and 11. 220 Thompson (2021).
221 Hansard HC Deb, vol 677, col 126, 8 June 2020.

4

PROTECTION FROM DOMESTIC ABUSE

CENTRAL ISSUES

1. Domestic abuse is a widespread problem, experienced particularly by women in mixed-sex couples. Tackling it is part of the government's broader violence against women agenda.
2. Historically, domestic abuse was regarded as a 'private' matter. The state failed to protect victims. But human rights law now imposes duties on states to act against abuse. Government policy clearly aims to prevent, reduce, and punish domestic abuse, and to support and protect victims.
3. A key issue is how to provide an effective response to domestic abuse, involving criminal, civil, and family law, whilst funding material and emotional support for victims and giving appropriate weight to their wishes and interests in any legal proceedings.
4. The civil law provides remedies principally under the Family Law Act 1996 (FLA 1996). The family courts can make non-molestation orders (NMOs) and occupation orders between parties to a wide range of domestic relationships. The family courts have strong powers to enforce orders made under the FLA 1996, but breach of an NMO is also a criminal offence.
5. The Domestic Abuse Act 2021 (DAA 2021) introduces a new type of order for which victims can apply—domestic abuse protection orders (DAPOs)—which covers much of the same ground as the FLA 1996 orders on a far simpler basis, particularly in regulating the occupation of property. Breach of a DAPO is a criminal offence. DAPOs are due to be rolled out nationwide in 2025.
6. The DAA 2021 considerably enhances the role of third parties to intervene on victims' behalf. Building on the model of the Crime and Security Act 2010 (CSA 2010, to be repealed), from 2025 police can issue domestic abuse protection notices (DAPNs), temporarily controlling alleged perpetrators' behaviour and requiring them to leave the home, and then apply to court for a DAPO to extend that protection potentially indefinitely. Police and other third parties can also apply directly for DAPOs. These actions can be taken without victims' consent, raising questions about respect for victim autonomy.
7. The FLA 1996 also provides civil remedies to combat forced marriage, a form of domestic abuse encountered in a wide range of communities in England and Wales.

4.1 INTRODUCTION

Every 30 seconds, someone contacts the police for assistance regarding domestic abuse.[1] Domestic abuse destroys many relationships, impairs the emotional, social, and psychological development of children who witness it, and can have devastating, long-term effects on the immediate victims. It has been estimated that domestic abuse costs public services, the wider economy, and victims around £74 billion annually (2022 prices), including £47 billion related to the resulting physical and emotional harm, and an estimated £14 billion lost from time off work, as well as direct costs to health and other services for victims.[2]

Domestic abuse impacts on many areas of family law. How should an allegation of domestic abuse made by one parent against the other be handled in the context of sorting out arrangements for the children where the parents live apart? We tackle this very pressing issue in some detail in chapter 11, at 11.7.3. Should the state intervene to protect children who are not the primary victims of abuse between adults in their household?[3] Should domestic abuse affect financial remedies on divorce? Can mediation safely be used where there has been domestic abuse? The presence of domestic abuse is now also a key route to obtaining legal aid for lawyers' services for all private family law matters, for which legal aid is now otherwise generally unavailable. That makes it increasingly important for victims to take action in relation to the abuse in order to obtain the evidence required to access legal aid.[4] This chapter focuses on what the law can do directly to punish and rehabilitate perpetrators and to protect adult victims.

Central to any discussion of domestic abuse is the dichotomy between the public and private spheres. Domestic violence used to be regarded as a private problem, largely ignored by the state and society. But from the 1970s, the state increasingly recognized its responsibility to tackle domestic violence and broader forms of domestic abuse. The state's role might initially appear obvious: domestic violence and other abuse is often criminal conduct. We might therefore expect offences committed in the domestic context to be treated like any other crime. Recent initiatives seek to improve the criminal justice system's response, in both dealing with perpetrators and supporting victims. However, the dynamics of domestic abuse raise complicated issues, particularly concerning the extent to which victims can, or should be able to, control any criminal proceedings. While domestic abuse is rightly recognized as a matter of grave public concern, victims still have legitimate private interests that might affect how the state should deal with perpetrators.

This chapter focuses mainly on the family courts' powers, alongside new 'hybrid' powers and orders available (in particular) to the police that blur the boundary between civil and criminal justice. 'Non-molestation orders' (NMOs) can be used to prohibit a wide range of abusive conduct. 'Occupation orders' can secure the victim's right to occupy a home shared by the parties and exclude the abuser; as well as tackling domestic abuse, occupation orders have wider significance regarding family members' rights to occupy the home, particularly in the event of relationship breakdown between family members other than spouses and civil partners.[5] The contemporary, increasingly hybrid, approach to domestic abuse in the civil sphere poses new questions for the public/private dichotomy. The criminalization of breach of NMOs has implications for victims' ability to control their family's fate, as do new powers

[1] HMIC (2014), 38. [2] HM Government (2022a), 83, based on Oliver et al (2019).

[3] NB CA 1989, s 31(9) definition of 'harm'; DAA 2021, s 3.

[4] Legal Aid, Sentencing and Punishment of Offenders Act 2012, Sch 1, paras 11 and 12, and Civil Legal Aid (Procedure) Regulations, SI 2012/3098, reg 33.

[5] See 7.3.3.

for police and other third parties to obtain 'domestic abuse protection orders' (DAPOs) without victim consent. Determining the proper legal response to domestic abuse is not easy.

4.2 BACKGROUND ISSUES: DOMESTIC ABUSE AND KEY POLICY QUESTIONS

4.2.1 DEFINING 'DOMESTIC ABUSE'

Terminology in this field is contested. The term used by government and, from 2021, in legislation is 'domestic abuse', an expression intended to encompass the wide range of concerning behaviours understood to fall within its ambit. Some commentators regret the loss of 'domestic violence' from the lexicon, concerned that this risks minimizing the physical and other forms of violence that are often involved;[6] they prefer 'domestic violence and abuse'. Nevertheless, the legal definition used across government[7]—applicable between two parties aged over 16 who are 'personally connected'[8]—is as follows:

Domestic Abuse Act 2021

1 Definition of "domestic abuse"

. . .

(3) Behaviour is "abusive" if it consists of any of the following —
- (a) physical or sexual abuse;
- (b) violent or threatening behaviour;
- (c) controlling or coercive behaviour;
- (d) economic abuse (see subsection (4));
- (e) psychological, emotional or other abuse;

and it does not matter whether the behaviour consists of a single incident or a course of conduct.

(4) "Economic abuse" means any behaviour that has a substantial adverse effect on [the victim's] ability to —
- (a) acquire, use or maintain money or other property, or
- (b) obtain goods or services.

(5) For the purposes of this Act [the perpetrator's] behaviour may be behaviour "towards" [the victim] despite the fact that it consists of conduct directed at another person (for example, [the victim's] child).

The inclusion of 'controlling or coercive' behaviour[9] (often referred to in the literature and in this chapter as 'coercive control'), albeit merely as one type of abuse rather than its defining concept,[10] acknowledges the many abusive activities deployed to exercise power in

[6] E.g. Aldridge (2021). [7] See generally HO (2022c). [8] DAA 2021, s 2—see 4.6.1.

[9] HO (2022c), from para 47; can include denial of religious divorce and refusal to contract civil marriage to protect parties to a religious-only marriage: from para 79. Contrast the specificity of the Domestic Abuse (Scotland) Act 2018, s 2.

[10] See Bishop (2021), 166–7 for criticism.

relationships. This is an issue highlighted by feminist analysis, which conceives of domestic abuse as a form of 'liberty crime'.[11] The catch-all reference to 'other' abuse ensures that novel methods of control and harassment can be tackled, including through social media and other technology, for example 'revenge porn', 'trolling', hacking, and spyware.[12] The definition's use of 'behaviour', which may entail 'a course of conduct', may help underscore how abuse can be an 'ongoing, "everyday" reality' for victims, rather than discrete, isolated 'incidents'.[13]

As we discuss at 4.2.2.b and 4.2.3, domestic abuse is widely regarded as a gender-based problem: most victims are women in mixed-sex relationships. 'Domestic abuse' may therefore be misleadingly gender neutral. The expression 'violence against women and girls' is sometimes preferred (and is used by government[14]); the inclusion of 'girls' reflects the growing problem of teen abuse.[15] But it may inhibit other victims—in same-sex relationships or men generally—from coming forward.[16]

However, family law's remedies for domestic abuse—and the statutory definition—apply to a broader range of more or less loosely 'familial' relationships, characterized by physical, emotional, and often financial closeness. The parties' proximity poses potential difficulties: it can make victims reluctant or unable to pursue remedies that objectively appear best suited to ending the abuse. We examine the scope of 'personal connection'—on which the DAA 2021 concept of domestic abuse rests—at 4.6.1, in the context of eligibility for DAPOs. The inclusion of various family members (as well as intimate partners) as perpetrators brings activities such as elder abuse,[17] forced marriages, and 'honour crimes'[18] within domestic abuse policy.[19]

The word 'domestic' is associated with historical trivialization of the problem. Police were particularly criticized: their expression 'it's just a domestic' betrayed a failure to take violence in the home as seriously as violence committed in public.[20] And some commentators object to 'victim', preferring 'survivor' (where apt).[21] Hoff described the women she met when researching domestic violence as:

> knowledgeable, capable people who developed strategies for coping within the violent relationship, as well as for eventually leaving it. Their ability to cope with life-threatening crises in spite of self-blame and intimidations from others that they were somehow responsible for their plight, reveals them more as survivors than as helpless victims.[22]

Throughout this chapter, we use various terms, including 'victim', the word used by the criminal justice system and the DAA 2021. In discussing civil remedies, we use 'applicant' and 'respondent'.

[11] Bishop (2016), 69 and 4.2.3.

[12] HO (2022c), para 70; see generally ch 3 for examples of all types of abuse listed in s 1. On use of tracking devices, see Hill (2020), 219–20.

[13] Cf Bishop (2021). [14] HM Government (2021). [15] HO (2022c), from para 22.

[16] Donovan et al (2006); government clumsily and confusingly refers to 'male victims of violence against women and girls': HM Government (2022b).

[17] See Herring (2011). [18] HO (2018), 10. [19] See generally: HO (2022c), ch 2.

[20] Mullender and Morley (1994), 11. [21] Hilder and Bettinson (2016), 5.

[22] Hoff (1990), 229; Hill (2020), ch 2.

4.2.2 EVIDENCE ABOUT DOMESTIC ABUSE

4.2.2.a The prevalence of domestic abuse

Measuring domestic abuse statistically is challenging: until recently, agencies used differing definitions of domestic abuse for data collection, and both survey and administrative (e.g. police and CPS) data still count 'incidents' of abuse and related distinct 'events', such as arrest or charge. This incident-based model is problematic, in particular, for capturing the lived experience of coercive controlling behaviour;[23] work to find a way of measuring that phenomenon and repeat victimization (as contrasted with isolated events) through the Crime Survey for England & Wales (CSEW) is ongoing.[24] There are also particular knowledge gaps about abuse of members of groups who are inhibited for various reasons from coming forward and for whom domestic abuse support service provision is also poor, including men and members of black, other minority ethnic communities, and LGBT+ communities.[25]

Domestic abuse is certainly under-reported and so under-recorded in justice system and other administrative data, which is why the CSEW is so important. The Covid-19 pandemic means that, at the time of writing, the latest CSEW data are for year-ending March 2020.[26] Only about a third of victims of partner abuse perceive themselves as having experienced domestic violence, and only a quarter perceive what happened to them as criminal.[27] Researchers are often the first people—and the police the last—to whom the abuse has been disclosed, if disclosed at all; well under a fifth of victims contact the police.[28] The CSEW collects information about abuse that never reaches the legal system; and the privacy of its self-completion questionnaire yields significantly higher reports of abuse than conventional interviews.[29] Since the CSEW is based on private households, those living in refuges, who might have experienced the worst abuse, are unrepresented. But even with these and other limitations,[30] the figures gathered are high.

In evaluating the data, particularly when analysing prevalence of abuse by gender of victim, we must distinguish between the different categories of abuse surveyed: the use and threat of physical violence, including threats against someone close to the victim; financial abuse (such as preventing the victim from having a fair share of the household money); emotional abuse (such as stopping the victim from seeing friends and relatives; repeatedly belittling the victim); and sexual violence and stalking by current and former partners and other family members.[31] Abuse by current/former partners and other 'family' abuse are distinguished. The following extract and Table 4.1 report on abuse experienced by survey respondents in the last year (to March 2020) and since age of 16, respectively.

ONS, *Domestic Abuse Victim Characteristics, England and Wales: Year Ending March 2020* (2020d)

> For the year ending 2020, the [CSEW] estimated that 1.6 million women and 757,000 men aged 16 to 74 years experienced domestic abuse in the last year. This is a prevalence rate of approximately 7 in 100 women and 4 in 100 men.

[23] Bishop (2021), 165–7. [24] ONS (2021a), following Walby et al (2016)'s criticism.

[25] House of Commons Select Committee on Home Affairs (2018), 10; HM Government (2022b); Martin (2016); Barnes and Donovan (2016); Turgoose (2016).

[26] ONS (2021b), section 3. [27] ONS (2020e), tables 16 and 17. [28] Ibid, table 12.

[29] ONS (2020c), heading 7. [30] ONS (2021c), (2021d). [31] ONS (2021c), section 5.

Women were significantly more likely than men to be victims of each type of abuse, with the exception of sexual assault by a family member where, although higher, the difference was not significant. . . .

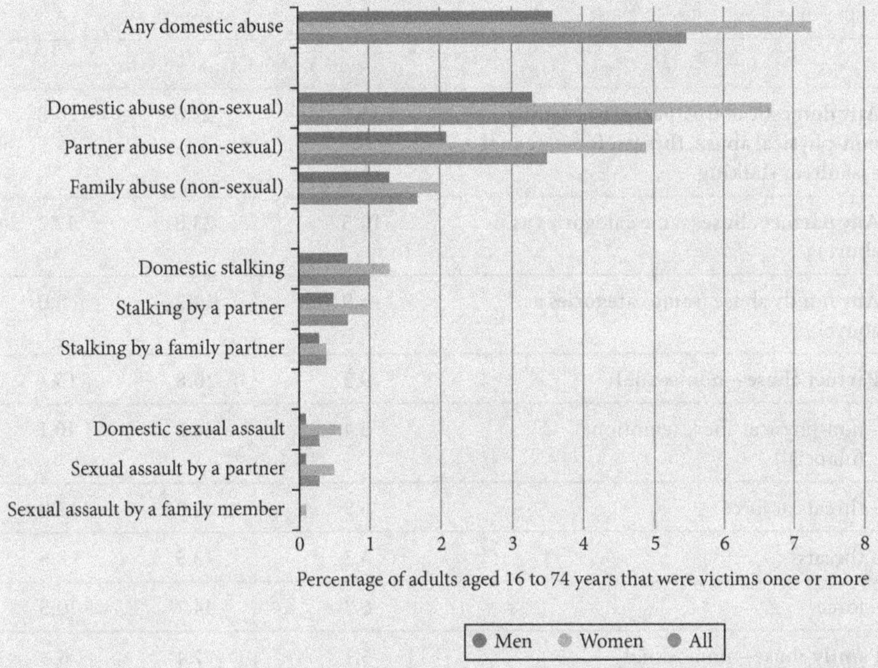

Prevalence of domestic abuse in the last year for adults aged 16 to 74 years, by sex and type of abuse, England and Wales, year ending March 2020.

When looking at [long-term] trends, the prevalence of domestic abuse experienced by men and women aged 16 to 59 years in the year ending March 2020 is significantly lower than reported in the year ending March 2005. For example, 4.0% of men and 8.1% of women aged 16 to 59 years had experienced domestic abuse within the last year in the year ending March 2020, compared with 6.5% of men and 11.1% of women in the year ending March 2005.

Whilst the proportion of respondents reporting domestic abuse in the CSEW has dropped since 2005, analysis of data regarding *violent* crime shows that the total *volume* of such crime against *women* has been increasing since 2009, *domestic* violence (specifically) being on a different trajectory from other types of violent crime.[32] In order words, whilst the number/proportion of *victims* may be falling, the *amount of violent domestic abuse* being experienced by some 'high frequency' victims is rising. Domestic abuse is the highest offence for

[32] Walby et al (2016) criticizing ONS's approach as seriously underestimating repeat victimization and so total volume of domestic abuse; see ONS (2021a).

Table 4.1 Prevalence of domestic abuse among adults aged 16 to 74 since the age of 16, by type of abuse and sex, year ending March 2020 CSEW, selected data extracted from ONS (2020c), table 1

Types of abuse	Men	Women	All
	% who were victims once or more		
Any domestic abuse (partner or family non-physical abuse, threats, force, sexual assault, or stalking	**13.8**	**27.6**	**20.8**
Any partner abuse (same categories as above)	**10.5**	**23.8**	**17.2**
Any family abuse (same categories as above)	**5.9**	**10.2**	**8.0**
Partner abuse—non-sexual	**9.3**	**20.8**	**15.1**
- non-physical abuse (emotional, financial)	5.4	14.7	10.1
- threats or force	6.9	17.0	12.0
- threats	3.3	13.5	8.5
- force	6.3	14.7	10.5
Family abuse—non-sexual	**5.1**	**7.4**	**6.3**
Any sexual assault (including rape/ penetration (and attempts), touching, exposure) by a partner	**0.6**	**6.4**	**3.5**
Any sexual assault (same categories) by a family member	**0.2**	**2.1**	**1.1**
Domestic stalking	**3.1**	**9.3**	**6.3**
Unweighted base—number of adults	*11,347*	*13,330*	*24,677*

repeat victimization: in 2012–13, 75 per cent of all domestic violence was a repeat incident;[33] over a fifth of victims reported abuse on three or more occasions, but over half declined to answer or did not know how often they had been abused.[34] However measured, domestic abuse clearly remains a 'volume crime', constituting about 15 per cent of all crime (excluding fraud)—and over a third of all crimes of violence against the person—reported to police in year ending March 2020.[35] And it is estimated that three to four million children live with an adult who has experienced domestic abuse, one in five of those seeing or hearing abuse perpetrated.[36]

[33] ONS (2014d), ch 1, table D7: latest data on this. [34] Ibid, ch 4, 16, and table 4.12.
[35] ONS (2020c), fig 7. [36] Victims' Commissioner (2020), 23.

4.2.2.b The gender dimension

CSEW data on the number of male victims may seem surprisingly high.[37] Accurately gauging the pattern and frequency of abuse by gender is challenging. Researchers using different methodologies have reached apparently contradictory conclusions about the incidence of women's violence against men, and gathering reliable evidence of male victimization through official records is especially problematic given male victims' reticence: half of male victims (a fifth of female victims) tell no one.[38]

However, closer inspection reveals a more subtle picture, supporting the view that domestic abuse is primarily experienced by female victims at the hands of male perpetrators,[39] particularly once coercive controlling behaviour is brought into account.[40] The CSEW data reported at 4.2.2.a reveal detailed differences between men and women's experiences, with twice as many women as men reporting any partner abuse since age 16. Moreover, women typically report abuse over longer periods and by more than one perpetrator.[41] Other studies have found that women's use of force is generally isolated and defensive or reactive, rather than sustained and controlling, and far less serious.[42] The vast majority of prosecutions for coercive control have been brought against men.[43] When domestic violence has fatal consequences, the gender difference is stark: the principal suspect in relation to 37 per cent of female homicide victims aged over 16 and 2.5 per cent of male victims in 2020–21 was a current or former partner; women were also far more likely to be killed by another family member than by some other acquaintance or a stranger.[44]

4.2.2.c Causes and risk factors

If gathering reliable data about the prevalence and experience of domestic abuse is difficult, identifying its causes is harder—the reality is complex, so individual cases cannot readily be pigeonholed into specific 'types'. Several suggested causal explanations, each controversial, indicate different strategies for tackling the abuse,[45] depending on whether the abuse can be regarded as 'instrumental' or 'expressive'.[46]

The latter views abuse as a manifestation of anger-management problems. These might stem from the psychology of the individuals involved: perpetrators having unusually aggressive, narcissistic, or jealous personalities, victims being unusually insecure or masochistic. Or from inter-generationally learned behaviour, parties acting in ways witnessed by them as children in their own families, including experience of child abuse.[47] Other theories focus on the effects of social and economic deprivation; others on alcohol and other substance abuse.

The former, 'instrumental' view, by contrast—underpinning the feminist theories explored at 4.2.3—sees domestic abuse as a manifestation of patriarchy, of male power being systematically exercised over women: an exercise in coercive control.

37 Men reported higher levels of force than female victims of partner abuse in year to March 2018: ONS (2018a), 19.

38 ONS (2020e), table 12.

39 See Kaganas (2006), 144–6; Hill (2020), ch 7.

40 Myhill (2015).

41 Roe (2010), tables 3.08 and 3.09; no more recent ONS data.

42 Dobash and Dobash (2004); Hester (2009).

43 ONS (2020f), table 1.

44 ONS (2022a), tables 13a and 13b.

45 Law Com (1992), from para 2.6.

46 Hilder and Freeman (2016). See also Madden Dempsey's typology, noted at 4.2.3.

47 Morley and Mullender (1994), 6–7; Hill (2020), chs 3 and 6; HM Government (2022a), 23.

No one theory can explain any one incident of domestic abuse, and correlations are far easier to identify than causes. Theories which in some way blame victims are highly controversial, inconsistent with findings about survivors' determination to escape and the barriers that they face.[48] It is easier to identify correlations or risk factors that heighten the probability of abuse than to isolate specific causes.[49] Various factors have been found to increase the likelihood of becoming a victim of partner abuse, including: being female; young (aged 16–19); separated, divorced, or single; living as a single parent; long-term sick or disabled; unemployed. Women of white and mixed race backgrounds are more likely to become victims than women from other ethnic groups.[50] Perpetrators tend to be: young males; with lower levels of education; histories of criminal behaviour; disadvantaged backgrounds; and poor role models for attitudes towards violence and gender equality. Substance abuse and mental health issues are also correlated with abuse.[51] There is increasing understanding of the problem of intersectionality: where possession of more than one of the risk factors heightens risk and may make tackling the abuse harder:[52]

Joint Committee on Human Rights, *Violence Against Women and Girls*.
HL Paper 106; HC 594 (2015), 8

We share the concern of the UN Special Rapporteur on violence against women, its causes and consequences, Rashida Manjoo:

It is crucial to acknowledge that violence, inequality and discrimination does not occur solely on the basis of gender, and that women and girls face multiple forms of discrimination on the basis of their race, ethnicity, class, sexuality, and other factors, including their immigration status. Multiple forms of discrimination have an impact on women's experiences of violence, their perceptions of those experiences, and their ability to seek and receive support.

However, whilst certain characteristics *increase* the risk, it is important to appreciate that domestic abuse occurs across all parts of society:

R. Morley and A. Mullender, *Preventing Domestic Violence to Women*
(London: Home Office, 1994)

Attempting to isolate particular groups of people prone to domestic violence may be defended as a way of furthering an understanding of the causes and hence cures of the problem. However, the message from research is clear. While class, ethnicity, drinking, childhood experiences and indeed other psychological/social factors may in some cases contribute to the establishment of violent relationships and/or their continuation, domestic violence to women is far too common throughout society to isolate specific groups as constituting *the* problem.

48 Edwards (1989), 164–72; Hoff (1990); Dobash and Dobash (1992), ch 7.
49 Walby and Myhill (2001). 50 See generally ONS (2020d).
51 HM Government (2022a), 23–4. 52 HO (2022c), from para 80.

4.2.2.d Why not just leave?

Two-thirds of victims who share accommodation with the perpetrator do not leave.[53] There can be a complex web of reasons for this. Some incline them to stay: many victims stay because they still love their partner and want to help them resolve their problems, perhaps not appreciating that they are victims of abuse at all. Others inhibit them (women, in particular[54]) from leaving: family responsibilities to children, the simple lack of anywhere to go, financial dependence on the perpetrator (exacerbated by any economic abuse), fear of what the perpetrator will do to them or their children if they do attempt to leave.[55] Indeed, as the statutory application of 'domestic abuse' to ex-partners recognizes,[56] ending the relationship does not always stop the abuse. It may actually precipitate or escalate it,[57] even to the point of homicide.[58] Many victims are abused in the context of contact arrangements for their children with the now ex-partner.[59]

C. Humphreys and R. Thiara, 'Neither Justice nor Protection: Women's Experiences of Post-Separation Violence', (2003) 25 *Journal of Social Welfare and Family Law* 195, 196

'Why doesn't she leave?' is probably one of the most frequently asked questions for those who witness a woman suffering domestic violence. Implicit in this question is frustration and mystification that women are failing to 'look after themselves', and often their children, by remaining caught in a web of violence and abuse. This individualizing discourse places the responsibility on the woman for leaving herself open to continued violence and abuse. It further implies that there is a clear line separating her life in the abusive relationship and the safety and security which awaits her once she separates.

Post-separation violence is a fear and frequently a reality for women and children who attempt to escape from abusive and violent relationships. However, it is often over-looked as a danger and remains an area where the failure of effective intervention leaves women and children vulnerable and unprotected. The effect of this failure is not neutral, but compounds the abuser's control and the woman's sense of entrapment.

Evidently, public funding cuts that remove sources of local support, especially refuge places and specialist services for particular groups, worsen victims' predicament.[60] The lockdowns of the Covid-19 pandemic posed unique problems.[61]

4.2.2.e The justice gap

There is clearly a vast 'justice gap' between the estimated 2.3 million victims each year, many of whom are repeat victims experiencing persistent abuse, and the number of cases in the legal system. Police figures for the year ending March 2020 record 1.28 million domestic

53 ONS (2020e), table 6.

54 ONS (2014d)'s finding of no difference in women and men's likelihood of leaving for at least one night gives no indication of longer-term outcomes. ONS (2020e) data on leaving is not disaggregated by gender.

55 ONS (2020e), table 7; Hill (2020) ch 2.

56 DAA 2021, s 2.

57 Walby and Allen (2004), 62–9. ONS (2020d), fig 7: abuse most prevalent amongst divorced and separated.

58 See the Femicide Census (undated), 2.8.

59 See 11.7.2–11.7.3.

60 Walby et al (2016), 1207.

61 ONS (2020g).

abuse-related incidents, of which 59 per cent were recorded as domestic-abuse related *crimes*, the remainder staying on file as domestic-abuse related *incidents* (an important marker of a safeguarding concern).[62] Those apparently high figures are put into stark relief by the fact that less than one in five victims contacts the police. But attrition beyond that point is even more profound. Only 33 in 100 domestic abuse-related crimes recorded by police in the year to March 2020 resulted in arrest.[63] Over half of the crimes were not progressed owing to evidential difficulties following victim withdrawal (see 4.3.2), and nearly a quarter more cases were dropped for that reason despite victims' support for prosecution.[64] In the same year,[65] the Crown Prosecution Service (CPS) received just 79,965 domestic-abuse flagged referrals from police (a 19 per cent drop on the previous year), and around a quarter of cases that reached the CPS did not result in a prosecution.[66] Of the 61,169 prosecutions for domestic abuse-related crimes that year (14 per cent of all CPS prosecutions), over three-quarters (47,534) were successful, mostly following a guilty plea; most failed prosecutions resulted from problems with the victim (withdrawal, non-attendance, or weak evidence).[67] While that represents a rising conviction rate (for cases that get that far), clearly the attrition earlier in the system means that the number of convictions is dwarfed by the number of victims identified by the CSEW, even before we factor in repeat victims. Meanwhile, just over 37,000 non-molestation orders (discussed at 4.5.2) were made by the family court in the calendar year 2020.[68]

4.2.3 FEMINIST PERSPECTIVES ON DOMESTIC ABUSE LAW, POLICY, AND PRACTICE

The data explored earlier indicate that domestic abuse may principally be viewed as a gendered problem. Feminist scholars have accordingly been at the forefront of critiques of the law and analyses of domestic abuse. While feminist theories specifically offer an explanation of women's abuse by men, they can be applied more widely to abuse of power by dominant parties in any unequal relationships, such as the abuse of vulnerable older people by family members or 'carers'.[69] Michelle Madden Dempsey has argued that in order properly to understand the phenomenon and so tailor appropriate responses, it is important to distinguish instances of domestic violence (and abuse) in its 'strong sense' of 'intimate terrorism'—where it carries this aspect of control and abuse of power in an unequal relationship[70]—from other instances of abuse between family members (sometimes referred to as 'situational violence').[71]

Central to feminist analysis of domestic abuse is the dichotomy between public and private spheres. The law and its agents have been accused of regarding domestic abuse as a private matter, not a concern for the state. The state and wider society have thus enabled abuse to continue free from outside interference, and so condoned it. Historically, those charges are unanswerable. The law paid no special attention to domestic abuse, instead placing wives

[62] ONS (2020f), heading 3: no data for Greater Manchester Police owing to IT problems.
[63] Ibid, heading 4. [64] Ibid, fig 4.
[65] Owing to inevitable time lags, police and CPS figures relate to different case-flows—e.g. convictions in one year will at least in part relate to offences referred earlier.
[66] ONS (2020f), heading 6. [67] Ibid, heading 7. [68] MOJ (2022a), table 16.
[69] Freeman (1989), 743–5. Cf concerns that an exclusively feminist focus may exclude atypical victims: Centre for Social Justice (2012).
[70] This analysis is adopted by HO (2022c), para 36.
[71] Madden Dempsey (2006); Douglas (2018a), ch 3; Hill (2020), 189–90.

in an inferior position: at common law, husbands could use 'reasonable' chastisement on their wives and confine them in order to control their behaviour and enforce the right to consortium.[72] These rights flowed from the law's understanding of the marital relationship:

***W. Blackstone, Commentaries on the Laws of England*, vol 1** (1765, Facsimile edn: Chicago: University of Chicago Press, 1979), 430, 432–3

By marriage, the husband and wife are one person in law: that is, the very being or legal existence of the woman is suspended during the marriage, or at least is incorporated and consolidated into that of the husband: under whose wing, protection, and *cover*, she performs every thing . . . Under this principle, of an union of person in husband and wife, depend almost all the legal rights, duties, and disabilities, that either of them acquire by marriage. . . .

The husband also (by the old law) might give his wife moderate correction. For, as he is to answer for her misbehaviour, the law thought it reasonable to intrust him with this power of restraining her, by domestic chastisement, in the same moderation that a man is allowed to correct his servants or children; for whom the master or parent is also liable in some cases to answer. But this power of correction was confined within reasonable bounds . . . But . . . this power of correction began to be doubted: and a wife may now have security of the peace against her husband; or, in return, a husband against his wife. Yet the lower rank of people, who were always fond of the old common law, still claim and exert their antient privilege: and the courts of law will still permit a husband to restrain a wife of her liberty, in case of any gross misbehaviour. . . .[73]

Husbands also held immunity from liability for rape:

M. Hale, *The History of the Pleas of the Crown* (1736, London: Professional Books, 1971), 629

. . . the husband cannot be guilty of a rape committed by himself upon his lawful wife, for by their mutual matrimonial consent and contract the wife hath given up herself in this kind unto her husband, which she cannot retract.

These rights were eroded over time, but it was not until 1891 and 1991, respectively, that the courts definitively declared each right no longer to exist.

The Queen v Jackson [1891] 1 QB 671, 678–9, 680

LORD HALSBURY LC:

I confess that some of the propositions which have been referred to during the argument are such as I should be reluctant to suppose ever to have been the law of England. More than a century ago it was boldly contended that slavery existed in England; but, if any one were

[72] See Cretney (2003a), ch 4.

[73] Doggett (1992), ch 2, argues that husbands' right to control wives was the very *essence*, not the mere consequence, of the doctrine of coverture.

to set up such a contention now, it would be regarded as ridiculous. In the same way, such quaint and absurd dicta as are to be found in the books as to the right of a husband over his wife in respect of personal chastisement are not, I think, now capable of being cited as authorities in a court of justice in this or any civilized country . . . The [case] seems to me to be based on the broad proposition that it is the right of the husband, where his wife has wilfully absented herself from him, to seize the person of his wife by force and detain her in his house until she shall be willing to restore to him his conjugal rights. I am not prepared to assent to such a proposition.

Regina v R [1992] 1 AC 599, 616

LORD KEITH OF KINKEL:

The common law is . . . capable of evolving in the light of changing social, economic and cultural developments. Hale's proposition reflected the state of affairs in these respects at the time it was enunciated. Since then the status of women, and particularly of married women, has changed out of all recognition in various ways . . . Apart from property matters and the availability of matrimonial remedies, one of the most important changes is that marriage is in modern times regarded as a partnership of equals, and no longer one in which the wife must be the subservient chattel of the husband. Hale's proposition involves that by marriage a wife gives her irrevocable consent to sexual intercourse with her husband under all circumstances and irrespective of the state of her health or how she happens to be feeling at the time. In modern times any reasonable person must regard that conception as quite unacceptable.

However, even once all adults *theoretically* enjoyed equal protection under the law, commentators continued to highlight the legal system's failure to treat domestic violence as seriously as other offences. This failure to intervene was attributed to a perception of domestic violence as a 'private' matter that, by implication, women just have to tolerate:[74]

J. Pahl, *Private Violence and Public Policy: The Needs of Battered Women and the Response of Public Services* (London: Routledge & Kegan Paul, 1985), 13–15

In a culture which, both explicitly and implicitly, assumes fundamental linkages between such concepts as 'woman', 'wife', 'family', 'home' and 'private', it is no accident that violence against a woman, perpetuated by her husband within their family home, is somehow seen as a different sort of crime from violence against a stranger in a public place. We can see these linkages exemplified in many different statements which have been made on the subject, most especially in the justifications for non-intervention given both by violent husbands, and also by people who might well have intervened had the violence occurred between strangers in a public place.

[74] E.g. Pizzey (1974); Edwards (1989); Dobash and Dobash (1992); Barnett (2014).

Pahl drew on two examples from evidence given to the 1975 Parliamentary Select Committee on Violence in Marriage. The first was from the Association of Chief Police Officers:

> It is important to keep 'wife battering' in its correct perspective and realise that this loose term is applied to incidents ranging from a very minor domestic fracas where no Police action is really justified, to the more serious incidents of assaults occasioning grievous bodily harm and unlawful woundings. Whilst such problems take up considerable Police time during say, 12 months, in the majority of cases the role of the Police is a negative one. We are, after all, dealing with persons 'bound in marriage', and it is important for a host of reasons, to maintain the unity of the spouses. (Select Committee Report, 1975, 366)

The second came from the Home Office, addressing the scope of criminal injuries compensation:

> It can perhaps be argued that the Government (or the police) cannot have the same day to day responsibility for the day to day behaviour of members of a household within their own walls. Some disagreement may be inevitable within a family. Even a degree of minor violence may be normal in some homes. It can perhaps be argued that the point at which the State should intervene in family violence should be higher than that which is expected in the case of violence between strangers. Or even that the State has no particular responsibility for compensating those who suffer violence in circumstances which are largely (in the case of adult members of a family) under their own control. (Select Committee Report, 1975, 418)

According to Pahl:

> Both these statements suggest that the intervention of the state is less appropriate when the individuals concerned are linked by family ties as opposed to being strangers, and when the incident takes place in a private rather than a public place. To question this is not to advocate that there should be a policeman in every bedroom nor is it to argue for the abolition of privacy or domestic life. However, for our topic it is important to consider more carefully the ways in which the public-private boundary is defined; more specifically, it is important to consider *whose* privacy is being respected or violated in particular circumstances. . . . [T]he notion of privacy is not an absolute value, . . . some people's privacy appears to be more inviolate than other people's privacy, and . . . by looking at how 'the private' is defined and maintained we can understand a great deal about the power relations in a particular society.

E. Schneider, 'The Violence of Privacy', in M. Fineman and R. Mykitiuk (eds), *The Public Nature of Private Violence* (New York: Routledge, 1994), 44

> Although social failure to respond to problems of battered women has been justified on grounds of privacy, this failure to respond is an affirmative political decision that has serious public consequences. The rationale of privacy masks the political nature of the decision. Privacy thus plays a particularly subtle and pernicious ideological role in supporting,

encouraging, and legitimating violence against women. The state plays an affirmative role in permitting violence against battered women by protecting the privileges and prerogatives of battering men and failing to protect battered women, and by prosecuting battered women for homicide when they protect themselves.

Domestic violence and other abuse—and the concept of privacy that allowed it to flourish—are the product of deep-seated, patriarchal ideology, still present throughout society, and within the legal system if no longer the substantive law itself:

M. Freeman, 'Legal Ideologies, Patriarchal Precedents, and Domestic Violence', in M. Freeman (ed), *State, Law, and the Family: Critical Perspectives* (London: Tavistock, 1984), 72

[G]iven the position of women in society the behaviour of violent husbands is rational, if extreme. It is not necessary for husbands to have formal rights such as to chastise their wives. That they once had this right and exercised it is sufficient. It helped to form and then to reinforce an ideology of subordination and control of women. The ideology remains imbricated in the legal system even if one of its grosser manifestations has virtually disappeared. Wife battering remains one of its legacies and if this too is to go the ideology must be dismantled. The legal system has been committed to a patriarchal ideology. It is this that must be challenged if violence against women is to diminish and ultimately to cease.

L. Hoff, *Battered Women as Survivors* (London: Routledge, 1990), 234, 241

Terms such as the 'battered wife syndrome' and 'domestic violence' reveal an interpretation of wife battering as only a 'family' or medical problem and tend to mask the political and broader social ramifications of the more explicit term 'violence against women' . . .

[W]oman abuse is more than a personal crisis. It is a public health problem which arises from traditional values that regard women as appropriate objects of violence and male control; from the chronic problem of women's continued economic disparity in a wealthy industrialized society; and from the gender-based division of labour regarding child-care.

On this view, improving the law's response to individual perpetrators may alleviate a symptom, but it will not destroy the underlying infection. Domestic abuse will not be prevented until the structural inequality of women in society, particularly marked in some communities,[75] is dismantled. This requires legal and policy measures designed to produce a more equal division of responsibilities within the home and to give men and women more equal economic power, such as fundamental reform of employment law and childcare practices. It also requires education of children and the public generally about healthy

[75] Joint Committee on Human Rights (2015), para 167; see also Judge Elósegui's dissenting remarks in *Kurt v Austria* (App No 62903/15, ECHR) (2021).

relationships and appropriate interpersonal behaviour,[76] countering the 'hyper-masculine' cultures evident amongst some perpetrators.[77] Current government strategy has multiple strands: prioritizing prevention; supporting victims; pursuing perpetrators; and delivering a strong response from all relevant public agencies.[78] The aim is to create a 'zero tolerance' environment in which domestic abuse is 'everyone's business', not a matter hidden in the private domain.[79] But the scale of that task should not be underestimated:[80]

HM Government, *Transforming the Response to Domestic Abuse: Government Consultation* (2018), 15

[W]e have to challenge the acceptability of violence and abusive behaviour and address underlying gender norms.

"To be honest, I never knew there were services that could support you and help people in my situation. Because to us, for me, it's like a normal thing: I've seen my grandmother, my aunties, my mother going through all that . . . people just think that is the way it is, that is the way that it's supposed to be. . . ."

4.2.4 THE HUMAN RIGHTS DIMENSION

Human rights law adds a further dimension to contemporary discourse about domestic abuse.[81] The European Court of Human Rights has held in several cases, notably *Opuz v Turkey*,[82] that inadequate state response to domestic violence constitutes a human rights violation, identifying several obligations on the state to protect victims whilst also ensuring proportionate and fair treatment of alleged perpetrators.[83] In this section, we outline the law set out in *Opuz* and other human rights arguments that may be made to protect victims. We identify particular issues in the English context throughout the chapter.

The applicant's husband in *Opuz* had over several years perpetrated serious attacks on the applicant and her mother, threatening to kill them. The police arrested but released him, the women withdrew their complaints (under threat from the husband), and the prosecutor dropped the charges. He was later convicted for a multiple stabbing of the applicant, but sentenced only to pay a fine. Despite the women's appeals for further action, nothing was done. Shortly afterwards, the husband killed the mother, claiming that it was necessary to protect his 'honour'. He was released pending an appeal, and again threatened to kill the applicant and her new partner. The police simply circulated his picture and fingerprints to facilitate an arrest should he appear near the applicant's home.

The applicant successfully claimed violations of Articles 2, 3, and 14 of the European Convention on Human Rights (ECHR), arguing that the Turkish state had breached its

[76] HM Government (2018); DFE (2019).
[77] Crowther-Dowey et al (2016); Aldridge (2021), 1834.
[78] HM Government (2022a).
[79] HM Government (2018).
[80] See HM Government (2022a), fig 2 on reasons why victim did not report partner abuse to police.
[81] See McQuigg (2016); Herring (2020).
[82] (App No 33401/02, ECHR) (2009).
[83] *Kurt v Austria* (App No 62903/15, ECHR) (2021), [182].

positive obligations to protect her and her mother, and that its lacklustre policing, prosecution, and sentencing of domestic violence constituted discrimination against women. The Court took a robust approach, drawing on its own case law concerning states' obligations regarding child protection and other international conventions and policies concerning the prevention of violence and discrimination against women. Turkish law and practice were found wanting. It should have been possible to prosecute the husband despite the victims' withdrawal given the seriousness of his offences and the continuing threat posed. The response of police and prosecutors was found 'manifestly inadequate', having no impact on the husband's behaviour; the few judicial interventions were chastised for exhibiting 'a certain degree of tolerance' of his conduct.[84]

4.2.4.a Article 2

The Court found that Article 2, the right to life, was breached in *Opuz*:

Opuz v Turkey **(App No 33401/02, ECHR) (2009)**

128. . . . Article 2§1 enjoins the State . . . to take appropriate steps to safeguard the lives of those within its jurisdiction . . . This involves a primary duty on the State to secure the right to life by putting in place effective criminal law provisions to deter the commission of offences against the person backed up by law enforcement machinery for the prevention, suppression and punishment of breaches of such provisions. It also extends in appropriate circumstances to a positive obligation on the authorities to take preventive operational measures to protect an individual whose life is at risk from the criminal acts of another individual . . .

129. Bearing in mind the difficulties in policing modern societies, the unpredictability of human conduct and the operational choices which must be made in terms of priorities and resources, the scope of the positive obligation must be interpreted in a way which does not impose an impossible or disproportionate burden on the authorities. Not every claimed risk to life, therefore, can entail for the authorities a Convention requirement to take operational measures to prevent that risk from materialising. For a positive obligation to arise, it must be established that the authorities knew *or ought to have known* at the time of the existence of a *real and immediate* risk to the life of an identified individual from the criminal acts of a third party and that they failed to take measures within the scope of their powers which, judged reasonably, *might have been expected to avoid* that risk. Another relevant consideration is the need to ensure that the police exercise their powers to control and prevent crime in a manner which fully respects the due process and other guarantees which legitimately place restraints on the scope of their action to investigate crime and bring offenders to justice, including the guarantees contained in Articles 5 and 8. [Emphasis added]

The third set of italicized words is significant. The applicant is not required to prove causation: that prompt action by the state *would have prevented* the death. It is enough that it *might* have done. Commentators had expressed concern that the *Opuz* test might be difficult to satisfy, given the need to prove 'immediate' risk[85] and the possibility that the assessment

[84] *Opuz v Turkey* (App No 33401/02, ECHR) (2009), [170].

[85] McQuigg (2020).

might be made only on the basis of information already available to police, rather than further information discoverable by more active investigation.[86] However, *Kurt v Austria* has since emphasized the need for risk assessments to be sensitive to the dynamics of domestic abuse and the authorities' obligation to respond immediately to alleged domestic abuse with an 'autonomous, proactive and comprehensive' risk assessment that is not reliant on the victim's account. The state must then have at its disposal a sufficient range of measures from which to choose in order to produce a response 'adequate and proportionate' to the assessed risk.[87]

4.2.4.b Article 3

The Court in *Opuz* recognized that sufficiently serious domestic abuse can constitute 'ill-treatment' within the scope of Article 3, whether it entails physical injury or psychological pressure, and so potentially trigger the state's positive duty under that Article to protect 'vulnerable individuals'.[88] The applicant here was vulnerable, not least because of the history of violence and fear of further violence from the husband.[89] Later case law notes that coercive control may also reach the Article 3 threshold.[90] States have discretion in deciding how to act given local conditions, but must operate within the ambit of common international values and understandings of states' duties 'relating to the eradication of gender-based violence'.[91] This the Turkish state had lamentably failed to do. Having the right policies on paper is insufficient: operational and systemic problems may breach the Convention, but only in case of 'egregious or significant' error or misconduct.[92]

4.2.4.c Article 14

The Court turned finally to the charge of discrimination on grounds of gender under Article 14 in conjunction with Articles 2 and 3. The Court here drew on growing international legal and political measures to combat violence against women, to which we can now add the Council of Europe's Istanbul Convention:[93]

Opuz v Turkey (App No 33401/02, ECHR) (2009)

186. . . . The [UN Convention on the Elimination of All Forms of Discrimination Against Women (CEDAW)] defines discrimination against women under Article 1 as '. . . any distinction, exclusion or restriction made on the basis of sex which has the effect or purpose of impairing or nullifying the recognition, enjoyment or exercise by women, irrespective of their marital status, on a basis of equality of men and women, of human rights and fundamental freedoms in the political, economic, social, cultural, civil or any other field.'

---

86 Burton (2009a) 287–8, criticizing remarks at para 86, *Chief Constable of the Hertfordshire Police v Van Colle* and *Smith v Chief Constable of Sussex Police* [2008] UKHL 50; cf *Michael v Chief Constable of South Wales* [2015] UKSC 2.

87 (App No 62903/15, ECHR) (2021), from [164]; *Y v Bulgaria* (App No 9077/18, ECHR) (2022).

88 *Opuz v Turkey* (App No 33401/02, ECHR) (2009), [158]–[161].

89 The Court also referred to the inferior position of women generally in that region of Turkey: ibid, [160].

90 *Volodina v Russia* (App No 41261/17, ECHR) (2019).

91 *Opuz*, [164]–[165].

92 *Commissioner of Police of the Metropolis v DSD* [2018] UKSC 11, [29].

93 Council of Europe Convention on preventing and combating violence against women and domestic violence, cited in *Kurt v Austria* (App No 62903/15, ECHR) (2021), ratified by UK in 2022.

187. The CEDAW Committee has reiterated that violence against women, including domestic violence, is a form of discrimination against women . . .

188. The UN Commission on Human Rights expressly recognised the nexus between gender-based violence and discrimination by stressing in resolution 2003/45 that 'all forms of violence against women occur within the context of *de jure* and *de facto* discrimination against women and the lower status accorded to women in society and are exacerbated by the obstacles women often face in seeking remedies from the State.' . . .

191. . . . [T]he State's failure to protect women against domestic violence breaches their right to equal protection of the law and . . . this failure does not need to be intentional.

The Court went on to find that, while the legislative framework in Turkey was not discriminatory, discrimination nevertheless arose from:

192. . . . the general attitude of the local authorities, such as the manner in which the women were treated at police stations when they reported domestic violence and judicial passivity in providing effective protection to victims.

It concluded that:

198. . . . the applicant has been able to show, supported by unchallenged statistical information, the existence of a prima facie indication that the domestic violence affected mainly women and that the general and discriminatory judicial passivity in Turkey created a climate that was conducive to domestic violence.[94]

4.2.4.d Article 8

Balancing rights

Owing to the seriousness of the abuse entailed, *Opuz* did not address the state's obligation to protect victims under Article 8. However, less serious abuse may fall within the scope of victims' right to respect for private and family life, and state inactivity may accordingly violate Article 8 (and Art 14 in conjunction with it).[95] The key difference between Article 8 and Articles 2 and 3, however, is that Article 8 is a qualified right. Respondents might seek to assert their rights under Article 8 to resist, for example (in the English context), removal from the parties' home (using an FLA 1996 occupation order or a DAA 2021 DAPO[96]), or civil injunctions or bail conditions that inhibit the relationship with their children. Two points raised by Choudhry and Herring should be noted here.[97] First, they

[94] Cf on the facts, *A v Croatia* (App No 55164/08, ECHR) (2010); *Y v Bulgaria* (App No 9077/18) (2022), from [122].

[95] *Bevacqua v Bulgaria* (App No 71127/01, ECHR) (2008); *Hadjuova v Slovakia* (App No 2660/03, ECHR) (2010); *R (Waxman) v CPS* [2012] EWHC 133, from [21].

[96] See 4.5.3 and 4.6.2.b. [97] Choudhry and Herring (2006).

have argued that Article 17 may preclude respondents from asserting their Convention rights in these cases:

Article 17

Nothing in this Convention may be interpreted as implying for any State, group or person any right to engage in any activity or perform any act aimed at the destruction of any of the rights and freedoms set forth herein or at their limitation to a greater extent than is provided for in the Convention.

On this basis, they argue, perpetrators of domestic abuse forfeit their right to respect for private life and home where necessary to protect victims' Article 8 rights from the threat posed by the abuse. Some support for this approach may be drawn from the remark in *Opuz* that 'in domestic violence cases perpetrators' rights cannot supersede victims' human rights to life and to physical and mental integrity',[98] the latter falling within Article 8. Secondly, where children are affected by the violence, their rights will often be determinative or at least highly influential in an Article 8 balancing exercise.

Balancing rights and victim withdrawal

Another aspect of Article 8 that was explored in *Opuz* is whether the state can justify relative inactivity if victims withdraw their complaints, on the basis that this respects their family life under Article 8—or can/should the state ignore victims' preference that it not intervene? The problem of victim withdrawal divides commentators.[99] Should legal proceedings be taken where the victim opposes such intervention? Should the criminal or civil law be used, or both? Is a *legal* response the most constructive one? Improvements to the *civil* justice response to domestic abuse might reinforce notions of domestic abuse as a *private* problem, when perpetrators should instead incur the public condemnation of criminal justice.[100] On the other hand, victims may wish to retain the control that the civil justice system (on the face of it) allows them. These are questions that we address in the English context at 4.7.4.b and 4.8.

Many victims seem reluctant to bring or cooperate with any legal proceedings, often for negative reasons: they may not perceive themselves as victims of crime or even wrongful behaviour;[101] they may blame themselves for their predicament;[102] they may fear reprisals in whatever form; indeed—as in *Opuz*—they may have been directly threatened. Some victims view legal intervention, particularly criminal justice, as detrimental to their and their family's interests. While it is important to help victims overcome these barriers to taking action, the state cannot simply ignore their aversion to using the law. Some argue that the state should aim to empower victims to make informed choices about whether and how to engage with the legal system, thus preserving their autonomy.[103] Otherwise, victims escape patriarchal control by their abusers only to be controlled by the state.[104] However, others caution against placing undue weight on 'victim autonomy', given some victims' difficulties in exercising truly free choice. The independent interests of children affected by the abuse, and of wider society, may also mean that victims' wishes cannot invariably be prioritized.[105]

98 *Opuz v Turkey* (App No 33401/02, ECHR) (2009), [147]. 99 Morris and Gelsthorpe (2000), 412.
100 E.g. Edwards (1989). 101 ONS (2020e), tables 16 and 17; see also extract at end of 4.2.3.
102 Hoff (1990). 103 Hoyle and Sanders (2000). 104 Schneider (1994).
105 Choudhry and Herring (2006); Dobash and Dobash (1992), ch 4.

In *Opuz*, the Turkish authorities were found to have breached Articles 2 and 3 through their approach to victim withdrawal: they had not explored why the victims withdrew their complaints and had not considered countervailing factors that favoured continuing the prosecution anyway, instead giving 'exclusive weight to the need to refrain from interfering in what they perceived to be a "family matter"'.[106] The Court specifically endorsed the English Crown Prosecution Service's approach to victim withdrawal, which weighs up several factors to decide whether prosecution remains in the public interest. The CPS starting point is that the public interest will normally require prosecution, given the seriousness of domestic abuse.[107] The current guidance specifies such factors as the ostensible reasons for the withdrawal, any suspicions of witness intimidation, what support the victim had prior to the withdrawal, identified risks to the victim, children, and others, and the likely impact on them of proceeding or not with the case.[108] The Court in *Opuz* supported this sort of approach on the basis that:

> 144. . . . in some instances, the national authorities' interference with the private or family life of the individuals might be necessary in order to protect the health and rights of others or to prevent commission of criminal acts.

Indeed, the victim's Article 2 rights might trump her *own* Article 8 right to respect for private and family life.[109]

4.3 THE CRIMINAL LAW AND DOMESTIC ABUSE

While its response to domestic abuse is far from unimpeachable, English law and practice is considerably further along the road mapped by the European Court in *Opuz* than Turkey's, not least given government recognition of domestic abuse as the exercise of power and control, reflecting a feminist-inspired, 'strong sense' of domestic violence.[110] In this section, we briefly outline the principal features of English criminal law and justice applicable to domestic abuse, in order to set the chapter's main focus on protective remedies in context. As we shall see, however, at 4.7.4 and 4.8, developments over the last twenty years (most recently under the DAA 2021) have created an increasingly 'hybrid' system in which police have been recruited to help ensure victim protection beyond their conventional criminal justice role.

4.3.1 THE CRIMINAL LAW

The criminal law now protects all adults, regardless of marital status. The *general* criminal law can deal with various forms of physical, sexual, psychological, and economic abuse: for example, offences against the person, including homicide, rape and other sexual offences, false imprisonment, kidnapping, blackmail, criminal damage, stalking and harassment,

[106] *Opuz v Turkey* (App No 33401/02, ECHR) (2009), [143].
[107] CPS (2022), 'Applying the Code' > 'Is it in the public interest to prosecute?'.
[108] Ibid, 'Case building and approach to prosecuting DA cases' > 'Victim withdrawals and withdrawal statements'.
[109] *Opuz v Turkey* (App No 33401/02, ECHR) (2009), [140].
[110] HO (2022c), para 36; Madden Dempsey (2006).

public order offences, malicious communications, and revenge porn.[111] Introducing our 'hybrid' theme, the Protection from Harassment Act 1997 (PHA 1997) empowers criminal courts to issue restraining orders, breach of which is an offence; these orders may be made both following conviction for *any* offence or even on acquittal.[112] Like civil injunctions, these orders prohibit specified behaviour to protect the victim. Moreover, some *specialist* offences now deal with domestic abuse. The Serious Crime Act 2015 created an offence of 'controlling or coercive behaviour' within intimate or family relationships, including between ex-partners.[113] And, as discussed at 4.7.4.b, breach of non-molestation orders granted by a *civil* court under the FLA 1996 is an offence. So too is breach of forced marriage protection orders (see 4.10), while the Anti-Social Behaviour, Crime and Policing Act 2014 directly criminalizes various activities related to forced marriage.

4.3.2 THE CRIMINAL JUSTICE SYSTEM

Despite the criminal law's potential, the criminal justice system has historically been accused of dismissing domestic abuse as a trivial, private matter. Police action has been described as 'lethargic',[114] particularly if victims are not perceived to be committed to pursuing the case; arrest and charge rates have been low; incidents have been 'down-crimed', that is, the abuser merely cautioned or charged with a less serious offence than that committed; and courts have been criticized for lenient sentencing.[115] Women have reported feeling 'more endangered than protected by the prosecution process',[116] their experience of using the system described as 'double victimization'.[117]

At the policy level, at least, matters are now far better, with all criminal justice agencies committed to tackling domestic abuse using research-led strategies.[118] Current initiatives aim to ensure a robust, effective, and consistent criminal justice response that protects victims and holds perpetrators responsible. Domestic abuse is emphatically regarded as criminal, the domestic context now considered an *aggravating* factor in both prosecution and sentencing.[119]

> [T]he days when courts sought to distinguish between violence within the home from violence on the streets are . . . long gone. Cases . . . [that attempted] to distinguish between situations of violence and breach of the peace in a domestic context and elsewhere are . . . not to be relied upon and hopelessly out of date.[120]

Police and CPS policies are pro-arrest and pro-prosecution, with or without victims' agreement.[121] Decisions about charges are for the CPS—based on evidential and public interest criteria—not for police or victims.[122] The victim is often the only witness, potentially jeopardizing the case if she withdraws her evidence. So police are encouraged to gather as

[111] CPS (2022), 'Offences available to prosecutors'.

[112] PHA 1997, s 5A; Sentencing Act 2020, ss 359–64. See also pre-conviction stalking protection orders: Stalking Protection Act 2019.

[113] Section 76; HO (2015); HO (2021c).

[114] Burton (2016), 38.

[115] See generally Pahl (1985); Edwards (1989); Dobash and Dobash (1992).

[116] Humphreys and Thiara (2003), 203.

[117] Edwards (1989), 153.

[118] Hester and Westmarland (2005).

[119] CPS (2022), 'Introduction'; Sentencing Council (2018a).

[120] *Demetriou v DPP* [2012] EWHC 2443, [8].

[121] College of Policing (online); CPS (2022).

[122] CPS (2022).

much other evidence as possible to reduce reliance on victim testimony,[123] and decisions to retract should be closely investigated to ensure they are not the product of pressure or threats. Where defendants are released, whether pre- or post-charge, they should ordinarily be bailed subject to conditions designed to protect victims (who are consulted about suitable conditions),[124] so that victims are not left to protect themselves by seeking civil orders of the sort we consider from 4.4.[125] Sentencing may include referral to accredited 'perpetrator programmes', designed to reform offenders' attitudes and behaviour through counselling and group work, though robust evidence for such programmes' effectiveness is still needed.[126] Meanwhile, *potential* victims can apply to police under the Domestic Violence Disclosure Scheme (known as Clare's Law) for information that may indicate whether they are at risk from a new partner—or they may receive that information on a 'right to know' basis, without making a request.[127]

However, if victims are to be encouraged[128] to engage with criminal justice, they need support and protection. The 'Best Practice Framework' for magistrates' courts handling domestic abuse cases emphasizes multi-agency working[129] and Independent Domestic Violence Advisers/Advocates, the 'central pivot',[130] whose role is to: support victims through the criminal justice process;[131] liaise between police, prosecutors, courts, other agencies, and victims; and help victims access material and emotional resources to start a new life free from abuse.[132] The ordeal of attending court can be alleviated somewhat through protections for 'vulnerable and intimidated' witnesses.[133]

Despite these positive developments on paper, entrenched working practices, attitudes, and cultures amongst some of those within the criminal justice system have hampered fully effective implementation of policy on the ground. The Joint Committee on Human Rights in 2015 condemned some police officers' 'lack of cultural literacy'[134] about domestic abuse, and researchers have found only around two-thirds of officers considered domestic abuse a public matter in relation to which positive action should be taken.[135] Unless practice on the ground matches policy on paper, the risk of ECHR violation in individual cases remains.[136] Following a 'not good enough' verdict in 2014,[137] the police inspectorate's 2017 report found some progress, but ample room for improvement:

HM Inspectorate of Constabulary, Fire and Rescue Services, *A Progress Report on the Police Response to Domestic Abuse* (2017), 5, 7, 10

Since the publication of [HMIC (2014)], there have been considerable improvements in the overall police response to victims of domestic abuse. Police leaders prioritise tackling domestic abuse within the wider context of supporting vulnerable people and keeping them

[123] HMCPSI and HMICFRS (2020).

[124] Police and Criminal Evidence Act 1984, as amended in 2022.

[125] HO (2021b), para 322.

[126] Hilder and Freeman (2016), 274; HO (2022c), from para 458.

[127] See Duggan and Grace (2018); DAA 2021, s 77; HMICFRS (2021), 12.

[128] Victims can, unusually, be compelled to testify: CPS (2022), 'Witness summonsing a victim'.

[129] Cook et al (2004); Vallely et al (2005); Bettinson (2016), on the Specialist Domestic Abuse Courts, which have been vulnerable to court closures etc.

[130] Robinson and Payton (2016), 265.

[131] Supplementing the Code of Practice for all crime victims: MOJ (2021).

[132] HO (2022c), from para 419 and ch 7 generally on multi-agency working with IDVAs.

[133] Youth Justice and Criminal Evidence Act 1999, Part II, Ch I; CPS (2022), 'Supporting victims'.

[134] (2015), para 175.

[135] Kelly et al (2013), 20.

[136] Choudhry and Herring (2006), 107; Burton (2010), 136–7.

[137] HMIC (2014), 6; see Burton (2016).

> safe. However, there are still areas where improvements are required in some forces . . . Some police forces are still failing to assess the risk and respond appropriately at the first point of contact. Others are inconsistent in the way they use their powers to keep people safe. Some forces are still not doing enough to pursue positive outcomes, where perpetrators are charged with an offence and brought before a court.

The Inspectorate found strong leadership, a big increase in recorded domestic abuse, and good training in some forces, but identified several areas of concern, not least the fact that:

> some officers still do not understand the dynamics of domestic abuse and coercive control, and underestimate how manipulative perpetrators can be.

There was evidence that some forces 'potentially suppress demand' by downgrading domestic abuse calls, perhaps because of a lack of frontline officers available to attend; considerable local variation in crime recording, arrest, charging, and referral to the CPS;[138] and, most disturbingly, falling arrest levels:

> Police officers have a duty to take positive action when dealing with domestic abuse incidents. Often this means making an arrest, provided that the grounds exist, and it is a necessary and proportionate response. The use of arrest is falling at an alarming rate, which can be explained in part by the misguided belief of some officers that their actions in not arresting the perpetrator are 'victim-focused' . . .

Concerns have also been raised about use of supposed 'restorative justice' approaches, in place of criminal prosecution.[139]

The 2019 report found a significant increase in victim reporting,[140] but the attrition rate from police call, to arrest, to charge, and on to conviction is far too high, as we saw at 4.2.2.e.[141] The suggestion that a slackening arrest rate may reflect lack of resources is dismaying but unsurprising given funding cuts.

However, 'improvement' of the criminal justice response may not be best, or solely, measured by reference to arrest and conviction rates. Nor is victim withdrawal necessarily a failure, *provided* the victim was properly supported—so not subject to intimidation, fear, or economic constraints—and had faith in a positive outcome, which it seems many victims lack.[142] Not all victims measure success in criminal justice terms.[143] The goal must be for victims to become abuse-free, something that arrest, victim withdrawal, charge, and conviction rates alone do not measure.[144] Some victims may not view prosecution and conviction as constructive steps towards that goal, particularly if they want the relationship to continue in some form—the immediate relief provided by the arrest may often meet their objective. But whether and when the system *should* respect victims' opposition to arrest or prosecution is controversial, and the question of victim consultation or consent to legal action was

138 These were still problems in 2019: HMICFRS (2019), 31, 35.
139 Westmarland et al (2018).
140 HMICFRS (2019), 3.
141 The 2020 data reflect a five-year trend: HMICFRS (2021), 2, 6–7.
142 Ibid.
143 Hoyle (1998); cf Hester (2005).
144 Women's Aid (2005); Robinson and Cook (2006).

notably absent from the government's major consultation paper in 2018.[145] This is a theme that we pursue at 4.8 when we consider victim consent to the new hybrid measures that enable police and others to instigate protective action in the civil law arena.

On any view, however, the criminal justice system is only one option for tackling domestic abuse, and perhaps not always the best, given the availability (funding permitting[146]) of housing/refuges, welfare, counselling, other social tools, and the civil law, to which we now turn.[147]

4.4 THE CIVIL LAW AND DOMESTIC ABUSE: INTRODUCTION

By contrast with criminal justice, the principal purpose of civil law is protection of the victim rather than punishment of the abuser,[148] its remedies dispensed on a lower standard of proof[149] in private hearings. Since the 1970s, when the Women's Aid Movement brought domestic violence to public attention,[150] prompting a Parliamentary Select Committee to examine the matter,[151] special family legislation has provided bespoke remedies for victims of domestic abuse in place of the general law.[152] That legislation,[153] criticized on various grounds,[154] was replaced by the FLA 1996 following a Law Commission review.[155] That Act, amended by the Domestic Violence, Crime and Victims Act 2004 (DVCVA 2004), creates non-molestation and occupation orders, available to different categories of applicant on various detailed grounds that we examine at 4.5. Meanwhile, the general law of tort's ability to respond to harassment was enhanced by the PHA 1997, which operates regardless of the nature of the relationship (if any) between the parties; we do not discuss that legislation in detail.

As we shall see at 4.8, later legislation has enabled third parties—notably, the police—to apply for civil orders that offer similar protection to the FLA 1996. The DAA 2021 significantly expands the scope and effect of those orders—now 'domestic abuse protection orders' (DAPOs)—which can be sought by both specified third parties and victims themselves. DAPOs, due to be rolled out nationally in 2025 following piloting from early 2023,[156] are intended to take over from FLA 1996 orders in cases involving domestic abuse.[157] But the latter Act is not being repealed and so remains available to victims, as well as to applicants in non-abusive cases. Given their dual aspect, we consider DAPOs in two locations– first, from 4.6, as 'private' measures alongside FLA 1996 orders; secondly, at 4.8, as 'public' protection sought by third parties, whether as free-standing orders or following the police giving the alleged perpetrator an emergency domestic abuse protection notice (DAPN).

By way of introduction, Table 4.2 provides a comparative overview of FLA orders and DAPOs as private measures. Table 4.3 compares the range of relationships in relation to which orders can be made under the two Acts.

145 HM Government (2018); cf, e.g., HO (2005). 146 See Turgoose (2016).

147 Hoyle and Sanders (2000); Robinson and Cook (2006); cf Lewis, R. (2004).

148 Law Com (1992), para 2.11. 149 Cf Edwards and Halpern (1991), 98–9. 150 Pizzey (1974).

151 Select Committee (1975).

152 On the limitations of the general law, see Law Com (1992), paras 3.13–3.17; see 7.3.3.b on the position of non-owners in non-formalized relationships.

153 Domestic Violence and Matrimonial Proceedings Act 1976; Domestic Proceedings and Magistrates' Courts Act 1978; see also Matrimonial Homes Act 1967; and the Homeless Persons Act 1977: housing law and domestic abuse are discussed in a supplement to this chapter in the online resources.

154 McCann (1985); Edwards (1989); Burton (2008), ch 3. 155 Law Com (1992).

156 HM Government (2022a), 53. 157 HO (2021a), 3.

Table 4.2 FLA 1996 and DAA 2021 orders compared

	FLA 1996		DAA 2021
Feature of each order	*Non-molestation orders, s 42—see 4.5.2*	*Occupation orders, ss 33–8—see 4.5.3*	*Domestic Abuse Protection orders—see 4.6 and 4.8*
Available between whom *see also Table 4.3*	'Associated persons', and any relevant child (u18): s 62(2)(3)—*see 4.5.1*	• all (ex) spouses, civil partners, and cohabitants—which section applies depends on parties' entitlement or not to occupy the property (ss 33–8); • for other types of 'associated person', only where A is 'entitled to occupy' the property (s 33)	Persons who are 'personally connected': s 2, where the victim is over 16 and R is aged over 18: ss 27, 32(5)—*see 4.6.1*
Function	To prohibit 'molestation' of A or any RC—*see 4.5.2.c*	To protect A's occupation of family home; to regulate R's occupation—compare, e.g., ss 33(3), 35(3)(4), 37(3)	To impose any requirements that the court considers necessary to prevent R from being abusive (s 1), whether by prohibiting R from doing/ requiring R to do specified things; may prohibit contact, protect A's occupation of family home, regulate R's occupation: ss 27, 35—*see 4.6.2*
Grounds	Discretion exercisable in light of all circumstances, including need to safeguard health, safety, and well-being of A or any RC: s 42(5)—*see 4.5.2.b*	• Discretion exercisable in light of checklist factors, varying by applicable section—compare, e.g., ss 33(6), 35(6), 36(6) • But, in some categories of case, may be obliged by 'balance of harm' test to make an order regulating R's occupation—compare, e.g., ss 33(7), 35(8), 36(7)(8)	• Preconditions: court satisfied on balance of probabilities that R has been abusive towards A, and that the order is necessary and proportionate to protect A from domestic abuse or its risk from R: s 32 • Then discretion exercisable in light of specified circumstances: s 33 *See 4.6.3*

(*Continued*)

Table 4.2 (Continued)

	FLA 1996		DAA 2021
Feature of each order	*Non-molestation orders, s 42—see 4.5.2*	*Occupation orders, ss 33–8—see 4.5.3*	*Domestic Abuse Protection orders—see 4.6 and 4.8*
Substantive limitations	None specified in legislation; but NB rights of R—*see 4.5.2.b*	None specified in legislation; but courts view ejection of R entitled to occupy the property as 'Draconian'—*see 4.5.3.g*	DAPO requirements must, as far as practicable, avoid conflict with specified rights and interests of R: s 36(1)—*see 4.6.3*
Duration	Fixed term or indefinite, as determined by court: s 42(7)—*see 4.5.2.c*	Depends on category of case: for some (s 33), any fixed term, until specified event, or indefinite; for others (ss 35, 37) successive terms of up to six months each; for others again (ss 36, 38) no more than two six-month periods	Fixed term, until specified event, or indefinite: s 38—*see 4.6.4*
On whose application	Victim, or made by court of its own motion: s 42(2)—*see 4.7.1 and 4.8.1*	Victim only—*see 4.7.1*	Victim, by court of its own motion, or on application by specified third parties, including police and anyone with leave of court: ss 28(2), 29, 31—*see 4.7.1 and 4.8*
In what proceedings	Any 'family proceedings': s 63(2)	Any 'family proceedings': s 63(2)	• On application by victim or non-police third-party applicant: s 28(5) • On police application, in magistrates' court: ss 28(2)(b), (6), 29 • By court of its own motion in any family proceedings, criminal proceedings (on conviction or acquittal of R), or specified civil proceedings between A and R: s 31
Enforcement for breach	As contempt of court (arrest by warrant: s 47(8)) or criminal offence (arrestable): s 42A—*see 4.7.4.b*	As contempt of court only; court can (sometimes must) attach power of arrest to original order or issue warrant later: s 47—*see 4.7.4.a*	As contempt of court (arrest by warrant: s 40) or criminal offence (arrestable): s 39—*see 4.7.4.b*

Table 4.3 Range of persons between whom orders can be made under FLA 1996 and DAA 2021

	FLA 1996: 'associated persons', s 62(3)		DAA 2021: 'personally connected' people, s 2
Relationship type	*NMO*	*OO*	*DAPO*
Are/have been spouses or civil partners	✓	✓	✓
Are/have been cohabitants	✓	✓	*[not as distinct class—but surely falls within 'intimate personal relationship', below]*
Live/have lived as members of shared household (domestic)	✓	Only if A is entitled to occupy the property at issue	✗
Are relatives—as listed in s 63(1) FLA 1996	✓	Only if A is entitled to occupy the property at issue	✓ Regardless of property rights
Have agreed to marry or become civil partners	✓	Only if A is entitled to occupy the property at issue	✓ Regardless of property rights
Are/have been in an intimate personal relationship with each other	✓ Only if of 'significant duration'	Only if A is entitled to occupy the property at issue, and if of 'significant duration'	✓ Whatever the duration, regardless of property rights
Share parenthood or PR for a child aged u18	✓	Only if A is entitled to occupy the property at issue	✓ Regardless of property rights
Are parties to same family proceedings	✓	Only if A is entitled to occupy the property at issue	✗

4.5 THE FAMILY LAW ACT 1996, PART 4

Until the national rollout of the DAA 2021 scheme in 2025, the FLA 1996 is the principal source of remedies for domestic abuse in the family court. It provides two types of order: non-molestation orders (NMOs) and occupation orders. These respectively protect victims from physical and other forms of abuse, and offer victims security in the home. The Act's procedures and enforcement provisions are particularly designed for the domestic abuse context.

4.5.1 THE RANGE OF RELATIONSHIPS COVERED

The FLA 1996 protects a wide range of 'associated persons', different in some respects (variously wider and narrower) than the DAA 2021 (see Table 4.3). NMOs are equally available to all categories of associated person. But the nature of the parties' relationship affects whether occupation orders are available at all and, if so, the basis on which they are made. Identifying the type of 'associated person' relationship between the parties, particularly whether they are 'cohabiting', is crucial.

Family Law Act 1996

62 Meaning of . . . 'associated persons'

(3) For the purposes of this Part, a person is associated with another person if—

(a) they are or have been married to each other;

(aa) they are or have been civil partners of each other;

(b) they are cohabitants or former cohabitants;

(c) they live or have lived in the same household, otherwise than merely by reason of one of them being the other's employee, tenant, lodger or boarder;

(d) they are relatives;

(e) they have agreed to marry one another (whether or not that agreement has been terminated);[158]

(eza) they have entered into a civil partnership agreement (as defined by section 73 of the Civil Partnership Act 2004) (whether or not that agreement has been terminated);[159]

(ea) they have or have had an intimate personal relationship with each other which is or was of significant duration;

(f) in relation to any child, they are both [parents or persons who have or have had parental responsibility for the child]; or

(g) they are parties to the same family proceedings (other than proceedings under this Part).

(4) A person falls within this subsection in relation to a child if—

(a) he is a parent of the child; or

(b) he has or has had parental responsibility for the child.

Some of the terms used in s 62(3) to define 'associated person' themselves require definition. 'Relatives' is broadly defined:

63 Interpretation of Part IV

(1) In this Part— . . .

'relative', in relation to a person, means—

(a) the father, mother, stepfather, stepmother, son, daughter, stepson, stepdaughter, grandmother, grandfather, grandson, granddaughter of that person or of that person's spouse, former spouse, civil partner or former civil partner, or

[158] See FLA 1996, ss 44, 42(4), 33(2).

[159] Ibid, ss 44, 42(4ZA), 33(2A).

(b) the brother, sister, uncle, aunt, niece, nephew[160] or first cousin (whether of the full blood or of the half blood or by marriage or civil partnership) of that person or of that person's spouse, former spouse, civil partner or former civil partner,and includes, in relation to a person who is cohabiting or has cohabited with another person, any person who would fall within paragraph (a) or (b) if the parties were married to each other or were civil partners of each other.

The definition of 'cohabitant' adopts the marriage analogy:

62 Meaning of 'cohabitants' . . .

(1) For the purposes of this Part—

(a) 'cohabitants' are two persons who are neither married to each other nor civil partners of each other but are living together as if they were a married couple or as if they were civil partners; and

(b) 'cohabit' and 'former cohabitants' are to be read accordingly, but the latter expression does not include cohabitants who have subsequently married each other or become civil partners of each other.

The facts of leading case *G v F (Non-Molestation Order: Jurisdiction)*[161] demonstrate the difficulties of categorizing relationships that are neither formalized in marriage or civil partnership nor based on blood relationship. When the parties' sexual relationship began, they had separate homes but spent most nights together. Two years later, they discussed marriage. When the man had to sell his home, he deposited the proceeds in the parties' joint account and most of that money was spent improving the woman's house, the anticipated matrimonial home. Initially, they continued to maintain separate homes, the man renting a flat, but he subsequently moved in with her. Only weeks later, he moved out, withdrawing his funds (and his name) from the joint account. The relationship ended shortly afterwards, having lasted just over three years. The woman sought an NMO, arguing that the parties were 'associated persons' as 'cohabitants'. The magistrates concluded that the parties were not 'cohabitants', applying the 'six signposts' from social security law.[162] Their decision was overturned:

G v F (Non-Molestation Order: Jurisdiction) [2000] Fam 186, 196

WALL J:

In my judgment, the evidence is sufficient to support the proposition that the applicant and the respondent were cohabitants within the meaning of section 62(3)(b) of the Act. Of the "admirable signposts" set out in *Crake v Supplementary Benefits Commission* . . ., three are present. There was plainly a sexual relationship; there is evidence that they lived in the same household, and there was substantial evidence . . . that the applicant and the respondent operated a joint account into which the proceeds of sale of the respondent's previous property were paid. The respondent asserts also that money was spent on the applicant's property.

[160] Not including the step-child of one's sibling: *M v D* [2021] EWHC 1351.

[161] [2000] Fam 186.

[162] *Crake v Supplementary Benefits Commission* [1982] 1 All ER 498; see 2.8.2.

> In my judgment . . . the respondent's evidence taken as a whole is sufficient to demonstrate that he and the applicant were, indeed, cohabitants. It is true that the relationship was not stable, although in one way or another it appears to have lasted [for three years] . . .
>
> [T]he message of this case . . . is that where domestic violence is concerned, [courts] should give the statute a purposive construction and not decline jurisdiction, unless the facts of the case . . . are plainly incapable of being brought within the statute. Part IV of the Family Law Act 1996 is designed to provide swift and accessible protective remedies to persons of both sexes who are the victims of domestic violence, provided they fall within the criteria laid down by section 62. It would, I think, be most unfortunate if section 62(3) were narrowly construed so as to exclude borderline cases where swift and effective protection for the victims of domestic violence is required. This case is, after all, about jurisdiction; it is not about the merits. If on a full inquiry the applicant is not entitled on the merits to the relief she seeks, she will not get it.

This case signals a generous approach to the interpretation and application of 'associated person'. But the relationship must fall within one of the prescribed categories of relationship. When *G v F* was decided, had the parties not been regarded as 'cohabitants' or as having 'lived in the same household' (s 62(3)(c)), and if the court had found no evidence of an agreement to marry, that would have been the end of it; the applicant would have been left to the general law, including the PHA 1997. However, s 62(3)(ea) now brings non-cohabiting but intimate relationships within the Act. The scope of 'intimate personal relationship of significant duration' remains unclear. The Explanatory Notes to the amending Act state that:

> It will be for the court to decide on whether the relationship meets these criteria. This covers a long-standing relationship which may, or may not, be a sexual relationship, but which is an intimate and personal one. It does not include long-term platonic friends or "one-night stands."[163]

It might be interpreted to include relationships between vulnerable adults and non-residential carers, as well as sexual relationships.[164]

The concept of 'associated person' is the widest concept of 'family' in law. Some of the relationships necessarily involve the parties living together: paras (b) and (c). Many others do not: paras (a), (aa), and (d)–(g). Some involve blood or other legal relationship: paras (a), (aa), (d), (e), (eza), and (f). Some categories turn on factual rather than legal factors: paras (b), (c), and (ea). The definition of 'relative' is particularly wide, not least given the inclusion of 'in-law' relationships based on cohabitation rather than marriage or civil partnership. However, there are arguable omissions. For example, the Act does not protect new partners of those whose former partners resent the new relationship and direct their frustration at the new partner. Although undoubtedly 'associated' with the person on the third side of this love triangle, the new and ex-partners are not associated with each other so no order can be made between them; resort must be had to the general law, notably restraining orders made under the PHA 1997.[165]

163 Explanatory Notes to the Domestic Violence, Crime and Victims Act 2004, para 24.

164 Such as *JM v CZ* [2014] EWHC 1125.

165 As Katie Price has discovered: Guardian (2022).

The rationale for the Act's initial coverage was described by the Law Commission, on whose recommendations the Act is largely based:

Law Commission, *Family Law: Domestic Violence and Occupation of the Family Home*, Law Com No 207 (London: HMSO, 1992)

3.17 The need to extend the scope of injunctions in family proceedings beyond the scope of the law of tort has been explained by reference to the special nature of family relationships. When problems arise in close family relationships, the strength of emotions involved can cause unique reactions which may at times be irrational or obsessive. Whilst these reactions may most commonly arise between spouses and cohabitants, they can also occur in many other close relationships which give rise to similar stresses and strains and in which the people concerned will often continue to be involved with one another . . .

3.19 . . . As we see it, there are three possible choices:

(i) [to extend the law to include *former* spouses and cohabitants, and possibly people with parental responsibility for the same child];

(ii) to remove all restrictions on applicants and throw the jurisdiction open to all . . .; or

(iii) to choose a middle path and widen the range of applicants to include anyone who is associated with the respondent by virtue of a family relationship or something closely akin to such a relationship.

On reflection, we have concluded that the third is the best alternative. The first might exclude people who have a genuine need for protection in circumstances which most people would regard as a family relationship in the broader sense . . . [for example] people who lived together on a long term basis whether as close friends or in a homosexual relationship.[166] We think that the second alternative goes too far. We do not think it is appropriate that this jurisdiction should be available to resolve issues such as disputes between neighbours, harassment of tenants by landlords or cases of sexual harassment in the workplace. Here there is no domestic or family relationship to justify special remedies or procedures and resort should properly be had to the remedies provided under property or employment law. Family relationships can, however, be appropriately distinguished from other forms of association. In practice, many of the same considerations apply to them as to married or cohabiting couples. Thus the proximity of the parties often gives unique opportunities for molestation and abuse to continue; the heightened emotions of all concerned give rise to a particular need for sensitivity and flexibility in the law; there is frequently a possibility that the relationship will carry on for the foreseeable future; and there is in most cases the likelihood that they will share a common budget, making financial remedies inappropriate.

The breadth of 'associated person' exemplifies a 'functional' approach that extends family law beyond its traditional confines. But critics are concerned about diluting the concept of domestic abuse as a phenomenon particularly experienced by women in marital and cohabiting relationships:[167]

166 Bear in mind that the Law Com was writing in 1992.

167 See also Aldridge (2021) and views collected by HMIC (2014), 36–7 re new definition of 'domestic abuse'.

H. Reece, 'The End of Domestic Violence', (2006) 69 *Modern Law Review* 770, 782, 790–1

Contrary to the Law Commission's rendition, the four features of proximity, heightened emotions, the possibility of a continuing relationship and the likelihood of a common budget had little to do with special protection against domestic violence for wives and female heterosexual cohabitants. Such protection was primarily associated with proximity only when coupled with isolation, controlled rather than heightened emotions in the context of unequal power, barriers to leaving the relationship rather than the mere possibility that the relationship would continue and financial dependence as opposed to a common budget . . .

In many contexts, there are progressive aspects to expanding our understanding of the concept of family. But if the boundaries of the family are also treated as the boundaries for enhanced protection against domestic violence then in this context expanding the boundaries of the family is regressive, because expansion endangers the specificity of the category of domestic violence. Domestic violence used to be treated as a problem specific to the traditional marital or quasi-marital union, caused partly by women's inferior position within the home and family, 'but now the violence between those in close emotional relationships is seen as a wider problem, being restricted not just to wives nor even to domestic situations'. Intimacy is replacing inequality as the touchstone of domestic violence law . . .

Feminist commentators have commonly interpreted the state's *apparent* concern to protect women from domestic violence as motivated by a *real* concern to preserve the status of the traditional nuclear family. They have suggested that the state achieves this objective by minimising domestic violence in various connected ways. The claim that domestic violence occurs in every type of relationship seems to be the reverse of minimising domestic violence, but in fact it is another method, because if domestic violence occurs everywhere then domestic violence occurs nowhere . . .

That said, structural inequalities do exist beyond spousal and quasi-spousal relationships.[168]

One other individual whom the courts must consider, and in favour of whom NMOs may be made, is the 'relevant child' (aged under 18):[169]

Family Law Act 1996

62 Meaning of . . . 'relevant child'

(2) . . . (a) any child who is living with or might reasonably be expected to live with either party to the proceedings;

(b) any child in relation to whom an order under the . . . Adoption and Children Act 2002 or the Children Act 1989 is in question in the proceedings; and

(c) any other child whose interests the court considers relevant.

[168] Burton (2008), 19; Barnes and Donovan (2016), 310.

[169] FLA 1996, s 63.

4.5.2 NON-MOLESTATION ORDERS

Family Law Act 1996

42 Non-molestation orders

(1) In this Part a "non-molestation order" means an order containing either or both of the following provisions—
  (a) provision prohibiting a person ("the respondent") from molesting another person who is associated with the respondent;
  (b) provision prohibiting the respondent from molesting a relevant child. . . .

(5) In deciding whether to exercise its powers under this section and, if so, in what manner, the court shall have regard to all the circumstances including the need to secure the health, safety and well-being—
  (a) of the applicant . . .; and
  (b) of any relevant child.

(6) A non-molestation order may be expressed so as to refer to molestation in general, to particular acts of molestation, or to both.

(7) A non-molestation order may be made for a specified period or until further order. . . .

63 Interpretation of Part IV . . .

'health' includes physical or mental health

NMOs are available on the same basis between all categories of associated person. They can be obtained by an applicant for the protection of a relevant child without also protecting the applicant herself.[170] In this section, we examine the concept of molestation and the court's discretion to make an order. We address issues relating to applications for and enforcement of NMOs at 4.7.

4.5.2.a Molestation

'Molestation' is undefined, as the Law Commission recommended.[171] Cases decided under the 1970s legislation remain instructive to some extent. Neither actual nor threatened violence is required, but 'such degree of harassment as to call for the intervention of the court'.[172] The range of conduct within 'molestation' is evident from the standard order template used by judges:

Family Standard Order 10.1: Non-Molestation Order (2022)

Non-Molestation Order – Applicant

11. The respondent, [respondent name], must not use or threaten violence against the applicant, [applicant name], and must not instruct, encourage or in any way suggest that any other person should do so.

[170] *Re A (Non-Molestation Proceedings by a Child)* [2009] NI Fam 22.
[171] Law Com (1992), para 3.1. [172] *Horner v Horner* [1982] Fam 90, 93.

12. The respondent, [respondent name], must not intimidate, harass or pester the applicant, [applicant name], and must not instruct, encourage or in any way suggest that any other person should do so.

13. The respondent, [respondent name], must not telephone, text, email or otherwise contact or attempt to contact the applicant, [applicant name], (including via social networking websites or other forms of electronic messaging) [except for the purpose of making arrangements for contact between the respondent and the relevant children] OR except through [his OR her] solicitors [respondent firm name], [respondent firm address], . . . [respondent firm email], [respondent firm phone], . . .

14. The respondent, [respondent name], must not damage, attempt to damage or threaten to damage any property owned by or in the possession or control of the applicant, [applicant name], and must not instruct, encourage or in any way suggest that any other person should do so.

15. The respondent, [respondent name], must not damage, attempt to damage or threaten to damage the property or contents of [the family home] OR [property short name] and must not instruct, encourage or in any way suggest that any other person should do so.

Non-Molestation Order – Zonal

16. The respondent, [respondent name], must not go to, enter or attempt to enter [the family home] OR [property short name] OR [any property where [he OR she] knows or believes the applicant, [applicant name], to be living], and must not go [within [number] metres of it OR [along the road[s] known as [road(s) name(s)] OR [anywhere within the territory of the map annexed hereto], except that the respondent may [go to the property [without entering it]] OR go along the road[s] known as [road(s) name(s)] for the purpose of collecting the relevant child[ren] for, and returning them from, such contact with the children as may be agreed in writing between the applicant and the respondent or in default of agreement ordered by the court.

Case law provides illustrations. In *Vaughan v Vaughan*,[173] after the wife had successfully petitioned for divorce on grounds of cruelty,[174] the husband followed her between home and workplace, despite constant requests not to and his knowing that she was frightened of him owing to his past violence; her health consequently suffered. The husband claimed that he simply wanted to ask her to see and speak to him. The court resorted to the dictionary:

Vaughan v Vaughan [1973] 1 WLR 1159 (CA), 1162–3, 1165

DAVIES LJ:

There are two different definitions . . .: "meddle hostilely or injuriously" . . . "to cause trouble to; to vex, annoy, put to inconvenience". It seems to me that, in the circumstances of this case, taking into consideration this lady's health, of which the husband was to some degree aware, and taking into consideration the fact that he knew she was frightened of him, molestation has plainly been made out in the present case.

[173] [1973] 1 WLR 1159.

[174] This was one of the grounds for divorce before 1969: see 3.4.

STEPHENSON LJ:

"Molest" is a wide, plain word which I should be reluctant to define or paraphrase. If I had to find one synonym for it, I should select "pester". Whether communication amounts to molestation is a question of fact and degree. I have no doubt that what this man did . . . to this woman, with the knowledge of his past conduct which both of them had, was to molest her.

Molestation was also found in *Horner v Horner*, where the husband accosted the wife in public, repeatedly telephoned the school where she worked, made demeaning comments about her to the school secretary, and displayed abusive posters about her on the school railings in sight of her pupils' parents.[175] The aggrieved ex-partner in *Johnson v Walton* was alleged to have engaged in old-style revenge porn, instigating newspaper articles about the parties' relationship illustrated by semi-nude photographs of the applicant. The court held that, if done with intent to distress the applicant,[176] this was clearly molestation.[177]

But it is clear from more recent authority that the focus is on the effect on the victim—there is no requirement of intention to molest.

Re Al-M (Non Molestation Application) [2020] EWHC 3305

SIR ANDREW MCFARLANE P:

31. . . . [I]n *C v C (Non-Molestation Order: Jurisdiction)* [1998] 1 FLR 554, Sir Stephen Brown P held that molestation:

> "implies some quite deliberate conduct which is aimed at a high degree of harassment of the other party, so as to justify the intervention of the court . . . It does not include enforcing an invasion of privacy per se;[178] there has to be some conduct which clearly harasses and affects the applicable to such a degree that the intervention of the court is called for." . . .

33. Although in *C v C* [2001] EWCA Civ 1625, an order was made controlling conduct which "was calculated to cause alarm and distress to the mother", the courts have held that the respondent's intention is not a necessary element in establishing conduct which amounts to molestation.

34. In *Re T (A Child)* [2017] EWCA Civ 1889, having referred to earlier authorities, I urged caution against attempts to narrow down the definition of "molestation":

> "27. In the decades that have followed those judicial utterances those siting in the Family Court have, on a day by case, case by case, basis, deployed good sense and judgment in determining whether or not particular conduct amongst to "molestation". In my view this court should continue to be very wary of offering any further precision in the definition."

[175] [1982] Fam 90. [176] Cf modern authorities discussed later. [177] [1990] 1 FLR 350.

[178] This was an issue in *C v C*, which concerned newspaper articles disparaging the applicant's marital conduct. The general law—of harassment, defamation, privacy, breach of confidence, etc.—may deny a remedy for good reason, e.g. to protect freedom of expression absent insufficiently strong countervailing interest: Art 10 ECHR; cf *R v Debnath* [2005] EWCA Crim 3472; *Hipgrave v Jones* [2004] EWHC 2901, [21].

Later in the same judgment I went on to state:

> "42. When determining whether or not particular conduct is sufficient to justify granting a non-molestation order, the primary focus . . . is upon the "harassment" or "alarm and distress" caused to those on the receiving end. It must be conduct of "such degree of harassment as to call for the intervention of the court". Although in *C v C* the phrase "was calculated to cause alarm and distress" was used, none of the authorities require that a positive intent to molest must be established."

35. What is needed to justify the intervention of the court is some form of deliberate conduct which has the effect on the applicant of harassment to such a degree that the court's protection is called for. The negative impact on the applicant can include elements of psychological and/or emotional harm. The conduct of the respondent, whilst being deliberate, does not need to have been with the intention of causing that harm.

However, the continuing requirement of 'deliberate' conduct raises interesting questions where the behaviour derives from mental health problems beyond the respondent's control. The wife's mental illness in *Banks v Banks*[179] caused her to abuse her husband verbally and physically. An NMO was refused; whether because the wife's behaviour could not be regarded as molestation or because the judge simply exercised his discretion against making an order is unclear.[180]

McFarlane LJ had supported his decision in *Re T* in part by reference to the fact that the FLA 1996 'aims to protect a victim from molestation, rather than . . . to convict and punish a perpetrator'.[181] But this overlooks the fact that, whilst the order itself is merely a civil injunction, that order may be criminally enforced. Earlier research suggested that it was harder to get NMOs for non-physical abuse.[182] The criminalization of breach of NMOs (discussed at 4.7.4.b) might have exacerbated this if courts are reluctant to expose respondents to the risk of criminal sanction.[183] But contemporary awareness of non-physical forms of abuse (not least as underscored by the DAPO regime, discussed at 4.6), together with the criminalization of controlling or coercive behaviour,[184] might encourage deployment of NMOs against non-physical abuse. Concerns about stretching the concept too far might be met by the courts' applying stricter standards at the enforcement stage. In a case concerning conviction for breach of an NMO, it was said that harassment 'cannot simply be equated with "causing alarm and distress"', on the basis that to do would risk criminalizing all conduct (including 'unattractive and unreasonable' conduct) that had that effect. It would therefore be necessary to direct the jury that the conduct was 'oppressive'.[185]

4.5.2.b The court's discretion

Even if molestation is found, the court has a discretion whether to make an order and, if so, in what terms and for what duration. Section 42(5), set out earlier, lists some factors to which the court must have regard, but, as usual, it is directed to have regard to 'all the circumstances'.

Chechi v Bashier[186] provides an unusual example. A family feud over land led to cross-allegations of violence to person and property, some attracting criminal charges. One brother sought an NMO against other relatives. The trial judge refused an order on various

179 [1999] 1 FLR 726.

180 Cf the less serious mental condition of the respondent in *Gull v Gull* [2007] EWCA Civ 900.

181 [2017] EWCA Civ 1889, [44].

182 Burton et al (2002), discussed by Burton (2008) from 39.

183 Cf *Majrowski v Guy's and St Thomas' NHS Trust* [2005] EWCA Civ 251, [83]; Noon (2008).

184 Serious Crime Act 2015, s 76.

185 *R v O'Neill* [2016] EWCA Civ 92, [39].

186 [1999] 2 FLR 489.

grounds, two of which were upheld. But the Court of Appeal rejected his first objection: that the existence of the family relationship was incidental to the dispute. Butler-Sloss LJ noted the Law Commission's rationale for covering a wide range of relationships, remarking that:

> Although the dispute between the parties is in origin about land, it is patently overlaid and magnified by the family relationship . . . The depth of the dissension and the violent reaction on both sides must owe a great deal to family ill-feeling.[187]

Where molestation is found, the court will usually grant an order. The standard order noted earlier indicates the range of behaviours that might be barred. The potentially criminal consequences of breach make the tight drafting of orders important to avoid ambiguity about the prohibition: better to prohibit specified behaviour, not just 'molestation' generally.[188]

The principal objective is to protect victims whose rights under Articles 3 and 8 (or even Article 2) are at stake. But, whilst Articles 2 and 3 create unqualified rights, the court must not impose any greater restriction on respondents' rights under Articles 8 and 10 than is necessary and proportionate to the objective of protecting applicants' and any relevant children's rights and interests.[189] As the standard order template extracted earlier reflects, where the parties are parents, the order may need to allow contact between the respondent and child,[190] without jeopardizing the applicant's safety and well-being. In particular, 'zonal' exclusions (clause 16 in the template) should not be made routinely, particularly given the criminalization of breach: they 'are serious infringements of a person's freedom of action and require special evidence to justify them'.[191] Indeed, zonal exclusions cannot be made pursuant to an NMO that would interfere with the respondent's property rights: that sort of intervention is the preserve of occupation orders, made on a far more tightly circumscribed basis (see 4.5.3).[192]

4.5.2.c Duration of orders

Orders may last for a specified time or indefinitely—but, as a matter of best practice, an end date should be specified, likely to be no more than a year from the making of the order.[193] In *Re B-J (Power of Arrest)*, an NMO was made indefinitely in the context of ongoing disputes regarding contact between the respondent father and the parties' 10-year-old daughter, C, who no longer wanted contact with her father and his new family:

In re B-J (A Child) (Non-Molestation Order: Power of Arrest) [2001] Fam 415 (CA)

> **HALE LJ:**
>
> 28. [Counsel for the father] argues that an indefinite order was wrong. [He relied on *M v W (Non-Molestation Order: Duration)* [2000] 1 FLR 107, in which Cazalet J said]:
>
> "... the object of non-molestation orders is designed to give a breathing space for the parties and, unless there are exceptional or unusual circumstances, it should be for a specified period of time. If this latter course is not taken then many years may go by

[187] Ibid, 493. [188] See Platt et al (2009), 6.69.

[189] Cf *R v Secretary of State for the Home Department, ex parte Craven* [2001] EWHC Admin 850.

[190] See 11.7.3.

[191] *R v R (Family Court: Procedural Fairness)* [2014] EWFC 48, [1](3); *Re T (A Child: Murdered Parent)* [2011] EWHC 1185, [79].

[192] *Re Al-M (Non Molestation Application)* [2020] EWHC 3305, [41]. Though contrast DAPOs: see 4.6.3.b.

[193] *Manjra v Shaikh* [2020] EWHC 1805.

> and a party may find himself or herself suddenly arrested under an order made many years previously when much has since changed and the original order has lost the substance of its main purpose."

29. In my judgment, that passage both underestimates the range of purposes for which non-molestation orders were designed and contains a serious fallacy. A non-molestation order is indeed sometimes, even often, designed to give a breathing space after which the tensions between the parties may settle down so that it is no longer needed. But in other cases it may be appropriate for a much longer period, and it is not helpful to oblige the courts to consider whether such cases are "exceptional" or "unusual." [The judge then set out s 42(5) and (7) and went on:] . . .

31. These provisions implemented the recommendations of the Law Commission [(1992), para 3.28]:

> ". . . protection should be available when and for as long as it is needed. Fixed time limits are inevitably arbitrary and can restrict the courts' ability to react flexibly to problems arising within the family. In particular, it is important that non-molestation orders should . . . be capable of enduring beyond the end of a relationship, although in some cases, short term relief will be all that is necessary or desirable."

Earlier, the Commission had rejected the idea of a two-tier system of short- and long-term remedies, with different criteria, at para 2.43:

> "The distinction between short and long term remedies certainly arises in practice . . . But this distinction does not always correspond to the requirements of particular categories of applicant and is not therefore a justification for requiring the courts to distinguish between short and long term orders in each case. Sometimes the need for a long term order may be apparent from the outset. Often, having solved the immediate problem the parties do not need to return. . . . In principle the criteria upon which a decision is based should be appropriate to the nature of the remedy sought: the duration of the remedy is simply a matter of judgment according to the circumstances of the particular case."

. . .

33. A non-molestation order rarely prohibits a person from doing something which would otherwise be completely unobjectionable. It is not usually appropriate to use or threaten violence, or to harass, pester or molest another person. There are obviously cases, of which this is one, in which the continuing feelings between parties who separated long ago are such that a long-term or indefinite order is justified. The order in this case was made for the benefit of C as much as for her mother: it is to C's benefit that her mother is not threatened or pestered.

However, whilst NMOs 'rarely prohibit . . . something . . . completely unobjectionable', the criminalization of breach—since *Re B-J* was decided (see 4.7.4.b)—raises the stakes somewhat. So, in measuring the order's initial duration or deciding whether to discharge it, the test is now whether the continuation of the order is necessary to protect the victim, not whether it would cause any prejudice to the perpetrator.[194]

[194] Ibid, [20]–[26].

4.5.3 OCCUPATION ORDERS

Occupation orders can be made in relation to a dwelling-house in which the parties have lived or do live together as their home or, in some cases, in which they intended to live together.[195] They can perform two basic functions: (i) confer a personal right to occupy on someone otherwise not entitled to (under contract or property law), or enforce a pre-existing right to occupy; and (ii) exclude from the property another party, or otherwise regulate that party's occupation of the home, even if that party is the sole owner. They can also support NMOs, physically separating the parties and so reducing opportunities for abuse. They also have uses outside the domestic abuse arena, to help unhappy families navigate the unravelling of their shared life on relationship breakdown before the final orders determining the fate of their home are made.

The rules governing occupation orders are more complex than those for NMOs, since the FLA 1996, departing to some extent from the Law Commission's scheme, differentiates sharply between different categories of applicant, depending on their marital status and entitlement to occupy the property. In consequence, five sections in the FLA 1996 deal with five types of case. As we shall see at 4.6, this differs starkly from the far more loosely drafted and more broadly accessible DAPO scheme (see Table 4.2), which makes none of the distinctions found in the FLA 1996:

- s 33: associated persons (of any category), where the applicant is 'entitled to occupy' the property or has 'home rights' under s 30;
- s 35: former spouses or former civil partners, where the applicant is not entitled to occupy the property, but the respondent is entitled;
- s 36: cohabitants or former cohabitants, where the applicant is not entitled to occupy the property, but the respondent is entitled;
- s 37: current and former spouses and civil partners, where neither party is entitled to occupy the property;
- s 38: cohabitants or former cohabitants, where neither party is entitled to occupy the property.

Figures 4.1 and 4.2 provide an overview of the five categories. Features on these diagrams such as the 'balance of harm' test are explained in the rest of this part of the chapter.

It is important to select the appropriate section, as each:

- has different qualifying criteria;
- confers different powers regarding the types of order that can be made and the terms that can be included;
- allows for different maximum duration of orders;
- requires the court to consider different factors in exercising its discretion to make an order, to define the order's terms, and to determine its duration;
- in some cases, constrains the court's discretion by *requiring* it to make an order in certain circumstances, under the 'balance of harm test'.

A hierarchy of property-ownership and family forms emerges from the occupation order scheme. The best protection is enjoyed by applicants who are entitled to occupy the property,

[195] FLA 1996, ss 33, 35–6; contrast ss 37–8. Law Com (1992), para 4.4.

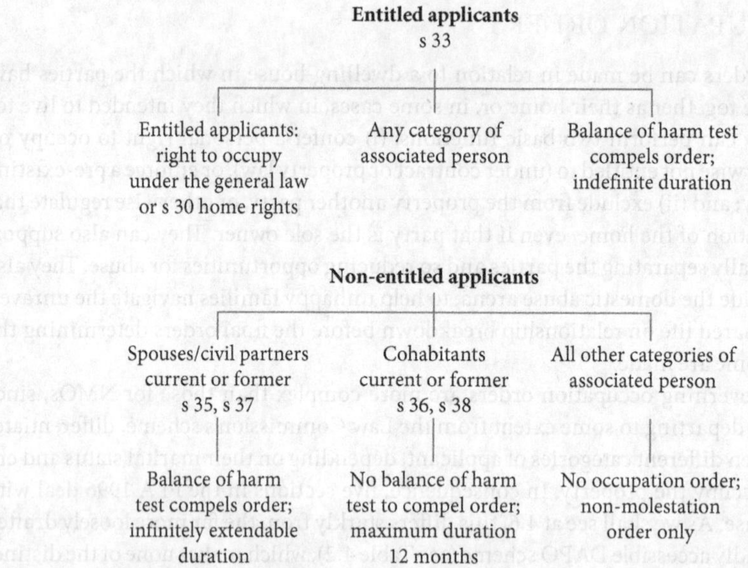

Figure 4.1 Features of different categories of occupation order

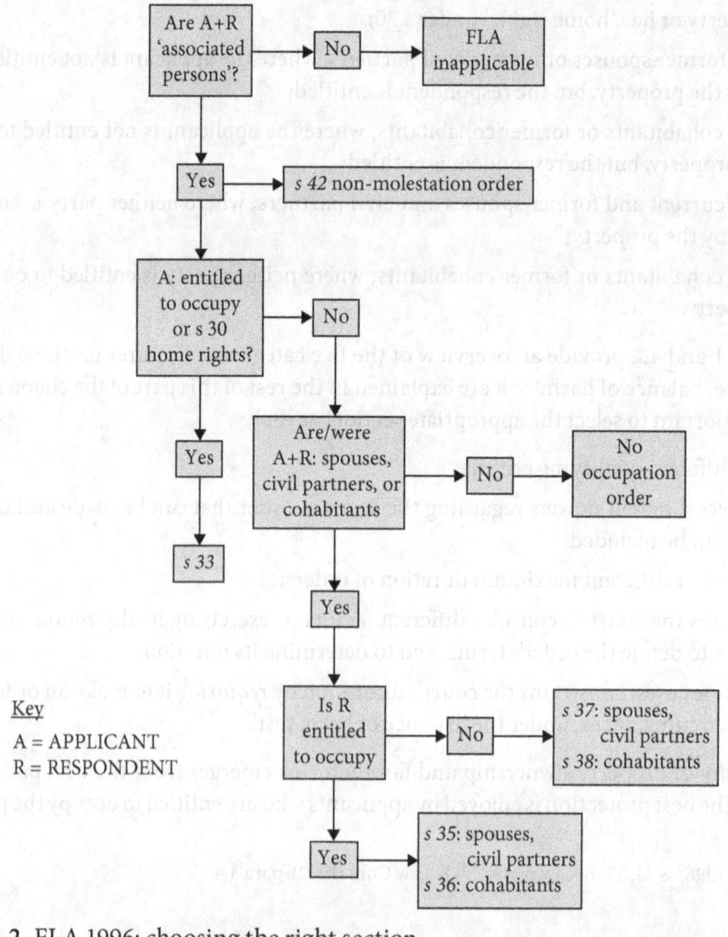

Figure 4.2 FLA 1996: choosing the right section

whatever the nature of their 'associated person' relationship with the respondent, and to spouses/civil partners with home rights under s 30. Applicants who are not entitled to occupy the property are ranked according to their relationship to the respondent: spouses and civil partners (current and former) secure the better treatment under ss 35 and 37; cohabitants (current and former) have a lesser measure of protection under ss 36 and 38. Other non-entitled individuals—such as adult children living at home with their parents, other 'home-sharers', even if related—cannot apply for an occupation order. Formerly left to remedies under the general law discussed in chapter 7 and to NMOs, most (not all[196]) of those individuals will be able to use DAPOs to deal with occupation matters. Indeed, DAPOs may become the preferred order by many applicants who *are* eligible under the FLA 1996: see 4.9.2.

We explore first the concept of entitlement to occupy, and then the components of each occupation order section: qualifying criteria; terms that the order may contain and its potential duration; and factors bearing on the court's discretion. Having set out the framework for each section, we then examine a key feature of the FLA 1996 scheme: the balance of harm test.

4.5.3.a 'Entitlement to occupy' in the occupation order scheme

Entitlement to occupy for the purposes of the FLA occupation order scheme flows from 'a beneficial estate or interest or contract or . . . any enactment giving . . . the right to remain in occupation'.[197] Beneficial owners or co-owners of property, contractual licensees, and statutory tenants all have relevant rights to occupy and so fall within s 33. Those occupying merely under a bare licence are not entitled for these purposes, so may only apply under ss 35–8. However, quite apart from those rights under the general law, spouses and civil partners (and some ex-spouses/civil partners) may also enjoy an entitlement to occupy by virtue of statutory 'home rights' under s 30, which (amongst other things) confer eligibility to apply for an occupation order against the other spouse/civil partner.[198]

Family Law Act 1996

30 Rights concerning home where one spouse or civil partner has no estate etc.

(1) This section applies if—
  (a) one spouse or civil partner ("A") is entitled to occupy a dwelling-house by virtue of—
    (i) a beneficial estate or interest or contract; or
    (ii) any enactment giving A the right to remain in occupation; and
  (b) the other spouse or civil partner ("B") is not so entitled.

(2) Subject to the provisions of this Part, B has the following rights ("home rights")—
  (a) if in occupation, a right not to be evicted or excluded from the dwelling-house or any part of it by A except with the leave of the court given by an order under section 33;

[196] Not those who are 'associated persons' only by virtue of FLA 1996, s 62(3)(c) and (g), who are not 'personally connected' under DAA 2021, s 2.

[197] E.g. FLA 1996, s 33(1)(a)(i). See 7.3.1 and 7.3.4.

[198] More information about the history and current law of home rights is provided in a supplement to chapter 6 in the online resources.

(b) if not in occupation, a right with the leave of the court so given to enter into and occupy the dwelling house.

. . . [Subsections (3)–(6): Provisions regarding payments by B of outgoings due from A to third parties; security of leasehold tenure; and cases where A is a beneficiary of trust property]

(7) This section does not apply to a dwelling-house which—

(a) in the case of spouses, has at no time been, and was at no time intended by them to be, a matrimonial home of theirs; and

(b) in the case of civil partners, has at no time been, and was at no time intended by them to be, a civil partnership home of theirs.

(8) B's home rights continue—

(a) only so long as the marriage or civil partnership subsists, except to the extent that an order under section 33(5) otherwise provides; and

(b) only so long as A is entitled as mentioned in subsection (1) to occupy the dwelling-house, except where provision is made by section 31 for those rights to be a charge on an estate or interest in the dwelling-house.

(9) It is hereby declared that a person—

(a) who has an equitable interest in a dwelling-house or in its proceeds of sale, but

(b) is not a person in whom there is vested (whether solely or as joint tenant) a legal estate in fee simple or a legal term of years absolute in the dwelling-house,

is to be treated, only for the purposes of determining whether he has home rights, as not being entitled to occupy the dwelling-house by virtue of that interest.

4.5.3.b Section 33: entitled applicants—associated persons

The qualifying criteria

Section 33 is in one sense the widest category, covering any type of 'associated person' relationship. However, that generosity extends only to applicants who are entitled to occupy the property or who have s 30 home rights over it. The order must relate to a dwelling that has been or is or has at any time been intended by both parties to be their home together.[199]

The order's terms and duration

Because the applicant already has the right to occupy the property, the order need not confer such a right, though the court might be asked to declare that the right exists.[200] The applicant may have been ejected from the property by the respondent or otherwise wish to enforce their right to occupy. The applicant may also want the respondent's occupation to be regulated, even terminated.

Family Law Act 1996, s 33

(3) An order under this section may—

(a) enforce the applicant's entitlement to remain in occupation as against the [respondent];

(b) require the respondent to permit the applicant to enter and remain in the dwelling-house or part of the dwelling-house;

[199] FLA 1996, s 33(1). [200] Ibid, s 33(4).

(c) regulate the occupation of the dwelling-house by either or both parties;
(d) if the respondent is entitled [to occupy, as defined earlier at 4.5.3.a], prohibit, suspend or restrict the exercise by him of his right to occupy the dwelling-house;
(e) if the respondent has home rights in relation to the dwelling-house and the applicant is the other spouse or civil partner, restrict or terminate those rights;
(f) require the respondent to leave the dwelling-house or part of the dwelling-house; or
(g) exclude the respondent from a defined area in which the dwelling-house is included.

. . .

(10) An order under this section may, in so far as it has continuing effect, be made for a specified period, or until the occurrence of a specified event or until further order.

It has been suggested that the power under para (c) to regulate the parties' occupation can govern specific details of their use of the home: allowing each party exclusive use of one bedroom; prohibiting communication by notes; requiring decision-making via consultation and not by dictation; requiring each party to give the other advance notice of intended overnight absences.[201] An exclusion zone can be obtained under para (g), in this context (unlike in the case of an NMO) interfering with property rights.[202]

The court's discretion to make s 33 orders and the balance of harm

The court's discretion is guided by a statutory checklist (in subsection (6)) and constrained by the 'balance of harm' test (in subsection (7)).

Family Law Act 1996, s 33

. . .

(6) In deciding whether to exercise its powers under subsection (3) and (if so) in what manner, the court shall have regard to all the circumstances including—
(a) the housing needs and housing resources of each of the parties and of any relevant child;
(b) the financial resources of each of the parties;
(c) the likely effect of any order, or of any decision by the court not to exercise its powers under subsection (3) . . . on the health, safety or well-being of the parties and of any relevant child; and
(d) the conduct of the parties in relation to each other and otherwise.

(7) If it appears to the court that the applicant or any relevant child is likely to suffer significant harm attributable to conduct of the respondent if an order under this section containing one or more of the provisions mentioned in subsection (3) is *not* made, the court *shall make* the order *unless* it appears to it that—
(a) the respondent or any relevant child is likely to suffer significant harm if the order *is* made; and
(b) the harm likely to be suffered by the respondent or child in that event is as great as, or greater than, the harm attributable to conduct of the respondent which is likely to be suffered by the applicant or child if the order *is not* made. [Emphasis added] . . .

[201] *G v G (Occupation Order)* [2000] 3 FCR 53, 59.
[202] *Re T (A Child: Murdered Parent)* [2011] EWHC 1185; cf text at n 192.

The effect of the balance of harm test in subsection (7) is that where the applicant 'wins' that test, the court has *no* discretion as to *whether* to make an order, but retains discretion regarding the order's precise terms and duration. In *Chalmers v Johns*, it was said that the court should first check whether the test in subsection (7) was met, before addressing the subsection (6) factors. If the test in (7) is satisfied, the court knows it must make an order. If not, it has a broad discretion under (6).[203] This suggests that subsection (6) has no function unless and until the balance of harm test has been applied. If the applicant wins the test, subsection (6) simply guides the court's decision as to the terms and duration of the order; if the applicant loses, subsection (6) helps the court to decide whether nevertheless to make an order, and (if so) in what terms and for how long. However, the balance of harm test cannot be conducted in a vacuum. Assessing likely harm may require an examination of subsection (6) factors, such as the parties' housing resources. It is also clear that an application may be made where there is no question of the balance of harm test being satisfied in favour of the applicant, but an occupation order is nevertheless desirable.[204]

4.5.3.c Section 35: non-entitled former spouse or civil partner; entitled respondent

The qualifying criteria

Section 35 applies to former spouses and civil partners where the respondent is entitled to occupy but the applicant need not be.[205] It applies only to *former* spouses and civil partners because *current* spouses or civil partners of respondents who are entitled to occupy the property enjoy home rights under s 30, and so fall within s 33. Since home rights ordinarily terminate on divorce, such individuals may require an alternative basis on which to seek occupation orders: hence s 35. The order must relate to a dwelling that has been or is or has at any time been intended by both parties to be their home together.[206]

The order's terms and duration

Section 35 cases involve non-entitled applicants and entitled respondents. Unlike applicants under s 33, these applicants have no right to be in the property themselves, never mind a right to exclude the entitled party. So, if any order is made at all, it must first confer on the applicant a right to occupy (stage 1). Different subsections apply according to the applicant's situation at the date of the hearing:

Family Law Act 1996, s 35

...

(3) If the applicant is in occupation, an order under this section must contain provision—
 (a) giving the applicant the right not to be evicted or excluded from the dwelling-house or any part of it by the respondent for the period specified in the order; and
 (b) prohibiting the respondent from evicting or excluding the applicant during that period.

203 [1999] 2 FCR 110, 114.

204 *Grubb v Grubb* [2009] EWCA Civ 976; *Dolan v Corby* [2011] EWCA Civ 1664.

205 Note FLA 1996, s 35(11)–(12) and equivalent provisions in s 36 allow applicants to use these sections without prejudicing any future claim they might wish to make regarding their entitlement to occupy and a consequent s 33 application.

206 Ibid, s 35(1).

(4) If the applicant is not in occupation, an order under this section must contain provision—
(a) giving the applicant the right to enter into and occupy the dwelling-house for the period specified in the order; and
(b) requiring the respondent to permit the exercise of that right. . . .

If the court decides to make an order in those terms, it additionally has the power under s 35(5) to regulate the respondent's occupation of the property (stage 2). Its powers here match those under paras (c), (d), (f), and (g) of s 33(3), set out earlier. The duration of any order made under s 35 is limited to six months, but it may be extended on one or more unlimited occasions for further specified periods not exceeding six months each.[207]

The court's discretion to make s 35 orders and the balance of harm

There are potentially two stages to any case under s 35: first, the court must consider whether to make an order giving the applicant a personal right to occupy the property for the order's duration; if it does that, the court must then consider whether to attach a provision regulating the respondent's occupation. Different considerations apply at each stage. Subsection (6) sets out the criteria for the first stage: determining whether it is appropriate to give a right to occupy to the non-entitled former spouse or civil partner:

Family Law Act 1996, s 35

. . .

(6) In deciding whether to make an order under this section containing provision of the kind mentioned in subsection (3) or (4) and (if so) in what manner, the court shall have regard to all the circumstances including—
(a) the housing needs and housing resources of each of the parties and of any relevant child;
(b) the financial resources of each of the parties;
(c) the likely effect of any order, or of any decision by the court not to exercise its powers under subsection (3) or (4), on the health, safety or well-being of the parties and of any relevant child;
(d) the conduct of the parties in relation to each other and otherwise;
(e) the length of time that has elapsed since the parties ceased to live together;
(f) the length of time that has elapsed since the marriage or civil partnership was dissolved or annulled; and
(g) the existence of any pending proceedings between the parties—
(i) for an order under section 23 . . . or 24 of the Matrimonial Causes Act 1973 (property adjustment orders in connection with divorce proceedings, etc.);
(ia) for a property adjustment order under Part 2 of Schedule 5 to the Civil Partnership Act 2004;[208]
(ii) for an order under paragraph 1(2)(d) or (e) of Schedule 1 to the Children Act 1989 (orders for financial relief against parents);[209] or
(iii) relating to the legal or beneficial ownership of the dwelling-house.[210] . . .

[207] Ibid, s 35(10). [208] See 6.4.3. [209] See 5.5.1. [210] See 7.2.

If the parties separated and divorced years ago, the case for giving the ex-spouse the right to occupy a dwelling that had been intended to be, but in the event never was, the matrimonial home is not obviously strong. However, orders will sometimes be appropriate, in particular where the children's needs require it. *S v F (Occupation Order)* provides an interesting example. The parties had divorced and both remarried. Their teenage children lived with the mother in the former matrimonial home. She decided to move to Somerset, without consulting the children or the father, then living in Malaysia. The son insisted on staying in London to complete his education. The mother (it might be said) effectively abandoned him, and he went to live with an aunt. The father applied for an occupation order to provide a home for his son in the former matrimonial home. He also sought financial provision from the mother under the Matrimonial Causes Act 1973 (MCA 1973); those proceedings were pending at the time of the occupation order application:

S v F (Occupation Order) [2000] 3 FCR 365 (Fam Div), 372

JUDGE CRYAN:

I must have regard to the length of separation, seven years, and the time since [the divorce], five years, and take those factors into account. . . . They are long periods and are together factors which have caused me to pause. But it seems to me that I have to see the timescale in the context of a continuing common parental responsibility and the use to which this property is put. It was still the children's home until they went to [Malaysia this summer].

I must also have regard to the present applications for [financial remedies on divorce].

Balancing all these [and other] factors I take the view that I should make an order permitting the father to return to the property forthwith for a period of six months, or until the [financial remedy] proceedings between the parties have been resolved, whichever is the shorter.

If an order is made at stage 1, the court may then be invited (stage 2) to regulate the respondent's occupation by making provision under s 35(5). From this point, the case proceeds as under s 33: the court must first apply the balance of harm test in s 35(8). As in s 33, if the applicant wins that test, provision regulating the respondent's occupation *must* be included, leaving the court with discretion only as to the order's particular terms and duration. Again, as in s 33, should the applicant *not* win the test, the court retains a discretion to make provision regulating the respondent's occupation. Wherever the court has a discretion, it must have particular regard to paras (a)–(e) of s 35(6).[211]

4.5.3.d Section 36: non-entitled current or former cohabitant; entitled respondent

The qualifying criteria

Like s 35, this section is available between applicants who are not entitled to occupy the property and respondents who are.[212] It too is limited to a particular class of 'associated person': current and former cohabitants. The order must relate to a dwelling that has been or is or has at any time been intended by both parties to be their home together.[213]

[211] FLA 1996, s 35(7). [212] See n 205. [213] FLA 1996, s 36(1).

The order's terms and duration

As under s 35, cases under s 36 have two potential stages: first, securing the applicant's occupation; and, secondly, regulating the respondent's occupation. The types of order that may be made are the same as under s 35. However, the duration of s 36 orders differs: in the first instance, it may be made for a period not exceeding six months, but only *one* extension (again, up to six months) is permitted.[214]

The court's discretion to make s 36 orders and the balance of harm

The two-stage pattern for orders under s 36 means that again there are different criteria for the two stages. The subsection (6) criteria for stage 1—giving the applicant the right to occupy—are different in some respects from those applying under s 35:

Family Law Act 1996, s 36

. . .

(6) In deciding whether to make an order under this section containing provision of the kind mentioned in subsection (3) or (4) and (if so) in what manner, the court shall have regard to all the circumstances including—

(a) the housing needs and housing resources of each of the parties and of any relevant child;

(b) the financial resources of each of the parties;

(c) the likely effect of any order, or of any decision by the court not to exercise its powers under subsection (3) or (4), on the health, safety or well-being of the parties and of any relevant child;

(d) the conduct of the parties in relation to each other and otherwise;

(e) the nature of the parties' relationship and in particular the level of commitment involved in it;

(f) the length of time during which they have cohabited;

(g) whether there are or have been any children who are children of both parties or for whom both parties have or have had parental responsibility;

(h) the length of time that has elapsed since the parties ceased to live together; and

(i) the existence of any pending proceedings between the parties—

(i) for an order under paragraph 1(2)(d) or (e) of Schedule 1 of the Children Act 1989 (orders for financial relief against parents);[215] or

(ii) relating to the legal or beneficial ownership of the dwelling-house.[216] . . .

At stage 2—regulating the respondent's occupation—there is another major difference between this section and ss 33 and 35. In those sections, the balance of harm can *require* the court to include provision regulating the respondent's occupation. By contrast, under s 36(7) and (8), the court is directed only to 'have regard to' the balance of harm 'questions', along with the first four factors in subsection (6). So, the court must consider whether the applicant or any relevant child is likely to suffer significant harm attributable to the respondent's

[214] Ibid, s 36(10). [215] See 5.5.1. [216] See 7.2.

conduct if such provision is not made; and whether the respondent or any relevant child is likely to suffer significant harm if such provision is made; and it must ascertain which side of the balance weighs more heavily. But even if the applicant's likely harm is clearly greater than the respondent's, the court is not obliged to regulate the respondent's occupation; it retains full discretion.

4.5.3.e Sections 37 and 38: current and former spouses, civil partners, and cohabitants, where neither party is entitled to occupy

The qualifying criteria

Both sections deal with cases where *neither* party is entitled to occupy the property in relation to which the order is sought. They may, for example, be living by personal licence in a third party's property, or even be squatting. The sections are limited to current and former spouses and civil partners (s 37), and current and former cohabitants (s 38). The property must be or have been the matrimonial or civil partnership home (s 37) or one in which the parties cohabit or have cohabited (s 38); no order can be made in relation to property merely intended to be a joint home.[217]

The order's terms and duration

The fact that neither party is entitled to occupy the property limits the type of order available:

Family Law Act 1996, ss 37(3) and 38(3)

. . .

(3) An order under this section may—

(a) require the respondent to permit the applicant to enter and remain in the dwelling-house or part of the dwelling-house;

(b) regulate the occupation of the dwelling-house by either or both of the parties;

(c) require the respondent to leave the dwelling-house or part of the dwelling-house; or

(d) exclude the respondent from a defined area in which the dwelling-house is included.

The duration of orders under each section differs as it does in ss 35 and 36: under s 37 (spouses and civil partners), an unlimited number of six-month orders may be made; under s 38 (cohabitants), only two six-month orders are available.[218]

The court's discretion in ss 37 and 38 and the balance of harm

Here too, the position largely corresponds with that under ss 35 and 36, respectively. Under s 37 (spouses and civil partners), the court is bound by the balance of harm test, and its remaining discretion is guided by the factors set out in s 33(6). Under s 38 (cohabitants), the court must merely have regard to the balance of harm 'questions' and a checklist matching that in s 33(6).[219]

[217] FLA 1996, ss 37(1) and 38(1). [218] Ibid, ss 37(5) and 38(6). [219] Ibid, s 38(4).

4.5.3.f Ancillary orders under s 40

Section 40 empowers the court to attach additional provisions dealing with incidental matters on making an occupation order under ss 33, 35, and 36 (only):

Family Law Act 1996, s 40

(1) The court may on, or at any time after, making an occupation order under section 33, 35 or 36—
  (a) impose on either party obligations as to—
    (i) the repair and maintenance of the dwelling-house; or
    (ii) the discharge of rent, mortgage payments or other outgoings affecting the dwelling-house;
  (b) order a party occupying the dwelling-house or any part of it (including a party who is entitled to do so [as defined earlier, 4.5.3.a]) to make periodical payments to the other party in respect of the accommodation, if the other party would (but for the order) be entitled to occupy the dwelling-house [as defined above];
  (c) grant either party possession or use of furniture or other contents of the dwelling-house;
  (d) order either party to take reasonable care of any furniture or other contents of the dwelling-house;
  (e) order either party to take reasonable steps to keep the dwelling-house and any furniture or other contents secure.

(2) In deciding whether and, if so, how to exercise its powers under this section, the court shall have regard to all the circumstances of the case including—
  (a) the financial needs and financial resources of the parties; and
  (b) the financial obligations which they have, or are likely to have in the foreseeable future, including financial obligations to each other and to any relevant child.

(3) An order under this section ceases to have effect when the occupation order to which it relates ceases to have effect.

To think that this appears to be rather petty detail would be to misunderstand the nature of domestic abuse:

H. Conway, 'Money and Domestic Violence—Escaping the *Nwogbe* Trap', (2002) 32 *Family Law* 61

The predominant feature of domestic violence is less physical assault than the exercise and maintenance of power held by one party over the other. . . . Often ill-treatment is manifested in a financial way, with the income and monetary arrangements for the family being in the sole domain of one of the parties, thus leading to unacceptable levels of control over the life of the other partner.

It is a further feature of domestic violence that in many cases an abuser will be imaginative and vindictive in seeking ways around the law to continue his abuse. Unless orders are drafted carefully, using the ability to specify particular forms of behaviour as molestation, a level of abuse may continue, although it might not legally form the basis for a power of arrest being activated or a committal application being founded.

[Hence s 40, which was] partly intended to prevent the undermining of occupation orders by such actions that would make continued occupation of the home under an order either impossible (for example, because of repossession) or intolerable (for example, because the property is stripped of all the furniture).

We shall see at 4.7.4.a that, insofar as it involves ordering payment of outgoings to third parties (e.g. landlords, local authorities, etc.), the effectiveness of s 40 is seriously limited by problems surrounding its enforcement.

4.5.3.g The balance of harm test and questions

The balance of harm test and the corresponding 'questions' that apply to ss 36 and 38 were intended to overcome deeply ingrained judicial reluctance to make 'Draconian' orders interfering with respondents' property rights and so to ensure that applicants needing protection receive it.[220] Breaking the test into separate steps helps us to see more clearly what it involves and how it is 'won' or 'lost' in sections 33, 35, and 37. We examine next the key components of the test, indicated in square brackets.

- Is the applicant or any relevant child [likely] to suffer [significant harm] [attributable to the respondent's conduct] if the relevant type of order is *not* made? If not, the test has not been satisfied, so the court is not *required* to make the order but may *choose* to do so.
- If such harm is likely, is the respondent or any relevant child [likely] to suffer [significant harm] if the order *is* made? If not, the applicant wins by default and so the court must, under ss 33, 35, and 37, make an order.
- If such harm is likely, the court must weigh the respective harm on each side of the balance.
- If the harm on the applicant's side of the balance is *greater than* the harm on the respondent's side, then an order *must be made.*
- If the harm on the respondent's side is greater, *or if the scales are evenly balanced*, then the court is not obliged to make an order, but may choose to do so.

In ss 36 and 38 (applications by non-entitled cohabitants), the court simply asks these questions, but is never obliged to make an order, retaining full discretion.

'Significant harm'

The core concept—'harm'—whilst broad in terms of the range of harms encompassed, requires more than mere 'hardship':

Family Law Act 1996, s 63(1)

. . . "harm"—

(a) in relation to a person who has reached the age of eighteen years, means ill-treatment or the impairment of health; and

(b) in relation to a child, means ill-treatment or the impairment of health or development; . . .

[220] See *Davis v Johnson* [1979] AC 264; *Richards v Richards* [1984] 1 AC 174; Burton (2008), 35.

"development" means physical, intellectual, emotional, social or behavioural development;
"health" includes physical or mental health;
"ill-treatment" includes forms of ill-treatment which are not physical and, in relation to a child, includes sexual abuse . . .

Noting contemporary 'changes in understanding and awareness of the nature and extent of domestic abuse', judges have recognized that 'controlling and intimidating' behaviour over the course of a long marriage could cause harm without any physical abuse.[221] The harm must be 'significant', which is taken here, as in the context of child protection law, to mean 'considerable, noteworthy or substantial'.[222] Harm in relation to children can include emotional harm suffered as a result of non-violent but acrimonious verbal feuding between separating parents;[223] indeed, children are now recognized as primary victims of domestic abuse if they witness or hear abuse of a relative.[224]

Likely

The significant harm must be 'likely'. By analogy with child protection law, this does not mean that the harm must be 'more likely than not' to occur—a greater than 50 per cent chance. It is sufficient that there is a 'real possibility' of that harm occurring. But that prognosis must be based on facts that have themselves been proved on the balance of probabilities, and not on mere suspicions.[225] By contrast with child protection law, the test is concerned only with future risk of harm. The fact that harm may have occurred in the past or present is irrelevant if it is unlikely to endure. But, as we shall see, by further contrast, jurisdiction to make a DAPO *only* arises if there is *both* proven abuse in the past *and* at least a risk of future harm.

It has been argued that this focus on the future and the courts' particular interpretation of the likelihood test in the FLA 1996 may deny remedies to worthy applicants. In *B v B (Occupation Order)*,[226] the respondent's serious violence caused the applicant to flee the parties' home with their baby. At the time of the application, they were safely (though unsatisfactorily) housed elsewhere. In asking whether the applicant and child were likely to suffer significant harm in the future, the court focused on their housing situation, not on the respondent's violence. Felicity Kaganas has criticized the court's approach: Parliament can hardly have intended that victims should be deprived of the protection of an occupation order by fleeing their home.[227] At what point should the likelihood of harm be assessed: the time of the hearing or some earlier point? Kaganas advocates an approach similar to that used for the threshold test in child protection cases,[228] whereby the court would ask whether significant harm was likely when the applicant took steps to protect herself, by calling the police, leaving the home, etc. Alternatively, Kaganas suggests that the courts should consider whether harm is likely should the applicant return home. Applicants otherwise face an invidious choice: remain in a violent home in order to satisfy the balance of harm test; or escape to safety, but thereby fail the test and so perhaps fail to secure an occupation order.

221 *PF v CF* [2016] EWHC 3117, [25].
222 *Chalmers v Johns* [1999] 2 FCR 110, 117, adopting *Humberside County Council v B* [1993] 1 FLR 257. See 12.5.3.
223 *Re L* [2012] EWCA Civ 721, [26].
224 DAA 2021, s 3.
225 *Re H and others (Minors) (Sexual Abuse: Standard of Proof)* [1996] AC 563.
226 [1999] 2 FCR 251.
227 Kaganas (1999a), 201.
228 Ibid; Children Act 1989 (CA 1989), s 31(2); see 12.5.3.

One further difficulty with the test is its hypothetical nature: the court must consider what is likely to happen should it make, or not make, an order. At that stage, the court does not know what precise terms any order that it might make would contain. For the test to make practical sense, the court should consider the harm in the light of specific possibilities. For example: what harm is the applicant likely to suffer if we do not regulate the respondent's occupation or, alternatively, suspend the respondent's right to occupy; and what harm is the respondent likely to suffer if we do make either sort of provision? In almost all cases, an NMO will also be sought and made. The court will then have to predict how effective that order will be. If an NMO has been made, will that stop the abuse and remove any real possibility of further harm?

'Attributable to the conduct of the respondent'

A further limitation is that it must be shown that the likely harm on the applicant's side of the scales is 'attributable to the conduct of the respondent'. This makes the test harder for applicants to win; it formed no part of the Law Commission's recommendations, which focused on need rather than conduct.[229] What sort of link between the conduct and the harm is required?

The first question is whether it must be shown that the respondent *intends* to harm the applicant or relevant child. In *G v G (Occupation Order)*,[230] the parties were divorcing but still living in the same household with their children. The wife sought an occupation order. The strain between the parents was found by the judge to be causing significant harm to the wife and children, but was it attributable to the husband's conduct? The first instance judge thought not. His remarks could describe the ending of many relationships:

G v G (Occupation Order: Conduct) [2000] 3 FCR 53 (CA), 57

Quoting the first instance judge:

. . . [T]o a great extent the conduct of the father is . . . unintentional. I do not believe . . . that this is a father who sets out to be unpleasant . . . [M]uch of the present strain and worry is the result of the meeting of two apparently incompatible personalities, and that the great differences between them are aggravated by this awful no-man's land in which they have now been living for a year. . . .

. . . [I]n all the circumstances of this thoroughly difficult case, bearing in mind the length of the marriage [15 years] and that much of the difficulties are to do with character and temperament and other factors unavoidable on an adult relationship breakdown, I am not persuaded that it would be appropriate . . . to make an occupation order.

On appeal, the wife successfully argued that unintended conduct and resulting harm should be considered:

THORPE LJ:

13. . . . Plainly, the word attributable on its proper construction could not dissociate the tension that the judge found evident in the complaint from the conduct by the husband that he had found proved. Plainly, the court's concentration must be upon the effect of conduct

[229] Law Com (1992), para 4.34. [230] [2000] 3 FCR 53.

rather than on the intention of the doer. Whether misconduct is intentional or unintentional is not the question. An applicant under s 33 is entitled to protection from unjustifiable conduct that causes harm to her or the children of the family. The effect is what the judge must assess. Tiny wounds may be inflicted with great malice: great blows may be struck unintentionally. Of course, lack of intent might support a plea of accidental injury. But where something is not done accidentally it is not to be dismissed on the grounds that it was not done deliberately.

Secondly, 'attributable' implies some causal relationship between conduct and harm. But how far can the 'chain of causation' stretch before harm can no longer be attributed to the respondent's conduct?

F. Kaganas, '*B v B (Occupation Order)* and *Chalmers v Johns*: Occupation Orders under the Family Law Act 1996', (1999) 11 *Child and Family Law Quarterly* 193, 198

Section 33(7) does not prevent the courts, in assessing the harm to a respondent or relevant child, from taking cognisance of factors such as their housing needs and resources; the provision does not limit the types of harm that are relevant here and it appears that any harm that would be likely to stem from the making of an order can be taken into account. Indeed, in explaining the operation of the balance of harm test, the Law Commission, while suggesting that this would not normally constitute significant harm, specifically cited as an example of potential hardship to a respondent difficulty of finding alternative accommodation. But doubts have been expressed as to whether considerations of this nature can be taken into account when determining whether there is a risk of significant harm to the applicant or child. In relation to the applicant or child, subsection 7 provides that it is only the likelihood of harm attributable to the conduct of the respondent that can be considered. It has accordingly been suggested that the harm suffered by an applicant or child as a result of having to flee to overcrowded or unsuitable accommodation because of the respondent's violence may be attributable to the inadequate provision of refuges and housing rather than to the conduct of the respondent. Against this, however, it could be argued that such harm can be attributed to both factors; although it is not the respondent's conduct that renders the available accommodation unsatisfactory, it is his conduct that forces the applicant and the child to occupy it. On this reasoning, the harm suffered by the applicant and child as a result of the move whether caused by inhabiting a dangerous environment or, say, by the disruption for a child of having to change schools, would fall within the purview of subsection 7.

This was the approach taken in *B v B (Occupation Order)*.[231] Having fled the family home owing to the husband's violence, the wife and baby were housed by the local authority in temporary, extremely poor, bed and breakfast accommodation: mother and child occupied one room with a shower and shared a bed; 12 other people lived in the house, with only one kitchen, one toilet, and two bathrooms; there was no garden, but a park ten minutes away. The judge found that, particularly in winter when poor weather would confine them to their room, this accommodation was likely significantly to impair the baby's health and development. The appeal court agreed that this was attributable to the father's conduct.

[231] [1999] 2 FCR 251.

Illustrations from the case law: applying the balance of harm test and statutory discretion

The appellate courts have been reluctant to make even short-term orders excluding a violent party who is entitled to occupy the property, particularly where ongoing family proceedings have implications for the home's future occupation. In *Chalmers v Johns*, the parties had had a long relationship, were joint tenants of their home, and had a child aged 7. Each party had assaulted the other over the years, causing only minor injury. The mother, in particular, had problems with alcohol. The father had called out the police on three occasions in the previous year, but although the mother had been arrested each time, she had not been charged.

Chalmers v Johns [1999] 2 FCR 110 (CA), 112, 115–16

THORPE LJ:

The final call out came on 5 May. On this occasion it was the mother who called the police. On this occasion she was observed to have minor injury. On this occasion the police seemed to have taken a more robust line, for they arrested the father and charged him with common assault. Apparently he was bailed on condition that he vacated the family home pending trial. That trial took place on 5 June. The justices acquitted the father and so he was free to return to the family home.

The mother's emotional reaction is not established but can be imagined. She exercised her right to leave, taking the youngest child with her and sadly that has to date constituted a final separation. I say that because it does seem very sad that this couple after 25 years of shared family life and obvious attachment each to the other should have determined, at least on one side, that a continuing relationship is impossible.

There have been a welter of applications to the court following the mother's departure. On 11 June she applied for a non-molestation and an occupation order. On 19 June the father applied for a residence order[232] and an occupation order. On 13 July she applied for a transfer of tenancy[233] and for a residence order. Those applications have been before the court either for directions, or for conciliation or for interlocutory application. . . . [At one hearing, an order was made allowing regular staying contact between the youngest child and the father in the family home.]

When with her mother [that child, A] is in unsatisfactory temporary council accommodation, which is said to be a mile and a half from school. The family home is about ten minutes' walk from the school . . .

The Children Act 1989 order determining which parent A would live with had not yet been made. The instant appeal had been brought by the father against an interim occupation order excluding him from the family home and allowing the mother to return with the daughter. Thorpe LJ overturned the judge's finding that the balance of harm test was satisfied, and turned to the exercise of the discretion. He remarked that this was 'a very slight' case as domestic violence cases go, such that it did not fall within the scope of the balance

[232] The forerunner of child arrangements orders specifying with whom the child should live: see chapter 11.

[233] See 7.3.4.

of harm test at all. That left the question whether to make an order to the court's discretion. The fact that the Children Act hearing was just a month away was considered highly relevant:

> On that occasion the court will have before it all the issues and principally which of these two parents, if they have to remain separate, should have the primary responsibility for A's care; which of the two, if they must be separate, should have the sole tenancy of the family home; and whether there should be orders of a more permanent character under the Family Law Act 1996 . . . As a matter of generality, . . . a court should be cautious to make a definitive order at an interlocutory stage with a final hearing only six or seven weeks distant. The gravity of an order requiring a respondent to vacate the family home, an order overriding proprietary rights, was recognised in cases under the [1970s legislation] and a string of authorities in this court emphasise the draconian nature of such an order, and that it should be restricted to exceptional cases. . . . [T]he wider statutory provisions contained in the Family Law Act [do not] obliterate that authority. The order remains draconian, particularly in the perception of the respondent. It remains an order that overrides proprietary rights and it seems to me that it is an order that is only justified in exceptional circumstances. Of course there will be cases where the character of the violence or the risk of violence and the harm to the victim or the risk of harm to the victim is such that the draconian order must be made, must be made immediately, and must be made at the earliest interlocutory stage. But I simply do not see this case on its facts approaching anywhere near that category. Conventionally the court has given careful consideration to the control of domestic disharmony by the imposition of [non-molestation] orders before resorting to the draconian order. It is to be noted that in the history of this case, there is clear evidence of such judicial management having proved highly effective . . .

It may have been difficult to satisfy the balance of harm test on these facts, and the violence was being controlled by NMOs. But there is something to be said for enabling the parties to live apart pending the final hearing and so removing the tension that would otherwise exist (even if NMOs are made). An order would also have enabled the mother and daughter to return to the family home, closer to the child's school. Kaganas considers that Thorpe LJ's focus on violence (specifically) and property rights undermines Parliament's intention to emphasize the broader interests of victims and children and to give the courts power to achieve 'sensible' solutions to the problems associated with relationship breakdown.[234]

This reluctance to use occupation orders as a matter of course on relationship breakdown was evident in other cases:[235]

Re Y (Children) (Occupation Order) [2000] 2 FCR 470 (CA), 478, 480

SEDLEY LJ:

> The purpose of an occupation order, however large its grounds may be, is not to break matrimonial deadlocks by evicting one of the parties . . . To use the occupation order as a weapon in domestic warfare is wholly inappropriate. Parliament has made provision for it as a last resort in an intolerable situation, not as a move in a game of matrimonial chess.[236]

[234] Kaganas (1999a), 197. [235] See also *G v G (Occupation Order)* [2000] 3 FCR 53.
[236] [2000] 2 FCR 470, 478, and 480.

By contrast, *B v B (Occupation Order)*,[237] aspects of which we have already considered, was an unusual case in which an order was withheld despite serious violence, and illustrates the importance of housing law to occupation order cases. The wife and baby had fled to temporary bed and breakfast accommodation following serious violence by the husband against the wife. He remained in the home with his 6-year-old son from a previous marriage. Having fled the home because of domestic violence, the wife was entitled to permanent rehousing by the local authority, as someone having a 'priority need' for accommodation and not 'intentionally homeless'.[238] The husband would also have priority need by virtue of having his son with him, but, if ejected from the home by an occupation order because of his violence, he would be regarded as intentionally homeless. As such, he and his son would be given only temporary accommodation and advice and assistance in seeking a home.[239] Since the husband was caring full-time for his son, he could not afford to rent private sector accommodation:

B v B (Occupation Order) **[1999] 2 FCR 251 (CA), 258–61**

BUTLER-SLOSS LJ:

The respective housing needs of the parties are, in one sense, equal. Each needs two-bedroom accommodation provided by the local authority; but the 'housing resources', using that term to include the duty owed to each by the local authority, were quite different. Unsatisfactory as [the wife's] current temporary accommodation is, there is every prospect that in the reasonably foreseeable future she and [the baby] will be rehoused by the local authority in suitable two-bedroomed accommodation. There is no such prospect for [the husband and his son, MB] if the occupation order stands.

As we discussed earlier, the Court of Appeal agreed with the judge that the baby was likely to suffer significant harm in the poor accommodation and that this could be attributed to the respondent's conduct. However, the Court of Appeal also found that were the husband and his son evicted to allow the wife and baby to return home, the son would suffer significant harm: he had already suffered from his parents' separation and would have to change schools for the fifth time in 18 months, further impairing his social, educational, and emotional development.

In our judgment, and whilst in no sense under-estimating the difficulties and frustrations of living with and caring for a toddler in bed and breakfast accommodation, the essential security for a child of [the baby's] age is being where her mother is. Furthermore, . . . on the evidence, Mrs B's residence in bed and breakfast accommodation is likely to be temporary.

For MB the position is much more complex. His security depends not just on being in the care of his father, but on his other day-to-day support systems, of which his home and his school are plainly the most important . . .

In our judgment, if, on the facts of this case, the respective likelihoods of harm are weighed so far as the two children are concerned, the balance comes down clearly in favour of MB suffering the greater harm if an occupation order is made.

[237] [1999] 2 FCR 251.

[238] Housing Act 1996, s 193; see the online resources for further information.

[239] Ibid, s 190.

However, Butler-Sloss LJ emphasized that this was an unusual case, and that the husband should not think that the court condoned his behaviour:

> . . . This case turns on its own very special facts. We have no sympathy for Mr B. He has behaved towards his wife in a manner which the judge found to be disgraceful. He treated her with serious domestic violence. Such conduct is unacceptable, and plainly falls to be considered within s 33(6) (d). Thus, were it not for the fact that he is caring for MB, and that MB has particular needs which at present outweigh those of [the baby], an occupation order would undoubtedly have been made.
>
> The message of this case is emphatically *not* that fathers who treat their partners with domestic violence and cause them to leave home can expect to remain in occupation of the previously shared accommodation. Equally, such fathers should not think that an application for a residence order in relation to a child or children of the relationship will prevent occupation orders being made against them.
>
> Part IV of the 1996 Act is designed to protect cohabitants from domestic violence and to secure their safe occupation of previously shared property. Nothing in this judgment should be read as weakening that objective.
>
> Each case will, of course, turn on its facts. The critical, and highly unusual facts of this case are (1) that MB is not a child of the parties; (2) that there is no question of MB being cared for by Mrs B or anyone other than Mr B; (3) that Mr B is thus the full-time care of a child who is likely to suffer greater harm that the harm which will be suffered by Mrs B and [the baby] if an occupation order is made. It is the position of MB alone which . . . makes it inappropriate for an occupation order to be made on the facts of this case.

The courts are alert to what they regard as undue reliance on public housing entitlements. In *Re Y (Children) (Occupation Order)*,[240] it had been suggested that the local authority would find it easier to rehouse the wife than the husband, who had special accommodation needs associated with his disability. But the authority might find the wife intentionally homeless if she were evicted by an occupation order and regard the husband as having a greater need. In any event, the Court of Appeal held that an occupation order was not merited: the home was large enough to share, and mutual undertakings made by the parties seemed to have brought their behaviour under control. The local authority's ability to reduce tension by housing one party was not regarded as a reason either to require that party to leave or to refuse to make an order in favour of that party. If a home can safely be shared, or if the applicant for an occupation order can make a good case for evicting the other party, the court considered that it should not engineer an outcome that throws the party with stronger housing entitlements on the local authority. As Sedley LJ pithily put it, 'the purpose of an occupation order . . . [is not] to use publicly-funded emergency housing as a solution for domestic strife'.[241]

Decisions such as *Re Y* have been criticized for underestimating the impact on children of living in a high-tension household.[242] Indeed, Mary Hayes long ago advocated a more expansive use of occupation orders:

[240] [2000] 2 FCR 481. [241] Ibid, [30]. [242] Choudhry and Herring (2010), 370.

M. Hayes, 'The Law Commission and the Family Home', (1990) 53 *Modern Law Review* 222, 223–4

. . . [I]t is a dangerous social policy which regulates the right to occupy the matrimonial home . . . only where there is proof of violence. . . . Such a rigid approach could provoke a wife, desperate to live apart from her husband, but needing to stay in the family home (perhaps because of the children) either falsely to accuse him of violence or, in an extreme case, to precipitate an act of violence against herself . . .

[I]s it reasonable to expect spouses to remain together under the same roof, where one of them has decided that the marriage has broken down to such a degree that he or she wants the other spouse to leave the home and is prepared to apply to a court to achieve this purpose? . . . [W]here one spouse is in an economically weak position, and especially where housing must be provided for the children, that spouse . . . may not be able to separate from her husband without recourse to, and the assistance of, the courts.

However, a series of non-violent cases, whilst acknowledging the seriousness of interfering with property rights,[243] has produced orders to alleviate pressures experienced on relationship breakdown, to help bridge the gap between separation and final financial remedies on divorce.[244] This aligns with the intention (with the advent of DAPOs) for non-abusive cases to become the standard fare for FLA 1996 orders.[245] In *Grubb v Grubb*,[246] an occupation order was made in favour of the wife pending the resolution of the parties' financial issues following their stressful, defended divorce. Crucially, the husband had adequate alternative accommodation and the wife was prepared to vacate the family home as soon as he provided somewhere else for her to live.[247] *Re L (Children)* provides a similar example, where it had been found that the children were likely to suffer significant emotional harm as a result of their parents' non-violent but acrimonious verbal feuding. The balance of harm test was not satisfied—both parents were responsible for the harm—but the court exercised its discretion to make an order excluding the husband from the home for three months. That order was upheld on appeal:

Re L (Children) [2012] EWCA Civ 721

BLACK LJ:

21. There is nothing in section 33(6) to limit the discretion to make an occupation order to cases in which there has been physical violence. Even in section 33(7), which deals with "significant harm", physical harm is not required as we can see from the definition of harm in section 63 . . ., which is wide. Section 33(6) requires the court to look at all the circumstances and by section 33(6)(c) it is directed to include in these "the likely effect of any order, or of any decision by the court not to exercise its powers under subsection (3), on the health, safety

[243] *PF v CF* [2016] EWHC 3117, [27].

[244] E.g. *BR v VT* [2015] EWHC 2727: terminating home rights to facilitate sale of the property during financial remedy proceedings.

[245] HO (2021a), 3.

[246] [2009] EWCA Civ 976.

[247] See also *PF v CF* [2016] EWHC 3117.

or well-being of the parties and any relevant child." This is broadly drafted covering not just cases in which there is violence but also all manner of other problems that can occur when a relationship has run into difficulties. This court dealt with this issue recently in *Dolan v Corby*, paragraph 27 of which includes the following passage.

"No finding of violence had been made by the [judge] against Mr Corby and the [judge] had that in mind. I do not read *Chalmers v Johns* . . . as saying that an exclusion order can only be made where there is violence or a threat of violence. That would be to put a gloss on the statute which would be inappropriate. *Chalmers v Johns* . . . stress[es] that it must be recognised that an order requiring a respondent to vacate the family home and overriding his property rights is a grave or draconian order and one which would only be justified in exceptional circumstances, but exceptional circumstances can take many forms and are not confined to violent behaviour on the part of the respondent or the threat of violence, and the important thing is for the judge to identify and weigh up all the relevant features of the case whatever their nature."

22. There is equally no authority establishing that a spouse can only be excluded from the home if reprehensible conduct on his or her behalf is found. It would be surprising if there were such an authority given the general terms of the relevant provisions of the Act and in particular the requirement of section 33(6) that there be consideration of all the circumstances.

Black LJ noted that the judge did not appear to have contemplated alternatives to exclusion, such as the parties being confined to separate areas of the large house, or—interestingly—an arrangement (facilitated by the husband's occasional absences) for what is now commonly called 'nesting': 'where the children lived in the house at all times but the parents alternated in the time they spent there with them'.[248] But the short-term order was upheld, such alternatives perhaps having already been ruled out by the parties as impractical.

In *Dolan v Corby*, the female partner was permitted to remain in the parties' rented home to the exclusion of the male partner under s 33 where there had been only verbal abuse, but the woman's greater vulnerability arising from her psychiatric condition made her less able to find alternative accommodation.

Dolan v Corby [2011] EWCA Civ 1664

BLACK LJ:

28. Exercising discretion under Section 33(6) is not a matter of considering the behaviour of the parties and awarding occupation of the property in question to the one who has behaved less inappropriately. All the circumstances must be considered, of which conduct is only one. The end of the relationship between these parties had given rise to a situation in which the [judge] had no choice but to exclude one of them from the house as it was clearly unworkable for them both to live there together . . .

[248] [2012] EWCA Civ 721, [30].

4.6 DOMESTIC ABUSE PROTECTION ORDERS UNDER THE DAA 2021, PART 3

In this section, we introduce the DAA 2021's DAPO regime as a further source of private protection accessible by victims. We address all aspects of applications and enforcement for both the FLA 1996 and private DAA 2021 orders together in 4.7. In 4.8, we examine the *public* aspect of the DAPO scheme, the new protective regime that is not dependent on victim action but is instead invoked by some third party. The general issues addressed in this section are equally applicable to the public cases discussed at 4.8. We flag differences between the 2021 and 1996 Acts as we go along, but readers may wish first to revisit Table 4.2 (see 4.4), which provides an overview comparison of the FLA 1996 orders and DAPOs, and we then consider at 4.9 what the future use of the two Acts might be.

4.6.1 THE RANGE OF RELATIONSHIPS COVERED

Table 4.3 (see 4.4) compares the list of 'associated persons' covered by the FLA 1996 with the DAA 2021's list of 'personally connected' individuals, found in s 2.

Domestic Abuse Act 2021

2 Definition of "personally connected"

(1) For the purposes of this Act, two people are "personally connected" to each other if any of the following applies—

(a) they are, or have been, married to each other;

(b) they are, or have been, civil partners of each other;

(c) they have agreed to marry one another (whether or not the agreement has been terminated);

(d) they have entered into a civil partnership agreement (whether or not the agreement has been terminated);

(e) they are, or have been, in an intimate personal relationship with each other;

(f) they each have, or there has been a time when they each have had, a parental relationship in relation to the same child (see subsection (2));

(g) they are relatives.

(2) For the purposes of subsection (1)(f), a person has a parental relationship in relation to a child if—

(a) the person is a parent of the child, or

(b) the person has parental responsibility for the child.

(3) In this section—

"child" means a person under the age of 18 years;

"civil partnership agreement" has the meaning given by [CPA 2004, s 73];

"parental responsibility" has the same meaning as in the [CA 1989, see s 3];

"relative" has the meaning given by [FLA 1996, s 63(1)].

While the list in s 2 looks familiar, there are notable (apparent) omissions: cohabitants; those who have shared a household other than in a commercial relationship (e.g. landlord/lodger); and those who are both parties to other family proceedings.[249] However, cohabitants clearly have an 'intimate personal relationship' under para (e). Many home-sharers and family litigants will be covered under another heading, such as para (f) or (g). But platonic, unrelated home-sharers with no shared child whose relationship cannot be described as 'intimate' are not included. As under the FLA 1996, it is unclear whether, and if so when, a platonic carer/dependant relationship will be considered 'intimate'. A government factsheet refers to 'intimate *partners*', language indicative of romantic relationships.[250] But draft statutory guidance gives the example of 'carers who are personally connected e.g. family carers';[251] while *family* carers would generally be 'relatives' under para (g) anyway, it is probably the case that any *non-commercial* carer counts, whether or not otherwise related.[252] Like the FLA 1996, the DAA 2021 cannot deal with the third point of a love-triangle situation—so the PHA 1997 retains a role there. On the other hand, unlike the FLA 1996, the DAA 2021 does not require 'intimate' relationships to be of 'significant duration' in order to fall within scope.

The other very significant feature of the DAA 2021, again noted in Table 4.3, is that—unlike the FLA 1996—there is no concept of being 'entitled to occupy' property as a passport to preferential protection in relation to occupation of the home; nor is access to such protection for non-entitled persons limited to spouses, civil partners, and cohabitants. All types of 'personally connected' individuals can access the full range of protection offered by DAPOs.

DAPOs cannot be made against under 18s.[253]

4.6.2 WHAT THE DAPO CAN DO

The DAPO is a powerful order, broadly defined:

Domestic Abuse Act 2021

35 Provision that may be made by orders

(1) A court may by a domestic abuse protection order impose any requirements that the court considers necessary to protect the person for whose protection the order is made from domestic abuse or the risk of domestic abuse.
"Requirement" includes any prohibition or restriction.

(2) The court must, in particular, consider what requirements (if any) may be necessary to protect the person for whose protection the order is made from different kinds of abusive behaviour.

(3) Subsections (4) to (6) contain examples of the type of provision that may be made under subsection (1), but they do not limit the type of provision that may be so made.

249 See FLA 1996, s 62(3)(b), (c), (g). 250 HO (2022a). 251 HO (2021a), 7.

252 This could have been made rather clearer, cf Inheritance (Provision for Family and Dependants) Act 1975, s 1(3).

253 DAA 2021, s 32(5). There is no similar provision in the FLA 1996, but those orders will probably not be made against under-18s: cf *Re L (Injunction and Committal: Guardian ad Litem)* (1997) 17 FL 91.

(4) A domestic abuse protection order may provide that the person against whom a domestic abuse protection order is made ("P")—
   (a) may not contact the person for whose protection it is made;
   (b) may not come within a specified distance of any premises in England or Wales in which that person lives;
   (c) may not come within a specified distance of any other specified premises, or any other premises of a specified description, in England or Wales."Specified" means specified in the order.

(5) If P lives in premises in England or Wales in which the person for whose protection the order is made also lives, the order may contain provision—
   (a) prohibiting P from evicting or excluding that person from the premises;
   (b) prohibiting P from entering the premises;
   (c) requiring P to leave the premises.

(6) A domestic abuse protection order may require P to submit to electronic monitoring in England and Wales of P's compliance with other requirements imposed by the order . . .

41 Notification requirements . . .

(2) [A person subject to a DAPO] must, within the period of three days beginning with the day on which the order is made, notify the police of the information in subsection (3).

(3) The information referred to in subsection (2) is—
   (a) the person's name and, if the person uses one or more other names, each of those names;
   (b) the person's home address . . .

The DAA 2021 draws none of the elaborate distinctions that we examined under the FLA 1996 in 4.5, as it does not have distinct orders providing different forms and levels of protection with different eligibility criteria: the universal DAPO is equally available between all 'personally connected' persons. For ease of exposition here, we shall discuss separately distinct types of measure: restrictions designed to protect, regulation of occupation, and positive requirements. But readers should not lose sight of the very wide range of negative restrictions and positive obligations that the court can impose with a DAPO: as s 35(3) emphasizes, the *examples* of provisions that might be included in a DAPO listed in the Act are *just examples*. The only limit on what the court can order is the subsection (1) test that the court considers the requirement 'necessary to protect' the victim from domestic abuse or its risk.

4.6.2.a Restrictions designed to protect from 'domestic abuse'

The DAPO can certainly do all the things that one could achieve with NMOs under the FLA 1996 by way of person protection, including (expressly on the face of the statute) the imposition of exclusion zones around victims' homes and other premises, which might include their place of work, their children's school, lawyer's office, doctor's surgery, and so on. The open-ended nature of the court's powers enable it to respond in a bespoke way to the varied types of domestic abuse—as defined in s 1, extracted at 4.2.1—being perpetrated or threatened. Draft statutory guidance for police (whose role we examine at 4.8) gives a useful non-exhaustive list of examples of activities that might be prohibited:

HO, *Domestic Abuse Protection Notices and Domestic Abuse Protection Orders: Draft statutory guidance for the police* (2021a), 22–3

- Contacting or interacting with the person to be protected via third parties. For example the children, partner, other family members, friends or co-workers of the person to be protected;
- Hacking, monitoring or controlling social media accounts, email, phone, computer, or other personal devices of the person to be protected;
- Engaging in any form of surveillance of the person to be protected by any means;
- Interfering with or restricting the person to be protected's access to goods, services or property;
- Damaging or threatening to damage property belonging to the person to be protected;
- Cancelling or procuring goods or services to the person to be protected, or intentionally running up bills or debts in the name of the person to be protected (with or without the knowledge of the person to be protected);
- Interfering with, restricting the person to be protected's access to, or deliberately frustrating the disposal of joint assets;
- Making of or threatening to make vexatious applications to the civil or family court with reference to the person to be protected;
- Sharing or publishing, or threatening to share or publish, personal information or images relating to the person to be protected;
- Making reference to the person to be protected on social media either directly or indirectly.

This list is not exhaustive.

4.6.2.b Regulation of occupation

The most striking feature of the DAPO, as compared with the FLA 1996, is its apparently indiscriminate provision of occupation order-style regulation across all categories of victim. Curiously, the government did not explain (or even acknowledge) this significant transition. Unlike the FLA 1996, DAPOs can only be made in relation to premises in which the two parties currently live—not past shared homes or intended future ones. But there is no statutory restriction on or hierarchy amongst the types of 'personally connected' persons between whom occupation of a shared home can be regulated, and no priority (on the face of the statute) for those whose proprietary or other legal right to occupy the shared home may be interfered with by DAPOs. Indeed, the DAA 2021 contains none of the technicality that we saw, for example, in s 33(3) of the FLA 1996[254] about the precise impact of the proposed order on the respondent's property rights or statutory home rights: it is simply provided that the respondent can be required to leave the home and prohibited from returning to it, and prohibited from evicting or excluding the victim.[255] Presumably, courts will—if they think it necessary—draft their orders in such a way as to make clear the technical impact on respondents' rights. Nor is there any direct equivalent of s 40 of the FLA 1996[256] to make ancillary orders around the occupation of the home—but the open-ended nature of the court's powers will presumably enable it to include such provision in its orders.

[254] See 4.5.3.b. [255] DAA 2021, s 35(5). [256] See 4.5.3.f.

4.6.2.c Other positive requirements

Compliance is supported by the court's power to add an electronic monitoring (tagging) requirement[257] and the automatic requirement that DAPO respondents notify the police of their name and address.[258] Other positive requirements can only be imposed where they can be supported by a nominated individual who will supervise compliance, overseen by the police.[259] The draft police guidance gives examples of possible requirements:

Home Office, *Domestic Abuse Protection Notices and Domestic Abuse Protection Orders: Draft statutory guidance for the police* (2021a), 24

- Attend an assessment for a perpetrator intervention programme;
- Attend a mental health assessment;
- Attend an assessment for a drugs or alcohol programme.

This list is not exhaustive.

4.6.3 SUBSTANTIVE BASIS FOR MAKING A DAPO

Whereas FLA 1996 NMOs are entirely discretionary[260] and occupation orders *must* be made in certain cases where the balance of harm dictates but are otherwise discretionary,[261] the power to grant DAPOs arises only if two preconditions are satisfied. There are then specified discretionary factors for the court to take into account, and constraints on what the order can do.

4.6.3.a Preconditions for making a DAPO

The cumulative preconditions are backward- and forward-looking:[262]

Domestic Abuse Act 2021

32 Conditions for making an order

(1) The court may make a domestic abuse protection order . . . against a person ("P") if conditions A and B are met.

(2) Condition A is that the court is satisfied on the balance of probabilities that P has been abusive towards a person aged 16 or over to whom P is personally connected.

(3) Condition B is that the order is necessary and proportionate to protect that person from domestic abuse, or the risk of domestic abuse, carried out by P . . .

'Abusive' conduct is as defined in the range of ways specified in s 1.

[257] DAA 2021, ss 35(6), 37. [258] Ibid, s 41. [259] Ibid, s 36(2)–(7), and HO (2021A), ch 9.
[260] See 4.5.2.b. [261] See 4.5.3.g.
[262] Contrast the 'threshold test' for child protection under CA 1989, Part IV, which offers alternative bases for jurisdiction to make those orders: see 12.5.3.

4.6.3.b Relevant factors and constraints

Those preconditions satisfied, the court then has a discretion to make an order (contrast the mandatory effect of the balance of harm test in some FLA 1996 cases[263]), bounded by the overarching test in s 35(1) that the court considers any requirements included in the order 'necessary' to protect the victim from abuse or the risk of same. The statute identifies some specific factors for the court to take into account, and some constraints on what the order can do, bearing in mind the respondent's rights and interests.

33 Matters to be considered before making an order

(1) Before making a domestic abuse protection order against a person ("P"), the court must, among other things, consider the following—
(a) the welfare of any person under the age of 18 whose interests the court considers relevant to the making of the order (whether or not that person and P are personally connected)
(b) any opinion of the person for whose protection the order would be made
(i) which relates to the making of the order, and
(ii) of which the court is made aware . . . .

For occupation-style orders, the court must also consider the known opinions of any 'relevant occupant' about the order; that is, someone else who lives in the property and is personally connected with either the victim or (if the property is also their home) the respondent.[264]

36 Further provision about requirements that may be imposed by orders

(1) Requirements imposed on a person by a domestic abuse protection order must, so far as practicable, be such as to avoid—
(a) conflict with the person's religious beliefs;
(b) interference with the person's work or with the person's attendance at an educational establishment;
(c) conflict with the requirement of any other court order or injunction to which the person may be subject.

A notable omission from this list of conflicts to be minimized—not least given the universal and equal access of all 'personally connected' persons to DAPO occupation requirements—is the respondent's property rights. Contrast the many limitations that hedge about the FLA 1996's occupation orders,[265] the judicial characterization of such orders as 'Draconian',[266] and the confinement of NMO exclusion zones to cases where respondents' property rights are not compromised.[267] Curiously, the government at no point commented on this apparently very sharp distinction between the two Acts. The judges' interpretation of their new statutory powers will be critical. Although property rights are not listed in s 36(1), the courts will doubtless consider the impact of proposed orders on those rights, especially in cases involving parties between whom no adjustive property remedies arise on relationship breakdown (i.e. any case not involving spouses or civil partners).[268] It would clearly defeat the

263 See 4.5.3.g.
264 DAA 2021, s 33(1)(c)(2).
265 See 4.5.3.
266 See 'Illustrations from the case law . . .' in 4.5.3.g.
267 See 4.5.2.b.
268 Compare chapters 6 and 7.

purpose of the legislation to conclude that, because (unlike the FLA 1996) the DAA 2021 does not *expressly* permit derogation from property rights, DAPOs may not do so at all. Victims' rights under Articles 2, 3, and 8 ECHR to be free from all forms of domestic abuse, as defined in s 1, readily justify interference with property rights.[269] But s 35(1) empowers the court only to impose such requirements as it considers 'necessary' to protect the victim. The question is how far the judges will be emboldened by the drafting of the new Act to depart from the traditional, 'Draconian' view of interference with property rights for the sake of victims' personal protection. Bear in mind here that a DAPO can *only* be made in cases of actual *and* apprehended domestic abuse; and, unlike the FLA 1996's balance of harm, satisfaction of that test allows but never requires an order.[270] By contrast, occupation orders may in theory be made in non-abusive cases: in the latter context, property rights properly attract more weight in the balance. One key factor in striking the appropriate balance between the parties' rights will be the duration of the order, to which we come next.

4.6.4 DURATION OF PROTECTION

Here again we find another striking contrast with the FLA 1996, again as regards the DAA 2021's universally generous approach, regardless of the type of relationship between the parties or the types of requirement being imposed:

38 Duration . . . of orders

. . .

(3) A domestic abuse protection order has effect—
  (a) for a specified period,
  (b) until the occurrence of a specified event, or
  (c) until further order.
  "Specified" means specified in the order

(4) A domestic abuse protection order may also specify periods for which particular requirements imposed by the order have effect.

(5) But a domestic abuse protection order may not provide for an electronic monitoring requirement to have effect for more than 12 months . . .

44 Variation and discharge of orders

. . .

(8) The court may make any order varying or discharging a domestic abuse protection order that it considers appropriate.
  This is subject to subsections (9) to (13).

(9) The court may include an additional requirement in the order, or extend the period for which the order, or a requirement imposed by the order, has effect, only if it is satisfied that it is necessary to do so in order to protect the person for whose protection the order was made from domestic abuse, or the risk of domestic abuse, carried out by P.

[269] See generally 4.2.4. [270] Cf 4.5.3.g.

(10) The court may not extend the period for which an electronic monitoring requirement has effect by more than 12 months at a time.

(11) The court may remove any requirement imposed by the order, or make such a requirement less onerous, only if satisfied that the requirement as imposed is no longer necessary to protect the person for whose protection the order was made from domestic abuse, or the risk of domestic abuse, carried out by P.

(12) If it appears to the court that any conditions necessary for a requirement to be imposed are no longer met, the court—

(a) may not extend the requirement, and

(b) must remove the requirement.

(13) The court may discharge the order only if satisfied that the order is no longer necessary to protect the person for whose protection it was made from domestic abuse, or the risk of abuse, carried out by P.

As elsewhere in the Act, the objective is clearly to give the court most flexibility to produce a bespoke order that does whatever is 'necessary'—but *only* what is necessary—to protect from the particular risk of abuse involved. The express limit on periods of electronic tagging reflects the seriousness of the interference with respondents' privacy of such measures. And so the (traditionally understood) seriousness of interfering with property rights—particularly where the victim has no proprietary claim in, or adjustive remedy in relation to, the home in question—might often result in occupation-related requirements having shorter duration than other requirements.[271]

4.7 APPLICATIONS, UNDERTAKINGS, AND ENFORCEMENT OF FLA 1996 AND PRIVATE DAA 2021 ORDERS

In this section, we consider applications, undertakings, and enforcement from the perspective of a case brought in the conventional 'private law' model by the victim. At 4.8, we shall see what scope there is for these protective orders to be made without application by the victim, and what implications that 'public' model has for victim autonomy. What we say here about without notice applications, enforcement, and sanctions applies equally to those 'public' cases.

4.7.1 ORDERS ON APPLICATION BY THE VICTIM

Applications for orders under both the FLA 1996 and DAA 2021 may be made by the victim, who must have a relevant relationship (associated person/personal connection) with the respondent.[272] Children aged under 16 can—with leave—apply for orders under the FLA 1996,

[271] Cf discussion of potentially indefinite NMOs at 4.5.2.c.

[272] FLA 1996, ss 33(1), 35(2), 36(2), 37(2), 38(2), 42(2)(a); DAA 2021, s 28(2)(a).

leave depending on the court's being 'satisfied that the child has sufficient understanding to make the proposed application'.[273] The more usual course, wherever possible, would be for an adult associated person to apply on the child's behalf.[274] By contrast, DAPOs are not available for the (direct) protection of persons under 16.[275]

4.7.2 'WITHOUT NOTICE' ORDERS

Ordinarily, respondents must have at least two days' notice of proceedings. But cases involving domestic abuse are often urgent. In 'exceptionally urgent' cases, where the victim's safety requires it,[276] the court must be able to provide immediate protection without the respondent's being tipped off about the application.[277] Orders under both Acts can therefore be obtained without giving notice—'ex parte'. But 'the default position of a judge faced with a without notice application should always be "*Why?*", not "*Why not?*"'.[278] The FLA 1996 provision is very similar to that in the DAA 2021:[279]

Family Law Act 1996, s 45

45 Ex parte orders

(1) The court may, in any case where it considers that it is just and convenient to do so, make an occupation order or a non-molestation order even though the respondent has not been given such notice of the proceedings as would otherwise be required by rules of court.

(2) In determining whether to exercise its powers under subsection (1), the court shall have regard to all the circumstances including—
   (a) any risk of significant harm to the applicant or a relevant child, attributable to conduct of the respondent, if the order is not made immediately
   (b) whether it is likely that the applicant will be deterred or prevented from pursuing the application if an order is not made immediately; and
   (c) whether there is reason to believe that the respondent is aware of the proceedings but is deliberately evading service and that the applicant or a relevant child will be seriously prejudiced by the delay involved [in commencing the proceedings].

(3) If the court makes an order by virtue of subsection (1) it must afford the respondent an opportunity to make representations relating to the order as soon as just and convenient at a full hearing [i.e. a hearing of which notice has been given to all parties in accordance with the rules of court]. . . .

[273] FLA 1996, s 43(2): see 8.5.6.b. [274] *Re A (Non-Molestation Proceedings by a Child)* [2009] NI Fam 22.
[275] DAA 2021, ss 1(2), 27(1)—but see ss 1(5) and 3. [276] *JM v CZ* [2014] EWHC 1125.
[277] Practice Guidance (2017), para 7; there is no equivalent guidance yet for ex parte DAPOs.
[278] *R v R (Family Court: Procedural Fairness)* [2014] EWFC 48, [1](1). [279] DAA 2021, s 34.

Many applications are made ex parte, but research has suggested that *occupation* orders are particularly difficult to obtain ex parte.[280] These applications do have drawbacks:

Law Commission, *Family Law: Domestic Violence and Occupation of the Family Home*, Law Com No 207 (London: HMSO, 1992)

5.6 The danger of a misconceived or malicious application being granted or the risk of some other injustice being done to the respondent is inevitably greater where the court has only heard the applicant's side of the story and the respondent has had no opportunity to reply. Also, on ex parte applications, the judge has no opportunity to try to resolve the parties' differences by agreed undertakings or otherwise to reduce the tension of the dispute. Equally, there is no opportunity to bring home the seriousness of the situation to the respondent and to underline the importance of complying with the order . . .

In many cases involving violence, 'reducing tension' is an inadequate response and an ex parte order will be appropriate.[281] But it is important that the procedure *as a whole* is fair to the respondent and complies with Article 6 ECHR. Compliance should be ensured by the fact that the legislation entitles the respondent to an inter partes hearing and to have an ex parte order set aside.[282] Practice guidance requires that ex parte orders under the FLA 1996 be of fixed duration and that they always specify a 'return day' (on which a normal inter partes hearing will be conducted) to be set normally no more than 14 days from the making of the order, even if the order's duration is longer.[283]

4.7.3 UNDERTAKINGS: FLA 1996 ONLY

The FLA 1996 allows courts—instead of making an order—to accept undertakings from one or both parties: a voluntary promise to the court, commonly to do what an order would otherwise have required. Undertakings have long been popular amongst some applicants and professionals,[284] but their use is controversial. This perhaps explains their omission from the DAA 2021 regime:

A. Kewley, 'Pragmatism before Principle: The Limitations of Civil Law Remedies for the Victims of Domestic Violence', (1996) 18 *Journal of Social Welfare and Family Law* 1, 3–6

[An applicant] who accepts . . . an undertaking in lieu of a court injunction, will not have to testify in court, an experience which the evidence suggests many women would prefer to avoid if an alternative option is available to them.

Undertakings appear to be popular with judges and lawyers . . . because the practice of accepting them means that an expensive, protracted and difficult hearing of the case is avoided and that the practical effect—[with the exception of the power of arrest: see later]—is much

280 Barron (2002); Burton et al (2002).
281 Kaganas (1999a), 196–7.
282 See generally *JM v CZ* [2014] EWHC 1125.
283 Practice Guidance (2017), para 5.
284 Burton (2008), 40.

> the same as if an . . . order is granted in that breach of the undertaking may theoretically be punishable [as] contempt of court. Some practitioners consider that in some ways such undertakings are likely to be more effective than orders . . . because they are given freely and voluntarily by the respondent to the judge rather than to an estranged ex-partner and that, having been given to the court, are the more likely to be honoured, because the judge has the authority to punish any future non-compliance. It is apparent that domestic violence victims may sometimes be subject to considerable pressure from their lawyers to accept an undertaking instead of a court order because lawyers' training and practical experience are characterized by the need to avoid lengthy and expensive disputes if at all possible by a process of negotiation and compromise between the parties. Moreover, there is evidence that a complainant may be subject to pressure to accept an undertaking from the respondent even where there has been a breach of a previous undertaking or court order . . . and where the woman has understandable doubts about the probable effectiveness of accepting the undertaking offered to her. . . .

It is one thing to accept an undertaking from the respondent instead of getting the vindication and protection of an order. But the victim might sometimes even be required to give a 'cross-undertaking' in return:[285]

> [I]t is viewed by some courts as a 'sensible' or 'fair' way of keeping the domestic peace in that blame is not being attached to either party's conduct but that each of the parties undertakes to behave reasonably in the future. . . . A victim of violence may feel understandably aggrieved in such a case where she infers that she is being held partly to blame for the abuse that she has had to endure.
>
> Finally, the acceptance of an undertaking denies the victim of violence a chance for the court formally to find fault and to condemn, through the granting of the injunction, the violence that has taken place. . . . By giving an undertaking on a purely voluntary basis, the respondent has not been required to accept any responsibility for his or her actions nor has he or she been required to acknowledge having been culpable of any wrongdoing. In such circumstances, failure to obtain the required court order . . . may also leave the [victim] understandably disillusioned with the whole legal process and reluctant to seek to obtain legal redress if, as experience has shown, it is likely that the violence or harassment will be repeated in the future.

While an undertaking can be enforced as if it were a court order, it is not possible to attach a power of arrest. The court may be unable to accept an undertaking in lieu of an order for that reason.[286]

4.7.4 ENFORCEMENT OF ORDERS UNDER THE FLA 1996 AND DAA 2021

Research into the early years of the FLA 1996 suggested that the family justice system was still failing victims in relation to enforcement,[287] and the enforcement of NMOs was reformed in 2004 to bring the weight of the criminal justice system behind the family court.

[285] If a cross-undertaking is given, then the applicant will not be eligible for legal aid: cf SI 2012/3098, Sch 1, para 8.

[286] FLA 1996, s 46(3A).

[287] Barron (2002); Burton et al (2002); Humphreys and Thiara (2003).

The criminalization model—despite being controversial—has been extended under the DAA 2021 to breach of all DAPO requirements, which leaves FLA 1996 occupation orders the only ones enforceable exclusively as a (civil) contempt of court.

4.7.4.a Occupation orders under the FLA 1996

Breach of an occupation order is a contempt of court, exclusively a matter for the family court. There are two routes to arrest: either the applicant may return to court for a warrant; or the court can attach a power of arrest to the original order. The latter permits arrest of the respondent where a police officer has reasonable cause to suspect a breach.[288] To issue a warrant, the court must be satisfied that there are reasonable grounds for believing that a breach has occurred.[289] Respondents must be brought to court within 24 hours of arrest; either the matter is dealt with then, or the respondent is remanded or released on bail until a later hearing.[290]

The FLA 1996 requires the attachment of powers of arrest in certain situations:

Family Law Act 1996

47 Arrest for breach of order

. . .

(2) If—

(a) the court makes an occupation order; and

(b) it appears to the court that the respondent has used or threatened violence against the applicant or relevant child,it shall attach a power of arrest to one or more provisions of the order unless satisfied that in all the circumstances of the case the applicant or child will be adequately protected without such a power of arrest.

(3) Subsection (2) does not apply [to ex parte orders], but in such a case the court may attach a power of arrest to one or more provisions of the order if it appears to it—

(a) that the respondent has used or threatened violence against the applicant or a relevant child; and

(b) that there is a risk of significant harm to the applicant or child, attributable to conduct of the respondent, if the power of arrest is not attached to those provisions immediately. . . .

Powers of arrest and undertakings

Since undertakings are voluntary, no power of arrest can be attached to them.[291] So in order to ensure that a power of arrest is available wherever one would be appropriate, the court cannot accept an undertaking if, were it to make an occupation order, it would be obliged to attach a power of arrest.[292] The court may only accept an undertaking, therefore, having determined that a power of arrest is unnecessary. It is very hard to obtain reliable data about the use of undertakings, though it seems likely that they are accepted in only a minority of cases,[293] and subject to regional variation.[294]

288 FLA 1996, s 47(6). 289 Ibid, s 47(9). 290 Ibid, s 47(7). 291 Ibid, s 46(2).
292 Ibid, s 46(3). 293 DCA (2006a), table 5.9: last reported official data.
294 Edwards (2001); Burton et al (2002).

Lawyers and courts must ensure that those needing the full protection of a court order are not left in a vulnerable position: the effectiveness of legislation can be, and has been, undermined by the attitudes of those responsible for implementing it.[295] Nevertheless, the FLA 1996 may have alleviated some of Kewley's concerns.[296] Notably, it is questionable whether a proper hearing can now be avoided, for without testing the evidence the court cannot decide—as it is required to—whether a power of arrest (and so an order) is necessary and so whether an undertaking may lawfully be accepted.

Duration of powers of arrest

Where a power of arrest is attached to an occupation order, the court must decide how long that power should last. The Act specifically provides that powers of arrest attached to ex parte orders may last a shorter period than the order itself[297] but says nothing about standard orders. Before breach of NMOs was criminalized, powers of arrest would commonly be attached to NMOs of indefinite duration. Should the power of arrest also be indefinite? The Court of Appeal, mindful of respondents' rights, decided that powers of arrest can operate for a shorter period than the orders to which they relate:

In re B-J (A Child) (Non-Molestation Order: Power of Arrest) [2001] Fam 415 (CA)

HALE LJ:

43. There is nothing inherently incompatible between the mandatory duty contained in section 47(2) and [the flexibility of allowing powers of arrest shorter than the order to which they are attached]. The court would have to be satisfied that the victim would be adequately protected with only a shorter power of arrest. The cases in which the court could be satisfied of this might be difficult but are not impossible to imagine. . . . The great variety of circumstances in which Part IV orders, especially perhaps occupation orders, may be required make this by no means impossible, although it may not be common. One thing, however, is clear from section 47(2): the criterion is whether or not the applicant or child will be adequately protected without the power of arrest, not whether its continued existence will be inconvenient for others.

44. Given the inherent difficulties of predicting the future, and in particular when people will be safe, however, it would usually be preferable to attach the power for the same time as the order. Once it can be shown that the victim will be adequately protected without it, or without a different power, the obvious course is to vary the order [under s 49] so as to remove the power of arrest or reduce its scope. . . .

47. . . . If there is a case in which an order is appropriate but the court is indeed satisfied that the victim will be adequately protected by a time-limited power of arrest, an order which gives a larger power of arrest without warrant might . . . be incompatible with Convention rights. The court would then have to read section 47(2) [under s 3 of the HRA 1998] so as to permit this.

49. . . . In the context of the liberty of the subject, statutes are normally to be construed in such a way as to limit rather than enlarge the powers of the state. Powers of arrest for breach of the orders of a civil court are themselves unusual, although amply justified by the

[295] Smart (1989), 164; Kewley (1996), 7. [296] Kewley (1996), 7 and extracted at 4.7.3.
[297] FLA 1996, s 47(4).

need effectively to secure the performance of the obligations contained in the order. . . . [T]o require the court to attach a power of arrest for a longer period than the court is satisfied is required for the protection of victims is manifestly unjust to the respondent; it may also indirectly lead to injustice to the victims if the court is thereby deterred, either from making an order for the appropriate period, or from attaching a power of arrest. . . .

Similar arguments may be made when deciding to which *parts* of the order a power of arrest should be attached; a power necessary only for some types of breach should not be applied to the whole order.

Sanctions from the family court for contempt

Contempt proceedings in the family court are 'criminal proceedings' for the purposes of Article 6 ECHR, carrying the rights to legal representation and against self-incrimination, and decided on a criminal standard of proof.[298] The family courts' maximum sanction for contempt of court is two years' imprisonment; they can also order fines and make mental health orders.[299] Any assessment of the adequacy of sanctions imposed for breaches of occupation and other family court orders has to bear in mind that two-year maximum imprisonment, quite low compared with sentencing for many criminal charges (including those arising from breaches of NMOs and DAPOs that we consider next). The family court therefore cannot hand down prison sentences comparable to those that the criminal court could deliver.[300] This might be a basis for preferring criminal prosecution for whatever offences are available over contempt proceedings.[301]

In *Hale v Tanner*, Hale LJ explored whether and when, and if so for how long, imprisonment might be deployed for breach of an FLA 1996 order. She considered the particular context in which the court's contempt jurisdiction is exercised:

Hale v Tanner [2000] EWCA Civ 5570

HALE LJ:

25. Family cases, it has long been recognised, raise different considerations from those elsewhere in the civil law. The two most obvious are the heightened emotional tensions that arise between family members and often the need for those family members to continue to be in contact with one another because they have children together or the like. Those two factors make the task of the court, in dealing with these issues, quite different from the task when dealing with commercial disputes or other types of case in which sanctions have to be imposed for contempt of court. . . .

29. . . . [T]he length of the committal [to prison] has to depend upon the court's objectives. There are two objectives always in contempt of court proceedings. One is to mark the court's disapproval of the disobedience to its order. The other is to secure compliance with that order

298 *Hammerton v UK* (App No 6287/10, ECHR) (2016).

299 Contempt of Court Act 1981, s 14. Minors cannot be imprisoned for contempt: see *Re H (Respondent Under 18: Power of Arrest)* [2001] 1 FCR 370.

300 Cf suggestion of Thorpe LJ, *Lomas v Parle* [2003] EWCA Civ 1804, [50].

301 *Robinson v Murray* [2005] EWCA Civ 935, [13].

in the future. Thus, the seriousness of what has taken place is to be viewed in that light as well as for its own intrinsic gravity. . . .

33. . . . [O]f course, the court has to bear in mind the context. This may be aggravating or mitigating. The context is often the break-up of an intimate relationship in which emotions run high and people behave in silly ways. The context of having children together, if that be the case, cannot be ignored. Sometimes that means that there is an aggravation of what has taken place, because of the greater fear that is engendered from the circumstances. Sometimes it may be mitigating, because there is reason to suppose that once the immediate emotions have calmed down, the molestation and threats will not continue.

That context might also include parallel proceedings relating to the same conduct before another court, such as a criminal prosecution arising from the behaviour that also constituted the contempt: the court would need to avoid effectively punishing twice for the same conduct.[302] But whilst sharing a deterrent objective, sentencing in those other proceedings would, to some extent, have a different aim from the family court: the contempt jurisdiction seeks to uphold the authority of the court whose order has been flouted.[303]

Enforcement of provisions ancillary to occupation orders under s 40

An important limitation on the courts' powers to enforce occupation orders was exposed in *Nwogbe v Nwogbe*.[304] The court had made an occupation order with s 40 provisions requiring the respondent to pay the rent and other outgoings on the property from which he had been excluded. He failed to pay. The wife brought contempt proceedings. The Court of Appeal reluctantly found itself powerless. The maze of relevant civil law statutes offers no way of enforcing payment of money to a third party in this context, whether by imprisonment or less serious measures, such as attachment of earnings. Without some other basis on which the respondent can be ordered to pay money directly to the applicant, who can then pass it on to the third party, this form of s 40 provision is useless. Where the parties are spouses or civil partners, the various matrimonial financial orders might provide an answer.[305] But cohabitants and other associated persons may have no such alternative. Two decades on, Parliament has yet to remedy this deficiency. However, assuming that a DAPO can include similar requirements—in order to avoid what could otherwise amount to economic abuse—this problem is avoided in that context by the criminalization of DAPO breaches.

4.7.4.b Non-molestation orders and DAPOs

The criminal law option

While NMOs were originally enforced like occupation orders, since 2004, breaches can be pursued either as a contempt of court (arrestable only by warrant[306] and otherwise as discussed in relation to occupation orders) or prosecuted as a criminal offence. This development was controversial, particularly for what it signalled about the treatment of domestic abuse as a public or private issue. But this twin model also applies to DAPOs, whatever sorts of requirement they impose on respondents.[307] Indeed, as we shall see in 4.8, the DAA

302 *Hale v Tanner* [2000] 1 WLR 2377, 2381; *Slade v Slade* [2009] EWCA Civ 748, [21]–[23].
303 *Lomas v Parle* [2003] EWCA Civ 1804, [47]. 304 [2000] 2 FLR 744. 305 See 6.4.
306 FLA 1996, s 47(8). 307 DAA 2021, ss 39–40, 43.

2021 takes the 'public' response to domestic abuse considerably further. And draft guidance underscores the police's role in monitoring and enforcing the privately obtained DAPOs that we are considering here.[308]

Family Law Act 1996

42A Offence of breaching non-molestation order

(1) A person who without reasonable excuse[309] does anything that he is prohibited from doing by a non-molestation order is guilty of an offence.

(2) In the case of an [ex parte order], a person can be guilty of an offence under this section only in respect of conduct engaged in at a time when he was aware of the existence of the order.

(3) Where a person is convicted of an offence under this section in respect of any conduct, that conduct is not punishable as contempt of court.

(4) A person cannot be convicted of an offence under this section in respect of any conduct which has been punished as a contempt of court.

(5) A person guilty of an offence under this section is liable—

(a) on conviction on indictment, to imprisonment for a term not exceeding five years, or a fine, or both; and

(b) on summary conviction, to imprisonment for a term not exceeding twelve months, or a fine . . ., or both. . . .

The Explanatory Notes accompanying the 2004 reform explained that its purpose was to permit police to arrest immediately for breaches of orders without needing the family court to have attached a power of arrest or to seek a warrant.[310] The criminal power of arrest endures for the lifetime of the order.

Early CPS guidance for the 2004 Act stated that the s 42A offence 'aims to place complainants at the heart of the criminal justice system' and so 'gives complainants a choice' about whether breach of an NMO will be dealt with criminally or as a contempt of the family court.[311] It suggested that where the conduct that breached the NMO was not otherwise criminal in nature, the public interest may be better served by letting the victim pursue the matter as contempt of the family court, rather than by criminal prosecution. But the possibility of parallel criminal and civil (family) proceedings was also contemplated: breaches can be prosecuted either for the s 42A offence only (with no contempt proceedings as well), for a substantive criminal offence (e.g. an offence against the person), or both. Sentencing guidelines for the s 42A offence require the sentencing court to decide on the level of culpability and the level of harm entailed in the breach, noting specifically that 'where a breach is committed in the context of a background of domestic abuse, the sentencer should take care not to underestimate the harm which may be present'. Specified aggravating factors for the sentencer to take into account are also carefully tailored to the domestic context: for example, the use of child contact arrangements to instigate the offence.[312]

[308] See HO (2021A), chs 9 and 10.

[309] The burden lies with the prosecution to prove there was no such excuse: *R v Richards* [2010] EWCA Crim 835; cf *R v Nicholson* [2006] EWCA Crim 1518 on the contents of the defence.

[310] Para 15. [311] CPS (undated), 'Background'. [312] Sentencing Council (2018b).

Evaluating the arguments for criminalization

The government strongly promoted criminalization of NMO breaches in 2004, arguing that it brought several advantages:

Hansard, *Official Report*—Domestic Violence, Crime and Victims Bill Debates, Hansard HL Deb, cols GC237–8, 240, 19 January 2004

Baroness Scotland of Asthal, Minister of State:

There are a number of reasons why contempt of court is not a sufficient or effective sanction. Contempt of court is of course a very serious matter and has always been so. However, many victims with whom we have spoken have stressed to us the disdain in which the offender holds the non-molestation order—even where a power of arrest is attached to that order. We are concerned that the sanction for breach of a non-molestation order must bring home to the respondent the seriousness of that breach. That is why we wish to make breach a criminal offence. . . .

Making breach a criminal offence would also extend the range of sanctions available to the courts to punish the offender. Contempt of court limits the sanctions to imprisonment or fine. Where a breach is a criminal offence, the courts would also be able to impose the usual range of community sentences. Sections 189 and 190 of [the Criminal Justice Act 2003] provide that, on conviction, conditions can [in certain cases] be imposed to do with curfew, mental health, drug treatment, voluntary activities, residence and supervision. If the person does not comply with those conditions, a suspended sentence can take effect. . . .

That gives the court an opportunity to deal with the offending behaviour. Many partners who find themselves involved in domestic violence are in need of anger management, drug treatment and a whole series of other interventions that will inure to the benefit not only of that partner, but of partners who may come afterwards. . . . [In] the analysis of partners who kill, it is very unusual indeed if those persons have not had a series of partners whom they have abused on the way to the murder that they eventually commit. It is not simply the complainant on the day whom we have to protect, but all the other partners who may come afterwards. That should exercise our attention, because of the nature of domestic violence. . . .

. . . Some women do not wish to criminalise their husbands but wish to have the abuse stopped. It will be possible to continue to do that through the civil route. But we should also take on board that the very abusive nature of domestic violence often erodes the will of the woman, who may need the greater support offered by the criminal court as well as that of the civil court, and that an intervention of that nature may prove necessary.

Many have said that they have benefited from having a police officer come to the door to arrest and remove the assailant. The courts can apply those provisions with flexibility and speed. We do not accept that they will be longer drawn-out as a result of the procedures. We will be assisted greatly by the way in which case management is currently dealt with and the fact that the CPS is working very closely with the police and the courts to get together protocols so that we have a holistic approach to domestic violence.

Hansard HC Deb, Proceedings of Standing Committee E, col 45, 22 June 2004

The Parliamentary Under-Secretary of State for the Home Department, Paul Goggins MP:

[Introducing s 42A would involve] a rebalancing between civil and criminal in the system. That is entirely in keeping with the spirit of this legislation, which is to empower and protect the victim on the one hand while also sending out a very clear message that Parliament—and the country—regards with increasing seriousness crimes associated with domestic violence and intends the penalties to be heavy and the protection to be stronger. There may be some rebalancing, and that would be entirely right.

The meaning of 'rebalancing' here is unclear and its wisdom debatable. The reforms tend to push domestic abuse towards the public realm of the criminal justice system, whilst 'further blur[ring] already muddied waters regarding the objectives of sanctions for breach of civil orders and criminal sanctions'.[313] The policy objectives need to be clarified. The choice between criminal and civil/family proceedings has many implications: for the sanctions available; for the degree of victim involvement in and control over the proceedings; for evidential rules; and for the public and police perception of these cases. Is the objective to protect the victim, or to punish the abuser? Criminal law has traditionally focused on the latter, family law on the former.

Criminalization of breach relieves victims of the financial and psychological burden of bringing enforcement proceedings themselves. Moreover, increased use of the criminal law sends out strong messages about society's disapproval of domestic abuse. However, criminalizing breach of civil orders as such may—ironically—undermine the message. Charging the s 42A FLA 1996—and, in future, DAPO—offence, instead of any 'ordinary' criminal charge applicable to the facts, might downgrade domestic abuse by giving the impression that it is not 'real crime'.

Opponents of the 2004 reform also raised questions about victim control.[314]

M. Burton, 'Criminalising Breaches of Civil Orders for Protection from Domestic Violence', [2003] *Criminal Law Review* 301, 305–6

Domestic violence is not just an individual matter but an offence against the state. The onus should not be on the victim to seek enforcement of the order, rather through criminal proceedings the state should mark society's disapproval of the defendant's conduct in breaching the order. The difficulty with this model is that the victim's interests may become supplanted by a wider public interest and the victim's views may become marginalised in relation to any decisions that may be taken by the prosecuting authorities about whether to prosecute for breach of a non-molestation order. If the conduct is grave enough to warrant criminalisation then it has been argued that it is right that the victim should lose control over the prosecution process, albeit that they should be kept informed of its progress. However, it can be questioned whether breach of a non-molestation order should result in the victim's wishes being subordinated to a wider public interest. It may be in practice that the police and CPS would not prosecute for breaches of a non-molestation order where the victim did not want them to, however, the possibility remains. . . . Perhaps prosecutors would feel that the victim should have more influence in relation to cases which came to them by the indirect route of breach of a civil order rather than the direct route of the police charging the defendant for assault or other general offences related to domestic violence. However, as far as victim decision-making in legal interventions is concerned, the victim has a more prominent role in civil interventions. There may be value in preserving that role and not, even theoretically, subordinating it to a wider public interest.

313 Burton (2003b), 305–8.

314 See in particular Hansard HL Deb, vol 656, cols GC229–30, 19 January 2004, Lord Thomas of Gresford.

Victims preferring to take civil proceedings cannot elect from the outset to have a power of arrest attached to an NMO or DAPO, so they have to return to the family court promptly to obtain a warrant if they wish to enforce their order as contempt and bring enforcement proceedings in the family courts before any criminal process has concluded; civil enforcement is otherwise barred by the rules against double punishment.[315] Victims might be deterred from seeking NMOs at all if they knew that their partners might gain a criminal record as a result of any breach and that decisions regarding charge and prosecution, in the public criminal courts, will be beyond their control.

Moreover, the fact that breach constitutes an offence might even deter courts from making orders in some cases. The prospect of a power of arrest instigating *contempt* proceedings dissuaded the court from making an NMO in *Chechi v Bashier*, the case involving brothers feuding over a land dispute.[316] It was felt that this would put too much power into the applicant's hands. The prospect of *criminal* proceedings might weigh even more heavily against making an order, though it may be hoped that in paradigm domestic abuse cases these sorts of considerations would not influence courts' decisions.

Furthermore, criminal punishment—if not carefully managed—may be counterproductive, prejudicing victims' safety rather than protecting them. Short prison sentences may simply aggravate the situation.[317] Fines are problematic where victim and abuser live in the same household; it has even been known for victims to pay fines themselves.[318] Note also that victims have no party status in criminal proceedings and are not directly represented by their own lawyer. However, their views can and should be conveyed to the court by an Independent Domestic Violence Advocate (IDVA), not least to share information about the family relevant to both the criminal and family courts, for example, as regards any arrangements for child contact, to try to avoid inconsistent orders being made by different courts. Without such liaison, important safeguarding and other welfare issues might get lost.[319]

An alternative approach, preferred by opponents of criminalization, would enhance the *family courts'* enforcement and sentencing powers—indeed, the advent of the DAPOs in a sense achieves this, by considerably expanding the range of things that the family court can order in the first place, notably including participation in perpetrator programmes. This may better align outcomes with victims' wishes. Family courts already hold some attractions with their more accommodating rules of evidence, the opportunity for proceedings to be held in private, and their speed of action, and victims are no longer exposed to the risk of cross-examination in person by the alleged perpetrator in family cases.[320]

Evidence about the impact of criminalization

Early anecdotal and survey evidence suggested that concerns about criminalization deterring victims/courts from seeking/making orders might have been well-founded,[321] and that police were not treating breaches seriously, not arresting or not charging, and issuing

[315] FLA 1996, s 42A(3), (4); DAA 2021, s 39(3)(4). [316] [1999] 2 FLR 489, 496; see 4.5.2.b.

[317] For sentencing decisions under s 42A: *R v Briscoe* [2010] EWCA Crim 373; *R v Franks* [2010] EWCA Crim 1030.

[318] Burton (2016), 48; Bettinson (2016), 98.

[319] See Hansard HC Deb, Proceedings of Standing Committee E on the Domestic Violence, Crimes and Victims Bill, 29 June 2004: discussion of amendments to cl 10.

[320] DAA 2021, s 65, inserting Matrimonial and Family Proceedings Act 1984, Part 4B; cf Munby (2018), 16–17.

[321] See generally Burton (2009b); Hester et al (2008); Platt (2008); Millward (2008).

cautions inappropriately.[322] Concern was also expressed about the delay attendant upon criminal prosecution (a problem that has only worsened), and the associated risk of victim withdrawal.[323]

The most recent evidence, several years on, is provided by the independent examination of a super-complaint raised by the Centre for Women's Justice alleging that 'police are failing to use the protective measures available to them in cases involving violence against women and girls', including NMOs.[324] There are clearly problems, though whether all of those are the responsibility of the police is less obvious:

College of Policing, HM Inspectorate of Constabulary and Fire & Rescue Services, and Independent Office for Police Conduct, *A duty to protect: police use of protective measures in cases involving violence against women and girls* (2021), 48–51

[T]here [are] limited published data on NMOs. Ministry of Justice data show that the number of NMOs granted [has] been increasing since 2012 and that the number of offenders sentenced for breaching NMOs has been going down since 2014. The number of offenders sentenced for breaching NMOs has not followed the same pattern as orders granted. The number of offenders sentenced for breaching an NMO in 2019 was 3 percent lower than in 2010. . . .

To fully understand the extent of any failure by the police to arrest for breaches of NMOs, the number of reports of breaches, together with their outcomes, is needed. The Home Office [only] started collating data on the number of arrests made for breaching NMOs in July 2019 . . .

[T]he Home Office collates [data on breaches of NMOs, which] have increased 37 percent from 2017/18 to 2019/20. The proportion of cases resulting in a suspect being charged is falling from around half in 2017/18 to a third in 2019/20. The number of cases that are not proceeding due to evidential difficulties, despite the victim supporting the action, is increasing (from 34 percent in 2017/18 to 42 percent in 2019/20).

Research from Bates and Hester [(2020)] found evidence of officers misunderstanding and/or 'trivialising'; and of not understanding threats and intimidation in the context of domestic abuse . . . In contrast our overall assessment from our fieldwork is that officers in nearly every force had a good understanding of NMOs and when to arrest for breach of an NMO. Some officers spoke of how they preferred to arrest for NMOs as it was considered an "easy" arrest. Several officers we spoke with were keen to emphasise that they did not "trivialise" the use of NMOs. Most were aware of the importance of NMOs to safeguard victims and recognised that child contact or being sent a single text message would be a breach.

Evidently, the criminal justice system only offers a useful enforcement mechanism for family court orders if the police know about those orders' existence and their terms. This is particularly so where the behaviour in question would not otherwise constitute an offence, and where very specific behaviour has been prohibited or positively required. Indeed, *failure*

322 House of Commons Select Committee on Home Affairs (2008).

323 Minute of evidence given by DJ Mornington to House of Commons Select Committee on Home Affairs (2008), Q55, 22 January 2008.

324 See College of Policing et al (2021), drawing on research by Bates and Hester (2020).

to arrest where breach has occurred can cause significant harm.[325] But information-transfer to police has proved problematic:

When asked about their understanding of what constitutes a breach, many officers said they were frustrated by ambiguous wording of NMOs provided by the civil courts, which they felt left NMOs open to interpretation . . . While this in itself is not conclusive, this may explain the view that minor breaches are sometimes not acted on, or that officers treat incidents in isolation. . . .

Our investigation found that police officers sometimes have problems accessing NMOs to check the provisions of orders, including the power of arrest. Being able to access this information is essential to enabling officers to assess whether the provisions have been breached. They told us accessing the information was often time-consuming and involved "digging around in police computer records". We were also told that despite their efforts, there were occasions when some officers couldn't find information on the NMO. . . .

This is supported by research by Bates and Hester [(2020)], who say the recording of NMOs is a problem. However, Bates and Hester argued that their evidence, from both victim reports and police data, suggests that there is still a lack of systematic communication of these NMOs to the police.

In the same article, Bates and Hester say that "in 307 out of 400 police domestic violence incidents (77 percent) analysed for the project, it was not known whether or not a protection order was in place. Given that at least a quarter of victims/survivors interviewed reported having one or more protection orders (26 percent), it is likely that police data [are] not capturing a swathe of cases where orders are in place."

Pilot projects are seeking to improve the effectiveness of the processes for conveying details of family court orders to the police, which will presumably apply equally to DAPOs.[326] This fits with the broader agenda to improve information-sharing between various agencies, including local authorities, regarding domestic abuse cases.[327]

4.8 ORDERS MADE WITHOUT APPLICATION BY THE VICTIM

While victims are clearly seeking NMOs in increasing numbers, the process is onerous, as a National Domestic Violence Helpline worker described in the super-complaint regarding police activity:

Centre for Women's Justice, *Super-complaint: Police failure to use protective measures in cases involving violence against women and girls* (2019), 32

". . . This is quite a demanding process for a woman to go through. Firstly, she may have to apply for legal aid which means providing bank statements, mortgage details and other financial documents. Some women obtain legal aid but then have to pay a contribution, which can

[325] College of Policing et al (2021), 10, and cases of femicide described at 51–2.
[326] HM Government (2022a), 43. [327] MOJ, HMCTS, and Wolfson (2022).

be quite large depending on their income. Those who cannot obtain legal aid have to either prepare the court application themselves or pay a solicitor. Many women represent themselves without solicitors. A detailed written statement must be prepared along with a court application form and these must be lodged with the court urgently. In many cases where an order is granted ex parte at the first hearing the perpetrator may challenge the order and the woman has to attend a second hearing where she must confront him in court. In some cases, such as those involving repeat e-mails and text messages it is unlikely that an order will be granted ex parte and she will face the perpetrator at a hearing."

If we can relieve victims of the burden of enforcement (by criminalizing breach, discussed at 4.7.4.b), why not also relieve them of the burden of making the initial application? Would such a step support or endanger victim autonomy?

4.8.1 ORDERS MADE OF THE COURT'S OWN MOTION

Both the FLA 1996 and the DAA 2021 empower courts to make orders without anyone's having applied for one. This facility is limited under the FLA 1996: only NMOs (not occupation orders) can be made without application, and then only by a family court in specified 'family proceedings':[328]

Family Law Act 1996, s 42

. . .

(2) The court may make a non-molestation order—. . .

(b) if in any family proceedings to which the respondent is a party the court considers that the order should be made for the benefit of any other party to the proceedings or any relevant child even though no such application has been made. . . .

(4A) A court considering whether to make an occupation order shall also consider whether to exercise the power conferred by subsection (2)(b) . . .

Whilst these victims did not apply for the NMO, they are at least already before the family court with a family problem.

The DAA 2021, by contrast, gives more power to more courts: the court can make any sort of DAPO—including requirements akin to occupation orders—and this power extends beyond the family court. Under s 31, the county court in (non-family) civil proceedings to which victim and respondent are parties can make an order. So too can the criminal court: following the example of restraining orders made under the PHA 1997, DAPOs can be made against defendants whether they are convicted or acquitted of the criminal charge.[329] When considering whether to make a DAPO in the latter context, the proceedings in the criminal court are classed as civil proceedings, and an accordingly wider range of evidence is admissible than was admissible in the criminal trial.[330]

[328] Identified in FLA 1996, s 63.

[329] DAA 2021, s 31(3)–(6); cf PHA 1997, s 5A and Sentencing Act 2020, ss 359–64.

[330] DAA 2021, s 48(1)–(2).

4.8.2 APPLICATIONS MADE BY POLICE AND OTHER THIRD PARTIES

The DAA 2021's most striking feature is its strong commitment to protective applications being made not by victims but by third parties. The concept of third party applications is not new. The FLA 1996 had empowered the making of regulations to permit third parties to apply for both NMOs and occupation orders, but this was never implemented.[331] However, the Crime and Security Act 2010 (CSA 2010) empowered police to issue 'domestic violence protection notices' (DVPNs) and apply for 'domestic violence protection orders' (DVPOs). These were a somewhat limited version of the new DAA 2021 scheme, for what are now called 'domestic *abuse* protection notices' (DAPNs), granted by the police, and DAPOs, for which the police, other specified third parties, and anyone with the leave of the court can apply.[332] We set out the details of that new scheme here, before evaluating the case for third party action at 4.8.3. The CSA 2010 scheme will be repealed once the DAA 2021 comes into force (expected in 2025 after piloting), so we mention it here only by way of contrast with the DAA 2021 scheme.

4.8.2.a Third party applications for DAPOs

The DAA 2021 for the first time allows third parties (police, other specified category of applicant, or person with leave[333]) to seek protective court orders—DAPOs—by way of free-standing application to the court.[334] The full extent of the DAPO jurisdiction (described at 4.6) is available in such cases, so is available on the basis of any type of domestic *abuse*, includes requirements that regulate occupation and positive requirements (not just enjoin molestation), and can be imposed for any duration, potentially indefinitely, with criminal consequences for breach. This contrasts markedly with the CSA 2010 scheme, for cases of domestic *violence*, which only permitted applications from police, and then only as a (compulsory) follow-up where the police had issued an emergency DVPN (discussed next). Any resulting DVPO could last only 28 days, and breach was a civil matter only.[335] So, where the DVPN/DVPO merely offered limited breathing space for victims then to make their own choices about the longer term, hopefully freed from perpetrators' influence,[336] DAPOs enable third parties to instigate much more comprehensive, long-term protection.

The criteria for grant of DAPOs in third party cases are the same as those in the 'private' applications that we discussed at 4.6. One obvious query is whether victims' wishes count at all. The Act's answer is clear:

Domestic Abuse Act 2021, s 33

(3) It is not necessary for the person for whose protection a domestic abuse protection order is made to consent to the making of the order.

[331] FLA 1996, s 60; MOJ (2007), 20. [332] DAA 2021, s 28(2)(b)–(d).

[333] Ibid. Police applications are made to the magistrates' court, all others to the family court: s 28(5)–(6).

[334] See also ibid, ss 40(4) and 44(3) on who can pursue breaches and who can seek variation and discharge, as to which see HO (2021a), 33.

[335] CSA 2010, ss 24–29; see Kelly et al (2013) for evaluation of the pilot scheme.

[336] See HO (2011), 1.3–1.5.

This is no different from the CSA 2010 scheme, but the degree of intrusion effected by a DAPO into the victim's (and perpetrator's) life is far more extensive than under DVPOs. Victims' opinions about what, if any, order should be made are merely a matter for the court to consider, where it is 'made aware' of them.[337]

4.8.2.b Police use of DAPNs

The other aspect of the DAA 2021 scheme is the separate facility for the police (only) themselves to grant what is the equivalent of an ex parte order,[338] in the form of a DAPN. The DAPN is very similar to its CSA 2010 precursor DVPNs. DAPNs can be 'given' in writing[339] to a perpetrator on the authority of a police inspector who has 'reasonable grounds for believing' that the two preconditions for DAPOs are met: that is, that the perpetrator ('P') has been abusive[340] towards an over-16 to whom he is 'personally connected'[341] and that it is necessary to give the DAPN to protect that person from domestic abuse or its risk.[342]

Like DAPOs, DAPNs can bar contact between P and the other party, impose an exclusion zone (though only around the other party's home), and regulate the parties' occupation of their shared home. The police officer must have regard to the same checklist of factors as apply to DAPOs, plus any representations made by P about the matter.[343] Again, victim consent is not required.[344]

Any breach of DAPNs can result in arrest without warrant, P being brought before the magistrates within 24 hours. But in any event, having given a DAPN, the police are required to apply to the magistrates for a DAPO, and that application must be heard within 48 hours of the DAPN being given.[345] The DAPN can then remain in place until the court decides what, if any, DAPO to make—that decision is made in the ordinary way.[346]

4.8.3 PROS AND CONS OF THIRD PARTY ACTION

Should third party applications be allowed and, if so, in what form? Are the police the right agency to be empowered to act in this way? What other third parties, if any, should be empowered under the DAA 2021? Does the scheme jeopardize the rights of either party?[347] Is it right that victims' consent to the application is not required?

4.8.3.a Victim protection versus victim autonomy?

The principal advantage of third party applications is relieving victims of the burden of protecting themselves, as this analysis of domestic abuse professionals' views about the introduction of such applications rehearses:

[337] DAA 2021, s 33(2)(b).

[338] This analogy is underscored by the fact that the required DAPO application that must follow cannot be ex parte: ibid, s 34(2). There is also a comparison to be made here with police powers in child protection cases: CA 1989, s 46, discussed at 12.6.1.

[339] Ibid, s 25(1), and thereafter for other procedural requirements.

[340] Ibid, s 1: see 4.2.1. [341] Ibid, s 2: see 4.6.1. [342] Ibid, s 22(1)–(4); cf s 32 for DAPOs.

[343] Ibid, s 24 and see 4.6.3.b. [344] Ibid, s 24(4). [345] Ibid, ss 28(3), 29. [346] See 4.6.

[347] See Crompton (2013), in relation to the CSA 2010 scheme.

M. Burton, 'Third Party Applications for Protection Orders in England and Wales: Service Provider's Views on Implementing Section 60 of the Family Law Act 1996', (2003) 25 *Journal of Social Welfare and Family Law* 137, 139

First, respondents felt that the confidence of some survivors may be so eroded by their experience of domestic violence that they would be unable to recognise that their situation called for a remedy, let alone undertake the daunting task of pursuing an order from a position of such low self-esteem. It was thought that the support of the third party could be beneficial in rebuilding the confidence of the survivor. Second, the survivor would know that she was believed by the third party, a boost to confidence in addition to that accruing from the order itself. Third, respondents also argued that third party applications would remove any blame attributed to the survivor for invoking the protection offered by the legal system against the perpetrator. It was felt that the survivor would be able to simply tell the perpetrator that the application had nothing to do with her; she could 'hide behind' the third party. Thus third party applications could deflect the blame coming from the perpetrator and also, in some situations, the extended family and wider community. This latter factor was considered to be particularly important for survivors in ethnic minority communities, where pursuing redress for domestic violence can lead to being ostracized by the whole community . . . An important consideration for women, in deciding whether to pursue a civil remedy, is weighing up the prospect of the remedy being effective against the chances that pursuing it may result in further violence. Many respondents in this study commented that women were put off pursuing civil protection by fear of reprisals. Respondents who favoured [these applications] saw third party applications as beneficial in reducing a survivor's fear of reprisals. It was thought that women would be less likely to be subjected to pressure by the respondent if a third party application was being made, because there would be no point in the respondent intimidating his partner with a view to getting her to withdraw the case.

Such considerations underpinned parliamentary support for the DAA 2021 scheme, albeit alert to the need for care about which third parties were allowed to apply:

Joint Committee on the Draft Domestic Abuse Bill, *Report* (14 June 2019)

85. Our witnesses were generally supportive of the provision that orders may be made without the victim's consent. . . .

87. . . . We believe it is a key strength of the proposed orders that they can be made by the police without the victim's consent: the nature of domestic abuse is such that pressure not to take action against the perpetrators will often be overwhelming and it would significantly weaken the protective effect of the orders if only victims were able to apply for them. We note the concerns about third parties being able to apply for orders and [to] potentially [be] subject to abuse by family members or others. We believe that the fact that any such application is at the discretion of the court will prevent instances of abuse.

But this is not uncontroversial. Burton's respondents in her study 20 years ago reported that:

M. Burton, 'Third Party Applications for Protection Orders in England and Wales: Service Provider's Views on Implementing Section 60 of the Family Law Act 1996', (2003) 25 *Journal of Social Welfare and Family Law* 137, 140, 146

the main objection [to third party applications] . . . was that [they] would reinforce a survivor's low self-esteem and confidence. It would reaffirm a survivor's belief that they are unable to obtain remedies themselves and deprive them of the benefits that may be gained by actively and fully engaging in the process of successfully pursuing a remedy. . . .

Indeed, most respondents then opposed applications without consent, as this would:

reinforce the lack of power and control that the survivor had already experienced due to the domestic violence. A comparison was . . . made with mandatory prosecutions . . . Even amongst respondents who supported mandatory prosecution, there were some who felt that there was a difference between pursuing a prosecution without the victim's consent and obtaining a protective order without her consent and cooperation.

Consent from victims brings pragmatic advantages—lack of victim cooperation may hamper collection of evidence and enforcement. But interfering with victim autonomy by bringing applications in the face of victim opposition raises human rights considerations, most obviously under Article 8 ECHR. However, the concept of victim autonomy in this area is complex. Consider these remarks from a case about whether social services (another potential third party for DAPO applications) could seek an injunction to protect an elderly couple from their abusive adult son:

DL v A Local Authority [2012] EWCA Civ 253

MCFARLANE LJ:

54. The appellant's submissions [against intervention] rightly place a premium upon an individual's autonomy to make his own decisions. However this point, rather than being one against the existence of the inherent jurisdiction in these cases, is in my view a strong argument in favour of it. The jurisdiction . . . is in part aimed at enhancing or liberating the autonomy of a vulnerable adult whose autonomy has been compromised by a reason other than mental incapacity because they are . . .:

a) Under constraint; or
b) Subject to coercion or undue influence; or
c) For some other reason deprived of the capacity to make the relevant decision or disabled from making a free choice, or incapacitated or disabled from giving or expressing a real and genuine consent.

As discussed at 4.2.4.d, victims' own need for protection might justify intervention against their wishes, and the Court of Appeal has justified equivalent intervention in forced marriage cases (discussed at 4.10.2.c) by reference to victims' rights under Article 3 ECHR.[348] Simply put, insisting on victim consent would deprive third party action of its chief advantage: protection of victims too petrified to protect themselves. Moreover, where children or other vulnerable individuals are affected by the abuse, state intervention might still be justified.[349] The challenge is finding a way of ensuring that victims feel empowered overall (not least via the provision of suitable support services and a sensitive approach in exploring their wishes[350]), rather than merely revictimized by being deprived of control by the state. As in relation to criminal proceedings following the breach of a privately obtained NMO or DAPO (discussed at 4.7.4.b), it is essential in these cases to ensure that victims' needs and wishes—and the contents of any existing court orders regarding the family—are properly understood by the court in these cases, and so again the role of the IDVA is key.[351] But as Burton has noted, the lack of any statutory mandate for provision of support services (or IDVAs) in these cases is a weakness of the English system, compared with some European jurisdictions, potentially undermining the effectiveness of these interventions.[352]

The government's view was that victims' ECHR rights would not be breached by the DAA 2021:

HO, MOJ, and Ministry of Communities, Housing and Local Government, *Draft Domestic Abuse Bill: European Convention on Human Rights Memorandum* (2019)

37. . . . The ability of the court to make orders where the victim is not supportive is to safeguard against the risk that a victim may be subject to coercion from or pressure by the perpetrator into withdrawing or withholding their consent. Making an order against the victim's wishes is likely to interfere with their Article 8 right for as long as the order remains effective. . . .

38. . . . [M]aking an order against the victim's wishes . . . is proportionate to meet the legitimate aims of protecting the victim from further acts of domestic abuse and preventing crime and disorder. [T]he interference with victim's rights will last only as long as the court deems it is both necessary and proportionate to protect the victim. The victim has the opportunity to explain their views to the court before the order is made. They may apply to vary or discharge the order, and they also have a right of appeal against the decision of a court following any such application. The Government considers that the Article 8 right of the victim, in cases where they do not consent to the order, is adequately protected.

4.8.3.b Symbol of public seriousness or risk of downgrading?

Third party applications carry a potential symbolic. Burton, writing in 2003, argued that permitting them:

[348] *Re K (Forced Marriage: Passport Order)* [2020] EWCA Civ 190, [37].

[349] Cf the exclusion requirements that can be attached to emergency protection and interim care orders, CA 1989, ss 38A and 44A: see 12.6.2 and 12.7. Cf remarks re lack of power to make a restraining order without victim consent: *R v Herrington* [2017] EWCA Crim 889, [7]–[9], but finding of such a power for forced marriage protection orders: *Re K (Forced Marriage: Passport Order)* [2020] EWCA Civ 190.

[350] See HO (2021A), Annex B.

[351] See Bettinson (2016).

[352] Burton (2015), (2016), 54.

> would affirm the responsibility of the state, through public bodies, to provide protection for survivors of domestic violence. . . . [A] clear message would be sent out by third party applications that domestic violence is a public matter not a private matter; it is a legitimate sphere of state intervention in the interests of society as a whole.[353]

But empowering police, specifically, in this hybrid civil/criminal law arena risks further 'decriminalizing' or at least 'downgrading' domestic abuse by avoiding using the *general* criminal law.[354] The Home Office's draft guidance for police states that:

> A DAPN should never be given as an alternative to charging [for a criminal offence] where the threshold for charging has been met – although a DAPN could be used in conjunction with a decision to charge. In these circumstances, full consideration should be given to protecting the needs of the victim and whether these can be fully addressed through the use of bail conditions.[355]

However, as ever, guidance is not always complied with in practice: Bates and Hester found examples of (purely civil) DVPNs and DVPOs both being used where more serious, criminal law intervention was required and not being used where they should have been.[356] While data on use of the CSA 2010 regime are hard to collate (itself problematic), it has clearly been underused, imperilling victims and children:

College of Policing, HM Inspectorate of Constabulary and Fire & Rescue Services, and Independent Office for Police Conduct, *A duty to protect: police use of protective measures in cases involving violence against women and girls* (2021), 61

> The number of DVPN/DVPOs applied for is very low in relation to the number of domestic abuse incidents, and varies significantly across forces. While not all incidents are eligible for a DVPN or DVPO, this strongly suggests that some forces are under-using them. It is essential that forces understand this variance and are taking steps to ensure they are being used where appropriate.
>
> Evidence gathered in our investigation shows that there are instances of misunderstanding by officers around DVPN/DVPOs. This . . . may explain why some forces may be underusing DVPN/DVPOs. This has the potential to cause harm.

Given this, careful piloting of and police training for the DAA 2021 scheme will be essential to maximize its effectiveness.[357]

[353] Burton (2003a), 141.
[354] Humphreys and Kaye (1997), 410–12; Burton (2003a), 142–3; Crompton (2014); Burton (2016), 49.
[355] HO (2021a), 8; see also at 16 on use of DAPOs.
[356] Bates and Hester (2020), 147–8.
[357] Cf Kelly et al (2013) on the CSA 2010 pilot.

4.9 THE FUTURE: WHICH ORDER, WHICH ROUTE?

The declared policy intention behind the DAA 2021 orders 'is to bring together the strongest elements of existing protective orders into a single, comprehensive, flexible order which will provide more effective and longer-term protection to victims of domestic abuse and their children'.[358] However, the Act repeals only the CSA 2010 scheme: NMOs and occupation orders remain available under the FLA 1996, as do restraining orders under the PHA 1997. The government's position is that the DAA 2021 orders 'are intended to be used instead of [the other orders] in all cases of domestic abuse where a protective order is being considered'.[359]

The government forecasts as many as 55,000 DAPOs being made each year.[360] This is an ambitious target when set against recent figures for FLA 1996 and CSA 2010 orders on which that estimate relies: in year ending March 2020 (so, pre-Covid-19 pandemic) just 6,267 DVPOs were granted,[361] while *c*. 39,600 FLA orders (over 37,000 NMOs, plus a smattering of occupation orders) were made in calendar year 2020.[362] The FLA 1996 numbers for 2020 and 2021—both pandemic years—were somewhat higher than previously, with *c*. 33,800 FLA 1996 orders made in 2019,[363] so these numbers might settle back. That being so, even taking into account restraining orders (as the government does) and a 5–10 per cent uplift, the 55,000 figure looks high.

Clearly much will depend, first, on how commonly police and other third parties exercise their new powers. The Joint Committee that scrutinized the draft Bill expressed concern that the DAPO scheme might not meet its objectives for various reasons, including the police's patchy use of the DVPN/DVPO scheme, the cost to the police of applying for orders (beyond the pilots), and the reluctance of some victims to engage with a process that would potentially criminalize their partner.[364] The second factor will be how many victims (and courts) shift their applications (and orders) from the FLA 1996 to DAPOs under the 2021 Act, bearing in mind the *choice* that many (but not all) victims will have here; and how many victims currently unable to access occupation orders under the FLA 1996 at all seek DAPOs for that purpose.[365] We now consider what factors might direct victims one way or another.

4.9.1 REASONS TO USE THE FLA 1996

Some victims will have no choice but to use the FLA 1996, because they are not (or may not be) eligible under the DAA 2021: those sharing a household on an unrelated, platonic, non-intimate basis; and parties whose only connection is that they are parties to the same family proceedings.[366] Even those who are clearly eligible under the DAA 2021 may be unable to pass—or wish to avoid the burden of passing—the 'domestic abuse' threshold (past and future) that applies to that Act.[367] Others, concerned to protect their autonomy in the conduct of the case, will be anxious to retain total or at least more control of their case, by applying for occupation orders (breach of which is not criminalized) and for NMOs, on the basis that while police can arrest and charge for breach, at least third parties cannot apply to vary NMOs and no other third parties can seek a *warrant* for arrest as they can under the DAA 2021.[368]

358 HO (2022b). 359 HO (2021a), 4. 360 HO (2022b). 361 Ibid.

362 MOJ (2022a), table 16. 363 Ibid.

364 Joint Committee (2019), para 115, and paras preceding.

365 Though note that the courts' powers to make DAPOs of their own motion in FLA 1996 proceedings can cut across the victims' chosen application.

366 See 4.6.1. 367 See 4.6.3.a. 368 See 4.8.2.a.

Of course, the court seized of the matter will be able (where the eligibility and other conditions were satisfied) to make a DAPO of its own motion, so retaining the FLA 1996's relative privacy will not be guaranteed—but at least it can be attempted.

4.9.2 REASONS TO USE THE DAA 2021

Other victims, able to meet the eligibility and threshold conditions, may be keen to secure the advantages of third party support and so hope to find a police or other applicant to pursue the matter for them under the DAA 2021, so being relieved of the onus of seeking protection.[369] DAPOs also offer a far wider range of interventions to help combat the abuse and its effects, including by the imposition of electronic monitoring and other positive requirements.[370] However, the effectiveness of all this is entirely dependent on adequate funding.

For all non-entitled, non-spouse/civil partner/cohabitant cases, of course, the DAA 2021 offers the only prospect of regulating occupation of a shared home. DAPOs may be particularly useful for multi-generation households. In the pre-FLA 1996 case, *Chaudhry v Chaudhry*, the judge declined to make an occupation order in favour of a blameless wife where the matrimonial home, owned by the husband with his father, was occupied by several other relatives who had allegedly attacked the wife. The judge found that requiring the husband to permit the wife to occupy the property would create a 'miserable situation which would lead to violence and . . . an impossible situation'. Divorce proceedings were in any event pending, and these would resolve the issue of the wife's accommodation in the longer term.[371] Under the FLA 1996, the court could now make NMOs against the husband's family. But an occupation order could only be made against the in-laws if the wife was entitled to occupy the property: see 4.5.3.a. If, unlike in *Chaudhry*, neither spouse had a beneficial interest in the home, the wife would have no 'home rights'[372] and so no order could be made. But a DAPO *could* now be made against relatives on such facts.

Indeed, the DAA 2021 is, on its face, far less protective of property rights, with no balance of harm test[373] and no regard to the nature of the parties' relationship. Where the 'domestic abuse' threshold is met, the DAPO scheme may be thought effectively to render redundant the FLA 1996's elaborate differentiation of occupation order cases.[374] The FLA 1996 has always been open to criticism for oversensitivity to proprietary rights and relationship status where basic safety from abuse is at stake. But it remains to be seen how the courts will exercise the DAPO jurisdiction: they retain full discretion over whether to make any order at all—satisfaction of the domestic abuse threshold permits but does not require an order;[375] and over the terms and duration of any order made. And, despite the lack of statutory signalling on this point, they may continue to consider restrictions on property rights 'Draconian', particularly given DAPOs' criminalization of breach: hence the concerns of the Joint Committee on the Bill that courts might be 'reluctant to impose [occupation DAPOs] in all but the most exceptional of circumstances'.[376] Time will tell.

369 HM Government (2022a), 8. 370 See 4.6.2. 371 [1987] 1 FLR 347.
372 FLA 1996, s 30; see 4.5.3.a. 373 See 4.5.3.g. 374 See 4.5.3 and 4.6.2.b.
375 Contrast the balance of harm test under FLA 1996, ss 33, 35, 37.
376 Joint Committee (2019), para 115.

4.10 FORCED MARRIAGE PROTECTION ORDERS

We first encountered forced marriage in chapter 2: lack of consent to marry owing to duress renders a marriage voidable.[377] Forced marriage is itself also a form of domestic abuse—another mode of patriarchal coercive control[378]—and a human rights violation,[379] engaging at least Articles 8 and 12 ECHR, and commonly connected with the commission of various criminal offices, such as kidnapping, rape, and assault.[380]

HM Government, *The Right to Choose: Multi-Agency Statutory Guidance for Dealing with Forced Marriage* (2014a), 1–2

The UK Government regards forced marriage as an abuse of human rights and a form of domestic abuse, and where it affects children and young people, child abuse. . . .

It can happen to both women and men, although many of the reported cases involve young women and girls aged between 16 and 25. There is no "typical" victim of forced marriage. [They] may be over or under 18 years of age, some may have a disability, some may have young children and some may also be spouses from overseas.

To address the increasing scale and extent of forced marriage, the UK Government established the Forced Marriage Unit (FMU) in 2005. The FMU is a joint Home Office and Foreign and Commonwealth Office Unit – the role of the FMU is to provide direct assistance, through information and support, to victims, as well as undertaking a full and comprehensive programme of outreach activity, raising awareness and providing advice to professionals and communities. . . .

In 2013, the [FMU] received calls in relation to a possible or actual forced marriage in over 1300 cases, involving 74 different countries.[381] A number of other cases also come to the attention of the police, children and adult social care services, health, education and voluntary organisations.

While the majority of cases report to the FMU to date have involved South Asian countries, this is in part reflective of the largely established South Asian diaspora in the UK. So we need to . . . remain extremely mindful that forced marriage is not solely a South Asian problem, as there have been numerous cases in recent years involving many other countries across the Middle East, Europe, Africa and North America to name but a few.

Despite the recorded numbers, forced marriage still remains a hidden practice, as many more cases remain unreported . . .

Debates about the proper legal response to forced marriage are in some respects a microcosm of domestic abuse debates generally:

- whether the criminal or civil law provides the better solution;
- how victims might be empowered within the legal system;

377 See 2.7.1.a. 378 Noack-Lundberg et al (2021).

379 *A Chief Constable, AA v YK and 5 others* [2010] EWHC 2438, [9].

380 See case analysis by Noack-Lundberg et al (2021); HO (2022c), from para 92.

381 For latest statistics, see Foreign & Commonwealth Office and HO (2022), bearing in mind the impacts of changed recording practices and the Covid-19 pandemic; the 2013 figure in the extract closely reflects the average number of cases 2011–19. But this will be a considerable under-count of all actual cases: see SafeLives (undated), 24.

- how to ensure that public agencies in contact with victims, or that suspect a forced marriage has occurred or might occur, take appropriate action; and
- what non-legal measures can be taken to prevent forced marriages and to protect potential victims.

Bespoke civil law remedies were created in 2007 to prevent forced marriage or protect those who have been subjected to it:[382] FLA 1996, Part 4A now aims to protect victims of intended or completed forced marriages with civil orders, essentially giving a statutory basis to powers developed under the inherent jurisdiction.[383] An offence of forced marriage was created in 2014, and extended in 2022 to *all* conduct (whether or not coercive) intended to cause a child to marry before age 18.[384]

4.10.1 WHICH MARRIAGES ARE AFFECTED?

The FLA 1996 provisions apply to marriages created by religious or civil ceremony, here or abroad, whether or not they create a marriage recognized under English law:[385] even if a marriage is not legally binding, the parties may 'still be treated by family and the wider community as though they were married, so the effect is just as damaging'.[386] The harm of forced marriage is not therefore necessarily or exclusively 'legal'—the imposition on one or both parties of an unwanted legal status—but also emotional, psychological, and (in the worst cases) physical.

4.10.2 FORCED MARRIAGE PROTECTION ORDERS

4.10.2.a What is a 'forced' marriage?

Family Law Act 1996

63A Forced marriage protection orders

(1) The court may make an order for the purposes of protecting—

(a) a person from being forced into a marriage or from any attempt to be forced into a marriage; or

(b) a person who has been forced into a marriage. . . .

(4) For the purposes of this Part a person ('A') is forced into a marriage if another person ('B') forces A to enter into a marriage (whether with B or another person) without A's free and full consent.

382 FLA 1996, Part 4A.

383 Ibid, ss 63A–S. The inherent jurisdiction and all other existing rights and remedies for victims of forced marriage remain available—ibid, s 63R.

384 Anti-Social Behaviour, Crime and Policing Act 2014, s 121, as amended by the Marriage and Civil Partnership (Minimum Age) Act 2022.

385 FLA 1996, s 63S, definition of 'marriage'. The Act therefore covers forced 'non-qualifying ceremonies', discussed at 2.5.1 and 2.6.2.b.

386 Hansard HL GC, vol 691, col 237, 10 May 2007, Baroness Ashton.

(5) For the purposes of subsection (4) it does not matter whether the conduct of B which forces A to enter a marriage is directed against A, B[387] or another person.

(6) In this Part—

'force' includes coerce by threats or other psychological means . . .

Concerns have been expressed about how the courts in reported cases have determined whether a marriage has been forced rather than 'arranged' in this context, setting a high bar for proof (by the victim) of a completed or threatened forced marriage, and so determined whether legal intervention is called for.[388]

K. Noack-Lundberg, A. Gill, and S. Anitha, 'Understanding Forced Marriage Protection Orders in the UK', (2021) 43 *Journal of Social Welfare and Family Law* 371, 377–8, 388

[M]arriages considered by judges to be arranged rather than forced included those where there was limited or no consultation with the bride-to-be, where the bride had no or limited opportunity to meet her future spouse and/or turn down the marriage, and those where the bride's consent was not sought for the marriage. In four cases of forced marriage and one case of a betrothal ceremony, the brides/brides-to-be were vulnerable: they were either very young or had limited capacity/severe mental illness. In cases such as M's [*AB v HT and others* [2018] EWCOP 2], where a marriage has already taken place, in order to rule that the marriage was forced because of inability to consent, it must be proven that the bride did not have capacity at the time of the marriage . . . This was difficult to prove in M's case, despite her very low IQ and the fact that she was being involuntarily held in a mental hospital during the court proceedings . . .

Despite the law's recognition of the role emotional pressure plays in consent versus coercion. . ., formulations of consent in civil cases still seem to rely on a passive construction whereby the mere absence of an expression of dissent to marriage at the time of the wedding is deemed to indicate consent, even in the context of vulnerabilities and significant barriers (including learning disabilities, mental illness and deprivation of liberty) to expressing such dissent. . . .

. . . This places the onus on vulnerable victims to provide proof of coercion instead of on perpetrators to provide proof of consent, . . . bringing in issues of standards of proof in civil versus criminal proceedings. The concept of 'affirmative' or 'active' consent in relation to sexual activity could be usefully applied to forced marriage, shifting the focus from the victim's resistance to marriage to the actions and words of the alleged perpetrators, demonstrating whether agreement to the marriage was sought and/or whether it could be obtained if the victim arguably lacked capacity to consent and/or understand any elements of what was involved.

4.10.2.b Content of the order

Designed to respond to the complex dynamics of forced marriage, FMPOs may contain a wide variety of provisions tailor-made for the individual case to meet the general purpose

[387] E.g. a family member of A threatens to kill herself unless the marriage occurs: ibid, col 234.

[388] See, in the context of the law of nullity, 2.7.1.a.

of protection: 'such prohibitions, restrictions or requirements . . . and . . . other terms . . . as the court considers appropriate for the purposes of the order'.[389] The order may be made for a specified period or to take effect until varied or discharged.[390]

A wide range of conduct, within the jurisdiction and/or abroad, may be covered, both: (i) conduct directly connected with forcing a marriage or attempting to do so; and/or (ii) otherwise becoming 'involved,' for example by aiding and abetting, encouraging, or assisting a forced or attempted forced marriage, or conspiring to force or attempt to force a marriage.[391]

The order may be directed at a wide range of people, who need not all be identified in the order. The order may be principally directed at: (i) respondents who force or attempt to force a marriage, or who *may* force or attempt to force a marriage; and/or at (ii) respondents who are or may become 'involved' in a forced or attempted forced marriage. But in either case, the order can also cover 'other persons' (not parties to the proceedings in which the order is made, and who need not be identified by name in the order), who are or may become so 'involved'.

The breadth of the courts' powers in this regard attracted comment during the parliamentary debates on the Bill. Concerns were expressed that, absent any requirement that such unidentified persons should *knowingly* become involved in a forced marriage, people might innocently find themselves subject to an order made in proceedings of which they were ignorant. However, the government argued that these powers are necessary to ensure maximum protection for victims, who may be unable, when seeking the order,[392] to prove who might become involved and who was aware of the situation, particularly where a wide range of relatives and members of the community might become involved. It was also emphasized that there would be no question of anyone's being punished in contempt proceedings unless that person 'had sufficient knowledge of the order to know that his actions would frustrate its intention'.[393]

The courts have, unsurprisingly, also noted the extraordinary breadth of the powers conferred (exercisable simply as deemed 'appropriate') and the lack of any threshold[394] or basic evidential test in the legislation that needs to be passed before the orders can be made. However, as discussed at 4.10.2.a, in practice, the courts need persuading that any actual or threatened marriage is or will be forced. And they have signalled that particular care must be taken with 'mandatory' provisions. It is one thing to *prohibit* certain conduct (commonly on an ex parte basis), quite another to *require* conduct, particularly where such an order prima facie interferes with the respondents' rights under the ECHR. And so it has been said that mandatory orders (e.g. requiring that a child be returned to the jurisdiction from overseas) should only be made where the court is 'satisfied on appropriate evidence that the making of such an order is a *necessary and proportionate* response' (emphasis added), bearing in mind the 'potentially penal consequences' of breach.[395]

[389] FLA 1996, s 63B(1). One commonly cited example of a 'requirement' that might be imposed is the surrender of a passport, preventing travel to the overseas location of an intended forced marriage. Exemplifying of the range of orders that might be made in one case, see *A Chief Constable, AA v YK and 5 others* [2010] EWHC 2438, [21]–[31].

[390] FLA 1996, s 63F. [391] Ibid, s 63B(2), (3).

[392] Particularly if doing so on an urgent ex parte basis.

[393] Hansard HC Deb, vol 463, col 643, 23 July 2007, Parliamentary Under-Secretary of State for Justice, Bridget Prentice MP. The criminal standard of proof would have to be satisfied: Hansard HL Deb, col 1758, 13 June 2007, Baroness Butler-Sloss.

[394] Cf care proceedings (see chapter 12), sometimes brought alongside proceedings for an FMPO, and the 'domestic abuse' threshold for DAPOs: see 4.6.3.a.

[395] *West Sussex CC & Chief Constable of Sussex Police v F, M, N, P and T* [2018] EWHC 1702, [18]–[20].

4.10.2.c The court's discretion

Having determined that 'forced' marriage has occurred or is at risk of occurring, the court has discretion to decide whether an order should be made at all and if so in what terms.

Family Law Act 1996, s 63A

(2) In deciding whether to exercise its powers under this section and, if so, in what manner, the court must have regard to all the circumstances including the need to secure the health, safety and well-being of the person to be protected.

(3) In ascertaining that person's well-being, the court must, in particular, have such regard to the person's wishes and feelings (so far as they are reasonably ascertainable) as the court considers appropriate in light of the person's age and understanding.

In relation to the victim's wishes, a former President of the Family Division made the following remarks:

A Chief Constable, AA v YK and 5 others **[2010] EWHC 3282**

SIR NICHOLAS WALL:

6. Nobody should underestimate the pressures which may, in certain circumstances, be placed upon [victims of suspected forced marriage]. It is therefore essential . . . if the court is to make a realistic assessment pursuant to s 63A(2) that the person to be protected is seen by someone who is aware of those pressures and is, in short, an expert in the field. It is also desirable . . . that the person to be protected is separately and independently represented.

Later Court of Appeal authority has confirmed that—despite the lack of statutory provision to this effect[396]—'the court can make an order protecting a person from themselves', that is to say, the wishes of competent adults cannot be 'an automatic trump card or determining factor'.[397] This arises from the state's positive obligations under Article 3 ECHR, which need to be 'accommodated' alongside its obligations under Article 8.[398] The court went on to provide a 'route map' for judges to use in determining applications for FMPOs in such cases:

Re K (Forced Marriage: Passport Order) **[2020] EWCA Civ 190**

SIR ANDREW MACFARLANE P:

46. Stage One is for the court to establish the underlying facts based upon admissible evidence and by applying the civil standard of proof. The burden of proof will ordinarily be upon the applicant who asserts the facts that are said to justify the making of a FMPO . . .

[396] Cf the express provision for DAPOs: DAA 2021, s 33(3).

[397] *Re K (Forced Marriage: Passport Order)* [2020] EWCA Civ 190, [65], [35].

[398] Ibid, [37].

50. At Stage Two, based on the facts that have been found, the court should determine whether or not the purpose identified in FLA 1996, s 63A(1) is established, namely that there is a need to protect a person from being forced into a marriage or from any attempt to be forced into a marriage, or that a person has been forced into a marriage.

51. At Stage Three, based upon the facts that have been found, the court must then assess both the risks and the protective factors that relate to the particular circumstances of the individual who is said to be vulnerable to forced marriage. This is an important stage and the court may be assisted by drawing up a balance sheet of the positives and negatives within the circumstances of the particular family in so far as they may relate to the potential for forced marriage.

52. At the conclusion of Stage Three, the court must explicitly consider whether or not the facts as found are sufficient to establish a real and immediate risk of the subject of the application suffering inhuman and degrading treatment sufficient to cross the ECHR, Article 3, threshold.

53. At Stage Four, if the facts are sufficient to establish a risk that the subject will experience conduct sufficient to satisfy ECHR, Article 3, the court must then undertake the exercise of achieving an accommodation between the necessity of protecting the subject of the application from the risk of harm under Article 3 and the need to respect their family and private life under Article 8 and, within that, respect for their autonomy. This is not a strict "balancing" exercise as there is a necessity for the court to establish the minimum measures necessary to meet the Article 3 risk that has been established under Stage Three.

54. In undertaking the fourth stage, the court should have in mind the high degree of flexibility which is afforded to the court by the open wording of FLA 1996, s 64A. In each case, the court should be encouraged to establish a bespoke order which pitches the intrusion on private and family life at the point which is necessary in order to meet the duty under Article 3, but no more. The length of the order, the breadth of the order and the elements within the order should vary from case-to-case to reflect the particular factual context; this is not a jurisdiction that should ordinarily attract a template approach.

4.10.2.d When—and on whose application—an order may be made

Like NMOs, FMPOs may be made by the court of its own motion where it considers such an order should be made to protect an individual where other family proceedings involving the respondent to the proposed order are before the court.[399] Otherwise, more like DAPOs, FMPOs may be made on the application of: (i) the person to be protected by the order; (ii) any person who has the leave of the court;[400] or (iii) by a 'relevant third party'.[401] The possibility of third party applications here is especially important given the prevalence in these cases of victims with disabilities and child victims, who may particularly struggle to bring their own application.[402] Only local authorities have been designated (as a class) as relevant third parties,[403] and statutory guidance has been issued to assist them in exercising this function.[404] In cases involving minors, the local authority may also commence child protection proceedings,[405] though providing adequate support can become complicated where the

[399] FLA 1996, s 63C(1)(b), (6).

[400] See ibid, s 63C(4). Examples of persons who might successfully obtain leave include headteachers, health-care professionals, social workers, police, and IDVAs.

[401] Ibid, s 63C(1), (2).

[402] Noack-Lundberg et al (2021).

[403] Family Law Act 1996 (Forced Marriage) (Relevant Third Party) Order 2009, SI 2009/2023.

[404] MOJ (2009a).

[405] E.g. *A v SM and HB* [2012] EWHC 435.

victims are on the cusp of adulthood.[406] Like other FLA 1996 orders and DAPOs, FMPOs may be made ex parte in urgent cases.[407]

4.10.2.e Enforcement of FMPOs, and free-standing criminal offences

Since 2014, FMPOs have been enforceable like NMOs and DAPOs: either by contempt proceedings in the family court, or by criminal prosecution under s 63CA. The latter avenue is based on the same model as the equivalent offence for NMOs and DAPOs, discussed at 4.7.4.b. The criminalization of breach provides an avenue for the police to become directly involved in FMPO enforcement, which may prove useful where the victim (particularly a child victim) is unable or unwilling to act.[408] However, third party-initiated enforcement in this arena involves the same sort of pros and cons as those discussed in relation to domestic abuse proceedings more generally at 4.8.3.

The criminalization of breach—and the creation of freestanding offences related to forced marriage—were both controversial and extensively debated.[409] Arguments in favour of criminalization highlighted the powerful symbolic impact and deterrent effect of criminalization, empowering victims. Arguments against focused on the difficulty of distinguishing between forced and arranged marriage in some cases, and concerns that criminalization might drive the practice further underground, inhibiting reporting by victims reluctant to see family members imprisoned or who feared reprisals.[410]

4.10.3 USE OF FMPOS

Research suggested that initial use of FMPOs was mixed.[411] One local authority area, led by local police, had made extensive use of FMPOs. But three of four local authority areas surveyed had made little use of FMPOs for various reasons, including: concern about their use 'against' particular minority ethnic communities; uncertainty about the nature and extent to which voluntary organizations and statutory agencies could or should be involved; and continued ambivalence about using the civil (rather than criminal) law in response to forced marriage. Many applications made in the first year were initiated (with leave) by police.[412] However, numbers of orders have been steadily rising, from the 101 orders made in the first year of the Act's operation (twice the predicted number) to a sudden peak of 596 in 2019 before numbers dropped back to *c.* 320 annually during Covid-19 pandemic years 2020–1.[413] Concerns have been expressed about the effectiveness of the monitoring of orders and enforcement.[414] But interestingly the marked rise in the numbers of orders per annum postdates the criminalization of breach.

4.11 CONCLUSION

A poor response from the justice system to domestic abuse can be worse than no legal response at all.

[406] Maclean (2013), 127–8. [407] FLA 1996, s 63D.
[408] Cf *Beds Police Constabulary v RU* [2013] EWHC 2350: police cannot bring proceedings for contempt for breach of a civil order.
[409] E.g. House of Commons Select Committee on Home Affairs (2011); HO (2012).
[410] HO (2012); Gill (2011); Pearce and Gill (2012). [411] Kazimirski et al (2009).
[412] MOJ (2009b); Maclean (2013). [413] MOJ (2022a), table 17.
[414] House of Commons Select Committee on Home Affairs (2011); see generally Pearce and Gill (2012).

C. Humphreys and R. Thiara, 'Neither Justice nor Protection: Women's Experiences of Post-Separation Violence', (2003) 25 *Journal of Social Welfare and Family Law* 195, 210

[In their research sample there was] a smaller group of chronic and serious offenders [who] were unresponsive to normative frameworks. 'Brushes' with the law which result in being charged with minor offences, cautions, binding over or short custodial sentences had no effect and in fact served to reinforce the abuser's belief that there are no effective constraints or sanctions on his behaviour. They can increase the dangers to women, who will be seen to have 'transgressed' having called the police or given evidence against the abuser. Moreover, poor and ineffective action from law enforcement and prosecution services may serve to confirm a woman's belief that she is outside help and, therefore, has no option other than to seek to appease the abuser.

The legal system must provide effective and timely protection for victims. However, the law's ability to deal with domestic abuse is limited. The vast majority of victims never reach a courtroom. The activities of other government and voluntary sector agencies are vital to victims' safety. Current policy emphasizes an integrated, multi-agency approach to promote awareness of domestic abuse, protect and support victims, and hold perpetrators to account.[415] It is also recognized that prevention must be a priority, and that education, particularly of young people, is vital to root out attitudes that tolerate or even support domestic abuse, and to encourage victims and others to speak out.[416] Social exclusion and other risk factors associated with domestic abuse must be tackled. Above all, proper resourcing for all agencies involved with families experiencing domestic abuse, including refuges, are essential, yet so easily lost in times of economic austerity. Only these non-legal measures will ultimately secure a significant reduction in the prevalence of domestic abuse.

ONLINE RESOURCES

Questions, suggestions for further reading, and supplementary materials for this chapter (including updates on developments in this area of family law since this book was published) may be found in the online resources at **www.oup.com/uk/familytcm5e.**

[415] HO (2022c), 16. [416] HM Government (2022a), 23 et seq.

5

FINANCIAL PROVISION FOR CHILDREN

CENTRAL ISSUES

1. The principal responsibility for maintaining minor children lies with their legal parents, whatever the nature of the parents' legal relationship to each other.
2. Financial and property provision for children who live apart from one or both parents is dealt with by the Child Maintenance Service (CMS) and the courts.
3. CMS has principal jurisdiction to secure payment of regular child support from 'non-resident parents', calculated by reference to a rule-based, statutory formula under the Child Support Act 1991 (CSA 1991).
4. The courts have residual jurisdiction to order periodical payments for children in certain circumstances. They also have exclusive jurisdiction to make capital and property adjustment orders for the benefit of children. They make their decisions pursuant to wide statutory discretion.
5. Parents are encouraged to make informal 'family-based arrangements' for child maintenance. This marks a significant change from the former policy of the state strictly enforcing the financial responsibility of 'non-resident parents' (paying parents) in order to save expenditure on public support (welfare benefits/tax credits). 'Parents with care' (receiving parents) now retain any amount of child maintenance on top of any state support they receive. But the emphasis on private ordering risks leaving more children's households without financial support.
6. There are concerns about the fairness (to both payers and recipients) of the formula used to calculate child support, and non-resident parents remain dissatisfied that child support is not more closely linked to the time they do (or do not) spend with their child.

5.1 INTRODUCTION

This chapter examines financial support for children who live apart from one or both parents, whether in a single-parent family, step-family, or with other carers.[1] The law in this area is highly technical and so can appear rather dry. But beneath the dry technicality lie interesting and important policy questions, some of general importance throughout family law—including the use of private ordering and the contrast between rule-based and discretionary decision-making. We tease out some of those issues in the last section of this chapter.

The development of the law has been driven by the rapid rise in parental separation and single-parent families. Single parents accounted for less than a tenth of families with dependent children in Britain in the early 1970s, but approaching a quarter (23 per cent) of such families (1.9 million) in the UK in 2021, mostly headed by single mothers.[2] Single-parent families also feature disproportionately amongst poorer households,[3] raising concerns about child poverty.[4] Single mothers are less likely to be employed than other mothers and single parents more likely than other parents to have low household income and to claim benefits or tax credits.[5] Since the vast majority of single parents are *mothers*, the poverty of these families has long been regarded as a matter of gender equity.[6] Analysis of survey data showed that, over six years, nearly a third of families with children had been single-parent families at some point, some single parents then repartnering.[7] The law discussed in this chapter is also relevant where one or both separated parents has a new partner. Including those cases together with lone-parent families gives 2.4 million separated families in Great Britain, comprising 3.6 million children.[8]

Child poverty in these cases—and generally—might be alleviated in three ways:

- by the state providing money for children's households, such as benefits and tax credits, and subsidized child-care facilities to enable parents to work;
- by parents boosting household income via paid employment;[9] and
- where children do not live with both parents, by the parent with whom the child does not mostly live (the 'non-resident parent') transferring resources to the child's primary household.[10]

All three routes may be adopted to varying degrees: how they are balanced depends on current political preferences.[11]

The initial question is whether principal responsibility for children's maintenance, in single-parent families and otherwise, lies with the state or private individuals. The state might have a direct interest in ensuring that parents maintain their children: if parents do not or cannot maintain their children from their own resources, the state might have to

[1] We do not address the position of children looked after by the state.

[2] ONS (2022b), table 3. [3] DWP (2021a), table 4_14ts.

[4] E.g. Hansard HC Deb, vol 714, col 1WH, 19 May 2022; Foley (2022), 9.2; Oppenheim and Milton (2021), 30–2.

[5] ONS (2021d), table 14; DWP (2021b), tables 2.5 and 2.9. See more generally 6.2.

[6] Barnes et al (1998), 71; Flaherty et al (2004), ch 6 on women and poverty.

[7] Rabindrakumar (2017). [8] National Audit Office (2022), 4.

[9] See Fortin (2009b), 337 et seq; Busby and James (2020).

[10] Cf where the other parent is deceased, unidentifiable, or untraceable. On cases of shared care, see 5.7.3.b.

[11] See Lewis (1998) and (2000), 94–6. On the state's role, see Eekelaar and Maclean (1986), 107–12.

step in financially or practically. However, international human rights instruments do not require the state to assume the whole burden. The United Nations Convention on the Rights of the Child 1989 (UNCRC) places primary responsibility on parents, envisaging only a 'safety net' function for the state,[12] to 'take all appropriate measures to secure the recovery of maintenance for the child from the parents or other persons having financial responsibility for the child'.[13]

Successive governments have therefore also sought to reinforce private responsibility by getting more single parents into paid employment, with increased availability of free pre-school child-care, tax-free child-care,[14] and changes to benefit/tax credit rules pushing single parents to seek work.[15] But while employment rates amongst single parents have increased, many of their jobs are part-time, low-skilled, and low-paid, and many parents' lack of access to affordable, flexible, good quality child-care acts as a barrier to any—or better paid—employment.[16] Moreover, employment-based strategies may be criticized for denying the social and economic value conferred on society by individuals caring for their own children, and the moral value of choosing to care rather than work.[17]

The key question within the private sphere—and the focus of this chapter—is how responsibility for supporting children should be allocated between separated parents. To what extent can 'non-resident parents' or other private individuals be expected to contribute to a child's financial support? On whom should private obligations to maintain children be imposed: should the duty arise from legal or social parenthood? What if the legal parent[18] has had no social relationship with the child or no formalized relationship with the other parent?[19] English law imposes principal private financial responsibility for children on their legal parents. That liability is enforced in various ways almost regardless of the parents' marital status. But the law provides remedies only for separated families. It generally does not permit children to obtain support from parents who are together—and, even when they are apart, limits the right of children themselves to apply for support.

The provision made for children is often just part of a larger puzzle of financial remedies between separated parents. The practical importance of financial remedies for the children differs markedly depending on the nature of the parents' relationship. Where the parents were spouses or civil partners, provision for children is part of the package of financial remedies available on divorce/dissolution. We shall see in chapter 6 that the courts generally[20] have substantial powers to order financial provision and property adjustment between such parents for their own benefit. Here, children will benefit indirectly from orders made for the parent(s) with whom they are living and so capital or property orders specifically for their own benefit are less necessary (and may not be affordable). However, child support will also

[12] See in particular Arts 18, 26, and 27 UNCRC; see Fortin (2009b), 334–5.

[13] Art 27(4) UNCRC, referred to in *Smith v Secretary of State for Work and Pensions* [2006] UKHL 35, [77]–[78]; Baroness Hale doubted whether Art 8 ECHR entailed the right to receive regular, reasonable maintenance; see also [65], Lord Walker.

[14] See DFE (2019), 6 and 11 for the various entitlements.

[15] E.g. Welfare Reform Act 2009; HM Government (2014b).

[16] Coleman et al (2022); DFE (2019).

[17] Fineman (2004).

[18] See chapter 9.

[19] See 5.7.3. On theories underlying parents' obligations, see Altman (2003); Eekelaar (1991a); Wikeley (2006a), ch 1.

[20] Where they have no jurisdiction under the Matrimonial Causes Act 1973 (MCA 1973) or Civil Partnership Act 2004 (CPA 2004), they may deploy Sch 1 to the Children Act 1989, discussed at 5.5: e.g. *DB v PB (Pre-Nuptial Agreement: Jurisdiction)* [2016] EWHC 3431.

be payable and, if there are surplus resources, additional provision for the children—such as payment of school fees—might also be made.

By contrast, as we shall see in chapter 7, where the parents were not spouses or civil partners, there are far fewer, if any, remedies between the adults themselves. This leaves parents who have been and will continue to be primary carers of children to shoulder alone the potential long-term economic effects of their role, such as reduced earning capacity owing to time taken out of the labour market. Remedies for the benefit of children assume huge significance here, as substantial indirect benefit can accrue to parents from financial remedies for the child. However, that indirect benefit ends once the child becomes independent, potentially leaving such parents in a precarious economic position.

This area of the law has been in flux for some time, and so we begin this chapter with a brief history, before examining the law. We address first the detail of the laws applied by the statutory child support agency (at 5.4) and by the courts (at 5.5). But, as we shall see, the current legal and policy environment strongly encourages private ordering, and so (at 5.6) we then discuss parties' options for making their own arrangements for financial support of children—arrangements which may or may not be influenced by the 'shadow of the law' discussed in 5.4 and 5.5. We use the terms 'child support' and 'child maintenance' interchangeably.

5.2 A BRIEF HISTORY OF FINANCIAL PROVISION FOR CHILDREN

The legal history of child maintenance is complex—we relate that history in more detail in the online resources, where full references for the following discussion are provided. It is helpful to know the history in outline in order to appreciate the policy choices available to the state in this arena.

While parents were understood to be obliged to maintain their children as a matter of natural law,[21] the common law offered no direct means of enforcing that duty and it was not until the nineteenth century that statute—forerunners of today's legislation—provided a mechanism in *private* law for doing so. Prior to that, however, the state had long sought to ensure that the burden of caring for children (and other indigent relatives) was not cast on the taxpayer, and so *public* law—originally, the Tudor-era Poor Laws, latterly the 'liable relative procedure'—sought to recoup from various relatives any public relief paid out to poor individuals. This included the non-resident father of any child, legitimate or not.

During the twentieth century, however, ideology about receipt of means-tested benefits changed substantially from one of stigma to one of entitlement. In time, use of the liable relative procedure fell away, both courts and benefit authorities more commonly leaving the financial burden with the state: mothers would be left to claim whatever benefits they could for themselves and their children, fathers would rarely be pursued by the state, and (despite authority to the contrary) courts tended to take mothers' benefits into account in deciding what (if any) maintenance to order from fathers. Since maintenance payments would simply reduce mothers' benefit entitlements and so (except in very high-value cases) do nothing to improve their household economy, there would often seem little point in

[21] Blackstone (1765), book 1, ch XVI.

ordering it—especially if that would risk impoverishing the father. So fathers were commonly relieved of maintenance liabilities.[22]

The 1980s brought a major shift in policy prompted by political concerns about supposed 'welfare dependency' and the (unevidenced) notion that the situation was incentivizing lone-motherhood. These worries aligned with moral concerns about supposedly 'feckless fathers' shirking the responsibilities attached to their procreative activities and leaving the burden on mothers.[23] And so the new policy, given effect by the CSA 1991, reasserted the pre-eminence of private responsibility and sought to reduce the cost to the state of growing lone parenthood.

The CSA 1991 created a new administrative body—the Child Support Agency (CSA)—to extract regular child maintenance from non-resident parents instead of the courts. The maintenance payable by 'absent parents' to 'parents with care' for their children was calculated using a statutory formula rather than on a discretionary, case-by-case basis. The intention was to achieve consistent, predictable maintenance payments, promptly collected and enforced by the Agency, largely confining the courts to making capital orders. Crucially, the Agency had *compulsory* jurisdiction over cases in which parents with care were claiming benefits with a view to ensuring that such welfare payments were reimbursed by liable non-resident parents. Parents with care receiving certain means-tested welfare benefits were accordingly compelled to cooperate with the CSA's efforts to secure maintenance, on pain of a substantial benefit cut if they failed to do so (absent 'good cause'). Under the original version of the scheme, any child support received simply reduced welfare benefits paid to parents with care pound for pound—so they derived no benefit from CSA involvement.[24] Benefits cases constituted the vast bulk of the CSA's caseload, suggesting that the priority lay in cutting welfare benefit expenditure.

This was the intention. In practice, the CSA was hampered by chronic administrative problems, diabolical IT, an over-complex formula, and opposition from both groups of parents, which resulted in significant arrears that were left uncollected and only around 30 per cent of parents with care receiving any maintenance.[25] Described as 'one of the greatest public administration disasters of recent times',[26] the CSA never met its creators' expectations and cost taxpayers more to run than was recouped from non-resident parents.[27]

After various changes, including the introduction of a new, simplified formula in 2003, radical reform was announced in 2006, following a major review (the Henshaw Report).[28] The Child Maintenance and Other Payments Act 2008 (CMOPA 2008) effected a 'virtual abandonment' of the original CSA policy,[29] profoundly altering the roles of non-resident parents and state in supporting children by effectively formalizing pre-CSA 1991 practice—and this remains the position today. The state now provides a basic level of support to parents with care via welfare benefits and/or tax credits;[30] and any contribution from non-resident parents, rather than reducing the state's burden, now supplements the child's household income. This is designed to incentivize parents with care to seek maintenance and non-resident parents to pay it. Yet in other ways, the reform sees the state retreat from the fray by no longer

[22] This summary is based on Baroness Hale's discussion in *R (Kehoe) v Secretary of State for Work and Pensions* [2005] UKHL 48.

[23] Cf contemporaneous discussion of unmarried fathers and parental responsibility: see 10.3.2.b.

[24] A 'maintenance disregard' was later introduced, permitting parents with care to retain the first £10 per week recovered from the non-resident parent; the balance (up to the value of their benefits) went to the state.

[25] Henshaw (2006), 12. [26] Family Law Week (2007). [27] Henshaw (2006), para 13.

[28] Henshaw (2006); DWP (2006). [29] Fehlberg and Maclean (2009).

[30] See CPAG (2019a) for the current year.

requiring *any* parents with care to cooperate with the statutory agency and encouraging parents to reach their own arrangements for child maintenance. The agency—now the Child Maintenance Service (CMS)—simply serves as a backstop for parents who cannot agree. It operates a new system that is intended to be easier to operate, with a much simpler formula adopted from 2012 (so commonly referred to as the '2012 scheme'). It is that latest iteration of child support law, contained in the heavily amended CSA 1991, that we discuss at 5.4.

The Secretary of State promoted the new policy as a way to make an immediate and significant contribution to child poverty-reduction targets:[31]

Hansard, *Official Report*—Ministerial Statement on Child Support Redesign, Hansard HC Deb, vol 449, cols 597–9, 24 July 2006

The Secretary of State for Work and Pensions (Mr. John Hutton):

Both those changes [full state support + full maintenance receipt] will help more families to receive more maintenance and reduce the risk of child poverty. They reflect both the rights of children to be properly maintained by their parents and the right of society to ensure that parental responsibilities are properly discharged.

Interestingly, unlike the Secretary of State's remarks, the 'four new principles' set out in the White Paper preceding the CMOPA Bill for a reformed child maintenance system contain no reference to a *right* of the *child* in this arena:

DWP, *A New System of Child Maintenance*, Cm 6979 (London: TSO, 2006), paras 15–16

- help tackle child poverty by ensuring that more parents take responsibility for paying for their children and that more children benefit from this;
- promote parental responsibility by encouraging and empowering parents to make their own maintenance arrangements wherever possible, but taking firm action – through a tough and effective enforcement regime – to enforce payment where necessary;
- provide a cost-effective and professional service that gets money flowing between parents in the most efficient way for the taxpayer; and
- be simple and transparent, providing an accessible, reliable and responsive service that is understood and accepted by parents and their advisers and is capable of being administered by staff.

These four principles refocus the child maintenance system on meeting the needs of children. They make tackling child poverty the first and most critical test for reform, and they establish and enforce clear rights and responsibilities – the right of a person to make a claim and the resulting responsibility of the non-resident parent to pay.

[31] Henshaw (2006), para 24; Bryson et al (2013).

Evidently, the success of the policy depends on how many non-resident parents actually pay maintenance under a scheme in which private agreements are the preferred mechanism. We shall examine at 5.7.2.c how successful—or not—the policy has been in practice.

ONLINE RESOURCES

Readers interested to know more about the history of child maintenance law will find further materials in the online resources for chapter 5 at **www.oup.com/he/familytcm5e.**

5.3 OVERVIEW OF THE CURRENT LAW

The law governing financial and property provision for children is contained in several statutes. Distinguishing between (i) the identity of the children involved and their relationship with the potential payer and (ii) the type of remedy sought gives a helpful overview: see Figure 5.1.

5.3.1 THE PARTIES' RELATIONSHIPS

Like most areas of contemporary child law, financial and property provision is almost blind to parents' marital status—an approach that aligns with public attitudes.[32] What matters is the legal parent–child relationship. Parents' liability for their own children is distinguished from the liability of step- and other social parents in relation to other 'children of the family'. Only spouses and civil partners may be liable to provide for children other than their own. Step-parental liability does not arise in cohabiting relationships,[33] or following a joint enterprise to create a child by artificial insemination from which legal parenthood for the non-gestational party did not arise,[34] even if that person has parental responsibility via a child arrangements order.

5.3.2 CMS OR COURT?

As we can also see from Figure 5.1, the law treats periodical payments and other forms of relief, such as lump sum and property adjustment orders, very differently. The courts have exclusive jurisdiction over the latter. CMS has principal jurisdiction over periodical payments for parents' *own* children under the CSA 1991. The court may only order periodical payments in limited circumstances: where CMS lacks jurisdiction in parent–child cases, in relation to step-children and others who are not the respondent's child, and where the CSA 1991 explicitly permits it. We examine the child support legislation at 5.4 and the courts' jurisdiction at 5.5.

[32] Clery et al (2021), 16–17.

[33] Children Act 1989 (CA 1989), s 105; MCA 1973, s 52; CPA 2004, s 72.

[34] *T v B* [2010] EWHC 1444; cf agreed parenthood provisions in the Human Fertilisation and Embryology Act 2008: see 9.4.3.b.

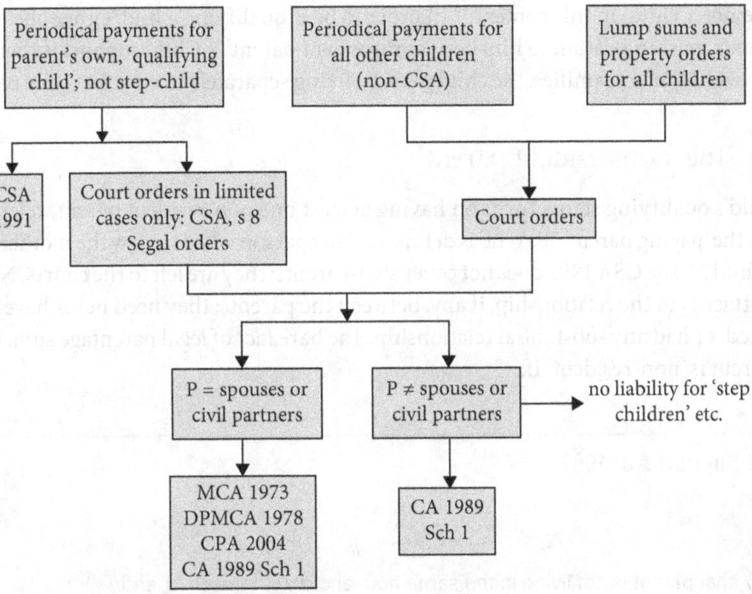

Figure 5.1 Financial and property provision for children

5.4 CHILD SUPPORT: THE CURRENT LAW

Child support law is highly technical.[35] It is contained in primary legislation—the heavily amended CSA 1991—and secondary legislation, most importantly the Child Support Maintenance Calculation Regulations 2012,[36] referred to in the footnotes as the CSMCR 2012. Where statutory materials refer to the 'Secretary of State' acting, those actions are in practice taken by CMS. Extracts in this chapter refer variously to the CSA and CMS, depending on which incarnation of the administrative body then existed.

5.4.1 THE RELEVANT PARTIES

Four categories of person are relevant to child support claims: the 'qualifying child'; the 'non-resident parent'; the 'person with care'; and 'relevant other children'. The Act ordinarily applies only where each of the first three is habitually resident in the UK.[37]

5.4.1.a The 'qualifying child'

The Act applies if the child for whom support is sought meets the definition in s 55. Otherwise, the courts may instead have jurisdiction over child maintenance.[38] In broad outline, a 'child' for these purposes is anyone under the age of 16; and anyone under the age of 20 who either is in full-time, non-advanced education (i.e. below degree level), or is undertaking certain types of training.[39] If the individual is or has been a spouse or civil partner (including in a void union),

[35] For detailed treatment, see CPAG (2019b) for the current year. [36] SI 2012/2677.
[37] CSA 1991, s 44. [38] See 5.5.
[39] CSMCR 2012, reg 76: the definition is linked to eligibility for child benefit.

they are not a 'child' in this context.[40] In order to be a 'qualifying' child, either one or both of his parents must in relation to him be a 'non-resident parent'.[41] Child support is therefore not payable within intact families: the child must be living separately from at least one parent.

5.4.1.b The 'non-resident parent'

The child's qualifying status turns on having at least one non-resident parent, referred to by CMS as the 'paying parent'. 'Parent' is defined as 'any person who is in law the mother or father of the child'.[42] The CSA 1991 does not cover step-parents; they are left to the courts. No significance attaches to the relationship, if any, between the parents; they need never have married, cohabited, or had any substantial relationship. The bare fact of legal parentage suffices.

A parent is 'non-resident' if:

Child Support Act 1991

3(2) . . .

(a) that parent is not living in the same household with the child; and

(b) the child has his home with a person who is, in relation to him, a person with care.

'Not living in the same household' includes living under the same roof as the child but in a separate household from the child and person with care.[43] Since the vast majority of non-resident parents are fathers, we refer to them as such, whilst acknowledging that there are cases where the roles are reversed or the parents are of the same gender.

5.4.1.c The 'person with care'

Referred to by CMS as the 'receiving parent', the '*person* with care' need not, in fact, be a parent:

3(3) A person is a "person with care", in relation to any child, if he is a person—
(a) with whom the child has his home;
(b) who usually provides day to day care for the child (whether exclusively or in conjunction with any other person); and
(c) who does not fall within a prescribed category of person.

(4) The Secretary of State shall not, under subsection (3)(c), prescribe as a category—
(a) parents;
(b) guardians;
(c) persons named, in a child arrangements order under s 8 of the Children Act 1989, as persons with whom a child is to live . . .

(5) For the purposes of this Act there may be more than one person with care in relation to the same qualifying child. . . .

[40] CSA 1991, s 55(2), (3). [41] Ibid, s 3.
[42] Ibid, s 54; see chapter 9. In case of dispute regarding parentage, see CSA 1991, s 26.
[43] See 2.8.1.b on the concept of a shared household.

The regulations made under s 3(3)(c) exclude local authorities and their foster parents from the scope of 'person with care'.[44] Who provides 'day to day care' depends not on the formal question of who holds parental responsibility but on who undertakes the mundane, hands-on practicalities of looking after the child: 'it is about who puts food on the table, washes the child's clothes, deals with the letters from school and reads a bedtime story'.[45] The designation of parents who *share* the care of the child is discussed at 5.4.4.f.

5.4.1.d The 'relevant other child'

A 'relevant other child' may affect the amount of child support payable in respect of qualifying children. A child is 'relevant' if the non-resident parent or his partner with whom he shares a household (whether as spouses, civil partners, or cohabitants) receives child benefit in relation to that child.[46]

5.4.2 GENERAL PRINCIPLES

Child Support Act 1991, s 1

The duty to maintain

(1) For the purposes of this Act, each parent of a qualifying child is responsible for maintaining him.

(2) For the purposes of this Act, a non-resident parent shall be taken to have met his responsibility to maintain any qualifying child of his by making periodical payments of maintenance with respect to the child of such amount, and at such intervals, as may be determined in accordance with the provisions of this Act.

(3) Where a maintenance calculation made under this Act requires the making of periodical payments, it shall be the duty of the non-resident parent with respect to whom the calculation is made to make those payments.

The Act closely defines non-resident parents' duties but says nothing about how parents with care discharge their maintenance responsibility. However, it is implicit in the Act—and in the apparent rationale of the formula for calculating non-resident parents' liability (discussed at 5.7.4)—that parents with care fulfil their duty by caring for the child.

Unlike the rest of child law, there is no general welfare principle in the CSA 1991. Given the rule-based rather than discretionary nature of the Act, that is perhaps unsurprising. Where CMS does have discretion, for example in making variations from the formula or in taking enforcement action, a welfare principle applies. The principle is relatively weak, requiring only that 'regard' be had to the child's welfare, not paramount or even first consideration. But it is wide-ranging: the welfare of *any* child likely to be affected must be considered, not just that of the qualifying child and relevant other children.[47]

[44] CSMRC 2012, reg 78; but see regs 51 and 53 for other situations involving the local authority.
[45] *GR v CMEC (CSM)* [2011] UKUT 101 (AAC), [48].
[46] Sch 1, para 10C and CSMCR 2012, reg 77.
[47] CSA 1991, s 2.

5.4.3 APPLICATION TO CMS

5.4.3.a Encouraging private agreement

A key policy of the current scheme is that, rather than apply to CMS, parents should wherever possible agree on arrangements for child support:

Child Support Act 1991

9(2A) The Secretary of State may, with a view to reducing the need for applications [to the CMS]—

(a) take such steps as the Secretary of State considers appropriate to encourage the making and keeping of maintenance agreements, and

(b) in particular, before accepting an application [to the CMS under s 4], invite the applicant to consider with the Secretary of State whether it is possible to make such an agreement.

Until June 2022, potential CMS applicants ordinarily[48] had to proceed through the 'mandatory gateway' of a telephone conversation with the Child Maintenance Options Service about alternatives to using the statutory agency. Now, potential applicants are simply led through a series of webpages that make them aware of the options—to reach agreement privately or apply to CMS—and provide other relevant information, including an online calculator to demonstrate how much would be payable under the statutory scheme.[49]

5.4.3.b Application to CMS where agreement fails

If one party so chooses from the outset, or if agreement cannot be reached, or one becomes dissatisfied with their agreement, either party can apply to CMS for a maintenance calculation under the CSA 1991, s 4. Consistently with the policy to encourage agreements, the law disincentivizes applications by charging applicants a fee of £20 for a formal maintenance calculation. Further fees are charged if CMS collects maintenance for the person with care ('Collect & Pay'), rather than the non-resident parent paying the person with care directly ('Direct Pay').[50] Indeed, CMS will only make a Collect & Pay arrangement if:

(a) the non-resident parent agrees to the arrangements, or

(b) the Secretary of State is satisfied that without the arrangements child support maintenance is unlikely to be paid in accordance with the calculation.[51]

If Collect & Pay is used, the non-resident parent is charged an additional 20 per cent on top of the child support due and 4 per cent is deducted from the child support before it is handed

[48] Those who identified as victims of domestic abuse were fast-tracked to CMS: DWP (2014), para 20.

[49] <https://child-maintenance.service.gov.uk/get-help-arranging-child-maintenance/>. The continuing possibility of talking to someone on the phone is hidden deep in the website at <https://child-maintenance.service.gov.uk/get-help-arranging-child-maintenance/get-more-information>.

[50] Child Support Fees Regulations 2014, SI 2014/612.

[51] CSA 1991, s 4(2A).

to the person with care.[52] Applicants under the age of 19 and victims of domestic abuse who have reported the abuse to an appropriate person[53] are exempt from the application fee, though not the collection fee.[54] We discuss at 5.7.2 the policy implications and potential practical effects of this regime.

5.4.4 THE MAINTENANCE CALCULATION

The maintenance calculation under the CMS scheme is based on a formula that, in its simplest form, requires only two pieces of information: the non-resident parent's gross earned income for the last tax year and the number of qualifying children. A fixed percentage of that income is usually payable, depending on the number of children. We discuss in this section add-ons to the formula used where there are 'relevant other children' or the qualifying child stays overnight with the non-resident parent. Special rates apply in particular circumstances.[55] Importantly, the person with care's income is irrelevant, as is the income of any new partner of either party. So the non-resident parent's liability is unaffected by the relative wealth of the person with care or her household. We discuss at 5.7.4 the rationale for the basic formula and the fairness of the assumptions on which it rests.

5.4.4.a Basing the calculation on gross historic earned income

For administrative ease, the formula is based on the non-resident parent's *gross* earned income for the *last* year,[56] information in theory available from the tax authorities (HMRC).[57] Historic income being a known, fixed amount, the calculation is unaffected by fluctuations in income.[58] However, historic income is not necessarily a reliable guide to what non-resident parents can afford to pay now: the income for the last tax year may be very different—higher or lower—than current income. Where the difference in income is 25 per cent or greater, current income data may therefore be used instead.[59] CMS's administrative burden may be eased by such a high threshold having to be passed before calculations have to be revised. But it may pose significant trouble for non-resident parents—especially low-earners—caught by the legacy of past 'riches' falling just below that threshold, who may find their payments unaffordable.[60]

[52] Child Support Fees Regulations 2014, SI 2014/612.

[53] See the list of persons prescribed in the Guidance on reg 4(3) of the Child Support Fees Regulations 2014, which includes police, medical professionals, lawyers and courts, refuges, employers, and certain other professionals/support services.

[54] SI 2014/612, reg 4.

[55] For default rates and voluntary payments made pending a formal calculation, see CSMCR 2012, reg 49 and the Child Support (Voluntary Payments) Regulations 2000, SI 2000/3177.

[56] For the definition of 'gross income', see CSA 1991, Sch 1, para 10 and CSMCR 2012, regs 34–42. Periodic current income checks and regular annual reviews are carried out to update the calculation; see CSMCR 2012, regs 19–22.

[57] DWP (2006), ch 4; cf the cautionary notes sounded by Wikeley (2007a), paras 19–21.

[58] DWP (2007), para 16.3.

[59] CSMCR 2012, reg 23; employed non-resident parents must report increases in income: Child Support Information Regulations 2008, reg 9A. The position is different for self-employed non-resident parents.

[60] See House of Commons Select Committee on Work and Pensions (2007), paras 125–34; DWP (2007), para 16; cf Gingerbread (2017), 24.

5.4.4.b The basic rate

The standard case

The basic rate[61] applies to non-resident parents with gross weekly incomes of £200 and above. For the first £800 of gross income, non-resident parents must pay 12 per cent of income for one qualifying child, 16 per cent for two qualifying children, and 19 per cent for three or more. Any additional income between £800 and £3,000 is subject to a 'basic plus' rate of 9 per cent for one, 12 per cent for two, and 15 per cent for three or more qualifying children.[62] Income over £3,000 per week is ignored entirely.[63] As we shall see at 5.5.2.a, however, income above that threshold can be accessed via court-ordered periodical payments.[64] These monetary thresholds—contained in the primary legislation and so amendable only by Act of Parliament—are not index-linked and have not been uprated since their introduction in 1998. Needless to say, increased costs of living makes £200 today worth much less than it was then, so the basic rate applies to parents who are in real terms poorer than was originally intended. This has raised concerns about the affordability of child maintenance for some non-resident parents.[65]

Cases where the non-resident parent has 'relevant other children'

Non-resident parents with one or more 'relevant other children' (see 5.4.1.d) are effectively permitted to reserve income for expenditure on children in their current household before the child support formula is used to calculate what they must pay to the qualifying child. This is achieved by reducing the gross income by 11, 14, or 16 per cent (depending on the number of relevant other children) before the basic rate percentage is applied to the remainder.[66] The non-resident parent broadly ends up paying a similar percentage of his total gross income to the qualifying child(ren) as is reserved for the relevant other children, though in fact pays out slightly less to the qualifying child than he is permitted to reserve for the others. It had been suggested that the basic rate should instead be applied to all qualifying and relevant children of the non-resident parent and the resulting maintenance award apportioned equally between them.[67] But the rule that has been adopted, whilst also aiming to provide roughly 'equal treatment' to the two sets of children,[68] gives the qualifying children much more than they would receive on the apportionment basis. For example, if one qualifying child and one relevant child were treated as two children under the basic rule, a father with gross income of £800 per month would notionally pay 16 per cent, £128; when apportioned equally between them, this would give the qualifying child just £64, rather than the £96 that he would have received on the basic rate of 12 per cent as one child. Under the rule adopted, that child receives £85.44, while a notional £88 is reserved for the relevant

[61] CSA 1991, Sch 1, para 2.

[62] This second set of percentages for the second tranche of income is necessary to accommodate the different tax rates being applied at different levels of income.

[63] CSA 1991, Sch 1, para 10(3). [64] See 5.5.2 on 'top-up' orders.

[65] See Social Security Advisory Committee, 22 and ch 4 generally re related concerns about the interaction of the formula with Universal Credit; National Audit Office (2022) from 2.23; Public Accounts Committee (2022a), recommendation 7.

[66] CSA 1991, Sch 1, para 2(3). [67] DSS (1999), paras 2.9–2.15.

[68] The rule adopted had originally been said to give a 'slight preference' to the first family (DSS (1999), ch 2, para 13), though the amount allocated for the relevant other children was greater than that payable to the qualifying child as the deductions were originally made at the same percentages as the basic rate. In advocating the move to the current percentages, the government acknowledged that, and preferred the new percentages as providing 'more equal treatment' of both sets of children: CMEC (2012), para 107.

other child. This means that the father is notionally 'paying' not just £128, but over £173 for both children—though, of course, he keeps the money allocated for the relevant other child, and those children benefit from his expenditure on the fixed costs of his household.

5.4.4.c The reduced rate

The reduced rate[69] applies to non-resident parents on gross incomes of between £100 and £200 per week, to whom neither the flat nor the nil rate applies. Again, these thresholds have not been updated since 1998. They pay £7 for the first £100, and then a set percentage (different from the basic rate percentages) over the remaining amount, depending on the number of qualifying children and any relevant other children.

5.4.4.d The flat rate

A flat rate[70] of £7 per week is payable by non-residents parents who earn less than £100 per week (again, not updated since 1998) or who (or whose partners) receive one of several welfare benefits, pensions, or allowances. Where the non-resident parent's partner[71] is also a non-resident parent in respect of whom a maintenance calculation is in force and receives one of the relevant benefits, each is required to pay half the flat rate. Even those living on benefits are required to accept some financial responsibility for their children.[72]

5.4.4.e The nil rate

No support is payable by non-resident parents with gross weekly incomes below £7, and those who fall into one of several categories prescribed in regulations, including children,[73] prisoners, and parents aged 16–17 receiving certain means-tested benefits.[74]

5.4.4.f 'Shared care'

The statutory terminology of 'non-resident parent' and 'person/parent with care' is a source of grievance where the child spends significant amounts of time with both parents; the language of 'paying parent' and 'receiving parent' is more neutral. Both might regard themselves as 'persons with care', and neither as 'non-resident', even if a court order specifies that the child 'lives with' one parent whilst merely 'spending time' with the other.[75] In these cases, whichever parent provides day-to-day care for the child to a 'lesser extent' is classed as the non-resident parent; unless there is evidence to suggest otherwise, whichever parent receives the child benefit for the child is deemed to provide more care.[76]

In some cases—still unusual—parents genuinely provide fully equal day-to-day care, in which case neither will be classed as non-resident. If so, no child support is payable by either

[69] CSA 1991, Sch 1, para 3 and CSMCR 2012, reg 43.
[70] CSA 1991, Sch 1, para 4 and CSMCR 2012, reg 44.
[71] CSA 1991, Sch 1, para 10(C)(4) and (5).
[72] Barnes et al (1998), 66 view this as an expensive public relations exercise: the costs of collection generally outweigh the income received.
[73] As defined in s 55(1), see earlier.
[74] CSA 1991, Sch 1, para 5 and CSMCR 2012, reg 45.
[75] See chapter 11.
[76] CSMCR 2012, reg 50; *C v Secretary of State for Work and Pensions* [2002] EWCA Civ 1854.

parent, whatever their respective incomes. Such cases involve more than the child simply spending the same number of nights per year with each parent, and require closer analysis of the care actually provided, including expenditure on larger items such as clothing and equipment.[77]

Where, as is usual, one parent is clearly the primary carer, the support payable is reduced by reference to the number of nights that the child spends with the 'non-resident' parent:[78]

Child Support Act 1991, Sch 1, para 7

(1) This paragraph applies where the rate of child support maintenance payable is the basic rate or a reduced rate [or is determined under special rules applicable to certain maintenance agreements, under para 5A].

(2) If the care of the qualifying child is, or is to be, shared between the non-resident parent and the person with care, so that the non-resident parent from time to time has care of the child overnight, the amount of child support maintenance which he would otherwise have been liable to pay the person with care [as calculated above] is to be decreased in accordance with this paragraph.

(3) First, there is to be a decrease according to the number of such nights which the Secretary of State determines there to have been, or expects there to be, or both during a prescribed twelve-month period.

(4) The amount of that decrease for one child is set out in the following Table—

Number of nights	Fraction to subtract
52 to 103	One-seventh
104 to 155	Two-sevenths
156 to 174	Three-sevenths
175 or more	One-half

(5) If the person with care is caring for more than one qualifying child of the non-resident parent, the applicable decrease is the sum of the appropriate fractions in the Table divided by the number of such qualifying children.

(6) If the applicable fraction is one-half in relation to any qualifying child in the care of the person with care, the total amount payable to the person with care is then to be further decreased by £7 for each such child.[79]

(7) If the application of the preceding provisions of this paragraph would decrease the weekly amount of child support maintenance (or the aggregate of all such amounts) payable by the non-resident parent to the person with care (or all of them) to less than £7, he is instead liable to pay child maintenance at the rate of £7 per week, apportioned (if appropriate) in accordance with paragraph 6.

[77] See Social Security Advisory Committee (2019), 34–5.
[78] Supplemented by CSMCR 2012, regs 46–7.
[79] See DSS (1999), para 7.17: this effectively shares the child benefit paid to the person with care.

Where parents agree that care is shared but cannot agree by how much, CMS will assume that the non-resident parent has the child for one night a week, attracting the one-seventh reduction.[80] In flat-rate cases, the fact of shared care for at least 52 nights over 12 months reduces the £7 assessment to nil.[81] We discuss the impact and fairness of the shared care rules further at 5.7.4.

5.4.4.g Apportionment

What happens where non-resident parents have qualifying children by two or more partners, and each child lives with their other parent?

Child Support Act 1991, Sch 1, para 6

(1) If the non-resident parent has more than one qualifying child and in relation to them there is more than one person with care, the amount of child support maintenance payable is (subject to [rules regarding shared care]) to be determined by apportioning the rate between the persons with care.

(2) The rate of maintenance liability is to be divided by the number of qualifying children, and shared among the persons with care according to the number of qualifying children in relation to whom each is a person with care.[82]

5.4.4.h Set-off

Sometimes, siblings are split between parents—some living with one parent, while others live with the other. Technically, both parents are liable to pay support for the children in the other's care. CMS can treat their liability as having been satisfied by setting off such counter-liabilities.[83] Similarly, CMS may also 'set-off' child support liability where the non-resident parent has made payments that the person with care agrees may be treated as satisfying the liability, for example payments made under certain mortgages, rent, utility bills, council tax, and the cost of essential repairs to the child's home.[84]

5.4.5 VARIATIONS

The basic formula and add-ons discussed in the previous section operate strictly mathematically.[85] However, CMS has discretion to vary the amount payable in cases falling in one of the categories specified in the Act and accompanying regulations.[86] Variations—up or down—are designed to relieve specific injustices that the formula might produce. Either party may apply for a variation at the outset or, once a maintenance calculation is in force,

[80] CSMCR 2012, reg 47. [81] CSA 1991, Sch 1, para 8.

[82] See para 5A and CSMCR, reg 48 for the inclusion in the apportionment of children subject to family-based arrangements.

[83] CSA 1991, s 41C and Child Support (Management of Payments and Arrears) Regulations 2009, SI 2009/3151, reg 5.

[84] Child Support (Management of Payments and Arrears) Regulations 2009, SI 2009/3151, reg 6.

[85] *R v Secretary of State for Social Security, ex parte Biggin* [1995] 1 FLR 851.

[86] See DSS (1995); CSA 1991, ss 28A–G, Schs 4A and 4B; CSMCR 2012, regs 47–75.

apply for a revision.[87] It must first be shown that one of the 'cases' for a variation applies, and then CMS has a discretion whether to allow any variation.

5.4.5.a The cases for a variation

Special expenses

The first case concerns 'special expenses' of the non-resident parent which, it is argued, should reduce the maintenance payable.[88] Regulations deal exhaustively with the nature and level of expenses that may be invoked here.[89] Broadly speaking, they include:

- average weekly travel and accommodation costs incurred regularly by the non-resident parent in maintaining contact with the qualifying child—in order to encourage regular contact, this includes costs connected with contact for which the non-resident parent receives a shared care deduction under the rules discussed earlier;[90]
- the maintenance element of boarding school fees, up to 50 per cent of the non-resident parent's income;[91]
- repayment of certain types of debts incurred when the non-resident parent and the person with care were still together for the benefit of specified family members (and not exclusively for the benefit of the non-resident parent). This includes mortgage payments over the home occupied by the parent with care and child, even if the non-resident parent retains an interest in that property, but not responsibility for other debts taken on by the non-resident parent as part of a financial settlement with the parent with care or court order;[92]
- repayment of limited other categories of mortgage, loan, and endowment insurance policies, but—by contrast with the previous case—not where the non-resident parent has any interest in the property over which the debt is secured;[93]
- additional costs necessarily incurred because of the long-term illness or disability of a relevant other child (less amounts received by way of relevant welfare benefits or other financial assistance received in respect of the illness or disability).[94]

In relation to the first four categories, a variation cannot be obtained if weekly expenses under any individual heading are below £10. But if they exceed £10, the variation can reflect the full amount, not just the excess.[95] If CMS considers any expenses to be unreasonably high or to have been unreasonably incurred, it may substitute such lower amount as it considers reasonable (potentially nil), though it must not put the non-resident parent in a position whereby he cannot continue to see the child as frequently as a court order permits.[96]

Unearned and diverted income

The second case aims to prevent non-resident parents paying less than they should, given the formula's exclusive focus on their *earned* income and failure to view their financial

[87] CSA 1991, s 16 and CSMCR 2012, regs 14–16. [88] CSA 1991, Sch 4B, para 2.
[89] CSMCR 2012, regs 63–8. [90] Ibid, reg 63 and CMEC (2012), Annex C, para 60.
[91] CSMCR 2012, reg 66. [92] Ibid, reg 65. [93] Ibid, reg 67. [94] Ibid, reg 64.
[95] Though see Social Security Advisory Committee (2019), 23 regarding use of travel allowances as basis for variation, rather than actual costs incurred.
[96] CSMCR 2012, reg 68.

circumstances in the round.[97] There are plans to change the law to include other sources of *taxable*[98] income in the basic formula (e.g. income from rental properties, share dividends),[99] but for the time being a variation under the second case[100] is needed. The following, in broad terms, may give grounds for a variation:

- the non-resident parent has unearned taxable income (e.g. from investments) exceeding £2,500 per annum;[101]
- the non-resident parent falls within the nil or flat-rate category, but has an income exceeding £100 per week;[102]
- the non-resident parent can control the amount of his income,[103] and CMS believe that he has unreasonably[104] reduced his income in order to reduce his child support liability by diverting it to other persons or for purposes other than providing his own income (e.g. by paying an unreasonably high salary to his partner for working in his business or making extra pension contributions).[105]

Parents with care are obviously hampered in using this ground, assuming that they even know it exists, without access to the non-resident parent's financial details necessary to substantiate their case. CMS will not give parents with care a breakdown of the non-resident parent's income.[106] And receiving parents are often inhibited from seeking a variation for fear of inflaming what may be an already difficult relationship with the paying parent.[107]

Moreover, this variation case does not deal with the problem of non-resident parents with high capital but low income, including those who are enjoying a lifestyle inconsistent with their declared income. The removal in 2008 of variation cases to deal with these scenarios[108] was widely criticized.[109] But government stood firm against reintroduction of the 'lifestyle' ground, arguing that it was difficult to use,[110] instead introducing legislation to create the next case, based on capital assets.

Notional income arising from assets exceeding a prescribed value

This new case for variation aims to catch 'the cultivation of a cash-poor but asset-rich lifestyle' as a means of avoiding child support liability.[111] It applies where the non-resident parent owns certain classes of assets worth over £31,250. These assets are then deemed to generate a weekly income based on a fixed percentage of their value—currently 8 per cent.[112]

[97] E.g. *Phillips v Peace* [1996] 2 FCR 237.

[98] This qualification—arising from reliance on HMRC data—means that income from savings and investments held in ISAs and other untaxed sources will remain excluded.

[99] DWP (2022b). [100] CSA 1991, Sch 4B, para 4 and CSMCR 2012, regs 69–71.

[101] CSMCR 2012, reg 69. [102] Ibid, reg 70.

[103] Self-employed non-resident parents who can divert income from earned into unearned sources pose significant challenges: *Smith v Secretary of State for Work and Pensions* [2006] UKHL 35; Wikeley (2007a), paras 19–21. See Public Accounts Committee (2022b), Q34 on the role of the Financial Investigation Unit—but its work generally requires a referral from the parent with care, as to which see Public Accounts Committee (2022a), recommendation 4 and National Audit Office (2022), 42–3.

[104] See *DW v CMEC* [2010] UKUT 196 (ACC). [105] CSMCR 2012, reg 71.

[106] Gingerbread (2012), paras 35–8. [107] National Audit Office (2022), para 2.7.

[108] See the old regulations: SI 2001/156, regs 18–20.

[109] *Green v Adams (No 2)* [2017] EWFC 52, [24]–[25], quoting Gingerbread (2017); House of Commons Select Committee on Work and Pensions (2017a).

[110] House of Commons Select Committee on Work and Pensions (2017b), 6.

[111] Hansard HC Deb, Delegated Legislation Committee, col 3, 12 November 2018, Parliamentary Under-Secretary of State for Work and Pensions.

[112] CSA 1991, Sch 4B, para 4; CSMCR 2012, reg 69A, introduced by SI 2018/1279.

The asset classes covered are restricted, and in any case the ground will not apply where, for example, the asset is being used in the course of the parent's trade or business; where it is held in joint names with one or more others; where it would have to be sold to meet the child support liability, and such sale would cause hardship to a child of that parent or otherwise be unreasonable; or where it is land that is the primary residence of that parent or a child of his.[113]

5.4.5.b The discretion

If one of the three 'cases' applies, the CMS has a discretion whether to allow a variation. The legislation identifies some specific factors to be considered in addition to the general welfare principle in s 2, which are instructive about the policies underpinning child support:

Child Support Act 1991

28E Matters to be taken into account

(1) In determining whether to agree to a variation, the Secretary of State shall have regard . . . to the general principles set out in subsection (2) . . .

(2) The general principles are that—
 (a) parents should be responsible for maintaining their children whenever they can afford to do so;
 (b) where a parent has more than one child, his obligation to maintain any one of them should be no less than his obligation to maintain any other of them.

(3) In determining whether to agree to a variation, the Secretary of State shall take into account any representation made to it—
 (a) by the person with care or non-resident parent concerned; . . .

(4) In determining whether to agree to a variation, no account shall be taken of the fact that—
 (a) any part of the income of the person with care concerned is, or would be if the Secretary of State agreed to a variation, derived from any benefit; or
 (b) some or all of any child support maintenance might be taken into account in some manner in relation to any entitlement to benefit. . . .

28F Agreement to a variation

(1) The Secretary of State may agree to a variation if—
 (a) the Secretary of State is satisfied that the case is one which falls within one or more of the cases set out in Part 1 of Schedule 4B or in regulations made under that Part [described earlier]; and
 (b) it is the Secretary of State's opinion that, in all the circumstances of the case, it would be just and equitable to agree to a variation.

(2) In considering whether it would be just and equitable[114] in any case to agree to a variation, the Secretary of State—
 (a) must have regard, in particular, to the welfare of any child likely to be affected if the Secretary of State did agree to a variation; and
 (b) [to factors specified in regulations] . . .

[113] Ibid, reg 69A(4).

[114] See *Green v Secretary of State for Work and Pensions and Adams* [2018] UKUT 377, [105].

Child Support Maintenance Calculation Regulations 2012, SI 2012/2677, reg 60

Factors not taken into account for the purposes of section 28F

The following factors are not to be taken into account in determining whether it would be just and equitable to agree to a variation in any case—

(a) the fact that the conception of the qualifying child was not planned by one or both of the parents;

(b) whether the non-resident parent or the person with care of the qualifying child was responsible for the breakdown of the relationship between them;

(c) the fact that the non-resident parent or the person with care of the qualifying child has formed a new relationship with a person who is not a parent of that child;

(d) the existence of particular arrangements for contact with the qualifying child, including whether any arrangements are being adhered to;

(e) the income or assets of any person other than the non-resident parent;

(f) the failure by a non-resident parent to make payments of child support maintenance, or to make payments under a maintenance order or maintenance agreement; or

(g) representations made by persons other than the parties.

Once CMS has decided to allow the variation, regulations govern how the variation affects the maintenance calculation. In particular, where the variation involves augmenting the income to which the formula applies, any income above £3,000 per week is, as normal, ignored. Where the income is reduced, the non-resident parent is required to pay at least the flat-rate amount.[115]

5.4.6 TERMINATION OF THE CALCULATION

The maintenance calculation ceases to have effect if: (i) the non-resident parent or person with care dies; (ii) there is no longer any qualifying child;[116] or (iii) the non-resident parent ceases to be a parent of the qualifying child (e.g. following adoption).[117]

5.4.7 ENFORCEMENT OF CHILD MAINTENANCE

As we discussed at 5.4.3, parties are encouraged not to rely on CMS. To this end, both parties must pay if CMS's collection service is used. Should non-resident parents need an additional incentive to comply, failure to pay may be met by an arsenal of enforcement tools.[118]

5.4.7.a 'Enforcement' via reliance on tax and benefit records

Whilst not an issue of enforcement as such, calculating maintenance by reference to historical gross income data obtained from HMRC—combined with information from CMS's

[115] CSMCR 2012, regs 72–5. [116] *SL v CMEC (CSM)* [2010] AACR 24.
[117] CSA 1991, Sch 1, para 16(1). [118] Ibid, ss 29–41A.

host department, the DWP, about benefits entitlements—in theory provides early-stage 'enforcement' in over 90 per cent of cases,[119] hampering non-resident parents' ability to frustrate matters by withholding income information (particularly when self-employed).[120] However, the tax information available to CMS is only as good as that available to (and obtained from[121]) HMRC, who have tended not to investigate the affairs of low-earning taxpayers.[122]

5.4.7.b Enforcement by CMS

Enforcement—available only in Collect & Pay cases (see 5.4.3.b)—is entirely for CMS to instigate. It has full discretion as to whether and how to pursue cases, and can accept part-payment or write off arrears in certain circumstances.[123] Unlike other financial liabilities (including court-ordered periodical payments), there is no limitation period during the child's minority on collection of child support arrears;[124] CMS can even chase defaulters beyond the grave.[125] Fees are payable by the non-resident parent for each type of enforcement action.[126] CMS may also impose penalty payments of up to 25 per cent of the sums due, which go to the state; the person with care gains no compensation or interest for late payment.[127] In flat-rate cases, the £7 owed can be deducted directly from paying parents' benefits/tax credits.[128]

In taking any enforcement action, CMS is subject to its general duty under s 2 of the CSA 1991 to have regard to the welfare of any child likely to be affected by its decision.[129] As a public authority, CMS has a duty to act compatibly with Convention rights in its enforcement activities.[130] Enforcement may engage several rights of non-resident parents, in particular those to respect for private life (Article 8), to a fair trial in the determination of civil rights and obligations (Article 6), and to peaceful enjoyment of possessions (Article 1 of Protocol 1).

Considerable policy attention has been focused on the array of enforcement powers that should be at CMS's disposal, government commonly proposing new powers, while critics observe that CMS makes only 'tentative' use of its existing powers.

House of Commons Select Committee on Work and Pensions, 14th Report of Session 2016–17, *Child Maintenance Service*, HC Paper 587 (2017), para 70

This enables non-resident parents to get away with not making appropriate contributions to their children's upbringing. It also signals to other non-resident parents that they may well be able to do the same. Faith in the statutory child maintenance system is fundamental to its effectiveness. The CMS ought to strike fear into would-be evaders of parental responsibility.

[119] National Audit Office (2022), 11.

[120] Note also the Child Support Information Regulations 2008, SI 2008/2551 and associated offences created by CSA 1991, s 14A.

[121] This is not always straightforward: Social Security Advisory Committee (2019), 26.

[122] Wikeley (2007a), para 20.

[123] CSA 1991, ss 41D–E.

[124] Cf Burrows (2010).

[125] CSA 1991, s 43A.

[126] Child Support Fees Regulations 2014, SI 2014/612, Part 4.

[127] CSA 1991, s 41A; SI 1992/1989, Part IIA.

[128] CSA 1991, s 43.

[129] *Brookes v Secretary of State for Work and Pensions and C-MEC* [2010] EWCA Civ 420.

[130] Human Rights Act 1998 (HRA 1998), s 6.

It must take a stronger approach to enforcement, comparable with the Government's approach to other areas of financial liability such as benefit fraud or tax. *We recommend the CMS adopt a presumption in favour of enforcement action when a payment has been missed, and proceed unless there is evidence of a valid reason why or a credible reparative payment plan is in place.*

ONLINE RESOURCES

Readers interested to know more about enforcement of child support by CMS, and mechanisms for challenging CMS's actions, will find further materials in the online resources for chapter 5.

5.4.7.c No enforcement of CMS calculations by person with care

Persons with care cannot take enforcement proceedings themselves in court or otherwise, and have no party status in proceedings brought by CMS. They may only empower CMS to act for them in Collect & Pay cases.[131] We examine the position of those who use private ordering at 5.6.

The exclusion of parents with care from enforcement was unsuccessfully challenged in *R (Kehoe) v Secretary of State for Work and Pensions*. The case raises fundamental questions about the nature of the child support obligation. The Kehoes had been married with four children. Following the divorce, Mrs Kehoe applied to the CSA. For ten years, it extracted some maintenance from Mr Kehoe, but substantial arrears accumulated. Mrs Kehoe felt that she could have done better at enforcing her child support assessment than the CSA was apparently able to do. She argued that the system violated Article 6 of the European Convention on Human Rights (ECHR) by preventing her from judicially enforcing her civil right, as the person with care, to receive child maintenance from the non-resident parent. The House of Lords, Baroness Hale dissenting, held that persons with care have no such civil right and that Article 6 was therefore not engaged. The majority view was based on its interpretation of the CSA 1991, in particular parts of s 4:

Child Support Act 1991, s 4

Child support maintenance

(1) A person who is, in relation to any qualifying child . . ., either the person with care or the non-resident parent may apply to the Secretary of State for a maintenance calculation to be made under this Act with respect to that child . . .

(2) Where a maintenance calculation has been made in response to an application under this section the Secretary of State may, if the person with care or non-resident parent with respect to whom the calculation was made applies to it under this section, arrange for—

(a) the collection of the child support maintenance payable in accordance with the calculation;

[131] CSA 1991, s 4(2)(b). Nor may they avoid CMS entirely by applying for a court order: ibid, s 8—see 5.5.2.a.

(b) the enforcement of the obligation to pay child support maintenance in accordance with the calculation. . . .

(3) Where an application under subsection (2) for the enforcement of the obligation mentioned in subsection (2)(b) authorises the Secretary of State to take steps to enforce that obligation whenever the Secretary of State considers it necessary to do so, the Secretary of State may act accordingly. . . .

The majority in *Kehoe* held that Parliament had thereby removed the right of the person with care to bring enforcement action. As we flag in this next extract, at the time, the state retained maintenance due to parents with care on benefits to recoup that outlay of public funds (see 5.2).

R (Kehoe) v Secretary of State for Work and Pensions [2005] UKHL 48

LORD BINGHAM:

6. That a caring parent in the position of Mrs Kehoe was given no right of recovering or enforcing a claim to child maintenance against a . . . non-resident parent was not a lacuna or inadvertent omission in the 1991 Act: it was the essence of the new scheme, a deliberate legislative departure from the regime which had previously obtained. The merits of that scheme are not for the House in its judicial capacity to evaluate. But plainly the scheme did not lack a coherent rationale. The state has an interest, most directly [at the time of *Kehoe*] in cases where public funds are disbursed, but also more generally that children should be adequately supported. It might well be thought that a single professional agency, with the resources of the state behind it and an array of powers at its commend, would be more consistent in assessing and more effective and economical in enforcing payment than individual parents acting in a random and uncoordinated way. It might also be thought that the interposition of an independent, neutral, official body would reduce the acrimony which had all too frequently characterised applications for child maintenance by caring against absent or non-resident parents in the past which, however understandable in the aftermath of a fractured relationship, rarely enured to the benefit of the children. For better or worse, the process was deliberately changed.

That seriously undermined Mrs Kehoe's argument under Article 6, which guarantees access to an impartial tribunal for the determination of substantive civil rights and obligations but does not itself decide *what* substantive rights and obligations individuals enjoy. Article 6 could not create a right to recover child maintenance to which Mrs Kehoe had no right in English law.

10. . . . Whether the scheme established by the 1991 Act is on balance beneficial to those whom it is intended to benefit may well be open to question, but it is a question for Parliament to resolve and not for the courts, since I do not consider that any article 6 right of Mrs Kehoe is engaged.

The majority decision that there is no 'civil right' for the purposes of Article 6 to receive maintenance for one's children under the CSA 1991 was branded 'disturbing'.[132] Nick Wikeley described the majority's reasoning as 'profoundly disappointing in their adoption of an unduly literalist and positivist approach to the question of statutory construction in *Kehoe*'.[133] But the government declined to pursue reform, apparently anxious that parents with care in difficult cases should not be burdened with the cost of enforcement.[134]

Enforcement therefore remains a matter exclusively for CMS. This seems particularly surprising now that the state no longer uses child support law as a means of recouping benefits paid out to parents with care.[135] Indeed, allowing parents to enforce maintenance would also be consistent with encouraging parents to take responsibility for child support through private arrangements, relieving the state of the burden to act.[136] Where parents enshrine their agreement on child support in a consent order made by the family court (see 5.5.2.a), the notion that the parent with care has no civil right to enforce is especially odd.[137] But it is doubtful that the European Court of Human Rights, to which Mrs Kehoe unsuccessfully appealed, would be swayed by this: the Court (somewhat doubtfully[138]) considered that, were Article 6 engaged, judicial review of the statutory agency's action constituted an adequate remedy.[139]

So the current law is clear, but it is worth briefly examining Baroness Hale's dissenting judgment for its distinctive approach. While she agreed that the scheme deprived *parents* of the right to *enforce* maintenance, she concluded that the underlying right (in her view, of the *child*) to *receive* maintenance was intact, raising an issue under Article 6.

BARONESS HALE (dissenting):

49. This is another case which has been presented to us largely as a case about adults' rights when in reality it is about children's rights. It concerns the obligation to maintain one's children and the corresponding right of those children to obtain the benefit of that obligation.

She then set out the history of the public and private law in this area, concluding from her survey that 'children have a civil right to be maintained by their parents' under Article 6 that exists beyond the CSA 1991 regime and that entitles the children to 'determination and enforcement of that right'.

72. The problem is that [the system] is trying to enforce the children's rights. It is sometimes, as this case shows, lamentably inefficient in so doing. It is safe to assume that there are cases, of which this may be one, where the children's carer would be much more efficient in enforcing the children's rights. The children's carer has a direct and personal interest in enforcement which the Agency, however good its intentions, does not. Even [pre-CMOPA 2008] in benefit cases, where the state does have a direct interest in enforcement, it is not

[132] Douglas (2004b), discussing the same decision of the majority in the Court of Appeal.

[133] (2006b), 292.

[134] DWP (2007), para 28; cf Burrows (2009). Most recently, see Hansard PQ 198381 [on Children: Maintenance], 3 December 2018.

[135] See Douglas (2009). [136] Henshaw (2006), para 67.

[137] Wikeley (2006b), 295, who catalogues various other incoherencies generated by *Kehoe*.

[138] Ibid, 293. [139] *Kehoe v UK* (App No 2010/06, ECHR) (2008).

the sort of interest which stems from needing enough money to feed, clothe and house the children on a day-to-day basis. Only a parent who is worrying about where the money is to be found for the school dinners, the school trips, the school uniform, sports gear or musical instruments, or to visit the "absent" parent, not only this week but the next and the next for many years to come, has that sort of interest. A promise that the Agency is doing its best is not enough. Nor is the threat or reality of judicial review. Most people simply do not have access to the Administrative Court in the way that they used to have access to their local magistrates' court. Judicial review may produce some action from the Agency, but what is needed is money from the absent parent. Action from the Agency will not replace the money which has been irretrievably lost as a result of its failure to act in time.

Having found that Article 6 was engaged, and that the Act's attempt to improve enforcement of the child's right to maintain was a legitimate aim, she then considered whether depriving the parent with care of the right to enforce maintenance assessed under the Act was proportionate, and found that it was not.[140]

However, while arguably reaching the better result, Baroness Hale's judgment is not unproblematic in suggesting that English law recognizes maintenance as a right of the *child*, rather than of the parent with care. Nick Wikeley's analysis of the legal history yields the opposite conclusion:

N. Wikeley, 'A Duty But Not a Right: Child Support after *R (Kehoe) v Secretary of State for Work and Pensions*', (2006b) 18 *Child and Family Law Quarterly* 287, 297–9, 301

If [the suggestion that children have a right to maintenance] is right, it requires a fundamental rethinking on the part of family law scholars. The traditional understanding was set out by J.C. Hall, writing in 1966: 'There was no civil obligation to maintain one's child at common law or in equity, but statute has imposed a duty'.

The common law cases provide scant support for the proposition that the common law clearly established a right of the child to maintenance, particularly where illegitimate. As for the pre-CSA 1991 legislation, the public law was always more concerned with protection of the public purse. What about the private law?

Admittedly, the private law legislative measures have historically made a sharp distinction between spousal maintenance and child maintenance. However, . . . these statutes . . . all proceed on the assumption that it is the parent with care who will institute proceedings to enforce the maintenance obligation. In effect, the default position in English law is that children have no personal right to sue for maintenance. This might simply be seen as indicative of a mere lack of legal capacity, but the weight of authority [including that relating to tax and social security] would suggest that it points to the absence of any underlying legal right. We are

140 [2005] UKHL 48, [76].

thus some way from the position in the USA, where it seems to be accepted that 'the right to support lies exclusively with the child, and that a parent holds the child support payments in trust for the child's benefit'. . . .

5.5 COURT-BASED PROVISION: THE CURRENT LAW

Where the courts have jurisdiction, they operate under various (broadly similar) statutes, depending on the nature of the proceedings and the parties' relationship. We must consider first whether the courts have jurisdiction at all. And for that purpose, we need to discuss periodical payments separately from other forms of order. Readers may wish to refresh their memory of Figure 5.1, at 5.3, before tackling this section.

5.5.1 LUMP SUM AND PROPERTY-RELATED ORDERS

The courts have exclusive jurisdiction, unaffected by the CSA 1991, to make lump sum orders and orders in relation to property: property adjustment orders, property settlements, and orders for sale.[141]

5.5.2 PERIODICAL PAYMENTS

More complicated is the courts' jurisdiction to order periodical payments to or for the benefit of children. It is necessary to distinguish between cases where CMS has jurisdiction to make a maintenance calculation and cases where it does not.

5.5.2.a Where CMS has jurisdiction

First, the general rule is that the courts have *no* power to order maintenance where CMS has potential or actual jurisdiction—that is, where there is a qualifying child in respect of whom a maintenance calculation could be or has been made, including a nil calculation.[142] The courts cannot order periodical payments for maintenance in these cases, nor may they use capital orders (e.g. lump sums or property adjustment) as a means of evading this general rule; capital orders should be confined to meeting the child's capital rather than day-to-day income needs—such as home and furnishings, or a car for the parent's use.[143] A lump sum order will not be regarded as a maintenance order for these purposes unless it expressly says so.[144]

However, there are some exceptions to the general rule set out in CSA 1991, s 8, and the courts have identified one other.

[141] MCA 1973, Part II; CPA 2004, Sch 5; CA 1989, Sch 1; Domestic Proceedings and Magistrates' Courts Act 1978 (DPMCA 1978), s 2(3); CPA 2004, Sch 6, para 2(2); CA 1989, Sch 1, para 5(2).

[142] CSA 1991, s 8.

[143] *Phillips v Peace* [1996] 2 FCR 237; *Dickson v Rennie* [2014] EWHC 4306, [38].

[144] *AMS v Child Support Officer* [1998] 1 FLR 955.

Consent orders

The most significant exception is that the courts can order periodical payments for the benefit of children with the consent of both parties.[145] Parties can thereby confer jurisdiction on the courts and avoid engaging with CMS. A standard practice has emerged to exploit this exception fully:

V v V (Child Maintenance) [2001] 2 FLR 799 (Fam Div)

WILSON J:

18. My experience . . . has been that, even when parties require the court to determine other claims for [financial remedies on divorce], they have often reached agreement upon the level of periodical payments for the benefit of the children; and that they are keen for the court to make an order in that respect with a view . . . to excluding the possibility of [a maintenance calculation under the CSA] and to securing the facility for the court to resolve any future issue about the level of such payments in the exercise of its variation jurisdiction. In that event the court proceeds without difficulty to make the order under s 8(5).

19. Even, however, when parties remain at odds as to the level of periodical payments for the children, they often wish the court to determine that issue as well as the other issues, thereby perhaps obviating the need for a return to court for a topping-up order[146] following [a maintenance calculation] and in any event securing the court's ongoing jurisdiction in the event of future such dispute. In my experience the court invariably wants to accommodate the parties in that regard. But, in the light of the general prohibition, how can it do so? Over the last 8 years the following mechanism, which I believe to be entirely legitimate, has evolved, namely that at the outset of the hearing the court makes an order by consent for periodical payments for the benefit of the children in the sum of five pence each and that at the end of the hearing it varies that order to the level of payments which it thinks fit.

20. It may be argued that, technically, such a mechanism requires the preparation of three documents:

(a) a written agreement between the parties for the husband to pay five pence for the benefit of each of the children;[147]

(b) a nominal order, duly perfected, which reflects that agreement;[148] and

(c) a notice of application, duly issued, to vary that order.[149]

21. My experience is that the written agreement at (a) and the notice of application at (c) rarely come into existence. I have no problem with that. My view is that, if the words 'by consent' appear above the nominal order, they satisfy the requirement of a written agreement and that any requirement for the issue of a notice of application can and should be waived.

[145] CSA 1991, s 8(5); Child Maintenance (Written Agreements) Order 1993, SI 1993/620. On consent orders generally, see 6.7.1.
[146] CSA 1991, s 8(6).
[147] Ibid, s 8(5) and Child Maintenance (Written Agreements) Order 1993, SI 1993/620 require a written agreement which is then reflected in the court order.
[148] Thus complying with s 8(5) and SI 1993/620.
[149] CSA 1991, s 8(3A) allows the courts to vary validly made maintenance orders.

However, we shall see at 5.6.1 that consent orders cannot be relied on long-term to exclude any possibility of an application to CMS.

Top-up orders

The next exception concerns wealthy non-resident parents. CMS's maintenance calculation only covers gross income of up to £3,000 per week. The CSA 1991, s 8(6) preserves a power for the courts, where a CMS maintenance calculation is in force in relation to the first £3,000, to order top-up periodical payments from the surplus. This does not automatically give the courts jurisdiction in 'big money' cases: parents with care must obtain a maintenance calculation before applying for this 'top-up'.[150]

Expenses connected with education and disability

The courts have jurisdiction to make orders designed to meet costs incurred in the child's education[151] or training for a trade, profession, or vocation,[152] and to cover expenses attributable to the child's disability.[153] Unlike 'top-up' orders, these orders may be made even if there is no maintenance calculation in force.

Butler-Sloss LJ has examined the purpose of the disability-related orders:

C v F (Disabled Child: Maintenance Orders) [1999] 1 FCR 39 (CA), 46

BUTLER-SLOSS LJ:

In general a court considering this difficult assessment should take into account in the broadest sense the expenses attributable to the child's disability. The additional help needed, the cost of feeding . . . additional help, a larger or better-appointed house, heating, clothing, car expenses, respite care are only some of the expenses which immediately spring to mind. The expenses attributable to the disability, broadly assessed, the income and allowances coming into the family housing the child under a disability have to be weighed in the balance against the income, assets, liabilities and outgoings of the person asked to meet some or all of those expenses.

'Segal' orders

The courts have carved out one further exception, where it is making financial orders following the parents' divorce but where, unlike in the consent order case considered previously, there is a contested application for child maintenance before CMS:

[150] *Dickson v Rennie* [2014] EWHC 4306, not following dicta in *CF v KM* [2010] EWHC 1754, [4]–[6].

[151] Including nanny and nursery fees: e.g. *G v W* [2022] EWHC 1101.

[152] CSA 1991, s 8(7).

[153] Ibid, s 8(8); 'disability' for these purposes is defined in s 8(9).

Dorney-Kingdom v Dorney-Kingdom [2000] 3 FCR 20 (CA), 24–5

THORPE LJ:

A practice has grown up, finding its origins before District Judge Segal in the Principal Registry,[154] to make an order for spousal maintenance under s 23(1)(a) of the Matrimonial Causes Act 1973 that incorporates some of the costs of supporting the children as part of a global order. When a Segal order is made an important ingredient is that the overall sum will reduce pro tanto from the date upon which [CMS] brings in a [maintenance calculation]. The utility of the Segal order is obvious, since in many cases the determination of the [financial remedy] claims will come at a time when [CMS] has yet to complete its assessment of liability. It is therefore very convenient for a district judge to have a form of order which will carry the parent with primary care over that interim pending [CMS's] determination.

The proscription on the court making orders for child periodical payments other than by agreement, expressed in s 8(3) of the statute, could be said to be challenged, if not breached, by the mechanism of the Segal order. However, it seems to me to be just within the bounds of legitimacy, since it is no sort of ouster of or challenge to the jurisdiction of [CMS], but merely a holding until such time as [CMS] can carry out its proper function. But it seems to me absolutely crucial that if legitimacy is to be preserved, there must be a substantial ingredient of spousal support in the Segal order. If in any case there is a determination that the primary carer has no entitlement to periodical payments on her own account, any form of order that is not an agreed order plainly circumvents the statutory prohibition.

Variation of a court order duly made

The final exception is an adjunct of the previous four: the courts may vary maintenance orders that they have made, provided no superseding maintenance calculation has been made by CMS.[155] While the extract from *V v V (Child Maintenance)* demonstrates how this facility can be used to maximize the consent order exception,[156] commentators are divided on whether variations of consent orders must themselves be made by consent.[157]

5.5.2.b Where CMS has no jurisdiction

Where CMS lacks jurisdiction to make a maintenance calculation, the courts have exclusive jurisdiction to order periodical payments for the benefit of a child (and lump sum orders capitalizing such liability[158]). These situations are:

- where maintenance is sought from a step-parent or other person who is not a 'parent', and so in relation to whom the child is not a 'qualifying child' under the CSA 1991;
- where the child is not a 'qualifying child' in relation to anyone—for example, if the child is older than the various age limits prescribed for the CSA 1991;

[154] Cf Judge Segal's own, extra-judicial views about the scope of this category, considered in *AB v CD (Jurisdiction: Global Maintenance Orders)* [2017] EWHC 3164.

[155] CSA 1991, s 8(3A). [156] [2001] 2 FLR 799. [157] See Wikeley (2006a), 209–10.

[158] *V v V* [2001] 2 FLR 799; *AZ v FM (Capitalisation of Child Maintenance)* [2021] EWFC 2; *Her Royal Highness Haya Bint Al Hussein v His Highness Mohammed Bin Rashid Al Maktoum* [2021] EWFC 94: only where agreed or in exceptional circumstances.

- where maintenance is sought from a person with care;[159]
- where any of the person with care, non-resident parent, and qualifying child is not habitually resident in the UK;[160]
- where CMS's jurisdiction is ousted by binding private ordering: see 5.6.1.[161]

It is important to distinguish between cases where CMS does not have jurisdiction at all, and those where it *does* have jurisdiction but has concluded or would conclude that the non-resident parent's situation warrants a nil calculation: that outcome cannot be circumvented by resort to court.[162]

5.5.3 THE STATUTORY SCHEMES

The courts' jurisdiction to make orders for the benefit of children arises from several statutes (see Figure 5.1 at 5.3). Their powers under these Acts can be broadly divided into three categories, the first two applying only between spouses and civil partners:

- failure to maintain a child during marriage or civil partnership: DPMCA 1978/CPA 2004, Sch 6; MCA 1973, s 27/CPA 2004, Sch 5, Part 9;
- financial provision on or following divorce/dissolution, nullity, or judicial separation: MCA 1973, Part II and CPA 2004, Sch 5;
- financial provision for the benefit of a child under the CA 1989, Sch 1, available whatever the nature of the parents' relationship.

For ease of exposition, we refer to each jurisdiction as proceedings or provisions relating to 'failure to maintain', 'divorce', and 'under the CA 1989, Sch 1', respectively. We refer collectively to provisions and proceedings within the first two jurisdictions as 'matrimonial'.

The extent of the courts' powers under each Act is slightly different.[163] The appropriate choice of statute turns on various factors, including the type of order sought and the identity of both parties. The parents' marital or civil partnership status is obviously significant. There is no need to show that one parent is 'non-resident' for the court to exercise its powers. But the statutes variously restrict or entirely preclude the making of orders (or limit their duration) where the parents are living together.[164] So these are jurisdictions aimed, specifically, at meeting the needs of children whose parents' relationship has broken down or never involved much if any relationship at all.[165] It has been held that the confinement of the courts' powers to such cases is not discriminatory against other children.[166]

In order to gain an overall impression of the nature and extent of the courts' powers, we approach the law thematically, rather than by statute, highlighting differences as they arise.

[159] CSA 1991, s 8(10); see Wikeley (2006a), 198; this provision appears to have been overlooked in *N v C* [2013] EWHC 399 in concluding that there was no jurisdiction to make periodical payments in favour of the non-resident parent (though there were good reasons not to do so in that particular case).

[160] CSA 1991, s 44. [161] Ibid, s 4(10). [162] Ibid, s 8(2).

[163] We do not address issues regarding the parties' domicile, habitual residence, etc.

[164] CA Sch 1, para 2(4); cf para 1, which permits such applications from specified third parties when the child lives apart from the parents; DPMCA 1978, s 25; CPA 2004, Sch 6, para 29 (failure to maintain cases in the magistrates' court; no equivalent restriction in MCA 1973, s 27/CPA 2004, Sch 5, Part 9, but such orders would be extremely unusual); in divorce cases, the parents' relationship is evidently ending.

[165] See *Siddiqui v Siddiqui* [2021] EWCA Civ 1572. [166] Ibid.

5.5.3.a The orders available

On applications for failure to maintain, only periodical payment (secured and unsecured) and lump sum orders may be made. In both other jurisdictions, several remedies are available: periodical payments; lump sums; property settlements; and property transfers.[167] In divorce proceedings, periodical payment and lump sum orders can require payment to a third party, for example direct payment of school fees.[168] The divorce court can also vary ante- and post-nuptial settlements for the benefit of the child, and order sale of property as an adjunct to secured periodical payment, lump sum, and property adjustment orders.[169] None of these additional powers arises under the CA 1989, Sch 1.[170] We examine what each type of order entails in chapter 6.[171]

5.5.3.b Who can be made liable for whom?

Orders can be made not only against parents for the benefit of their own children but also, where the parties are spouses or civil partners, against certain other adults for the benefit of 'children of the family':

> 'child of the family', . . . means—
> (a) a child of both of those parties; and
> (b) any other child, not being a child who is placed with those parties as foster parents by a local authority or voluntary organisation, who has been treated by both of those parties as a child of their family.[172]

When determining whether a child is a 'child of the family', it is irrelevant that a husband had so treated a child mistakenly believing that he was the father;[173] the court can consider those circumstances in deciding what, if any, order to make. But the definition of 'child of the family' depends on the relevant adults having formalized their relationship: cohabitants have no liability for each other's children.[174]

5.5.3.c Who can apply?

We consider the standing of persons other than the child in the different categories of case, before examining what scope there is for applications by children for themselves.

[167] MCA 1973, ss 23 and 24; CPA 2004, Sch 5, Parts 1 and 2; CA 1989, Sch 1, para 1: see *Phillips v Peace* [2004] EWHC 3180; cf *B v B* [2007] EWHC 789.

[168] MCA 1973, s 23(1)(d)–(f); CPA 2004, Sch 5, para 2(d)–(f); the same applies in proceedings for failure to maintain, though not under the DPMCA 1978/CPA 2004, Sch 6.

[169] 'Property adjustment' here includes transfers, settlements, and variation of settlements: MCA 1973, s 24A, CPA 2004, Sch 5, Part 3.

[170] See Pollock et al (2022), on orders available to meet housing needs under CA 1989, Sch 1.

[171] A series of cases have considered the use of CA 1989, Sch 1 orders to cover the applicant's legal costs: e.g. *PG v TW (No 1) (Child: Financial Provision: Legal Funding)* [2012] EWHC 1892.

[172] E.g. MCA 1973, s 52; CPA 2004, Sch 5, para 80(2); CA 1989, Sch 1, para 16(2): cognate definition of 'parent'.

[173] *W (RJ) v W (SJ)* [1972] Fam 152. [174] *T v B* [2010] EWHC 1444.

Matrimonial cases

In matrimonial proceedings, a current or former spouse or civil partner may apply against the other for an order in relation to a child of the family of whatever age.[175] The child's guardian,[176] and a person who has (or is entitled to apply for) a child arrangements order naming that person as someone with whom the child is to live[177] may also apply.[178]

Schedule 1 cases

A broader range of persons may apply under the CA 1989, Sch 1. With most births in 2021 for the first time involving unmarried parents,[179] this Act potentially has substantial practical importance.[180] It covers disputes arising between spouses, civil partners, cohabitants, or those connected only by shared parenthood; and between parents and other individuals who enjoy certain other legal relationships with the child. A parent, guardian,[181] special guardian,[182] or person with whom a child is to live under a child arrangements order[183] may apply for an order against a parent or, where the applicant is not a parent, against both parents. 'Parent' here includes those in relation to whom a child is a 'child of the family', so spouse or civil partner step-parents may be applicants and respondents.[184] An application may be brought against a child's primary carer by the non-resident parent in order to cover costs incurred for the child's benefit, such as costs to travel to see the child or to accommodate the child when in the care of the non-resident parent, but these will be unusual cases.[185] A spouse who has a 'clean break' financial settlement on divorce[186] can apply under the CA 1989, Sch 1 for the child's benefit, but awards in such cases will be exceptional.[187]

Applications by the child?

As we have seen, the CSA 1991 gives children no standing to apply for a maintenance calculation from CMS for themselves.[188] Children's opportunities to apply to *court* for provision are limited, and the fact that applications can only be brought where the parents' relationship is not intact deprives most children of the right to apply at all, however inadequately they feel their parents are supporting them.[189]

If granted leave, children of the family (of any age) may intervene in *divorce* proceedings to apply for financial provision.[190] Only a spouse or civil partner can apply for an original order in *failure to maintain* cases, but children over 16 may apply to *vary* existing orders[191] and to revive orders that expire between the ages of 16–18, provided (as we shall see at 5.5.3.d) they are required to meet educational needs or special circumstances.[192]

Opportunities for children to apply under the CA 1989, Sch 1 are entirely reserved for older teenagers whose parents are living apart.[193] Children over 18 may in certain circumstances

[175] *J and K v L* [2021] EWFC B104. [176] CA 1989, s 5. [177] Ibid, ss 8 and 10(4).
[178] FPR 2010, SI 2010/2955, r 9.10. [179] ONS (2022c), worksheet 1.
[180] *Re P (Child: Financial Provision)* [2003] EWCA Civ 837. [181] CA 1989, s 5: see 10.3.7.
[182] Ibid, s 14A: see 10.3.6. [183] Ibid, s 8: see chapter 11. [184] Ibid, Sch 1, para 16(2).
[185] *N v C* [2013] EWHC 399; but see n 159 regarding maintenance. [186] See 6.6.1.
[187] *PK v BC (Financial Remedies: Schedule 1)* [2012] EWHC 1382.
[188] Cf the position in Scotland: CSA 1991, s 7.
[189] *Siddiqui v Siddiqui* [2021] EWCA Civ 1572, dismissing any claim of discrimination.
[190] FPR 2010, r 9.10; inapplicable to failure to maintain and Sch 1 cases: *Siddiqui v Siddiqui* [2021] EWCA Civ 1572, approving [2020] EWFC 63, [44].
[191] DPMCA 1978, s 20(12); MCA 1973, s 27(6A); CPA 2004, Sch 5, para 55, and Sch 6, para 39.
[192] MCA 1973, s 27(6B). [193] CA 1989, Sch 1, para 2.

apply for lump sum or periodical payments orders—not property adjustment orders—against their parents,[194] but not against step-parents or others. No such application can be made where a periodical payments order was in force when the child attained 16—the route here, instead, is for the child over 16 to apply for variation of that order, provided that the order: (i) is not due to expire after the child attains 18; and (see 5.5.3.d) (ii) is required for educational needs or special circumstances.[195] It has been assumed—though not authoritatively decided—that the Sch 1 'baton passes' from adult to child once the child attains 18, such that only the latter can bring a fresh application.[196]

5.5.3.d The child's age and the duration of orders

Ordinarily, no application[197] for financial provision or property adjustment may be made in favour of children aged 18 or above. However, orders may be made to endure beyond 18 (and beyond the age limit of the CSA 1991[198]) or be made after the child has reached majority if: (i) the child is receiving instruction at an educational establishment or is training for a trade, profession, or vocation; or (ii) there are special circumstances that justify the order.[199] The courts have held that, while there is no rule against property orders extending into adulthood, they should be made only exceptionally: see further 5.5.5.b.

Whilst orders commonly last until the end of an undergraduate degree, including a gap year, they will not be made to last beyond that, notwithstanding the increasing trend for children to remain at home post-university.[200]

C v F (Disabled Child: Maintenance Orders) considered the 'special circumstances' exception as applied by the courts (most commonly) in relation to disability. Butler-Sloss LJ observed that:

> It is part of the philosophy of the Children Act that a young person in [the child's] position with a total dependence upon others for the rest of his life should look for continuing financial support from his parents for whatever period may be necessary.[201]

Butler-Sloss and Thorpe LJJ concluded, obiter, that once the child ceased to be a 'qualifying child' for the purposes of the CSA 1991, the restriction on the courts' powers imposed by s 8(8) of that Act—that its periodical payments order could only cover expenses connected with the disability, and not with any other needs—would also cease, freeing the court to make orders for any purpose.

Periodical payments orders terminate on the payer's death.[202] If the parents are living together, payments may cease to be payable or not be ordered at all. While an order may be

[194] It is unclear whether the parents' standing to apply under the Sch 1 jurisdiction survives once the child reaches 18: see Harrison and Benson (2019); cf *J and K and L* [2021] EWFC B104, [26], [34] assuming that it does not and that the adult-child can apply instead.

[195] CA 1989, Sch 1, para 6(4).

[196] *J and K v L* [2021] EWFC B104, [26], [34]; cf Harrison and Benson (2019).

[197] An order can be made under Sch 1 on a parent's application even for children aged 18, provided they were under 18 at the date of the application: *UD v DN* [2021] EWCA Civ 1947, [68].

[198] See discussion in *C v F (Disabled Child: Maintenance Orders)* [1999] 1 FCR 39.

[199] DPMCA 1978, s 5; CPA 2004, Sch 6, para 27; MCA 1973, ss 27(6) and 29; CPA 2004, Sch 5, para 49; CA 1989, Sch 1, para 3.

[200] *Re N (A Child)* [2009] EWHC 11.

[201] [1999] 1 FCR 39, 42.

[202] DPMCA 1978, s 5(4); CPA 2004, Sch 6, para 27(6); CA 1989, Sch 1, para 3(3); MCA 1973, s 29(4); and CPA 2004, Sch 5, para 49: save for arrears due.

made for the child's benefit while the parents are living together under some of the 'failure to maintain' jurisdiction and the CA 1989, Sch 1, it will terminate after the parties have lived together, or resumed cohabitation, for over six months.[203]

5.5.4 THE GROUNDS FOR ORDERS AND THE COURTS' DISCRETION

The failure to maintain provisions specify the ground on which orders under those Acts may be made for the child's benefit: that the respondent has failed to provide, or make a proper contribution towards, reasonable maintenance for the child.[204] The other legislation stipulates no specific ground for the exercise of the courts' powers. Nevertheless, the courts tend to confine themselves to providing for the child's 'maintenance', however broadly construed.[205] Each statute prescribes a checklist of factors for the courts to consider in exercising their discretion, very similar to those applying to financial remedies between spouses on divorce. The checklists are broadly identical, but we highlight differences below.[206]

Only in proceedings on divorce is it expressly stated that 'first consideration' must be given to the welfare while a minor of any child of the family.[207] The welfare principle in the CA 1989 does not apply to decisions about children's maintenance,[208] but it has nevertheless been held that the child's welfare is at least a relevant consideration.[209]

Re P (A Child: Financial Provision) [2003] EWCA Civ 837

THORPE LJ:

44. . . . I would only wish to amplify [that] by saying that welfare must be not just 'one of the relevant circumstances' but, in the generality of cases, a constant influence on the discretionary outcome. I say that because the purpose of the statutory exercise is to ensure for the child of parents who have never married and who have become alienated and combative, support and also protection against adult irresponsibility and selfishness, at least insofar as money and property can achieve those ends.

In deciding whether and, if so, how to exercise their powers under the Acts, the courts must consider all the circumstances,[210] particularly:[211]

- the child's financial needs;
- the child's income, earning capacity (if any), property, and other financial resources;

[203] DPMCA 1978, s 25(1); CPA 2004, Sch 6, para 29; CA 1989, Sch 1, para 3(4).

[204] DPMCA 1978, s 1(b); CPA 2004, Sch 6, para 1; MCA 1973, s 27(1); CPA 2004, Sch 5, para 39(1).

[205] *A v A (Financial Provision for Child)* [1995] 1 FCR 309. CA 1989, Sch 1, para 5 expressly permits lump sums to cover expenses incurred in connection with the child's birth.

[206] DPMCA 1978, s 3; CPA 2004, Sch 6, para 6; MCA 1973, ss 25(1), (3)–(4), and 27(3A); CPA 2004, Sch 5, paras 20 and 22; CA 1989, Sch 1, para 4.

[207] MCA 1973, s 25(1) and CPA 2004, Sch 5, para 20.

[208] See ss 1 and 105, definition of 'upbringing'.

[209] *J v C (Child: Financial Provision)* [1998] 3 FCR 79.

[210] Including egregious conduct: *O v P* [2014] EWHC 2225, [128].

[211] See n 206.

- in matrimonial proceedings: the current or former spouses'/civil partners' income, earning capacity (including earning capacity that it would be reasonable to expect each party to take steps to acquire), property, and other financial resources; and their financial needs, obligations, and responsibilities, both now and likely in the foreseeable future;
- under the CA 1989, Sch 1: those same aspects of the parents' financial situation; and, where the applicant is not a parent of the child, the financial situation of that person, save that the court is not directed to consider any earning capacity that it would be reasonable to expect a party to take steps to acquire;
- any physical or mental disability of the child (and, in matrimonial proceedings, of either spouse/civil partner);
- the standard of living enjoyed by the family before: (i) the failure to make reasonable provision for the child (failure to maintain cases); (ii) the breakdown of the marriage/civil partnership (divorce cases). This factor is not listed in the CA 1989, Sch 1, where the parents may never have lived together or with the child;[212]
- the manner in which the child was being, or was expected to be, educated or trained.

Where orders are sought for the benefit of a 'child of the family' who is not in law the respondent's child, the court must also consider:

- whether the respondent assumed any responsibility for the child's maintenance; and, if he did, the extent to and the basis on which he assumed that responsibility; and for how long he discharged it;
- whether in assuming and discharging that responsibility the respondent did so knowing that the child was not his own;
- the liability of any other person to maintain the child: for example, the child's legal parent, who may be liable to make child support payments.

5.5.5 PRINCIPLES FROM THE CASE LAW

Most reported cases involve extremely wealthy respondents (so-called 'big money' cases) and unmarried parents. In 'everyday' divorce cases,[213] child support liability generally consumes respondents' free income and the parties cannot afford to litigate, so very few reported cases address their situation. Capital and property orders on divorce, particularly regarding the former matrimonial home, will be made for the benefit of the parent-spouse rather than for children, but the children obtain substantial indirect benefit from such orders. By contrast, where the respondent is wealthy and/or the parties were not spouses or civil partners so there is no jurisdiction to adjust capital or make income orders between the adults, orders for the child may be financially feasible and vital for the economy of the child's household.[214] As it does when granting financial remedies on divorce, the court must ensure that the orders made achieve overall fairness for both parties. Where funds are limited, finances may be quite tight for both:[215]

[212] But see *N v D* [2008] 1 FLR 1629.
[213] Hitchings (2009).
[214] Cf Law Com (2006), paras 4.34–4.46 on the under-use of the CA 1989, Sch 1.
[215] *DE v AB* [2011] EWHC 3792, [41].

***DE v AB* [2010] EWHC 3792**

BARON J:

46. Neither of these parties seems sufficiently to have considered or expected that a sexual relationship would lead to the birth of a child. However, that is a known consequence. If a child arrives, then parenthood brings with it significant financial and other responsibilities. Both these parties have to make a continuing contribution in that regard for the good of their son. Both will suffer financially because the new circumstances mean that they do not have the freedom and the financial flexibility that they once had. But that is a consequence of their own actions. As adults, they have to bear responsibility for such.

5.5.5.a Unwanted births and births to unmarried parents

As the opening of that extract from *DE v AB* suggests, applications for financial provision sometimes prompt respondents to claim that the conception was accidental, the birth unwanted, and the relationship between the parents, and between respondent parent and child, insubstantial.

***J v C (Child: Financial Provision)* [1998] 3 FCR 79 (Fam Div), 81–3**

HALE J:

. . . [A]lthough para 4(1) of Sch 1 to the 1989 Act tells me to consider all the circumstances, I do not consider that any great weight should be attached either to the circumstances of T's birth or to the length or quality of her [parents'] relationship. There is nothing in the private law provisions to distinguish between different children on such grounds. The policy of the Child Support Act 1991 was that people who had children should support them, whether or not those were wanted children. As a general proposition children should not suffer because their parents are irresponsible or uncaring towards them. I note that there is an example of an order being made against a father who had wanted the mother to have a termination in the case of *Phillips v Peace* [1996] 2 FCR 237. . . .

. . . The underlying principle [is] that children should not suffer just because their parents had, for whatever reason, not been married to one another.

Equally of course they should not get more . . .

5.5.5.b The basic objective: meeting the child's needs

The courts view their objective as being simply to cater for the child's needs, however wealthy the respondent parent. By contrast with spouses and civil partners, who can generally claim a form of entitlement to share family assets on divorce,[216] children are merely dependants to be maintained until adulthood.[217] However, in assessing the extent of the child's needs,

[216] See 6.5.5.
[217] *A v A (Financial Provision for Child)* [1995] 1 FCR 309; *Kiely v Kiely* [1988] 1 FLR 248; *Re A (A Child)* [2014] EWCA Civ 1577.

the courts have regard to the resources and standard of living of the respondent parent (and, where applicable, the standard of living enjoyed by the family during the parents' relationship[218]), considering that the child's situation should bear some reasonable resemblance to the respondent's.[219] Determining the extent of the child's 'needs' is an uncertain art.[220] Whilst orders must be 'for the benefit of the child', it is enough for a 'welfare' benefit, rather than a financial benefit, to accrue to the child.[221] So orders may be made transferring property from one parent to the other in order for the child to occupy with that parent.[222]

Orders are, however, ordinarily intended only to benefit the child during minority or until completion of education, not for life.[223] It would therefore ordinarily be improper to order an outright transfer of property (e.g. a home), rather than a settlement of that property during the child's dependence.[224] It would, similarly, generally be inappropriate to order periodical payments that would not be exhausted in meeting the child's needs during the term of the order.[225] As discussed at 5.5.3.d, 'special' circumstances generating some financial need[226]—related to disability or otherwise[227]—are required for orders to endure beyond 18.

5.5.5.c Indirect benefit for others

Orders may only be made 'for the benefit of the child'. Applicants who were not the respondent's spouse or civil partner cannot obtain financial remedies for their own benefit. However, orders made for the benefit of the child can provide such individuals (and any other children living with them for whom the respondent is not liable[228]) with substantial indirect benefit. The courts have generally been happy to contemplate such indirect benefit, considering it to be in children's best interests that those living with them enjoy comparable standards of living.[229] In particular, the child's need for a carer requires that that carer's needs, particularly regarding accommodation, be considered, but only whilst the child is dependent.[230] The non-resident parent may also need accommodation adequate for the child to stay overnight regularly. However, the courts are alert to claims that are, in substance, for the benefit of the adult applicant or her other children rather than the respondent's child.[231] In *Morgan v Hill*, the Court of Appeal noted that it was difficult to disentangle the indirect costs (e.g. of housing, running a car, and so on) pertaining to each individual in the household (contrast the identifiable direct costs of food and clothing for each person).

[218] *N v D* [2008] 1 FLR 1629, [23]. [219] *J v C (Child: Financial Provision)* [1998] 3 FCR 79, 87.

[220] Gilmore (2004a), 112; compare 'needs' on divorce: see 6.5.3.

[221] This includes legal costs of proceedings taken for the child's benefit: e.g. *PG v TW (Child: Financial Provision: Legal Funding) (No 1)* [2012] EWHC 1892.

[222] *K v K (Minors: Property Transfer)* [1992] 1 WLR 530.

[223] *A v A (Financial Provision for Child)* [1995] 1 FCR 309. Cf *Tavoulareas v Tavoulareas* [1998] 2 FLR 418; criticized by Gilmore (2004b).

[224] *UD v DN* [2021] EWCA Civ 1947.

[225] *Re P (A Child: Financial Provision)* [2003] EWCA Civ 837, [49], in relation to the carer's allowance.

[226] *UD v DN* [2021] EWCA Civ 1947, [76], [81]–[82].

[227] E.g. the truly exceptional circumstances in which justification for lifetime orders was conceded (see [23]) in *Her Royal Highness Haya Bint Al Hussein v His Highness Mohammed Bin Rashid Al Maktoum* [2021] EWFC 94; cf lack of finding of ongoing dependency (mere 'vulnerability' insufficient) to justify an award in *UD v DN* [2021] EWCA Civ 1947, [76].

[228] *Morgan v Hill* [2006] EWCA Civ 1602; cf the child born later in *Phillips v Peace* [2004] EWHC 3180, [11].

[229] *A v A (Financial Provision for Child)* [1995] 1 FCR 309; *J v C (Child: Financial Provision)* [1998] 3 FCR 79.

[230] *Haroutunian v Jennings* (1980) 1 FCR 62; *Re A (A Child)* [2014] EWCA Civ 1577.

[231] *J v C (Child: Financial Provision)* [1998] 3 FCR 79; *Re S (Unmarried Parents: Financial Provision)* [2006] EWCA Civ 479; and in the case of application by non-resident parent: *N v C* [2013] EWHC 399.

But it was emphasized that it was important in principle not to lose sight of the extent of the respondent's liability. We explore this issue insofar as it relates to the 'carer element' of periodical payments in this section. It has been suggested that where the applicant's children have different second parents, it might be fairest to bring consolidated actions against all respondents and apportion the liability for the children between them.[232]

5.5.5.d Property orders

The following extract exemplifies the courts' approach to capital orders, here regarding a child's housing under the CA 1989, Sch 1. As is typical of reported cases, the respondent was wealthy. Ward J considers the factors in para 4 of Sch 1:

A v A (Financial Provision for Child) [1995] 1 FCR 309 (Fam Div), 315–16

WARD J:

The father is so rich he could transfer this property and not even be aware that he had done so. His obligations and responsibilities are to provide for the maintenance and education of his child until she has completed that education, including her tertiary education, and reached independence. There is no special circumstance which imposes on him any moral duty to advance capital or income to her once he has fulfilled that duty. Her financial needs are to be considered, and it is noticeable that they are the "financial needs of the child", which again suggests that adult needs are not ordinarily relevant. The child has no income. She has no physical or mental disability. I must have regard to the manner in which she was being or was expected to be educated or trained, and the implication in those words is once more that the obligation to maintain ceases when that educational training ceases. . . . There is no special circumstance I can find which would require this father to do more than maintain his daughter until she is independent. I therefore reject her claim for the transfer of the property to her absolutely.

The judge refused simply to accept an undertaking from the father that he would allow the child to occupy the property: the child needed the security of a beneficial interest in the home, and so a property settlement order was made:[233]

The terms of the trust . . . should be that the property be conveyed to trustees . . . to hold the same for A for a term which shall terminate six months after A has attained the age of 18, or six months after she has completed her full-time education, which will include her tertiary education, whichever is latest. I give her that period of six months to find her feet and arrange her affairs. The trustees shall permit her to enjoy a reasonable gap between completing her school education and embarking upon her further education.

I have regard to para. 4(1)(b) which requires me to consider the financial needs, obligations and responsibilities of each parent and also subpara. (c) which requires me to have regard to the financial needs of the child. The mother's obligation is to look after A, and A's financial need is to provide a roof over the head of her caretaker. It is, indeed, [the] father's obligation to provide the accommodation for the living-in help which A needs. Consequently, it must

[232] *Morgan v Hill* [2006] EWCA Civ 1602, [38]–[39].
[233] See also *Re P (A Child: Financial Provision)* [2003] EWCA Civ 837, [45].

be a term of the settlement that while A is under the control of her mother and thereafter for so long as A does not object, the mother shall have the right to occupy the property to the exclusion of the father and without paying rent therefor, and for the purpose of providing a home and care and support for A.

5.5.5.e Periodical payments

How to determine the level of periodical payments

The court has complete discretion in this matter, subject to the focus of the remedies being on meeting the child's needs. However, *GW v RW (Financial Provision: Departure from Equality)* exemplifies one approach to fixing periodical payments.[234] In this big-money case, the court had full jurisdiction over child maintenance because the parent with care and children were not habitually resident in the UK. The parents were divorcing, so their financial issues had been dealt with under the MCA 1973; the wife, broadly speaking, was awarded 40 per cent of the substantial assets. We examine s 4(10) of the CSA 1991, referred to in this extract, at 5.6.1. The judge identified two main principles:

GW v RW [2003] EWHC 611

NICHOLAS MOSTYN QC (sitting as a deputy High Court judge):

74. . . . First, I am of the view that the appropriate starting point for a child maintenance award should almost invariably be the figure thrown up by the . . . child support rules. The Government's express policy in making awards of child maintenance susceptible to abrogation and replacement by a maintenance calculation by the CSA (see 4(10)(aa) Child Support Act 1991) was that child maintenance orders should be negotiated:

'. . . in the shadow of the CSA. All parties will know that either parent can turn to the CSA in future, and that it will therefore be sensible to determine child maintenance broadly in line with CSA assessment rates.' [See DSS (1999), ch 8]

If a child maintenance order, whether made by consent or after a contest, is markedly at variance with the calculation under the [child support] regime then there will be a high temptation for one or other party after the order has been in force for a year, and . . . to approach the CSA [as it then was] for a calculation. Quite apart from the obvious acrimony that this would engender, a calculation in a different amount to the figure originally negotiated or awarded may cast doubt on the fairness of the original . . . settlement [of financial remedies on divorce] between the parties, leading to further litigation. These spectres should be avoided at all costs.

75. The second principle is that notwithstanding that the income of the parent with care is disregarded in the calculation of child support . . . it is reasonable to expect the parent with care who has received a substantial share of the parties' assets to contribute to the support of the children. . . . It should be noted that the Government justified the omission of the parent with care's income in the new formula on the ground that she would from her own resources be making a substantial contribution to the support of the children. . . .

[234] See also *E v C (Calculation of Child Maintenance)* [1996] 1 FLR 472; *A v M* [2005] EWHC 1721; *Re M-M (Schedule 1 Provision)* [2014] EWCA Civ 276.

77. Having regard to these principles my decision is as follows:

77.1. I am satisfied that there should be some increase on the starting point of the maximum CSA calculation that would be applicable here. The husband has an income well in excess of the capped amount of [£2,000 per week—the then ceiling for the CSA]. I am also of the view that where a proportionate division of the main assets has been effected [60% to H, 40% to W] then that proportion should inform the division of the child maintenance costs. . . . I therefore award general maintenance of [60% of those costs] per child per annum payable quarterly in advance . . . to continue until each respective child attains 18 years of age or completes full time tertiary education if later. . . . Once a child enters tertiary education the payments will be made, as H has suggested, as to two-thirds to the child direct and one-third to W.

77.2. In addition H will pay all the educational costs of the children, to include reasonable extras until the conclusion of full-time tertiary education.

77.3. H will also pay all the costs of travel for contact, to include the cost of an accompanying nanny until the younger child's seventh birthday.

Mostyn J has since suggested that, in top-up cases, the formula should provide the starting point all the way up to gross incomes of £650,000 pa, well beyond the CSA 1991 scheme's cap of £156,000. Above £650,000, he still advocates that starting point, albeit with 'full discretionary freedom to depart from it having regard to the scale of the excess'.[235] While the child support formula offers a guide to determining the extent of the child's needs, as measured by reference to the non-resident parent's living standard (as roughly reflected in his income level), it must be remembered that the legislation requires the courts to consider a wider range of circumstances, and so they must be free to depart from the formula as fairness requires.

A carer's allowance?

Where the courts have jurisdiction in relation to periodical payments, for example in 'top-up' cases under s 8(6) of the CSA 1991, and where the available funds are extensive, they include an allowance to cover the needs of the child's carer. This extract, from the Court of Appeal's first decision under the CA 1989, Sch 1, describes the approach that should be taken in high-value cases to capital provision, and then turns to the question of maintenance and the carer's allowance. The parents had not married, so the non-resident parent had no responsibility to support the parent with care in her own right.

Re P (A Child: Financial Provision) [2003] EWCA Civ 837

THORPE LJ:

47. . . . [T]he judge [must] determine what budget the mother reasonably requires to fund her expenditure in maintaining the home and its contents and in meeting her other expenditure external to the home, such as school fees, holidays, routine travel expenses,

[235] *CB v KB* [2019] EWHC 78, [49].

> entertainments, presents, etc. In approaching this . . . decision, the judge is likely to be assailed by rival budgets . . . Invariably the applicant's budget hovers somewhere between the generous and the extravagant. Invariably the respondent's budget expresses parsimony. . . . But it is worth emphasising the trite point that . . . an order for periodical payments is always variable and will generally have to be revisited to reflect both relevant changes of circumstance and also the factor of inflation. Therefore . . . the court should discourage undue bickering over budgets. What is required is a broad commonsense assessment. What the court first ordains may have a comparatively brief life before a review is claimed by one or other party.
>
> 48. In making this broad assessment how should the judge approach the mother's allowance, perhaps the most emotive element in the periodical payments assessment? The respondent will often accept with equanimity elements within the claim that are incapable of benefiting the applicant (for instance school fees or children's clothing) but payments which the respondent may see as more for the benefit of the applicant than the child are likely to be bitterly resisted. Thus there is an inevitable tension between the two propositions, both correct in law, first that the applicant has no personal entitlement, second that she is entitled to an allowance as the child's primary carer. Balancing this tension may be difficult in individual cases. In my judgment, the mother's entitlement to an allowance as the primary carer (an expression which I stress) may be checked but not diminished by the absence of any direct claim in law.
>
> 49. Thus . . . the court must recognise the responsibility, and often the sacrifice, of the unmarried parent (generally the mother) who is to be the primary carer for the child, perhaps the exclusive carer if the absent parent disassociates from the child. In order to discharge this responsibility the carer must have control of a budget that reflects her position and the position of the father, both social and financial. On the one hand she should not be burdened with unnecessary financial anxiety or have to resort to parsimony when the other parent chooses to live lavishly. On the other hand whatever is provided is there to be spent at the expiration of the year for which it is provided. There can be no slack to enable the recipient to fund a pension[236] or an endowment policy or otherwise to put money away for a rainy day. In some cases it may be appropriate for the court to expect the mother to keep relatively detailed accounts of her outgoings and expenditure in the first and then in succeeding years of receipt. Such evidence would obviously be highly relevant to the determination of any application for either upward or downward variation.

Whilst keeping accounts may be sensible, these observations have been questioned: requiring that accounts be regularly reported to the respondent may be intrusive, cause friction, and so be counterproductive.[237] As to making savings, it was noted in *Re C (Financial Provision)* that the parent with whom the child is living should be allowed to save up for recurrent expenditure that arises less frequently than annually: it is *personal* saving which is barred.[238]

Thorpe LJ made the following observations in quantifying the carer element (note that this father had 'unlimited means' and the court had approved budgets of £1 million to acquire central London accommodation for the child and mother and £100,000 for its furnishing):

[236] See *CA v DR* [2021] EWFC 21, [64]–[70].

[237] *Re P* [2003] EWCA Civ 837, [75] per May LJ; *Re C (Financial Provision)* [2007] 2 FLR 13; cf accounting for the expenditure of a lump sum paid for a specific purpose: *Re N (A Child)* [2009] EWHC 11, [32]–[33].

[238] [2007] 2 FLR 13.

42. . . . [In] *A v A* [see earlier, decided in 1995], in explaining his quantification of an allowance for the mother's care Ward J said:

"I bear in mind a broad range of imprecise information from the extortionate demands (but excellent service) of Norland nannies, to au pair girls and mother's helps, from calculations in personal injury and fatal accident claims and from the notice-boards in the employment agencies I pass daily. I allow £8,000 under this head. It is almost certainly much less than the father would have to pay were he to be employing staff, but to allow more would be—or would be seen to be—paying maintenance to the former mistress who has no claim in her own right to be maintained."

43. I cannot agree with that reservation. I believe that a more generous approach to the calculation of the mother's allowance is not only permissible but also realistic. Nor would I have regard to calculations in either personal injury or fatal accident claims. It seems to me that such cross-references only risk to complicate what is an essentially broad-brush assessment to be taken by family judges with much expertise and experience in the specialist field of ancillary relief. . . .

54. In making an independent assessment [of the periodical payments order] in the exercise of my own discretion, I have regard to the likely cost of running the home that the trustees will buy for the mother and L [the child]. I have regard to the fact that the mother is to be L's primary carer. I would not relate that to the cost of a Norland nanny. That would be to demean the mother's role. Mothers provide 24-hour care for children. That level of care would be difficult to buy in, even for a father as rich and resourceful as this. In the real world nannies are entitled to days off, weekends off and holidays. . . . I would take a broad-brush figure of £70,000 per annum from which the father is entitled to deduct the amount of state benefits that the mother receives for L. Of course it is easy to say that that represents a liability of approximately £1,500 a week for a two-year-old child. But that is a distortion of the reality that £70,000 is a budget to enable the mother to run the home for [the child] and to provide her additional needs. . . .

As May LJ noted, cases involving sums such as these are atypical and so should not be used as a benchmark for future cases.

In *F v G (Child: Financial Provision)*, a full carer's allowance was made even though the mother worked full-time. The court considered that she should be able to choose whether to spend that allowance on hiring child-care and continue to work, securing her own financial future, or alternatively to work part-time and care for the child herself.[239] This was not considered to offend *Re P*'s prohibition on any 'slack' being made available to the recipient: any savings would derive from her own earnings, should she choose to work.

A carer's allowance can also be justified in relation to teenage children, even when at university: they still need someone to provide a home, and can in their way be as demanding of a carer's time and attention as younger children.[240]

5.5.6 ENFORCEMENT OF COURT ORDERS

The courts have broad powers to enforce their own orders, corresponding with those available in matrimonial and civil partnership cases.[241]

[239] [2004] EWHC 1848, [44]–[54].

[240] *N v D* [2008] 1 FLR 1629, [24]–[25]; *H v C* [2009] EWHC 1527.

[241] See 6.4.6.

5.6 'FAMILY-BASED ARRANGEMENTS' AND OTHER PRIVATE ORDERING

As we saw at 5.2, a key feature of current child maintenance policy is that all parents should be free and encouraged to make their own arrangements for child support without any state intervention. Various provisions in the CSA 1991 and accompanying regulations support this policy:

- s 9(2A) empowers the state to encourage private maintenance agreements, and to explore that possibility with a person with care before she makes any application to CMS;
- s 4(2A) allows the state to collect maintenance for the person with care only if either the non-resident parent agrees or it is satisfied that payment will otherwise not be made;
- an application fee is charged for a formal CMS maintenance calculation; further charges for collection of child support are levied against both parties.

In this section, we consider the legal framework within which such private arrangements are made. We consider the policy implications of the new emphasis on private ordering at 5.7.2.

5.6.1 PRIVATE ORDERING OF MAINTENANCE

The statutory provisions governing the legal effect of private ordering of child maintenance (i.e. matters falling within the jurisdiction of CMS) are quite difficult to follow, but their overall effect—which we explain in this section—is clear:

Child Support Act 1991

4 Child support maintenance . . .

(10) No application [to CMS] may be made at any time under this section with respect to a qualifying child or any qualifying children if—. . .

(aa) a maintenance order made on or after [6th April 2002] is in force in respect of them, but has been so for less than the period of one year beginning with the date on which it was made; . . .

8 Role of courts with respect to maintenance for children . . .

(11) In this Act "maintenance order", in relation to any child, means an order which requires the making or securing of periodical payments to or for the benefit of the child and which is made under—

(a) Part II of the Matrimonial Causes Act 1973;

(b) the Domestic Proceedings and Magistrates' Courts Act 1978; . . .

(e) Schedule 1 to the Children Act 1989;

(ea) Schedule 5, 6 or 7 to the Civil Partnership Act 2004; or

(f) any other prescribed enactment,[242] and includes any order varying or reviving such an order.

[242] Child Support (Maintenance Arrangements and Jurisdiction) Regulations 1992, SI 1992/2645, reg 2.

9 Agreements about maintenance

(1) In this section "maintenance agreement" means any agreement for the making, or for securing the making, of periodical payments by way of maintenance . . . to or for the benefit of any child.

(2) Nothing in this Act shall be taken to prevent any person from entering into a maintenance agreement. . . .

(3) Subject to section 4(10)(a) . . ., the existence of a maintenance agreement shall not prevent any party to the agreement, or any other person, from applying for a maintenance calculation with respect to any child to or for whose benefit periodical payments are to be made or secured under the agreement.

(4) Where any agreement contains a provision which purports to restrict the right of any person to apply for a maintenance calculation, that provision shall be void . . .[243]

Parents are free to make 'family-based arrangements' (as government sometimes calls them), which may be theoretically enforceable as contracts.[244] However, like separation agreements made between spouses on divorce,[245] the existence of such agreements cannot prevent either party at any time applying to CMS for a maintenance calculation. That calculation then replaces the agreement, which is no longer enforceable.[246]

Parties who want greater certainty should enshrine their agreement in a consent order, but the status of such orders in this arena is complex. Whilst theoretically capable of variation and enforcement for their duration, once that order has been in place for one year, either party is free to apply to CMS for a maintenance calculation, which will supplant what the parties agreed and deprive the court of jurisdiction.[247] So, for their first year of operation, consent orders offer more security than mere agreements; but after that year, they are as vulnerable as agreements to CMS's intervention.[248] The bar in s 4(10)(aa) on applying for child support during the first year of a consent order for maintenance does not apply to orders made for special expenses associated with the child's education or disability: such orders are designed to deal with matters other than the child's basic maintenance.[249]

It follows that parties' ability to avoid using CMS through private ordering requires ongoing, mutual consent. As was observed in *GW v RW (Financial Provision: Departure from Equality)*,[250] parties seeking to avoid CMS should consider what the CSA 1991 formula would provide if it were applied to their case. Then neither party will have any incentive to apply to CMS. A court invited to enshrine in a consent order a maintenance agreement that departs substantially from the CMS calculation may ask careful questions before making the order.

It has often been recommended that the 12-month rule rendering consent orders vulnerable to attack via CMS be dropped, leaving such cases entirely within the court system.[251] Some have even argued for a return to an entirely court-based system so that child

243 Further subsections relate to courts' powers to vary certain maintenance agreements.

244 *Darke v Strout* [2003] EWCA Civ 176.

245 See 6.7.2.

246 CSA 1991, s 10(2); SI 1992/2645, reg 4.

247 CSA 1991, s 10(1); SI 1992/2645, reg 3.

248 Practitioners seek to avoid this rule by use of 'Christmas orders': periodical payments orders for the benefit of children expressed to start and end on Christmas Day each year, only to be automatically replaced by a new such order: Resolution (2009), 138. No reported decision has yet confirmed their effectiveness, but compare term 88 in Standard order 2.1 – Financial remedy order (omnibus) precedent for orders that automatically vary in line with a prescribed index on a given date each year.

249 Child Support Act 1995, s 18(6).

250 [2003] EWHC 611, [74].

251 E.g. Henshaw (2006).

maintenance could be addressed alongside all the other issues over which the courts have jurisdiction on relationship breakdown.[252] But others were concerned that the emphasis on court-based private ordering might be detrimental to children and their primary carers where there was an imbalance of power, and costly to those who cannot readily access the courts.[253] The government firmly opposed both ideas:

DWP, *Report on the Child Maintenance White Paper: Reply by the Government*, Cm 7062 (London: TSO, 2007)

7.1 . . . The Government wants to give parents the choice of resolving child maintenance either by private agreement, or by recourse to a straightforward and transparent administrative process. It is the Government's view that providing a further parallel State child maintenance system operating on very different principles and with the ability to set very different levels of child maintenance would add a further level of complexity that would not, for the vast majority of clients, lead to a better service.

8.1. . . . The 12-month rule ensures that Consent Orders contain fair and consistent levels of child maintenance and provides parents with a route back into the assessment, collection and enforcement services of [CMS] if their order breaks down. Removal of the 12-month rule would keep parents locked into the court system and would enable the courts to make awards that were not consistent with the formula.

8.2 We want parents to agree fair and sustainable child maintenance arrangements, and to ensure that, if agreements do break down or circumstances change, children can continue to receive maintenance because their parents will still have the opportunity to access the services provided by [CMS].

One of the faults of the past was that courts authorised clean-break settlements leaving children stranded in poverty without any ongoing child maintenance. The Government does not want to return to this past scenario and the 12-month rule appears to be effectively discouraging this type of settlement.

Mrs Kehoe (see 5.4.7.c) may well ask whether being 'locked into' the court system would be preferable to being locked into the CMS system.

5.6.2 PRIVATE ORDERING OF OTHER FINANCIAL ISSUES FOR CHILDREN

Parents are free to reach private agreements regarding all matters falling *outside* CMS's jurisdiction for the benefit of children: for example, an agreement to hold a house on trust for the child and parent to occupy, or regarding school fees. Again, parents may simply conclude an agreement or—for greater certainty—obtain a consent order. The latter option is fully binding—and variable—like any other order.[254] An agreement not so formalized may be binding as a contract, save that the courts' powers over the matters for which they have jurisdiction cannot be ousted by agreement. Either party may therefore apply to court for provision different from that agreed, or ask the court to vary the agreement either because of a change of circumstances or because the agreement 'does not contain proper financial

[252] Pirrie (2006). See also DWP (2018a), [91]–[94]. [253] CPAG (2006). [254] See 6.7.1.

arrangements with respect to the child'.[255] The Court of Appeal held in *Morgan v Hill* that the same principles apply whichever route is taken.[256] The applicant need only show lack of proper financial arrangements; no higher threshold of inadequacy need be crossed. But any court order varying or departing from what had been agreed must be just having regard to all the circumstances, and the existence and terms of the agreement are a 'very important circumstance'.[257] This approach, similar to that taken to agreements made between spouses on divorce, discourages applications made merely because parties become dissatisfied with their bargain.

5.7 POLICY QUESTIONS RELATING TO FINANCIAL PROVISION FOR CHILDREN

The law in this area raises several important policy questions. In this section, we explore five issues: child support as a matter of children's rights or parents' responsibilities; public intervention, family privacy, and private ordering; the relevance of legal and social parenthood to child support liability; the theoretical basis of child support formulae; and the contrast between rules and discretion as tools for determining the extent of financial responsibility for children.

5.7.1 CHILDREN'S RIGHTS OR PARENTS' RESPONSIBILITIES?

Key government papers on child support have had child-centred titles: 'Children Come First', 'Children First: a new approach to child support', 'Children's Rights and Parents' Responsibilities'. The Henshaw Report in 2006 asserted that 'children have a right to appropriate support', whilst also using the language of 'welfare'.[258] Various questions arise when attempting to formulate a rights-based approach to financial provision for children, not least: what is the content of the right and against whom is it exercisable? We should pause and note that the law discussed in this chapter offers nothing to children whose families are intact, whose parent with care is widowed, or whose non-resident parent is untraceable. To that extent, the current law protects the rights of only a specific subset of children. To set the scene of this next extract, readers may wish to read the extracts at 8.5.2 from the theoretical work of Eekelaar and others on whom Nick Wikeley relies in developing his rights-based approach:

N. Wikeley, *Child Support: Law and Policy* (Oxford: Hart Publishing, 2006a), 8–10

> [C]hildren's basic interests mean that children have a right that their essential needs for food, shelter and clothing are satisfied. This right may be conceptualised in two parallel and complementary ways. First, it might be characterised as a fundamental human right, which is vested in children by virtue of their membership of the wider community and irrespective of their own parents' particular circumstances. In the United Kingdom, the availability of child

[255] CA 1989, Sch 1, para 10; MCA 1973, s 35.
[256] [2006] EWCA Civ 1602, [34].
[257] Ibid, [28]; cf *Edgar v Edgar* [1980] 1 WLR 1410, discussed at 6.7.2.
[258] Henshaw (2006), 2; see also Hutton (2006).

> benefit as a universal[259] social security benefit may be seen as a tangible manifestation of this principle, in that it reflects a (modest) contribution by society at large to assist all parents (for the most part) in meeting the costs of raising their children. The resource implications for the state of the child's fundamental human right to support may be more extensive in some circumstances: [e.g. orphans]. Secondly, the child's right to support might be construed as a correlative claim-right, in the sense that failure to satisfy those needs would amount to a breach of duty by an individual subject to corresponding obligations. The decision to impose such a duty on a particular individual – for example, the child's parent(s) – will be the outcome of a process of weighing up a range of considerations drawn from the realms of moral insight and social policy. These factors will also influence the priority which is accorded within society to the child's correlative right to (private) child support, as against the contribution made by (public) child support.
>
> One undoubted benefit of such a twin-track approach to understanding the child's right to support is that it would appear to command widespread popular support. A further advantage of this framework is its universality in that it is not predicated on family breakdown; in principle it applies just as much to children who live in intact families as to those whose parents have separated (or indeed whose parents have never lived together at all). Yet in practice . . . the state is inhibited from seeking to regulate the distribution of resources within the private domain of the intact family. For this reason, the problems of identifying and quantifying a child's basic needs remain largely hidden from view. It is the public fact of separation that throws these questions into sharp relief: even if we assume that child support is first and foremost a call on parental income, how do we define a child's basic needs?

The options range from securing a minimum, uniform subsistence level of support for all children, or relating maintenance to the standard of living of the particular family, an approach which departs further from the needs-based paradigm and so from a fundamental human right:

> [I]t may be possible to resolve this dilemma by returning to Eekelaar's analysis of children's rights in terms of basic, developmental and autonomy interests. Applying this taxonomy, we might argue that children enjoy a fundamental human right to child support in terms of having their basic living needs met, and that these are to be satisfied by a combination of public and private resource (the precise balance between those two sources to be determined by both value judgments and social policy considerations). On top of this, we might also contend that children have at the very least a legitimate expectation that they will benefit from the standard of living enjoyed by both their parents, irrespective of with which parent they actually happen to reside. This is, admittedly, a question of values and political choices rather than fundamental human rights. Obviously, the state itself cannot fund such expectations . . . One may, however, suggest that it is not unreasonable for the state to create the legal structures within which such expectations may be realised. The nomenclature of legitimate expectations, rather than rights, is deliberate, in that it implies that such expectations may be subject to compromise where there are other compelling interests to take into account. Its importance, however, lies in the message that child support is not simply a question of ensuring that food is put on the table and clothes on the child's back. Rather, child support is about improving the child's overall life chances – a matter in which society at large has a considerable interest and investment.

[259] But see now the High Income Child Benefit Tax Charge: CPAG (2019a), ch 27.9.

Current English law cannot readily be explained in rights-based terms, notwithstanding Baroness Hale's speech in the *Kehoe* case[260] and the radical change in the state's interest in recovery of child support post-CMOPA 2008. Pre-CMOPA, when the state was the principal beneficiary of child support in public law cases, the notion that this was a child's rights measure was problematic.[261] But even now that child support fully supplements children's household income, the matter remains doubtful. There is no reference in governmental policy documents to the UNCRC's guarantees.[262] The legislation does not conceptualize financial provision as a children's rights issue: attempts to affirm the child's right to maintenance on the face of CMOPA 2008 failed.[263] As we have seen, children have no right to apply to CMS and only limited opportunities to apply to court for financial provision. It was held in *Treharne v Secretary of State for Work and Pensions* that Article 8 created no economic right to receive regular, reasonable maintenance.[264] While family and private life may be tougher (in that case) owing to the state's failure to recover unpaid maintenance, that 'cannot be said to affect the core values attached to those concepts'.[265]

The new focus on private ordering leaves children dependent on parents' actions: whether maintenance is paid at all, in what form and amount, depends on adults' agreement or on the person with care applying to CMS or court. CMOPA 2008's reinstatement of family privacy in this sphere, discussed at 5.7.2, detracts from any notion that the child has an independent right to be maintained. As Stephen Parker has observed, if anyone has a right here it is the person with care.[266] Moreover, it is perhaps an odd fundamental human right which applies only to the children of parents who are living apart:

S. Parker, 'Child Support in Australia: Children's Rights or Public Interest?', (1991) 5 *International Journal of Law and the Family* 24, 55

> What particular class of children is intended as the class of right-holder? It cannot be children in one-parent families because, for example, a child whose father has died or disappeared is not covered by the Scheme. The obvious counter to this is that the putative right is to share in *parental* income and that the establishment of a guaranteed maintenance scheme for *all* children (which would belong to the more contestable class of welfare rights) was never intended. Whilst this might be true, it is difficult to see what exactly the child gains in insisting that the *parent* provides the money,[267] when set alongside the advantage of simply having the benefit of that amount of money from somewhere. A Scheme more obviously in line with this theory of children's rights would guarantee to all children the same sort of income as in the normal case [of children living with two parents] but quite separately institute a reimbursement mechanism for those absent parents who can be tracked down.[268]

[260] *R (Kehoe) v Secretary of State for Work and Pensions* [2005] UKHL 48: see Wikeley (2006b), extracted at 5.4.7.c.
[261] Parker (1991); cf *R (Kehoe) v Secretary of State for Work and Pensions* [2005] UKHL 48.
[262] Henricson and Bainham (2005), 44.
[263] E.g. Hansard HL Deb, vol 698, cols GC275–80, 29 January 2008.
[264] [2008] EWHC 3222. [265] Ibid, [31]. [266] Parker (1991), 53–5.
[267] Cf Altman (2003); Eekelaar (1991a).
[268] Compare the Finer Committee proposals (DHSS (1974)) for a guaranteed maintenance allowance for all lone-parent families: Lewis (1998); Douglas (2000a).

It may be more appropriate to focus on the second part of the title of the government's 1999 paper: 'Parents' Responsibilities'. Indeed, more recent titles place the emphasis here—for example, 'Strengthening families, promoting parental responsibility'.[269] Rebecca Bailey-Harris's comments on the Australian system are apposite to the UK context:

R. Bailey-Harris, 'Child Support: Is the Right the Wrong One?', (1992) 6 *International Journal of Law and the Family* **169, 171**

> [A]rguably *any* rights analysis is inappropriate: the scheme is more properly viewed as being based on obligation ie the enforcement of parental *obligations* to support their children. The language employed in the [Australian legislation—compare CSA 1991, s 1] is of symbolic significance: it is framed entirely in terms of parental duty. It is not suggested that an obligations analysis is necessarily less capable of promoting the child's interests than a rights analysis;[270] nevertheless the two approaches must be recognized as conceptually distinct. If the Child Support Scheme is to be analyzed in obligation terms, the nature of the parental obligation it creates merits analysis. It arises from procreation and not from nurturing; it is not necessary for a liable parent to have lived with the custodian. It is an obligation which may exist without any correlative benefit . . ., the legislation having set its face squarely against any necessary link between access [i.e. time spent by the non-resident parent with the child] and financial support.

But while 'parental responsibility' has been in the foreground of child support debates, its meaning has changed over time. In promoting the original CSA 1991, Margaret Thatcher was concerned about the irresponsibility of 'feckless fathers' who paid nothing towards their children's upbringing,[271] but the latest reforms adopt a rather different approach. The meaning of 'parental responsibility' here does not correspond with the term as used in s 3 of the CA 1989, discussed in chapter 10, not least because child support is payable by 'parents' whether or not they have 'parental responsibility' (as defined by s 3) for the child. The concept is being deployed here in a wider sense[272] that echoes the 'responsibility' featured in divorce law and policy debates.[273] Just as government wishes spouses to 'divorce responsibly', so it is desirous that parents make 'responsible' arrangements for child maintenance and act 'responsibly' by endeavouring to make private agreements rather than by relying on the state to do it for them.[274] And so we see a shift also in the nature of the state's role: not 'government'—strictly enforcing legal duties in all cases—but 'governance'—seeking to nudge[275] private individuals' behaviour to conform to a desirable norm.[276]

However, it is doubtful to what extent parents do or can reach private arrangements for child maintenance that provide a proper level of financial support—and so contribute to child poverty targets—without a more assertive role for the state. We examine the latest data on that at 5.7.2.c. The rhetoric of 'parental responsibility' may be rather empty. But if the child support regime is as weak on parental responsibility as it is on children's rights,

[269] DWP (2011). [270] See O'Neill (1992). [271] Cretney (2003a), 474.
[272] Cf Fox Harding (1991a), (1991b); Eekelaar (1991c). [273] See chapter 3.
[274] Cf discussion of this theme at 3.6.1 and 3.6.3.
[275] See the government-sponsored 'Nudge Unit', the Behavioural Insights Team, applying theories from behavioural economics and psychology to public policy and services: <www.bi.team/>.
[276] Compare Smart's analysis of divorce reforms at 3.6.1.

then what is it about? Some might argue that it is driven by pragmatic, operational efficiency concerns of the state, and not by rights, interests, or concerns of the individuals involved, least of all the child.[277]

5.7.2 PUBLIC AND PRIVATE

The dichotomy between public and private spheres, and the justification for state (public) intervention in family (private) life, is a prevalent theme in family law.[278] Several issues pertaining to that theme arise in relation to financial provision for children: the state's role in intact and separated families; the nature of the privacy afforded to families; and the impact of family privacy and private ordering on vulnerable family members.

5.7.2.a Protecting the private sphere

Financial provision cannot be sought for or by children living with both parents. Only where one or both parents live apart from the child or are severing their legal relationship does the law offer any remedy. The private realm of the nuclear family is immune from state interference. But we must beware of viewing family law in purely negative terms: in defining what is 'dysfunctional' and therefore warrants legal intervention, the law implicitly promotes 'accepted', and so private, family forms and behaviours.[279] The non-intervention of law in intact families has implications for the status and rights of children.

A. Diduck, *Law's Families* (London: Butterworths, 2003), 166

> When children and parents live in the same household, the law says very little about how they carry out their financial obligations to each other. It is clear, however, that children have no right to share in the overall family wealth, but simply the right to be supported during their dependence. . . . Law thus does not assume democracy or children's economic 'citizenship' within the family, but rather relies upon an idea of children's status to endorse their (economic) dependency.

This can produce strange inequalities. For example, the restrictions on children's right to apply against their own parents place children of separated parents in a stronger position than those living with both parents. While the former may apply for support during university, the latter ordinarily may not, even if their parents are not supporting them adequately, and even though their eligibility for student loans and grants is generally determined by reference to parental resources.[280]

As we discussed at 5.2, pre-CMOPA 2008, the public/private line was drawn very differently where the parent with care was on benefits. The state actively intervened in family life to recoup welfare benefit payments from child support received, requiring parents with care to cooperate in this exercise despite the very limited personal benefit (up to £10 per week)

277 Fortin (2009b), 354; Wikeley (2007b). 278 See 1.2.7. 279 O'Donovan (1985).

280 Education (Student Support) Regulations 2011, SI 2011/1986, Sch 4; cf 'independent eligible students', including orphans and those irreconcilably estranged from both parents, para 4; Maclean and Eekelaar (1997), 43.

that would accrue to them. Meanwhile, the privacy of families not reliant on state support was preserved, not required to engage with the CSA regime unless one party wished to do so. But the 2008 reforms reinforced the privacy of *all* families, by removing compulsion in benefit cases, creating a full maintenance disregard, and abolishing the old liable relative rule as it applied to children.

5.7.2.b A limited form of privacy?

However, the privacy available is somewhat limited. As we saw at 5.6.1, on the face of it, the law gives parents good reason both to fix periodical payments at levels prescribed by the CSA formula and also to view periodical payment, so calculated, as the only—or at least the primary—means of discharging the child support obligation. Some parents might have preferred to do this some other way in order to achieve a clean break:[281] that is, to make capital transfers now in lieu of maintenance and so terminate the parties' financial relationship.[282] But because private ordering over maintenance cannot be guaranteed to stick beyond the first year of any consent order (see 5.6.1), non-resident parents may be unwilling to make such settlements. On this view, parents should take full account of potential CMS support obligations when negotiating other aspects of their financial settlement on divorce. 'Private ordering' so understood seems to have (limited) procedural rather than substantive content: the parties' freedom is to behave amicably within the substantive framework set down by the law, not to agree their own terms.

But in promoting 'family-based arrangements', the state is sending parents mixed signals. The government website introduced in 2022[283] encourages such arrangements in the following terms:

> You can make your own maintenance arrangements between parents. No else has to be involved. You and the other parent can organise everything yourselves.[284]

The site goes on to suggest various things that parents might agree, some not directly financial:

> This might cover their living costs and care. For example, you could both agree that one parent:
>
> - does the school or nursery pick-ups
> - looks after the children in the holidays
> - pays a proportion of their income to the parent with the day-to-day care
> - pays for things like school clothes instead of giving money
> - pays a regular set amount directly to the parent with care.

[281] See 6.6, in case of divorce.

[282] This had been common pre-CSA 1991: *R (Kehoe) v Secretary of State for Work and Pensions* [2005] UKHL 48, [64] extracted at 5.4.7.c. For the problems encountered when the CSA 1991 was implemented, see *Crozier v Crozier* [1994] Fam 114; *Smith v McInerney* [1994] 2 FLR 1077, and the introduction of a special variation ground for such cases in 1995.

[283] <https://child-maintenance.service.gov.uk/get-help-arranging-child-maintenance/>.

[284] <https://child-maintenance.service.gov.uk/get-help-arranging-child-maintenance/make-your-own-arrangement>.

Of the items in that list, only the third resembles what the CSA 1991 formula would prescribe. It is suggested that parents might use the CMS online calculator as a basis for discussion, though parents 'do not have to use it'. The website suggests that a private arrangement 'might be a good option if . . . you think the other parent will stick to an agreement'. But it is not made clear that arrangements not reflecting the CSA formula are vulnerable to being upset by an application by either party to CMS for a formal calculation, or that private agreements are not straightforwardly enforceable (see 5.6.1). Were parents made aware of that, they might be less keen on using a private arrangement.[285] Similarly, the suggested inclusion of non-financial matters such as holiday time might make parents believe—erroneously—that child support liability can readily be traded for time spent with the child: contrast the restrictive 'shared care' rules, and the basis for identifying the 'non-resident parent', discussed at 5.4.4.f. The freedom of family-based arrangements may prove to be something of a trap for the unwary (and uninformed) in such cases.[286]

As we saw at 5.4.7.c, if either parent applies to CMS, they cede even procedural privacy: enforcement falls entirely under state control.[287] The government justified its policy on the basis that parents whose private arrangement fails should—on payment of an application fee (see 5.4.3.b)—have easy access to CMS, which, it said, would provide 'swift intervention'. In echoes of past child support debates, the new administrative body was repeatedly portrayed in the parliamentary debates as hyper-efficient, by contrast (at least implicitly) with the courts to which parties might otherwise have to turn (and get 'stuck') were the 12-month rule relating to enforcement of consent orders abolished (see 5.6.1).[288] As it transpires, CMS has attracted plenty of familiar criticism.[289]

So, child support is privatized insofar as liability rests with private individuals and family-based arrangements are strongly encouraged (despite their legally insecure foundations), but 'publicized' insofar as the state, in theory, ultimately controls nearly all aspects of that liability. This undermines what one commentator describes as the 'important principle of autonomy for parents in whom the state has no direct financial interest (other than the raising of taxes)'.[290]

5.7.2.c Whose privacy? The dangers of private ordering

Private ordering is not risk-free, and only a minority (42 per cent) of the British public agrees that parents should be left to agree child maintenance themselves (i.e. without the support of a government agency, lawyer or court, or some other advice service).[291] Most fundamentally, making private individuals rather than the state primarily responsible for organizing child maintenance may be said to ensure women's dependence on men.[292] When parents with care on benefit were obliged to participate in recovery of child support, the dysfunctional, fatherless family was forced by the state to 'reconnect' via the enforcement of financial obligations.[293] However, greater dangers might arise from private ordering, particularly where application to CMS depends entirely on private action and ability to pay the fee.

[285] Wikeley (2007b), 446–7.

[286] No variation ground accommodates such cases, cf the old variation ground to achieve fair outcomes for clean break settlements made pre-CSA 1991.

[287] *R (Kehoe) v Secretary of State for Work and Pensions* [2005] UKHL 48.

[288] E.g. Hansard HL Deb, col GC525, 5 February 2008; HC Public Bill Committee, cols 246–7, 9 October 2007; and see extract at 5.6.1 from DWP (2007).

[289] E.g. National Audit Office (2022). [290] Mostyn (1999), 97.

[291] Clery et al (2021), 'Child maintenance', 6–8. [292] Lewis (1998), 275. [293] Diduck (1995), 539.

Freeing parents to make their own arrangements does not necessarily mean that satisfactory—or any—child support will be paid. Outcomes may be dictated by the preferences of the more powerful party,[294] particularly where there is an imbalance of power or information.[295] Withholding child support is a recognized form of economic abuse.[296] It is striking that a survey of separated parents just before the CMOPA 2008 reforms found that parents with care who were using the CSA to obtain maintenance were much less enthusiastic than non-resident parents about the move to private agreements.[297] If a non-resident parent does not want to pay, or to pay at the level requested by the parent with care, he may just refuse to reach any such agreement. The onus will then be on the parent with care to remove the dispute from the private sphere by applying to CMS.

The government was confident that offering full information and support to parents with care would empower them to seek the child maintenance to which they are entitled, if not by agreement then via CMS. But there is an important distinction between simply providing information and support, and providing *independent advice* tailored to the circumstances of each family. The controversial CMS £20 application fee magnifies the difficulties. In this extract, written shortly before the new scheme came into effect, the NGO Gingerbread—which provides expert advice, practical support, research, and campaigning for single parents—outlines some of the problems.

Gingerbread, *Strengthening Families, Promoting Parental Responsibility – Government Plans for Child Maintenance: Gingerbread Briefing* (2011)

8. . . . Voluntary agreements can work well. For example, families with a voluntary agreement are more likely to receive the full amount of child maintenance on time than those receiving maintenance through the CSA . . . But a moment's reflection reveals the obvious: that if parents are in agreement, by definition the money is more likely to be paid. The success figures for those with voluntary arrangements are always likely to be good, because where an agreement breaks down, the parent with care is likely to move from a voluntary arrangement to using the CSA instead. It is not the fact that an arrangement is voluntary which makes it work; rather this is down to the circumstances of the parents who entered into the agreement.

9. Research indicates that only some parents are likely to be able to make successful voluntary arrangements for maintenance, and that their success is associated with certain characteristics. Analysis shows, for example, that private agreements are less likely where the mother and father have never lived together, or they separated some time ago. Factors shown to facilitate successful private agreements include:

- Amicable relations between the parents . . .
- Higher household incomes . . .
- The parent with care being in work . . .
- A continuing engagement of the non-resident parent with the children . . .

[294] House of Commons Select Committee on Work and Pensions (2007), para 179; see also Hansard, Public Bill Committee, col 49, Nick Wikeley, and cols 70, 72, Janet Allbeson, 17 July 2007; Hansard HL Deb, cols GC382–3. On factors impacting on behaviour around child support, see Andrews et al (2011).

[295] Parents negotiating privately do not have the benefit of courts' powers to require disclosure.

[296] Domestic Abuse Commissioner (2022a).

[297] Wikeley et al (2008).

> 10. The profile of parents who use the Child Support Agency is considerably different. Their circumstances are likely to make achieving private voluntary arrangements less likely.
>
> - Only 28 per cent of parents with care using the CSA reported friendly relations with the other parent, compared to 41 per cent of parents not using the CSA.
> - Parents with care using the CSA were more likely than those not using the CSA to say that their relationship had ended because they argued all the time (36 per cent compared to 24 per cent).
> - More parents with care using the CSA said violence towards them from an ex-partner was the cause of their break-up (24 per cent), compared to those not using the CSA (18 per cent).
> - 39 per cent of parents with care using the CSA had an income under £10,000 compared to 30 per cent of parents with care not using the CSA.
> - Only 23 per cent of the former were working full-time, compared to 38 per cent of the latter.
>
> 11. There is an over-simplistic view in the government's Green Paper [DWP (2011)] that, somehow, if parents were pushed down the road of voluntary arrangements, all the characteristics associated with voluntary arrangements would happen as well. The paper says, for example, that "parents report higher levels of contact between non-resident parents and their children when they have made their own maintenance arrangements". In reality, all experts agree that the associated link between contact and maintenance or vice versa, or between parental relations and the engagement of the non-resident parent with the children – is a complex one, where what is cause and what effect is difficult to discern. . . . Using financial and procedural pressure to push parents into making their own child maintenance arrangements will not necessarily result in reduced conflict and more engaged non-resident parents as the Green Paper hopes; but it will certainly make many children poorer. . . .

Yet despite critics' repeatedly observing that the assumption that family-based arrangements cause good relationships—rather than the other way around—is ill-founded,[298] government has continued to promote its charging policy and emphasize private ordering on the basis that 'family-based arrangements' will make for better relationships, including increased contact between non-resident parent and child.[299]

The next issue addressed by Gingerbread is how the power dynamics between parents may play out in the private sphere:

> 13. The key feature of a purely private agreement is that it is one voluntarily entered into by both parties, which cannot be enforced by the courts or the CSA. The government fails to acknowledge that what may seem advantageous to the paying parent about private arrangements – that they are flexible as to amount and timing and do not involve interference from the state – may be seen as potential disadvantages to the recipient parent, with day-to-day care of the child: payments are not regular, may be for lower amounts than the statutory formula, and if not paid, there is no redress. Much therefore depends on the degree of trust between the parents in question when reaching an agreement, and their mutual commitment to the best interests of their children.

[298] E.g. McKay (2014).

[299] E.g. DWP (2017a); Public Accounts Committee (2022b), Q43.

14. DWP research looking at private arrangements between separated parents prior to the involvement of the CSA noted that "overall, non-resident parents appear to wield a disproportionate amount of power over establishing financial arrangements following separation, regardless of the type of arrangement adopted" . . .

17. The proposed procedural and financial barriers to use of the statutory system would bite first on parents with care wishing to use the statutory child maintenance system. The explicit aim is to turn them towards attempting to negotiate a voluntary child maintenance arrangement with the other parent instead. At this point, this is no equivalent mechanism pushing the non-resident parent to actively engage in reaching a mutually agreeable arrangement. It is only after a parent with care has paid [an] application fee[300] that financial 'encouragement' to the non-resident parent to reach a private agreement kicks in. In effect, the charging regime proposed weakens the negotiating position of the parent with care still further; knowing of the charges a parent with care would have to pay, an unwilling non-resident parent may use them as an excuse to offer less. . . .

19. Paradoxically, even for many of those who don't use the statutory system, its existence is important. It is precisely because a parent with care can easily access the state child support service that non-resident parents are more likely to agree good private arrangements in its shadow. . . .

The new government website does acknowledge that parents' being able to communicate well and the parent with care's feeling safe dealing with—and able to rely on—the other parent may be reasons to use private ordering, and—if the facts are otherwise—to use CMS.[301] However, Gingerbread reported that the advent of CMS charges had done little to encourage agreement and created an unfair barrier for parents with care who have no choice but to apply to CMS where non-resident parents refuse to agree (any) reasonable maintenance. It also found that the application fee disproportionately impacted vulnerable individuals, such as those on low incomes and victims of domestic abuse (who should in theory have the fee waived, but who experienced inconsistent treatment).[302] The government and House of Commons Work and Pensions Select Committee disagreed on whether the CMS fees were preventing parents from applying to the statutory service. The latter concurred with Gingerbread's view; yet the government claimed that, while independent survey data showed that some parents find the application fee 'difficult to afford', there was nevertheless no evidence that this was preventing applications.[303] In fact, most CMS clients now have a fee waiver, almost all owing to domestic abuse[304]—but an unknown number may fail to secure a waiver and find the fee unaffordable.

Evidently, parents with care may be unable or unwilling, for all sorts of reasons, to secure child maintenance, and patterns of behaviour have defied government predictions. Estimates of the prevalence of different types of maintenance arrangements in the

[300] At the time Gingerbread were writing, the proposed fee for applicants not on benefits was £100. That proposal suffered a spectacular parliamentary defeat, led by former Conservative Lord Chancellor, Lord Mackay, during the Report stage on the Welfare Reform Bill 2012. The fee as introduced, £20, is still a lot for many single parents.

[301] <https://child-maintenance.service.gov.uk/get-help-arranging-child-maintenance/make-your-own-arrangement>, and following page.

[302] Gingerbread (2016).

[303] DWP (2017a), para 28. Cf House of Commons Select Committee on Work and Pensions (2017a), paras 25–9, 33.

[304] DWP (2022a), table 2.

population in 2019–20[305] record that under 20 per cent of the 2.4 million separated families in Britain (comprising 3.6 million children) had a CMS arrangement in place (nearly two-thirds of those using Direct Pay, and over a third relying on Collect & Pay). Roughly 38 per cent had a family-based arrangement. But around 44 per cent (over a million families) had no arrangement at all.[306] The situation is more dire when one looks at whether 'all' maintenance due (defined as more than 90 per cent) was provided in those cases where an arrangement was in place, or just 'some', or none. Overall (i.e. including both CMS and private arrangements) barely 1 in 3 families received 'all' maintenance due, while 27 per cent received 'some', leaving the majority receiving no *financial* support.[307] Interestingly, Direct Pay cases were most likely to see 'all' maintenance being paid (nearly two-thirds of such cases), compared with just over half of private arrangements, indicating that the private group are, contrary to expectations, less reliable. Collect & Pay cases were, perhaps unsurprisingly given their nature (but disappointingly in terms of CMS performance), least successful, only 37 per cent achieving 'full' payment, and 44 per cent none. If we combine the 'no arrangement' cases with the 'nothing paid' cases, children in around half of separated families were not receiving any of the child support owed to them. These figures are well short of government's expectations.[308] It seems highly likely that many of the some-payment and no-payment cases were ones where the non-resident parent found the required payment unaffordable.[309]

It is laudable that government does now measure, specifically, cases where 90 per cent or more of the maintenance due is paid. But the government's definition of 'effective'—or their now preferred-term 'functioning'—maintenance arrangements (those falling in the 'some' category) is rather underwhelming:

> Effective family-based arrangements . . . can be:
>
> a. Regular payments where *at least some* of the agreed amount is always/*usually* received on time and the surveyed parent thinks that the arrangement is working very well or *fairly* well.
>
> b. *Occasional* financial payments or transactions in kind (e.g. school uniform) where the surveyed parent thinks the arrangement is working very well or *fairly* well.[310] [Emphases added]

So, a parent with care may receive only some of the money some of the time, and sometimes late, and the arrangement will still be regarded by government as 'effective'. For low-income households, there is a world of difference between reliable payment in full on time and patchy, late, incomplete payment.

[305] National Audit Office (2022), fig 25, with figures for *only* 'some' and 'none' extrapolated from the data provided.

[306] The percentage will not tally to 100 per cent as they are drawn from different sources, but they provide the best impression of the overall trends in current arrangements.

[307] But it is possible that some private arrangements (19 per cent of those cases, 144,000 families) entail *non*-financial support: see fn 4 to National Audit Office (2022) fig 25.

[308] See National Audit Office (2017) for comparison with DWP projections for the destination of old CSA cases.

[309] See text to n 65.

[310] DWP (2017b), 2; see now DWP (2018b), 2.

Clearly, then, many cases are 'slipping through the net': neither using the statutory service nor coming to (effective) family-based arrangements. The failure to revise the thresholds at which the different child support rates apply, discussed at 5.4.4.b, clearly means that some non-resident parents are genuinely struggling to pay. But that does not account for all the non-payment and absence of arrangements. And the data show that vulnerable and low-income families, cases with higher levels of parental conflict, and families with disabilities are more likely than others to have no child support arrangement—that is to say, it is children in more vulnerable households and who would therefore most benefit from child support who are not receiving it.[311]

The National Audit Office attributes some of the blame to the lack of integrated support for those attempting to reach family-based arrangements.[312] Concerns have also been expressed about DWP's failure to investigate the obstacles many sub-groups of parents face in reaching agreements or applying to CMS.[313] In some cases—for example, where payment would be at the flat rate—a contribution from the non-resident parent might seem small in raw terms. Some parents with care may decide it is not worth the potential aggravation or cost to pursue that payment. But others may be left below the poverty line without it,[314] and survey data suggest that 35 per cent of parents with care without an arrangement want to have one.[315]

It is laudable to encourage agreement where agreement is attainable, but one cannot legislate with only easy cases in mind. A policy aimed to increase 'parental responsibility' and promote family autonomy may ironically mark increased abdication from that responsibility and allow imbalances of power within families to damage children's economic well-being.

House of Commons Select Committee on Work and Pensions, *Fourteenth Report of Session 2016–17: Child Maintenance Service*, HC Paper 587 (2017a), para 52

In seeking to encourage separated parents to take more responsibility for their children, the Government must not abdicate its own duties to them. Monitoring must be improved to establish the extent to which parents are adequately supported in making child maintenance choices and whether incentives intended to result in better support for children are in fact having the opposite effect. Only then can it have confidence in meeting its commitment to increase the number of children receiving maintenance.

5.7.3 LEGAL AND SOCIAL PARENTHOOD

Parents have differing views about linking child support obligations to the social relationship between the liable party and the child. Should child support liability inexorably flow from legal, rather than social, parenthood? And what links, if any, should there be between financial support and the time the child spends with each parent?

311 National Audit Office (2022), 1.23.
312 (2022), 23; see also Public Accounts Committee (2022a), rec 1.
313 National Audit Office (2022), 10; Public Accounts Committee (2022a), rec 2.
314 See Bryson et al (2013). 315 National Audit Office (2022), 1.24.

5.7.3.a Who should pay for whom?

Much opposition to the CSA 1991 has arisen from differing perceptions about who should be liable for whom, and which children should have priority call on adults' income. This issue particularly affects step-families. Establishing such new family bonds has long been recognized as an optimum way for mothers and children to improve their economic lot after breakdown of the parents' relationship.[316] Because the law places primary responsibility for children's maintenance on legal parents, some families are in a chain of households along which money is passed: the father of children in one household pays child support to children from his first relationship, while the step-father of his children in turn sends money to yet another household for children from his earlier relationship, and so on.[317] Inevitable breaks in the chain leave some individuals supporting two sets of children.[318] As Jane Millar astutely observes, 'people's lives are far messier in reality than [the Child Support Act] policy can easily allow for'.[319] Sustaining two households is a costly exercise. Mavis Maclean even asks, 'If society accepts serial partnering, should it bite the bullet and pay for the children out of public funds?'[320]

In the early days of the CSA 1991, commentators considered the likely impact of its reinforcement of obligations deriving from legal parenthood:

M. Maclean and J. Eekelaar, 'Child Support: The British Solution', (1993) 7 *International Journal of Law and the Family* 205, 226

The creation of children is now more likely to have lasting effect on the lives of men, as it always has for women. We are less certain, however, about the extent to which the scheme subordinates the social family to the biological principle. Whether this will enhance individual responsibility as is hoped is unpredictable and, in a society where so many family relationships cross households, it may not make good economic sense to shift resources across families to such an extent and with such cost.

R. Boden and M. Childs, 'Paying for Procreation: Child Support Arrangements in the UK', (1996) 4 *Feminist Legal Studies* 131, 156

This biological determinism as the basis for financial obligations indicates how heavily involved the state is in defining the private realm of the family and family obligations. In their real lives people may have assumed kinship responsibilities with regard to step-children and new partners. Yet here the state is retrospectively redetermining obligations based on biological parentage, refusing to recognise the private realm social relationships which may exist. One type of kinship, that based on biology, is privileged over that based on social or cultural foundations. The state is not reasserting the rightful role of the private realm of the family, it is imposing its own definition of that role in an attempt to relieve itself

316 Marsh and Vegeris (2004).

317 Barton (1999), 705 advises non-resident parents to join such households in order to reduce their own liability whilst their new household also enjoys that income from the other non-resident parent.

318 Davis et al (1998), 229. 319 (1996), 189. 320 Maclean with Kurczewski (2011), 54.

> of a public expenditure commitment [pre-CMOPA 2008]. One result may be an adverse effect on women whose partners are deemed to have more important financial commitments to previous children.

Research confirmed that emphasis on biological (legal) parenthood clashes with some social perceptions. As with private ordering, parents with care and non-resident parents held different views:[321]

M. Maclean and J. Eekelaar, *The Parental Obligation: A Study of Parenthood Across Households* (Oxford: Hart Publishing, 1997), 149–50

> [T]he "social" dimension of parenthood plays a far more important part in the performance of the parental role (and therefore probably in the perception of parental obligations) than the policy underscoring the Child Support Act allowed. This is seen in the following major findings: *first*, a strong association between the maintenance of contact with and support by the "outside" parent and the age of the child at separation; *secondly*, the strong negative effect which the presence or subsequent acquisition of a partner by either parent had on the maintenance of contact with and support by the "outside" parent of children with whom they had not lived, or with whom they had lived only for a relatively short time; and *thirdly*, the strong association between payment of support and the exercise of contact.
>
> However, the attitudinal survey showed that there was a strong gender factor lying behind people's perceptions of their cross-household support obligations. The fathers [non-resident parents] related their obligations much more closely to the exercise of social parenthood both by themselves and by another man who may have joined the mother's household than the mothers would have allowed. In view of such a division, we should perhaps not speak of *a* social rule, but of *two conflicting* social rules. The empirical data strongly showed the fathers acting consistently with the viewpoints they expressed in the attitudinal survey. They can be said to assume a social rule which can be formulated in three stages: (i) a prior social parenthood developed in a household can be extended beyond that household after parental separation; (ii) social parenthood so extended can create a social obligation to provide support; and (iii) such social obligations can co-exist with the social obligations associated with subsequently acquired social parenthood. Since each stage is dependent on the preceding stage for its existence, *if an initial social parenthood had not existed, or, if it had existed, if it was not extended after separation*, the men will be reluctant to view any support obligation based solely on their natural fatherhood as co-existing with subsequent social parenthood and will be inclined to assume that the obligation attaches to a man who later takes on social parenthood with respect to their child.

The researchers concluded that the implications of their findings for the scope of child support obligations were complicated:

> It could not be right to conclude that fathers . . . should have no support obligations towards the children they have procreated simply because they have not lived with them. It also

[321] See also the gendered differences in the British Social Attitudes survey on these issues: Clery et al (2021), 12–13.

> seems dangerous to say that only those fathers who have looked after their children should have continuing obligations towards them, for this seems to punish virtue. Furthermore, the mothers saw that natural fatherhood, at least when initiated in marriage, created in itself a strong support obligation and were less likely than fathers to see this as lapsing if the child acquired a stepfather. It is not surprising that mothers should place more weight on natural parenthood and fathers more weight on social parenthood because, for almost all mothers, but by no means all fathers, natural parenthood and social parenthood coincide.
>
> . . . A support obligation which accompanies or arises from social parenthood is embedded in that social parenthood; thus the payment of support can be seen as part of the relationship maintained by continued contact. But an obligation based on natural parenthood rests on the policy of instilling a sense of responsibility for individual action and equity between fathers who do and fathers who do not exercise social parenthood.

This aligns with DWP's 2021 finding that the absence of any child maintenance arrangement is more likely where non-resident parent and child have little contact, or where the parents had never had a relationship.[322]

But this re-emphasis of the obligations of legal parenthood reversed the courts' previous 'pragmatic policy' of allowing men to move on, economically, to new families, and attracted huge opposition.[323] Some fathers claimed (unsuccessfully on the facts) that their Article 8 ECHR rights were being interfered with insofar as child support obligations contributed to the break-up of second families.[324] As we saw when examining the significance of 'relevant other children' to the basic rate formula at 5.4.4.b, the CSA 1991 scheme now makes quite significant allowance for children in the non-resident parent's new family. Indeed, it may be argued that the formula goes too far to accommodate them by giving insufficient weight to the substantial material benefits that accrue to those children from living with the non-resident parent, for example sharing the fruits of his expenditure on the fixed costs of providing a home which are not increased by their presence in the household. Certainly, a clear majority of the British public (76 per cent—81 per cent of women, 72 per cent of men) agree that child maintenance should continue to be payable after he starts a new family.[325] We explore these issues further at 5.7.4 when we examine the basis of the formula.

5.7.3.b The relationship between the child's living arrangements and child support

A perennial issue in child support policy has been the link—or lack of it—made between child support liability and whether the non-resident parent spends any time with—and how much time he spends with—the child for whom he is paying.

How to deal with shared care

Overnight stays can reduce child support liability under the shared care modification to the basic rate formula and a variation can be made to reflect contact costs,[326] though some non-resident parents are unaware that liability can be varied for these contact-related expenses.[327]

[322] National Audit Office (2022), 36. [323] Diduck (2003), 181.
[324] *Burrows v United Kingdom* (App No 27558/95, ECHR) (1996). [325] Clery et al (2021), 18.
[326] See 5.4.4.f and 5.4.5.a. [327] Atkinson and McKay (2005), 113.

J. Wallbank, 'The Campaign for Change of the Child Support Act 1991: Reconstituting the "Absent" Father', (1997) 6 *Social and Legal Studies* 191, 197

This . . . can be interpreted in a number of ways: it might be viewed as consolidating the government's commitment to ensuring that parental contact with children is maintained; alternatively [it] might be considered as part of a package of changes which attempted to appease the mass of middle-class fathers who voiced their grievances about the Act in a vociferous manner; less cynically perhaps it could have been a very real attempt to respond to the problems caused by the inflexibility of the formula. Whatever the motivation . . . the change has the effect of highlighting the desirability of maintaining links between a father and his child(ren). . . .

One feared disadvantage of allowing reductions in child support to reflect overnight stays is an increase in disputes over child arrangements under the CA 1989, s 8. Non-resident parents have clear financial (as well as emotional) incentives to maximize time spent with the child overnight; parents with care conversely have financial incentives to try to minimize such arrangements.

However, as Wikeley has explained, the shared care rules—aimed to encourage contact and improve compliance in payment of child support—do not match the expectations of non-resident parents, who tend to view shared care rules as a way of reflecting their direct expenditure on the child by discounting their maintenance liability more fully than the rules permit.[328] It is unusual for care to be so fully shared that no child support liability arises at all. More commonly, even if the child stays overnight with the non-resident parent for half the nights in the year, the liability will at most be halved.

But the rules can also appear unfair to parents who provide substantial day-time care but not extensive overnight care. When *R (Plumb) v Secretary of State for Work and Pensions*[329] was decided, the then rules only permitted a deduction if the child spent at least 104 nights per annum with the non-resident parent. The child's mother—the parent with care—had a new partner and was earning £15,000 full-time, with accommodation provided. Mr Plumb was less well-off than the mother, but provided substantial amounts of care for the child as non-resident parent: there were frequent overnight stays (but fewer than 104 nights) and considerable after-school and weekend day-care and meals—an estimated 1,600 hours and 260 meals per annum. Despite all this, his liability could not be reduced. Even now, his deduction would be based exclusively on the fact of overnight stays: save in those cases where it can be argued that the parents provide equal care, no account is taken of each parent's level of care for or expenditure on the child, including on costly items such as clothing. So non-resident parents whose child stays overnight as often as Mr Plumb's but who provided *no* day-care or evening meals would receive the same deduction as him.

It is questionable whether this rough-and-ready mechanism produces just results for either parent, even putting aside Mr Plumb's complaint. The marginal costs (e.g. on meals) saved by parents with care on those nights when the child is with the non-resident parent may be dwarfed by the reduction in the maintenance they receive as a result of the shared care rules. But similarly, the additional fixed costs to the non-resident parent of having to provide accommodation adequate to have the child stay overnight may far exceed the

[328] Wikeley (2006a), 313–14. [329] [2002] EWHC 1125.

deduction he is granted, making such stays impossible for low-income parents.[330] Non-resident parents are not assisted by the fact that social security rules operate on the basis that there is just one carer (the receiving parent in these cases), so the paying parent gets no state support in meeting these additional costs.[331] A daytime-hours rule was rejected on the basis that hours could not be reliably counted.[332] But it may not be possible to count nights much more reliably, particularly on the boundaries between bands, where one night more or fewer makes a big difference.

The issue of shared care is regularly debated. One group in particular, Families Need Fathers, have argued that the shared care rules should be abolished in favour of new rules that better recognize and promote shared parenting and the costs incurred by 'non-resident' parents,[333] and two influential public bodies advocated no liability in cases where care is shared 50:50.[334] That is currently only the case, as explained at 5.4.4.f, where the parents are providing qualitatively equal day-to-day care—not based only on counting overnight stays—such that there is no non-resident parent at all.[335]

It is doubtful whether extinguishing liability entirely in equally shared care cases is right. Where the parents have more or less equal financial resources, such that both are able to provide similar standards of living for the child, that outcome makes sense. However, more commonly one parent has greater resources than the other, in which case—even where care is fully shared—there is a strong case for some resource-transfer between the two households, in order to share the economic burden of child-care more equitably between the parents. Indeed, as we discuss at 5.7.4, where (unusually) a person with care has greater resources than a non-resident parent with whom the child spends time, arguably the former parent should pay maintenance to the latter.

The irrelevance of contact

The shared care rules and contact-cost variation aside, the law makes no link between contact and child support. The non-resident parent must pay child support at the prescribed rate whether or not he has any sort of contact with the child. No discount is applied where the parent with care refuses to allow the non-resident parent to spend time (or otherwise have contact), with the child, even if she is breaching a court order in doing so. Whether the non-resident parent has contact is a factor expressly not to be taken into account when CMS decides whether the grant a variation (see 5.4.5.b). A father's *failure* to pay maintenance is not given substantial weight in courts' decisions to grant parental responsibility (in the strict sense), at least where he has otherwise demonstrated devotion to the child.[336] And it was held in *Re B (Contact: Child Support)*[337] that it would be inappropriate when making orders for *contact* to consider the impact of different arrangements on child support liability, in particular under the shared care rules:[338] that would introduce a factor unrelated to the child's welfare into the CA 1989 decision-making process. Stephen Gilmore has criticized that decision, arguing that—reflecting a wider trend[339]—it neglects parents' rights

[330] Social Security Advisory Committee (2019), 23. [331] Ibid, 11. [332] DSS (1999), para 7.20.

[333] Families Need Fathers (2007). Note also that child benefit and child tax credit cannot be shared. See also Gilmore (2007).

[334] Henshaw (2006); House of Commons Select Committee on Work and Pensions (2007).

[335] In theory, the court would have full jurisdiction here, there being no 'qualifying child', but it is doubtful—given the high levels of cooperation required to operate a fully shared care system—that parents in such a case would litigate; they might, of course, transfer resources between households voluntarily.

[336] *Re H (Parental Responsibility: Maintenance)* [1996] 1 FLR 867.

[337] [2006] EWCA Civ 1574. [338] See 5.4.4.f. [339] See 8.4.4.

to respect for family life with their children under Article 8 ECHR. While those rights may frequently be outweighed by the child's interests, they cannot be simply ignored. If a decision about contact so increases the non-resident parent's child support liability that exercising contact becomes problematic, an Article 8 issue arises and cannot be sidelined as 'irrelevant'.[340]

The lack of link has been debated several times owing to non-resident fathers' frustration with cases where mothers (to their eyes) unreasonably refuse contact. The Family Justice Review team initially considered that the court should have the option, if in the child's best interests, to alter or suspend child support payments as a way of enforcing contact orders. But following its consultation exercise, they recommended no change, concluding that it:

> would be wrong to risk strengthening the view that it is acceptable not to pay maintenance when there are contact difficulties or for that matter, that contact can be withheld when maintenance is not being paid.[341]

The Review felt any other approach could encourage litigation and undermine private arrangements. Douglas et al expand on that concern:

G. Douglas and Members of the Network on Family, Regulation and Society, 'Contact is not a Commodity to be Bartered for Money', (2011) 41 *Family Law* 491, 495

> Far from promoting private resolution the result would be to trigger recourse either to the child support system, or to the courts. Issues of 'fault' as well as 'mere' matters of whether contact did or did not take place, and why, would have to be examined. The law would have to prescribe what kinds of contact arrangements would 'count' for the purposes of a reduction (direct only or to include indirect forms?); it would have to determine how much contact would be required to trigger a reduction (would the loss of one day per month suffice to do so, or would the contact have to be more than de minimis?); it would have to set out whether a single breach of contact would trigger a reduction or whether repeat breaches of the arrangement would be required; and it would have to decide what to do if the evidence showed that the refusal of contact was the child's decision rather than that of the parent. It can be seen that the issue raises precisely the kinds of emotionally-charged and highly conflictual matters that the courts and government have sought to hard to remove from the arena of post-separation parenting.

But not all parents agree with the formal legal position. A large-scale survey of CSA clients made the following findings:

[340] Gilmore (2007). The argument in *Logan v United Kingdom* (App No 24875/94, ECHR) (1996) that this violated Art 8 failed the facts.

[341] Norgrove (2011), 171.

N. Wikeley et al, *National Survey of Child Support Agency Clients*, DWP Research Report No 152 (Leeds: Corporate Document Service, 2001), 153

A question which underpins much of the discussion concerning the expectation that NRPs [non-resident parents] pay significant sums in child support concerns the appropriateness of requiring such payments in circumstances where the father (as it usually is) has little, if any, contact with his children and so does not derive any benefit from his 'investment'. . . . [It] is important to acknowledge that a survey methodology cannot possibly do justice to the complexities of this issue.

As one might have expected, NRPs were more likely to assert as an absolute principle that payment of 'full' maintenance should entitle the NRP to have regular contact with his children. Only 16 per cent dissented. A majority of PWCs [parents with care] likewise seemed willing to sign up to this as an absolute principle, although 25 per cent equivocated, suggesting (wisely) that the answer to this question would depend on the particular circumstances of the case.

We gave this theme a somewhat sharper edge by asking whether, in circumstances where the NRP is denied contact with his children, he should pay less maintenance. (This, needless to say, is to oversimplify the 'contact' issue, certainly as it would be perceived by many parents with care.) The question nonetheless exposed sharp differences between the attitudes of NRPs and PWCs . . . NRPs were much more likely to assert that a denial of contact should lead to a reduced maintenance obligation. Over 50 per cent supported this proposition without any qualification. Less than 20 per cent of PWCs took the same view.

Researchers have found correlations between frequency of contact and both payment rates and parents' perception of the child support system as fair.[342] However, Maclean and Eekelaar concluded that fathers do not exercise contact *because* they are paying support—the status of the previous relationship between the parents is more important both to contact being exercised and child support being paid.[343] Much of the British public also appears to link contact and child support in determining how much child support should be paid, particularly where the parent with care is unreasonably refusing contact and, interestingly, where the non-resident parent is unreasonably refusing to see the child.[344] Moreover, survey data indicate that (whatever the law may say) contact and child support *are* in fact linked in many families, with very high levels of non-payment amongst fathers who have no contact with their children.[345] As ever, what happens on the ground does not necessarily correspond with what the law says ought to happen. The move to private ordering may exacerbate non-payment amongst this group, as well as other contact-related departures from what the CMS scheme would prescribe, particularly for 'shared care'.

[342] Wikeley et al (2001); Davis and Wikeley (2002); McKay (2014), who also notes a link with social class: contact and child support payment both higher in middle-class families.

[343] (1997), 128; cf Bradshaw et al (1999) and Wilson (2006) on the complex social inter-relationship of contact and maintenance.

[344] Bryson et al (2015); see also Clery et al (2021), 14, 18, finding a gendered difference of view.

[345] Poole et al (2013), table 20; National Audit Office (2022), 36.

5.7.4 THE POLICY CHOICES BEHIND THE FORMULA

One of the most complex but important issues in child support is the formula for calculating liability. It is easy to lose sight of the fact that there are policy questions behind all the maths, as Ellman et al have observed:

> The mechanical and precise nature of the support calculation creates the illusion that the numbers reflect some objective, scientific fact, when they actually reflect important policy choices about which people may differ.[346]

The formula design partly depends on whether the aim is to achieve 'collective justice' between the parents (and child) or 'distributive justice' between parents and state, the parents compensating the state for benefits paid for the child.[347] The latter type of scheme might not be responsive to facts that might be relevant to achieving justice between the private individuals involved: for example, capital settlements already made for the benefit of children, contact costs, obligations to new families, and resources of the parent with care's new partner.[348] The level of support would evidently also be fixed by reference to the costs the state was trying to recoup. The child support scheme is clearly no longer concerned with the state's expenditure; the focus is on justice as between the private parties. But what conception of justice? What is it fair to require a non-resident parent to pay, and how should that be measured? Commentators identify two principal types of formula.[349]

- Cost-sharing: the cost of raising the child should be shared between the parents. This type of formula requires answers to two basic questions: (i) what are those costs—are we concerned only with basic necessities, or is a more subjective assessment of the child's needs to be used, having regard to the parties' standard of living; and (ii) how should they be shared—equally between the parents, or on some other basis, for example in proportions reflecting their respective incomes? A cost-sharing model must be careful not to underestimate the 'true' costs of child-rearing or to overestimate either parent's ability to contribute towards these.
- Resource-sharing: the child should share a given proportion of the non-resident parent's resources. Most generously, this might aim to achieve equivalent household standards of living for non-resident parent and child, regardless of whether that involves support being paid at a level which exceeds the needs-related costs of raising the child, however measured. Less generously, it might be capped at some level of parental income so as not to extend too far beyond a needs-based measure.

The rationale of the current statutory formula, calculated as 'fraction of gross income per child', is less than clear and certainly open to criticism.[350] The percentages of non-resident parental income that are payable were apparently based on evidence not about the cost of raising children (as such), but rather on evidence about *expenditure* on children by intact families. It was suggested that intact families on average spend around 30 per cent of their joint net income on a child; and that therefore the non-resident parent should pay half of that

346 Ellman et al (2014), 295. 347 Maclean and Eekelaar (1997), 42.
348 Ibid, 39 and 42; Davis et al (1998), 217.
349 Eekelaar and Maclean (1986), ch 7; Parker (1991); Wikeley (2006a), ch 1.
350 Fortin (2009b), 347–8.

now the family is separated—15 per cent under the net scheme rules, 12 per cent in the new gross scheme.[351] Ellman et al identified an immediate problem: if 30 per cent of *joint* income was spent directly on the child while the family was intact, should that not mean (assuming similar earnings) each parent continuing to contribute 30 per cent of their own income post-separation to ensure the equivalent level of expenditure now?[352] However, there is a more profound difficulty with the notion that child support levels for separated families should be based on expenditure on children in *intact* families, involving many policy choices. For starters, what counts as 'expenditure on children'?

I. Ellman et al, 'Child Support Judgments: Comparing Public Policy to the Public's Policy', (2014) 28 *International Journal of Law, Policy and the Family* 274, 295–6

The standard method . . . imagines a hypothetical childless couple at some income level, and then asks how much *more* they would need to spend to maintain their living standard when a child or children are added to their household. But additional expenditures occasioned by the new child do not, of course, include things the parents also spent money on when childless, even though many of these continuing expenditures benefit the newly added children. So the cost of any changes in housing required to maintain the same living standard—perhaps, for example, the additional cost of a larger home—counts as an expenditure on children, but the base cost of having a home in the first place does not. Such a system thus assumes the father should share, for example, in the additional cost of the extra bedroom, but not in the cost of the kitchen, bathroom, or living room, since the childless couples already had those. Additions to the food or clothing budget are counted, but not the cost of a car (except to the extent it is greater after children than before, which is not especially likely).

In short, the intact family makes many expenditures that confer benefits on children that are not included in the standard child expenditure estimates upon which most support guidelines are based, because they are 'joint expenditures' that benefit *everyone* in the household. The necessary premise of such a calculation is that the parents are equally capable, after separation, of providing the foundational living standard that the intact family enjoyed before separation, so that the child support system need only address how parents should share the *additional* expenditures the couple incurs by having a child. But where the mother earns less than the father, this premise is wrong. Providing her with the father's share of the cost of an extra bedroom does not help much if, now on her own, she cannot afford the rest of the home to which it is attached. A spousal maintenance order, if there were one, could deal with that discrepancy; a child support schedule based on estimates of 'child-only' expenditures, excluding joint expenditures that benefit children along with other household members, cannot.

There is no problem in focusing on the extra marginal costs of the child where the parents earn about the same amount: those parents are in similar financial positions post-separation, similarly equipped to meet their basic fixed costs. Not so where they earn at different levels:

[351] DSS (1999), para 2.5, citing Middleton et al (1997), para 16.

[352] Ellman et al (2014), fn 28.

The lower-income parent [then] suffers a more precipitous drop in living standard from the separation than does the higher-income parent. And as the lower-income parent is most often also the mother with whom the child primarily lives, that steeper fall becomes a matter that the child support law should reasonably be expected to address. Of course, income transfers between parents through the child support system are not the only potential source of assistance for the low-income mother, and can in any event provide little real help in the common case in which the father is also low-income. Benefits provided through public programmes necessarily play a critical role. But they are alone often inadequate, and are not intended to and in fact cannot provide children of higher-income fathers with the amenities these children were accustomed to and some of which, at least, their fathers are still able to provide after separation.

A system requiring the father to pay his share of just the child-only expenditures might be explained as maintaining the status quo: he is then contributing, after separation, precisely the same amount toward his children that he did before separation. But it is the same amount of only the additional 'child-only' expenditures. He retains all he contributed to the foundational joint expenditures, even though these must be duplicated after separation when the parents need two kitchens rather than one. In effect, this system shields the higher-income father from contributing his share to the duplicated costs that are the inevitable consequence of separation, leaving the lower-income mother to bear them on her own.

It is worth contrasting the basis of the child support formula and limited nature of the remedy (periodical payments)—which makes no provision for the 'fixed' costs incurred by the parent with care in providing the child's principal home—with the discretion under the CA 1989, Sch 1 (in particular), for courts to make orders providing a home for the child and parent, together with (in high-value cases) a carer's allowance. Such orders can help primary carers to meet their fixed costs,[353] though only, of course, if there are resources available to do so.

Meanwhile, under the child support formula, 'relevant other children' living with the father are amply catered for by what he spends on his own home, as well as being protected by the reduced formula applied in such cases (see 5.4.4.b where 'relevant other child'). It may be asked whether they are over-provided for—certainly, their situation may be more comfortable than that of the qualifying child where the non-resident father has a higher income than the parent with care.

Equally, however, in other cases, the current formula's failure to take into account the income of the parent with care or any new partner she has may mean some non-resident parents are paying more than is fair. (And note also the basic concern outlined at 5.4.4.b regarding the failure to revise the current child support rates in line with increased costs of living.) Currently, non-resident parents must pay regardless of their economic standing relative to the parent with care, and so regardless of whether the parent with care needs any payment to help cover her household expenditure.[354] Such cases may be few,[355] and disregarding the income of parents with care may act as a work incentive, thus increasing the income of the child's household. But non-resident parents may regard this failure to consider the parent with care's household income as unfair, and the attitude survey indicates that the British public shares those misgivings.

[353] On concerns regarding the 'hidden alimony' effect of this, see Ellman and Braver (2011).

[354] Douglas (2004a), 206. [355] Wikeley (2000), 822.

Ellman et al deduced a set of 'principles' from the public's responses to their large-scale attitude survey. That what the non-resident parent should have pay: (i) should be dependent on both parents' incomes; (ii) should—all else being equal—increase with the non-resident parent's income, not just in raw monetary terms, but as a percentage of the non-resident parent's income; (iii) should—all else being equal—be reduced (in raw and percentage terms) as the parent with care's income increases; and (iv) should be aimed not just at lifting the child from poverty, but should continue to increase with the non-resident parent's income so as to allow the child to benefit from that higher standard of living.[356] A formula based on these criteria would look very different from that currently used in English law.

5.7.5 RULES OR DISCRETION?

Child support law provides a powerful example of family law operated on the basis of rules, in preference to discretionary decision-making. This is a theme that we introduced at 1.2.2 and on which readers will find further materials in the online resources. Many jurisdictions have adopted more rule-based child support laws, some applied by courts rather than by an administrative body.[357] There are arguments both ways.

Discretion claims some advantages over rule-based systems, certainly as manifested by the original, highly complex CSA 1991 formula before variations were introduced:

Phillips v Peace [1996] 2 FCR 237 (Fam Div), 239

JOHNSON J:

It is of the essence of the policy underlying the Child Support Act 1991 that child support is to be assessed according to a mathematical formula which is to be applied rigorously, seemingly without any significant element of discretion to cater for the needs of a child in the circumstances of the child with whom I am concerned. . . . This is quite contrary to the practice of the court which for generations, in seeking to assess entitlements to financial support for former spouses or children, has sought to achieve a result which is fair, just and reasonable, based on the realities and the practicalities.

Mostyn J has been scathing about the statutory scheme, in a long-running case that highlighted the repeal of the 'lifestyle' and 'assets' variation grounds, noting ministerial remarks recorded in a Gingerbread report:[358]

Green v Adams (No 2) [2017] EWFC 52

MOSTYN J:

24. . . . [T]he minister [said] that "[the child maintenance scheme] does not attempt to provide a unique, bespoke solution in respect of the care of each child whose parents live apart,

356 Ellman et al (2014), 292.
357 E.g. in Canada and the United States, where judges use the formulae/guidelines: see Rogerson (2014).
358 Gingerbread (2017).

as it would be prohibitively expensive and time-consuming to do so." This is dispiriting. The scheme should surely strive to provide a just solution in all cases; for the few as well as the many. Justice surely should not be sacrificed on the altar of managerial efficiency. Ease of administration surely does not furnish an objectively reasonable justification for a process that allows a multi-millionaire father to get away with paying child support for his son of a mere £7 per week.

But court-based discretion carries disadvantages too:

G. Davis, S. Cretney, and J. Collins, *Simple Quarrels* (Oxford: OUP, 1994), 256

. . . along with discretion goes *uncertainty: the elevation of professional judgment* (because only lawyers, who deal with these matters all the time, have the necessary knowledge and skill to weigh up the competing factors); *an almost limitless need for information about family finances* (because discretion, if it is to be justified at all, has to be based on a minute examination of differing circumstances); and *the demand for large amount of professional time* (because the discretion, if it is not to be exercised arbitrarily, takes time). In practice, of course, there is a limit to the amount of lawyer-time which divorcing couples can purchase, and also a limit to the amount which the State is prepared to support. Court-time is likewise expensive and has, somehow, to be rationed.

As we see in chapter 6, similar arguments play out in relation to financial remedies between spouses on divorce, where child support is one part of the wider economic package:

E. Jackson et al, 'Financial Support on Divorce: The Right Mixture of Rules and Discretion?', (1993) 7 *International Journal of Law and the Family* 230, 231–2

In any child support system which depends on discretion, there will tend to be public dissatisfaction if one father finds out that he pays twice as much as his neighbour, or one mother discovers that she receives half as much as hers. In a situation where dissatisfied payers can and do just cease payments without much fear of recourse, it is important to minimize public mistrust. In addition to the problems of inconsistency, a system of discretion will make it very difficult for lawyers to predict the outcome of an adjudication. This may mean that more couples will fight full adversarial battles, and have to bear increasing legal costs and the strain of protracted litigation. Alternatively they may accept unsatisfactory settlements in preference to the high-cost, high-risk strategy of litigation. . . .

On the other hand, taking decisions more formulaically creates problems too:

It might be thought that, in making the 'ancillary' matters part of an administrative process, divorce can cease to be a time for conflict and instead simply be the civilized ordering of a couple's affairs. Nonetheless, the rush to simplicity and certainty may underestimate the complexity of the issues to be resolved and fail to do justice to them. The divorce represents a substantial upheaval for the spouses and their children, and it takes a great deal of time to work out how their domestic arrangements should be restructured. Indeed, there are so many complex issues that it is difficult to envisage a formula that could encompass them all. Most couples just want to sort out a workable solution and not become embroiled in protracted legal battles. If thoroughness is sacrificed in the interests of administrative efficiency, simplicity and cost-cutting, problems may not be addressed adequately at the time of the divorce and may re-emerge later with extra complications.

. . . As family law continues to move towards interlocking systems, rules, and formulae, it might be timely to question if there should be limits to these trends. What, if anything, is worth retaining from a discretion-based system? Can the trend towards rules go too far? To what extent does discretion . . . allow divorcing people to be flexible, responsive to need, and open to compromise? Will formula-based approaches to maintenance gain in predictability, generosity, and consistency but at a cost of greater rigidity and an inability to make adjustments to the overall financial package?

Even though discretion may not facilitate the resolution of disputes without the need for legal representation and may lead to inconsistencies, it might nevertheless be fairer for the decision-maker to examine each case individually before deciding how much this father should pay.

Rule-based systems are not a panacea, and discretion is not perfect. But we do not have to choose between them. Rule-based systems can be more or less complex, demanding more or less information for their operation.[359] There are some (limited) discretionary components to the current CMS scheme, and the emphasis on family-based arrangements now affords increased scope for 'discretion', albeit exercised by the parties and not necessarily in accordance with legal criteria. Yet there is also growing interest in England and Wales in moving financial remedies on divorce towards a more formulaic model, as we note at 6.8.1. Getting the balance between 'individualized justice' and 'average justice'[360] right is a difficult exercise.

5.8 CONCLUSION

Child support provides a valuable case study for several key debates in contemporary family law. The nature of family obligations—should responsibility attach to legal status, or to the actual performance of social family roles? The relationship between family and state—should financial obligations be for families to agree wherever possible, or should the state regularly intervene? Family law techniques—are family disputes better dealt with by way of wide discretion or more certain rules, and by courts or administrative agencies? Ironically, the figure who often fades into the background is the child. What combination of private law obligations and state-based provision would best meet children's needs, and what *rights* of children should we recognize here?

[359] For criticism of the original CSA scheme, see Horton (1995); cf influential Canadian support guidelines: Rogerson (2020).

[360] Rogerson (2002), 6.

ONLINE RESOURCES

Questions, suggestions for further reading, and supplementary materials for this chapter (including updates on developments in this area of family law since this book was published) may be found in the online resources at **www.oup.com/he/familytcm5e.**

6

FINANCIAL REMEDIES ON DIVORCE

CENTRAL ISSUES

1. English law has no special regime of property ownership *during* marriage and civil partnership. However, on relationship breakdown, spouses and civil partners can apply for extensive financial remedies.
2. On divorce/dissolution, judicial separation, and nullity, the courts have wide discretionary powers under the Matrimonial Causes Act 1973 (MCA 1973) and Civil Partnership Act 2004 (CPA 2004) to make financial orders (formerly known as 'ancillary relief') adjusting the parties' property rights and requiring ongoing financial provision between them in order to achieve a 'fair' result, regardless of property ownership.
3. *Miller; McFarlane* [2006] UKHL 24 identified three elements of a 'fair' outcome: meeting need; compensating for 'relationship-generated disadvantage'; and equal sharing. The statute requires that first consideration be given to the welfare of minor children of the family. It is usually possible only to meet the parties' needs, insofar as limited resources allow.
4. The 'clean break' principle encourages the courts where appropriate to terminate ongoing financial ties between the parties, for example by ordering one-off capital transfers and no periodical payments.
5. The law is ambivalent about private ordering in this sphere. Parties can make agreements binding on divorce only by converting them into an order by consent and cannot by agreement deprive each other of the right to apply to court. But a court invited to grant orders inconsistent with an agreement will have regard to the agreement's terms and may determine that fairness requires that its order should reflect what the agreement provides.
6. Reform remains a live issue following a Law Commission project. Key debates concern the basis and scope of the remedies that should be available, the proper balance between certainty and flexibility in the law, and between protection of the economically vulnerable and party autonomy.

6.1 INTRODUCTION

Media coverage of financial settlements on divorce provides a distorted impression of the real world. The media relate stories about the wives of premiership footballers, entrepreneurs, and rock stars seeking multi-million pound 'pay-outs'. The reality for thousands of families affected by divorce each year is 'just about keeping heads above water'. Divorcing couples, some with the aid of solicitors and/or mediators, and in the last resort the courts, must conjure as beneficial (or as least detrimental) an outcome as possible for all parties from limited assets. We discussed in chapter 5 the various financial remedies for children whose parents live apart, whatever the legal status of the parents' relationship. Our focus here is on remedies for the benefit of the adults at the end of formalized relationships. We address the very different position of cohabitants and parties to other non-formalized relationships in chapter 7.

Spouses and civil partners have access to powerful financial remedies on divorce/dissolution, enabling the courts to adjust property rights and order ongoing financial provision, regardless of the parties' property rights.[1] These financial orders[2] are still sometimes referred to as 'ancillary relief', reflecting a time when the main issue would be whether the marriage should be dissolved, and the grant of financial orders was a subsidiary consequence.[3] The main dispute is now more likely to concern the financial settlement, since spouses can no longer challenge the breakdown of their marriage in court.

6.2 THE SOCIAL CONTEXT: THE FAMILY ECONOMY

Economic problems on relationship breakdown, marital or not, are most acutely felt where the parties are parents.[4] Many couples adopt specialized roles within the family economy, at least for some periods of their relationship, one party concentrating on breadwinning and paying the mortgage, while the other gives up or limits paid employment (whether for a few years or longer -term) to look after home and family. The issue presents in a starkly gendered form in mixed-sex relationships, but similar role divisions may also occur between same-sex couples.

Women's employment patterns, particularly following motherhood, have changed markedly over the last 40 years, as increasing numbers of women, including mothers, have entered the workforce. Over 70 per cent of women in the UK aged 16–64 are now employed,[5] including 75.6 per cent of mothers of dependent children.[6] Social attitudes have also moved markedly away from support for traditional gender roles.[7] But it is essential to go behind those headlines and look at the detail of couples' behaviour. In 2022, 34.4 per cent of women with dependent children worked part-time, compared with 6.3 per cent of men with dependent children.[8] Although the Covid-19 pandemic catalysed a trend towards working from home,[9] more female than male employees have opted for flexible working patterns.[10] This can enable work to be balanced alongside child-care, but as research has found, can also reinforce traditional gendered divisions of domestic labour.[11] Indeed, statistics show

[1] Cf *Tee v Hillman* [1999] 2 FLR 613; *Miller Smith v Miller Smith* [2009] EWCA Civ 1297.
[2] Family Procedure Rules 2010 (FPR 2010), r 2.3. [3] Cretney (2003a), 396, 402.
[4] Hale (2004); Douglas (2018b). [5] ONS (2022k), table 1a. [6] ONS (2022e), 3.
[7] Attar Taylor and Scott (2018); Albakri et al (2019) 12. [8] ONS (2022k), table 1a.
[9] ONS (2022e), 14. [10] Ibid, 12. [11] Chung and Booker (2022).

the persistence of such inequalities. While 580,000 women (664,000 men) were unemployed from July to September 2022,[12] more than 5.33 million working age women (3.62 million working age men) were 'economically inactive'. The most common reason for women's economic inactivity was that they were looking after family or home: 30 per cent of economically inactive working age women (1.6 million) gave that reason in 2022, compared with only 8 per cent of men (302,000).[13] Moreover, as Figure 6.1 shows, the younger the youngest child, the less likely the mother is to work. The child's age has no impact on fathers' employment.[14] Given these data, and the gender pay gap,[15] it is unsurprising that general population survey data for England and Wales show that wives who later divorce contributed only 36 per cent of the combined household income during marriage.[16] Yet UK wives on average are still responsible for most of the unpaid work in their households.[17] Though men have undertaken 18 per cent more unpaid child-care in 2022 than in 2014–15, women consistently spend considerably more time on child-care and housework;[18] worth an estimated £1.24 trillion to the UK economy.[19]

Some parents positively choose a traditional division of roles. However, for mothers who want to play a greater role in the workforce, employment-related rights are crucial. Employment legislation has become increasingly family-friendly and registered child-care places have increased, though complaints about the lack of accessible and affordable child-care (beyond the initial free entitlement) persist.[20] However, not enough has been done to enable and encourage *men* to shoulder more caring responsibilities, achieving better

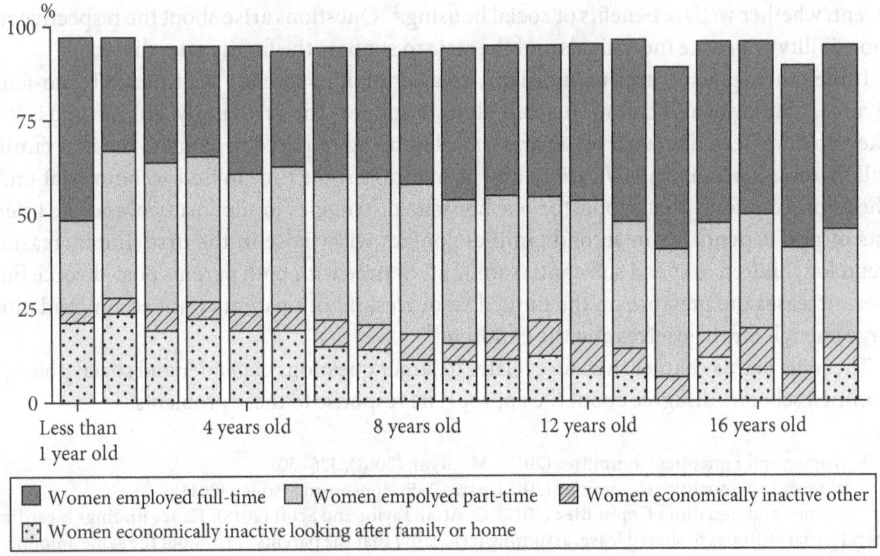

Figure 6.1 Percentage of mothers living with dependent children by economic activity by single year of age of youngest dependent child, April–June 2021, UK

Source: Reproduced from ONS (2022e), by Crown copyright ©.

[12] ONS (2022k), table 1a. [13] Ibid. [14] ONS (2022e), 5.
[15] Women and Equalities Committee (2017), para 8; Costa Dias et al (2018).
[16] Fisher and Low (2016), table 1. [17] McFall et al (2012), 7–8; Scott and Dex (2009).
[18] ONS (2022e) 15. [19] ONS (2018b). [20] DFE (2017).

work/life balance for both parents.[21] Many men want to work fewer hours to care for children, but encounter legal, economic, and cultural obstacles to doing so.[22] New initiatives, such as rules for shared parental leave introduced in 2015, have had little impact thanks to various structural limitations with the rules and workplace culture that discourage take-up by fathers.[23] Unlike some other jurisdictions, English law has no 'daddy quota' that has to be taken by the father or lost.[24] Until men are equally able to take time off work to care for children, the burden of juggling work and family responsibilities is likely to rest predominantly with women, both during and after marriage and other relationships.[25]

So although far more women are working now than in the 1960s, men's and women's engagement with the labour market remain very different, not least given most women's primary role in undertaking unpaid caring responsibilities in the family. While the relationship is intact, all will usually appear to be well: the couple have a home, an income, and may be accumulating savings and pensions for later life that will support both spouses. The fact that technically each party owns their 'separate property' (see 6.3) and has no claim over the other's assets may not seem to matter. But relationship breakdown exposes the economic vulnerabilities created by role-specialization, particularly for those who worked unpaid in the home. Despite the existence of the special statutory remedies discussed in this chapter, the negative economic impact of divorce is often great and often gendered.[26] With reduced earning capacity, reduced personal pension[27] and other savings of their own, and often with continuing child-care obligations that limit opportunities to maximize earning capacity, many women (and the children living with them) experience substantial drops in their standard of living.[28] At least one party may often have to rely on state support to some extent, whether welfare benefits or social housing.[29] Questions arise about the respective responsibility of private individuals and the state to support the family after divorce.[30]

If the other spouse wants to 'move on', an aspiration apparently legitimized by no-fault divorce,[31] it may be difficult for (usually) him to support the first family. His income is less likely to have been damaged by separation,[32] but being required to support the first family will increase his financial *obligations* and he may take some time to find accommodation.[33] The family economy that supported one household struggles to support two, and the interests of new dependants in second families conflict with those in the first. The increasing trend for children to spend substantial amounts of time with both parents post-divorce further increases the pressure on the limited resources, if both parents want accommodation large enough for themselves and the children.[34]

The topic of this chapter therefore relates to larger questions of gender and social policy.[35] Feminist scholars disagree about the appropriate response to these problems:

[21] Women and Equalities Committee (2017); McGlynn (2001), 326–30.

[22] Women and Equalities Committee (2017), paras 3–5; Hobson and Fahlén (2011).

[23] Women and Equalities Committee (2017). Cf Attar Taylor and Scott (2018), 12: see findings regarding liberal social attitudes to shared leave, assuming (critically) that the parents earn about the same amount.

[24] See Hobson and Fahlén (2011).

[25] Indeed, data suggest that when both men and women with dependent children are employed, women spend more time on all work combined (including paid work, unpaid child-care, and unpaid household work): ONS (2022e), 2.

[26] Rake (2000); Fisher and Low (2009), (2016), (2018b). [27] Price (2009); Douglas (2018b), 115–16.

[28] Fisher and Low (2009), (2016), (2018b).

[29] In 2007–8, 34 per cent of entrants to the social rented sector who had previously owned their home cited divorce/separation as their reason for moving: DCLG (2009), 108, table 4.5.

[30] Ferguson (2008); Miles (2011a). [31] Symes (1985), 52–3.

[32] Fisher and Low (2009), (2016), (2018b). [33] Perry et al (2000). [34] See chapter 11.

[35] See Herring (2005a); Miles (2011a).

J. Carbone, 'Feminism, Gender and the Consequences of Divorce', in M. Freeman (ed), *Divorce: Where Next?* (Ashgate: Dartmouth, 1996), 181–2

As a descriptive undertaking, there is near unanimity, both within feminist circles and without, as to the role of gender in accounting for the economic consequences of divorce. Women generally, for reasons attributable to gender, earn less than men. Marriage increases the gap as married women, who bear the overwhelming responsibility for child-rearing, earn less than single women, while married men increase their earnings over single men. At divorce, mothers overwhelmingly retain physical custody of their children, and the pressures of single parenthood interfere with labour force participation . . . Accordingly, divorce almost inevitably lowers the standard of living of the custodial family and, for systemic reasons related to gender, leaves the vast majority of divorced women in a financially more precarious position than their former husbands.

Despite the near unanimous embrace of this picture of divorce, there is considerable disagreement, both within feminist circles and without, as to the implications. The disagreement starts with the central feature of the gendered division of family responsibilities: what Mary Becker describes as mothers' greater, and qualitatively different, attachment to their children . . .

Nonetheless, feminists have been slow to call attention to this central difference in men and women's approach to family. When feminist scholarship does acknowledge it, it is without agreement on cause and effect. And although the source of women's greater attachment to children may well be irrelevant to the determination of public policy, feminists are no closer to agreement on possible solutions. 'Liberal' feminists believe that it is the gendered division of labour itself that ensures women's subordination to men and that, unless there is genuinely shared responsibility for childbearing, equality is impossible. 'Cultural feminists' or 'feminists of difference' believe that the principal problem is not that women disproportionately care for children, but that society so undervalues child-rearing. In between are many feminists who believe that equality requires both greater sharing of the responsibility for child-rearing *and* greater support for the child-rearing role.

At least in the matrimonial/civil partnership context, there are financial remedies available to help share and mitigate the economic consequences of divorce. We shall see in chapter 7 how very limited is the law's ability to deal with the equivalent problem in cases involving cohabitants and other non-formalized relationships.

6.3 A BRIEF HISTORY OF FINANCIAL REMEDIES ON DIVORCE

Since the late nineteenth century, marriage has had no impact on spouses' property rights during marriage: unlike jurisdictions that operate systems of 'community property', each spouse is—as a matter of *law*—equally free during marriage to acquire their own 'separate' property, independently of the other. However, as Katherine O'Donovan put it, 'So long as equality remains a formal notion, like the Ritz hotel which is open to all, structural obstacles will prevent those for whom opportunities are opened from taking advantage of them.'[36]

[36] O'Donovan (1985), 167.

Despite the increasing numbers of wives and mothers who engage in paid employment, discussed at 6.2 above, full gender equality is some way off and so these problems remain, their detrimental impact on women (in particular) exposed by relationship breakdown. This legal and socio-economic context makes financial remedies on divorce so important.

> **ONLINE RESOURCES**
>
> For related information about the history of marriage, its impact on property, and husbands' related common law duty to maintain and provide a home for their wives *during* marriage, see the supplement to this chapter in the online resources at **www.oup.com/he/familytcm5e.**

The history of financial remedies on divorce is closely related to the history of divorce itself.[37] Fault-based divorce law pre-1969 was accompanied by fault-based financial provision:

Law Commission, *The Financial Consequences of Divorce: The Basic Policy*, Law Com No 103 (London: HMSO, 1980)

> 13. Prior to 1971 . . . the main features of the law governing the financial consequences of divorce were based on the assumption that (subject perhaps to the exception that a wife who was technically "guilty" might nevertheless expect some financial provision) the function of divorce was to give relief where a wrong had been done. The right and duty of maintenance was related to the performance of reciprocal maintenance obligations; a husband who was at fault should continue to support his wife, but conversely it would be unjust to require a husband who had "performed substantially all his matrimonial obligations to continue to provide maintenance for a wife who had substantially repudiated hers." The concept of a life-long right to and duty of support was thus inextricably linked with the concept of divorce as a relief for wrongdoing.

As discussed in chapter 3, the Divorce Reform Act 1969 replaced the concept of matrimonial offence with irretrievable breakdown of marriage as the sole ground for divorce. This might have been expected to affect the basis on which financial relief should be granted. However, the Law Commission report underpinning the financial relief legislation of 1970 did not examine basic principles.[38] The abandonment of the contractual, fault-based model left a 'normative vacuum'.[39] Orders could now be made in favour of *either* party, regardless of who had petitioned for divorce. Importantly, the courts' powers were considerably enhanced: they were empowered not just to order spousal maintenance or to make lump sum awards of cash,[40] but also to order the transfer of specific assets between the parties, in order to ensure that the financial consequences of divorce for wives—made newly vulnerable by no-fault divorce—could be dealt with comprehensively.[41] As for the substantive basis on which those powers were to be exercised, the legislation required courts to consider a checklist of factors,

[37] See Cretney (2003a), ch 10. [38] Law Com (1969). [39] Dewar (2003), 426.
[40] Only possible since 1963. [41] See Cretney (2003a), 416–20.

of which the parties' conduct was just one. And, adopting the stance of pre-1969 case law, the court was directed by statute:

> . . . so to exercise [its] powers as to place the parties, so far as it is practicable and, having regard to their conduct, just to do so, in the financial position in which they would have been if the marriage had not broken down and each had properly discharged his or her financial obligations and responsibilities towards the other.[42]

The practical problems with this 'minimal loss' principle[43] quickly became apparent.[44] The objective was usually unattainable as resources were insufficient to meet the parties' basic needs: the principle was more aptly described as 'equal misery' than 'minimal loss'.[45] There were concerns that continuing obligations caused financial hardship to husbands and their new families, but equally that wives were receiving inadequate provision and relying on welfare benefits.[46] Fundamentally, the minimal loss objective seemed incompatible with no-fault divorce.

Law Commission, *The Financial Consequences of Divorce: The Basic Policy*, Law Com No 103 (London: HMSO, 1980)

> 30. We think that the arguments against the retention of a principle of life-long support at the standard enjoyed during the marriage can most easily be analysed and considered under four heads:
>
> (i) A duty of life-long support is now out of date because it is rooted in the concept of marriage as a life-time union.[47] If marriage were indeed still a life-long institution, it might perhaps be reasonable that the parties should expect that the benefits and burdens incident to the status of marriage would not be affected by divorce; but (it is said) in modern conditions it is unrealistic for married couples not to accept that there is a very real possibility that their marriage will break down. It is thus correspondingly unrealistic for them to suppose that if this should happen their financial position would remain unaffected.
>
> (ii) The change in the juristic basis of divorce from matrimonial offence to irretrievable breakdown has fundamentally altered the validity of the law's approach to support obligations. On this argument the obligation to provide life-long support is based on the analogy between marriage and contract, under which compensation would be available for its breach. Consequently, it is argued that now that divorce is available whenever the marriage has broken down, irrespective of whether one or other of the parties is in breach of his or her matrimonial obligations, it is inappropriate for the law to continue to found the parties' respective financial obligations after divorce on the now largely irrelevant notion of breach of duty; and it is unjust to do so since the present law may require a man to maintain his wife when she has herself been entirely responsible for the breakdown.
>
> (iii) The objective of life-long support is almost invariably impossible to attain because in most cases one man's resources are insufficient to support two households.

[42] Matrimonial Proceedings and Property Act 1970, s 5(1), now repealed.
[43] Eekelaar (1978), 173.
[44] See Cretney (2003a), 427–8.
[45] *Miller; McFarlane* [2006] UKHL 24, [126].
[46] Law Com (1980), paras 25–8.
[47] For clarification on the common law duty to maintain, see *Villiers v Villiers* [2022] EWCA Civ 772.

(iv) The concept of a life-long support obligation is based on wholly out of date views of the division of function between husband and wife as well as of the economic status of women.

The first and fourth of these arguments could be overstated. While divorce was no longer rare, many wedding couples might still expect or intend theirs to be a lifelong union.[48] While wives were more economically active, large differences in spouses' employment patterns, particularly following the birth of children, meant that men and women were far from being on an equal economic footing and many wives could not be self-sufficient on divorce.[49] The second argument had more weight, the courts having decided that detailed investigation of conduct other than in extreme cases would subvert the aims of no-fault divorce.[50] As the Law Commission asked, 'If . . . the essence of the obligation of life-long support on divorce is that it represents compensation for a wrong done to the financially weaker party, yet the courts no longer investigate the question of blame, how (it is asked) can the obligation to support still be justified?'[51] The policy represented by the minimal loss principle no longer commanded support.[52] The MCA 1973, Part II was accordingly amended in 1984,[53] giving us the statute in force today.[54]

6.4 THE CURRENT LAW: THE TOOLBOX OF ORDERS AND RESOURCES AVAILABLE

The MCA 1973 provides the courts with a flexible toolkit for transferring resources on divorce. The choice of tools and the amounts transferred in each case depend on the *basis* for exercising the powers—in what circumstances and for what purpose should orders be made? We address that in the next section. Here, we ask the mechanical question—what orders is the court able to make and in relation to what resources?

The aim is produce a financial 'package' achieving the optimum outcome for the parties and their children, using whatever powers are available.[55] Child maintenance is often an important component, dealt with either via a consent order, informally in a private agreement, or via the statutory agency.[56] Given the extensive powers to make orders between the adults themselves on divorce, capital orders for the benefit of dependent children may seldom be required.[57]

6.4.1 THE RESOURCES AVAILABLE TO THE COURT

The first step is always to identify and value the resources[58] available for distribution: the 'computation' stage.[59] It is essential to this process that the parties provide the court with

48 Law Com (1980), paras 31–4. 49 Ibid, paras 45–57; Thompson (2022).
50 *Wachtel v Wachtel* [1973] Fam 72; see 6.5.6. 51 Law Com (1980), para 41.
52 Law Com (1981), para 17. 53 Matrimonial and Family Proceedings Act 1984.
54 For more recent history, see Law Com (2011), Part 3. 55 Jackson et al (1993), 244–5.
56 See chapter 5, and 5.5.2 on consent orders.
57 Cf cases involving unmarried parents, discussed in chapter 7. 58 MCA 1973, s 25(2)(a).
59 *Charman v Charman* [2007] EWCA Civ 503, [67]. Cf difficulties encountered in *Hart v Hart* [2017] EWCA Civ 1306 and concerns of Balfour (2017).

full and frank disclosure regarding their resources.[60] The court can draw adverse inferences about the resources of parties who fail to disclose,[61] but doing even that depends on the court knowing that something is not being disclosed.[62]

The computation stage is usually straightforward, but high-value cases, in particular, can involve complex legal questions that lie beyond the scope of this book. In short, the courts' powers are exercisable only in relation to resources belonging to one or both spouses. They cannot make orders over property owned beneficially by third parties, whether family members,[63] companies,[64] or discretionary trusts[65] (other than 'nuptial settlements', which the matrimonial court can vary[66]). Nor will the courts assume that a third party will make resources available, either to enable the respondent to satisfy an order that he cannot meet alone or to support either party, whether to relieve the respondent of his obligations to the applicant[67] or to restore the respondent's position after paying over the bulk of the assets to the applicant. But it may make findings about the likelihood of support from third parties occurring and take such resources into account.[68]

Having identified the resources, what can the court do with them?

6.4.2 FINANCIAL PROVISION ORDERS

6.4.2.a Periodical payments

The first type of financial provision order[69] is periodical payments orders, often referred to as 'spousal maintenance', but may be used for any purpose.[70] Commonly paid from income to help meet the recipient's day-to-day needs, they are simply a mechanism for transferring money, weekly, monthly, or on some other timetable. They may be expressed as a fixed sum (perhaps index-linked, to increase automatically with costs of living) or as a percentage of some resource of the payer's, such as a bonus.[71] We address the potential duration of periodical payments orders in discussing the 'clean break' principle at 6.6.1; notably, the court can *dismiss* one or both parties' applications for spousal periodical payment orders with the result that no such payments may ever be required.

The order may require that payments be 'secured':[72] a capital sum is set aside from which payments can continue should the payer default or die, avoiding the need to take enforcement proceedings or to seek continued support from the deceased's estate.[73] Periodical payments orders can be varied at any point, as to the amount payable, the timetable for payment, and the duration of the liability.[74] They terminate automatically if the recipient marries or forms a civil partnership.[75]

[60] On the potential consequences of failure to do so, see *Sharland v Sharland* [2015] UKSC 60; *Gohil v Gohil* [2015] UKSC 61.

[61] *Prest v Petrodel Resources Ltd* [2013] UKSC 34, [45].

[62] Cf *Tchenguiz v Imerman* [2010] EWCA Civ 908; Probert (2011c).

[63] *TL v ML (Ancillary Relief: Claim Against Assets of Extended Family)* [2005] EWHC 2860.

[64] *Prest v Petrodel Resources Ltd* [2013] UKSC 34; George (2013).

[65] *Charman v Charman* [2007] EWCA Civ 503.

[66] MCA 1973, s 24(1)(c): *Ben Hashem v Ali Shayif* [2008] EWHC 2380; see also 6.7.

[67] *Alireza v Radwan* [2017] EWCA Civ 1545.

[68] *Thomas v Thomas* [1995] 2 FLR 668.

[69] MCA 1973, s 23.

[70] *Miller; McFarlane* [2006] UKHL 24, [31].

[71] Percentage payments from a bonus intended just to meet income needs should be subject to a cap to prevent excessive payments: *Parr v Parr* [2013] EWHC 4105.

[72] MCA 1973, s 23(1)(b).

[73] Inheritance (Provision for Family and Dependants) Act 1975.

[74] MCA 1973, s 31.

[75] Ibid, s 28(3).

6.4.2.b Lump sums

The court can order one party to pay the other a capital sum or sums, whether expressed as a monetary amount or as a percentage of the future proceeds of sale of a given asset,[76] payable either immediately in full or by instalments.[77] An order for a discrete lump sum or sums cannot be varied. However, a lump sum payable by instalments can be varied both as to the timetable for instalments and quantum.[78] Lump sums remain payable despite the recipient's subsequent marriage or civil partnership.

6.4.3 PROPERTY ADJUSTMENT ORDERS AND ORDERS FOR SALE

The courts have various powers to adjust the parties' rights over capital assets:[79] transfer of any sort of property from one to the other (whether the former matrimonial home or other land, shares, investments, chattels, etc.); settlement of property for the benefit of one or both parties; varying or extinguishing the parties' interests under existing nuptial settlements.[80] These one-off orders cannot be varied, though there is limited scope for them to be set aside and appealed against outside the normal time limits.[81] The courts can order the sale of property to facilitate the performance of property adjustment orders, orders for lump sums, and secured periodical payments.[82]

6.4.3.a Orders relating to owner-occupied homes

The family home is commonly the most valuable asset at stake, subject to any mortgage debt. There are various ways in which it can be used on divorce. Pending a final determination of the home's fate, it may be appropriate to make occupation orders under the Family Law Act 1996 (FLA 1996).[83]

The home could be sold immediately[84] and the proceeds (after any mortgage debt has been paid) divided in defined shares, providing each party with resources to fund new accommodation. However, the net equity in the home (even combined with each party's ability to raise fresh mortgage finance) may not be enough to enable both to rehouse. The home could alternatively be transferred outright to one spouse, perhaps in return for a lump sum payment or for that spouse foregoing other claims. These appear to be the two most common options used in practice, achieving a clean break as regards this key asset.[85]

Apparently much less common in practice,[86] but in theory a good way of maximizing the 'use value' of the parties' assets, is the option to make the house the subject of a settlement allowing one spouse and any children to occupy it until a specified date or event following which it will be sold and the proceeds split. A similar effect can be achieved by an outright

[76] Commonly the former matrimonial home, but also assets such as shares: *B v B (Lump Sums on Deferred Realisation of Shares)* [2015] EWHC 210. This will delay payment pending the sale, but may sometimes be the fairest way of dealing with uncertain valuation or price fluctuation.

[77] MCA 1973, s 23(1)(c). [78] Ibid, s 31(2)(d); *Hamilton v Hamilton* [2013] EWCA Civ 13.

[79] MCA 1973, ss 24–24A. [80] E.g. *P v P (Variation of Post-Nuptial Settlement)* [2015] EWCA Civ 447.

[81] See 6.6.3. [82] MCA 1973, s 24A. [83] See 4.5.3.

[84] Interim orders for sale must be sought under other legislation, e.g. the Trusts of Land and Appointment of Trustees Act (TOLATA) 1996: *WS v HS (Sale of Matrimonial Home)* [2018] EWFC 11, *SR v HR* [2018] EWHC 606.

[85] Miles and Hitchings (2018). [86] Ibid.

transfer subject to a charge in the other party's favour to be realized on sale. Various events can be used as the trigger for sale, as illustrated by '*Mesher*' and '*Martin*' orders. A *Mesher* order[87] settles the property on the parties in defined shares to be realized on sale once the youngest child reaches a particular age, or finishes a specified level of education, or (earlier) on further order; until then, the children and nominated spouse occupy the property. This may be feasible only if: (i) the other parent can obtain alternative accommodation without immediate access to their share of the capital; (ii) the occupying spouse will be able to fund new accommodation following the sale, bearing in mind the continuing impact on earning capacity of ongoing child-care responsibility until sale;[88] and (iii) the parties can maintain mortgage or other outgoings on the former matrimonial home whilst also funding the other party's new home. A *Mesher* order may be an unattractive option, simply 'postpon[ing] the evil day' for the party left in occupation.[89] A *Martin* order[90] triggers sale on the occurrence of some event in the life of the occupying spouse, such as remarriage, cohabitation, death, or that spouse electing to leave the property. This potentially further delays the other party's access to their capital share with no clear sense of when it might be released, but provides greater protection for the occupying spouse, who may otherwise struggle to find alternative accommodation without public assistance. However, that 'protection' may seriously restrict the occupying party's freedom: that spouse might wish to move, for example to take up a new job or to be near family, but that spouse's share following the required sale might be insufficient to acquire a home in the new location.[91] The apparent unpopularity of these options may be attributed to various factors, including the potential for the operation of these arrangements to generate conflict[92] and their simply delaying the clean break that many couples prefer.[93]

Whilst broad, however, the court's powers are not unlimited. Crucially, although the court can order one party to pay the mortgage on that property and/or to indemnify the other party in the event of non-payment,[94] it cannot adjust the parties' liabilities under the mortgage. Any mortgagee must receive notice of the proceedings and have an opportunity to be heard;[95] their consent may be required to any transfer of the property; even if the property is transferred, the original mortgagor(s) remain liable to repay the loan unless the mortgagee consents to transfer the liability.[96] There are various ways of coping with these restrictions. Parties commonly 'undertake' to do or to use best endeavours to achieve *x*, *x* being something that the court cannot order, for example to secure the lender's agreement to transfer the mortgage. Such undertakings—solemn promises to the court—can be enforced like court orders, though the court cannot order specific performance.[97] Where aspects of the court's order are premised on the undertakings, the order could, to that extent, be set aside or varied if the undertakings were breached.

6.4.3.b Orders relating to rented homes

The courts can transfer various types of tenancy to one party, whether the property was previously rented by one or both parties. Many types of tenancy can be transferred under the

[87] [1980] 1 All ER 126. [88] *S v B* [2004] EWHC 2089. [89] *Harvey v Harvey* [1982] Fam 83, 89.
[90] [1978] Fam 12. [91] Deech (1982), 633. [92] *S v B* [2004] EWHC 2089.
[93] Miles and Hitchings (2018).
[94] *CH v WH* [2017] EWHC 2379. Cf concerns re enforcement of such orders made under the FLA 1996 in *Nwogbe v Nwogbe*, discussed at 4.5.3.
[95] FPR 2010, r 9.13. [96] *Livesey v Jenkins* [1985] AC 424, 444.
[97] Ibid; *L v L* [2006] EWHC 956, [61]; cf Law Society (2003), para 293, doubting the enforceability of undertakings.

MCA 1973, s 24, but there are also relevant powers under the FLA 1996.[98] The FLA 1996 sets out a checklist of factors which the court must consider in exercising its discretion.[99] The landlord is entitled to be heard before an order is made.[100] Where the landlord is a housing authority, it may allocate new housing to one or both parties without a court order, at least where they are in agreement.[101] Access to social housing is a matter for the local authority, whose hands cannot be tied by court orders, for example orders arranging for children to live with both parties.[102]

6.4.4 PENSION ORDERS

Pensions are important forms of tax-free saving to provide for retirement.[103] Pensions are an immensely complex area, even before one adds the complication of divorce, so we can provide only the briefest overview here.[104]

The courts have two main powers over pension funds on divorce: pension attachment and pension sharing. Pension attachment is a type of financial provision order,[105] addressed not to the pension-holder but to that spouse's pension provider. When the pension (or relevant death-in-service benefit) falls due, the order directs that some defined portion of the pension or benefit be paid to the other spouse. Neither the court nor the other spouse can control whether and when the pension will fall due, or how valuable it will be. Partly for that reason, pension attachment is little used. The preferred order is pension sharing,[106] available in relation to almost all except the basic state pension.[107] The court orders that a specified percentage of one party's pension fund be debited and immediately transferred to establish an independent fund for the other spouse. This approach avoids the difficulties associated with pension attachment and helps achieve a clean break. If the pension share will generate sufficient income in later life for the recipient, there may be no need for periodical payments beyond retirement.

Alternatively, and far more common in practice than either type of pension order,[108] the overall package seeks to 'offset' the value of the pension against other assets, for example giving a greater share in the value, or all, of the house to one spouse in return for lower or no share of the pension.[109] But this is a deeply problematic exercise, given the difficulties of valuing some types of pensions in a way that permits any ready comparison with the value of non-pension capital in order to calculate an appropriate bargain.[110] Rules introduced in 2015 now also enable holders of certain types of pension to turn their pension savings into cash at aged 55 (subject to payment of tax). Whilst it is generally prudent to keep pension assets as a pension in order to fund retirement, in some cases this added flexibility to liquidize a pension may help achieve a fair divorce settlement.[111]

[98] Sch 7. [99] Ibid, para 5. [100] Ibid, para 14(1).

[101] Law Com (2006), para 3.58. [102] *Holmes-Moorhouse v Richmond LBC* [2009] UKHL 7.

[103] See generally Woodward with Sefton (2014).

[104] For detail, see the work of the Pension Advisory Group: <www.nuffieldfoundation.org/pensions-divorce-interdisciplinary-working-group>; Woodward (2019).

[105] MCA 1973, ss 25B–D. [106] Ibid, ss 21A, 24B–D. [107] Now the New State Pension.

[108] Woodward with Sefton (2014); Miles and Hitchings (2018).

[109] *Martin-Dye v Martin-Dye* [2006] EWCA Civ 681, [85].

[110] *Maskell v Maskell* [2003] 1 FLR 1138; Woodward with Sefton (2014), 4 and ch 8; Taylor and Woodward (2015).

[111] Morris (2015); *W v H (Divorce: Financial remedies)* [2020] EWFC B10; *KM v CV* [2020] EWFC B22; *RH v SV* [2020] EWFC B23; Hay (2022).

6.4.5 WHEN MAY ORDERS BE MADE?

All orders are available on divorce and nullity, and all except pension sharing on judicial separation. Orders may be made[112] at any time following the grant of a conditional order,[113] but will not take effect until after the final order.[114] It is not possible to make orders in relation to capital under the MCA 1973 at an interim stage,[115] but the intervening period can be covered by orders for maintenance pending suit and interim maintenance,[116] and legal services payment orders to enable the economically weaker party to fund legal advice and assistance for the divorce and related financial proceedings.[117] Orders may also be made after the final order; there is no formal limitation period, though applications brought years after divorce may be difficult to sustain.[118] A party who has remarried or formed a new civil partnership cannot make an application,[119] but can pursue an application made in the original divorce application.[120]

6.4.6 ENFORCEMENT

The courts have wide-ranging powers to enforce financial orders against defaulters. Key powers include attachment of earnings; warrants of control (the seizure and sale of goods to pay the debt); orders requiring a third party holding funds belonging to the liable party (e.g. a bank) to pay them to the applicant; charging orders, giving the applicant a security interest in property belonging to the respondent realizable on sale; and committal to prison for up to six weeks—the last resort to be used where the defaulting party can pay but is wilfully refusing or culpably neglecting to do so. Failure to execute relevant documentation for property adjustment or to give up vacant possession prior to sale can be rectified by the court executing the documents or making an order for possession.[121] The law in this area is notoriously labyrinthine and procedurally complex and the Law Commission has recommended reform.[122] The government has planned non-legislative changes to help rationalize and streamline the process.[123]

6.5 THE CURRENT LAW: THE PRINCIPLES GOVERNING THE GRANT OF REMEDIES

Having identified the tools, we now examine the basis on which they may be used.

[112] Consent order applications can be *approved* prior to conditional order: *Pounds v Pounds* [1994] 1 WLR 1535.

[113] *K v K (Financial Remedy Order Prior to Decree Nisi)* [2016] EWFC 23; cf *JP v NP (Financial Remedies: Costs)* [2014] EWHC 1101.

[114] MCA 1973, ss 23(5) and 24(3); see 3.7.

[115] Cf jurisdiction under other legislation to make interim orders for sale: see n 84.

[116] MCA 1973, s 22; *BD v FD (Maintenance)* [2014] EWHC 4443.

[117] MCA 1973, ss 22ZA–B; *Rubin v Rubin* [2014] EWHC 611.

[118] *Wyatt v Vince* [2015] UKSC 14, reversing a decision to strike out an application made nearly 20 years after the decree absolute (final order): see discussion of late applications at 6.5.6.

[119] Save, oddly, for a pension sharing order—this is probably a case of legislative oversight.

[120] MCA 1973, s 28(3); *Whitehouse-Piper v Stokes* [2008] EWCA Civ 1049.

[121] *Constantinides v Constantinides* [2013] EWHC 3688.

[122] For detailed discussion, see Black et al (2015), ch 33; Law Com (2016); Douglas (2022).

[123] MOJ (2018b).

6.5.1 INTRODUCTION: THE STATUTORY DISCRETION AND THE CASE LAW PRINCIPLES

English law allocates resources on divorce not in accordance with statutory rules but following the exercise of a wide judicial discretion. The basic principles are uniform, whether the case involves spouses or civil partners.[124] However, features of at least some same-sex relationships (such as a more equal division of labour during the relationship) may mean that one tends to see different *outcomes* from those typical of many mixed-sex divorces and dissolutions. But like cases should be treated alike, regardless of their form and gender pattern. Application of the principles between same-sex couples may provide a valuable, gender-neutral, and ahistorical context in which to re-evaluate the principles as they apply in the ideologically loaded, traditionally gendered context of marriage.[125] So too may contemplating the principles' use in mixed-sex relationships where the 'traditional' roles have been reversed.[126]

Any examination of the current law must begin with the statute. In this extract, we have italicized key wording that was added, along with the clean break provision, s 25A, in 1984:

Matrimonial Causes Act 1973

25 Matters to which the court is to have regard in deciding how to exercise its powers [to order financial provision, property adjustment, sale, and pension sharing]

(1) It shall be the duty of the court in deciding whether to exercise its powers [to order financial provision, property adjustment, sale, or pension sharing] and, if so, in what manner, to have regard to all the circumstances of the case, *first consideration being given to the welfare while a minor of any child of the family who has not attained the age of eighteen.*

(2) As regards the exercise of the powers of the court [to make such orders] in relation to a party to the marriage, the court shall in particular have regard to the following matters—
   (a) the income, earning capacity, property and other financial resources which each of the parties to the marriage has or is likely to have in the foreseeable future, *including in the case of earning capacity any increase in that capacity which it would in the opinion of the court be reasonable to expect a party to the marriage to take steps to acquire;*
   (b) the financial needs, obligations and responsibilities which each of the parties to the marriage has or is likely to have in the foreseeable future;
   (c) the standard of living enjoyed by the family before the breakdown of the marriage;
   (d) the age of each party to the marriage and the duration of the marriage;[127]
   (e) any physical and mental disability of either of the parties to the marriage;
   (f) the contributions which each of the parties has made or is likely in the foreseeable future to make to the welfare of the family, including any contribution by looking after the home or caring for the family;
   (g) the conduct of each of the parties, *if that conduct is such that it would in the opinion of the court be inequitable to disregard it;*

[124] *Lawrence v Gallagher* [2012] EWCA Civ 394. Cf Leckey (2013) questioning the aptness of this.
[125] Wilson (2007), 37; see also Lind (2004), extracted at 2.3.4.d.
[126] Parkinson (2011), 256; Diduck (2011b), 313–14; Bendall (2014), 269–70.
[127] Case law additionally includes cohabitation that moves seamlessly into marriage: *GW v RW* [2003] EWHC 611; *IX v IY* [2018] EWHC 3053, [68].

(h) in the case of proceedings for divorce or nullity of marriage, the value to each of the parties to the marriage of any benefit which, by reason of the dissolution or annulment of the marriage, that party will lose the chance of acquiring.[128] . . .

25A Exercise of the court's powers in favour of party to marriage on decree of divorce or nullity of marriage

(1) Where on or after the grant of a decree of divorce or nullity of marriage the court decides to exercise its powers [to make such orders] in favour of a party to the marriage, it shall be the duty of the court to consider whether it would be appropriate so to exercise those powers that the financial obligations of each party towards the other will be terminated as soon after the grant of the decree as the court considers just and reasonable. . . .

52 Interpretation

(1) In this Act—
"child" in relation to one or both of the parties to a marriage, includes an illegitimate child of that party or, as the case may be, of both parties;
"child of the family", in relation to the parties to a marriage, means—
(a) a child of both of those parties; and
(b) any other child, not being a child who is placed with those parties as foster parents by a local authority or voluntary organisation, who has been treated by both of those parties as a child of their family.

Similarly, on applications to vary orders, the court must give first consideration to the welfare of minor children of the family, and have regard to all the circumstances, including any relevant change of circumstance and the clean break principle,[129] discussed at 6.6.

The most striking feature of these provisions is that no ultimate objective is identified. The 1984 legislation removed the minimal loss principle, but the 'replacements'—first consideration to the welfare of minor children, and the clean break principle—do not perform an equivalent function.[130] If anything, they clash: the individualism implicit in the clean break principle jars with the idea of continuing obligations and constraints where there are dependent children.[131] But they perhaps signal a new focus on the parties' ongoing relationship as parents, as opposed to their concluded relationship as spouses.[132] The factors in the statutory checklist point in different directions, some suggesting forward-looking, needs-based awards, others encouraging a retrospective evaluation of parties' contributions. Since English law operates separate property during marriage, there must be some rationale for redistributing the parties' resources on divorce.[133] But the legislation provides none. As one Australian judge has described it, the family judge's situation is like that of:

> . . . a bus driver who is given a large number of instructions about how to drive the bus, and the authority to do various actions such as turning left or right. There is also the occasional advice or correction offered by three senior drivers. The one piece of information which he or

[128] I.e. benefits that would have been enjoyed had the party remained married, e.g. a widow's pension.
[129] MCA 1973, s 31(7).
[130] Cf Family Law (Scotland) Act 1985; Scot Law Com (1981); Deech (1982).
[131] Diduck (2003), 142.
[132] Douglas (2012), 223.
[133] *Miller; McFarlane* [2006] UKHL 24, [137], citing a lecture by Ward LJ.

she is not given is where to take the bus. All he or she is told is that the driver is required to drive to a reasonable destination.[134]

The courts have been left to decide for themselves where to go, and their direction has changed over time, generating a vast academic literature seeking both to explain what the law is (which is less than straightforward) and to debate the principles which *should* govern financial orders.[135] As one practitioner put it:

There is something in the work of archaeologists that reflects the current difficulties faced by family lawyers. The excavation requires a large group of people to pick through the rubble to find a few nuggets, which are delivered to a learned few, who develop a theory to unlock the mysteries of the investigation.[136]

The basic principle identified by the judges is that outcomes must be 'fair'. But as Lord Nicholls remarked in *White v White*, 'fairness, like beauty, lies in the eye of the beholder'.[137] He went further in *Miller; McFarlane*:

Miller v Miller; McFarlane v McFarlane [2006] UKHL 24

LORD NICHOLLS:

4. Fairness is an elusive concept. It is an instinctive response to a given set of facts. Ultimately it is grounded in social and moral values. These values, or attitudes, can be stated. But they cannot be justified, or refuted, by any objective process of logical reasoning. Moreover, they change from one generation to the next. It is not surprising therefore that in the present context there can be different views on the requirements of fairness in any particular case . . .

6. . . . Implicitly the courts must exercise their powers so as to achieve an outcome which is fair between the parties. But an important aspect of fairness is that like cases should be treated alike. So, perforce, if there is to be an acceptable degree of consistency of decision from one case to the next, the courts must themselves articulate, if only in the broadest fashion, what are the applicable if unspoken principles guiding the court's approach . . .

9. The starting point is surely not controversial. In the search for a fair outcome it is pertinent to have in mind that fairness generates obligations as well as rights. The financial provision made on divorce by one party for the other, still typically the wife, is not in the nature of largesse. It is not a case of 'taking away' from one party and 'giving' to the other property which 'belongs' to the former. The claimant is not a supplicant. Each party to a marriage is *entitled* to a *fair* share of the available property. The search is always for what are the *requirements* of fairness in the particular case.

[134] Chisolm J, quoted in Parkinson (1999), 53; Law Com (2012), para 3.3.

[135] E.g. Eekelaar (1991b), ch 4; Diduck and Orton (1994); Eekelaar and Maclean (1997); Eekelaar (1998a); Diduck (2003), ch 6, (2011a), (2011b); Bailey-Harris (2005); Miles (2005), (2008), 2011a); Cooke (2007); articles in Fehlberg and Miles (2018).

[136] Pirrie (2007). [137] [2001] 1 AC 596, 599.

Miller; McFarlane identified three broad principles, rationales, or 'strands' underpinning the 'fair' result: need, compensation, and (equal) sharing. The outcomes generated by these principles in individual cases vary substantially, depending on factors such as the scale of the parties' resources and when they were acquired, whether they have children, the degree of financial interdependence between the parties, and the length of their cohabiting or marital relationship. But all three principles have something important to tell us about the law's understanding of the economic relationship created by marriage and civil partnership. Baroness Hale summarized the 'ultimate objective' as being 'to give each party an equal start on the road to independent living'.[138]

Our discussion is chiefly organized around those three principles. However, some judges are clearly more comfortable than others with the principled approach.[139] Judges regularly reiterate that the exercise remains discretionary, guided by the s 25 factors and focused on obtaining a 'fair' result. The three principles are not 'separate heads of claim', and should not be routinely argued in everyday cases, which (as we discuss later) focus on needs.[140] It is often said that the court is engaged in a holistic, 'intuitive' pursuit of fairness,[141] informed but not constrained by the principles, or whichever of them is deemed most relevant.[142] In particular, having reached a provisional view under the principles, the court must then 'determine that its proposed award is a fair outcome having regard to all the relevant section 25 factors'.[143]

But while these cases are fact-specific, in that many different circumstances fall to be examined, 'fairness' cannot be the sole criterion:

Waggott v Waggott [2018] EWCA Civ 727

MOYLAN LJ:

119. The overarching question . . . is whether the award made by the judge was fair. However, to provide an answer to this question requires more than the simple, almost pantomime, response of, "Yes, it is" or "No, it isn't". The answer needs to have a principled basis of sufficient substance to explain why any specific award is to be regarded as fair or unfair. . . . This is not . . . the same as saying that the application of [the *Miller; McFarlane*] principles will lead to one answer. Discretion and evaluation remain important elements which will inform the judge's determination. However, . . . it is incumbent on the courts to seek to provide sufficient clarity as to the relevant legal principles and the manner in which they should be applied so that the outcome in any specific case can be identified as being within a reasonably circumscribed range of potential awards.

That is particularly important to enable parties to settle their cases without resort to the courts. Otherwise, the exercise becomes unacceptably arbitrary (like sticking a pin in a map

[138] *Miller; McFarlane* [2006] UKHL 24, [144].

[139] Compare the emphasis on strong discretion in *B v B* [2008] EWCA Civ 543, *Robson v Robson* [2010] EWCA Civ 1171; and the exercise of discretion within principled guidelines in *Jones v Jones* [2011] EWCA Civ 11, *K v L* [2011] EWCA Civ 550.

[140] *R v R* [2011] EWHC 3093, [9], [55]–[56].

[141] E.g. *RP v RP* [2006] EWHC 3409, [58]; *VB v JP* [2008] EWHC 112, [45], [52].

[142] *B v B* [2008] EWCA Civ 543, [50]–[51].

[143] *Hart v Hart* [2017] EWCA Civ 1306, [95].

blindfold)[144] and settlement (or not) dictated more by individual parties' risk-aversion than by any sense of their legal entitlements.[145] So we must try to develop a coherent view of the case law, analysing the principles and their inter-relationship, considering when one principle or feature of the case might assume 'magnetic importance',[146] and trying to chart where the courts' sense of 'fairness' takes them. However, 'It is prudent to remember that [the House of Lords' speeches] are explanations of and expansions upon the statute, not the statute itself.'[147] So we begin with the factor that statute requires be given first consideration.

6.5.2 FIRST CONSIDERATION: THE WELFARE OF MINOR CHILDREN

Children's income requirements are dealt with primarily via child support, but their interests may influence provision between the adults in various ways:

Miller v Miller; McFarlane v McFarlane **[2006] UKHL 24**

BARONESS HALE:

128. . . . [S]ection 25(1) . . . is a clear recognition of the reality that, although the couple may seek to go their separate ways, they are still jointly responsible for the welfare of their children. The invariable practice in English law is to try to maintain a stable home for the children after their parents' divorce. Research indicates that it is more successful in doing this than in securing a comparable income for them in future (see, eg [Arthur et al (2002)]). Giving priority to the children's welfare should also involve ensuring that their primary carer is properly provided for, because it is well known that the security and stability of children depends in large part upon the security and stability of their primary carers (see eg [Lewis (2001a)] p 178).

Children's welfare in this context is only the first, not paramount, consideration,[148] and only during the children's minority. However, the courts acknowledge that children remain financially dependent and live at home long after reaching 18.[149] Other children's interests (such those from a previous or subsequent relationship) may be relevant insofar as they affect parties' needs and obligations.[150] Children's interests frequently affect decisions about housing, and may also impact on whether and when it is reasonable to expect a primary carer spouse to undertake paid employment.

6.5.3 MEETING THE PARTIES' MATERIAL NEEDS

The first of the House of Lords' three principles derives from the second factor in s 25(2): financial needs.

[144] Cf *Robertson v Robertson* [2016] EWHC 613, [69]. See generally Hitchings and Miles (2019).
[145] Hitchings and Miles (2016). [146] E.g. *McCartney v Mills McCartney* [2008] EWHC 401, [301].
[147] *Charman v Charman* [2006] EWHC 1879, [114].
[148] *Suter v Suter* [1987] Fam 111, 123–4; cf chapter 8.
[149] *Richardson v Richardson (No 2)* [1994] 2 FLR 1051. [150] *Roberts v Roberts* [1970] P 1.

Miller v Miller; McFarlane v McFarlane [2006] UKHL 24

LORD NICHOLLS:

11. This element of fairness reflects the fact that to a greater or lesser extent every relationship of marriage gives rise to a relationship of interdependence. The parties share the roles of money-earner, home-maker and child-carer. Mutual dependence begets mutual obligations of support. When the marriage ends fairness requires that the assets of the parties should be divided primarily so as to make provision for the parties' housing and financial needs, taking into account a wide range of matters such as the parties' ages, their future earning capacity, the family's standard of living, and any disability of either party. Most of these needs will have been generated by the marriage, but not all of them. Needs arising from age or disability are instances of the latter.

In what Emma Hitchings has dubbed the 'everyday' cases[151]—where the resources do not exceed the parties' needs—the needs of both parties (and associated pragmatic issues) are the only real consideration, to the exclusion of compensation and equal sharing. In many cases, it is impossible, given the limited resources and debts, even to cover both parties' needs fully.[152] 'Creativity and common sense'[153] are required to stretch the resources as far as possible.

6.5.3.a What is 'need'?

The courts interpret 'need' by reference to the marital standard of living.[154] This generates surprising results in high-value cases, as the 'needs' of the rich are more substantial than those of the rest, extending, for example, to a 'need' to keep horses.[155] But the marital standard of living is merely a 'starting point' by which to assess needs—not 'a ceiling or a floor' for provision. Not least given the objective of parties' living independent lives, there is no absolute right to be maintained indefinitely at that level by the other party, either at all or beyond a fixed period (rather than for life).[156] In particular, the level and duration of any periodical payments order will turn on various factors. The longer the marriage and the contributions made by the applicant to the welfare of the family (including post-divorce), 'the more likely the court will decide that the applicant's . . . needs should be provided for at a level . . . similar to the standard of living during the marriage' (provided resources permit). The longer the duration of both marriage and contributions, 'the more likely that those needs will be assessed on a lifetime's basis'. But equally, the longer the period over which the applicant's needs are to be met, the more likely it is that the *level* of provision will reduce over time.[157] After a short marriage,[158] the court will seek to enable that party to transition back to a standard of living that they can sustain.[159]

There is very little case law illustrating resolutions of 'everyday' cases; Gillian Douglas goes as far as to say that the focus on high-value cases means that we have ended up with a 'fantasy

[151] Hitchings (2009), (2010). [152] *AL v AL* [2011] EWHC 3150, [50].
[153] *R v R* [2011] EWHC 3093, [9]. [154] *Miller; McFarlane* [2006] UKHL 24, [138]; s 25(2)(c).
[155] *S v S* [2008] EWHC 519. [156] *BD v FD* [2016] EWHC 594, [114]–[116]. [157] Ibid, [120]–[122].
[158] Duration including immediately preceding period of stable cohabitation: *GW v RW* [2003] EWHC 611.
[159] *G v G* [2012] EWHC 167, [136].

family law'.[160] This is especially concerning given judicial assertions that 'small money cases can be infinitely more difficult than cases involving larger sums'.[161] But, absent much case law, the Law Commission's work offers valuable insight into how the everyday cases are dealt with. Surprisingly, perhaps, the law on needs is rather unclear: '[M]ost family lawyers are confident that needs is something they know when they see it; none can offer a definition, although all can offer explanations and descriptions of what "needs" can include.'[162]

Law Commission, *Marital Property Agreements*, Law Com CP 198 (London: TSO, 2011)

2.28 . . . We can identify a number of distinctive features of the courts' interpretation:

(1) In looking at the parties' income needs the courts are aware of the difficulties experienced by those who have given up work, wholly or in part, to look after children. It is not assumed that people can readily return to work in later years, nor that they can recover economically from years out of employment. Orders for periodical payments reflect this.

(2) Needs encompasses the value of a home. We live in a society where owner-occupation is highly valued, and where the market for private rented accommodation is nowhere near so plentiful or so acceptable as it is, for the most part, in continental Europe. Considerable emphasis is therefore placed on the division of the capital value of the family home, whether immediately or at a later stage when the children leave home.

(3) In assessing the parties' housing needs the courts are mindful of the ability of each party to obtain and support a mortgage loan. Someone who has given up work to care for children will often receive a larger share in the capital value of the family home when it is sold than will a parent who has not given up work and has therefore had a continuing (and perhaps growing) mortgage capacity.

(4) So far as possible, the courts try to avoid allowing either party to leave the other dependent on state benefits, on the basis that it is not acceptable to pass on one's individual responsibilities to the state. However, on occasions that is not possible,[163] and the courts will avoid making an order that leaves someone in a position where he or she would be better off not working.[164]

(5) The concept of needs is sufficiently long-term to encompass provision for retirement. . . . [T]he courts . . . have the power to make [pension sharing] orders and so can share an asset that was intended by the spouses originally as a joint provision for their old age.

Against that backdrop, we now examine some specific issues related to need, dealing in more detail with the duration of income-based provision through periodical payments when we examine the 'clean break' principle at 6.6.1.

[160] Douglas (2018b), 108. [161] *JM v KK* [2021] EWFC 54, [49]. [162] Law Com (2012), para 3.25.
[163] *Delaney v Delaney* [1990] 2 FLR 457. [164] *Furniss v Furniss* (1982) 3 FLR 46.

6.5.3.b Housing first

Wherever there are minor children living with a primary carer, the court's priority is securing accommodation for them, that spouse, and (if possible)[165] the other parent:

M v B (Ancillary Proceedings: Lump Sum) [1998] 1 FCR 213 (CA), 220

THORPE LJ:

In all these cases it is one of the paramount considerations, in applying the s 25 criteria, to endeavour to stretch what is available to cover the need of each for a home, particularly where there are young children involved. Obviously the primary carer needs whatever is available to make the main home for the children, but it is of importance, albeit it is of lesser importance, that the other parent should have a home of his own where the children can enjoy their contact time with him. Of course, there are cases where there is not enough to provide a home for either. Of course, there are cases where there is only enough to provide one. But in any case where there is, by stretch and a degree of risk-taking, the possibility of a division to enable both to rehouse themselves, that is an exceptionally important consideration and one which will almost invariably have a decisive impact on outcome.

Here the judge had the opportunity to make a division which would just about enable each to rehouse. True, if the wife was to go for [the house she preferred] it would require some sacrifice on the part of her family and some burden of future mortgage. True, on the husband's side it would entail taking advantage of his ability to defer the [legal aid authority's] charge in respect of his costs.[166] But those are the sort of methods to which the court regularly has to have recourse in cases where the money is only just enough . . .[167]

Even if the home is retained for occupation by the children and one parent (commonly their primary carer) during the children's minority, it might be appropriate for the other spouse to retain a share in its capital value under a *Mesher* order.[168] But the parties' respective needs and resources may indicate that the primary carer should retain the property either on a *Martin* basis or outright.[169] Indeed, *Mesher* orders have become rare, primary carers placing such weight on retaining the family home and obtaining a 'clean break' that they forego periodical payments or the long-term security offered by a pension share in order to secure the home outright.[170] This sort of trade-off may be economically unwise in the long term.[171] In other cases, resources may be so tight that the house may have to be sold and the proceeds divided between the parties to rehouse, one or both potentially having to rent rather than buy.

6.5.3.c The source of available resources

Under s 25(2)(a), the court must have regard to all available financial resources of the parties. All assets may, in principle, be used to meet the parties' needs, including assets that (for the purposes of the sharing principle, discussed at 6.5.5) would be classed as 'non-matrimonial':

165 E.g. *B v B (Financial Provision: Welfare of Child and Conduct)* [2002] 1 FLR 555.
166 The statutory charge recovering public funding for legal services: Black et al (2015), ch 2.
167 See also *Fisher-Aziz v Aziz* [2010] EWCA Civ 673.
168 *Elliott v Elliott* [2001] 1 FCR 477; see 6.4.3.
169 *B v B (Mesher Order)* [2002] EWHC 3106.
170 Perry et al (2000); Miles and Hitchings (2018).
171 Woodward with Sefton (2014).

for example, wealth accumulated prior to the marriage; acquired by gift or inheritance during it;[172] years after separation;[173] or from a personal injury claim.[174] The parties' ability to borrow is also relevant, whether to release the value of otherwise illiquid assets or to acquire new property.[175] But if all or most of the property available for division is 'non-matrimonial' (for the purposes of the sharing principle), it may be appropriate to moderate the level of need to be catered for,[176] unless the marriage was long.[177]

Public benefits and housing have an important role in resolving low-value cases.[178] Tax credits are especially important, as their means-testing rules take no account of child or spousal[179] maintenance payments; by contrast, entitlement to key means-tested welfare benefits is reduced pound for pound by receipt of *spousal* maintenance.[180] The mere fact that one party is likely to become reliant on state support following divorce may not itself justify a financial order, particularly if the marriage was short or childless.[181] But, although a former spouse is not a 'liable relative' from whom benefits payments may be recouped by the state, it is generally considered undesirable that the state should pick up the bill if the ex-spouse can and should reasonably be expected to provide support.[182] The law must therefore determine when, on what basis, and for how long[183] an ex-spouse, rather than the state, should have to provide support.

6.5.3.d The source of the parties' needs

This brings us to a key question: the particular needs for which an ex-spouse can be made responsible.[184]

North v North **[2007] EWCA Civ 760**

THORPE LJ:

32. . . . There are of course two faces to fairness. The order must be fair both to the applicant in need and to the respondent who must pay. . . . But it does not follow that the respondent is inevitably responsible financially for any established needs. He is not an insurer against all hazards nor, when fairness is the measure, is he necessarily liable for needs created by the applicant's financial mismanagement, extravagance or irresponsibility. The prodigal former wife cannot hope to turn to a former husband in pursuit of a legal remedy, whatever may be her hope that he might out of charity come to her rescue.

An ex-spouse may clearly be required to help meet needs generated by the relationship: for example, where one spouse gave up paid employment to raise the children and so is

172 *White v White* [2001] 1 AC 596, 610.
173 *Schuller v Schuller* [1990] 2 FLR 193; *Vaughan v Vaughan* [2010] EWCA Civ 349, [42].
174 *Mansfield v Mansfield* [2011] EWCA Civ 1056. 175 *Arbili v Arbili* [2015] EWCA Civ 542, [25].
176 *N v F* [2011] EWHC 586, [16]–[19]; *B v B* [2012] EWHC 314, [89].
177 *Robson v Robson* [2010] EWCA Civ 1171, [8]. 178 See CPAG (2018); Black et al (2015), ch 25.
179 Cf new Universal Credit rules, which do include spousal maintenance in means-testing: see Miles and Hitchings (2018), 72.
180 Contrast the full maintenance disregard in relation to child support payments: see 5.7.2.a.
181 *SRJ v DWJ (Financial Provision)* [1999] 3 FCR 153, 160.
182 *Peacock v Peacock* [1984] 1 All ER 1069; cf *Delaney v Delaney* [1991] FCR 161. 183 See 6.6.
184 See Eekelaar and Maclean (1986), 39–41.

not self-sufficient; or where domestic abuse caused some disability impairing the victim's earning capacity.[185] It is less clear whether and when responsibility may extend to needs which have not been produced by the marriage: for example, arising from long-term unemployment, illness, disability, or old age, particularly where those problems arise following separation.[186] Although not necessary for their decision, both Lord Nicholls and Baroness Hale considered this issue in *Miller; McFarlane*. While Lord Nicholls referred generally to needs arising from disability without qualification,[187] Baroness Hale's view required at least a 'temporal' link to the marriage:[188]

Miller v Miller; McFarlane v McFarlane [2006] UKHL 24

BARONESS HALE:

137. . . . The cardinal feature is that each [of the three principles: need, sharing, and compensation] is looking at factors which are linked to the parties' relationship, either causally or temporally, and not to extrinsic, unrelated factors, such as a disability arising after the marriage has ended.

138. . . . The most common rationale is that *the relationship has generated needs* which it is right that the other party should meet . . . This is a perfectly sound rationale where the needs are the consequence of the parties' relationship, as they usually are. The most common source of need is the presence of children, whose welfare is always the first consideration, or of other dependent relatives, such as elderly parents. But another source of need is having had to look after children or other family members in the past. Many parents have seriously compromised their ability to attain self-sufficiency as a result of past family responsibilities. Even if they do their best to re-enter the employment market, it will often be at a lesser level than before, and they will hardly ever be able to make up what they have lost in pension entitlements. A further source of need may be the way in which the parties chose to run their life together. Even dual career families are difficult to manage with completely equal opportunity for both. Compromises often have to be made by one so that the other can get ahead. All couples throughout their lives together have to make choices about who will do what, sometimes forced upon them by circumstances such as redundancy or low pay, sometimes freely made in the interests of them both. The needs generated by such choices are a perfectly sound rationale for adjusting the parties' respective resources in compensation.

The Scottish Law Commission examined this area when recommending that awards should be possible on the grounds of 'grave financial hardship', one of five principles on which relief can be based under the Family Law (Scotland) Act 1985. But they felt that the principle should have limited operation:[189]

[185] *Jones v Jones* [1976] Fam 8; *FF v KF* [2017] EWHC 1093.

[186] E.g. *Ashley v Blackman* [1988] Fam 85; *Re G (Financial Provision: Liberty to Restore Application for Lump Sum)* [2004] EWHC 88. See Law Com (2012), case study 3 and para 4.42.

[187] See [11], in extract at 6.5.3. [188] See also *Radmacher v Granatino* [2010] UKSC 42, [187].

[189] See also Law Com (1980), para 72.

Scottish Law Commission, *Report on Aliment and Financial Provision*, Scot Law Com No 67 (Edinburgh: HMSO, 1981)

3.110 . . . We do not think, for example, that a man who suffers hardship on being made redundant at the age of 52 should have a claim for financial provision against a former wife whom he divorced thirty years before. We think that the general principle should be that after the divorce each party bears the risk of *supervening* hardship without recourse against the other. It should therefore be made clear in the legislation that it is only where the likelihood of grave financial hardship is established at the time of the divorce that a claim will arise [on that basis]. We recognise that if the principle is framed in this way there will be cases falling narrowly on the "wrong" side of the line. The man or woman paralysed as a result of a road accident six months before the divorce would have a claim for financial provision. The man or woman who suffered a similar injury six months after the divorce would not. We consider, however, that a line has to be drawn somewhere and that the right place to draw the line is the date when the legal relationship between the parties comes to an end. After that each should be free to make a new life without liability for future misfortunes which may befall the other.

On this view, a former spouse cannot be expected to meet all needs, howsoever arising, however short the marriage, and however long ago the divorce.[190]

Unlike the clarity of the Scottish position, the English cases do not clearly delineate the extent of responsibility for need. The Supreme Court has suggested that:

In order to sustain a case of need, *at any rate if made after many years of separation,*[191] a wife *must* show not only that the need exists but that it has been generated by her relationship with her husband.[192] [Emphasis added]

At least one first instance judge (echoing the Scottish position) considers that needs not causally related to the marriage should be met only to 'alleviate significant hardship':

SS v NS [2014] EWHC 4183

MOSTYN J:

31. . . . I find it difficult to see why it is just and reasonable that an ex-husband should have to pay spousal maintenance . . . by reference to factors which are not causally connected to the marriage, unless one is looking at the issue in a macro-economic utilitarian way and deciding that in such circumstances it is better that the ex-husband picks up the cost of the ex-wife's support rather than the hard-pressed taxpayer. This . . . is a matter of social policy.

[190] Cf Diduck (2011a), (2011b); Miles (2011a).

[191] See 6.5.6 re late applications.

[192] *Wyatt v Vince* [2015] UKSC 14, [33].

But other judges have—without discussion of the point of principle—made substantial awards directed at needs connected with a serious illness that arose late in the marriage: temporally related to the marriage only.[193]

It may sometimes be proper to require an ex-spouse to provide support following some misfortune even where that occurs long after divorce. While the unmet need may be triggered by an event unrelated to the marriage, the applicant's inability to be self-supporting at that point may be because she lacks any financial cushion, having given up paid employment to make domestic contributions during and after the marriage.[194] But in *North v North*, the ex-husband was required to make modest annual payments to his ex-wife of 14 years, some 20 years post-divorce, when her position became precarious following her emigration and unwise investment decisions.[195] The Court of Appeal rejected the husband's argument that the wife should be required, as a matter of principle, to prove that 'despite her best efforts, her attempts at self-help had failed' before being able to proceed with her application, instead factoring the point into its broad discretion to achieve a fair result. On the facts, and given Thorpe LJ's statement of principle extracted earlier, it is surprising that any periodical payment was awarded.[196]

6.5.3.e The needs and resources of second families

The court must also consider the needs and obligations of the respondent and any new dependants, whether the respondent is legally or, as in the case of step-children or a cohabiting partner, only morally obliged to maintain them.[197] In *Vaughan v Vaughan (No 2)*, it was said that 'although [the court] should not go so far as to give priority to the claims of the first wife, it should certainly not give priority to the claims of the second wife'.[198] In *Delaney v Delaney*, the wife was renting the former matrimonial home with the two children; the husband had bought a new three-bedroomed property with his girlfriend on a shared equity basis, wishing to start a family. Any obligation to the first family would leave the husband's household with an amount 'barely adequate to sustain any reasonable way of life'.[199] The Court of Appeal balanced support for the primary carer against the needs of the husband's new family.

Delaney v Delaney [1991] FCR 161 (CA), 165–6

WARD J:

[T]he approach of this court in this case must be, first, to have regard to the need of the wife and the children for proper support. Having assessed that need, the court should then consider the ability of the husband to meet it. Whilst this court deprecates any notion that a former husband and extant father may slough off the tight skin of familial responsibility and

[193] E.g. *HC v FW* [2017] EWHC 3162. See also *Fisher v Fisher* [1989] 1 FLR 432; cf approach in *Wyatt v Vince* [2015] UKSC 14; *Seaton v Seaton* [1986] 2 FLR 398.

[194] E.g. *Whiting v Whiting* [1988] 1 WLR 565, 580.

[195] Cf *Yates v Yates* [2012] EWCA Civ 532.

[196] Cf *Mills v Mills* [2018] UKSC 38: where provision is already made for housing, 'very good reason' is needed to justify an uplift in periodical payments to cover accommodation costs.

[197] *Roberts v Roberts* [1970] P 1.

[198] [2010] EWCA Civ 349.

[199] Note that the husband would now remain technically liable to pay child support at the relevant rate: chapter 5.

may slither into and lose himself in the greener grass on the other side, nonetheless this court has proclaimed and will proclaim that it looks to the realities of the real world in which we live, and that among the realities of life is that there is a life after divorce. The . . . husband is entitled to order his life in such a way as will hold in reasonable balance the responsibilities to his existing family which he carries into his new life, as well as his proper aspirations for that new future.

In the circumstances, it was appropriate to bring the wife's welfare benefit entitlements into account.

Can the resources of a respondent's new partner be considered in deciding what, if any, order to make against that spouse? If working, the partner can be expected to contribute to shared household costs, thereby reducing that spouse's expenditure and freeing up resources for the first family. But the court will not ordinarily make orders that can only be satisfied by using the resources of the payer's new partner, or other third party, or by making orders that leave payers dependent on a third party.[200]

Elsewhere, the question is whether and how a new partner of the (would-be) *recipient* of periodical payments is relevant.[201] Where the recipient marries or forms a civil partnership before any order has been made, any application is statute-barred and any existing order for periodical payments automatically terminates.[202] Cohabitation does not have the same effect. Orders commonly provide that periodical payments will cease if the recipient cohabits with a third party for six months. But if no such term was included, the payer wishing to cease or reduce payment must seek a variation under the MCA 1973, s 31. A cohabitant or other committed life partner[203] who can afford to contribute to the recipient's household should do so to the extent that they have capacity to pay;[204] orders have been reduced, discharged, or rendered nominal accordingly.[205]

But there is disagreement about the weight that should, in principle, be attached to cohabitation. In *Atkinson v Atkinson*,[206] the Court of Appeal held that cohabitation should not be equated with marriage, a position affirmed in *Grey v Grey*,[207] despite the 'heretical' reservations of Coleridge J in *K v K*.[208] Coleridge J had argued that given the rise in cohabitation and births outside marriage, and the functional and social equivalence to marriage of lengthy, settled cohabitation, it was too easy for an ex-spouse to avoid periodical payments terminating automatically by cynically not marrying the new partner, leaving the payer to seek a variation of the order.[209] But the Court of Appeal is clear that the matter must be left to Parliament. For now, cohabitation is just another factor to weigh in the balance of fairness, albeit one that can attract considerable weight. This clash between law and social practice is difficult. While many cohabiting relationships are akin to marriage, others are less stable. Moreover, as the wife in *K v K* argued, cohabitants—unlike spouses—have no legal obligations of mutual support, whether during their relationship or following separation.[210]

[200] *Macey v Macey* (1982) 3 FLR 7.

[201] See also *Chadwick v Chadwick* [1985] FLR 606: whether *Martin* order is more appropriate than outright transfer.

[202] MCA 1973, s 28(1)(a), (3). [203] *Grey v Grey (No 3)* [2010] EWHC 1055.

[204] *Grey v Grey* [2009] EWCA Civ 1424, [28]. [205] E.g. *Suter v Suter* [1987] Fam 111.

[206] [1988] Fam 93. [207] [2009] EWCA Civ 1424. [208] [2005] EWHC 2886.

[209] Cf Diduck (2011b), 307–8. [210] See chapter 7.

6.5.3.f Criticism of the law relating to needs

The Law Commission has made several criticisms of the current law relating to 'need'. It lacks principle, offering no consistent explanation for when and why one ex-spouse should have to meet the other's needs and it is inaccessible to the lay person, being ascertainable only from close scrutiny of the case law. It is said also to be crucially unclear regarding the use of periodical payments, both as to how much should be paid and for how long; and there is dissatisfaction with the level of awards, some being regarded as too high, others far too low.[211] Insofar as this debate relates to whether and when 'clean break' settlements are made, we explore it at 6.6.

6.5.3.g Contribution-based awards in non-sharing, non-needs cases?

Before we leave the needs principle, we must briefly note how the courts emphasize a spouse's contributions to the welfare of the family, for example where a needs-based award is inappropriate (as the applicant's needs cannot be related to the marriage) but the 'sharing' principle is inapplicable (as the assets are non-matrimonial, discussed later).[212] This was so in *Wyatt v Vince*, a case complicated by the lateness of the wife's application. When the parties had divorced years earlier, they had no assets. The husband subsequently became hugely successful while the wife struggled. In seeking a financial remedy, she relied on her care of the two children of the family and the husband's lack of significant financial or other contribution to their upbringing, leaving her to raise them in 'hand to mouth' conditions:

Wyatt v Vince **[2015] UKSC 14**

LORD WILSON:

34. . . . In the discharge of its duty under section 25 . . . the court will be required, by subsection (2)(f), to have regard to "the contributions which each of the parties has made . . . to the welfare of the family, including any contribution by looking after the home or caring for the family". Such contributions are not limited to those made prior to the separation or even during the marriage. . . . Her case is no more than that, for whatever reason, the heavy burden fell upon her and, in effect, upon her alone.

The Supreme Court gave no clear guidance about how such an order should be quantified, but the parties ultimately agreed a relatively modest lump sum that would enable the wife to house herself mortgage-free.[213] Whilst not 'needs-based', the contribution-based remedy[214] ultimately secured her basic housing needs. Insofar as it sought to recognize her contributions over the years, it might also be said to have a compensatory aspect, which brings us to the next *Miller; McFarlane* principle.

[211] Law Com (2012), from para 3.30.
[212] Cf concern to reflect wife's contributions in needs case *Alireza v Radwan* [2017] EWCA Civ 1545, [86].
[213] [2015] UKSC 14, [36]; *Wyatt v Vince* [2016] EWHC 1368.
[214] For commentary, see Ferguson (2015b), 202–5.

6.5.4 COMPENSATION: RELATIONSHIP-GENERATED ECONOMIC DISADVANTAGE

***Miller v Miller; McFarlane v McFarlane* [2006] UKHL 24**

LORD NICHOLLS:

13. Another strand, recognised more explicitly now than formerly, is compensation. This is aimed at redressing any significant prospective economic disparity between the parties arising from the way they conducted their marriage. For instance, the parties may have arranged their affairs in a way which has greatly advantaged the husband in terms of his earning capacity but left the wife severely handicapped so far as her own earning capacity is concerned. Then the wife suffers a double loss: a diminution in her earning capacity and the loss of a share in her husband's enhanced income. This is often the case. Although less marked than in the past, women may still suffer a disproportionate financial loss on the breakdown of a marriage because of their traditional role as home-maker and child-carer . . .

15. Compensation and financial needs often overlap in practice, so double-counting has to be avoided. But they are distinct concepts, and they are far from co-terminous. A claimant wife may be able to earn her own living but she may still be entitled to a measure of compensation.

Mrs McFarlane's circumstances were the paradigm case for this principle: she had given up a very good professional job in order to raise their three children and support her husband, who acquired a high earning capacity and accumulated all of the couple's assets during their 16-year marriage. With occasional exceptions,[215] the compensation strand received a cool reception from practitioners and the lower courts, perceived (rightly or wrongly) to lack statutory foundation,[216] to be impractical, speculative, and potential costly to operate, unless very tightly circumscribed,[217] and to be unprincipled.[218] Like arguments about conduct and 'stellar contributions',[219] the argument seems to be one that the courts only rarely entertain,[220] and there is considerable overlap between compensation and the other two principles. Since the available resources are often insufficient even to cover the parties' needs, there is no room for any distinct element of 'compensation'.

The speeches of Lord Nicholls and Baroness Hale identified two distinct potential issues: (i) loss of earning capacity sustained by a spouse who reduced or gave up paid employment in order to care for the family; and (ii) enhancement of one spouse's income and earning capacity which is partly attributable to the other's support. They touched only briefly on the latter. Some earlier big-money cases had seen awards of periodical payments exceeding needs, ostensibly made as part of a 'bridging period' prior to a clean break,[221] but perhaps better understood as recognizing the applicant's contribution to the respondent's earning

[215] Notably *Lauder v Lauder* [2007] EWHC 1227.

[216] But see *Charman v Charman* [2007] EWCA Civ 503, [71]; Miles (2005).

[217] E.g. *RP v RP* [2006] EWHC 3409, [59]–[64]; *SA v PA* [2014] EWHC 392, [36].

[218] E.g. *CR v CR* [2007] EWHC 3334, [79]; Deech (2009c); Parkinson (2011), 257–8; cf Miles (2008), esp 391–2.

[219] See 6.5.6. [220] Viney and Brunsdon-Tully (2014).

[221] E.g. *Q v Q (Ancillary Relief: Periodical Payments)* [2005] EWHC 402.

capacity.[222] But the Court of Appeal has rejected the idea that the compensation principle applies to the second type of case.[223] Insofar as any version of this argument might be sustainable, this is addressed at 6.5.5 with the sharing principle, and we focus here on the first idea: compensation for 'relationship-generated disadvantage'.[224]

6.5.4.a Compensation: a distinct principle?

In theory, where resources permit, the compensation principle could justify an award exceeding need or an equal share of the assets in an appropriate case: the scale of Mrs McFarlane's career disadvantage 'went well beyond the compensation afforded by a generous interpretation of her needs'.[225] But the idea of compensation for earning capacity impaired by past and/or future child-care responsibility predates *Miller; McFarlane*:

SRJ v DWJ (Financial Provision) **[1999] 3 FCR 153 (CA), 160**

HALE LJ:

This was a long marriage. The couple had 27 years together. There were four children. It was a classic example of the sort of case where the wife could have continued to work as a teacher; indeed, she did for some of the time. But she gave up her place in the world of work to concentrate upon her husband, her home and her family. That must have been a mutual decision from which they both benefited. It means that the marriage has deprived her of what otherwise she might have had. Over the many years of that marriage she must have built up an entitlement to some compensation for that. It is not only in her interests but in the community's interests that parents, whether mothers or fathers, and spouses, whether wives or husbands, should have a real choice between concentrating on breadwinning and concentrating on home-making and child rearing, and do not feel forced, for fear of what might happen should their marriage break down much later in life, to abandon looking after the home and the family to other people for the sake of maintaining a career.

Short marriages that produce children may also generate compensation-based arguments, as may childless marriages in which one spouse gives up a lucrative career so that the parties can relocate for the sake of the other's career.[226] In *B v B (Mesher Order)*, the parties had been married for only one year, but had a child, Will. A lump sum was ordered to allow the wife to buy a house for herself and Will. Should this be done on a *Mesher* basis, reserving a portion of the capital for the husband on Will's independence, or transferred outright? Munby J agreed with the 'common sense view of the future realities', depicted by counsel for the wife, that:

[222] E.g. *Parlour v Parlour* [2004] EWCA Civ 872; cf *M v M* [2004] EWHC 688: award based on the wife's future contributions to caring for their special needs child.

[223] *Waggott v Waggott* [2018] EWCA Civ 727, [139].

[224] *Miller; McFarlane* [2006] UKHL 24, [140].

[225] *VB v JP* [2008] EWHC 112, [60]; *Miller; McFarlane* [2006] UKHL 24, [15].

[226] *Murphy v Murphy* [2009] EWCA Civ 1258.

B v B (Mesher Order) **[2002] EWHC 3106**

MUNBY J:

. . . the wife's major contribution to this marriage . . . is the fact that she, for the next 16 years or so (and I put it that way because Will is now approximately two years old), will have the very considerable burden of looking after him and bringing him up . . .

Furthermore . . . in the nature of things the performance by the wife of her obligations . . . will inevitably impact adversely upon her earning capacity. Not merely her capacity to earn an income during that part of her life, during Will's early years when she will not be able to work at all; not merely during that part of Will's later childhood during which she will be able to work part-time perhaps on an increasing scale. But even after Will is off her hands, her continuing earning capacity, even when she is free to work full-time, will be significantly reduced . . . by the fact that for a number of years she will have been out of the job market. She will therefore find herself, when Will is 18, in her mid-40s, even if free to work full-time, not able to get the kind of job which will generate the kind of income which by then she could realistically have hoped to obtain had she not had the interruption of looking after Will.

Moreover . . . that impacts not merely upon her earning ability in the sense of her income, it impacts seriously (and he suggests decisively) upon her ability . . . ever to generate capital, whether by way of acquiring a property on a mortgage, or more particularly by way of building up a pension fund.

Meanwhile, the husband would readily make back the capital and had substantial pension funds that were untouched by the order. The outright transfer of the house to the wife was therefore upheld.

Failing to recognize career sacrifice such as Mrs McFarlane's would often leave an imbalance between the parties. In theory, such cases call for close examination of the quantum of appropriate compensation,[227] especially where the full and final settlement of a clean break is contemplated.[228] But the order should not create a new imbalance that operates unfairly against the respondent. There are only limited assets available for distribution and these are not tort claims: the respondent is not paying damages for injury sustained owing to his blameworthy conduct, regardless of his own needs and legitimate claims. The sacrifice of curtailing paid employment should ordinarily be viewed as the product of a joint decision made as part of the spouses' lifestyle choices for their relationship. The economic consequences of that choice should be fairly shared, given the finite resources that their partnership has generated and both parties' interests; there should be no question of the applicant emerging with a superior standard of living.[229]

However the award is measured, fairness to respondents also dictates that applicants should be expected to 'mitigate' their disadvantage, for example by returning to paid employment once child-care obligations permit. In assessing what earning capacity it would be reasonable to expect such parties to acquire,[230] courts consider their ages and the duration of their absence from the labour market.[231] But, as *SRJ v DWJ* indicates,[232] there are

[227] [2008] EWHC 112, [60]; see criticism of the judge's reasoning in *H v H* [2014] EWCA Civ 1523.

[228] [2008] EWHC 112, [61], [66]. Since periodical payments terminate on remarriage, only a capital award will guarantee full compensation unaffected by that possibility.

[229] See *McFarlane v McFarlane (No 2)* [2009] EWHC 891, [44]–[45], [113]–[114]; Miles (2008).

[230] See the reference to future earning capacity in MCA 1973, s 25(2)(a).

[231] *Leadbeater v Leadbeater* [1985] FLR 789.

[232] [1999] 2 FLR 176, 182.

important social questions about what can reasonably be expected of parents: some parents wish to work, or feel they have to do so; others prefer to undertake child-care personally as far as possible and so limit paid work commitments. Hale LJ assumed that the parties' decisions in *SRJ v DWJ* about employment and child-care were mutual—but what if one party contends otherwise? Respondents may also wish to make lifestyle choices after divorce that reduce their income and so limit their ability to make periodical payments.[233]

Career sacrifice or downscaling has sometimes been characterized not as a 'relationship-generated disadvantage', but rather a lifestyle choice by that spouse for which they alone should bear responsibility.[234] There was a stark divergence of view in *Radmacher v Granatino* between the majority and Baroness Hale, dissenting, regarding the husband's decision in that case to move from merchant banking to a less lucrative academic career.[235] While the majority categorized this decision as a personal lifestyle choice, Baroness Hale viewed his decision as one made in the context of his marriage with his wife's support. As Alison Diduck has argued, the difference here lies between viewing parties as exercising 'abstract agency' as autonomous individuals, or viewing their decisions contextually, within a mutually supportive relationship.[236]

Radmacher v Granatino [2010] UKSC 42

BARONESS HALE:

188. . . . Most spouses want their partners to be happy—partly, of course, because they love them and partly because it is not much fun living with a miserable person. So, choices are often made for the sake of the overall happiness of the family. The couple may move from the city to the country; they may move to another country; they may adopt a completely different lifestyle; one of them may give up a well-paid job that she hates for the sake of a less lucrative job that she loves; one may give up a dead-end job to embark upon a new course of study. These sorts of things happen all the time in a relationship. The couple will support one another while they are together. And it may generate a continued need for support once they are apart. Whether this is seen as needs or compensation may not matter very much. It can only be for this reason that the husband in this case had any real claim upon his wife apart from his claims as the father of her children.

6.5.4.b Compensation: need in disguise?

However, for all the theoretical discussion, these cases may in fact best be understood not as introducing an entirely separate rationale for the financial order, but rather as underscoring the justification for generous needs-based awards:[237]

233 Moor and Le Grice (2006).
234 E.g. Mostyn J's analysis of Mrs McFarlane's decision: *SA v PA* [2014] EWHC 392, [28].
235 [2010] UKSC 42, [121], cf [186]–[188]. 236 (2011b), from 306. See also Bendall (2014), 269.
237 E.g. *Lauder v Lauder* [2007] EWHC 1227; *VB v JP* [2008] EWHC 112, [59], [82].

Law Commission, *Marital Property Agreements*, Law Com CP 198 (London: TSO, 2011)

2.56 The introduction of compensation as a distinct concept has made no difference in the level or the nature of the awards made. We think that it may be best regarded as a way of spelling out something that has always been regarded as an element of needs. . . . Having compensation articulated separately is useful because it draws attention to financial consequences that may not be obvious . . .

2.58 The recognition that an award focused on this type of disadvantage is a form of compensation may help the courts to focus their attention upon the real value of what has been lost. It is arguable that the introduction of compensation as a separate concept is simply a teasing out of the complex notion of "needs generously interpreted", at least in the way that the courts have applied it so far.

This view is supported by various judicial remarks: the concept of 'relationship-generated disadvantage . . . is intended principally to ensure that the court does not overlook the effect on a spouse of a loss of career';[238] the point merits separate attention from the other principles 'to ensure that the courts adopt a non discriminatory approach in the exercise of the discretion',[239] achieving overall equality of outcome between the parties.[240]

Close examination of *McFarlane*—the supposedly paradigm case—also supports this view. Both spouses had successful professional careers, but they decided the wife should stop work to look after the home and family. By the divorce, the husband was earning over £750,000 net annually, a sum far exceeding the family's needs. The House of Lords held that annual periodical payments of £250,000 should be paid both to meet the wife's needs and to compensate her for foregone earning capacity. There was no explanation of how that figure was reached, or to what extent it compensated rather than met need. When *McFarlane* returned to court on a variation application,[241] Charles J considered that, given the parties' long marriage and its character as a joint enterprise, fairness required that the wife should maintain her current standard of living for life, with no drop on retirement, as might otherwise have been expected. It could at least be said that, had she not given up her career, she would have been able to maintain that standard herself, but instead the parties had so conducted themselves that they would depend on the husband's income. However, rather than try to estimate the wife's earnings losses, the order effectively provided a *very* generous assessment of need.[242]

6.5.4.c Compensating for what?

John Eekelaar argues that the *McFarlane* formulation of compensation is misguided:[243]

238 *W v W* [2009] EWHC 3076, [97].
239 *H v H* [2014] EWCA Civ 1523, [41]; *SA v PA* [2014] EWHC 392, [36](iv).
240 *Vaughan v Vaughan* [2007] EWCA Civ 1085, [50]; *CR v CR* [2007] EWHC 3334, [95].
241 [2009] EWHC 891. 242 See also *H v H* [2014] EWCA Civ 1523.
243 See also Ellman (2007); Douglas (2018b).

J. Eekelaar, 'Property and Financial Settlements on Divorce—Sharing and Compensating', (2006) 36 *Family Law* 754, 756

Baroness Hale described the compensation as being for 'relationship-generated disadvantage' . . . Does this mean that *any* loss, or opportunity foregone, as a result of entering the relationship should be (fully?) compensated? Lord Hope remarked that it would be unfair if 'a woman who has chosen motherhood over her career in the interests of her family' were to be 'denied a fair share of the wealth that her husband has been able to build up . . . out of the earnings that he is able to generate when she cannot be compensated for this out of capital' . . . Yet there are strong arguments against approaching the compensation issue in this way. Some are practical. In many cases the financial benefits of an 'alternative life' are too speculative to provide an appropriate measure. But also, there must be a high possibility that, had the applicant not had the relationship with the respondent, he or she will have had one with another person. The 'alternative life' may never have happened anyway. As the [American Law Institute] put it:

> '[The wife] has not lost a career, for that is not what she had sought. She instead lost the opportunity to have her children with someone with whom she would enjoy an enduring relationship. The most direct measure of her financial loss would compare her situation at divorce to the hypothetical situation had she married a different man'. . . .

The compensation is, therefore, for the consequences of the differential risk between the parties of the consequences of the separation. As Lord Nicholls said, the compensation element would be 'aimed at redressing any significant prospective economic disparity between the parties arising from the way they conducted their marriage' (at para [13]). This must refer to the disparity after the separation, not before it. Suppose the respondent earns less than the applicant after separation, but the applicant would nevertheless have earned more were it not for the relationship. Surely there should be no claim against the respondent.[244] If there is no disparity, so the risk has turned out even, there again seems no case for compensation . . .

In summary, while it is likely that most couples will experience relationship-generated economic disadvantage post-separation, the distinct question of compensation will only be considered in exceptional circumstances. First, there must be sufficient resources available for this argument to be made. As noted at the beginning of this section at 6.5.4, there will be no space to consider a separate compensation-based claim in needs cases. Secondly, compensation-based claims require evidence of the spouse having given up a 'proven track record',[245] resulting in assets greater than the financial award to which they would otherwise be entitled:

Waggott v Waggott [2018] EWCA Civ 727

MOYLAN LJ:

139. In practice it is a claim which appears very rarely to have been established and I do not intend to encourage any more extensive or expensive exploration of the issue. However, as

[244] See Miles (2008).

[245] *Miller v Miller; McFarlane v McFarlane* [2006] UKHL 24, [92].

a necessary factual foundation the court would have to determine, on a balance of probabilities, that the applicant's career would have resulted in them having resources greater than those which they will be awarded by application of either the need principle or the sharing principle. Further, the court must separately determine whether, and if so how, this factor should be reflected in the award so as to ensure that it is fair to both parties.

As we discuss further at 6.5.5.e, it is rare that compensation-based claims will succeed even when these apparent prerequisites are satisfied, although there are some exceptions.[246]

6.5.5 ENTITLEMENT: EQUAL SHARING

The equal sharing principle originates in *White v White*. The Whites had been married for over 30 years and had three children, all adult by the divorce. They had built a successful farming business, the wife working as an active business partner and raising the family. The assets exceeded the parties' financial needs:

White v White [2001] 1 AC 596, 605–6, 608

LORD NICHOLLS:

In seeking to achieve a fair outcome, there is no place for discrimination between husband and wife and their respective roles. Typically, a husband and wife share the activities of earning money, running their home and caring for their children. Traditionally, the husband earned the money, and the wife looked after the home and the children. This traditional division of function is no longer the order of the day. Frequently both parents work. Sometimes it is the wife who is the money-earner, and the husband runs the home and cares for the children during the day. But whatever the division of labour chosen by the husband and wife, or forced upon them by circumstances, fairness requires that this should not prejudice or advantage either party when considering [s 25(2)] (f), relating to the parties' contributions. This is implicit in the very language of paragraph (f): ". . . the contribution which *each* . . . has made or is likely . . . to make to the *welfare of the family*, including any contribution by looking after the home or caring for the family." (Emphasis added.) If, in their different spheres, each contributed equally to the family, then in principle it matters not which of them earned the money and built up the assets. There should be no bias in favour of the money-earner and against the home-maker and the child-carer . . .

A practical consideration follows from this. Sometimes, having carried out the statutory exercise, the judge's conclusion involves a more or less equal division of the available assets. More often, this is not so. More often, having looked at all the circumstances, the judge's decision means that one party will receive a bigger share than the other. Before reaching a firm conclusion and making an order along these lines, a judge would always be well advised to check his tentative views against the yardstick of equality of division. As a general guide, equality should be departed from only if, and to the extent that, there is good reason for doing so. The need to consider and articulate reasons for departing from equality would help the parties and the court to focus on the need to ensure the absence of discrimination.

[246] *RC v JC* [2020] EWHC 466.

He found that the established case law, which confined wives in high-value cases to awards satisfying their 'reasonable requirements', leaving the surplus to the money-making husband, was not supported by the statute or the objective of fairness:

> If a husband and wife by their joint efforts over many years, his directly in his business and hers indirectly at home, have built up a valuable business from scratch, why should the claimant wife be confined to the court's assessment of her reasonable requirements, and the husband left with a much larger share? Or, to put the question differently, in such a case, where the assets exceed the financial needs of both parties, why should the surplus belong solely to the husband? On the facts of a particular case there may be a good reason why the wife should be confined to her needs and the husband left with the much larger balance. But the mere absence of financial need cannot, by itself, be a sufficient reason. If it were, discrimination would be creeping in by the back door. In these cases, it should be remembered, the claimant is usually the wife. Hence the importance of the check against the yardstick of equal division.

The facts of *White* fell squarely within the premise for Lord Nicholls' equality yardstick. But there was held to be good reason to depart from equality in recognition of financial help given by Mr White's father.[247]

White had particular significance for older spouses. The needs associated with old age may be substantial but are time-limited. Pre-*White*, an elderly wife who needed only a small capital sum to generate income for the rest of her life might receive less following a decades-long marriage than a younger applicant after a shorter marriage. *White* offered such applicants a substantial award reflecting their contributions over a long marriage.[248]

However, *White* left many questions unanswered. Did the 'yardstick' of equal division apply only where assets exceeded the parties' needs? Did it apply only to long marriages? What if one party was already very wealthy before the marriage? What if one party inherited assets during the marriage? Could it ever be argued that the parties had not 'contributed equally' to the family's welfare, entitling the party who had made a 'stellar' or otherwise 'unmatched contribution' to a larger share? And how (if ever), for these purposes, should the ostensibly incommensurable contributions of homemaker and breadwinner be compared?

Miller returned the question to the House of Lords on facts very different from *White*'s: a short, childless marriage to which the husband brought considerable wealth. How, if at all, should the equality yardstick apply here? And to what property should it apply? Their Lordships parted company on the latter point, albeit reaching the same outcome on the facts: £5 million to Mrs Miller (the matrimonial home and capital to generate nearly £100,000 per annum). This award, under a third of the value of the wealth acquired during the marriage, less than one-sixth of Mr Miller's total estimated wealth, recognized that the gains made during the marriage derived largely from pre-marital business endeavours. The main speeches were delivered by Lord Nicholls and Baroness Hale. Lord Hoffmann agreed with Baroness Hale; Lord Hope agreed with both on all points relevant to the disposal of the case; Lord Mance did likewise, but preferred Baroness Hale's analysis of some points. Regrettably, *Miller; McFarlane* left several questions unanswered, and posed new problems, to which subsequent Court of Appeal authorities give mixed answers.

247 See Cooke (2011b).

248 *White v White* [2001] 1 AC 596, 609, criticizing the '*Duxbury* paradox'.

***Miller v Miller; McFarlane v McFarlane* [2006] UKHL 24**

LORD NICHOLLS:

16. A third strand [after need and compensation] is sharing. This 'equal sharing' principle derives from the basic concept of equality permeating a marriage as understood today. Marriage, it is often said, is a partnership of equals. In 1992 Lord Keith of Kinkel approved [the] observation that 'husband and wife are now for all practical purposes equal partners in marriage': *R v R* [1992] 1 AC 599 [the marital rape exemption case]. This is now recognised widely, if not universally. The parties commit themselves to sharing their lives. They live and work together. When their partnership ends each is entitled to an equal share of the assets of the partnership, unless there is a good reason to the contrary. Fairness requires no less. But I emphasise the qualifying phrase: 'unless there is good reason to the contrary'. The yardstick of equality is to be applied as an aid, not a rule.

17. This principle is applicable as much to short marriages as to long marriages: see *Foster v Foster* [2003] EWCA Civ 565 . . . A short marriage is no less a partnership of equals than a long marriage. The difference is that a short marriage has been less enduring. In the nature of things this will affect the quantum of the financial fruits of the partnership.

18. A different approach was suggested in *GW v RW (Financial Provision: Departure from Equality)* [2003] 2 FLR 108 . . . There the court accepted the proposition that entitlement to an equal division must reflect not only the parties' respective contributions 'but also an accrual over time' . . . It would be 'fundamentally unfair' that a party who has made domestic contributions during a marriage of 12 years should be awarded the same proportion of the assets as a party who has made the domestic contributions for more than 20 years. . . .

19. I am unable to agree with this approach. This approach would mean that on the breakdown of a short marriage the money-earner would have a head start over the home-maker and child-carer. To confine the *White* approach to the 'fruits of a long marital partnership' would be to re-introduce precisely the sort of discrimination the *White* case . . . was intended to negate.

BARONESS HALE:

141. A third rationale [after needs and compensation] is *the sharing of the fruits of the matrimonial partnership*. One reason given by the Law Commission for not adopting any one single model was that the flexibility of section 25 allowed practice to develop in response to changing perceptions of what might be fair. There is now a widespread perception that marriage is a partnership of equals. The Scottish Law Commission found that this translated into widespread support for a norm of equal sharing of the partnership assets when the marriage ended, whatever the source or legal ownership of those assets . . . A decade earlier, the English Law Commission had found widespread support for the automatic joint ownership of the matrimonial home, even during marriage . . . [T]he authors of *Settling Up* [Arthur et al (2002)] p 56, found that "there appeared to be a relatively widespread assumption that an 'equal' or 50/50 division was the normal or appropriate thing to do", alongside a recognition of needs and entitlements (but their respondents' views on entitlements might not be quite the same as the lawyers' . . .).

143. . . . [T]here are many cases in which the approach of roughly equal sharing of partnership assets with no continuing claims one against the other is nowadays entirely feasible and fair. One example is *Foster v Foster* [2003] EWCA Civ 565 . . ., a comparatively short childless

marriage, where each could earn their own living after divorce, but where capital assets had been built up by their joint efforts during the marriage. Although one party had earned more and thus contributed more in purely financial terms to the acquisition of those assets, both contributed what they could, and the fair result was to divide the product of their joint endeavours equally. Another example is *Burgess v Burgess* [1996] 2 FLR 34, a long marriage between a solicitor and a doctor, which had produced three children. Each party could earn their own living after divorce, but the home, contents and collections which they had accumulated during the marriage could be equally shared. Although one party might have better prospects than the other in future, once the marriage was at an end there was no reason for one to make further claims upon the other.

So the principle of equal sharing is available whatever the duration of the marriage.[249] In cases where the moneyed spouse sought a departure from equality on the basis that the marriage was short and childless, the court has reaffirmed that these factors in themselves do not constitute an exception to the equal sharing principle.[250] Cases where such a departure may be justified 'will be as rare as a white leopard', as Mostyn J put it in *E v L*.[251] But beyond that, the scope and application of equal sharing are unclear. Several related questions arise.

- Does the principle operate as a presumption or starting point?
- To what property does it apply?
- What constitutes 'good reason' to divide that property other than equally?
- What is its relationship with the other principles?

6.5.5.a Does the equal sharing principle provide a starting point?

Lord Nicholls in *White* was adamant that judges must not curtail the wide discretion conferred by the MCA 1973 by treating equal sharing as a presumption or starting point. He deployed it instead as a final 'check', having provisionally decided what outcome would be fair given the s 25 checklist.[252] However, in *Charman v Charman*, the Court of Appeal interpreted *Miller; McFarlane* as treating equal sharing as an appropriate—though not mandatory—starting point. In their view, the equal sharing principle means that 'property should be shared in equal proportions unless there is good reason to depart from such proportions'.[253] This difference—examining the checklist first or applying the sharing principle first—reflects the deeper difference in approach to the s 25 exercise that we noted at the start of 6.5, in which certain judges emphasize the strongly discretionary nature of the exercise whilst others seek to contain the exercise within principled bounds. Indeed, we shall see later that, in similar vein, different judges approach the sharing principle itself differently—some more loosely, some more formulaically.

[249] Crowe-Urbaniak (2022). [250] *VV v VV* [2022] EWFC 41. [251] [2021] EWFC 60 (Fam), [45].
[252] See also *B v B* [2008] EWCA Civ 543, [50]–[60]; *Robson v Robson* [2010] EWCA Civ 1171.
[253] [2007] EWCA Civ 503, [65].

6.5.5.b To what property does equal sharing apply?

'Matrimonial' and 'non-matrimonial' property introduced

Where the equal sharing principle is applicable, a key question is what property falls within the equal sharing pool. Lord Nicholls took a broad view:

Miller v Miller; McFarlane v McFarlane **[2006] UKHL 24**

LORD NICHOLLS:

20. . . . The rationale underlying the sharing principle is as much applicable to 'business and investment' assets as to 'family' assets . . .

Matrimonial property and non-matrimonial property

22. . . . The statute requires the court to have regard to all the circumstances of the case. One of the circumstances is that there is a real difference, a difference of source, between (1) property acquired during the marriage otherwise than by inheritance or gift, sometimes called the marital acquest but more usually the matrimonial property, and (2) other property. The former is the financial product of the parties' common endeavour, the latter is not. The parties' matrimonial home, even if this was brought into the marriage at the outset by one of the parties, usually has a central place in any marriage. So it should normally be treated as matrimonial property for this purpose.[254] As already noted, in principle the entitlement of each party to a share of the matrimonial property is the same however long or short the marriage may have been.

23. The matter stands differently regarding property ('non-matrimonial property') the parties bring with them into the marriage or acquire by inheritance or gift during the marriage. Then the duration of the marriage will be highly relevant. The position regarding non-matrimonial property was summarised in the *White* case [2001] 1 AC 596, 610:

> 'Plainly, when present, this factor is one of the circumstances of the case. It represents a contribution made to the welfare of the family by one of the parties to the marriage. The judge should take it into account. He should decide how important it is in the particular case. The nature and value of the property, and the time when and circumstances in which the property was acquired, are among the relevant matters to be considered. . . .' . . .

Flexibility

26. This difference in treatment of matrimonial property and non-matrimonial property might suggest that in every case a clear and precise boundary should be drawn between these two categories of property. This is not so. Fairness has a broad horizon. Sometimes, in the case of a business, it can be artificial to attempt to draw a sharp dividing line as at the parties' wedding day. Similarly the "equal sharing" principle might suggest that each of the party's assets should be separately and exactly valued. But . . . [the] costs involved can quickly become disproportionate . . .

27. Accordingly, where it becomes necessary to distinguish matrimonial property from non-matrimonial property the court may do so with the degree of particularity or generality

[254] Cf *FB v PS* [2015] EWHC 2797: matrimonial, but not shared equally given history as H's family's home; *JL v SL (No 2) (Financial Remedies: Rehearing: Non-Matrimonial Property)* [2015] EWHC 360, [29]; cf *WA v Executors of the Estate of HA* [2015] EWHC 2233, [61].

appropriate in the case. The judge will then give to the contribution made by one party's non-matrimonial property the weight he considers just. He will do so with such generality or particularity as he considers appropriate in t.he circumstances of the case.

By contrast, Baroness Hale contemplated a potentially smaller sharing pool:

BARONESS HALE:

149. The question . . . is whether in the very big money cases, it is fair to take some account of the source and nature of the assets, in the same way that some account is taken of the source of those assets in inherited or family wealth. Is the 'matrimonial property' to consist of everything acquired during the marriage (which should probably include periods of pre-marital cohabitation and engagement) or might a distinction be drawn between "family" and other assets? Family assets were described by Lord Denning MR in the landmark case of *Wachtel v Wachtel* [1973] Fam 72, at 90:

> "It refers to those things which are acquired by one or other or both of the parties, with the intention that there should be continuing provision for them and their children during their joint lives, and used for the benefit of the family as a whole."

Prime examples of family assets of a capital nature were the family home and its contents, while the parties' earning capacities were assets of a revenue nature. But also included are other assets which were obviously acquired for the use and benefit of the whole family, such as holiday homes, caravans, furniture, insurance policies and other family savings. To this list should clearly be added family businesses or joint ventures in which they both work. It is easy to see such assets as the fruits of the marital partnership. It is also easy to see each party's efforts as making a real contribution to the acquisition of such assets. . . .

150. More difficult are business or investment assets which have been generated solely or mainly by the efforts of one party. The other party has often made some contribution to the business, at least in its early days, and has continued with her agreed contribution to the welfare of the family (as did Mrs Cowan [*Cowan v Cowan* [2001] EWCA Civ 679]). But in these non-business-partnership, non-family asset cases, the bulk of the property has been generated by one party. Does this provide a reason for departing from the yardstick of equality? On the one hand is the view, already expressed, that commercial and domestic contributions are intrinsically incommensurable. It is easy to count the money or property which one has acquired. It is impossible to count the value which the other has added to their lives together. One is counted in money or money's worth. The other is counted in domestic comfort and happiness. If the law is to avoid discrimination between the gender roles, it should regard all the assets generated in either way during the marriage as family assets to be divided equally between them unless some other good reason is shown to do otherwise.

151. On the other hand is the view that this is unrealistic. We do not yet have a system of community of property, whether full or deferred. Even modest legislative steps towards this have been strenuously resisted. Ownership and contributions still feature in divorcing couples' own perceptions of a fair result, some drawing a distinction between the home and joint savings accounts, on the one hand, and pensions, individual savings and debts, on the other (*Settling Up*, [Arthur et al (2002)] chapter 5). Some of these are not family assets in the way that the home, its contents and the family savings are family assets. Their value may well be speculative or their possession risky. It is not suggested that the domestic partner should share in the risks or potential liabilities, a problem which bedevils many community of property regimes and can give domestic contributions a negative value. It simply cannot be

demonstrated that the domestic contribution, important though it has been to the welfare and happiness of the family as a whole, has contributed to their acquisition. If the money maker had not had a wife to look after him, no doubt he would have found others to do it for him. Further, great wealth can be generated in a very short time, as the *Miller* case shows; but domestic contributions by their very nature take time to mature into contributions to the welfare of the family.

How to approach 'matrimonial' and 'non-matrimonial' property: divergent views

Since *Miller; McFarlane*, Court of Appeal judges have articulated two different approaches to the sharing principle and its scope, particularly as it concerns non-matrimonial property.

In *Charman v Charman*, the court preferred the view that, subject to narrow exceptions, the principle applies to *all* of the parties' property, whether 'matrimonial' or not. It felt that any alternative risked being discriminatory and undermining the sharing principle. But the presence of 'non-matrimonial' property would be likely to provide a 'good reason' for unequal sharing of the total asset pool, particularly after shorter marriages.[255] By contrast, the court in *Jones v Jones*[256] preferred to separate 'non-matrimonial' assets from 'matrimonial' assets at the outset. The latter would ordinarily be shared equally, but the former would ordinarily not be shared at all (save as required by reference to needs/compensation). This approach gives effect to the concept of sharing the 'fruits of the partnership' (the matrimonial property), whilst clearly not sharing assets such as those acquired by one spouse before the marriage,[257] inherited by one of them,[258] or generated post-separation (the non-matrimonial property). Which approach is better?

Jones v Jones [2011] EWCA Civ 41

WILSON LJ:

35. Criticism can easily be levelled at both approaches. In different ways they are both highly arbitrary. Application of the sharing principle is inherently arbitrary; such is, I suggest, a fact which we should accept and by which we should cease to be disconcerted . . . The exercises, on the one hand, of adopting A and of testing against B and, on the other, of adopting B and testing against A may indeed have subtly different consequences. At all events in this case, particularly in circumstances in which a central valuation mandated by it has been crystallised by sale, I prefer in the first instance to adopt [the approach which deals separately with matrimonial and non-matrimonial assets].

The Law Commission prefers the *Jones* approach for its clarity and predictability, both useful aids to settlement.[259] A prominent critic of the looser approach puts the matter this way:

255 [2007] EWCA Civ 503, [66].

256 [2011] EWCA Civ 41; see also *K v L* [2011] EWCA Civ 550; *Scatliffe v Scatliffe* [2016] UKPC 36, [25].

257 E.g. *Jones v Jones* [2011] EWCA Civ 41; *N v F* [2011] EWHC 586.

258 E.g. *B v B* [2008] EWCA Civ 543; *K v L* [2011] EWCA Civ 550.

259 Law Com (2014), para 8.81.

WM v HM **[2017]** EWFC 25

MOSTYN J (quoting from his judgment in an unreported case):

11 . . . [The *Jones* approach] is logically pure, morally sound, easy to understand, and limits individual judicial caprice. I recognise that not everyone agrees with this approach. For example, the Hong Kong Court of Appeal . . . described it as "not helpful at all" apparently because it encroaches on the exercise of a wide discretion. Even so, I continue to oppose the school of thought that plucks a random percentage out of the air where the pool of assets is a mixture of matrimonial and non-matrimonial property.

However, that Wilson LJ specified in *Jones* that the formulaic approach was right 'in this case' makes clear that he was not propounding this approach as a rule. The more formulaic *Jones* approach works best where the court can ascribe a clear value to each pool of property;[260] it may also suggest that the party wishing to establish the existence *and value* of non-matrimonial assets should have to discharge a burden of proof on that issue.[261] It should surely be the court's preferred approach.[262] On the other hand, where the *existence* of non-matrimonial property is clear but its *valuation* problematic, the alternative 'broad-brush' approach[263] might be preferable, even necessary. And the Court of Appeal has made it clear that the formulaic approach is not required, mindful of the acute difficulties of valuing some assets and the very high costs that can be incurred seeking a valuation:

Hart v Hart **[2017]** EWCA Civ 1306

MOYLAN LJ:

96. If the court has not been able to make a specific factual demarcation but has come to the conclusion that the parties' wealth includes an element of non-matrimonial property, the court will . . . have to fit this determination into the section 25 exercise. The court will have to decide . . . what award of such lesser percentage than 50% makes a fair allowance for the parties' wealth in part comprising or reflecting the product of non-marital endeavour. In arriving at this determination, the court does not have to apply any particular mathematical or other specific methodology. The court has a discretion as to how to arrive at a fair division and can simply apply a broad assessment of the division which would affect "overall fairness". This accords with what Lord Nicholls said in *Miller*. . .

This extract perhaps demonstrates why the Law Commission might prefer a more formulaic approach—there are a number of reported cases where it is difficult to discern why a particular percentage division was selected rather than another. More problematic, however,

260 See Mostyn J's suggested linear approach to difficult valuation questions arising from growth of pre-acquired assets during marriage: *WM v HM* [2017] EWFC 25: [14]–[20]; cf *XW v XH* [2017] EWFC 76, [241].

261 *N v F* [2011] EWHC 586, [14]. Cf the rules of continental European sharing systems: e.g. German Civil Code §1377: a spouse wishing to assert the equivalent of non-matrimonial assets must prove both their existence and value, failing which it will be presumed that there were no such assets, leaving all available for sharing.

262 See *Hart v Hart* [2017] EWCA Civ 1306, [93].

263 *K v L* [2011] EWCA Civ 550, [22].

was the application of this approach in *Hart* itself, where one reason for the impossibility of valuing the non-matrimonial assets was the husband's inadequate disclosure, despite which the judge settled on the lowest of the various possible awards for the applicant wife, an award in fact no greater than her needs. In upholding that award, the Court of Appeal offered no explanation why *she* should have been the one to bear to burden of the factual uncertainty created by the husband.[264]

Whichever approach is taken, in no reported case has property classed as non-matrimonial been shared under this principle.[265] To that extent, the theoretical scope of the sharing principle is clear.

The impact on 'non-matrimonial' property of the passage of time or changed circumstances

Reflecting the two different approaches to non-matrimonial property outlined above, there are two different views about when originally non-matrimonial property, such as pre-acquired assets brought to the marriage or assets inherited during it, may become available for sharing.

Courts that treat the equal sharing principle as applicable to the entire asset pool are inclined to depart from equal sharing after short marriages in recognition of any 'non-matrimonial' property. By contrast, after long marriages, the case for crediting the owner of non-matrimonial property may wane, especially if the property has been used to the family's benefit, such as to buy their home:[266]

Miller v Miller; McFarlane v McFarlane **[2006] UKHL 24**

LORD NICHOLLS:

24. In the case of a short marriage fairness may well require that the claimant should not be entitled to a share of the other's non-matrimonial property. The source of the asset may be a good reason for departing from equality. This reflects the instinctive feeling that parties will generally have less call upon each other on the breakdown of a short marriage.

25. With longer marriages the position is not so straightforward. Non-matrimonial property represents a contribution made to the marriage by one of the parties. Sometimes, as the years pass, the weight fairly to be attributed to this contribution will diminish, sometimes it will not. After many years of marriage the continuing weight to be attributed to modest savings introduced by one party at the outset of the marriage may well be different from the weight attributable to a valuable heirloom intended to be retained in specie. . . . To this non-exhaustive list should be added, as a relevant matter, the way the parties organised their financial affairs.[267]

Where the marriage is long, courts adopting this view have tended to take a broad-brush approach to the treatment of non-matrimonial property in their awards.[268]

[264] Cf concerns expressed in *Versteegh v Versteegh* [2018] EWCA Civ 1050, [135] and resort to '*Wells* sharing' of the hard-to-value assets: see 6.5.5.c.

[265] Cf its use to meet needs: see 6.5.3.c.

[266] *L v L* [2008] EWHC 3328.

[267] See also Baroness Hale, [147], [152].

[268] E.g. *C v C* [2007] EWHC 2033; *H v H* [2008] EWHC 935.

By contrast, those courts that view non-matrimonial property as prima facie excluded from any equal sharing may sometimes bring such property into the sharing pool, but not merely because of the passage of time:

K v L **[2011] EWCA Civ 550**

WILSON LJ:

18. . . . I believe that the true proposition is that the importance of the source of the assets *may* diminish over time. Three situations come to mind:

(a) Over time matrimonial property of such value has been acquired as to diminish the significance of the initial contribution by one spouse of non-matrimonial property.

(b) Over time the non-matrimonial property initially contributed has been mixed with matrimonial property in circumstances in which the contributor may be said to have accepted that it should be treated as matrimonial property or in which, at any rate, the task of identifying its current value is too difficult.[269]

(c) The contributor of non-matrimonial property has chosen to invest it in the purchase of a matrimonial home which, although vested in his or her sole name, has – as in most cases one would expect – come over time to be treated by the parties as a central item of matrimonial property.

The situations described in (a) and (b) above were both present in *White*. By contrast, there is nothing in the facts of the present case which logically justifies a conclusion that, as the long marriage proceeded, there was a diminution in the importance of the source of the parties' entire wealth, at all times ring-fenced by share certificates in the wife's sole name which to a large extent were just kept safely and left to reproduce themselves and to grow in value.

Those last observations leave room for a different conclusion to be reached where an increase in assets' value arises from positive investment activity ('active growth') and so can be classed as a product of the parties' joint endeavours in the marriage, rather than simply 'passive growth' in the market.[270]

Resources acquired post-separation

If originally non-matrimonial property can sometimes become matrimonial during the marriage, can assets not acquired until after the parties' separation ever fall within the sharing principle? The courts have taken a very clear line on post-marital earning capacity and the resultant income:[271]

[269] E.g. *AC v DC (No 2)* [2012] EWHC 2420.

[270] Cf Law Com (2012), para 6.10(4); *Robertston v Robertson* [2016] EWHC 613, [30]–[34].

[271] Permission for the wife to appeal to the Supreme Court was refused.

Waggott v Waggott [2018] EWCA Civ 727

MOYLAN LJ:

121. . . . [I]s an earning capacity capable of being a matrimonial asset to which the sharing principle applies and in the product of which, as a result, an applicant spouse has an entitlement to share?

122. In my view, there are a number of reasons why the clear answer is that it is not.

123. Any extension of the sharing principle to post-separation earnings would fundamentally undermine the court's ability to effect a clean break. In principle, . . . the entitlement to share would continue until the payer ceased working (subject to this being a reasonable decision), potentially a period of many years. If the court was to seek to effect a clean break this would, inevitably, require the court to capitalise its value [a course of action ruled out by Wilson LJ in *Jones*].

124. Looking at its impact more broadly, it would apply to every case in which one party had earnings which were greater than the other's, regardless of need. This could well be a very significant number of cases. Further, if this submission was correct, I cannot see how this would sit with Lady Hale's observations in *Miller* that, even confined to "(i)n general", "it can be assumed that the marital partnership does not stay alive for the purpose of sharing future resources unless this is justified by need or compensation" (para 144) . . .

125. Additionally, it would inevitably require the court to assess the extent to which earning capacity had accrued *during* the marriage. This would require the court to undertake the exercise to which there are powerful objections referred to by Wilson LJ in *Jones v Jones*. Where would the court start and by reference to what factors would the court determine this issue?

126. . . . This lack of clarity supports the conclusion that to apply the sharing principle in this way would significantly undermine the "important aspect of fairness" referred to by Lord Nicholls . . ., namely to achieve an "acceptable degree of consistency of decision". This is in part because this branch of the road to achieving a clean break would be devoid of clear signposts.

So the 'sharing' of earning capacity generally is ruled out. The partnership principle has no force once the marriage is over: the other spouse can then no longer be said to be making a present 'contribution' to the earning spouse's ability to earn, at least not by reference to the partnership rubric that supports equal sharing of income during the marriage.[272] The impact of the other spouse's continuing, post-divorce contributions to the welfare of the family, for example through child-care, must instead be dealt with by needs- or compensation-based provision. However, there is scope to share bonuses that are not paid until after the parties' separation where the recipient's entitlement to the bonus was (if only in part) earned during the marriage: the bonus, to that extent, may then fall within the sharing pool as matrimonial property.[273]

[272] See *H v H* [2007] EWHC 459, [82]–[87].
[273] E.g. *C v C* [2018] EWHC 3186, and *Waggott* itself: [2018] EWCA Civ 727, [5].

6.5.5.c When will there be good reason to divide matrimonial property unequally?

Aside from cases where another principle—such as need—dictates unequal shares, unequal shares may be ordered as a result of departures made 'within' the sharing principle itself.[274] As Elizabeth Cooke has argued, these departures betray an ambiguity in the sharing principle's rationale: is it based on the idea of marriage as a partnership that of itself justifies equal sharing of matrimonial property; or is it based more or less precisely on the notion that the parties have actually made contributions of equal value and that these contributions justify the equal share? The 'partnership' approach makes it harder to argue against equal sharing. By contrast, the 'valuation' approach invites dispute about what each party contributed (financially or otherwise) to the marriage and over what period. In the following sections, we consider 'stellar' contributions, 'unilateral assets', and risky or illiquid assets.

Stellar contributions

Equal sharing of matrimonial property is grounded in part on the assumption that the parties' contributions are equal: 'Absent reliance on exceptional contribution and/or on conduct, evidence is not required about the nature of each party's contribution during the marriage beyond a broad history of the marriage.'[275]

Miller v Miller; McFarlane v McFarlane [2006] UKHL 24

BARONESS HALE:

146. . . . Following *White v White* . . ., the search was on for some reason to stop short of equal sharing, especially in 'big money' cases where the capital had largely been generated by the breadwinner's efforts and enterprise. There were references to exceptional or 'stellar' contributions . . . These, in the words of Coleridge J in *G v G (Financial Provision: Equal Division)* [2002] EWHC 1339 (Fam) . . ., opened a 'forensic Pandora's box'. As he pointed out . . .:

> "[W]hat is 'contribution' but a species of conduct? . . . Both concepts are compendious descriptions of the way in which one party conducted him/herself towards the other and/or the family during the marriage. And both carry with them precisely the same undesirable consequences. First, they call for a detailed retrospective at the end of a broken marriage just at a time when parties should be looking forward, not back . . . But then, the facts having been established, they each call for a value judgment of the worth of each side's behaviour and translation of that worth into actual money. But by what measure and using what criteria? . . . Is there such a concept as an exceptional/special domestic contribution or can only the wealth creator earn the bonus? . . . It is much the same as comparing apples with pears and the debate is about as sterile or useful."

A domestic goddess self-evidently makes a 'stellar' contribution, but that was not what these debates were about. Coleridge J's words were rightly influential in the later retreat from the concept of special contribution in *Lambert v Lambert* [2002] EWCA Civ 1685 . . . It had already been made clear in *White v White* . . . that domestic and financial contributions should be treated equally. Section 25(2)(f) of the 1973 Act does *not* refer to the contributions which

[274] *Charman v Charman* [2007] EWCA Civ 503, [65].

[275] *AR v AR* [2011] EWHC 2717, [75].

each has made to the parties' *accumulated wealth*, but to the contributions they have made (and will continue to make) to the *welfare of the family*. Each should be seen as doing their best in their own sphere. Only if there is such a disparity in their respective contributions to the *welfare of the family* that it would be inequitable to disregard it should this be taken into account in determining their shares.

Or as Lord Nicholls put it, in order to justify unequal sharing:

68. . . . The wholly exceptional nature of the earnings must be, to borrow a phrase more familiar in a different context [conduct—see 6.5.6], obvious and gross.

Contributions that directly led to the acquisition of the assets being divided are perhaps easier to recognize and measure in financial remedy terms than more intangible domestic contributions; and the argument tends only to arise where there is considerable wealth available by which to acknowledge it. Very few reported claims of stellar contribution have succeeded. Accumulation of wealth does not of itself make a financial contribution 'stellar';[276] there must be some 'exceptional and individual quality' in the wealth-creator[277] that has 'a striking evidential foundation which so clearly stands out that the question almost answers itself'.[278] There is no specific monetary threshold that must be exceeded before wealth-creation becomes 'special': that would encourage a presumption of special contribution wherever the threshold was exceeded.[279]

It is hard to envisage a stellar 'domestic' contribution, even (as is common) where one spouse is both engaging in paid employment and doing the larger share of the housework,[280] and it appears impossible to defend a breadwinner's claim of stellar contribution by reference to domestic efforts, however many children must be cared for and however dependent they may be.[281] Moreover, arguing 'stellar' domestic contributions may tend to denigrate the other spouse's efforts at home, so might be ruled out as an attempt to impugn the respondent's 'conduct'.[282] In consequence, it has been argued—unsuccessfully[283]—that the stellar contribution argument should be expunged from the law as inherently discriminatory. As Mostyn J put it: 'The problem with the whole concept of special contribution is that it gives rise to the Orwellian oxymoron that "all contributions are equal but some are more equal than others".'[284] But while the principle remains available, the judges are clearly concerned to avoid discrimination in practice:

[276] Cf *XW v HW* [2017] EWFC 76, [242].
[277] *Work v Gray* [2017] EWCA Civ 270, [103].
[278] *Evans v Evans* [2013] EWHC 506, [132].
[279] *Charman v Charman* [2007] EWCA Civ 503, [87]–[88].
[280] E.g. *X v X (Application for a Financial Remedies Order)* [2016] EWHC 1995; Scully (2003).
[281] E.g. *Cooper-Hohn v Cooper-Hohn* [2014] EWHC 4122; *XW v XH* [2017] EWFC 76, [234]–[235], [242]–[243].
[282] *Sorrell v Sorrell* [2005] EWHC 1717; see 6.5.6.
[283] *Work v Gray* [2017] EWCA Civ 270; criticized by Bailey-Harris (2018).
[284] *WM v HM* [2017] EWFC 25, [28].

Robertson v Robertson [2016] EWHC 613

HOLMAN J:

55. . . . [I]t is fundamental to a successful claim to special contribution that it be unmatched,[285] and the court must be astute to avoid discrimination against a party, usually a wife, who was the home-maker and had the daily role of caring for the children. . . . [T]he husband agreed in his oral evidence that during their marriage they had been 'a team', in which he was the money maker and she was 'an excellent home-maker', and 'an excellent mother and still is'. He agreed in his evidence that the wife ran the family life effectively, while he was very effective at money making. That was the 'partnership' they had. He agreed that the fact that the wife looked after the children left him free to concentrate on [his business], and that he knew that his daughters were well cared for while he dealt with a myriad business problems.

56. Against that background I ask rhetorically: what more could the wife have done or contributed to the marriage or to the welfare of the family? It is relatively easy to express the earnings or the wealth of the money earner and wealth creator in financial terms. What price can be put on the role within the 'partnership' or 'team' of the wife and mother who fulfilled her role to the full in the home, and thereby freed up the husband, as he agreed, to make the money? Any outcome which treated some special contribution of the husband in this case as 'unmatched' would, in my view, be highly discriminatory.

57. . . . It is an obvious feature of cases and families with higher resources that some staff may be employed. It is nit-picking whether the staff (to put it pictorially) wash the dishes while the mother changes the nappies, or change the nappies while the mother washes the dishes. I completely reject that the wife of a successful and high-earning husband should somehow receive less just because his success has enabled staff to be employed, if . . . the wife remained an excellent home-maker and an excellent mother.[286]

In the rare cases where the stellar contribution argument has succeeded, the courts have alighted on a percentage division to reflect that this is considered 'fair'—providing a 'meaningful and significant' rather than 'token' adjustment,[287] somewhere between a 55:45 and 66.6:33.3 split. Patently, these outcomes have no measurable, scientific basis and so seem inherently arbitrary.[288]

'Unilateral assets'

Baroness Hale and Lord Mance in *Miller; McFarlane* had considered, with some caution, the possibility that there might be cases in which the fruits of one spouse's sole business activity, which would ordinarily be classed as matrimonial, could nevertheless be excluded from sharing—deemed 'unilateral'—where they had not been used for the family's benefit during the marriage. It was suggested that this would apply, as in *Miller* itself, to 'short' marriages and also (obiter) to dual-career marriages where the parties deliberately kept their assets separate.

[285] *Work v Gray* [2017] EWCA Civ 270, [102] has since ruled out this term in favour of focus on whether the disparity of contributions is such that it would be inequitable to disregard it.

[286] See also *XW v XH* [2019] EWCA Civ 2262, [122]–[124].

[287] *Charman v Charman* [2006] EWHC 1879, [125].

[288] Ibid, [2007] EWCA Civ 503, [90]–[91].

Miller v Miller; McFarlane v McFarlane [2006] UKHL 24

BARONESS HALE:

153. . . . [I]n a matrimonial property regime which still starts with the premise of separate property, there is still some scope for one party to acquire and retain separate property which is not automatically to be shared equally between them. The nature and the source of the property and the way the couple have run their lives may be taken into account in deciding how it should be shared. . . . However, one should be careful not to take this approach too far. What seems fair and sensible at the outset of a relationship may seem much less fair and sensible when it ends.

LORD MANCE:

170. . . . [T]here can be marriages, long as well as short, where both partners are and remain financially active, and independently so. They may contribute to a house and joint expenses, but it does not necessarily follow that they are or regard themselves in other respects as engaged in a joint financial enterprise for all purposes. Intrusive inquiries into the other's financial affairs might, during the marriage, be viewed as inconsistent with a proper respect for the other's personal autonomy and development, and even more so if the other were to claim a share of any profit made from them. . . . Once needs and compensation had been addressed, the misfortune of divorce would not of itself, as it seems to me, be justification for the court to disturb principles by which the parties had chosen to live their lives while married.

These ideas lay fallow, courts and practitioners apparently adopting Lord Nicholls' unqualified distinction between matrimonial and non-matrimonial assets.[289] But the concept of unilateral assets was revived in the paradigm case of *Sharp*: a short (six-year), child-free marriage of a couple who had developed professional careers prior to marrying and in which they continued to work full-time, keeping their finances entirely separate. Their two homes, bought in joint names, were funded from part of the extraordinary bonuses earned by the wife during the marriage. The Court of Appeal accepted the wife's argument that not allowing—exceptionally—for this class of 'unilateral assets' ignored the true ratio of *Miller; McFarlane*:

Sharp v Sharp [2017] EWCA Civ 408

MACFARLANE LJ:

86. If, as the court was told by [counsel for the husband], the equal sharing principle of 50/50 allocation is now applied by courts and practitioners, in cases which are not predetermined by 'needs', to all relevant assets [i.e. presumably, matrimonial property], without exception, from the moment the couple leaves the church or the Register Office, this would seem to be a very significant and wholly unjustified development from the approach so carefully described by Lord Nicholls. An automatic or blind application of a 50/50 split in every case can only be an impermissible gloss on the statute, which expressly requires the court to consider all the circumstances of the case . . .

[289] *Sharp v Sharp* [2017] EWCA Civ 408, from [62].

93. . . . If, as the speeches of the majority contemplate, some grounds for departure from the equal sharing principle may lie in the littoral zone along its outer edges, these will require careful, fact-specific, evaluation and cannot be fairly determined by the blind application of an arithmetic formula.

The award made to the husband in *Sharp* (a half-share in the two homes—clearly 'matrimonial' in character, plus £700,000[290]) is hard to rationalize; another reported outcome that seems to some extent to be plucked out of the air. The court sought to emphasize that unilateral assets exist only in a 'very narrow . . . fringe' of cases,[291] but it is easy to see how litigants in various high-value cases might seek to argue the point. However, it has been held that it would be discriminatory to exclude unilateral assets from equal sharing in cases involving children.[292] Moylan LJ has since decisively confined *Sharp*'s departure from equality in the case of unilateral assets to short,[293] childless, dual-career marriages.

XW v XH [2019] EWCA Civ 2262

MOYLAN LJ:

106. I would note that we were referred to no authority in the approximately 13 years since the decisions in *Miller* and *Charman* in which the concept of unilateral assets, in other words, assets that are the product of one party's endeavour during the marriage has been applied to support an unequal division of such assets beyond short childless marriages.

It might, more generally, be objected that parties wishing to remove themselves from the equal sharing norm should be expected to do so by express agreement (see 6.7), rather than by seeking an *ex post facto* judicial determination that theirs was not a sharing marriage.[294]

Risky and illiquid assets

Even if they fall within the equal sharing pool, the nature of some assets may justify unequal sharing. Where assets are 'illiquid', for example because they are tied up in a family farm or private company, the courts do not insist on an equal division immediately, if at all. To facilitate an 'orderly redistribution of wealth',[295] courts may effect equal sharing via periodical payments, pending release of the capital.[296] A fair distribution of 'copper-bottomed' and 'risk-laden' assets is generally also necessary.[297] But what is 'fair' here? The former, such as land and cash, have a reliable value, are readily saleable, but may yield a more modest income. The latter, such as shares, may yield a higher income but be less readily saleable, more

[290] Ibid, [114]. [291] Ibid, [75]. [292] *XW v XH* [2017] EWFC 76, [174]–[175].

[293] It was suggested that a marriage of seven years was not short: *XW v XH (Financial Remedies: Business Assets)* [2019] EWCA 2262, [33]. On this basis, Kelly (2021), 95 has interpreted the cut-off period for short marriages as being six years. It is important to note, however, that this is not a set definition of a short marriage, as such definition does not exist.

[294] Cf [2017] EWCA Civ 408, [109]. [295] *N v N (Financial Provision: Sale of Company)* [2001] 2 FLR 69, 71.

[296] *F v F (Clean Break: Balance of Fairness)* [2003] 1 FLR 847.

[297] *Wells v Wells* [2002] EWCA Civ 476; cf *Myerson v Myerson* [2009] EWCA Civ 282, noted at 6.6.3.

susceptible to loss of capital value or income potential, or be difficult to value as capital at all and better treated as a source of income.[298] Sharing such assets equally (so-called '*Wells* sharing') may be a way of avoiding the problems of valuation—but that may undesirably tie parties together financially, precluding a clean break. So if one party is to have a larger share of the risk-laden assets (e.g. a shareholding in a private company), it may be appropriate, given the extra risk thereby taken on, for that party to retain what may appear to be a larger share of the total sharing pool.[299]

6.5.5.d The indeterminacy of the equal sharing principle

Having reviewed some of the key questions arising under the sharing principle, it is worth revisiting Cooke's question about its rationale:[300] is it based on partnership theory or valuation of contributions? Somewhat incoherently, the answer seems to be both:

J. Miles, '*Charman v Charman (No 4)*: Making Sense of Need, Compensation and Equal Sharing after *Miller/McFarlane*', (2008) 20 *Child and Family Law Quarterly* 378, 385–6

For example, a starting point of equal sharing in relation to (almost) the entire asset pool implies a deep, universal partnership. Yet the grounds on which equal sharing might be denied 'within' that principle suggest alternative rationales. Either a rough valuation approach, which responds to the claim that one party has made an 'unmatched' contribution, whether a stellar contribution or some form of non-matrimonial wealth. Or a more sophisticated form of partnership, whereby the increasing duration of the marriage reduces scope for arguing that the partnership should take a shallower form. . . .

Again, the partnership view is supported by the . . . exception to equal sharing in relation to 'unilateral' assets: the short duration (how short?) or the spouses' financial independence makes universal partnership too intense. (Though . . . the shallower partnership entailed in the sharing of core 'matrimonial' assets is countenanced even in those cases). Equally, however, these cases could be presented as illustrations of the need for non-owner spouses to make some plausible claim that they have indirectly contributed to the acquisition of those assets: a valuation approach.

Other cases seem firmly to adopt valuation, for example, where applicants seek to share in post-separation earning capacity. Here the question has been framed in terms of whether the applicant can demonstrate the continuing influence of her contribution to the welfare of the family as a factor contributing to an enhancement in the respondent's earnings post-separation. At the very least, the termination of the marital partnership on separation excludes a partnership model, and requires that a valuation approach be taken to claims in relation to property acquired after that point. The court's remarks in *Charman* about the rare cases where one would permit a stellar contribution argument also lie with the 'valuation of contributions' rather than 'partnership' rationale:

> 'the statutory requirement in every case to consider the contributions which each party has made to the welfare of the family . . . would be inconsistent with a blanket rule that their past contributions to its welfare must be afforded equal weight.'

[298] *A v A* [2004] EWHC 2818.
[299] *N v N (Financial Provision: Sale of Company)* [2001] 2 FLR 69.
[300] Cooke (2007).

Unsurprisingly, it is in cases perceived to lie further from the paradigm of marital partnership – for example, short marriages or where property is acquired post-separation – that we apparently no longer feel comfortable with the implications of a partnership-based sharing principle, and so fall back on a valuation approach, insisting on concrete demonstration of actual contribution to rebut the unmatched[301] contribution argument.

6.5.5.e What is the relationship of equal sharing to the other principles?

In most cases, as Lord Nicholls indicated, equal sharing will not determine the outcome, or even carry much weight. Other concerns—whether need, compensation, conduct (see 6.5.6), or the desirability of a clean break (6.6.1)—may dictate unequal sharing of matrimonial property.

Departing from equal sharing in 'everyday' and other needs-based cases

In the vast majority of divorces—where the assets do not exceed the parties' combined needs (construed liberally by reference to the parties' standard of living)—the equal sharing principle might be thought largely irrelevant. An equal share of the matrimonial property might leave one party in a situation of need that should be alleviated by the other spouse, and so the needs principle operates as the trump card, mandating an unequal division of assets in that spouse's favour, even resorting to non-matrimonial assets if necessary.[302] Even in high-value cases, need is the key principle where all or most of the assets are classed as 'non-matrimonial' and so not susceptible to 'sharing'.

The applicant in many such cases, typically a wife who reduced paid employment to raise the children of whom she remains primary carer, may therefore receive rather *more* than half of the assets in order to secure the children's welfare and to cater for her needs as their carer, in both the short and longer term. Such unequal division (with or without periodical payments to assist with income-needs) may be necessary to give the parties an 'equal start on the road to independent living'.[303]

Miller v Miller; McFarlane v McFarlane **[2006] UKHL 24**

BARONESS HALE:

136. . . . Giving half the present assets to the breadwinner achieves a very different outcome from giving half the assets to the homemaker with children . . .

142. . . . [A]n equal partnership does not necessarily dictate an equal sharing of the assets. In particular, it may have to give way to the needs of one party or the children. Too strict an adherence to equal sharing and the clean break can lead to a rapid decrease in the primary carer's standard of living and a rapid increase in the breadwinner's. The breadwinner's unimpaired and unimpeded earning capacity is a powerful resource which can frequently repair any loss of capital after an unequal distribution . . . Recognising this is one reason why English law has been so successful in retaining a home for the children.

301 In the context of stellar contributions, *Work v Gray* [2017] EWCA Civ 270, [102] rejects this term in favour of focus on whether disparity of contributions such that it would be inequitable to disregard.

302 See 6.5.3.c. 303 *Miller; McFarlane* [2006] UKHL 24, [144].

But the fact that the conclusion is likely to be needs-driven, unequal sharing of capital in the homemaker's favour does not mean that there is no point taking equal shares as a starting point, even if one will quickly depart from that in order to ensure that the applicant's needs are met. Something vital may be gained from acknowledging that the applicant is *entitled* to *at least* half of the matrimonial property, and not merely a 'needy supplicant'. This may be particularly important where parties are negotiating privately, where the concept of entitlement may help reduce any imbalance in power where the respondent owns most of the assets.[304]

The relationship between equal sharing and need in high-value cases

It is only where the matrimonial assets exceed the parties' combined needs to the extent that both parties' needs would be met by an equal share that equal sharing assumes potentially determinative significance, and the interaction between all three principles becomes important.[305]

The relationship between equal sharing and need is straightforwardly explained in *Charman*.[306] As discussed earlier, equal sharing may be departed from where need in fairness requires it. But, conversely, an applicant is not to be denied an equal share on the basis that it exceeds their needs.[307] Where each spouse's equal share is itself sufficient to cover needs, the equal sharing principle will simply subsume any needs-based claim. On this view, one does not first meet the parties' needs and then apply the equal sharing principle only to whatever surplus remains: that would encourage 'trial by budget' by each party, attempting to secure a larger overall share based on need.[308] Moreover, a spouse can be expected to use 'free' capital (not required for housing) from their equal share to generate income on an amortizing basis,[309] even if the other spouse will be able to preserve his capital and live off earned income.[310] This might be said to prioritize formal equality over the notion that we are seeking to give the parties an 'equal start on the road to independent living'.[311] But alternatively, it might be said that that objective, in a high-value case, is amply met by an equal share of capital under the partnership principle that fully reflects the wife's contributions to the partnership, an investment from which she is then able to live independently for life. The issue has to be addressed very differently in the lower value cases discussed previously.

And compensation?

The place of compensation appears to be more difficult,[312] but the reality may be straightforward. There are concerns about the risk of double-counting:[313] that is, 'compensating' the applicant for the same disadvantage under more than one of the principles. Just as equal sharing may subsume 'need', so need will generally subsume compensation: as we have seen, the courts essentially use compensation as a justification for generously assessed needs-based awards. The adequacy of an equal share to meet compensation has been acknowledged in relation to wives with 'ordinary career prospects' where that equal share will leave them

304 Diduck (1999); cf Hunter et al (2018).
305 See Miles (2008).
306 Cf Law Com (2012), from para 4.96.
307 [2007] EWCA Civ 503, [73].
308 Ibid, [73], [77](c).
309 I.e. the capital fund that will generate income but will gradually reduce until being exhausted on death, e.g. a *Duxbury* fund: *Duxbury v Duxbury* [1990] 2 All ER 77.
310 *Waggott v Waggott* [2018] EWCA Civ 727, from [129].
311 Heenan (2018).
312 Not addressed in *Charman* [2007] EWCA Civ 503, [73].
313 *RP v RP* [2006] EWHC 3409, [64].

with a very comfortable standard of living.[314] If the capital is insufficient for an equal share to achieve that outcome, fairness may then require either that the wife receive more capital on a clean break,[315] or that she receive periodical payments (as in *McFarlane*). But the trend of the cases, discussed at 6.5.4, clearly indicates that even in the case of a high-flying wife with an apparent case for compensation, any 'extra' beyond equal sharing will normally be calculated on a generous needs basis. Nevertheless, there are some exceptions to this approach which confirm that compensation for relationship-generated disadvantage still exists as a distinct principle.

The case of *RC v JC*[316] involved the husband—a partner at a law firm—and his wife, who was also a qualified solicitor but was now a homemaker and primary carer for the couple's two children, aged 10 and 8. Their relationship lasted around ten or eleven years. The wife had been doing extremely well in her City firm, and—as the judge found—'might well have become a partner with the huge financial rewards that would have brought'.[317] But that did not happen, for 'the Husband's career took precedence'; he 'did not want [the wife] to remain at the firm if they were to marry and she accepted that she could not remain'.[318] Significantly, the judge found that the wife gave up the chance 'of far higher remuneration'[319] and instead of reflecting this in an augmented award based upon her needs and sharing entitlement, he made a separate compensatory award of £400,000; a sum he considered to be 'relatively modest' given the capital assets totalled £9.7 million:

RC v JC [2020] EWHC 466

MOOR J:

72. Exceptionally, in this case, I have found there to have been relationship generated disadvantage sufficient to justify an award of compensation. I continue to be of the view that such cases will be very much the exception rather than the rule. It is rare to be able to make the findings of fact that I have made in this case. Even having done so, I have been clear that the case remains a suitable one for a clean break with, by the standards of such cases, a relatively modest additional award. . . . [I]n many of these cases, the assets will be such that any loss is already covered by the applicant's sharing claim. In other cases, the assets/income will be insufficient to justify such a claim in the first place. It follows that litigants should think long and hard before launching a claim for relationship generated disadvantage and they should not take this judgment as any sort of "green light" to do so unless the circumstances are truly exceptional.

Thus, compensation claims are exceptional, and even where they are argued successfully—as in *RC v JC*—the resulting award ultimately may be far short of what is sought by the party seeking compensation for relationship-generated disadvantage. In short, even post *RC v JC*, if needs (generously assessed) subsume compensation, and equal sharing subsumes needs in high-value cases, compensation is still more likely to drop out of the picture as a truly independent principle.

[314] E.g. *CR v CR* [2007] EWHC 3334, [92]; endorsed in *VB v JP* [2008] EWHC 112, [59]; see also *Miller; McFarlane* [2006] UKHL 24, [154]; *Charman* [2007] EWCA Civ 503, [76](b).

[315] E.g. *CR v CR* [2007] EWHC 3334, [92].

[316] [2020] EWHC 466.

[317] Ibid., [51].

[318] Ibid., [52].

[319] Ibid., [53].

6.5.6 THE PARTIES' CONDUCT

Conduct provides a distinctive reason for departing from equal sharing, or for curtailing[320] or increasing[321] awards based on need or compensation. Conduct was central to financial remedies under fault-based divorce, but under no-fault divorce is rarely relevant.

Wachtel v Wachtel [1973] Fam 72 (CA), 89–90

LORD DENNING MR:

Parliament has decreed: "If the marriage has broken down irretrievably, let there be a divorce." It carries no stigma, but only sympathy. It is a misfortune which befalls both. No longer is one guilty and the other innocent. No longer are there long contested divorce suits. Nearly every case goes uncontested. The parties come to an agreement, if they can, on the things that matter so much to them. They divide up the furniture. They [make arrangements for] the children, the financial provision for the wife, and the future of the matrimonial home. If they cannot agree, the matters are referred to a judge in chambers.

When the judge comes to decide these questions, what place has conduct in it? Parliament still says that the court has to have "regard to their conduct" . . . Does this mean that the judge in chambers is to hear their mutual recriminations and to go into their petty squabbles for days on end, as he used to do in the old days? Does it mean that, after a marriage has been dissolved, there is to be a post mortem to find out what killed it? We do not think so. In most cases both parties are to blame—or, as we would prefer to say—both parties have contributed to the breakdown.

It has been suggested that there should be a "discount" or "reduction" in what the wife is to receive because of her supposed misconduct, guilt or blame (whatever word is used). We cannot accept this argument. In the vast majority of cases it is repugnant to the principles underlying the new legislation, and in particular the [Divorce Reform] Act of 1969. There will be many cases in which a wife (though once considered guilty or blameworthy) will have cared for the home and looked after the family for very many years. Is she to be deprived of the benefit otherwise to be accorded to her by section [25(2)(f)] because she may share responsibility for the breakdown with her husband? There will no doubt be a residue of cases where the conduct of one of the parties is in the judge's words . . . "both obvious and gross." so much so that to order one party to support another whose conduct falls into this category is repugnant to anyone's sense of justice. In such a case the court remains free to decline to afford financial support or to reduce the support which it would otherwise have ordered. But, short of cases falling into this category, the court should not reduce its order for financial provision merely because of what was formerly regarded as guilt or blame. To do so would be to impose a fine for supposed misbehaviour in the course of an unhappy married life. [Counsel for the husband] disputed this and claimed that it was but justice that a wife should suffer for her supposed misbehaviour. [The parties had been found equally responsible for the marital breakdown]. We do not agree. Criminal justice often requires the imposition of financial and indeed custodial penalties. But in the financial adjustments consequent upon the dissolution of a marriage which has irretrievably broken down, the imposition of financial penalties ought seldom to find a place.

320 *R v B and Capita Trustees* [2017] EWHC 33, [85].

321 *Jones v Jones* [1976] Fam 8, 15.

The House of Lords affirmed this restrictive approach in *Miller; McFarlane*. Mrs Miller argued that the shortness of the marriage should not reduce her award where its shortness was caused by Mr Miller's affair. Her argument found favour with the lower courts, but was unanimously dismissed by the House of Lords.[322] They also dismissed the associated argument that a spouse should have their 'expectation' loss remedied on divorce, as if it were an action for breach of contract:[323]

Miller v Miller; McFarlane v McFarlane [2006] UKHL 24

LORD NICHOLLS:

'Legitimate expectation'

56. . . . The judge [in *Miller*] said the key feature was that the husband gave the wife a legitimate expectation that in future she would be living on a higher economic plane.

57. By this statement I doubt whether the judge was doing more than emphasise the importance . . . of the standard of living enjoyed by Mr and Mrs Miller before the breakdown of their short marriage. This is one of the matters included on the statutory check list. The standard of living enjoyed by the Millers during their marriage was much higher than the wife's accustomed standard and much higher than the standard she herself could afford.

58. If the judge meant to go further than this I consider he went too far. No doubt both parties had high hopes for their future when they married. But hopes and expectations, as such, are not an appropriate basis on which to assess financial needs. Claims for expectation losses do not fit altogether comfortably with the notion that each party is free to end the marriage. Indeed, to make an award by reference to the parties' future expectations would come close to restoring the 'tailpiece' which was originally part of section 25. By that tailpiece the court was required to place the parties, so far as practical and, having regard to their conduct, just to do so, in the same financial position as they would have been had the marriage not broken down. It would be a mistake indirectly to re-introduce the effect of that discredited provision.

While surveys of the legal profession find strong support for the exclusion of conduct arguments in this context,[324] it is not popular with the divorcing public[325] and some parliamentarians.[326] Even some judges have expressed disquiet about the amorality implied by the exclusion of fault.[327] Recognizing fault, or responsibility for deciding to end marriage without good cause, is regarded by some commentators as a basic aspect of justice on divorce.[328] Nevertheless, fault seems destined to play only a peripheral role.

Where it is taken into account, like the parties' contributions, 'conduct' poses a challenge: how is the financial significance of conduct to be measured? In one case, the husband was convicted for attempted murder of the wife in front of the children. This was at the top end of the scale of conduct that should be taken into account:[329]

322 [2006] UKHL 24, [59]–[63], [145], [164].

323 Cf the history of fault-based divorce and the minimum loss principle: Law Com (1980), paras 10–12.

324 E.g. Solicitors Journal (2006).

325 Law Com (1981), para 36; media reaction to *Miller*.

326 An amendment to the FLA 1996 designed to give conduct greater prominence was never implemented.

327 Davis and Murch (1988), 16–17.

328 E.g. economists such as Rowthorn (1999); Dnes (1998); cf Eekelaar (2017); Ellman (1997): see 3.10.1.

329 See also *K v L* [2010] EWCA Civ 125.

H v H (Financial Relief: Attempted Murder as Conduct) [2005] EWHC 2911

COLERIDGE J:

44. How is the court to have regard to his conduct in a meaningful way? I agree with [counsel for the husband] that the court should not be punitive or confiscatory for its own sake. I therefore consider that the proper way to have regard to the conduct is as a potentially magnifying factor when considering the wife's position under the other subsections and criteria. It is the glass through which the other factors are considered. It places her needs, as I judge them, as a much higher priority to those of the husband because the situation the wife now finds herself in is, in a very real way, his fault. It is not just that she is in a precarious position, which she might be for a variety of medical reasons, but that he has created this position by his reprehensible conduct. So she must, in my judgment and in fairness, be given a greater priority in the share-out.

The offence had impacted directly on the wife's mental health and destroyed her career and earning capacity; she had had to move away from the area and would obviously receive no financial or other support from the husband in raising the children.

46. Those are the ways, in my judgment, in which this conduct has impacted directly on the wife's life and it is against that that I turn now to consider the needs of the parties, and first the needs of the wife and the children. It seems to me that so far as practical she should be free from financial worry or pressure. So far as housing is concerned, by far the most important aspect of her security is a decent and secure home for herself and the children. If she feels she is in a nice, new home of her choosing that will be beneficial therapeutically to her. . . .

48. The husband too would like a home when he is released from prison. He would like a home, he says, similar to that of the wife's. . . . If it is possible to achieve that, then of course it is reasonable as well. But as I have indicated, because of his conduct, he has to come very much second place in the queue.

49. So far as incomes are concerned, again the wife should, in my judgment, be as secure as possible and not be under pressure to have to work more than she can really cope with. She wants no recourse to the husband so this will be on a clean break basis. . . .

The judge awarded the wife three-quarters of the assets.

Relevant conduct is 'the elephant in the room; incapable of definition but easy to recognise'.[330] It induces not a 'gulp' but a 'gasp'.[331] 'Ordinary' instances of 'behaviour' and adultery are insufficient.[332] It is not necessary to show that the 'victim' was entirely blameless before it will be equitable to take account of the other spouse's conduct.[333] Conduct after marital breakdown is relevant, even if several years after the divorce.[334] Cases in which conduct has been taken into account have been extreme. They include inciting third parties to murder the other spouse,[335] assisting the other spouse's attempted suicide

[330] *Charman v Charman* [2006] EWHC 1879, [115] per Coleridge J.

[331] *S v S* [2006] EWHC 2793, [57].

[332] *Miller; McFarlane* [2006] UKHL 24, [145].

[333] *Kyte v Kyte* [1988] Fam 145, 155.

[334] *Evans v Evans* [1989] 1 FLR 351.

[335] Ibid.

for personal gain,[336] other serious domestic violence,[337] and abduction of the parties' child.[338] In *K v K (Conduct)*, the court took into account the husband's serious drinking problem, his unreasonable failure to seek employment following redundancy, and his neglect of the house, which forced its sale; meanwhile, the wife supported the household and endeavoured to pay the mortgage from her earnings. Since the separation, the wife had made considerable efforts to improve her financial situation, and the husband's application for financial relief was largely rejected.[339] In *Clark v Clark*, a younger woman heavily in debt married a millionaire approaching his 80s; exercised undue influence over him to persuade him to pay her debts, spend vast sums of money, and transfer substantial assets to her; refused to consummate the marriage or cohabit; and confined him at times to a caravan in the grounds or an annexe in the property, while she resided in the main house with her boyfriend. Six years on, the old man, by then reduced to a 'pitiful' state, was rescued by relatives. The wife was perhaps lucky to receive the £175,000 that she did.[340]

6.5.6.a Financial misconduct and anti-avoidance powers

The courts also take into account financial misconduct in the form of dissipating the assets available for division,[341] for example by gambling the family assets and diverting funds from payment of the mortgage on the matrimonial home to a mistress;[342] or fraudulently remortgaging the family home,[343] or sheer extravagant spending. Unlike other forms of misconduct, this behaviour is more readily measurable in financial terms.

The MCA 1973, s 37 creates anti-avoidance powers to deal with conduct where a purpose[344] of the respondent was to 'defeat' the other party's claim, whether by preventing it from being made, reducing its amount, or frustrating or impeding its enforcement.[345] The court can recover assets disposed of by the respondent,[346] restrain such transactions before they go ahead, and prevent the transfer of assets out of the jurisdiction.[347] It is not possible to challenge a completed disposition if it was made for valuable consideration (other than marriage or civil partnership[348]) to a person acting in good faith and without actual or constructive notice[349] of any intention on the part of the transferor to defeat their spouse's claim for financial relief. But any other past or proposed disposition[350] by a spouse while the case is

336 *Kyte v Kyte* [1988] Fam 145.

337 *H v H (Financial Provision: Conduct)* [1994] 2 FLR 801; cf *S v S* [2006] EWHC 2793, criticized by Choudhry and Herring (2010), 410.

338 *B v B (Financial Provision: Welfare of Child and Conduct)* [2002] 1 FLR 555.

339 [1990] 2 FLR 225.

340 [1999] 2 FLR 498, 509.

341 E.g. *Clark v Clark* [1999] 2 FLR 498.

342 Suspected in *M v M (Third Party Subpoena: Financial Conduct)* [2006] 2 FCR 555.

343 *Le Foe v Le Foe and Woolwich plc* [2001] 2 FLR 970.

344 It need not be the sole or main intention: *Kemmis v Kemmis* [1988] 1 WLR 1307.

345 On the preservation of joint periodic tenancies in anticipation of tenancy transfer, see: *Newlon Housing Trust v Al-Sulaimen* [1999] 1 AC 313; *Muema v Muema* [2013] EWHC 3864.

346 Cf *Ansari v Ansari* [2008] EWCA Civ 1456.

347 See generally *AC v DC (Financial Remedies: Effect of s 37 Avoidance Orders)* [2012] EWHC 2032; *UL v BK (Freezing Orders: Safeguards: Standard Examples)* [2013] EWHC 1735. Injunctive relief may be available against other financially prejudicial behaviour: *R v R* [2013] EWHC 4244.

348 Curiously, the MCA 1973 and CPA 2004 refer, respectively, to 'marriage' and 'civil partnership', and neither to both; it might have been expected that each statute would encompass both possibilities, which are of equivalent significance.

349 *Kemmis v Kemmis* [1988] 1 WLR 1307.

350 Except provision in a will or codicil: MCA 1973, s 37(6).

ongoing[351] is 'reviewable'. If made with the intention to defeat a claim, a reviewable disposition may be set aside. If made less than three years before the claim for financial relief, and it would defeat the claim, it will be presumed (and so for the respondent to prove otherwise) that the disposition was made with that intention.[352]

Where these powers cannot be relied upon to recover and return property to the pool of assets awaiting distribution (e.g. because the third party to whom the assets were transferred acted in good faith and without notice), the court can instead take the relevant conduct into account when deciding how to divide the assets.[353] The spouse who disposed of the assets is likely to be penalized to some extent in that division.[354]

6.5.6.b Litigation misconduct

One spouse's conduct of the financial remedy litigation may cause the other to incur unnecessary legal costs. Examples include failing to make full and prompt disclosure,[355] concealing or disposing of assets, making groundless allegations or exaggerated claims, pursuing clearly futile legal points, or failing to accept a reasonable offer. Litigation misconduct can be taken into account either by reducing the offending party's share of the assets,[356] or more usually by making a costs order.[357] The costs rules are intended to encourage reasonable and proportionate conduct of litigation.[358] But many practitioners are dissatisfied with the way that current rules operate,[359] and in any event costs orders are not always the better option. In *Clark v Clark*, since the husband had effectively been funding both sides' legal costs, a costs order would have imposed no real penalty on the wife, and so her litigation misconduct was properly reflected in the quantification of her award.[360] Proceedings for contempt of court may also be brought to deal with litigation misconduct.[361]

6.5.6.c Delayed or late applications

Another form of 'conduct' associated with the litigation itself is the making of the application long after the divorce. In *Wyatt v Vince*, the wife applied nearly 20 years after decree absolute. The Supreme Court confirmed that, there being no limitation period for financial remedy claims, there is no basis to strike out such applications. But the court will take into account the passage of time and intervening events in exercising its discretion to decide what, if any, provision to make:

351 *Nightingale v Nightingale* [2014] EWHC 77, including where the order is made but not yet performed; cf *Ahmed v Mustafa* [2014] EWCA Civ 277.

352 Equivalent tests apply to planned dispositions.

353 The wife was ordered to contribute to the husband's costs as a result of her conduct in *VV v VV* [2022] EWFC 46.

354 *Le Foe v Le Foe and Woolwich plc* [2001] 2 FLR 970. On 'add-backs', e.g. *MAP v MFP (Financial Remedies: Add-Back)* [2015] EWHC 627.

355 Cf *Hart v Hart* [2017] EWCA 1306 and concerns of Balfour (2017).

356 *F v F* (2008) 38 FL 183.

357 *Young v Young* [1998] 2 FLR 1131, 1140; Edwards and Calver (2022), 42.

358 FPR 2010, Part 28.

359 E.g. Edwards and Doherty (2015).

360 [1999] 2 FLR 498.

361 E.g. *Young v Young* [2012] EWHC 38, [2013] EWHC 34.

***Wyatt v Vince* [2015] UKSC 14**

LORD WILSON:

32. Consistently with the potentially lifelong obligations which attend a marriage, there is no time limit for seeking orders for financial provision or property adjustment for the benefit of a spouse following divorce. Sections 23(1) and 24(1) of the 1973 provide that such orders may be made on granting a decree of divorce 'or at any time thereafter'. Yet there is a prominent strain of public policy hostile to forensic delay. The court will look critically at explanations for it; and, even irrespective of its effect upon the respondent, will be likely, by reason of it and subject to the potency of other factors, to reduce or even to eliminate its provision for the applicant. Nevertheless it remains important to address its effect upon the respondent. In some cases, albeit not in the present, a respondent can show that he has assumed financial obligations or otherwise arranged his financial affairs in the belief that the applicant would make no claim against him and that he has done so in a way which, even if it were possible, it would not be reasonable for him to put into reverse. Sometimes, instead, he can point to factual issues of which the dimming of memories or the disappearance of witnesses over the period of the delay no longer permits accurate determination. . . .

It seems that delay may particularly reduce the quantum of orders based on the sharing principle, rather than on need.[362] However, as in *Wyatt* itself, extensive delay may complicate an applicant's claim that present needs arise from the now long-distant marriage.[363] Cases where the respondent had been supporting the applicant informally (i.e. not pursuant to a court order) may also be dealt with rather differently from those where no sort of support or provision had been made in the intervening years.[364]

6.5.6.d Nullity cases: criminal offences relating to the marriage or civil partnership

Special issues arise in relation to marriages or civil partnerships that are void in circumstances potentially involving commission of a criminal offence by one or both parties,[365] whether bigamy[366] or perjury on some issue material to the validity of the union. There is clearly no obstacle to the innocent spouse applying for financial relief on the nullity application. But should the 'guilty' spouse effectively be able to profit from their crime by making an application?

In *Whiston v Whiston*, it was held that a bigamist could be barred as a matter of public policy from seeking financial relief from the innocent spouse.[367] But it has since been held in relation both to bigamy[368] and perjury (regarding the spouse's gender)[369] that such criminal behaviour does not necessarily bar an application by the guilty party. Instead, it should

[362] E.g. *Briers v Briers* [2017] EWCA Civ 15; cf Ferguson (2015b), 204, 206–7.
[363] See the contribution-based solution to *Wyatt*, discussed at 6.5.3.
[364] E.g. *A v B (No 2)* [2018] EWFC 45; cf *Hill v Hill* [1998] 1 FLR 198, where parties had resumed cohabitation.
[365] Cf where the marriage was merely void: *Mendal v Mendal* [2007] EWCA Civ 437.
[366] There is no offence of bigamy in the case of civil partnership, though the 'bigamist' may be guilty of perjury.
[367] [1995] Fam 198.
[368] *Rampal v Rampal* [2001] EWCA Civ 989, [2002] Fam 85.
[369] *S-T (formerly J) v J* [1998] Fam 103.

be one factor for the court to consider in its discretion, albeit one that may yield a nil award in appropriate circumstances. Where, as in *Whiston*, the respondent is entirely innocent, they should not be required to satisfy any claims by the bigamist/perjurer. But where, as in *Rampal v Rampal (No 2)*, the respondent knew of the impediment to the marriage, and engineered the marriage despite it, orders against them are less obviously unjust. While acknowledging that *Whiston* would permit a claim by bigamists as culpable as the applicant in *Whiston* to be struck out, the court in *Rampal* preferred the discretionary route.[370] The same approach may be taken where it is clear that the twice-married applicant was not guilty of the offence of bigamy.[371]

6.5.6.e 'Positive' conduct

Relevant conduct may also be positive: for example, an argument that one party has made stellar contributions to the family. We have addressed this issue in relation to equal sharing, where contributions and conduct are regarded as two sides of the same coin.[372] The relevance of parties' agreements is considered at 6.7.

6.6 ACHIEVING FINALITY ON DIVORCE

In this section we explore two issues related to finality on divorce: the clean break principle; and the grounds on which an order designed to provide a once-and-for-all settlement may be undone. It is important to note at the outset that a clean break can only ever be effected between the spouses themselves: where there are dependent children, the theoretical ongoing requirement to pay child maintenance precludes a full economic break between the parties' households.[373]

6.6.1 ENDING ONGOING FINANCIAL TIES BETWEEN THE PARTIES

The statutory clean break principle was introduced in 1984 on repeal of the minimum loss principle following heated debate about what maintenance obligations, if any, should survive divorce.[374] Some complained that ex-wives were becoming 'alimony drones', permitted to live a life of 'parasitic'[375] idleness at the expense of their ex-husbands and their second families.[376] Women's groups and others strongly opposed the introduction of the clean break.[377] Subsequent research demonstrated that the concept of the alimony drone was unreal: most ex-wives received such low maintenance that, unless they were employed, it would simply be diverted to the state to recoup welfare benefit payments; ex-wives therefore had a clear incentive to work in order for maintenance payments to augment their income.[378] Similar debates continue today.[379]

370 [2001] EWCA Civ 989; applied in *Hashem v Shayif* [2008] EWHC 2380.

371 *Azizi v Aghaty* [2016] EWHC 110.

372 *Miller; McFarlane* [2006] UKHL 24, [164].

373 See chapter 5.

374 See Douglas (2018a), ch 4 for the history.

375 Deech (1977), 232; cf O'Donovan (1982).

376 For accounts of the Campaign for Justice on Divorce, see Eekelaar (1991b), 34–6.

377 Including the Law Society: Symes (1985), fn 10.

378 Eekelaar and Maclean (1986).

379 Miles and Hitchings (2018).

6.6.1.a The statutory provisions

The clean break principle is manifest in several statutory provisions (some of which are extracted at 6.5.1). Section 25(2)(a) requires the court to have regard not only to current resources but also resources available to each party in the foreseeable future, including any increase in earning capacity which it would be reasonable to expect them to acquire. Section 25A requires the court to consider whether it would be appropriate to exercise its powers so as to terminate the parties' financial obligations to each other as soon as is just and reasonable after the divorce. Essentially, the court should ask itself whether it can produce a package of orders that achieves fairness without periodical payments or other ongoing ties. If assets are very extensive, cash and investments can generate income to meet living costs.[380] In lower value cases, a larger share of capital to the economically weaker party may offset the need for periodical payments, for example if that party can then service alone the smaller mortgage required given the larger deposit on a new home. Or more capital may offset periodical payments if the other party, despite having higher income, simply cannot afford to pay,[381] or may be an unreliable payer.[382]

If the court decides to effect an immediate clean break, it will dismiss any periodical payment application under s 25A(3). If it decides that no payments are needed currently but wants to leave the door open, it can make a nominal order that can be varied in future if circumstances change. Periodical payments orders always cease if the recipient marries or forms a civil partnership,[383] but may otherwise last for the parties' joint lives,[384] until further order, until some specified event, or for a fixed period (a 'term order'),[385] which may or may not be extendable. Section 25A(2) requires the court to consider whether it would be appropriate to make the order only for a term long enough for the recipient 'to adjust without undue[386] hardship to the termination of their financial dependence on the other party'.[387] If the court is confident that no extension should be permissible, the order can bar that option upfront under s 28(1A).[388] The order can be structured so that the payments reduce yearly in line with anticipated increases in the recipient's earnings.[389] Where pension sharing has been ordered, any periodical payment order may be structured so as to end (or reduce) when the recipient's pension becomes payable.[390]

If the order has no fixed end point and circumstances change, the onus will be on the payer to seek a variation under s 31 reducing or extinguishing the order. If a fixed term is imposed, the onus will be on the recipient to seek an extension of that term before the order expires under s 31; leading authority requires 'exceptional justification' to extend the term.[391] On addressing an application to vary a periodical payments order, s 31(7) requires the court to revisit its original decision under s 25A(2) in light of the current circumstances. So if a clean break was impossible on divorce for want of resources but there are now sufficient

[380] A '*Duxbury* fund' does this on an amortizing basis: *Duxbury v Duxbury* [1990] 2 All ER 77; see Hitchings (2021).

[381] *A v L* [2011] EWHC 3150.

[382] *Robson v Robson* [2010] EWCA Civ 1171, [86].

[383] MCA 1973, s 28(3).

[384] The order may survive the payer's death if secured: ibid, s 28(1)(b).

[385] Ibid, s 28(1).

[386] Emphasized in *SS v NS* [2014] EWHC 4183, [28].

[387] Cf if periodical payments ordered for compensatory purposes rather than need, as in *McFarlane* [2006] UKHL 24, [38]–[39], [97]: order made for joint lives.

[388] *Mutch v Mutch* [2016] EWCA Civ 370.

[389] *Murphy v Murphy* [2014] EWHC 2263, [22].

[390] *Roxar v Jaladoust* [2017] EWHC 977.

[391] *Fleming v Fleming* [2003] EWCA Civ 1841, endorsed (despite its incompatibility with *Flavell v Flavell* [1997] 1 FLR 353) in *Miller; McFarlane* [2006] UKHL 24, [97], [155]; cf e.g. *SS v NS* [2014] EWHC 4183, [44] proposing an approach based on whether the original rationale of the order has been fulfilled.

assets, a clean break can be effected later (e.g. on the payer's retirement) with fresh capital orders.[392] The clean break can extend beyond the grave by barring any application by the ex-spouse under the Inheritance (Provision for Family and Dependants) Act 1975, s 15.

6.6.1.b The courts' approach

Some Court of Appeal panels had construed the Act as *requiring* a clean break wherever possible.[393] But the House of Lords in *Miller; McFarlane* held that the 'principle' is not a prima facie universal requirement, but a practical consideration to bear in mind when structuring the settlement that fairness—judged by reference to the three principles and s 25 checklist—demands in the individual case.

Miller v Miller; McFarlane v McFarlane **[2006] UKHL 24**

BARONESS HALE:

133. Section 25A is a powerful encouragement towards securing the court's objective by way of lump sum and capital adjustment (which now includes pension sharing) rather than by continuing periodical payments. This is good practical sense. Periodical payments are a continuing source of stress for both parties. They are also insecure. With the best will in the world, the paying party may fall on hard times and be unable to keep them up. Nor is the best will in the world always evident between formerly married people. It is also the logical consequence of the retreat from the principle of the life-long obligation. Independent finances and self-sufficiency are the aims. Nevertheless, section 25A does not tell us what the outcome of the exercise required by section 25 should be. It is mainly directed at how that outcome should be put into effect.

134. Hence, these . . . pointers [including the requirement that first consideration be given to the welfare of the children] do make it clear that a clean break is not to be achieved at the expense of a fair result . . .

While a clean break must always be considered, the courts in reported cases have often been cautious about imposing it where dependent children's needs continue to inhibit one spouse's ability to undertake paid employment, or might do so in future, even after a short marriage.[394] A clean break may also be inappropriate where the children are independent but one spouse's earning capacity has been impaired by past child-care responsibilities,[395] or where children of the marriage have special needs demanding long-term care well into adulthood.[396]

Deciding whether and when a clean break can be achieved requires an evaluation of applicants' prospects of increased earning capacity, at least (where any award would be based on need) to the point of becoming self-sufficient, bearing in mind costs of child-care necessary to let them pursue paid employment.[397] Applicants must take reasonable steps to become self-sufficient[398] and, presumably, to mitigate any loss of earning capacity that underpins

392 MCA 1973, s 31(7B); *Miller; McFarlane* [2006] UKHL 24, [131].
393 *Fleming v Fleming* [2003] EWCA Civ 1841; *McFarlane; Parlour* [2004] EWCA Civ 872.
394 E.g. *B v B (Mesher Order)* [2002] EWHC 3106; cf *Chiva v Chiva* [2014] EWCA Civ 1558.
395 *Flavell v Flavell* [1997] 1 FLR 353. 396 *V v C* [2004] EWHC 1739.
397 *Murphy v Murphy* [2014] EWHC 2263, [26]. 398 *Wright v Wright* [2015] EWCA Civ 201.

a compensation argument.[399] Ex-wives cannot 'freeload' on ex-husbands, but nor can respondents offload their responsibility on the state (though applicant's benefit and tax credit entitlements are commonly an important part of the package).

The courts have warned against unduly optimistic or speculative forecasts, particularly where the applicant is middle-aged and would have to retrain: orders should not be made 'more in hope than in serious expectation'.[400] However, going against the grain of older authorities, some recent cases have appeared to require *applicants* to bear the risk of future uncertainty, either taking a fixed-term rather than joint lives order[401] or having to accept an immediate clean break rather than a nominal order 'safety net'.[402] As the Law Commission has noted, whilst the objective 'should be to enable a transition to independence', in many cases that 'is not possible, usually because of age but sometimes for other reasons arising from choices made during the marriage'.[403] The Court of Appeal has acknowledged that the 'meal ticket for life' critique of joint lives orders 'can be used as an unfair trope': fairness sometimes demands long-term maintenance.[404] Indeed, as Baroness Hale has observed extra-judicially that, 'To refer to [such orders] as a "meal-ticket for life" is . . . patronising and demeaning, but making an award [of joint-lives periodical payments to reflect the permanent disadvantage caused to the recipient's earning capacity by choices made during the marriage] is not.'[405] Ultimately, the question is whether the applicant *can* adjust and become self-sufficient, not whether she *should* do so:[406]

Murphy v Murphy **[2014] EWHC 2263**

HOLMAN J:

36. I do not know, nor do the parties know, what the future will bring. It may be that this wife will find another partner with whom she chooses to share her life and the maintenance will all end. It may be that she will be able later, if not sooner, to obtain well remunerated employment, carrying with it a good pension, and any dependence will end. But at the moment this lady [who had twins aged 3] is in a precarious position. She is very largely dependent on her husband, and it is frankly impossible for me to form the opinion that section 25A(2) requires as the trigger to then making a term order.

But if she *can* become self-sufficient, she *should*—she cannot choose not to work and just seek periodical payments instead.[407]

6.6.2 THE CLEAN BREAK IN PRACTICE

In high-value cases, a clean break is usually readily achievable using the capital assets. The difficulties arise in normal cases, where the capital is insufficient to cover the parties' needs,

[399] See Eekelaar (1991b), 86–7. [400] *Flavell v Flavell* [1997] 1 FLR 353, 358.
[401] *SS v NS* [2014] EWHC 4183, [46](v); cf *C v C* [1997] 2 FLR 26, 46, (8) (Court of Appeal).
[402] *WD v HD* [2015] EWHC 1547. [403] Law Com (2014), 3.67.
[404] *Waggott v Waggott* [2018] EWCA Civ 727, [156]. On the impact of this trope, see Thompson (2019) and on the related 'gold-digger' trope, see Thompson (2016).
[405] Hale (2018), 14. [406] *C v C* [1997] 2 FLR 26, adopted in *Murphy v Murphy* [2014] EWHC 2263, [32].
[407] *G v G* [2012] EWHC 167, [139].

including their income needs. However, the Law Commission has noted apparent geographical inconsistency in outcomes, particularly regarding the likelihood of a clean break (immediate or deferred) being ordered. Both practitioners' accounts of the situation and empirical research indicate that orders for spousal periodical payments are uncommon in many regions, even between couples with dependent children.[408]

Law Commission, *Matrimonial Property, Needs and Agreements*, Law Com No 343 (London: TSO, 2014)

2.45 First, there is evidence of significant regional differences in the levels of support likely to be awarded in different courts. This is not so much about amounts as about duration. . . .

2.50 In 2010, the Law Reform Committee of the General Council of the Bar said to us:

> There exists an almost "policy based" approach by the courts as to whether they provide for joint lives, or term orders. For example, the Principal Registry of the Family Division [now the Central Family Court in London] and High Court tend to make joint lives orders, other major court centres do not. The impact is that clients and solicitors openly forum shop and an element of geographical lottery is introduced to these orders. . . .

2.52 One of the questions asked in the Resolution survey, conducted specifically to support this project, was whether practitioners had ever issued proceedings in a particular court, or area of the country, because of a belief that the outcome to their client would be more favourable than issuing elsewhere. The majority of the 234 practitioners who responded (57%) indicated that they had issued proceedings in particular location or court because they thought that it would yield a more favourable outcome for their client.

2.53 There is sufficient evidence of regional inconsistency, and of its being used strategically by legal advisers, for us to regard it as problematic. . . .

2.54 Second, there is a lack of transparency. Certainly, family lawyers are familiar both with the law and with the practice of their local courts, and they can advise on the most likely outcome of litigation and so enable their clients to settle. But most people cannot afford lawyers. Many who previously had access to legal advice are no longer entitled to legal aid. They are able to access the courts, of course; but the process is more difficult without lawyers (for both the parties and the judiciary) and there is great concern that the court system will not be able to cope. In any event, at present most divorces are not accompanied by litigation about financial orders, and the court system does not have the capacity to accommodate the adjudication of a greater proportion of disputes; so it is no answer to the problem of the withdrawal of legal aid to say that the parties always have access to judicial discretion. This is not a reality.

On the Law Commission's recommendation, the Family Justice Council has produced plain English guidance for lay people to help them understand the law in this area,[409] and guidance addressed to judges and practitioners to try to achieve greater consistency of outcome.[410]

As regards the apparent geographical inconsistency, one study suggests that this is at least in part a result of the very different levels of resources at stake and housing costs in different areas of the country, rather than ideological differences between judges.[411] Where money

[408] Miles and Hitchings (2018); Woodward with Sefton (2014).

[409] Advice Now (online). [410] Family Justice Council (2018).

[411] Hitchings and Miles (2019); see also Douglas (2018b), 116–18.

is tight, paying child support may exhaust respondents' disposable income. In low-cost housing areas, primary carers may be able to rehouse with whatever capital they obtain in the settlement (or by renting), increasing their income with benefits and tax credits, as well as any earnings, and preferring not to seek spousal maintenance as well.[412] Indeed, financial remedy orders are only made at all following about a third of all divorces,[413] and we know nothing directly about the outcomes for those individuals who do not obtain orders.

But it cannot be assumed from this that wives (the principal recipients of periodical payment orders) are self-sufficient on divorce. Analysis of general population data shows that women's household income on average drops substantially following divorce whereas men's on average rises, and that, while wives partially recover their position post-divorce, this is driven by their re-partnering rather than through the labour market.[414] As Gillian Douglas has noted, contemporary preference for the clean break—'the modern emphasis on marriage as a vehicle for achieving emotional self-fulfilment', and so the notion that a spouse has the right to leave a failed marriage 'unencumbered by continuing financial as well as emotional ties'—leaves many women shouldering the economic burden of the marriage alone.[415]

6.6.3 APPLICATIONS TO VARY, SET ASIDE, AND FOR LEAVE TO APPEAL FINAL ORDERS

Evidently, circumstances may change post-divorce. Either party's fortunes might improve or deteriorate making the orders made on divorce now seem unfair. Or new evidence may emerge, suggesting that the order was unfair when made. The dilemma is to balance the competing virtues of fairness and finality, though finality might sometimes be considered an aspect of fairness.

6.6.3.a Orders that may be varied

Periodical payment orders and a limited range of other orders can be varied under the MCA 1973, s 31 at any point. The legislation does not require that there be a change of circumstance before variation can be considered, but it is hard to imagine when one would otherwise vary an order.[416] So, for example, if it becomes difficult for the payer to afford the payments or the payee becomes self-sufficient sooner than expected, an order for periodical payments may be varied downwards or discharged. The courts will consider applications to release parties from undertakings on similar grounds.[417]

6.6.3.b Other orders

By contrast, 'one-off' orders such as property transfers and lump sums seek to dispose of the parties' affairs once and for all in order to achieve finality. These orders cannot be varied and the court's jurisdiction ordinarily ceases once an order is made and executed.[418] They can only be altered later if there are grounds either: (i) for the order to be 'set aside' because it is tainted at the outset by some underlying flaw;[419] or (ii) for one party to be granted

412 Ibid. 413 MOJ (2022b), table 13. 414 Fisher and Low (2009), (2016), (2018b).

415 Douglas (2018a), 99. This is not a new problem: see also Smart (1984).

416 *Birch v Birch* [2017] UKSC 53, [15]. 417 Ibid.

418 Cf *Thwaite v Thwaite* (1981) 2 FLR 280; *Bezeliansky v Bezelianskaya* [2017] EWCA Civ 76, [30]–[39]; cf Horton (2018); *SR v HR* [2018] EWHC 606.

419 FPR 2010, rr 4.1(6) and 9.9A, Practice Direction 9A.

leave to appeal outside the usual time limit in the light of changed circumstances (akin to frustration).[420]

Setting orders aside

Orders can be set aside on limited grounds, including fraud, mistake, and non-disclosure or misrepresentation of facts, but only where knowledge of the truth would have made a substantial difference to the order made.[421] This reflects the parties' 'duty of full and frank' disclosure owed to each other and the court.[422] Examples include the concealment of an impending remarriage[423] or lucrative new job,[424] or of the existence, value, and marketability of key assets.[425] Where the order is based on the parties' agreement, issues may arise regarding the validity of that agreement. But it has been held that undue influence will not provide grounds for setting aside a consent order.[426] Nor will bad legal advice.[427] But lack of capacity to agree to a consent order will.[428]

Appealing out of time

Late appeals brought in light of new events are only exceptionally permitted: the clean break achieved by capital orders would be undermined if parties were free to seek some alteration given changes in their fortunes. If leave is granted, the case is reconsidered in light of all the circumstances at the time of the appeal.[429] The leading authority involved the most dramatic change of circumstance conceivable: shortly after the court had ordered a clean break settlement, transferring the matrimonial home to the wife for her to occupy with the children, she killed the children and committed suicide. On what grounds could leave be granted to appeal against the order?

Barder v Calouri **[1988] AC 20, 41, 43**

LORD BRANDON:

My Lords, the question whether leave to appeal out of time should be given on the ground that assumptions or estimates made at the time of the hearing of a cause or matter have been invalidated or falsified by subsequent events is a difficult one. The reason why the question is difficult is that it involves a conflict between two important legal principles and a decision as to which of them is to prevail over the other. The first principle is that it is in the public interest that there should be finality in litigation. The second principle is that justice requires cases to be decided, so far as practicable, on the true facts relating to them, and not on assumptions or estimates with regard to those facts which are conclusively shown by later events to have been erroneous . . .

A court may properly exercise its discretion to grant leave to appeal out of time from an order for financial provision or property transfer made after a divorce on the ground of new

420 *Cornick v Cornick* [1994] 2 FLR 530; for full review of these mechanisms, see *L v L* [2006] EWHC 956.

421 *Livesey v Jenkins* [1985] AC 424; see *Sharland v Sharland* [2015] UKSC 60; *Gohil v Gohil* [2015] UKSC 61 on the burden of proof, whether non-disclosure intentional or inadvertent.

422 *Livesey v Jenkins* [1985] AC 424.

423 Ibid.

424 *Bokor-Ingram v Bokor-Ingram* [2009] EWCA Civ 412.

425 *Vicary v Vicary* [1992] 2 FLR 271.

426 *Tommey v Tommey* [1983] Fam 15, doubted in *Livesey v Jenkins* [1985] AC 424, 440.

427 *L v L* [2006] EWHC 956, [47]–[53].

428 *MAP v RAP* [2013] EWHC 4784.

429 *Smith v Smith (Smith and others Intervening)* [1992] Fam 69.

> events, provided that certain conditions are satisfied. The first condition is that new events have occurred since the making of the order which invalidate the basis, or fundamental assumption, upon which the order was made, so that, if leave to appeal out of time were to be given, the appeal would be certain, or very likely, to succeed.[430] The second condition is that the new events should have occurred within a relatively short time of the order having been made. While the length of time cannot be laid down precisely, I should regard it as extremely unlikely that it could be as much as a year, and that in most cases it will be no more than a few months. The third condition is that the application for leave to appeal out of time should be made reasonably promptly in the circumstances of the case. To these three conditions . . . I would add a fourth, which it does not appear has needed to be considered so far, but which it may be necessary to consider in future cases. That fourth condition is that the grant of leave to appeal out of time should not prejudice third parties who have acquired, in good faith and for valuable consideration, interests in property which is the subject matter of the relevant order.

The supervening event must have been both unforeseen and unforeseeable.[431] Whether death invalidates the order's fundamental assumption will now turn on whether provision was based on needs or sharing.[432] The intention of the parties at the time the order was approved will also be deemed to be important.[433] It was clear in *Barder* that a fundamental assumption of the order, shared by the parties and the court,[434] was that the wife and children would indefinitely need a suitable home. That was invalidated by their sudden deaths, and the order was set aside. Contrast the impact of a spouse's death on provision based on sharing—as an entitlement of that spouse, it survives the spouse's untimely demise.[435]

Situations to which these criteria have been applied include: the death[436] or remarriage of one party;[437] major change in the children's living arrangements;[438] inheritance by one spouse;[439] mis-valuation of key assets; significant changes in value generated by subsequent events (not mere market conditions or natural price fluctuations, however unforeseeable);[440] and changes in financial remedies law.[441] The parties' reconciling after the divorce and cohabiting long term seems not to constitute a *Barder* event.[442] Nor, at a time when few jobs are wholly secure, does redundancy.[443] The Covid-19 pandemic 'probably' does not constitute

430 On the basis that had the event been foreseen *at the time of the original order*, a different order would have been made: *Williams v Lindley* [2005] EWCA Civ 103.

431 *Cornick v Cornick* [1994] 2 FLR 530.

432 For a useful illustration, see *WA v Executors of the Estate of HA* [2015] EWHC 2233.

433 *Goodyear v Goodyear (Deceased)* [2022] EWFC 96. The order would not have been agreed had the parties known the wife would die six months after it was entered into.

434 *Dixon v Marchant* [2008] EWCA Civ 11, [25].

435 *Richardson v Richardson* [2011] EWHC 79. See also *Goodyear v Goodyear (Deceased)* [2022] EWFC 96, where the order was not set aside in its entirety because of the wife's earned share.

436 E.g. *Smith v Smith (Smith and other Intervening)* [1992] Fam 69.

437 *Dixon v Marchant* [2008] EWCA Civ 11; cf *Nasim v Nasim* [2015] EWHC 2620, [9]. Cohabitation would probably also be relevant: cf *Cook v Cook* [1988] 1 FLR 521.

438 *Nasim v Nasim* [2015] EWHC 2620.

439 *Critchell v Critchell* [2015] EWCA Civ 436.

440 See *Cornick v Cornick* [1994] 2 FLR 530, and cases reviewed therein; *Middleton v Middleton* [1998] 2 FLR 821.

441 *S v S (Ancillary Relief: Consent Order)* [2002] EWHC 223: *White v White* [2001] 1 AC 596 not a *Barder* event because foreseeable at the relevant time.

442 *Hill v Hill* [1997] 1 FLR 730 (FD), rvsd on different grounds in [1998] 1 FLR 198 (CA).

443 *Maskell v Maskell* [2001] EWCA Civ 858, [4].

a *Barder* event either.[444] The uncertain times of global recession generated several attempts to appeal out of time by respondents who had elected to take the risky assets and lost out,[445] and by applicants who regretted having deliberately foregone a stake in speculative assets that later appreciated.[446] The courts rejected these applications under *Barder*: if you deliberately choose risk over certainty, or certainty over risk, you cannot later complain that you struck the wrong deal. While the scale of loss may be unforeseeable, the fact of a change in value is not.[447]

6.7 PRIVATE ORDERING: MARITAL AGREEMENTS

Financial disputes on divorce are rarely resolved by contested litigation.[448] Agreement is the norm, whether reached by lawyer-led negotiation,[449] mediation, or privately.[450] A small number of couples are now also agreeing to use arbitration; as we noted at 1.2.7, this is a rather different sort of agreement—not to specific terms, but rather to a non-court-based process that will decide those terms for them. If the case is contested, the court process provides incentives and opportunities for settlement, in particular: the requirement to attend a mediation information and assessment meeting before starting proceedings;[451] the requirement of full and frank disclosure;[452] 'first directions appointments' to define the issues in dispute;[453] settlement-oriented 'financial dispute resolution' appointments;[454] costs rules;[455] and various codes of conduct and protocols.[456] Less than 10 per cent of all financial orders made following divorce are made following adjudication of contested proceedings, the vast majority of proceedings entailing a consent order, discussed in the following section (6.7.1); only around a third of all divorces have any sort of financial order at all.[457]

However, two basic questions arise: (i) are financial agreements made on separation legally enforceable; and (ii) can parties reach a binding agreement in advance, whether before or during marriage, about how their assets and income will be shared (or not shared) in the event of any future divorce?

The short answer is that no form of purely private arrangement is straightforwardly enforceable. The key underlying principle emanates from *Hyman v Hyman*:[458] parties cannot oust the jurisdiction of the matrimonial court by agreement, including an agreement to go to arbitration. As King LJ affirmed in *Haley v Haley*,[459] agreements to arbitrate do not carry more weight than agreements reached between the parties themselves, and the court retains residual discretionary power when such agreements are enforced. So no agreement can prevent the court from considering what provision would be fair; and the court is not bound to determine that the parties' agreement produces a fair outcome—it can impose its own,

444 *BT v CU* [2021] EWFC 87, [22].
445 *Myerson v Myerson* [2009] EWCA Civ 282.
446 *Walkden v Walkden* [2009] EWCA Civ 627.
447 *DB v DLJ (Challenge to Arbitral Award)* [2016] EWHC 324.
448 See generally, Hitchings et al (2013).
449 Including collaborative law, see *S v P (Settlement by Collaborative Law Process)* [2008] 2 FLR 2040.
450 On problematic aspects of settlement, see Diduck (2003), 153–8; and 1.2.7.
451 See 1.2.7.
452 *Livesey v Jenkins* [1985] AC 424; *Sharland* and *Gohil* [2015] UKSC 60 and 61.
453 FPR 2010, r 9.15.
454 Ibid, r 2.61D–E; *Rose v Rose* [2002] EWCA Civ 208; see generally Black et al (2015), ch 30.
455 FPR 2010, Part 28; including Ungley orders, potentially imposing a costs sanction on a party who unreasonably refuses to engage in mediation.
456 E.g. Law Society (2015); Resolution (2012).
457 MOJ (2022b), tables 13 and 15.
458 [1929] AC 601.
459 [2020] EWCA Civ 1369.

different order. With that principle in mind, we shall work backwards from the point of divorce, starting with the only really secure form of private ordering—consent orders—and ending with the most controversial—pre-nuptial agreements.

6.7.1 CONSENT ORDERS

Most parties agree how to divide their property and finances. However, to achieve certainty and finality they should enshrine that agreement in a court order: a 'consent order'.[460] Most financial orders are made by consent, rather than contested, around 70 per cent following simple consent order applications (i.e. no contested application is made at all) and around 20–5 per cent following settlement of contested proceedings.[461] To obtain the order, parties present prescribed information to the court, essentially an overview of key financial and other data relevant to s 25, including a summary of their income and capital positions, the parties' and children's accommodation, their ages, the duration of the marriage, and any re-partnering plans. The court then determines whether their draft order should be made, or whether further inquiry is necessary.[462] Once the agreement is transposed into an order, the parties' rights and obligations flow directly from the order itself.[463] A consent order is as binding as one made following contested litigation, so can only be varied, appealed against, or set aside on the grounds discussed earlier.[464] Some decisions indicate that because a consent order is based on agreement, the court considering an application for variation or appeal out of time should be particularly slow to intervene.[465] Consent orders cannot include provisions that the court could not have ordered in contested litigation, except as undertakings.[466]

The court's role in making a consent order in financial remedy cases is distinctive, lying somewhere between 'rudimentary rubber stamp' and 'forensic ferret', 'a watchdog, but not a bloodhound', 'entitled but not obliged to play the detective':[467]

Pounds v Pounds [1994] 1 WLR 1535 (CA), 1537–41

WAITE LJ:

In most areas of our law, parties to litigation who are sui juris and independently advised can settle their differences on terms which are included by agreement in an order or rule of court . . . with the authority of a judge who may not be aware of the terms of the deal at all . . ., still less be concerned with any question as to their suitability or fairness. That is not so in financial proceedings between husband and wife, where the court does not act, it has been said, as a rubber-stamp: the judge will be concerned, whether the order be made by consent or imposed after argument, to be satisfied that the criteria of sections 25 and 25A of the Matrimonial Causes Act 1973 have been duly applied . . .

When the House of Lords ruled in *Livesey (formerly Jenkins) v Jenkins* [1985] A.C. 424 . . . that the duty of disclosure of assets was owed by spouses not only to each other but to the

[460] On the process, see Hitchings et al (2013), ch 1. On whether agreement has been reached, see *Xydhias v Xydhias* [1999] 1 FLR 683; *Radmacher v Granatino* [2010] UKSC 42, [148]–[149] per Baroness Hale.

[461] MOJ (2022b), table 15.

[462] MCA 1973, s 33A; FPR 2010, r 9.26: see *Pounds* extract, below.

[463] *De Lasala v De Lasala* [1980] AC 546, 560.

[464] See 6.6.3.

[465] *Richardson v Richardson (No 2)* [1996] 2 FLR 617.

[466] *Livesey v Jenkins* [1985] AC 424, 444.

[467] *B-T v B-T (Divorce: Procedure)* [1990] 2 FLR 1, 17; *L v L* [2006] EWHC 956, [73].

court, it did so upon the basis that it was the function of the court in every case, whether it was proceeding by consent of the parties or after a contested hearing, to be satisfied that the provision made by the order fulfilled the criteria laid down by section 25 . . . It is clear, however, that this was intended to be an assertion of general principle only, and not to impose on the court the need to scrutinise in detail the financial affairs of the parties who came to it for approval of an independently negotiated bargain. It could not be otherwise, for earlier that year Parliament had specifically enacted a more cursory regime for the scrutiny of consent orders [in the MCA 1973, s 33A] of which subsection (1) reads as follows:

> "Notwithstanding anything in the preceding provisions of this Part of this Act, on an application for a consent order for financial relief the court may, unless it has reason to think that there are other circumstances into which it ought to inquire, make an order in the terms agreed on the basis only of the prescribed information furnished with the application."

The "prescribed information" is that required by [FPR 2010, r 9.26.

Forms for use in supplying those particulars . . . run to no more than two pages, and the space allowed in the boxes for financial information is very restrictive indeed [see currently Form D81[468]].

The effect of section 33A and the Rules and Directions made under it is thus to confine the paternal function of the court when approving financial consent orders to a broad appraisal of the parties' financial circumstances as disclosed to it in summary form, without descent into the valley of detail. It is only if that survey puts the court on inquiry as to whether there are other circumstances into which it ought to probe more deeply that any further investigation is required of the judge before approving the bargain that the spouses have made for themselves.

In the case of applications based on arbitrated outcomes, the court's approach had been to approve the order based on that decision 'unless something has gone seriously wrong in the arbitral process'.[469] But the court has since clarified that an order can be declined 'where there are good and substantial grounds for concluding that an injustice will be done' if the terms of the arbitral award are given effect.[470]

It has been doubted whether the paternalism underpinning the rule in *Hyman v Hyman*, requiring parties to submit to the authority of the court in order to secure a binding settlement, is exercised in practice:

S. Cretney, 'From Status to Contract?', in F. Rose (ed), *Consensus ad Idem* (London: Sweet & Maxwell, 1996b), 277

[T]he question of whether a court can sensibly discharge [the function described by Waite LJ] . . . is self-evidently difficult; and it may well be that different judges approach their tasks

[468] <www.gov.uk/government/publications/form-d81-statement-of-information-for-a-consent-order-in-relation-to-a-financial-remedy>.

[469] *S v S (Financial Remedies: Arbitral Award)* [2014] EWHC 7, [21]. For criticism, see Ferguson (2015a); Diduck (2016), 139–42.

[470] *Haley v Haley* [2020] EWCA Civ 1369, [69]. See also *DB v DLJ (Challenge to Arbitral Award)* [2016] EWHC 324.

in different ways . . . [I]t is difficult to be confident that the investigation which the court is able to carry out is sufficient to ensure that the terms embodied in its order do not take advantage of the vulnerability of one of the parties. . . . [Given the limited information available to it,] it seems questionable how far the court is really in a position to make any informed judgment about the fairness of the agreement to which it is asked to give effect.[471]

On the other hand, significant investigation by the court may be undesirable: 'Officious inquiry may uncover an injustice, but it is more likely to disturb a delicate negotiation and produce the very costly litigation and the recrimination which conciliation is designed to avoid.'[472]

Judges' ability to exercise meaningful scrutiny will evidently be affected by their familiarity with the detailed facts and issues between the parties, which will differ considerably depending on whether the consent order application follows contested proceedings:

Hamilton v Hamilton **[2013] EWCA Civ 13**

BARON J:

29. [T]he modern approach is that the court endeavours to give effect to fair agreements reached by the parties with the assistance of proper legal advice. In practice most cases settle and the bulk of agreements reached will fall to be approved by the Court . . . as a piece of box work by a District Judge. In this event, save for the necessary forms and draft order, the court will have little information as to the objective or the true underlying structure of the deal. In contrast, if a case is settled at a Financial Dispute Resolution hearing, then the Judge may well have a direct input with the result that the essential causal matrix of the agreement will be known and understood.

Empirical research has found a mixed picture, with some judges (at least) prepared to intervene to query the substantive fairness of proposed orders in correspondence, sometimes requiring the parties to appear in person to explain the agreement (or to check that parties acting without a lawyer understand what they are agreeing to), and even very occasionally refusing to make orders in the terms proposed where not satisfied that they are fair.[473]

E. Hitchings, J. Miles, and H. Woodward, *Assembling the Jigsaw Puzzle: Understanding Financial Settlement on Divorce* (University of Bristol, 2013), 54, 57–8

Many applications pass through the court straightforwardly with no query. Most obviously, where the proposed order is within the expected parameters for a case of that nature (given type and size of assets / length of marriage / presence of children) the judge will perceive

[471] See also Davis et al (2000), 48 and 63–4.
[472] *Harris v Manahan* [1997] 1 FLR 205, 213.
[473] Hitchings et al (2013), 60–1.

> no need to query the application, at least not on substantive grounds. By contrast, where the agreement appeared to be outside the normal range of settlement options, [solicitor] interviewees anticipated judicial intervention. [One solicitor's] most recent case involved an uneven split – 20:80 [wife:husband]: "*I guess, on the face of it, you may say that this was outside the parameters because that's exactly what the judge is saying. But one person's interpretation of what's outside the parameters compared to another – it's grey, isn't it?*" The judge queried whether the settlement was fair, particularly in relation to the wife and children's housing needs, and her income position and needs. Both parties' solicitors wrote to explain why the agreement was structured as it was (parties wanting a clean break, wife made limited contributions and now living with a new partner earning a decent salary sufficient to meet her needs, former matrimonial home pre-acquired with work done on it before the marriage). They were waiting to hear whether it had been approved. . . .

But it seems that not all judges would view the same order in the same way:

> Interviewees suggested that particular expectations about the paperwork depend[ed] on the court or the particular judge. To some extent, this was something that practitioners could anticipate in order to try to ensure the smooth passage of their application. . . . [One] solicitor suggested that knowledge of the local court and of the local judge enabled their more recent consensual case to go through without a hitch: "*(W)hat he likes is a lovely long letter to go with the Statement of Information that says what's the logic behind this order.*" . . . This practitioner also raised the issue of variation in the level of judicial scrutiny at different courts: "*You might as well toss a coin . . . I'm quite disillusioned at the inconsistency. That's a nice way of saying it.*" . . .
>
> When explaining possible inconsistencies in approach to clients, [another solicitor] suggested that they explain to clients that, on one day, one judge will look at the consent application and give you a tick, and another judge will say that "*there's absolutely no way I'm agreeing to this*". This solicitor suggested that this disparity in approach reflected differing levels of experience amongst the judiciary in family law (without elaborating on what level of experience yielded a more inquisitive and challenging approach).

Given the inherent limitations on the court's ability to review applications, it has been said that the parties' lawyers (if any[474]) have a corresponding responsibility to secure fair outcomes and to minimize scope for subsequent challenge.[475] But the interests of securing finality in emotionally fraught financial litigation following divorce dictate that orders cannot be set aside because of bad legal advice.[476] Conversely, increasing numbers of unrepresented parties place greater burdens on the judge when they seek consent orders, but the judge's function in such cases is necessarily limited—they cannot adopt the function of the missing legal representatives:

[474] On litigants in person in these cases, see ibid, ch 5.

[475] *Dinch v Dinch* [1987] 1 WLR 252, 255. Cf the limited scope of the lawyer's duty if on a limited retainer: *Minkin v Landsberg* [2015] EWCA Civ 1152.

[476] *L v L* [2006] EWHC 956. Contrast the position applying to separation agreements, 6.7.2. The lawyers might be liable in negligence: *Arthur JS Hall and Co (A Firm) v Simons et al* [2002] 1 AC 615; cf *Minkin v Landsberg* [2015] EWCA Civ 1152, [38].

Minkin v Landsberg [2015] EWCA Civ 1152

KING LJ:

73. The District Judges, more than any other level of the judiciary, are finding their lists are overwhelmed as a consequence of the increase in court time taken by each case where (as is now routinely the case) the parties appear as litigants in person.

74. Following a contested financial remedy case where there are no lawyers representing the parties, the District Judge will draft an order which reflects his or her decision; there is no scope for ambiguity or misunderstanding as he or she knows precisely what he [or she] wishes to achieve and drafts the order accordingly. When however two unrepresented parties come before the judge with an agreement, the situation is entirely different. The district judge has neither the time, nor should he or she attempt, to interpret the minutiae of the agreement and draft/redraft the proposed consent order. That is not to say that he [or she] will not correct obvious errors or technical defects, but his [or her] task is to approve the order, not to sit with the parties and painstakingly work through with them every possible parameter of the draft in order to ensure they have considered every angle and future eventuality; to do so runs the risk that the judge will be seen to be giving advice or is seeking to interfere or undermine an otherwise unimpeachable agreement reached between the parties.

6.7.2 SEPARATION AND MAINTENANCE AGREEMENTS

What about agreements made at the point of divorce that have not been enshrined in a consent order? Separation agreements do not offer certainty and finality because, unless and until a consent order is obtained, *Hyman* leaves both parties free to apply for financial orders inconsistent with their agreement. Even if the parties intend to obtain a consent order, there is often a delay between agreement and order,[477] since the court cannot make most types of order until the conditional order is granted[478] (a minimum of 20 weeks from the date of the initial divorce application).[479]

Insofar as separation agreements deal with an actually impending separation or divorce, they may be contractually valid.[480] Specifically, written agreements making financial arrangements 'between the parties to a marriage' before or after divorce[481] are binding (save insofar as they purport to oust the court's jurisdiction) under s 34 of the MCA 1973. The ordinary requirement of consideration from the payee may be dealt with by the use of a deed.[482] The need to prove an intention to create legal relations, problematic if the parties are apparently in domestic harmony,[483] will not be difficult where the agreement is in writing and made with legal advice, particularly where divorce is pending.[484] However, although

[477] Cf the circumstances in *Rose v Rose* [2002] EWCA Civ 208.

[478] Save maintenance pending suit, s 22, legal services orders, s 22ZA, and financial provision: s 27, MCA 1973.

[479] This was a more pressing issue before the enactment of the Divorce, Dissolution and Separation Act 2020: *T v T (Agreement not Embodied in Consent Order)* [2013] EWHC B3.

[480] *Hyman v Hyman* [1929] AC 601; compare pre-nuptial agreements, 6.7.4.

[481] Including recitals to court orders: *T v R (Maintenance After Remarriage: Agreement)* [2016] EWFC 26.

[482] Cf *Bennett v Bennett* [1952] 1 KB 249, which prompted enactment of the precursor of s 34. Cf *Xydhias v Xydhias* [1999] 1 FLR 683 on the compromise of a financial remedy claim not concluded in a deed: *MacLeod v MacLeod* [2008] UKPC 64, [26]. [483] *Balfour v Balfour* [1919] 2 KB 571.

[484] *Merritt v Merritt* [1970] 1 WLR 1211.

binding to that extent in contract, maintenance agreements falling within s 34 and other separation agreements may be challenged via two routes.

First, s 35 empowers the court to alter s 34 agreements where:

> by reason of a change in the circumstances in the light of which any financial arrangements contained in the agreement were made or, as the case may be, financial arrangements were omitted from it (including a change foreseen by the parties when making the agreement), the agreement should be altered so as to make different, or, as the case may be, so as to contain, financial arrangements.[485]

The court has the discretion, to be exercised as appears 'just having regard to all the circumstances', to vary existing terms or insert wholly new terms into the agreement (e.g. by making provision for the making of periodical payments where none had originally been agreed). However, s 35 is rarely if ever used.[486]

Far more important in practice is the second route. The MCA 1973 preserves the *Hyman* principle that maintenance agreements cannot prevent an application to court for alternative provision.[487] So parties seeking greater provision—or those no longer wishing to pay what they agreed—can apply for financial orders on divorce in the ordinary way. However, the court hearing that application will take account of the agreement's existence[488] and circumstances surrounding it when deciding under s 25 what financial orders would be 'fair'.[489]

The leading case on the courts' approach to financial applications made despite a separation agreement is *Edgar v Edgar*. Contrary to her lawyers' advice that she was entitled to substantially more, the wife had agreed by deed to a capital sum and periodical payments and covenanted not to apply for further capital provision. She applied to the court, claiming that she had made the agreement because she was desperate to leave the husband, by whose wealth and position she felt overpowered:

Edgar v Edgar [1980] 1 WLR 1410 (CA), 1417–18

ORMROD LJ:

> To decide what weight should be given, in order to reach a just result, to a prior agreement not to claim a lump sum, regard must be had to the conduct of both parties, leading up to the prior agreement, and to their subsequent conduct, in consequence of it. It is not necessary in this connection to think in formal legal terms, such as misrepresentation or estoppel; *all* the circumstances as they affect each of two human beings must be considered in the complex relationship of marriage. So, the circumstances surrounding the making of the agreement are relevant. Und[ue] pressure by one side, exploitation of a dominant position to secure an

485 MCA 1973, s 35(2)(a). Following the death of one party, see MCA 1973, s 36. The court may also alter agreements insofar as they '[do] not contain proper financial arrangements with respect to any child of the family': s 35(2)(b): see 5.6.

486 *Radmacher v Granatino* [2009] EWCA Civ 649, [134]. A rare example: *T v R (Maintenance After Remarriage: Agreement)* [2016] EWFC 26.

487 MCA 1973, ss 34(1), 35(1), (6).

488 Decided not by reference to contractual principles, but in the exercise of the court's discretion: *Xydhias v Xydhias* [1999] 1 FLR 683; *DN v HN* [2014] EWHC 3435; see Cretney (1999).

489 *Hyman v Hyman* [1929] AC 601, 609, and 629.

> unreasonable advantage, inadequate knowledge, possibly bad legal advice,[490] an important change of circumstances, unforeseen or overlooked at the time of making the agreement, are all relevant to the question of justice between the parties. *Important too is the general proposition that formal agreements, properly and fairly arrived at with competent legal advice, should not be displaced unless there are good and substantial grounds for concluding that an injustice will be done by holding the parties to the terms of their agreement.* [emphasis added] There may well be other considerations which affect the justice of this case; the above list is not intended to be an exclusive catalogue . . .
>
> Eastham J. in the present case, approached the problem on these lines. He summarised the law in five propositions:
>
> "(1) . . . (and this is not contested) notwithstanding the deed . . ., the wife is entitled to pursue a claim under section 23 of the Act. (2) If she does pursue such a claim, the court not only has jurisdiction to entertain it but is bound to take into account all the considerations listed in section 25 of the Act. (3) The existence of an agreement is a very relevant circumstance under section 25 and in the case of an arm's length agreement, based on legal advice between parties of equal bargaining power, is a most important piece of conduct to be considered under section 25. (4) Providing that there is equality above, the mere fact that the wife would have done better by going to the court, would not generally be a ground, for giving her more as, in addition to its duty under section 25, the court had a duty also to uphold agreements which do not offend public policy. (5) If the court, on the evidence, takes the view that having regard to the disparity of bargaining power, it would be unjust not to exercise its powers under section 23 (having regard to the considerations under section 25), it should exercise such powers even if no fraud, misrepresentation or duress is established which, at common law, would entitle a wife to avoid the deed."
>
> I agree with these propositions, subject to two reservations. First, as to proposition (4), I am not sure that it is helpful to speak of the court having "a duty" to uphold agreements, although I understand the sense in which the word was used. Secondly, the reference to "disparity of bargaining power" in proposition (5) is incomplete. . . . [What is required is a situation] where one spouse takes an unfair advantage of the other in the throes of marital breakdown, a time when emotional pressures are high, and judgment apt to be clouded. . . . There can be no doubt in that in this case, as in so many, there is a disparity of bargaining power. The crucial question, however, for present purposes, is not whether the husband had a superior bargaining power, but whether he exploited it in a way which was unfair to the wife, so as to induce her to act to her disadvantage.

As Oliver LJ pithily put it:

> [I]n a consideration of what is just to be done in the exercise of the court's powers under the Act of 1973 in the light of the conduct of the parties, the court must, I think, start from the position that a solemn and freely negotiated bargain by which a party defines her own requirements ought to be adhered to unless some clear and compelling reason, such as, for instance, a drastic change of circumstances, is shown to the contrary.[491]

[490] *Camm v Camm* (1983) 4 FLR 577: 'bad' does not connote 'negligent', 580.
[491] [1980] 1 WLR 1410, 1424.

The court found that it was fair to hold her to the agreement: the husband had not abused his position and the wife was driven by her desire to achieve independence.[492]

Cases vary in their description of the approach to be taken to separation agreements and the *Edgar* criteria, though differences of emphasis may simply reflect the facts of the individual cases. Sometimes, the approach seems to be that, unless the party seeking to depart from the agreement can show that the case satisfies one of the *Edgar* criteria, the court will give effect to the agreement without reviewing the parties' current circumstances.[493] At other times, the courts have emphasized that agreements are just one factor in the global s 25 analysis.[494] Amendments to the 1973 Act since *Edgar* requiring that first consideration be given to the welfare of minor children of the family deprive agreements of primary status in such cases.[495] Clearly, more weight will generally be given to agreements concluded with independent, good quality legal advice, and full disclosure.[496] But as *Radmacher v Granatino* (discussed later) shows, neither is necessary for a court to attach decisive weight to an agreement.

The Privy Council held in *MacLeod v MacLeod* that the same approach should be taken whether the agreement is challenged via s 35 or by a straightforward application for financial orders.[497] So the court hearing the latter application may decide, in the exercise of its s 25 discretion, to depart from the agreement given a change of circumstance. Baroness Hale suggested that what was needed was 'the sort of change which would make those arrangements manifestly unjust', though in *Radmacher* she retracted the word 'manifestly' as imposing too strict a test.[498] Crucially, going beyond what s 35 allows, the court under *Edgar* principles may also depart from the agreement because of the circumstances in which the agreement was made. However, the mere fact that a court would have made different provision will not of itself justify departure from the agreement.[499] Baroness Hale also noted the general point of public policy that, regardless of any change of circumstance, an obligation that ought to be met by a family member should not be cast onto the public purse.[500]

The 'limbo' status of separation agreements—neither straightforwardly binding nor irrelevant—has attracted judicial criticism:

Pounds v Pounds [1994] 1 WLR 1535 (CA), 1550–1

HOFFMANN LJ:

[I]t does seem to me that the law is in an unsatisfactory state. There are in theory various possible answers to the problem. One might be that an agreement between the parties, at least where each has independent legal advice, is binding upon them subject only to the normal contractual remedies based on fraud, misrepresentation, undue influence, etc. At present, the policy of the law as expressed in *Hyman v Hyman* . . . is against such a solution. The court retains its supervisory role and only its order gives finality. Another answer might be that when parties are negotiating with a view to an agreement which will be embodied in

[492] Cf *Camm v Camm* (1983) 4 FLR 577, in which the wife was also found to have received bad legal advice.

[493] *Smith v McInerney* [1994] 2 FLR 1077; *X v X (Y and Z Intervening)* [2002] 1 FLR 508; *T v T* [2013] EWHC B3.

[494] *Smith v Smith* [2000] 3 FCR 374: Black J held that *Smith* did not indicate a different approach: *A v B (Financial Relief: Agreements)* [2005] EWHC 314.

[495] *Richardson v Richardson (No 2)* [1994] 2 FLR 1051.

[496] See generally *X v X (Y and Z Intervening)* [2002] 1 FLR 508, [103].

[497] [2008] UKPC 64, [41]; cf *Simister (No 1)* [1987] 1 FLR 194.

[498] [2010] UKSC 42, [168]. [499] Ibid, [42]. [500] Ibid, [41].

> a consent order, everything should be treated as without prejudice negotiation until the order is actually made. In the latter case, the parties would know that until the court had given its imprimatur, nothing which they had negotiated was legally binding or even admissible. If one of them changed his or her mind, they would have either to go back to the negotiating table or litigate the matter de novo. This may be tiresome, as in the case of a house purchase where one party changes his or her mind before contracts are exchanged. But the parties would at least know where they stood. The result of the decision of this court in *Edgar v Edgar* . . . and the cases which have followed is that we have, as it seems to me, the worst of both worlds. The agreement may be held to be binding, but whether it will be can be determined only after litigation and may involve . . . examining the quality of the advice which was given to the party who wishes to resile. It is then understandably a matter for surprise and resentment on the part of the other party that one should be able to repudiate an agreement on account of the inadequacy of one's own legal advisers, over whom the other party had no control and of whose advice he had no knowledge. The husband's counsel, who has considerable experience of these matters, told us that he reckoned that in Northampton an agreement has an 80 per cent chance of being upheld but that attitudes varied from district judge to district judge. In our attempt to achieve finely ground justice by attributing weight but not too much weight to the agreement of the parties, we have created uncertainty and . . . added to the cost and pain of litigation.

The only guarantee of finality is to obtain a consent order based on the agreement.

6.7.3 POST-NUPTIAL AGREEMENTS

We turn now to agreements not made at the point of divorce, but earlier in the marriage—possibly during a 'rocky' patch[501] and/or affirming or varying an earlier pre-nuptial agreement[502]—setting out what would happen in the (hypothetical) eventuality of a future divorce.

Until the Privy Council decision in *MacLeod v MacLeod*, 'post-nuptial' agreements ('post-nups') were widely considered void on grounds of public policy for improperly contemplating and so potentially encouraging divorce. The Privy Council held that any such objection no longer applies, concluding that post-nuptial agreements fall within s 34, which applies to agreements made 'between the parties to a marriage'. So, provided they were made in writing with an intention to create legal relations and consideration (or by a deed), post-nuptial agreements would—like separation agreements—be valid and binding by statute,[503] but could be challenged via s 35 or, more likely, an application for financial orders subject to *Edgar* principles.

However, the Supreme Court in *Radmacher* by majority (only obiter, as that case concerned a *pre*-nuptial agreement) considered this interpretation of s 34 erroneous: Parliament in 1973 cannot have intended to include within s 34 agreements then considered void on grounds of public policy.[504] The majority of the court therefore preferred to align post-nups with pre-nuptial agreements. In short, neither type of agreement is now void on grounds of public policy (including agreements that simply exclude all claims, explicitly or implicitly leaving the parties with whatever they own at the point of divorce). The *Hyman* principle entitles the matrimonial court to order provision different from that agreed (including making

[501] E.g. *NA v MA* [2006] EWHC 2900. [502] E.g. *MacLeod v MacLeod* [2008] UKPC 64.
[503] Ibid, [35]–[39]. For criticism, see Parker (2015). [504] [2010] UKSC 42, [54]–[55].

provision that the agreement was for *none*), but that court will give the agreement decisive weight where freely entered into with full appreciation of its implications unless it would not be fair to hold the parties to it.[505]

Given *Radmacher*, little may now turn on the type of marital agreement: all are subject to *Hyman*, all are examined in a fact-sensitive way in pursuit of a fair outcome, and all agreements reached as a true exercise of the parties' autonomy are upheld unless it would be unfair to do so.[506] But there is at least one important factual difference between the different types of agreement: separation agreements generally deal with known circumstances prevailing at the time of the impending divorce;[507] by contrast, pre-nuptial agreements and post-nups concluded early in the marriage try to cater for what will happen 'in an uncertain and unhoped for future'.[508] Whether that agreement is 'fair' will depend on what that future brings. We examine the courts' approach to 'fairness' in this context in the next section.

6.7.4 PRE-NUPTIAL AGREEMENTS

Pre-nuptial agreements, sometimes called 'ante-nuptial' agreements or less formally 'prenups', had the most tenuous status of all types of marital agreement.

6.7.4.a The public policy objection removed

Like any other marital agreement, pre-nuptial agreements are subject to the *Hyman* principle, but until recently their status (like post-nuptial agreements) was further weakened by the fact that they were entirely *void* as a matter of contract law on grounds of public policy.[509] This public policy objection had been stated in various ways over the years, but essentially it was considered objectionable that couples should reach agreements that potentially encouraged either party to instigate divorce. Baroness Hale described the argument in the following terms:

Radmacher v Granatino [2010] UKSC 42

143. . . . This rule was developed in the context of agreements or settlements which made some or better financial provision for the wife if she were to live separately from her husband. Such an agreement could be seen as encouraging them to live apart – for example, by encouraging her to leave him, if it was sufficiently generous or more than she would get if she stayed with him, or encouraging him to leave her, or to agree to her going, if it were not so generous. Such encouragement was seen as inconsistent with the fundamental, life-long and enforceable obligation of husband and wife to live with one another.

[505] Ibid, [75].

[506] Compare the italicized words in the extract from Ormrod LJ's judgment in *Edgar* in the previous section with *Radmacher v Granatino* [2010] UKSC 42 at [75], extracted at 6.7.4.b.

[507] *Radmacher v Granatino* [2010] UKSC 42, [65].

[508] Ibid, [59]; cf if the marriage is very short: *BN v MA* [2013] EWHC 4250, [25].

[509] *MacLeod v MacLeod* [2008] UKPC 64, [31]–[33].

Such agreements were therefore simply unenforceable as contracts. However, somewhat confusingly,[510] despite being contractually void, pre-nuptial agreements were not ignored and, in certain circumstances, came to be given substantial—even decisive—weight.[511]

The current law was definitively stated by the Supreme Court in *Radmacher v Granatino*, a decision commonly described as effecting major change,[512] though arguably it simply extended a pre-existing trend to give determinative weight to pre-nuptial agreements in appropriate circumstances.[513] The court, by majority (Baroness Hale dissenting in certain key respects), held first—and obiter—that the public policy objections to pre-nuptial agreements are obsolete and so no longer apply.[514] Since spouses' duty to cohabit is no longer legally enforceable[515] the basis for the public policy argument against both types of agreement has disintegrated.

The Privy Council had suggested in *MacLeod* that parties to pre-nuptial agreements need protection from pressures to which parties to post-nups are not subject: the agreement might be 'the price which one party may extract for his or her willingness to marry' at all.[516] But parties to post-nuptial agreements might be susceptible to equally powerful if different pressure, as *NA v MA* illustrates. Here the wife, who was entirely dependent on the husband and his family, was bullied into signing the agreement after her adultery was discovered. The agreement was a non-negotiable condition of the marriage continuing (and of her returning home). He knew that she felt overwhelmingly guilty and was desperate to save the marriage for the children's sake. Baron J had no difficulty in departing from this agreement on *Edgar* grounds given the wife's evident subjection to undue influence.[517] In view of these similarities between the pre- and post-nuptial context, the Supreme Court in *Radmacher* therefore rejected a sharp distinction between pre- and post-nuptial agreements, preferring to treat them in the same way.

6.7.4.b The *Hyman* principle: the treatment of agreements in the matrimonial court

However, whilst all forms of nuptial agreements are now understood to be contractually valid, a majority regarded their contractual enforceability to be a 'red herring':[518] because they are all subject to the *Hyman* principle, and so can all be departed from in the exercise of the matrimonial court's discretion under the MCA 1973 following divorce.[519] The key question is what the court will do when faced with an application for financial orders between parties who made a pre- or post-nuptial agreement—including agreements for no provision to be made, as in *Radmacher*. From this point, Baroness Hale largely agreed with

510 *Radmacher v Granatino* [2009] EWCA Civ 649, [64].

511 Ibid; *Crossley v Crossley* [2007] EWCA Civ 1491; *M v M (Pre-Nuptial Agreement)* [2002] 1 FLR 654; *K v K* [2003] 1 FLR 120.

512 E.g. *KA v MA (Pre-Nuptial Agreement: Needs)* [2018] EWHC 499, [48]; *Versteegh v Versteegh* [2018] EWCA Civ 1050, [44].

513 E.g. *Crossley v Crossley*; cf the needs-based provision made in *M v M (Prenuptial Agreement)* and *K v K (Ancillary Relief: Prenuptial Agreement)* [2003] 1 FLR 120: n 510.

514 [2010] UKSC 42, [52].

515 Since, in particular, the abolition of decree for restitution of conjugal rights: Matrimonial Proceedings and Property Act 1970, s 20.

516 *MacLeod v MacLeod* [2008] UKPC 64, [36].

517 [2006] EWHC 2900; see also the bizarre circumstances in *Kremen v Agrest (No 11)* [2012] EWHC 45.

518 Cf Miles (2011b), 439–40 on contexts in which contractual validity matters.

519 *Radmacher* [2010] UKSC 42, [62]–[63]; cf Lord Mance [128] and Baroness Hale [159].

the substance of the majority's position, but adopted a different emphasis (regarded by Lord Mance as unlikely to make any practical difference[520]). The majority, in describing their approach, essentially providing a new starting point for cases involving agreements:

Radmacher v Granatino [2010] UKSC 42

LORD PHILLIPS ET AL:

75. *White v White* and *Miller v Miller* establish that the overriding criterion to be applied to ancillary relief proceedings is that of fairness and identify the three strands of need, compensation and sharing that are relevant to the question of what is fair. If an ante-nuptial agreement deals with those matters in a way that the court might adopt absent such an agreement, there is no problem about giving effect to the agreement. The problem arises where the agreement makes provisions that conflict with what the court would otherwise consider to be the requirements of fairness. The fact of the agreement is capable of altering what is fair. It is an important factor to be weighed in the balance. We would advance the following proposition, to be applied in the case of both ante- and post-nuptial agreements . . .:

> "The court *should give effect* to a nuptial agreement that is freely entered into by each party with a full appreciation of its implications *unless* in the circumstances prevailing it *would not be fair* to hold the parties to their agreement." [italics added]

Baroness Hale preferred to formulate the test the other way around,[521] asking 'Did each party freely enter into an agreement, intending it to have legal effect and with full appreciation of its implications. If so, in the circumstances as they now are, *would it be fair* to hold them to their agreement?'[522] But whether expressed negatively or positively, what does 'fairness' consist of in this context? The majority went on:

76. . . . This will necessarily depend upon the facts of the particular case, and it would not be desirable to lay down rules that would fetter the flexibility that the court requires to reach a fair result. There is, however, some guidance that we believe that it is safe to give directed to the situation where there are no tainting circumstances attending the conclusion of the agreement. [See below]

There are, therefore, two stages to the inquiry, though the court may in practice examine their combined effect in its pursuit of fairness.[523] The first stage achieves what Jens Scherpe calls 'protection *of* autonomy', seeking to ensure that both parties really did agree: are there any 'tainting circumstances' present at the outset that detract from the weight to be accorded to the agreement? If not, the court then moves to the second stage in which the parties—or one of them—is 'protected *from*' the consequences of that exercise of their autonomy: would it nevertheless now be unfair to hold the parties to the agreement?[524]

[520] Cf Thompson's analysis of Hale's approach as more compliant with a feminist relational contract theory: (2015), 185 et seq.

[521] See Scherpe (2011b), 526 on the impact on the burden of proof.

[522] *Radmacher* [2010] UKSC 42, [169]. Cf Lord Mance [129]. [523] Ibid, [73].

[524] Scherpe (2011a), (2011b).

BN v MA [2013] EWHC 4250

MOSTYN J:

17. . . . [G]iven the important notice in its prominent font at the beginning of the [pre-nuptial agreement] stating that it is intended to confirm separate property interests and to be determinative of the division of their assets, it must be obvious that the principal object of the exercise in this case (as indeed in every case where a nuptial agreement is signed) is to avoid subsequent expensive and stressful litigation; and it is for this reason . . . that the law adopts a strict policy of requiring demonstration of something unfair before it will open the Pandora's Box of litigation . . .

Step 1: factors tainting the agreement from the outset

The court in *Radmacher* identified several issues that might undermine an agreement from the outset, going beyond what contract law would regard as a vitiating factor (e.g. fraud, duress, and so on).[525]

Radmacher v Granatino [2010] UKSC 42

LORD PHILLIPS ET AL:

71. In relation to the circumstances attending the making of the nuptial agreement, this comment of Ormrod LJ in *Edgar v Edgar* at p 1417, although made about a separation agreement, is pertinent:

> "It is not necessary in this connection to think in formal legal terms, such as misrepresentation or estoppel; all the circumstances as they affect each of two human beings must be considered in the complex relationship of marriage."

The first question will be whether any of the standard vitiating factors: duress,[526] fraud or misrepresentation,[527] is present. Even if the agreement does not have contractual force, those factors will negate any effect the agreement might otherwise have. But unconscionable conduct such as undue pressure (falling short of duress) will also be likely to eliminate the weight to be attached to the agreement, and other unworthy conduct, such as exploitation of a dominant position to secure an unfair advantage, would reduce or eliminate it.

Both parties must have entered into the agreement 'of their own free will, without undue influence and pressure, and informed of its implications'. The absence of independent legal advice or full disclosure of each party's assets will not necessarily undermine the agreement: while both might be 'obviously desirable', what matters is that 'each party should have all the information that is *material* to his or her decision, and that each party should intend

[525] *Radmacher* [2010] UKSC 42, [71]–[72].

[526] E.g. *Hopkins v Hopkins* [2015] EWHC 812; failed post-nup duress case.

[527] Exaggerated misrepresentation of wealth by the economically weaker party will not permit that spouse later to resile from the agreement: *WW v HW (Pre-Nuptial Agreement: Needs: Conduct)* [2015] EWHC 1844.

that the agreement should govern the financial consequences of the marriage coming to an end'.[528] Mr Granatino had received no disclosure and foregone the opportunity to take independent legal advice, but, as a financially literate man, he clearly understood the German pre-nuptial agreement, insisted on by his fabulously wealthy wife, that neither spouse would have any sort of claim against each other on divorce; the lack of advice and disclosure had no impact on his decision.[529] Indeed, *Radmacher* was like many cases in that it involved 'globe-trotting' parties who made their agreement under a foreign law that allows agreements to be binding without independent advice or disclosure and operates an entirely different financial remedy regime on divorce: that different context, and the absence of any advice about English law, will not of itself reduce the weight to be given to the agreement should the parties divorce in England and Wales.[530] But the parties must surely appreciate that the agreement purports to govern their financial positions *on divorce* and not, for example, simply during the marriage.[531]

In considering whether the parties were under undue pressure, the court will consider a wide range of factors. To the list provided here, we might add whether one party is pregnant:

Radmacher v Granatino [2010] UKSC 42

72. The court may take into account a party's emotional state, and what pressures he or she was under to agree. But that again cannot be considered in isolation from what would have happened had he or she not been under those pressures. The circumstances of the parties at the time of the agreement will be relevant. Those will include such matters as their age and maturity, whether either or both had been married or been in long-term relationships before their experience of previous relationships may explain the terms of the agreement, and may also show what they foresaw when they entered into the agreement. What may not be easily foreseeable for less mature couples may well be in contemplation of more mature couples. Another important factor may be whether the marriage would have gone ahead without an agreement, or without the terms which had been agreed. This may cut either way.

Analysis of these issues requires close scrutiny of the interpersonal dynamics, viewed from both parties' perspectives.[532] But the hurdle to be crossed in order to undermine an agreement at step 1 is clearly high. A finding of coercive control can justify an agreement having no weight on divorce.[533] However, signing an agreement a short time before the wedding does not necessarily meet the threshold of undue pressure.[534] In *KA v MA*, where the parties had already cohabited for some years and had a child together, the pre-nup—discussed over a long period—was a clear 'but for' precondition of the husband marrying at all, concerned as he was to preserve his wealth for children from his previous marriage. The wife's motivation to marry was founded on a wish to build a stable family unit for their son's

[528] *Radmacher* [2010] UKSC 42, [68]–[69]. In purely English cases, such intention will more readily be found for agreements concluded post-*Radmacher*: [70].

[529] Ibid, [114]–[117], upholding the Court of Appeal decision; see Miles (2009). See subsequently *Z v Z (No 2)* [2011] EWHC 2878; *V v V* [2011] EWHC 3230; cf the lack of understanding in *GS v L* [2011] EWHC 1759.

[530] *Versteegh, v Versteegh* [2018] EWCA Civ 1050, [62]–[64], [182].

[531] *Y v Y (Financial Remedy: Marriage Contract)* [2014] EWHC 2920.

[532] Cf Thompson's concern that insufficient attention is paid to this: (2015), (2018).

[533] *Traharne v Limb* [2022] EWFC 27. [534] *WC v HC* [2022] EWFC 22.

welfare (e.g. shared surnames) rather than financial issues. The husband's wealth far exceeded £20 million:

KA v MA (Pre-Nuptial Agreement: Needs) [2018] EWHC 499

ROBERTS J:

60. This is not a case where this husband made overt threats to the wife. I do not regard his stated position of principle that there would be no marriage absent a signed prenuptial agreement to be capable of constituting duress or exploitation of a dominant position for these purposes *in the context of this particular case*. These were mature, consenting adults, each of whom had been married for a number of years prior to meeting one another. The wife had an established career when they met. She worked full-time in a professional environment and owned her own property. She was financially independent to all intents and purposes. Each had travelled through the vicissitudes of an ultimately unhappy marriage which had resulted in divorce. Whilst the wife appears to have steered a path through a relatively trouble-free (although, no doubt, painful) disengagement from her first husband, this husband's experience of divorce had been very different. That experience had left a lasting scar . . . and informed his attitude in relation to future personal relationships. Having become a couple, they had made the decision to have a child together. They had chosen to live together as a family unit, sharing the same home, and had been cohabiting as a family unit for four years prior to their decision to marry. That does not in any sense dilute the impact of the wife's clear wish to elevate their cohabitation to the status of marriage but it informs to a significant extent the court's enquiry into the dynamics of their personal relationship at that particular point in time. . . .

61. . . . He had made clear to her that he was unwilling to take that final legal step . . . without the quid pro quo of a legal agreement which, so far as the law would allow, restricted his financial exposure in the event of a subsequent divorce. . . . [T]hat was a position which had been known to this wife throughout the entire course of their relationship . . .

62. . . . [S]he told her solicitor that part of the pressure which she felt flowed from her perceived inability to negotiate effectively with the husband. I accept that her solicitor did not appear to suggest any alternative figures, or even a bracket, which she might take back to the husband as an alternative proposal. Nonetheless she received advice in the clearest terms to the effect that, whatever the ongoing evolution of the law in relation to marital agreements, she should consider that she would be bound by any agreement into which she entered.

63. Does the 'furious row' (per the wife) [following W's first visit to the solicitors and discussion of the draft agreement with H] constitute the sort of pressure or unconscionable conduct which might enable the court to reach a clear finding that when she authorised the release of the signed agreement the following Tuesday, *her free will had by then been overborn[e]* by the husband's conduct? . . . [S]he was clearly upset and in tears when she spoke to her solicitor that morning about the prenuptial agreement . . . I have no doubt that she was psychologically torn between her wish to proceed with the plans she had been making for the wedding and the husband's request to agree to a potentially binding document which might well, at some point in the future, operate to her significant financial detriment. That said, the evidence in this case does not lead me to a conclusion that this wife was *effectively disabled* from negotiating with the husband supported as she was by the legal advice she had received from her solicitor. . . .

64. . . . It may well be that she had placed some reliance on what she may have interpreted as the husband's reassurance that the weight which a court would attach to any signed agreement would recede over time once they were married. However, . . . *I cannot in this*

case reach a conclusion that, by the time she authorised the release of the signed agreement, the wife's free will was completely overborne by any action or inaction on the part of the husband. It is clear to me that at that moment in time the celebration of the marriage was uppermost in her mind. That was what she wanted to achieve and she accepts quite candidly that she knew full well that the agreement was the condition precedent to achieving that end. *I cannot accept that she was prevented by anything said or done by the husband from balancing the alternative options* which were open to her at that point in time. [Emphases added]

If the agreement fails at step 1, it will not attract the benefit of *Radmacher*'s para 75 presumption, but may (depending on the nature and strength of the 'tainting' factor) attract some weight in the exercise of the court's discretion.[535]

Step 2: the 'fairness' of upholding the agreement at the point of divorce

The next step is to examine the 'fairness' of giving effect to the agreement at the point of divorce. Elaborating on the remarks made at paras 75 and 76 (extracted earlier), the court identified several relevant factors. The agreement cannot 'prejudice the reasonable requirements of any children of the family', whose welfare is by statute the 'first consideration' on granting financial relief.[536] Beyond that, however, the court should respect the parties' autonomy and their choice about how to regulate their financial affairs: 'It would be paternalistic and patronising to override their agreement simply on the basis that the court knows best.' This will especially be the case where the agreement dealt with known circumstances, unlikely in the case of a pre-nuptial agreement preceding a long marriage. Agreements that simply preserve a particular item of 'non-matrimonial property', such as an inheritance, may also attract more weight.[537] Contrast an agreement dealing with 'the contingencies of an uncertain future',[538] where changed circumstances over the course of decades may have rendered the agreement unfair.[539] Baroness Hale was particularly eloquent in her treatment of the last point:

Radmacher v Granatino **[2010] UKSC 42**

BARONESS HALE:

175. The focus both of my test and that of the majority is upon whether it is now fair to give effect to the agreement. The longer it is since the agreement was made, the more likely it is that later events will have overtaken it. Marriage is not only different from a commercial relationship in law, it is also different in fact. It is capable of influencing and changing every aspect of a couple's lives: where they live, how they live, who goes to work outside the home and what work they do, who works inside the home and how, their social lives and leisure pursuits, and how they manage their property and finances. A couple may think that their futures are all mapped out ahead of them when they get married but many things may happen to push them off course – misfortunes such as redundancy, bankruptcy, illness, disability, obligations to other family members and especially to children, but also unexpected opportunities and unexplored avenues. The couple are bound together in more than a business

[535] *Versteegh v Versteegh* [2018] EWCA Civ 1050, [178]. [536] *Radmacher* [2010] UKSC 42, [77].
[537] Ibid, [78]–[79]. [538] Ibid, [78]. [539] Ibid, [80].

relationship, so of course they modify their plans and often compromise their individual best interests to accommodate these new events. They may have no choice if their marriage is to survive. There may be people who enter marriage in the belief that it will not endure, but for most people the hope and the belief is that it will. There is also a public interest in the stability of marriage. Marriage and relationship breakdown can have many damaging effects for the parties, their children and other members of their families, and also for society as a whole. So there is also a public interest in encouraging the parties to make adjustments to their roles and life-styles for the sake of their relationship and the welfare of their families.

176. All of this means that it is difficult, if not impossible, to predict at the outset what the circumstances will be when the marriage ends. It is even more difficult to predict what the fair outcome of the couple's financial relationship will be . . .

The most significant part of the court's decision, following on from these concerns, is that if one party is left in a 'predicament of real need, while the other enjoys a sufficiency or more' at the end of the marriage, a court may readily find an agreement making no provision for that party to be unfair; likewise where one spouse's devotion to the domestic sphere freed the other to accumulate wealth: there too, allowing the breadwinner to keep all is likely to be considered unfair. In those circumstances, provision based on *need* and/or *compensation* is *likely* to be ordered, notwithstanding any agreement. But provision based on *equal sharing* is *unlikely* to be ordered. Indeed, where neither party is in need on divorce (so that needs-based provision would not be warranted anyway), it may be fair to make no provision at all.[540]

In short, while a nuptial agreement is likely to displace the equal sharing principle, provision for needs (and compensation) on divorce appears to constitute an irreducible core obligation of marriage, such that agreements should provide for each party's needs in order to be upheld.

Radmacher could therefore be viewed as a coda to the sharing principle,[541] the agreement providing another 'good reason' to 'depart from' equal sharing on the basis that the parties have clearly signalled that their marriage is not one to which the premise of the equal sharing principle applies at all or with full force,[542] or simply on the basis that the parties are themselves clearly defining what property counts as 'non-matrimonial' and so beyond the reach of that principle. But this differential treatment of sharing and needs/compensation also places significant weight on an issue which, as we discussed at 6.5.3, English law has yet satisfactorily to address: when does a former spouse come under an obligation to meet the other's needs, and how extensive (in terms of quantum and duration) is that obligation? And how, if at all, is the concept of 'real need' more limited than our ordinary understanding of 'needs' in these cases?

Radmacher and subsequent cases suggest that agreements purporting to exclude *all* provision may have more a emphatic impact on the outcome than agreements purporting only to govern property division, displacing only the equal sharing principle.

In the latter circumstances, courts have tended to disapply the sharing principle while varying the extent of needs-based provision. The wife in *Z v Z (No 2)*,[543] whose French

[540] Ibid, [81]–[82], and [178]. [541] *Versteegh v Versteegh* [2018] EWCA Civ 1050, [82].

[542] See Miles (2012), 101; cf the potential for *ex post facto* judicial determination of this in cases like *Sharp* [2017] EWCA Civ 408, discussed at 6.5.5.

[543] [2011] EWHC 2878.

pre-nuptial agreement created separate property (excluding equal sharing) but did not exclude maintenance, received full, 'generously assessed' needs-based provision following a long marriage and three children, the husband having conceded that such provision should be made. However, in *V v V*,[544] Charles J was prepared to allow a Swedish agreement precluding sharing of pre-acquired and gifted/inherited property to limit the extent of the wife's needs-based provision. Compared with *Z v Z (No 2)*, this marriage was shorter, the wife younger, and much of the property pre-acquired. But Charles J's approach, curtailing the extent of outright provision to the wife, indicates that an agreement dealing only with property may nevertheless affect the court's approach to needs.[545] This might be explicable on the basis that 'generous assessment' of needs is itself a manifestation of the sharing/partnership ideology of marriage, to be disapplied where the parties have excluded or significantly modified the application of sharing in their case.[546] In *Hopkins*, the wife was held to the (relatively modest) level of needs-based provision that she had herself specified for the agreement.[547] By contrast, in *KA v MA*, extracted earlier, Roberts J's needs-based award to the wife was greater than the agreed sum, though rather less than what the wife sought and less than she would otherwise have awarded for needs, in recognition of the agreement.[548]

This series of cases would seem to suggest that when it is appropriate for the agreement to be given effect, the courts are only willing to intervene to ensure the needs of the parties have been met. However, this rather neat proposition has since been complicated by the Court of Appeal:

Brack v Brack [2018] EWCA Civ 2862

KING LJ:

103. In my judgment, in the ordinary course of events, where there is a valid prenuptial agreement, the terms of which amount to the wife having contracted out of a division of the assets based on sharing, a court is likely to regard fairness as demanding that she receives a settlement that is limited to that which provides for her needs. But whilst such an outcome may be considered to be more likely than not, that does not prescribe the outcome in every case. Even where there is an effective prenuptial agreement, the court remains under an obligation to take into account all the factors found in s25(2) MCA 1973, together with a proper consideration of all the circumstances, the first consideration being the welfare of any children. Such an approach may, albeit unusually, lead the court in its search for a fair outcome, to make an order which, contrary to the terms of an agreement, provides a settlement for the wife in excess of her needs. It should also be recognised that even in a case where the court considers a needs-based approach to be fair, the court will as in *KA v MA*, retain a degree of latitude when it comes to deciding on the level of generosity or frugality which should appropriately be brought to the assessment of those needs.

This decision is likely to have disappointed spouses keen to rely on their pre-nup to protect their assets from sharing-based claims. It also differentiates the current law more from

[544] [2011] EWHC 3230. [545] Ibid, [95].
[546] Miles (2011c), 443; see also cases suggesting narrower needs-based provision from non-matrimonial property at 6.5.3.
[547] [2015] EWHC 812. [548] [2018] EWHC 499, [111], [125].

the Law Commission's recommendations for statutory reform (6.8.2), which would only permit needs-based provision in the face of a qualifying nuptial agreement. However, *Brack* is also cognizant of the current legal status of pre-nups; such agreements cannot override the courts' discretionary exercise. And so, if there were cases where a judge decided an award exceeding needs were appropriate, the pre-nup should not oust their power to make such a determination. Where the agreement purports to exclude *all* claims, by contrast, the courts have been more restrictive, deploying the 'predicament of real need' concept strictly—though more generously than at 'just above destitution' level.[549] In *Radmacher* itself, where the parties would be sharing child-care, the majority considered it fair to hold the parties to the agreement to the extent that no provision should be made for the husband in his own right once the children reached independence. The wife had discharged the husband's substantial debts and the Court of Appeal had ordered ample provision for the children from which the husband would indirectly benefit throughout the children's minority (e.g. the provision of accommodation and substantial maintenance, including a carer allowance). But the husband had earning capacity, there was no evidence that he would at any point struggle to meet his own needs, and he had no claim for 'compensation'.[550] It would therefore be fair to hold him to his agreement to have no share in his wife's property—indeed, it would be unfair to depart from that agreement.[551] By contrast, the husband in *Luckwell v Limata* was found to be in a predicament of real need—with no home, no capital, substantial debts, no real income or substantial earning capacity, no borrowing capacity, and less time (given his age) to rebuild his position. The court held that *lifetime* provision was fair—but, crucially, not *outright* provision (save again to discharge his debts). A home would therefore be made available for his occupation, initially sufficient to accommodate the children too, but once they attained independence, in a more modest property, again with only the right to occupy.[552]

6.7.5 CRITICISM OF THE CURRENT LAW

Baroness Hale has suggested that we now 'have the worst of all worlds':

Lady Hale, Keynote Speech, Resolution National Conference (Bristol, 2018)

> The common law public policy rule has gone. Theoretically, agreements are valid and enforceable by the parties, but without any of the safeguards which have invariably been introduced in other countries when legislating to abolish the common law rule: typically, full disclosure of assets and independent legal advice and a breathing space before the wedding. But at the same time they are not binding on the divorce court, so the parties cannot easily predict whether they will be regarded as 'magnetic' and dictate the result or whether they will be taken into account at all and if so to what extent.

The Law Commission had begun a project on marital property agreements before the Supreme Court decision in *Radmacher*. Despite that decision, reform remains a live issue

549 *WW v HW (Pre-Nuptial Agreement: Needs: Conduct)* [2015] EWHC 1844, [53].
550 See 6.5.4. 551 *Radmacher* [2010] UKSC 42, [123]. 552 [2014] EWHC 502.

because the *Hyman* principle (which only Parliament could remove) means that in theory the court retains full jurisdiction despite the agreement. Should couples ever be able to exclude that jurisdiction entirely by agreement? Or does even the current law give too much weight to some agreements?

Radmacher is grounded in respect for party autonomy:

Radmacher v Granatino **[2010] UKSC 42**

LORD PHILLIPS ET AL:

78. The reason why the court should give weight to a nuptial agreement is that there should be respect for individual autonomy. The court should accord respect to the decision of a married couple as to the manner in which their financial affairs should be regulated. It would be paternalistic and patronising to override their agreement simply on the basis that the court knows best. This is particularly true where the parties' agreement addresses existing circumstances and not merely the contingencies of an uncertain future.

Yet Anne Barlow argues that this assumes an equality of power between the parties both at the point of making the agreement and throughout the marriage. That assumption may be unrealistic:

A. Barlow, 'Solidarity, Autonomy and Equality: Mixed Messages for the Family?', (2015) 27 *Child and Family Law Quarterly* 223, 226

Even if power is equally held at the point of the marriage, how possible is it to act in accordance with one's own interests under the agreement (for example, not to give up work to preserve one's earning capacity), in the face of competing needs to act in the wider family interests (for example, to move abroad with your children to enable you to live together as a family while your spouse pursues their own advantageous career opportunity)?

Contrast Baroness Hale's alertness to potential concerns about autonomy:

Radmacher v Granatino **[2010] UKSC 42**

LADY HALE:

135. . . . Some may regard freedom of contract as the prevailing principle in all circumstances; others may regard that as a 19th century concept which has since been severely modified, particularly in the case of continuing relationships typically (though not invariably) characterised by imbalance of bargaining power (such as landlord and tenant, employer and employee). Some may regard people who are about to marry as in all respects fully autonomous beings; others may wonder whether people who are typically (although not invariably) in love can be expected to make rational choices in the same way that businessmen can. Some may regard the recognition of these factual differences as patronising or paternalistic;

others may regard them as sensible and realistic. . . . Perhaps above all, some may think it permissible to contract out of the guiding principles of equality and non-discrimination within marriage; others may think this a retrograde step likely only to benefit the strong at the expense of the weak.

A growing academic literature[553] argues that the capacity of conventional contract law theory to deal with the context of marital agreements is limited, questioning whether the family courts' evaluation of party autonomy in these cases is sufficiently nuanced:

L. Buckley. 'Autonomy and Prenuptial Agreements in Ireland: A Relational Analysis', (2018) 38 *Legal Studies* 164, 166

In classical liberal theory, individuals are seen as rational and atomistic actors, who make agreements based on considerations of personal utility. Enforcing agreements therefore not only respects personal decision making, but enhances overall efficiency, since (in the absence of duress or undue influence) individuals would not agree to bargains that they did not regard as personally beneficial. Accordingly, state intervention with personal bargains should be minimised. These views are taken further by neo-liberalism, which emphasises the role of the individual as a responsible citizen-actor. Stressing the individual's duty to make responsible, self-reliant choices, neoliberalism effectively assigns accountability for disadvantageous bargains to the poor choice of the affected party . . .

These views have been strongly challenged by relational theorists, including many feminists, who have highlighted the effects of economic inequalities, socialised gender roles, race, class, cultural location and connection on the development of personal preferences and bargaining capacities. The actor is conceived as embedded in his or her cultural, social, economic and familial role, with a wide range of considerations, including emotions and relational connections, which may influence personal choices. Feminists have also highlighted the significance of gender in personal decision making: women generally earn less and are excluded from the labour market for long periods, or have their earning capacity reduced, because of their social role as caregivers. This affects their ability to bargain. Accordingly, ascribing poor economic decisions to 'personal choice' ignores the gendered nature of the bargaining context, and the impact of economic and social power disparities, as well as the pressures that may derive from other relational contexts. In this view, liberalism and neoliberalism screen out the effects of structural conditions, and help to maintain and foster a context of gender disadvantage. . . .

Alison Diduck picks up this theme in arguing that the focus on party autonomy entails a 'dejuridification of financial issues on divorce', whereby relationship-generated economic disadvantage arising on divorce can be ascribed to that party's own (poor) choices, rather than to the relationship and the social structures within which that relationship was conducted.[554] This, in turn, tends to privatize the issues, making them merely a matter for party agreement rather than a publicly adjudicated determination of justice:

[553] Notably Thompson (2015), (2018), (2020); Fox O'Mahony (2014).
[554] See also Gordon-Bouvier (2020); Heenan (2021).

A. Diduck, 'Autonomy and Vulnerability in Family Law', in J. Wallbank and J. Herring (eds), *Vulnerabilities, Care and Family Law*, (Abingdon: Routledge, 2014), 112–13

> But the court, the public gaze of the law, must be able to influence what justice means in intimate relationships. By permitting courts to review disputes about the financial consequences of relationship decisions we bring into the public eye the relational nature and context of choices to care or not to care, not to mention their social and financial consequences. Care thus becomes a public issue. Its value is made visible which could have both distributional and recognitional consequences. As Herring reminds us, '[w]e already live in a society in which care work goes largely unrecognised and unvalued. The making of financial orders on divorce is one of the few areas in which care work is recognised.' . . . While women continue to perform the majority of care work in society and while care work itself is linked to gender no matter who does it, this is a real concern, both for the women involved and for society generally.

Indeed, others have argued that by effectively permitting parties to exclude the equal sharing principle, *Radmacher* undermined key advances effected by *White* and *Miller; McFarlane*:[555]

J. Herring, P. Harris, and R. George, 'Ante-Nuptial Agreements: Fairness, Equality and Presumptions', (2011) 127 *Law Quarterly Review* 335, 338

> In *White v White* . . . and *Miller; McFarlane* . . . the House of Lords developed the law on ancillary relief to ensure that orders met the needs of the parties; provided compensation for any losses caused by the marriage; and shared, at least, the fruits of the partnership. These were important principles needed to combat gender discrimination and prevent exploitation of the wife's labour. Yet in *Radmacher*, the Supreme Court tells us that the couple can agree to bypass this protection. This is remarkable. There are few, if any, other areas of law where a person can engage in gender discrimination because the other person has consented to the treatment. For so long, marriage has been a vehicle for oppression and disadvantage for women, and it is unfortunate that, so soon after having amended the law on ancillary relief so that marriage can be a tool for protecting women's interests, the court should allow men to create agreements which remove that protection . . .

On the other hand, it might be said in response that at least those men may now be offering to marry. Before *Radmacher*, some legal advisers of the wealthy advised them not to marry at all—now, they are advised to marry with a pre-nup.[556] If a wealthy individual refuses to marry their partner, the parties might nevertheless continue to cohabit and have children (or indeed, as in *KA v MA*,[557] already be parents) with very little legal protection in case of separation.[558] Those who insist on a pre-nup as a precondition of marriage may feel badly

555 See also Diduck (2011a).
556 Vardag and Miles (2015).
557 [2018] EWHC 499.
558 See chapter 7.

done by if that agreement is readily overridden after they have contracted the marriage on the faith of the agreement. Understanding the context of their consent to the *marriage* is arguably as important to achieving a fair conclusion in these cases as is understanding the context of the other party's consent to the *pre-nup*. Moreover, it is notable that jurisdictions which operate systems of community of property or other sharing systems on divorce permit couples to opt out of that regime, but few permit opting out of maintenance.[559] *Radmacher* has brought English law closer to that position.

On another level, there are concerns about the impact on relationships of the process of negotiating pre-nups. Some supporters of pre-nups consider that negotiating one's own marriage contract could, at best, 'foster the norms of commitment, reciprocity and openness in personal relationships, norms which are integral to egalitarian and democratic relationships'.[560] But the experience could, at first sight at least, be less beneficial:[561]

B. Fehlberg and B. Smyth, 'Binding Pre-Nuptial Agreements in Australia: The First Year', (2002) 16 *International Journal of Law, Policy and the Family* 127, 135

According to family lawyers, one of the major factors inhibiting entry into agreement is difficulty experienced at a personal level between couples during the process of negotiating agreements. Relationship tension reportedly increased when the parties and their legal representatives began formal negotiations regarding the terms of the agreement. Family lawyers, mindful of the agreement's central purpose of offering certainty for the future, were evidently keen to sort out the fine details and to 'reality test' agreements (by asking 'what if?' questions). Yet this process was often confronting for clients as they sat with their beloved and their respective legal representatives around the negotiating table. One practitioner, for example, said that the three clients who had contacted her regarding entry into a pre-nuptial agreement had not gone ahead and entered an agreement due to 'difficulties in negotiation leading to abandonment of the agreement, and sometimes of the relationship'.

But might parties driven to separate by that experience in any event have had short-lived marriages, owing to fundamental disagreements about financial issues?[562] We discuss possible reform at 6.8.2.

6.8 REFORM

6.8.1 REFORM OF THE SUBSTANTIVE LAW

In 2023, following an earlier commitment by the government,[563] the Law Commission launched a review of financial remedies law.[564] However, legislative reform will be challenging, as Hitchings and Miles have explained:

[559] See generally Scherpe (2011a).
[560] Kingdom (2000), 24; see also Vardag and Miles (2015).
[561] See also Reece (2015).
[562] Vardag and Miles (2015); cf Hitchings (2011), 28.
[563] Hansard, HC Deb, vol 677, col 96, 8 June 2020.
[564] <www.lawcom.gov.uk/review-to-examine-50-year-old-laws-on-finances-after-divorce-and-the-ending-of-a-civil-partnership>.

E. Hitchings and J. Miles, 'Rules Versus Discretion in Financial Remedies on Divorce', (2019) 33 *International Journal of Law, Policy and The Family*, 24, 46

> In order to make any appreciable [legislative] advance on the current law, this would require a willingness to accept a more tightly specified, homogenously applicable set of legal norms, and so perhaps to adopt a more average (but uniform) substantive sense of justice, than the MCA on its face currently provides. Even if it can be agreed that the law should have clearer principles, agreeing what governing norms to adopt may prove harder, as different legislative members endorse different ideologies of marriage and how they should be reflected in financial remedies on divorce.

This goes some way towards explaining why the task of reforming financial remedies law is so complex. Indeed, such reform had been under consideration before *White* and *Miller; MacFarlane*.[565] Those cases prompted renewed calls for legislative reform amongst those concerned about lack of predictability of outcomes, disquiet about the scale of awards in 'big money' cases,[566] and disquiet about the potential implications of joint-lives support.[567] The Law Commission's last project addressed only some aspects of the current law.[568] A comprehensive review would have to consider both: (i) what the principles underpinning financial remedies on divorce should be; and (ii) whether a discretionary system is too unpredictable and uncertain, particularly for parties acting without lawyers. Should statute set out clear objectives, principles, or guidelines for the courts, or even prescribe rules determining how resources should be divided on divorce?[569] And, if so, what would those principles or rules be?

English law could take the more formulaic sharing case law to its logical conclusion and adopt a rule-based system of deferred community of property on divorce: 'matrimonial property' (as defined by the rules of the scheme) would be shared, 'non-matrimonial property' would not be.[570] Any such system would have to be accompanied by spousal support, which could involve capital transfers and occupation rights, as well as periodical payments, but the calculation of that component might itself be rendered more predictable. In criticizing the compensation principle, John Eekelaar has suggested that awards be determined by reference to a formula based on the disparity in the parties' incomes and the duration of the marriage.[571] The Law Commission has sympathy for moving to such an approach,[572] which could be underpinned by a theory of financial provision aimed to 'unravel the merger over time', rather than to reflect either 'need' or 'compensation' as currently understood:

565 Ancillary Relief Advisory Group (1998): see (1998) FL 380; HO (1998), (1999).

566 E.g. *Charman v Charman* [2007] EWCA Civ 503, [106]–[126].

567 Notably Baroness Deech: see Divorce (Financial Provision) Bill (HL) 2021–22 and associated debates from when the Bill was before Parliament in previous sessions, discussed by Miles and Hitchings (2018) and more generally Hitchings and Miles (2019); Thompson (2019).

568 Law Com (2011), (2012), (2014).

569 Hitchings and Miles (2019); Miles (2018); contributions to Fehlberg and Miles (2018); Eekelaar (2006), (2010); Law Society (2003); Douglas and Perry (2001). Cf the Deech Bill, n 566.

570 Scherpe (2012); Cooke (2009); Cretney (2003b); Cooke, Barlow, and Callus (2006).

571 (2006). 572 Law Com (2014), from para 3.121.

Law Commission, *Matrimonial Property, Needs and Agreements*, Law Com CP 208 (London: TSO, 2012)

4.52 A compensatory theory, based on the idea of reversing losses generated by the marriage or civil partnership, has some very hard edges; as well as generating evidential difficulties it can be said to be individualistic and unduly financial in its focus. A very different approach is to be found in the group of theories which build on the idea of "merger over time" and make proposals that focus on the unravelling of that merger without an assessment of individual economic contributions to the marriage. These theories are also known as "income-sharing theories" because that is the mechanism they advocate for the calculation of spousal support.

4.53 "Merger over time" is a description of what happens within a marriage:

> [An approach to spousal support] is to see the spouses as merging into each other over time. In this model, the longer they are married, the more their human capital should be seen as intertwined rather than affixed to the individual spouse in whose body it resides. This idea is consistent with the notion that human capital needs constant renewal – a regular tune-up, repair, and parts replacement model, if you like. After a while, one can less and less distinguish between what was brought into the marriage and what was produced by the marriage. Moreover, the longer the marriage, the longer the spouse in a dependent role has likely submerged her or his identity and earning capacity into the marital collective.
>
> One way to implement such a concept would be to give each spouse a percentage interest in the other's human capital/future earnings based upon the duration of the marriage.[573]

The Canadian spousal support advisory guidelines, which received close attention from the Law Commission, offer an example of how such a 'formula' can—quite unlike the child support formula that we examined in chapter 5—provide a flexible range of figures within which the award in an individual case may be fixed.[574]

But the challenges are significant, not least given the strong attachment of many (but not all[575]) family lawyers to broad discretion:[576]

E. Jackson et al, 'Financial Support on Divorce: The Right Mixture of Rules and Discretion?', (1993) 7 *International Journal of Law and the Family* 230, 252–3

Ultimately it is the outcome of negotiations regarding financial arrangements on divorce which is important for the parties. Nonetheless, concentration on the final settlement disguises the importance of the reasoning process. The theoretical framework on which the issues are pinned is of great significance. If the legal regulation of economic distribution is underpinned by a belief in the importance of the satisfaction of rights-based claims, then clear rules are essential so that those rights may be prospectively evaluated. If, on the other

573 Sugarman (1990), 159–60.
574 Law Com (2012), from para 4.69; Law Com (2014), from para 3.121.
575 Hitchings and Miles (2019). 576 Cf 1.2.2.

hand, the law attempts to fulfil needs and expectations, discretion must be used to assess their relative importance in the light of competing claims and available resources.

One approach is not necessarily better than the other. The issues raised by the economics of divorce are many and diverse. . . . [T]he most complex decision which must be made involves the family home. Here a settlement must deal with the settling-up of property rights in a substantial capital sum, while being sensitive to the importance of the continuing use-value of the home. The matter is further complicated by the fact that a decision concerning the property rights of two adults must also take account of the needs of the children for a stable and satisfactory home environment. If rights are best served by clear rules and needs best served by the sensitive exercise of discretion, we appear to have reached an impasse. Perhaps it is best to acknowledge that the process is not susceptible to a clear and elegant exegesis. We should gain reassurance from the obvious care taken by solicitors in trying, as nearly as possible, to resolve the irresolvable.

However, as the Law Commission observes in the extract at 6.6.2, in the current setting of family justice (not least the removal of legal aid), that 'reassurance' may be absent from most cases. The establishment of specialist financial remedies courts, ensuring that only expert judges handle money cases, may in time help alleviate problems of inconsistency and unpredictability.[577]

Most importantly, any substantive reform to the basis on which financial remedies are granted must be grounded in an appreciation of the demographic data surveyed earlier at 6.2. In particular, financial remedies law must reflect a realistic view about the enduring wider structural obstacles to women's financial independence and men's sharing of caring responsibilities. Unless and until men and women share the benefits and burdens of parenting and other domestic responsibilities more equitably, financial remedies law must be equipped to respond to the substantive economic inequality experienced at the point of relationship breakdown.[578]

6.8.2 REFORM OF THE LAW RELATING TO AGREEMENTS

The difficulty of adjudicating between the various concerns expressed in the academic literature on marital agreements discussed at 6.7.5 is reflected in a public survey on pre-nuptial agreements, which yielded the ostensibly contradictory findings that 58 per cent of respondents agreed that 'binding pre-nuptial agreements are a good way of allowing couples to decide privately what should happen in the event of divorce', while 65 per cent agreed that 'binding pre-nuptial agreements are a bad idea because it is too difficult to predict what will be fair at the end of a marriage'.[579]

Following extensive consultation, the Law Commission recommended reform:

[577] President of the Family Division (2018); Hess and Miles (2017); Farquhar Committee (2021).

[578] Miles and Hitchings (2018), Eekelaar (2018b), criticizing Baroness Deech's justification of her Divorce (Financial Provision) Bill (HL) 2017–19 (later reintroduced in the 2021–22 parliamentary session), which would significantly curtail remedies; cf Douglas (2018b) for an alternative reform proposal.

[579] Barlow and Smithson (2012), 307–8.

Law Commission, *Matrimonial Property, Needs and Agreements*, Law Com No 343 (London: TSO, 2014)

Autonomy

5.28 Why should it not be possible for a couple to choose the financial consequences of the ending of their relationship, rather than having those consequences imposed upon them? Those who enter into marital property agreements have the capacity for marriage or civil partnership, and indeed to enter into other contracts between themselves; why should they not have capacity to enter into an agreement about their future financial status? It has been suggested that the paternalism of the law of financial orders is inappropriate in a modern world. In 2009 the Court of Appeal [in *Radmacher*] said that to assume one party is "unduly susceptible to . . . demands . . . is patronising, in particular to women". Lord Justice Wilson suggested that it would be preferable for the "*starting point* to be for both parties to be required to accept the consequences of whatever they have freely and knowingly agreed" . . .

5.30 However, we accept . . . that the argument for autonomy has to be regarded with caution: those who marry or form civil partnerships are adults and can take their own decisions, but it is a matter of experience that people are willing to agree, when they are in love, to things that they would not otherwise contemplate. . . . [W]e know that people tend to be unrealistically optimistic about both the likelihood that they will divorce and their future fortunes. A fiancé(e) may enter into an agreement at the other's request in the firm belief that the relationship will never end. He or she may not really want the agreement to take effect, or may not have thought through the consequences of entering into it.

5.31 Furthermore there may be pressure. Practitioners in a study by Dr Emma Hitchings talked of the pressures their clients may face when being encouraged to sign a pre-nuptial agreement. Dr Hitchings reported that:

> Time and again practitioners raised the "typical scenario" of the financially stronger party exerting emotional pressure upon their client (normally the financially weaker party), through the "I won't marry you if you don't sign the agreement" argument.

Indeed, the law already recognises the possibility of pressure within a close relationship, in the context of the law relating to undue influence in contracts . . .

5.32 We think that it is possible, to some extent, for the law to counteract pressure by imposing certain pre-conditions for the validity of a qualifying nuptial agreement and we have attempted to ensure that our suggested reform would do so. For example, . . . we recommend that the parties to a qualifying nuptial agreement must take legal advice and receive disclosure, and that qualifying nuptial agreements should not be concluded within the 28 day period leading up to the day of the wedding. We accept, however, that legal pre-conditions cannot entirely eliminate the probability that some people may agree qualifying nuptial agreements that they would later regret.

5.33 The other reason for caution is that we have to be very clear about what the autonomy, or freedom, in question is. All couples, under the current law, have the freedom to agree whatever they like by way of financial settlement when their relationship comes to an end. The autonomy that is prayed in aid of binding marital property agreements is not simply the freedom to make an agreement, nor simply the freedom to do as one wishes. It is the freedom to force one's partner to abide by an agreement when he or she no longer wishes to do so. It is freedom of contract, but it is therefore freedom to use a contract to restrict one's partner's choices.

5.34 So the autonomy argument is a strong one but it raises concerns as well. These concerns . . . have led to our decision . . . to limit the scope of qualifying nuptial agreements.

We recognise that there may be pressure on one party to sign an agreement, and that that party may enter the agreement unwillingly or with unrealistic optimism. Thus, whilst a party may regret the agreement, or have his or her choices restricted, we have decided that the court's jurisdiction to make provision for needs should not be ousted by a qualifying nuptial agreement and so no party will be left without resources following separation.

Certainty and the cost of discretion

5.35 Much stronger, we feel, than the argument for autonomy is the argument for certainty. As one member of the public put it [in their consultation response]:

> Surely the most important point of a pre-nuptial agreement is to provide both parties with a high degree of certainty as to the outcome in the event of a breakdown of their forthcoming marriage and to reduce the need to resort to expensive legal redress in the event of the breakdown.

5.36 Again, of course, that freedom exists under the current law, provided there is agreement at the point when the relationship ends. What is being argued is that it is important for the parties to have certainty in advance that a partner will not be able to re-open the financial agreement by resorting to the court, and that that limitation upon one partner's freedom is justified in the interests of both by ensuring that neither will be involved in the uncertainty, stress and cost of litigation. The fact that the terms of a marital property agreement are always subject to the court's review means that it is currently never possible to be certain, in advance, that an agreement will determine the outcome of the financial relief process.

5.37 Certainty may be particularly important for those who are remarrying and have children from a previous marriage, and for those who wish to protect inherited or "family" wealth from division upon divorce. Under the current law there is no guarantee that a party who has children from a previous relationship will be able to preserve assets to pass on to those children, whilst a binding qualifying nuptial agreement would allow a party to do just that. . . . [T]he law on non-matrimonial property is unclear, both in terms of what property can be considered "non-matrimonial" and in terms of the effect that the existence of non-matrimonial property will have on the eventual division of assets by the court. A qualifying nuptial agreement would allow the parties to define, from the outset of the relationship, what property should be split between them and the way in which it should be split. . . . [T]hese two situations are ones in which the public feel that a pre-nuptial agreement may be sensible and pragmatic [see Barlow and Smithson (2012)].

5.38 It may be argued that couples can, following *Radmacher v Granatino*, already be reasonably sure that pre-nuptial agreements will be upheld. However, the fact that the terms of a marital property agreement are always subject to the court's review means that it is currently never possible to be certain, in advance, that an agreement will determine the outcome of the financial relief process.

The Commission therefore recommended a new statutory regime for all categories of marital agreement—pre-nups, post-nups, and separation agreements—that would be binding provided preconditions for 'qualifying' status were satisfied. These preconditions would impose specific procedural requirements on the parties in place of the broader-based inquiry into the parties' knowledge and freedom to agree (theoretically broader than vitiating grounds in contract law) adopted by *Radmacher*'s 'step 1' (the factors tainting the agreement from the outset). So to attract 'qualifying' status, the agreement would have to be: valid in contract law; made by deed more than 28 days before the wedding or civil partnership; and contain a statement signed by both parties that each understood the agreement's nature and its effect in removing the court's discretion to make financial orders on divorce, save insofar as the agreement left either party without provision for their financial needs. Each party, at the time of making the agreement, would have had to have received disclosure of material information about the other's financial situation and independent legal advice explaining the nature of the agreement and its effect on that party's rights.[580] Critics argue that even these requirements could not *guarantee* that both parties will be fully autonomous in making the agreement—but they would go some way to mitigate against abuse of position by the more powerful spouse and at least provide greater certainty about when an agreement would be prima facie binding.

Thereafter, at step 2 (the 'fairness' of upholding the agreement at the point of divorce), the courts would retain the power to provide for the parties' needs (understood in the normal sense, rather than a narrower, 'real need' sense[581]), notwithstanding the agreement. That recommendation is intended to provide an appropriate balance between autonomy and protection against the dangers of pressure, imbalance of power, and optimism bias.[582] Parties would therefore be able to protect their financial interests but not at the expense of disturbing the core obligation to provide for a spouse's needs. The 'primary function of family law' to protect the vulnerable would thus continue to be met.[583] The government has yet to issue a final response to the report. Meanwhile, reflecting a very different balancing of autonomy and protection, Baroness Deech's Divorce (Financial Provision) Bill 2021–22 would have introduced a far tougher regime, under which procedurally compliant agreements (with lower procedural preconditions[584]) would be fully binding in contract law—and with no step 2 review at all.[585]

6.9 CONCLUSION

The law relating to financial remedies on divorce and civil partnership dissolution is highly technical in practice and conceptually sophisticated. However, beneath that complexity lie fundamental questions about the nature of marriage and civil partnership. Are they relationships of dependency and support, joint ventures between equal partners, or associations between economically independent individuals? And what is the role of the state in all this: (i) to intervene to protect the economically vulnerable, to stand back and allow parties freedom to make their own arrangements; or (ii) to make structural changes in the workplace and elsewhere in the public sphere to help improve women's economic position generally and so reduce the economic disparities experienced on relationship breakdown? Or both?

ONLINE RESOURCES

Questions, suggestions for further reading, and supplementary materials for this chapter (including updates on developments in this area of family law since this book was published) may be found in the online resources at **www.oup.com/he/familytcm5e**.

[580] See Law Com (2014), ch 6. [581] Ibid, para 5.82. [582] Ibid, from para 5.42.

[583] Ibid, para 5.81.

[584] Notably, a requirement only to have had reasonable opportunity to obtain independent legal advice, not a requirement to have done so.

[585] Clause 3. Thompson (2019).

7

PROPERTY AND FINANCES WHEN NON-FORMALIZED RELATIONSHIPS END

CENTRAL ISSUES

1. While spouses and civil partners have access to special statutory financial remedies on divorce, parties to other relationships that break down—for example, cohabitants, blood relatives, platonic home-sharers—must use a patchwork of common law and statutory rights and remedies. These offer no comprehensive or coherent, substantive, or procedural response to the financial and property-related problems associated with family breakdown.
2. The courts have no power to order financial provision, property adjustment, or pension sharing for the benefit of the adults involved. Remedies for the benefit of any dependent children involved (discussed in chapter 5) are therefore particularly important here as a means of providing indirectly for a parent with whom such children live.
3. The general law of property, trusts, and contract determines all issues regarding ownership, occupation, and use of the family home, and ownership and use of other assets within families on relationship breakdown.
4. The judicial development of specific principles of implied trusts law for family-related cases is controversial, creating new problems and uncertainties. That law is still criticized for failing adequately to respond to the demands of the family context.
5. By contrast with the Matrimonial Causes Act 1973 (MCA 1973) regime that applies on divorce, particular difficulties arise from implied trust law's focus on parties' intentions around property ownership and on financial contributions, rather than on any carefully articulated idea of 'fairness' that acknowledges the value of domestic contributions and the parties' needs and sacrifices for the family.
6. Limited statutory family law remedies are available between cohabitants in relation to occupation of the home (as discussed in chapter 4) and for the transfer of tenancies over rented homes. Save in cases of domestic abuse, occupation remedies are only available between other family members where the applicant is entitled to occupy the property as a matter of property law.
7. Despite persistent calls for reform from senior judiciary and others, reform

recommendations that would create a statutory scheme of financial remedies between cohabitants have yet to be adopted, leaving England and Wales out of step with Scotland, Ireland, and many other jurisdictions.

7.1 INTRODUCTION

Much of family law deals with family 'pathology': the consequences of family breakdown. This chapter is no different. But much of the law addressed in this chapter—the general law of property and trusts—applies as much to intact relationships as it does to those that have ended. Indeed, that general law applies to spouses and civil partners unless and until the family courts' matrimonial/civil partnership jurisdiction is invoked. This reflects the fact that 'there is really no such thing in English law as "family property"'.[1] In particular, as we noted at 6.3, unlike in some European jurisdictions where a 'community of property' regime arises, marriage in English law has no impact on the parties' property rights. Indeed, until what we now know as the MCA 1973 regime was introduced,[2] even divorce courts had no power to adjust the spouses' property rights and so the general law of property determined which spouse left the marriage with what assets. The general law remains important for spouses and civil partners when disputes with third parties (such as mortgagees) require ascertainment of the parties' beneficial ownership of particular assets, and so some cases discussed in this chapter involve spouses.

But our focus is on what happens to the economic resources of cohabitants and parties to other non-formalized relationships when they separate during the parties' lifetimes,[3] since—unlike marriage and civil partnership—they attract no comprehensive set of specialist remedies that empower the family courts to redistribute the parties' income, capital, and pension assets on a discretionary basis on relationship breakdown. This includes parties to non-qualifying marriage ceremonies, discussed at 2.5.1 and 2.6.2.b. Instead, when these relationships end, the general law very largely dictates what will happen to the parties' resources: the parties' shared home, its contents, other chattels, bank accounts, and so on. While the court can in many cases take decisions about the continued occupation or sale of the home, it cannot adjust the parties' property rights or pension entitlements, and neither party can be ordered to make periodical payments to the other. In short, each party will leave with what the general law says that person owns, and nothing more.

There is an important qualification to that statement in cases involving dependent children, where remedies will be available for their benefit under the Child Support Act 1991 (CSA 1991) and the Children Act 1989 (CA 1989), Sch 1, discussed in chapter 5. These remedies are of greater practical importance here than in the matrimonial/civil partnership context, as they potentially offer significant indirect benefit to parents with whom dependent children live that is not available to those adults in their own right. Such parents' household income may be increased by receipt of child support, and they will clearly benefit from

[1] Law Com (1971), para 0.1.

[2] And cognate provisions of the Civil Partnership Act 2004 (CPA 2004).

[3] In the event of death, many of these relationships are covered by either or both of the statutory schemes that apply on intestacy (Administration of Estates Act 1925) and to challenge dispositions made by the intestacy rules or by the deceased's will (Inheritance (Provision for Family and Dependants) Act 1975).

accommodation provided for the children. However, orders under the CA 1989 are unusual outside the 'big money' context, and various limitations on the court's powers—not least its inability to adjust the adults' capital entitlements or to order sale—inhibit their usefulness. Moreover, since these remedies offer protection ordinarily only during the children's minority, any benefit obtained by the parent ceases with the order's termination. The former parent with care of the child, who—like a similarly situated spouse—may have been out of paid employment for years, will have no remedy (direct or indirect) to address any ongoing economic vulnerability.[4]

The occupation order regime of the Family Law Act 1996 (FLA 1996; see 4.5.3) may also provide some protection for cohabitants who are not entitled under the general law to occupy the parties' home. But it will not protect non-entitled parties to other non-formalized relationships. Only in cases of domestic abuse would protection be available in the latter situations, under the Domestic Abuse Act 2021 (see 4.6).

Lastly, if the parties had reached any contractual agreement about their resources, that will govern—provided it is binding as a matter of contract law.

Evidently, without a 'one-stop-shop' like the MCA 1973, separated parties to non-formalized relationships have to sew together a patchwork of rights and (relatively limited) remedies to settle their property matters. This may not be easy, not least because—if the parties have not formally declared a trust determining the matter—ascertaining ownership of the home can be forensically demanding, operating trusts law that the courts have (with only mixed success) adapted to the family context. Unlike the MCA 1973, focused on principles of partnership-based sharing, relief of need, and compensation for relationship-generated disadvantage, the general law of property and trusts focuses on the parties' intentions about the ownership of each asset and (as a facet of that inquiry) on their financial contributions to its acquisition.[5] Moreover, while the divorce court can throw all of the parties' economic resources into one big pot to produce one overall economic settlement under the MCA 1973, the general law only deals with specific, individual assets: there is no holistic evaluation of the parties' respective positions. The resulting outcome may be 'fair' by reference to orthodox *property law* criteria. But whether this outcome seems 'fair' measured by criteria that might be adopted by *family lawyers* will be the fortuitous product of happenstance, not design.

The following extract (from a case involving separated cohabitants who had no children, so for whom the CA 1989, Sch 1 offered no remedy) highlights these core differences between the MCA scheme and property law, and the resulting difference in the court's function:

Dobson v Griffey [2018] EWHC 1117

HHJ PAUL MATTHEWS (sitting as a Judge of the High Court):

4. Because this case arises in the wake of the break-up of the personal relationship between the parties, it is important to emphasise the limited function of the court. In the case of a divorce, or dissolution of a civil partnership, the court has extensive powers to allocate to either of the parties assets belonging to either or both of them, as the court things fit, taking

[4] See Law Com (2006), paras 4.34–4.46.

[5] See Fox O'Mahony (2014) for a general critique of property law's focus.

into account the criteria set out in the legislation. In such circumstances, it does not matter very much which of the parties as between themselves owned the assets in question. As a result, there is generally no enquiry by the court into the strict *legal* property rights of each party. Instead there is an intense *factual* examination of all the circumstances in which the court's discretion can or should be exercised. These will include what happened during the course of the relationship and its breakdown.

5. However, in the present case the parties were not married and the family law jurisdiction to allocate assets according to the statutory criteria simply does not apply. The fall-back in such a case is to the rules of property law. This is a common occurrence. For example, *James v Thomas* [discussed later] . . . was another case of a broken intimate (but non-marital) relationship, where the claimant claimed a beneficial interest in a property of which the defendant was the sole registered proprietor, and in which she had lived with him. She had worked for some time in his business as an agricultural building and drainage contractor, doing heavy physical labour. Sir John Chadwick . . . said of the claimant:

> "38. . . Her interest in the property (if any) must be determined by applying principles of law and equity which (however inadequate to meet the circumstances in which parties live together in the twenty-first century) must now be taken as well-established. Unless she can bring herself within those principles, her claim in the present case must fail."

6. The rules of property law, like those of family law, also provide for the allocation of available resources. However, they do not operate at all in the same way as the family law jurisdiction which I have referred to. Property rights have important effects on third parties, and also have an important role to play in a functioning market economy. For these reasons, they are inherently more stable than judicial discretion and operate in predictable and well-known ways.

7. The matters which are important in considering the acquisition and the disposal of property rights are the methods and the formalities for the transfer of such rights between persons. These are comparatively few in number, and in some cases involve requirements as to publicity or notice to third parties. Moreover, and importantly, they are nearly all *consensual*, in the sense that a property owner will not generally lose an existing property right unless he or she expressly or impliedly agrees to do so.

8. It is important to notice that, unless it bears on the question of consent to transfer, what happened during the course of a personal relationship and its breakdown is not of itself relevant to the question of who (in property law terms) owns what at the end of it. . . .

9. Some forms of property right in English law, in particular those relating to the ownership of land, have highly formal and public methods of transfer, involving the making of deeds before witnesses and the registration of dispositions at HM Land Registry. But, in some circumstances, it is possible to get over the lack of compliance with such formality and publicity requirements. . . .

10. . . . [This can be done using the rules] relating to common intention constructive trusts and proprietary estoppel. These rules . . . provide for a method of creating or transferring rights which is both private and relatively informal. But nevertheless in each case they are still consensual, in that the owner of the property rights concerned must first manifest an intention to share the beneficial ownership with or transfer it to another person or persons. If there is such an intention manifested, . . . there must then be some further conduct in reliance which makes it unconscionable (in a special legal, rather than layman's, sense) for the person manifesting that intention not to share or transfer the asset. . . .

We examine that law in detail from 7.2, where we shall also begin to evaluate the statement that the property law rules invariably operate in 'predictable and well-known ways'.

The growth in couples cohabiting outside marriage or civil partnership means that this array of general law and limited statutory remedies is increasingly relied upon. Empirical data indicate that cohabiting relationships are more heterogeneous than marriages, which makes them harder to regulate as a group.[6] Many involve young couples with no children who cohabit only for a short time: there is no evident need for any special financial remedies there. Others involve older couples who have been divorced from earlier marriages and who are now deliberately seeking to avoid the MCA scheme in order to preserve assets recovered from the previous relationship. Others again cohabit long-term, have children, and may function in a manner—and consider themselves to be—indistinguishable from many marriages, pooling resources and investing in the relationship in anticipation that it will last for life. Many of those relationships may entail the sorts of economic inequalities arising on parental separation from the division of responsibility for child-care that we discussed in 6.2: those data relate to parents generally, not just spouses. It is these last cases that arouse most concern and prompt calls for reform that have thus far gone unheeded.

As we discuss at 7.6.3.a, it is commonly argued that reform would intrude on couples' autonomy—their right to choose not to be subject to matrimonial-style remedies and obligations. However, as in other spheres of family life, protecting 'autonomy' may be counterproductive for economically weaker family members. It is important to examine the implications of the law not just for couples but for *individuals*, some of whom the law may serve better than others. Leaving economic resources where the general law has put them may create or sustain dependency and poverty for family members, particularly women in mixed-sex relationships.[7] At 7.6.3.b, we examine reform recommendations made by the Law Commission over a decade ago but recently revived by a parliamentary committee.

7.2 ASCERTAINING OWNERSHIP OF THE SHARED HOME AND OTHER LAND

Different rules determine the ownership of freehold land[8] and of other assets. The law ordinarily insists on compliance with certain formal requirements for the creation and transfer of interests in land, whereas interests in other forms of property can be created and transferred orally. However, interests in land may arise informally under the laws of implied trust and by proprietary estoppel. We cannot know how many cases are litigated or settled under the law of implied trusts, but such trusts have generated a large (and in places confused) corpus of case law seeking to ascertain their parameters and they have accordingly attracted extensive academic debate, so we give them most attention here.

It is impossible to provide a full account of this area of law here; readers needing more should consult a specialist textbook on land law.[9] The following discussion assumes a basic understanding of English law's concepts of land, estates, and interests in land; the distinction between legal and equitable ('beneficial') ownership; the concepts of joint tenancy and tenancy in common; the system of land registration; and the concept of overreaching.

[6] See Law Com (2006), Part 2.
[7] See generally O'Donovan (1985); various chapters in Miles and Probert (2009).
[8] For rented homes, see 7.3.4.
[9] E.g. McFarlane et al (2021).

7.2.1 TRANSFERS AND EXPRESS TRUSTS: FORMAL REQUIREMENTS

The express creation and transfer of interests in land requires compliance with specific formalities.

All transfers of *legal* estates and interests in land are void unless made by deed.[10] When property is transferred into the name of *one* person, prima facie that individual—once registered as proprietor with HM Land Registry[11]—is absolute owner (legally and beneficially). Survey data addressing the ownership patterns of couples' owner-occupied homes show that such sole-name legal ownership is far more common amongst cohabiting couples (over a third such cases) than amongst spouses (around a tenth).[12]

Where ownership by *two* (or more) people is desired, legal title to the property will usually be transferred into the parties' joint names—necessarily as joint tenants—so that they are both legal owners (once registered as proprietors).[13] Joint legal ownership of homes is more common amongst spouses (nearly 90 per cent of owning spouses) than amongst cohabiting couples (nearly two-thirds).[14] Since jointly owned property must be held on trust, the joint *legal* owners (the trustees) should, ideally, also expressly declare the basis on which they, and any others, hold the *beneficial* (equitable) interest in the property: who has beneficial shares; if more than one person, are they joint tenants or tenants in common; and if tenants in common, what size share does each party have?[15] The declaration of such a trust of land (since it creates an equitable estate) must ordinarily be manifested and proved by some signed writing of the settlor(s)[16] that uses legally effective language.[17] Any such expressly declared trust determines the shares in which the beneficial interest is held.[18] Land Registry data indicate that only around 7 per cent of joint-name registrations fail to declare the beneficial ownership.[19]

As we discuss from 7.2.2, the law permits some important exceptions to these formal requirements, allowing beneficial interests to arise by implied (resulting and constructive) trusts and proprietary estoppel.[20] These allow individuals who may or may not be on the legal title to acquire a beneficial share in property without any validly executed express declaration of trust in their favour. However, since the operation of implied trust and estoppel law can generate forensic complexity and unpredictable outcomes, it is preferable that parties decide how the beneficial title of property is to be held and declare an express trust. The courts' exasperation with those who fail to do so is exemplified in *Carlton v Goodman*. Mr Goodman and Ms Carlton had bought a house in joint names with a joint mortgage to be occupied only by Mr Goodman, he alone paying the mortgage instalments. They had not

[10] Law of Property Act 1925 (LPA 1925), s 52. [11] Land Registration Act 2002 (LRA 2002), s 27.

[12] Miles (2023), table 2, using data derived from Lersch and Vidal (2016) and associated work.

[13] LRA 2002, s 27. The legal title may be held by up to four people: Trustee Act 1925, s 34(2), LPA 1925, s 34(2).

[14] Miles (2023), table 2.

[15] A clause providing that the survivor of the trustees can give a valid receipt for the proceeds of sale or other disposition of the property does not constitute an express declaration of a beneficial joint tenancy: *Stack v Dowden* [2007] UKHL 17.

[16] LPA 1925, s 53(1)(b). [17] *Singh v Heer* [2016] EWCA Civ 424.

[18] *Goodman v Gallant* [1986] Fam 106; subject, e.g., to vitiating grounds such as fraud; the possibility of a subsequent express variation of their interests: *Singla v Browne* [2007] EWHC 405; a remedy arising in proprietary estoppel: *Stack* [2007] UKHL 17 [49], *Clarke v Meadus* [2010] EWHC 3117; or a supervening constructive trust arising (at least on facts postdating the express trust): *Qayyum v Hameed* [2009] EWCA Civ 352, cf *Pankhania v Chandegra* [2012] EWCA Civ 1438—see Bevan (2019); Maniscalco (2020), from 134.

[19] See Miles (2023), table 1. [20] LPA 1925, s 53(2).

expressly declared how the beneficial title was to be held, so the case was decided under the law of resulting trust (a complex exercise in cases of mortgage-financed purchase):

Carlton v Goodman [2002] EWCA Civ 545

WARD LJ:

44. I would add only this. The conveyancer who acted for these parties thought at one time that she had discussed with Mr Goodman whether or not he wished to declare their beneficial interest in the conveyance and record that they held as joint tenants, the rules of survivorship having been explained to him [i.e. that where property is held on a joint tenancy, in the event of the death of one of two joint tenants, the survivor is immediately sole owner of the whole property]. When she gave evidence she eventually concluded that she did not have any such discussion with Mr Goodman and the judge had no hesitation in concluding that no such discussion had taken place. It was common ground that Anita [Carlton] was not involved in any such discussion. I ask in despair how often this court has to remind conveyancers that they would save their clients a great deal of later difficulty if only they would sit the purchasers down, explain the difference between a joint tenancy and a tenancy in common, ascertain what they want and then expressly declare in the conveyance or transfer how the beneficial interest is to be held because that will be conclusive and save all argument. When are conveyancers going to do this as a matter of invariable standard practice? This court has urged that time after time. Perhaps conveyancers do not read law reports. I will try one more time: ALWAYS TRY TO AGREE ON AND THEN RECORD HOW THE BENEFICIAL INTEREST IS TO BE HELD. It is not very difficult to do.

In theory, HM Land Registry's process prompts joint purchasers to think about beneficial ownership: question 10 on the form that must be completed by the *transferor* directs them—where the property is being transferred to more than one person—to state how the beneficial interest is to be held.[21] If duly completed, this will constitute an express declaration of trust. It has been held that this is so even where (as will be usual) the *transferees* themselves do not sign that form, on the basis that the transferor is the settlor in such cases, acting on the instructions of the transferee(s)' solicitor.[22] A further form—Form JO—can also be used by transferees themselves to set out their beneficial interests in the property that they are acquiring.

However, question 10 (like Form JO) is optional[23] and not always answered.[24] Land Registry will register transfers even if question 10 is not answered; but, as a non-conclusive, default measure, will enter a restriction on the register, a step that ensures—in case the parties are beneficial tenants in common (rather than joint tenants)—that no future transfer can go ahead unless there are at least two legal owners (trustees) in place, in order to ensure

[21] LRA 2002, s 44(1), and Land Registration Rules 2003, r 95(2)(a); Form FR1 in the case of first registration, and Form TR1 in the case of a transfer of registered land: <www.gov.uk/government/publications/registered-titles-whole-transfer-tr1>.

[22] *Taylor v Taylor* [2017] EWHC 1080, [44]—this despite the fact that the TR1 guidance notes state that transferees 'must' sign where qu 10 is answered; cf reasoning in *Roy v Roy* [1996] 1 FLR 541.

[23] [2007] UKHL 17, [52]; cf Cooke (2011a) on failure of Land Registry to change the rules.

[24] See Miles (2023), table 1.

overreaching occurs. If the parties cannot agree how they hold the beneficial estate, they have to ascertain their respective rights under the law of implied trusts (7.2.2).

Conversely, research suggests that some purchasers who *do* answer question 10 (thereby making a binding express declaration of trust) may not fully appreciate the significance of their choice and get an unpleasant surprise later. Many couples appear to select a beneficial joint tenancy on the basis that, in the event of their relationship ending by *death*, the survivor will automatically acquire title to the whole property under the doctrine of survivorship.[25] It seems to be less well appreciated (or optimism bias blinds people to this possibility) that if their relationship instead ends by *separation*, the equity in the property (the capital value remaining after the mortgage loan has been repaid) will (after severance of the joint tenancy) be divided 50:50, however much each party contributed financially to the property's acquisition. By contrast, if parties select a tenancy in common, they can specify whatever lifetime shares in the property they like and—if they want to—ensure that the survivor will inherit by drafting wills to that effect.[26]

At the very least, purchasers should be alerted to the significance of their choices by information and legal advice provided at the point of conveyancing, particularly where potentially conflicting interests mean that parties should receive independent advice.[27] There are many advantages to parties' agreeing at the outset how they wish to deal with their property, not least the avoidance of litigation under the law of implied trusts. However, as in the matrimonial context, we should applaud reliance on private ordering only where we can be satisfied that the parties reached their agreements autonomously, with sound basic knowledge of the relevant law and facts, and with equal bargaining power.[28] Moreover, the Land Registry form and associated advice is only likely to draw people's attention to the question of beneficial ownership if they purchase land *together*. It will not help where either the property is bought during the relationship in one party's sole name or one party moves into property pre-acquired by the other.[29]

There are therefore many cases where the law of implied trusts and estoppel must be used: either to determine whether someone who is not a legal owner has acquired a beneficial interest in the property, potentially some years after the property's acquisition; or to determine the beneficial interests of joint owners who have not expressly declared a trust.

7.2.2 IMPLIED TRUSTS OF LAND AND PROPRIETARY ESTOPPEL: INTRODUCTION

The law of implied trusts identifies the extent of the beneficial interests, if any, held by joint legal owners who failed to declare an express trust, and enables individuals not on the legal title to acquire a beneficial interest. The law of proprietary estoppel (see 7.2.5) may also generate an interest in property for a claimant. Before embarking on an examination of this

[25] Douglas et al (2007a), (2007b).

[26] Cf the construction placed on the declaration of trust in *Chopra v Bindra* [2009] EWCA Civ 203, which purported to create survivorship in what was otherwise a tenancy in common: the court construed the survivorship clause as conferring a contingent remainder interest on the survivor in the other party's share. The parties thus achieved separate, unequal interests during their joint lives, but with survivorship (in effect) on death. For comment, see (2009) FL 584.

[27] Douglas et al (2007a), (2007b).

[28] Cf Diduck (2016).

[29] Equally common scenarios: Lersch and Vidal (2016).

area, comments from a Court of Appeal judge—prompted by the morass of complex and often apparently contradictory case law—deserve repetition:

Stack v Dowden [2005] EWCA Civ 857

CARNWATH LJ:

75. To the detached observer, the result [of this case law] may seem like a witch's brew, into which various esoteric ingredients have been stirred over the years, and in which different ideas bubble to the surface at different times. They include implied trust, constructive trust, resulting trust, presumption of advancement, proprietary estoppel, unjust enrichment, and so on. These ideas are likely to mean nothing to laymen, and often little more to the lawyers who use them.

That statement was made before the three major House of Lords/Supreme Court decisions that now direct this area. As we saw in our introduction, one judge has more recently described property law as operating in 'predictable and well-known ways'. It may be questioned whether the law of implied trusts now entirely merits that description—and whether the results it produces are 'fair'.

7.2.3 IMPLIED TRUSTS OF LAND: THE PRESUMPTIONS OF RESULTING TRUST AND ADVANCEMENT

We must first briefly examine two presumptions, one of which (resulting trust) is considerably less relevant now in disputes between family members than formerly, the other of which (advancement) is long due to be abolished. Both presumptions are (or were) based on what the courts assume—in the absence of an express trust—to be the 'common sense' view of what parties would intend in particular circumstances. The law of implied trusts is—notionally, at least—based on what the parties actually intended. Presumptions such as these help to fill the gap by providing a starting point—and, absent conclusive evidence, an ending point—for inquiring into the parties' intentions.[30] We shall see that these two presumptions have been largely displaced in the family cases with which we are concerned, thanks to the rise of the common intention constructive trust, which reflects a new judicial understanding of probable party intention in this context.

7.2.3.a The presumption of resulting trust

If property is transferred into the name of A but B funded the purchase, the law will generally presume that the parties intended that A would hold the land on a resulting trust for B to the extent of B's contribution. So, for example, if A and B buy property together that is put in A's sole name, but they contributed 40 per cent and 60 per cent of the purchase price, respectively, A is presumed to hold the property on resulting trust for A and B in shares of 40:60. The presumption only applies where B makes some direct financial contribution to the property's acquisition, for example by paying a deposit, assuming personal liability under a

[30] Cf difficult remarks in *Marr v Collie* [2017] UKPC 17, [53]–[54], discussed in the supplement to this chapter in the online resources.

mortgage,[31] or—depending on the circumstances and type of mortgage—paying mortgage instalments.[32] Indirect financial contributions (e.g. paying other household bills or contributing to a common pool from which household expenses are met) and non-financial contributions to the parties' relationship (e.g. home-making and child-rearing) are irrelevant.[33] To the extent that B's financial contribution was in fact intended as a gift or a loan to A, the presumption is rebutted.[34]

The resulting trust's exclusive focus on financial contributions to the acquisition of the land in question makes it difficult for some family members to acquire a share in land under this presumption, and the Supreme Court has held that:

> 53. The assumptions as to human motivation, which led the courts to impute particular intentions by way of resulting trust, are not appropriate to the ascertainment of beneficial interests in a family home.[35]

7.2.3.b The presumption of advancement

The presumption of advancement—due to be abolished by the still-unimplemented s 199 of the Equality Act 2010 and in any event rarely if ever determinative[36]—was an interesting relic of the law's historical treatment of certain family relationships.[37] It will remain good law for cases arising from events occurring or obligations arising before s 199 comes into force. For these cases, where a husband or father made a transfer to his wife or child—but not where a wife or mother did so[38]—the law presumed not a resulting trust, but a gift.[39] This presumption was not replicated in civil partnership law (unsurprisingly, given its gendered nature—so it cannot apply to same-sex marriages). Nor—importantly for this chapter—did it apply between cohabitants.[40]

The presumption was based on an increasingly dubious assumption that a husband or father would intend to make a gift, given his natural and moral obligation to his wife or child[41] and their economic dependence on him.[42] By contrast, no wife or mother would be taken to intend a gift in such cases, but rather to retain an interest under resulting trust. As early as 1970, the House of Lords in *Pettitt* considered that the force of the presumption was much weakened in contemporary conditions,[43] and it is widely thought to be incompatible with human rights law related to equality between spouses.[44] In any event, there was almost always evidence, however slight, from which the parties' actual intentions could be deduced, readily rebutting the presumption.[45]

31 Cf *Stack v Dowden* [2007] UKHL 17, [120] per Lord Neuberger.

32 *Huntingford v Hobbs* [1993] 1 FLR 736; *Carlton v Goodman* [2002] EWCA Civ 545; *Curley v Parkes* [2004] EWCA Civ 1515; *McKenzie v McKenzie* [2003] 2 P&CR DG6.

33 *Gissing v Gissing* [1971] AC 886.

34 *Re Sharpe (A Bankrupt)* [1980] 1 WLR 219; *Chapman v Jaume* [2012] EWCA Civ 476.

35 *Jones v Kernott* [2011] UKSC 53.

36 Not in force February 2023; see Glister (2010).

37 See generally Gray and Gray (2009), from 7.2.33.

38 Gender inequality in the parental context was questioned in *Gross v French* (1976) 238 EG 39; note also developments in some Commonwealth jurisdictions: Gray and Gray (2009), 7.2.37.

39 *Dyer v Dyer* (1788) 2 Cox Eq Cas 92; extended to fiancés by Law Reform (Miscellaneous Provisions) Act 1970, s 2(1), *Mossop v Mossop* [1989] Fam 77; cf *Mercier v Mercier* [1903] 2 Ch 98.

40 *Soar v Foster* (1858) 4 K&J 152, 162.

41 *Bennet v Bennet* (1879) 10 Ch D 474, 477.

42 *Pettitt v Pettitt* [1970] AC 777, 793.

43 For criticism, see Auchmuty (2007), 180–3.

44 See Art 5 of Protocol No 7 to the ECHR; Andrews (2007); cf Glister (2010).

45 *Pettitt v Pettitt* [1970] AC 777, 793, 811, 814, and 824.

7.2.4 IMPLIED TRUSTS OF LAND: 'COMMON INTENTION' CONSTRUCTIVE TRUSTS

Following *Stack v Dowden*[46] and *Jones v Kernott*,[47] the common intention constructive trust is the principal form of implied trust applied in the family context, notably where parties buy a home together or where one moves into the other's home. The voluminous case law has given property and trust lawyers considerable doctrinal difficulty, generating a vast literature. It is not entirely easy to state the law. Many commentators consider that *Stack* and *Jones* significantly relaxed the requirements of the common intention constructive trust, increasing its ability to produce 'fair' outcomes in family cases.[48] However, that has not obviously been the effect of those decisions (or, on key points, of obiter dicta), and few if any subsequent cases have reached outcomes strikingly different from those that would previously have been expected. Moreover, it is questionable whether trusts law *should* be used to reach the 'fair' outcomes that are sought: a specifically tailored statutory scheme may be far safer, doctrinally, as a means of achieving this.[49]

7.2.4.a When should the common intention constructive trust be deployed?

We need to begin by defining the sphere of operation of the common intention constructive trust: with what sort of cases are we dealing? The *Stack/Jones* approach was originally predicated on a distinction between the 'domestic'/'consumer' and 'commercial' contexts.[50] In *Stack*, Baroness Hale noted:

Stack v Dowden [2007] UKHL 17

42. . . . the recognition in the courts that, to put it at its lowest, the interpretation to be put on the behaviour of people living together in an intimate relationship may be different from the interpretation to be put upon similar behaviour between commercial men. To put it at its highest, an outcome which might seem just in a purely commercial transaction may appear highly unjust in a transaction between husband and wife or cohabitant and cohabitant.

Lord Hope agreed:

3. . . . Where the parties have dealt with each other at arms' length it makes sense to start from the position that there is a resulting trust according to how much each party contributed . . . But cohabiting couples are in a different kind of relationship. The place where they live together is their home. Living together is an exercise in give and take, mutual co-operation and compromise. Who pays for what in regard to the home has to be seen in the wider context of their overall relationship. A more practical, down-to-earth, fact-based approach is called for in their case. . . .

46 [2007] UKHL 17. 47 [2011] UKSC 53.
48 Most enthusiastic are Gardner (2013); Gardner and Davidson (2012); Auchmuty (2016).
49 See Mee (2011), (2012); Miles (2023), and 7.6. 50 See Hopkins (2011) for criticism.

Stack thus exemplifies what Dewar has called the 'familialization' of trusts law: developing trust law doctrine in a way that better accommodates the family context.[51] But Lord Neuberger, dissenting, doubted the wisdom, propriety, and necessity of judges developing specific principles for domestic cases:

> 101. The determination of the ownership [of] the beneficial interest in a property held in joint names primarily engages the law of contract, land and equity. The relevant principles in those areas have been established and applied over hundreds of years, and have had to be applied in all sorts of circumstances. While both the nature and the characteristics of the particular relationship must be taken into account when applying those principles, the court should be very careful before altering those principles when it comes to a particular type of relationship . . .
>
> 102. . . . A change in the law, however sensible and just it seems, always carries a real risk of new and unforeseen uncertainties and unfairnesses. That is a particular danger when the change is effected by the court rather than the legislature, as the change is influenced by, indeed normally based on, the facts of a particular case, there is little room for public consultation, and there is no input from the democratically elected legislature.

What is the scope of this 'familial' trusts law?[52] *Stack* involved a long-term couple cohabiting with four children in their shared home, purchased in joint names. What about: the purchase of a holiday home,[53] or of a pied-à-terre occupied by only one party during the working week; blood relatives who live together; the joint purchase by an adult child and their parent of a home to be occupied for the foreseeable future by the parent alone;[54] or a purchase by friends?[55] What if cohabitants or spouses are business partners—is the case nevertheless 'domestic'?[56] Early cases held that the 'domestic' approach applied to a home bought in joint names by mother and adult son that both occupied for some years before the mother's death,[57] but not, in *Laskar v Laskar*, where a similar pair made a joint-names purchase of the mother's former home as an investment (to be rented out).[58] These cases suggested that it was the use of property as a home by the parties together that attracted the 'domestic' approach. However, a Privy Council decision has given the common intention constructive trust broader application. Whilst not technically binding on English courts, since the panel included four of the judges involved in *Stack*, *Jones*, and *Laskar*, it must be regarded as highly persuasive.

The case concerned a couple of 17 years' standing who had acquired several properties in joint names for investment/development purposes. Did that investment purpose take the case out of the 'domestic' arena and compel a resulting trust approach?

51 Dewar (1998b); Hayward (2012). 52 Cf Law Com (2002).

53 *Rowland v Blades* [2021] EWHC 426: non-cohabiting couple, agreed that *Stack* applied to their case.

54 Cf *Abbey National Bank v Stringer* [2006] EWCA Civ 338; *Ledger-Beadell v Peach and Ledger-Beadell* [2006] EWHC 2940.

55 *Gallarotti v Sebastianelli* [2012] EWCA Civ 865.

56 Lord Walker suggested that the doctrine of resulting trust might remain relevant here: [2007] UKHL 17, [32].

57 *Adekunle v Ritchie* [2007] EW Misc 5 (EWCC).

58 [2008] EWCA Civ 347. See also *Erlam v Rahman* [2016] EWHC 111, investment by spouses; *Wodzicki v Wodzicki* [2017] EWCA Civ 95, property bought as home for deceased's adult daughter put in joint names of deceased and his second wife, who had no close relationship with the deceased's daughter.

Marr v Collie [2017] UKPC 17

LORD KERR:

48. In *Laskar*, of course, the co-funding of the purchase was required because the mother could not have afforded to buy the house herself. This was a joint investment impelled by her circumstances. Although the relationship was familial, the financial venture on which the parties had embarked *was not associated with a mutual commitment to each other for the future.* [emphasis added] The investment could therefore be characterised as a purely financial one, designed to pay dividends to each of the participants but shorn of any aspiration for a future equal sharing of proceeds [as joint-name owners]. Further, . . . the judge had found that there were no discussions between the parties as to the ownership of the beneficial interest in the property, and it does not appear to have been suggested that the court could or should infer any intention in that connection on the part of the parties.[59]

49. The Board does not consider, therefore, that *Laskar* is authority for the proposition that the principle in *Stack v Dowden* (that a conveyance into joint names indicates legal and beneficial joint tenancy unless the contrary is proved) applies only in "the domestic consumer context". Where a property is bought in the joint names of a cohabiting couple, even if that is as an investment, it does not follow inexorably that the "resulting trust solution" must provide the inevitable answer as to how its beneficial ownership is to be determined. . . . It is entirely conceivable that partners in a relationship would buy, as an investment, property which is conveyed into their joint names with the intention that the beneficial ownership should be shared equally between them, even though they contributed in different shares to the purchase. Where there is evidence to support such a conclusion, it would be both illogical and wrong to impose the resulting trust solution on the subsequent distribution of the property.[60]

The advice of the Board in *Marr v Collie* is not entirely easy to understand in places. But the key point is the importance of the parties' intentions to implied trusts law. In the following sections, we set out the law relating to common intention constructive trusts expounded in *Stack* and *Jones*. We do so on the footing that, where the acquisition of or later dealing with the property at stake in some way reflects the parties' 'mutual commitment to each other for the future' (most commonly, but not exclusively, as a shared home), the common intention constructive trust—not the presumption of resulting trust—provides the appropriate framework for ascertaining the parties' intentions and so the beneficial ownership of that property. But one can anticipate factual disputes on whether an investment or other purchase was indeed a joint venture of the sort contemplated by *Marr* (triggering the common intention constructive trust presumption), or a business proposition, albeit between intimate partners (attracting the resulting trust presumption).

ONLINE RESOURCES

Readers wishing to read about problems interpreting some aspects of *Marr v Collie* should visit the supplement to this chapter in the online resources at **www.oup.com/he/familytcm5e.**

[59] See 7.2.4.b for why this is significant to the common intention constructive trust.

[60] See also *Gallarotti v Sebastianelli* [2012] EWCA Civ 865, [5].

7.2.4.b Common intention constructive trusts: the basics

The three key ingredients

On an orthodox understanding of the law, three inter-related ingredients must be proved in establishing a common intention constructive trust: (i) a common (i.e. shared) intention between the parties that the claimant each has[61] a beneficial share in the property (or more than a half-share in a joint-names case); (ii) on which the claimant has detrimentally relied, such that it would be unconscionable for the owner to deny the claimant's interest; and finally (iii) that interest must be quantified. The detailed discussion that follows is organized around the categories of case identified in *Stack/Jones* in which those ingredients are differently interpreted and applied: first, cases in which the legal title is held jointly (joint-names cases); and, secondly, those in which it is held by one party (sole-name cases). But we start with some general remarks about the nature and basis of the common intention constructive trust.

The leading overarching statement of the law applicable in 'domestic' cases (as understood after *Marr*: 7.2.4.a) is found in *Jones v Kernott*, supplemented by key passages of Lady Hale's judgment in *Stack v Dowden*. The judges start by considering the case of property owned jointly at law, but then address the equivalent issue for cases where the property is held in the sole-name of one party:

Jones v Kernott [2011] UKSC 53

LORD WALKER AND LADY HALE:

51. In summary, therefore, the following are the principles applicable in a case such as this, where a family home is bought in the joint names of a cohabiting couple who are both responsible for any mortgage,[62] but without any express declaration of their beneficial interests.

(1) The starting point is that equity follows the law and they are joint tenants both in law and in equity.

(2) That presumption can be displaced by showing (a) that the parties had a different common intention at the time when they acquired the home, or (b) that they later formed the common intention that their respective shares would change. [See further below]

(3) Their common intention is to be deduced objectively from their conduct: "the relevant intention of each party is the intention which was reasonably understood by the other party to be manifested by that party's words and conduct notwithstanding that he did not consciously formulate that intention in his own mind or even acted with some different intention which he did not communicate to the other party" (Lord Diplock in *Gissing v Gissing* [1971] AC 886, 906). Examples of the sort of evidence which might be relevant to drawing such inferences are given in *Stack v Dowden*, at para 69. [Extracted later in this section]

(4) In those cases where it is clear either (a) that the parties did not intend joint tenancy at the outset, or (b) had changed their original intention, but it is not possible to ascertain by

[61] Now, not at some future point: *O'Neill v Holland* [2020] EWCA Civ 1583, [40].

[62] See 7.2.4.a re the wider range of cases to which this trust may be applied after *Marr*.

direct evidence or by inference what their actual intention was as to the shares in which they would own the property, "the answer is that each is entitled to that share which the court considers fair having regard to the whole course of dealing between them in relation to the property": Chadwick LJ in *Oxley v Hiscock* [2005] Fam 211, para 69. In our judgment, "the whole course of dealing . . . in relation to the property" should be given a broad meaning, enabling a similar range of factors to be taken into account as may be relevant to ascertaining the parties' actual intentions.

(5) Each case will turn on its own facts. Financial contributions are relevant but there are many other factors which may enable the court to decide what shares were either intended (as in case (3)) or fair (as in case (4)).

52. This case is not concerned with a family home which is put into the name of one party only. [There the] starting point is different. The first issue is whether it was intended that the other party have any beneficial interest in the property at all. If he does, the second issue is what that interest is. There is no presumption of joint beneficial ownership. But their common intention has once again to be deduced objectively from their conduct. If the evidence shows a common intention to share beneficial ownership but does not show what shares were intended, the court will have to proceed as at para 51(4) and (5) above.

Stack v Dowden [2007] UKHL 17

BARONESS HALE:

68. The burden will . . . be on the person seeking to show that the parties did intend their beneficial interests to be different from their legal interests, and in what way. This is not a task to be lightly embarked upon. In family disputes, strong feelings are aroused when couples split up. These often lead the parties, honestly but mistakenly, to reinterpret the past in self-exculpatory or vengeful terms. They also lead people to spend far more on the legal battle than is warranted by the sums actually at stake. A full examination of the facts is likely to involve disproportionate costs. In joint names cases it is also unlikely to lead to a different result unless the facts are very unusual . . . It cannot be the case that all the hundreds and thousands, if not millions, of transfers into joint names using the old forms[63] are vulnerable to challenge in the courts simply because it is likely that the owners contributed unequally to their purchase.

How is the court to ascertain what the parties intended? Having indicated that the relevant starting point would rarely be departed from, the range of relevant factors appears to provide considerable room for parties to attempt to do just that. Note again some differences of approach for joint-names cases:

69. In law, "context is everything" and the domestic context is very different from the commercial world. Each case will turn on its own facts. Many more factors than financial contributions may be relevant to divining the parties' true intentions. These include: any advice

[63] I.e. forms containing the 'valid receipt' clause, discussed at n 15, which was held in *Stack* not to constitute an express declaration of trust, hence the resort to implied trusts.

> or discussions at the time of the transfer which cast light upon their intentions then;[64] the reasons why the home was acquired in their joint names; the reasons why (if it be the case) the survivor was authorised to give a receipt for the capital monies; the purpose for which the home was acquired; the nature of the parties' relationship; whether they had children for whom they both had responsibility to provide a home; how the purchase was financed, both initially and subsequently; how the parties arranged their finances, whether separately or together or a bit of both; how they discharged the outgoings on the property and their other household expenses. When a couple are joint owners of the home and jointly liable for the mortgage, the inferences to be drawn from who pays for what may be very different from the inferences to be drawn when only one is owner of the home. The arithmetical calculation of how much was paid by each is also likely to be less important. It will be easier to draw the inference that they intended that each should contribute as much to the household as they reasonably could and that they would share the eventual benefit or burden equally. The parties' individual characters and personalities may also be a factor in deciding where their true intentions lay. In the cohabitation context, mercenary considerations may be more to the fore than they would be in marriage, but it should not be assumed that they will always take pride of place over natural love and affection. At the end of day, having taken all this into account, cases in which the joint legal owners are taken to have intended that their beneficial interests should be different from their legal interests will be very unusual.
>
> 70. This is not, of course, an exhaustive list. There may also be reasons to conclude that, whatever the parties' intentions at the outset, these have now changed. An example might be where one party has financed (or constructed himself) an extension or substantial improvement to the property, so that what they have now is significantly different from what they had then.

In relation to cases where intentions are claimed to have changed over time, Baroness Hale said:

> 62. . . . [A]lthough the parties' intentions may change over the course of time, producing . . . an "ambulatory" constructive trust, at any one time their interests must be the same for all purposes. They cannot at one and the same time intend, for example, a joint tenancy with survivorship should one of them die while they are still together, a tenancy in common in equal shares should they separate on amicable terms after the children have grown up, and a tenancy in common in unequal shares should they separate on acrimonious terms while the children are still with them.

Curiously, perhaps, this exposition of the law (like other passages extracted here) makes no reference to detrimental reliance, the second of the three ingredients required on the orthodox view. But it would be odd were this requirement dispensed with in common intention constructive trust cases—certainly without any justifying commentary, and Lord Walker in *Stack* cited without qualification a key passage from the leading case *Gissing v Gissing* that rehearses the need for detrimental reliance.[65] It is the detrimental reliance that makes it unconscionable for the respondent to insist that the parties' interests simply mirror

[64] E.g. the draft declaration of trust considered in *Williamson v Sheikh* [2008] EWCA Civ 990; the claimant was a minor at the date of purchase, so could not take the legal title.

[65] [2007] UKHL 17, [19]–[21].

the legal title. In *Stack*, at least, the court was not called on to consider *whether* the claimant had a beneficial share *at all*—that was agreed, and the issue was quantification: the issue of detrimental reliance did not arise for decision.[66] Court of Appeal decisions have since confirmed that detrimental reliance remains a requirement in both sole name[67] and joint name cases.[68]

Inferring intention, imputing intention, and the role of 'fairness'

Jones v Kernott identifies two stages: (i) the *acquisition* stage—do the parties have a common intention to have interests different from those which the relevant starting point supplies? and has there been detrimental reliance by the claimant?; if so, (ii) the *quantification* stage—in what other shares do the parties hold the beneficial title? Although there is some ambiguity in the lead judgment,[69] the Supreme Court clearly requires stage (i) to be answered by reference to the parties' actual intentions, either evidenced directly from express discussions or inferred from their conduct. The court cannot at this stage 'impute' to the parties an intention that they never had or to impose the answer it regards as 'fair'.[70] Nor is the court determining here whether the parties' actions:

> generate a moral obligation by one of them to the other. It is not an objective process of that kind. Instead, it is to consider whether that course of dealing provides a basis, in the absence of express agreement, for *inferring* that the parties intended to undertake obligations towards one another, even though they did not express them as such. It is a process which seeks to ascertain the genuine intentions of the parties . . .[71]

Contrast the suggestion some years earlier, in *Midland Bank v Cooke*, that a constructive trust could be found even where the parties 'had been honest enough to admit that they never gave ownership a thought or reached any agreement about it', thinking it 'unrealistic' to expect them to have had such conversations.[72] True as that view of the world may be, the orthodox position rejects use of imputed intentions at stage (i), certainly in a sole-name case.

Lord Neuberger, dissenting in *Stack*, rejected *any* resort to imputation:

Stack v Dowden [2007] UKHL 17

LORD NEUBERGER:

126. An inferred intention is one which is objectively deduced to be the subjective actual intention of the parties, in the light of their actions and statements. An imputed intention is one which is attributed to the parties, even though no such actual intention can be deduced

66 *Stack v Dowden* [2007] UKHL 17, [63]. Gardner (2008) and Etherton (2009) go too far in suggesting that detrimental reliance is no longer required given the absence of any express discussion of the point.

67 E.g. *Curran v Collins* [2015] EWCA Civ 404, [77]–[78]; *O'Neill v Holland* [2020] EWCA Civ 1583, [35].

68 *Hudson v Hathaway* [2022] EWCA Civ 1648.

69 [2011] UKSC 53, end of [31], opening of [48]; cf views of Lords Collins [64], Kerr [68], and Wilson [84].

70 *Geary v Rankine* [2012] EWCA Civ 555, [19]; *Thompson v Hurst* [2012] EWCA Civ 1752, [22]; *Capehorn v Harris* [2015] EWCA Civ 955, [17]; *Barnes v Phillips* [2015] EWCA Civ 1056, [25].

71 *Dobson v Griffey* [2018] EWHC 1117, [81].

72 [1995] 4 All ER 562, 575; *Kernott v Jones* [2010] EWCA Civ 578, [90].

from their actions and statements, and even though they had no such intention. Imputation involves concluding what the parties would have intended, whereas inference involves concluding what they did intend.

127. To impute an intention would not only be wrong in principle and a departure from [*Pettitt v Pettitt* [1970] AC 777 and *Gissing v Gissing* [1971] AC 886] in this very area, but it would also involve a judge in an exercise which was difficult, subjective and uncertain. . . . It would be difficult because the judge would be constructing an intention where none existed at the time, and where the parties may well not have been able to agree. It would be subjective for obvious reasons. It would be uncertain because it is unclear whether one considers a hypothetical negotiation between the actual parties, or what reasonable parties would have agreed. The former is more logical, but would redound to the advantage of an unreasonable party.

However, despite Lord Neuberger's reservations, once we reach quantification at stage (ii), *Jones* decides that if the parties' actual intentions regarding the size of their respective beneficial interests cannot be ascertained, or were non-existent, the court must substitute an answer based on what is fair. Earlier in their judgment,[73] Lord Walker and Lady Hale had used the language of 'imputed intention' to describe this decision. There is no obvious difference between a decision described in terms of 'imputed intention' and one expressed in terms of what is fair in the circumstances. Where the parties' *actual* intention—most obviously a lack of *common* intention—requires a result that is considered objectively *unfair*, the court must follow it.[74] By contrast, where no actual intention can be found, it is difficult to imagine a court imputing to the parties an objectively unfair intention, certainly not if the parties are taken to be 'reasonable people'.[75] But the language of fairness is more transparent:[76]

Jones v Kernott **[2011] UKSC 53**

LORD KERR:

74. The reason that I question the aptness of the notion of imputing an intention is that, in the final analysis, the exercise is wholly unrelated to ascertainment of the parties' views. It involves the court deciding what is fair in light of the whole course of dealing with the property. That decision has nothing to do with what the parties intended, or what might be supposed would have been their intention had they addressed that question. In many ways, it would be preferable to have a stark choice between deciding whether it is possible to deduce what their intention was and, where it is not, deciding what is fair, without elliptical references to what their intention might have – or should have – been. But imputing intention has entered the lexicon of this area of law and it is probably impossible to discard it now.

[73] E.g. [2011] UKSC 53, [31]. [74] See *James v Thomas* [2007] EWCA Civ 1212, [38].

[75] *Jones v Kernott* [2011] UKSC 53, [48].

[76] Not least to keep the distinction clear: cf the view of Lord Walker and Lady Hale that there may be little practical difference between inferring and imputing intention, ibid, [38]; Piška (2009).

However described, the greater difficulty is the lack of criteria for deciding *what* is 'fair'. In the matrimonial finance sphere (chapter 6), the courts have conceded that 'fairness is an elusive concept', and that in order to achieve consistency 'the courts must . . . articulate, if only in the broadest fashion, what are the applicable if unspoken principles guiding the court's approach'.[77] We await any such principles for the operation of trusts law, having had only limited guidance thus far from the courts, save to highlight the relatively narrow focus of the exercise.[78]

Graham-York v York [2015] EWCA Civ 72

TOMLINSON LJ:

22. It is essential . . . to bear in mind that, in that deciding in such a case what shares are fair, the court is not concerned with some form of redistributive justice. Thus it is irrelevant that it may be thought a "fair" outcome that a woman who has endured years of abusive conduct by her partner to be allotted a substantial interest in his property . . . The plight of Miss Graham-York attracts sympathy, but it does not enable the court to redistribute property interests in a manner which right-minded people might think amounts to appropriate compensation. Miss Graham-York is "entitled to that share which the court considers fair having regard to the whole course of dealing between them in relation to the property." It is these last words, which I have emphasised, which supply the confines of the enquiry as to fairness.[79]

In the next two sections, we look more closely at how the *Stack/Jones* approach has been applied, first in 'joint-names' cases[80] and then where legal title is in the name of one party.

7.2.4.c Cases where the legal title is in the parties' joint names

The decision in Stack v Dowden

Mr Stack and Ms Dowden, parents of four children, were legal co-owners of a home purchased ten years into their 20-year cohabiting relationship. The purchase was funded by capital from Ms Dowden, the proceeds of sale of their previous home held in her name, and a joint mortgage. Throughout the relationship, she was the higher earner. They had separate bank and savings accounts. He paid the mortgage interest; she paid all other household bills; both helped pay off the capital sum due under the mortgage. Overall, her financial contribution to the acquisition of this property and their previous home had been greater. There was no express declaration of the parties' beneficial shares in the property.

The House of Lords held that where the property is held in the parties' joint names (which means that there must be *a* trust) but no beneficial interests have been expressly created, the fact of putting title in joint names will 'at least in the vast majority of cases' demonstrate

[77] *Miller; McFarlane* [2006] UKHL 24, [4]–[6]: see 6.5.1. [78] See Miles (2023).

[79] Though compare *Barnes v Phillips* [2015] EWCA Civ 1056, discussed at 7.2.4.c.

[80] Where the property is in the joint names of A and B and the claimant is C, A and B are effectively a sole owner vis-à-vis C: see n 113.

that the parties intended that both would have a beneficial share.[81] The majority, not called on to make a decision regarding the acquisition stage, appear to assume detrimental reliance on this initial, *presumed* intention by whichever party most benefits from it;[82] or, put another way, equity simply follows the law. As to the size and nature of those shares, it is *strongly* presumed in such cases that the parties intended to create a beneficial joint tenancy.[83] This would give the parties equal shares on sale of the property following their separation (at which point the joint tenancy would in practice be severed) or the survivor would take all if the other owner(s) died without severance having occurred. This effectively creates a highly valuable, gender- and relationship status-neutral presumption of advancement in favour of whichever party made the lesser (or even no) financial contribution to the purchase.[84] The basis of this presumption was further explained in *Jones v Kernott*:

Jones v Kernott **[2011] UKSC 53**

LORD WALKER AND LADY HALE:

19. The presumption of a beneficial joint tenancy is not based on a mantra as to "equity following the law" . . . There are two much more substantial reasons (which overlap) why a challenge to the presumption of beneficial joint tenancy is not lightly to be embarked upon. The first is implicit in the nature of the enterprise. If a couple in an intimate relationship (whether married or unmarried) decide to buy a house or flat in which to live together, almost always with the help of a mortgage for which they are jointly and severally liable, that is on the face of things a strong indication of emotional and economic commitment to a joint enterprise. That is so even if the parties, for whatever reason, fail to make that clear by any overt declaration or agreement . . .

22. The notion that in a trusting personal relationship the parties do not hold each other to account financially is underpinned by the practical difficulty, in many cases, of taking any such account, perhaps after 20 years or more of the ups and downs of living together as an unmarried couple. That is the second reason for caution before going to law in order to displace the presumption of beneficial joint tenancy . . .

The onus then lies with whichever party wishes to claim a *larger* share to *rebut* the presumption of beneficial joint tenancy by bringing evidence to show that (i) the parties had a *different* common intention on which, as the Court of Appeal has confirmed (see 7.2.4.b), (ii) the claimant had relied to her detriment Ms Dowden had done this through her greater financial contribution. One might have thought it could be rebutted simply where parties had made different levels of financial contribution to the acquisition of the property, triggering the presumption of resulting trust instead.[85] However, the majority rejected this approach, arguing that in contemporary circumstances 'the importance to be attached to who paid for what in a domestic context may be very different from its importance in other contexts or long ago'. Baroness Hale, for the majority in *Stack v Dowden*, claimed that only

[81] *Stack v Dowden* [2007] UKHL 17, [56], [63]. [82] Ibid, [63].
[83] Ibid, [53]–[56]. [84] Ibid, [112].
[85] Lord Neuberger would take this approach where the only additional evidence is different levels of financial contribution: ibid, [110]–[122].

rarely would the presumption be rebutted by a finding that other beneficial shares were intended; but such a finding turns on the parties' 'whole course of conduct in relation to the property', by reference to the factors set out in para 69, extracted at 7.2.4.b.[86] If a common intention to hold the beneficial interest other than as joint tenants can be found, the court then quantifies the shares by references to the parties' intentions or (after *Jones v Kernott*) absent such intentions, by reference to what is 'fair'.

Far from discouraging arguments attempting to rebut the presumption, the wide range of relevant factors identified in *Stack* and the result itself encouraged practitioners to suggest that it might often be worth trying to rebut the presumption.[87] Stack and Dowden emerged with 35:65 shares, essentially reflecting their respective financial contributions to the purchase. Baroness Hale concluded that they intended to hold in those proportions because they had: contributed unequally to the purchase price;[88] kept their money in separate accounts, not pooling it; and divided responsibility for household outgoings rigidly (as described earlier). This financial separation, and Mr Stack's apparent failure to commit at least 'to do what he could' towards family expenditure,[89] persuaded Baroness Hale that this relationship was not a 'partnership' in which a beneficial joint tenancy was intended. This despite the parties' having chosen to put *this* asset in joint names, the length of their relationship, their raising four children together (albeit with the help of nannies and childminders), and the fact that they contributed equal *proportions* of their earnings to the purchase.[90] We examine at 7.2.6.a empirical evidence about cohabitants' money-management practices that suggests that such cases are less unusual than Baroness Hale supposes.[91]

The outcome suggests that the presumption of resulting trust remains close by:[92] the presumption of beneficial joint tenancy seems to yield quickly to unequal financial contributions. As Lord Neuberger has observed extra-judicially, 'If the presumption of equality is to be rebutted because the contributions are significantly different, it is a pretty useless presumption: the only time you need it, it isn't there.'[93]

Applying Stack v Dowden

One later case paints a different picture. In *Fowler v Barron*,[94] the parties had cohabited for 23 years and had two children. Mr Barron, a retired fireman on a pension, looked after the children while Ms Fowler worked. Without any legal advice or express discussion, they put their house in joint names (with no declaration of trust) and took out a joint mortgage, despite having no intention that Ms Fowler would help repay the debt. Mr Barron contributed the deposit and paid the mortgage, and all of the utility, council tax, and other general household bills. Ms Fowler made no financial contribution to the house or general household costs. Her wages were used to buy her clothes and to meet the children's various expenses. When they separated, Ms Fowler sought to establish that she had an interest in the property, but the trial judge found that the beneficial title was

[86] Ibid, [60]. [87] See, e.g., Barnes (2007).

[88] This appeared to be sufficient for Lord Hope [2007] UKHL 17, [11], which indicates, despite his approval of Baroness Hale's reasoning, sympathy for Lord Neuberger's minority approach.

[89] Ibid, [91]. [90] George (2008a). [91] See also *Kernott v Jones* [2010] EWCA Civ 578, [75].

[92] See in particular Lord Hope: [2007] UKHL 17, [11]; *Jones v Kernott* [2011] UKSC 53, [25].

[93] Neuberger (2008), para 15. [94] [2008] EWCA Civ 377.

Mr Barron's alone under the presumption of resulting trust, having found that the parties had no actual intention to share beneficial ownership equally. The Court of Appeal, overturning that decision, set out its general approach to *Stack*'s presumption of beneficial joint tenancy as follows:

Fowler v Barron [2008] EWCA Civ 377

ARDEN LJ:

34. At this point it may be appropriate to make some observations about the effect of the presumption. It provides a default rule that, unless and until the contrary is proved, joint tenants in this context are treated as joint legal and beneficial owners. If the contrary were not proved, the mere fact that the property was transferred into their joint names would be enough to give both parties an equal beneficial share.

35. In determining whether the presumption [of beneficial joint tenancy] is rebutted, the court must in particular consider whether the facts as found are *inconsistent* with the inference of a common intention to share the property in equal shares to an extent sufficient to discharge the civil standard of proof on the person seeking to displace the presumption arising from a transfer into joint names. [Emphasis added]

This elaboration of how the presumption works is important. Evidence *consistent* with a beneficial joint tenancy does *not necessarily* mean that parties *intended* a beneficial joint tenancy—the facts may be equally consistent with a tenancy in common (quite possibly in shares other than 50:50) or sole beneficial ownership. That will not displace the presumption. The party seeking to rebut the presumption, here Mr Barron, must establish facts positively *inconsistent* with a beneficial joint tenancy. Viewed in this way, Mr Barron's task looks daunting (and *Stack*'s outcome perhaps too favourable to Ms Dowden).

In *Fowler*, there was only circumstantial evidence of the parties' common intention regarding ownership of the property. The trial judge found that Mr Barron had intended that Ms Fowler should become sole owner of the property on his death: this is consistent with joint tenancy's doctrine of survivorship. But the judge also found that he had not intended that she should get an equal share should they separate: this is evidently inconsistent with a beneficial joint tenancy. However, this 'secret' intention had not been communicated to Ms Fowler, so could not form the basis of a *common* intention.[95] The parties had executed mutual wills, leaving each other their interests in the property: this implied that both thought each had *a* share (at least) during their lifetime.[96] But despite being party to the mortgage, Ms Fowler, unlike Mr Stack, had made no financial contribution to the mortgage or other regular household expenditure. Like Stack and Dowden, the parties had no joint bank account. *Perhaps* like Mr Stack (we know relatively little about these aspects of *Stack v Dowden*), Ms Fowler had not been the children's primary carer since she was working. Nevertheless, the Court of Appeal upheld the presumption of beneficial joint tenancy, rejecting Mr Barron's claim for more, and so giving each party an equal share after severance.

95 Ibid, [36]–[37]. 96 Ibid, [6], [42].

Fowler v Barron [2008] EWCA Civ 377

ARDEN LJ:

41. . . . Mr Barron paid some items properly described as household expenses, such as the council tax and utilities bills, whereas she paid for other such items. The division was perfectly logical if . . . she did most of the shopping for the children. The further inference that . . . it is appropriate to draw is that the parties intended that it should make no difference to their interests in the property which party paid for what expense. Those payments also throw light on their intentions in this respect. The inference from this, especially when taken with the evidence as to mutual wills . . . was that the parties simply did not care about the respective size of each other's contributions. . . .

45. In a case where the parties have made unequal contributions to the cost of acquiring their home, it is obvious that in some cases there may be a thin dividing line between the case where the parties' shared intention is properly inferred to be ownership of the home in equal shares, and the case where the parties' shared intention is properly inferred to be that the party who has contributed less should have a smaller interest than the other. The resolution of such cases must however all depend on the facts. In my judgment it is important to return to the ratio in *Stack*. The essential reasoning of the House was (1) that, where parties put their home in joint names, the burden is on the one asserting that they own the property other than in equal shares to rebut the presumption of beneficial joint ownership that arises from their legal co-ownership, and (2) that the court must have regard to all the circumstances which would throw light on their shared intentions and not just their financial contributions to the cost of acquiring the property. It is necessary to consider the resolution of the facts in *Stack* with these principles in mind. In other words, it was not the fact that the parties made unequal contributions to the cost of acquiring their property . . . that mattered so much as the inferences as to their shared intentions to be gleaned from the evidence overall.

Arden LJ sought to justify upholding the presumption of beneficial joint tenancy on the basis of factual differences from *Stack* that, with respect, do not obviously *favour* Ms Fowler: for example, the mutual wills; the lack of other substantial assets; the fact that she had made no financial contribution; that, without a share, she might become reliant on state support, which—in Arden LJ's view—the parties could not reasonably be inferred to have intended;[97] and their treatment of their money as a common pool (despite the lack of a joint account).[98] The outcome is perhaps more convincing without seeking forensic points of distinction from *Stack*:

TOULSON LJ:

53. In *Stack v Dowden* the House of Lords regarded the facts as very unusual. In the present case there was nothing at all unusual about the circumstances in which the property was acquired. It was bought and conveyed into the parties' joint names . . . at a time when they had a 9 month old baby . . . They had been in a relationship for 4 years. They had not been cohabiting, but Miss Fowler said . . . that the birth . . . "was the spur for us to become a proper family unit". The judge found that the property was bought in order to provide a home for themselves and their son. . . . They were joint borrowers and jointly liable [on the

[97] See Miles (2011), 101. [98] [2008] EWCA Civ 377, [46].

mortgage]. The judge found that whatever either of them thought about the question of ownership of the property at the time of the transfer, nothing was ever said. Looking at the matter at the time of acquisition, there was in my judgment nothing to rebut the ordinary presumption in such circumstances that the parties were intended to be joint beneficial owners in equal shares. . . .

56. . . . [He summarizes the factors listed in [69] of Baroness Hale's judgment in *Stack*, and goes on:] The judge in his analysis of the facts looked only at financial matters. That is too narrow an approach when addressing issues of inferred common intention. In this case the property served as a family home for the parties and their children from the time of its acquisition until the time of the breakdown of the relationship. During those 17 years Miss Fowler contributed to the life and wellbeing of the family in financial and other ways . . . In that family context I would reject any argument that a common silent intention should be inferred from the parties' conduct that their property interests were to be varied so as to reduce Miss Fowler's original share.

If anything, therefore, the difficulty lies not in Ms Fowler's having a half-share, but in Mr Stack's not doing so. The analysis in *Fowler v Barron* may therefore be more typical, and *Stack extremely* unusual.[99] Indeed, another court showed a strong attachment to the equal shares starting point in a case where a couple (romantically attached but not cohabiting) had deliberately chosen to put their holiday home in joint names, despite one party supplying all the purchase money.[100] But equally, there are examples going the other way, including cases involving actual or intended matrimonial homes, facts over which one might have assumed the joint starting point would hold particular sway.[101]

'Ambulatory' common intention constructive trusts

Jones v Kernott proved to be another unusual case, but here the question of beneficial ownership arose 14 years after the parties' separation, during which time Ms Jones alone had funded the mortgage without any significant child support payments from Mr Kernott, who had acquired his own home and paid no attention to the property.[102] The Supreme Court reinstated the trial judge's decision that the presumption of beneficial joint tenancy could be rebutted. While the presumption would have held had the issue arisen on separation, it was inferred that the parties' intentions had changed over the intervening period—*Jones* thus exemplifies a so-called 'ambulatory trust', which changes over time. By majority, it was further inferred[103] that the parties intended that Mr Kernott's share in the property should crystallize *in value* on separation: they liquidated some other assets at that point to help him buy a new home, which had since increased in value. The value of his crystallized share on a rough-and-ready basis justified 90:10 shares of the current value in favour of Ms Jones.[104]

[99] See *Kernott v Jones* [2010] EWCA Civ 578, [72] and [75].

[100] *Rowland v Blades* [2021] EWHC 426; see also *Wall v Munday* [2018] EWHC 879, where the court proposed to undertake equitable accounting (see supplement in the online resources), on facts where departure from 50:50 might have been thought justified on an 'ambulatory' basis—see next heading.

[101] E.g. *S v J* [2016] EWHC 559 (fiancés); *Premium Jet AG v Sutton* [2017] EWHC 186 (spouses).

[102] [2010] EWCA Civ 578. Cf the sole-name case, *Holman v Howes* [2007] EWCA Civ 877.

[103] Lords Kerr and Wilson reached the same outcome via imputation.

[104] See also *Quaintance v Tandan* [2012] EWHC 4416: 100:0 where defendant left very shortly after purchase, having contributed nothing.

Barnes v Phillips similarly entailed a substantial post-separation 'ambulation' in the parties' shares, in light (in particular) of money received by the male partner on moving out and the female partner then paying the mortgage alone for six years.[105] More problematically, and inconsistently with the focus in *Graham-York* on the parties' dealings 'in relation to the property',[106] the court also brought into account Mr Barnes's failure to pay child support 'as part of the financial history of the parties'.[107] The court was rightly alert to the need to avoid the double-counting that would result were Ms Phillips's property rights inflated on that basis whilst the child support arrears remained recoverable. But considerable caution should be taken in attempting to take such a holistic view of 'financial fairness' in fixing the parties' property rights. Where the court has only one of the parties' assets at its disposal, it can do only so much, and using ownership of the former family home as a proxy battleground for other financial disputes between the parties may imperil third parties' interests in the property.[108] Contrast the truly holistic jurisdiction of the matrimonial court, which—ironically, save for contested child support—can seek a 'once and for all', comprehensive settlement encompassing all of the parties' assets and financial resources.

Other family relationships

Going beyond the cohabitants' context, in *Adekunle v Ritchie*,[109] the presumption of beneficial joint tenancy was rebutted where mother and son had purchased a property in joint names which both occupied for some years until the mother's death. The judge held that the circumstances were sufficiently unusual to depart from the presumption.[110] The primary purpose of this purchase had been to acquire a home for the mother, who could not use the 'right to buy' option over her council house without the son's help to get a mortgage; the parties had kept their finances separate; the mother had nine other children with whom she had good relations, and so it was inconceivable that she would have intended to have a beneficial joint tenancy with the son such that he would take the house (her only sizeable asset) under the doctrine of survivorship on her death.[111] However, the son was clearly intended to have *some* interest, since the property had been put in joint names with a joint mortgage; he had lived in the house when it was bought; and he had contributed to the mortgage payments. The judge found that the parties' financial contributions justified at most a 25 per cent share for the son, but (for reasons that were not closely articulated) increased his share to a third pursuant to the 'holistic' examination required by *Stack*. HHJ Behrens was clearly less than comfortable in conducting that exercise, acknowledging the 'subjectivity and uncertainty' of the task highlighted by Lord Neuberger.[112]

7.2.4.d Cases where the legal title is in the sole name of one party

The starting point here is simply that the property belongs solely to the party in whose name it is registered. The onus is on the party *not* on the legal title to prove that they have

105 [2015] EWCA Civ 1056.
106 [2015] EWCA Civ 72, [22], extracted previously.
107 Ibid, [38]–[41].
108 Though they often have access to various mechanisms by which to secure priority: see McFarlane et al (2021), ch 17.
109 [2007] EW Misc 5 (EWCC). See also *Gallarotti v Sebastianelli* [2012] EWCA Civ 865: platonic home-sharers.
110 [2007] EW Misc 5 (EWCC), [65]. Dixon suggests that rather than being unusual this may simply feel 'unfair': (2007), 459–60.
111 At [66]–[67].
112 At [68].

a beneficial interest and that there is therefore a trust.[113] The three analytical stages of orthodox common intention constructive trust doctrine—intention, detrimental reliance, quantification—are clearly evident. The first two map on to the 'acquisition' stage in *Stack/Jones*. As noted earlier, sole ownership is more common amongst cohabitants than spouses (affecting over a third of owner-occupied cohabitants' homes),[114] so this area of law—and the hurdles it puts in front of claimants—have particular importance here.

Acquisition step 1: finding a 'common intention' to share beneficial ownership

The first stage is to establish a common intention—express or inferred—that the claimant should have a beneficial share at all. The leading case on sole-name cases remains the House of Lords decision in *Lloyds Bank v Rosset*:

Lloyds Bank v Rosset [1991] 1 AC 107, 132–3, 131

LORD BRIDGE:

The first and fundamental question which must always be resolved is whether, independently of any inference to be drawn from the conduct of the parties in the course of sharing the house as their home and managing their affairs, there has at any time prior to acquisition, or exceptionally at some later date, been any agreement, arrangement or understanding reached between them that the property is to be shared beneficially. The finding of an agreement or arrangement to share in this sense can only, I think, be based on evidence of express discussions between the partners, however imperfectly remembered and however imprecise their terms may have been. Once a finding to this effect is made it will only be necessary for the partner asserting the claim to a beneficial interest against the partner entitled to the legal estate to show that he or she has acted to his or her detriment or significantly altered his or her position in reliance on the agreement in order to give rise to a constructive trust or a proprietary estoppel.

On some facts, the judge may find an **express** common intention where the sole-name owner has given some excuse for not putting the claimant on the legal title. Whilst those owners may subjectively have had no intention that their partners should have any share, what matters is the objective impression and so whether the claimant reasonably understood what was said to reflect a common intention to share.[115] Such a finding will not always or even usually arise in such 'excuse' cases: what is needed is an understanding that the legal title *would have* been in joint names, *but for* some impediment—and that the sole-name registration covers what in substance is agreed (informally) to be joint beneficial ownership.[116] This has been criticized as allowing 'mere sophistry', giving unduly 'formal force' to the words people happen to use, an approach that is 'in itself . . . an irony as we are dealing with doctrines designed to deal with informality'.[117] Gardner considers that finding a common intention to share the beneficial ownership here may recognize the owner's moral obligation, but is

[113] *Stack v Dowden* [2007] UKHL 17, [56]. This includes cases where the claimant seeks an interest in property held by two others: e.g. *Wodzicki v Wodzicki* [2017] EWCA Civ 95.
[114] Miles (2023), table 2.
[115] E.g. *Eves v Eves* [1975] 1 WLR 1338; *Grant v Edwards* [1986] Ch 638.
[116] *Curran v Collins* [2015] EWCA Civ 404, [69]–[72].
[117] Cowan et al (2016), 229.

nonetheless problematic: as he puts it, someone who gives a bogus excuse for declining an invitation to a boring party does not thereby indicate an intention to attend.[118] Indeed, it will sometimes be objectively clear from the parties' discussions that the owner has no intention that the other should have a share: if so, clearly no *common* intention can be found.[119]

Lord Bridge's exposition in *Rosset* continued with the possibility of '**inferring**' the required intention:

> In sharp contrast with this situation is the very different one where there is no evidence to support a finding of an agreement or arrangement to share, however reasonable it might have been for the parties to reach such an arrangement if they had applied their minds to the question, and where the court must rely entirely on the conduct of the parties both as the basis from which to infer a common intention to share the property beneficially and as the conduct relied on to give rise to a constructive trust. In this situation direct contributions to the purchase price by the partner who is not the legal owner, whether initially or by payment of mortgage instalments, will readily justify the inference necessary to the creation of a constructive trust. But, as I read the authorities, it is at least extremely doubtful whether anything less will do.

This was bad news for Mrs Rosset. The Rossets had been married for 12 years and had two children. Their newly acquired home was in his sole name, there was no express common intention to share, and she had made no direct financial contribution to the acquisition or renovation of the property. What she had done was to supervise the renovations, carried out decorating work herself daily, and obtained building materials while her husband was working abroad:

> [T]he judge based his inference of a common intention that Mrs Rosset should have a beneficial interest . . . essentially on the basis of what Mrs Rosset did in and about assisting the renovation of the property . . . Yet by itself this activity . . . could not possibly justify any such inference. It was common ground that Mrs Rosset was extremely anxious that the new matrimonial home should be ready for occupation before Christmas if possible. In these circumstances it would seem the most natural thing in the world for any wife, in the absence of her husband abroad, to spend all the time she could spare and to employ any skills she might have, such as the ability to decorate a room, in doing all she could to accelerate progress of the work quite irrespective of any expectation she might have on enjoying a beneficial interest in the property. The judge's view that some of this work was work "upon which she could not reasonably have been expected to embark unless she was to have an interest in the house" seems to me, with respect, quite untenable.

In *Stack v Dowden*, Lord Walker opined that whether or not Lord Bridge's doubts about the adequacy of anything other than direct financial contributions were rightly held at that time, 'the law has moved on'.[120] Baroness Hale acknowledged that Lord Bridge might arguably have set the hurdle 'rather too high'.[121] They did not directly revisit the issue in *Jones v Kernott*, but commentators seized upon the fact that the exposition of the law in paras 51–2 of their judgment, extracted at 7.2.4.b, simply states that the parties' common intention

[118] Gardner (1993), 265.

[119] E.g. *Geary v Rankine* [2012] EWCA Civ 555; *Curran v Collins* [2015] EWCA Civ 404, from [69].

[120] [2007] UKHL 17, [26]; see also [34]–[36].

[121] Ibid, [63]; see also dicta in *Abbott v Abbott* [2007] UKPC 53.

may be inferred from their *conduct*, noting Baroness Hale's expansive list of factors in para 69 of *Stack* to herald a liberalized trusts regime.[122] Yet neither *Stack* nor *Jones* was a sole-name case, so the necessarily obiter remarks provide slim foundations for reversing the well-established *Rosset* position.

Later sole-owner cases appear to accept that it is appropriate to look at the parties' wider conduct—not just direct financial contributions to acquisition—in seeking to infer their common intention at the acquisition stage.[123] The *Rosset* line is not therefore a rule of law that *bars* looking at such evidence—what matters is what inferences the judges feel able, on the balance of probabilities, to draw from it. And so, crucially, we need to look at the *results* of those cases, which provide little evidence that the law has loosened up in practice. Successful claimants have made direct financial contributions to the acquisition of the property[124] or something very close to it, such as the significant financial and labour contribution towards the creation of a dwelling from a barn in *Aspden v Elvy*—contributions of a rather different order of magnitude from Mrs Rosset's activities.[125] There can be very little hope that *purely* domestic contributions, such as looking after the home and caring for children,[126] or general financial contributions to some household costs that are not required to enable the other party to pay the mortgage,[127] will generate a beneficial share. This is because the sole-name cases are as strict as *Fowler v Barron*—here to the *disadvantage* of the party who made little or no financial contribution—in identifying evidence from which a common intention rebutting the relevant presumption may in practice properly be inferred.[128]

For example, in *James v Thomas*,[129] the parties had cohabited for 15 years in a property previously acquired in his sole name by Mr Thomas with mortgage finance. Miss James worked unpaid in his business throughout the relationship (that work including heavy labour[130]), only latterly becoming a formal business partner. The parties were reliant on the business for their livelihood; the mortgage and all outgoings on the property were paid from the business profits. When their relationship ended, Miss James claimed a beneficial share of the home.[131] The court found no evidence of an express common intention to share the beneficial title: Mr Thomas's remarks (regarding improvement to the property) that 'this will benefit us both' were construed as statements regarding shared use and enjoyment of the property, not shared beneficial ownership.[132] And, despite accepting that it was entitled to survey the parties' whole course of dealing for this purpose, the court declined to infer an intention to share, despite Miss James's substantial non-financial contribution to the

[122] E.g. Gardner (2008), (2013); Dixon (2012); Sloan (2015a), who expresses some caution; Lees (2012); Newnham (2013).

[123] E.g. *Curran v Collins* [2015] EWCA Civ 404, [44]–[50].

[124] E.g. *Abbott v Abbott* [2007] UKPC 53; *CPS v Piper* [2011] EWHC 3570; *Rubin v Dweck* [2012] BPIR 854; *Lord Chancellor v Farooqi* [2018] EWHC 3638; *Oberman v Collins* [2020] EWHC 3533.

[125] [2012] EWHC 1387.

[126] *Burns v Burns* [1984] Ch 317; *R v Thayaparan* [2019] EWCA Crim 247 (confiscation proceedings), from [22]. Cf Gardner's optimism (2013) and Mee's more sanguine view (2011). *Bank of Scotland v Brogan* [2012] NICh 21 is best viewed as a case of express intention, essentially corroborated by other factors, including significant financial contribution to extension of the property; thanks to John Mee for discussion of this.

[127] Cf *Webster v Webster* [2008] EWHC 31, [33]: common intention to share inferred, without close analysis, from indirect contributions to general family expenditure, in a case ultimately decided on a completely different basis; cf *Le Foe v Le Foe* [2001] 2 FLR 970: such contributions sufficing if they *enable* the other to pay the mortgage.

[128] Piška (2009), 229.

[129] [2007] EWCA Civ 1212.

[130] Cf *Eves v Eves* [1975] 1 WLR 1338.

[131] She was in any event entitled to her share of the business assets on dissolution of the partnership.

[132] [2007] EWCA Civ 1212, [33].

business (and so, it might be argued, indirectly to the mortgage repayments) and to the property's renovation.[133]

James v Thomas **[2007] EWCA Civ 1212**

SIR JOHN CHADWICK:

27. Although it is possible to envisage circumstances in which the fact that one party began to make contributions to capital repayments due under a mortgage might evidence an agreement that that party was to have a share in the property, the circumstances of this case are not of that nature. On the facts found by the judge, the only source of funds to meet Mr Thomas' commitments under the mortgage, as well as all other household and personal expenses, was the receipts of the business. While the parties were living together they were dependent on the success of the business to meet their outgoings. It was not at all surprising that, in the early days of their relationship, Miss James should do what she could to ensure that the business prospered. That is not to undervalue her contribution, which, as Mr Thomas recognised, was substantial. But it is to recognise that what she was doing gives rise to no inference that the parties had agreed (or had reached a common understanding) that she was to have a share in the property: *what she was doing was wholly explicable on other grounds*. [Emphasis added]

Similarly, in *Morris v Morris*[134] a wife unsuccessfully claimed a beneficial interest in the family farm, owned at law by the husband's mother.[135] Here too the Court of Appeal emphasized the need for 'exceptional circumstances'[136] before any common intention to share beneficial ownership could be inferred from conduct, particularly conduct after the property had already been acquired. Sir Peter Gibson talked in terms of conduct which 'can only be explained on the footing that [the claimant] believes that she was acquiring an interest in the land'.[137] The wife's apparently full (and unpaid) involvement in a joint business venture on the farm was insufficient. And in *Dobson v Griffey*: 'Her labour and commitment were understandable in the context of their relationship and their intended long-term future together with children . . . It is unnecessary to suppose some quasi-commercial bargain between them to explain it.'[138]

The courts have also been reluctant to infer a common intention to share beneficial ownership where the parties were cohabiting when the sole-name property was purchased. In *Thomson v Humphrey*,[139] the court emphasized that previous properties had also been held in the defendant's sole name, and attached significant weight to a cohabitation agreement confirming that the claimant had no interest but which she had refused to sign; the unsigned agreement made it harder to show that her partner, the legal owner, intended that she should have a share at all. But even without that striking feature, for a home to be bought in the name of just one party *during* a relationship strongly suggests there is no common

[133] Ibid, [19]. This same caution denied the woman's claim in *Aspden v Elvy* [2012] EWHC 1387, [110]–[112]. The adequacy, in principle, of the woman's activities to infer an intention in *Geary v Rankine* [2012] EWCA Civ 555 was not argued, the case failing on the basis that the man clearly had no intention that she should share.

[134] [2008] EWCA Civ 257.

[135] The wife's case was made more difficult to sustain by the various business and property-holding structures between the parties.

[136] At [23]. [137] [2008] EWCA Civ 257, [25]; see also *Walsh v Singh* [2009] EWHC 3219.

[138] [2018] EWHC 1117. [139] [2009] EWHC 3576.

intention to share beneficial ownership. Even if that legal sole ownership is imposed by external circumstances—for example, a mortgagee's insistence that only the creditworthy party take on the responsibility—the courts will not readily make assumptions about what the parties would have intended about the beneficial ownership in other circumstances and so infer an intention to share after all.[140]

For very different reasons, a common intention to share may seem implausible in the context of controlling, abusive relationships where the property is in the sole name of the perpetrator.[141]

Acquisition step 2: detrimental reliance

If a common intention to share beneficial ownership can be found, the claimant must then show detrimental reliance on that intention. Some decisions—in which the claimants made financial contributions that would readily suffice—are silent on the issue. But, absent the formal requirements for an express trust's having been executed, the continuing need for detrimental reliance to secure the intention to share is confirmed by Court of Appeal authority.[142] As noted at 7.2.4.b, it would be extraordinary—particularly in a sole-name case—if the requirement had evaporated from the law without explanation.

Where common intention is *inferred* from direct financial contributions to acquisition of the property or something akin to it, those contributions also readily constitute detrimental reliance. But in *express* common intention cases, the claimant must show detrimental reliance separately. In two recent cases, agreeing to go along with sole-name legal ownership instead of joint names was found to constitute detrimental reliance.[143] Indeed, a wider range of conduct has sometimes been admitted as detrimental reliance in *express* intention cases than would provide a basis for *inferring* an intention to share.[144] But while financial contribution, direct or indirect, to the purchase is not required, the courts have commonly required that the conduct constituting detrimental reliance be 'referable' to the acquisition of an interest in the property, and not something that the claimant would have done anyway. This approach effectively excludes 'normal' domestic contributions to family life from consideration. More recent cases have taken this harder line, excluding even quite extensive domestic and business conduct that was explicable for other reasons:

James v Thomas [2007] EWCA Civ 1212

36. It would unreal to think that Miss James did what she did in reliance on such a promise. The true position . . . is that she worked in the business, and contributed her labour to the improvements to the property, because she and Mr Thomas were making their life together as

[140] Cf *Thompson v Hurst* [2012] EWCA Civ 1752: an express common intention to share was found, but the court would not infer an intention to share *equally*, despite the mortgagee's position having prevented joint-names purchase.

[141] *Graham-York v York* [2015] EWCA Civ 72, [16].

[142] E.g. *James v Thomas* [2007] EWCA Civ 1212; *Curran v Collins* [2015] EWCA Civ 404, [77]–[78]. See generally, Mee (2011), 192.

[143] *O'Neill v Holland* [2020] EWCA Civ 1583; *Hussain v Hussain* [2021] EWHC 1954.

[144] E.g. *Grant v Edwards* [1986] Ch 638, 657A–B, per Browne-Wilkinson V-C, effectively requiring the defendant in an express case to show that the claimant's conduct was *not* detrimental reliance—see also *Wayling v Jones* [1995] 2 FLR 1029; cf the stricter approach of Nourse LJ in *Grant*, at 648G–H; *Hammond v Mitchell* [1991] 1 WLR 1127; *Eves v Eves* [1975] 1 WLR 1338; *Cox v Jones* [2004] EWHC 1486.

> man and wife. The Cottage was their home: the business was their livelihood. *It is a mistake to think that the motives which lead parties in such a relationship to act as they do are necessarily attributable to pecuniary self-interest.* [Emphasis added]

This approach may be said to privilege the mercenary-minded over those who simply get on with life.[145]

Quantification

If intention and detrimental reliance are proved, the court moves to quantifying the parties' beneficial shares. As discussed at 7.2.4.b, here the *Stack/Jones* approach prescribes that if the parties have no actual intention (expressed or inferred) the court may impute an intention or, in other words, impose a fair outcome. Reported outcomes reveal a spectrum from the full partnership of marriage where a 50:50 outcome is likely[146] (though not inevitable[147]) through cases where the parties' domestic relationship is considered less of a joint venture,[148] to increasingly more business-like cases where the property is purchased as an investment[149] or for some other reason 'mercenary considerations' are found to be 'to the fore'.[150] Even an investment case can, on the right facts, be found to justify 50:50 shares.[151] But the closer the case to this end of the spectrum, the closer the outcomes to parties' financial contributions, even to the point of finding sole beneficial ownership in the legal non-owner who provided all of the funding.[152] The judge in *Aspden v Elvy* can be forgiven for regarding the outcome of his deliberations as somewhat 'arbitrary',[153] given the absence of guiding principles determining the content of 'fairness' at this stage.

Before exploring criticisms of the common intention constructive trust, we complete the picture of land ownership by examining a closely related claim that may also be available.

7.2.5 PROPRIETARY ESTOPPEL

The ingredients of a proprietary estoppel claim are superficially similar to common intention constructive trusts and the courts often elide the two,[154] but there are key differences.[155] Indeed, it has been remarked that proprietary estoppel is generally the lesser remedy, in terms of likely outcomes for claimants.[156]

[145] Compare Gray and Gray's analysis of more generous, earlier case law: (2009), 7.3.46.

[146] E.g. *Abbott v Abbott* [2007] UKPC 53; *CPS v Piper* [2011] EWHC 3570; *Rubin v Dweck* [2012] BPIR 854; *Bank of Scotland v Brogan* [2012] NICh 21.

[147] E.g. *R v Thayaparan* [2019] EWCA Crim 247; *Amin v Amin* [2020] EWHC 2675 (religious-only marriage); *Hussain v Hussain* [2021] EWHC 1954.

[148] E.g. the platonic flat-sharers in *Gallarotti v Sebastianelli* [2012] EWCA Civ 865; but see also the cohabitants in *Thompson v Hurst* [2012] EWCA Civ 1752, and the on-off cohabitants in *Aspden v Elvy* [2012] EWHC 1387.

[149] *Agarwala v Agarwala* [2013] EWCA Civ 1763, [13]; cf *Marr v Collie* [2017] UKPC 17, remitted to the local court for decision on the facts.

[150] E.g. *Graham-York v York* [2015] EWCA Civ 72, [16].

[151] *Oberman v Collins* [2020] EWHC 3533, where the court decided the case on a 'whole portfolio' basis, rather than asset by asset.

[152] *Agarwala v Agarwala* [2013] EWCA Civ 1763. [153] [2012] EWHC 1387, [128].

[154] Lord Walker in *Stack v Dowden* [2007] UKHL 17 retracted from that position: [37]. Cf *Dobson v Griffey* [2018] EWHC 1117, [25].

[155] For a useful survey, see *Culliford v Thorpe* [2018] EWHC 426, [68]–[69].

[156] Lord Walker, *Stack* [2007] UKHL 17, [37]; *Q v Q* [2008] EWHC 1874, [113].

It must be shown: (i) that the legal owner has made some representation, assurance, or promise to the claimant that the latter has or will have an interest in or right over property. That interest/right may be something less than beneficial ownership, for example secure occupation rights—so estoppel may succeed where a claim based on common intention constructive trust would fail for want of an intention to share the beneficial title.[157] The claimant must: (ii) have relied on that to their detriment; and (iii) the circumstances must make the legal owner's later repudiation of the assurance or promise unconscionable.[158] Repudiation will usually be unconscionable, but the particular factual context, as it has developed since the assurance/promise was given, may mean otherwise; we say no more about this here.[159] The court then: (iv) determines what remedy is 'necessary to satisfy the equity' that has arisen—to 'undo' the unconscionability. It is often said that those ingredients are interconnected, with unconscionability the overarching issue.[160]

7.2.5.a Finding an assurance, representation, or promise

The defendant must have offered some assurance or made some representation regarding the claimant's current entitlements in relation to the former's property or made some promise as regards a future entitlement (e.g. that the property would be left to the latter in the former's will).

As in the constructive trust context, judges have distinguished between 'domestic' and 'commercial' contexts in proprietary estoppel cases[161]—not to decide *what* rules to apply, but *how* the rules apply in the particular factual situations that arise:[162]

Yeoman's Row Management Ltd v Cobbe [2008] UKHL 55

LORD WALKER:

68. . . . In the commercial context, the claimant is typically a business person with access to legal advice and what he or she is expecting to get is a *contract*. In the domestic or family context, the typical claimant is not a business person and is not receiving legal advice. What he or she wants and expects to get is an *interest* in immovable property, often for long-term occupation as a home. The focus is not on intangible legal rights but on the tangible property which he or she expects to get. The typical domestic claimant does not stop to reflect (until disappointed expectations lead to litigation) whether some further legal transaction (such as a grant by deed, or the making of a will or codicil) is necessary to complete the promised title.[163]

The nature of domestic cases is such that it is more likely to be reasonable for parties to rely on informal statements where a business person should insist on legal formality. Writing extra-judicially, Lord Neuberger has noted that emotional or social factors in domestic relationships may impede parties from insisting that any assurance/promise be formalized, and that it would be 'unreal' to expect that they should. He argues that there is therefore more

157 E.g. *Southwell v Blackburn* [2014] EWCA Civ 1347.

158 *Guest v Guest* [2022] UKSC 27, [8], [70].

159 Ibid, [74].

160 E.g. *Davies v Davies* [2016] EWCA Civ 463, [38].

161 Cf *Marr v Collie* [2017] UKPC 17. For criticism in the estoppel context, see Mee (2009), 374; Hopkins (2011).

162 Hopkins (2011), 176.

163 See also Lord Neuberger, *Thorner v Major* [2009] UKHL 18, [96]–[97].

room for proprietary estoppel to operate in domestic cases than in the commercial context, where parties can be expected formally to protect their legal position rather than rely on informal statements.[164]

In domestic cases, the courts may more readily find that an assurance/promise was intended to be taken seriously and that the claimant's reliance on it was therefore reasonable. As Lord Walker remarked in *Thorner v Major*, whether an assurance/promise has sufficient clarity is 'hugely dependent on context': it need only be 'clear enough'.[165] In *Thorner*, the claimant had worked unpaid for decades on his taciturn cousin's farm, the cousin having given several somewhat oblique, allusive indications that he would leave the farm to the claimant. He died intestate, leaving the claimant with nothing. In the context of the parties' relationship and the deceased's character, those remarks and conduct were regarded as sufficiently clear to underpin a proprietary estoppel claim to the farm, a finding that would never be made in a commercial case. Proprietary estoppel, like the common intention constructive trust, is therefore responsive to the familial context.

Nevertheless, the assurance/promise underpinning the claim must actually exist and be reasonably understood by the claimant—in the particular factual context—to be intended to be acted on. Even in a domestic case, the assurance must relate to a particular asset or ascertainable pool of assets.[166] A general promise that the respondent will support the claimant or that the claimant will be 'financially' secure in the future is not enough,[167] though an assurance that the claimant 'would always have a home and be secure in this one' was.[168]

7.2.5.b Detrimental reliance

The detrimental reliance requirement raises problems similar to those experienced in constructive trust cases for claimants who have made domestic, rather than financial, contributions to family life. Non-financial contributions are not necessarily insufficient;[169] giving up secure accommodation elsewhere is a good example.[170] But, while the evaluation of detrimental reliance in the domestic context has been held not to be 'an exercise in financial accounting',[171] it may be hard to show that domestic contributions were not simply explicable as a normal aspect of family life (often in return for which the claimant received a benefit such as rent-free accommodation). As such, they will not constitute detrimental reliance on the assurance.[172] However, such contributions may suffice if, the assurance having been made, the claimant would not then have continued to make them had the assurance then been withdrawn.[173]

7.2.5.c Remedying the unconscionability of repudiation

Proprietary estoppel diverges from constructive trust on deciding what remedy is necessary to satisfy the equity, first, in the wide range of remedial tools available to the court. Given

[164] Neuberger (2009), 542, contrasting the decisions in *Yeoman's Row Property Ltd v Cobbe* [2008] UKHL 55 and *Thorner v Major* [2009] UKHL 18.

[165] [2009] UKHL 18, [56]; e.g. *Liden v Burton* [2016] EWCA Civ 275.

[166] *Jennings v Rice* [2002] EWCA Civ 159; *Thorner v Major* [2009] UKHL 18.

[167] *Lissimore v Downing* [2003] 2 FLR 308; *Layton v Martin* [1986] 2 FLR 227.

[168] *Southwell v Blackburn* [2014] EWCA Civ 1347; see also *Liden v Burton* [2016] EWCA Civ 275.

[169] *Greasley v Cooke* [1980] 1 WLR 1306; *Campbell v Griffin* [2001] EWCA Civ 990.

[170] *Southwell v Blackburn* [2014] EWCA Civ 1347, [17].

[171] Ibid, [18].

[172] *Lissimore v Downing* [2003] 2 FLR 308; *Coombes v Smith* [1986] 1 WLR 808; cf *Grant v Edwards* [1986] Ch 638, 656; *Henry v Henry* [2010] UKPC 3.

[173] *Wayling v Jones* [1995] 2 FLR 1029.

that the assurance or promise may have related to *any* sort of interest in or right over property, the court in proprietary estoppel cases is clearly not confined to awarding a beneficial share in the relevant property (as will always arise from a successful common intention constructive trust claim). It can instead award some other sort of interest[174] or monetary compensation,[175] or even conclude that no remedy is required because benefits enjoyed by the claimant during the relationship counterbalance any disadvantage sustained such that the owner's repudiation of the original assurance/promise may, in fact, not be regarded as unconscionable.[176]

But where some remedy is called for, how does the court decide *what* remedy to grant? Here again the two doctrines part company: where constructive trust claimants always obtains the 'commonly intended' beneficial share (of the intended or, failing proof of that, fair quantum), estoppel claimants are not guaranteed to have their expectation met. Recent years had seen a 'lively controversy', at least amongst academics,[177] about the doctrinal basis of proprietary estoppel's remedy: should the court be seeking to meet the claimant's expectation in full, or simply to compensate outstanding losses incurred in reliance on it, or something in between?[178] The question has now been answered (not uncontroversially) by a majority of the Supreme Court in *Guest v Guest*.[179]

Guest v Guest [2022] UKSC 27

LORD BRIGGS:

94. [N]either expectation fulfilment nor detriment compensation is the aim of the remedy. The aim remains what it has always been, namely the prevention or undoing of unconscionable conduct. In many cases, once the equity is established, then the fulfilment of the promise is likely to be the starting point, although considerations of practicality, justice between the parties and fairness to third parties may call for a reduced or different award. And justice between the parties may be affected if the proposed remedy is out of all proportion to the reliant detriment, if that can easily be identified without recourse to minute mathematical calculation, and proper regard is had to non-monetary harm.[180]

Lord Briggs had earlier described the approach to fashioning the remedy thus:

75. The [remedy] stage will normally start with the assumption (not presumption) that the simplest way to remedy the unconscionability constituted by the repudiation is to hold the promisor to the promise. The promisee cannot (and probably would not)

---

174 E.g. the entire freehold: *Pascoe v Turner* [1979] 1 WLR 431; a life interest: *Greasley v Cooke* [1980] 1 WLR 1306; a reversionary interest: *Guest v Guest* [2022] UKSC 27.

175 *Dodsworth v Dodsworth* (1973) 228 EG 1115; *Jennings v Rice* [2002] EWCA Civ 159.

176 *Sledmore v Dalby* (1996) 72 P&CR 196. Unlikely where, e.g., rent-free occupation of the family home was a natural aspect of the parties' personal relationship: *Anaghara v Anaghara* [2020] EWHC 3091; cf approach in *Lissimore v Downing* [2003] 2 FLR 308, [54].

177 Cf [2022] UKSC 27, [52]; see scholarship identified at [170]–[172].

178 For useful discussion, see *Culliford v Thorpe* [2018] EWHC 426, from [70].

179 [2022] UKSC 27. For the start of the controversy, see Lords Leggatt and Stephen's dissent.

180 The majority consider this impossible where the promise and reliance were such as to have had 'whole life' consequences for the claimant: ibid, [72]–[73].

complain, for example, that his detrimental reliance had cost him more than the value of the promise, were it to be fully performed. But the court may have to listen to many other reasons from the promisor (or his executors [where the promisor has died]) why something less than full performance will negate the unconscionability and therefore satisfy the equity. They may be based on one or more of . . . real-life problems . . . [for example, that the parties' relationship has broken down and they cannot be expected to continue to live together in the property; or the promise would not have taken effect until death (which may be many years off), and has been repudiated sooner because the promisor now wishes to benefit other dependants or requires the property to meet his later-life needs; or the property has been sold to a third party[181]]. The court may be invited by the promisor to consider one or more proxies for performance of the promise, such as the transfer of less property than promised or the provision of a monetary equivalent in place of it, or a combination of the two.

7.2.6 CRITICISMS OF THE CURRENT LAW RELATING TO OWNERSHIP OF LAND

The position is at least (or should be[182]) certain where parties have declared their beneficial interests in the required form to create an express trust. But where no such declaration has been made by joint legal owners, the law of implied trusts (and/or proprietary estoppel) must fill the gap to determine their beneficial shares. And sole-name owners may always be vulnerable to attempted claims to beneficial interests or estoppel equities by others. Many commentators have criticized that law as unfair and uncertain, both in terms of the substantive requirements and the result they will—or might—yield in individual cases.[183] Property ownership is now theoretically equally open to all,[184] but the preconditions required for property ownership to arise where there is no express trust may often—certainly in sole-name cases—prevent individuals not engaged in paid employment from acquiring ownership of the assets on which family life is based. Particular problems with common intention constructive trusts arise from the need to base the trust on the parties' intentions regarding property ownership, and—despite dicta in *Stack* and *Jones*—the lower courts' continuing reluctance to infer such intentions from anything other than financial contributions to the acquisition of the property. As more couples cohabit outside marriage/civil partnership,[185] this law acquires increased significance given cohabitants' reliance on the general law to determine the fact of their property.

In this section, we address five inter-linked problems relating particularly to constructive trusts: (i) problems with the starting point for the *Stack/Jones* approach: its empirical basis and its heavy, fortuitous influence on outcomes; (ii) problems surrounding 'intention'; (iii) the scope of detrimental reliance; (iv) the situation of homemakers; and (v) the uncertainty of the law and some of its outcomes.

[181] For this and other examples, see ibid, [16], [32], [47], [62]–[65].

[182] Subject to arguments identified at n 18 previously, and to any claim for equitable accounting or TOLATA compensation for occupation rent: see supplement in the online resources.

[183] For a useful survey pre-*Stack v Dowden*, see Law Com (2006), Part 4. The extent of the post-*Stack* and *Jones* literature does not suggest certainty has been achieved.

[184] Cf wives' historical disabilities, discussed in the supplement to chapter 6 in the online resources.

[185] See 2.2.2.

7.2.6.a The *Stack/Jones* starting point

Doubtful empirical basis

Legal presumptions in these cases fill the gaps where there is no formalized evidence of what parties intended, on the basis that, given circumstance *y*, individuals can (the courts think) generally be expected to intend *x*. We start these cases with a presumption but can rebut it with evidence that the parties actually intended *something* else.[186] If we do not know precisely what that 'something else' was (or they did not get as far as thinking about that detail—here, about the size of the claimant's beneficial interest), we fill that gap with an imputed intention—or decision about what is fair—based on the wider circumstances beyond the basic facts that generated the starting presumption.

In *Stack v Dowden*, both Baroness Hale and Lord Neuberger sought to describe what people may, or may not, be taken to intend in particular circumstances. But, crucially, they offered differing assessments of the same facts.[187] The majority's presumption of beneficial joint tenancy for joint-names cases, reinforced in para 56 of *Jones v Kernott* extracted at 7.2.4.b, assumes that putting the house in joint names is a meaningful and conscious[188] decision denoting a 'joint enterprise' between parties in a 'materially communal relationship'.[189] But as Baroness Hale acknowledged in *Stack*, parties' actions regarding house purchase are not necessarily as deliberate or even voluntary as we might assume:

Stack v Dowden [2007] UKHL 17

BARONESS HALE:

67. This is not to say that the parties invariably have a full understanding of the legal effects of their choice: there is recent empirical evidence from a small scale qualitative study to confirm that they do not [Douglas et al (2007b)]. But that is so whether or not there is an express declaration of trust and no-one thinks that such a declaration can be overturned, except in cases of fraud or mistake . . . Nor do they always have a completely free choice in the matter. Mortgagees used to insist upon the home being put in the name of the person whom they assumed would be the main breadwinner. Nowadays, they tend to think that it is in their best interests that the home be jointly owned and both parties assume joint and several liability for the mortgage. (It is, of course, a matter of indifference to the mortgagee where the beneficial interests lie.) Here again, this factor does not invalidate the parties' choice if there is an express declaration of trust, nor should it automatically count against it where there is none.

However, it is one thing *not to ignore* the fact of purchase in joint names, quite another to *erect a strong presumption* that the parties thereby intended a beneficial joint tenancy. If parties who *expressly* declared a beneficial joint tenancy often fail to appreciate its significance, it is difficult to presume that parties who bought a home together *without* making such a

[186] Cf dicta in *Marr v Collie* [2017] UKPC 17 discussed in the supplement to this chapter in the online resources.

[187] Contrast [2007] UKHL 17, [66]–[67], Baroness Hale with [113]–[116], Lord Neuberger.

[188] *Stack v Dowden* [2007] UKHL 17, [66].

[189] [2011] UKSC 53, [19] and quoting Gardner and Davidson (2011) at [21].

declaration nevertheless intended to create a beneficial joint tenancy or even equal shares as tenants in common, particularly (perhaps) where they contributed different amounts to acquisition.[190] In practice, evidence of clear, *common* intention about property ownership seems scarce:

G. Douglas, J. Pearce, and H. Woodward, 'Money, Property, Cohabitation and Separation: Patterns and Intentions', in J. Miles and R. Probert (eds), *Sharing Lives, Dividing Assets* (Oxford: Hart Publishing, 2009), 159

In our study, we found that the type of ownership of property – joint or sole, joint tenancy or (rarely) tenancy in common – established at the point of purchase was selected for a variety of reasons or no conscious reason at all. Whilst one would expect that cohabitants might have poor recollections of conversations and advice which had taken place several years before they were interviewed, our discussions with practitioners confirmed that, even at the time, most couples are not interested in such matters. Moreover, as some cohabitant respondents explained, a joint meeting with a conveyancer may not be the right time or setting in which to consider coolly how to protect one's individual interests. At the same time, other, more wily (or more astute) cohabitants may be able to mislead partners so that they fail to assert their own interests or may not have any to protect. The complexity of the law and the opacity of the legal jargon may contribute to the parties' lack of understanding of their positions, and explanations written by lawyers for whom such language is commonplace may not be sufficiently clear to overcome the difficulties.

Baroness Hale and Lord Neuberger also attached different significance to parties' money-management practices as reflecting intentions regarding beneficial ownership of the home.[191] Research shows that more spouses than cohabitants pool their resources, but that cohabiting *parents* act more like spouses in their money management than childless cohabitants.[192] That Stack and Dowden, long-term cohabiting parents, did *not* pool their resources may thus seem 'unusual'. However, researchers caution against making assumptions about the nature and commitment of couples' relationships—never mind their intentions regarding ownership of their *home*—from simplistic analysis of their general money management.[193] There are many pragmatic reasons for keeping money separate (e.g. access to extra credit and tax-free allowances, management of personal debts, even sheer inertia) that do not necessarily indicate that parties regard themselves as separate financial entities; as in *Fowler v Barron*, separate bank accounts may conceal a de facto pooling arrangement.[194] Lord Neuberger remarked that 'there is a substantial difference, in law, in commercial terms, in practice, and almost always in terms of value and importance, between ownership of a home and the ownership of a bank account or, indeed, furniture, furnishings and other chattels'.[195] For him, parties' treatment of their household finances, whether pooled or separate, does not necessarily cast light on their intentions regarding home ownership where the parties have made

[190] Lord Neuberger: [2007] UKHL 17, [113].
[191] Compare [2007] UKHL 17, [86]–[92] and [131]–[137], [143].
[192] Vogler (2009); Kan and Laurie (2014).
[193] Barlow, Burgoyne, and Smithson (2007), 62–3; Fisher and Low (2018a).
[194] Burgoyne and Sonnenberg (2009).
[195] [2007] UKHL 17, [133].

different financial contributions to its purchase. Conversely, if they generally keep their finances separate but put the *home* into joint names (as Stack and Dowden had), that might suggest they had different intentions regarding the home. But even there, Lord Neuberger would be cautious about drawing any inference about joint ownership;[196] as Baroness Hale notes in the extract here, the selection of joint names (or sole name) may have been dictated by the lender.

Empirical research can improve our understanding of how people behave in relation to their property and finances, and what they think about them, and so inform courts and policy-makers. Real life is more complicated than neat legal presumptions can accommodate. Gillian Douglas and colleagues drew the following conclusions from their study of cohabitants' property disputes, having analysed their data in light of Baroness Hale's 'paragraph 69' factors:

G. Douglas, J. Pearce, and H. Woodward, 'Money, Property, Cohabitation and Separation: Patterns and Intentions', in J. Miles and R. Probert (eds), *Sharing Lives, Dividing Assets* (Oxford: Hart Publishing, 2009), 159

Couples' relationships vary infinitely, in terms of why they cohabit initially and why they remain cohabiting, their economic and domestic positions, their personalities, the dynamics of their relationship, the changes they undergo as life proceeds, and how far they can or do make financial contributions to keeping the relationship going and acquiring property during it. The way they hold property, and the way they organise their finances, as our study and others' demonstrate, may in turn reflect this myriad of circumstances and does not always conform to what one might logically or rationally predict or assume. It is arguable whether, on the breakdown of their relationship, a couple should be held to arrangements which have arisen during their relationship in response to circumstances as if they were by common intention.

Baroness Hale's list of factors was intended to capture and encapsulate this variety and to indicate which elements might be relevant to establishing the parties' 'true intentions', but our study gives little encouragement to the belief that it will provide a clear pointer towards those cases which are 'unusual' enough to warrant departure from the legal title. On the basis of our findings, we are more inclined to agree with the view of Lord Neuberger:

> 'To say that factors such as a long relationship, children, a joint bank account, and sharing daily outgoings of themselves are enough, or even of central importance, appears to me not merely wrong in principle, but a recipe for uncertainty, subjectivity, and a long and expensive examination of the facts.'

The starting point's fortuitous influence on outcome

Following on from this, we should notice how the outcome of a case can be determined more or less by happenstance—disconnected from the dynamics of the parties' relationship—thanks to two factors. First, absent proof of an *express* common intention at variance with the starting point, the relative difficulty of *inferring* some other intention—given the courts' insistence on evidence of conduct that can *only* be explained on the basis that different beneficial ownership was intended—gives the starting point (joint names or

[196] Ibid, [134].

sole name) an 'anchoring' effect. Secondly, however, as just discussed, the reasons (such as they may be) why the property was held in joint names or the sole name of one party may have no bearing on the parties' true intentions (see further 7.2.6.b). And, as we explore at 7.2.6.d, the net result may bear particularly harshly on claimants in sole-name cases who have made no relevant contribution:

J. Miles, 'The Politics and Principle of Pursuing "Fairness" in Family Property Matters', in J. Gardner et al (eds), *Politics, Policy and the Private Law: Tort, Land & Equity* (Oxford: Hart Publishing, 2023)

The party who has made no financial contribution to acquisition in a joint-names case may well hold fast to their half-share, it being clear . . . that the mere fact of the other's greater financial contribution to acquisition cannot, itself, justify an inference of the required intention [to depart from joint beneficial ownership]. But an *identically situated party* in a case indistinguishable from that joint-names case save for the fact of a sole-proprietor will emerge empty-handed. . . .

The stark difference of outcome in otherwise identical joint- and sole-name cases is all the more concerning to a family lawyer (at least) because it may often be said to turn on happenstance. Certainly, some parties do make careful decisions on this matter. But whether the property is in joint-names is frequently *not* the result of an informed decision by the parties to elect that mode of property-holding for their shared home. . . . And what of . . . the cases where one party moves into the other's pre-acquired (sole-name) home? What if that property was already mortgage-free at that point? What if it was the mortgagee who had insisted on joint names? Or had been prepared to accept only a sole-name application? Or some other perceived convenience or external constraint effectively dictated the choice made? . . .

But whatever the reason . . . the state of the proprietorship may not be reliably informative about the parties' conception of their *relationship* . . . [T]he result is that anyone who wants the parties' relationship to be the central determining factor will be disappointed by many sole-name cases [in particular].

7.2.6.b The problem of intention

Parties' intentions about beneficial ownership are central to the law of trusts. But proving their intentions can be problematic in this family context once we leave the predictable ground of express trusts[197] and try to navigate through the altogether more tricky forensic terrain of common intention constructive trusts. It is hard enough to discern what each party individually might have intended, harder to divine *commonly* held intentions, assuming that they ever existed.[198] But simply abandoning that inquiry, as some would wish,[199] in favour of 'imputing' to the parties an intention that they never had, or simply deciding for them what is 'fair', would take us into doctrinally troubling waters—at least, if that task were notionally undertaken within the law of trusts.[200]

197 Subject to factors noted previously at n 18.

198 Probert (2008b), 345.

199 Notably Gardner (2013) and, in relation to estoppel, (2014).

200 Mee (2011), (2013); see further 7.2.6.e.

Finding express evidence of common intention

Happy families rarely think about what each individual's entitlements in relation to the home may or may not be, and are even less likely to discuss them expressly:

Lloyds Bank v Rosset [1991] 1 AC 107, 127–8

LORD BRIDGE:

Spouses living in amity will not normally think it necessary to formulate or define their respective interests in property in any precise way. The expectation of parties to every happy marriage is that they will share the practical benefits of occupying the matrimonial home whoever owns it. But this is something quite distinct from sharing the beneficial interest in the property asset which the matrimonial home represents. These considerations give rise to special difficulties for judges who are called on to resolve a dispute between spouses who have parted and are at arm's length as to what their common intention or understanding with respect to interests in property was at a time when they were still living as a united family and acquiring a matrimonial home in the expectation of living in it together indefinitely.

One judge has described as 'grotesque' the idea of 'a normal married couple spending the long winter evenings hammering out agreements about their possessions'.[201] But failure to devote at least one or two evenings to that exercise may cause uncertainty and insecurity in the longer term, especially within non-formalized relationships given the lack of remedies on relationship breakdown. These cases can devolve into a 'painfully detailed retrospect':

Hammond v Mitchell [1991] 1 WLR 1127 (Fam Div), 1139

WAITE J:

The primary emphasis accorded by the law in cases of this kind to express discussions between the parties ("however imperfectly remembered and however imprecise their terms") means that the tenderest exchanges of a common law courtship may assume an unforeseen significance many years later when they are brought under equity's microscope and subjected to an analysis under which many thousands of pounds of value may be liable to turn on fine questions as to whether the relevant words were spoken in earnest or in dalliance and with or without representational intent. This requires that the express discussions to which the court's initial inquiries will be addressed should be pleaded in the greatest detail, both as to language and as to circumstance.

Proof of an express common intention different from the starting point can therefore be hard to establish.

[201] *Pettitt v Pettitt* [1970] AC 777, 810.

The subjective and gendered nature of intention

But *inferring* an actual common intention is also not straightforward. Several items on Baroness Hale's para 69 list are inherently subjective: for example, the 'nature of the parties' relationship'; the parties' 'individual characters and personalities'. In neither case is it clear what specific issue she has in mind and what, if anything, each might suggest about the parties' intentions about the ownership of their home.[202] All depends on the judge's analysis of the facts and their decision about what inferences regarding the parties' intentions may properly be drawn from them, rendering outcomes unpredictable, and quite possibly unrelated to whatever the parties actually did intend.[203]

Anne Bottomley has argued that 'intentions' are often construed differently by men and women, creating an emotional (if not also economic) vulnerability for women.[204] She bases her argument on an analysis of reported cases:[205]

A. Bottomley, 'Self and Subjectivities: Languages of Claim in Property Law',
(1993) 20 *Journal of Law and Society* 56, 61–3

Evidence given in [*Lloyds Bank v Rosset*] is not, in my opinion, unusual and illustrates this point:

> *As soon as we heard he was likely to get the money, we looked round, looked for a suitable home for us and children. I always understood we were going to share whatever we had, big or little. We always discussed it as being ours. The only discussion was in very general terms. We needed a house; we would go out and look for one we could own as a couple for a family. When we found [the house], he said he was glad he would be able to provide a proper home, a place where we could be secure. I understood it would be jointly ours. He'd always indicated it would be a joint venture. Everything we did in the past had been jointly done. If you live with someone, you don't 'dissect'. It was the accepted thing.*

This was enough for the trial judge and Court of Appeal, but the more 'orthodox' Lord Bridge was less easily satisfied:

He wanted explicit evidence that there was an agreement about ownership.

> *I pause to observe that neither a common intention by spouses that a house is to be renovated as a 'joint venture' nor a common intention that the house is to be shared by parents and children as the family home throws any light on their intentions with respect to beneficial ownership of the property.*

[She also quotes the extract of Lord Bridge's judgment, set out towards the start of 7.2.6.b.]

. . . It seems to me that this is not only a requirement of a certain jurisprudential approach but also a mode of reasoning and language use which is more conducive to men than women. This may in part be due to material factors and differences in socio-economic

[202] See Lord Neuberger's analysis: [2007] UKHL 17, [131]–[139]; and Douglas et al (2009).
[203] See Mee (2012), 176–7, criticizing this process.
[204] Bottomley (2006).
[205] Probert (2001) cautions against drawing generalizations from this source.

strengths and roles, but evidence drawn from psychoanalytical material would suggest that this division derives from the construction of gender identity. In other words, it is far more deeply embedded than a simple analysis of economic difference and consequent relative power relations would reveal.

. . . There is some evidence from the case material to suggest that women too often read silence as positive assent and lack of specificity as covering a number of issues with equal firmness rather than evading the particular issue.[206]

There is also evidence of the great difficulty some women experience in raising issues about property as well as their difficulty in persuading their partners to confront the issue through discussions.

The high hurdle for claimants in sole-name cases

The courts continue to be conservative in finding a common intention that the claimant should have a share in sole-name cases. Yet as Simon Gardner once observed,[207] what is odd is not so much the refusal to infer a common intention to share from non-financial contributions in those cases, but rather that the courts should be so quick to assume the existence of such an intention where there is a direct financial contribution to property acquisition. Such contributions might equally be motivated by other intentions, yet there the law assumes 'pecuniary self-interest'.[208] The otherwise conservative approach deprives many claimants of a share where either the intention to share might well have existed (albeit unexpressed and not evidenced by sufficiently probative conduct) or where no intention was held at all, because normal people in intimate relationships seldom consider *beneficial ownership* of their home. It may simply be that we cannot expect property law to provide 'fair' outcomes that respond to the economic situation of vulnerable individuals in some of these cases.

Abandoning intention?

While Bottomley would nevertheless retain a concept of intention in this context, other commentators have argued that intention provides the wrong starting point in the family sphere. The focus should instead be on the parties' relationship:

S. Gardner, 'Rethinking Family Property', (1993) 109 *Law Quarterly Review* 263, 282–3

A doctrine centred on the parties' own thinking ostensibly takes its stand on the recognisable individualist platform that the law should not impose obligations on persons other than by their consent. However, it has long been a commonplace that palpable thinking on the subject of property rights is unlikely to be forthcoming on the part of those who are emotionally committed to one another. So if the true facts are adhered to, it is natural that individualist doctrines will give a remedy only infrequently in such cases.

A doctrine centred on the fact of the relationship would allow the law to bypass such specific reference to the parties' thinking, and so give remedies more freely—as indeed seems to be the courts' instinct. The challenge now is to point to some defensible analysis which proceeds on the strength of the parties' relationship rather than of their thinking. . . . [One]

206 E.g. *Dobson v Griffey* [2018] EWHC 1117, [54], [59].

207 Gardner (1993), 264–5; cf his more recent writing.

208 *James v Thomas* [2007] EWCA Civ 1212.

possible analysis . . . argues that in at least some cases, the intrinsic logic of trust and collaboration is that the parties should be seen not as keeping separate accounts, . . . but as pooling their efforts and their rewards: each operating on joint behalf of both. Being thus in effect mutual fiduciaries, they would hold the relevant property on a trust whose obligations follow from the ideas of trust and collaboration: either, simply, to share the property equally, or to provide for the adequate future support of each.

Following *Stack v Dowden*, Gardner refined this approach to argue that the court's task in implied trust cases is to 'effectuate the implications of the parties' relationship'. Thus, where the relationship is found to be 'materially communal'—as it was in *Fowler v Barron*[209]—the parties pooling their financial and other resources in a common endeavour in life, the outcome should be equal sharing of the beneficial interest; otherwise, as in *Stack v Dowden*, a resulting trust analysis should determine the parties' shares.[210] Attractive as this approach may seem, it suffers from empirical and evidential problems similar to the current intention-based test, given its reliance on judicial characterization of the parties' relationship. And as John Mee has observed:[211]

The essential problem is that an approach which conscientiously focuses on genuine intentions would provide a remedy in a very limited set of circumstances, while an approach which moves beyond real intentions seems to involve impermissible judicial law-making.

7.2.6.c The problem of detrimental reliance

The law regarding detrimental reliance in both common intention constructive trusts and proprietary estoppel has been accused of gender bias, to the potential disadvantage of both female and male claimants, in generally requiring 'conduct on which the [claimant] could not reasonably have been expected to embark, unless she was to have an interest in the house'.[212] So how do the courts construe parties' conduct?

L. Flynn and A. Lawson, 'Gender, Sexuality and the Doctrine of Detrimental Reliance', (1995) 3 *Feminist Legal Studies* 105, 116–18

In their construction of normality, the decisions of the courts display the tenacious hold of the 'separate spheres' ideology [i.e. that woman's place is in the home, and man's place out in the labour market]. All the behaviour which is placed in the realm of the domestic, no matter how arduous, will not amount to detriment because it can be expected of any woman in an intimate relationship with a man. Behaviour which takes the [female] claimant outside the domestic realm is categorised as abnormal, and, in order to explain it, must be placed in

[209] [2008] EWCA Civ 377.

[210] Gardner (2008), (2013), and Gardner with Davidson (2011), (2012); see also Harding (2009) on the communitarian aspects of *Stack v Dowden*; Newnham (2013).

[211] (2012), 179; see also (2011), 191–2.

[212] *Grant v Edwards* [1986] Ch 638, 648G–H per Nourse LJ; cf the more generous test at 657A–B, per Browne-Wilkinson LJ and the reasoning in *Wayling v Jones* [1995] 2 FLR 1029.

the context of a market-like transaction giving rise to a property interest [rather than the product of love or desire to live in a comfortable home]. According to the authorities one cannot expect women, out of the love they have for their partners or of the desire to live in a comfortable place, to pay towards mortgage instalments.[213] Nor is it reasonable to expect to them to spend small sums on improvements, at least when those small sums represent a quarter of all their worldly wealth and their partner is a comparatively rich man.[214] A woman cannot be reasonably expected to wield 14-lb. sledge-hammers[215] or work cement mixers[216] out of love or the desire for more pleasant surroundings. Prompted by such motives, however, it is reasonable to expect women to leave their husbands, move in with their lovers, bear their babies, refrain from seeking employment,[217] wallpaper, paint and generally decorate and design their lovers' houses, and to organize builders working on those same houses, even when this includes the purchase and delivery of building materials.[218] In order to succeed, female claimants must show that they "did much more than most women would do",[219] or rather that they did more than the judges would expect most women to do. If the claimant's conduct is of a type regarded by judges as "the most natural thing in the world for a wife"[220] to have done, she will not succeed. The use of the stereotype as a norm, from which deviation has to be established, is an almost inevitable consequence of adopting Nourse LJ's test [in *Grant v Edwards*]. [Footnotes from the original]

Similarly, as Lawson observes,[221] men may not be regarded as incurring detriment by undertaking stereotypically 'male' tasks, such as gardening, DIY, and house decoration.[222] How the courts would react to the male partner in a mixed-sex relationship who undertook childcare and looked after the house while his partner went out to work remains to be seen.[223] More problematic and revealing for this test are same-sex relationships. *Wayling v Jones*,[224] a proprietary estoppel case that long predates civil partnership and same-sex marriage,[225] involved a 20-year-long gay partnership, in which the younger man (Wayling) acted as the other's companion and gave him substantial professional assistance (as a trained chef) in running his hotel and restaurant businesses.

L. Flynn and A. Lawson, 'Gender, Sexuality and the Doctrine of Detrimental Reliance', (1995) 3 *Feminist Legal Studies* 105, 118–19

Homosexuality is a troubling presence in such a scheme. One of the problems with same-sex sexual relations is that they call into question the inevitability of basic social norms which underlie patriarchy. While this is not to suggest that homosexuality cannot be appropriated by patriarchal modes of representation, homosexuality is always, to some extent, a challenge. At a basic level it upsets the images of the 'real man' or the 'authentically feminine',

[213] *Grant v Edwards* [1986] Ch 638. [214] *Pascoe v Turner* [1979] 1 WLR 431.
[215] *Eves v Eves* [1975] 1 WLR 1338. [216] *Cooke v Head* [1972] 1 WLR 518.
[217] *Coombes v Smith* [1986] 1 WLR 808. [218] *Lloyds Bank v Rosset* [1991] 1 AC 107.
[219] *Cooke v Head* [1972] 1 WLR 518, 519. [220] *Lloyds Bank v Rosset* [1991] 1 AC 107, 131.
[221] Lawson (1996). [222] *Pettitt v Pettitt* [1970] AC 777.
[223] The female claimant in *Fowler v Barron* [2008] EWCA Civ 377 benefited from the joint-names case presumption.
[224] [1995] 2 FLR 1029.
[225] Query whether a contemporary court would exhibit the attitudes described here.

disrupting strongly held codes of masculinity and femininity. For the most part, the anxiety which this provokes results in hostility to lesbians and gay men. But when the normalcy-dependent test of detriment is applied to male-male relationships the unnatural qualities of these relations between men can operate in favour of the cohabiting claimant. In the separate spheres ideology which resurfaces in this field, it is not normal for a man to undertake caring, domestic duties. As a result, it is necessary for Balcombe LJ to explain (and to elevate) Wayling's domestic behaviour in the description of him acting as companion and chauffeur in exchange for monetary support. Wayling's activities have a visibility here which no woman's would possess. However, the Court of Appeal does not dwell on this aspect of the case because it can turn to a more conventional pattern of behaviour. Wayling has also engaged in non-domestic activity with Jones, and his work in the various hotels and restaurants which they ran is deemed to constitute detrimental behaviour. Wayling, a man who lives with another gay man, who works inside and outside the domestic sphere, is visible in a way in which a woman living with Jones would not have been. All of his private behaviour is unnatural and so could amount to detriment in the eyes of a court. All of his public behaviour in the market is conventional and familiar; he does the type of things which men do which are the foundations of contracts and property transactions.

7.2.6.d The position of the homemaker and other non-financial contributors

Where legal title to the property in question is in joint names, family members who have devoted themselves to raising children and looking after the home now benefit from the strong presumption of beneficial joint tenancy that arises following *Stack v Dowden*. Should the other party seek to rebut that presumption, the result in *Stack* itself might suggest that financial contributions have a magnetic effect on the outcome, and the lack of attention to the issue of responsibility for child-care in that case may suggest that the homemaker is vulnerable to losing the benefit of the presumption.[226] However, *Fowler v Barron* (where the applicant happened to be female) augurs considerably more favourably for this type of case.[227]

Far more problematic is the position of claimants who have been homemakers, or participated extensively in business or renovation activities, and whose partners are sole legal owner. Without proof of an express common intention to share, such claimants will struggle to establish any share in the property.

The case most commonly used to illustrate the law's perceived unfairness is *Burns v Burns*,[228] which would be decided identically today.[229] Mrs Burns and her partner (who were unmarried, but she took his name), lived together for nearly 20 years in a house purchased in his sole name. Mrs Burns raised their children and looked after the home. When the children were older, she took up employment, but did not earn significant income until 15 years into their relationship. From her earnings, she paid some household bills and bought household items, including 'white goods' and furniture. Her partner paid the mortgage instalments. When they separated, she was able to keep the washing machine and other items that

226 Probert (2008b), 349 is concerned that this augurs badly for homemakers.

227 Cf the unusual division of responsibilities in *Fowler v Barron* [2007] EWCA Civ 377; *Abbott v Abbott* [2007] UKPC 53, a sole-name case.

228 [1984] Ch 317.

229 Cf Gardner (2013); Auchmuty (2016), who overlook *James v Thomas* [2007] EWCA Civ 1212, *Morris v Morris* [2008] EWCA Civ 257, and other later cases; cf the orthodox view of Mee (2011) and Lady Hale's continued urging of reform, referring to *Burns: Gow v Grant* [2012] UKSC 29, [50]. See further Miles (2023).

she had bought, but was held to have no share in the home. There was no express common intention to share the beneficial interest, and in the absence of any financial contribution to the acquisition of the house, no such intention could be inferred. She had little to show for nearly 20 years' contribution to her family, despite her having 'worked just as hard as the man' in her domestic sphere.[230] But Fox LJ concluded that 'the unfairness of that is not a matter which the courts can control. It is a matter for Parliament.'[231]

True, the world has changed somewhat since Mrs Burns's day. As we saw at 7.2.1, nearly two-thirds of cohabitants live in jointly owned homes, and most joint registrations are accompanied by an express trust, so most couples do not depend on the law of implied trusts and estoppel. Where beneficial ownership was not declared on a joint-names acquisition, *Stack v Dowden* goes some way to protect homemakers' presumptive half-share, given the anchoring effect of the starting point (see 7.2.6.a, second sub-heading). Meanwhile, sex equality legislation and more family-friendly employment leave entitlements have opened up the labour market to more women, who are therefore now more likely to make the financial contributions recognized in sole-name cases.[232] However, it is important not to overstate the position. As we discussed at 6.2, full economic gender equality is far from being achieved. Many mothers of young children (in particular) are not in paid employment or are only employed part-time, struggling to find affordable child-care, punished by the enduring gender pay gap, and so contributing much less money to the household economy.[233] This will matter for many of the 36 per cent of cohabitant-claimants in sole-name owned homes.

John Eekelaar's strong criticism of the law—opening here with a quotation from *Burns*[234]—still has force:

J. Eekelaar, 'A Woman's Place—A Conflict Between Law and Social Values',
(1987) 51 *Conveyancer and Property Lawyer* 93, 94

"The mere fact that the parties live together and do the ordinary domestic tasks is, in my view, no indication at all that they intended to alter the existing property rights of either of them." The "mere" fact that the bearing and upbringing of a child is the decisive event which for most women permanently reduces their earning capacity, throwing them into dependency on men for their security in both the short and long term is to count as nothing when considering whether the parties may have intended that some form of such security may have been provided. The very activity which deprives a woman of her independent means of acquiring security and saving capital is excluded when deciding whether an alternative form of security was intended. A woman's place is often still in the home, but if she stays there, she will acquire no interest in it.

7.2.6.e The problems of uncertainty, destabilization, and democratic legitimacy

In the extract from *Dobson v Griffey* at the start of this chapter, HHJ Matthews said that the rules of property law 'operate in predictable and well-known ways', certainly more so than the MCA 1973 discretion.[235] Readers will now have their own view about that. Clearly, the

[230] [1984] Ch 317, 345. [231] Ibid, 332. [232] Probert (2001).
[233] Miles (2023). Cf Bannister's (2021) arguments for the commodification of domestic contributions' to underpin an unjust enrichment informed approach to these cases.
[234] [1984] Ch 317, 331. [235] [2018] EWHC 1117, [6].

law of express trusts operates predictably.[236] There is at least predictability in the (harsh?) fact that someone who has made no financial contribution to acquisition in a sole-name case will very probably have no interest in the property. But there remains doctrinal dispute about the precise requirements and operation of the common intention constructive trust and proprietary estoppel, particularly at the remedial stage.

Common intention constructive trusts

In the case of the common intention constructive trust, there is ample scope for argument, increased by *Marr v Collie*, about whether the case is one to which the *Stack v Dowden* approach applies at all, and then in undertaking the wide-ranging, forensically detailed factual survey necessary to identify the parties' intentions. With so much turning on the judges' findings of fact and their evaluation of them, it may be hard to anticipate whether and when the court will be prepared to infer a common intention different from the applicable starting point. It may be impossible to anticipate whether the case is a 'very unusual' one—in which the presumption of beneficial joint tenancy will be rebutted—unless and until you have examined the 'paragraph 69 factors'.[237] Contrary to Baroness Hale's hopes, this may simply promote litigation.

The uncertainty persists if we reach the quantification stage, where—absent party intention on the matter—the court has broad discretion to identify a 'fair' quantum without clear principles by which to give 'fairness' substantive content.[238] Contrast the clear articulation of principles for the MCA/CPA context by *Miller; McFarlane*.[239]

Judges might be tempted to try to resolve these problems through further case law development, particularly given government's apparent disinclination to support reforming legislation to protect economically vulnerable cohabitants (see 7.6). But John Mee argues that radical judicial development of trusts law would have doubtful democratic legitimacy,[240] and risks sacrificing doctrinal coherence[241] and increasing uncertainty:

J. Mee, '*Burns v Burns*: The Villain of the Piece?', in S. Gilmore et al (eds), *Landmark Cases in Family Law* (Oxford: Hart Publishing, 2011), 191, 194

In thinking about the role of the law of trusts as a possible location for law reform in this area, it is crucial to remember that the law of trusts, like all areas of the law, has its own function to perform within the legal system. Like impatient visitors to a distant country, irritated at the locals' inability to speak the visitors' language, lawyers concerned only with the achievement of the goal of affording cohabitants greater remedies may chafe at the limitations of equity and trusts. The problem is that the law of trusts is important for reasons other than its role in respect of resolving disputes between cohabitants. We are not talking here about abstract theoretical purity and logic which could appeal only to anorak-clad property-law scholars. Rather, having a sensible law of equity and trusts is important because it impacts on people's lives (as do all areas of law). . . .

[236] But see n 18. [237] Probert (2008b), 345.

[238] Cf *Graham-York v York* [2015] EWCA Civ 72 and other cases considered on quantification, discussed previously.

[239] [2006] UKHL 24; see Miles (2023).

[240] Contrast *statutory* trusts law reform: but the Law Commission's attempt to devise such reform suitable for all 'family' cases ended in failure: Law Com (2002); see Miles (2003); Fox (2003); Mee (2004).

[241] See also Hopkins (2011), 193–8.

The creation of more sweeping (and more invasive) rules, involving a higher level of discretion, has the effect of diminishing predictability, potentially involving more people in litigation and the threat of litigation, setting family members against each other in a context of heightened tension, and risking remedies being unjustly granted in favour of claimants who can exploit the open-endedness of the law to present an unmeritorious claim in a plausible way.

Contrast the view of Lorna Fox O'Mahony, here specifically discussing *Rosset*, that certainty and other conservative values attract too much weight:

L. Fox O'Mahony, 'The Politics of *Lloyd's Bank v Rosset*', in S. Douglas et al (eds), *Landmark Cases in Property Law* (Oxford: Hart Publishing, 2015), 194–5, 196–7

[*Rosset*] provides a timely reminder that the values that are 'ingrained into the property lawyer's psyche' . . . are politically borne, learned, internalised, and not inherent. While Dewar suggested that the 'attempt to accommodate the resolution of family disputes within the land law framework has significantly disturbed the conceptual orderliness of land law itself'[,] it is important to be aware that the characterisation of trusts of the family home as a contest between 'property law values' (stylised, and therefore accepted, as certainty, stability, security, coherence) and 'family law values' (read as fact-, context- and outcome-sensitivity, flexibility) is prone to lead us down the path of accepting the conservative vision of property uncritically. A more nuanced view recognises that property law – like any field of common law – is not fixed but evolves. . . .

While the common intention constructive trust does not explicitly portray the claimant who has not secured joint legal title, obtained an express declaration of trust or made direct financial contributions as greedy or self-dealing, it does imply normative expectations about acquisitive-individualism over family-communitarianism, self-interest over trust, and the 'tidy lives' of consent, private ordering, and capital investment over non-financial contributions and the messy realities of family life. Conservative property protagonists might argue that – at least so far as third parties are concerned – we have a 'duty' to be 'tidy' in our affairs, although this line of discourse can also be viewed as a strategy for closing down discussion of differential impacts [of particular rules on different classes of party in these cases] in favour of the presumption that property outsiders [e.g. the claimants such as Mrs Rosset] should be held to a standard calibrated to the interests of property insiders [e.g. the legal owner]. This also tends to by-pass the practical question of whether third parties are adequately equipped to protect themselves in any event.[242] From this perspective, the commitment to a strict approach might be revealed to be both regressive and unnecessary.

She also critiques the view that legal certainty is essential to guide people's decision-making about property:

[A]rguments based on the signalling function of property law's 'hard-edged doctrines that tell everyone where they stand' tend to assume that legal advice has a meaningful influence

[242] They may be said to have 'ample tools at their disposal to manage the risks of undiscovered claims': Fox O'Mahony (2014), 433; see McFarlane et al (2021), Part E.

on the process in which people buy houses, a premise that was called into question by Douglas, Pearce and Woodward's findings of disconnect between law, and the process of receiving and responding to advice in the conveyancing process, on the one hand, and real life on the other. Even if we accept, for the sake of argument, that there is a supportive relationship between the advice given by practising lawyers and the arrangements made by cohabiting partners, is there any real difference in the 'certainty' cost between cases where a claimant makes a small direct financial contribution to gain access through the gates of property, only for the quantification process to inflate his share of the equity; and those in which the claimant makes a large indirect financial contribution [probably excluded by *Rosset* as a basis for inferring intention]? Even if we agree – further – to take at face value the operational claim that the law must prioritise certainty, coherence and predictability, the benefit of such a regime remains open to question. . . . [Addressing the argument that the law must give people confidence in property rights by upholding settled expectations,] Davidson highlighted the 'morale' value of a property system that allows parties to be confident that the law will ensure fair treatment, arguing that, in some circumstances:

> stability is less important than the assurance that the legal system will respond when external forces threaten to overwhelm the value owners will create, that the rules will provide a fair process of adjustment over time, and that the property regime will ensure inclusion.

As for the argument that certainty is necessary to avoid litigation, Fox O'Mahony notes that 'this is countered by the argument that litigation is sometimes necessary to ensure that certain types of cases (for examples, cases which reveal the existence, or perhaps the extent, of specific injustices) reach a public forum'.[243]

For the time being, unless a Supreme Court decision in a sole-name case takes the law decisively in a more progressive direction[244] and gives more principled 'meat' to the 'fairness' inquiry, we are left with the law as it is.

Proprietary estoppel

As for estoppel cases, here we might be particularly concerned about uncertainty surrounding the nature and extent of the potential remedy that might be obtained, assuming that the requirements to set up the claim are met. But Lord Briggs for the majority, perhaps sharing ground with Fox O'Mahony in the extract here, was unconcerned:

Guest v Guest [2022] UKSC 27

LORD BRIGGS:

81. In the present case the criticism has not been that there are no sufficient principles to govern the circumstances when a judge may intervene [i.e. the requirements of assurance/promise, detriment, and unconscionable repudiation]. Rather the complaint is that there is insufficient principle to guide the judge as to an appropriate remedy, once the equity has

[243] (2014), 431.

[244] There is clearly no judicial appetite for any of the Commonwealth models: Miles (2023); see Gray and Gray (2009), 7.3.77 et seq; Rotherham (2004); Mee (1999); Gardner (1993); McInnes (2011).

arisen, so that practitioners find it hard to advise their clients as to likely outcome, with the result that cases go to court at great expense and family bitterness whereas otherwise they would settle.

82. I am not persuaded by this. The repudiation of promises of this kind made between family members is likely to be causative of, or at least accompanied by, such bitterness that settlement is always going to be difficult. Since the relevant promises are likely to have been made orally, or even by conduct, the propensity for fundamental disputes of primary fact are themselves likely to be the greatest enemy of any predictability of outcome. Nor is unpredictability of remedy necessarily a bar to settlement, because the increased risks of a trial for both sides can be a spur to settlement before the litigation becomes a battle purely about costs. But even if it is, that is no reason for the court to invent artificial rules about remedy where this is in truth no underlying supportive principle beyond those which I have described.

Whilst much of what Lord Briggs says here about the bitterness attendant on these highly fact-sensitive disputes may be true, it is important not to overlook the fact that the parties' ability to bear the risks of trial—both financial and psychological—may be very different and so distort the settlement process to the disadvantage of the 'weaker' party. The simple fact of settlement is not necessarily a good in its own right.[245]

7.3 OCCUPATION AND SALE OF THE OWNED FAMILY HOME

Establishing beneficial ownership of the home is just the first stage of dealing with disputes about a home that is owned by one or more of the parties. Next is resolving disputes regarding its future. One party may want to sell up now to realize their capital share in it, but the other may want to carry on living in the property (without the other party, perhaps with their children) for a few years before any sale. What difference does it make whether only one or both parties own the home? What difference does the presence of children make? We first address the basis of parties' rights to occupy and to make decisions about sale, and then consider the courts' powers to decide these disputes.[246]

7.3.1 RIGHTS TO OCCUPY THE FAMILY HOME

7.3.1.a The general law

Rights attached to property interests

Where property is co-owned and so subject to a trust, the beneficial owners have a statutory right to occupy the trust property if a purpose of the trust is to make the property available for their occupation and the property is in fact available and suitable for their occupation.[247] Since the right to occupy flows from ownership of an estate in the land, those claiming that right must be able to demonstrate that they are a beneficial freehold owner or tenant under a lease. A proprietary estoppel claim may also generate a right to occupy.[248]

245 Diduck (2016).
246 We do not address whether any rights are binding on third parties: see McFarlane et al (2021).
247 TOLATA 1996, s 12; McFarlane et al (2021), 13.5.3.
248 E.g. *Greasley v Cooke* [1980] 1 WLR 1306.

Contractual rights

A right to occupy property may also be conferred by written or oral, express or (more problematically) implied contract.[249] If the contract does not grant a lease, it takes effect simply as a contractual licence. There are statutory constraints on terminating contractual licences, but these do not apply to licences to share property with the resident owner or a member of the owner's family.[250] While a contractual licence cannot lawfully be terminated other than in accordance with the agreement,[251] the court will not enforce a licence of a shared home by injunction;[252] the wrongfully ejected licensee will be left to a remedy in damages.

Bare licensees

A 'bare' licence to occupy may be granted, expressly or impliedly, without the intention to create legal relations and the valuable consideration necessary to create a contract. This is the most tenuous basis for occupation, easily terminated by the licensor withdrawing the permission. The right to respect for the home under Article 8 of the European Convention on Human Rights (ECHR) requires that reasonable notice be given to terminate a licence to occupy property as a home, but the owner's right to terminate a bare licence is otherwise unqualified; no reason need be given.[253] The Law Society's recommendation that cohabitants with children or whose relationships have lasted two years should have statutory 'home rights' of the sort enjoyed by spouses—discussed at 4.5.3.a—has not been adopted.[254]

7.3.1.b The case of children

Save for those who have a right to occupy by virtue of a beneficial interest in the property,[255] the status of children is unclear. Case law, perhaps surprisingly, suggests that even minor children occupy their parents' home under only a bare licence.[256] Parents could in theory therefore withdraw permission for their own children to live with them. That may be appropriate for adult children living at home, but it sits somewhat incongruously alongside parents' responsibilities to minor children: a parent who evicts their minor child may be guilty of child neglect and attract child protection proceedings.[257] It has therefore been argued that these obligations, together with Article 8 ECHR and Article 16 of the United Nations Convention on the Rights of the Child (UNCRC)—no child 'shall be subjected

[249] E.g. *Tanner v Tanner* [1975] 1 WLR 1346; cf *Horrocks v Foray* [1976] 1 WLR 230. *Coombes v Smith* [1986] 1 WLR 808. On the various categories of licensee, see McFarlane et al (2021), ch 7.

[250] Protection from Eviction Act 1977, s 3A(2)–(3).

[251] The court may have to imply terms regarding termination, e.g. reasonable notice: *Chandler v Kerley* [1978] 1 WLR 693.

[252] *Thompson v Park* [1944] KB 408.

[253] *Parker v Parker* [2003] EWHC 1846, [276]. 'Home' rights under Art 8 can be asserted even by those with no legal right to occupy the property: *Prokopovich v Russia* (App No 58255/00, ECHR) (2006).

[254] Law Society (2002). See also *Hannaford v Selby* (1976) 239 EG 811.

[255] Such interest must be registered to bind third parties, since a minor cannot be in 'actual occupation' for the purposes of establishing an overriding interest under LRA 2002, Sch 3, para 2: *Hypo-Mortgage Services Ltd v Robinson* [1997] 2 FLR 71; McFarlane et al (2021), 16.4.2.4. A minor cannot hold a legal estate in land: LPA 1925, s 1(6). In the leasehold context, see *Kingston upon Thames BC v Prince* [1999] 1 FLR 593.

[256] E.g. *Metropolitan Properties Co Ltd v Cronan* (1982) 44 P&CR 1.

[257] E.g. Children and Young Persons Act 1933, s 1; on child protection, see chapter 12. 17-year-olds are in a particularly vulnerable position, and may end up in voluntary accommodation as 'looked after' children in need.

to arbitrary or unlawful interference with his or her ... home'—demand that children should attract a protected occupation status in their home, at least vis-à-vis their parents or de facto carers.[258]

7.3.2 DECISION-MAKING ABOUT SALE AND OTHER TRANSACTIONS RELATING TO THE FAMILY HOME

7.3.2.a Disputes involving legal and beneficial owners

Under the general law, decisions about sale, mortgage, and other dispositions of property are for the legal owner(s). Where all occupiers of the property are legal owners, all must consent to any disposition, so each has a right of veto. Adults who are not legal owners but who have beneficial shares in the property have no right of veto, unless the trust specifically requires that their consent be obtained.[259] A beneficiary of property held by a sole-name legal owner can at least delay dispositions by registering a restriction that, in effect, will prevent dispositions from going ahead without a second trustee being appointed;[260] but if the owner can find someone else willing to become a trustee, the disposition may proceed, overreaching the beneficiary's interest.[261] Beneficiaries of trusts created post-1996 have a statutory right to be consulted, so far as is practicable. Trustees must give effect to the majority view, so far as that is consistent with the general interest of the trust.[262] But any party to a dispute can refer the case to the court under the Trusts of Land and Appointment of Trustees Act 1996 (TOLATA 1996), discussed at 7.3.3.a.

7.3.2.b The position of non-owners

Given the tenuous occupation status of non-owning family members, it is unsurprising that English law does not straightforwardly provide them with a right to be consulted about transactions regarding the family home. We discuss at 7.3.3.b what statute-based protection they might be able to obtain from the family court.

7.3.3 RESOLVING DISPUTES ABOUT THE FUTURE OF THE FAMILY HOME

We turn next to the court's jurisdiction to resolve disputes about continued occupation versus sale. Which tools are available to the court depends on: (i) whether the property is owned or rented by the parties and, if owned, whether it is beneficially owned solely or jointly; (ii) whether there are any children in whose favour an order might be made under the CA 1989, Sch 1; (iii) whether the parties are 'personally connected' and there is domestic abuse between them, in terms of the Domestic Abuse Act 2021 (DAA 2021); and (iv) whether the parties are 'associated persons' and, if so, what sort, in terms of the FLA 1996. Figure 7.1 seeks to give readers a basic map through this legal thicket, identifying all the legislation

[258] Gray and Gray (2009), 10.2.16. *Sed quaere* whether this right is enforceable horizontally between private parties.

[259] TOLATA 1996, s 10, likely only to be the case with express trusts.

[260] LRA 2002, s 40.

[261] See Hopkins (2009), 320–1: overreaching conceptualizes the home as an investment.

[262] TOLATA 1996, s 11. The 'majority' is calculated by the size of the parties' interests.

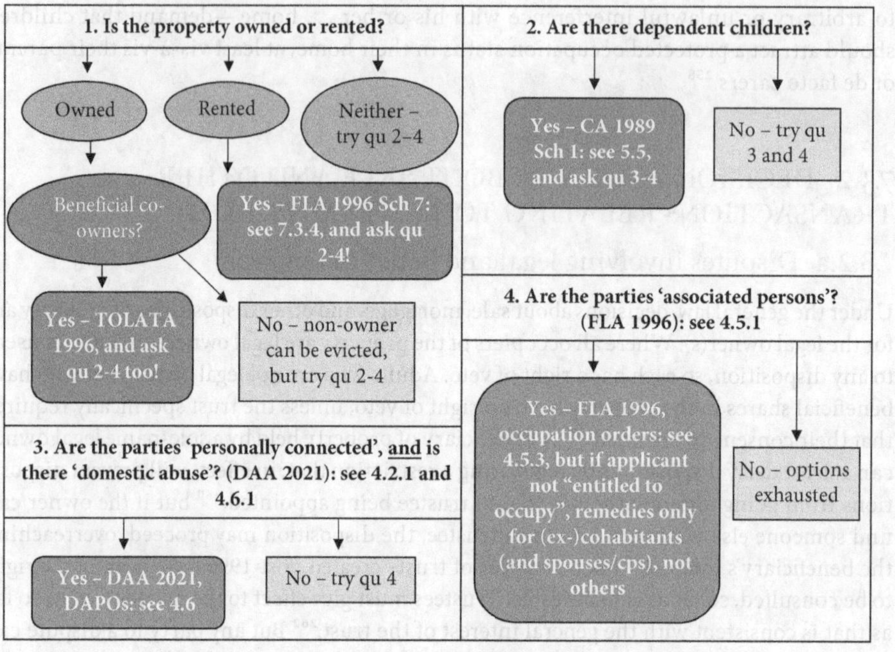
1. Is the property owned or rented?
2. Are there dependent children?
Owned
Rented
Neither – try qu 2–4
Yes – CA 1989 Sch 1: see 5.5, and ask qu 3-4
No – try qu 3 and 4
Beneficial co-owners?
Yes – FLA 1996 Sch 7: see 7.3.4, and ask qu 2-4!
4. Are the parties 'associated persons'? (FLA 1996): see 4.5.1
Yes – TOLATA 1996, and ask qu 2-4 too!
No – non-owner can be evicted, but try qu 2-4
Yes – FLA 1996, occupation orders: see 4.5.3, but if applicant not "entitled to occupy", remedies only for (ex-)cohabitants (and spouses/cps), not others
No – options exhausted
3. Are the parties 'personally connected', and is there 'domestic abuse'? (DAA 2021): see 4.2.1 and 4.6.1
Yes – DAA 2021, DAPOs: see 4.6
No – try qu 4

Figure 7.1 Coming at the family home problem from four directions

potentially in play. We discuss the interaction of those statutes in the following sections, which divide the terrain into two categories:

(i) disputes between beneficial co-owners; and
(ii) disputes between a beneficial owner and a party with no continuing general law right to occupy the property (a 'non-entitled' party).

7.3.3.a Disputes between beneficial co-owners

Suppose two or more family members who both have beneficial interests disagree about their home's continued occupation. For example, one might wish to remain living there alone while the other wishes to sell up and so release their capital share.[263] Various court applications can break the deadlock.

TOLATA 1996

First, disputes regarding occupation and sale can be heard under TOLATA 1996, s 14, under which the court can also ascertain and declare the parties' beneficial interests.[264] The court's powers under TOLATA 1996, though not unlimited, are wider than trustees' powers. For example, although the court cannot simply order one beneficiary to transfer his interest to the other(s) (as the divorce court *can*[265]), it can direct the trustees to *sell* the trust property

[263] See generally Hopkins (2009).

[264] The same power arises under the Married Women's Property Act 1882, s 17 between engaged couples: Law Reform (Miscellaneous Provisions) Act 1970, s 2(1)—see, e.g., *S v J (Beneficial Ownership)* [2016] EWHC 586; and cognate provisions of the CPA 2004. The same principles of property and trusts law apply either way.

[265] MCA 1973, s 24(1)(a): see 6.4.3.

to one or more particular beneficiaries without the consent of the other(s) at a price determined by the court (rather than on the open market).[266] Trustees are required by equity 'single-mindedly to advance the interests of the beneficiaries as a class' and to give effect to the unanimous wishes of the beneficiaries,[267] but the court resolving a dispute amongst co-owners is directed by s 15(1) to consider a wider range of factors:

Trusts of Land and Appointment of Trustees Act 1996, s 15(1)

(a) the intentions of the person or persons (if any) who created the trust,
(b) the purposes for which the property subject to the trust is held,
(c) the welfare of any minor who occupies or might reasonably be expected to occupy any land subject to the trust as his home, and
(d) the interests of any secured creditor of any beneficiary.

In considering disputes regarding *occupation*, the court must also have regard to the circumstances and wishes of each beneficiary who is in principle entitled to occupy.[268] In disputes regarding *sale*, the circumstances and wishes of all adult beneficiaries entitled to an interest in possession must be addressed.[269] The court can require the occupant to pay 'rent' to the excluded party[270]—but where the property is to be occupied by one party with the children, the parties' obligations to those children may make such an order inappropriate.[271]

The Court of Appeal has held that the relevant 'intention' for para (a) must be that held at the time the trust arose (usually on acquisition of the home), not one that the parties' developed later, for example once they had had children.[272] But this much-criticized[273] decision seems unduly narrow, not least given the 'ambulatory' common intention constructive trust (see 7.2.4.c), which responds precisely to the fact that intentions (there, more profoundly, about the beneficial ownership itself) might change over time.

As for para (b), the main purpose of the trust will often have been to provide a family home for the children. Even after the adults have separated, that purpose may still be fulfilled by providing a home for the children, whose welfare in any event commands independent attention under para (c).[274]

CA 1989, Sch 1

If the parties have dependent children, an application may be made under CA 1989, Sch 1 for orders relating to the occupation of the parties' home and transfer or settlement of other assets for the benefit of the children,[275] discussed at 5.5.[276] The court cannot order sale under

[266] *Bagum v Hafiz* [2015] EWCA Civ 801; cf TOLATA 1996, s 6.
[267] *Bagum v Hafiz* [2015] EWCA Civ 801, [23]–[25].
[268] TOLATA 1996, s 15(2).
[269] Ibid, s 15(3).
[270] Ibid, s 13, subject to s 15 factors. See also the use of 'equitable accounting' to require balancing payments between co-owners, discussed in supplement to this chapter in the online resources.
[271] *Stack v Dowden* [2005] EWCA Civ 857, [61]–[63]; cf [2007] UKHL 17, [94] and [155].
[272] *W v W (Joinder of Trusts of Land Act and Children Act Applications)* [2003] EWCA Civ 924, [23].
[273] Gray and Gray (2009), 7.5.98, fn 1; Probert (2007b); earlier editions of this book.
[274] Though see again the unduly narrow approach taken in *W v W* [2003] EWCA Civ 924, [24].
[275] The courts only have limited jurisdiction to make periodical payments orders for children: see 5.5.2.
[276] For further detail on the various property structures that might be deployed, see Pollock et al (2022).

this legislation, but sale can be postponed and the child (with their primary carer) permitted to occupy to the exclusion of the other party, for example until the children leave home or reach a prescribed age,[277] or until the occupying party marries or cohabits with a third party, dies, or no longer requires the property.[278]

DAA 2021 and FLA 1996

If the applicant has been the victim of domestic abuse and the parties are 'personally connected', domestic abuse protection orders (DAPOs) under the DAA 2021 are also available, discussed at 4.6. Even without domestic abuse, if the co-owners are 'associated persons',[279] disputes regarding *occupation* can be dealt with by an order under the FLA 1996, s 33, discussed at 4.5.3.

Where more than one Act can be used, how do they interact?

Competing claims under these three Acts should be heard together,[280] but combining them is not straightforward, either procedurally (TOLATA claims are civil matters, the others family proceedings)[281] or substantively (each confers different powers exercisable on different criteria). As such, they compare unfavourably with the 'one-stop-shop' of the MCA 1973.

Where there are dependent children, the CA 1989, Sch 1 should be considered first in any combined TOLATA/CA case because it gives particular prominence to the needs of the children. Applications concerning the children's future living arrangements should ideally be determined by the same judge,[282] but this is not always possible and it may be necessary to deal with the property questions before a child arrangements application is decided.[283]

Where there are no dependent children and so CA 1989, Sch 1 does not apply, s 33 of the FLA 1996, tailored specifically for the family context, is the preferred framework for dealing with occupation disputes between 'entitled' applicants, rather than TOLATA 1996. But TOLATA 1996 must be used to resolve the timing of any sale.[284] The DAA 2021 may now be preferred where applicable, not least as DAPOs can provide extensive protection to victims beyond just regulating occupation.

So, despite the procedural maze, this legislation can collectively provide outcomes regarding the family home not entirely dissimilar to those achievable under the MCA 1973 on divorce. However, the crucial *difference* between these cases and the matrimonial context is that here the court *cannot adjust* the parties' beneficial shares in the property: those are fixed by the law of trusts. Any property made available for the child to occupy (with primary carer) under CA 1989, Sch 1 will therefore ultimately revert to its beneficial owners strictly in accordance with their property entitlements once the children are independent.[285]

An illustration from the case law

The following extract from a Circuit Judge's decision usefully illustrates a first instance Family Court judge working her way through a combined TOLATA/CA 1989, Sch 1 case.

[277] *Parkes v Legal Aid Board* [1997] 1 WLR 1547.
[278] Cf *Holman v Howes* [2007] EWCA Civ 877, where an estoppel had arisen in the occupant's favour.
[279] FLA 1996, s 62(3): see 4.5.1.
[280] *W v W (Joinder of Trusts of Land Act and Children Act Applications)* [2003] EWCA Civ 924, [5].
[281] Cf *Seabrook v Sullivan* [2014] EWHC 4110, [24].
[282] Ibid, [15] and [17].
[283] *V v W* [2020] EWFC B25, [24].
[284] *Chan v Leung* [2002] EWCA Civ 1075, [46]–[48].
[285] See 5.5.5.d; *Norris v Hudson* [2005] EWHC 2934.

It also reminds us of the stark reality that individuals who could afford to *own* property *together* might each end up having to *rent* once separated. The separated parents of two children—aged 19 (now at university) and 14, for whom they effectively had a shared care arrangement[286]—co-owned the four-bedroomed family home in equal shares. Various practical constraints inevitably influenced the possible outcomes. The applicant mother sought sale; the respondent father wanted to occupy the home with the younger child, E, for another seven or so years.

V v W [2020] EWFC B25

HHJ VINCENT:

67. . . . While the ToLATA and Schedule 1 applications place emphasis on different factors, both require the Court to consider all the circumstances. I therefore consider the applications together. . . .

69. The Respondent accepts that he owns only half the property, but he wishes the Applicant to have no benefit from her half share for another seven or eight years. He asks that she continues to pay for half the mortgage, yet has no intention of her deriving any benefit from that, for example by receiving an occupation rent either from him or a lodger.

70. If the property were not sold, the Respondent would effectively hold the property on trust for the Applicant for seven or eight years. Even if for the minimum period up to E's eighteenth birthday, there is a real risk that the Respondent [who was unable to work owing to illness] would be unable to maintain the mortgage payments and keep the property in a good state of repair and upkeep, thereby putting his ability to safeguard the Applicant's share at risk.

71. If the property were to be sold then the Respondent would be able to use his share of the equity, combined with his continuing income, to rent an alternative smaller property with lower living and maintenance costs. He is in a worse position than the Applicant so far as obtaining a mortgage is concerned, because he has been out of work for so long. However, on either a ToLATA or Schedule 1 Application, I am not directed as I might be had the parties been married, to strive to achieve an outcome where a lower earner in the partnership may effectively be compensated by the other to achieve parity, but to look in the round at the financial situations of the parties, the needs of the children and to take that into account when considering what if any orders should be made in respect of the property they both own in equal shares.

72. If the Applicant is prevented from realising her share in it for a period of four, seven or eight years her financial stability is at risk. She is unlikely to be released from the mortgage account. The Respondent has been unable to make mortgage payments consistently, she has been exposed to the adverse consequences of a poor credit rating and will continue to face that risk, as he does not have a job and cannot meet the payments. Approaching her sixtieth birthday [in seven–eight years' time], even if with the benefit of a lump sum [from her share of the net proceeds of the eventual sale], she is highly unlikely to be able to obtain a mortgage at that time.

73. If the property were sold, the Applicant could use the [capital] to improve her current situation and rent, or in time apply for a mortgage for, a new property in which she and the children could spend time together.

[286] See *V v W* [2020] EWFC B25, [77].

> 74. The parents would both be able to rehouse themselves within a reasonable distance of E's school. . . . There is no requirement for him to live only ten minutes away from his school [as is the case in the family home]. There is no necessity for him to live in the same village as his grandparents, although of course it would be to his and their continuing benefit if they were able to live nearby. . . .
>
> 76. There is in my judgment no good reason to require the parties to provide E with accommodation in his current four bedroom home . . .
>
> 78. For all these reasons, . . . the property should be put on the open market as soon as reasonably practicable and sold for the best price that can be obtained. If the partes are able to negotiate with one another so that one buys out the other's share then that may provide a sensible way forward.

ONLINE RESOURCES

Readers wishing to read about the personal remedy of equitable accounting, designed to balance the books between co-owners at the end of their relationship, should visit the supplement to this chapter in the online resources.

7.3.3.b Occupation remedies for non-entitled claimants

What if the party wishing to remain in occupation is a non-entitled party, that is, has no beneficial interest in the property or other relevant entitlement under the general law? That person is likely to be a bare licensee, whose occupation can be terminated with reasonable notice.[287]

The presence of dependent children makes all the difference in these cases, as the CA 1989, Sch 1 may provide much longer-term protection of occupation for the children (and their primary carer), as well as other financial provision for the children's benefit (and maintenance under the CSA 1991); but, of course, there can be no capital or income payment for the non-entitled primary carer in her own right. Readers should refer to the discussion immediately above and in chapter 5 for details of that jurisdiction.

Absent dependent children, the non-entitled party is left to the DAA 2021 and FLA 1996 (see chapter 4).[288] Where the applicant has been the victim of domestic abuse, the former Act has the most to offer, given the DAPO's universal availability between all types of 'personally connected' parties and offer of occupation (and other) protection on a potentially indefinite basis (which may, of course, also be valuable in cases with children). By contrast, under the FLA 1996 (putting spouses and civil partners aside), non-entitled applications can only be brought by current and former cohabitants (not parties to other non-formalized relationships), under ss 36 and 38. And the protection offered even to them is limited, in terms both of the basis on which the court makes its decision and the short-term duration of any potential order (at most, 12 months).[289]

[287] E.g. *Hannaford v Selby* (1976) 238 EG 811.

[288] Note FLA 1996, ss 35(11)–(12), 36(11)–(12): can apply as a non-entitled applicant without prejudicing any subsequent claim to a beneficial interest.

[289] FLA 1996, ss 36 and 38.

But that is at least better than the position for other non-entitled family members (such as relatives and unrelated home-sharers) who, absent domestic abuse, are left to the general law governing licences, outlined at 7.3.1.a.

7.3.4 THE CASE OF RENTED HOMES

We have focused principally on the owner-occupied home, but cohabitants are more likely than spouses to be living in rented accommodation than in owner-occupied homes, with as many as a third doing so.[290] The occupation order regime of the FLA 1996 applies to rented property as it does to owner-occupied property,[291] so a sole or joint tenant may apply for an occupation order under s 33 and a non-entitled cohabitant under s 36/s 38. The general law of licences also applies. The DAPO regime of the DAA 2021 would also apply in case of domestic abuse, and the CA 1989, Sch 1 where there are dependent children.

However, where the case involves separating cohabitants (not other home-sharers), the courts have the same powers under the FLA 1996, Sch 7 to order a transfer of that tenancy as they do between spouses and civil partners.[292] Jurisdiction arises when the parties 'cease to cohabit'.[293] The landlord of the property has a right to be heard before any such order is made.[294] The party to whom the transfer is made may be required to compensate the other.[295] Schedule 7 sets out the criteria to which the court must have regard in exercising its discretion, including the circumstances in which the tenancy was granted and several of the factors pertinent to the grant of occupation orders, notably the parties' respective housing needs, housing and financial resources, and health, safety, and well-being.[296]

Since many *private* sector tenancies now offer limited security of tenure, the practical benefit offered by Sch 7 may be limited to the *social housing* context,[297] as illustrated by the Court of Appeal decision in *Guerroudj v Rymarczyk*.[298] The parties were contesting the future of a joint secure tenancy over a ground-floor flat granted to them by the local housing authority. A critical feature of this case was Mr Guerroudj's back condition, which prevented him from working and had been a significant factor in the council's decision to offer the couple the flat. Ms Rymarczyk was employed, but only in low-paid shift work. In deciding finally to transfer the tenancy to her, the judge was conscious of the parties' housing resources: Mr Guerroudj's back condition gave him much better prospects of being rehoused by the local authority, which would probably have a duty to rehouse him under homelessness legislation,[299] whereas Ms Rymarczyk would be owed no such duty and could not afford private rental costs.

7.4 OWNERSHIP AND USE OF OTHER PROPERTY

While the courts rarely wish to get involved in disputes regarding chattels, some forms of property other than land—including cars[300]—have significant value and so it may be important to resolve disputes regarding their ownership and use.

290 Miles (2023), table 2, using data from Lersch and Vidal (2016).
291 E.g. *Chalmers v Johns* [1999] 2 FCR 110. 292 FLA 1996, Sch 7.
293 Cf *Gully v Dix* [2004] EWCA Civ 139. 294 FLA 1996, Sch 7, para 14(1). 295 Ibid, para 10.
296 Ibid, para 5.
297 Note also problems regarding notice to quit joint periodic tenancies: Law Com (2006), para 3.61; *Sims v Dacorum BC* [2014] UKSC 63.
298 [2015] EWCA Civ 743. 299 See supplement to chapter 4 in the online resources.
300 E.g. *Montalto v Popat* [2020] EWHC 810, from [131].

7.4.1 CREATING AND TRANSFERRING OWNERSHIP: THE BASICS

Title to most forms of property other than land can be acquired without completing onerous formalities, but not purely on the basis of intention. The Law Commission concluded that creating co-ownership (specifically) can be hard:

Law Commission, *Family Law: Matrimonial Property*, Law Com No 175 (London: HMSO, 1988b)

2.4 . . . [E]ven when a married couple have thought about it and wish their property to be co-owned, creating co-ownership may present difficulties. In what we suspect is the more usual case, where the couple have not thought about it at all, but if asked would say that they *assumed* much of their property was co-owned, they would be wrong.

There are various ways—in the vast majority of cases, determined by the general law—in which ownership or co-ownership of property other than land can arise within a family.[301] First, unless the presumption of advancement applies (see 7.2.3.b), paying for an item generates beneficial ownership under the doctrine of resulting trust (7.2.3.a). The general law discussed here applies between all family members, not just spouses.

Law Commission, *Family Law: Matrimonial Property*, Law Com No 175 (London: HMSO, 1988b)

2.1 In deciding who owns property acquired by the spouses during the marriage the law at present places great weight on who paid for the property. Superficially this may seem reasonable but two examples may serve to show how the results may not reflect the spouses' wishes.

(i) Husband and wife decide to buy a washing machine; one Saturday they look together at various makes and decide to discuss it over the weekend. They decide upon the make they want and on Monday, the husband, who happens to pass on his way to work a shop which has the particular machine in stock, goes and buys the machine. On sale, ownership of the machine passes to the husband.

(ii) A husband is paid in cash, and his wife receives a monthly salary cheque. Because of this, they use his money for rent, food and other day to day necessities, and her money for bills and larger purchases. Consequently all the furniture in the house belongs to her.

Further, the emphasis on who pays creates great disadvantage for a non-earning spouse, who, whatever other contributions he or she may be making to the couple's life together, is likely to end up owning very little of the property which both of them may well regard as "joint."

2.2 It might be thought that the couple could avoid these results by choosing co-ownership. However, co-ownership cannot arise simply because the parties intend to own property in this way. Intention alone is insufficient; there must be some act which is effective to create the co-ownership. . . .

[301] The following discussion is taken largely from Law Com (1988b), para 2.2.

So one party purchasing an item for joint use does not of itself generate joint ownership.[302] But property purchased using funds pooled, either in cash or in a bank account held jointly both legally and beneficially,[303] will belong to both parties.

Secondly, ownership of chattels can be transferred either by using a deed or by the property being delivered to the new (co-)owner with an intention to transfer ownership. But it can be difficult to prove delivery between family members,[304] especially so as to create co-ownership.

Thirdly, an owner of property can orally[305] declare himself to hold the asset on trust for another, provided it is made clear that he intends to become a trustee and does not just indicate a wish that the other party should have an interest. As with common intention constructive trusts of land founded on expressly articulated intentions,[306] this creates scope for litigation over conversations held long ago. In one case, a yacht bought with the man's funds in which the parties intended to sail the world was found to be owned by the parties in half-shares, owing to conversations in which he had repeatedly referred to the boat as 'ours':

Rowe v Prance [1999] 2 FLR 787 (Ch Div), 792–5

NICHOLAS WARREN QC (sitting as a deputy judge of the High Court):

In his witness statement, [Mr Prance] says that he meant this in the sense that people might refer to the hotel or restaurants they visit together as 'our' hotel or restaurant; and that he would refer to the previous boats he had owned as 'our' boat to the crew he had on board. In oral evidence, he gave a rather different explanation. He said he did not like to boast, and preferred to refer to the boat as 'our' boat so as to remove the spotlight—my word not his—as it were from him. . . . I found all that very unconvincing. I consider that Mr Prance's use of the word 'our' on many occasions was a reflection of how he wanted Mrs Rowe to think things were. It was the only expression of his intention and it is the effect of those words with which I am concerned. . . .

. . . There was . . . a conversation in which Mrs Rowe raised the issue of her security [She had given up her rented accommodation and put her furniture in storage to live on the boat.] . . . [The] response from Mr Prance . . . was that her security was his ability to sail the boat *and her interest in it*.

Unlike many assets, ownership of boats has to be registered.[307] In this case, the boat was registered in Mr Prance's sole name. What bearing did that have?

[Ms Rowe] asserts that she was told by Mr Prance that the boat could not be registered in their joint names because she did not hold an Ocean Master's certificate. . . . Of course, no such certificate is necessary for yacht ownership at all. But if Mr Prance *did* say something to that effect, it is strong evidence of ownership on the part of Mrs Rowe: otherwise Mr Prance

[302] Ibid, para 2.3 considers how the law of agency might apply. [303] See further at 7.4.2.

[304] *Re Cole* [1964] Ch 175. [305] Cf the writing requirement for land: see 7.2.1.

[306] That law can also be used in relation to property other than land: *Montreuil v Andreewitch* [2020] EWHC 2068; e.g. *Parrott v Parkin* [2007] EWHC 210, in relation to a boat.

[307] See also cars: the registered keeper is not necessarily the owner.

would not have made such a statement but would have said—if there was an occasion for him to need to say anything at all—that the boat was entirely his. . . .

I am satisfied that Mr Prance effectively constituted himself an express trustee of the boat. . . .

The judge then addressed the size of the parties' shares:

Nothing express was said to that effect, but the regular use of the word 'our' indicates to me an intention that there was no distinction to be drawn by Mr Prance between himself and Mrs Rowe so far as concerned ownership of the boat. Moreover, the discussion about security indicates that Mrs Rowe was intended to have a substantial interest. If I am reading too much into the first of these factors (the use of 'our') in deciding that it points to equality, and given also that the second factor (the reference to security) does not necessarily require equality, I consider that I should apply the maxim that equality is equity and hold that the shares are equal.

Since the property at stake was not land, Mrs Rowe did not need to prove any detrimental reliance on Mr Prance's unformalized oral statements about ownership of the boat in order to make them binding as an express trust. Those who live in houseboats and caravans[308] may therefore acquire a stake in their homes more readily than those who live between bricks and mortar.

7.4.2 INCOME AND BANK ACCOUNTS

The law relating to income and savings from earnings and investments is similar to that governing ownership and use of property. Ownership of such funds is determined by the general law: earners/investors are prima facie exclusively entitled to their income, and are under no general obligation to share it with any family member. Crucially, even though means-testing rules for key state benefits treat cohabitants (like spouses and civil partners) as a single economic unit, assuming that they support each other,[309] there are no maintenance obligations between cohabitants or other non-formalized family members, either during their relationships or on separation.[310]

Windeler v Whitehall [1990] 2 FLR 505, 506

MILLETT J:

If this were California, this would be a claim for palimony, but it is England and it is not. English law recognises neither the term nor the obligation to which it gives effect. In this country a husband has a legal obligation to support his wife even if they are living apart. A man has

[308] Unless the caravan constitutes a fixture: see McFarlane et al (2021), 2.3.1.
[309] See, e.g., Social Security Contributions and Benefits Act 1992, s 137(1).
[310] *Windeler v Whitehall* [1990] 2 FLR 505.

no legal obligation to support his mistress even if they are living together. Accordingly, the plaintiff does not claim to be supported by the defendant but brings a claim to a proprietary interest in his business and his home.

The courts can make financial orders to secure payments relating to property subject to an occupation order under the FLA 1996,[311] but these powers are 'not intended as a disguised form of maintenance for those who are not entitled to it'.[312] So although that power is exercisable in favour of a cohabitant, it cannot be used as a means of requiring the respondent to support that individual.

An individual's income will usually be paid directly into a bank account. Like land held in the name of one party, the credit balance of a sole-name bank account may be subject to a trust giving rise to a beneficial interest in favour of another person. Since a bank account is personal property, an express trust over the credit balance may arise orally. In *Paul v Constance*, the repeated statement that 'the money is as much yours as mine'—made in relation to funds in a bank account held in the name of one party but on which the other had the right to draw—was held to confer on her a half interest in those funds.[313] Conversely, the fact that an account is held in joint names does not necessarily mean that both parties are beneficially entitled to the funds, either at all or to the same degree. This depends first (and, if done, determinatively) on whether the parties had executed a written banking agreement dealing with beneficial ownership, for example via the bank's account-opening application form:

Whitlock v Moree [2017] UKPC 44

29. . . . [W]here two or more holders of a joint account all sign an account opening document (or separately sign identical documents) which, on their true [objective] construction, declare or set out their respective beneficial interests in the property constituted by the account (loosely, the money in the account), then those are the beneficial interests of the account holders, pending any subsequent variation of them by agreement or otherwise, and an examination of the subjective intentions of the account holders, or of those of them who place money in the joint account, is neither relevant nor permissible. Still less is recourse to the doctrine of presumed resulting trusts permissible, because the potential beneficial owners have declared what are their beneficial interests by signed writing.

Failing such an express declaration of the beneficial interests, implied trust principles apply:

Law Commission, *Cohabitation: The Financial Consequences of Relationship Breakdown*, Law Com CP 179 (London: TSO, 2006)

Ownership of funds in bank accounts

3.38. . . . If the account is fed from the resources of one party, A, but is held in joint names with B merely for convenience—for example, to give B access to funds—B has no beneficial interest in the money in the account until he or she actually exercises the right to draw funds

311 FLA 1996, s 40; see 4.5.3.f. 312 Law Com (1992), para 4.41. 313 [1977] 1 WLR 527.

from it. While it remains in the account, the money will belong, under resulting trust principles, to A as the party who fed the account. If B has made no contribution to the account, A will be entitled to terminate B's access to the funds at any time.[314]

3.39 Where both parties contribute to the account, pooling their resources, they will at least be found to own the funds on a resulting trust basis in accordance with their contributions. However, both in pooling cases and in cases where A has provided all the funds, the presumption of resulting trust might be displaced, for example, where there is . . . a common intention to the effect that the parties should share the account in some other proportions. Indeed, the court might find that the parties intended to be joint tenants of the beneficial interest, each equally entitled to the whole of the fund.

3.40 Property purchased with funds from a joint account will ordinarily belong to whoever acquires title to that property, even if that person had no or only a part-share in the funds when they were in the account.[315] If, unusually, there is evidence that the assets acquired were intended to be held in the same way as the funds in the account, then that property will be held accordingly.[316] [Some footnotes retained from original]

In this context, as with land, the courts may be quicker to imply an intention to pool both funds in the account and property acquired from those funds in cases involving spouses and civil partners than with others.[317]

Research examining financial practices within mixed-sex relationships suggests that, in practice, cohabiting *parents* are much more like spouses than other cohabitants in being more likely to operate as a single economic unit, adopting a 'pooling' system of money management. Where couples do not pool their resources and give each party equal decision-making power over and access to the funds, there can be marked imbalances between the parties, prejudicing the lower-earning party (often the woman).[318]

7.4.3 USE-RIGHTS OVER THE CONTENTS OF THE FAMILY HOME

Ownership of the contents of the family home—furniture, furnishings, kitchen equipment, crockery and cutlery, household linen, and so on—is again a matter for the general law. Ordinarily, the use and possession of that property flows from ownership. In the course of normal family life, of course, the technical owner of the spoons, towels, and sofa, whoever it is (the parties may have no idea), will implicitly allow other family members to use that property. But once the relationship is over, the owner is entitled to remove their property.

Aside from remedies available under the CA 1989, Sch 1 for the benefit of children, the only family law expressly addressing use of such property outside the MCA/CPA context is an adjunct to the occupation order regime discussed in chapter 4. When making an occupation order under the FLA 1996, the court can include provisions granting either party possession or use of furniture or other contents.[319] The reach of this protection is governed by the width of the FLA 1996 regime, so only family members who have a beneficial interest in the home, spouses/civil partners, and cohabitants can access this provision. No other

314 *Stoeckert v Geddes (No 2)* [2004] UKPC 54.
315 Ibid.
316 *Jones v Maynard* [1951] Ch 572.
317 E.g. ibid.
318 Vogler (2005), (2009).
319 FLA 1996, s 40; see generally 4.5.3.f.

property, such as the family car,[320] attracts similar protection. But, where available, the courts might use their extensive powers to fashion DAPOs under the DAA 2021 to regulate such matters.

7.5 PRIVATE ORDERING FOR RELATIONSHIP BREAKDOWN

Parties can try to avoid the problems that might be encountered under the general law to determine disputes arising on separation by expressly creating their own solution by agreement, either in advance or on separating.[321] What is the governing law, and what is the reality?

7.5.1 THE LAW

As we have already seen, any two or more people can readily regulate the ownership of property via express declarations of trust, and the courts have repeatedly entreated couples to do so.[322]

By contrast, question marks may arise over the enforceability of *contracts* making financial arrangements between cohabitants.

First, courts may hesitate to find an intention to create legal relations between parties to any ongoing relationship, unlike parties clearly dealing at arm's length following relationship breakdown.[323] Moreover, just as domestic contributions struggle to count as detrimental reliance for the purpose of the laws of implied trusts and estoppel, it may be hard to establish consideration by promising to undertake such tasks.[324] However, these problems can be overcome with an appropriately drafted deed.

Another factor has (at least historically) bedevilled cohabitants' contracts: a contract for which the performance of extra-marital sexual relations appears to form part of the consideration is void on public policy grounds. While that is not a problem for contracts made following separation (where the provision being agreed is clearly a consequence of the relationship, rather than a condition of it), it is *potentially* problematic for contracts made earlier.[325] However, it is now widely accepted that a contract between cohabitants governing their property and financial entitlements, whether during the relationship or following its future demise, will be upheld.[326] This view was reinforced from the unlikely source of a case involving a 'Swedish sex slave'. A negligence action was brought against solicitors in connection with the drafting of an agreement for a 'master/slave' relationship between two men that provided, inter alia, that the property of the 'slave' would be transferred absolutely to the 'master'. In the course of striking out the claim on the merits, the judge considered the agreement's validity. Was it void because 'meretricious'? This agreement was, but

[320] Occupation orders can be made over caravans or houseboats used as the family home: FLA 1996, s 63.

[321] Insofar as the common intention constructive trust rests on shared party intentions, this might also be viewed as a form of private ordering, but the lack of formalized or any express evidence about intention readily creates disputes of the sort examined previously. Our focus here is on agreements catering expressly (and usually in writing) for the eventuality of separation.

[322] See 7.2.1.

[323] E.g. *Jones v Padavattan* [1969] 1 WLR 328, 332.

[324] *Horrocks v Foray* [1976] 1 WLR 230, 239.

[325] Probert (2004d) for analysis of the old cases.

[326] E.g. Lowe et al (2021), 92.

others—simply governing cohabitants' property rights—could be valid. In considering the 'unlawfulness' of cohabitants' sexual relationships, the judge started by quoting from Tony Honoré's 1978 book, *Sex Law*:

Sutton v Mishcon de Reya and another [2003] EWHC 3166, [2004] 3 FCR 142

HART J:

22. . . . 'Whatever the reason, and however stable the relation, sexual intercourse between an unmarried couple is "unlawful" though it is not in general a crime . . . A contract for which the whole or part of the consideration is sexual intercourse (or any other sexual relation) outside marriage is void, as is a contract which tends to promote unlawful sexual intercourse. So, if Jack agrees to support Jill to whom he is not married on condition that she keeps house for him and that they have sexual intercourse, the whole agreement is void even if they mean it to be a legally binding one. It makes no difference that the agreement to have sex is understood rather than expressed.'

But, as [Honoré] went on to point out, that analysis does not prevent the cohabitors from entering into perfectly valid legal relations concerning their mutual property rights, or even (he suggests) as to other ancillary matters such as how they will divide up the work. Such a contract will not be a contract of cohabitation but a contract between cohabitors. He suggested that there was no reason why such a contract should not be upheld even though its tendency in fact might be to encourage the continuation of the "unlawful" sexual relationship.

23. If that is the right distinction to draw (ie a distinction between a contract *for* sexual relations outside marriage and a contract *between* persons who are cohabiting in a relationship which involves such sexual relations), it is not, in my judgment, difficult even for a moron in a hurry . . . to see on which side of the line the cohabitation deed in this case falls. It was not a property contract between two people whose sexual relationship involved them in cohabitation. It was itself an attempt to express the sexual relationship in the property relations contained in the contract (or, as [counsel for the claimant] himself put it, the property relation "sprang from" the desire to give the sexual role-play verisimilitude). It was an attempt to reify an unlawful ideal.

While the remarks of Hart J are welcome (if colourful), there is still no contemporary decision upholding a contract between cohabitants.[327] The Law Commission recommended that clarifying legislation would remove any lingering doubts.[328]

To the extent that such agreements (like deeds) are binding, it is important to bear in mind that the courts have no overriding supervisory jurisdiction of the sort exercised under the MCA/CPA to displace them.[329] Neither the *Hyman* principle nor anything like it applies here, so no court order is required to achieve finality.[330] But the flipside of this is that a deed or contract will be determinative, absent any grounds to avoid it under the general law (such

[327] Though note contractual licence cases such as *Tanner v Tanner* [1975] 1 WLR 1346, *Chandler v Kerley* [1978] 1 WLR 693 involving 'mistresses' set up in a home by their partners.

[328] Law Com (2007), para 8.25.

[329] Including informal agreements to settle a dispute that have become binding by estoppel: *Ely v Robson* [2016] EWCA Civ 774.

[330] Cf 6.7.

as fraud, undue influence, and so on). No broader grounds for intervention akin to those enjoyed in the matrimonial court under *Edgar/Radmacher* are available.[331] Applications might remain open under the CA 1989, Sch 1 or the FLA 1996, but the basic property issues would be governed by the parties' contract, the existence of which would doubtless be a factor that the family court would take into account in hearing an application under one of those Acts.

7.5.2 THE REALITY?

However, it is questionable how many couples do or, if the law were further clarified, would regulate their affairs by contract:

R. Probert, '*Sutton v Mishcon de Reya and Gawor & Co*—Cohabitation Contracts and Swedish Sex Slaves', (2004d) 16 *Child and Family Law Quarterly* 453, 461–2

> In a study by Lewis . . ., only one-quarter of respondents agreed with the statement that 'people who are going to live together or get married should write down beforehand how they will divide their finances in case they split up'. In the accompanying qualitative study, 20 of the 73 respondents were in favour of contracts: those opposed suggested that contracts were 'too cold', 'defeatist', and inappropriate in view of the way that relationships change over time and demand flexibility. Barlow and James [(2004)] have suggested that their more recent research suggests greater enthusiasm for a contractual solution. Certainly, their respondents were positive about the idea of a partnership register . . . but such a scheme confers status as well as regulating the rights of the parties, and may be more attractive for that reason. In any case, their enthusiasm was not matched by formal arrangements. The number who actually enter into a contract is likely to be considerably smaller than those who are willing to contemplate one in theory: first, both parties must agree in theory that a contract is a good idea, secondly, they must agree on what the terms of the contract are to be, and thirdly, they must actually get round to entering into such a contract. The failure of couples thus to regulate their lives is well documented.

Indeed, a precondition to use of contract is the parties' appreciation that such a step is necessary or desirable, a requirement that continued belief in the 'common law marriage myth', in some form, continues to obscure (see 2.8.2.b). Moreover, even when individuals are armed with the right legal knowledge, imbalances of power within couples may deprive the economically weaker party of the chance to secure their position through agreement.[332]

But from a psychological perspective, it may be undesirable to encourage contracting between couples whose relationship is good. Couples are commonly accused of suffering from 'optimism bias'—assuming that *their* relationship will not founder despite statistical evidence indicating that many relationships do end in separation, and so failing to protect their position against that risk in advance. But should we burst the bubble by encouraging them to sit down and contract for that possibility?

[331] See 6.7.2 and 6.7.4; Chandler (2017).

[332] Women and Equalities Committee (2022a), paras 19–21.

H. Reece, 'Leaping without Looking', in R. Leckey (ed), *After Equality* (Abingdon: Routledge, 2015), 123–4

Although diverse roots of the optimism bias have been suggested it is commonly accepted that at least part of the explanation is that we base our predictions on a mental simulation of ourselves engaging in the actions necessary for the outcome, and our simulation tends to dwell on the positive, not negative, possibilities. Once we have conjured up a positive mental picture of the future event, we see that picture as more likely, especially because imagining that picture crowds out any other . . . Moreover, our mental picture of a positive future event is rich and vivid, this clear picture reinforcing our belief that the positive event is probable. In contrast, when Sharot [a researcher] . . . asked people to visualize separation from their partner, their mental picture was blurry. We make a close connection between clarity and probability and between fuzziness and improbability; we have a fuzzy picture of an event that we believe is unlikely, and, if our picture is fuzzy, then we believe that the event is unlikely.

Crucially, if we make ourselves conjure up clearer pictures of negative events, then we regard those negative events as more likely. Explaining a negative event makes for a clearer picture, to such an extent that explaining the negative event may affect us similarly to experiencing the negative event, altering our behaviour. . . . Moreover, just like a positive picture, generating a negative picture also crowds out alternative, positive scenarios. Once cohabitants focus in on the potential failure of their relationship, they may believe their relationship is more likely to fail, which may, in turn, cause them to act as if the relationship is failing, causing the relationship to fail.

Those who wish to persuade cohabitants to reach agreement may find it necessary to dent unrealistic optimism, with negative impact on cohabiting relationships. Moreover, the process of reaching cohabitation agreements may dent unrealistic optimism, with negative impact on cohabiting relationships. The more seriously cohabitants take the process, the more their optimism may be damaged. The less seriously cohabitants take the process, the less their optimism will be dented, and the worse an agreement they may make.

7.6 REFORM FOR COHABITANTS

If couples cannot or simply do not protect their own positions through property/trusts law and contract, should the law ensure better protection of economically vulnerable parties by providing financial remedies on separation? If a cohabiting relationship ends on one party's death, the survivor can seek reasonable financial provision under the Inheritance (Provision for Family and Dependants) Act 1975, even if the deceased made no will or made a will in favour of others. But there is no equivalent scheme on separation in England and Wales, even though several other jurisdictions, including Scotland[333] and Ireland,[334] now have such laws. We address cohabitants (specifically) here, rather than other, non-conjugal relationships, as they are the ones that have been in the spotlight for possible reform. Within that category, however, note one unique sub-group: parties to non-qualifying religious marriage ceremonies (discussed at 2.6.2.b), who (on one level at least) regard themselves as married but who are not regarded as spouses by domestic law

[333] Family Law (Scotland) Act 2006.

[334] Civil Partnership and Certain Rights and Obligations of Cohabitants Act 2010.

and so are, at best, classed as cohabiting. Reform of wedding law to accommodate more such marriages would be the better solution.[335] But, pending that, this area of law matters acutely to them too.[336]

7.6.1 A STOCK-TAKE OF THE CURRENT POSITION

Before considering reform options, it is worth regrouping and evaluating how the position of cohabitants,[337] using the patchwork of rights and remedies described in this chapter, differs from that of divorcing spouses under the MCA 1973:

- The most important point is that the court cannot interfere with the parties' property rights or redistribute the capital value of assets, such as the family home, cash savings, and investments.
- Instead, the destination of assets on separation is determined by the law of property, the rubric of which—unlike the MCA jurisdiction—is focused largely on intention regarding ownership and financial contributions towards the acquisition of assets.
- Moreover, the courts can only address ownership and use of individual assets, not adopt a holistic approach designed to achieve economic justice in the round between the parties, bringing all of their resources into account.
- Where (as is common) the parties purchased the house in joint names and declared their beneficial interests, that declaration will generally be determinative of their shares. But where they failed to declare the beneficial interests or the house was owned in law by just one of them, the law of implied trusts may be invoked in order to determine how the beneficial title to the property is held. We explored some of the problems with that law at 7.2.6.
- There is no basis under the general law on which one party can acquire an interest in the other's pension assets, and the courts have no pension-sharing powers.[338]
- There is no obligation of maintenance between cohabitants or power for the courts to order periodical payments between former cohabitants. But the CSA 1991 and the CA 1989, Sch 1 will apply for the benefit of any dependent children.
- Cohabitants' agreements about property, whether formed as contracts or trusts, will be legally binding; the courts can only disapply them on grounds available under the general law.
- Where the parties have access to TOLATA 1996 as co-owners or to the CA 1989, Sch 1 for the benefit of dependent children, the courts can create solutions regarding the occupation of a home that are not dissimilar to *Mesher* orders under the MCA 1973, to the extent that they can make that home available for the occupation of one party (and children) to the exclusion of the other for a defined period.
- Parents of children for whom orders are made under the CA 1989, Sch 1 can derive no lasting personal benefit once the child reaches independence: for example, any home

[335] Law Commission (2022): see 2.5.3.d and 2.6.2.b.

[336] Women and Equalities Committee (2022a), from para 27.

[337] The position of parties to other non-formalized relationships is different to the extent that some statutory remedies are specific to cohabitants.

[338] Cf dependants' benefits that might arise on death of the pension-holder.

made available for the child's occupation will revert to the owner(s) in line with the beneficial ownership and the parent is not allowed to save money from a Sch 1 order to provide for her long-term security. Contrast the availability of outright property transfers, *Martin* orders, joint-lives spousal periodical payments, and pension sharing for a spouse's benefit under the MCA 1973.

- The courts can only make orders regarding the use of other assets as an adjunct to occupation orders made under the FLA 1996, (probably) as an aspects of DAPOs under the DAA 2021, or the CA 1989, Sch 1; in the latter case, the court can make orders requiring that the respondent purchase or make available certain items (e.g. a car, washing machine, furniture, etc.) for the child's benefit.
- The only situation where the court has an adjustive power for the direct benefit of a cohabitant is the transfer of tenancies over rented homes under the FLA 1996, Sch 7.

In many cases, the outcomes generated by this array of laws may seem perfectly clear and 'fair'. For example, following a short-term or child-free cohabitation in which neither party's economic situation was impacted negatively by contributions or sacrifices made for the sake of the relationship, we may feel that these economically independent parties can readily go their separate ways with whatever each owns. Contrast other cases, especially those where child-care or other domestic responsibilities (such as caring for a dependent older relative) have impaired one party's economic position and economic interdependency between the parties has arisen.[339] As we discussed at 7.2.6.a, whether the outcome generated by the general law does anything to protect the position of that party may turn on what might be the pure happenstance of whether the property was held in joint or sole names. We might think that some of the results generated—albeit 'fair' in terms of the rubric of property and trusts law—are not 'fair' measured by some other set of criteria.

J. Miles, 'The Politics and Principle of Pursuing "Fairness" in Family Property Matters', in J. Gardner et al (eds), *Politics, Policy and the Private Law: Tort, Land & Equity* (Oxford: Hart Publishing, 2023)

[Whether the outcome in sole-name cases, in particular, is 'unfair'] depends entirely on the criteria by which that normative question is to be measured. . . . As HHJ Matthews put it in *Dobson v Griffey*, 'the purpose of considering the whole course of dealing between the parties [in a common intention constructive trust case—CICT] is not to evaluate their respective actions and decide whether they generate a moral obligation by one of them to the other'. . . .

The focus of property law is . . . entirely backward-looking, concerned with how the parties conducted themselves . . . *specifically* in relation to the property at issue. This contrasts strikingly with matrimonial law's largely forward-looking focus . . . [G]iven the CICT criteria, it is clearly no part of the court's role in these cases – by contrast with the matrimonial cases – to examine the parties' economic position going forward, whether viewed in terms of the parties' needs or of ongoing relationship-generated disadvantage created by economic sacrifices made during the relationship (notably, in relation to future earning- and pension-saving capacity). Property law therefore brings to these cases a very different lens from that which a family law statute would generally have.

This being so, what—if anything—should be done?

339 See Arthur et al (2002); Douglas et al (2007b).

7.6.2 DOES CIVIL PARTNERSHIP SOLVE THE PROBLEM?

Some have suggested that the advent of mixed-sex civil partnerships causes concerns about cohabitants to fall away: all couples, after all, now have a choice to marry or to form a civil partnership.[340] But does that—theoretical—choice address the problems? Many would say not.

J. Miles and R. Probert, 'Civil Partnership: Ties That (Also) Bind?', (2019) 31 *Child and Family Law Quarterly* 303, 306–7

[T]here is a very real danger that framing the introduction of civil partnerships as a solution for cohabiting couples diverts attention from the development of other, more suitable solutions.

There is a considerable body of research into the reasons why couples cohabit. Anne Barlow and Janet Smithson classified cohabitants into 'ideologues' [who are ideologically opposed to marriage], 'pragmatics', 'romantics' and 'uneven couples'. Setting aside what is probably only the small group of 'ideologues' . . ., it is difficult to see how the availability of civil partnerships will encourage or enable any of these cohabiting couples to formalise their relationship. The 'pragmatics' who would marry if they perceived any benefit in doing so would have no greater reason to enter into a civil partnership. This group is likely to be particularly affected by the continuing prevalence of the 'common law marriage myth' – if the majority of couples already believe that cohabitants have the same rights as married couples, they are unlikely to see the need to formalise their relationship, whether by marriage or civil partnership. The romantics who are holding out for the perfect wedding are unlikely to be attracted to what they are likely to perceive (at least in symbolic and possibly also in commitment terms) as an inferior relationship form that would call for a more pared-down ceremony than the one they want to have. And those in uneven relationships [where there is an imbalance of power] are not in a position to persuade their partner to enter into either a marriage or a civil partnership, and so will be unable to protect themselves by either route.

And, of course, parties to religious-only marriages may think that they are already married.

7.6.3 FUNCTIONAL, REMEDIAL, 'FAMILY LAW' REFORM?

If we want to ensure economic justice measured by 'family law' criteria at the end of cohabiting relationships, neither the general law nor formalization into a status-based relationship provides an obvious answer. Instead of hoping that the general law will morph itself into such a shape that it more reliably generates outcomes that—from a family law perspective—seem 'fair', it might seem better to devise bespoke remedies and principles specifically for the familial context that respond to that fairness measure directly.[341] In other words, rather than start from the 'form' of parties' dealings or relationships and expect that to produce the answers that we want, start at the other end of the equation: work out what 'functions' of relationships we want the law to be recognizing and design a legal regime that fits the brief.

[340] See sources discussed by Hayward (2019).

[341] See Dewar (1998b); Law Commission (2002); Miles (2003); Fox (2003); Miles (2023); Women and Equalities Committee (2022a), [14]–[15].

This brings us to the Law Commission's cohabitation project of the mid-2000s. The Commission was tasked with identifying options for reform that would provide financial remedies between cohabitants on separation. The terms of reference for the Commission's project explicitly excluded other home-sharers and non-formalized relationships, despite concerns that have also been raised (not least during parliamentary debates on civil partnership) about situations such as the Burden sisters or adult children caring for elderly parents.[342]

7.6.3.a The parameters of the reform debate

Discussion of cohabitation reform provokes strong responses.[343] The first question is whether there should be reform at all, and if so, for which cases. This is a large question of social policy.

Some flatly oppose the introduction of statutory remedies for cohabitants on relationship breakdown. Rather than giving cohabitants the remedies that many mistakenly believe they already have,[344] the state should endeavour to educate them about the substantial legal differences between marriage/civil partnership and cohabitation.[345] Then, it is said, those who continue to cohabit can confidently be said to have rejected marriage and it would be unjustifiable to impose on them similar legal regulation.[346] Other opponents of reform fear that any legal recognition of cohabitation would undermine the institution of marriage by removing an incentive to marry.[347] Others query the conclusion that property law fails cohabitants, arguing that Mrs Burns's predicament is now far from the norm, and fear the loss of freedom of choice around the conduct of domestic relationships that they consider subjection to a family law scheme would entail.[348] Some even assert that provision of financial remedies on separation would discourage women from securing their own financial independence within their relationships.[349]

At the opposite end of the debate are those who argue that all or some cohabitants should be brought fully within the MCA 1973. The economic vulnerability experienced by many cohabitants and their children on separation is no different from that encountered on divorce. These commentators regard the flexible MCA regime as the best tool to deal with these practical problems, enabling the courts to differentiate those short-term, childless relationships at the end of which no remedy is called for from longer term, more economically interdependent partnerships that merit relief. It is argued that this would bring the law into line with people's expectations and social practices.[350]

The Law Commission recommended a middle path, which we summarize at 7.6.3.b, seeking to respect the autonomy of those couples who wish to keep the law out of their relationships, whilst providing some level of protection to those left economically vulnerable on separation owing to their contributions to the relationship. But we start with some extracts from the Commission's Report that provide a flavour of some of the arguments made by consultees about the idea of pursuing *any* reform and the Commission's evaluation of them.

[342] See Law Com (2006), Part 1 on the genesis of the project; and see 2.8.3.

[343] Cf the history of the Family Violence and Domestic Homes Bill 1995, which preceded the FLA 1996: Hale (2004), 419; and see 2.8.2.

[344] See the common law marriage myth: 2.8.2.b.

[345] Cf Reece (2015).

[346] E.g. Deech (1980).

[347] E.g. generally, Morgan (2000).

[348] E.g. Bottomley (2006); Auchmuty (2016); cf 7.2.6.d.

[349] E.g. Auchmuty (2016); Deech (1980).

[350] E.g. Barlow et al (2005); Bailey-Harris (1996).

The institution of marriage

We start with perennial concerns about how reform might affect the institution of marriage:[351]

Law Commission, *Cohabitation: The Financial Consequences of Relationship Breakdown*, Law Com No 307 (London: TSO, 2007)

2.37 . . . [O]ur consultees expressed a wide range of views about marriage and cohabitation. A few took issue with the emphasis that we placed . . . on supporting marriage. But others were concerned that any further legal recognition of cohabitants would undermine the institution of marriage. . . .

2.38 The Evangelical Alliance [a non-denominational Christian organization] . . . observed that they were:

> not persuaded . . . that reform is necessary. Naturally, there are individuals who suffer from the current absence of specific legislation to cover the situation when an uncommitted relationship breaks up. The church recognises and sympathises with the very human and tragic consequences of such live events. Nevertheless, we doubt that new legislation is the answer. The fact remains that the UK already has an established legal arrangement that couples can opt into if they want to create mutual rights and obligations. This is called marriage. We concur with those who express fears that imposing rights and duties on cohabiting couples – which would amount to a "cut price" or "reduced" version of marriage – will undermine the crucial institution of marriage itself and will result in fewer couples actually marrying. This in turn will continue to have serious consequences for society.

. . .

2.40 The potential effects on social behaviour of legal change of the sort being contemplated in this project are difficult to predict.

2.41 Take, for example, last year's highly publicised House of Lords' decision on the law governing [financial remedies] on divorce [*Miller; McFarlane*—see chapter 6]. Reaction to that decision highlighted how the current law, by providing financial relief between spouses but not between cohabitants, may provide the economically stronger party with compelling reasons to shun marriage in preference to cohabitation. Some consultees suggested that introducing new remedies between cohabitants would, in turn, reduce the numbers of cohabiting couples and increase single-person households.

2.42 The law is clearly not an irrelevant factor, and the incentive structure it creates may affect individuals' decisions about their personal relationships, at least where other considerations are finely balanced. However, we think that it is important not to over-estimate the influence that the law has on people's behaviour in relationships. . . . [R]esearch suggests that even where individuals are provided with accurate information about their legal position, the law may have relatively little effect on what people do: in particular, in deciding whether to start of end a relationship, and whether to cohabit or to marry or register a civil partnership. Indeed, recent research finds that some cohabitants think that it would be wrong to take on what they view as the serious commitment of marriage for legal or financial reasons.

[351] A large number of responses to the Women and Equalities Committee consultation in 2022 were centred on this worry: see Women and Equalities Committee (2022a).

This view is shared by Relate, the UK's largest provider of relationship counselling, who made the following observation in their consultation response:

> We support a change in legislation simply because it is necessary in a world where cohabitation is on the increase. We do not believe that it would provide a disincentive to marriage, as our experience is that people rarely get married for financial reasons. The argument that they do is even less plausible when we consider the still common misconception that there is such a thing as a 'common law marriage'. Nor do we believe a change in the law would encourage cohabiting people to separate – another decision rarely propelled by money.

...

2.44 . . . [B]oth the institution of marriage and individual marriages can be supported whilst also recognising and responding to the factual reality of cohabitation and the hardship that can arise when such relationships end. It seems to us that marriage does not need to be supported by perpetuating the hardship experienced by others when alternative forms of personal relationships end.

2.45 Cohabiting relationships are currently more prone to breakdown than marriage. But we do not accept that new remedies would inevitably aggravate that trend; they may even help to stem it. One factor contributing to the present fragility of cohabiting relationships may be precisely the current law's failure to ensure a fair distribution between the parties of the economic consequences of separation. Cohabitation may therefore be viewed by some individuals as a "responsibility-free" option, from which they can walk away without any financial consequences. The introduction of a scheme of financial relief may prompt couples to consider more carefully whether and on what basis they should cohabit. But it may also help to reinforce the commitment which cohabitants make to each other, not least by protecting the position of the party who was or would be more economically vulnerable should the parties separate. Indeed, the introduction of remedies between cohabitants may even lead some couples to formalise their relationship. If financial responsibility attached not only to marriage and civil partnership but also to cohabitation, the economically stronger party's current incentive to refuse to marry[352] . . . may to some extent be reduced.

Promoting autonomous decision-making

What of the argument that public information and education to explode the 'common law marriage myth'[353] provide the answer, enabling individuals to make informed, responsible choices about their relationships? Here, the Commission reviewed the findings of research into one such campaign, which found that very few of those who had received the information had taken any action:[354]

2.51 . . . Various reasons were offered for this inactivity. Over a third "hadn't yet got around to it", but almost as many had encountered an obstacle which was preventing them acting on the information: lack of agreement from their partner (where needed); concern that legal advice was required but could not be afforded; and concern that taking any further steps might cause problems with their partner. A significant minority felt that they did not need to take any action; it appears that some of them were banking on the hope that the need for legal protection would not arise or found thinking about the legal aspects of their relationship "negative".

[352] For a case law example of this, see *Southwell v Blackburn* [2014] EWCA Civ 1347.
[353] See 2.8.2.b. [354] Barlow, Burgoyne, and Smithson (2007).

> 2.52 These findings suggest that too much weight can be placed on the potential of information to solve the problems encountered by cohabitants. The researchers conclude that taking legal action:
>
> > is often inhibited by practical barriers . . . and is often a long piecemeal process rather than a single event, leaving cohabitants legally vulnerable [often] for . . . long periods of time.
>
> 2.53 Some of our consultees might respond to the suggestion that education often does not lead to action by arguing that . . . the role of the State should begin and end with the provision of information; thereafter it is for individuals to take responsibility for themselves within the existing legal framework.
>
> 2.54 This is a justifiable standpoint. However, many other consultees would take issue with it. Many would consider the harshness of the consequences in some cases too stiff a penalty for disadvantaged individuals' failure to take legal steps that were theoretically open to them. In reality, many cohabitants' options are narrower than the theory would suggest. As a result, even if they were made aware of the dangers of their current position, they would not be practically able to do anything to improve it.

But the Commission did not dismiss the need to respect party autonomy. The question is how best to balance that with the concern to protect the vulnerable. That turns largely on whether a new scheme of remedies should be available on an 'opt-in' basis (covering only those who proactively register their relationship in some way) or by default (applying automatically to all eligible couples, subject to an opt-out by agreement between the parties).[355]

> 2.87 We appreciate that, at least in theory, the choice between opt-in and opt-out should make no difference to outcomes. Equipped with the same information, parties ought to reach the same destination (within the scheme or outside it), whether positive action is required in order to come within, or to remain outside, the scope of the scheme. If so, an opt-out scheme would do no better at protecting the vulnerable than an opt-in: the individual who would fail to persuade his or her partner to opt in would equally come under pressure to opt out. However, we consider that such arguments underestimate the practical significance of the default position, combined with the likelihood that many couples who do not actively intend to fall outside the scheme would either not address their minds to the issue or postpone taking action for the sorts of reasons discussed earlier. Only an opt-out scheme would ensure protection in the absence of positive action by the parties; and because of the tendency of people not to get around to things, an opt-in scheme, just like the current law, would leave many unprotected. Moreover, conferring eligibility to apply for financial relief by default may improve the bargaining position of the more vulnerable party where the other party would prefer that the relationship continue on that basis than not continue at all. . . .
>
> 2.92 However, we do place considerable weight on the concerns of those who preferred some form of opt-in solution: facilitating and protecting party autonomy. . . .
>
> 2.93 . . . [W]e agree with the majority who favoured a scheme of general application, but which would permit couples who wished to do so to agree to disapply the scheme. They would then be able, if they wished to do so, to make their own financial arrangements determining how their resources would be divided in the event of separation. We consider that this model strikes the appropriate balance between, on the one hand, the need to provide a fairer means of resolving the property and financial disputes that can arise between cohabitants

[355] Cf 6.7 on private ordering in the matrimonial context.

on separation than that provided by the current law, and, on the other hand, the importance of preserving individuals' freedom to conduct their private relationships on their own terms.

Assimilation with spouses and civil partners?

But should the default scheme be that provided by the MCA 1973 for spouses? The Commission recommended not:

4.9 Recent research has indicated that, in particular situations, a majority of the public would like to see couples with children, whether married or unmarried, treated in the same way on separation, whatever that treatment might be. It also seems that a majority would support financial relief being granted between couples without children, at least following a long relationship, and in light of such factors as their contributions to the relationship. However, it is by no means clear that all members of that majority would support the specific application of the MCA regime to cohabitants with children, let alone to those without. Cohabiting relationships differ widely in terms of duration, commitment and degree of economic interdependence. Case law on the MCA has advocated the treatment of a divorcing couple as a "partnership of equals" to which the yardstick of equality may be applied. This approach may generate enormous awards even after very short marriages, and we believe that there would be significant public disquiet if cohabitants were to be treated similarly.

Such disquiet might flow from a perception that 'strong' principles such as sharing—which require the distribution of property on divorce regardless of any practical impact of the marriage on the parties' economic positions—are unsuited to non-formalized relationships. But if not a sharing principle, then what about need or compensation?[356] The following extract surveys the arguments that any jurisdiction contemplating cohabitation law reform needs to canvas in relation to this fundamental issue.

J. Miles, 'Unmarried Cohabitation in a European Perspective', in J. Scherpe (ed), *European Family Law, Vol III* (Cheltenham: Edward Elgar, 2016), 99–100

Certain provision available between spouses might be deemed on normative grounds to be inapplicable to cohabitants. For example, a [sharing principle] may be understood to be based on the partnership created by the formal step of marriage, which mere informal cohabitation cannot parallel; so too rights of support might be regarded as dependent upon the . . . assumption of responsibility made expressly on marrying. Such arguments reflect both a concern to protect the institution of marriage and the choices made by autonomous individuals to marry or not and so to come within that specific regime or not. Alternatively, however, it might be argued that property sharing or other spousal remedies are ultimately justified not on the exercise of choice regarding marriage but rather on protective grounds reflecting the dynamics of financially interdependent relationships, and that those grounds have equal force in the case of cohabitants who find themselves in functionally identical circumstances at the end of their relationships. Or one might adopt an intermediate position, regarding some spousal rights (such as fixed entitlements to property sharing [or the MCA sharing principle]) as properly confined to the partnership of marriage whilst considering that other remedies, particularly those which seek to respond directly to the actual economic

[356] See 6.5.

situation of the claimant arising from the relationship, find their justification in the practical situation of that individual regardless of the legal form of the relationship.

7.6.3.b The Law Commission's recommended approach

The Commission adopted that sort of intermediate position:

Law Commission, *Cohabitation: The Financial Consequences of Relationship Breakdown*, Law Com No 307 (London: TSO, 2007)

4.24 We consider that, while respondents should not have responsibility to meet all categories of need, it is appropriate to recommend a scheme that would respond to needs arising from the parties' contributions to the relationship. However, . . . we consider that such needs are better viewed as a sub-set of a wider principle, focusing on the economic impact of the parties' contributions to the relationship [regardless of whether the parties are in a situation of need as a result]. We have therefore framed our recommended scheme in terms of "retained benefit" and "economic disadvantage" rather than "need".

The key aspects of the Commission's recommendations were as follows.

- A new statutory scheme should provide financial relief between 'eligible' cohabitants on separation, without requiring the parties to have 'opted in' by prior registration or agreement.
- Cohabitants would be 'eligible' to apply under a new scheme if they had been living as a couple in a joint household; and had either:
  - had a child together (born during, before, or following their cohabitation), or
  - had lived together for a minimum duration, which should be set by statute somewhere within a range between two and five years.[357]
- Couples should be able to 'opt out' of the scheme and make their own binding arrangements at any time.
- Such agreements would be enforceable if in writing, signed by the parties, and made clear the parties' intention to disapply the statute; independent legal advice would not be a precondition of enforceability.
- But the court should be entitled to set aside an otherwise binding opt-out agreement if enforcement would cause 'manifest unfairness' given the circumstances at the time the agreement was made or changed circumstances unforeseen when the agreement was made.
- For eligible couples with no binding opt-out agreement, the courts should have a discretion to grant the same types of orders as under the MCA 1973, save that periodical payments orders should only be available in respect of future child-care costs.
- But those orders should be granted on a basis different from that applying between spouses on divorce,[358] corresponding most closely with the 'compensation' strand from

[357] Separate recommendations were made regarding eligibility where a couple have a child living with them who is not in law the child of both of them.

[358] Appendix C to the Report explains the Commission's reasons for rejecting alternative schemes, including the MCA 1973.

Miller; McFarlane:[359] the exercise of the court's discretion should be focused on addressing the economic impact of contributions arising from the parties' relationship and made by the applicant to the parties' shared lives or to the welfare of members of their families.

- Specifically, an applicant would have to prove that following separation:
  - the respondent retained an economic benefit (whether in the form of capital, income, or earning capacity) arising from contributions made by the applicant during the relationship (e.g. financial contributions to the acquisition of property held in the respondent's name or physical labour increasing the value of the respondent's property), and/or
  - the applicant sustained an economic disadvantage (in the form of lost future earnings or earning capacity, or reduced savings, including pension savings) flowing from economic sacrifices made because of that party's contribution to the relationship (typically, giving up paid employment to care for dependants), or as a result of continuing child-care responsibilities following separation.[360]

7.6.3.c Reception of the Commission's scheme

The Law Commission's recommendations attracted various criticisms. Some disagreed with the basic policy: wanting cohabitants to be assimilated with spouses, or opposing *any* reform,[361] or promoting alternative schemes. Others criticized the scheme's theoretical basis and/or its apparent complexity, and problems that might be encountered attempting to prove and quantify claims under it.[362] The Labour Government deferred any final decision pending research into the costs and efficacy of Scottish reform introducing similar remedies between cohabitants in the Family Law (Scotland) Act 2006. Research into the first three years of operation of those provisions was duly published,[363] but the Coalition Government claimed that the findings did 'not provide . . . a sufficient basis for change in the law'.[364]

However, there has been no let-up from proponents of reform. The public strongly supports reform,[365] Lord Marks has promoted a Private Member's Bill that would implement the Commission's scheme,[366] and the need for reform has been recognized at the highest level:

Gow v Grant [2012] UKSC 29

LADY HALE:

50. Responding to the Government's announcement . . . Professor Elizabeth Cooke, the Law Commissioner who leads the Commission's work in family and property law, said this:

"We hope that implementation [of the Commission's recommendations] will not be delayed beyond the early days of the next Parliament, in view of the hardship and

[359] See *Gow v Grant* [2012] UKSC 29, [45].

[360] Appendix B to the Report illustrates the operation of the recommended scheme with examples.

[361] See, strikingly, Auchmuty (2016) and Baroness Deech: e.g. Hansard HL Deb, vol 757, cols 2072–75, 12 December 2014.

[362] Probert (2007b), (2009d); Douglas et al (2008); Sverdrup (2015).

[363] Wasoff, Miles, and Mordaunt (2010).

[364] Hansard HC Deb, cols 15–16WS, 6 September 2011; see also Hansard HL Deb, vol 730, cols 118–20, 6 September 2011, Lord McNally.

[365] Barlow et al (2008).

[366] Most recently, Cohabitation Rights Bill (HL) 2019–21.

injustice caused by the current law. The prevalence of cohabitation, and the birth of children to couples who live together, means that the need for reform of the law can only become more pressing over time."

As Professor Cooke also pointed out, the "existing law is uncertain and expensive to apply and, because it was not designed for cohabitants, often gives rise to results that are unjust." The reality is that the "sufficient basis for changing the law" had already been amply provided by the long-standing judicial calls for reform (dating back at least as far as *Burns v Burns* [1984] Ch 317, at 332); by the Law Commission's analysis of the deficiencies in the present law and the injustices which can result; by the demographic trends towards cohabitation and births to cohabiting couples . . .; and by the widespread belief that cohabiting couples are already protected by something called "common law marriage" . . . There was no need to wait for experience north of the border to make the case for reform.

Most recently, the parliamentary Women and Equalities Committee held an inquiry to take stock of the policy arguments and the state of the law 15 years on from the Law Commission's work. As well as promoting further public information campaigns—including ones targeted at members of communities in which religious-only marriages are common, and urging reform of weddings law to help resolve that problem—the Committee supported the Law Commission's scheme:

Women and Equalities Committee, *The Rights of Cohabiting Couples*, HC 92 (2022a), 26–7

1. The current law applicable to cohabitants on relationship breakdown can be costly, complicated and unfair. Complex property law and trusts principles often require the financially weaker partner – often women – to demonstrate direct financial contributions to the acquisition of the family home, while childcare and other non-financial contributions go largely unrecognised. Schedule 1 to the Children Act 1989 is out-dated, mostly benefits the children of wealthy parents and is in need of reform . . .

2. It is staggering that so many people in England and Wales believe in the common law marriage myth. This misplaced belief in legal protections can have profound consequences for cohabiting partners – many of whom do not realise the reality of their situation until it is too late . . .

3. The lack of comprehensive legal protections for cohabitants upon relationship breakdown means that women, especially women from ethnic minority backgrounds and those who have had a religious-only marriage, can suffer relationship-generated disadvantage. . . .

4. The law should fully recognise the social reality of modern families and protect people regardless of whether they are married, in a civil partnership, or in long-term cohabiting relationships. However, law reform should recognise that marriage continues to hold an important social and religious status in England and Wales. We believe that the Law Commission's 2007 proposals for an opt-out cohabitation scheme are a pragmatic approach for reforming cohabitation law . . .

5. The Government should reform family law to better protect cohabiting couples and their children from financial hardship in the event of separation. . . . The Government should

make a commitment to publishing draft legislation for pre-legislative scrutiny in the 2023-24 Session of Parliament. In the meantime, the Ministry of Justice should commission a refresh review of the Law Commission's *2007* proposals to see if they need updating.

The government, however, seems largely unmoved, so reform remains distant.[367]

7.6.4 BUT DOES FUNCTIONALISM REQUIRE BOLDER REFORM?

Several commentators have argued that debates about remedies for cohabitants have continued to be distorted by a preoccupation with relationships' formal status rather than their functions (exacerbated by the introduction of mixed-sex civil partnerships: see 7.6.2), hence, for example, the perceived need to give cohabitant applicants 'less' than an equivalent divorce applicant. This would involve individuals in functionally similar circumstances receiving very different treatment:[368]

L. Glennon, 'The Limitations of Equality Discourses on the Contours of Intimate Obligations', in J. Wallbank, S. Choudhry, and J. Herring (eds), ***Rights, Gender and Family Law*** (Abingdon: Routledge, 2010), 197–8

The result is that familial caregiving is not considered as a valued activity in its own right, but is conceptualised through the lens of the relationship form in which it takes place. As such, it can be said that these mutually informing equality discourses [about the recognition of non-traditional family forms and about non-discrimination between breadwinner and home-maker], whilst having transformative potential, have failed to generate a root and branch approach to family law development which would strip back the assumptions upon which current norms are based and encourage a deeper connection between the functions which a family (family members) perform(s) and the obligations to which it (they) are subjected.

By contrast, a preferable approach to the construction of legal obligations between adults would de-emphasise relationship form and encourage a more direct consideration of relationship functions. In this way, the focus on actual interdependencies, such as those arising through shared parenthood, would encourage a more direct and positive value to be placed on familial caregiving. It would also allow more accurate demarcations to replace the current bright line distinctions drawn between the married and unmarried which prevents a proper evaluation of the mutual dependencies which can arise in couple-based relationships of varying forms. Such an approach . . . would help to bring legal ideology into line with the emerging social view, revealed in the recent British Social Attitudes Report, that 'most people seem to place the emphasis on successfully "doing" family in practice, whatever situation people find themselves in, rather than on the supposed functionality of different family forms'.

Indeed, on this basis, cohabitants should not be the only beneficiaries of reform. Australian states have extended financial relief to other 'domestic' or 'personal' relationships, in

[367] See Women and Equalities Committee (2022b), and Hayward (2022).

[368] See also Wong (2009); Bottomley and Wong (2006). But compare Probert's reservations (2009c) about such arguments, noted at 2.8.1.

some instances even without requiring that the parties shared a household.[369] English law recognizes some such relationships in the event of death: as well as cohabitants, 'dependants' of the deceased—those who were being maintained, wholly or partially, by the deceased immediately before their death—may apply for provision under the Inheritance (Provision for Family and Dependants) Act 1975. But for the time being, should their relationship founder during the parties' joint lives, these families, like cohabitants, remain reliant on the general law and limited statutory remedies.

7.7 CONCLUSION

The issues discussed in this chapter engage several core questions in family law:

- what weight we should give to party autonomy and private ordering;
- how we should respond to widespread legal misunderstanding (the common law marriage myth), optimism bias, and uneven relationships that deflect or prevent people from making what may appear to be 'rational' decisions;
- what protection, if any, should be offered to those who are economically vulnerable on separation and, if *some* protection should be provided, on what *basis*—a formal basis only (i.e. based on marriage/civil partnership or express agreements) or on a functional basis (i.e. extending remedies by default to relationships that meet prescribed criteria);
- whether it is the presence of children that is most critical.

For the time being, property and trusts law have to provide most of the answers. Whether they have the right tools with which to do so is debatable.

D. Cowan, L. Fox O'Mahony, and N. Cobb, *Great Debates in Land Law* (London: Palgrave, 2016), 222

> [The issues raised in implied trusts cases involving cohabitants] highlight the problematic nature of land law's rational search for intention when the parties themselves may not have expressed it. The first flush of love leads people to do extraordinary things without thought; it is only when, inevitably, that love turns to bitterness and hatred, or, more mundanely, the cohabitants part company, that the issues for land law arise. It is at that latter point, the bitter end, that land law requires the re-construction – or, perhaps, the better word is translation – of events around the tools it provides . . .

ONLINE RESOURCES

Questions, suggestions for further reading, and supplementary materials for this chapter (including updates on developments in this area of family law since this book was published) may be found in the online resources at **www.oup.com/he/familytcm5e**.

[369] Property (Relationships) Act 1984 (NSW); Domestic Relationships Act 1994 (ACT); Relationships Act 2003 (Tas); see Mee (2004), 427–9.

8

FUNDAMENTAL PRINCIPLES IN THE LAW RELATING TO CHILDREN

CENTRAL ISSUES

1. The welfare of the child is the paramount consideration in most court-adjudicated disputes about children's upbringing. This means the rights and interests of others are relevant only insofar as they bear upon the child's interests. This has led to debate about the compatibility of the paramountcy principle with Article 8 of the European Convention on Human Rights (ECHR).
2. The paramountcy principle only applies where the 'upbringing' of a child is *directly* in issue before a *court*. In cases which affect children less directly, or where a state body other than a court is determining the issue, the child's welfare is 'a primary consideration' under the United Nations Convention on the Rights of the Child.
3. The welfare principle is criticized for its indeterminacy and lack of transparency. Measures to curtail judicial discretion, such as statutory checklists and scientific evidence, only partially address these problems.
4. Alternatives to the welfare principle remain closely wedded to its basic premises: that children should be afforded special consideration in the decision-making process.
5. Children's rights play an increasingly important role in English family law. Although difficult to uphold when children seek to act in ways considered inimical to their welfare, the rights of children are now widely recognized and respected.
6. The Children Act 1989 (CA 1989) enshrines a policy of non-intervention in private family life. The relationship between this policy, parental autonomy, and the paramountcy principle is debatable.
7. Away from its statutory powers, the High Court also has power to protect children under its so-called inherent jurisdiction. The appropriate role for this ancient power in the modern law is debatable.

8.1 INTRODUCTION

The law relating to children covers many issues. Who, as a matter of law, should be recognized as being a parent, and what does it mean to be a parent? In what ways, if any, should the rules be different for mothers and for fathers, for married and for unmarried parents, for mixed-sex and for same-sex parents? Can a child have only two parents? What about cases involving artificial insemination, surrogacy, or adoption?

Separately, there are questions about who should have the responsibilities and powers associated with raising a child, which English law terms 'parental responsibility' (PR). Often the answer will be 'the child's parents' (once we work out what the law means by that), but not always. The questions of who should have PR, how they should get it, and whether they can have it removed from them, are all important and difficult. At the same time, we need to grapple with children's own autonomy and rights, particularly when important decisions have to be made about their lives. What if a child disagrees with the view of those with PR? Should we answer that question differently in the case of children at different ages?

Two particular factual contexts in family law provide a focus for examining the legal approach to children. One is the situation when parents have separated or divorced, and they are unable to agree about the arrangements that should be put in place for their children. These disputes involve questions about which parent the child should live with (which may be both, of course), and what time they should spend with the other parent. We also address more specific questions, such as disputes about a proposed change of the child's surname, about schooling, or about where, geographically, the child should live.

The second factual issue that we address in detail is the situation when children are being abused or neglected. When should the state take action to protect children from harm, and from what sorts of harm should children be protected? When, if ever, should children be removed from their birth families, and in what circumstances should this take place? Moreover, once children are removed, what should happen next?

These are all difficult and important questions, and we address them (and many more) over the course of the following chapters. There are many different approaches to these issues, and the topics which we discuss are controversial, giving rise to strong feelings on all sides of the debate. The purpose of this chapter is to introduce some of the core ideas and legal approaches which underpin the later chapters, and to examine the ways in which different perspectives can be seen to have influenced the development of English law.

We begin by exploring the welfare principle and its central role in child law today. The problems and limitations of the principle are addressed, before the chapter considers the alternatives to a welfare-orientated approach. Contemporary challenges to the welfare principle are explored, particularly the pressure from advocates of parental rights who now find vital support for their approach in the Human Rights Act 1998 (HRA 1998). We then consider children's rights within, and as an alternative to, a welfare-orientated approach. The different theoretical perspectives on the concept of children's rights are explored, before looking at the extent to which this approach has gained acceptance within domestic family law; we use contested medical decision-making about children as an example to explore these issues. The chapter considers the importance of the 'non-intervention' principle and the possible tension between a commitment to maximizing children's welfare whilst supporting only a minimalist role for the state, including recognition of the value of parental decision-making and promoting family dispute resolution in the private realm. Finally, we look at the High Court's so-called inherent jurisdiction in relation to children, offering protection to children outside the statutory frameworks that we explore elsewhere in the book.

8.2 THE WELFARE PRINCIPLE

The welfare principle is at the core of all aspects of child law in England and Wales. Although commonly referred to as 'the welfare principle', there are also statutory and judicial references to a child's 'best interests'. Because the child's welfare is said to be 'paramount' under the legislation, the phrase 'paramountcy principle' is also used. The courts use these terms interchangeably,[1] though it can be argued that welfare and best interests should be seen as separate concepts.[2]

8.2.1 THE PARAMOUNTCY OF THE CHILD'S WELFARE

The welfare principle is central to the resolution of child-related disputes under English law. It is enshrined in s 1 of the Children Act 1989 (CA 1989):

Children Act 1989, s 1

(1) When a court determines any question with respect to—
  (a) the upbringing of a child; or
  (b) the administration of a child's property or the application of any income arising from it,

the child's welfare shall be the court's paramount consideration.

The same principle is enshrined in s 1 of the Adoption and Children Act 2002 (ACA 2002):

Adoption and Children Act 2002, s 1

(1) This section applies whenever a court or adoption agency is coming to a decision relating to the adoption of a child.
(2) The paramount consideration of the court or adoption agency must be the child's welfare, throughout his life.

This means that whenever a court determines any question relating to the upbringing of a child, whether concerning adoption, living arrangements after parental separation, medical treatment, or taking a child into state care, the child's welfare must be the paramount consideration. The child's welfare is also paramount in relation to decisions about any property that the child owns (such as by way of inheritance or when received as compensation for an injury).[3]

[1] *Re Pippa Knight* [2021] EWCA Civ 362, [69].
[2] Hollingworth and Stalford (2017), 62–4. Furthermore, as we will see, the child's best interests can be a significant factor without being 'paramount' (see 8.2.1.c and 8.5.5)—so although we refer to 'the' welfare principle, there are in fact several, with this version merely being the most central to domestic child law.
[3] Such cases are comparatively rare, but see, e.g., *Re B (A Child: Inherited Property)* [2022] EWFC 7.

8.2.1.a The meaning of 'paramount'

In *J v C*, the House of Lords had to interpret the word 'paramount' as then found in s 1 of the Guardianship of Infants Act 1925.[4] Lord MacDermott gave the clearest judgment as to the meaning to be attributed to the term:

J v C **[1970] AC 668, 710–11**

LORD MacDERMOTT:

The second question of construction is as to the scope and meaning of the words "shall regard the welfare of the infant as the first and paramount consideration." Reading these words in their ordinary significance . . . it seems to me that they must mean more than that the child's welfare is to be treated as the top item in a list of items relevant to the matter in question. I think they connote a process whereby, when all the relevant facts, relationships, claims and wishes of parents, risks, choices and other circumstances are taken into account and weighed, the course to be followed will be that which is most in the interests of the child's welfare as that term has now to be understood. That is the first consideration because it is of first importance and the paramount consideration because it rules upon or determines the course to be followed.

It is widely accepted that 'paramount' means that factors are relevant to the court when determining any aspect of the child's upbringing only if and insofar as they affect the child's welfare in some way, whether directly or indirectly. The child's welfare is thus determinative, with other potentially relevant factors, such as the rights, wishes, or feelings of the child's parents, taken into account only insofar as they have a bearing upon the best interests of the child.

8.2.1.b The meaning of 'welfare'

In order to give some substantive content to the welfare principle, both the CA 1989 and the ACA 2002 contain a 'checklist' of factors that the judge should take into account when trying to determine the welfare of any particular child.[5] The checklists provide valuable guidance as to the most important matters to be considered. The checklist applied under the CA 1989 is contained in s 1(3):

Children Act 1989, s 1

(3) In the circumstances mentioned in subsection (4), a court shall have regard in particular to—

(a) the ascertainable wishes and feelings of the child concerned (considered in the light of his age and understanding);

[4] For commentary on the history of, and subsequent reaction to, *J v C*, see Lowe (2011).

[5] For an argument that the courts make generalizations and category-based assumptions about who 'the child' is when considering welfare decisions, see Krutzinna (2022).

checklist

(b) his physical, emotional and educational needs;
(c) the likely effect on him of any change in his circumstances;
(d) his age, sex, background and any characteristics of his which the court considers relevant;
(e) any harm which he has suffered or is at risk of suffering;
(f) how capable each of his parents, and any other person in relation to whom the court considers the question to be relevant, is of meeting his needs;
(g) the range of powers available to the court under this Act in the proceedings in question.

The application of the welfare checklist is mandatory only in the circumstances specified in s 1(4):

- a *contested* application to make, vary, or discharge a s 8 order (i.e. a child arrangements, specific issue, or prohibited steps order);
- an application to make, vary, or discharge a special guardianship order or an order under Part IV of the Act (i.e. care and supervision orders), whether contested or not.

A similar checklist to be applied in the context of adoption is set down in s 1(4) of the ACA 2002.[6]

The Children and Families Act 2014 (CFA 2014) also added an important (but linguistically complicated) provision to the CA 1989 about the importance of parents being involved in their children's lives after parental separation. The following provision applies in contested private law disputes when the court is considering making or discharging a s 8 order or a parental responsibility order:

Children Act 1989, s 1

(2A) A court . . . is as respects each parent within subsection (6)(a) to presume, unless the contrary is shown, that involvement of that parent in the life of the child concerned will further the child's welfare.
(2B) In subsection (2A) "involvement" means involvement of some kind, either direct or indirect, but not any particular division of a child's time.
(6) In subsection (2A) "parent" means parent of the child concerned; and, for the purposes of that subsection, a parent of the child concerned—
(a) is within this paragraph if that parent can be involved in the child's life in a way that does not put the child at risk of suffering harm; and
(b) is to be treated as being within paragraph (a) unless there is some evidence before the court in the particular proceedings to suggest that involvement of that parent in the child's life would put the child at risk of suffering harm whatever the form of the involvement.

[6] See 13.4.1.

The welfare checklist sets out relevant factors in a value-neutral way, telling the court what to think about, but giving no guidance about the relevance that each factor will have to the decision. The parental involvement provision, on the other hand, directs the court to presume that it will be in the child's interests for each parent to be involved in the child's life (though the form of the involvement is left open) unless there is evidence to show that the parent cannot be involved without putting the child at risk.[7]

The courts have interpreted the concept of the child's 'welfare' or 'best interests' broadly, as illustrated by Munby LJ's judgment in *Re G (Education: Religious Upbringing)*.[8]

Re G (Education: Religious Upbringing) [2012] EWCA Civ 1233

MUNBY LJ:

26. 'Welfare', which in this context is synonymous with 'well-being' and 'interests' . . . extends to and embraces everything that relates to the child's development as a human being and to the child's present and future life as a human being. The judge must consider the child's welfare now, throughout the remainder of the child's minority and into and through adulthood. . . . How far into the future the judge must peer – and with modern life expectancy a judge dealing with a young child today may be looking to the 22nd century – will depend upon the context and the nature of the issue.

27. . . . Evaluating a child's best interests involves a welfare appraisal in the widest sense, taking into account, where appropriate, a wide range of ethical, social, moral, religious, cultural, emotional and welfare considerations. Everything that conduces to a child's welfare and happiness or relates to the child's development and present and future life as a human being, including the child's familial, educational and social environment, and the child's social, cultural, ethnic and religious community, is potentially relevant and has, where appropriate, to be taken into account. The judge must adopt a holistic approach.

Re G is also important for the Court of Appeal's discussion of other elements relating to the understanding of welfare. For example, it is clear from Munby LJ's judgment that the understanding of welfare has to keep pace with changing ideas in society, whether informed by new understanding of science or technology, or whether simply based on changes to social attitudes.[9] Munby LJ linked his reference to the child's happiness to the Aristotelian notion of 'the good life': it is not about hedonistic pleasure, but rather 'such things as the cultivation of virtues and the achievement of worthwhile goals'.[10] The judge also emphasized that a child's welfare cannot be assessed in isolation, because the child's relationships with others are crucial: 'a child's relationships, both within and without the family, are always relevant to the child's interests; often they will be determinative'.[11] However, the secular values

[7] The parental involvement presumption was being reviewed by the Ministry of Justice at time of going to press.

[8] Further extracts from *Re G* can be found at 11.6.4.

[9] *Re G (Education: Religious Upbringing)* [2012] EWCA Civ 1233, [33]. For discussion and criticism, see Taylor (2013).

[10] Ibid, [29].

[11] Ibid, [30]. The relational nature of welfare is central to a number of Jonathan Herring's works: see, e.g., discussion at 8.3.1.

promoted by Munby LJ have little by way of democratic credentials, nor is there much explanation of where the values to be ascribed to the 'reasonable parent' come from.

R. Taylor, 'Secular Values and Sacred Rights: *Re G (Education: Religious Upbringing)*', (2013) 25 *Child and Family Law Quarterly* 336

It is quite clear that reasonable people in 2012 disagree on what welfare may mean. . . . It is questionable whether any society, particularly one as diverse as modern Britain, has anything approaching generally accepted standards. There is also a danger that generally accepted standards can be a shorthand for the imposition of majority values . . .

These are noble aims and no doubt many would subscribe to the vision of parental values held out by Munby LJ. They are, however, not uncontroversial. Laudable as many will think these values are, nowhere does Munby LJ explain their derivation as values that may be attributed to the reasonable parent or ought to be so attributed. . . .

Further, there is a serious risk that these aims may conflict with the values of broad-minded tolerance attributed to the reasonable person. The uncomfortable truth is that not all religious minorities do subscribe to equality of opportunity between, for example, men and women. Further, not all religious minorities consider that aspiration within the secular world is a worthwhile pursuit and may fear that bringing the child to the cusp of adulthood with maximum opportunity to pursue those goals may well be at odds with the child's ability to integrate within the religious community and to maintain religious purity. To choose these values as the values that determine the application of welfare, creates a significant disadvantage for those religious minorities that are based on fundamentally different visions of life.

ONLINE RESOURCES

We examine more of the literature about *Re G* in the online resources, available at **www.oup.com/he/familytcm5e**.

The principles set out in *Re G* received strong endorsement from the Court of Appeal five years later in *Re M (Ultra-Orthodox Judaism: Transgender)*,[12] when Munby P quoted at length from his earlier judgment in setting out the relevant approach. He also offered a summary of one of the core principles that informs the court's approach.

Re M (Ultra-Orthodox Judaism: Transgender) **[2017] EWCA Civ 2164**

MUNBY P:

60. [T]he function of the judge in a case like this is to act as the 'judicial reasonable parent', judging the child's welfare by the standards of reasonable men and women today, 2017, having regard to the ever changing nature of our world including, crucially for present purposes, *changes in social attitudes*, and always remembering that the reasonable

[12] [2017] EWCA Civ 2164.

man or woman is receptive to change, broadminded, tolerant, easy-going and slow to condemn. We live, or strive to live, in a tolerant society. We live in a democratic society subject to the rule of law. We live in a society whose law requires people to be treated equally and where their human rights are respected. We live in a plural society, in which the family takes many forms, some of which would have been thought inconceivable well within living memory.

The idea of the judge as 'judicial parent' first arose in the concept of wardship, where the child comes under the legal protection of the High Court and no significant decisions may be made in the child's life without the court's approval.[13] Whether it makes any difference to the analytical process, or whether it is helpful to extend it beyond the wardship context, is a matter of debate.[14]

In a number of recent decisions, the courts have stressed that a welfare analysis requires an assessment of all the realistic proposals for the outcome of the dispute, with the court conducting a holistic and parallel analysis of each option before reaching a conclusion. As Ryder LJ has put it, '[a] proposal that may have no particular merit on its own may still be better than the only other alternative which is worse',[15] so all options have to be considered before reaching a conclusion.

A further important point in considering what a child's welfare requires is to consider the child's own perspective. This factor is included within the welfare checklist, mandating the court to consider 'the ascertainable wishes and feelings of the child concerned (considered in the light of his age and understanding)'.[16] In an important analysis, John Eekelaar considered how children's voices should be heard as part of decision-making, bearing in mind the way that children's capacity to understand and participate changes as they get older. Eekelaar explains that there needs to be an additional element added to the decision-making process about children's welfare:

J. Eekelaar, 'The Interests of the Child and the Child's Wishes: The Role of Dynamic Self-Determinism', (1994b) 8 *International Journal of Law, Policy and the Family* 42, 47-49

The additional element is 'dynamic self-determinism'. This severely blurs the normally sharply focused conclusions of an objectivized determination. Instead, the child is placed in an environment which is reasonably secure, but which exposes it to a wide range of influences. As the child develops, it is encouraged to draw on these influences in such a way that the child itself contributes to the outcome. The very fact that the outcome has been, at least partly, determined by the child is taken to demonstrate that the outcome is in the child's best interests. The process is dynamic because it appreciates that the optimal course for a child cannot always be mapped out at the time of the decision, and may need to be revised as the child grows up. It involves self-determinism because the child itself is given scope to influence the outcomes.

13 Wardship is part of the court's inherent jurisdiction: see 8.7.
14 Eekelaar (2018a).
15 *Re F (International Relocation Cases)* [2015] EWCA Civ 882, [30].
16 CA 1989, s 1(3)(a).

> A characteristic feature of this strategy is that initial dispositions may often not be determinative. The court decrees no *final* outcome . . . Instead, the directions in which the child's relationships may move are left open-ended. . . .
>
> As applied in some of the cases, this approach may put considerable strain on resources. But that will only be so in the most conflicted of cases, where the costs are high in any case . . . More importantly, these solutions may find their way into the informal settlements reached between parents.

The importance of children having a voice within decision-making has gained traction since Eekelaar was writing about this issue,[17] and his ideas now have broad application in many areas of child law.[18]

8.2.1.c When will the welfare principle apply?

Although the welfare principle is of central importance in most family law disputes concerning children, there are some important limitations on when it applies.

'When a court determines any question'

The mandate in s 1 of the CA 1989 is only directed at the *courts*. It does not apply to any other decision-making body, public or private, exercising power and responsibility over children. Parents are free to prioritize other needs and interests, including their own or those of siblings, when making decisions in the ordinary course of family life. Similarly, local authorities taking decisions with respect to 'looked after' children do not have to prioritize the best interests of any individual child: they can take into account wider considerations, such as their own limited financial resources.

'Upbringing of the child'

The welfare principle under the CA 1989 only applies to questions where the 'upbringing of the child' is *directly* in issue. There is no definition of 'upbringing', but it seems to be connected with the scope of parental responsibility,[19] covering issues like where the child lives and with whom, how much time they spend with other people, education, health care, religion, the child's name, and so on. However, one or more of these issues must be directly before the court for determination for the welfare principle to apply, and several questions which clearly affect a child's interests have been held to be only *indirectly* concerned with upbringing, including:

- applications for an occupation or non-molestation order under Part 4 of the Family Law Act 1996;[20]
- applications for financial remedies after divorce;[21]

[17] UN Committee on the Rights of the Child (2009), para 74, suggesting that it is not possible to understand what a child's welfare requires without giving the child the opportunity to express their own views about the issue.

[18] See Daly, Kilkelly, and O'Mahony (2022). [19] See chapter 10. [20] See chapter 4.

[21] See chapter 6.

- applications for the use of scientific tests to determine the parentage of a child under s 20 of the Family Law Reform Act 1969;[22]
- applications for leave *to apply* for a s 8 order (e.g. child arrangements orders) under s 10 of the CA 1989, if the person seeking to make an application is not automatically entitled to do so;[23]
- disputes concerning publication of potentially damaging details about a child's background where the publicity does not relate directly to some aspect of the child's upbringing.[24]

There are also numerous decisions which *affect* children, but which are not about their upbringing—decisions about immigration, social security payments for a parent, society's allocation of housing, health care or educational resources, and so on. The welfare principle in s 1 of the CA 1989 does not apply to such situations.[25] However, there is also another version of the best interests principle which has broader application, coming from the United Nations Convention on the Rights of the Child, which the UK (and almost every other country in the world) has signed.

United Nations Convention on the Rights of the Child 1989

3(1) In all actions concerning children, whether undertaken by public or private social welfare institutions, courts of law, administrative authorities or legislative bodies, the best interests of the child shall be a primary consideration.

Whereas the paramountcy principle in s 1 of the CA 1989 applies only to *courts* making decisions about children's *upbringing*, the best interests principle in Article 3 applies much more broadly—*all actions* concerning children and covering a much wider range of bodies, including private institutions.[26] However, the 'trade-off' for such broad application of the welfare principle is that the obligation imposed on state authorities is significantly weakened: the welfare of the child is only *a primary* as opposed to *the paramount* consideration. Making the child's welfare only 'a primary consideration' allows considerable scope for the decision-maker to take into account a wide range of factors other than the particular interests of the child.[27] Article 3 is important across all areas of law, and has particular importance in family law for those decisions which affect children but which are not directly concerned with an aspect of their upbringing within the scope of s 1 of the CA 1989.[28]

[22] *Re H (A Minor) (Blood Tests: Parental Rights)* [1997] Fam 89, 104. See 9.3.3.b.

[23] *Re A (Minors: Residence Order)* [1992] Fam 182. See 11.3.2.

[24] *Re Z (A Minor) (Freedom of Publication)* [1997] Fam 1; *Re S (A Child) (Identification: Restrictions on Publication)* [2004] UKHL 47.

[25] *ZH (Tanzania) v Secretary of State for the Home Department* [2011] UKSC 4.

[26] On the distinction between actions *affecting* children and decisions *about* children, see Eekelaar (2015).

[27] The meaning of Art 3 of the Convention on the Rights of the Child was discussed by Lady Hale in *ZH (Tanzania) v Secretary of State for the Home Department* [2011] UKSC 4, an immigration case to which the paramountcy principle in the CA 1989 did not apply. See also *R (SG) v Secretary of State for Work and Pensions* [2015] UKSC 16; Fenton-Glynn (2015a); Hollingsworth (2015).

[28] See 8.5.5 and 8.5.6.

Best interests of more than one child relevant

A third important limitation on the application of the welfare principle is where the upbringing of two or more children is in question in court proceedings. While the court may consider the effect of imposing different solutions on a sibling group, it is essential that the welfare of each child be considered separately.[29] In situations where the best interests of each child, when taken individually, point to a different and irreconcilable outcome, it can be impossible for the court to fulfil its duty to give effect to the best interests of each child. Whichever approach the court adopts, the paramountcy principle will be compromised.

It is important to note that the problem only arises where *both children* are to be the subject of the proposed orders and all the proposed orders are to be determined in accordance with the paramountcy principle. Even though two or more minors are involved, if only one child is the *subject* of the proceedings before the court then the issue will not arise.[30] The correct approach where two children are the subject of proposed orders was confirmed by the Court of Appeal in *Re A (Children) (Conjoined Twins: Surgical Separation)*.[31] The court held that should a conflict develop between the paramount interests of two children, a balancing exercise weighing up the potential benefits and detriments of the possible outcomes to each of the two children must be undertaken and whichever course of action believed to cause the least overall harm adopted.[32] The case concerned an application for a declaration that it would be lawful for doctors to undertake surgical separation of conjoined twins, Jodie and Mary, against the wishes of the twins' parents and with the inevitable consequence that Mary, the weaker twin, would die. Without the separation both twins would die within a few months.

Re A (Children) (Conjoined Twins: Surgical Separation) [2001] Fam 147 (CA), 181–97

WARD LJ:

[T]he operation will be in Jodie's interests [it would give her the chance of a normal life] but not in Mary's [the operation would hasten her certain death]. Can that conflict be resolved and if so how?

. . . [T]he question arises directly in this case and because it is the right to life of each child that is in issue, the conflict between the children could not be more acute. If the duty of the court is to make a decision which puts Jodie's interests paramount and that decision would be contrary to the paramount interests of Mary, then, for my part, I do not see how the court can reconcile the impossibility of properly fulfilling each duty by simply declining to decide the very matter before it. That would be a total abdication of the duty which is imposed upon us. Given the conflict of duty, I can see no other way of dealing with it than by choosing the lesser of the two evils and so finding the least detrimental alternative. A balance has to be struck somehow and I cannot flinch from undertaking that evaluation, horrendously difficult though it is . . .

[29] *Re LC (Children) (Abduction: Habitual Residence: State of Mind of Child)* [2014] UKSC 1; *Re S (Relocation: Interests of Siblings)* [2011] EWCA Civ 454.

[30] *Birmingham City Council v H (A Minor)* [1994] 2 AC 212, 218–23. Note that the rights and interests of a non-subject child who is potentially affected by a decision must still be respected and given due weight by the court: see *Re Y (Removal from Jurisdiction: Failure to Consider Family Segmentation)* [2014] EWCA Civ 1287, [40].

[31] [2001] Fam 147.

[32] Ibid, 181–97. *Re A* is discussed further at 8.6.2.

Having conducted the required balancing exercise, Ward LJ concluded that the scales came down heavily in favour of giving Jodie the chance of a normal life. Permission was thus granted for the operation to be carried out.[33]

8.2.2 CRITICISMS OF THE WELFARE PRINCIPLE

8.2.2.a Indeterminacy

The concept of the child's welfare is notoriously vague, leaving considerable scope for individual judges to determine what they consider to be in a child's best interests. This indeterminacy has been the subject of considerable criticism. In particular, it is argued that the nebulous nature of the principle allows cases to be determined in accordance with nothing more principled than the personal prejudices and untested assumptions of individual judges.

R. Mnookin, 'Child-Custody Adjudication: Judicial Functions in the Face of Indeterminacy', (1975) 39 *Law and Contemporary Problems* 226, 229–61

[T]he determination of what is "best" or "least detrimental" for a particular child is usually indeterminate and speculative. For most custody cases [i.e. disputes about children's living arrangements], existing psychological theories simply do not yield confident predictions of the effects of alternative custody dispositions. Moreover, even if accurate predictions were possible in more cases, our society today lacks any clear-cut consensus about the values to be used in determining what is "best" or "least detrimental."

B. The Indeterminacy of Present-Day Standards

. . . When a judge must resolve a custody dispute, he is committed to making a choice among alternatives. The very words of the best-interests-of-the-child principle suggest that the judge should decide by choosing the alternative that "maximizes" what is best for a particular child. Conceived this way, the judge's decision can be framed in a manner consistent with an intellectual tradition that views the decision process as a problem of rational choice. In analyzing the custody decision from this perspective, my purpose is not to describe how judges in fact decide custody disputes nor to propose a method of how they should. Instead, it is to expose the inherent indeterminacy of the best interests standard.

1. Rational Choice

Decision theorists have laid out the logic of rational choice with clarity and mathematical rigor for prototype decision problems. The decision-maker specifies alternative outcomes associated with different courses of action and then chooses that alternative that "maximizes" his values, subject to whatever constraints the decision-maker faces. This involves two

[33] Brooke LJ agreed with Ward LJ on the issue of the children's best interests and how the conflict between them should be resolved. Robert Walker LJ disagreed, finding that the operation would be in Mary's best interests as well as Jodie's, because it would give them both back their bodily integrity. On his analysis, no conflict therefore arose between the best interests of the two children. For alternative ways in which the case might have been decided, giving greater weight to the views of the twins' parents or to children's rights, see respectively Hastings (2010) and Alghrani (2017).

critical assumptions: first, that the decision-maker can specify alternative outcomes for each course of action; the second, that the decision-maker can assign to each outcome a "utility" measure that integrates his values and allows comparisons among alternative outcomes. Choice does not require certainty about the single outcome that will in fact flow from a particular action. Treating uncertainty as a statistical problem, models have been developed that allow decisions to be made on the basis of "expected" utility . . .

2. A Custody Determination under the Best-Interests-of-the-Child Principle

Assume that a judge must decide whether a child should live with his mother or his father when the parents are in the process of obtaining a divorce. From the perspective of rational choice, the judge would wish to compare the expected utility for the child of living with his mother with that of living with his father. The judge would need considerable information and predictive ability to do this. The judge would also need some source for the values to measure utility for the child. All three are problematic.

a. The Need for Information: Specifying Possible Outcomes

In the example chosen, the judge would require information about how each parent had behaved in the past, how this behavior had affected the child and the child's present condition. Then the judge would need to predict the future behavior and circumstances of each parent if the child were to remain with that parent and to gauge the effects of this behavior and these circumstances on the child. He would also have to consider the behavior of each parent if the child were to live with the other parent and how this might affect the child . . .

One can question how often, if ever, any judge will have the necessary information. In many instances, a judge lacks adequate information about even the most rudimentary aspects of a child's life with his parents and has still less information available about what either parent plans in the future . . .

b. Predictions Assessing the Probability of Alternative Outcomes

Obviously, more than one outcome is possible for each course of judicial action, so the judge must assess the probability of various outcomes and evaluate the seriousness of possible benefits and harms associated with each. But even where a judge has substantial information about the child's past home life and the present alternatives, present-day knowledge about human behavior provides no basis for the kind of individualized predictions required by the best-interests standard. There are numerous competing theories of human behavior, based on radically different conceptions of the nature of man, and no consensus exists that any one is correct. No theory at all is considered widely capable of generating reliable predictions about the psychological and behavioral consequences of alternative dispositions for a particular child . . .

c. Values to Inform Choice: Assigning Utilities to Various Outcomes

Even if the various outcomes could be specified and their probability estimated, a fundamental problem would remain unsolved. What set of values should a judge use to determine what is in a child's best interests? If a decision-maker must assign some measure of utility to each possible outcome, how is utility to be determined?

For many decisions in an individualistic society, one asks the person affected what he wants. Applying this notion to custody cases, the child could be asked to specify those values or even to choose. In some cases, especially those involving divorce, the child's preference is sought and given weight. But to make the child responsible for the choice may jeopardize his future relationship with the other parent. And we often lack confidence that the child has the capacity and the maturity appropriately to determine his own utility.

Moreover, whether or not the judge looks to the child for some guidance, there remains the question whether best interests should be viewed from a long-term or short-term perspective. The conditions that make a person happy at age seven to ten may have adverse consequences at age thirty. Should the judge ask himself what decision will make the child happiest in the next year? Or at thirty? Or at seventy? Should the judge decide by thinking about what decision the child as an adult looking back would have wanted made? In this case, the preference problem is formidable, for how is the judge to compare "happiness" at one age with "happiness" at another age?

Deciding what is best for a child poses a question no less ultimate than the purposes and values of life itself. Should the judge be primarily concerned with the child's happiness? Or with the child's spiritual and religious training? Should the judge be concerned with the economic "productivity" of the child when he grows up? Are the primary values of life in warm, interpersonal relationships, or in discipline and self-sacrifice? Is stability and security for a child more desirable than intellectual stimulation? These questions could be elaborated endlessly. And yet, where is the judge to look for the set of values that should inform the choice of what is best for the child? Normally, the custody statutes do not themselves give content or relative weights to the pertinent values. And if the judge looks to society at large, he finds neither a clear consensus as to the best child rearing strategies nor an appropriate hierarchy of ultimate values.

8.2.2.b Lack of transparency and irrelevant considerations

Helen Reece has made a similarly strong attack on the welfare principle. Her concern focuses not on indeterminacy, but the way in which untested policies and principles which have little or nothing to do with the best interests of the child (some based on little more than ignorance or prejudice), are able to find their way into child-related disputes through the medium of the welfare principle.[34]

H. Reece, 'The Paramountcy Principle: Consensus or Construct?', (1996) 49 *Current Legal Problems* 267, 273 and 293–8

The indeterminacy and value-laden nature of custody decisions lead critics to characterise the ultimate results as subjective, individualistic, and idiosyncratic, arbitrary, and capricious. A more extreme version of this criticism is that adjudication under the paramountcy principle yields something close to a random pattern of outcomes. Slightly more radical variants of this argument suggest that judges' decisions may be informed by their middle and upper-class backgrounds, by their patriarchal values, or simply by their personal prejudices . . .

[These criticisms of the welfare principle] miss the mark. It is true that the paramountcy principle itself is indeterminate, but this indeterminacy has enabled a determinate policy to take over; where one parent does not fit into the traditional mould, the results of residence disputes can be predicted with as much accuracy as can legal cases generally. It is true that these decisions are value-dependent, but they depend on a value rather than on values. It follows that the claim that results in children's cases are subjective and depend on the views of the individual judge is false . . .

[34] Reece's later work examines this theory in the broader context of what she terms 'deviant' parents. See Reece (2017).

It emerges that the indeterminacy of children's welfare has allowed other principles and policies to exert an influence from behind the smokescreen of the paramountcy principle. I am referring here to principles and policies which are extraneous to children's welfare . . . [such as the principle that a child should live with the parent who is best able to create a 'normal' family environment].

[O]nce we have recognised that children's welfare does not really determine the course to be followed, the paramountcy principle becomes even less sacred: not only is the principle impossible to justify when taken at face value, the reality is that it is not even applied. We are now in a position to challenge the argument that the paramountcy principle is a harmless statement of intent. . . . Its danger lies in impeding open debate, open debate about which principles and which policies other than children's welfare should be given what weight in children's cases . . .

Indeed, this smothering of debate may not be so much the danger of, but rather the very purpose of, the paramountcy principle. King has argued that the paramountcy principle has an important symbolic function in legitimating the resolution of disputes. Whatever the contestants' view of the eventual decision, they unite with the judge in accepting the principle that the child's interests are paramount.

Not everyone agrees that the discretionary nature of the welfare principle with its attendant uncertainty and unpredictability is a problem. In fact, some perceive it as a positive strength.[35] However, there are various ways in which the law could try to address the concerns raised by Mnookin and Reece. One option would be to take a more 'scientific' approach to determining what will maximize the child's welfare, relying on 'objective' scientific evidence, drawn from a range of disciplines such as paediatrics, psychology, and sociology. The ready justification that expert scientific evidence can provide for difficult and often controversial decisions has obvious attractions for the courts. Greater reliance on scientific evidence is not, however, without its problems. Mnookin doubts the value of this type of evidence in trying to predict future outcomes for an individual child.

R. Mnookin, 'Child-Custody Adjudication: Judicial Functions in the Face of Indeterminacy', (1975) 39 *Law and Contemporary Problems* 226, 258–60, and 287

While psychiatrists and psychoanalysts have at times been enthusiastic in claiming for themselves the largest possible role in custody proceedings, many have conceded that their theories provide no reliable guide for predictions about what is likely to happen to a particular child. Anna Freud, who has devoted her life to the study of the child and who plainly believes that theory can be a useful guide to treatment has warned: "In spite of . . . advances there remain factors which make clinical foresight, i.e. prediction, difficult and hazardous," not the least of which is that "environmental happenings in a child's life will always remain unpredictable since they are not governed by any known laws . . ."

Various studies have attempted to trace personality development to specific antecedent variables to show that these variables have the same effects on different children. This connection is now widely questioned by experimental psychologists . . . who think that infants experience external events in individual ways. The implication of this for prediction is

[35] Herring (2005b), 161; George (2012a), ch 7.

described very well by Skolnick: "[I]f the child selectively interprets situations and events, we cannot confidently predict behaviour from knowledge of the situation alone" . . .

Having custody disputes determined by embracing more and more of the niceties of psychological and psychiatric theories requires careful analysis of the limits of these theories, their empirical bases, and the capacity of our legal system to absorb this new doctrine. In cases where, from the child's perspective, each claimant has a psychological relationship with the child, I doubt whether there would often be widespread consensus among experts about which parent would prove psychologically better (or less detrimental) to the child. Often each parent will have a different sort of relationship with the child, with the child attached to each. One may be warm, easy-going, but incapable of discipline. The other may be fair, able to set limits, but unable to express affection. By what criteria is an expert to decide which is less detrimental? Moreover, even the proponents of psychological standards have acknowledged how problematic it is to evaluate relationships from a psychological perspective unless a highly trained person spends a considerable amount of time observing the parent and child interact or talking to the child. Superficial examinations by those without substantial training may be worse than nothing. And yet, that is surely a high risk.

Even with the best trained experts, the choice would be based on predictions that are beyond the demonstrated capacity of any existing theory. While the psychologists and psychiatrists have made substantial therapeutic contributions, they are not soothsayers capable of predicting with any degree of confidence how a child is likely to benefit from alternative placements. When the expert does express a preference, it too often is based on an unexpressed value preference. What is psychologically least detrimental will usually be no more determinate for expert and nonexpert alike than what is in a child's best interests; and to reframe the question in a way that invites predictions based on the use of labels and terminology developed for treatment is both demeaning to the expert and corrupting for the judicial process.

The current limitations of scientific disciplines in trying to predict future outcomes is not the only concern. Commentators writing from a feminist perspective have noted how the legal process makes selective use of scientific evidence, often to provide apparently unqualified support for a particular ideological position or policy. Writing about the law's regulation of children's relationships with a parent with whom they do not live (then termed 'contact'), Felicity Kaganas is highly critical of the use of 'child welfare science' to reinforce an ideology on post-divorce parenting which prioritizes the importance of contact with non-resident fathers at the expense of the legitimate concerns and interests of mothers. As she points out, the scientific research on this issue is not straightforward.

F. Kaganas, 'Contact, Conflict and Risk', in S. Day Sclater and C. Piper (eds), *Undercurrents of Divorce* (Aldershot: Ashgate, 1999b), 99

The version of the research studies that has shaped the dominant discourse about divorce and contact is clearly a simplified one. In this version, divorce damages children and, in order to limit that damage it is essential to ensure that conflict is reduced or eliminated and that contact is maintained. The more nuanced and complex features of the research are absent . . . A recent review of research in the field confirms that it is characterised by greater complexity and greater uncertainty than the law allows. Rodgers and Pryor observe that, 'there is no simple or direct relationship between parental separation and children's adjustment, and poor outcomes are far from inevitable.' Nor can it be assumed, they say, that the disadvantages to children identified by researchers are attributable to the separation. And although they ultimately favour contact, they note that the loss or absence of a parent does not appear to have a very significant effect on children and that it is the quality and not the frequency of contact that matters. Furthermore, they identify factors such as the ability of parents to recover from the psychological distress as being important for children's ability to adjust.

Moreover, there is conflicting research in this field. Yet little credence is attached to studies that contradict what Maclean and Eekelaar term the 'new orthodoxy' . . .

Thus, whilst the scientific disciplines have an important contribution to make in improving understanding about how best to maximize children's welfare, the use of scientific evidence in the judicial process is not without significant difficulties.[36]

An alternative way in which the judge's discretion could be curtailed is to move towards a more transparent, rule-based system in which the guiding principles and values to be applied in determining a child's interests are more clearly articulated. However, to develop such rules or principles is a value-laden exercise fraught with just the same difficulties as more individualized decision-making. Mnookin doubts whether a rule-based system would prove any more successful than the current discretionary model.

R. Mnookin, 'Child-Custody Adjudication: Judicial Functions in the Face of Indeterminacy', (1975) 39 *Law and Contemporary Problems* 226, 262

[A]djudication by a more determinate rule would confront the fundamental problems posed by an indeterminate principle. But the choice between indeterminate standards and more precise rules poses a profound dilemma. The absence of rules removes the special burdens of justification and formulation of standards characteristic of adjudication. Unfairness and adverse consequences can result. And yet, rules that relate past events or conduct to legal consequences may themselves create substantial difficulties in the custody area. Our inadequate knowledge about human behavior and our inability to generalise confidently about the relationship between past events or conduct and future behavior make the formulation of rules especially problematic. Moreover, the very lack of consensus about values that make the best-interests standard indeterminate may also make the formulation of rules inappropriate: a legal rule must, after all, reflect some social value or values. An overly ambitious and indeterminate principle may result in fewer decisions that reflect what is known to be desirable. But rules may result in some conspicuously bad decisions that could be avoided by a more discretionary standard . . .

8.2.2.c Why should the child's welfare be paramount?

As Reece remarks, 'the paramountcy principle rests on an astonishingly solid consensus, both inside and outside the discipline of Family Law'.[37] It may be thought that given the strong support for the welfare principle, the justification for prioritizing the interests of

[36] See also Barnett (2000), 137–40.

[37] Reece (1996), 268.

one child over all other interests would be self-evident. However, articulating a convincing reason why children should always take priority is not necessarily straightforward. Reece outlines the most common arguments, none of which she finds convincing.

H. Reece, 'The Paramountcy Principle: Consensus or Construct?', (1996) 49 *Current Legal Problems* 267, 276–81

Children are more vulnerable

This is the most common justification for the paramountcy principle. For example, Cretney writes that the 'welfare principle is widely supported because . . . children who are necessarily vulnerable and dependent must be protected from harm'. A variation of this argument is that children's welfare should be paramount as a way of 'bending the stick', that in a world run by adults, there would otherwise be a danger that children's interests would be completely overlooked.

This argument holds the key to the consensus behind the paramountcy principle. Resting as it does on vulnerability, it has great resonance in the current political climate, in which vulnerability generally attracts priority . . . Even on its own terms this argument is flawed: in a case under the Children Act, the child will not necessarily be the most vulnerable individual . . .

Since the argument explains the consensus behind the paramountcy principle, it could not be more crucial to recognise the fallacy contained at the heart of the argument. The fallacy lies in the equation of priority with protection. It is self-evident that, as a general rule, children need more protection than adults. From this statement it does not follow that children should be prioritized over adults . . .

Children must be given the opportunity to become successful adults

'[T]he care of our children must be a prime priority. Within each child is the person he will one day become. Inside each of us is the child we once were' [Baroness Strange]. According to this argument, childhood is important because of its psychological significance; unless we do what is best for children, they will not be able to flourish into adults. The argument is self-defeating because it makes the importance of childhood contingent on, and subordinate to, the importance of adulthood: if decisions are made which sacrifice adults' interests to children's interests, there is little point becoming a successful adult.

More broadly, this argument is self-defeating because it promotes the future at the expense of the present, and indeed Leach argues explicitly that children are important because they are our future. The resonance of this yearning for the future reflects a social malaise. Although a preoccupation with the future is often favourably contrasted with a preoccupation with the past, the reality is that both represent an attempt to escape the present. A society which puts its hope in simply reproducing itself is a society which has lost its sense of purpose. It reduces the destiny of humans to ensuring that others take their place.

Adults create children

'Grown-ups . . . make free decisions, pooled their genes, created a baby and have to take the consequences . . . Children come first. We invited them to life's party' [Libby Purves]. It is not self-evident that the creation is more important than the creator; the opposite argument is equally plausible and indeed forms the basis of most religions. Moreover, the argument only achieves coherence in relation to parents; when the paramountcy principle ignores the interests of anyone other than a natural parent, it ignores the interests of someone who had no control over whether the child was born.

Argument from Solomon

This argument, which again could only conceivably justify the paramountcy principle in its application to parents, is that the desire to sacrifice one's own interests to those of one's child is the very mark of being a parent. If the argument is that this is how things are, then it stands defeated by legal disputes between parents and children. If the argument is that this is what it means to be a good parent, first, this is not self-evident, and secondly . . . there are more important values than being a good parent.

Utilitarian arguments

. . . All the previous arguments have justified the importance attached to children's welfare as a primary good. Two final arguments return to the utilitarian premises which initiated the discussion, but cast the net more broadly to include effect on society. More specifically, Barton and Douglas argue that children are important for the continuity of order in society and Parker suggests that giving greater weight to children's welfare maximises the welfare of society. However, . . . when we raise the discussion to the social level, as indeed we should, the reasons to reject the paramountcy principle are far stronger than any reasons to retain it.

Reece argues that prioritizing the interests of children over all other relevant parties simply cannot be justified.[38]

Along similar lines, it is sometimes said that the paramountcy principle means that the child is being viewed in isolation from their family,[39] and that welfare is the 'single deciding factor'.[40] Not everyone accepts these criticisms, however.[41]

R. George, 'The Child's Welfare in a European Perspective' in J. Scherpe (ed), *European Family Law, Vol III: Family Law in European Perspective* (London: Elgar, 2016)

When a judge, or anyone in fact, says that *x* is in the child's welfare, that statement represents the conclusion of an analysis of many factors – indeed, of all factors which bear on the decision about the child's upbringing, either directly or indirectly. This analysis expressly includes the rights of parents, and expressly requires a careful balancing of the competing considerations. . . .

So, 'when all the relevant facts, relationships, claims and wishes of the parents, risks, choices and other circumstances *are taken into account and weighed*',[42] the course of action to be followed is the one that most promotes the child's welfare. Does that mean that the courts assess welfare 'without regard for' the rights, interests or welfare of others? Surely not. The fact that A's (qualified) rights do not prevail in the analysis does not mean that there

[38] Ibid, 275. It may be noted that children are the 'subjects' of proceedings about their upbringing, but are rarely participants in those disputes: see 11.3.3.

[39] Herring (1999a), 225.

[40] Choudhry and Fenwick (2005), 456.

[41] For consideration of a similar issue from a children's rights perspective, see Ferguson (2013b), 197–9.

[42] Quoting *J v C* [1970] AC 668, 710.

was no 'regard' given to them. One might note that the child's (qualified) rights have not necessarily prevailed either. Consider, for example, a court order authorising a child to be taken into local authority care. The article 8 rights of each parent are, of course, involved in such a decision; but so too are some of the child's article 8 rights. Welfare is a composite idea, whereas rights can be atomised. I have a right to *x*, to *y* and to *z*, all of which are separate and freestanding, and which may indeed conflict with one another at times. My welfare interest, on the other hand, is always made up of many considerations: those considerations may well be conflicting, but the welfare conclusion sits above such conflict, and reflects the end result of the analysis rather than a discussion about which factors should be included.

For these reasons, I would respectfully suggest that to say that welfare 'displaces' all other considerations risks conflating 'a welfare decision' with 'the factors which are used to make a welfare decision'. The conclusion of any gestalt, complex, multi-factorial analysis like a welfare analysis will overtake (or displace) the individual considerations which feed into it, but that does not mean that those considerations are unimportant, nor that they are not given their due weight and respect. It is the result of a balance . . .

Another possible answer to the criticism is that the paramountcy principle applies only to questions about the *upbringing* of a child, where the child is at the very heart of the case. In other areas, where the child is merely *part* of the case, their welfare is not paramount.[43] Does the fact that the dispute is about the child offer a justification for focusing attention on the child's interests, even if that approach might not be acceptable in other contexts?[44]

8.3 ALTERNATIVES TO THE WELFARE PRINCIPLE

For those who are critical of the welfare principle, the question inevitably arises as to whether there is a better approach to decision-making about children. There are several alternatives, reflecting Reece's view that decision-making in family law needs to be more transparent and disciplined and that automatically prioritizing the child's interests is wrong. The alternatives thus seek to find a way to identify the legitimate rights and interests of all affected parties and to bring those interests fairly into the decision-making process.

8.3.1 RE-CONCEPTUALIZING THE WELFARE PRINCIPLE

Reece's concerns regarding the 'unduly individualistic' nature of the welfare principle are shared by Herring.[45] In light of these concerns, he has developed an alternative theory which he terms 'relationship-based welfare'.[46] This approach is based on the principle that a child should not be seen as an isolated individual but as an integral part of a wider family network. In his view, the interdependence of the child on this wider family network should constitute a core consideration in the decision-making process: not least because teaching the child the importance of respecting the needs and interests of others is core to the child's welfare.[47]

[43] See 8.2.1. [44] Eekelaar (2015). [45] Herring (1999a), 233. [46] Herring (1999a), (1999b).
[47] See also Herring and Foster (2012).

J. Herring, 'The Welfare Principle and the Rights of Parents', in A. Bainham, S. Day Sclater, and M. Richards (eds), *What is a Parent? A Socio-Legal Analysis* (Oxford: Hart Publishing, 1999b), 89, 101–3

The conception of the welfare principle adopted by the courts is often too narrowly individualist and focuses on a self-centred approach to welfare. A broader version of the welfare principle could allow consideration of the parent's interests. There are two elements to the argument for pursuing a wider understanding of the welfare principle. The first is that it is part of growing up for a child to learn to sacrifice as well as claim benefits. Families, and society in general, are based on mutual co-operation and support. So it is important to encourage a child to adopt, to a limited extent, the virtue of altruism and an awareness of social obligation. It needs to be stressed that it is a very limited altruism that is being sought. Children should only be expected to be altruistic to the extent of not demanding from parents excessive sacrifices in return for minor benefits.

The second element of this approach is that the child's welfare involves ensuring that the child's relationships with the other family members are fair and just. A relationship based on unacceptable demands on a parent is not furthering a child's welfare . . .

It is in the child's welfare to be brought up in a family whose members respect each other and so, on occasion, sacrifices may be required from the child . . .

The effect of this approach is to move away from conceiving the problem as a clash between children and parents and in terms of weighing two conflicting interests, and towards seeing it rather as deciding what is a proper parent-child relationship. The child's welfare is promoted when he or she lives in a fair and just relationship with each parent. Understood in this way, the welfare principle can protect children while properly taking into account parent's rights.

The argument can also operate where a child's welfare may require a sacrifice for the obtaining of some greater social good . . .

As Herring notes, one advantage of his approach is that it does not entail abandoning the centrality of the paramountcy principle. Herring has the more limited objective of 're-conceptualizing' what we mean by welfare. However, it could be argued that this is not a marked departure, if a departure at all, from the approach that the courts take in practice already.

R. George, *Ideas and Debates in Family Law* (Oxford: Hart Publishing, 2012), 118

[W]hile the welfare principle might, on occasion, require an outcome which did indeed "cause a huge level of harm to others", such a solution will be exceptional, because the harm to others—particularly a parent or other family member—will in itself impact adversely on the child, which will be a significant factor to take into account when deciding what is in the child's best interests in the first place.

In *J v C* itself, the House of Lords explained that the welfare principle involved

> "a process whereby, when all the relevant facts, relationships, claims and wishes of the parents, risks, choices and other circumstances *are taken into account and weighed*, the course to be followed will be that which is most in the interests of the

child's welfare as that term has now to be understood. That is the first consideration because it is of first importance and the paramount consideration because it rules upon or determines the course to be followed."

The suggestion that the welfare principle requires the child to be viewed in isolation from his or her family and community would seem to ignore the first part of this explanation of the process. . . .

J v C remains the leading explanation of the process involved in the welfare principle, and shows that only factors which have *no bearing whatever* on the child's welfare need be discounted. This approach is somehow morphed in some critics' analysis to suggest that welfare is a stand-alone factor, as if the child's welfare were unaffected by those around him or her. Of course some factors will be more important to the child's welfare than others, and part of the court's job is to assess the relevance of each factor—but factors which are of indirect relevance to welfare may still be important in the overall assessment of an individual case.

Herring's approach may also prove problematic from the child's perspective, in that once it is conceded that the rights and interests of the parents are relevant to the child's welfare, the child's welfare may be subsumed within the parents' interests. Eekelaar is critical of Herring's approach for this reason, pointing out that it was not so long ago that the view was taken that 'recognition of the pre-eminence of the father was in the child's interests'.[48] Arguably this problem continues today, though different groups might argue about whether it is mothers' or fathers' interests with which children's interests are more aligned.

Eekelaar proposes a more radical alternative which, in seeking to ensure that proper regard is paid to the interests of others, abandons the paramountcy of welfare.

J. Eekelaar, 'Beyond the Welfare Principle', (2002) 14 *Child and Family Law Quarterly* 237, 242–5

It might appear that many dilemmas in family law involve resolving issues at which the future well-being . . . of various people are at stake. How are these issues best resolved? A crude utilitarian attempt at maximising the well-being of the greatest number could not be accepted, since this would pay insufficient regard to extreme adverse affects of certain outcomes on the well-being of particular individuals. The best solution is surely to adopt the course that avoids inflicting the most damage on the well-being of any interested individual. The methodology can be illustrated in this way. Suppose one could assign a value to the degree of benefit and detriment to the well-being of all interested parties under various possible solutions. The following would be a simple case. C is the child. X and Y are adult participants. Minus values indicate an outcome that has more detriment than benefit for the party:

- Solution 1: C (+15); X (+10); Y (–30).
- Solution 2: C (+10); X (+10); Y (–20).
- Solution 3: C (+5); X (–5); Y (–10).

Solution 1 would be chosen under the best interests test. Solution 2 would be chosen under general utilitarianism (since the overall benefit/detriment scores are: –5 (solution 1);

[48] Eekelaar (2002), 238.

> 0 (solution 2); and −10 (solution 3)). Under the suggested methodology, solution 3 should be chosen, for although it reduces the benefit to C (and to X), the detriment to Y is far less . . .
>
> It seems very difficult to advocate a solution that is, on these assumptions, the least beneficial to the child of all three solutions. But on closer examination, some merits appear. It *considerably* reduces the detriment for Y. It may be that the disadvantage to the child is a price worth paying . . . Of course, the evaluation of the benefits and detriments on various parties is a matter of judgment in each case, but this is true in all matters of adjudication, including, of course, the welfare test. It is a delusion to believe that such matters can be evaluated with scientific objectivity. Nevertheless, it is safe to say that special care must be taken in evaluating the impact or potential impact, of a solution on the well-being of children, for it is always necessary to remember children's vulnerability and the potential longer term effects on them, than on adults, of many decisions . . .

Although Eekelaar rejects the paramountcy principle, he still affords the child a privileged position within the decision-making process:

> Qualifications—privileges and appropriateness
>
> Unfortunately, this does not conclude the matter. It might be difficult (but not impossible) to envisage solutions that hold nothing but detriment to the child. It is easier to imagine this for an adult. Yet it is possible to imagine an outcome for a child where detriments exceed benefits. How, then, would a decision be made between the following two solutions?
>
> - Solution 1: C (+10); X (+10); Y (−30).
> - Solution 2: C (−10); X (−15); Y (−15).
>
> Here the price paid in solution 2 for reducing Y's detriment is to spread the hardship around relatively equally. It certainly would not satisfy general utilitarianism. Should it satisfy anyone? I think the answer must be to hold that no solution should be adopted where the detriments outweigh the benefits for the child unless that would be the result of *any* available solution, so that it is unavoidable. There should be no negative quantity for C. In this way, the interests of children would be *privileged* in the calculus, but not given priority. This could be justified on the basis that, whatever we might say about future generations, they at least have no control whatsoever over our actions. It behoves us, therefore, when considering the consequences of our actions, to treat our successors as always innocent and to allow them to start their lives, as far as possible, without deficits from what we have done. For the same reason, the privilege should allow resolution in favour of children where the value of benefits and detriments between them and other parties is minimal or very speculative.

Eekelaar's approach has the advantage that, by separating out the individual rights and interests of all affected parties, it brings much greater transparency to the decision-making process. This is preferable to concealing those interests behind the obscurity of the welfare principle. Eekelaar also provides some comfort for strong adherents to a welfare-centred approach by continuing to privilege the children's interests in the form of a long-stop guarantee that no solution will ever be adopted which results in a net detriment to the child. The child's basic interests are thus safeguarded, whilst creating a better balance between

the rights and interests of all parties. However, as Eekelaar acknowledges, the downside of his approach is its complexity, making it difficult to apply in practice.[49] This is perhaps inevitable. Family life is complex and disputes about a child are rarely easy to resolve. It is perhaps better to face this complexity than to hide behind the apparent safety of the welfare principle.

Whether one finds these alternatives to the welfare principle convincing, the question is no longer merely a matter for academic speculation. Following the implementation of the HRA 1998, there is a very real question whether the welfare-orientated approach of the CA 1989 and the ACA 2002 can be sustained in the face of the rights-based approach of the ECHR.

8.4 THE ECHR AND CHILD-RELATED DISPUTES

In considering the relationship between the welfare principle and the rights protected under the ECHR, the potential relevance of the Convention to disputes concerning children must first be explored.[50] Anyone seeking to take advantage of the ECHR and its rights-based approach in a family dispute must first establish that they fall within the scope of the ECHR's protection. The most important provision of the ECHR here is the right to respect for private or family life, guaranteed under Article 8.

8.4.1 ESTABLISHING A 'RIGHT' UNDER ARTICLE 8(1)

In order to fall within the scope of Article 8(1), the applicant must first establish the existence of 'family life'. A well-established line of authority makes it clear that Article 8 affords respect only to existing family relationships: it does not safeguard the 'mere desire' to found a family or create new familial relationships.[51] Establishing the existence of family life is not always straightforward. The European Court has generally favoured the traditional, heterosexual, married unit where the existence of family life between both the parents and the child is established automatically by virtue of the marital tie.[52] Establishing family life between parent and child where the parents are not married is more difficult.

The relationship between unmarried mothers and their children was dealt with in the seminal case of *Marckx v Belgium*.[53] At the time of the application, illegitimate children suffered a number of disadvantages under Belgian law when compared with legitimate children, including the fact that no legal bond was automatically created between illegitimate children and their mothers by the mere fact of birth. The European Court held that Article 8 protects the family life of both the 'legitimate' and the 'illegitimate' family, thereby bringing the position of an 'illegitimate' child into line with that of a 'legitimate' child as regards the mother–child relationship.

[49] Ibid, 248. [50] Fenton-Glynn (2021).

[51] See, e.g., *Fretté v France* (App No 36515/97, ECHR) (2003), [32]; *Paradiso and Campanelli v Italy* (App No 25358/12, ECHR) (2017), [141].

[52] *Al Nashif v Bulgaria* (App No 50963/99, ECHR) (2003); see also *Kosmopoulou v Greece* (App No 60457/00, ECHR) (2004), [42].

[53] (A/31, ECHR) (1979–80), [31].

The European Court has not, however, taken the same step with respect to the relationship between an unmarried father and his children. Although *Marckx* states unequivocally that Article 8 'makes no distinction between the "legitimate" and the "illegitimate" family', the European Court has resisted assuming the existence of family life between an unmarried father and his children on the basis of a mere biological bond. The Court therefore has tended to require unmarried fathers to demonstrate the existence in practice of 'close personal ties' between himself and the child, or at least between himself and the child's mother, before he can claim the protection of Article 8. The Court has held that factors relevant to determining whether de facto family life has been established include cohabitation (usual but not essential), the nature of the relationship between the parents, and the father's demonstrable commitment to the child both before and after the birth.[54] However, in *Anayo v Germany*,[55] the European Court held that 'family life' may extend to the '*potential*' relationship between an unmarried father and his child where the absence of an established relationship cannot be attributed to the father. While reiterating that '[a]s a rule, cohabitation is a requirement for a relationship amounting to family life', the Court acknowledged that there may be exceptional cases in which family life is established without this element.[56] The Court suggested that 'relevant factors' in making this assessment would 'include the nature of the relationship between the natural parents and a demonstrable interest in and commitment by the father to the child before and after the birth'.[57]

Although the European Court has treated the traditional married unit more favourably than the unmarried family, its willingness to embrace de facto as well as de jure family life has enabled unconventional family relationships to benefit from the protection of the ECHR. Importantly, this has included the relationship between transgender parents and their children, and gay and lesbian parents and their children.[58]

Outside the immediate family unit of parents and child, the Court has suggested that the protection of 'family life' under Article 8 may extend to include near relatives such as grandparents, siblings, aunts, uncles, and cousins,[59] though this depends on there being 'sufficiently close family ties' to trigger Article 8.[60] Rather oddly, the Strasbourg jurisprudence suggests that it may be easier for grandparents to establish 'family life' for the purposes of Article 8 than the child's father.[61]

8.4.2 ESTABLISHING A BREACH OF ARTICLE 8(1)

Once the existence of family life has been established, the inquiry moves on to consider whether the state is, prima facie, in breach of any of its obligations under Article 8. The specific obligations imposed on the state by Article 8 are many and varied. We give just a flavour here.

Perhaps the most fundamental obligation imposed on the state under Article 8 is to respect the 'mutual enjoyment by parent and child of each other's company', what the

[54] *Lebbink v Netherlands* (App No 45582/99, ECHR) (2004).

[55] (App No 20578/07, ECHR) (2010).

[56] Ibid, [56].

[57] Ibid, [57]. Note the similarity between these factors and those used by the domestic courts when determining application for parental responsibility orders from unmarried fathers: see 10.3.2.

[58] *X, Y and Z v United Kingdom* (App No 21830/93, ECHR) (1997); *da Silva Mouta v Portugal* (App No 33290/96, ECHR) (1999).

[59] *Marckx v Belgium* (A/31, ECHR) (1979–80), [45].

[60] Fenton-Glynn (2021), 232–3.

[61] *C v XYZ County Council* [2007] EWCA Civ 1206, [31] and [39].

European Court describes as a 'fundamental element of family life'.[62] Any state action in the public or private sphere which prevents or hinders the parent and child from exercising this right, such as refusing an order for a parent to spend time or have contact with their child, or taking a child into state care, constitutes a prima facie violation of Article 8(1).[63]

The primary object of Article 8 is thus to protect individuals against arbitrary intervention by public authorities. However, as held in *Marckx v Belgium*, Article 8 also imposes positive obligations on the state, one of the most important of which is to ensure the integration of a child into their family.[64] A second positive obligation imposed on the state is to take all reasonable measures to reconcile parent and child where family life, for whatever reason, has broken down. This is now well established in both the public and private law context.[65]

Finally, Article 8 offers procedural as well as substantive protection, requiring that the decision-making process is both transparent and fair. In particular, the public authority (whether a local authority, an adoption agency, or the court) must ensure that 'the parents have been involved in the decision-making process, seen as a whole, to a degree sufficient to provide them with the requisite protection of their interests'.[66]

8.4.3 JUSTIFYING A BREACH UNDER ARTICLE 8(2)

If the applicant is able to establish a prima facie breach of Article 8(1), the next question is whether the breach can be justified in accordance with Article 8(2): (i) that the act in question was 'in accordance with the law'; (ii) that it pursued a legitimate aim; and (iii) was 'necessary in a democratic society'.[67] This last requirement gives rise to the most difficult questions, requiring a careful balancing exercise between the various rights and interests at stake. It is at this stage of the decision-making process that we reach the crux of the issue: in carrying out this balancing exercise, what weight is to be attributed to the child's interests? In particular, are the child's interests to be regarded as the paramount or determining factor, such that any interference with the adult applicant's rights will be deemed 'necessary in a democratic society' provided the measure in question was taken with the aim of protecting the child? It is the answer to this question which determines whether the welfare-orientated approach of English law can survive implementation of the HRA 1998.

8.4.4 THE RELATIONSHIP BETWEEN THE WELFARE PRINCIPLE AND ARTICLE 8

Academic commentators were divided on whether the implementation of the HRA 1998 would necessitate change to the paramountcy principle. It was suggested that pursuant to

[62] *KA v Finland* (App No 27751/95, ECHR) (2003), [92]. See also *Venema v Netherlands* (App No 35731/97, ECHR) (2003), [71].

[63] *KA v Finland* (App No 27751/95, ECHR) (2003), [45]. *Hoffman v Austria* (A/255-C, ECHR) (1994).

[64] (A/31, ECHR) (1979–80), [31].

[65] *Haase v Germany* (App No 11057/02, ECHR) (2005), [93]; *Glaser v United Kingdom* (App No 32346/96, ECHR) (2000).

[66] *W v United Kingdom* (App No 9749/82, ECHR) (1988), [62]–[64].

[67] These requirements are discussed more generally at 1.2.1.

s 3 of the HRA 1998 the welfare principle, as traditionally understood in English law, would have to be 're-interpreted' in order to give greater recognition to the independent rights and interests of parents. It was also suggested that if such re-interpretation of the word 'paramount' was considered impossible, the paramountcy principle would find itself subject to a declaration of incompatibility under s 4 of the HRA 1998.[68]

8.4.4.a The domestic courts' approach

Prior to the HRA 1998 coming into force, there were clear indications that the domestic courts did not see any incompatibility between the welfare principle in s 1 of the CA 1989 and the rights protected under the ECHR. Indeed, in one of the more significant challenges to the welfare principle shortly before the enactment of the CA 1989,[69] the House of Lords had said that any difference that might exist between the two approaches was 'semantic only'.[70]

The courts adopted much the same approach following the implementation of the HRA 1998.[71] The clear message was that the HRA 1998 did not challenge the previously understood interpretation of the welfare principle.

More recently, the Supreme Court has given further thought to the way in which Article 8 interacts with domestic law. *Re B (Care Proceedings: Appeal)* was a child protection case in which the child—whom the Justices named Amelia—was removed from her parents at birth because of concerns about the standard of care which she would receive if left with her mother. The trial judge found the threshold test in s 31 of the CA 1989 to be crossed (Amelia was at risk of suffering significant harm) and determined that her welfare demanded that she be freed for adoption. While the Supreme Court reiterated the earlier view that there is no incompatibility between the welfare principle and Article 8, the reasons which the Justices identified as supporting this view may be more developed than in some of the earlier case law.[72]

Re B (Care Proceedings: Appeal) [2013] UKSC 33

LORD WILSON:

32. [The] care order in relation to Amelia with a view to her adoption represented an interference with the exercise by Amelia, by M and by F of their rights to respect for their family life. It was therefore lawful only if, within the meaning of article 8(2) of the Convention, it was not only in accordance with the law but also "necessary" in a democratic society for the protection of the right of A to grow up free from harm. In *Johansen v Norway* (1997) the European Commission of Human Rights observed, at para 83, that "the notion of necessity implies that the interference corresponds to a pressing social need and, in particular, that it is proportional to the legitimate aim pursued."

[68] See, e.g., the discussion in Herring (1999a).

[69] The welfare principle was substantively the same under the previous legislation.

[70] *Re KD (A Minor (Ward: Termination of Access)* [1988] 1 AC 806.

[71] See, e.g., *Payne v Payne* [2001] EWCA Civ 166 and *Re B (A Minor) (Adoption: Natural Parent)* [2001] UKHL 70; for discussion, see Harris-Short (2002).

[72] Further extracts from *Re B* are found at 13.4.3.

33. In a number of its judgments the European Court of Human Rights, "the ECtHR", has spelt out the stark effects of the proportionality requirement in its application to a determination that a child should be adopted. Only a year ago, in *YC v United Kingdom* (2012), it said:

> "134. The Court reiterates that in cases concerning the placing of a child for adoption, which entails the permanent severance of family ties, the best interests of the child are paramount. In identifying the child's best interests in a particular case, two considerations must be borne in mind: first, it is in the child's best interests that his ties with his family be maintained except in cases where the family has proved particularly unfit; and secondly, it is in the child's best interests to ensure his development in a safe and secure environment. It is clear from the foregoing that family ties may only be severed in very exceptional circumstances and that everything must be done to preserve personal relations and, where appropriate, to 'rebuild' the family. It is not enough to show that a child could be placed in a more beneficial environment for his upbringing. However, where the maintenance of family ties would harm the child's health and development, a parent is not entitled under article 8 to insist that such ties be maintained."

Although in that paragraph it did not in terms refer to proportionality, the court had prefaced it with a reference to the need to examine whether the reasons adduced to justify the measures were relevant and sufficient, in other words whether they were proportionate to them.

34. In my view it is important not to take any one particular sentence out of its context in the whole of para 134 of the *YC* case: for each of its propositions is interwoven with the others. But the paragraph well demonstrates the high degree of justification which article 8 demands of a determination that a child should be adopted or placed in care with a view to adoption. Yet, while in every such case the trial judge should . . . consider the proportionality of adoption to the identified risks, he is likely to find that domestic law runs broadly in parallel with the demands of article 8. Thus domestic law makes clear that:

(a) it is not enough that it would be *better* for the child to be adopted than to live with his natural family (*Re S-B (Non-Accidental Injury)* [2009] UKSC 17); and

(b) a parent's consent to the making of an adoption order can be dispensed with only if the child's welfare so *requires* (section 52(1)(b) of the Adoption and Children Act 2002); there is therefore no point in making a care order with a view to adoption unless there are good grounds for considering that this statutory test will be satisfied.

LORD NEUBERGER P:

73. . . . As Lady Hale (who knows more about this than anybody) says in para 194, the 1989 Act was drafted with the Convention in mind; in any event, with the coming into force of the Human Rights Act 1998 ("the 1998 Act"), the 1989 Act must now, if possible, be construed and applied so as to comply with the Convention. So too the Adoption and Children Act 2002 ("the 2002 Act") must, if possible, be construed and applied so as to comply with the Convention. It also appears to me that the 2002 Act must be construed and applied bearing in mind the provisions of the UN Convention on the Rights of the Child 1989 ("UNCRC").

75. As already mentioned, it is clear that a judge cannot properly decide that a care order should be made in such circumstances, unless the order is proportionate bearing in mind the requirements of article 8.

76. It appears to me that, given that the Judge concluded that the section 31(2) threshold was crossed, he should only have made a care order if he had been satisfied that it was

necessary to do so in order to protect the interests of the child. By "necessary", I mean, to use Lady Hale's phrase in para 198, "where nothing else will do". I consider that this conclusion is clear under the 1989 Act, interpreted in the absence of the Convention, but it is put beyond doubt by article 8. The conclusion is also consistent with UNCRC.

Put another way, the judges appear to be saying that not only was the CA 1989 drafted so as to be compatible with the ECHR, but that its application in practice is informed by developments in the Strasbourg jurisprudence. The argument is that same result is reached whether under the CA 1989 or under Article 8, not because the two approaches are necessarily identical in theory, but because the welfare principle is applied in such a way as to make them identical in practice.

8.4.4.b The Strasbourg Court's approach

The European Court has not always spoken with one voice in terms of its approach to the welfare principle, and there are numerous examples of judgments using the terms 'primary' and 'paramount' somewhat interchangeably—certainly the Court does not see such a sharp line between them as has been drawn by the domestic courts.[73]

For many years, the approach of the European Court to child welfare and Article 8 was set down by *Johansen v Norway*, which concerned a mother's challenge to the Norwegian authorities' decision to take her child into care and terminate her parental rights and responsibilities with a view to placing the child for adoption. The Norwegian government expressly argued that in a case of this nature 'rather than attempting to strike a "fair balance" between the interests of the natural parent and the child', the best interests of the child should be paramount. The European Court clearly rejected this interpretation of the required balancing exercise.

Johansen v Norway (App No 17383/90, ECHR) (1997)

78. The Court considers that taking a child into care should normally be regarded as a temporary measure to be discontinued as soon as circumstances permit and that any measures of implementation of temporary care should be consistent with the ultimate aim of reuniting the natural parent and the child . . . In this regard, a fair balance has to be struck between the interests of the child in remaining in public care and those of the parent in being reunited with the child . . . In carrying out this balancing exercise, the Court will attach particular importance to the best interests of the child, which, depending on their nature and seriousness, may override those of the parent. In particular, as suggested by the Government, the parent cannot be entitled under Article 8 of the Convention . . . to have such measures taken as would harm the child's health and development.

In the present case the applicant had been deprived of her parental rights and access in the context of a permanent placement of her daughter in a foster home with a view to adoption by the foster parents . . . These measures were particularly far-reaching in that they totally

[73] See *ZH (Tanzania) v Secretary of State for the Home Department* [2011] UKSC 4.

deprived the applicant of her family life with the child and were inconsistent with the aim of reuniting them. Such measures should only be applied in exceptional circumstances and could only be justified if they were motivated by an overriding requirement pertaining to the child's best interests . . .

Much of the subsequent case law faithfully followed the *Johansen* approach, often quoting directly from the judgment and emphasizing the need to strike a 'fair balance' between, on the one hand, the rights and interests of the child's parents and, on the other, the rights and interests of the child. This approach was adopted in both the public and private law contexts,[74] and some commentators argued strongly that it was difficult to reconcile the *Johansen* approach with the welfare principle as understood in English law.[75]

However, a number of later authorities have departed from the *Johansen* approach and provide some scope for seeing the paramountcy principle as compatible with Article 8.[76] The most significant is the Grand Chamber decision in *Neulinger and Shuruk v Switzerland*,[77] which arose out of international child abduction proceedings in relation to children taken to Switzerland.

Neulinger and Shuruk v Switzerland (App No 41615/07, ECHR) (2010)

134. In this area the decisive issue is whether a fair balance between the competing interests at stake – those of the child, of the two parents, and of public order – has been struck, within the margin of appreciation afforded to States in such matters . . . bearing in mind, however, that the child's best interests must be the primary consideration . . . The child's best interests may, depending on their nature and seriousness, override those of the parents . . . The parents' interests, especially in having regular contact with their child, nevertheless remain a factor when balancing the various interests at stake . . .

135. The Court notes that there is currently a broad consensus – including in international law – in support of the idea that in all decisions concerning children, their best interests must be paramount (see the numerous references in paragraphs 49–56 above, and in particular Article 24 § 2 of the European Union's Charter of Fundamental Rights). As indicated, for example, in the Charter, "[e]very child shall have the right to maintain on a regular basis a personal relationship and direct contact with both his or her parents, unless that is contrary to his or her interests."

136. The child's interest comprises two limbs. On the one hand, it dictates that the child's ties with its family must be maintained, except in cases where the family has proved particularly unfit. It follows that family ties may only be severed in very exceptional circumstances and that everything must be done to preserve personal relations and, if and when appropriate, to "rebuild" the family (see *Gnahoré* [*v France* (App No 40031/98) (2000)]). On

[74] See, e.g., *Buchberger v Austria* (App No 32899/96, ECHR) (2003), [40]; *Sahin v Germany; Sommerfeld v Germany* (App No 30943/96, ECHR) (2003), [66]; and *Görgülü v Germany* (App No 74969/01, ECHR) (2004), [43].

[75] See, e.g., Bonner, Fenwick, and Harris-Short (2003), 582–3.

[76] The first of these cases was *Yousef v Netherlands* (App No 33711/96, ECHR) (2002), though at the time it appeared to be an outlier from the general approach.

[77] (App No 41615/07, ECHR) (2010).

the other hand, it is clearly also in the child's interest to ensure its development in a sound environment, and a parent cannot be entitled under Article 8 to have such measures taken as would harm the child's health and development . . .

139. In addition, the Court must ensure that the decision-making process leading to the adoption of the impugned measures by the domestic court was fair and allowed those concerned to present their case fully . . . To that end the Court must ascertain whether the domestic courts conducted an in-depth examination of the entire family situation and of a whole series of factors, in particular of a factual, emotional, psychological, material and medical nature, and made a balanced and reasonable assessment of the respective interests of each person, with a constant concern for determining what the best solution would be for the abducted child in the context of an application for his return to his country of origin.

It can be seen here that the Grand Chamber, while starting with language taken from the *Johansen* judgment, moved away from that position. Whereas the Court in *Johansen* spoke of the child's interests being given 'particular consideration', the *Neulinger* judgment stated that the child's best interests 'must be the primary consideration', and then that there is a broad consensus that in decisions concerning children their best interests 'must be paramount'.[78]

While *Neulinger* and similar cases seemed to suggest a central place for children's welfare in the European Court's approach to Article 8 cases,[79] more recent cases may have taken a different turn:

C. Fenton-Glynn, *Children and the European Court of Human Rights*
(Oxford: OUP, 2021), 307–8

[The *Neulinger* approach] appeared to represent the start of a new era for the Court, and for the decade following there was a consistent emphasis on children at the centre of decision-making in child protection cases. However, in the recent case of *Strand Lobben v Norway*,[80] . . . the Court seems to have rowed back on this position. This case involved a challenge brought by a biological mother whose child had been removed from her care and adopted. In undertaking its analysis under Article 8, the Court criticised the domestic authorities for focusing on the interests of the child, at the expense of the mother. While acknowledging the 'primordial interest' of the child's interests in the decision-making process, the Court held that the authorities had failed to 'perform a genuine balancing exercise between the interests of the child and his biological family'.

This judgment, coming as it does from the Grand Chamber, sets a new and concerning precedent. To criticise a state for focusing too much on the interests of the child is an astounding position, turning the clock back on the position of children before the Court. As [the dissenting judgment] made clear . . ., the Convention is premised on the balancing of

[78] The same juxtaposition of language is used in *X v Latvia* (App No 27853/09, ECHR GC) (2013), [95]–[96].

[79] See also *YC v United Kingdom* (App No 4547/10, ECHR) (2012); *R and H v United Kingdom* (App No 35348/06, ECHR) (2011).

[80] (App No 37283/13, ECHR) (2019).

family rights, and the effect of this on children is particularly pernicious: the particular importance given to children's best interests is for the very reason that they are more vulnerable and dependent—their rights are already balanced because of their position in society, and in the family.

It is to be hoped that this case is nothing but an anomaly; a brief deviation from which the Court will soon recover . . . However, early indications are not good. In *AS v Norway*,[81] decided three months after *Strand Lobben*, the Court had reverted to using the *Johansen* test of 'a fair balance' and 'depending on their nature and seriousness'. The term 'paramount' was not mentioned at any stage.

In light of this, it appears to be a case of two steps forward, one step back for the court when it comes to protecting children's interests.

Where this leaves the debate about the interrelationship between Article 8 and the welfare principle in domestic law is unclear. Whereas under the *Neulinger* approach, it is possible to argue that there is little substantive difference between the two,[82] that argument is harder to sustain if the European Court reverts to its earlier approach. Earlier academic argument raised significant questions about the compatibility of the welfare principle with Article 8, particularly in private law disputes.[83]

J. Herring, 'The Human Rights Act and the Welfare Principle in Family Law—Conflicting or Complementary?', (1999a) 11 *Child and Family Law Quarterly* 223, 231

In a case based on the Convention, concerning, say, denying a parent access to a child, the starting point is the parent's right to contact. In order to justify a breach there must be clear and convincing evidence that the contact would infringe the rights and interests of the child to such an extent as to make the infringement necessary and proportionate. However, an approach based on the Children Act's welfare principle might start with a factual presumption that the welfare of the child is promoted by contact with parents, but this could be rebutted by evidence that the welfare is not thus enhanced in the particular case.

The difference is twofold. First, less evidence is required to rebut the factual presumption of welfare than to demonstrate that the breach of a right is *necessary* in a democratic society. Secondly, the nature of the question is different. It is essentially an evidential question in the welfare approach. The law is clear—the order which should be made is that which best promotes the child's welfare. The question is then a factual one—which order will actually promote the child's welfare? Whereas in the European Convention approach, it is a question of judgment—whether the harm to the child is sufficient to make the breach 'necessary' as understood by the law.

There is no definitive answer as to whether these arguments remain valid or not, and it remains to be seen whether, as Fenton-Glynn suggests, there is a change of approach underway or not.

[81] (App No 60371/17, ECHR) (2019).

[82] See, e.g., Simmonds (2012); George (2016).

[83] E.g., Herring (1999a); Choudhry and Fenwick (2005); Harris-Short (2005).

8.5 CHILDREN'S RIGHTS

The rights protected under the ECHR apply to 'everyone',[84] including children. Consequently, while challenges brought under the ECHR tend to be brought by adults, a great many of the claims in cases relating to children are brought also on behalf of the children concerned. In theory, there is nothing to prevent a claim being brought to the European Court by a child, though in practice there are a number of obstacles to such claims in many cases and most such applications are brought by adults on behalf of children.

Both within and alongside the ECHR, though, there is also the issue of children's own rights. In addition to the rights under the ECHR, the main international source of children's rights comes from the UN Convention on the Rights of the Child 1989 (UNCRC), which has been almost universally ratified. While the Convention is binding on the UK, the rights contained within it have not been directly incorporated into domestic law.[85] As we will see later, this means that their application to individual cases is inevitably more indirect than ECHR rights.

In part because the UNCRC is not incorporated into domestic law, and in part because of the inadequacies of the ECHR as a vehicle for the protection of children's rights, the focus of arguments in the cases has been on parents' rights, with relatively little attention given to children's rights. Additionally, there has been deep ambivalence about the concept of children's rights within contemporary legal, political, and social thinking.[86] However, despite struggling to gain a secure foothold in mainstream family law, the idea of children's rights provides a potentially important perspective alongside—or in contrast to—the welfare principle. Many children's rights are based on a very different understanding of childhood from that of a welfare-orientated approach. Whereas the latter tends to emphasize the incapacity and vulnerability of children, much of children's rights discourse tends to emphasize the autonomy of children and their capacity for independent thought and action. The paternalism of the welfare principle and the 'liberationist' tendencies of a children's rights approach are not, however, mutually exclusive: indeed, there is considerable overlap between the concept of welfare and rights.[87] Adherents to the welfare approach will readily concede that for children entering their teenage years it is often in their best interests that they should begin to take responsibility for their own futures, to become self-determining beings.[88] Similarly, proponents of children's rights would agree that children, particularly young children, have a right to special protection and care thereby ensuring their future welfare is maximized. As is evident from the case law, difficulties tend to arise when teenagers begin to struggle for independence from those in authority, wanting to determine for themselves how their future welfare will be secured.

We begin this section by looking at the theoretical foundations of children's rights and why the protection of children's rights, as opposed to children's welfare, may be important. We then move on to consider the extent to which children's rights have gained acceptance in English law.

[84] Art 1 ECHR.

[85] For an argument that the UNCRC should be seen as having direct effect despite this lack of incorporation, see Lord Kerr's dissenting judgment in *R (SG) v Secretary of State for Work and Pensions* [2015] UKSC 16.

[86] Fortin (2014); Stalford and Hollingsworth (2017).

[87] For more detailed discussion, see Fortin (2006), 311–12 and 317–18. [88] Ibid, 317–18.

8.5.1 ARE CHILDREN'S RIGHTS IMPORTANT?

There are a number of reasons why people have been traditionally sceptical about the importance of children's rights. For some commentators, such as Onora O'Neill, rights can only ever offer a partial understanding of the obligations and duties owed by society to children, and a focus on rights may be distracting.[89] Believing children's situation to be fundamentally different from other oppressed groups (because being a child is both a universal and a time-limited experience), she argues that rights-based discourse is an inappropriate legal and political tool to empower and protect this particularly vulnerable and often disadvantaged group.

O. O'Neill, 'Children's Rights and Children's Lives', (1992) 6 *International Journal of Law and the Family* 24, 36–9

Appeals to children's rights might have political and rhetorical importance if children's dependence on others is like that of oppressed social groups whom the rhetoric of rights has served well. However, the analogy between children's dependence and that of oppressed groups is suspect. When colonial peoples, or the working classes or religious and racial minorities or women have demanded their rights, they have sought recognition and respect for capacities for rational and independent life and action that are demonstrably there and thwarted by the denial of rights . . . But the dependence of children is very different from the dependence of oppressed social groups on those who exercise power over them.

Younger children are completely and unavoidably dependent on those who have power over their lives. Theirs is not a dependence which has been artificially produced (although it can be artificially prolonged); nor can it be ended merely by social or political changes, nor are others reciprocally dependent on children . . . It is not surprising that oppressors often try to suggest that they stand in a paternal relation to those whom they oppress: in that way they suggest that the latter's dependence is natural and irremediable and their own exercise of power a burden which they bear with benevolent fortitude. The vocabulary and trappings of paternalism are often misused to mask the unacceptable faces of power. It is not mere metaphor but highly political rhetoric, when oppressors describe what they do as paternalistic . . .

The crucial difference between (early) childhood dependence and the dependence of oppressed social groups is that childhood is a stage of life, from which children normally emerge and are helped and urged to emerge by those who have most power over them. Those with power over children's lives usually have some interest in ending childish dependence. Oppressors usually have an interest in maintaining the oppression of social groups . . .

Children are more fundamentally but less permanently powerless; their main remedy is to grow up.

O'Neill can be criticized for underestimating the similarity of children's oppression at the hands of patriarchal and/or matriarchal authority to that of other oppressed groups. O'Neill portrays the incapacity, dependence, and vulnerability of children as a natural and inevitable state, a state from which a child will 'naturally' emerge upon reaching majority. It is

[89] O'Neill (1992), 25–9.

questionable, however, whether the perceived incapacity and dependence of children is any more 'natural' than the 'natural' dependence of slaves and women was once thought to be. It can be argued that rather than a natural state, childhood as currently depicted in western societies is socially constructed, created to serve some wider societal interest.[90] Smith suggests that one such interest is that of the state in ensuring that children grow up to be responsible citizens.[91] The interests of individual adults, and in particular parents, are also served by a conception of childhood dominated by ideas of dependency and vulnerability, in which a protective role for the adult is guaranteed.

It can also be noted that alongside this protective role for adults, such a position might also simply serve adults' interests. O'Neill perhaps underestimates the extent to which adults, and particularly parents, do have a clear self-interest in maintaining control over their children's lives, adopting an idealistic conception of parent–child relationships. Many parents have strong aspirations about the type of people they want their children to be. Very often they have invested heavily, emotionally and financially, in their futures. Recognizing children's capacity for autonomous decision-making, giving them the freedom to determine their own path in life, can jeopardize strongly held parental hopes and dreams.

In seeking to convince a sceptical public of the importance of children's rights, children's rights advocates have tried to focus on the realities of children's lives, challenging some of the more idealistic assumptions about childhood, including the parent–child relationship.

M. Freeman, 'Taking Children's Rights More Seriously', (1992) 6 *International Journal of Law and the Family* 52, 55–6

The arguments put [against children's rights] tend to take one or more of three forms.

First, there is the argument that the importance of rights and rights-language themselves can be exaggerated. That there are other morally significant values, love, friendship, compassion, altruism, and that these raise relationships to a higher plain than one based on the observance of duties cannot be gainsaid. This argument may be thought particularly apposite to children's rights, particularly in the context of family relationships. Perhaps in an ideal moral world this is true. Rights may be used to resolve conflicts of interest and in an ideal world there would be harmony and these would not exist. But it is not an ideal world—certainly not for children. Children are particularly vulnerable and need rights to protect their integrity and dignity. 'Solitary, poor, nasty, brutish and short' (Hobbes, 1651) may not be a description of a state of nature . . . but it may come close to describing what a world without rights would look like for many children . . .

The second argument is in one sense related to the first. It assumes that adults already relate to children in terms of love, care and altruism, so that the case for children's rights becomes otiose. This idealizes adult-child relations: it emphasises that adults (and parents in particular) have the best interests of children at heart. There is a tendency for those who postulate such an argument to adopt a *laissez-faire* attitude towards the family. Thus, the only right for children . . . is the child's right to autonomous parents . . .

The third argument equally rests on a myth. It sees childhood as a golden age, as the best years of our life. Childhood is synonymous with innocence. It is the time when, spared the rigours of adult life, we enjoy freedom, experience play and joy. The argument runs: just as

[90] Smith (1997), 109, 133. [91] Ibid, 132.

> we avoid the responsibilities and adversities of adult life in childhood, so there should be no necessity to think in terms of rights, a concept which we must assume is reserved for adults. Whether or not the premise underlying this were correct or not, it would represent an ideal state of affairs, and one which ill-reflects the lives of many of today's children and adolescents . . .

For children's rights advocates, children's rights are important because of their potential to protect children from suffering and exploitation at the hands of others. Rights give children's interests, regardless of age, a status equal to the interests of adults, meaning they cannot be easily disregarded: the child, as person, as individual, has to be respected. Freeman continues:

> Rights are important because those who lack rights are like slaves, means to the ends of others, and never sovereigns in their own right. Those who may claim rights, or for whom rights may be claimed, have a necessary pre-condition to the constitution of humanity, of integrity, of individuality, of personality.

8.5.2 THE THEORETICAL FOUNDATIONS OF CHILDREN'S RIGHTS

There are two main competing approaches to children's rights: (i) the 'will' or 'power' theory; and (ii) the 'interest' theory. These two theories have very different implications for the law's approach to childhood and, in particular, differ in the extent to which they challenge the paternalism of the welfare principle. Tom Campbell provides a detailed explanation of both theories, beginning with the will or power theory of rights.

8.5.2.a The will or power theory of rights

T. Campbell, 'The Rights of the Minor: As Person, as Child, as Juvenile, as Future Adult', (1992) 6 *International Journal of Law and the Family* 1, 4–5

> On the power theory, a right is a normative capacity that the bearer may choose to use for the furtherance of his or her own interests or projects, a sanctioned exercise of legitimate control over others . . . In its limited forms, the power theory is that the formal analysis of the structure of rights must be carried out in terms of the mechanisms available for invoking, waiving and enforcing rights, all of which are said to depend on the exercise of will by the right-bearer. Thus a right may give a normative control over others which may be used at the discretion of the right-holder to activate those obligations the performance of which she judges to be advantageous to herself or her projects. It follows that only those capable of claiming, demanding or waiving a right can be the bearers of rights. Hence, for instance, small children, being in no position to exercise this sort of control over the obligations of others, have no rights.
>
> The embarrassment for the power theorists of denying rights to children may seem to be avoided by allowing that a proxy, such as a parent, may exercise, on behalf of a child, the

discretionary powers which constitute the rights in question. However, on the power theory, this must be less than a full possession of a right since the bearer's will, the exercise of which is definitive for the existence of the right, is not involved. Indeed, it would appear, on the assumptions of the theory, that the proxy is the right-holder. After all, it is she who possesses the power which is said to constitute the right. In other words, children's rights exercised by proxies are certainly less than full rights as defined by the power theory. Moreover, at least for some theorists, the process of choosing to exercise one's rights is part of what gives importance to rights, for it is the exercise of choice in matters of importance to the individual that enhances the dignity and exhibits the autonomy of the right-holder. On this view, while the natural capacity to make choices of this sort comes to minors in the course of their normal development, it is only in so far as the individual minor has come to possess these capacities, and hence to resemble an adult, that he or she can have rights. For young children there can be no such choices, and hence, no genuine rights.

In the fuller version of the power theory, rights are related substantively to capacities for choice and rational action in that, at least as far as fundamental rights are concerned, all rights relate to the exercise of practical rationality and self-determination, in that rights have the function of protecting and furthering these capacities. In its purest form, the fuller version of the power theory is that all rights are materially based in the presupposition of the value pre-eminence of the distinctively rational elements of human nature. It is because human beings have the power of reasoned self-determination that they can have rights, these rights being for the protection of the exercise of these capacities or related to the prerequisites of rational action, such as life itself. In this way, the whole rights viewpoint is a working out of some ideal of Kantian rationalism as the distinctive value-basis of human existence.

Clearly, on the fuller version of the power theory, minors can have rights only to the extent that they have acquired adult-like capacities for reasoned decision-making and willed conduct under the control of rational moral agency. To some people this is an outrageous denial of the value significance of young children which exposes the intellectual and moral limitations of the power theory. Children are no less precious on account of the immaturity of their characteristically adult capacities.

As Campbell argues, the will or power theory of rights can lead to a complete denial that children, particularly young children, can be sensibly regarded as rights-holders. However, there is scope within this particular theory of rights for a more radical interpretation. The will or power theory does not necessarily exclude children as rights-holders. What it requires from children is the capacity for reasoned, rational thought. Once a child has that capacity, there can no longer be any objection to that child being accorded the same rights as others. The crux of the issue thus becomes at what point it can be said that a child acquires the necessary skills and maturity to hold and exercise rights. In response, the so-called 'child liberationists' argue that children have the capacity for rational, reasoned, decision-making from a much earlier age than western society has generally been willing to acknowledge, a fact attributable to adults' self-interest in retaining control over children.[92] They thus contend that children, even very young children, have the capacity to be self-determining, autonomous beings capable of holding and exercising rights.

[92] Smith (1997), 106. See also Fortin (2009b), 4–5.

However, whilst this theory does not entirely exclude children as rights-holders, it does have important limitations. Attributing rights to children on the basis of their adult-like capacities tends to conceptualize children as 'little adults', making their respective rights and interests virtually indistinguishable. Children's rights to various forms of autonomy and freedom, such as the right to freedom of expression or the right to determine their own health care, are emphasized at the potential expense of other core interests, particularly of young children. This, according to Campbell, is to adopt only a partial view of childhood. It attributes no value to the distinctive interests of children, 'as children'. This leads him to prefer the much broader, interest theory of rights.

8.5.2.b The interest theory of rights

T. Campbell, 'The Rights of the Minor: As Person, as Child, as Juvenile, as Future Adult', (1992) 6 *International Journal of Law and the Family* 1, 5–6

According to this—the interest—theory of rights, children have rights if their interests are the basis for having rules which require others to behave in certain ways with respect to these interests. It is enough that there are ways of identifying these interests and arranging and enforcing duties which meet the requirements that they set. There is no presupposition that these interests are expressions of rational capacities, although some of them may be. Nor is there any assumption that the performance of the correlative interest-saving duties must be triggered or set aside by the choice of the right-bearer, although this may often be the preferred way to protect the interests concerned. . . .

Taking the offensive, interest theorists claim to be able to explain a wider range of rights than the power theorists who have to resort to subtle reconstructions of those specific rights where there is no evident link to capacities of choice. Thus, the right not to be tortured has to be interpreted by a full power theorist as being grounded in something like the fact that torture interferes with the processes of rational decision-making. The interest theorist may retort that it also hurts. Similarly, the interest theorist can persuasively argue that there is nothing particularly indirect about the ascription of rights to mentally handicapped adults and small children, whereas the power theorist . . . has difficulty with these classes of persons.

The concept of childhood embraced by the interest theory of rights is much broader and allows for the core interests of even very young children to be elevated to the status of rights. Campbell argues that children's interests change throughout childhood, with different rights being particularly important at different stages of children's development. During the latter stages of childhood, as the child develops the capacity for independent decision-making, the autonomy or freedom interests identified with the will or power theory become of increasing importance. However, during very young childhood, needs-based rights, more closely identified with a traditional welfare approach, predominate.

It can be difficult to identify the core interests of children which are of such fundamental importance that they should be elevated to the status of rights. Identifying those rights that children, as children, would value raises particular difficulties. Eekelaar has developed one possible solution to this dilemma.

J. Eekelaar, 'The Emergence of Children's Rights', (1986) 6 *Oxford Journal of Legal Studies* 161, 169–71

We here meet the problem that children often lack the information or ability to appreciate what will serve them best. It is necessary therefore to make some kind of imaginative leap and guess what a child might retrospectively have wanted once it reaches a position of maturity. In doing this, values of the adult world and of individual adults will inevitably enter. This is not to be deplored, but openly accepted. It encourages debate about these values. There are, however, some broad propositions which might reasonably be advanced as forming the foundation of any child's (retrospective) claims. General physical, emotional and intellectual care within the social capabilities of his or her immediate caregivers would seem a minimal expectation. We may call this the 'basic' interest. What a child should expect from the wider community must be stated more tentatively. I have elsewhere suggested the formulation that, within certain overriding constraints created by the economic and social structure of society (whose extent must be open to debate), all children should have an equal opportunity to maximize the resources available to them during their childhood (including their own inherent abilities) so as to minimize the degree to which they enter adult life affected by avoidable prejudices incurred during childhood. In short, their capacities are to be developed to their best advantage. We may call this the 'developmental' interest . . .

There is a third type of interest which children may, retrospectively, claim. A child may argue for the freedom to choose his own lifestyle and to enter social relations according to his own inclinations uncontrolled by the authority of the adult world, whether parents or institutions . . . We may call them the 'autonomy' interest.

Campbell criticizes this reliance on 'retrospective judgment', arguing that such an approach is inevitably adult-centred.[93] He points out that Eekelaar relies exclusively on an adult perspective and that adults considering childhood with hindsight tend to minimize the sufferings and sacrifices made, dismissing such misery as unimportant in light of the benefits and advantages they now enjoy.[94] This is a clear problem with any 'substituted judgment' approach. Giving children a much more direct voice in defining their own interests would help achieve a better balance.

8.5.2.c Children's rights and paternalism

The interest theory of rights is not unproblematic. On the positive side, the strong correlation between interests and rights means that children's rights are more easily reconciled with the welfare principle, which in turn renders children's rights less challenging for policy-makers and more easily integrated into mainstream family law. Indeed, Fortin argues that there is no conflict between children's rights and children's welfare.[95] However, on the negative side, tying children's rights so closely to children's interests makes children's rights vulnerable to the paternalism of a welfare-centred approach. As noted earlier, there is a danger that

[93] Campbell (1992), 20–1. [94] Ibid.

[95] Fortin (2006), 311–12. The existence of Art 3 UNCRC, making children's best interests a primary consideration in all actions concerning them, supports the idea that rights and welfare are not inherently incompatible: see 8.5.5.

children will only be accorded such rights as adults deem to be consistent with welfare. Thus, whilst children will readily be accorded the right to special protection and care, they may be denied the right to refuse life-saving medical treatment, such a right being regarded as inimical to their best interests.

The danger of slipping back into adult paternalism is not just a problem for the interest theory of rights. In fact, faced with the stark realities of allowing even older children to determine their own path in life, Campbell emphasizes that both the interest theory and the power/will theory of rights can be appropriately qualified with paternalistic interventions where necessary.[96]

Freeman, a strong proponent of children's rights, agrees that an element of paternalism is often necessary in order to protect children from themselves.[97]

M. Freeman, 'Taking Children's Rights More Seriously', (1992) 6 *International Journal of Law and the Family* 52, 65–6

To respect a child's autonomy is to treat that child as a person and as a rights-holder. It is clear that we can do so to a much greater extent than we have assumed hitherto. But it is also clear that the exercising of autonomy by a child can have a deleterious impact on that child's life chances. It is true that adults make mistakes too (and also make mistakes when interfering with a child's autonomy). Having rights means being allowed to take risks and make choices. There is a reluctance to interfere with an adult's project. This reluctance is tempered when the project pursuer is a child by the sense that choice now may harm choice later . . .

If we are to make progress we have to recognize the moral integrity of children. We have to treat them as persons entitled to equal concern and respect and entitled to have both their present autonomy recognized and their capacity for future autonomy safeguarded. And this is to recognize that children, particularly younger children, need nurture, care and protection. Children must not, as Hafen (1977) put it, be 'abandoned' to their rights.

The difficult question in seeking to reconcile the competing demands of autonomy and protection is where the line justifying adult intervention should be drawn. Freeman suggests that intervention will be justified to protect children against irrational actions. Which simply begs the question: what will constitute an irrational action? In particular, will any action with which an adult disagrees be labelled irrational?

M. Freeman, 'Taking Children's Rights More Seriously', (1992) 6 *International Journal of Law and the Family* 52, 67–9

[W]hat is to be regarded as 'irrational' must be strictly confined. The subjective values of the would-be protector cannot be allowed to intrude . . . Nor should we see an action as irrational unless it is manifestly so in the sense that it would undermine future life choices, impair interests in an irreversible way. Furthermore, we must tolerate mistakes . . . But we also would be failing to recognize a child's integrity if we allowed him to choose an action, such as using

[96] Campbell (1992).

[97] See also Fortin (2004), 259–60.

heroin or choosing not to attend school, which could seriously and systematically impair the attainment of full personality and development subsequently. The test of 'irrationality' must also be confined so that it justifies intervention only to the extent necessary to obviate the immediate harm, or to develop the capacities of rational choice by which the individual may have a reasonable chance of avoiding such harms.

The question we should ask ourselves is: what sort of action or conduct would we wish, as children, to be shielded against on the assumption that we would want to mature to a rationally autonomous adulthood and be capable of deciding on our own system of ends as free and rational beings? We would, I believe, choose principles that would enable children to mature to independent adulthood. One definition of irrationality would be such as to preclude action and conduct which would frustrate such a goal. Within the constraints of such a definition we would defend a version of paternalism: not paternalism in its classical sense for, so conceived, there would be no children's rights at all . . .

To take children's rights more seriously requires us to take seriously nurturance and self-determination. It demands of us that we adopt policies, practices, structures and laws which both protect children and their rights. Hence the *via media* of 'liberal paternalism'.

Whichever theory of rights is preferred, it is difficult to escape the attractions of adult paternalism. And, perhaps not surprisingly, this will emerge as a dominant theme as we explore the current approach to children's rights in English law.

8.5.3 THE DEVELOPMENT OF CHILDREN'S RIGHTS IN ENGLISH LAW

The twentieth century witnessed a fundamental shift in understanding about the parent–child relationship. At the turn of the nineteenth century, this relationship was governed by the historic concept of 'guardianship', which conferred on the father of his legitimate children complete authority over their person and property.[98] By the early part of the twentieth century, 'paternal authority' had been transformed into 'parental authority', but the nature of the parent–child relationship had not undergone significant change.[99] Parents were understood to possess all the necessary power and authority over a child that would enable them to control every aspect of the child's upbringing. This power and authority was enshrined in the parental right or bundle of rights often simply referred to as the 'right to custody and control'. The primary concern of the law was to protect this right from any outside interference.

During the twentieth century, attitudes towards children began to change with important consequences for the parent–child relationship. Growing concern with the welfare of children initiated the gradual liberation of children from their parents, with the result that children were no longer regarded as their parents' possessions. The control and authority that parents enjoyed over their children was gradually replaced with the embryonic idea that children were also autonomous individuals with enforceable rights of their own. The emerging concept of children's rights had far-reaching significance for the concept of

[98] *In re Agar-Ellis* (1883) 24 Ch D 317.

[99] The statutory process of placing mothers in a position of equality with fathers began with the Guardianship of Infants Act 1886, s 5.

parenthood. If children possess rights then somebody must hold the corresponding duty or responsibility to protect them. That person is the parent. It is these duties and responsibilities that now dominate the concept of parenthood in English law.[100]

Whilst the general concept of parental rights is currently undergoing a certain renaissance, the parental right to custody and control has been fundamentally transformed. This right is now understood as a *conditional* right. It inheres for the benefit of the child and not the parent.[101] Thus, the right to custody and control is of only instrumental value: that is, it exists only insofar as necessary for the fulfilment of parental duties. This understanding of the relationship between children's rights and parental rights and duties was usefully summarized by L'Heureux-Dubé J in the Canadian Supreme Court.

Young v Young **[1993] 4 SCR 3**

L'HEUREUX-DUBÉ J:

The power of the custodial parent is not a "right" with independent value which is granted by the courts for the benefit of the parent, but is designed to enable that parent to discharge his or her responsibilities and obligations to the child. It is, in fact, the child's right to a parent who will look after his or her best interests . . . It has long been recognized that the custodial parent has a duty to ensure, protect and promote the best interests of the child. That duty includes the sole and primary responsibility to oversee all aspects of day to day life and long-term well-being, as well as major decisions with respect to education, religion, health and well-being.

It is this view of parenthood which underpins the House of Lords' decision in *Gillick v West Norfolk and Wisbech Area Health Authority*,[102] discussed at 8.5.6.b. As will be seen, it has important implications as to the scope of the parents' decision-making authority within the parent–child relationship, and in relation to the child's interactions with the state.[103]

8.5.4 CHILDREN'S RIGHTS AND THE ECHR

Children have rights under the ECHR in the same way as adults. Of the greatest potential significance in protecting the welfare and autonomy rights of children are Articles 3 (the right not to be subjected to torture or to inhuman or degrading treatment), 5 (the right to liberty and security of the person), and 8 (the right to respect for private and family life).[104] As understood under English law, rights are qualitatively different from other legal interests. They have an assumed weight and importance. To talk of children's *rights* thus underlines their significance. This is essential given the current preoccupation with parents' rights under the ECHR. If parents' interests are to be routinely articulated in terms of rights, it is

[100] See chapter 10.

[101] This contrasts with parental rights as enshrined in Art 8 ECHR which are properly conceptualized as autonomous rights which inhere for the benefit of the parent.

[102] [1986] AC 112. [103] See 8.6.

[104] For a detailed discussion of how rights protected under the HRA 1998 could strengthen the claims of autonomous teenagers, see Fortin (2006), 314–17, 320–1.

important that children's interests are similarly conceptualized. Otherwise, there is a danger that should the parents' and child's interests conflict (e.g. should parents claim the right to discipline their children using physical force in accordance with their religious beliefs), the child's interests (to physical and mental integrity) will be treated as somehow less weighty and important than those of the parents—as simply welfare-based exceptions to the parents' rights as opposed to rights with equal standing.[105] Children's rights, even in areas where the welfare approach would also apply, are thus important. They ensure that children's interests are taken equally seriously in the decision-making process.

One of the potential drawbacks in routinely articulating children's interests as rights is the potential complexity it introduces into the decision-making process. Most child-related disputes involve many potentially conflicting rights, both between the rights of the parents and child and between the child's own rights. Such conflicts should not, however, deter the courts from fully engaging with rights-based reasoning. Building on House of Lords authority in the sphere of media freedom,[106] academics have developed a 'discipline'—termed a 'parallel analysis'—to resolve such conflicts while seeking to give proper weight and value to all the rights engaged.[107]

As Fortin notes, 'the domestic courts have responded to the demands of the HRA in an extraordinarily haphazard manner when dealing with children's cases'.[108] However, it is not in children's interests for the courts to prevaricate on the question of children's rights. A rights-based approach has the potential to strengthen rather than weaken the court's focus on the child.[109] A principled, transparent, and fair approach to resolving inevitable conflicts of rights can be utilized. It is thus to be hoped that the limited and 'patchy' progress made by the courts in advancing children's interests through the discourse of rights in certain child-related disputes can be developed and extended into areas of child law that currently remain dominated by adult-centred concerns and perspectives on 'welfare'.[110]

8.5.5 THE UN CONVENTION ON THE RIGHTS OF THE CHILD (UNCRC)

The UNCRC is the single most significant expression of children's rights in a global context. In addition to numerous rights relating to different areas of children's lives (such as education, health, and family) and rights providing specific protections to children (from violence and abuse, trafficking, participation in armed conflict, and so on), the Convention sets out four 'core principles'.

United Nations Convention on the Rights of the Child 1989

Article 2

1. States Parties shall respect and ensure the rights set forth in the present Convention to each child within their jurisdiction without discrimination of any kind, irrespective of the child's or his or her parent's or legal guardian's race, colour, sex, language, religion, political or other opinion, national, ethnic or social origin, property, disability, birth or other status.

[105] Ibid, 310.

[106] *Re S (A Child) (Identification: Restrictions on Publication)* [2003] EWCA Civ 963; *Campbell v MGN Ltd* [2004] UKHL 47.

[107] See Choudhry and Fenwick (2005); Fortin (2006). [108] Fortin (2006), 300.

[109] Ibid, 313–14. [110] Fortin (2004), 271; Fortin (2006).

2. States Parties shall take all appropriate measures to ensure that the child is protected against all forms of discrimination or punishment on the basis of the status, activities, expressed opinions, or beliefs of the child's parents, legal guardians, or family members.

Article 3

1. In all actions concerning children, whether undertaken by public or private social welfare institutions, courts of law, administrative authorities or legislative bodies, the best interests of the child shall be a primary consideration. . . .

Article 6

1. States Parties recognize that every child has the inherent right to life.
2. States Parties shall ensure to the maximum extent possible the survival and development of the child.

Article 12

1. States Parties shall assure to the child who is capable of forming his or her own views the right to express those views freely in all matters affecting the child, the views of the child being given due weight in accordance with the age and maturity of the child.
2. For this purpose, the child shall in particular be provided the opportunity to be heard in any judicial and administrative proceedings affecting the child, either directly, or through a representative or an appropriate body, in a manner consistent with the procedural rules of national law.

As noted earlier, a key difference between the ECHR and the UNCRC is that the latter does not have direct effect in English domestic law, meaning that its rights cannot be directly enforced. There is also no supranational court equivalent to the European Court of Human Rights, though there is a UN Committee on the Rights of the Child which writes country reports on how states are performing in relation to their obligations under the UNCRC, and issues general guidance on rights protected by the Convention.[111]

Despite the fact that it has not been incorporated into domestic law, the UNCRC appeared to be gaining increased recognition and importance in recent years. The courts had previously commented on the need to interpret domestic law in compliance with the UK's international legal obligations as far as possible,[112] and an important 'back door' for the UNCRC into domestic law comes from its use by the European Court of Human Rights to inform and interpret Article 8 ECHR claims relating to children.[113]

More recently, though, the UNCRC had begun to gain ground more directly in the English case law. In *ZH (Tanzania) v Secretary of State for the Home Department*,[114] *R (SG) v Secretary of State for Work and Pensions*,[115] *R (DA) v Secretary of State for Work and Pensions*,[116] and other cases, the Supreme Court specifically discussed the potential importance of Article 3 UNCRC in domestic law, both in its own terms and via Article 8 ECHR. Various decisions

[111] The status of these General Comments is limited: *R (SC) v Secretary of State for Work and Pensions* [2021] UKSC 26, [64]–[67].

[112] *Smith v Secretary of State for Work and Pensions* [2006] UKHL 35, [78].

[113] Kilkelly (2014). See also *HH; PH v Deputy Prosecutor of the Italian Republic, Genoa* [2012] UKSC 25, [155]; *ZH (Tanzania) v Secretary of State for the Home Department* [2011] UKSC 4, [33].

[114] [2011] UKSC 4. [115] [2015] UKSC 16. [116] [2019] UKSC 21.

of lower courts also demonstrated some of the practical ways in which UNCRC rights could affect family court decisions.[117]

However, it seems unlikely that this approach to using international children's rights in domestic cases can survive the Supreme Court's apparent retreat from allowing the UNCRC (and other unincorporated international human rights instruments) to influence domestic decision-making. In *R (AB) v Secretary of State for Justice*[118] and *R (SC) v Secretary of State for Work and Pensions*,[119] the Supreme Court explicitly rejected its earlier approach in decisions that 'represent a temporary blow to children's rights and legal human rights more generally'[120]—though how 'temporary' this shift proves to be remains to be seen. It seems likely that the family courts will take a more cautious and conservative approach to these issues in future decisions, given the steer received from the Supreme Court.

8.5.6 CHILDREN'S RIGHTS IN THE DOMESTIC COURTS

8.5.6.a Children's welfare-based rights to care and protection

The courts have had relatively little difficulty embracing children's rights where there is no inconsistency between the child's rights and the child's welfare. To talk of a child's right to be protected from parental abuse or neglect, or to be provided with the basic necessities of life, is uncontentious and raises no challenge to a welfare-orientated approach.

Many rights that children have from international law relate primarily to their protection in one form or another. The application of Articles 2 and 3 ECHR to children in relation to family law, for example, is primarily directed to protecting children from the most serious forms of harm that they might suffer at the hands of abusive parents—domestic law protects these rights primarily through care proceedings,[121] and (often indirectly) through protections against domestic abuse.[122]

Similarly, the UNCRC has a great many rights directed primarily towards protecting children. To take some examples:

- Article 6—one of the 'core principles' of the Convention—recognizes the child's 'inherent right to life' and requires states to 'ensure to the maximum extent possible the survival and development of the child';
- Article 11 protects children against being illicitly transferred abroad;
- Article 19 protects children from all forms of physical and mental abuse;
- Article 20 guarantees 'special protection and assistance' to children who are not able to remain in their family environment.

However, while there is no immediate suggestion of a change of approach in relation to ECHR-based rights[123]—and the UNCRC can influence the interpretation of

[117] For a useful analysis of how the English courts have use the UNCRC in family cases, see Gilmore (2017). Notable examples include *Re G (Declaration of Parentage: Removal of Person Identified as Mother from Birth Certificate) (No 1)* [2018] EWHC 3379, [37] (Arts 7 and 8 UNCRC); *Re Z (Egyptian Fostering: UK Adoption)* [2016] EWHC 2963, [95]–[100] (Arts 20 and 21 UNCRC); *Re D (International Recognition)* [2016] EWCA Civ 12, [40] (Art 12 UNCRC and Art 23 of the Charter of Fundamental Rights of the European Union 2000).

[118] [2021] UKSC 28. [119] [2021] UKSC 26. [120] Tan (2022). [121] See chapter 12.

[122] See chapter 4.

[123] The courts do seem increasingly to suggest that litigants should seek to rely first on rights under the common law or contained in statutes, rather than turning to ECHR rights: in the family law context, see, e.g., *Re A (Withdrawal of Treatment: Legal Representation)* [2022] EWCA Civ 1221.

those rights[124]—we noted earlier that there appears to have been a retreat from direct consideration of UNCRC rights in the domestic courts.[125] How this is likely to impact the consideration of rights that provide protection to children remains to be seen. Historically, though, because an analysis of the child's welfare is easily reconcilable with children's rights that are focused on protection, the courts have not struggled with incorporating these rights into their analysis under s 1 of the CA 1989.

8.5.6.b Children's autonomy rights

The Gillick *decision*

As expected, the real test of judicial commitment to children's rights came in a case which raised the more challenging issue of a child's right to self-determination.[126] Many cases in this area concern questions about medical treatment of children; understandably, these important decisions have often been the site of court adjudication, but the principles can apply equally to other areas in relation to a child's upbringing.

Gillick concerned a challenge to a memorandum of guidance issued by central government to local health authorities containing a section on the provision of contraceptive advice and treatment to children under the age of 16. In essence, the guidance suggested that contraceptive advice and treatment could be provided without informing the child's parents or obtaining parental consent. Mrs Gillick, a mother of five girls, wrote to her local health authority requesting assurance that no contraceptive advice or treatment would be given to any of her daughters whilst under the age of 16 without her knowledge and consent. The health authority refused to give such assurance, arguing that such a decision would be a matter of clinical judgement for the individual doctor. Mrs Gillick consequently sought a declaration that the guidance was unlawful, in particular, that it unlawfully interfered with her parental rights and duties. The House of Lords, by a majority, dismissed her complaint, and in the process gave rise to the idea of a '*Gillick*-competent child'.

Gillick v West Norfolk and Wisbech Area Health Authority [1986] AC 112, 166–75, 181–90

LORD FRASER:

[P]arental rights to control a child do not exist for the benefit of the parent. They exist for the benefit of the child and they are justified only in so far as they enable the parent to perform his duties towards the child, and towards other children in the family . . .

From the parents' right and duty of custody flows their right and duty of control of the child, but the fact that custody is its origin throws but little light on the question of the legal extent of control at any particular age . . .

It is, in my view, contrary to the ordinary experience of mankind, at least in Western Europe in the present century, to say that a child or a young person remains in fact under the complete control of his parents until he attains the definite age of majority, now 18 in the United Kingdom, and that on attaining that age he suddenly acquires independence. In practice most wise parents relax their control gradually as the child develops and encourage him or

[124] Kilkelly (2014). [125] See 8.5.5. [126] See generally, Fortin (2009b), ch 5.

her to become increasingly independent. Moreover, the degree of parental control actually exercised over a particular child does in practice vary considerably according to his understanding and intelligence and it would, in my opinion, be unrealistic for the courts not to recognise these facts. Social customs change, and the law ought to, and does in fact, have regard to such changes when they are of major importance . . .

[T]he view that the child's intellectual ability is irrelevant cannot, in my opinion, now be accepted. It is a question of fact for the judge (or jury) to decide whether a particular child can give effective consent to contraceptive treatment.

In times gone by the father had almost absolute authority over his children until they attained majority. . . .

Once the rule of the parents' absolute authority over minor children is abandoned, the solution to the problem in this appeal can no longer be found by referring to rigid parental rights at any particular age. The solution depends upon a judgment of what is best for the welfare of the particular child. Nobody doubts, certainly I do not doubt, that in the overwhelming majority of cases the best judges of a child's welfare are his or her parents. Nor do I doubt that any important medical treatment of a child under 16 would normally only be carried out with the parents' approval. That is why it would and should be "most unusual" for a doctor to advise a child without the knowledge and consent of the parents on contraceptive matters. But, as I have already pointed out, Mrs Gillick has to go further if she is to obtain the first declaration that she seeks. She has to justify the absolute right of veto in a parent. But there may be circumstances in which a doctor is a better judge of the medical advice and treatment which will conduce to a girl's welfare than her parents . . .

The only practicable course is to entrust the doctor with a discretion to act in accordance with his view of what is best in the interests of the girl who is his patient. He should, of course, always seek to persuade her to tell her parents that she is seeking contraceptive advice, and the nature of the advice that she receives. At least he should seek to persuade her to agree to the doctor's informing the parents. But there may well be cases, and I think there will be some cases, where the girl refuses either to tell the parents herself or to permit the doctor to do so and in such cases, the doctor will, in my opinion, be justified in proceeding without the parents' consent or even knowledge provided he is satisfied on the following matters: (1) that the girl (although under 16 years of age) will understand his advice; (2) that he cannot persuade her to inform her parents or to allow him to inform the parents that she is seeking contraceptive advice; (3) that she is very likely to begin or to continue having sexual intercourse with or without contraceptive treatment; (4) that unless she receives contraceptive advice or treatment her physical or mental health or both are likely to suffer; (5) that her best interests require him to give her contraceptive advice, treatment or both without the parental consent . . . For those reasons I do not consider that the guidance interferes with the parents' rights.

LORD SCARMAN:

Parental right and the age of consent . . .

Parental rights clearly do exist, and they do not wholly disappear until the age of majority. Parental rights relate to both the person and the property of the child . . . But the common law has never treated such rights as sovereign or beyond review and control. Nor has our law ever treated the child as other than a person with capacities and rights recognised by law. The principle of the law, as I shall endeavour to show, is that parental rights are derived from parental duty and exist only so long as they are needed for the protection of the person and property of the child. The principle has been subjected to certain age limits set by statute for certain purposes: and in some cases the courts have declared an age of discretion at which a child acquires before the age of majority the right to make his (or her) own decision. But these limitations in no way undermine the principle of the law, and should not be allowed to obscure it.

Let me make good, quite shortly, the proposition of principle.

First . . . when a court has before it a question as to the care and upbringing of a child it must treat the welfare of the child as the paramount consideration in determining the order to be made. There is here a principle which limits and governs the exercise of parental rights of custody, care and control. It is a principle perfectly consistent with the law's recognition of the parent as the natural guardian of the child; but it is also a warning that parental right must be exercised in accordance with the welfare principle and can be challenged, even overridden, if it be not.

Secondly, there is the common law's understanding of the nature of parental right . . . It is abundantly plain that the law recognizes that there is a right and a duty of parents to determine whether or not to seek medical advice in respect of their child, and, having received advice, to give or withhold consent to medical treatment. The question in the appeal is as to the extent, and duration, of the right and the circumstances in which . . . it can be overridden by the exercise of medical judgment . . .

The principle is that parental right or power of control of the person and property of his child exists primarily to enable the parent to discharge his duty of maintenance, protection and education until he reaches such an age as to be able to look after himself and make his own decisions. . . . Although statute has intervened in respect of a child's capacity to consent to medical treatment from the age of 16 onwards, neither statute nor the case law has ruled on the extent and duration of parental right in respect of children under the age of 16. More specifically, there is no rule yet applied to contraceptive treatment . . . It is open, therefore, to the House to formulate a rule. The Court of Appeal favoured a fixed age limit of 16 . . . They sought to justify the limit by the public interest in the law being certain. Certainty is always an advantage in the law, and in some branches of the law it is a necessity. But it brings with it an inflexibility and a rigidity which in some branches of the law can obstruct justice, impede the law's development, and stamp upon the law the mark of obsolescence where what is needed is the capacity for development. The law relating to parent and child is concerned with the problems of the growth and maturity of the human personality. If the law should impose upon the process of "growing up" fixed limits where nature knows only a continuous process, the price would be artificiality and a lack of realism in an area where the law must be sensitive to human development and social change. If certainty be thought desirable, it is better that the rigid demarcations necessary to achieve it should be laid down by legislation after a full consideration of all the relevant factors than by the courts confined as they are by the forensic process to the evidence adduced by the parties and to whatever may properly fall within the judicial notice of judges. Unless and until Parliament should think fit to intervene, the courts should establish a principle flexible enough to enable justice to be achieved by its application to the particular circumstances proved by the evidence placed before them.

The underlying principle of the law was exposed by Blackstone and can be seen to have been acknowledged in the case law. It is that parental right yields to the child's right to make his own decisions when he reaches a sufficient understanding and intelligence to be capable of making up his own mind on the matter requiring decision . . .

In the light of the foregoing I would hold that as a matter of law the parental right to determine whether or not their minor child below the age of 16 will have medical treatment terminates if and when the child achieves a sufficient understanding and intelligence to enable him or her to understand fully what is proposed. It will be a question of fact whether a child seeking advice has sufficient understanding of what is involved to give a consent valid in law.

Until the child achieves the capacity to consent, the parental right to make the decision continues save only in exceptional circumstances . . .

I am, therefore, satisfied that the department's guidance can be followed without involving the doctor in any infringement of parental right.

[On the issue of consent and the purported interference with parental rights and duties, Lord Bridge agreed with both Lord Fraser and Lord Scarman.]

It is difficult to discern the ratio of *Gillick* on the question of the existence and scope of children's rights vis-à-vis the rights of the parents. The issue has sparked considerable academic debate. However, both Lord Fraser and Lord Scarman appear to confirm that the parental right to custody and control is wholly derived from the parents' duties and responsibilities to the child and thus depends on the continuing existence of those duties. Furthermore, they hold that the parental right to custody and control is forever dwindling and diminishing in importance as the child grows older because, as children mature, they become increasingly capable of exercising their own rights and decision-making powers. It follows logically from this that parents' rights cannot be ascertained by reference to any particular fixed age, but depend on the degree of intelligence and understanding of the child in question. Essentially, the question is whether the child has sufficient maturity and understanding of the particular issue to make their own decisions—the idea of being '*Gillick* competent'. Lord Scarman also appears to go one step further than Lord Fraser in holding in unequivocal terms that the child's right and the corresponding parental right cannot coexist. He thus suggests that parents' and children's rights exist on a continuum such that once a child reaches the required level of '*Gillick* competency', the purpose behind the parental right is exhausted and must yield to the right of the child.

The scope and meaning of the *Gillick* decision was considered by the Court of Appeal in recent litigation about medical treatment to provide so-called 'puberty-blockers' and other interventions to children experiencing gender dysphoria; that is, an individual's distress at a mismatch between their perceived identity and their natal sex. The claimants were respectively a young person previously treated by the clinic, and the mother of a young person who was concerned that her child might be treated by the clinic; they sought a declaration that the practice of prescribing puberty blockers to children under 18 was unlawful as they lacked capacity to give valid consent to that treatment. The Divisional Court gave a judgment that, amongst other things, purported to set out particular ages at which a child was likely (or not) to be able to consent to treatment for gender dysphoria.[127] The Court of Appeal rejected this approach.

Bell v Tavistock and Portman NHS Trust [2021] EWCA Civ 1363

THE COURT OF APPEAL:

76. The ratio decidendi of *Gillick* was that it was for doctors and not judges to decide on the capacity of a person under 16 to consent to medical treatment. Nothing about the nature or implications of the treatment with puberty blockers allows for a real distinction to be made

[127] For insightful commentary on the limitations of the Divisional Court's approach, with critique from a children's rights perspective in particular, see Hirst (2021).

between the consideration of contraception in *Gillick* and of puberty blockers in this case bearing in mind that, when *Gillick* was decided 35 years ago, the issues it raised in respect of contraception for the under 16s were highly controversial in a way that is now hard to imagine. A similar conclusion was reached by Silber J in connection with abortion in *R (Axon) v Secretary of State for Health* [2006] QB 539 at para [86]. . . .

80. . . . Both Lords Fraser and Scarman in *Gillick* expressed views about the matters which a clinician would have to explore with a patient, without being prescriptive and recognising that it was for the clinicians to satisfy themselves, in their own way. . . . It would have been inconsistent with the ratio of the case that clinicians must be trusted to make the decisions for the court effectively to give them a manual about how to do so. It is instructive to consider the language of Lord Scarman on the main issue in *Gillick* at pages 188H to 189A:

> "I would hold that as a matter of law the parental right to determine whether or not their minor child below the age of 16 will have medical treatment terminates if and when the child achieves a sufficient understanding and intelligence to enable him or her to understand fully what is proposed. It will be a question of fact whether a child seeking advice has sufficient understanding of what is involved to give consent valid in law."

81. His conclusion on the law is found in the first sentence but the second recognises that the question whether valid consent is given in any case is a question of fact. That depends upon the individual circumstances of any child and the surrounding circumstances of the clinical issues. Both he and Lord Fraser identified at a high level what they could expect a clinician to take into account in making a clinical decision. . . .

89. We conclude that it was inappropriate for the Divisional Court to give the guidance concerning when a court application will be appropriate and to reach general age-related conclusions about the likelihood or probability of different cohorts of children being capable of giving consent.

For children's rights advocates, these decisions seem to hold enormous promise. An interpretation of the *Gillick* decision in line with Lord Scarman's judgment would significantly erode parental authority and control over children, particularly as they enter their teenage years. For this reason, many commentators hailed *Gillick* as a landmark decision in securing children's basic autonomy rights. In line with the power or will theory, Lord Scarman's approach suggested that as soon as children were deemed to have the necessary rational will, they would be regarded as autonomous rights-holders, able to make decisions free from parental control. They also allow children to be seen as autonomous individuals. As Moscati comments with respect to the *Bell* decision, 'the Court of Appeal departed from sterile generalisations about trans children, recognised trans children's agency, and encouraged respectful attention for each trans child'.[128]

However, to champion children's autonomy when it enables the child to make decisions many would deem in the child's best interests, such as receiving confidential contraceptive advice and treatment before embarking on a sexual relationship, is one thing. To continue to champion that right when the child is refusing life-saving treatment is more difficult, even for the most ardent supporter of children's autonomy rights.

[128] Moscati (2022), though she is also critical of the Court of Appeal for failing to 'engage with children's rights discourse and . . . acknowledge that the [right] to identity is indeed a child right'.

It is perhaps for this reason that the more radical interpretation of *Gillick* and its promise of delivering real autonomy for older children has not been realized. In what many regard as a retreat from *Gillick*, children's autonomy rights have been consistently qualified by a return to a more paternalistic approach, seen both in relation to parents' rights and the court's own power to override the child's wishes.

Resistance to the Gillick *decision*

The first sign that *Gillick* would be subjected to a conservative application came in *Re E (A Minor) (Wardship: Medical Treatment)*.[129] *Re E* concerned a 15-year-old boy ('A') with leukaemia who urgently required a blood transfusion. Both the boy and his parents were devout Jehovah's Witnesses and therefore refused to consent to treatment, blood transfusions being contrary to the tenets of their faith. Ward J accepted that a *Gillick*-competent child could validly withhold consent to treatment. However, he avoided the difficult consequences of such a conclusion by refusing to find that the child had sufficient understanding and maturity to be regarded as *Gillick* competent, despite his 'obvious intelligence'. The child was thus deemed incapable of refusing treatment.

Re E (A Minor) (Wardship: Medical Treatment) [1992] 2 FCR 219, 224–7

WARD J:

I am quite satisfied that A does not have any sufficient comprehension of the pain he has yet to suffer, of the fear that he will be undergoing, of the distress not only occasioned by that fear but also—and importantly—the distress he will inevitably suffer as he, a loving son, helplessly watches his parents' and his family's distress. They are a close family, and they are a brave family, but I find that he has no realization of the full implications which lie before him as to the process of dying. He may have some concept of the fact that he will die, but as to the manner of his death and to the extent of his and his family's suffering I find he has not the ability to turn his mind to it nor the will to do so. Who can blame him for that?

If, therefore, this case depended upon my finding of whether or not A is of sufficient understanding and intelligence and maturity to give full and informed consent, I find that he is not.

The boy who was the subject of the application in *Re E* refused to give his consent to continuing treatment upon reaching the age of 18 and died shortly thereafter.[130] However, the approach of finding young people not to have *Gillick* competence in significant medical decision-making cases was to continue in numerous cases, offering judges an easy (if often disingenuous) way out of situations where an older child's wishes conflicted with the court's own protectionist approach.

The Gillick *decision and the court's own powers*

Crucial to these cases is the idea that the court itself has power to make decisions about a child's medical treatment. In itself, that is not a controversial proposition: the court clearly

[129] [1992] 2 FCR 219. [130] Fortin (2009b), 154.

has power under s 8 of the CA 1989 to make a specific issue order or prohibited steps order to authorize or prohibit medical treatment where a parent could otherwise give (or refuse) consent in the exercise of their parental responsibility, and the court claims that its powers under its inherent jurisdiction are more wide-ranging than those of a parent in any case.[131] If, for example, the court is concerned with a dispute between parents, or between the parents and medical authorities, the court therefore plainly has power to determine that dispute and make orders about the child's medical treatment.[132] However, there is a separate question of whether the court's powers permit it to override the decision of a *Gillick*-competent child.

The Court of Appeal considered this issue in *Re R (A Minor) (Wardship: Consent to Treatment)*. The case concerned a 15-year-old girl who was suffering from a psychotic illness manifesting itself from time to time in periods of violence, paranoia, hallucinations, and suicidal tendencies. When rational and stable, she refused to consent to anti-psychotic drugs being administered to her. On the question of whether her refusal to consent to treatment should be treated as determinative of the matter, Lord Donaldson held that it could not be.

Re R (A Minor) (Wardship: Consent to Treatment) [1992] Fam 11 (CA), 22–6

LORD DONALDSON MR:

It is trite law that in general a doctor is not entitled to treat a patient without the consent of someone who is authorised to give that consent. If he does so, he will be liable in damages for trespass to the person and may be guilty of a criminal assault. This is subject to the necessary exception that in cases of emergency a doctor may treat the patient notwithstanding the absence of consent, if the patient is unconscious or otherwise incapable of giving or refusing consent and there is no one else sufficiently immediately available with authority to consent on behalf of the patient. However consent by itself creates no obligation to treat. It is merely a key which unlocks a door. Furthermore, whilst in the case of an adult of full capacity there will usually only be one keyholder, namely the patient, in the ordinary family unit where a young child is the patient there will be two keyholders, namely the parents, with a several as well as a joint right to turn the key and unlock the door. If the parents disagree, one consenting and the other refusing, the doctor will be presented with a professional and ethical, but not with a legal, problem because, if he has consent of one authorised person, treatment will not without more constitute a trespass or a criminal assault . . .

In the instant appeal [counsel], appearing for the Official Solicitor, submits that (a) if the child has the right to give consent to medical treatment, the parents' right to give or refuse consent is terminated and (b) the court in the exercise of its wardship jurisdiction is only entitled to step into the shoes of the parents and thus itself has no right to give or refuse consent. . . .

The key passages upon which counsel relies are to be found in the speech of Lord Scarman . . .

What [counsel's] argument overlooks is that Lord Scarman was discussing the parent's right "to *determine* whether or not their minor child below the age of 16 will have medical treatment" . . . A right of determination is wider than a right to consent. The parents can

131 *Re R (A Minor) (Wardship: Consent to Treatment)* [1992] Fam 11 (CA).
132 See, e.g., *Yates v Great Ormond Street Hospital* [2017] EWCA Civ 410.

only have a right of determination if *either* the child has no right to consent, that is, is not a keyholder, *or* the parents hold a master key which could nullify the child's consent. I do not understand Lord Scarman to be saying that, if a child was "*Gillick* competent", to adopt the convenient phrase used in argument, the parents ceased to have an independent right of consent as contrasted with ceasing to have a right of determination, that is, a veto. In a case in which the "*Gillick* competent" child refuses treatment, but the parents consent, that consent *enables* treatment to be undertaken lawfully, but in no way determines that the child shall be so treated. In a case in which the positions are reversed, it is the child's consent which is the enabling factor and again the parents' refusal of consent is not determinative. If Lord Scarman intended to go further than this and to say that in the case of a "*Gillick* competent" child, a parent has no right either to consent or to refuse consent, his remarks were obiter, because the only question in issue was Mrs Gillick's alleged right of veto. Furthermore I consider that they would have been wrong.

One glance at the consequences suffices to show that Lord Scarman cannot have been intending to say that the parental right to consent terminates with the achievement by the child of "*Gillick* competence". It is fundamental to the speeches of the majority that the capacity to consent will vary from child to child and according to the treatment under consideration, depending upon the sufficiency of his or her intelligence and understanding of that treatment. If the position in law is that upon the achievement of "*Gillick* competence" there is a transfer of the right of consent from parents to child and there can never be a concurrent right in both, doctors would be faced with an intolerable dilemma, particularly when the child was nearing the age of 16, if the parents consented, but the child did not. . . . I do not believe that that is the law . . .

Both in this case and in *In Re E*, the judges treated *Gillick* . . . as deciding that a "*Gillick* competent" child has a right to refuse treatment. In this I consider that they were in error. Such a child can consent, but if he or she declines to do so or refuses, consent can be given by someone else who has parental rights or responsibilities. The failure or refusal of the "*Gillick* competent" child is a very important factor in the doctor's decision whether or not to treat, but does not prevent the necessary consent being obtained from another competent source.

The wardship jurisdiction

In considering the wardship jurisdiction of the court, no assistance is to be derived from *Gillick*'s case, where this simply was not in issue . . . It is, however, clear that the practical jurisdiction of the court is wider than that of parents . . . It is also clear that this jurisdiction is not derivative from the parents' rights and responsibilities, but derives from, or is, the delegated performance of the duties of the Crown to protect its subjects and particularly children who are the generations of the future.

. . . I see no reason whatsoever why [the court exercising its wardship powers] should not be able, and in an appropriate case willing, to override decisions by "*Gillick* competent" children who are its wards or in respect of whom applications are made . . .

Conclusion

1. No doctor can be required to treat a child, whether by the court in the exercise of its wardship jurisdiction, by the parents, by the child or anyone else. The decision whether to treat is dependent upon an exercise of his own professional judgment, subject only to the threshold requirement that, save in exceptional cases usually of emergency, he has the consent of someone who has authority to give that consent. In forming that judgment the views and wishes of the child are a factor whose importance increases with the increase in the child's intelligence and understanding.

2. There can be concurrent powers to consent. If more than one body or person has a power to consent, only a failure to, or refusal of, consent by all having that power will create a veto.
3. A "*Gillick* competent" child or one over the age of 16 will have a power to consent, but this will be concurrent with that of a parent or guardian.
4. "*Gillick* competence" is a developmental concept and will not be lost or acquired on a day to day or week to week basis. . . .
5. The court in the exercise of its wardship or statutory jurisdiction has power to override the decisions of a "*Gillick* competent" child as much as those of parents or guardians. . . .

[Staughton LJ agreed with Donaldson MR as to the scope of the court's wardship jurisdiction but expressed no opinion on the question of whether the parent's right to consent to treatment continued to exist alongside that of the competent child. Farquharson LJ decided the case on the basis that the child lacked *Gillick* competency.]

Lord Donaldson MR therefore expressed the clear view, supported by Staughton LJ, that the court is not restricted by the decision of a *Gillick*-competent child, and can override that child's decision (even if the parents agree) if the court considers that doing so will be in the child's best interests.

The strong swing back in favour of paternalism, even in the case of *Gillick*-competent children or children *over the age of 16*, was taken a step further by Lord Donaldson MR in *Re W (A Minor) (Medical Treatment: Court's Jurisdiction)*.[133] In this case, Lord Donaldson held that, despite a 16-year-old having a clear statutory right to consent to treatment under s 8 of the Family Law Reform Act 1969 (FLRA 1969), a 16-year-old's *refusal* to consent could be overridden by anyone holding parental responsibility or by the court.

The approach of *Re R* and *Re W* was subjected to a strong challenge before Sir James Munby in *An NHS Trust v X*.[134] X was a girl of 15, but about to turn 16; she was a Jehovah's Witness, and had sickle cell syndrome. This condition on occasion produced a medical crisis which, in the opinion of her doctors, required a blood transfusion. On two earlier occasions the court had authorized this, while on other occasions alternative medical management had resolved the crisis without transfusion being necessary. It was not disputed that X was *Gillick* competent, and she did not consent to transfusion (though she did consent to other forms of treatment). It was argued on her behalf that, whatever may have been said in *Re R*, X's refusal of consent should be determinative of the matter.

Sir James noted that an adult with capacity has the absolute right to give or refuse consent to a medical procedure. The judge posed the question in this way:

An NHS Trust v X [2021] EWHC 65

SIR JAMES MUNBY:

27. . . . Is the decision of a *Gillick* competent child determinative in the same way as the decision of a capacitous adult? If not, are there any, and if so what, circumstances in which

[133] [1993] Fam 64. For a partial defence of *Re W* and *Re R*, see Gilmore and Herring (2011), where the authors draw a distinction between a refusal to consent and a refusal of treatment. For a response, suggesting that this approach is unworkable in practice, see Cave and Wallbank (2012).

[134] [2021] EWHC 65.

the decision of a *Gillick* competent child is determinative? The question could hardly be more important, for on the answer depends whether the *Gillick* competent child is autonomous in the same way as a capacitous adult is autonomous. No doubt, if a child is *Gillick* competent, her wishes and feelings and decision will, on any view, carry significantly more weight than those of a child who is not *Gillick* competent, but that does not meet [counsel for X's] point which is that the *Gillick* competent child is autonomous and her decision is in all circumstances determinative.

[After quoting extensively from *Re R* and *Re W*, Sir James drew two interim conclusions]

53. . . . (1) that in relation to medical treatment neither the decision of a *Gillick* competent child nor the decision of a child 16 years old or more is determinative in all circumstances; and (2) that there are circumstances in which the decision of such a child can be overridden by the court.

After a comparison with the approach in relation to incapacitous adults under the Mental Capacity Act 2005, the approach of the Canadian courts to these issues, and the relevant rights under the ECHR, Sir James concluded that there was nothing that 'even begins to suggest the need for any judicial re-evaluation' of the *Re R* and *Re W* decisions; any change, he said, 'is a matter for Parliament, not the courts'.[135] The same conclusion was reached by the Court of Appeal in *Re E (Minors: Blood Transfusion)*, where Sir Andrew McFarlane P endorsed the analysis in *Re X*, and concluded with regard to the *Re W* decision:

Re E (Minors: Blood Transfusion) [2021] EWCA Civ 1888

SIR ANDREW McFARLANE P:

57. . . . Each member of the court [in *Re W*] expressed himself somewhat differently, but in our view there is no real difference in their reasoning. They each asserted the primacy of the welfare principle, while emphasising the importance of the decision of a capacitous young person. Such decisions will doubtless prevail in the great majority of situations, whether or not in the medical context, and the court will simply not be involved. At the same time, each member of the court explicitly referred to cases where the irreparable and disproportionate consequences of a refusal of treatment places the court under a duty to intervene. In our view, this approach remains good law. It survives the Human Rights Act 1988 and the Mental Capacity Act 2005, and it has not been overtaken by subsequent decisions, by the passage of time, or by the evolution of societal values.

It is therefore beyond doubt, as the law currently stands, that the court can and will override a *Gillick*-competent child's decision if the court is persuaded that that decision is not in the child's best interests.

The Gillick *decision and parental rights*

A different issue that arises in relation to *Gillick* competence is about the interrelationship between the child's rights and the parent's rights. Just because the court has reserved to itself the right to make the final determination if it considers the child to have made the wrong

[135] Ibid, [84] and [162]. For commentary, see Cave (2021).

choice, it does not necessarily follow that a parent has the same prerogative to impose their views on their child once the child gains competence.

In *Re R*, as extracted earlier, and *Re W*, Lord Donaldson MR discussed this issue extensively, though the question was not before the court and therefore his comments were all obiter (and the other judges did not agree about this aspect of his judgments). Lord Donaldson's influential judgment, despite these limitations, led to a view that parents do not lose their independent right to consent upon the child becoming *Gillick* competent—it was said that the two rights coexist. This led to the view that provided the doctor obtains the consent of *either* the child or the parent, the treatment can proceed.[136]

This approach has also been subjected to recent challenge, this time with rather more success. In *AB v CD, The Tavistock and Portman NHS Foundation Trust and others*,[137] Lieven J was considering a case about whether a hospital could lawfully treat young people at its Gender Identity Development Service, in particular by the prescribing of puberty blockers, in cases where the parents and the young person concerned *were in agreement* about that course of action. In considering the situation where a parent might seek to consent to treatment that their *Gillick*-competent child refused to agree to receive, Lieven J rejected the approach set out by Lord Donaldson.

AB v CD, The Tavistock and Portman NHS Foundation Trust and others
[2021] EWHC 741

LIEVEN J:

60. To the degree that Lord Donaldson was seeking to find that a parent retains the right to consent to treatment which a *Gillick* competent child has refused, in my view that analysis does not fit with what the House of Lords, and in particular Lord Scarman, said in *Gillick*. It would now also be very difficult to accept in the light of article 8 of the ECHR. . . .

67. . . . The very essence of *Gillick* is, in my view, that a parent's right to consent or "determine" treatment cannot trump or overbear the decision of the child. Therefore, the doctors could lawfully advise and treat the child without her mother's knowledge or consent. In *Gillick*, the parent did not have the right to know that the treatment was being given, so it makes little sense to assume that the parent could act to stop the child's decision being operative on whether the treatment takes place or not. I cannot accept that Lord Scarman was drawing the distinction between the child making the decision and the parent being able to give legally operative consent that Lord Donaldson seems to have drawn in Re R. Mrs Gillick was asserting a right to "decide" whether her daughter could be given advice and treatment without her knowledge, and thus without her consent. Therefore, the distinction that Lord Donaldson seeks to draw between the parent retaining a right to consent, but not being in a position to determine the treatment, does not accord with the issue in *Gillick*.

68. However, in the present case, the parent and the child are in agreement. Therefore, the issue here is whether the parents' ability to consent disappears once the child achieves *Gillick* competence in respect of the specific decision even where both the parents and child agree. In my view it does not. The parents retain parental responsibility in law and the rights and duties that go with that. One of those duties is to make a decision as to consent in

136 Applied in *Re K, W and H (Minors) (Medical Treatment)* [1993] 1 FLR 854.
137 [2021] EWHC 741.

medical treatment cases where the child cannot do so. The parent cannot use that right to "trump" the child's decision, so much follows from *Gillick*, but if the child fails to make a decision then the parent's ability to do so continues. At the heart of the issue is that the parents' "right" to consent is always for the purpose of ensuring the child's best interests. If the child does not, for whatever reason, make the relevant decision then the parents continue to have the responsibility (and thus the right) to give valid consent.

69. This might arise if the child is unable to make the decision, for example is unconscious. However, it could also arise if the child declines to make the decision, perhaps because although *Gillick* competent she finds the whole situation too overwhelming and would rather her parents make the decision on her behalf. In the present case, . . . it has not been possible to ascertain whether the child is competent. In this case, there are two options. If the child is *Gillick* competent, she has not objected to her parent giving consent on her behalf. As such, a doctor can rely on the consent given by her parents. Alternatively, the child is not *Gillick* competent. In that case, her parents can consent on her behalf. It is not necessary for me or a doctor to investigate which route applies to give the parents authority to give consent. Therefore, in my view, whether or not XY is *Gillick* competent to make the decision about [puberty blockers], her parents retain the parental right to consent to that treatment.

Lieven J therefore drew a distinction between a *Gillick*-competent child actively refusing treatment, where the parent's right to give consent would not apply and a court application would have to be made, and a situation where a *Gillick*-competent child either simply wished the parent to make the decision despite the child's own technical competence to do so, or where that child did not in fact make any decision, in which case the parent's right to consent continued.

Wider considerations from Gillick

In many ways, the post-*Gillick* era can seem disappointing for children's rights advocates, but it is worth bearing in mind that the wider consequences of the decision in terms of children's autonomy are likely mainly to be seen away from the courts—after all, the whole point of *Gillick* is that children with sufficient understanding of the issues should be making decisions about their own lives, and the courts generally should not become involved.[138] Understanding the overall impact of *Gillick* and the later case law therefore requires us to step back from court judgments and consider the law as it is applied on the ground, such as by doctors when seeing their patients.[139] The concept of '*Gillick* competency' is now a central idea in considering children's right to self-determination, and is particularly important in fixing the legal right to make decisions not to age, but to the child's ability to understand and process the relevant issues.

It is also important to note the wider application of ideas first set out in *Gillick*. The courts consider children's maturity and understanding in a number of other circumstances. One example is where a child is separately represented in court proceedings, the child can give instructions directly to their lawyer—rather than having a guardian or litigation friend to act on their behalf—if 'a solicitor considers that the child is able, having regard to the child's

138 *Bell v Tavistock and Portman NHS Trust* [2021] EWCA Civ 1363 emphasizes this point in particular.

139 There are numerous examples, but see, e.g., CQC (2020) for an example of reference to the need for doctors to bear in mind that 'Children under 16 may be competent to consent to treatment (Gillick competence)'.

understanding, to give instructions in relation to the proceedings' and the solicitor has done so.[140] Thorpe LJ considered this provision in the *Mabon* case.

Mabon v Mabon [2005] EWCA Civ 634

THORPE LJ:

29. In testing the sufficiency of a child's understanding I would not say that welfare has no place. If direct participation would pose an obvious risk of harm to the child arising out of the nature of the continuing proceedings and, if the child is incapable of comprehending that risk, then the judge is entitled to find that sufficient understanding has not been demonstrated. But judges have to be equally alive to the risk of emotional harm that might arise from denying the child knowledge of and participation in the continuing proceedings . . .

32. In conclusion this case provides a timely opportunity to recognise the growing acknowledgement of the autonomy and consequential rights of children, both nationally and internationally. . . .

It can be noted that the UN Committee on the Rights of the Child has said that there is an inherent link between autonomy rights and best interests, and that it is not possible to understand best interests properly without giving appropriate weight to the child's views[141]—though, of course, that is not the same thing as saying that children should be able to make the decisions themselves. Overall, despite the potential of the *Gillick* decision, it remains the case that the courts are more comfortable with children's rights when they relate to the protection of children than when they promote children's autonomy.[142]

ONLINE RESOURCES

The supplementary materials for chapter 10 in the online resources at **www.oup.com/he/familytcm5e** provide further information on this topic.

8.6 THE COURT, THE STATE, AND PRIVATE FAMILY LIFE

Any decision by a court in relation to a child represents an interference by the state in the private life of the child and of their family. To reflect the importance of these rights, the role of the state (including the court) is restricted in a number of important ways. The most significant restriction applies when the state, in the guise of the local authority children's services department, seeks to interfere by taking children into care: here, the CA 1989 sets up a specific threshold of harm that must be met—the court may not make any order unless the child is

[140] FPR 2010, r 16.6(3). [141] UN Committee on the Rights of the Child (2009), para 74.
[142] On ways to balance these concerns, see, e.g., Eekelaar (1994b); Freeman (2007).

suffering, or is at risk of suffering, significant harm.[143] However, across all areas of child law, there are general principles which govern the interaction of the state with the family. Two of the most important are discussed here. They are: the principle that courts should not make any orders about children unless doing so is better than making no orders at all; and the general idea that parents should normally be the ones responsible for making decisions about children.[144]

8.6.1 THE CHILDREN ACT'S 'NO ORDER' PRINCIPLE

The idea that the court should not interfere in relation to children unless there is reason to interfere with private family life is encapsulated in s 1(5) of the CA 1989. This so-called 'no order' principle is central to the legislative scheme set out in the Act.

Children Act 1989, s 1

(5) Where a court is considering whether or not to make one or more orders under this Act with respect to a child, it shall not make the order or any of the orders unless it considers that doing so would be better for the child than making no order at all.

While the application and interpretation of this provision in the courts has been somewhat haphazard,[145] s 1(5) has commonly been interpreted to constitute a *presumption* against making formal orders in matters relating to the upbringing of children unless it can be positively shown that such an order is in the child's best interests. This interpretation could be a fundamentally important philosophical commitment to a particular relationship between the family and the state.[146] Arguably inspired by the policies of the Thatcher era, in which a minimalist state and the self-sufficiency and autonomy of the family unit were core ideals, it is argued that s 1(5) represents a policy of non-intervention in family life whereby parents are to be left to the task of raising their children free from scrutiny and intervention by the state. These aims are reflected in an article written by the Law Commissioner responsible for the reports which led to the Children Act.

B. Hoggett, 'The Children Bill: The Aim', (1989) 19 *Family Law* 217, 217–18

The Bill assumes that bringing up children is the responsibility of their parents and that the State's principal role is to help rather than to interfere. To emphasize the practical reality that bringing up children is a serious responsibility, rather than a matter of legal rights, the conceptual building block used throughout the Bill is 'parental responsibility'. . . .

[143] CA 1989, s 31. See chapter 12.
[144] For discussion in general about whether parents know what is best for their children, see Eekelaar (2020).
[145] Bailey-Harris, Barron, and Pearce (1999a); Harris and George (2010).
[146] Harris and George (2010), 154–5.

Non-intervention

In keeping with reinforcing rather than undermining parental responsibility, the Bill seeks to keep compulsory intervention to a minimum. Courts, therefore, should not make any order at all unless doing so would be better for the child than making none. In the public law sphere, this means that even if the required conditions for making a care order or a supervision order exist, the court has to ask itself what such an order will do to improve the child's overall welfare. . . .

In the private law sphere, it is intended to remove any assumption that the court should make an order simply because the parents are separated or divorced. Often, a custody order under the [pre-1989] law is seen as 'part of the package'.

While it is not without its critics,[147] a 'non-interventionist' approach to the family has deep foundations in legal and political thought. The principle is grounded in a certain belief about the family and its role in society, in particular, that parents are better placed than the state to know what is best for their children and therefore should be trusted to raise them as they see fit.[148] Allied to this strong faith in the institution of the family, those in favour of a non-interventionist approach (or what Lorraine Fox Harding terms a laissez-faire approach) often harbour a deep mistrust of the state and question the legitimacy of any purported interference into the privacy of family life.

L. Fox Harding, 'The Children Act 1989 in Context: Four Perspectives in Child Care Law and Policy (I)', (1991a) 13 *Journal of Social Welfare and Family Law* 179, 182–6

(1) Laissez-faire and patriarchy

Underlying the *laissez-faire* perspective lies a mistrust of the state and its powers. There is a strong undercurrent of feeling in this view that the state should in general keep out of certain "private" areas of citizens' lives, with restricted exceptions. In particular, domestic and family life are seen as a relatively private arena which should not be invaded by the agents of the state except with due cause, such cause usually being associated with criminality . . .

The most notable child care authors associated with the *laissez-faire* position are Goldstein *et. al.*, who set out their views in two works, *Beyond the Best Interests of the Child* and *Before the Best Interests of the Child*. In the earlier work, the authors used psychoanalytical theory to develop child placement guidelines which would safeguard the child's psychological needs. Of importance were two "value preferences": that the law must make the child's needs paramount, and a value preference for privacy and minimum state intervention. This stems from the need to safeguard the child's need for continuity, and therefore to safeguard the right of parents to raise their children as they see fit, free of state intrusion, except in cases of neglect and abandonment. The value preference is reinforced by the view that the law is a crude instrument, incapable of effectively managing complex parent-child relationships.

[147] See, e.g., Bainham (1998).

[148] *B (R) v Children's Aid Society of Metropolitan Toronto* [1995] 1 SCR 315.

. . . In their later work, *Before the Best Interests of the Child*, they developed further their theme of parental control undisturbed by state intervention except in extreme cases. The question posed in their book is essentially when the state *is* justified in overriding the autonomy of families. They consider that: "the child's need for safety within the confines of the family must be met by law through its recognition of family privacy as the barrier to state intrusion upon parental autonomy in child rearing". The authors' position is that "A policy of minimum coercive intervention by the state thus accords not only with our firm belief as citizens in individual freedom and human dignity, but also with our professional understanding of the intricate developmental processes of childhood". In every case the law should ask "whether removal from an unsatisfactory home is the beneficial measure it purports to be" . . .

The main elements of this perspective therefore appear to be a belief in the benefits for society of a minimum state which engages in only minimal intervention in families; and a complementary belief in the value to all, including children, of undisturbed family life where adults can get on with bringing up their children in their chosen way. It is argued that adults have a right to do this, and it is better for the children too. The bearing and rearing of a child produces a special bond between parents and child and it is damaging to disrupt it, though it is accepted that it may be necessary to do so *in extreme cases* to avert a greater evil . . .

It may be hypothesised that the thinking of the "new right" on autonomous (and probably patriarchal) families, and on the drawbacks of state intervention in general, had some influence, if only indirectly, on the non-intervention aspect of the [Children] Act. As already noted, it is consonant with other aspects of Conservative policy in the 1980s, and with new right ideology on the issues of family and state.

A non-interventionist approach to family life as enshrined in s 1(5) has important implications in both the public and private law context. A 'hands-off' approach to the family has perhaps the most obvious impact in public law proceedings aimed at protecting the child from parental neglect and abuse. The CA 1989 thus demands that a threshold of significant harm is crossed before state intervention can be justified.[149] In private law proceedings, a non-interventionist approach is particularly important in the context of family breakdown. One manifestation of the 'privatizing' trend in family law has been the emphasis on promoting 'privately' negotiated agreements rather than relying on state-adjudicated outcomes.[150] However, the question is whether the state should intervene to regulate disputes over essentially 'private' matters where the parties have been able to reach their own agreement. If the state respects the privacy of the family when it is intact, can state intervention on the sole basis of the parent's separation be justified? In attempting to provide such justification, some commentators simply question whether parents can be trusted to promote the child's, as opposed to their own, best interests when the family is in crisis. It is argued that there is a legitimate public interest and even duty to protect the interests of children subject to the risks of family breakdown. Adopting this approach, the non-intervention principle not only compromises commitment to the welfare principle, particularly if the issue has been brought before the court, but is an irresponsible abdication of responsibility. Intervention to protect the child, even in the sphere of private family matters, is thus regarded as legitimate.

[149] See chapter 12, esp 12.5.3. [150] See generally 1.2.7.

G. Douglas et al, 'Safeguarding Children's Welfare in Non-Contentious Divorce: Towards a New Conception of the Legal Process', (2000) 63 *Modern Law Review* 177, 179–80

As divorce has become increasingly common and the concept of 'parental responsibility' has come to underpin modern child law, the question of whether it is appropriate for the state, through the court, to scrutinise parents' decisions for their children in the absence of any dispute has been raised. One argument in favour of some sort of 'welfare check' is that given by Gerald Caplan:

> By voluntarily approaching the courts to dissolve their marriage, parents explicitly open up their private domain to public scrutiny and intervention. Their request for divorce is a formal statement that their marriage has broken down and constitutes an invitation to the representatives of society to assess the consequences for themselves and their children . . .

But this view begs several questions. First, it by no means follows that, just because a couple seeks a divorce, they thereby willingly lay themselves open to state scrutiny. After all, there is no alternative to engaging with whatever is required of them by the legal system if they wish to obtain a licence to remarry. Secondly, no 'marker' is flagged up if parents merely separate and do not take divorce proceedings (or if the parents are unmarried), but the needs of the child may be no different. Thirdly, the form and efficacy of intervention must be assessed. 'Intervention' for its own sake may be at best, irrelevant and at worst, iatrogenic. Further, one must query whether, in the age of mass divorce, there are the resources to permit any meaningful and beneficial legal 'intervention' to occur. Indeed, one can trace over the last half century, a progressive withdrawal from any attempt to scrutinise divorces . . .

Nonetheless, there is very good reason for the state to be concerned about the interests of children when their parents' relationship breaks down and to use the legal system as well as other mechanisms and services, to try to address these. There is a considerable body of research evidence suggesting that children may face detrimental outcomes from parental separation and divorce . . . Given the level of divorce and separation in this country and the numbers of children affected, there is a strong justification in ensuring that social—and legal—policies and practices are designed to tackle and reduce this risk.

Bainham has expressed similar concern about the trend towards private ordering on divorce. He suggests a normative framework reflecting accepted societal standards should be enshrined within the law to guide the family in post-separation decision-making. In his view, the absence of such normative standards from the CA 1989 is a serious omission.

A. Bainham, 'The Privatisation of the Public Interest in Children', (1990) 53 *Modern Law Review* 206, 207, and 210–14

A basic philosophy enshrined in the 1989 Act is that the state's role in the family is a primarily supportive one and that it should not intervene at all unless it is necessary to do so. There is nothing in the reformed legislation which contradicts (and a great deal which supports) the notion that the family, and specifically child care, is an area which ought to remain unregulated by law unless the need for regulation can be positively demonstrated . . .

. . . I have no quarrel with either the intended marginalisation of the judicial role or with the view that child care arrangements brought about by agreement are more likely to work than those which result from attempts at compulsion. But I want to suggest that this scheme, by regarding private agreements as sacrosanct, fails to give adequate recognition to the *public* interest in children. In developing this argument it must be conceded that, on one interpretation, the Act has simply re-defined the public interest and has not diluted it. On this view, the public interest is seen as best served by facilitating parental agreements. In other words, the theory would be that it is in children's best interests (and consequently the public interest) that parents should agree on their future care. But . . . whichever way the policy shift is described there can be little doubt that an area which hitherto was thought appropriate for legal regulation will in future be substantially de-regulated.

The crucial point is that there has been no attempt in the legislation to influence the nature or content of parental agreements following divorce other than through the somewhat nebulous and indirect notion of continuing parental responsibility. Parental agreement would arguably have been a more acceptable means of meeting the public interest if the legislation had also established some normative standards for child rearing, both in the context of united families and on divorce, to act as a benchmark or basis for private ordering. Yet the legislation tells us nothing about what is involved in the discharge of parental responsibility . . .

It is disconcerting that the model apparently believed to be representative of what society considers desirable should be one in which private ordering is seen as an end in itself whatever the quality or nature of the agreements reached.

In practice, research carried out by Bailey-Harris, Barron, and Pearce suggests s 1(5) received a mixed response from the judiciary.

R. Bailey-Harris, J. Barron, and J. Pearce, 'Settlement Culture and the Use of the "No Order" Principle under the Children Act 1989', (1999a) 11 *Child and Family Law Quarterly* 53, 59–61

[S]ection 1(5) receives a very mixed response in practice at county court level . . . [T]he evidence from our study could be interpreted as suggesting two themes. First, the 'no order principle' is invoked by judges to reinforce the concept of parental autonomy and the vigorous promotion of agreement, this results in the court declining or refusing to make an order even when parties have sought one. It is highly questionable whether this use of the principle accords with the original intention of the legislature, and we found that it could be productive of acute dissatisfaction on the part of parents who were expecting an adjudicated outcome. Secondly, and in complete contrast, the principle is very commonly breached or not observed by judges, particularly when legal practitioners press for resolution by consent order . . . Our file survey showed that, overall, a substantive order was made in 67 per cent of cases, no substantive order in 27 per cent, and an order of 'no order' in 5 per cent. The extent of non-observance of the principle by the courts we sampled is thus immediately apparent.

To pursue the first theme: it is possible to argue from the evidence of our study that in practice the courts are using the 'no order principle' in cases to which it was never intended to apply. In many cases where there is originally real conflict between parents who have invoked the court's jurisdiction specifically to resolve their dispute, the principle is invoked by judges to reinforce the promotion of parental autonomy and agreement as the preferred mode of resolution: the court asserts that no order is needed where parents can eventually agree, even though their preferred original intention was to obtain an order.

Our study reveals many examples of judges using the rhetoric of parental autonomy to justify the refusal to make an order, even in proceedings where there is real dispute and where proceedings are protracted . . .

There is considerable evidence of the dissatisfaction of parents with the outcome of 'no order' when they consider that they have invoked the court's jurisdiction precisely for the exercise of its authority in a matter which they find difficult to resolve themselves. In other words, the use of the 'no order' approach by the court to reinforce its promotion of parental autonomy is often at odds with parental expectations of the process . . .

There is, perhaps unsurprisingly, little reported authority on the use of s 1(5)—after all, if the court considers that the principle is engaged, it will not have made any order in the case.[151] The House of Lords in *Dawson v Wearmouth* interpreted the provision as meaning that an applicant 'has to make out a positive case . . . that it is in the interests of the child that the order should be made. If he fails to make out that positive case, his application will fail.'[152] However, while the courts have later said that they do not consider s 1(5) to create any kind of presumption against the making of an order,[153] it has been reiterated that 'in conducting its welfare analysis the court *has to* have in mind the "no order principle" which applies under section 1(5)'.[154]

8.6.2 THE STATE AND PARENTAL DECISION-MAKING

Another key limitation on the role of the state in children's lives is the CA 1989's concept of *parental responsibility*. Parental responsibility is defined in s 3(1) as being 'all the rights, duties, powers, responsibilities and authority which by law a parent of a child has in relation to the child and his property'. We explore the meaning and application of parental responsibility in chapter 10. The focus here is on the interrelationship between parental responsibility and the role of the state in children's lives.[155]

Current policy generally dictates that parents should generally be left to raise their children as they see fit. Parental autonomy and protecting the privacy of the family unit against unnecessary intervention are seen as serving the child's rights or interests (and thereby those of the state). With respect to the vast majority of decisions regarding a child's upbringing, the state plays no role at all and parents are left to raise their children in the way that they wish—the state is involved only in an indirect way, but setting broad limitations on the range of decisions that parents can legitimately take. A good example is educational provision: parents are required to 'cause [their child] to received efficient full-time education suitable (a) to his age, ability and aptitude, and (b) to any special educational needs . . .

[151] See, e.g., the conclusion to *Re B (Role of Biological Father)* [2007] EWHC 1952, [27], that '[the] making of no order must be treated as a final order'.

[152] [1999] 2 AC 308, 326 (Lord Hobhouse); see also at 321 (Lord Mackay LC).

[153] *Re G (Children)* [2005] EWCA Civ 1283, [10]. Harris and George (2010), 165 suggest that this approach leaves s 1(5) 'add[ing] nothing of substance to the general welfare principle in s 1(1)'.

[154] *Re S and Re W (Section 20 Accommodation)* [2023] EWCA Civ 1, [43] (emphasis added).

[155] See also the discussion of children's rights at 8.5.

he may have, either by regular attendance at school or otherwise'.[156] Most parents discharge this duty by sending their child to state school, but it is equally permitted for them to select a private school, to arrange a personal tutor, or to educate their child themselves at home.

The law does, of course, set limits. There are numerous criminal offences relating to cruelty, neglect, or failure to protect a child,[157] and—as we will explore in detail in chapter 12—family law provides a mechanism for children to be removed from the care of their parents if their parenting causes the child to suffer or be at risk of suffering 'significant harm'.[158] Within these broad limitations, however, parents are granted a wide discretion about how to raise their children, which inevitably means that many forms of parenting are seen as acceptable without the state stepping in.

Re L (Care: Threshold Criteria) [2007] 1 FLR 2050

HEDLEY J:

50. . . . [S]ociety must be willing to tolerate very diverse standards of parenting, including the eccentric, the barely adequate and the inconsistent. It follows . . . that children will inevitably have both very different experiences of parenting and very unequal consequences flowing from it. It means that some children will experience disadvantage and harm, while others flourish in atmospheres of loving security and emotional stability. These are the consequences of our fallible humanity and it is not the provenance of the state to spare children all the consequences of defective parenting. In any event, it simply could not be done.

The policy of the law in one sense is therefore clear, at least when it comes to the possibility of the parents being removed from the care of their children entirely—the state will only step in when there are serious concerns about the child's welfare, assessed against a threshold of 'significant harm' actually occurring or being a demonstrable risk.[159]

But what about situations where the overall parenting that a child is receiving is good, but there is a particular issue where the decision of the parents appears not to be in the child's best interests? If the parents (or other holders of parental responsibility) disagree with each other about the appropriate course of action, the court becomes involved—as we discuss in chapter 10, the courts are well used to resolving disputes between parents in these situations.[160] The bigger challenge concerns cases where the parents are agreed, but someone else—a teacher, a doctor, a wider family member—thinks that the parents have made the wrong decision. Should the state get involved in those cases, or are parents simply to be left to it?

Depending on the nature of the issue, some cases in this category might technically allow a local authority to bring care proceedings in relation to a child, which would (if successful) grant the local authority parental responsibility (PR) in relation to the child and the right to determine the extent to which the parents could exercise their own PR.[161] However,

[156] Education Act 1996, s 7.
[157] See, e.g., Children and Young Persons Act 1933, s 1; Domestic Violence, Crime and Victims Act 2004, s 5.
[158] CA 1989, s 31. [159] We discuss this in detail in chapter 12. [160] See 10.5.
[161] See 12.5.6.

Sir James Munby P expressed significant doubt about both the appropriateness and legal effectiveness of taking such an approach:[162]

Re AB (Medical Treatment: Care Proceedings) [2018] EWFC 3

MUNBY P:

24. (iii) Whatever its strict rights may be, a local authority will usually be ill-advised to rely upon its parental responsibility under section 33(3)(a) of the 1989 Act as entitling it to authorise medical treatment opposed by parents who also have parental responsibility: see *Barnet London Borough Council v AL* [2017] EWHC 125, para 32, and the discussion in Re C *(Child in Care: Choice of Forename)* [2016] EWCA Civ 374, paras 92-95. For a local authority to embark upon care proceedings in such a case merely to clothe it with parental responsibility is likely to be problematic and may well turn out to be ineffective.

Concerns about a specific aspect of parenting where there are not wider concerns that might justify care proceedings cannot, at least in most cases, therefore be addressed by way of care proceedings. But that does not mean that the court has no role, and the court has consistently held that it has the power—originally under its inherent jurisdiction,[163] and now under the CA 1989's private law orders[164]—to intervene and override parents' decisions.[165]

Re A (Children) (Conjoined Twins: Surgical Separation) [2001] Fam 147 (CA), 178–9

WARD LJ:

There is, however, this important safeguard to ensure that a child receives proper treatment. Because the parental rights and powers exist for the performance of their duties and responsibilities to the child and must be exercised in the best interests of the child, ". . . the common law has never treated such rights as sovereign or beyond review and control": per Lord Scarman in *Gillick* case . . .

Overriding control is vested in the court. This proposition is well established and has not been the subject of any challenge in this appeal. Because of the comment in the media questioning why the court should be involved, I add this short explanation. Long, long ago the sovereign's prerogative to protect infants passed to the Lord Chancellor and through him to the judges and it forms a part of the inherent jurisdiction of the High Court. The Children Act 1989 now contains a statutory scheme for the resolution of disputes affecting the upbringing of children. If a person having a recognisable interest brings such a dispute to the court, the court must decide it.

[162] In *Re B (Medical Treatment)* [2008] EWHC 1996, Coleridge J doubted that a local authority's parental responsibility would give it the power to consent to the withdrawal of life-sustaining treatment for a child against the parents' wishes; cf obiter comments from King LJ in *Re C (Child in Care: Choice of Forename)* [2016] EWCA Civ 374, [93].

[163] See 8.7. [164] See chapter 11.

[165] See also 10.5.2.b on when the state can intervene in the exercise of parental responsibility.

While the court's claim to be able to step in to protect a child's welfare is therefore clearly established, the question remains as to *when* and *in what circumstances* the court will exercise this jurisdiction. Most of the cases that test these issues involve disputes about medical treatment for a child, but it is important to note that although the legal principles are largely discussed in that context, there are other issues that can require court intervention.[166]

8.6.2.a When will the court intervene?

As we will see in chapter 12, when a local authority seeks orders in child protection cases, the court can make a care or supervision order only if it is first satisfied that the child is suffering or is at risk of suffering significant harm,[167] *and* then that the order sought is in the child's best interests. The first part of this test is known as the *threshold* stage.

If a *local authority* makes an application under the High Court's inherent jurisdiction, there is a similar threshold whereby the court must be satisfied that there is 'reasonable cause to believe that if the court's inherent jurisdiction is not exercised with respect to the child he is likely to suffer significant harm';[168] but this threshold does not apply to an application brought by anyone else, such as a hospital trust or a teacher, and anyone with a 'proper interest' in the child's welfare can apply.[169] Similarly, when an application is made under the private law provisions of the CA 1989, there is no such threshold. Anyone who is not an 'entitled' applicant will need the court's leave to make an application, but this is not a high hurdle;[170] and a local authority can apply for these orders on the same basis as any other non-entitled applicant, with no threshold of significant harm.[171] But should the state, whether through the local authority, a hospital trust, or anyone else, be able to apply to the court to override parents' decisions without some kind of threshold to be met first? The court had to engage with this question in litigation about contested medical treatment of a young child called Charlie Gard.[172]

Charlie was born with a severe mitochondrial condition that caused worsening brain damage which left him unable to hear, move, or breathe independently. His condition had no cure, and his doctors considered that it was not in his best interests for life-sustaining treatment to be continued. Charlie's parents disagreed, and wanted to try an experimental treatment being offered by a doctor in the USA. With no agreement possible, the hospital sought declarations from the court that it would be lawful for them to stop providing life-sustaining treatment for Charlie. The High Court and Court of Appeal agreed with the medical professionals, and the Supreme Court refused the parents' application for permission to appeal. In the Court of Appeal, the parents ran a strong argument based in part on parental autonomy, in effect saying that the court should not be able to interfere with their exercise of parental responsibility unless their decisions would cause significant harm to Charlie.

[166] An example is *Re C (Child in Care: Choice of Forename)* [2016] EWCA Civ 374, where the issue was whether the mother should be permitted to name her twin children 'Preacher' and 'Cyanide'. The children were the subject of care proceedings from birth, and the local authority objected to the names, and so brought the matter to court.

[167] CA 1989, s 31. [168] Ibid, s 100(4)(b).

[169] *Re D (A Minor) (Wardship: Sterilisation)* [1976] Fam 185. [170] See 11.3.2.b.

[171] *Re R (A Minor) (Blood Transfusion)* [1993] 2 FLR 757.

[172] On the medical treatment of children generally, see Bridgeman (2020).

Yates v Great Ormond Street Hospital [2017] EWCA Civ 410

McFARLANE LJ:

110. It is also argued that where there is a viable, alternative treatment available, then, absent the court being satisfied that the carrying out of the treatment would cause the child significant harm, the parents' view must prevail, even if their proposed course of treatment is not in the child's best interests. That must be the submission that is made to the court in this case given the judge's finding. The judge has held that to travel to America is not in Charlie's best interests, yet it is submitted that the parents' views to the contrary must prevail in the absence of significant harm.

111. It is neither necessary nor appropriate, in my view, to import such a test or to create a new category of case. There is no justification for it in any previously decided authority . . .

112. It goes without saying that in many cases, all other things being equal, the views of the parents will be respected and are likely to be determinative. Very many cases involving children with these tragic conditions never come to court because a way forward is agreed as a result of mutual respect between the family members and the hospital, but it is well recognised that parents in the appalling position that these and other parents can find themselves may lose their objectivity and be willing to 'try anything', even if, when viewed objectively, their preferred option is not in a child's best interests. As the authorities to which I have already made reference underline again and again, the sole principle is that the best interests of the child must prevail and that must apply even to cases where parents, for the best of motives, hold on to some alternative view.

In thinking about the role of the courts, though, it is worth asking why parents do not get to make the decisions, given that the state entrusts them as the holders of parental responsibility for their child. In order to understand this issue, it is helpful first to think about the role of parental responsibility.

R. Taylor, 'Parental Decisions and Court Jurisdiction: Best Interests or Significant Harm?', (2020) 32 *Child and Family Law Quarterly* 141, 144–5, 150, 151, 154

The first important principle of parental responsibility is that the parental role is one of responsibility to children rather than proprietary rights over them. . . .

The second important principle of parental responsibility is that responsibility for children's upbringing is primarily that of parents rather than the state. Reasonable people will frequently disagree on what is best for children; the fact that parents are obliged to exercise their authority in line with children's best interests does not often yield a single right answer to a particular decision. Instead parents are generally granted a broad discretion to exercise their responsibilities as they see fit, for example in naming, educating, feeding and disciplining their children. There are many good reasons for giving parents this zone of discretion. . . . The reality for many parents is that they may have to compromise in some of the decisions that they make for their children in order to meet the competing interests of other family members and to balance demands on their resources. Parents often need flexibility in order to meet all of these responsibilities in practice. There are also important considerations of freedom

> and diversity: in a free society, the state should be cautious in imposing a particular view as to what is best for children without good reason and clear evidence to support that view. . . . The challenge for the law is how to accommodate these two important aspects of parental responsibility: recognising the primary role of parents whilst also requiring that they protect the interests of their children. As Lady Hale observes [in *Williamson*[173]], whilst parents have the primary role, the state also has a legitimate role in regulating parental decisions in the interests of children and society.

The challenge brought by the parents in the *Gard* litigation was concerned with this final issue: when does the state, through the court, have a legitimate role in regulating parental decisions? They argued that there should be the same threshold of 'significant harm', but as Taylor goes on to explain, this idea is not founded in an analysis of the CA 1989.

> There is nothing in the Children Act 1989 to suggest that the jurisdiction of the court is limited in the manner proposed on behalf of Charlie Gard's parents. Instead the Act facilitates the court's use of its protective jurisdiction in order to protect the welfare of the child. The 'significant harm' test is not the boundary that demarcates legitimate court intervention into mutual parental decisions; instead it is the boundary that must be crossed to allow ongoing state involvement in the life of the child, and particularly to allow local authorities to obtain ongoing discretionary authority over the child's life through a care order. This may, however, appear a rather fine distinction to parents seeking to resist state intervention in the treatment of their terminally ill child. As Mostyn J noted in *Re JM (A Child)*,[174] section 8 [of the CA 1989] was primarily drafted to address parental disputes rather than cases in which the state sought to impose medical treatment against the wishes of the child's parents. Nonetheless, the balance between the two aspects of parental responsibility comes not through restrictions on the jurisdiction of the court but through judicial restraint and sensitivity to the important role of parents in securing their children's welfare. . . .

Taylor then turns to consider the alternative approach to these cases, where the CA 1989 is not used and instead recourse is had to the High Court's inherent jurisdiction.[175]

> The argument that the court should only permit intervention [under the inherent jurisdiction] in such cases if significant harm is shown is, however, clearly unsupported by current law. The inherent jurisdiction is a protective jurisdiction that is routinely and invariably deployed on the basis of the 'best interests' test. As each of the courts in *Gard* agreed, there was simply no authority for the argument that a significant harm test should apply. To the extent that the court had the freedom to choose to introduce further self-restraint in the cases that it would receive under the jurisdiction, there was little to commend the use of significant harm as the means of doing so. The legislative choice to use significant harm as a threshold for local authority applications but not for other parties would

[173] *R (Williamson) v Secretary of State for Education and Employment* [2005] UKHL 15, [72].

[174] [2015] EWHC 2832.

[175] As both Bridgeman (2017a) and George (2019a) argue, it is questionable whether the courts are justified in using the inherent jurisdiction in these cases.

seem to be a clear indication that Parliament did not intend to impose that limit on the jurisdiction. Further, such a test would be inconsistent with the approach of the Children Act 1989 which, as we have seen, reserves significant harm for the threshold at which local authorities might acquire ongoing discretionary authority over the life of the child. Given that cases routinely combine applications under the Children Act and the inherent jurisdiction, it would be undesirable to apply substantially different tests in those applications. . . .

The importance of parents' responsibility for their children is recognised in law not by hard barriers to prevent judicial intervention but by careful respect for the relationship between parents and children in determining children's welfare. It is in this way that the tension between the two meanings of parental responsibility, identified [in the first extract above], are best reconciled by the courts.

8.6.2.b The role of the parents' views

The court had previously made clear that its role was to make an independent assessment of the child's welfare, rather than to conduct a 'review' of the parents' own decision-making.[176] However, that is not to say that the parents' views are not a significant factor in the court's assessment of the child's welfare.

Re T (A Minor) (Wardship: Medical Treatment) [1997] 1 WLR 242 (CA), 253–4

WAITE LJ:

All these cases depend on their own facts and render generalisations—tempting though they may be to the legal or social analyst—wholly out of place. It can only be said safely there is a scale, at one end of which lies the clear case where parental opposition to medical intervention is prompted by scruple or dogma of a kind which is patently irreconcilable with principles of child health and welfare widely accepted by the generality of mankind; and that at the other end lie highly problematic cases where there is genuine scope for a difference of view between parent and judge. In both situations it is the duty of the judge to allow the court's own opinion to prevail in the perceived paramount interests of the child concerned, but in cases at the latter end of the scale, there must be a likelihood (though never of course a certainty) that the greater the scope for genuine debate between one view and another the stronger will be the inclination of the court to be influenced by a reflection that in the last analysis the best interests of every child include an expectation that difficult decisions affecting the length and quality of its life will be taken for it by the parent to whom its care has been entrusted by nature.

Consequently, there is a clear suggestion that, where there is room for genuine debate as to the child's interests and the parents adopt an entirely reasonable position within that

[176] *Re T (A Minor) (Wardship: Medical Treatment)* [1997] 1 WLR 242 (CA). The Court of Appeal overturned a High Court judge's decision and, in agreement with the parents, refused to permit a young child to have a liver transplant that his doctors wished to perform and which would have saved his life. It is difficult to understand how the court came to think that certain death was in this child's best interests when a treatment was available. See Freeman (2017); Peleg (2017).

debate, their views will be treated with greater respect.[177] This was put to the test in *Re A*, the case of the conjoined twins. The hospital treating the twins wished to undertake separation surgery to save the life of the stronger twin, Jodie, with the inevitable result that the weaker twin, Mary, would die. Without surgery, the prognosis for both twins was very poor, with the doctors predicting both would die within a few months. The parents, who were Roman Catholics with strong religious views on the matter, as well as practical concerns about raising a severely disabled child on the remote island where they lived, opposed the operation. This was a case with enormous scope for genuine disagreement amongst reasonable people as to what course of action would best serve the interests of the children. This was therefore one of those difficult, marginal cases in which deference to the parents' views might have been expected.

Re A (Children) (Conjoined Twins: Surgical Separation) [2001] Fam 147 (CA)

WARD LJ:

9.3 The weight to be given to these parents' wishes

I would wish to say emphatically that this is not a case where opposition is "prompted by scruple or dogma." The views of the parents will strike a chord of agreement with many who reflect upon their dilemma. I cannot emphasise enough how much I sympathise with them in the cruelty of the agonising choice they had to make. I know because I agonise over the dilemma too. I fear, however, that the parents' wish does not convince me that it is in the children's best interest:

(i) From Jodie's point of view they have taken the worst possible scenario that she would be wheelchair bound, destined for a life of difficulty. They fail to recognise her capacity sufficiently to enjoy the benefits of life that would be available to her were she free and independent.

(ii) She may indeed need special care and attention and that may be very difficult fully to provide in their home country. This is a real and practical problem for the family, the burden of which in ordinary family life should not be underestimated. It may seem unduly harsh on these desperate *parents* to point out that it is the *child's* best interests which are paramount, not the *parents'*. Coping with a disabled child sadly inevitably casts a great burden on parents who have to struggle through these difficulties. . . .

(iii) They are fully entitled to recoil at the idea, as they see it, of killing Mary. That is wholly understandable. This lies at the core of their objection. Yet they came to this country for treatment. They were aware of the possibility that Mary might be stillborn and they seemed reconciled to an operation which would separate Jodie from her. They seemed to have been prepared . . . [to] agree to the operation if Mary predeceased Jodie. The physical problems for Jodie would be the same, perhaps even worse in such an event. The parents appear to have been willing to cope in any event, and the burdens for parents and child cannot have changed. Mary is lost to them anyway.

[177] Viewed from a child's rights perspective, this approach has difficulties, though it is not straightforward. Art 5 UNCRC requires states to 'respect the responsibilities, rights and duties of parents' in giving direction and guidance in relation to the exercise of the child's rights under the Convention, though Art 6 provides in clear terms that 'every child has the inherent right to life' and that the state 'shall ensure to the maximum extent possible the survival and development of the child'.

(iv) In their natural repugnance at the idea of killing Mary they fail to recognise their conflicting duty to save Jodie and they seem to exculpate themselves from, or at least fail fully to face up to, the consequence of the failure to separate the twins, namely, death for Jodie. In my judgment, parents who are placed on the horns of such a terrible dilemma simply have to choose the lesser of their inevitable loss. If a family at the gates of a concentration camp were told they might free one of their children but if no choice were made both would die, compassionate parents with equal love for their twins would elect to save the stronger and see the weak one destined for death pass through the gates.

This is a terribly cruel decision to force upon the parents. It is a choice no loving parent would ever want to make. It gives me no satisfaction to have disagreed with their views of what is right for their family and to have expressed myself in terms they will feel are harshly and unfairly critical of them. I am sorry about that. It may be no great comfort to them to know that in fact my heart bleeds for them. But if, as the law says I must, it is I who must now make the decision, then whatever the parents' grief, I must strike a balance between the twins and do what is best for them.

[The Court of Appeal held that it would be in the twins' best interests for the operation to separate them to be performed.]

Some judges are plainly uncomfortable with having to override parents' decisions, though, as this judgment from Hedley J demonstrates:

Re Wyatt (A Child) (Medical Treatment: Parents' Consent) [2004] EWHC 2247

HEDLEY J:

33. There is no doubt that the law places final responsibility on the judge. This is not because parliament has expressly said so . . . but because the court is discharging its historic duty of overseeing the best interests of those who, for whatever reason, cannot make decisions for themselves. So although I have no doubt about the law, it leaves me a little uncomfortable. . . . I am being asked to override the views of these parents as to what is best for their daughter and undoubtedly I have the jurisdiction to do so.

34. I think the only way I can allay my discomfort is to remind myself in my consideration of Charlotte's best interests that Mr and Mrs Wyatt know her best. I should pay proper attention to their intuitive feelings whilst reminding myself that they may project those on to Charlotte. In approaching the case in this way, bearing in mind the breadth of the concept of best interests, I think I come closest to giving proper weight to their views whilst discharging the responsibility placed on the court.

Although the courts clearly strive to reassure parents that considerable weight will be afforded to their views, the great deference which is shown to the medical authorities in these cases has led to concern that in reality it is the health-care professionals, and not the parents or the courts, who are determining the future of these children, even if the views of the children's parents are reasonable.[178] As Huxtable and Forbes suggest, when determining

[178] Huxtable and Forbes (2004), 352.

the child's welfare, the courts are prone to fall back on the objective, scientific evidence provided by the medical experts—though there are notable exceptions.[179]

Cases like these raise a particular challenge in relation to the welfare principle, and—as in other contexts—have led some to ask whether a rights-based approach might be preferable. There are clearly arguments to be made in relation to Article 8 ECHR, particularly in relation to the state's interference in parental decision-making and their exercise of parental responsibility. In relation to medical decision-making, there are also important rights under the UNCRC, such as the child's right to life, survival, and development under Article 6, the rights of disabled children to 'enjoy a full a decent life' under Article 23, and the right of all children 'to the enjoyment of the highest attainable standard of health' under Article 24. Sometimes these rights will support the parents' position, and other times they may be in conflict with them. However, whether these rights are adequately addressed within the welfare assessment and whether an explicit rights-based analysis would be preferable is a matter of debate.[180]

8.7 THE INHERENT JURISDICTION OF THE HIGH COURT

In a very small minority of cases, the courts find that the statutory remedies that they have do not provide any way to deal with a problem that has arisen with regard to a child. One solution is for the High Court to invoke what is called its 'inherent jurisdiction'. The inherent jurisdiction stems from the Crown's innate power and responsibility to protect its subjects, that power having been vested in the court. It is said that the power of the court under the inherent jurisdiction is theoretically limitless,[181] but there are 'extensive limitations on the exercise by the High Court of that jurisdiction'.[182] Quite what those limitations are, though, is less clear.

Anyone with a genuine interest in the child may make an application,[183] and the orders that can be made are widespread and flexible. Most issues that engage the inherent jurisdiction concern the upbringing of a child, and so engage the welfare principle.[184] Local authorities can apply for orders under the inherent jurisdiction, but need the court's permission to bring such an application;[185] and irrespective of who applies, the inherent jurisdiction powers cannot be used to cause a child to be accommodated by or on behalf of a local authority.[186] Beyond the express limitations of the CA 1989, though, the inherent jurisdiction is restricted only by general constitutional principles such as not interfering with the operation of other statutory bodies.[187]

One common tool within the inherent jurisdiction is *wardship*. When a child becomes a ward of the court,[188] a number of immediate and important things happen. The child comes

[179] See, e.g., *Raqeeb v Barts NHS Foundation Trust* [2019] EWHC 2530.
[180] See 8.4.
[181] See, e.g., *Re E (SA) (A Minor) (Wardship)* [1984] 1 WLR 156.
[182] *Tameside MBC v AM (DOLS Order for Children Under 16)* [2021] EWHC 2472, [52].
[183] *Re D (A Minor) (Wardship: Sterilisation)* [1976] Fam 185. [184] CA 1989, s 1(1).
[185] Ibid, s 100(3). [186] Ibid, s 100(2)(a).
[187] *Re A Ward of Court* [2017] EWHC 1022; *Re NY (Abduction: Inherent Jurisdiction)* [2019] UKSC 49.
[188] The child becomes a ward immediately someone makes an *application* for wardship, which the court must then either affirm or discharge at a hearing.

under the protection of the court: no significant decision about the child's upbringing can be made without the court's permission (in particular, the child may not be removed from England and Wales without High Court approval), and parental rights over the child are effectively superseded by the court's own powers. In exercising these powers, the child's welfare is the court's paramount concern, and the court must 'act in the way best suited in its judgment to serve the true interest and welfare of the ward'.[189]

Despite the availability of orders under the CA 1989 which were intended to reduce the need to draw on the High Court's inherent jurisdiction,[190] those powers remain important in a number of areas. Some areas where the inherent jurisdiction is often used do not seem to require it at all: disputes concerning the medical treatment of children is a particular example, and it is questionable why it continues to be used for those cases.[191] International child abduction is another area that sees the inherent jurisdiction used frequently: while the Supreme Court held that this was permissible despite the availability of a suitable statutory remedy under the CA 1989,[192] it is hard to see what the justification is for not using the statutory scheme.[193] A particularly notable case that drew on the inherent jurisdiction when the CA 1989 could have been used just as well was *Re H (Parental Responsibility: Vaccination)*,[194] where the Court of Appeal seemed not even to consider whether it could achieve the desired outcome using statutory remedies.[195]

A particularly difficult area where the court has had frequent recourse to the inherent jurisdiction in recent years is in providing secure accommodation for young people who present a serious risk to the well-being of themselves or others. There is a statutory power to make orders that restrict a child's liberty under s 25 of the CA 1989, but there are two key limitations to that power. The first is that the eligibility criteria are narrowly framed, and not all young people thought to be in need of what amounts to protective custody will fall within the scheme. The other limitation is that the s 25 power allows the child to be placed only in secure accommodation that meets specific criteria, and there is an enormous shortage of such places. There is an endless list of reported judgments where courts are unable to make orders for a child to be placed in secure accommodation because there is no applicable accommodation available.[196]

The issue has been to the Supreme Court in *Re T (Secure Accommodation of Child)*,[197] where the Justices confirmed that the inherent jurisdiction can be used in circumstances where either the statutory criteria are not met or, more commonly, when there is no placement available in which the young person can be placed. However, Parliament simultaneously passed new Regulations that provide that local authorities may not place any child under the age of 16 in any unregistered accommodation (whether secure or otherwise).[198] Curiously, though, the Court of Appeal held that these Regulations do not, in fact, limit the court's powers under the inherent jurisdiction to authorize the placement of children under the age of 16 in secure accommodation.[199]

[189] *Re E (SA)* [1984] 1 WLR 156. [190] Law Commission (1988c).
[191] Bridgeman (2017a); George (2019a). [192] *Re NY (Abduction: Inherent Jurisdiction)* [2019] UKSC 49.
[193] This view is shared by Mostyn J: *Re N (Abduction)* [2020] EWFC 35.
[194] [2020] EWCA Civ 664. [195] George (2020).
[196] There are sadly many judgments from High Court judges expressing in strong terms about how unacceptable this situation is. Some examples are cited by the Supreme Court in *Re T (Secure Accommodation of Child)* [2021] UKSC 35.
[197] [2021] UKSC 35.
[198] Care Planning, Placement and Case Review (England) (Amendment) Regulations 2021, r 4.
[199] *A Mother v Derby CC* [2021] EWCA Civ 1867.

R. George, 'Vulnerable Children in Unregulated Care: The Unstoppable Inherent Jurisdiction', (2022a) 44 *Journal of Social Welfare and Family Law* 254, 257

That raises the question of what the court's power is to authorise a placement that is otherwise contrary to the Act. . . . [T]he Regulation explicitly limits the local authority's ability to place a child in this way, and the court's authorisation simply cannot circumvent the statutory scheme. . . .

These cases raise acute difficulties, and the immediate and often critical needs of the vulnerable teenagers concerned is not to be underestimated. It is obvious why the judiciary do not wish to allow the only remedy at their disposal to be limited or removed, but the courts are acting in a constitutionally concerning manner, failing to comply with their role in applying the law. It is hard to see how Parliament could have been clearer. It is not permissible to place children under 16 in these unregulated placements, and the court's continued complicity in allowing the use of such placements is unacceptable. The answer to these cases is for the state to make proper provision for its most vulnerable young people, not for the court to permit the continued use of sub-standard unregulated accommodation.

ONLINE RESOURCES

We discuss the inherent jurisdiction of the High Court in more detail in the online resources.

8.8 CONCLUSION

The various approaches to child-related disputes are not, of course, mutually exclusive. Finding an acceptable balance or compromise between them is one of the greatest challenges for family lawyers. From the following chapters it will be clear that, despite the recent trend towards a more rights-based culture in family law, the welfare principle predominates. However, despite this, parents' rights, children's rights, and a non-interventionist ethos are all important and will be evident, to varying degrees, in the discussion to follow. So, with these underlying principles in mind, we turn to our first substantive question: who are a child's legal parents?

ONLINE RESOURCES

Questions, suggestions for further reading, and supplementary materials for this chapter (including updates on developments in this area of family law since this book was published) may be found in the online resources at **www.oup.com/he/familytcm5e.**

9

BECOMING A LEGAL PARENT AND THE CONSEQUENCES OF LEGAL PARENTHOOD

CENTRAL ISSUES

1. There are many possible answers to the question 'who are a child's parents?' Genetic, gestational, and social parents may all have convincing claims to the status of 'legal parenthood'.
2. Legal parenthood confers a fundamentally important status on both parent and child, making the child a member of the parent's family and bringing with it a core bundle of rights and responsibilities.
3. In the context of natural procreation, the crucial factor in determining a child's legal parents is the genetic tie between parent and child. This is easily established in the case of the mother. Determining the identity of a child's genetic father is more difficult. Disputes focus today on whether scientific tests should be ordered to put the parentage of a child beyond doubt. Establishing genetic truth is now regarded as a centrally important consideration.
4. In the context of assisted reproduction, the intended social parents are generally accorded legal parenthood. Freed from biological constraints, this opens up a much more flexible concept of parenthood. For a long time, English law remained faithful to the heterosexual norm that a child should have one legal father and one legal mother. However, the Human Fertilisation and Embryology Act 2008 (HFEA 2008) revolutionized this position by allowing a child, from birth, to have two legal parents of the same sex.
5. Where genetic parentage does not coincide with legal parenthood, the continuing role of the genetic progenitors must be addressed. The right of donor-conceived children to information about their genetic background has been a particularly contentious issue.
6. Surrogacy remains a 'grey' area, neither condemned nor approved by law. Although the HFEA 2008 facilitates surrogacy in a wide range of circumstances, not all arrangements are covered and considerable uncertainty remains where the surrogacy arrangement breaks down. The Law Commissions have proposed reform of this area.

9.1 INTRODUCTION

One might have thought becoming a parent was a relatively straightforward matter. However, even with the assistance of new fertility treatments, becoming a parent can be anything but straightforward and, whether or not one conceives through natural means, gaining legal recognition of one's status as a parent can prove an even more difficult and complicated process.

Who are a child's parents? If you posed this question to a group of passengers on the Clapham omnibus, you would probably elicit a wide variety of responses. One passenger might respond that it is the man and woman who are linked by blood to the child: the genetic parents. Another passenger might respond that it is the woman who gives birth to the child: the gestational mother, and perhaps her husband or partner.[1] Yet another passenger might respond that it is the people who intend to be the parents: the intended parents. Another might suggest it is those who actually love, nurture, and care for the child: the social parents. The concept of parenthood and who should be regarded as a child's parents is thus a strongly contested question. Disagreement as to the identity of a child's parents may be further intensified when the question of assisted reproduction is raised. The passengers who confidently asserted that the blood tie should form the basis for determining parenthood may feel less sure of their position when the scenario of a married couple receiving fertility treatment using donated sperm (termed 'artificial insemination by donor', or AID) is put to them. Would our passengers still consider that the sperm donor, the person with the genetic link to the child, and not the husband receiving fertility treatment with his wife, should be regarded as the father? How would they respond to the challenges raised by surrogacy? Would they consider that the man and woman who can claim a genetic link to the child (who may or may not be the intended parents)[2] should be regarded as the parents? Would they remain of that view when faced with the possibility that the genetic and gestational mothers may be different? Would they now consider that the gestational, not the genetic, mother should prevail? Alternatively, could they both be recognized as the child's mother? Does the child have to be limited to just two legal parents? And do those legal parents have to be based on the heterosexual norm of one mother and one father?

And what are the legal consequences of all this? Passengers who think that the genetic tie should determine the identity of a child's parents may not agree that any legal rights and responsibilities should flow from that status. They may, for example, baulk at the idea that a man who raped a married woman, whilst correctly described as the father of any resulting child, should have any *legal* status in relation to the child. Our passengers may again begin to waiver in their original conviction that it should be the person with the genetic tie, rather than the person who loves, nurtures, and cares for the child, who should be regarded in law as the parent. If, for example, the husband of the raped woman has accepted the child as his own and intends to raise the child, with his wife, as part of their family unit, should he be accorded the legal rights and responsibilities of parenthood? One response to this dilemma would be to separate the status of being a 'parent' from holding any legal rights and responsibilities with respect to the child. Could the law not recognize that several people may

[1] The genetic and/or gestational parents are often referred to as the 'natural' parents. Cf Baroness Hale's judgment in *Re G (Residence: Same-Sex Partner)* [2006] UKHL 43, [32]–[37] extracted at 9.2.1 where she includes social or intentional parents within this term.

[2] The couple for whom the surrogate carries the child.

play different but complementary 'parenting' roles in relation to a child, with different legal rights and responsibilities attaching to each?

Our passengers may by now be feeling somewhat bewildered. These are complex and difficult questions. And they are questions that become increasingly difficult to answer as the diversity and fluidity in modern family life intensifies and innovations in assisted reproduction continue to stretch the boundaries of possibility. The fluidity of modern family life and the relentless march of 'scientific progress' will require us to find increasingly nuanced answers to the deceivingly simple question, who are a child's parents?

The principal aim of this chapter is to examine how one acquires the status of 'being a parent' under English law, what we shall refer to as 'legal parenthood'. We begin by examining differing concepts of 'parenthood' and possible approaches to determining legal parenthood. We then move on to consider the current legal framework for identifying a child's legal parents where a child is conceived through natural procreation, before examining the challenges raised by use of assisted reproduction techniques, including surrogacy. Finally, we briefly consider adoption, a unique means of acquiring the legal status of parenthood under English law.[3]

9.2 CONCEPTS OF PARENTHOOD AND POSSIBLE APPROACHES TO DETERMINING LEGAL PARENTHOOD

9.2.1 WHAT IS A 'PARENT'?

Martin Johnson has identified four possible components to parenthood.

M. Johnson, 'A Biomedical Perspective on Parenthood', in A. Bainham, S. Day Sclater, and M. Richards (eds), *What Is a Parent? A Socio-Legal Analysis* (Oxford: Hart Publishing, 1999), 47–8

First there is a genetic component to parenthood. We now know that biologically the production of a viable human conceptus *requires* two distinctive subsets of chromosomes, one of which *must* be derived from a woman and the other from a man. The mother's egg alone also contributes a much smaller additional and essential chromosome (<1 per cent of total genetic material) in a non-nuclear structure called a mitochondrion, whilst the father's sperm contributes a non-chromosomal structure which is, however, essential for cell survival and proliferation in the embryo. Thus, genetic parents of both sexes are required and make non-equivalent contributions to their off-spring.

Secondly, there is a coital component to parenthood. Since fertilisation occurs inside the body, an act of coitus or mating is required between male and female . . .

Thirdly, there is a gestational or uterine component to parenthood, which is exclusively the province of the female. The mother provides a uterus and there is accumulating evidence that her behaviour, mental state, diet and health during pregnancy may affect enduringly the health, traits and well-being of the child that is subsequently born. The tendency to overlook this important parental contribution to the child may have over-emphasised the significance of the genetic component to parenthood.

[3] Adoption is considered in detail in chapter 13.

Finally, there is a post-natal component to parenthood. Higher primates such as humans transmit not just their genes, but also their culture from one generation to another. Post-natal parenthood is sometimes called "social parenthood", but since this component of parenthood has evolved it does have an important biological component to it.

These four aspects of parenthood—genetic, coital, gestational, and social—may be performed by various people. Leaving aside possible future developments in assisted reproduction, a child must currently have two genetic parents: one male and one female. In most cases, the child's genetic parents will have engaged in an act of coitus to achieve fertilization. However, the development of assisted reproduction techniques means that coitus is no longer an essential element of parenthood and will be absent in a significant minority of cases. In addition to two genetic parents, all children must have a gestational mother. Although the gestational mother will generally also be the genetic mother, the advent of in vitro fertilization (IVF) means that again this will not necessarily be the case. The possibility of using donated eggs (whether in the context of fertility treatment or for the purposes of surrogacy) means that genetic and gestational motherhood can now be located in two different women. Post-natal or social parenthood is the most open component of parenthood. It is often equated with intentional parenthood because it results from an act of will on the part of the parent. Social parents can be identified as those individuals who care for and nurture a child day-to-day. The crucial post-natal or social aspect of parenthood is usually performed by the genetic (and gestational) parents. Social parenthood can, however, be divorced from both genetic and gestational parenthood. Typical situations where this will occur include assisted reproduction using AID, surrogacy, adoption, and cohabitation between a genetic and non-genetic parent, such as step-parents. Once parenthood is freed from genetics, it opens up endless possibilities. Social parenthood can be performed by an infinite number of people, at different times in the child's life, and with no limitation as to gender or status. Thus a child's social parents may range from the child's genetic and gestational mother and her husband to a gay couple who have neither a genetic nor gestational link to the child.

Baroness Hale tried to unpack the complexity and potential significance of these various components of parenthood in *Re G (Children) (Residence: Same-Sex Partner)*,[4] though it is important to note that she is not talking about *legal* parenthood in this passage.

Re G (Children) (Residence: Same-Sex Partner) [2006] UKHL 43

BARONESS HALE:

33. There are at least three ways in which a person may be or become a natural parent of a child, each of which may be a very significant factor in the child's welfare, depending upon the circumstances of the particular case. The first is genetic parenthood: the provision of the gametes which produce the child. This can be of deep significance on many levels. For the parent, perhaps particularly for a father, the knowledge that this is "his" child can bring a very special sense of love for and commitment to that child which will be of great benefit

[4] For the facts and further extracts from *Re G*, see 11.6.5.

to the child . . . For the child, he reaps the benefit not only of that love and commitment, but also of knowing his own origins and lineage, which is an important component in finding an individual sense of self as one grows up. The knowledge of that genetic link may also be an important (although certainly not an essential) component in the love and commitment felt by the wider family, perhaps especially grandparents, from which the child has so much to gain.

34. The second is gestational parenthood: the conceiving and bearing of the child. The mother who bears the child is legally the child's mother, whereas the mother who provided the egg is not . . . While this may be partly for reasons of certainty and convenience, it also recognises a deeper truth: that the process of carrying a child and giving him birth (which may well be followed by breast-feeding for some months) brings with it, in the vast majority of cases, a very special relationship between mother and child, a relationship which is different from any other.

35. The third is social and psychological parenthood: the relationship which develops through the child demanding and the parent providing for the child's needs, initially at the most basic level of feeding, nurturing, comforting and loving, and later at the more sophisticated level of guiding, socialising, educating and protecting . . .

36. Of course, in the great majority of cases, the natural mother combines all three. She is the genetic, gestational and psychological parent. Her contribution to the welfare of the child is unique. The natural father combines genetic and psychological parenthood. His contribution is also unique . . .

37. But there are also parents who are neither genetic nor gestational, but who have become the psychological parents of the child and thus have an important contribution to make to their welfare. Adoptive parents are the most obvious example, but there are many others.

Whilst some commentators welcomed Baroness Hale's apparent inclusion of psychological/social parenthood within her understanding of 'natural' parenthood, her suggestion that genetic parenthood, and genetic/gestational motherhood in particular, should be regarded as of unique importance proved considerably more contentious.[5] Indeed, Lady Hale herself has acknowledged that it is 'a fair criticism of my opinion that it appeared to attach too much weight to the carrying mother's role'.[6]

9.2.2 THE IMPORTANCE OF LEGAL PARENTHOOD

Legal parenthood confers an important legal status on both parent and child. Andrew Bainham argues that it represents the most fundamental relationship between parent and child.[7] Unlike parental responsibility (the legal authority to make decisions with respect to a child's upbringing),[8] which can be conferred on a succession of different social carers during the child's minority, legal parenthood can be held by only two individuals at any one time—usually, but no longer necessarily, the child's 'mother' and the child's 'father'. Legal parenthood is also permanent, non-alienable, and has legal consequences for an individual throughout life, not just during childhood.[9] As Bainham argues, legal parenthood makes

[5] For an excellent critique, see Diduck (2007), and for an alternative way in which the case could have been decided, Diduck (2010); but cf Bainham (2007b). For further discussion, see 11.6.5.

[6] Hale (2014), 30. [7] Bainham (1999), 32–3. [8] See chapter 10.

[9] Legal parenthood can only be terminated by adoption or the making of a parental order under s 54/54A of the HFEA 2008.

the child a member of a family. The legal consequences that attach to legal parenthood therefore represent a core body of rights and responsibilities that flow from the fact that X is Y's child and belongs to Y's family. Although for many parents, particularly those deprived of parental responsibility, the authority to make decisions about a child's upbringing may seem more important and meaningful, the rights and responsibilities attaching to legal parenthood are also significant. For example:

- a child's core familial relationships for the purposes of determining restrictions on marriage and criminal prohibitions relating to incest are determined in accordance with the child's legal parenthood,[10] as are broader ideas of kinship (who are your grandparents, aunts and uncles, cousins, and so on);
- entitlements on intestacy are determined by reference to legal parenthood, and a child's legal parents are the ones who have the default right (unless overridden by court order) to make arrangements for disposing of a child's body in the event of the child's death;[11]
- citizenship rights under the British Nationality Act 1981 flow from legal parenthood;
- the duty to maintain a child financially rests with the legal parents.[12]

There are also aspects of parental responsibility (PR) that, as we will see in chapter 10, apply only where the holder of PR is *also* the child's legal parent.[13]

9.2.3 POLICY ARGUMENTS ABOUT LEGAL PARENTHOOD

In determining legal parenthood, the law has to make a choice, as a matter of policy, which aspects of parenthood should be given priority: a case can be made for focusing on genetic, gestational, intentional, or social aspects.[14] The law has not always taken a consistent approach, and there might be reasons for focusing on different elements for different reasons.

Historically, legal parenthood under English law was strictly gendered, the law insisting on the heterosexual norm that every child at birth should have precisely two legal parents: one legal mother and one legal father.[15] Until relatively recently, the law also gave little focus to genetic ties, with the primary tool being the legal relationship of the parents: 'It was the sociological institution of marriage and *not* the biological tie that made men and women into parents.'[16] More recently, though, as we will see,[17] there is—in the context of natural reproduction, away from the special rules of the HFEA 2008—a strong focus on genetics as the basis of legal parenthood.

However, there is nothing, in principle, that requires legal parenthood to be limited to two people; nothing, in principle, that requires a child's parents to be exclusively one man and

[10] See Marriage Act 1949, Sch 1 and Sexual Offences Act 2003, ss 64–5.

[11] Non-contentious Probate Rules 1987, r 22. This is a function of legal parenthood and *not* of parental responsibility, as is apparent from *Re E (A Child: Burial Arrangements)* [2019] EWHC 3639, where the father had never had parental responsibility.

[12] Child Support Act 1991, s 1(1); Children Act 1989 (CA 1989), Sch 1. See chapter 5.

[13] See 10.2.2.

[14] As the coital aspect of parenthood is no longer present in all cases, it is excluded as an appropriate basis for determining legal parenthood.

[15] In some circumstances, adoption, surrogacy, and some provisions of the HFEA 2008 allow a child to have only one legal parent.

[16] Willekens (2022), 568, who sets out the historical development of the law in this regard.

[17] See 9.3.

one woman; and nothing, in principle, that requires genetics to be the determiner of which people are a child's legal parents. Strong arguments can be made both in support of, and against, these positions.

However, Day Sclater, Bainham, and Richards argue that in the wake of scientific advances in DNA testing, the genetic model of parenthood has become even more firmly entrenched.[18]

S. Day Sclater, A. Bainham, and M. Richards, 'Introduction', in A. Bainham, S. Day Sclater, and M. Richards (eds), *What Is a Parent? A Socio-Legal Analysis* (Oxford: Hart Publishing, 1999), 15

Developments in the technologies and procedures for DNA testing, used to establish paternity, have undoubtedly contributed to the new constructions of fathers in biological rather than social terms. As Neale and Smart argue, the newly emerging model of family life . . . is one which venerates biological kin ties and has entailed a refashioning of the legal status of biological parenthood; parenthood has begun to supersede marriage as the bedrock of "the family" and as the central mechanism for the legal regulation of domestic life. If marriage is no longer for life, then (biological) parenthood is. Biology now provides the main basis upon which claims to parental status rest. The increasing availability of genetic testing for a range of inherited conditions, as well as for paternity, and the increasing visibility of the microstructures which make up our bodies, have given added impetus to the salience of "biology" and "genetics" in relation to the question of "what is a parent?"

Whilst arguing that the law must afford appropriate recognition to the importance of social parenthood by conferring on social parents the legal rights and duties required to raise a child (parental responsibility), Bainham supports the approach whereby legal parenthood is based exclusively on the genetic tie. His reasons focus on the unique significance of genetic parentage.

A. Bainham, 'Parentage, Parenthood and Parental Responsibility', in A. Bainham, S. Day Sclater, and M. Richards (eds), *What Is a Parent? A Socio-Legal Analysis* (Oxford: Hart Publishing, 1999), 27

In allocating parental responsibility to more and more social parents, is it necessary or desirable to go the extra mile and confer on them legal parenthood? It will be my strong contention that this is neither necessary nor desirable and that legal parenthood, with some exceptions, ought to be confined to genetic parents. This is because those legal effects, which are peculiar to parenthood, are fundamental to the genetic link . . .

What are these fundamental effects of legal parenthood which do not pass with parental responsibility? The first is arguably the most important and is also the most frequently neglected. This is that legal parenthood, but not parental responsibility, makes the child a

[18] Other commentators have also noted the increasing trend towards the 'geneticization' of parenthood (particularly fatherhood), albeit they are more critical of this approach. See especially Sheldon (2009).

member of a family, generating for that child a legal relationship with wider kin going well beyond the parental relationship . . . [T]he social or psychological value of belonging to a particular family is a nebulous subject for lawyers and is more the terrain of the anthropologist or psychologist. What the lawyer *can* point out is that the loss of the legal status of parent will entail the loss, at least in law, of these wider relationships . . .

Other effects which arise specifically from legal parenthood are financial liability for child support, the right to object or consent to adoption (though this also depends on possessing parental responsibility), and the right to object to a change of the child's surname and to removal of the child from the jurisdiction, the right to appoint a guardian (although . . . the parent must possess parental responsibility), a presumption of contact where a child is in care and an automatic right to go to court . . .

Are these distinctive legal effects just anomalies, historical accidents of the piecemeal development of the law? . . . It is my contention that on the contrary, they continue to serve a vital purpose in that they give expression to the continuing importance of the genetic link. What they all have in common is that they relate to fundamentals which go beyond the everyday decisions involved in upbringing . . . If we are to move in the direction of giving effect to a child's right to knowledge of genetic origins we are going to need some legal means of preserving the genetic connection and it is the concept of legal parenthood which currently achieves this . . .

Bainham suggests that three key principles should guide the law's approach to determining legal parenthood: (i) a commitment to truth; (ii) individual autonomy; and (iii) priority for the rights and interests of those primarily affected—the individuals who result from reproduction.[19] In his view, conferring legal parenthood on the basis of biological truth, rather than the 'fiction' of social parenthood, best protects these core values.[20]

Others are more cautious about a genetic approach. Willekens argues that a child's birth mother 'is in a unique position, incomparable to all others, before birth', and that this must give her a preferential position for the allocation of parenthood at birth—but his reason for taking this view is not about genetics, but rather about gestation and the predisposition towards post-birth care of the child.[21] However, he continues:

H. Willekens, 'What (If Anything) Can Justify the Use of Biological Criteria for Allocating Parental Rights and Obligations?', in J. Scherpe and S. Gilmore (eds), *Family Matters: Essays in Honour of John Eekelaar* (Cambridge: Intersentia, 2022), 579–80

As to the parental rights and obligations of all others, the only persuasive argument we have encountered for taking the genetic tie as the foundation of parental rights is that genetic kinship predisposes persons to invest in their offspring. The strength of this argument is mitigated by the observation that this predisposition is actualised only in the presence of a

[19] Bainham (2008a), 323–4.

[20] Ibid. It is not clear from Bainham's argument why genetic truth can only be adequately protected through the attribution of legal parenthood to the genetic parents.

[21] Willekens (2022), 579 (and the reasoning at 574–5). For further discussion about legal mothers, see Jackson (2022).

social relationship between the child and the genitor. There is some kind of argument here for considering genetic ties as relevant to the formulation of rules pertaining to the allocation of parental rights, but that is all there is. . . . The only thing we can safely conclude from the arguments discussed . . . is that we ought to be suspicious of too-easy claims for the priority of genetic ties.

Barton and Douglas are also sceptical about a focus solely on genetics, arguing that there has been a perceptible swing in the law towards according precedence to intentional or social parenthood, particularly in the wake of the statutory regime introduced by the HFEA 1990 (now further entrenched by the HFEA 2008) for determining legal parenthood in the context of assisted reproduction.[22]

A model of legal parenthood based on the *intention* to parent or the 'function' or 'doing' of parenting has always had the potential to revolutionize English law's historical approach to determining a child's legal parents—and also, at least potentially, to allow a uniform approach to all children, whether born following natural reproduction, donor gametes, or surrogacy.[23] Freed from the biological imperative, legal parenthood need not be restricted to two people of different sexes, or indeed to only two people.[24] The HFEA 1990 and HFEA 2008 have seen this revolutionary potential at least partially realized (but also create a system whereby the rules for allocation of parental status are radically different as between children who are born under the HFEA's rules and those who are not).

The first inroad into the gendered heterosexual model of legal parenthood was made by the Adoption and Children Act 2002 (ACA 2002) which, for the first time, enabled a same-sex couple to adopt. Thus, since 2002, a child need not have precisely one legal mother and one legal father. The HFEA 2008 took this considerably further by permitting the deliberate creation of a child who will be born into a family consisting of two parents of the same sex. A child with two legal mothers[25] but no legal father is thus possible, as is a child with no legal mother but two legal fathers[26] following a surrogacy arrangement. The legitimacy of same-sex parenting has been accepted in law. This considerable liberalization of the law on parenthood in the context of assisted reproduction clearly embraces intentional (rather than genetic) parenthood and accepts the equal worth of a diverse range of family relationships. Parenthood has moved a step closer to being a gender-neutral activity.

So do these radical changes fundamentally undermine the genetic or biological basis of legal parenthood in English law? As we examine the current legal framework for determining legal parenthood, it will become apparent that there is no clear answer to this question, English law drawing upon both the genetic and social models of parenthood depending on the particular social need. Those searching for a coherent policy underlying the law's approach will be disappointed. Indeed, Jackson describes the law as 'spectacularly confused and confusing'.[27] The choice as to which model should predominate in any particular context has been driven by pragmatic considerations as much as by matters of policy and principle.[28]

[22] Barton and Douglas (1995), 51. [23] Kessler (2019).

[24] Ontario in Canada introduced a law in 2016 allowing up to four legal parents when specified criteria are met; see Leckey (2019).

[25] Strictly, the child will have one 'mother' and a second female 'parent'.

[26] Strictly, two male 'parents'. [27] Jackson (2006), 60.

[28] For an argument that 'intention' and 'care' should be the determining factors in allocating legal parental status, with a separate category of 'progenitor' to record genetic origins, see Kessler (2019).

In the context of natural procreation, and until the recent advances in DNA testing, difficulties in establishing genetic parentage with any certainty influenced legal policy, as did social and legal considerations concerning illegitimate children. However, as the accuracy of genetic testing has improved, and the legal category of illegitimacy has been purged from English law, genetic parentage has become increasingly important in the determination of legal parenthood for children conceived through natural reproduction. In stark contrast, in the context of assisted reproduction different pragmatic considerations, such as the desire to avoid the seemingly nonsensical result of a sperm donor acquiring legal responsibility for financially maintaining his genetic offspring, have driven legal policy, with the result that social or intentional parenthood has become the central determining principle under the HFEA.

9.3 DETERMINING PARENTHOOD IN THE CONTEXT OF NATURAL REPRODUCTION

9.3.1 ESTABLISHING MATERNITY

In the context of *natural reproduction*, English law's approach to ascribing the legal mother of a child is straightforward. As Lord Simon explained in the *Ampthill Peerage* case, '[m]otherhood, although a legal relationship, is based on a fact, being proved demonstrably by parturition'.[29] The woman who gives birth to the child is the child's legal mother. In the context of *natural reproduction*, the woman who gives birth to the child is also, inevitably, the child's genetic mother as well.[30]

However, a significant challenge to this 'obvious' approach arose in the case of *R (McConnell) v The Registrar General for England and Wales.* Mr McConnell had been assigned female at birth, but in around 2009 had transitioned to live as a man. He undertook hormone therapy and a double mastectomy. In 2016, he suspended hormone therapy and began fertility treatment. In 2017, Mr McConnell received a gender recognition certificate. A few days later, he underwent further fertility treatment, with donor sperm being placed inside his uterus, leading to a pregnancy. His son, YY, was born in 2018. The Registry Office informed Mr McConnell that he would have to be registered as YY's mother, though he could do so with his (male) name. Mr McConnell applied for judicial review, on the basis that he wished to be registered as YY's father or, failing that, as his parent. His claim was rejected by the High Court,[31] and by the Court of Appeal,[32] both courts finding that there was no breach of the applicant's human rights by the Registrar General's decision that he had to be registered at the child's legal mother. Sir Andrew McFarlane P's judgment in the High Court engaged more explicitly with the issue of what makes 'a mother' as a matter of law.

[29] [1977] AC 547, 577. In *Re G (Declaration of Parentage: Removal of Person Identified as Mother from Birth Certificate) (Nos 1 and 2)* [2018] EWHC 3379 and [2018] EWHC 3361, a heterosexual couple, M and F, entered an informal surrogacy arrangement using an egg from an anonymous donor. The surrogate gave birth at hospital having presented herself under M's name, and M was subsequently registered as the mother on the child's birth certificate. The court held that M was not the child's legal mother, despite the hospital records and birth certificate naming her as such. For comment, see Brown (2019b).

[30] See further Willekens (2022).

[31] *R (TT) v Registrar General for England and Wales* [2019] EWHC 2384.

[32] *R (McConnell) v The Registrar General for England and Wales* [2020] EWCA Civ 559. Permission to appeal to the Supreme Court was refused.

R (TT) v Registrar General for England and Wales [2019] EWHC 2384

SIR ANDREW McFARLANE P:

279. The principal conclusion . . . can be shortly stated. It is that there is a material difference between a person's gender and their status as a parent. Being a 'mother', whilst hitherto always associated with being female, is the status afforded to a person who undergoes the physical and biological process of carrying a pregnancy and giving birth. It is now medically and legally possible for an individual, whose gender is recognised in law as male, to become pregnant and give birth to their child. Whilst that person's gender is 'male', their parental status, which derives from their biological role in giving birth, is that of 'mother'.

280. [My conclusions] can now be firmly stated as:

a) At common law a person whose egg is inseminated in their womb and who then becomes pregnant and gives birth to a child is that child's 'mother';

b) The status of being a 'mother' arises from the role that a person has undertaken in the biological process of conception, pregnancy and birth;

c) Being a 'mother' or a 'father' with respect to the conception, pregnancy and birth of a child is not necessarily gender specific, although until recent decades it invariably was so. It is now possible, and recognised by the law, for a 'mother' to have an acquired gender of male, and for a 'father' to have an acquired gender of female;

d) GRA [Gender Recognition Act] 2004, s 12 is both retrospective and prospective. The status of a person as the father or mother of a child is not affected by the acquisition of gender under the Act, even where the relevant birth has taken place after the issue of a [gender recognition] certificate.

While the Court of Appeal reached the same conclusion, the President's judgment at first instance 'evinces a more sensitive, contextual approach' and showed a 'willingness to re-evaluate fundamental notions of family law' that was not seen on appeal, where the approach was more technical.[33]

McConnell tells us important things about what English law thinks it means by the term 'mother', but also raises some wider considerations, as Emily Jackson explains.[34]

E. Jackson, 'When Is a Mother Not a Mother?', in J. Scherpe and S. Gilmore (eds), *Family Matters: Essays in Honour of John Eekelaar* (Cambridge: Intersentia, 2022), 589, 592–3

Perhaps the bigger and more interesting question raised by the *McConnell* case is whether the law needs to use the terms 'mother' and 'father' at all. Would it be sufficient for the law to instead identify a child's 'parents'? In order to answer this question, we need to consider

[33] Bremner (2020), 525. See also Fenton-Glynn (2020); Brown (2021a).

[34] See also Margaria (2020) on wider considerations of trans men giving birth and what this may say about the idea of 'fatherhood'.

when and why the law currently distinguishes between mothers and fathers. Are these gendered terms for parents capturing an important legal difference that would be lost if the law simply identified a child's parents instead?

. . .

The law uses the terms 'mother' and 'father', not in order to ascribe differential parental roles to men and women, but rather, in order to distinguish between the parent who gave birth (the mother) and the parent who did not give birth (the father or second parent). It would, however, be possible to distinguish between [these] . . . without requiring the use of gendered terms . . . It is worth reminding ourselves, as Claire Fenton-Glynn (2020) explains, that Freddy McConnell's objection was not to the recording on [his child's] birth certificate of his role in the birth, 'but to the use of a highly (socially) gendered term to do so'.

. . . From the point of view of families themselves the legal definition of motherhood [given by the courts in *McConnell*], by insisting that motherhood is not female parenthood, and that a child's social father is his legal mother, 'flies in the face of their actual family lives'. Or, as Claire Fenton-Glynn (2020) puts it:

> the attribution of 'motherhood' to a legal male creates a discord between law and identity, and an inconsistency between the legal meaning of the term 'mother', and its common understanding.

Some may argue that this does not matter, and that it is more important for the law to reaffirm that only mothers give birth. But if it is undesirable for the legal meaning of 'mother' to be substantially different from its social meaning, might there be advantages to degendering legal parenthood? It could be, for example, that the legal institution of marriage has already been degendered: it used to be regarded, in law, as the union of one man and one woman, but as Timothy Murphy puts it, 'the sex of the people coming forward to marry is now a *matter of indifference* to the state'. Might the logical next step be to degender legal parenthood as well?

ONLINE RESOURCES

We discuss *McConnell* further in the online resources, available at **www.oup.com/he/familytcm5e.**

9.3.2 ESTABLISHING PATERNITY

Determining a child's father is potentially more complicated. Establishing the genetic link between father and child has, in the past, proved difficult. Without the incontrovertible proof of parturition and, in the absence of accurate genetic testing, the law has had to rely on certain presumptions in order to establish paternity. The current law is more straightforward, but differences remain between fathers who are in a formalized relationship with the mother,[35] and those who are not.

[35] We use this phrase to include those who are married to or in a civil partnership with the mother; for these purposes, there is no difference between the two.

9.3.2.a Fathers in a formalized relationship with the mother: the presumption of legitimacy

In the case of children born to parents who are in a formalized relationship with each other,[36] the common law *presumes* that the mother's husband or civil partner is the child's genetic father and thus the legal parent. This presumption applies if the man was in a formalized relationship with the mother either at the date of conception or at the date of birth.[37]

Where the parents of a child are in a formalized relationship, both parents are obliged to register the child within 42 days of the birth.[38] Either the child's mother or her spouse can attend at the registrar's office and enter the man's name as the child's father without producing any further evidence of his paternity. As Bainham points out, despite the operation of the *pater est* presumption, the birth register is supposed to reflect biological truth—but it is assumed the mother's spouse is indeed the biological father,[39] and it is a criminal offence to register someone as the child's father if it is known that he is not in fact the biological father.[40] However, it is estimated that in 2–10 per cent of cases the mother's husband is wrongly named as the child's genetic father on the birth certificate.[41]

The common law presumption that the mother's husband is the father has, in the past, been difficult to displace. Until the law was amended by the Family Law Reform Act 1969, s 26, the presumption could only be rebutted by evidence establishing beyond reasonable doubt that the husband could not be the father.[42] This restrictive approach was explained by the fact that the child's legitimate status depended on the presumption that the mother's husband was the legal father. Given the significance of legitimacy, the courts were extremely reluctant to 'bastardize' a child without the strongest possible proof.[43]

However, following scientific, social, and legal changes, the courts' reluctance to disturb the common law presumption has changed. Whereas previously, legal fatherhood really turned not genetics but on the status of his relationship with the mother,[44] now the law seems firmly committed to upholding the importance of biological truth. Consequently, the *presumption* is relevant only if there is no challenge to the paternity of the mother's spouse; if his paternity is contested, the court will usually order testing to determine the issue conclusively,[45] and the presumption will have no significance.

9.3.2.b Unmarried fathers and prima facie evidence based on registration of the birth

Just over half of children are born to unmarried[46] parents.[47] As with fathers who are in a formalized relationship with the child's mother, the determination of paternity for unmarried

[36] Legitimacy Act 1976, s A1(2) (introduced by the Civil Partnership (Opposite-Sex Couples) Regulations 2019) extends the presumption of legitimacy to heterosexual civil partners.

[37] Family Law Reform Act 1987, s 1(4). Bainham (2008b) argues that if the mother is married to one man at the date of conception and a different man at the date of birth, she will be able to register her second husband as the father unless challenged by the first. Lowe et al (2021) argue that the wife should be afforded the presumption of fidelity during marriage and thus her husband at the date of conception should be deemed the legal father.

[38] Births and Death Registration Act 1953, s 2. [39] Bainham (2008b), 452–3.

[40] Perjury Act 1911, s 4. [41] Bainham (2008b), fn 108.

[42] Cretney (2003a), 534. [43] Ibid, 533.

[44] Barton and Douglas (1995), 53; Bainham (2008b), 451; Willekens (2022).

[45] See 9.3.3. Note that the court can refuse to order testing, in which case the presumption will continue, as in *MS v RS and BT (Paternity Testing)* [2020] EWFC 30, extracted at 9.3.3.b.

[46] We use this term to mean neither married nor in a civil partnership.

[47] ONS (2022c), Table 1. 2021 was the first year when more than half of children were born to parents who were not in a formalized relationship, but the number has been close to half for several years.

parents turns on the simple question: who is the genetic father of the child? The man who is the genetic father is, as a matter of fact, the child's legal father, and most of the time that issue is not contested and creates no difficulty. If there is a dispute, however, the *presumption* that applies to parents in a formalized relationship does not apply.

For these fathers, the starting point is registration on the child's birth certificate, which is regarded as good prima facie evidence that the man named is the child's father,[48] because it is a criminal offence 'wilfully' to enter incorrect information on a child's birth certificate.[49] In 2020, 89 per cent of births outside marriage were registered jointly by both parents, and in 76 per cent of those cases the parents were registered as resident at the same address.[50] While there are cases where the wrong man is named as the father (either intentionally or otherwise),[51] birth registration is an extremely important tool in helping to evidence the child's paternity in the majority of cases.

There remains, however, a small minority of cases (5.2 per cent of all births in 2020) in which the birth of a child is registered solely by the child's mother.[52] In these cases, there is not even prima facie evidence as to the child's paternity.

As a matter of law, only the child's mother, where she is unmarried, has a duty to register the child.[53] Registration of the child's father requires the active agreement of both parents or the production of an appropriate court order.[54] This means that where the child's mother does not want the child's father registered on the birth certificate she can simply withhold her consent to joint registration.

The law's approach to birth registration—and in particular the questions of whether the mother should be able to *veto* the father's registration, or conversely whether she should be *required* to register him[55]—brings into sharp relief some of the most contentious issues in the law relating to parents and children. At the heart of the strongly opposing views are fundamentally competing visions as to the importance of genetic, as opposed to functional or social, parenthood. As mothers typically fulfil the requirements of both genetic and social parenthood, this debate inevitably focuses on the position of genetic fathers. This raises key questions for family lawyers: should the fact of genetic fatherhood itself be sufficient to confer legal rights and responsibilities on the father? Does a children's rights perspective demand legal recognition of the genetic father? Does equality demand that genetic fathers are accorded exactly the same legal rights as genetic (and social) mothers regardless of whether the father intends to meet the responsibilities of social fatherhood—or does 'real equality' demand something more nuanced? Is active and involved fathering by the biological father

[48] In the absence of an entry in favour of the putative father on the birth register, the making of a parental responsibility order may also constitute good prima facie evidence as to the child's paternity. It was held in *R v Secretary of State for Social Security, ex parte W* [1999] 2 FLR 604 that, because the court can only make a parental responsibility order under s 4 of the CA 1989 in favour of the child's father, it must be implicit in making the order that the man is 'found or adjudged' to be the child's father. The same reasoning might apply to the existence of a parental responsibility agreement between the child's parents, which has to be signed on oath before a court official.

[49] Perjury Act 1911, s 4. [50] ONS (2022d), Table 1.

[51] It is important to stress that if the birth certificate is wrong, it will have no effect on the man's legal status: he does not *become* the father by being named on the birth certificate. The birth certificate acts only as *evidence*, and can be rebutted by stronger evidence, e.g. from a DNA test.

[52] Ibid (authors' calculations).

[53] Births and Deaths Registration Act 1953, s 10. [54] Ibid.

[55] In order to try to reduce the number of sole registrations, part of the Welfare Reform Act 2009 aimed to make joint registration in effect compulsory. However, the relevant provisions have never been implemented.

of such central importance to securing better outcomes for children that it should be promoted and supported by the law even if the welfare of the mother, and possibly the immediate welfare of the child, will be compromised? We will meet these questions repeatedly throughout the following chapters.

9.3.3 COURT PROCEEDINGS TO DETERMINE THE PARENTAGE OF A CHILD

Where the parentage of a child is disputed,[56] s 55A of the Family Law Act 1986 (FLA 1986) provides that the child, the child's mother, the putative father, the Child Maintenance and Enforcement Commission, or any other sufficiently interested person can make a free-standing application to the court for parentage to be determined.[57] A declaration made pursuant to s 55A is binding on all persons and for all purposes, including the Child Support Act 1991.[58]

Slightly curiously, s 55A can be used to declare a person's *factual* parental status even in circumstances where that person is not the child's *legal* parent. In *H v R (No 1)*,[59] MacDonald J held that the court had the power to make a declaration of parentage in relation to a birth parent whose child has been made the subject of an adoption order, despite the fact that the child is, as a result of the adoption order, 'to be treated in law as if born as the child of the adopters'.[60] The father in that case had come to know of his child's existence some months after birth, when care proceedings were already well underway. Those proceedings concluded with the child being adopted, and the father sought a declaration of parentage. MacDonald J considered the purposes of the declaration under s 55A:

H v R (No 1) [2020] EWFC 74

MacDONALD J:

45. Section 55A(1) of the Family Law Act 1986 deals with the identity of a child's parent as a matter of *fact*. The purpose of Part III of the Family Law 1986 is to make provision for declarations regarding status, dealing as it does with marital status (s 55), parentage (s 55A), legitimacy and legitimation (s 56) and adoptive status under a foreign adoption order (s 57). Within this context, s 58(1) of the 1986 Act makes clear that on an application under Part III of the Act for a declaration of status, the court is concerned with proof of matters of fact.

[56] In practice, s 55A is almost always about determining a child's paternity, but the wording makes clear that it applies to either parent, and there are exceptional cases where maternity may be in doubt: see, e.g., *Re G (Declaration of Parentage: Removal of Person Identified as Mother from Birth Certificate) (Nos 1 and 2)* [2018] EWHC 3379 and [2018] EWHC 3361. For comment, see Brown (2019b).

[57] A child may also apply under FLA 1986, s 56 for a declaration as to their legitimacy, though legitimacy rarely has any relevance following the Family Law Reform Act 1987.

[58] FLA 1986, s 58(2). Generally, cases under s 55A concern declarations that flow from a parent's *genetic* connection with a child, and the factual declaration is a legal affirmation that the two individuals are factually, and therefore legally, related. However, these are not necessary elements of a s 55A declaration. In *Osborne v Arnold* [2022] EWHC 1983, s 55A was used to declare that a person is a parent when they have acquired that status as a result of the provisions of the HFEA 2008, not as a result of genetics. On parenthood under the HFEA, see 9.4.3.

[59] [2020] EWFC 74. [60] ACA 2002, s 67(1).

A declaration as to status made under Part III of the Family Law Act 1986 is intended to be an authoritative statement of the fact so declared. Within this context, the term 'parent' in s 55A(1) of the Family Law Act 1986 refers to someone who is a parent of the child as a matter of *fact*.

46. By contrast, s 67 of the Adoption and Children Act 2002 deals with the identity of a child's parent or parents as a matter of *law*. Pursuant to ss 67(1), 67(2) and 67(3) of the Adoption and Children Act 2002, once a person is made the subject of an adoption order, as a matter of *law* that person ceases to be the child of his or her birth parents and is to be treated in law as not being the child of any person other than the adoptive parents, the child being treated in law as if born as the child of the adopters and the legitimate child of the adopters. Section 67 has effect from the date of the adoption, but is retrospective in its effect on the *legal* status of the child and the adoptive parents. . . .

47. Within this context, s 67 of the Adoption and Children Act 2002 concerns the question of who are the parents of the child as a matter of law and not wider questions of fact such as the child's biological parentage. This is made clear in the explanatory notes attached to the Adoption and Children Act 2002 that deal with the operation of s 67 of the Act:

> 193. The provisions in this section are intended only to clarify how an adopted child should be treated in law. They do not touch on the biological or emotional ties of an adopted child, nor are they intended to.

. . .

50. . . . I am satisfied that it is possible to read the words "any person" in s 55A(1) of the Family Law Act 1986 as encompassing a birth parent in the position of Mr H whose child has been made the subject of an adoption order pursuant to s 46 of the Adoption and Children Act 2002 without the risk of conflicting decisions being arrived at due to the terms of s 67 of the 2002 Act. Within the context of these two statutory frameworks, it remains possible for a birth parent to establish the truth of the proposition contended for, namely that he or she is as a matter of *fact* the parent of the adopted child, without that factual determination coming into conflict with the status in *law* of the child and the adoptive parents under s 67 of the Adoption and Children Act 2002. Within this context, a declaration as to status under s 55A(1) of the 1986 Act does not conflict with the question of legal status established by the operation of s 67(1) of the 2002 Act.

However, despite reaching the conclusion that the court *could* make a declaration of parentage in such a case, on consideration of the particular circumstances, MacDonald J refused to make the declaration sought.[61]

The principles identified by MacDonald J were later applied in the joined cases of *Re Ms L; Re Ms M (Declaration of Parentage)*.[62] There, both cases concerned applicants who had been adopted at birth in the 1960s, and who had made contact with their birth families many years later. In both cases, the original birth certificates did not record their fathers' names, but the applicants had been able to trace their identities. Cobb J recorded the purpose of the applications was 'to correct the historical record on their original birth certificates, so as to add to that document the name and identity of their *birth* father and thus formally complete their *birth* history';[63] there was no suggestion of altering the adoption orders. Cobb J, in granting the declarations, recorded that the declarations sought would 'represent both an acknowledgment of their true identity, and a degree of stability in that identity'.[64]

[61] *H v R (No 2)* [2021] EWHC 1943. [62] [2022] EWFC 38. [63] Ibid, [46]. [64] Ibid, [47].

9.3.3.a Rebutting the presumptions and the advent of DNA testing

If a child has been born to unmarried parents and the birth register is silent as to paternity, the applicant will simply have to prove their case on the balance of probabilities.[65] Where the presumption applies (for fathers who are in a formalized relationship) or where the birth certificate provides good prima facie evidence of parentage, the person seeking to challenge that position must adduce sufficient evidence on the usual civil standard of proof.

Family Law Reform Act 1969, s 26

Any presumption of law as to the legitimacy or illegitimacy of any person may in any civil proceedings be rebutted by evidence which shows that it is more probable than not that that person is illegitimate or legitimate, as the case may be, and it shall not be necessary to prove that fact beyond reasonable doubt in order to rebut the presumption.

The effect of this provision has been explained by Lord Reid.

S v McC and M; W v W **[1972] AC 24 (HL), 41**

LORD REID:

That means that the presumption of legitimacy now merely determines the onus of proof. Once evidence has been led it must be weighed without using the presumption as a makeweight in the scale for legitimacy. So even weak evidence against legitimacy must prevail if there is not other evidence to counterbalance it. The presumption will only come in at that stage in the very rare case of the evidence being so evenly balanced that the court is unable to reach a decision on it. I cannot recollect ever having seen or heard of a case of any kind where the court could not reach a decision on the evidence before it.

Presumptions about a child's paternity and the standard of proof required to rebut them remain technically relevant to determining disputes over parentage. However, the advent of widely accessible, accurate DNA testing means that paternity can now be established with virtual certainty. Where the court makes a direction for DNA tests to be taken, legal niceties about the onus and standard of proof required to rebut a presumption are therefore of little, if any, continuing significance: the DNA tests will be determinative and if a person refuses to be tested then adverse inferences may be drawn against them. Because of this, the continuing relevance of the presumption of legitimacy has been explicitly questioned by Thorpe LJ, who considered that 'the paternity of any child is to be established by science and not by legal presumption or inference'.[66]

[65] FLA 1986, s 58(1).

[66] *Re H and A (Children) (Paternity: Blood Test)* [2002] EWCA Civ 383.

The key question in present-day paternity disputes is thus whether the court should make the direction for tests so that the truth about a child's genetic parentage can be established with the certainty science now offers.

9.3.3.b Directing tests under the FLRA 1969, s 20

The relevant statutory provisions governing the use of scientific tests in disputes over parentage are found in ss 20–25 of the Family Law Reform Act 1969 (FLRA 1969).

Family Law Reform Act 1969, s 20

(1) In any civil proceedings in which the parentage of any person falls to be determined, the court may, either of its own motion or on an application by any party to the proceedings, give a direction—

(a) for the use of scientific tests to ascertain whether such tests show that a party to the proceedings is or is not the father or mother of that person; and

(b) for the taking, within a period specified in the direction, of bodily samples from all or any of the following, namely, that person, any party who is alleged to be the father or mother of that person and any other party to the proceedings;

and the court may at any time revoke or vary a direction previously given by it under this subsection.

Section 20 confers discretion on the court as to whether a direction for tests should be made. Several factors could influence the court's decision.

The rights of the child

First, it could be argued that children have a fundamental right to know the truth about their genetic origins.

United Nations Convention on the Rights of the Child, 1989

7. The child shall be registered immediately after birth and shall have the right from birth to a name, the right to acquire a nationality and, as far as possible, the right to know and be cared for by his or her parents . . .
8. State Parties undertake to respect the right of the child to preserve his or her identity, including nationality, name and family relations as recognised by law without unlawful interference.

Although the word 'parent' in Article 7 is open to differing interpretations, Bainham argues that it should be taken to refer to genetic, as opposed to social, parentage.

A. Bainham, 'Parentage, Parenthood and Parental Responsibility', in A. Bainham, S. Day Sclater, and M. Richards (eds), *What Is a Parent? A Socio-Legal Analysis* (Oxford: Hart Publishing, 1999), 37–8

First, the history of Articles 7 and 8 reveals that the concern of the international community was with the rights of children from the moment of birth and in relation to their birth parents. It was precisely the threat of removal of the child from the birth parents by others which was the *raison d'etre* of Article 8. Secondly, we must remember that the Convention is a *legal* document. In 1989, when it was adopted, there was, for example, no legislation anywhere in the world regulating assisted reproduction which has been the engine for the re-evaluation of traditional definitions of parenthood. Leaving aside adoption, legislation worldwide has traditionally defined parenthood as genetic parenthood. The legal tie has closely followed the genetic connection. Thirdly . . . the jurisprudence generated under another international Convention, the European Convention on Human Rights, again supports the notion of "family life" from birth and has confirmed that this includes the potential relationship of a child with his or her genetic father even where unmarried. Finally . . . the conventional interpretation was adopted by the Court of Appeal in the one reported decision which directly invokes Article 7. For all these reasons it is submitted that "parents" in the Convention was intended to mean genetic parents and thus the onus is very firmly on those who would argue for an unconventional interpretation.

The principle that children have a fundamental right to know the truth about their genetic parentage has found favour amongst some English judges. *Re R (A Minor) (Contact: Biological Father)* concerned a dispute between the child's mother and her former husband in relation to a child who had been raised to believe, incorrectly, that the mother's new partner was her father; Butler-Sloss LJ held in unequivocal terms that the child 'has a right in this case to know the truth'.[67]

Further support for a children's rights approach can be found in Article 8 of the European Convention on Human Rights (ECHR). It has been held that individuals have a 'private life' interest in ascertaining, through paternity proceedings, the identity of their genetic parents.

C. Fenton-Glynn, *Children and the European Court of Human Rights* (Oxford: OUP, 2021), 242–3

[The European Court] has made clear that children have a vital interest, protected by the Convention, in receiving the information necessary to uncover the truth about their biological origins and have their paternity recognised, as an important aspect of their personal identity.

This was first established in *Mikulić v Croatia*[68] concerning a child and her mother who were seeking to establish the identity of the child's father. Despite a court order, the putative father refused to undergo a DNA test, and as a result, the domestic authorities concluded that paternity could not be established. The Court acknowledged that protection for third parties may prevent them from being compelled to make themselves available for medical tests that they did not want to undertake. However, this protection for third parties must be balanced against the right of the child to have any uncertainty as to her personal identity

[67] [1993] 2 FLR 762, 768. [68] (App No 53176/99, ECHR) (2002).

eliminated without unnecessary delay. As such, it would only be proportionate to allow a refusal to undergo tests if there was an alternative mechanism to enable an independent authority to determine the issue of paternity, absent DNA results.

The principle in *Mikulić* was further expanded in *Jäggi v Switzerland*,[69] where the Court recognised that the right to establish one's biological parentage is an integral part of the notion of private life, and therefore particularly rigorous scrutiny is called for when weighing up competing interests. Importantly, this right does not end when a child reaches majority, but continues to be granted protection as long as it continues to be individual.

An approach focused on the child's rights is not, however, necessarily always in favour of the child knowing their genetic origins. An important question is whether a child can have the right *not* to know their biological parentage, and how the court should respond if it is not the parent, but the child, who is opposing testing. Fenton-Glynn notes that the European Court decisions on this issue have gone both ways.[70]

C. Fenton-Glynn, *Children and the European Court of Human Rights* (Oxford: OUP, 2021), 247

These cases again demonstrate the 'hands-off' approach of the Court in this area: it is within the margin of appreciation of states to decide whether and how paternity may be established or challenged, as long as the child's best interests have been taken into consideration. The problem lies with the concept of the child's best interests itself: it can mean whatever the domestic decision-makers want it to mean, with apparently no oversight by the Court. Only Judge Nussberger in dissent in *Mandet* [*v France*[71]] was willing to challenge the assessment of the domestic courts in this respect. . . . She stressed that finding out information about one's genetic origins is a *right* of a child, not an *obligation*. This means that a child should also have the right to ignore the truth of his biological paternity if he or she so wishes.

In *L v P (Paternity Test: Child's Objections)*,[72] a '*Gillick* competent' 15-year-old child objected to having a DNA test; Hedley J took the view that, although the child's views were not determinative, the child had good reasons for taking that position and therefore testing was refused. More recently, though, the views of the child in objecting to testing have been given more weight.

MS v RS and BT (Paternity Testing) [2020] EWFC 30

MacDONALD J:

92. The authorities are clear that, with respect to children under 16 who are considered *Gillick* competent, if a child is of sufficient understanding he or she may refuse to submit to medical examination or other assessment and that it is therefore generally unwise to subject

[69] (App No 58757/00, ECHR) (2006).
[70] Fenton-Glynn (2021), 244–7.
[71] (App No 30955/12, ECHR) (2016).
[72] [2011] EWHC 3399.

a child who is able to understand the purpose and implications of testing to testing against that child's will. In the circumstances, I am satisfied that to press further forensic DNA testing of the children at this time would not only heap further and damaging emotional pressure onto the children and be antithetic to their clearly expressed wishes and feelings, it would also be wrong in principle in my judgment to impose such forensic DNA testing on *Gillick* competent children who clearly object to it. . . .

95. However, . . . it must be acknowledged that the decision of the court leaves the father in the position of being the legal father of the children for a further period, with all the legal consequences that flow from that status, including a not insignificant financial obligation under the current child maintenance order. . . . In addition, it would be unfair on the father, and arguably a further breach of his Art 8 rights, to remain indefinitely as the children's legal father by virtue of a presumption if that is not the biological reality. Beyond these factors, there is a wider public interest in the children's status being, eventually, formally settled and recorded in properly maintained records, not least to address potential future questions with respect to, for example, consanguinity. With respect to the children, . . . in the medium to long term I am satisfied that it is likely to be in the children's best interests to know the identity of their biological father. . . .

97. . . . [W]hilst satisfied it would be wrong to press the question of testing with an order taking effect immediately, I am satisfied that an order stayed without limit of time coupled with the children being told that the court understands and sympathises with their position, believes that it would be best to determine the question of paternity scientifically as soon as possible but that it will not force the children to do so, has the best chance of bringing a final resolution to this sad case.

The rights of the putative father

A second factor that may incline the court to make a direction for tests is again rights-based but broadens the scope of the inquiry to include other family members. The European Court of Human Rights has held that under Article 8 ECHR the putative father's right to respect for his private and family life includes the right to have his paternal status and any potential relationship with his child recognized and protected under domestic law or, indeed, to have his paternity excluded.[73] This may require the state to have some mechanism in place whereby the putative father can establish or challenge his legal paternity by, for example, DNA testing and registration/de-registration on the birth register. In *Kroon v Netherlands*, it was held that the applicant's inability to obtain recognition of his paternity because the child had been born whilst the mother was still married and was therefore presumed to be the legitimate child of her former husband, constituted a breach of the genetic father's right to respect for family life under Article 8. Under Dutch law, only the husband could challenge the presumption of paternity in his favour.

Kroon v Netherlands (App No 18535/91, ECHR) (1994)

32. According to the principles set out by the Court in its case-law, where the existence of a family tie with a child has been established, the State must act in a manner calculated to enable that tie to be developed and legal safeguards must be established that render

[73] See Fenton-Glynn (2021), 236–42.

possible as from the moment of birth or as soon as practicable thereafter the child's integration in his family . . .

40. In the Court's opinion, "respect" for "family life" requires that biological and social reality prevail over a legal presumption which, as in the present case, flies in the face of both established fact and the wishes of those concerned without actually benefiting anyone. . . . There has accordingly been a violation of Article 8.

The guiding principle to emerge from *Kroon* (that 'biological and social reality' should prevail over legal presumptions) is consistent with the child's right to know the truth of genetic paternity as established in *Mikulić*.[74] It was, however, subsequently held in *Rozanski v Poland* that this principle will be accorded less weight where the parents do not agree about the desirability of establishing the putative father's status.[75] It is, moreover, clear that the right to biological certainty suggested by *Kroon* is not absolute but must be balanced against other competing interests.[76] Thus the interests of the child—and, in particular, the importance of preserving stability and certainty in the child's legal relationships, along with a focus on the importance of the functioning and quality of actual relationships already formed—have been found by the Court to constitute a *potential* justification for imposing various restraints, such as time limits, on adults challenging the child's paternity.[77] The competing Article 8 right of the child's mother not to be subjected to unwanted and potentially destabilizing interference with her existing family life is also a relevant consideration.

The child's best interests

A third approach that may influence the court's determination of the question of DNA tests rejects rights-based arguments in favour of prioritizing the child's welfare. Adopting this approach, it is argued that the question should simply be determined by asking what is in the child's best interests. If making a direction for DNA testing will secure the child's future welfare, tests should be ordered. If the tests may jeopardize the child's future security and happiness, they should be refused.

The problem is that disputes inevitably arise as to whether tests are in the child's best interests. As discussed in chapter 8, the indeterminacy of the welfare principle renders it subject to differing interpretations depending on prevailing social attitudes and trends, and the individual preferences of the decision-maker. Consequently, whilst at one time protecting the child against the detrimental consequences of illegitimacy may have been the court's overriding consideration, the declining social stigma surrounding illegitimacy and the final abolition of any legal distinction between a legitimate and illegitimate child[78] opened the way for competing discourses concerning the child's welfare to enter the field. Thus today's debates tend to centre on issues such as whether determining the truth about parentage risks destabilizing the child's existing family unit, how likely it is that the mother's partner is the father, the stability of the mother's existing relationship, the likelihood of the child being able to develop a meaningful relationship with the putative father, and whether doubts concerning the child's parentage have already entered the public arena.

[74] See also *Tavli v Turkey* (App No 11449/02, ECHR) (2006), [34]–[36].

[75] (App No 55339/00, ECHR) (2006), [67].

[76] See Bainham (2007a), esp at 280–1.

[77] See *Kautzor v Germany* (App No 23338/09, ECHR) (2012).

[78] FLRA 1987, s 1.

The public interest in the smooth administration of justice

Finally, the issue of whether the court should make a direction for DNA tests can be looked at from a completely different perspective. This fourth approach does not focus on the rights and interests of the parties to the dispute but on the wider public interest. It is argued that once court proceedings have been initiated there is a legitimate public interest in establishing the truth. Consequently, in order to ensure the fair and just administration of justice, the best available evidence should be brought before the court, even if it prejudices the particular rights and interests of the individuals concerned.

Case law under the FLRA 1969, s 20

There is evidence of all the arguments considered in this section being considered in the case law. In seeking to resolve the conflicts created, the courts have not always adopted a consistent approach. In recent years, the preferred approach has been to make a direction for tests, the rationale tending to focus on the child's right to know the truth about their genetic parentage, an approach which is considered consistent with the child's best interests.

In *S v McC and M; W v W*,[79] the House of Lords attempted to lay down authoritative guidance as to when a direction for tests should be made under s 20(1) of the FLRA 1969. The conjoined cases both concerned an attempt by the wife's husband to rebut the presumption of legitimacy following the wife's adultery. In making a direction for tests, the House of Lords made clear the declining importance being placed on the child's legitimacy and the court's primary concern, not with the child's welfare, but with the wider public interest in establishing the truth. The principles derived from the House of Lords' judgments have been effectively summarized by Balcombe LJ:

Re F (A Minor) (Blood Tests: Parental Rights) [1993] Fam 314 (CA), 318

BALCOMBE LJ:

From the speeches in the House of Lords the following principles can be derived: (1) The presumption of legitimacy merely determines the onus of proof . . . (2) Public policy no longer requires that special protection should be given by the law to the status of legitimacy . . . (3) The interests of justice will normally require that available evidence be not suppressed and that the truth be ascertained whenever possible . . . In many cases the interests of the child are also best served if the truth is ascertained . . . (4) However, the interests of justice may conflict with the interests of the child. In general the court ought to permit a blood test of a young child to be taken unless satisfied that that would be against the child's interests; it does not need first to be satisfied that the outcome of the test will be for the benefit of the child . . . (5) "It is not really protecting the child to ban a blood test on some vague and shadowy conjecture that it may turn out to be to its disadvantage: it may equally well turn out to be for its advantage or at least do it no harm."

Given the House of Lords' strong guidance that a direction for blood tests should ordinarily be made, it is somewhat surprising that the Court of Appeal in *Re F* managed to reach the

[79] [1972] AC 24.

opposite conclusion. *Re F* concerned a typical paternity dispute. The child was conceived whilst the wife was having sexual relations with both her husband and the putative father. The mother's relationship with the putative father ended before the child was born and the child was being raised as the child of the husband within the existing family unit. The putative father applied for parental responsibility and contact under the CA 1989. Paternity was disputed. Although paying lip-service to the requirement that blood tests must be shown to positively harm the child's interests (the approach adopted in *S v McC and M*),[80] in determining whether a direction for blood tests should be made, the Court of Appeal appeared to apply the different test of whether the tests would promote the child's interests. In determining this question, the Court of Appeal held that the child's interests lay not in ascertaining the 'abstract' truth about her true genetic parentage, but in providing support and protection to the existing family unit.

The Court of Appeal's apparent departure from the strict focus on genetic truth met with a mixed academic reaction. Barton and Douglas welcomed the court's preference for the presumed legal parenthood of the mother's husband, as evidence of the 'growing importance of the social, as opposed to genetic aspect of parenthood'.[81] Fortin was more critical, arguing, based on evidence from the field of adoption, that the court 'should have given far greater weight to the psychological value to E of knowing the truth about her origins'.[82] She also criticized the court for failing to keep the issue of the child's genetic parentage separate from that of the putative father's prospects of establishing a meaningful social relationship with the child.[83] However, as discussed in the following section, later cases prompted Fortin to reconsider these views.[84]

The apparent departure from the House of Lords' preference for determining the truth of parentage was, however, short-lived. The issue returned to the Court of Appeal in *Re H (A Minor) (Blood Tests: Parental Rights)*. The case was very similar on its facts to *Re F* although it was very unlikely the mother's husband could be the child's genetic father as he had had a vasectomy and sexual relations between them were very poor at the time of conception. The mother, nevertheless, disputed the putative father's paternity. In making a direction for scientific tests, Ward LJ reasserted and refined the House of Lords' principles from *S v McC and M*. On the question of welfare, the Court of Appeal confirmed that 'welfare does not dominate this decision', although most of the judgment is devoted to whether tests would be in the child's best interests. The decision is also distinctive for the emphasis placed on the child's right to know the truth about their genetic parentage, an approach Ward LJ clearly considered entirely consistent with the child's welfare.

Re H (A Minor) (Blood Tests: Parental Rights) [1997] Fam 89 (CA)

WARD LJ:

5. In my judgment every child has the right to know the truth unless his welfare clearly justifies the cover up. The right to know is acknowledged in the United Nations Convention on the Rights of the Child . . . there are two separate rights, the one to know, and the other to be cared for by, one's parents . . .

[80] See also *Re L* [2009] EWCA Civ 1239, [11]–[14].
[81] Barton and Douglas (1995), 61.
[82] Fortin (1994), 298.
[83] Ibid.
[84] Fortin (2009a). See 9.3.3.c.

> 9. Given the real risk bordering on inevitability that [the child] will at some time question his paternity, then I do not see how this case is not concluded by the unassailable wisdom expressed by Lord Hodson [in *S v McC and M*] . . .:
>
> > "The interests of justice in the abstract are best served by the ascertainment of the truth and there must be few cases where the interests of children can be shown to be best served by the suppression of truth."
>
> If, as she should, this mother is to bring up her children to believe in and to act by the maxim, which is her duty to teach them at her knee, that honesty is the best policy, then she should not sabotage that lesson by living a lie.
>
> 10. If the child has the right to know, then the sooner it is told the better. The issue of biological parentage should be divorced from psychological parentage. Acknowledging the applicant's parental responsibility should not dent the husband's social responsibility for a child whom he is so admirably prepared to care for and love irrespective of whether or not he is the father. . . .
>
> 11. If [the child] grows up knowing the truth, that will not undermine his attachment to his father figure and he will cope with knowing he has two fathers. Better that than a time-bomb ticking away.

The wider public interest in the smooth administration of justice does not feature in the Court of Appeal's reasoning.

The judgment in *Re H* is also significant for the clear distinction drawn between the child's genetic and social parents. It is thus emphasized that it is perfectly possible for a child to have two 'fathers'—one genetic and one social—and that the two parental roles are not necessarily mutually exclusive. Ward LJ does, however, make it clear that the two parents may serve quite different functions in relation to the child, and whilst the child has a right to know their genetic parentage, this does not necessarily involve trying to foster a personal relationship between them. The child's right to know should therefore not be seen as threatening or detracting from the parenting role of the social or psychological parent.

The impact of the Human Rights Act 1998

Re H is now regarded as the leading authority on when it is appropriate to make a direction for DNA tests. Although the child's welfare is not the paramount consideration, the child's rights and interests are very much the focus of concern. However, one argument which was not dealt with by the Court of Appeal in *Re H*, but could not be avoided following the implementation of the Human Rights Act 1998 (HRA 1998), was whether the putative father could rely on any rights under Article 8 to disturb what was now, essentially, an exclusively child-centred approach. Until this point, arguments focusing on the Article 8 rights of the putative father had been absent from the case law. However, the issue was tackled in *Re T (A Child) (DNA Tests: Paternity)*, Bodey J's judgment making it clear that the HRA 1998 did not change the approach set out in *Re H*. The facts of *Re T* were somewhat unusual. The mother, who was married but unable to conceive a child with her husband, had engaged in sexual intercourse with several men, including the putative father, at around the same time, in the hope of becoming pregnant. It was always intended that the resulting child would be raised within the existing family unit. However, the putative father, who had had some contact with the child, applied for parental responsibility and to spend time with the child. The husband responded by asserting his paternity. Having confirmed that the child's welfare was not paramount and that the child's interests had to be balanced against the competing interests of the adults, Bodey J went on to address the arguments flowing from the HRA 1998.

Re T (A Child) (DNA Tests: Paternity) [2001] 3 FCR 577 (Fam Div), 583–6

BODEY J:

There is no significant dispute that T [the child] has a right to respect for his private life (in the sense of having knowledge of his identity, which encompasses his true paternity) and a right to respect for his family life with each of his natural parents, all things being equal.

T also has what may (as here) be mutually 'competing' rights to respect for his private and family life, in the *other* sense that the stability of his present de facto family life should not be put at risk, except as may otherwise be held to be in his interests, and pursuant to art 8(2).

It is further common ground that the mother and her husband have a right to respect for their private and family life, comprising a right that the same should not be intruded upon, or interfered with, except as may be necessary to give effect to T's and (if he has them) the applicant's rights.

So far as the applicant is concerned, he may or may not (depending on the facts and on whether he is in truth the biological father) have a right to respect for a family life encompassing—all things being equal—the society of, and a relationship with T, and/or a knowledge of T's progress.

It is accepted between the parties that if and when these various Convention rights pull in opposite directions, then the crucial importance of the rights and best interests of the child fall particularly to be considered . . .

I am entirely satisfied that in evaluating and balancing the various rights of the adult parties and of T under art 8, the weightiest emerges clearly as being that of T, namely that he should have the possibility of knowing, perhaps with certainty, his true roots and identity.

I find any such interference as would occur to the right to respect for the family/private life of the mother and her husband, to be proportionate to the legitimate aim of providing T with the possibility of certainty as to his real paternity, a knowledge which would accompany him throughout his life.

Applying art 8 in this way (regardless of whether or not the applicant has established what, if he is the father, would constitute family life with T) confirms my previous view that I should grant the applicant's application.

9.3.3.c Consent requirements for the taking of samples

When parentage is disputed, the court will almost always make a direction for scientific tests to determine the issue. There is, however, a further hurdle to be negotiated. Regardless of any direction the court might make, a bodily sample cannot be taken from any party to the litigation for the purpose of carrying out the tests without consent.[85]

[85] FLRA 1969, s 21(1).

The child's consent to the taking of samples

In the case of a minor who is 16 years or over, s 21(2) of the FLRA 1969 provides that the minor can give an effective consent to the taking of bodily samples in the same way as a person of full age and capacity. For minors who are under 16, the consent of the person with 'care and control' is required. If consent is withheld, the court can override the refusal if satisfied that taking the sample would be in the child's best interests.

Family Law Reform Act 1969, s 21

(3) A bodily sample may be taken from a person under the age of sixteen years, not being a person as is referred to in subsection (4) of this section,

(a) if the person who has the care and control of him consents; or

(b) where that person does not consent, if the court considers that it would be in his best interests for the sample to be taken.

This appears to set down a straightforward welfare test for determining whether samples should be taken if the person with care and control does not consent. This is different from the qualified welfare test set down in *S v McC and M* and *Re H* for determining whether a direction for tests should be made under s 20(1). It is not yet clear how the courts will deal with the slightly differing demands of the two provisions. Although the child's welfare is not the only consideration in determining whether a direction for tests should be made, before making a direction under s 20(1) the court will have given detailed consideration to the issue and reached a firm conclusion as to whether or not DNA tests are in the child's best interests or at least not adverse to them. Section 21 may therefore be rendered a mere formality, the court invariably ordering that samples be taken once the direction for testing is made. Indeed, there is a clear trend in the current case law, at least where consent to the taking of samples is in issue, to conflate the requirements of ss 20 and 21 of the FLRA 1969 and decide the case by means of an unqualified application of the welfare principle.[86] This will invariably lead both to a direction for DNA tests to be carried out and an order for the taking of samples. This was the approach adopted in the case of *Re D (Paternity)* which unusually involved the vehement opposition of an 11-year-old child to the taking of samples.[87] Hedley J's analysis focused exclusively on the child's best interests with no distinction drawn between the requirements of ss 20 and 21 of the FLRA 1969. Despite the child's clear and determined opposition, Hedley J ordered that a sample be taken for the purposes of testing, albeit he stayed the order to remove the immediate pressure on the child.[88]

The decision in *Re D* generated concern that the emphasis on genetic truth is such that it is being dogmatically pursued even where, on the particular facts, it is strongly arguable that it may be better for the child to preserve stability and security in their current relationships. Fortin, who previously supported the child's right to know, has voiced concerns about this trend. She argues that the preoccupation with biological truth has more to do with serving the rights and interests of the adults than those of the child, particularly where paternity disputes are being driven, not by the child's right to information about their genetic origins,

[86] *Re T (A Child) (DNA Tests: Paternity)* [2001] 3 FCR 577; *Re H and A* [2002] 1 FLR 1145.

[87] [2006] EWHC 3545. [88] Ibid, [29]–[30].

but by the putative father's desire to establish a social relationship with the child based on nothing more than the genetic tie.

J. Fortin, 'Children's Right to Know Their Origins: Too Far, Too Fast?', (2009a) 21 *Child and Family Law Quarterly* 336, 338–54

When writing my critique of *Re F* [see 9.3.3.b], I had perhaps overlooked the dangers for children of the assumption that they all have a right to knowledge of their origins . . . The decision in *Re D* provokes a feeling of unease . . . Surely a child has a right *not* to know the identity of his father if he himself believes, with some grounds, that his entire life would be disrupted by such knowledge? Indeed, the view that *all* children have a right to know their parents' identity may sometimes achieve more harm than good, given the danger of the two issues being confused—the child's need to know about his origins and his possible need for a social relationship with his biological parent . . . When dealing with applications from putative fathers, it is arguable that the domestic courts are extending a child's right to know beyond its appropriate boundaries . . . [T]he disputes being litigated have little to do with children's right to knowledge of their origins. The DNA testing applications brought by putative fathers are not brought to provide the child with information alone, they are the initial stages of attempts to establish a social relationship between father and child based on assumptions about biological connectedness. The putative fathers' assumption that once the biological ties between father and child have been clearly identified, they should be fulfilled by a social relationship produces an elision of the right to know the parent's identity, with the right to know and have a relationship with that parent. Whether or not claims can be justified by reference to the child's own rights, such an elision concentrates the court's attention on the putative father's position and his own interests—countered by those of the mother . . . These are adult-centred arguments which spring from adult-centred disputes over children who are treated as the property of those who can establish biological connectedness. There are dangers that such an approach, unsupported by research will not benefit some children. Indeed, in some cases like *Re D (Paternity)* where the child himself rejects the need to know the identity of his father, it may psychologically damage him. That case reinforces Smart's warning . . . about the dangers of allowing the law to insist on only one kind of truth—'the truth of science' above those other claims concerned with 'caring, relationality and the preserve of kinship bonds'.

The consent of adult parties and the drawing of adverse inferences

Under s 21(3), the problem of a lack of consent with respect to the child can now usually be avoided. The need for consent is more difficult where one of the adults refuses to cooperate. This is most likely to arise where the putative father is denying paternity to avoid paying child support. There is no statutory equivalent to s 21(3) giving the court the authority to override the putative father's refusal. The courts have, however, made it clear that they will not allow themselves to be dictated to by intransigent parties and the stated intention of one party to withhold consent will not preclude them from making a direction for tests.[89] A refusal to submit to the tests does not amount to contempt of court and cannot be met by the court's punitive powers.[90] To withhold consent is, however, to play a dangerous game. The court can draw whatever inferences it feels appropriate from a party's refusal to cooperate,[91]

[89] *Re H (A Minor) (Blood Tests: Parental Rights)* [1997] Fam 89, 101.
[90] *Re G (A Minor) (Blood Test)* [1994] 1 FLR 495, 499–500. [91] FLRA 1969, s 23.

including an inference as to the actual paternity of the child.[92] As was made clear in *Re A (A Minor) (Paternity: Refusal of Blood Test)*, this is an effective weapon against an intransigent party. The facts of *Re A* are fairly typical of paternity disputes where liability to provide financial support for the child is at stake. At the time of the child's conception, the mother was having sexual relations with three different men. She claimed maintenance against just one, a man the Court of Appeal described as being 'of some substance'.[93] The man refused to comply with a direction for blood tests, arguing that it would be unjust to compel him to submit to a test and risk paternity being conclusively established against him when two other men who were equally likely to be the child's father were not being exposed to the same risk. The argument was dismissed.

Re A (A Minor) (Paternity: Refusal of Blood Test) [1994] 2 FLR 463 (CA), 472–3

WAITE LJ:

Any man who is unsure of his own paternity and harbours the least doubt as to whether the child he is alleged to have fathered may be that of another man now has it within his power to set all doubt at rest by submitting to a test. It has ceased, therefore, to be possible for any man in such circumstances to be forced against his will to accept paternity of a child whom he does not believe to be his.

Against that background of law and scientific advance, it seems to me to follow, both in justice and in common sense, that if a mother makes a claim against one of the possible fathers, and he chooses to exercise his right not to submit to be tested, the inference that he is the father of the child should be virtually inescapable. He would certainly have to advance very clear and cogent reasons for this refusal to be tested—reasons which it would be just and fair and reasonable for him to be allowed to maintain.

It is open to the party withholding consent to show good cause why his refusal to co-operate is justified. Absent such justification, however, the drawing of an adverse inference against the party disputing paternity seems virtually inevitable, even if one of the other putative fathers is married to the child's mother and a presumption of legitimacy therefore applies.[94]

9.3.3.d Telling the child the 'truth' about parentage

If scientific tests are ordered and the truth about parentage established, the next question is whether, and if so how, the child should be told. Not surprisingly, many mothers who oppose DNA testing are equally resistant to telling the child the result, particularly where it threatens the child's security within the existing family unit. It is, however, clear that the court can compel a parent to tell the child the truth about their parentage. In *Re F (Paternity Jurisdiction)*,[95] Thorpe LJ held that the question of whether a child should be told the truth is a question relating to the exercise of an aspect of

[92] *Re A (A Minor) (Paternity: Refusal of Blood Test)* [1994] 2 FLR 463, 472. [93] Ibid, 464.
[94] *F v Child Support Agency* [1999] 2 FLR 244. [95] [2007] EWCA Civ 873.

parental responsibility which can be controlled by a specific issue order or under the court's wardship jurisdiction.[96] Moreover, he made it clear that concerns over the enforceability of such orders were unfounded: if the parent refuses to cooperate, the court can put in place alternative mechanisms for ensuring the children are told, possibly involving mental health professionals.[97]

9.4 DETERMINING PARENTHOOD IN THE CONTEXT OF ASSISTED REPRODUCTION

9.4.1 THE BRAVE NEW WORLD OF ASSISTED REPRODUCTION

For family lawyers, post-war developments in assisted reproduction raised a number of challenging new questions. One of the key difficulties for policy-makers is the number of different treatments available and the vast range of circumstances in which people may seek to take advantage of them. Nearly 75,000 IVF 'treatment cycles' took place in 2019, and nearly 20,000 children were born that year, amounting to 3.1 per cent of all children born in the UK.[98]

Whilst scientific advances in reproductive medicine have generally been welcomed for giving much needed hope to infertile couples, there have also been strong voices of dissent. Concern tends to focus on what is perceived as the potential use of these treatments for social, as opposed to medical, reasons. Single women and same-sex couples are typically targeted as the most likely 'deviants' to seek to exploit the developments.[99] A married couple unable to conceive for medical reasons are likely to engender considerable sympathy. IVF using their own gametes to assist in conception raises relatively few problems for our traditional concepts of 'family' and 'parenthood'. By contrast, a same-sex male couple using a donor egg and having their child carried to term by a surrogate creates more challenges for these conventional ideas of what being a 'parent' means. Although artificial insemination using donor sperm has probably been practised on an informal 'DIY' basis for years, the ability to create an embryo in vitro raises the spectre of a previously unknown fragmentation of parenthood. There are now several individuals who can contribute to the creation of a single embryo and who are able to point to equally credible but competing claims to parenthood of the resulting child. Out of the complications is that there is no easy answer to the question of who the law should regard as the child's legal parents. Should priority be given to genetics, gestation, intention, or social parenting? The possibilities created by assisted reproduction dramatically expose the extent to which English family law is willing to embrace unconventional family forms.

However, before turning to consider how the law on parenthood has responded to these developments in assisted reproduction, we will consider an increasingly important and closely related issue: the right of an individual to access fertility treatment.

[96] Ibid, [8], [14]. [97] Ibid, [17]–[18].

[98] HFEA (2021b). We use 2019 data as treatments in 2020 were substantially interrupted by the Covid-19 pandemic, with virtually all services suspended between April and June 2020, and an overall decrease in treatments of 20 per cent compared to 2019: HFEA (2022).

[99] As to the concerns expressed in the parliamentary debates preceding the HFEA 1990, see: Jackson (2002), 195; Douglas (1993), 57–8; Roberts (2000), 49.

9.4.2 ACCESS TO TREATMENT: IS PARENTHOOD A RIGHT OR A PRIVILEGE?

Infertility can be devastating for those affected but developments in assisted reproduction mean that there are now several ways in which couples can be helped. However, whilst one may feel considerable sympathy for these couples, it does not necessarily follow that they have a right to demand access to treatment, and that argument may be even stronger for individuals and couples who are not infertile but seek access to assisted reproductive techniques for other, perhaps social, reasons. There are several arguments against allowing individuals to access fertility treatment, as the Warnock Committee set out:

DHSS, *Report of the Committee of Inquiry into Human Fertilisation and Embryology*, Cm 9314 (London: HMSO, 1984)

> 2.3 Arguments have been put to us both for and against the treatment of infertility. First, we have encountered the view that in an over-populated world it is wrong to take active steps to create more human beings who will consume finite resources. However strongly a couple may wish to have children, such a wish is ultimately selfish. It has been said that if they cannot have children without intervention, they should not be helped to do so. Secondly, there is a body of opinion which holds that it is wrong to interfere with nature, or with what is perceived to be the will of God. Thirdly, it has been argued that the desire to have children is no more than a wish; it cannot be said to constitute a need. Other people have genuine needs which must be satisfied if they are to survive. Thus services designed to meet those needs must have priority for scarce resources.

The Warnock Committee was unpersuaded by these arguments,[100] and following its recommendations, the UK has taken a fairly liberal approach to the provision of fertility treatment. Clinics specializing in assisted reproduction have been established in both the private and the public sector, albeit subject to the strict licensing conditions set down in the HFEA 1990 and closely regulated by the Human Fertilisation and Embryology Authority (HFEA). The wide availability of fertility treatment does not, however, translate into a right to treatment.

The right to access fertility treatment can be conceptualized as a right to found a family or, more broadly, as a right to reproductive freedom. Emily Jackson makes a strong case as to why those who wish to have children should be afforded the freedom to do so, focusing her arguments on the right of individuals to a protected 'zone of privacy' in which decisions concerning reproduction can be made.[101]

E. Jackson, 'Conception and the Irrelevance of the Welfare Principle', (2002) 65 *Modern Law Review* 176, 177–8

> Of course for the vast majority of people, deciding whether or not to conceive is not susceptible to legal control. People who conceive through heterosexual sexual intercourse do so without any external scrutiny of the merit or otherwise of their decision. Monitoring these

[100] DHSS (1984), para 2.4. [101] See also Alghrani and Harris (2006), 192 and 195–6.

exceptionally personal choices in order to identify ill-judged or improper conception decisions would be unreservedly condemned as an unacceptably intrusive abuse of state power . . . I would suggest that there are broadly two different justifications for the presumption that normally exists in favour of privacy in procreative decision-making. First, interfering with a particular individual's decision to conceive a child would usually involve violating their bodily integrity and sexual privacy . . . The second and I would argue equally important reason for respecting people's conception choices is that the freedom to decide for oneself whether or not to reproduce is integral to a person's sense of being, in some important sense, the author of their own life plan. For most people, these two justifications for reproductive privacy mesh together in the requirement that we treat both their body and their life plan with respect. We should, however, remember that those individuals whose procreative preferences can be disregarded without simultaneously violating their bodily integrity and sexual privacy nevertheless retain their interest in being able to make exceptionally personal and important decisions according to their own conception of the good.

In considering the right to reproductive freedom, a distinction needs to be made between what Jackson terms 'positive and negative liberty'.[102] There is an important difference between, on the one hand, the state interfering with the decision of an individual to seek fertility treatment in the private sphere and, on the other, the state refusing to provide unfettered access to state-funded treatment. The former seeks to impose a negative obligation of non-interference on the state, whilst the latter seeks to impose a positive obligation on the state to guarantee access to treatment for all. The argument in favour of recognizing the former right is considerably stronger than the latter, where other considerations such as the rationing of resources and prioritization of medical treatment within the NHS are legitimate considerations.[103] Where, however, there are no resource issues at stake, the legitimacy of the state seeking to scrutinize and restrict an individual's procreative freedom is harder to sustain.

E. Jackson, 'Conception and the Irrelevance of the Welfare Principle', (2002) 65 *Modern Law Review* 176, 177–8

My claim is that we should refrain from scrutinising the pre-conception decisions of adults who intend to bring about a child's creation just as we would if they had happened to be able to conceive naturally. Notice that this is not the same as saying that people have a *right* to be provided with fertility treatment. On the contrary, my argument here is much more modest. It is simply that we should each have the liberty to shield certain personal decisions from public scrutiny. The decision to conceive a child goes to the heart of an individual's identity and is precisely the sort of choice that we all ought to be able to make within the privacy of our most intimate relationship. I argue that it is therefore unfair to take advantage of the opportunity afforded by their biological incapacity in order to assess the wisdom of an infertile couple's decision to start a family. We may not be able to fund their treatment, or there might be no treatment that is clinically appropriate for them. But evaluating an infertile couple's fitness to parent deprives them of the decisional privacy that the majority of people are rightly able to take for granted.

[102] Jackson (2002), 184. [103] Ibid, 184–5.

9.4.2.a The right to reproductive freedom under Article 8 ECHR

In order to assist an individual seeking access to fertility treatment, the right to reproductive freedom must first be recognized under English law. The prevailing approach, before and after the HRA 1998, was that an individual had the right to seek investigation and advice concerning their infertility and a right to be considered for treatment. There was, however, no unfettered right to treatment in either the public or private sector.[104]

The issue of whether there is a Convention right to access fertility treatment arose in *Evans v United Kingdom*.[105] *Evans* did not concern a straightforward claim to treatment. Ms Evans was attending a clinic for fertility treatment with her partner, Mr Johnston, when it was discovered she had cancerous tumours in both ovaries. As a result, she underwent the first stage of IVF treatment to remove as many eggs as possible for use in future treatment. The eggs were fertilized using Mr Johnston's sperm and the resulting embryos frozen whilst Ms Evans underwent treatment for cancer. Before she recovered sufficiently for an embryo transfer to be carried out, the couple separated and Mr Johnston withdrew his consent to the further storage and use of the embryos. This meant that under the terms of the HFEA 1990, Sch 3, the embryos had to be removed from storage and destroyed. Ms Evans claimed that Mr Johnston's right to withdraw his consent violated her Article 8 right to respect for private and family life. In line with the approach adopted by the Court of Appeal hearing the case at the domestic level,[106] the Grand Chamber of the European Court held that the right to decide whether to become a genetic parent (and to realize that right by accessing fertility treatment) fell within the ambit of the Article 8 right to respect for private life, this right being broadly interpreted to incorporate any aspect of one's personal liberty and freedom.

Evans v United Kingdom **(App No 6339/05, ECHR) (2007)**

71. It is not disputed between the parties that Article 8 is applicable and that the case concerns the applicant's right to respect for her private life. The Grand Chamber agrees with the Chamber that "private life", which is a broad term encompassing, *inter alia*, aspects of an individual's physical and social identity including the right to personal autonomy, personal development and to establish and develop relationships with other human beings and the outside world . . . incorporates the right to respect for both the decisions to become and not to become a parent.

72. It must be noted, however, that the applicant does not complain that she is in any way prevented from becoming a mother in a social, legal, or even physical sense, since there is no rule of domestic law or practice to stop her from adopting a child or even giving birth to a child originally created *in vitro* from donated gametes. The applicant's complaint is, more precisely, that the consent provisions of the 1990 Act prevent her from using the embryos she and J [her former partner] created together, and thus, given her particular circumstances, from ever having a child to whom she is genetically related. The Grand Chamber considers that this more limited issue, concerning the right to respect for the decision to become a parent in the genetic sense, also falls within the scope of Article 8.

[104] DHSS (1984), para 2.12; *R v Ethical Committee of St Mary's Hospital (Manchester), ex parte H* [1988] 1 FLR 512.

[105] (App No 6339/05, ECHR) (2007).

[106] *Evans v Amicus Healthcare Ltd* [2004] EWCA Civ 727, [108].

It was subsequently confirmed in *Dickson v United Kingdom* that state-imposed restrictions on accessing assisted reproduction engages Article 8 and the right to respect for the decision to become a genetic parent.[107] It is, however, equally clear from *Evans* and *Dickson* that Article 8 is a qualified right: it does not confer an absolute right to become a parent using any technological means possible.

9.4.2.b Legitimate restrictions on the right to reproductive freedom: Article 8(2)

Procreative liberty and the need for unequivocal consent

The state can legitimately regulate and restrict the right to fertility treatment in order to safeguard the rights and interests of others. In *Evans*, the Court of Appeal held that the interference with Ms Evans' Article 8 rights was justified to protect the competing Article 8 rights of Mr Johnston, in particular, his *equal* right to procreative liberty including his right to choose not to become a father.

Evans v Amicus Healthcare Ltd [2004] EWCA Civ 727

ARDEN LJ:

109. The next question is whether the interference is justified under article 8(2). In the 1990 Act Parliament has taken the view that each genetic parent should have the right to withdraw their consent for as long as possible. It was not inevitable that Parliament should take that view. Subject to the possible effect of the Convention, Parliament could have taken the view that, as in sexual intercourse, a man's procreative liberty should end with the donation of sperm but that, in the light of the woman's unique role in making the embryo a child, she should have the right to determine the fate of the embryo. But Parliament did not take that view. Nor did Parliament take the view that the court should have any power to dispense with the requirement for consent of both parties, even when circumstances occur which were not envisaged when the original arrangements were made.

110 . . . I consider that the imposition of an invariable and ongoing requirement for consent in the 1990 Act in the present type of situation satisfies article 8(2) of the Convention. . . . As this is a sensitive area of ethical judgment, the balance to be struck between the parties must primarily be a matter for Parliament . . . Parliament has taken the view that no one should have power to override the need for a genetic parent's consent. The wisdom of not having such a power is, in my judgment, illustrated by the facts of this case. The personal circumstances of the parties are different from what they were at the outset of treatment, and it would be difficult for a court to judge whether the effect of Mr Johnston's withdrawal of his consent on Ms Evans is greater than the effect that the invalidation of that withdrawal of consent would have on Mr Johnston. The court has no point of reference by which to make that sort of evaluation. The fact is that each person has a right to be protected against interference with their private life. That is an aspect of the principle of self-determination or personal autonomy. It cannot be said that the interference with Mr Johnston's right is justified on the ground that interference is necessary to protect Ms

[107] *Dickson v United Kingdom* (App No 44362/04, ECHR) (2007).

Evans's right, because her right is likewise qualified in the same way by his right. They must have equivalent rights, even though the exact extent of their rights under article 8 has not been identified.

111. The interference with Ms Evans's private life is also justified under article 8(2) because, if Ms Evans's argument succeeded, it would amount to interference with the genetic father's right to decide not to become a parent. Motherhood could surely not be forced on Ms Evans and likewise fatherhood cannot be forced on Mr Johnston, especially as in the present case it will probably involve financial responsibility in law for the child as well.

The Grand Chamber of the European Court agreed that the HFEA 1990's strict provisions on consent were a proportionate response to the legitimate need to protect the procreative liberty of *both* parties embarking upon fertility treatment.[108]

This strict approach to consent was retained when the legislative framework governing assisted reproduction was reformed in 2008. The HFEA 2008 amends Sch 3 to the HFEA 1990 to introduce a 12-month 'cooling off' period.[109] This allows the embryos to be stored for 12 months following the withdrawal of consent by one party in the hope that an amicable agreement about their future use and storage can be reached. However, if the parties cannot reach agreement the embryos must still be destroyed on the expiration of the 12-month period.

The best interests of the child

The most important way in which the state regulates access to fertility treatment is through the welfare principle, the mechanism by which the rights and interests of any future child can be protected.

Human Fertilisation and Embryology Act 1990, s 13

(5) A woman shall not be provided with treatment services unless account has been taken of the welfare of any child who may be born as a result of the treatment (including the need of that child for supportive parenting), and of any other child who may be affected by the birth.

The child's welfare constitutes a legitimate qualification on the right of the prospective parents to procreative liberty under Article 8(2).[110] However, restricting access to fertility treatment on the basis of the child's welfare has been fiercely criticized. In practice, it is intrinsically difficult to apply the best interests principle to such an abstract question as the welfare of a child who does not yet exist. Indeed, Emily Jackson, one of the strongest critics, argues that to attempt to do so is 'disingenuous and essentially meaningless'.

[108] *Evans v United Kingdom* (App No 6339/05, ECHR) (2007), [89]–[92].

[109] HFEA 1990, Sch 3, para 4A.

[110] *Dickson v United Kingdom* (App No 44362/04, ECHR) (2007), [76].

E. Jackson, 'Conception and the Irrelevance of the Welfare Principle', (2002) 65 *Modern Law Review* 176, 193

Unlike factors that go to the heart of whether infertility treatment is, for example, clinically advisable or publicly affordable, the pre-conception welfare principle represents an invidious and opportunistic invasion of infertile people's privacy. Deciding to try to conceive a child through sexual intercourse is usually assumed to be a *self-regarding* decision that takes place within the privacy of a couple's intimate relationship. Yet biological infertility somehow serves to convert this choice into an *other-regarding* decision that must be judged according to its likely impact upon this 'other', namely the child that might be born . . . [R]egardless of whether the child's welfare is described as a medical or social outcome, for several interconnected reasons I believe that attempting to ration treatment using section 13(5) is both tautologous and unjust. First if the alternative is non-existence, it will in fact invariably be in the particular future child's best interests to be conceived. It is therefore simply illogical for the HFEA to insist that treatment should . . . be refused if the centre believes that it would not be in the interests of any resulting child, because, as John Robertson has explained, from the child's perspective, the risk-creating activity is welcome, since there is no alternative way for this child to be born.

The HFEA is responsible for issuing guidance on how fertility clinics are to apply s 13(5). The HFEA has taken a broadly permissive approach, effectively enshrining a presumption in favour of treatment unless there is evidence that any resulting child would be at risk of significant harm.[111] Indeed, Smith argues that this 'light touch' approach has rendered s 13(5) almost redundant.[112] The European Court added its voice to the debate in *Dickson v United Kingdom*.[113] *Dickson* concerned the right of a prisoner serving life imprisonment to access assisted insemination services so that he and his partner, who would be too old to conceive naturally by the time of his anticipated release, could attempt to begin a family. The Home Secretary, applying the policy then in force, refused permission for Mr Dickson to access such services. Although it was accepted by the court that the child's welfare was, in principle, a legitimate restriction on the applicants' rights to access artificial insemination facilities, it was clear that such is the importance of the procreative right at stake under Article 8 that significant welfare concerns, going beyond those which were evident on the facts of this particular case, would be needed in order for the state to successfully justify its interference.

Dickson v United Kingdom (App No 44362/04, ECHR) (2007)

76. [T]he Government argued that the absence of a parent for a long period would have a negative impact on any child conceived and, consequently, on society as a whole.

The Court is prepared to accept as legitimate, for the purposes of the second paragraph of Article 8, that the authorities, when developing and applying the Policy, should concern themselves, as a matter of principle, with the welfare of any child: conception of a child was

[111] See Alghrani and Harris (2006), 196–201. [112] Smith (2010), 51.
[113] (App No 44362/04, ECHR) (2007).

the very object of the exercise. Moreover, the State has a positive obligation to ensure the effective protection of children . . . However, that cannot go so far as to prevent parents who so wish from attempting to conceive a child in circumstances like those of the present case, especially as the second applicant was at liberty and could have taken care of any child conceived until such time as her husband was released.

In balancing the private and public interests engaged under Article 8, the Court seemed to place a much more onerous obligation on the state when seeking to justify restrictions imposed on access to reproductive treatment, particularly if the sole ground on which it purported to do so was the welfare of the child.

The question of whether access to treatment should continue to be regulated on the basis of a welfare test was thoroughly reviewed prior to the reforms enshrined in the HFEA 2008. However, the government decided to amend s 13(5) in only one respect. As originally enacted in the HFEA 1990, s 13(5) required clinics to have particular regard not to the need of the child for *supportive parenting* but to the need of the child for a *father*. This amendment was controversial at the time, both due to the symbolism of what the amendment might say about the importance of fathers, and about the practical consequences when read alongside other reforms within the 2008 legislation. As amended, s 13(5) not only permits the deliberate creation of fatherless children but confers legal approval on non-conventional family forms that present a direct challenge to the normative heterosexual foundations of family life.[114] And whilst this approach was welcomed by many, s 13(5) did not sit well with the previous Labour Government's strong commitment to promoting and supporting genetic fatherhood in other key areas of family law.[115] These contradictions and tensions at the heart of contemporary family policy are drawn out by Smith.

L. Smith, 'Clashing Symbols? Reconciling Support for Fathers and Fatherless Families after the Human Fertilisation and Embryology Act 2008', (2010) 22 *Child and Family Law Quarterly* 46, 54–5, 56–7

In recent years the government has placed its support behind same-sex parenting by initiating various pieces of legislation . . . The provisions contained in the HFE Act represent a further attempt to remove legal obstacles to the recognition of same-sex parenting arrangements. Each of these developments marks a departure from law's historical support for the heterosexual family unit. As such each also implicitly endorses both existing and prospective fatherless families. Moreover, these legislative developments have been bolstered by policy level rhetoric indicating an intention to support diversity rather than conventionality in family life . . .

In parallel with these developments, however, the government has repeatedly emphasised its commitment to the idea that the traditional married family is the best environment in which to bring up children . . . These and other, similar, tributes to the hetero-normative family have given opponents of the Act ample opportunity to criticise countervailing efforts to facilitate the establishment of families by same-sex couples. Given that the government

[114] Smith (2010), 51–2.

[115] See, especially, disputes about children's upbringing, discussed in chapter 11.

has intimated on multiple occasions that being brought up in a traditional heterosexual family unit is inherently advantageous to children, it is no small wonder that its attempts to support same-sex parenting in the present context have been the subject of criticism. Furthermore, the force of the message in support of the marital, necessarily heterosexual family is repeatedly reinforced by more specific and widespread promotion of the importance of fathers in children's lives. . . .

[W]hile lobbyists and judges eulogise the contributions made by fathers to their children's welfare and invoke the powerful language of rights, policy makers have referred to 'the *vital* role played by fathers'. Such statements present the connection between child well-being and father presence as absolute and this gives the government's suggestion that lesbian parents—who by definition will normally form fatherless families—can bring up children satisfactorily a hollow ring. It begins to look as if the government is indeed clashing its own symbols in terms of its various expressions of support for fathers and support for fatherless families.

9.4.2.c The right to reproductive freedom under Article 12 ECHR

At least on the face of the ECHR, Article 12 may seem a more promising route to establishing a right to reproductive treatment because, unlike Article 8, Article 12 appears to establish an unqualified right. The 'right to found a family' under Article 12 has, however, been subjected to a conservative interpretation by the European Court,[116] and '[r]eferences to Article 12 have been ignored or, possibly, avoided [by the European Court], and Article 12 hardly plays any role in the cases concerning reproduction'.[117] The Court has rejected the argument that Article 12 guarantees 'a right to procreation', taking a more traditionalist interpretation of the right to found a family.[118] However, the argument that the right to utilize assisted reproductive techniques, such as IVF, *should* fall within the right to 'found a family' is not obviously flawed, particularly as it has been held that adoption, which is arguably not as close to natural reproduction as IVF, has been found to fall within the scope of the provision.[119] That said, even if the right to artificial reproduction is found, in principle, to fall within the scope of Article 12, the right remains expressly subject to 'national laws governing the exercise of the right'. A state could thus legitimately restrict its treatment to couples who have formalized their relationship and who experience infertility, particularly as the right to marry and the right to found a family under Article 12 are closely linked in the Strasbourg case law.[120]

9.4.3 DETERMINING PARENTHOOD UNDER THE HFEA 2008

The common law's traditional emphasis on genetic parenthood can be inappropriate when applied in the context of assisted reproduction. For example, when determining the paternity of a child born through the use of AID, it cannot be right for a sperm donor who is unaware of the child's existence to be regarded as the child's legal father, particularly if that status involves a duty to maintain the child. It seems equally illogical for the husband of a

[116] Eijkholt (2010), 134–5. [117] Ibid, 128.

[118] E.g. *SH v Austria* (App No 57813/00, ECHR) (2007).

[119] *X and Y v United Kingdom* (App No 7229/75, ECHR) (1978) and *X v Netherlands* (App No 8896/80, ECHR) (1981).

[120] Eijkholt (2010), 136.

woman receiving AID treatment to be regarded in law as a stranger to the child he intends to raise as his own. In the case of disputes over maternity, the law has to contend not only with a potential split between genetic and social motherhood but the further complication of a split between genetic and gestational motherhood. As assisted reproduction became more widely available, it became clear that the common law's emphasis on genetic parenthood could not be sustained in this particular context. The HFEA 1990 was intended to provide a comprehensive scheme for determining the legal parenthood of children conceived via assisted reproductive techniques. This scheme was comprehensively revised by the HFEA 2008, which introduced quite radical changes to the way in which legal parenthood is determined in this context. Most notably, Parliament made it much easier for same-sex couples to acquire legal parenthood following fertility treatment by introducing provisions comparable to those in place for heterosexual couples.

The scheme set out in Part 2 of the HFEA 2008 is not straightforward, and can require consideration of various alternatives, some of which are phrased as negative requirements, or where there are subtle but crucial differences of wording between apparently similar provisions. Figure 9.1 offers a simplified guide through the HFEA 2008 provisions, indicating both the circumstances in which the statute's rules do not apply, and the outcomes when they do.[121] It is important to note that only cases that meet the criteria of the Act will lead

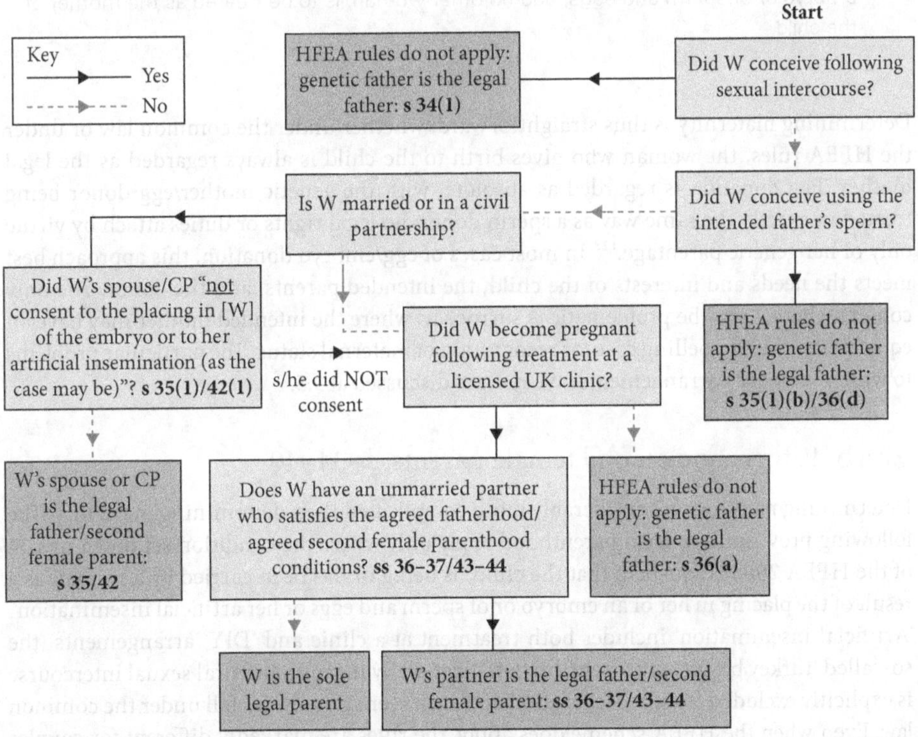

Figure 9.1 Simplified diagram of legal parentage under the HFEA 2008

[121] There are special rules that can apply in cases where W's partner has died prior to an embryo being created (in cases where the father's own sperm are used) or prior to the embryo being placed in W (when donor sperm are used), but these more niche provisions are not included in Figure 9.1. See HFEA 2008, ss 39, 40, 41, and 46, discussed at 9.4.3.b.

to the statutorily-determined outcomes; any case that falls outside the legislative regime is treated as natural reproduction, and the common law rules apply. Sometimes that is as intended, such as in the case of a heterosexual couple using their own gametes (they have no need for special rules), but it can create unintended consequences in some situations. Figure 9.1 is inevitably simplified, and we set out the details of the regime in the sections that follow.

9.4.3.a Mothers: s 33

Genetic, gestational, and social motherhood may now be located in three different women. The Warnock Committee considered that in the interests of certainty the gestational mother should, for all legal purposes, be accorded the legal status of motherhood.[122] This recommendation was enshrined in s 27(1) of the HFEA 1990 and retained without being reconsidered in s 33(1) of the HFEA 2008.

Human Fertilisation and Embryology Act 2008, s 33

(1) The woman who is carrying or has carried a child as a result of the placing in her of an embryo or of sperm and eggs, and no other woman, is to be treated as the mother of the child.

Determining maternity is thus straightforward: whether under the common law or under the HFEA rules, the woman who gives birth to the child is always regarded as the legal mother. Egg donation is regarded as absolute, with the genetic mother/egg donor being treated in exactly the same way as a sperm donor: no legal rights or duties attach by virtue only of her genetic parentage.[123] In most cases of egg/embryo donation, this approach best meets the needs and interests of the child, the intended parents, and the donor. The only context where it may be problematic is surrogacy, where the intended mother may have an equally or more compelling case for recognition of maternal status. The particular problems to which surrogacy arrangements give rise are discussed at 9.5.

9.4.3.b Fathers and second female parents: ss 34–40

Determining paternity is considerably more complicated than determining maternity. The following provisions on legal parenthood apply only where the condition set down in s 34 of the HFEA 2008 is satisfied: that the child 'is being or has been carried by a woman as a result of the placing in her of an embryo or of sperm and eggs or her artificial insemination'. 'Artificial insemination' includes both treatment at a clinic and 'DIY' arrangements (the so-called 'turkey baster' approach), but fertilization by means of natural sexual intercourse is explicitly excluded from the legislation and such scenarios always fall under the common law. Even when the HFEA scheme does apply, the rules are markedly different for couples who are in a formalized relationship compared to those who are not.

[122] DHSS (1984), para 6.8. [123] Ibid.

Fathers who are in a formalized relationship with the mother: s 35

The most straightforward scenario is where a heterosexual couple in a formalized relationship uses the man's own sperm: here, the common law will apply and, as the genetic father, he will be the legal father (as well as having the benefit of the presumption of paternity). Where it is clear that the husband is not the genetic father, s 35(1) provides that he will still be regarded as the child's legal father unless he did not consent to the treatment.[124]

Human Fertilisation and Embryology Act 2008, s 35

35 Woman married to or civil partner of a man at time of treatment

(1) If—

(a) at the time of the placing in her of the embryo or of the sperm and eggs or of her artificial insemination, W [the woman] was a party to a marriage with a man or a civil partnership with a man, and

(b) the creation of the embryo carried by her was not brought about with the sperm of the other party to the marriage or civil partnership,

then, subject to section 38(2) to (4) [the common law presumption of legitimacy], the other party to the marriage is to be treated as the father of the child unless it is shown that he did not consent to the placing in her of the embryo or the sperm and eggs or to her artificial insemination (as the case may be).

The onus to prove the absence of consent is on the mother's spouse. The law 'creates a rebuttable presumption that consent exists in cases of marriage or civil partnership. The presumption can be rebutted by evidence which shows that consent has *not* been given.'[125] However, *any* evidence will suffice: 'even weak evidence against consent having been given must prevail if there is no other evidence to counterbalance it'.[126]

Nevertheless, in determining whether the husband has given his consent, the question of what the husband must have consented to in order for legal parenthood to be conferred, has, under the identical provision in the previous legislation, been strictly construed. The issue was dealt with in the difficult case of *Leeds Teaching Hospital NHS Trust v A*. Two couples, Mr and Mrs A (a white couple) and Mr and Mrs B (a black couple), were receiving fertility treatment at the same clinic. Neither couple consented to treatment using donated gametes. By mistake, Mr B's sperm was used to fertilize Mrs A's eggs. The embryos were implanted in Mrs A, resulting in the birth of mixed-race twins. The mistake was immediately apparent and DNA tests confirmed Mr B was the twins' genetic father. Mr B applied for a declaration of parentage under s 55A of the FLA 1986. The legal position was relatively clear. Mrs A was the twins' mother and if Mr A could bring himself within the terms of s 28(2) (the precursor

[124] This rule is 'subject to' s 38(2), which provides that nothing in s 35 affects the presumption of legitimacy at common law. The purpose of this provision is set out in the Explanatory Notes, which envisage a scenario where the mother has already undergone treatment prior to entering a marriage or civil partnership. The new husband or civil partner would fall outside s 35 (they were not spouses *at the time of treatment*), but would still be the legal father under the presumption of legitimacy unless someone challenged his paternity.

[125] *Re the Human Fertilisation and Embryology Act 2008 (Case G)* [2016] EWHC 729, [26](ii).

[126] Ibid, [26](iii).

to s 35(1) of the HFEA 2008) he would be deemed the twins' legal father. If, however, he fell outside the scope of the HFEA 1990, the common law position would prevail and Mr B, as the twins' genetic father, would be regarded as the legal father. The application of s 28(2) turned on whether, given the mistake, Mr A could be said to have consented to his wife's treatment. Mr and Mrs A argued that a valid consent had been given.

Leeds Teaching Hospital NHS Trust v A and others [2003] EWHC 259

DAME ELIZABETH BUTLER-SLOSS P:

25. . . . Subsection (2) applies unless it is shown that Mr A 'did not consent to . . . her insemination'. It is obvious that s 28 is not relevant if the sperm given by Mr A was used since he is then the biological father and the twins are the legitimate children of Mr and Mrs A. The question is whether Mr A consented to the insemination of Mrs A by a third person (for the purposes of this argument, 'a donor').

26. . . . [Counsel] argued that Mr A gave a broad consent to the placing of an embryo sufficient to treat him as the father unless it could be shown that Mr A had not consented. He did not raise the issue nor seek to set aside the presumption.

27. The insurmountable problem, in my view, to that approach, is the question—to what did he consent? . . . The 'course of treatment' to which he consented was that outlined in Mrs A's consent form. . . . Mrs A consented to her eggs being used and mixed with her husband's sperm. She did not consent to her eggs being mixed with named or anonymous donated sperm. She consented to the placing of not more than two resulting embryos in her uterus.

28. Mr A certainly gave his consent to the placing in his wife of 'an embryo'. The embryo actually placed in Mrs A was a fundamentally different embryo from one that might have been created by the use of Mr A's sperm . . . The question whether the husband consented is a matter of fact which may be ascertained independently of the views of those involved in the process. On the clear evidence provided in the consent forms Mr A plainly did not consent to the sperm of a named or anonymous donor being mixed with his wife's eggs. This was clearly an embryo created without the consent of Mr and Mrs A.

[Butler-Sloss P refused to make a declaration of parentage in favour of Mr A and adjourned the application of Mr B. It was agreed by the parties that the twins should remain living with Mr and Mrs A.]

It is thus clear that if it is shown that the husband/civil partner did not consent to the particular treatment that is given, he cannot be regarded as the legal father under s 35.[127]

Assuming that absence of consent is not shown, s 35(1) prioritizes the intended social father over the genetic father. This again reflects the intentions of all the parties and will usually best serve the child's interests, the intended parents, and the donor. Section 35(1) is, however, far from revolutionary in negating the importance of the genetic tie. As we have seen, attaching children to their fathers through the fact of marriage to the mother is, in

[127] The court's rather unimaginative approach in the *Leeds Teaching Hospital* case stands in stark contrast to later cases on other aspects of the HFEA 2008. As we will see in relation to surrogacy, in particular, the courts have taken a far more creative approach to statutory interpretation, deploying s 3 of the HRA 1998 when a literal reading to the Act's wording would lead to the 'wrong' outcome. See 9.5.3.b.

effect, nothing more than what the common law has been doing for centuries through the presumption of legitimacy (albeit irrebuttable under s 35).

Unmarried fathers: ss 36–8

Where the man's own sperm is used in treatment, he will be the legal father of the child.[128] Where donor sperm is used, unmarried fathers are dealt with under ss 36–8. Although overshadowed by the more radical provisions on same-sex parents, s 36 remains in many ways a remarkable provision. It confers the status of legal parenthood on a man who is neither related to the child by blood or by marriage to the child's mother, provided the fatherhood conditions set down in s 36 are satisfied.

Human Fertilisation and Embryology Act 2008, ss 36–7

36 Treatment provided to woman where agreed fatherhood conditions apply

If no man is treated by virtue of section 35 [mother's husband or male civil partner] as the father of the child and no woman is treated by virtue of section 42 [mother's wife or female civil partner—see later] as a parent of the child but—

(a) the embryo or the sperm and eggs were placed in W [the woman], or W was artificially inseminated, in the course of treatment services provided in the United Kingdom by a person to whom a licence applies,

(b) at the time when the embryo or the sperm and eggs were placed in W, or W was artificially inseminated, the agreed fatherhood conditions (as set out in section 37) were satisfied in relation to a man, in relation to treatment provided to W under the licence,

(c) the man remained alive at that time, and

(d) the creation of the embryo carried by W was not brought about with the man's sperm,

then, subject to section 38(2) to (4) [presumption of legitimacy], the man is to be treated as the father of the child.

37 The agreed fatherhood conditions

(1) The agreed fatherhood conditions referred to in section 36(b) are met in relation to a man ("M") in relation to treatment provided to W under a licence if, but only if,—

(a) M has given the person responsible a notice stating that he consents to being treated as the father of any child resulting from treatment provided to W under the licence,

(b) W has given the person responsible a notice stating that she consents to M being so treated,

(c) neither M nor W has, since giving notice under paragraph (a) or (b), given the person responsible notice of the withdrawal of M's or W's consent to M being so treated,

[128] This applies even if he did not, in fact, consent to the embryo being implanted: *ARB v IVF Hammersmith* [2018] EWCA Civ 2803.

(d) W has not, since the giving of the notice under paragraph (b), given the person responsible—

(i) a further notice under that paragraph stating that she consents to another man being treated as the father of any resulting child, or

(ii) a notice under section 44(1)(b) stating that she consents to a woman being treated as a parent of any resulting child, and

(e) W and M are not within prohibited degrees of relationship in relation to each other.

(2) A notice under subsection 1(a), (b) or (c) must be in writing and must be signed by the person giving it.

Several conditions must be satisfied in order for s 36 to confer legal parenthood on the putative father.

(i) The putative father's sperm must not have been used (if it was, he does not need the HFEA 2008: common law rules make him the legal father).

(ii) The mother must have no husband or male civil partner who falls within the terms of s 35 and no wife or female civil partner who falls within the terms of s 42. Priority in determining legal parenthood therefore continues to be accorded to formal legal relationships, though a woman who is separated from her spouse or civil partner can still use s 36 as long as the spouse or civil partner did not consent to the treatment.

(iii) Treatment must have been provided by a licensed clinic *in the UK*. This means that unlike married couples or civil partners falling within the terms of s 35 or 42, an unmarried couple making a 'DIY' attempt at AID at home will not be able to rely on the determination of parenthood under s 36. If a couple does embark upon DIY treatment, the common law will apply and the donor, as the genetic father, will be regarded as the child's legal father. This requirement to attend at a licensed clinic allows the state, in the absence of a formalized relationship, to exercise greater control over access to treatment.

(iv) The agreed fatherhood conditions must be satisfied at the point at which the embryo or the sperm and eggs were placed in the mother or at which the mother was artificially inseminated.[129] The putative father must also have been alive at this point.

The agreed fatherhood conditions are set down in s 37, which establishes a straightforward process of notification: the mother and the putative father must both have notified the licensed provider in writing that they consent to the man being treated as the legal father of any resulting child. That notification can be withdrawn by either the mother or the putative father at any point up to the point of embryo transfer or insemination of the woman with the eggs and/or sperm. If consent is withdrawn by either party then legal fatherhood cannot be conferred on that man. The putative father is also prevented from being accorded legal fatherhood if, before the point of embryo transfer or insemination, the mother provides a further notice to the clinic, in writing, that she consents to another man or woman being treated as the legal father or second parent of the child. Provided this second man or woman

[129] HFEA 2008, s 36(b).

is able to satisfy the agreed fatherhood or agreed female parenthood conditions, then they will be deemed the legal parent.

Although s 37(1)(e) prevents legal parenthood from being conferred on a man and woman falling within the prohibited degrees of relationship, legal fatherhood is otherwise conferred on the putative father by a simple process of agreement. There is no requirement for the mother and father to be cohabiting or indeed involved in any kind of intimate relationship. It is perfectly possible for two friends to decide to parent a child together—subject to being able to satisfy the licensed provider that the arrangement gives rise to no welfare concerns under s 13(5).

Where these conditions are satisfied, the man will be treated for all legal purposes as the father of the child.[130]

Second female parents: ss 42–7

Sections 42–7 of the Act contain provisions on determining parenthood where a woman receives fertility treatment together with her female partner. The provisions for determining the legal status of the second female parent are identical to those for determining fatherhood but 'father' is replaced with 'second parent'.

Human Fertilisation and Embryology Act 2008, ss 42–4

42 Woman in civil partnership or marriage to a woman at time of treatment

(1) If at the time of the placing in her of the embryo or the sperm and eggs or of her artificial insemination, W [the woman] was a party to a civil partnership or a marriage with another woman, then subject to section 45(2) to (4) [presumption of legitimacy], the other party to the civil partnership or marriage is to be treated as a parent of the child unless it is shown that she did not consent to the placing in W of the embryo or the sperm and eggs or her artificial insemination (as the case may be). . . .

43 Treatment provided to woman who agrees that second woman to be parent

(1) If no man is treated by virtue of section 35 [woman husband or male civil partner] as the father of the child and no woman is treated by virtue of section 42 [woman's wife or female civil partner] as a parent of the child, but—

(a) the embryo or the sperm and eggs were placed in W, or W was artificially inseminated, in the course of treatment services provided in the United Kingdom by a person to whom a licence applies,

(b) at the time when the embryo or the sperm and eggs were placed in W, or W was artificially inseminated, the agreed female parenthood conditions (as set out in section 44) were met in relation to another woman, in relation to treatment provided to W under that licence, and

(c) the other woman remained alive at that time,

then, subject to section 45(2) to (4), the other woman is to be treated as a parent of the child.

[130] Ibid, s 48(1).

44 The agreed female parenthood conditions

(1) The agreed female parenthood conditions referred to in section 43(b) are met in relation to another woman ("P") in relation to treatment provided to W under a licence if, but only if,—

(a) P has given the person responsible a notice stating that P consents to P being treated as a parent of any child resulting from treatment provided to W under the licence,

(b) W has given the person responsible a notice stating that W agrees to P being so treated,

(c) neither W nor P has, since giving notice under paragraph (a) or (b), given the person responsible notice of the withdrawal of P's or W's consent to P being so treated,

(d) W has not, since the giving of the notice under paragraph (b), given the person responsible—

(i) a further notice under that paragraph stating that W consents to a woman other than P being treated as a parent of any resulting child, or

(ii) a notice under section 37(1)(b) stating that W consents to a man being treated as the father of any resulting child, and

(e) W and P are not within prohibited degrees of relationship in relation to each other.

(2) A notice under subsection (1)(a), (b) or (c) must be in writing and must be signed by the person giving it.

Where either s 42 or s 43 applies, the woman is treated as the second parent of the child for all legal purposes.[131] The Act further provides that where there is a second female parent, no man is treated as the child's father.[132] Thus, a child can be born into a family consisting of two female parents and no legal father.

Deceased fathers and female parents: ss 39–40 and 46

Under the HFEA 1990, Sch 3, para 8(1), it is clear that gametes cannot be preserved and stored, save in tightly defined circumstances, without the gamete provider's written consent.[133] It is, however, possible for a woman to use the frozen sperm or an embryo created using the gametes of her deceased husband/partner after his death, unless the consent stated otherwise.[134] Provided that the conditions in HFEA 2008, s 39 are met, the man's name may also then be entered 'as the particulars of the child's father in a relevant register of births',[135] though he is 'not [otherwise] to be treated as the father of the child' (such as for inheritance or obtaining a nationality from the man).[136]

Similar provisions for being named on the birth certificate apply to a partner who did not provide sperm (whether male or female) where an embryo is transferred into the mother after the partner's death, allowing the partner to be named as father or, as the case may be, second female parent on the birth certificate (though again, that person is not a parent for

131 Ibid, s 48(1). 132 Ibid, s 45(1).

133 See *R v HFEA, ex parte Blood* [1999] Fam 151 and *L v Human Fertilisation and Embryology Authority* [2008] EWHC 2149.

134 HFEA 1990, Sch 3, paras 2(2) and 2(2A). 135 HFEA 2008, s 39(3). 136 Ibid, s 41(2).

any other purpose).[137] Again, various criteria have to be met for these provisions to apply, including that the deceased person gave consent before their death to the use of the embryo after their death.[138]

Sperm and egg donors

Where either s 35, 36, 42, or 43 applies, no other person is to be treated as the father of the child.[139] In most cases, this will be sufficient to protect a sperm donor from legal parenthood. However, further protection is provided by s 41 which stipulates that provided a donor has given the requisite consent and his sperm was used in accordance with that consent, the man is not to be treated as the child's father. Where s 41 applies and there is no man who qualifies for legal fatherhood under s 35 or 36, the child will be legally fatherless. For the sake of completeness, s 47 similarly provides that an 'egg donor' is not to be treated as the parent of a child unless parenthood is conferred under s 42, 43, or 46 or the donor has adopted the child. This reiterates the position made clear in s 33 that the genetic mother is to have no claim to 'legal *motherhood*', which exclusively vests in the gestational mother.

9.4.3.c Reflections on the parenthood provisions in the HFEA 2008

At first sight, the HFEA 2008 is revolutionary. Having rejected the biological imperative that a child must have one legal father and one legal mother, the Act embraces a strong model of social parenthood unconstrained by genetics, gender, or heterosexuality. Thus an unmarried man or lesbian partner not tied to the child through blood or marriage (or civil partnership) can acquire legal parenthood by virtue of intention alone. A legally fatherless child with two female parents is therefore possible in English law, as is a child who has a legal mother but no other legal parent at all. This 'radical' departure from the traditional heterosexual foundations of family life was inevitably controversial. Critics argued that this attempt to deny the reality that a child must have two biological parents of different sexes betrays the needs of the child.

T. Callus, 'First "Designer Babies", Now À La Carte Parents', (2008) 38 *Family Law* 143, 143, 145, 146–7

[Current legislation] appears to suggest that parental status itself may be dependent upon the mere intention of the would-be (wannabe?) parent. This is not wholly unprecedented. We have recognised the importance of intention in the process of adoption and more recently in the use of donated gametes in assisted conception techniques. However, giving effect to

[137] Ibid, ss 40 and 46.

[138] While the Act appears to require written consent, in a related context the court has held that '[t]he reference to written consent is an evidential rule with the obvious benefits of certainty but it is not inviolable where the circumstances may require the Court to intervene': *Jennings v Human Fertilisation and Embryology Authority* [2022] EWHC 1619, [101]. In *Jennings*, a couple attended for fertility treatment together. The woman unexpectedly died, and her partner sought to use their remaining embryo to have a child by surrogacy. Although the woman has not signed the relevant form to authorize surrogacy pursuant to Sch 3 to the HFEA 1990, Theis J accepted that she had in fact consented to the use of her gametes in that way and allowed the surrogacy to proceed.

[139] HFEA 2008, s 48(1).

intention has been circumscribed within the heterosexual model, ideally of two parents to reflect the biological reality that a child is created by the fusion of male and female gametes. But the de-sexualisation of procreation through the use of assisted conception has resulted in a diversity of family forms and, in particular, the possibility of same-sex couples to 'parent' children. This has led to confusion between the parental role and parental status . . .

[The HFEA 2008] is remarkable because [it] grant[s] legal status to wider family forms based on the sole intention of the would-be parents who undergo treatment at a licensed clinic. Moreover, the proposals legally enshrine family models which deny the very basic fact that gametes of complementary sex are required to create the child. According to the Family Education Trust, they represent the 'lego-kit model of family construction' . . .

By recognising the status of two female parents, the child's identity is thrown into disarray because the recognition of two female parents conceals the necessary heterosexual element of human existence. Admittedly, even the present provisions on the use of donor gametes can lead to deception insofar as the parents may conceal their use of donated gametes, but the proposals double that deception.

[T]he [Act's] provisions are merely one example of a move towards recognising legal parental status on the basis of individual choice. Yet this choice may be transient and exercised in complete ignorance of the interest of the child.

Unquestionably, for some commentators the HFEA 2008 constitutes a step too far from the 'natural' biological imperatives of parenthood. However, others have criticized the Act, not for exploding the heterosexual parenting paradigm, but for its inherent conservatism. It is argued that the HFEA 2008 remains firmly wedded to a gendered, heterosexual model of parenthood that is binary, structured around the central and exclusive role of the legal 'mother', and precludes a more radical re-visioning of parenthood capable of embracing gay fatherhood, the fragmentation of motherhood and fatherhood into multiple biological and social components, and parenting outside the sexual norm.[140]

J. McCandless and S. Sheldon, 'The Human Fertilisation and Embryology Act (2008) and the Tenacity of the Sexual Family Form', (2010) 73 *Modern Law Review* 175, 188, 190–2, 193, 197

[T]he sexual family ideal has retained a significant hold . . . This can be seen in the ongoing significance of the formally recognised adult couple; law's continued adherence to a two-parent model; what we describe as 'parental dimorphism' (which, within the two-parent model, allows only for one mother plus one father or female parent); and the notion that the couple must be (at least potentially) in a sexual relationship . . .

In the context of widespread political and cultural disagreement regarding on what grounds parents should be recognised, acceptance of the fact that we can have two—and only two—'real' parents has proved a unifying article of faith. The two parent model retains a grip on

[140] See generally Diduck (2007); Lind and Hewitt (2009); McCandless and Sheldon (2010). Broader concerns about the consequences for minorities of adapting the heterosexual 'ideal' model of parenthood without a more fundamental reassessment of how that impacts on all kinds of modern families are set out by Bracken (2017). On the approach in Ontario, Canada, which has allowed up to four legal parents since 2016, see Leckey (2019).

the law which appears to have outlived any inevitable relationship between legal parenthood and either biological fact or marital convention . . . [T]his reform process saw no discussion of the question of whether if two parents are better than one, three parents might be better than (or, at least, as good as) two . . . [L]ack of further attention to this issue signals just how ingrained in our collective imagination is the notion that a child has only two parents, even in the context of assisted reproduction where more than two people may contribute biologically to the reproductive process . . .

[T]he sexual family model continues to resonate in a steadfast resistance to the possibility that a child can have two 'mothers' (or indeed two 'fathers'). The two parent model thus appears to encompass an assumption of what might be loosely termed 'parental dimorphism', by which we mean that the two parents are seen as occupying complementary yet different legal roles. This was seen . . . in the fact that a lesbian co-mother is not to be legally recognised as a 'mother' . . . but as a 'female parent' (a status awarded on grounds which closely parallel those by which men obtain fatherhood) . . .

It seems not to have been considered that the status provisions might be further adapted to allow two men to be recognised as parents from the moment of birth . . . [T]o recognise two gay men as parents under the status provisions would be a significant step further again, and one which simply stretches the current legal imagination too far, as it would involve moving beyond the idea that the birth mother is a legal mother (or, alternatively, recognising three parents from the moment of birth) . . .

Alison Diduck captures the essence of these concerns, concluding:

A. Diduck, '"If Only We Can Find the Appropriate Terms to Use the Issue Will Be Solved": Law, Identity and Parenthood', (2007) 19 *Child and Family Law Quarterly* 458, 466–7

It thus seems to me that the new legal status 'parent' does not overcome either the biological or 'proper' nuclear family privilege that attaches to the concept of legal parenthood which has underpinned the Human Fertilisation and Embryology Act 1990 since its inception. Like fatherhood under the Human Fertilisation and Embryology Act 1990, lesbian parenthood is acquired on a basis that mimics rather than overcomes traditional norms and biology. It applies a type of presumption of paternity to partnered lesbian women and instantiates rather than challenges hetero normativity and 'nature'. It both biologises and heterosexes 'parent' by ascribing that status on the basis of a person forming an exclusive sexual link with the biological parent . . . [W]e are left with a situation in which legal parenthood remains limited in number and subtly gendered.

The latest development in this area is the ability to create embryos using genetic material from more than two people. The reason for doing this is to prevent mitochondrial disease, which is a form of genetic disorder caused by unhealthy mitochondria (which are part of human cells, required to make them function properly, but comprising only about 0.1 per cent of our total DNA).[141] There are many forms of mitochondrial disease, some entirely

[141] DH (2014), 8.

asymptomatic and others fatal. The mitochondria form part of the egg itself, but separate from the so-called 'maternal spindle' which contains the woman's main DNA material. It is possible to remove the chromosomes from one woman's egg and implant them in another woman's egg, such that the unhealthy mitochondria are left behind but virtually all the DNA comes from the original egg. Since February 2015, this has been permitted in the UK where medically justified.[142]

9.4.4 THE CHILD'S RIGHT TO KNOW THEIR GENETIC PARENTAGE

Assisted reproduction presents a direct challenge to the common law's preference for genetics. A policy choice had to be made and the legislation favours social over genetic parenthood. Whilst this may be welcomed as affording greater recognition to the importance of social parenthood, it leaves open the question of what, if any, role genetic parents play in the child's future. The preference for social parenthood in the legislation is arguably at variance with moves elsewhere in English law to recognize the right of children to know the truth about their genetic parentage.[143] In recent years, the government has therefore faced increasing pressure to protect this right of children conceived using donated gametes.

9.4.4.a Why is the right to know important?

The importance of knowing the truth about one's genetic background is described in moving terms by Joanna Rose, an AID child, as quoted by the court in *R (Rose)*.

R (Rose) v Secretary of State for Health [2002] EWHC 1593

SCOTT BAKER J:

7. . . . Ms Rose describes the importance of the information to her in the following terms:

'I feel that these genetic connections are very important to me, socially, emotionally, medically, and even spiritually. I believe it to be no exaggeration that non-identifying information [information about the genetic parents that cannot lead to their identity becoming known] will assist me in forming a fuller sense of self identity and answer questions that I have been asking for a long time. I am angry that it has been assumed that this would not be the case, and can see no responsible logic for this (given the usual pre-eminence accorded to the rights and welfare of the child), unless it is believed that if we are created artificially we will not have the natural need to know to whom we are related. I feel intense grief and loss, for the fact that I do not know my genetic father and his family . . .

I need to find out more about my medical, genealogical and social heritage. Other people who come from families, where they have known both of their natural parents are able to discover this through the process of time. This includes

[142] Human Fertilisation and Embryology (Mitochondrial Donation) Regulations 2015, SI 2015/572.

[143] E.g. *Re H (A Minor) (Blood Tests: Parental Rights)* [1997] Fam 89, discussed at 9.3.3.b.

information about their background and religion, where certain of their talents and skills may come from (eg parents or relations with musical or artistic skills), why they look the way they do etc. I have a strong need to discover what most people take for granted. While I was conceived to heal the pain of others (ie my parents' inability to conceive children naturally), I do not feel that there are sufficient attempts to heal my pain.'

There is a growing body of research, largely conducted in the field of adoption, providing strong support for the argument that knowledge of one's genetic background is crucial to the development of a secure sense of identity and sense of self. As Michael Freeman explains, 'identity as what we know and what we feel is an organizing framework for holding together our past and our present and it provides some anticipated shape to future life'.[144] Denying children the truth about their genetic parentage can lead to a sense of 'genealogical bewilderment'.[145] O'Donovan highlights just some of the problems that can result.

K. O'Donovan, 'Interpretations of Children's Identity Rights', in D. Fottrell (ed), *Revisiting Children's Rights* (The Hague; Boston: Kluwer Law International, 2000), 75

Effects of identity confusion have been documented as long term. Low self-esteem, loss of trust in others, inability to form intimate relationships, depression, anxiety, lack of parenting skills, have all been noted. Security about identity is the basis for self-confidence.

There is, however, an important distinction between the need for knowledge about one's genetic background and establishing a social relationship with the genetic parents. As Fortin observes, research in the field of adoption suggests that whilst adopted children may experience a strong need for the former, this is not necessarily accompanied by any desire for the latter.[146] Recognition of the right of children to know the truth about their genetic background does not therefore involve any necessary revision of the *legal status* or *social role* of the genetic parent.[147]

There is not, however, complete consensus surrounding the child's right to know. The analogy often drawn with adoption has been questioned, with commentators suggesting that the secrecy surrounding AID may not be as damaging as that surrounding adoption given the very different circumstances in which they operate. In these circumstances, it is suggested that revealing the truth about genetic parentage may not be in the child's best interests, certainly as perceived by the parents.[148]

144 Freeman (1996), 290. 145 Van Bueren (1998), 123; Fortin (2009b), 469.
146 Fortin (2009b), 467.
147 This is the same point made in *Re H (A Minor) (Blood Tests: Parental Rights)* [1997] Fam 89, discussed at 9.3.3.b.
148 Turkmendag, Dingwall, and Murphy (2008), 302.

I. Turkmendag, R. Dingwall, and T. Murphy, 'The Removal of Donor Anonymity in the UK: The Silencing of Claims by Would-Be Parents', (2008) 22 *International Journal of Law, Policy and the Family* 283, 289

Adoption is a family-building activity that involves pre-existing individuals, whereas donor conception is directed towards creating a child in order to create a family. In other words, adoption is a *substitute* for procreation whereas donor conception is a *form* of procreation: the act has its own integrity and completeness—it is the would-be parent(s)' act and the child is unquestionably their child . . . In this act, social links are established between the procreator and the child, not with the donor.

Unlike an adopted child, a donor-conceived child usually has a biological connection with one of their social parents as a result of pregnancy and birth. In (traditional) adoption, both parents are biologically unrelated to the child. The donor conceived child usually has access to full genetic information about one of his/her biological parents. In addition, the donor's medical history is available for the resultant child on the HFEA registers. Adopted children are usually deprived of such information unless it is provided on their birth registers.

In gamete donation, it is easy for the parents to hide the method of their child's conception whereas 'adoption can only be the worst-kept "secret" around' . . . Despite the difference between adoption and donor conception, much of the evidence on the harm caused by secrecy and the importance for a child to know her/his origins is drawn from the literature on adoption. If the child knows that he/she was adopted, the feeling of relinquishment and the desire to seek reasons for being 'given up' may well cause emotional distress. By contrast, donor offspring were desired by their parents, parents have often contributed gametes, and their birth stories do not involve relinquishment. It is then questionable whether donor offspring's interest in knowing their origins is identical to that of adopted children and whether the research findings on the latter can simply be read across.

There has also been some criticism of the importance these arguments place on the role of genetics in determining 'who we are' and 'what we become'. The nature versus nurture argument has long polarized scholars. Some argue that the current emphasis on genealogical background is simply crude genetic determinism. It is also suggested that the desperate need expressed by some to know the truth about their genetic background is socially constructed. In other words, it is the emphasis placed by society on the importance of genetics that creates the strongly held need to know the truth.[149] Changing social attitudes may therefore be a more effective solution than further entrenching these attitudes by enshrining the right to know in legislation. Melanie Roberts disagrees.

M. Roberts, 'Children by Donation: Do They Have a Claim to their Genetic Parentage?', in J. Bridgeman and D. Monk (eds), *Feminist Perspectives on Child Law* (London: Cavendish, 2000), 47, 63

As the importance which society places on the genetic tie is socially constructed, it could be argued that information about the donor's identity should not be provided, as this reinforces the importance of the genetic link. However, denying children information about genitors is

[149] Ibid, 291.

not the way in which to diminish the importance placed on the genetic tie and to raise the importance of the social family. Concepts of anonymity and secrecy reinforce the importance of the blood tie. These concepts fuel the notion that the genetic family is the 'norm' and any other family formation is 'unnatural' and must be hidden. Recognition of, and respect for, the different ways in which families can be formed is needed, and the way to achieve this is to be honest and open about the formation and structure of families.

Furthermore, as O'Donovan points out, telling AID or adopted children that their perceived need for knowledge about their genetic origins is socially constructed does nothing to lessen the very real pain and profound sense of loss and bewilderment they are currently suffering.[150]

9.4.4.b The right to know in the HFEA 1990

Background to the HFEA 1990

Originally, the HFEA 1990 guaranteed complete secrecy concerning the conception of a child using donated gametes. The complex reasons behind this approach have been strongly criticized by Roberts. She suggests that the medical underpinnings of assisted reproduction have led to the privileging of the prospective parents' interests (the patients being treated) at the expense of the child.

M. Roberts, 'Children by Donation: Do They Have a Claim to their Genetic Parentage?', in J. Bridgeman and D. Monk (eds), *Feminist Perspectives on Child Law* (London: Cavendish, 2000), 47, 49, 53–4

Donation is surrounded with secrecy. When artificial insemination by donor was first introduced, it was assumed that secrecy was the best stance to take and was taken for granted. Secrecy stems from fear: fear that the child will reject the social parent in favour of the genitor; fear that the genitor will interfere; and fear of societal disapproval. As use of donor sperm far outweighs the use of donor ova, it is the infertile man in particular who is protected by a policy of secrecy. There is some evidence that there may be particular problems in relation to openness and male infertility. Western culture attaches much significance to the association between fertility and power. Male infertility is thus seen as a source of shame and weakness, with feelings of masculinity being damaged by the discovery of infertility. The myth that fertility and virility are related and the attitudes of others means that couples often wish to keep the problem of infertility and the means of conception secret. A quest for 'normality' can result in secrecy and dishonesty. For men, parenthood means genetic parenthood. Secrecy stems from patriarchal concern to protect male pride in hiding male infertility and what is considered a failure: the inability to pass on one's genetic heritage.

However, the secretive approach that marked the initial years of the HFEA 1990 was not inevitable given the somewhat mixed and inconsistent messages from the Warnock Committee. On the one hand, the Committee expressed great concern about the secrecy surrounding

[150] Cited in Van Bueren (1998), 123.

AID children, with a worry that secrets 'may undermine the whole network of family relationships'; but the Committee unequivocally endorsed preserving the 'absolute anonymity of the donor'. The rationale was to 'give legal protection to the donor' and protect the integrity of the family unit by 'minimizing the invasion of the third party into the family'.[151]

The legal framework in the HFEA 1990

Although donor anonymity was initially firmly entrenched in the HFEA 1990 as originally enacted, that anonymity was removed in 2004 (although not retrospectively) and greater openness further extended by the HFEA 2008. Now, the legal framework governing the collection, storage, and disclosure of information relating to the conception of a child is found in ss 31–5 of the 1990 Act, as amended. Sections 31–31ZE are the core provisions on information to be provided to the child and donor. Under s 31(1)–(2), the HFEA is required to keep a register of any identifiable individual who has received treatment services using donated gametes, details of any individual whose gametes have been kept or used in the provision of treatment services, and details of any identifiable individual who was, or may have been, born as a result of treatment services using donated gametes. Under s 31ZA, a donor-conceived child has the right, upon reaching the age of 16, to have access to non-identifying information about their genetic parentage and/or any genetically related siblings (specifically the number of such siblings, the sex of each, and the year of birth). Upon reaching the age of 18, the child has the right to access identifying information about the donor. Since the new right is not retrospective, children born by AID before 1 April 2005 are restricted to receiving non-identifying information. The exact information to be provided to the child is specified in regulations. Under s 31ZD, a donor-conceived child may obtain identifying information about any donor-conceived genetic siblings who have also attained the age of 18 and who have agreed to identifying information being released to a genetically related sibling requesting such information. Finally, the child has the right, upon reaching the age of 16, to know (with the specified person's consent) whether they may be related to a specified person with whom they intend to: (i) enter into a marriage; (ii) enter into a civil partnership; or (iii) engage in an intimate physical relationship.[152] Before any of this information is disclosed, the donor-conceived child and any other affected person (genetic sibling and 'specified person') must have been given the opportunity to receive proper counselling about the implications of the disclosure.[153]

One innovation of the 2008 reforms was the introduction of the right of donors to access non-identifying information about any children (specifically the number of children, the children's sex, and the year of the children's birth) conceived through the use of their donated gametes.[154] The donor may also be notified when a donor-conceived child has made a request for information about the donor. The donor will not, however, be informed about the child's identity.[155] The HFEA is also authorized to establish a voluntary contact register which may assist children, donors, and genetic siblings to make contact with one another where all relevant parties consent but there is no right to identifying information under the legislation.[156]

Despite the child's right to know now being entrenched in the legislation, children conceived using donated gametes may still face several obstacles in acquiring information about

151 DHSS (1984), para 4.22. 152 HFEA 1990, s 31ZB.
153 Ibid, ss 31ZA(3)(b), 31ZB(3)(c), 31ZE(3)(c). 154 Ibid, s 31ZD.
155 Ibid, s 31ZC. 156 Ibid, s 31ZF.

their genetic background. The first and most difficult to overcome through legal change alone is that many parents who conceive using donated gametes may still prefer to conceal the facts about the child's conception.[157] With no legal obligation on the parent (or the state) to tell children about their conception, some will remain ignorant about their genetic background—though research is clear that openness at an early age is usually a better approach.

S. Golombok, *We Are Family: What Really Matters for Parents and Children* (London: Scribe Publications, 2020), 261–2, 263–4

> Research on families formed through adoption shows that parents who are open with their children, who acknowledge the differences between their family and other families, but don't over-emphasise them, and who convey this information in ways that are appropriate for their [children's] age, are more likely to have children who are accepting of how they came to be. Our own studies of families formed by assisted reproduction have led to the same conclusions. Not one set of parents [in our studies] who told their children about their origins at an early stage regretted their decision to tell.

Moreover, deciding to try to keep the child's origins secret is a risky strategy, as Golombok explains.

> [T]oday, people can find out that they have been conceived using donor eggs, sperm or embryos through genetic testing kits in combination with online genealogy databases . . . All it can take is a saliva sample for someone to discover over the internet whether they are the genetic child of their parents, and if not, who their genetic relatives are. Donor-conceived people, some of whom were unaware of their origins, are finding themselves matched with their donor and donor-siblings, and inadvertently discovering that their mother, their father, or both parents, are genetically unrelated to them. Sometimes children figure it out for themselves, from genetics lessons at school. Parents who are not open with their children about their genetic origins from the start, run the risk of their children discovering this information for themselves. We have reached an age when secrecy about donor conception cannot be guaranteed . . .

There remains no legal requirement for donor-conceived children to be told of their genetic origins, an approach about which the Joint Parliamentary Committee scrutinizing the draft Human Tissue and Embryos Bill expressed deep concern, commenting that the authorities 'may be colluding in a deception'.[158] In response, whilst acknowledging the importance of donor-conceived children having access to information about their genetic background, the government argued that it is 'preferable that parents are educated about the benefits of telling children that they were donor-conceived rather than forcing the issue through the annotation of birth certificates'.[159] Although the government agreed to keep the issue under review,[160] there is no indication that the law will be reconsidered any time soon. While there

[157] Turkmendag, Dingwall, and Murphy (2008), 298.
[158] DH (2007), 19, Recommendation 28. [159] Ibid, para 69. [160] Ibid, para 70.

are differences of opinion on this issue, some argue that the law perpetuates a 'deception' and undermines the child's right to know their genetic origins.

A. Bainham, 'What is the Point of Birth Registration?', (2008) 20 *Child and Family Law Quarterly* 449, 463–4

> Our concern here . . . is with the process of birth registration in cases where donation has taken place. Here the position stands in stark contrast to the position which we saw in relation to adoption. In the case of donor-conceived children there is only *one* birth certificate. This records as the legal parents the birth mother and her husband or, where the mother is unmarried, her partner who joins in the registration with her . . . At the point of registration, the registration officer will be completely unaware of the fact that donation has taken place . . . [T]he baby will be registered as the presumptive biological child of both parties (except in the case of same-sex partners where it will be clear that one cannot be), as is the case with the registration of births which do not involve donation. The birth certificate which is issued will record the legal, and apparently biological, parents of the child. The concern that legal parentage should correspond with biological parentage, which as we have seen is a central feature of birth registration, is absent here except to the extent that the Registration Service has no reason of course to believe or suspect that it is doing anything other than registering two biological parents.
>
> In common with adopted children (who have no legal right to be told that they are adopted), donor conceived persons have no legal right to be told that they are donor conceived. But because of the way the registration system works, this is a far more serious matter for the latter than it is for the former. There is no attempt in the context of donation to maintain a clear distinction between genetic and social parents even though many of those registering the birth will be clear that this distinction in fact exists . . . While it is true that from April 2005 donors have lost their right to anonymity and the child will be able to access identifying information about them at 18, unless there is a revolution in current practice, the great majority will never discover that they are donor-conceived and hence will effectively be unable to exercise these rights to knowledge about biological origins.

A second potential difficulty lies in the consistency of information provided by donors. Since 1991, the HFEA has collected personal information about donors such as name at time of donation, name at time of birth, place of birth, sex, and whether the donor has children. It has also recorded donors' physical characteristics such as height, weight, ethnic group, eye colour, hair colour, and skin colour. Information about donors' religion, occupation, and interests was optional, as was the provision of a pen portrait. Clinics are advised to encourage donors to record as much non-identifying information about themselves as they are happy to provide but studies suggest the information provided was sparse.[161] Following reforms removing donor anonymity, applicable to children conceived after 2004, regulations make the provision of information about the donor's religion, occupation, interests, skills, and reasons for donating compulsory, but provision of a pen portrait remains optional.[162] The available information therefore remains limited in scope.

[161] Roberts (2000), 52.

[162] Human Fertilisation and Embryology Authority (Disclosure of Donor Information) Regulations 2004, SI 2004/1511, reg 2(2)(f)–(h).

The downside of reform

One of the strongest arguments against removing anonymity was the perceived risk that it would cause a drop in donors. Evidence from Sweden, where donor anonymity was removed in 1985, suggested that such fears may be unfounded: whilst numbers declined immediately following the change in the law, over time they recovered to their former level.[163] Unfortunately, the emerging picture in the UK following the removal of anonymity is not encouraging. Whereas most sperm used to be sourced from British donors, thousands of sperm samples are now imported, primarily from the USA and Denmark.[164] Many couples are having to wait months for treatment or are even being denied treatment altogether. This has led some commentators to observe that the 'frustration, despair and anxiety' of those seeking treatment has been ignored in a misplaced, and ultimately vain, attempt to promote greater openness.[165]

9.5 SURROGACY

Surrogacy is an arrangement whereby the woman who carries the child through pregnancy does so on behalf of the child's intended parents, and does not intend to become the child's parent. So-called 'traditional' surrogacy involves using the surrogate's own egg; more common now is what is termed 'full' surrogacy, where either the egg of the intended mother or a donor egg is used, such that the surrogate has no genetic connection to the child.

Surrogacy is a difficult area on which to legislate, and Lady Hale has commented that 'UK surrogacy law is fragmented and in some ways obscure'.[166] The policy arguments are also complex, particularly since surrogacy arrangements take place both domestically and internationally. On the one hand, the practice is now well established,[167] and is increasingly seen as a legitimate way of 'building families', as the Law Commissions' 2023 final report termed it;[168] surrogacy is used both by couples and single women who experience infertility, and by same-sex male couples and single men who cannot carry a child for reasons of gender.[169] However, against these perspectives, others consider surrogacy to be of dubious moral and ethical standing,[170] and therefore resist allowing it to be seen as a fully accepted alternative way of having children. Parliament has taken the middle ground, restricting some aspects of surrogacy while also facilitating the legal transfer of parental status to intended parents when certain criteria are met. The current law on surrogacy is found in the Surrogacy Arrangements Act 1985 (SAA 1985) and the HFEA 2008, ss 54–5. However, it is important to understand some of the background and policy debates before we turn to the current law.

[163] Roberts (2000), 57.

[164] DHSC (2018). See also Turkmendag, Dingwall, and Murphy (2008), 284 and 296–7.

[165] Ibid, 304–5.

[166] *Whittington Hospital NHS Trust v XX* [2020] UKSC 14, [9].

[167] The number of parental orders rose from 117 in 2011 and over 400 each year in 2019 and 2020: Horsey (2021). However, this says nothing about how many informal arrangements exist where no parental order is sought. E.g. no parental order had been sought in *Re Z (Surrogacy)* [2022] EWFC 18 until the fact of the surrogacy was discovered during unrelated care proceedings.

[168] Law Commissions (2023). See 9.5.5.

[169] Ibid, para 1.7. On the importance of surrogacy for gay men in particular, see Marsh (2022a).

[170] E.g. the UN Special Rapporteur on the sale and sexual exploitation of children said in 2018 that surrogacy arrangements, particularly international and commercial ones, can amount to the sale of children and/or to child trafficking: United Nations (2018).

9.5.1 EARLY ATTITUDES TO SURROGACY

The Warnock Committee found surrogacy particularly difficult and were divided over the correct approach. Having rehearsed the main arguments, the majority of the Committee was swayed by the arguments against surrogacy, particularly in a commercialized form, and strongly opposed introducing any measures that appeared to sanction or encourage the practice.

DHSS, *Report of the Committee of Inquiry into Human Fertilisation and Embryology*, Cm 9314 (London: HMSO, 1984)

8.10 The objections turn essentially on the view that to introduce a third party into the process of procreation which should be confined to the loving partnership between two people, is an attack on the value of the marital relationship . . . Further, the intrusion is worse than in the case of AID, since the contribution of the carrying mother is greater, more intimate and personal than the contribution of a semen donor. It is also argued that it is inconsistent with human dignity that a woman should use her uterus for financial profit and treat it as an incubator for someone else's child. The objection is not diminished, indeed it is strengthened, where the woman entered an agreement to conceive a child, with the sole purpose of handing the child over to the commissioning couple after birth.

8.11 Again, it is argued that the relationship between mother and child is itself distorted by surrogacy. For in such an arrangement a woman deliberately allows herself to become pregnant with the intention of giving up the child to which she will give birth and this is the wrong way to approach pregnancy. It is also potentially damaging to the child, whose bonds with the carrying mother, regardless of genetic connections, are held to be strong, and whose welfare must be considered to be of paramount importance. Further it is felt that a surrogacy agreement is degrading to the child who is to be the outcome of it, since for all practical purposes, the child will have been bought for money.

8.12 It is also argued that since there are some risks attached to pregnancy, no woman ought to be asked to undertake pregnancy for another, in order to earn money. Nor, it is argued should a woman be forced by legal sanctions to part with a child, to which she has recently given birth, against her will.

8.13 If infertility is a condition which should, where possible, be remedied, it is argued that surrogacy must not be ruled out, since it offers to some couples their only chance of having a child genetically related to one or both of them. In particular, it may well be the only way that the husband of an infertile woman can have a child. Moreover, the bearing of a child for another can be seen, not as an undertaking that trivialises or commercialises pregnancy, but, on the contrary, as a deliberate and thoughtful act of generosity on the part of one woman to another. If there are risks attached to pregnancy, then the generosity is all the greater.

8.14 There is no reason, it is argued, to suppose that carrying mothers will enter into agreements lightly, and they have a perfect right to enter into such agreement if they so wish, just as they have a right to use their own bodies in other ways, according to their own decision. Where agreements are genuinely voluntary, there can be no question of exploitation, nor does the fact that surrogates will be paid for their pregnancy of itself entail exploitation of either party to the agreement.

8.17 . . . In the first place we are all agreed that surrogacy for convenience alone, that is, where a woman is physically capable of bearing a child but does not wish to undergo pregnancy, is totally ethically unacceptable. Even in compelling medical circumstances the

> danger of exploitation of one human being by another appears to the majority of us far to outweigh the potential benefits in almost every case. That people should treat others as a means to their own ends, however desirable the consequences, must always be liable to moral objection. Such treatment of one person by another becomes positively exploitative when financial interests are involved. It is therefore with the commercial exploitation of surrogacy that we have been primarily, but by no means exclusively, concerned.

The majority thus recommended that any agency, profit- or non-profit-making, creating and supporting surrogacy agreements should be subject to criminal sanctions.[171] They also recommended that professionals knowingly assisting in establishing a surrogacy should be made criminally liable.[172] The Committee held back from recommending that the intended parents and the surrogate mother should be liable to criminal prosecution, concerned that children should not be 'born to mothers subject to the taint of criminality'.[173] They did, however, recommend that all surrogacy agreements be designated illegal contracts, unenforceable in the courts.

The minority was less hostile, accepting that there may be rare circumstances where surrogacy could be beneficial to couples as a very last resort.[174] They therefore felt that the door to surrogacy should 'be left slightly ajar'[175] and that medical practitioners should be able to recommend such a course to their patients without acting unlawfully. Whilst agreeing that surrogacy for mere convenience was totally unacceptable and that commercial agencies should be subject to criminal prohibitions, they argued in favour of bringing surrogacy within the remit of the regulatory authority and allowing the licensing of non-profit-making agencies to provide proper advice and support to those for whom surrogacy was deemed appropriate.[176] They also recommended that in order to regularize the legal relationship between the child and the intended parents some form of adoption procedure should be made available.[177] Given their view that surrogacy should not stand outside the law, they also disagreed with the majority's recommendation that all surrogacy arrangements should be unenforceable, arguing that each case should be dealt with on its own facts.[178]

9.5.2 SURROGACY ARRANGEMENTS ACT 1985

The SAA 1985 targets the commercial aspects of surrogacy. Surrogacy agreements are made unenforceable but neither the intended parents nor the surrogate commit a criminal offence by entering into such an arrangement. However, those who engage in surrogacy for financial gain are liable to criminal prosecution. The scope of the legislation is broad, covering, for example, the distributor of a newspaper that the distributor knows contains an advertisement relating to the making of surrogacy agreements.

The key provisions of the SAA 1985 can be summarized as follows. First, it makes surrogacy arrangements unenforceable by or against any party to those agreements.[179] Secondly, the Act makes it a criminal offence to initiate or take part in (or even to offer to take part in) negotiations about a commercial surrogacy arrangement,[180] though because the aim is

[171] DHSS (1984), para 8.18. [172] Ibid. [173] Ibid, para 8.19.
[174] Ibid, Expression of dissent, para 1. [175] Ibid, para 9. [176] Ibid, paras 3–5.
[177] Ibid, para 7. [178] Ibid, para 8. [179] SAA 1985, s 1A. [180] Ibid, s 2(1).

to prevent commercial enterprises from engaging in surrogacy arrangements, women who might be potential surrogates and individuals who might be intended parents are exempted from criminal sanction.[181] Non-profit organizations are also exempted, so long as any payments received by it are a reasonable reflection of its costs.[182] The SAA 1985 also criminalizes the advertising of surrogacy services in certain circumstances.[183]

The exclusion of non-profit organizations from the remit of the criminal sanctions has allowed such agencies to facilitate surrogacy arrangements and support and advise infertile couples seeking to enter into such arrangements. Agencies that make arrangements for surrogacies on a non-profit basis, whilst operating within the law, are unregulated as they fall outside the regulatory framework of the HFEA. If, however, the parties to a surrogacy agreement seek treatment from a licensed clinic, the clinic is subject to the HFEA's Code of Practice.[184]

9.5.3 DETERMINING PARENTAGE IN SURROGACY ARRANGEMENTS: THE HFEA 2008

The SAA 1985, apart from making surrogacy agreements unenforceable, does not deal with the legal consequences of such agreements, in particular as regards the parental status of the intended parents and their legal relationship with the child. These aspects of surrogacy are dealt with in the HFEA 2008, which seeks to strike a balance between protecting the surrogate whilst protecting the legal position of the intended parents and the child where all parties are happy to honour the original agreement.

9.5.3.a The child's legal parents

The surrogate is given strong protection by the HFEA 2008. Section 33 provides that having given birth to the child, the surrogate and on other woman, will be regarded as the child's legal mother, even if the intended mother is the genetic mother. The position of the intended father is more complicated. If the surrogate is unmarried and the intended father is the genetic father, he will be able to rely on the common law principle that the genetic parent is accorded legal parenthood. If, however, the surrogate is in a formalized relationship, the intended father will have to rebut the common law presumption that the surrogate's husband is the child's legal father. Similarly, if assisted reproduction techniques are used to bring about the pregnancy, even if the intended father's sperm is used in the treatment, the surrogate's husband will be deemed the legal father under s 35 unless it can be shown that he did not consent. Finally, if the surrogate is unmarried and donor sperm is used, the intended father may fall within the terms of s 36, provided he can satisfy the agreed fatherhood conditions under s 37. The weakest party is the intended mother who, whether under the common law or under s 33, will be regarded as a complete legal stranger to the child.

9.5.3.b Parental orders

Sections 54 and 54A of the HFEA 2008 provide the only means by which the intended parents can secure their status as legal parents with respect to the child without resorting to complicated and lengthy adoption proceedings. Under these provisions, the court can make a 'parental order'

[181] Ibid, s 2(2). [182] Ibid, s 2A. [183] Ibid, s 3. [184] HFEA (2021a), part 14.

in favour of the intended parents, with s 54 applying to applications by couples and s 54A applying to sole-applicant cases. A 'parental order' has the same legal effect as an adoption order, conferring legal parenthood on the intended parents and extinguishing the legal parenthood of the surrogate (and her husband, if applicable).[185] The making of a parental order is subject to a number of conditions which, for an application by a couple, are set out in s 54:

Human Fertilisation and Embryology Act 2008, s 54

54 Parental orders

(1) On an application made by two people ("the applicants"), the court may make an order providing for a child to be treated in law as the child of the applicants if—
   (a) the child has been carried by a woman who is not one of the applicants, as a result of the placing in her of an embryo or sperm and eggs or her artificial insemination,
   (b) the gametes of at least one of the applicants were used to bring about the creation of the embryo, and
   (c) the conditions in subsections (2) to (8) are satisfied.

(2) The applicants must be—
   (a) husband and wife,[186]
   (b) civil partners of each other, or
   (c) two persons who are living as partners in an enduring family relationship and are not within prohibited degrees of relationship in relation to each other.

(3) Except in a case falling within subsection (11), the applicants must apply for the order during the period of 6 months beginning with the day on which the child is born.

(4) At the time of the application and the making of the order—
   (a) the child's home must be with the applicants, and
   (b) either or both of the applicants must be domiciled in the United Kingdom or in the Channel Islands or the Isle of Man.

(5) At the time of the making of the order both the applicants must have attained the age of 18.

(6) The court must be satisfied that both—
   (a) the woman who carried the child, and
   (b) any other person who is a parent of the child but is not one of the applicants (including any man who is the father by virtue of section 35 or 36 or any woman who is a parent by virtue of section 42 or 43), have freely, and with full understanding of what is involved, agreed unconditionally to the making of the order.

(7) Subsection (6) does not require the agreement of a person who cannot be found or is incapable of giving agreement; and the agreement of the woman who carried the child is ineffective for the purpose of that subsection if given by her less than six weeks after the child's birth.

[185] HFEA 2008, s 55(1).

[186] Unlike other references to husband and wife in primary legislation, s 54(2)(a) was not amended by the Marriage (Same Sex Couples) Act 2013, but 'it should be read down to include a same-sex marriage': *Re W and X (Surrogacy)* [2022] EWFC 120, [26].

(8) The court must be satisfied that no money or other benefit (other than for expenses reasonably incurred) has been given or received by either of the applicants for or in consideration of—

(a) the making of the order,

(b) any agreement required by subsection (6),

(c) the handing over of the child to the applicants, or

(d) the making of arrangements with a view to the making of the order,

unless authorised by the court.

Assuming that these conditions are satisfied, the decision that the court must take is a welfare decision. Since 2010, this welfare determination has been informed by the same list of welfare considerations as exists in the adoption context.[187]

The s 54/s 54A conditions

Under the 1990 Act, a parental order could be made only in favour of a married couple. The 2008 Act extended the category of eligible persons. Initially, only *couples* who were married, civil partners, or 'two persons who are living as partners in an enduring family relationship' could apply under the 2008 legislation. However, following a successful HRA 1998 challenge from a single man who sought a parental order,[188] this rule was amended and s 54A added to the 2008 Act. The legislation is materially identical to s 54, but allows single applicants to seek a parental order (there is no equivalent of s 54(2) in terms of any relationship requirements for the applicant[189]).

The remaining conditions for making a parental order were reproduced from the 1990 legislation. The requirement that the surrogate must have been impregnated by artificial means (s 54(1)(a)) is probably aimed at discouraging the 'adultery' involved in basic 'DIY' surrogacy. Section 54(1)(b) requires that the gametes of at least one of the intended parents were used in creating the embryo; this is likely a safeguard against child trafficking, and against private fostering or adoption arrangements happening under the guise of surrogacy outside the regulatory framework for adoption (both domestic and international).[190]

Sections 54(4)(a) and 54(6) afford strong protection to the surrogate. The requirement that the child must be living with the intended parents at the time of the application means that the surrogate must have physically handed the child to the intended parents, though this

[187] The Human Fertilisation and Embryology (Parental Orders) Regulations 2010, SI 2010/985, import a modified version of s 1 of the ACA 2002 into s 54: the checklist in its adoption form is set out at 13.4.1. Consequently, the balance to be struck between public policy and the child's welfare, as discussed in some of the pre-2010 cases, is now weighted 'decisively in favour of welfare': *Re L (Surrogacy: Parental Order)* [2010] EWHC 3146, [10].

[188] *Re Z (A Child: Human Fertilisation and Embryology Act: Parental Order)* [2015] EWFC 73.

[189] An early draft of s 54A would have made it a requirement that the applicant *not* be in an enduring family relationship at the time of the order, but that proposed restriction was dropped on the recommendation of the Joint Committee on Human Rights.

[190] For discussion of the requirement for a genetic link in surrogacy cases, see Bracken (2020) and Tesfaye (2022).

could be achieved by court order if she refused to do so. However, the consent requirement in s 54(6) is absolute; unlike adoption cases, the court has no discretion to override the consent requirements: it is 'an absolute veto'.[191] The surrogate (and any other legal parent who is not one of the applicants) must therefore freely consent to the order being made.[192] Any consent given within six weeks of the birth, when the surrogate is deemed physically and emotionally vulnerable, is invalid.[193] The intended parents cannot therefore use s 54 where the surrogate reneges on the agreement and wishes to keep the child. Where consent is not obtained, a parental order cannot be made, and the only way that the intended parents can become the child's legal parents is to pursue an adoption order under the ACA 2002.[194] They can alternatively apply for a child arrangements order by which the child is to live with them under s 8 of the CA 1989, or for orders under the court's inherent jurisdiction,[195] but neither of these routes affects the child's legal parentage.

Consequently, while the surrogate can therefore veto the making of a parental order, that does not mean that she can necessarily stop the intended parents from having care of the child. As noted in *Re H (A Child: Surrogacy Breakdown)*, 'while the six-week "cooling off" period protects a [surrogate] mother in relation to the important issue of consent to a parental order, it tells one nothing about what the best welfare arrangements for the child will be after birth'.[196] We discuss these disputes in the following section,[197] but it should be emphasized that the majority of surrogacy arrangements proceed without difficulty in relation to the consent requirement.

The other 'conditions' in subsections (2) to (8) have been given a wide interpretation in the case law, to the point where some of them appear to have been disregarded entirely by the courts. The court has described its approach as being to take a 'broad and purposive construction of s 54 to achieve the transformative effect to the parental order [which has] required the court to read the provisions of s 54 to give effect to the right to [respect for] family life in accordance with Art 8(1) [of the ECHR]'.[198] As Brown and Wade argue, 'judgments in the parental order cases suggest that reflecting the "identity" of the child is crucial to the determination of legal parenthood'.[199]

Regarding the relationship requirements in subsection (2), the court in *Re F and M (Thai Surrogacy: Enduring Family Relationship)* noted that an 'enduring family relationship' is not defined under the Act, and so should not be given any particular definition in terms of longevity.[200] The couple began their relationship after one of the parties had already entered into the surrogacy agreement; however, the relationship had been stable since then and they planned to marry, and both were living with the twin children born from the surrogacy. The court made the order. Whether parties are in an 'enduring family relationship' or not is a question of fact, and the court has noted that—unlike under s 54(4)—the subsection (2) condition does not contain any time specification, and so '[t]here is no requirement in s 54(2)

[191] *Re X and Y (Foreign Surrogacy)* [2008] EWHC 3030, [13]; a renewed suggestion that the court should 'read in' a power to dispense with the surrogate's consent was 'unhesitatingly reject[ed]' in *Re C (Surrogacy; Consent)* [2023] EWCA Civ 16, [61].

[192] HFEA 2008, s 54(6). [193] Ibid, s 54(7). [194] See chapter 13.

[195] See 8.7. [196] [2017] EWCA Civ 1798, [12]. [197] See 9.5.4.

[198] *Re N (Surrogacy: Enduring Family Relationship: Child's Home)* [2019] EWFC 21, [27]. In summarizing the law, Lady Hale described the statutory provisions as having been 'liberally interpreted': *Whittington Hospital NHS Trust v XX* [2020] UKSC 14, [14].

[199] Brown and Wade (2023), 11. [200] [2016] EWHC 1594.

that the applicants must be in an enduring family relationship at the time of the making of the application and the making of the order'.[201] A formally valid marriage, even if it involves an entirely platonic relationship between a heterosexual woman and a homosexual man, also meets the criteria.[202]

Similarly, despite the wording of subsection (4), in *A v P (Surrogacy: Parental Order: Death of Applicant)*, Theis J held that an order could be made where one of the applicants had died between the application being lodged and the order being made, on the basis that to say otherwise would be an undue interference with Article 8 rights under the ECHR.[203] Perhaps unsurprisingly, given these developments, it has subsequently been held that applicants who separate during the application process can still obtain a parental order where the child is spending time in both households.[204]

Perhaps more remarkably, the court has held that subsection (3)—that the application must be made within six months of the child's birth—does not impose a strict limitation. Earlier authority had suggested that there was no discretionary power to extend the time limit set,[205] but in *Re X (Surrogacy: Time Limit)*,[206] Sir James Munby P took a different view. The President concluded, both as a matter of general principle and when considering the requirements of the ECHR, that the time limit was not strict and could be extended by the court in an appropriate case (which, in *Re X*, allowed an order to be made where the application was not made for 26 months after the child's birth). Later cases have stretched the time limit much further, including orders being made in relation to children aged 12 and 13[207]—and, more remarkably, in relation to a 23-year-old, despite the legislation allowing orders to be made in relation to 'a child'.[208] Whatever the merits of this approach, it is difficult to see how this interpretation can be reconciled with the plain wording of the Act.

The prohibition on financial reward set down in s 54(8) has been interpreted[209] following the approach taken in adoption cases,[210] that payments made to the surrogate in excess of reasonable expenses could be retrospectively authorized by the court. The development of the law is set out by Lady Hale in the *Whittington Hospital* case.[211]

[201] *Re N (Surrogacy: Enduring Family Relationship: Child's Home)* [2019] EWFC 21, [25]. There is some irony in Theis J's comment, at [34], that the court 'should be alert not to read in any requirement that is not there in the primary legislation', given the court's willingness to disregard the conditions that *are* there in the legislation.

[202] *Re X (A Child: Foreign Surrogacy)* [2018] EWFC 15.

[203] [2011] EWHC 1738. See also *Re X (Surrogacy: Death of Applicant)* [2020] EWFC 39 and *Re X (Foreign Surrogacy: Death of Intended Parent)* [2022] EWFC 34: in both cases, one of the applicants died after the embryo was implanted but before the child was born; as he was the intended parent with the genetic link to the child, s 54A could not be used by the surviving spouse. Theis J made the parental orders.

[204] See, e.g., *Re B (Foreign Surrogacy)* [2016] EWFC 77. See also *Re X (A Child: Foreign Surrogacy)* [2018] EWFC 15, where the applicants were married but lived separately; the child was spending time in both households, which the court held to satisfy the requirements of subsection (4).

[205] *JP v LP* [2014] EWHC 595.

[206] [2014] EWHC 3135. See Trimmings (2015).

[207] *A v C (Surrogacy: Parental Order)* [2016] EWFC 42.

[208] *X v Y (Parental Order: Adult)* [2022] EWFC 26. See Brown and Wade (2022).

[209] *Re C; Application by Mr and Mrs X under s 30 of the Human Fertilisation and Embryology Act 1990* [2002] EWHC 157.

[210] *Re Adoption Application (Payment for Adoption)* [1987] Fam 81.

[211] For arguments about payments to surrogates in the context of proposed reforms, see Brown (2021b).

Whittington Hospital NHS Trust v XX [2020] UKSC 14

LADY HALE PSC:

16. The court must also be satisfied that no money or other benefit, other than for expenses reasonably incurred, has been given or received by any applicant for making the arrangements, handing over the child, giving agreement, or making the order, unless authorised by the court. This might be thought to discourage the making of parental orders following a foreign (or indeed any) commercial surrogacy. But what is the court to do when confronted with a fait accompli? It was soon held that payments other than reasonable expenses could be authorised retrospectively, after they had been made . . . In *Re X and Y (Foreign Surrogacy)* [2008] EWHC 3030, which was the first case dealing with payments for a foreign commercial surrogacy, Hedley J asked himself whether the sums paid were disproportionate to reasonable expenses, whether the applicants were acting in good faith in their dealings with the surrogate, and whether they were party to any attempt to defraud the authorities. This set the tone. The Law Commissions are not aware of any case in which a parental order has been refused on the basis of payments which exceed reasonable expenses . . . This is not surprising: the deed has been done, the child is here living with the commissioning parents,[212] and his welfare will almost always require that he is not left legally parentless (and possibly also stateless). This has led one academic commentator to remark that: "English law, as developed through the jurisprudence of the High Court in the 30 years since [the Warnock Report] does not view commercial surrogacy as an intrinsic wrong".[213]

17. Certain provisions in the Adoption and Children Act 2002 . . . are applied to parental order applications by Regulations . . . These include the requirement that the court treat the welfare of the child as its paramount consideration: the court is required to have regard to the welfare of the child, not only during childhood, but throughout his life. As the Law Commissions comment, although laudable, this creates a tension: welfare considerations will almost always point towards making a parental order but this makes it difficult for the court to police even the requirements of sections 54 and 54A, let alone to enforce any public policy against commercial surrogacy arrangements which might be deduced from the Surrogacy Arrangements Act 1985.

Curiously, Lady Hale's concerns about the child being left 'legally parentless' seem misplaced: the child will have legal parents if a parental order is refused, it is just that the 'wrong' people will be the child's legal parents. However, while the *Whittington Hospital* case merely involves the Supreme Court summarizing the case law, there is no indication of disapproval, and the court's determination not to allow children (and intended parents) to be denied the 'transformative' effect of a parental order is clear.

Indeed, the court has gone to considerable effort to fit surrogacy arrangements into the existing legislation, giving the various provisions as wide an interpretation as possible. However, it is worth noting that some surrogacy arrangements cannot be brought within the framework of s 54, even when all those involved wish a parental order to be made. For instance, in *AB v CD (Surrogacy)*, the biological parents of twins born as a result of a surrogacy arrangement

[212] The term 'commissioning parents' is increasingly rare; the Law Commissions (2023), 5, says it prefers 'intended parents' because 'the parties' intentions are one of the defining features of a surrogacy arrangement'.

[213] Fenton-Glynn (2016).

had never applied for a parental order while their relationship continued, and following their separation and divorce the court was not able to grant an order. Keehan J commented that he was 'extremely frustrated, as no doubt are the [intended parents], that I am prevented, without any obvious good, legal or policy reason from making orders which explicitly recognise them as the legal mother and the legal father of these children'.[214] The judge made orders under the court's inherent jurisdiction to secure the children's placement with the mother, but noted that these 'fall very far short of the transformative effect of a parental order'.[215]

9.5.3.c Revoking parental orders

The HFEA itself provides no mechanism for revoking a parental order. However, in *G v G (Parental Order: Revocation)*,[216] the High Court considered that there was nonetheless a power to revoke a parental order. In *G v G*, the intended parents separated shortly after the parental order had been made and contact between the father and the child became the subject of litigation. The child had lived since birth with the intended mother. The father applied for the parental order to be revoked as a result of which the intended mother would be rendered a legal stranger to the child. However, the father, as the biological father, would retain parental responsibility. The father argued that the intended mother had deceived him, the surrogate mother, the parental reporter, and ultimately the court at the time the parental order was made in that she had already decided to leave him but concealed her intentions in order to secure the order. He therefore contended that the order had been made on a false premise, it being his position that had he known of his wife's true intentions he would not have proceeded and the order could not have been made.

In his judgment, Hedley J noted that a parental order, like an adoption order, confers a lifelong legal status on both the child and the intended parents,[217] and thus the bar for challenging such an order once made 'is set very high'.[218] In making that assessment, the judge suggested that guidance can be taken from the authorities that relate to applications to revoke an adoption order.[219] Furthermore, Hedley J made clear that in determining the application, the child's welfare is a relevant consideration. Taking into account the consequences of revocation for the legal relationship between the child and the intended mother (his primary carer) and the grave difficulty in finding a suitable alternative order to secure the mother's position should the parental order be set aside, Hedley J concluded, despite the serious concerns, that the father's application should be refused.

9.5.4 DISPUTES WHEN SURROGACY AGREEMENTS BREAK DOWN

Very few surrogacy arrangements break down such that the surrogate challenges the intended parents' wish to have the child live with them.[220] However, where the surrogacy agreement does break down, there is rarely an easy answer as to whether the surrogate should be able

[214] [2018] EWHC 1590, [76]. See also *Y v Z* [2017] EWFC 60, where the application failed due to lack of domicile in the UK, required by s 54(4)(b). Compare *Re Z and Y (Leave to Withdraw Application for a Parental Order)* [2019] EWFC 43, where the intended parents withdrew their application under s 54, seemingly on the basis that they were dissatisfied with the length of time that the process was taking and the amount of evidence that they were being asked to provide.

[215] Ibid. [216] [2012] EWHC 1979. [217] Ibid, [33]. [218] Ibid, [43]. [219] See 13.2.

[220] Marsh (2022b) notes that there have been only six reported cases on this issue in the last 15 years.

to keep the child and, if so, the role if any that should be played by the intended parents. The courts have tended to take each case on its facts, applying the welfare principle as best they can. This has led to very different outcomes in individual cases, depending on such factors as the circumstances surrounding the surrogacy agreement, the reasons for the surrogate's refusal to proceed with the arrangement, and the court's general attitude towards surrogacy. The following two cases provide extreme examples of the difficult circumstances that can face the court and their reactions in trying to secure, as best they can, the child's interests.

In the early case of *A v C*,[221] the Court of Appeal made no secret of its intense disapproval of the intended couple and the circumstances surrounding the surrogacy agreement. The Court of Appeal made it clear that, in the circumstances, a mere genetic link between father and child was not sufficient to justify an ongoing social relationship, and refused the application for contact between the intended parents and the child.

By contrast, in *Re N (A Child)*[222] the court disapproved just as strongly of the behaviour of the surrogate mother and transferred the child's residence from the surrogate and her husband to the intended parents, even though the child had been living with the surrogate and her husband for the 18 months since her birth. The case was unusual given the surrogate mother's deliberate intention to obtain sperm for insemination by deceiving the intended parents into entering the surrogacy arrangement when she had no intention to relinquish the child. This deliberate deception led the court to conclude that the child's long-term interests would be better served with the intended parents, despite the high standards of care the surrogate and her husband had provided and the strong bond they had formed with the child. The Court of Appeal upheld this decision, paying little regard to whether the surrogate and her husband or the intended parents were to be regarded as the legal parents. However, whilst Thorpe LJ approached the case as one between two 'natural' parents—the surrogate mother and the intended father[223]—Lloyd LJ noted that under the HFEA 1990, the surrogate's husband would be the legal father.[224] Whilst this did not affect his assessment of the child's welfare, it makes the decision notable as the child was placed to live with two people who were legal strangers to him.[225]

Under the current law, while there is no sense in which the courts are 'enforcing' surrogacy agreements, the intentions of the adults and what that says about the identity of the child concerned can be relevant. At first instance in *Re H (A Child: Surrogacy Breakdown)*, Theis J favoured an arrangement where the child would live with the intended parents and have limited contact with the surrogate and her husband.

Re H (A Child: Surrogacy Breakdown) [2016] EWFC 80

THEIS J:

93.(1) That placement [with the intended parents], in my judgment, will best meet [the child's] identity and needs. I accept the rationale set out by [the Cafcass reporter]; that is [the child's] identity in the wider sense of her being a child of intended gay parents with a genetic relationship with A, who is from country X, and a Spanish egg donor. It would be for her a lived experience on a day to day basis which would meet her welfare needs

[221] [1985] FLR 445. [222] [2007] EWCA Civ 1053. [223] Ibid, [13]–[14]. [224] Ibid, [19].
[225] See also the remarkably similar facts of *H v S (Surrogacy Agreement)* [2015] EWFC 36.

This decision was upheld on appeal. Reviewing the authorities, the Court of Appeal noted that if the criteria for a parental order cannot be met—here, because the surrogate would not consent to it—the court then fell back on private law orders.[226]

Re H (A Child: Surrogacy Breakdown) **[2017] EWCA Civ 1798**

McFARLANE LJ:

4.(i) We reaffirm the position stated by this court in the surrogacy case *Re N (A Child)* [2007] EWCA Civ 1053. The essential question in every case is: all things considered, which outcome will be best for the child? The law does not take a special approach to decisions about surrogacy breakdown or other disputes within unconventional family structures. The welfare principle applies with full force in such cases; indeed, the more unusual the facts, the greater the need to keep the child at the heart of the decision, and to ensure that the interests of others prevail only where they are in harmony with the interests of the child.

Whilst this pragmatic approach which seeks to protect each child's welfare has some advantages, it also has the major disadvantage of uncertainty, particularly for the intended parents, and potential for significant disruption for the child in the early months and years of their life. The alternative approach of making surrogacy agreements enforceable, like any other contractual arrangement, would give much better protection to the intended parents and much greater certainty to all parties in the vast majority of surrogacy agreements that work.

A further consequence of the breakdown of relations between the surrogate and the intended parents is that, because of the surrogate's absolute veto over the making of a parental order, legal parenthood cannot be transferred to the intended parents if she does not consent. As we noted earlier,[227] legal parenthood has significant consequences, not least in terms of kinship, which last throughout a person's lifetime (and not just through childhood, unlike court orders under the CA 1989 or the inherent jurisdiction).

Some amount of challenge to the power of the surrogate and her husband to prevent a parental order being made was brought by the intended parents in *Re H*, though they framed their case narrowly as a challenge to the inability to have the genetic father's name on their child's birth certificate (the surrogate was married, and so her husband was the legal father under s 35 of the HFEA 2008, even though neither he nor the surrogate was genetically related to the child). The High Court dismissed this application,[228] and a further application to the European Court of Human Rights was declared to be 'manifestly ill-founded'.[229] But the case could have been argued in broader terms.

[226] McFarlane LJ envisaged orders under s 8 of the CA 1989, but other cases have used the High Court's inherent jurisdiction: see, e.g., *AB v CD (Surrogacy)* [2018] EWHC 1590.

[227] See 9.2.2.

[228] *R (H) v Secretary of State for Health and Social Care* [2019] EWHC 2095.

[229] *H v United Kingdom* (App No 32185/20, ECHR) (2022).

R. Marsh, 'Surrogacy Breakdown, Birth Registration and Article 8: A Missed Opportunity in Strasbourg', (2022b) 44 *Journal of Social Welfare and Family Law* 529, 531

. . . *H* could instead have been argued as a challenge to the requirement for 'both' the surrogate and her husband to agree to the parental order (s 54(6) HFEA 2008). Framing the case thus could have recognised the parental role played by H's non-genetic intended parent, 'B'. He too lacked legal parental status for H and was missing from the birth certificate.

Such a legal challenge would have been transparent—the real reason the intended parents were not named on H's birth certificate was because the surrogate and her husband refused their agreement . . .—and more focused, requiring the courts to engage with the parental order scheme rather than the parental status provisions which also apply to other forms of ART. Moreover, it would have been more readily substantiated.

Under section 54(6), even if the surrogate agrees to the parental order, her partner can prevent the intended parents becoming their child's legal parents. H could have argued that prioritising the Article 8 rights of the surrogate's partner—who may have played little to no role in the surrogacy arrangement—over those of the child serves no legitimate aim. As for the surrogate, section 54(6) serves the legitimate aim of protecting women from handing over legal parental status where they have been exploited or coerced into a surrogacy arrangement. But in its present form, section 54(6) prevents courts overriding her refusal to agree where it would be in the child's best interests. H could therefore have argued that section 54(6) does not strike a fair balance between the Article 8 rights of surrogate-born children and surrogates, as surrogates' rights automatically prevail, including in circumstances where there are no concerns of exploitation or coercion.

H could also have pointed out that the social landscape has changed since surrogacy policy was last considered by UK Parliament in 2008. The Law Commissions (2019) have provisionally recommended that the surrogate and her partner's ability to veto a parental order application should be capable of judicial override (in some circumstances) in the child's best interests.

9.5.5 REFORM OF SURROGACY LAW

There is widespread criticism of the current law on surrogacy. The criteria which the law imposes for the making of a parental order are widely seen as inadequate,[230] and the courts—particularly since the importation of the welfare principle into s 54 determinations—have stretched the language of the legislation to breaking point. At the same time, arguments can be made that the law is so focused on reacting to the situation of the adults involved that it wholly fails to give proper regard to the rights of the children who are the subjects of these cases.[231]

In a joint project, the Law Commissions of England and Wales and of Scotland have been reviewing surrogacy law; their 2023 report identified a number of concerns about the present law, including the fact that the surrogate and her spouse or civil partner are the child's legal parents at birth, with the legal process for obtaining a parental order typically taking six to 12 months, and the fact that the court has no ability to override a veto on the parental order being made from the surrogate or her spouse / civil partner.[232] The Law Commissions'

[230] Alghrani and Griffiths (2017). [231] Wade (2017); Bridgeman (2017b).
[232] Law Commissions (2023), paras 1.10-1.24.

report addresses the concerns identified by the suggested creation of what they term 'a new pathway for domestic surrogacy agreements', and proposed reforms to the existing parental order process for international cases and domestic surrogacies that do not fall within the new pathway.

Law Commissions, *Building Families Through Surrogacy: A New Law—Core Report*, Law Com 411 (London: TSO, 2023)

2.1 We think that the most effective way of tackling the problems with the current law is to introduce a new surrogacy pathway. The new pathway will introduce essential safeguards before conception, so that state regulation comes before, not after, the birth of the child. If these safeguards are complied with, and eligibility conditions are met, then the intended parents and surrogate will be eligible for admission to the new pathway, which will enable the intended parents to become the child's legal parents at birth.

. . .

2.9 We recommend that a surrogacy agreement must meet a number of eligibility conditions, whether it is on the new pathway or if it is the subject of a parental order application. These conditions are there to protect the surrogate, the intended parents and any child born from the agreement. They are an essential first step to surrogacy.

. . .

2.11 The eligibility conditions for surrogacies to proceed on the new pathway are:

(1) the surrogate is over the minimum age required for surrogates, which is 21;

(2) the intended parents are over the minimum age, which is 18;

(3) at least one of the intended parents has a genetic link to the child;

(4) where the intended parents are in a couple, they are married, in a civil partnership, or living as partners in an enduring family relationship with each other; and

(5) the intended parents and surrogate are domiciled or habitually resident in the UK when they sign the Regulated Surrogacy Statement (the document which must be completed for an agreement to proceed on the new pathway) and at the birth of the child, and the assisted reproduction procedure is carried out in the UK.

. . .

2.30 Central to our recommendations for the new pathway is the introduction of RSOs [Regulated Surrogacy Organisations]. . . . One of the most important functions of RSOs will be to carry out the required screening and safeguarding checks in respect of the surrogate and the intended parents. . . .

2.49 The ability of the intended parents to hold legal parental status from the birth of the child in the new pathway is based on the agreement of the surrogate and the intended parents, with the oversight of the RSO. It is important to have a clear and unambiguous record of this agreement, and evidence that all the screening and safeguarding requirements of the new pathway have been met. Accordingly, the surrogate, intended parents, and RSO will need to complete and sign a specific document, called a 'Regulated Surrogacy Statement'. This is not a contract and will not be enforceable.

Under the new pathway, therefore, for domestic surrogacy cases that meet the criteria, the intended parents would be the child's legal parents immediately on birth, and there would be no court process required. A particular concern has been whether the surrogate should retain a right to challenge the transfer of legal parenthood under the new pathway. In their consultative work, the Law Commissions had termed this a 'right to object', but the final report uses the language of a 'right to withdraw her consent'. They propose that this right exists from the time of treatment commencing until six weeks after the birth of the child, but the effect of withdrawing consent would differ depending on whether it occured before or after the child's birth.

Law Commissions, *Building Families Through Surrogacy: A New Law—Core Report*, Law Com 411 (London: TSO, 2023)

2.65 . . . The legal parents of the child will be fixed at the time the child is born, and any change of legal parents after the birth can only be done through a court order.

2.66 If the surrogate withdraws her consent before the child is born, the surrogacy agreement exits the new pathway. That means that the surrogate will be the child's legal parent at the point of their birth, not the intended parents – just like in agreements which are not on the new pathway. The intended parents would then have six months to apply to the court for a parental order recognising them as the child's legal parents, in the same way as if they were not on the new pathway. The court would make a decision as to what would secure the child's lifelong welfare.

2.67 If the surrogate has not withdrawn her consent before the child's birth, the intended parents will be the child's legal parents at birth. The surrogate can withdraw her consent in the six-week period after birth. If she does so, the intended parents remain legal parents, but the surrogate can apply to the court for a parental order recognising her as the child's legal parent. She has six months from the date of birth to make this application. Again, the court would make a decision as to what is in the interests of the child's lifelong welfare.

For international cases, domestic cases where the new pathway criteria were not met, or if the surrogate in a new pathway case withdraws her consent before the birth of the child (or after birth, if she actively seeks to be the child's legal parent), there would be a court process where a judge could still make a parental order. The Law Commissions' proposals go on to suggest reform of the parental order route as well, including: (i) giving the court specific power to dispense with the six-month time limitation on applications;[233] and (ii) granting the court power to override the surrogate's refusal to consent to the parental order, in circumstances where either the surrogate has agreed to the child living with the intended parents or where the court has made an order to that effect.[234] They further recommend that in all cases, whether under the new pathway or not, the surrogate's spouse or civil partner should not be the child's legal parent, and therefore not be formally involved in the process.[235]

It remains to be seen whether the government will accept some or all of the recommendations, and whether parliamentary time will be found to enact new legislation if it does.

[233] Ibid, paras 3.14–3.16. [234] Ibid, paras 3.17-3.20. [235] Ibid, paras 2.103-2.104.

9.6 ADOPTION

Adoption is the one method of acquiring legal parenthood in English law that does not require one or other of the parents to have a biological link (genetic or gestational) with the child. It permanently extinguishes the legal parenthood of the child's original parents (usually the genetic/biological parents) and replaces them with the adoptive parents (the social/intended parents) as if the child had been born their legitimate child.[236] Adoption thus provides unique recognition of the value of social parenthood. The absence of a genetic tie between parent and child means, however, that this method of acquiring legal parenthood is subject to the most detailed and rigorous scrutiny by the state. It is covered in detail in chapter 13.

9.7 CONCLUSION

This chapter has been primarily concerned with how one determines the identity of a child's legal parents under English law. As Douglas and Lowe point out, one can situate the various methods of acquiring legal parenthood on a sliding scale, with natural procreation at one end, adoption at the other, and the various methods of assisted reproduction located at different points in the middle.[237] As one progresses along the scale from natural to adoptive parenthood, one moves from a strong emphasis on genetic parenthood to greater acceptance of the value of social parents. However, as the genetic tie weakens, one also moves from no regulation of an individual's attempts to become a parent, to detailed and rigorous scrutiny of one's parenting credentials by the state. Such scrutiny reflects the law's long-standing preference for genetic parenthood and the ambivalence, and even suspicion, in which it holds 'mere' social parents.

Legal parenthood is clearly central to defining the child's core family relationships. However, it is not the only 'parent' or 'parent-like' relationship that is of importance to children. Advances in reproductive technology and the increasing fluidity and diversity in modern family life, have led to 'parenthood' becoming an increasingly fragmented concept. Three distinct concepts of 'parenthood' have thus emerged in English law: genetic parentage, legal parenthood, and social parenthood. This chapter has considered legal parenthood and, where legal parenthood is divorced from genetic parentage, the continuing role, if any, of the genetic parents. In the next chapter, we consider the child's social parents: those individuals who provide care and nurture for a child. Although in most cases the child's social parents will also be the child's legal (and probably genetic) parents, this is no longer necessarily the case: social parenting can be, and often is, located in someone other than the legal parents. The extent to which English law is able to accommodate this additional level of complexity forms the subject matter of the next chapter. It is to the concept of parental responsibility that we now turn.

ONLINE RESOURCES

Questions, suggestions for further reading, and supplementary materials for this chapter (including updates on developments in this area of family law since this book was published) may be found in the online resources at **www.oup.com/he/familytcm5e**.

[236] ACA 2002, ss 46 and 67. [237] Douglas and Lowe (1992), 416–17.

10

PARENTAL RESPONSIBILITY

CENTRAL ISSUES

1. Understanding of the parent–child relationship has changed dramatically in recent years. From a concept dominated by rights, parenthood is now largely understood in terms of the parents' duties and responsibilities. Parental rights exist only insofar as they are necessary for parents to perform their parental duties.
2. Parenthood and parental responsibility (PR) are distinct legal concepts. Although largely undefined in the Children Act 1989 (CA 1989), PR gives an individual the power and authority to make decisions regarding the child's upbringing. Arguably, it is PR that reflects the real legal status of parenthood.
3. PR is conferred *automatically* on all mothers, fathers who are in a formalized relationship with the mother, and second female parents who gain parenthood under s 42 of the Human Fertilisation and Embryology Act 2008 (HFEA 2008).
4. Unmarried fathers (and second female parents accorded legal parenthood under s 43 of the HFEA 2008) must *acquire* PR in accordance with the legislative provisions. The difference in treatment between fathers who are in a formalized relationship and those who are not is controversial but, in practice, of diminishing significance. Indeed, some commentators are now suggesting that the balance has swung too far in conferring parental rights and responsibilities on disengaged fathers based on nothing more than the genetic tie.
5. A number of individuals can hold PR at any one time. In addition to the child's legal parents, PR may be held by social parents, such as step-parents and guardians, and 'corporate parents', such as the state. This raises the important question whether each individual holding PR can act unilaterally or whether the agreement of all members of the 'parenting team' must be obtained. Despite the clear statutory basis for unilateral action, the courts have suggested that there is a duty to consult and agree on a growing list of important issues.

6. The exercise of PR can be limited both by the child (upon reaching *Gillick* competence) and by the state. The state's intervention into the private decision-making realm of the parents is controversial, particularly when those holding PR are acting reasonably. The courts have been criticized for the limited weight given to parents' views once a dispute reaches court.
7. The PR of those listed in para 3 cannot be terminated, other than by way of adoption (or a parental order in surrogacy cases). For these parents, 'parenthood is for life'. The PR of anyone else can be terminated by the court. Arguably, in order to ensure the equal treatment of all parents, it should be possible to terminate the PR of any irresponsible and uninterested parent.

10.1 INTRODUCTION

Establishing the legal parenthood of a child under English law can be a complex and difficult process. However, establishing legal parenthood is only half the story. Although, as we have seen in chapter 9, a number of important rights and responsibilities attach to the mere fact of the parent–child relationship, in order to hold the full ambit of rights and responsibilities commonly associated with 'being a parent' and raising a child, an individual must also hold 'parental responsibility'. Indeed, it has been emphasized in the case law that it is parental responsibility (PR) that really confers the legal 'status of parenthood'.[1] PR is thus a distinct legal concept. It is both narrower and wider than parenthood, in that, whilst some enduring rights and responsibilities attach exclusively to the parent–child relationship, other rights and responsibilities relating to the care and upbringing of the child attach exclusively to the concept of PR. For most parents, this disjunction between parenthood and PR poses no problems as the law both confers on them the status of legal parenthood and automatically regards them as holding PR. However, for some, particularly unmarried fathers, the legal distinction is of enormous significance as they will not *automatically* hold PR for their children. Conversely, some social parents who have no genetic links with the child and do not hold the status of legal parenthood can acquire PR in accordance with the legislative provisions. PR therefore plays an important role in the legal recognition of social parenthood, such that it is a 'potentially radical legal construct'.[2]

In understanding the parent–child relationship in English law, it is important to keep in mind this crucial distinction between the two legal concepts of parenthood and PR. Whilst chapter 9 dealt with the concept of parenthood, the focus of this chapter is on PR. We begin by exploring the concept of PR and its legal significance, before considering the various legislative provisions dealing with who automatically holds PR, and how, and by whom, it may be acquired. We then examine the exercise of PR and the various restrictions that may be imposed on the decision-making authority of those who hold it. The final section briefly considers the rights and responsibilities of those who care for a child but do not have PR.

[1] *Re S (A Minor) (Parental Responsibility)* [1995] 3 FCR 225, 234.

[2] Diduck (2007), 462.

10.2 WHAT IS PARENTAL RESPONSIBILITY?

Section 3(1) of the CA 1989[3] defines PR:

Children Act 1989, s 3

(1) In this Act 'parental responsibility' means all the rights, duties, powers, responsibilities and authority which by law a parent of a child has in relation to the child and his property.

Before considering the meaning of this deceptively simple provision, it is worth thinking a little about its origins.

10.2.1 FROM RIGHTS TO RESPONSIBILITY

10.2.1.a The parent–child relationship

'Parental responsibility' as a distinct legal concept was an innovation in the CA 1989. It was intended to mark a fundamental shift in understanding about the parent–child relationship from one dominated by rights to one dominated by duties and responsibilities. However, the same concept of parenthood underpinned *Gillick v West Norfolk and Wisbech AHA*.[4]

Gillick v West Norfolk and Wisbech Area Health Authority **[1986] AC 112 (HL), 170, 183–5**

LORD FRASER:

[P]arental rights to control a child do not exist for the benefit of the parent. They exist for the benefit of the child and they are justified only in so far as they enable the parent to perform his duties towards the child, and towards other children in the family.

LORD SCARMAN:

Parental rights clearly do exist, and they do not wholly disappear until the age of majority. Parental rights relate to both the person and the property of the child—custody, care, and control of the person and guardianship of the property of the child. But the common law has never treated such rights as sovereign or beyond review and control. Nor has our law ever treated the child as other than a person with capacities and rights recognised by law. The principle of the law, as I shall endeavour to show, is that parental rights are derived from parental duty and exist only so long as they are needed for the protection of the person and property of the child . . .

The principle is that parental right or power of control of the person and property of his child exists primarily to enable the parent to discharge his duty of maintenance, protection, and

[3] Unless otherwise stated, all references to statutory provisions in this chapter are to the CA 1989.

[4] The facts of *Gillick* and further extracts are found at 8.5.6.

education until he reaches such an age as to be able to look after himself and make his own decisions . . . [Blackstone] accepts that by statute and by case law varying ages of discretion have been fixed for various purposes. But it is clear that this was done to achieve certainty where it was considered necessary and in no way limits the principle that parental right endures only so long as it is needed for the protection of the child . . .

The *Gillick* approach to parenthood was heralded and later unequivocally endorsed by the Law Commission,[5] before being enshrined in s 3. The language of parental rights has not, however, been erased entirely from the statute books. Indeed, the 'rights' of parents are expressly included within the statutory definition of PR. It is, however, clear from the preparatory work of the Law Commission that such parental rights as are enshrined in the CA 1989 are meant in the *Gillick* sense. That is, they are instrumental: they exist only insofar as they are necessary for parents to perform their parental duties and responsibilities. It is therefore parental duties and responsibilities, not parental rights, which *should* be regarded as standing at the heart of parenthood. The Court of Appeal has reiterated the centrality of the responsibilities and burdens of PR in the practice of raising children.

Re W (Direct Contact) [2012] EWCA Civ 999

McFARLANE LJ:

74. . . . I have stressed that, along with the rights, powers and authority of a parent, come duties and responsibilities which must be discharged in a manner which respects similarly-held rights, powers, duties and responsibilities of the other parent where parental responsibility is shared.

75. In all aspects of life, whilst some duties and responsibilities may be a pleasure to discharge, others may well be unwelcome and a burden. Whilst parenting in many respects brings joy, even in families where life is comparatively harmonious, the responsibility of being a parent can be tough. Where parents separate, the burden for each and every member of the family group can be, and probably will be, heavy. It is not easy, indeed it is tough, to be a single parent with the care of a child. Equally, it is tough to be the parent of a child for whom you no longer have the day-to-day care and with whom you no longer enjoy the ordinary stuff of everyday life because you only spend limited time with your child. . . .

76. Where parental responsibility is shared by a child's parents, the statute is plain (CA 1989, s 3) that each of those parents, and both of them, share 'duties' and 'responsibilities' in relation to the child, as well as 'rights . . . powers . . . and authority'. Where all are agreed, as in the present case, that it is in the best interests of a child to have a meaningful relationship with both parents, the courts are entitled to look to each parent to use their best endeavours to deliver what their child needs, hard or burdensome or downright tough though that may be. The statute places the primary responsibility for delivering a good outcome for a child upon each of his or her parents, rather than upon the courts or some other agency . . .

McFarlane LJ's approach in *Re W* received strong endorsement from Sir James Munby P in *Re H-B (Contact)*, who emphasized that 'parental responsibility is more, much more, than a

[5] Law Com (1988c), para 2.4.

mere lawyer's concept or a principle of law. It is a fundamentally important reflection of the realities of the human condition, of the very essence of the relationship of parent and child'.[6]

10.2.1.b The parent–state relationship

The change in emphasis from focusing on parental rights to focusing on parental responsibilities also reflects a wider political agenda concerning the appropriate relationship between the child, the parent, and the state. As expressed by the government in its 1987 review of the public law on children, 'the prime responsibility for the upbringing of children rests with parents'.[7] In other words, in a policy which was typical of the privatizing trend of the Conservative Government of the time, caring for and supporting children was seen to be an individual, not a state, responsibility. It served to emphasize the enduring nature of the individual responsibility of *both* parents for their children's upbringing, a responsibility that could not be transferred or surrendered to the state and would not be affected by the parents' changing relationship.[8]

Two distinct ideas therefore underpin the concept of PR in the CA 1989: one focuses on the parent–child relationship, the other on the parents' relationship with the state.[9] Eekelaar argues that, by the time the CA 1989 was enacted, there had been a decisive shift in emphasis from the Law Commission's initial concern with the duties and obligations owed by parents to their children, to the more politically contentious issue of the appropriate relationship between the parents and the state.[10] This was fuelled by the government's growing anxiety over the breakdown of the traditional family unit and the resulting growth in single motherhood. Traditionally, men had been legally tied to their children through the institution of marriage. Changing social trends challenged the effectiveness of this approach. It was widely perceived that the declining popularity of marriage, rising divorce rates, and the ever-increasing number of children born to unmarried mothers was resulting in a gradual transfer of responsibility from 'the husband' to the state. The growing 'irresponsibility' of men towards their children, and the wider social consequences of this phenomenon, was a matter of increasing concern.

J. Lewis, 'Family Policy in the Post-War Period', in S. Katz, J. Eekelaar, and M. Maclean (eds), *Cross Currents: Family Law and Policy in the United States and England* (Oxford: OUP, 2000), 81, 91–3

By the early 1990s, the political debate was dominated by those who stressed the irresponsibility and selfishness of men as well as of women. Michael Howard, then Home Secretary, said in a speech to the Conservative Political Centre in 1993: 'If the state will house and pay for their children the duty on [young men] to get involved may seem removed from their shoulders . . . And since the State is educating, housing and feeding their children the nature of parental responsibility may seem less immediate.' . . .

The prime concern of political commentators about men's obligation to maintain was often allied with a more generalised concern on the political Right, and the political Left, among politicians and the media, about an increase in male irresponsibility. All argued that the

6 [2015] EWCA Civ 389, [72]. 7 DHSS et al (1987), para 5.
8 See generally Lindley (1999) and Eekelaar (1991c), 42–3.
9 Eekelaar (1991c), 38–9. See also Freeman (2000), 452. 10 Eekelaar (1991c), 40.

successful socialization of children required the active involvement of two parents. Dennis and Erdos sought to trace the rise of the 'obnoxious Englishman' to family breakdown. Their chief concern was the effect of lone motherhood on the behaviour patterns of young men. Lone parenthood was in their view responsible for at best irresponsible and at worst criminal behaviour in the next male generation.

The state was anxious to find a way of attaching children to their fathers other than through the traditional mechanism of marriage.[11] The most obvious legal status to which parental duties and responsibilities could be attached was parenthood.[12] However, the government has not always been consistent in its attitude towards the parenting role of unmarried fathers. As evidenced by the decision to withhold *automatic* PR from unmarried fathers,[13] suspicion about the 'value' of this particular group of men as parents has persisted. In the debates leading up to the CA 1989, a strong image of the unmarried father as a feckless, irresponsible individual emerged. Whilst successive governments have taken a clear and unequivocal position on the financial responsibilities of men towards their children,[14] they have shown considerably more ambivalence towards unmarried fathers and the *non-financial* responsibilities of parenthood. However, whilst financial considerations clearly remain important, during the 1997–2010 Labour Government there was a discernible shift in attitude which has largely persisted since. Ambivalence about unmarried fathers gave way to a strong belief in the value of active engaged fathering to securing the best possible outcomes for children.[15] Suspicion was thus replaced by steadfast optimism, with the government keen to support and encourage fathers to embrace all aspects of their parenting responsibilities. The Labour Government's new-found faith in the worth of the unmarried father was strongly reflected in its reforms to the birth registration system. No longer feckless and irresponsible, unmarried fathers were portrayed as crucial to children's welfare, and it was therefore seen as essential that they exercise PR in its broadest sense.[16]

R. Collier and S. Sheldon, *Fragmenting Fatherhood: A Socio-Legal Study* (Oxford: Hart Publishing, 2008), 191–2

Given the broader policy context around the promotion of 'active fathering' . . . unmarried fathers' failure to obtain PR has been of growing concern to a government keen to foster men's commitment to their families in a more general sense. Granting automatic PR is thus seen as a way of entrenching paternal duty to provide for the child's emotional development, as well as their financial needs. Denying this 'stamp of approval' to unmarried fathers, it was suggested, risked alienating them and refusing the vital encouragement necessary for them to take on board family responsibilities, destabilising the family unit and further contributing to the creation of lone-parent families.

[11] Lewis (2000), 96. [12] See Douglas (2000b), esp at 223–7. [13] See 10.4.2.

[14] As enshrined in the Child Support Act 1991, s 1.

[15] The assumed value of fatherhood is a strong feature of the current debate over private law orders about children: see 11.7.2.

[16] DCSF and DWP (2008).

10.2.2 DEFINING PARENTAL RESPONSIBILITY

Parental responsibility has proved difficult to define with any specificity. The definition in s 3(1) raises more questions than it answers—indeed, as we will see in a moment, in some ways it is actively misleading. However, s 3(1) is the only express definition of PR, and we are otherwise left to work out the substantive content from other statutory provisions and from the common law. The Law Commission opposed attempts to articulate any kind of definitive list of parental rights and duties, citing impracticality, incompleteness, and a lack of flexibility as potential drawbacks of such an approach.[17]

However, whilst the formulation of a comprehensive list would be difficult, Lowe et al attempt to identify the most important rights and duties enshrined within PR.[18]

N. Lowe et al, *Bromley's Family Law*, 12th edn (Oxford: OUP, 2021), 443–4

- Bringing up the child.
- Having contact with the child.
- Protecting and maintaining the child.
- Disciplining the child.
- Determining and providing for the child's education.
- Determining the child's religion.
- Consenting to the child's medical treatment. . . .
- Consenting to the child's adoption.
- Vetoing the issue of a child's passport.
- Taking the child outside the United Kingdom and consenting to the child's emigration.
- Administering the child's property.
- Naming the child.
- Representing the child in legal proceedings. . . .
- Appointing a guardian for the child.[19]

This list is frequently cited by other commentators. Despite the absence of a clear statutory definition of PR, there is fairly widespread consensus about what is core to the concept. In short, PR encapsulates all the decision-making power and authority that parents need to provide effective long-term care for a child.

It is less clear where the *limits* of PR are or, to draw on the language of Lady Black, where the 'the ambit or zone of the parent's parental responsibility' ends.[20] The criminal law

[17] Law Com (1985b), para 1.9.

[18] This closely reflects the tentative list put forward by the Law Commission (1985b), para 2.25. For detailed discussion of various of the matters listed, see Probert, Gilmore, and Herring (2009).

[19] We omit 'consenting to the child's marriage', as the age for marriage is now 18 regardless of parental consent after the Marriage and Civil Partnership (Minimum Age) Act 2022, and 'disposing of the child's body' because this is an aspect of legal parenthood, and *not* of PR: see 9.2.2.

[20] *Re D (Residence Order: Deprivation of Liberty)* [2019] UKSC 42, [89].

imposes some limitations—a parent cannot exercise their PR to kill their child, nor to assault,[21] ill-treat, or neglect them,[22] to give some obvious examples. There are also positive requirements, such as ensuring that a child receives efficient full-time education.[23] Other limitations are less obvious, though, as can be seen from the 3:2 division of opinion in the Supreme Court about whether a parent can exercise their PR so as to detain an older child in such a way as would deprive the child of their liberty, and so engage Article 5 of the European Convention on Human Rights (ECHR). Lady Hale PSC held that 'it was not within the scope of parental responsibility for [an older child's] parents to consent to a placement which deprived him of his liberty'—but even the majority did not fully agree about the reasons for that conclusion, including the key issue of what the scope of PR was in this area.[24]

ONLINE RESOURCES

Further consideration of *Re D (Residence Order: Deprivation of Liberty)* [2019] UKSC 42 can be found in the online resources at **www.oup.com/he/familytcm5e.**

A further complication arises from the fact that although, on its face, PR appears to be a free-standing legal concept, giving any holder *all* the rights, duties, etc of a parent without qualification, the reality is significantly more complex. First, and most straightforwardly, the CA 1989 itself provides various limitations on certain holders of PR as to the scope of their decision-making powers—for example, a local authority that holds PR cannot change a child's religion, give consent to their adoption, or appoint a guardian for the child.[25]

Secondly, and less obvious, there are various intersections between the legal concept of PR and legal parenthood. The Act defines PR as being all the rights, etc that, by law, a parent '*has*'—but, in fact, a parent who does not have PR does *not* have most of the rights, etc that are bundled within PR.[26] But moreover, there are various examples that can be identified where the interaction of PR and legal parenthood requires further consideration.

J. Eekelaar, 'Rethinking Parental Responsibility', (2001) 31 *Family Law* 426, 426–7

The fact that s 3(1) . . . states that parental responsibility means 'all the rights, duties, powers, responsibilities and authority which by law a parent of a child has in relation to the child and his property' does not prevent some such rights etc being held by persons who do not have

[21] So-called 'reasonable chastisement' remains legal in England, but has been illegal in Wales since the Children (Abolition of Defence of Reasonable Punishment) (Wales) Act 2020 entered force.

[22] Children and Young Persons Act 1933, s 1.

[23] Education Act 1996, s 7.

[24] *Re D (Residence Order: Deprivation of Liberty)* [2019] UKSC 42, [48]. Lady Arden agreed with Lady Hale. Lady Black also agreed with Lady Hale, but addressed what she saw to be a prior question about the scope of parental authority at common law; Lady Hale and Lady Arden reserved their position on Lady Black's analysis. Lord Carnwath and Lord Lloyd-Jones dissented, preferring Munby P's approach in the Court of Appeal and rejecting both majority analyses. For critique of Lady Black's approach, see Gilmore (2022).

[25] S 33(6). Another limitation is found in s 13: whenever a 'live with' CAO is in force, no one may remove the child from the UK for more than one calendar month or change the child's surname without the consent of all holders of PR or permission from the court. See 11.8.

[26] Legal parenthood has its own legal consequences though: see 9.2.2.

parental responsibility. One has to look to statute and common law to find out what these rights are. In other words, having parental responsibility is not a necessary condition for possessing some important attributes of parenthood. Nor, it turns out, despite the word 'all' in s 3(1), is it a sufficient condition for holding some such attributes.

(A) Parental Responsibility Neither a Necessary nor a Sufficient Condition

It is well known that the duty to support a child [financially] . . . is imposed on 'any person who is in law the mother or father of the child' (Child Support Act 1991, s 54); having parental responsibility is neither necessary, nor (if the person with it is not in law the mother or father) sufficient. The same is true with respect to succession rights . . .

(B) Parental Responsibility a Sufficient but not Necessary Condition

Sometimes, having parental responsibility confers certain rights etc, but those rights could be held quite apart from it. In such cases, either having parental responsibility is sufficient, or being a legal parent is sufficient; neither is necessary. For example, either a legal parent (with or without parental responsibility), or someone who is not a legal parent, but who has parental responsibility, may apply, without leave, for certain orders with respect to the child (Children Act 1989, ss 10(4) and 12(2)). Similarly, parents (with or without parental responsibility) and non-parents with parental responsibility have the right to be kept in reasonable contact with children who are in local authority care (Children Act 1989, ss 34(1)(a) and 12(2)) and to be consulted by a local authority when it reviews the position of a child it is looking after (Children Act 1989, ss 26(2)(d) and 12(2)). The same is true with respect to education: either a parent or someone with parental responsibility is under a duty to ensure the child receives efficient full-time education (Education Act 1996, ss 7 and 576).

In these examples, PR either is irrelevant or adds nothing in the case of a person who is also a legal parent. The example of child support shows how the s 3(1) definition can be misleading. Financially maintaining the child is a core duty of being a legal parent, and applies to any parent whether they have PR or not—but does not apply to anyone who is not a legal parent even if they hold PR. However, as Eekelaar goes on to show, in other cases, holding PR is necessary:

(C) Parental Responsibility a Necessary but not a Sufficient Condition

Rarely will it be necessary to have both parental responsibility and legal parenthood to exercise a right, etc. The most important example is the right to consent, or to refuse consent, to adoption. A person with parental responsibility who is not the legal parent does not have this right (Children Act 1989, s 12(3)), but being the legal parent without parental responsibility is not enough either (Adoption Act 1976, ss 16 and 72. This is maintained in the Adoption and Children [Act 2002, s 52(6)]). Another example is the right to appoint a guardian (Children Act 1989, ss 5(3) and 12(3)).

(D) Parental Responsibility both a Necessary and Sufficient Condition

Sometimes, holding parental responsibility alone not only will be necessary to exercise a right but also will be enough. This is the case with respect to the right to object to the issue of a passport to a child . . . and to consent to the marriage of a child under the age of 18 (Marriage Act 1949, s 3(1A)(a) and (b)). Other examples are the right to apply for a discharge of a care order (Children Act 1989, s 39(1)(a)) and the right to object to a local authority providing accommodation on a voluntary basis to a child and the right to remove the child from such accommodation (Children Act 1989, s 20(7) and (8)). Like the case of adoption, these are rather unusual circumstances. A more common one is where, usually after the separation of the parents, a residence order is made. Then a child cannot be known by a new surname or removed from the country without the written consent of every person who has parental responsibility, or with the leave of the court (Children Act 1989, s 13(1)).

From all this, it can be seen that there is significant complexity to the idea of PR, and one might wonder whether Black LJ was right to say in *T v T* that s 3(1) 'gives a very clear exposition of the broad concept'.[27]

10.3 HOW IS PARENTAL RESPONSIBILITY OBTAINED?

Unlike parenthood, where the law can only recognize a maximum of two legal parents, one of the distinguishing features of PR is that it can be held simultaneously by more than two people.

Children Act 1989, s 2

(5) More than one person may have parental responsibility for the same child at the same time.

(6) A person who has parental responsibility for a child at any time shall not cease to have that responsibility solely because some other person subsequently acquires parental responsibility for the child.

There are two routes by which individuals may come to hold PR: (i) they hold it automatically; or (ii) it has been acquired in accordance with the CA 1989.

10.3.1 MOTHERS

Regardless of marital status, the child's mother will *always* have *automatic* PR.

Children Act 1989, s 2

(1) Where a child's father and mother were married to each other at the time of his birth, they shall each have parental responsibility for the child.

[27] [2010] EWCA Civ 1366, [23].

(2) Where a child's father and mother were not married to each other at the time of his birth—

(a) the mother shall have parental responsibility for the child . . .

10.3.2 FATHERS AND SECOND FEMALE PARENTS UNDER SS 42 AND 43 OF THE HFEA 2008

In legal terms, there is no material difference between the approach taken to fathers and to 'second female parents' under ss 42 and 43 of the HFEA 2008, so we deal with them together here. However, since the vast majority of cases involve a father rather than a second female parent, we refer primarily to 'fathers'.

10.3.2.a Fathers and second female parents who are married to, or are in a civil partnership with, the mother

Fathers and second female parents *automatically* acquire PR for their children provided they were in a formalized relationship[28] with the child's mother 'at the time of [the child's] birth'.[29] This phrase is interpreted to include any time between conception and birth.[30] It also includes any child whose parents enter a formalized relationship after the birth, with the effect of 'legitimating' the child from the date of the marriage/civil partnership.[31] These provisions apply to void marriages/civil partnerships, provided one or both of the parties reasonably believed that the formalized relationship was valid.[32]

10.3.2.b Unmarried fathers and second female parents

The position of an unmarried[33] father (or second female parent) is considerably more complicated. If not in a formalized relationship with the child's mother 'at the time of the child's birth', these parents do not automatically have PR. They must therefore acquire it in accordance with the legislative provisions.[34] Section 4 provides for three ways in which the child's *father* may acquire PR (with s 4ZA providing equivalent provisions for second female parents). It is crucial to note that s 4 applies *only* to a person who is, in fact, the child's legal father.[35]

Children Act 1989, s 4

(1) Where a child's father and mother were not married to each other at the time of his birth, the father shall acquire parental responsibility for the child if—

[28] We use this term as shorthand for being married or in a civil partnership—there is no legal difference between the two for these purposes.

[29] CA 1989, s 2(1). [30] Family Law Reform Act 1987 (FLRA 1987), s 1(4).

[31] Ibid, s 1(3)(b) and Legitimacy Act 1976, ss 2, 3, and 10.

[32] FLRA 1987, s 1(3)(a) and Legitimacy Act 1976, s 1(1). With respect to the status of a transgender marriage and its effect on parenthood, see *J v C (Void Marriage: Status of Children)* [2006] EWCA Civ 551.

[33] We use this term to mean not married or in a civil partnership.

[34] CA 1989, s 2(2). [35] See 9.3.2.b.

(a) he becomes registered as the child's father . . .;
(b) the father and the child's mother make an agreement (a "parental responsibility agreement") providing for him to have parental responsibility for the child; or
(c) the court, on his application, orders that he shall have parental responsibility for the child.

Registration

Section 4 of the CA 1989 was amended by the Adoption and Children Act 2002 (ACA 2002) to enable unmarried fathers who are entered as the child's father on the birth register[36] to acquire PR.[37] This is subject to the qualification that PR will not be acquired by means of registration if the father has previously made an unsuccessful application to the court for a parental responsibility order (PRO) or, having previously held PR, the court had ordered that his PR should cease.[38] In 2020, only 5.2 per cent of children born in England and Wales were registered by the mother alone.[39] This means that all but a small minority of unmarried fathers now acquire PR by the simple act of registration.[40]

Being named on a birth certificate will not, as a matter of law, confer PR on someone who is not the child's legal father[41]—though in reality, unless challenged, it is likely that everyone would assume that a man named on the birth certificate and who purported to be the child's father did indeed have PR.[42]

Parental responsibility agreements

A 'parental responsibility agreement' (PRA) is a formal agreement entered into by the child's parents that the father is to have PR alongside the mother. The PRA must be made on the prescribed form and registered at the Central Family Court in London.[43] In practice, they are rarely used,[44] probably due to a combination of the decreasing number of fathers who need

[36] The registration must comply with the Births and Deaths Registration Act 1953, ss 10 and 10A, so a foreign birth certificate will not be sufficient. However, if PR was obtained under the domestic law of the foreign country, it will likely be recognized here: this is automatic between countries that are signatories to the 1996 Hague Convention on Jurisdiction, Applicable Law, Recognition, Enforcement and Co-operation in Respect of Parental Responsibility and Measures for the Protection of Children, but usually applies even outside the Convention's structures.

[37] ACA 2002, s 111. The new registration provisions came into effect on 1 December 2003, with no retrospective effect. Fathers whose children were born before this date could not take advantage of them.

[38] S 4(1C).

[39] ONS (2022d), Table 1 (authors' calculations). Just over half of all births are to parents who were not in a formalized relationship with each other; nearly 90 per cent of children born to unmarried parents are registered with both parents' names on the birth certificate.

[40] This was an intended benefit of the birth registration reforms: DCSF and DWP (2008), para 9.

[41] *Re Z (Embryo Adoption: Declaration of Non-Parentage)* [2018] EWFC 68, [34]. *Re C and A (Children: Acquisition and Discharge of Parental Responsibility by an Unmarried Father)* [2023] EWHC 516 is wrong in law to suggest that registration confers PR on a non-parent until a declaration of non-parenthood is made by the court.

[42] Any reasonable steps taken by such a person in relation to the child's upbringing will likely be covered by s 3(5), which permits someone who has care of a child but who does not have PR to take such steps as are reasonable to safeguard or promote the child's welfare. See 10.7.

[43] S 4(2).

[44] In 2004, 5,831 agreements were registered, but the number fell after the 2002 reforms took effect, with 1,581 agreements registered in 2013, 737 in 2017, and only 97 in 2021. Thanks to staff at the Central Family Court for providing this information.

such agreements following the reforms to the birth registration system, together with a lack of knowledge about the relevant provisions.

Parental responsibility orders (PRO)

For those small number of fathers unable to take advantage of the provisions on birth registration and who have not entered into a PRA, the only means by which they may acquire PR is by obtaining a court order under s 4 of the CA 1989. Many PROs under s 4 come about from the father making a free-standing application for PR, but it is important to note that the court is *required* to make an order under this section if it is making a child arrangements order (CAO) under which the child is to *live with* the father if he does not otherwise have PR.

Children Act 1989, s 12

(1) Where—

(a) the court makes a child arrangements order with respect to a child,

(b) the father of the child, or a woman who is a parent of the child by virtue of section 43 of the Human Fertilisation and Embryology Act 2008, is named in the order as a person with whom the child is to live, and

(c) the father, or the woman, would not otherwise have parental responsibility for the child,

the court must also make an order under section 4 giving the father, or under section 4ZA giving the woman, that responsibility.

Conversely, if there is to be a CAO under which the child is to *spend time or otherwise have contact with* the father, and the father does not otherwise have PR, then the court has discretion to make a s 4 order if the court considers that 'it would be appropriate, in view of the provision made in the order with respect to the father or the woman, for him or her to have PR for the child'.[45] In other words, a PRO is *compulsory* if the child is to *live with* the father or second female parent, and must be *considered* if the child is to spend time or otherwise have contact.

In practical terms, an unmarried father's lack of PR often becomes a problem only when his relationship with the mother breaks down (if such a relationship ever existed) and a dispute develops over the child. Indeed, it is often at this point that the father learns for the first time that he lacks the necessary legal status to make key decisions with respect to his child's upbringing. Given the ease with which parents who were in agreement could either register the father's name on the birth certificate or enter into a PRA, it is unsurprising that most free-standing applications for a PRO are opposed.

The Court of Appeal has provided guidance on the factors that should be taken into account on an application for a PRO.[46] *Re H (Minors) (Local Authority: Parental Rights) (No 3)* concerned an application for a parental rights order under s 4(1) of the FLRA 1987 (the precursor to a PRO) but the criteria it set down have been approved and applied to applications under s 4 of the CA 1989.

[45] S 12(1A).

[46] For a more detailed discussion of the case law on applications for PROs, see Gilmore (2003).

Re H (Minors) (Local Authority: Parental Rights) (No 3) [1991] Fam 151 (CA), 158

BALCOMBE LJ:

In considering whether to make an order . . . the court will have to take into account a number of factors of which the following will undoubtedly be material (although there may well be others, as the list is not intended to be exhaustive): (1) the degree of commitment which the father has shown towards the child; (2) the degree of attachment which exists between the father and the child, and (3) the reasons of the father for applying for the order.

In subsequent case law, Balcombe LJ emphasized that these three factors provide only a *starting point* for the court.[47] Satisfying the *Re H (No 3)* criteria does not give rise to a presumption in favour of making the order,[48] and on the other hand in some cases satisfying the criteria may not be necessary, depending on the circumstances.[49] All applications for PR remain subject to the overriding principle of the child's best interests.[50]

Re RH (A Minor) (Parental Responsibility) [1998] 2 FCR 89 (CA), 94

BUTLER-SLOSS LJ:

15. The three requirements set out by Balcombe LJ in *Re H* are, undoubtedly, the starting point for the making of an order but it is clear . . . that he did not intend them to be the only relevant factors in considering a parental responsibility order and that his list was not exhaustive. In any event, such an approach would be contrary to s 1 of the 1989 Act, which applies to parental responsibility orders and the welfare of the child is therefore paramount. The court has the duty in each case to take into account all the relevant circumstances and to decide whether the order proposed is in the best interests of the child. Of course, it is generally in a child's interests to know and have a relationship with his father but the appropriateness of the order has to be considered on the particular facts of each individual case. If, reviewing all the circumstances, the judge considers that there are factors adverse to the father sufficient to tip the balance against the order proposed, it would not be right to make the order, even though the three requirements can be shown by the father.

When determining the child's best interests in relation to an application for a PRO, several factors have proved particularly persuasive. The courts have generally taken the position that it is in the child's interests to have a father who is 'sufficiently concerned and interested' that he wishes to acquire the formal recognition that PR represents. In support of this approach, the courts have placed great weight on the nature of a PRO, emphasizing that it confers a status on the unmarried father that a father in a formalized relationship would enjoy as of right. Moreover, it is argued that granting PR and giving the father the court's 'stamp of

[47] See *Re G (A Minor) (Parental Responsibility Order)* [1994] 1 FLR 504.

[48] Cf *Re P (Parental Responsibility)* [1997] 2 FLR 722, where Ward LJ held that 'the practice had developed where good reason had to be advanced why orders should not be granted in a committed father's favour'.

[49] *Re M (Parental Responsibility Order)* [2013] EWCA Civ 969.

[50] *Re W (Parental Responsibility Order: Inter-Relationship with Direct Contact)* [2013] EWCA Civ 335.

approval' helps promote a positive image of him, a vital factor in developing the child's own secure sense of identity.[51] It is also stressed that PR is not about conferring rights on fathers, but imposing duties and responsibilities, something which is said invariably to work to the child's advantage.[52]

Re S (A Minor) (Parental Responsibility) [1995] 3 FCR 225 (CA), 234–6

WARD LJ:

It would . . . be helpful if the mother could think calmly about the limited circumstances when the exercise of true parental responsibility is likely to be of practical significance. It is wrong to place undue and therefore false emphasis on the rights and duties and the powers comprised in "parental responsibility" and not to concentrate on the fact that what is at issue is conferring upon a committed father the status of parenthood for which nature has already ordained that he must bear responsibility . . .

I have heard, up and down the land, psychiatrists tell me how important it is that children grow up with good self-esteem and how much they need to have a favourable positive image of the absent parent. It seems to me important, therefore, wherever possible, to ensure that the law confers upon a committed father that stamp of approval, lest the child grow up with some belief that he is in some way disqualified from fulfilling his role and that the reason for the disqualification is something inherent which will be inherited by the child, making her struggle to find her own identity all the more fraught.

BUTLER-SLOSS LJ:

It is important for parents . . . to remember the emphasis placed by Parliament on the order which is applied for. It is that of duties and responsibilities as well as rights and powers. Indeed, the order itself is entitled "parental responsibility". A father who has shown real commitment to the child concerned and to whom there is a positive attachment, as well as a genuine *bona fide* reason for the application, ought, in a case such as the present, to assume the weight of those duties and cement that commitment and attachment by sharing the responsibilities for the child with the mother. This father is asking to assume that burden as well as that pleasure of looking after his child, a burden not lightly to be undertaken.

In my judgment, this father should be allowed to share the burden of caring for his daughter which does not remove from the mother the day-to-day control of her daughter's welfare. But it gives to the father the status in which he can share in the responsibility for the child's upbringing and demonstrate that he will be as good a parent as he can make himself to this little girl.

Applying these principles, the Court of Appeal granted a PRO to the father of a 7-year-old girl, despite his recent conviction for the possession of obscene literature including paedophilic photographs of young girls.

The courts' emphasis on the *status* conferred by PR has been accompanied by a general tendency to downplay its *practical* significance. Although it is recognized that PR confers important rights on the father,[53] the courts have made it clear that a PRO does not give the

[51] *Re G (A Minor) (Parental Responsibility Order)* [1994] 1 FLR 504, 508 and *Re C and V (Contact and Parental Responsibility)* [1998] 1 FLR 392, 397.

[52] *Re C and V (Contact and Parental Responsibility)* [1998] 1 FLR 392.

[53] See 10.2.2.

father a general licence to interfere in the day-to-day upbringing of the child. Fears concerning the father potentially misusing his PR to interfere in the mother's day-to-day care have therefore generally been regarded as insufficient to prevent the order being granted, particularly as such potential misuse can be controlled by the court under s 8.[54]

An alternative means by which the father's use of PR may be restricted is by subjecting the order to express conditions (though whether these are actually different from restrictions by way of s 8 orders is unclear). This approach has sometimes been used when dealing with applications by known sperm donors, and we discuss it in detail later.[55] These decisions are consistent with earlier authority holding that the fact that certain parental rights, duties, and responsibilities are currently incapable of being exercised or enforced by the father, whilst relevant, is no bar to the granting of a PRO.

Re C (Minors) **[1992] 2 All ER 86 (CA), 88–9, 93**

MUSTILL LJ:

This appeal has required us to consider another possible factor, namely enforceability. The question can be posed in this way: is the court, when considering a PRO application, entitled or bound to take into account the fact that under the circumstances at the date of the application one or more or all of the parental rights may be valueless in practice because they are incapable of being exercised by force of circumstances or by order of the court?

Looking at that question as one of first impression without reference to authority, we would think that the answer must be Yes. The enforceability of the rights which he is being invited to confer is something that any judge would be entitled and bound to regard as relevant to the exercise of his discretion . . .

Given, therefore, that the prospective enforceability of parental rights is a relevant consideration for a judge deciding whether or not to grant them, there is, in our judgment, nothing in the 1987 Act to suggest that it should be an overriding consideration. It would be quite wrong, in our view, to assume that just because few or none of the parental rights happen to be enforceable under conditions prevailing at the date of the application it would necessarily follow as a matter of course that a PRO would be refused. That can be illustrated by looking—as the legislation clearly requires one to look—at the position of a lawful father in analogous circumstances. Conditions may arise (for example in cases of mental illness) where a married father has, regretfully to be ordered, in effect, to step out of his children's lives altogether. In such a case his legal status as a parent remains wholly unaffected, and he retains all his rights in law although none of them may be exercisable in practice. This does not mean that his parental status becomes a dead letter or a mere paper title. It will have real and tangible value, not only as something he can cherish for the sake of his own peace of mind, but also as a status carrying with it rights in waiting, which it may be possible to call into play when circumstances change with the passage of time. It is not difficult to imagine situations in which similar considerations would apply in the case of a natural father. Though existing circumstances may demand that his children see or hear nothing of him, and that he should have no influence upon the course of their lives for the time being, their welfare may

[54] See, e.g., *Re P (A Minor) (Parental Responsibility Order)* [1994] 1 FLR 578; *Re C And V (Contact and Parental Responsibility)* [1998] 1 FLR 392; but cf *A Father v A Mother* [2020] EWFC B57. See 11.8 on specific issue and prohibited steps orders.

[55] See 10.3.3.

require that if circumstances change he should be reintroduced as a presence, or at least as an influence, in their lives. In such a case a PRO, notwithstanding that only a few or even none of the rights under it may currently be exercisable, may be of value to him and also of potential value to the children. Although there may be other factors which weigh against the making of a PRO in such circumstances, it could never be right to refuse such an order out of hand, on the automatic ground that it would be vitiated by the inability to enforce it.

It is, however, important to note that the case law does not all point the same way and a PRO has been refused in a few cases where PR would be devoid of any practical meaning or effect.[56] There are also cases where PROs are refused due to the conduct of the applicant parent. Amongst the reported cases, abusive behaviour towards the child or the mother,[57] repeated imprisonment,[58] and 'demonstrably improper and wrong' motives for making the application,[59] have all been held to justify refusing a PRO.

However, these somewhat exceptional cases aside, the courts have shown a strong propensity towards granting a PRO. Despite the initial view of the Law Commission that successful applications would be rare,[60] the vast majority of applications for a PRO are granted (though numbers are low).[61]

As with PRAs, the number of PROs has been dropping over the years—again, the likely cause is that fewer fathers *need* a PRO, as they have gained PR automatically by being named on the birth certificate. Nonetheless, it is notable that whereas nearly 5,500 children were the subject of PRO applications in 2011, by 2021 the number had dropped to 925.[62]

10.3.3 LESBIAN MOTHERS AND KNOWN FATHERS/DONORS

In recent years, there have been a number of cases reaching the courts involving disputes between a lesbian co-parenting couple and a person usually termed a 'known sperm donor'. In most of these cases, the man has 'donated' the sperm to allow one of the women to conceive, but later wishes to develop or maintain a meaningful parental or quasi-parental role in the child's life. This involvement is often opposed by the co-parenting couple on the basis that it was never intended that the man would act as a father to the child, and that regular involvement could destabilize the child's primary care-giving unit.[63]

[56] See, e.g., *M v M (Parental Responsibility)* [1999] 2 FLR 737 (Fam Div), where a PRO was refused in relation to a father who suffered a significant mental impairment after a bicycle accident which left him lacking the capacity to exercise PR. See also *Re G (Parental Responsibility Order)* [2006] EWCA Civ 745.

[57] *Re RH (A Minor) (Parental Responsibility)* [1998] 2 FCR 89; *A Father v A Mother* [2020] EWFC B57.

[58] *Re P (Parental Responsibility)* [1997] 2 FLR 722.

[59] *Re P (Parental Responsibility)* [1998] 2 FLR 96. See also *W v Ealing London Borough Council* [1993] 2 FLR 788 (sole purpose of application to prevent adoption of the child) and *Re M (Contact: Parental Responsibility)* [2001] 2 FLR 342 (the father perceived the order as giving him the right to interfere in the child's upbringing which would destabilize and undermine the mother's care of the child).

[60] Law Com (1982), para 7.27.

[61] In 2011 (the final year for which this level of detail was reported by the MOJ), 93.8 per cent of applications were granted; 4.6 per cent were withdrawn; and only 1.6 per cent were refused or 'no order' made: MOJ (2012), table 2.4 (authors' calculations).

[62] MOJ (2022b), table 3; <www.gov.uk/government/statistics/family-court-statistics-quarterly-april-to-june-2022>.

[63] For lesbian parents' views on these and other issues, see Smith (2006).

One of the first cases to address this situation in detail was *Re D (Contact and PR: Lesbian Mothers and Known Father) (No 2)*.[64] The sperm donor, Mr B, had understood that he was to have a continuing role in the child's upbringing, seeing her frequently and participating on an equal basis in important decisions. Conversely, the lesbian couple, Ms A and Ms C, had envisaged a more limited role: that he would be a 'real father' and enjoy regular contact, but he would not be a 'parent' involved in decisions regarding her upbringing. A and C feared that granting B PR would give him 'increased visibility' as 'a third parent', thereby compromising the security of their family unit and exacerbating the problems they faced in gaining social acceptance of their equal parenting roles. In trying to find a solution which recognized and affirmed the child's place within the primary care of A and C, yet also acknowledged the love and commitment of her biological father, Black J took what she described as a 'creative' approach.

Re D (Contact and PR: Lesbian Mothers and Known Father) (No 2) [2006] EWHC 2

BLACK J:

89. I confess that I have been anxious about whether making a parental responsibility order would be in D's interests for the sort of reasons that have influenced [the expert child and adolescent psychiatrist], notably the potential threat to the stability of D's immediate family from what I may loosely call "interference" from Mr B as well as the impact on society's perception of the family if he were, in fact, to use it to become more visible in D's life. On the other hand, I am very mindful of the authorities which stress the status aspect of parental responsibility and those which indicate that it is not appropriate to refuse to grant it because of a feared misuse which should more properly be controlled by s 8 orders. I am also mindful of the fact that such matters as those for which I have criticised Mr B in relation to his actions towards D's family fall far short of the sort of activity that has, in the past, been seen as sufficient to found a refusal of parental responsibility. Perhaps most importantly of all, I am considerably influenced by the reality that Mr B is D's father. Whatever new designs human beings have for the structure of their families, that aspect of nature cannot be overcome. It is to be hoped that as society accepts alternative arrangements more readily, as it seems likely will happen over the next few years, the impulse to hide or to marginalise a child's father so as not to call attention to an anomalous family will decline, although accommodating the emotional consequences of untraditional fatherhood and motherhood and of the sort of de facto, non-biological parenthood that is experienced by a step-parent or same sex partner will inevitably remain discomfiting.

90. The dilemma facing me has been greatly eased by Mr B's offer to be bound by conditions which would prevent him from being intrusive in the obvious situations which might be anticipated as problem areas, namely D's schooling and health care. It has rightly been argued on behalf of Ms A and Ms C that it is not possible to anticipate all the situations that may arise and to guard against them but the course that Mr B proposes would cover the obvious ones. The court has power to regulate others, should they arise, through Children Act orders. Given that Mr B will know, following this judgment, the sort of context that the court anticipates there will be for his involvement in D's life, he will be able to forecast the likely consequences of attempts to become involved in areas of her life not covered by the proposed conditions and it is my judgment that that ought to be a brake upon his conduct.

[64] [2006] EWHC 2.

The judge went on to accept the father's proposal that he have PR, but conditional on his not visiting or contacting the child's school or any health professional involved in the child's care without the written consent of the child's mothers. The grant of PR in this case thus had nothing to do with the actual 'doing' of parenthood; the imposition of conditions on the father's decision-making capacity stripped his PR of its meaningful practical effect. The order was made for purely symbolic reasons, to reflect the importance Black J attributed to the fact of B's biological fatherhood and to confer a sense of enhanced parental status.

However, other judges have refused to adopt the approach taken by *Re D*. For example, *TJ v CV* concerned a known 'sperm donor' (TJ) who had assisted his sister (S) and her civil partner (CV) to conceive a child and who wished to play a continuing parental role.[65] Hedley J considered it would be in the child's best interests to maintain a relationship with his father. However, he was equally clear that TJ should not have the status of a parent or play any kind of 'parental' role. In such circumstances, he held that granting PR would be inappropriate.[66]

In the later case of *MA v RS (Contact: Parenting Roles)*, Hedley J commented on the inadequacy of the available language to deal with these cases.

MA v RS (Contact: Parenting Roles) [2011] EWHC 2455

HEDLEY J:

9. The girls were conceived by IVF with the agreement and co-operation of all parties. This case provides a vivid illustration of just how wrong these arrangements can go. There are perhaps two particular issues that this case raises. The first is the need for precise agreement as to the roles that each is to play before any attempt is made to achieve a pregnancy; and secondly, this case, like others that I have been involved with, is bedevilled by a lack of a sufficient vocabulary to explain the true nature of the relationships. It is all too easy in these cases for biological fathers to see themselves in the same position as in separated parent cases in heterosexual arrangements, whereas this arrangement is, and was always intended to be, quite different. . . .

16. . . . The reason why this case is not equivalent to a separated parent is that there was a clear agreement that the respondents would do the principal parenting and that they would provide the two-parent care to these children. The second respondent clearly believes that her role in this regard has been brought into question, and it is certainly my view that her role in the concept of principal parenting, as one of the two principal parents, needs to be clearly affirmed and respected.

17. By the same token, I am satisfied that the applicants were acknowledged as having a parenting role, albeit in a secondary capacity. That parenting role was to fulfil at least three purposes. The first was indeed to give a clear sense of identity to the child or children in due course. The second was to provide the male component of parenting which all must be taken to have acknowledged. Thirdly, there was a more general role of benign involvement which would have, but would certainly not be confined to, an avuncular aspect.

[65] [2007] EWHC 1952.

[66] See also *R v E and F (Female Parents: Known Father)* [2010] EWHC 417. Bennett J similarly refused a known 'sperm donor' PR, holding that where it was not intended that the donor would 'parent' the child (meaning not just caring emotionally and physically for the child but taking responsibility for all the day-to-day decisions) conferring PR would not be appropriate.

To some extent, at least, these cases can be seen as fitting with the law's general pro-father approach of recent years, and it is arguable that the child may benefit from a legally recognized relationship with more than two parents.[67] On the other hand, some are critical of the courts precisely because they equate the sperm donor with a father, imposing heteronormative expectations on same-sex parents. It can be said that the courts' decisions in these cases give insufficient respect to the nuclear family that the lesbian couple has formed, and place the stability and well-being of that family at risk in order to promote a relationship with a man who was never intended to be a 'father'. It remains the case that the language available is inadequate and unhelpful in these cases—though it seems doubtful that finding better labels would help to resolve the underlying challenges.[68]

10.3.4 STEP-PARENTS

The CA 1989 was amended by the ACA 2002 and the Civil Partnership Act 2004 to allow 'stepparents' (which includes spouses and civil partners, but not cohabitants) to acquire PR for the children of their spouse or civil partner.

Children Act 1989, s 4A

(1) Where a child's parent ("parent A") who has parental responsibility for the child is married to, or a civil partner of, a person who is not the child's parent ("the step-parent")—
   (a) parent A or, if the other parent of the child also has parental responsibility for the child, both parents may by agreement with the step-parent provide for the step-parent to have parental responsibility for the child; or
   (b) the court may, on the application of the step-parent, order that the step-parent shall have parental responsibility for the child.

This allows a step-parent to acquire PR through agreement with the child's parents or by order of the court. The agreement of the child's father or second female parent will only be required if they hold PR. If a parent holding PR withholds consent, an application to the court will be necessary.

Section 4A is an important provision. Before its introduction, step-parents wishing to formalize their legal relationship with their step-children had to resort to the sometimes artificial mechanism of obtaining a 'live with' CAO or adopting the child. As there was usually no dispute over where the child lived, adoption was often preferred. However, step-parent adoption has a drastic effect on the legal position of the child: in addition to conferring PR on the step-parent, the adoption order terminates both the PR *and* the parental status of the non-adopting parent.[69] Indeed, once the adoption order has been made the child is to be

[67] *A v B and C (Contact: Alternative Families)* [2012] EWCA Civ 285.

[68] See generally Diduck (2007).

[69] Under the Adoption Act 1976, the child's parent (parent A) had to make a joint application with their spouse (the step-parent), to adopt their own child. The ACA 2002 removed this wholly artificial requirement, providing that the partner of a child's parent can make a sole application to adopt the child and that the adoption will have no effect on parent A's own PR: ss 46(3)(b) and 51(2). However, the position of the child's other parent (the non-adopting parent) remains unchanged.

treated for all purposes 'as if born as the child of the adopters or adopter'.[70] This effectively removes 'the very parenthood' of the non-adopting parent—usually the child's father—terminating any legal relationship between him and the child, as well as broader kinship relationships.

Growing awareness of the importance of genetic parentage and, wherever possible, preserving the child's familial links with *both* parents, regardless of whether the parents are divorced, separated, or have never lived together, has rendered step-parent adoption deeply problematic.[71] Section 4A thus provides an effective means of recognizing and supporting the social parenting role played by many step-parents, without undermining the importance of the child's relationship with both legal parents. It is thus a more measured response to the realities and complexities of modern families. There remains, however, an apparent anomaly: s 4A is specifically limited to a person who is in a formalized relationship with the child's parent, so cohabitants cannot acquire PR for their partner's children via this route. This sits uneasily with the ACA 2002 which permits the unmarried 'partner' of a child's parent to apply for an adoption order.[72] It seems regrettable that cohabitants in what the law elsewhere terms 'enduring family relationships'[73] are excluded from gaining PR in this way.

10.3.5 HOLDERS OF A CHILD ARRANGEMENTS ORDER

An alternative route by which step-parents, cohabitants, and others may PR for a child is by applying for a CAO.[74] There are two mechanisms.

10.3.5.a Orders that the child live with a person

If a CAO is made *under which the child is to live with a person* then, if that person does not already have PR, they get it automatically under s 12(2), but only for the duration of the order.

Children Act 1989, s 12

(2) Where the court makes a child arrangements order and a person who is not a parent or guardian of the child concerned is named in the order as a person with whom the child is to live, that person shall have parental responsibility for the child while the order remains in force so far as providing for the child to live with that person.

In theory, anyone can acquire PR via this route, as s 10 of the CA 1989 provides that *any person* may apply for this kind of CAO with respect to any child, although those falling outside certain defined categories will require permission from the court.[75] It is important to remember, though, that the primary purpose of this form of CAO is to determine the person

[70] ACA 2002, s 67(1).

[71] That said, it is clearly a matter of degree, and where the parent opposing the adoption has little or no involvement in the child's life, the balance of factors in the welfare assessment may still favour step-parent adoption: see *Re P (Step-Parent Adoption)* [2014] EWCA Civ 1174. Extracts from *Re P* can be found at 13.6.3.

[72] ACA 2002, s 51(2).

[73] Ibid, s 144 (definition of a 'couple'); HFEA 2008, s 54.

[74] Child arrangements orders are discussed in chapter 11.

[75] See 11.3.2.

or persons with whom a child is to live, and the conferral of PR is a necessary aside to enable the person with the order to provide for the child's care. Note that if the person is the child's father or second female parent, s 12(2) does not apply and instead a PRO *must* be made under s 4 (or 4ZA).[76]

10.3.5.b Orders that the child spend time or otherwise have contact with a person

Since 2014, the court has also had power under s 12(2A) to grant PR to a person with whom a child is to *spend time or otherwise have contact*.[77]

Children Act 1989, s 12

(2A) Where the court makes a child arrangements order and—

(a) a person who is not the parent or guardian of the child concerned is named in the order as a person with whom the child is to spend time or otherwise have contact, but

(b) the person is not named in the order as a person with whom the child is to live,

the court may provide in the order for the person to have parental responsibility for the child while paragraphs (a) and (b) continue to be met in the person's case.

This provision allows (but does not require) the court to make a free-standing order giving PR to a person who is named in a CAO but who is not a person with whom the child is to live. In other words, anyone who will be spending time or otherwise having contact with a child under a CAO is able to be given PR for that child for the duration of the order, if the court considers that appropriate. Again, where the person is the child's father or second female parent, if the court decides that PR should be granted then s 12(2A) does not apply and PR must be granted under s 4 (or 4ZA).[78]

10.3.5.c Limitations on parental responsibility arising from a child arrangements order

PR acquired by a non-legal parent under either of these provisions is subject to important limitations. First, the non-legal parent's PR is contingent on the continuation of the CAO. If the CAO terminates, so does PR.[79] This differs from the PR of a father or second female parent who acquires a PRO under s 4 or s 4ZA (whether following a free-standing application or as an adjunct to the grant of a CAO). In this situation, the PRO has life independent from the CAO, and continues (unless terminated[80]) even if the CAO ends. Secondly, there

[76] See s 12(1), discussed at 10.3.2.b. The reason is to ensure that the PR of the father or second female parent does not terminate if the child arrangements order ends, and to avoid the limitations discussed later.

[77] Prior to 2014, 'contact' orders (as they were termed) could not underpin an order for PR, and the court was often asked to make rather artificial 'shared residence orders' in favour of someone with whom the child was not really 'living' in any meaningful sense, in order to open up the possibility of granting the relevant person PR under s 12(2). Some judges saw this as a pragmatic solution to a lacuna in the law; others saw it as an inappropriate use of a residence order if the child's care was not actually being shared.

[78] S 12(1A). [79] S 12(2). [80] See 10.6.2.

are two specific limits on the scope of a non-legal parent's powers if PR is acquired under s 12(2) or 12(2A).

Children Act 1989, s 12

(3) Where a person has parental responsibility for a child as a result of subsection (2) or (2A), he shall not have the right—

(b) to agree, or refuse to agree, to the making of an adoption order, or an order under section 84 of the Adoption and Children Act 2002 with respect to the child; or

(c) to appoint a guardian for the child.

Decisions relating to adoption and guardianship are amongst the most important with respect to a child's future and Parliament has chosen to reserve such questions exclusively to legal parents.

10.3.6 SPECIAL GUARDIANS

Special guardianship orders (SGOs) confer PR on the applicants for the duration of the order.[81] A unique feature of SGOs is that whilst the PR of others is not terminated by the order, special guardians are entitled to exercise PR to the exclusion of any other person with PR.[82] Special guardianship is discussed in more detail in chapter 13.

10.3.7 GUARDIANS

A child's guardian has PR for the child for the duration of the appointment.[83] A guardian may be appointed by the court, a parent with PR, a previous guardian, or a special guardian.[84] Appointment by someone other than the court takes effect upon the death of the appointer, and may be revoked or disclaimed by the appointed person.[85] The appointment of an inter-testamentary guardian by a parent, guardian, or special guardian is the only mechanism available for conferring PR on an individual other than a parent or step-parent that does not require judicial scrutiny and approval.

10.3.8 ADOPTION

An adoption order confers PR on the adopter(s).[86] However, unlike other orders which confer PR on someone, an adoption order terminates the PR of any other person holding PR.[87] PR is thus transferred from the legal parents to the adoptive parent(s) who stand in relation to the child as if the child had been born their natural legitimate child.[88] In accordance with this approach, PR conferred by an adoption order is permanent and irrevocable save for a further adoption. The acquisition and exercise of PR by means of adoption is discussed in chapter 13.

[81] S 14C(1)(a). [82] S 14C(1)(b). [83] S 5(6). [84] S 5(3) and 5(4). [85] S 6.
[86] ACA 2002, s 46(1). [87] Ibid, s 46(2). [88] Ibid, s 67(1).

10.3.9 LOCAL AUTHORITIES

The state in the guise of the local authority automatically acquires PR for a child with respect to whom a care,[89] interim care,[90] or emergency protection order is made.[91] However, to reinforce the lifelong responsibilities of the child's parents, the parents' PR is not terminated but is shared with the local authority. Whilst PR is shared, the local authority has the power to determine the extent to which the parents are actually able to exercise their legal responsibility for the child.[92] The acquisition and exercise of PR by a local authority is discussed in chapter 12.[93]

10.4 WHO SHOULD HAVE PARENTAL RESPONSIBILITY?

Since the CA 1989 was originally enacted, the provisions for conferring PR on people who do not have it automatically have expanded considerably. The position of unmarried fathers, in particular, has changed a lot, but as regards their legal relationship with the child unmarried fathers do not enjoy complete equality with the child's mother or a father who is in a formalized relationship with the mother. There remains a small minority of unmarried fathers who, because they are not registered on the birth register or have not entered into a PRA with the mother, must still go to the expense and inconvenience of 'proving their worth' to the court before being accorded the full legal status of fatherhood. Furthermore, the PR of all unmarried fathers remains subject to termination by the court.[94] These anomalies are a continuing source of grievance for paternal rights activists who argue that all distinctions between the child's parents, whether based on sex or marital status, should be removed. On the other hand, whilst these technical distinctions remain, the reality following the birth registration reforms is that, save for a very small minority, all unmarried fathers will acquire PR. Debates continue about whether the less secure nature of PR for unmarried fathers amounts to a concerning and unjustified discrimination,[95] or whether PR is given too easily to men who may in reality have no active involvement in their children's lives.

10.4.1 THE ARGUMENTS FOR FURTHER REFORM

The continuing distinction between fathers who are, or are not, in a formalized relationship with the child's mother, even if largely symbolic, raises an important point of principle about the extent to which a diversity of family forms should be accorded equal respect under the law. There are strong public policy arguments in favour of recognizing and supporting a wide range of family relationships, particularly where the rights and interests of children are involved. There is now widespread agreement that children should not be disadvantaged because of their parents' marital status. What is important to children is the quality of the parent–child relationship, not whether their parents are in a formalized relationship.

The growing influence of human rights discourse in domestic law and policy provides further impetus for ensuring the children of unmarried parents are treated just the same

[89] S 33(3). [90] S 31(11). [91] S 44(4)(c). [92] S 33(3)(b).
[93] See 12.5.6 in particular. [94] See 10.6.
[95] The inability to remove the PR from a married father was unsuccessfully challenged on grounds of discrimination in *MZ v FZ* [2022] EWHC 295. The case was due to be heard on appeal when this book went to press.

way as children of parents whose relationship has been formalized. From a children's rights perspective, the UN Convention on the Rights of the Child (UNCRC) appears to promote the importance of the child's relationship with *both* parents, regardless of marital status.[96] With particular reference to parental responsibility, Article 18 emphasizes the importance of *equality* between the child's parents.[97]

United Nations Convention on the Rights of the Child 1989, Article 18

1. States Parties shall use their best efforts to ensure recognition of the principle that both parents have common responsibilities for the upbringing and development of the child. Parents or, as the case may be, legal guardians have the primary responsibility for the upbringing and development of the child. The best interests of the child will be their basic concern.

A particularly strong argument in favour of affording equal legal status to all fathers is the importance of eradicating any continuing legal distinction between 'legitimate' and 'illegitimate' children. This was acknowledged by the Law Commission during its review of illegitimacy in the 1980s—in its initial analysis, the Commission argued that the abolition of the concept of illegitimacy would be meaningful only if there were no practical or legal differences between children born to married and unmarried parents.[98]

Despite that initial view, the Law Commission finally recommended that fathers should not be accorded automatic parental rights. By retaining these differences between married and unmarried fathers, all legal distinctions between 'legitimate' and 'illegitimate' children have not therefore been removed from English law. The term 'illegitimate' may no longer be an acceptable part of legal discourse, but that should not disguise the fact that the legal relationship between children and unmarried parents is different from that enjoyed by children and their married parents. The Law Commission rationalized this continuing 'discrimination' on the basis that withholding automatic PR from unmarried fathers did not disadvantage the child, a conclusion with which not everyone would agree.

10.4.2 ARGUMENTS AGAINST CONFERRING EQUAL STATUS ON UNMARRIED FATHERS

The issue of whether unmarried fathers should be treated equally with mothers and married fathers highlights a basic tension in successive government policies on family life. Whilst wishing to ensure that responsibility for children, particularly those living outside the traditional married family unit, falls on the parents and not the state, successive governments have remained committed to promoting marriage as the preferred basis of family life. Reform that could undermine the status of marriage is thus treated cautiously. It is clear from the various consultation papers on PR that there was deep-seated resistance to fully embracing a diversity of family forms, with suspicion about the value of unmarried fathers

[96] See, e.g., Arts 7, 8, and 9. [97] For commentary, see Lowe (1997), 201–2.

[98] Law Com (1982), paras 4.23 and 4.44. Those in a civil partnership are now treated the same as married parents.

being particularly strong. Thus, whereas the commitment and worth of the married father has been simply assumed, the unmarried father, having failed to demonstrate his commitment to the mother and child through entering a formalized relationship, has been an uncertain figure, tainted by fears as to his reckless, irresponsible, and possibly even dangerous behaviour.[99] As the Law Commission's review of illegitimacy reveals, these concerns about the unmarried father were widely held. Although attitudes have undoubtedly moved on since the Law Commission was writing in the early 1980s, negative assumptions about the unmarried father remain a key part of the debate.

Law Commission, *Family Law: Illegitimacy*, Law Com No 118 (London: HMSO, 1982)

4.24 In the Working Paper we summarised the case against automatically extending parental rights to the father of an illegitimate child in the following words—

"3.9 . . . It may be argued that [it is right that the father of a child born out of wedlock should have neither rights nor duties unless and until the court so orders] because of the very wide range of possible factual relationships between the father on the one hand and the mother and the child on the other. If the father wishes to participate in the child's upbringing and can make a substantial contribution to his welfare, the court can make appropriate orders even if the mother wishes to exclude him. If, on the other hand, he has nothing to offer it would, on this view, be wrong to give him rights (albeit rights of which the court would be able to divest him if the child's welfare so required). One can think of extreme and no doubt unrealistic examples. For instance, should a rapist, even in theory, be entitled to rights equal to those of the mother in relation to a child conceived as the result of the rape? If so, the rapist would in theory be entitled to ask whether he agreed to the child being adopted, and would have equal rights to the child's custody unless and until proceedings were taken formally to divest him of such rights. If such an issue were brought before a court it would of course be resolved by reference to the child's welfare, but, unless and until this was done, the rapist father would as a matter of law have the right to exercise full parental rights over the child and might in theory do so.

3.10 We have used the case of the rapist because it provides the most dramatic example of the consequences of abolishing discrimination not only against the child but also against his genetic father. There will, however, be other cases in which the father's relationship with the mother and her child is such that it might seem wrong to give him any, even *prima facie*, legal recognition, as where a child has been conceived as the result of a casual encounter.

3.11 It may be questioned whether this problem is of any real importance since in practice such a father would not seek to exercise rights. Even if he did, the court would be bound to override his rights if to do so would be in the child's interests. Looking at the position pragmatically, this may well be the right approach, but there are two reasons why it may be thought not to be an entirely satisfactory answer. First, the necessity to take legal proceedings to divest the father of his rights may in itself be distressing to the mother—so much so that it could, for example, affect her decision about placing the child for adoption if the result were that the father had to be made a party to the proceedings. Secondly, it would be necessary for the mother to take legal proceedings if she wanted to secure herself and the child against the risk of intervention by the father. Unless and until she did so, the father could (on

[99] As to family law's construction of fathers, see Collier (2001), (2003).

the hypothesis that he had the same rights as the father of a legitimate child) properly exercise any of the parental rights over the child . . . Hence, to avoid this risk, mothers would no doubt often be advised to take steps to remove the father's rights, thus increasing not only the amount of litigation but also the mother's distress. These consequences must therefore be weighed in the balance in deciding whether or not the law should cease to discriminate against the genetic father."

Responses to the Law Commission's Working Paper identified a number of particular concerns with respect to conferring *automatic* PR on unmarried fathers. For example, it was said that mothers might be reluctant to identify the fathers of their children if the consequence was necessarily that the fathers would gain parental rights, and that significant distress and disruption might be caused in cases where mothers had subsequently married another man who was acting as the father to the child (possibly unaware that he was not the child's biological father).[100] There was also a concern about men being put in a position where they 'might be tempted to harass or possibly even to blackmail the mother at a time when she might well be exceptionally vulnerable to pressure', and that the way the law was interpreted by the ordinary person (as opposed to lawyers or social workers, for example) was an important consideration—in other words, the messages that the law sends are one of its important functions.[101]

As these responses to the Law Commission indicate, many commentators at the time were of the view that 'unmeritorious', unmarried fathers should be excluded from holding PR. Furthermore, as the Law Commission went on to point out, the term 'unmeritorious fathers' was not necessarily restricted to a particularly deviant group of men, such as those convicted of a criminal offence.[102] Even men who had cohabited with the child's mother were still viewed as potentially problematic, as were men who had voluntarily acknowledged their paternity through, for example, registration on the birth register.[103] A similarly negative image of the unmarried father emerges from the writings of Deech, a particularly strong opponent of the focus on father's rights (rather than responsibilities) within these debates, at what she perceives to be the risk of marginalizing concern for the mother's autonomy and the welfare of the child.

R. Deech, 'The Unmarried Father and Human Rights', (1992) 4 *Journal of Child Law* 3

Applying a contractual approach, if the father wants all the rights appertaining to a married father, he should marry the mother. If he does not want to make that permanent connection, then he is asking for rights without the *quid pro quo* of responsibilities. If she does not want to marry him, she should not be forced into a quasi-marital situation by being subjected to fathers' rights, such as they are, save where imposed by court in the interests of the child. It is also taken as self-evident here that the law alone cannot make a father assume parental responsibilities that he does not want. It can make him pay support but it cannot make him visit or stay at home or care for his child. . . .

Writers, mostly men, have argued for more fathers' rights, especially unmarried fathers', allegedly for the sake of the child's welfare. This connection can represent a confusion of

[100] Law Com (1982), para 4.26. [101] Ibid, para 4.26. [102] Ibid, para 4.30.
[103] Ibid, para 4.35.

thought. The basic rights of the child are not furthered by delivering more choice to the unmarried father. Legal rights which he may acquire are choices for him; that is, he may or may not choose to exercise them. Such choice is a limitation on the rights of the child. Moreover, the call for fathers' rights confuses abstract legal rights to have a say in long-term decisions about the child, with the existence of actual family contact with the child . . . If one sees parental rights as including protective rights, for example, the parent's right to consent to medical treatment, which gradually cedes with age to the child's choice, it is not clear that the absent unmarried father has any part to play. The proper exercise of a right such as consent to medical treatment of a minor depends fundamentally on intimate knowledge of the condition and maturity of the child and cannot sensibly be exercised otherwise . . .

Discrimination against [the unmarried father] is rooted in the perceived habits of fathers, married or not, who are absent from home, uncommunicative and unable to give guidance even when visiting . . . Criticism of absent fathers is to recognise, not to decry, the importance of a father's involvement . . .

The result of the intense consideration of fathers' rights internationally and in domestic policies has been seen in new legislation. Many of the rights claimed by men have been given to them. Has the movement gone too far? Has sufficient consideration been given to the need to plan for a child and the child's welfare? . . . The pressure for father's rights which has had so much effect is not directed towards making men take responsibility but only to allowing absent fathers to plant their name and the occasional visit on their children, as if they were pieces of property.

Deech goes on to argue that the question to ask was not whether fathers had too few rights, but rather whether they had too few responsibilities. Noting that the CA 1989 focuses on the term 'responsibilities', Deech asks rhetorically whether most fathers are aware of this shift in emphasis, and whether they were accepting of their consequent responsibility to do all in their power to provide for their children. Having observed that the CA 1989 does not define any of the responsibilities of parenthood, Deech suggests that they include 'feeding, washing and clothing the child, putting her to bed, housing her, educating and stimulating her, taking responsibility for arranging babysitting and daycare, keeping the child in touch with the wider family circle, checking her medical condition, arranging schooling and transport to school, holidays and recreation, encouraging social and possibly religious or moral development'.[104] A lack of involvement in these everyday responsibilities should be seen, in Deech's view, as disqualifying a parent from participating in making more significant decisions, thus drawing a distinction between the 'absent father' and the 'cohabiting father'—the former should not, in Deech's argument, have automatic PR.

In stark contrast to the negative view of unmarried fathers, the unmarried mother is generally portrayed as an inherently worthy parent, however the child was conceived. The perceived vulnerability of the unmarried mother is a further striking feature of the debates.

Law Commission, *Family Law: Illegitimacy*, Law Com No 118 (London: HMSO, 1982)

4.39 It may, however, be argued that the father should be entitled to parental rights in cases where *both* parents of the child agree that he should. After all (it might be argued) the

[104] Deech (1992), 4.

law already accords parental rights to all married parents without any prior scrutiny of what is in the child's best interests. Why should it not equally accord such rights to unmarried parents who are in agreement? We see force in this argument, but have nevertheless rejected it. The most powerful factor influencing our decision was the strong body of evidence from those best acquainted with the problems of the single parent family about the vulnerable position of the unmarried mother in many cases. Such mothers may well be exposed to pressure and even harassment, on the part of the natural father; and it would, in our view, give unscrupulous natural fathers undesirable bargaining power if they were to be placed in a position where they might more easily extort from the mother a joint "voluntary" acknowledgment, having the effect of vesting parental rights in the father, perhaps as the price of an agreement to provide for the mother or her child, or even as the price of a continuing relationship with the mother.

Concern for the mother has remained prominent in the debate over unmarried fathers and their 'right' to PR. All reforms to extend the rights of unmarried fathers have been qualified by the need to secure effective safeguards both for mother and child against the behaviour of 'irresponsible' fathers. This approach to the issue has found favour in the European Court of Human Rights, which considered whether it was discriminatory to withhold automatic parental rights from unmarried fathers in *McMichael v United Kingdom*.

McMichael v United Kingdom (A/308, ECHR) (1995)

97. According to the Court's well established case-law, a difference of treatment is discriminatory if it has no reasonable and objective justification, that is, if it does not pursue a legitimate aim or if there is not a reasonable relationship of proportionality between the means employed and the aim sought to be realized . . .

98. . . . As the Commission remarked, "it is axiomatic that the nature of the relationships of natural fathers with their children will inevitably vary, from ignorance and indifference at one end of the spectrum to a close stable relationship indistinguishable from the conventional matrimonial-based family unit at the other" . . . As explained by the Government, the aim of the relevant legislation, which was enacted in 1986, is to provide a mechanism for identifying "meritorious" fathers who might be accorded parental rights, thereby protecting the interests of the child and the mother. In the Court's view, this aim is legitimate and the conditions imposed on natural fathers for obtaining recognition of their parental role respect the principle of proportionality. The Court therefore agrees with the Commission that there was an objective and reasonable justification for the difference of treatment complained of.

99. In conclusion, there has been no violation of Article 14 taken in conjunction with Article 6 para. 1 or Article 8 . . . in respect of the first applicant.

The Court's reasoning in *McMichael* was applied to the specific issue of withholding automatic PR from unmarried fathers under the CA 1989 in *B v United Kingdom*.[105]

Despite attracting the support of the European Court, the purported justifications for withholding equal status from all unmarried fathers have been criticized on several

[105] (App No 39067/97, ECHR) (1999). See also *Sporer v Austria* (App No 35637/03, ECHR).

grounds. It can be argued that unmarried fathers are being denied equal status on the basis of a negative stereotype that is unsupported by any kind of objective evidence.[106] To deny all unmarried fathers full legal responsibility for their children on the basis of unsubstantiated concerns about the behaviour of a small minority of men is arguably manifestly unjust. There are, after all, many irresponsible and uninterested fathers, and indeed mothers, who happen to have formalized their relationship and who are nevertheless 'given the benefit of the doubt' and encouraged to take an active role in their children's upbringing by the automatic grant of PR. Similarly, if the government is committed to encouraging active and meaningful relationships between children and fathers, there is a good case for saying that it should use PR positively to support that policy. As Pickford argues, denying unmarried fathers PR undermines attempts to promote fathers' involvement with their children.[107]

These arguments feed into the wider debate about the cultural and social value of fatherhood in contemporary society. By making all men financially responsible for their children but denying them the full responsibilities of parenthood, the law not only constructs a negative image of the unmarried father but perpetuates outdated stereotypes of fathers as 'breadwinners' and 'providers', rather than 'nurturers' and 'carers', in contrast to mothers who are depicted as the *automatic* natural carers for their children.[108] If one is committed to true equality in parenting, perpetuating these outdated, gendered stereotypes is deeply problematic. As Nigel Lowe has argued, the law needs to foster a 'culture of responsibility' whereby 'fathers have a duty to provide for their children's emotional and moral development as well as their financial needs'.[109]

In order to remove all legal distinctions between parents, there are two further steps the government could take:

- place unmarried fathers in exactly the same position as mothers and fathers in formalized relationships: give them automatic PR which, like that of other parents, cannot be terminated or revoked (or create a mechanism for a married parent's PR to be terminated);
- confer automatic PR on all unmarried fathers but retain the provisions on termination as an appropriate safeguard in extreme cases. This option could be pursued without compromising the principle of equality by rendering the PR of all parents subject to termination.[110]

Both of these options would address continuing concerns about the inequalities faced by unmarried fathers, whilst sending out a strong message to counter the problematic gendered stereotypes which arguably continue to pervade this area of law.

10.4.3 REVIEWING THE CURRENT POSITION

The 2002 reforms which enabled an unmarried father to acquire PR by registration clearly took much of the heat out of the debate. It is arguable that registration on the birth register provides an effective mechanism for identifying those 'meritorious' fathers who have some form of continuing relationship with the child's mother, whilst requiring the minority of

106 Bainham (1989), 227 and 230–1.
107 Pickford (1999), 158.
108 See, e.g., Collier (2001), (2003) and McGlynn (2000), (2001).
109 Lowe (1997), 207. See also Bainham (1989), 226–7.
110 On terminating PR, see 10.6.

remaining fathers (who could be assumed to be more likely to fall into the category of 'irresponsible' or 'dangerous') either to apply to the court or enter into a PRA.

Sheldon and Collier suggest that the image of the unmarried father which has come to dominate family policy in recent years has changed dramatically.

R. Collier and S. Sheldon, *Fragmenting Fatherhood: A Socio-Legal Study* (Oxford: Hart Publishing, 2008), 175–6

[T]he image of unmarried fathers as unworthy, irresponsible and uninterested in their children has been increasingly supplemented (in many contexts even supplanted) by a very different depiction: of men who are often deeply committed to their children, yet find themselves subject to discrimination, denied access to their children and unfairly dependent on the whims of selfish, sometimes hostile mothers.

Against the background of this emerging image of the unmarried father as inherently worthy, it is argued that the tendency to use PROs to confer mere parental status (or 'legitimation'[111]) on unmarried fathers is shifting PR further away from its original purpose of providing legal recognition and support to those carrying out the actual work of parenting. This trend might have the effect of leaving PR devoid of any substantive meaning or purpose. Helen Reece is particularly critical of the decision in *Re D (Contact and PR: Lesbian Mothers and Known Father) (No 2)*, arguing that it represents the 'nadir' of a line of cases in which PR has become detached from parental decision-making. In her view, by awarding PR simply on the basis of biological fatherhood the distinction between parenthood and PR has become blurred,[112] leaving PR 'meaning nothing whatsoever'.[113] As Reece points out, 'if almost all unmarried fathers are compelled to hold parental responsibility, their parental responsibility will no longer even imply official approval of them, as least as individual fathers'.[114] Harris and George echo these concerns.

P. Harris and R. George, 'Parental Responsibility and Shared Residence Orders: Parliamentary Intentions and Judicial Interpretations', (2010) 21 *Child and Family Law Quarterly* 151, 161, 163

From the high point of compliance with the scheme intended by Parliament there has been a consistent trend in the case law downplaying both the potency and primacy of parental responsibility, with the concept being constructed as a form of status recognition with limited or no practical effect . . . [T]he pattern that can be seen is that parental responsibility is increasingly granted to men who are going to play no real part in their children's upbringing, primarily as a means of placating them . . . [W]e would suggest that the courts have robbed parental responsibility of its substantive content. Granting parental responsibility to fathers who are to have little if any involvement in their children's lives, makes it almost impossible to argue that parental responsibility can be something of substantive significance.

[111] Reece (2009), 85. [112] Ibid, 94, 101, and 102. [113] Ibid, 85. [114] Ibid, 97.

In addition to these concerns over devaluing PR, it is doubtful that the government's objectives will be achieved: that conferring PR on all unmarried fathers will encourage them to undertake the responsibility and work of caring for their children. Insofar as the birth registration reforms are intended to effect a change in fathers' parenting behaviour, several commentators suggest they are naïvely optimistic and thus deeply flawed.[115]

L. Smith, 'Clashing Symbols? Reconciling Support for Fathers and Fatherless Families after the Human Fertilisation and Embryology Act 2008', (2010) 22 *Child and Family Law Quarterly* 46, 55, 62–4, 69

[Joint birth registration] is motivated by the intention 'to develop a culture in which the welfare of children is paramount and people are clear that fatherhood as well as motherhood always comes with rights as well as responsibilities'. The White Paper sets out the optimistic view that the act of birth registration will, somehow, in and of itself, result in more fathers exercising their rights and responsibilities towards their children. This policy document too is supported by statements about the various unique advantages that children allegedly derive from the presence of an involved father, thus implicitly linking fathers with child welfare.

The position as a result of the reform is that the rights, duties, powers and responsibilities that comprise parental responsibility now follow upon the simple acknowledgement of genetic paternity. This creates an artificial link between biological and social fatherhood which assumes that the latter act follows the former fact . . .

These legislative and policy developments echo common law developments which have seen parental responsibility degraded from a mechanism for conferring rights and responsibilities to committed and attached fathers, to a simple recognition of status. Whereas, for the purpose of granting parental responsibility, the importance of unmarried fathers was once measured according to the role they actually played, it is now taken as a given. This once again shows a step backwards towards locating the importance of fatherhood in the genetic connection rather than the social relationship.

Smith concludes by suggesting that if the intention is to encourage more fathers to take an active interest in their children, the law would be better remaining faithful to the original purpose of PR and acknowledging and supporting the actual care a father provides rather than valorizing the genetic tie.

The irony of these developments is that the importance of genetic and social fatherhood has been fused using a tool which was designed to recognize that the two are not necessarily linked. The very existence of parental responsibility as a tool with which to graft practical aspects of parenting onto, or separate from, the duties and rights inherent in legal parenthood has always implied legal recognition that genetic and social parenthood may not always coincide. Moreover, when the concept of parental responsibility was introduced into English law, it encapsulated a view of parenthood as a care-giving role. More importantly . . . the *problem* with these developments is that merging the significance of genetic and social

[115] See also McCandless (2008) and Wallbank (2009).

fatherhood makes it possible to assert that all fathers are valuable. By blurring the distinction between fathers who make an active and valuable contribution to their children's upbringing and those who do not, the trend makes it difficult to separate the former from the latter and thus to reject the importance of any father in terms of his potential contribution to his child's welfare . . .

[G]enuinely promoting the value of fatherhood actually depends on distinguishing genetic paternity from social parenting. Failing to distinguish between uninvolved genetic fathers and attentive social fathers devalues the care devoted by the latter. In that sense the confusion which suggests that it is simply a father, rather than the supportive parenting a father can provide, that is intrinsically valuable not only undermines fatherless families, but also undermines efforts to promote fatherhood itself. This means that the drive in family law and policy to promote the idea of responsible (ie involved) parenting to fathers has been undermined because the way in which the message has been presented has been counter-productive. By contrast, an approach to parenthood which emphasized the distinction between the fact of genetic parentage and the act of socially parenting could further the goal of promoting active fatherhood by encouraging more men to focus on the value of parenting their children, rather than just genetically fathering them.

According to this approach, legal parenthood should be left to deal with issues of parental status; PR should deal with those who actually undertake the job of parenting.[116]

10.5 EXERCISING PARENTAL RESPONSIBILITY

10.5.1 A DUTY TO CONSULT OR A RIGHT OF UNILATERAL ACTION?

The Children Act's approach to the acquisition of PR means that at any one time there may be several adults who hold PR for a particular child. While a child's 'parenting team' can cooperate over decisions relating to the child's upbringing, the fact that decision-making is shared poses no particular problems. However, difficulties develop where cooperation breaks down and different members of the 'parenting team' hold different views about what will best serve the child's interests. Disputes may arise over the child's school, medical treatment, surname, and in which religion, if any, the child should be raised.[117] The possibility of disagreement raises the important question of whether individuals holding PR can act unilaterally without consulting or seeking the agreement of the other members of the 'parenting team'. This is also an important issue where an individual holding PR has little or no contact with the child and that person's whereabouts may be unknown, but can be more problematic in cases where both parents are involved in their child's upbringing but do not agree about various aspects of parenting.

These potential difficulties were anticipated by the Law Commission. Their proposed solution was to allow unilateral action by individual holders of PR.

[116] Lind and Hewitt (2009).

[117] For detailed discussion of these various aspects of PR, see Probert, Gilmore, and Herring (2009).

Law Commission, *Family Law, Review of Child Law: Guardianship and Custody*, Law Com No 172 (London: HMSO, 1988c)

(b) The power to act independently

2.10 . . . [W]hether or not the parents are living together, a legal duty of consultation seems both unworkable and undesirable. The person looking after the child has to be able to take decisions in the child's best interests as and when they arise. Some may have to be taken very quickly. In reality, . . . it is that person who will have to put those decisions into effect and that person who has the degree of practical control over the child to be able to do so. The child may well suffer if that parent is prevented by the other's disapproval and thus has to go to court to resolve the matter, still more if the parent is inhibited by the fear that the other may disapprove or by the difficulties of contacting him or of deciding whether what is proposed is or is not a major matter requiring consultation. In practice, where the parents disagree about a matter of upbringing the burden should be on the one seeking to prevent a step which the other is proposing, or to impose a course of action which only the other can put into effect, to take the matter to court. Otherwise the courts might be inundated with cases, disputes might escalate well beyond their true importance, and in the meantime the children would suffer. We recommend, therefore, that the equal and independent status of parents be preserved and, indeed, applied to others . . . who may share parental responsibility in future. This will not, of course, affect any statutory provision which requires the consent of each parent, for example, to the adoption of the child.

This recommendation was enshrined in s 2(7) of the CA 1989.[118]

Children Act 1989, s 2

(7) Where more than one person has parental responsibility for a child, each of them may act alone and without the other (or others) in meeting that responsibility; but nothing in this Part shall be taken to affect the operation of any enactment which requires the consent of more than one person in a matter affecting the child.

The only general statutory restriction on this right of unilateral action is that a person exercising PR must not act incompatibly with a court order.[119]

Although a right of unilateral action avoids potential difficulties in trying to locate and obtain the agreement of an estranged parent, such an approach creates the possibility of members of the 'parenting team' taking contradictory decisions and undermining one another's care of the child. Parents may present opposing concerns about this approach. On the one hand, a parent may consider that without the ability to make unilateral decisions, they may be unable to deal with even day-to-day matters effectively if the other parent does not agree, and that this will be contrary to the child's welfare (as well as their own!).

[118] Specific provision is made for those holding PR under a special guardianship order: see s 14C(1)(b), (2), and (3).

[119] S 2(8). Note the specific restrictions in s 13, discussed at 11.6.6 and 11.8.

Conversely, a parent who is perhaps less involved in the daily care of the child may feel that their PR is of little practical value if the other parent is free to make all the parenting decisions without agreement.

Despite the statutory basis for unilateral decision-making under s 2(7), the courts have imposed a duty to *consult* and, in effect, *agree* on certain important matters regarding the child's upbringing. The first case to suggest such a duty was *Re G (Parental Responsibility: Education)*. The case concerned a dispute between the child's parents over which school the child should attend. The father, with whom the child had lived since the parents' separation, wished the child to attend a local authority boarding school. The mother, who only became aware of the father's intentions at the eleventh hour, was strongly opposed to this course of action. She applied for a prohibited steps order[120] preventing the father from sending the child to the school until her own application for a CAO could be determined. The application was dismissed, but, on appeal, the Court of Appeal made it clear that the mother should have been properly consulted over such an important decision.

Re G (Parental Responsibility: Education) [1995] 2 FCR 53 (CA), 56

GLIDEWELL LJ:

The great difficulty is, of course, on the one hand that the mother was not informed of the decision to send the boy to the boarding school and there is no doubt she should have been. Under s. 2 of the Children Act 1989 she has parental responsibility for both children, even though they are not living with her . . .

So far no order has been made in respect of which the father is acting incompatibly, but equally there is no doubt, to my mind, that the mother, having parental responsibility, was entitled to and indeed ought to have been consulted about the important step of taking her child away from the day school that he had been attending and sending him to a boarding school. It is an important step in any child's life and she ought to have been consulted.

Support for imposing a duty to consult was taken a step further in *Re C (Minors) (Change of Surname)*, which concerned the mother's wish to change the children's surname from that of their father to that of her new husband. Following the parents' divorce, it was agreed that the children would live with their mother and no CAO was therefore made. The children's contact with their father ceased just before the mother remarried. The fact that there was no 'live with' order in force was significant because under s 13(1) of the CA 1989, had such an order been made, the mother would not have been able to change their surname without the written consent of everyone with PR or without first obtaining leave of the court.[121] However, following her remarriage, and on the advice of her solicitor, the mother attempted to change the children's surnames by deed poll without consulting her former husband or obtaining his agreement. Steps were then taken for the new surname to be used at official levels such as at school and on medical files. However, the headteacher and the local education authority requested confirmation that everyone with PR had consented to the change before being prepared to amend their records. Consequently, the mother applied for a specific issue order[122] requiring them to acknowledge and adopt the children's new surname.

[120] Prohibited steps orders are discussed at 11.8.

[121] See 11.8.3.

[122] Specific issue orders are discussed at 11.8.

Holman J held that despite the various legislative provisions suggesting a unilateral right of action, on a matter as important as changing the child's surname, all those with PR should have been *consulted and their agreement obtained.*[123]

Re C (Minors) (Change of Surname) [1997] 3 FCR 310 (Fam Div), 312–19

HOLMAN J:

The argument for the mother

[Counsel's] argument was, in essence, as follows. Section 2(7) provides that where two or more people have parental responsibility each of them may act alone subject to any enactment which requires the consent of more than one person. In relation to a change of name the only relevant enactments are s. 13(1) and s. 33(7) [where the child is in the care of the local authority subject to a care order]. They do not apply to this case since there is no residence or care order in force. Further, in private law cases, s. 13 provides an exhaustive statutory "code" of the circumstances in which the consents of all people having parental responsibility is required. Accordingly the mother had the right and power to change the surname . . .

In my judgment the conclusion and consequences of this argument are little short of bizarre. Where parents have not agreed about their child or not been able to trust each other so that a residence order has had to be made . . . the "rights" of both parents in relation to a change of name are carefully preserved; whereas where parents have been able to agree and have not caused or risked harm to their children, the "rights" of either parent can be unilaterally overborne by the other. Further, there would technically, and unless the mother obtained a court order, have been nothing to stop the father in the present case subsequently exercising *his* parental responsibility and executing another deed of name change, which would of course lead to chaos and be potentially very damaging to the children.

Moreover the argument, if correct, would run totally counter to the philosophy of the Children Act, for it would be likely to lead to an insistence on formal residence orders even when the parents were in complete agreement about the issue of with whom the child should live . . . In my judgment, Parliament neither intended nor enacted the result which the mother contends for . . .

Holman J went on to hold that the scope of PR as enshrined in the CA 1989 should be understood in light of any pre-existing limitations on parents' rights and responsibilities contained in the case law and/or legislation. He thus turned to examine the legal position on changing a child's surname as derived from the case law prior to the enactment of the CA 1989, which he held to set out a common law limitation on a parent's ability to make a unilateral change to a child's surname, at least (under the old law) where the child was legitimate. That rule, Holman J held, survived the introduction of the CA 1989, despite the wording of s 2(7).

Eekelaar strongly criticized this decision, fearing it could be of much wider application.

[123] It has subsequently been suggested that where one parent seeks to change the surname by which a child is known (usually the registered surname), the obligation to obtain the consent of all parents will apply regardless of whether a child arrangements order determining where the child should live is in force and regardless of which of the parents has PR. If the parent withholds consent, the leave of the court will be required. See *Dawson v Wearmouth* [1998] Fam 75.

J. Eekelaar, 'Do Parents Have a Duty to Consult?', (1998b) 114 *Law Quarterly Review* 337, 337–40

When two parents have parental responsibility, must one consult the other over important decisions regarding the child? . . . In 1988 the Law Commission thought it had resolved the question. "Whether or not the parents are living together, a legal duty of consultation seems both unworkable and undesirable" said the Law Commission, and recommended accordingly, but added that "this will not, of course, affect any statutory provision which requires the consent of each parent, for example, to the adoption of the child." . . .

[In *Re C*] Holman J held that [s 2(7)] did not "preclude that the consent of more than one person may also be required by some other source of law than an enactment, notwithstanding the first limb of s. 2(7)". He found such a source in the law as it existed prior to the implementation of section 2(7) which, in his view, prevented the parent of a legitimate child from changing its surname without the consent of the other parent.

. . . [I]t is certainly arguable that under a combination of statute and common law prior to the Children Act 1989 there was a legal duty to consult over "important" matters and that, if the second parent disagreed, the parent with the children could not act without permission of the court.

But this can hardly sustain the basis of Holman J's conclusion in [*Re C*]. For the Children Act 1975 was repealed by the Children Act 1989 and cannot form the source of rights thereafter and to hold that the common law position (whatever it was immediately before the implementation of the 1989 Act) overrides section 2(7) is to make the statute subject to the prior law it purported to replace and deprives it of all effect. An argument might be attempted that section 2(7) is consistent with the perpetuation of a duty to consult on the ground that all it does is to clarify that, should consultation fail to bring about agreement, either parent may take action "without the other" leaving the aggrieved party to seek eventual resolution of the dispute in court. Such an interpretation would depart from the intentions of the Law Commission . . . but there must now be some danger that it could be accepted . . .

It is suggested that the Law Commission was right in thinking that a general duty to consult would be unworkable. Apart from the problem of defining the range of issues upon which consultation would be required (what are "serious" issues? choice of school, probably; choice of curriculum, of extra-curricular activities? perhaps, perhaps not), what amounts to consultation or attempts at consultation? It cannot be sound policy to provide parties with increased opportunities for legal conflict and dispute . . . In most cases the best safeguard against surprise decisions lies in the hands of the outside parent. If he sees his children regularly, he will normally know about these "important issues", or will discover them quickly. It is striking that in [*Re C*] the attempt to change the children's name occurred only after direct contact between the father and the children had stopped for over a year. It is difficult to justify imposing a general duty to consult on the parent who is looking after the children when the other parent is not under a legally enforceable duty to involve himself with (or even visit) the children (and nor could such a duty be realistically imposed).

Holman J commented that if the parents retained the right to independent action, there would have been nothing to stop the father from exercising *his* parental authority and executing another deed of name change, causing "chaos" and being potentially very damaging to the children. This argument against independent action could be made with respect to any exercise of parental responsibility, but is a red herring. Parental responsibility can best be understood as the legitimation of *practical actions* in exercising parenthood. A parent who is not actively involved in a child's life cannot effectively bring about a change in the name by which the child is known. Of course, should he attempt to do so and thus come into conflict with the other parent, the matter would need to be resolved by a court. But that would equally be the case if there was a requirement for his consent.

Indeed, Eekelaar's concern that, following *Re C*, a more general duty to consult and obtain agreement on a wide range of 'important' decisions might be imposed, was borne out by the subsequent case law. Circumcision and immunization[124] were added to the 'small group of important decisions'[125] on which consultation is necessary.

The problem with this approach is the considerable uncertainty it causes. Whilst it is now clear that certain specific issues—schooling; change of surname; circumcision; sterilization; and immunization—fall within the class of case where consultation and agreement is necessary, other decisions potentially falling within this group will have to be determined on a case-by-case basis. The case law provides little guidance as to whether any particular decision will be regarded as sufficiently important as to require consultation. The Court of Appeal has suggested that 'in general terms, it must be the case that where two parents share parental responsibility, it will be the duty of one parent to ensure that the rights of the other parent are respected',[126] which suggests that the limitation on the exercise of PR may be very sizeable indeed. Wall J once set out some examples in three categories, but the suggestion does not seem to have been adopted more generally.

A v A (Shared Residence) [2004] EWHC 142

WALL J:

1. Decisions that could be taken independently and without any consultation or notification to the other parent.

   - How the children are to spend their time during contact
   - Personal care for the children
   - Activities undertaken
   - Religious and spiritual pursuits
   - Continuance of medicine treatment prescribed by GP

2. Decisions where one parent would always need to inform the other parent of the decision, but did not need to consult or take the other parent's views into account.

   - Medical Treatment in an emergency
   - Booking holidays or to take the children abroad in contact time
   - Planned visits to the GP and the reasons for this

3. Decisions that you would need to both inform and consult the other parent prior to making the decision.

[124] *Re C (Welfare of Child: Immunisation)* [2003] EWHC 1376. This approach is maintained in *private law* cases by *M v H (Private Law: Vaccination)* [2020] EWFC 93, where MacDonald J held that 'where two parents with parental responsibility disagree as to the proper course of action with respect to vaccination, the court becomes the decision maker through the mechanism of a specific issue order'. By contrast, in *public law* cases, if a child is in the care of a local authority, the local authority is entitled to rely on its own PR to override any objection from parents to standard immunizations: *Re H (Parental Responsibility: Vaccination)* [2020] EWCA Civ 664.

[125] Ibid, [16]–[17].

[126] *Re W (Direct Contact)* [2012] EWCA Civ 999, [47]. See also *Re C (Welfare of Child: Immunisation)* [2003] EWHC 1376, discussed by O'Donnell (2004).

- Schools the children are to attend, including admissions applications. With reference to which senior school C should attend this is to be decided taking into account C's own views and in consultation and with advice from her teachers.
- Contact rotas in school holidays
- Planned medical and dental treatment
- Stopping medication prescribed for the children
- Attendance at school functions so they can be planned to avoid meetings wherever possible
- Age that children should be able to watch videos. ie videos recommended for children over 12 and 18.

The law also provides no clear indication of what the consequences may be for failing to consult and agree in advance of a 'significant decision' being taken.[127] In some contexts—a change of school, or a relocation elsewhere within the UK—the decision may be technically reversible, but by the time the matter reaches a judge, a new status quo for the child may have been established, and it will need to be shown that a reversal of the decision is now in the child's best interests, bearing in mind the s 1(5) 'no order' principle.[128] Where reversal is not possible or not in the child's interests, the likely consequences may not go much further than a judicial 'slap on the wrist'. It is open to question, therefore, whether the duty to consult in fact has much in the way of teeth; the burden is on the parent opposing the decision both to know of it in advance and to make a court application to that effect.[129]

The proper mechanism for resolving disputes between those holding PR is to apply for a specific issue or prohibited steps order under s 8 of the CA 1989.[130] In determining the dispute the child's welfare is the paramount consideration.

10.5.2 LIMITATIONS ON THE EXERCISE OF PARENTAL RESPONSIBILITY

The need for consultation and agreement between the holders of PR can serve as an important limitation on the decision-making authority of a parent. However, even where there is agreement their authority may still be subject to challenge by a third party. There are two major sources of external restraint on the decision-making authority of those holding PR: (i) the child and (ii) the state.

[127] The exception to this is removal of a child internationally without consent (or the court's permission), where the law provides serious criminal and civil sanctions under the Child Abduction Act 1984 and the Hague Convention on the Civil Aspects of International Child Abduction 1980.

[128] See, e.g., our discussion of 'unilateral relocation' at 11.8.2.

[129] Scherpe (2022) suggests that a duty to *inform* would be more workable, as well as being more in line with the Law Commission's intentions and the wording of s 2(7).

[130] See 11.8. There is a small exceptional class of case where the issue in question does not fall within the limits of PR. An example is *Re JS (Disposal of Body)* [2016] EWHC 2859, where a terminally ill teenager wished to make arrangements for her body to be cryogenically preserved following her death. Her mother agreed with this proposal but her father did not. Because the issue was going to affect the child only after her death, it fell outside the scope of PR. The court, on the child's own application, made orders under the inherent jurisdiction to allow her wishes to be fulfilled. See generally 8.7.

10.5.2.a The *Gillick*-competent child

Following the decision of the House of Lords in *Gillick v West Norfolk and Wisbech Health Authority*,[131] it is now well established that where children are of sufficient understanding to be deemed capable of making their own decisions, the child's parents lose their *exclusive* decision-making powers with respect to the care and upbringing of the child. As interpreted in the subsequent case law, *Gillick*-competent children have the right, alongside their parents, to provide a valid consent on a range of important matters, such as contraception and medical treatment. As we discuss in detail in chapter 8,[132] while there was previously some suggestion that a parent could continue to give valid consent to medical treatment even when a *Gillick*-competent child had refused it, more recent authorities have disagreed. Lieven J in *AB v CD, The Tavistock and Portman NHS Foundation Trust and others* held that a parent could not use their PR to override a *Gillick*-competent child's refusal of treatment, but that the parent could still make the decision if such a child was unable to or declined to make the decision.[133] How far this principle applies outside the medical treatment context is unclear—for example, how a local education authority would react to a *Gillick*-competent child's application to change school without the support of their parents is unknown.

10.5.2.b The state

A second and potentially more powerful constraint on the decision-making authority of those with PR is the state. One obvious way in which this can happen is with prohibited steps orders restricting a parent's use of their PR.[134] General restrictions are not common, but can include prohibitions regarding particular issues (where a parent is not allowed to make decisions about schooling, for example, but can otherwise exercise their parental responsibility)[135] or, in rare and extreme cases, a complete restriction on a parent exercising any aspect of their PR.[136]

More generally, the CA 1989 gives the primary responsibility for decision-making about children to those with PR, and supports that with the 'no order' principle in CA 1989, s 1(5).[137] If it is proposed that children be taken into local authority care, the law protects family autonomy by providing that the state can only accommodate children if the parents choose voluntarily to delegate their PR to the local authority children's services department, or if a court order is obtained.[138] In terms of an order, the CA 1989 sets down that the court may only make a care or supervision order if the child is suffering, or is likely to suffer, significant harm.[139] Consequently, parents are given significant protections against interference by the state.

However, that does not mean that parents have completely free rein, even if they agree. While *local authorities* seeking a care or supervision order (or orders under the High Court's inherent jurisdiction) have to cross a threshold of demonstrating at least the risk of significant harm to the child, in other contexts there is no such restriction. Consequently, applications can be brought by an NHS Trust, for example, where they consider that the decision which parents are making is not in the best interests of the child, so long as they can show a sufficient interest in the child to justify giving them standing.[140] Local authorities can also

[131] [1986] AC 112. [132] For detailed discussion, see 8.5.6.b. [133] [2021] EWHC 741.
[134] See 11.8.
[135] *Re D (Contact and Parental Responsibility: Lesbian Mothers and Known Father) (No 2)* [2006] EWHC 2.
[136] See 10.6. [137] See 8.6.1. [138] *Williams v London Borough of Hackney* [2018] UKSC 37.
[139] CA 1989, s 31. See chapter 12. [140] See 8.6.2.

apply for private law orders under the CA 1989 without having to meet the 'significant harm' threshold,[141] though it is hard to square this general position with the obiter discussion in *Re H (Parental Responsibility: Vaccination)*.[142]

Re H was about whether a local authority needed court authorization to arrange for standard immunization injections to be provided to an infant in its care under a care order, where the parents objected. The Court of Appeal held that the local authority could exercise its existing PR, held by virtue of the care order,[143] and did not need to apply to court despite the parents' objection. King LJ went on, though, to consider the question of what the local authority could do in a situation where there was no care order, and so the local authority did not already hold PR. The court had previously held that it would not be appropriate for a local authority to seek a care order *only* to deal with such a limited issue without wider concerns about the child's welfare (even assuming that such a case would meet the 'significant harm' threshold).[144] But King LJ's obiter comments go further, holding that the local authority was not *permitted* to make any free-standing application in relation to vaccination at all.

The analysis in *Re H* is therefore rather confused. On the one hand, if a child happens to be in local authority care, the parents cannot interfere with the local authority's decision to have the child vaccinated—but if King LJ is right, if a child is not in local authority care and the parents do not agree to vaccination, the local authority is entirely powerless to intervene. As George explains, the second part of that analysis makes little sense, and the reasoning underpinning it overlooks the obvious statutory remedy that is available.

R. George, 'Parental Responsibility, Vaccination, and the Role of the State',
(2020) 136 *Law Quarterly Review* 559, 561–3

[T]he local authority cannot bring an application for a care order in order to obtain parental responsibility for a child where failure to vaccinate is the sole issue. It follows that the local authority cannot obtain and rely on its own parental responsibility in such a case, even though if it had parental responsibility already it could legitimately use that parental responsibility to authorise the child's vaccination.

The Court of Appeal then goes on to say, therefore, that the local authority cannot in fact obtain orders for vaccination at all if the child is not subject to a care order for other reasons, because the threshold under s 100(4) cannot be met. King LJ puts it this way:

> "If a parent in respect of whom there are no care proceedings cannot be considered to be causing a child to be likely to suffer significant harm when they decide not to vaccinate their child, I cannot see how can it be said now, for the purposes of s100(4)(b), that that very same refusal on their part provides reasonable cause to believe that the child is likely to suffer significant harm if the inherent jurisdiction is not exercised." (at [90].)

That logic is impeccable, but it only arises because the court is asking the wrong question, premised on the court's need to invoke the inherent jurisdiction rather than making a statutory order. Why should the question be: can the local authority invoke the inherent jurisdiction? The only reason for doing so is if the remedy sought cannot be obtained in some other way under the Children Act: s 100(4)(a) . . . Is this such a case?

[141] *Re R (A Minor) (Blood Transfusion)* [1993] 2 FLR 757.
[142] [2020] EWCA Civ 664.
[143] S 33(3).
[144] *Re AB (Medical Treatment: Care Proceedings)* [2018] EWFC 3.

King LJ is right that where a child is subject to a care order, the court is barred from making private law orders under s 8 of the CA 1989.[145] If, therefore, a court order is needed to regulate an aspect of PR where a child is in care, the local authority has no option but to seek an order under the High Court's inherent jurisdiction,[146] because the statutory route is blocked.[147]

> This outcome appears to be an anomaly, resulting from the court's view that Article 8 rights under the European Convention on Human Rights prevent the local authority from relying on its PR where the decision involves a significant interference in family life (*Re DE (Care Order: Change of Care Plan)* [2014] EWFC 6).
>
> Where a child is not subject to a care order or interim care order already, however, the restriction in s 9(1) does not apply. Anyone who can get the court's leave under s 10 of the Act can apply for a specific issue order or a prohibited steps order under s. 8 including . . . a local authority. The threshold for obtaining leave to apply under s 10 has no 'significant harm' element to it: it is a simple assessment by the court taking into account the factors highlighted in s 10(9) and any other relevant considerations in the particular case (*Re B (Care Proceedings: Joinder)* [2012] EWCA Civ 737, [48]). There is no reason at all why even the most serious dispute about medical treatment cannot be resolved by way of a specific issue order or a prohibited steps order (*Re JM (A Child) (Medical Treatment)* [2015] EWHC 2832), so the issue of vaccination can certainly be determined by the making of such an order. But because the court focuses only on its inherent jurisdiction, it seems to lose sight entirely of the more obvious remedy, and ends up imposing on local authorities an unnecessary and logically unobtainable threshold for intervention—significant harm.

10.6 TERMINATING PARENTAL RESPONSIBILITY

10.6.1 MOTHERS, FATHERS WHO ARE IN A FORMALIZED RELATIONSHIP, AND SECOND FEMALE PARENTS UNDER HFEA 2008, S 42

There are very restrictive circumstances under which the PR of mothers, fathers who are in a formalized relationship with the mother, and second female parents under HFEA 2008, s 42 can be terminated. This approach emphasizes that—despite the occurrence of other events affecting the parties, such as divorce, separation, or the removal of the children into care—the responsibilities of raising a child are lifelong, and that changes in the parents' relationship, in particular, do not impact the parental role that each of them plays. This is in contrast to the position for unmarried fathers, where the court has a mechanism for removing PR, as we set out in the following section.[148]

Consequently, the only way in which the PR of a child's mother, father in a formalized relationship, or second legal parent under the HFEA 2008, s 42 can be terminated, however

[145] S 9(1). The reason for this, somewhat ironically, is to prevent interference with the local authority's decision-making once a child is in care and the local authority has PR!

[146] See 8.7. [147] See *Re C (Child in Care: Choice of Forename)* [2016] EWCA Civ 374.

[148] See 10.6.2.

uninterested or unsuitable they are, is by making an adoption order.[149] Under these orders the 'parenthood' of the child, including PR, is transferred to the adopters who, like natural parents, can only be divested of their PR by a second adoption order.

An adoption order in favour of one legal parent can be used to divest the other legal parent of their PR. However, as noted previously, adoption has far-reaching effects on the child's core family relationships beyond the termination of PR. This use of adoption to deprive an absent, irresponsible, or uninterested parent of PR is therefore an extreme measure. The issue was considered by the House of Lords in *Re B (A Minor) (Adoption: Natural Parent)*.[150] The child's father, who was worried about the security of his position as the child's residential carer, was seeking an adoption order with the sole purpose of permanently excluding the mother from the child's life.[151] Controversially, Lord Nicholls allowed the adoption order to stand, thereby making the child 'legally motherless', even though the father's position could have been consolidated using alternative, less drastic measures under the CA 1989.[152] The controversy surrounding this case highlights the important question of whether specific provision needs to be made for terminating the PR of mothers, fathers in formalized relationships, and second female parents under s 42 of the HFEA 2008, akin to the measures in place for terminating the PR of unmarried fathers, second female parents under s 43 of the HFEA 2008, and step-parents.

However, the court has rejected the suggestion that the inability to remove PR from a married father amounted to unjustified discrimination on the basis of the parents' marital status. In rejecting a mother's challenge to the inability to remove her former husband's PR, the High Court in *MZ v FZ* held that there were legitimate reasons why the legislature might continue to differentiate between parents who are in a formalized relationship with each other and those who are not.[153] The case was due to be heard by the Court of Appeal when this book went to press. Introducing the power to revoke PR from anyone, regardless of marital status, would accommodate the somewhat transient nature of parenting in modern family life, recognizing the reality that there are absent, uninterested parents, who do not have a relationship with their children—or, indeed, whose involvement in their children's lives may be positively harmful—and should not have to be consulted on important decisions regarding their upbringing. It would also formally acknowledge that the problem of the absent parent is not one restricted to the unmarried father: it is a problem of parenthood, not fatherhood.

In the absence of such a provision allowing PR to be revoked, the court has had to improvise. The practical approach alighted on has been to make sweeping prohibited steps and specific issue orders which prohibit one parent from exercising any aspect of their PR and allowing the other to make all decisions about the child unilaterally and without consultation.[154] While such cases are rare, it is clear that the court's power 'extends, in very exceptional circumstances, to making an order prohibiting a parent from taking any steps in the exercise of parental responsibility'.[155]

[149] In surrogacy cases, PR is lost (along with legal parental status) when a parental order is made under HFEA 2008, s 54/54A, but the criteria for making such an order are premised on the arrangement having been intended as a surrogacy pre-conception. See 9.5.3.

[150] [2001] UKHL 70.

[151] This decision is discussed in detail at 13.6.4.

[152] For commentary, see Harris-Short (2002).

[153] [2022] EWHC 295.

[154] *Re B and C (Change of Names: Parental Responsibility: Evidence)* [2017] EWHC 3250.

[155] *Re D (Domestic Violence: Court Orders)* [2014] EWHC 2355, [109].

10.6.2 UNMARRIED FATHERS, SECOND FEMALE PARENTS UNDER HFEA 2008, S 43, AND STEP-PARENTS

10.6.2.a Unmarried fathers

The position of unmarried fathers regarding the acquisition of PR has improved considerably. However, unlike the PR of fathers in formalized relationships, the PR of unmarried fathers may still be terminated on application to the court by another holder of PR or even, with leave, by the child.

Children Act 1989, s 4

(2A) A person who has acquired parental responsibility under subsection (1) [methods by which unmarried fathers may acquire parental responsibility] shall cease to have that responsibility only if the court so orders.

(3) The court may make an order under subsection (2A) on the application—

(a) of any person who has parental responsibility for the child; or

(b) with the leave of the court, of the child himself,

subject, in the case of parental responsibility acquired under subsection 1(c), to section 12(4).

(4) The court may only grant leave under subsection (3)(b) if it is satisfied that the child has sufficient understanding to make the proposed application.

If the court has made a PRO in favour of an unmarried father or a second female parent made under s 4 or 4ZA because a child arrangements order was made under which the child was to live with that parent, the PRO cannot be terminated while the relevant child arrangements order remains in force.[156]

The principles to be applied in determining an application under ss 4(2A) and 4(3) are set down in *Re D (Withdrawal of Parental Responsibility)*. The father had PR by virtue of having been named on the child's birth certificate. He was subsequently convicted for sexual offences against the mother's two daughters by a previous relationship and sentenced to 48 months' imprisonment. On his release from prison, the mother sought an order revoking the father's PR. The father sought a specific issue order requiring the mother to provide him with annual reports about the child's progress, but indicated that he did not intend to seek any other orders. At first instance, Baker J followed the approach set out by Singer J in *Re P (Terminating Parental Responsibility)*,[157] which was then the only reported decision setting out any principles for such applications. The father appealed on the basis that the principles set out by *Re P* in 1994 needed to be revised following the Human Rights Act 1998 and the modifications that had been made to the CA 1989 with respect to PR.

[156] S 12(4). [157] [1995] 1 FLR 1048.

Re D (Withdrawal of Parental Responsibility) [2014] EWCA Civ 315

RYDER LJ:

12. When a court is considering an application relating to the cessation of parental responsibility, . . . the child's welfare will be the court's paramount consideration. By section 1(4), there is no requirement upon the court to consider the factors set out in section 1(3) (the 'welfare checklist') but the court is not prevented from doing so and may find it helpful to use an analytical framework not least because welfare has to be considered and reasoned. Given that the cessation of parental responsibility is an order of the court, the court must also consider whether making such an order is better for the child than making no order at all (the 'no order' principle in section 1(5)).

13. The paramountcy test is overarching and no one factor that the court might consider in a welfare analysis has any hypothetical priority. Accordingly, factors that may be said to have significance by analogy or on the facts of a particular case, for example, the factors that the court considers within the overarching question of welfare upon an application for a parental responsibility order (the degree of commitment which the father has shown to the child, the degree of attachment which exists between the father and the child and the reasons of the father for applying for the order) may be relevant on the facts of a particular case but are not to be taken to be a substitute test to be applied . . .

14. An unmarried father does not benefit from a 'presumption' as to the existence or continuance of parental responsibility. He obtains it in accordance with the statutory scheme and may lose it in the same way. In both circumstances it is the welfare of the child that creates the presumption, not the parenthood of the unmarried father. The concept of rival presumptions is not helpful . . . There is also ample case law describing the imperative in favour of a continuing relationship between both parents and a child so that ordinarily a child's upbringing should be provided by both of his parents and where that is not in the child's interests by one of them with the child having the benefit of a meaningful relationship with both. A judge would not be criticised for identifying that, as a very weighty, relevant factor, the significance of the parenthood of an unmarried father should not be under estimated.

Having rejected the father's claim on this issue, Ryder LJ went on to reject the father's other grounds of appeal, including that Baker J had not considered the proportionality of the order made. Permission to appeal to the Supreme Court was refused.[158]

Although *Re P* and *Re D* emphasize that the courts will be reluctant to terminate the PR of an unmarried father without very good grounds, the fact that the PR of an unmarried father (but not that of a mother or of a father in a formalized relationship) can be terminated at all is a potential source of grievance for paternal rights advocates. However, the argument that it constitutes discrimination against unmarried fathers has been dismissed by the European Court of Human Rights.[159]

[158] UKSC 2014/0172, 12 November 2014. For critical commentary, see Gilmore (2015). See also *C v D (Parental Responsibility)* [2018] EWHC 3312.

[159] *B v United Kingdom* (App No 39067/97, ECHR) (1999).

10.6.2.b Second female parents under HFEA 2008, s 43

The PR of a second female parent under s 43 of the HFEA 2008 can be terminated on exactly the same basis as that of an unmarried father.[160]

10.6.2.c Step-parents

The PR of step-parents is also subject to termination on the same basis as that of unmarried fathers and second female parents under s 43 of the HFEA 2008.[161] However, the possibility that the PR of a step-parent may be terminated on application to the court is considerably less controversial. A step-parent's relationship with a child will usually be very different from that of an unmarried father or second female parent under s 43 of the HFEA 2008, the marriage between the step-parent and one of the child's parents constituting the principal link between them. It therefore seems sensible to provide for the termination of the step-parent's PR should the step-parent's relationship with the child change upon their separation or divorce from the child's parent.

10.6.3 GUARDIANS, SPECIAL GUARDIANS, AND OTHERS

Guardians, special guardians, and those holding PR through a child arrangements order do not have a separate PRO in their favour: the holding of PR is regarded as an integral part of the appointment or order made. There are therefore no specific provisions for the termination of PR where it is acquired through one of these mechanisms: it terminates automatically when the relevant appointment or order comes to an end.[162] Similarly, the PR of a local authority is automatically extinguished when the care order terminates.

10.7 CARING FOR CHILDREN WITHOUT PARENTAL RESPONSIBILITY

There will be many occasions when a child will be cared for by someone who does not have PR, such as an unmarried father, a step-parent, a grandparent, a teacher, a foster carer, or a family friend. Without PR, these carers have no legally recognized decision-making authority. As regards the mundane, day-to-day decisions respecting the child, the carer's lack of PR poses no particular difficulties. Again, however, there may be problems if more important questions arise. For example, if the child is injured whilst in the care of one of these individuals, decisions may have to be made regarding the child's medical treatment. The position of a carer without PR is governed exclusively by s 3(5) of the CA 1989.

Children Act 1989, s 3

(5) A person who—
  (a) does not have parental responsibility for a particular child; but
  (b) has care of the child,

[160] S 4ZA(4)–(5). [161] S 4A. [162] Ss 12(2) and 14C(1)(a).

> may (subject to the provisions of this Act) do what is reasonable in all the circumstances of the case for the purpose of safeguarding or promoting the child's welfare.

This confers sufficient authority on the carer to make any decisions necessary to safeguard or promote the child's welfare. As there is little case law providing authoritative guidance on the correct interpretation of this provision, its exact meaning is unclear. In practice, it most probably means that where the child is being cared for by individuals on a short-term basis, they will only be able to make urgent decisions regarding, for example, whether the child should receive emergency medical treatment. In *Re S (Abduction: Hague and European Conventions)*,[163] Butler-Sloss LJ said that s 3(5) 'does not clothe the carers with control over the child other than the minimum necessary to provide for the day-to-day welfare of the child'.

Where, however, the child is in the longer-term care of an individual without PR, s 3(5) may confer on the child's carer the necessary authority to make longer-term decisions regarding such things as the child's education or religious upbringing. It depends on the context of the case.

10.8 CONCLUSION

Parenthood is a very complex issue with different rights and responsibilities attaching to the two core concepts of legal parenthood and PR. In many ways, the complexity of the law on this issue is a positive factor. It provides scope for the legal recognition of a range of 'parents'—genetic, intentional, and social—who play an important role in the life of the child. In a social context where family life, including parenting, is increasingly transient, this flexibility in the regulation of the parent–child relationship is a great strength. Whilst the child's immediate family environment may be subject to unsettling changes, English law is able to provide positive support for the child's core relationships.

There are, however, some issues of concern. In recent years, the position of unmarried fathers has generated most debate. However, reforms to the birth registration system and s 4 of the CA 1989 have considerably improved the overall picture, such that the argument that unmarried fathers face an unjust struggle to achieve recognition of their parenting role is no longer as strong. Indeed, with the vast majority of unmarried fathers now able to acquire PR by the mere act of registration (or failing that by a relatively straightforward application to the court), the concern may now be the other way. There are clear signs that PR is losing its distinct identity as a legal mechanism for providing legal recognition and support to those actively involved in raising a child and becoming no more than a useful device to confer enhanced parental status on (for the most part) unmarried fathers in the hope that it will encourage them to assume their parenting responsibilities. By routinely conferring PR on unmarried fathers, some of whom will play only a limited role in the life of the child, genetic fatherhood is being valorized whilst social parenthood and the actual work of parenting is marginalized. This has particularly worrying implications for mothers who still shoulder the bulk of the actual work and responsibility of parenting.[164] From a position in which the

[163] [1997] 1 FLR 958, 962, aff'd [1998] 1 FLR 122, 127.

[164] For some data on the impact of the Covid-19 pandemic on caring responsibilities, see Margaria (2022).

law was dominated by overwhelmingly positive images of mothers as natural committed carers alongside negative stereotypes of unmarried fathers as irresponsible and dangerous, we have moved to a position in which the law on parenthood and PR is now dominated by assumptions as to the value of genetic fatherhood alongside suspicions about obstructive mothers. As we will see in the next chapter, whilst these changing attitudes towards motherhood and fatherhood and the gendered assumptions which underpin them now permeate family law, they are deeply problematic.

ONLINE RESOURCES

Questions, suggestions for further reading, and supplementary materials for this chapter (including updates on developments in this area of family law since this book was published) may be found in the online resources at **www.oup.com/he/familytcm5e.**

11

PRIVATE DISPUTES OVER CHILDREN

CENTRAL ISSUES

1. When determining any private law dispute over a child's upbringing, the child's welfare is the paramount consideration. However, the application of that principle has been informed to varying degrees by the use of 'assumptions' or 'de facto presumptions' when resolving disputes about children's upbringing.
2. Many more mothers become the main carers of their children than fathers. However, when resolving disputes about children's living arrangements, the courts deny that they are applying a presumption in favour of mothers.
3. Claims that the judiciary discriminate against fathers in their approach to disputes about children's living arrangements must be examined carefully. The existing division of labour within intact families and the difficulties of 'co-parenting' post-separation make such claims difficult to sustain.
4. The courts are making increased use of orders for shared living arrangements as a solution to the problems of post-separation parenting. However, there are strong reasons to doubt whether requiring children to split their time equally between the two parents will commonly prove workable or fair. The use of shared orders for symbolic or psychological reasons has also attracted strong academic criticism.
5. When resolving disputes about children's upbringing between parents and non-parents, the courts have more openly applied a 'de facto presumption' in favour of the natural parent. Views differ as to whether any privileging of 'genetic' over 'social' parenting can be justified.
6. When resolving disputes about children spending time or having contact with a parent, the courts again apply a strong presumption in favour of making such orders, here reinforced by statute. Some say that this presumption is sometimes being applied inappropriately, so that abusive men are being granted contact at the expense of the safety and welfare of women and children.
7. Enforcing these orders is fraught with difficulty. The courts have sometimes adopted a 'hard-line' approach to 'intransigent' mothers, but many question whether punishing the mother for disobeying a contact order is in the child's interests.

8. Successive governments have introduced important reforms aimed at moving private law disputes out of the courts. Using both 'soft' and 'hard' tools of persuasion, the aim is to transform the 'culture' such that it becomes 'socially unacceptable' to deny children a relationship with both parents following separation or divorce.

11.1 INTRODUCTION

Private law disputes are typically, although not exclusively, concerned with disagreements between parents over some aspect of their child's upbringing. Disputes of this kind following the parents' separation or divorce are extremely common: while the majority of parents who separate do not go to court regarding their children,[1] nearly 85,000 children are the subject of private law applications every year.[2] These cases are often bitter, heart-wrenching, and protracted,[3] frequently involving high levels of hostility between the parents or serious allegations about domestic abuse or substance misuse.[4] Court users have above average levels of mental health concerns and other vulnerabilities,[5] and are disproportionately from the more deprived parts of society.[6] Perfect solutions which safeguard the welfare of the child whilst satisfying the wishes of both parties are rarely possible. Children cannot be physically split between two parents, and avoiding a win–lose mentality is difficult. Anger, betrayal, bitterness, and suspicion are just some of the emotions which make these disputes so hard to resolve—this is family law at its most raw.

Private law disputes over children have increasingly attracted the media spotlight, prompted by the activities of groups such as Fathers4Justice. It has become popularly portrayed as the modern-day 'battle of the sexes'. The gender dimension of intra-parental disputes has certainly added a heat and ferocity to the debate which has not always been helpful. Fathers' rights groups launched highly successful media campaigns against what they perceive to be the strong bias in favour of women in this area. Anecdotal 'tug-of-love' stories in which fathers and children are victimized by malevolent, spiteful, selfish mothers, determined to deprive their children of any meaningful relationship with their fathers, are used to maximum impact. Policy-makers, government ministers, even the judiciary have, to varying degrees, been receptive to these complaints. On the other hand, women's rights groups have responded with their own accusations of violent and abusive men who have no genuine interest in their children simply using family court disputes to exercise power and control over their former partners. Cutting through the highly charged, and increasingly politicized, rhetoric to get a more balanced perspective on the important gender dimensions of this debate is not easy.[7]

[1] Dabhi, Anand, and Tu (2022) surveyed 2,489 separated parents. Around 20 per cent reported using the family court for private law children issues (our calculations from figs 32 and 34). However, some of those parents will have reached agreement within the court process, rather than having a court-imposed outcome: earlier research suggested that only around 11 per cent of separating parents had child arrangements made by the court: ONS (2008), table 2.9.

[2] MOJ (2022a), table 2. After a dip to around 65,000 children per year in 2014 and 2015 (following the introduction of the Legal Aid, Sentencing and Punishment of Offenders Act 2012 (LASPO) and the CFA 2014), numbers are now back to their previous level and have been stable for the last three years.

[3] The mean duration of private law cases is now 44 weeks: MOJ (2022a), Table 9.

[4] Trinder et al (2005); Hunt and Macleod (2008); Newnham and Harding (2016), 177.

[5] Cusworth, Hargreaves et al (2021).

[6] Cusworth, Bedston et al (2021).

[7] See Collier (2005).

This chapter explores the current legal framework for resolving private law disputes over children. We begin by considering procedural issues germane to all private law disputes, including the extent to which children are able to participate in these proceedings. The three main private law orders available under the Children Act 1989 (CA 1989)—child arrangements orders, specific issue orders, and prohibited steps orders—will then be considered, as well as recent initiatives to try and improve the way in which these cases are handled.

11.2 PRIVATE LAW ORDERS UNDER THE CHILDREN ACT 1989

In 2014, substantial changes were made to the orders that are available in private law proceedings under s 8 of the CA 1989, which are referred to collectively as 's 8 orders'. Following amendment by the Children and Families Act 2014 (CFA 2014), s 8(1) states:

Children Act 1989, s 8

(1) In this Act—

"[a] child arrangements order" means an order regulating arrangements relating to any of the following—

(a) with whom a child is to live, spend time or otherwise have contact, and

(b) when a child is to live, spend time or otherwise have contact with any person;

"a prohibited steps order" means an order that no step which could be taken by a parent in meeting his parental responsibility for a child, and which is of a kind specified in the order, shall be taken by any person without the consent of the court; and

"a specific issue order" means an order giving directions for the purpose of determining a specific question which has arisen, or which may arise, in connection with any aspect of parental responsibility for a child.

The child arrangements order (CAO) replaced two different orders which existed previously:

- *residence orders*, which were orders settling the arrangements as to the person or persons with whom a child was to live; and
- *contact orders*, which required the person with whom the child lived to allow the child to visit or stay with the person named in the order, or for the person and the child otherwise to have contact with each other.

In practical terms, there is little difference between the different kinds of CAO and the two previous orders, all of which regulate the child's living arrangements and relationships with other people (usually parents and other family members). The rationale for the change was to remove the sense that some parents (especially fathers) perceived, that residence orders were 'better' than contact orders, or that the parent with a residence order was the 'main' parent.[8] By removing the labels 'resident parent' and 'contact parent', and making a single order which covers all the main arrangements and both parents, the government hoped that any sense of

[8] Norgrove (2011).

'winners' and 'losers' would be removed. Given that CAOs are routinely referred to as 'live with' and 'spend time with' orders, it is doubtful that this shift of language in fact changed anything.

There are provisions within Part II of the CA 1989 governing particular issues—removal of a child from the UK and change of the child's surname, for example—that we discuss later.[9] There are also other orders available under Part II—special guardianship orders,[10] orders for financial relief,[11] and family assistance orders[12]—that are not discussed here in detail.

11.3 PROCEDURAL MATTERS GERMANE TO ALL SECTION 8 ORDERS

11.3.1 WHEN MAY A SECTION 8 ORDER BE MADE?

A s 8 order may be made in any 'family proceedings' in which a question arises with respect to the child's welfare.[13] The court may act upon its own motion or upon an application being made.[14] While s 8 orders normally come into effect immediately, it is possible for the court to make an order which does not come into effect for a period of time, though the court must bear in mind that circumstances might change if a significant amount of time passes.[15]

11.3.2 WHO MAY APPLY FOR A SECTION 8 ORDER?

Sections 10(1) and 10(2) identify two categories of applicant who can apply for a s 8 order: 'entitled applicants', and those who have obtained the court's leave.

11.3.2.a Entitled applicants

Entitled applicants are divided into three groups. First, under s 10(4), any parent, guardian, or 'person who is named, in a child arrangements order that is in force with respect to the child, as a person with whom the child is to live' is entitled to apply for *any s 8 order*.[16] In this context, 'parent' includes both legal parents regardless of whether they hold parental responsibility.[17]

The second group of entitled applicants, specified in s 10(5), are entitled to apply as of right *only for a CAO*.

Children Act 1989, s 10

(5) The following persons are entitled to apply for a child arrangements order with respect to a child—

(a) any party to a marriage (whether or not subsisting) in relation to whom the child is a child of the family;

(aa) any civil partner in a civil partnership (whether or not subsisting) in relation to whom the child is a child of the family;

[9] See 11.8.1 and 11.8.2.
[10] CA 1989, s 14A; see 13.8. Unless stated otherwise, all statutory references in this chapter are to the CA 1989.
[11] S 15 and Sch 1; see 5.5.
[12] S 16.
[13] S 8(3)–(4).
[14] S 10(1).
[15] *L v L (Anticipatory Child Arrangements Order)* [2017] EWHC 1212.
[16] S 10(4).
[17] *M v C and Calderdale Metropolitan Borough Council* [1994] Fam 1.

(b) any person with whom the child has lived for a period of at least three years;

(c) any person who—

(i) in any case where a child arrangements order in force with respect to the child regulates arrangements relating to [any person] with whom the child is to live or when the child is to live with any person, has the consent of each of the persons named in the order as a person with whom the child is to live;

(ii) in any case where the child is in the care of a local authority, has the consent of that authority; or

(iii) in any other case, has the consent of each of those (if any) who have parental responsibility for the child;

(d) any person who has parental responsibility for a child by virtue of provision made under section 12(2A).

'Child of the family' is defined to include: (i) a child of the parties to a marriage or civil partnership; and (ii) any other child who has been treated by the parties to a marriage or civil partnership as a child of their family (except children placed with them as foster carers).[18]

The third category of entitled applicants can apply *only for a 'live with' CAO* (previously called a residence order).

Children Act 1989, s 10

(5A) A local authority foster parent is entitled to apply for a child arrangements order to which subsection (5C) applies with respect to a child if the child has lived with him for a period of at least one year immediately preceding the application.

(5B) A relative of a child is entitled to apply for a child arrangements order to which subsection (5C) applies with respect to the child if the child has lived with the relative for a period of at least one year immediately preceding the application.

(5C) This subsection applies to a child arrangements order if the arrangements regulated by the order relate only to either or both of the following—

(a) with whom the child concerned is to live, and

(b) when the child is to live with any person.

A 'relative' is defined as 'a grandparent, brother, sister, uncle or aunt (whether of the full blood or half blood or by marriage or civil partnership) or a step-parent'.[19] If an applicant does not fall within one of the categories of entitled applicant, the leave of the court will be required.

11.3.2.b Applicants requiring leave

Any person, including a child, who is not entitled under either s 10(4), (5), (5A), or (5B) may apply for *any s 8 order* if the court grants them leave to do so. This 'open door' policy is subject to specific restrictions imposed on local authority foster carers—they may not apply for

[18] S 105(1). See *Re A (Child of the Family)* [1998] 1 FLR 347.

[19] S 105(1).

leave unless they have the consent of the local authority, they are a relative of the child, or the child has been living with them for at least one year preceding the application.[20] The Court of Appeal has held that where foster carers are precluded from applying for a s 8 order by virtue of these restrictions, the court can nevertheless act of its own motion.[21]

11.3.2.c Principles to be applied on an application for leave

Applicants under s 10(9)

The principles to be applied on an application for leave, other than by the child who is the subject matter of the application, are set down in s 10(9).

Children Act 1989, s 10

(9) Where the person applying for leave to make an application for a section 8 order is not the child concerned, the court shall, in deciding whether or not to grant leave, have particular regard to—
(a) the nature of the proposed application for the section 8 order;
(b) the applicant's connection with the child;
(c) any risk there might be of that proposed application disrupting the child's life to such an extent that he would be harmed by it; and
(d) where the child is being looked after by a local authority—
(i) the authority's plans for the child's future; and
(ii) the wishes and feelings of the child's parents.

The question of whether considerations beyond those specified in s 10(9) can be taken into account has caused some difficulty. Initially, the courts observed that an application for leave was not a question relating to the upbringing of a child, and therefore that the child's welfare was not the paramount consideration.[22] Then it was said that an applicant had to have 'a good arguable case' on the merits before leave would be granted;[23] however, the Court of Appeal later queried this 'gloss' on the statutory wording, particularly in the light of Articles 6 and 8 of the European Convention on Human Rights (ECHR).[24] The Court of Appeal gave further guidance in *Re B (A Child) (Care Proceedings: Joinder)*.[25] Black LJ made clear that s 10(9) does not contain a 'test' as such, but merely picks out some relevant considerations for judges to assess. There is no limitation on any *other* considerations that might be relevant. Although 'leave will not be given for an application that is not arguable', the fact that an application is arguable is not in itself enough to justify allowing the application because all factors need to be taken together.[26] The extent of any investigation required to make the

[20] S 9(3). Where a child is placed with prospective adopters by a local authority adoption agency, the prospective adopters will be regarded as falling within the restrictions imposed on local authority foster carers by s 9(3). See *Re C (Adoption: Notice)* [1999] 1 FLR 384.

[21] *Gloucestershire County Council v P* [2000] Fam 1.

[22] *Re A and W* [1992] 2 FLR 154.

[23] See, e.g., *Re A (A Minor) (Residence Order: Leave to Apply)* [1993] 1 FLR 425; *Re S (Contact: Application by Sibling)* [1999] 1 Fam 283.

[24] *Re J (Leave to Issue Application for Residence Order)* [2002] EWCA Civ 1364.

[25] [2012] EWCA Civ 737.

[26] Ibid, [48]–[49].

decision will vary depending on the case, with a focus on 'ensur[ing] in each case that there is a fair determination of the claims of the parties and the issues in the case'.[27]

Obtaining leave does not give rise to any presumptions in favour of the applicant at the substantive hearing.[28]

Where the applicant is 'the child concerned': s 10(8)

Children are able to bring and defend Children Act proceedings in their own name.[29] In order to apply for a s 8 order, the child requires the court's leave under s 10(8).[30] In determining the application, the court must be satisfied that the child is of sufficient understanding to make the application.[31] Again, the child's welfare is not the court's paramount consideration and proceedings which are 'doomed to failure' will not be allowed to commence.[32] The application must also be sufficiently serious to merit intervention by the court.[33]

In determining a child's application for leave, the courts have been reluctant to allow children to make their own applications due to concerns about children being overly or inappropriately involved in litigation against their parents,[34] though there are exceptions.[35] However, while children rarely initiate proceedings as applicants, there are other circumstances where they can become parties to existing proceedings, as we discuss later.[36]

11.3.2.d Prohibited applicants

Section 9(2) prohibits a local authority from applying for a CAO. This restriction is based on the important principle that a local authority seeking to intervene in the private realm of family life should be required to use its public law powers under Part IV of the CA 1989,[37] rather than invoking private law proceedings. This prevents the local authority from circumventing the strict requirement under Part IV of the Act that the child must be suffering or likely to suffer significant harm before the state can intervene by way of compulsory measures. The local authority is permitted, if it obtains leave under s 10(9), to apply for a specific issue or prohibited steps order but the court cannot make a specific issue order or prohibited steps order with a view to achieving a result which could be achieved by making a CAO,[38] and the court may not make specific issue or prohibited steps orders in relation to a child who is in local authority care.[39] This leaves very little room for a local authority to make use of s 8 orders, even if it believes such orders would be a more nuanced response to the problems of a particular family than invoking its more confrontational powers under Part IV.[40]

[27] Ibid, [51]. See also the summary in *A County Council v M* [2021] EWFC 35, [24].

[28] *Re W (Contact: Application by Grandparent)* [1997] 1 FLR 793.

[29] Family Procedure Rules 2010 (FPR 2010), r 12.3(1).

[30] In order to fall within the terms of this provision, the child must be applying for an order where they are 'the child concerned', meaning they must be the intended subject matter of the order. See *Re S (Contact: Application by Sibling)* [1999] Fam 283. A child applying for a s 8 order with respect to another child will have their application for leave determined in accordance with s 10(9).

[31] *Re SC (A Minor) (Leave to Seek Residence Order)* [1994] 1 FLR 96.

[32] Ibid. See also *Re H (Residence Order: Child's Application for Leave)* [1994] 1 FLR 26.

[33] *Re C (A Minor) (Leave to Seek Section 8 Orders)* [1994] 1 FLR 26.

[34] See, e.g., *Re H (Residence Order: Child's Application For Leave)* [2000] 1 FLR 780.

[35] See, e.g., *Re JS (Disposal of Body)* [2016] EWHC 2859; *Re A and B (Recission of Order: Change of Circumstances)* [2021] EWFC 76. [36] See 11.3.3.c. [37] See chapter 12.

[38] S 9(5)(a).

[39] S 9(1). The prohibition applies only to children in care under s 31 or 38; see chapter 12.

[40] See further discussion at 12.5.2.

11.3.2.e Restricted applicants under section 91(14)

An important tool in the armoury of the judiciary is s 91(14), which empowers the court to prohibit a particular individual from making any further applications to the court in relation to a particular child without first obtaining the court's leave. The purpose of making restrictions of this kind is to protect the child and the child's carers from endless or vexatious litigation by requiring an applicant to obtain the court's leave before an application can be brought. Restrictions can be made for specified periods or until further order, and can relate either to applications for all orders in relation to a child or to specified types of application.

Judges have been cautious about the use of s 91(14) orders, and the Court of Appeal laid down guidelines about when they should be made in *Re P (A Child) (Residence Order: Child's Welfare)*.[41] A s 91(14) order will most commonly be made where there has been protracted litigation between the parties and it is in the child's best interests to bring proceedings to an end. In such cases, the prohibited applicant will usually have made repeated unmerited applications or will have conducted the litigation in an unreasonable manner,[42] though this is not a necessity as long as the court has a clear evidential basis to justify the order.[43] However, s 91(14) orders are not to be used simply to give the parties breathing space from litigation or to allow time for new child arrangements to settle.[44] An important amendment was made to the CA 1989 by the Domestic Abuse Act 2021, which clarifies that a s 91(14) order can be made where future applications by the named person would put either the child concerned or another individual at risk of harm.[45] This clarification is intended to ensure that the courts do not allow ongoing litigation to be a source of continued harm in cases of domestic abuse or other harms caused by one parent, though whether this will lead to greater use of s 19(14) orders remains to be seen.

It is sometimes said that s 91(14) orders are controversial because they deny a person access to the court, which is a fundamental right protected by Article 6 ECHR. However, the precise nature of the restriction needs to be remembered.

Re P (A Child) (Residence Order: Child's Welfare) [2000] Fam 15 (CA), 38

BUTLER-SLOSS LJ:

The applicant is not denied access to the court. It is a partial restriction in that it does not allow him the right to an immediate *inter partes* hearing. It thereby protects the other parties and the child from being drawn into the proposed proceedings unless or until a court has ruled that the application should be allowed to proceed. On an application for leave, the applicant must persuade the judge that he has an arguable case with some chance of success. That is not a formidable hurdle to surmount. If the application is hopeless and refused the other parties and the child will have been protected from unnecessary involvement in the proposed proceedings and unwarranted investigations into the present circumstances of the child.

If an order has been made under s 91(14), the applicant requires leave before making any further applications to the court. The principles to be applied on an application for leave

[41] [2000] Fam 15. These guidelines were reaffirmed in *Re M (A Child) (Parental Responsibility Order)* [2013] EWCA Civ 969.

[42] *B v B (Residence Order: Restricting Applications)* [1997] 1 FLR 139.

[43] *Re T (Suspension of Contact: Section 91(14) CA 1989)* [2015] EWCA Civ 719.

[44] *Re G (A Child) (Order: Restriction on Applications)* [2008] EWCA Civ 1468, [13]–[14]; *Re A (A Child) (Order: Restriction on Applications)* [2009] EWCA Civ 1548, [16]–[17].

[45] S 91A(2).

were considered by the Court of Appeal in *Re A (Application for Leave)*.[46] The court held that the application was not to be determined in accordance with the principles set down under s 10(9), but on the basis of the simple question: 'does the application demonstrate that there is any need for renewed judicial investigation?'[47] However, this approach must now be read with s 91A(4) of the CA 1989, which requires the court to '*consider* whether there has been a material change of circumstances since the [s 91(14)] order was made'.[48] The Court of Appeal has previously said that it is impermissible to attach conditions to a s 91(14) order, such as requiring a report from a psychiatrist demonstrating that the applicant has satisfactorily addressed his damaging behaviour, as such conditions would fetter the judge's discretion when hearing any future application and may, in effect, constitute a bar to the applicant seeking leave.[49] However, the court can give guidance as to what is expected of the parent before a new application is likely to be allowed,[50] and it is likely now that greater attention will be paid to whether there has been a change of circumstances since the original order was made.

11.3.3 THE PARTICIPATION OF CHILDREN IN PRIVATE LAW DISPUTES

Although many children in private family law disputes are very young,[51] in 2021 over 20,000 children aged 10 to 14 and over 2,500 young people aged 15 to 17 were involved in Children Act cases concerning private law issues.[52] This range of age, experience, and maturity makes the question of how children should participate in private law disputes about their upbringing difficult to answer in a straightforward way, and there remain strong differences of opinion about the best approach.

On the one hand, a children's rights approach emphasizes the importance of listening to and respecting the autonomous, decision-making abilities of children in all matters affecting them. Article 12 of the United Nations Convention on the Rights of the Child provides an underpinning of support for this approach, albeit qualified by reference to the 'age and maturity' of the child.[53]

United Nations Convention on the Rights of the Child 1989, Article 12

1. States Parties shall assure to the child who is capable of forming his or her own views the right to express those views freely in all matters affecting the child, the views of the child being given due weight in accordance with the age and maturity of the child.
2. For this purpose, the child shall in particular be provided the opportunity to be heard in any judicial and administrative proceedings affecting the child, either directly, or through a representative or an appropriate body, in a manner consistent with the procedural rules of national law.

[46] [1998] 1 FLR 1. [47] Ibid, 4. [48] Emphasis added.

[49] *Re S (Children) (Restrictions on Applications)* [2006] EWCA Civ 1190, [72]–[80]. Subject now to the effect of s 91A(4), *Re S* remains the leading authority on applications for leave once a s 91(14) order is in place: *Re P and N (Section 19(14): Application for Permission to Apply: Appeal)* [2019] EWHC 421.

[50] *Re M-D (A Child)* [2014] EWCA Civ 1363, [18].

[51] In 2021, over 30 per cent were under 5, with another 40 per cent between the ages of 5 and 9: MOJ (2022a), Table 5 (authors' calculations).

[52] Ibid.

[53] Mol (2019) compares ways that this provision is implemented in various countries. Tisdall, Morrison, and Warburton (2021) look at the practical hurdles that children face to participating in private law cases.

On the other hand, there remains deep-seated concern amongst some family practitioners about exposing children to the burdens and responsibilities of the adult world of decision-making in matters as difficult and sensitive as family court proceedings.[54] However, as Fortin notes, there is a crucial difference between allowing the views of children to determine the outcome of court proceedings—in effect, 'delegating the decision-making process to them'—and consulting children on matters that affect them.[55]

English law is clearly far from adopting the former, more radical approach, so where the child's views are before the court, they are relevant,[56] but they will not be determinative.[57] The weight to be accorded to the child's wishes is highly dependent on the child's age and understanding. May and Smart found that whereas younger children were generally regarded as incapable of forming a view, children over 7 years of age were routinely asked their preferences and they appeared to have no difficulty weighing up the various factors and expressing a clearly articulated view.[58] When it comes to older children—particularly those nearing the end of the court's jurisdiction to make orders about them—the court is generally more reluctant to impose its own views except in cases where the child's welfare would be seriously compromised.[59] The courts have recognized that there must come a point, particularly with older children, when it is counterproductive for the court to continue to force the issue.[60]

There are various ways in which the court can allow children to participate in proceedings.

11.3.3.a Section 7 reports

The most common way for children's voices to be heard in private law cases is by way of a welfare report prepared by a social worker, usually termed 'a s 7 report' in reference to the provision of the CA 1989 under which it is ordered. Most s 7 reports are prepared by a welfare officer employed by the Children and Family Court Advisory and Support Service (Cafcass), but they can also be prepared by a social worker from a local authority or by a privately-paid Independent Social Worker if the parties have the money to employ one and the court considers the appointment to be necessary.[61] However, a s 7 report will not be ordered in every case.[62] If the court does order a report, the welfare officer must have regard to the welfare checklist in s 1(3), which includes the child's wishes and feelings,[63] but any recommendations reflect the author's assessment of the child's overall welfare. As a mechanism for child participation, therefore, a s 7 report is a limited tool. Indeed, young adults looking back at their experiences of parental separation were not satisfied with the way in which their views were taken into account, both in the welfare report and by the court.[64]

[54] E.g. *Re LC (Children) (Abduction: Habitual Residence: State of Mind of Child)* [2014] UKSC 1, [55].

[55] Fortin (2009b), 291. [56] S 1(3)(a). [57] *Re M (Family Proceedings: Affidavits)* [1995] 2 FLR 100.

[58] May and Smart (2004), 314–15.

[59] On medical decision-making and the court's power to override the child's view, see 8.5.6.b.

[60] See *Re S (Contact: Children's Views)* [2002] EWHC 540, [114]–[121]; *Re C (Older Children: Relocation)* [2015] EWCA Civ 1298, [63] where Peter Jackson J cautioned of the need 'to recognise the proper limits on the court's exercise of its powers in the case of a mature and intelligent older child who is now 17 years of age'.

[61] CFA 2014, s 13(6).

[62] Around 45 per cent of cases include a s 7 welfare report (about 75 per cent of these are from Cafcass, with almost all the rest prepared by a local authority): Jay et al (2019), 17; Hargreaves et al (2022), 8–9.

[63] S 1(3)(a); FPR 2010, r 16.33(4). See 11.4.

[64] Fortin, Ritchie, and Buchanan (2006), 220–1. Fewer than a third of the young people felt that the court took proper account of their views and less than a third felt that they had been able to say everything they wanted to the welfare reporter.

11.3.3.b Giving evidence as a witness

It is extremely rare, but possible, for children to be called as witnesses in private family law cases.[65] The principles are set out by the Supreme Court in *Re W (Children) (Abuse: Oral Evidence)*.[66] Lady Hale explained that there could be no presumptions about children giving evidence or not, but noted that the likely outcome of the assessment of whether it was appropriate would be that only rarely would children be called as witnesses. In general, the courts consider that the harm caused a child from involvement in the court process to outweigh the benefits. As Lord Wilson once warned, '[t]he intrusion of the children into the forensic arena, which enables a number of them to adopt a directly confrontational stance towards the applicant parent, can prove very damaging to family relationships even in the long term and definitely affects their interests'.[67]

11.3.3.c Children as parties to proceedings

As noted previously,[68] while it is rare, children can initiate Children Act proceedings themselves if they get leave of the court. If a solicitor assesses the child as being competent to give instructions on the issues concerned,[69] they can accept the child as a client and the child can apply to commence proceedings or to intervene in existing proceedings.

More common, accounting for about 5 per cent of all private law cases,[70] is for the child to be joined as a party to existing proceedings, but represented by a children's guardian pursuant to r 16.4 of the Family Procedure Rules 2010. The guardian is usually a Cafcass social worker, though the court may allow a solicitor to act as guardian where an older child is able to give instructions directly.[71] The approach to joinder of a child is governed by r 16 of the Family Procedure Rules 2010 and by Practice Direction 16A.[72]

Practice Direction 16A—*Representation of Children* (2017)

7.1 Making the child a party to the proceedings is a step that will be taken only in cases which involve an issue of significant difficulty and consequently will occur in only a minority of cases. Before taking the decision to make the child a party, consideration should be given to whether an alternative route might be preferable, such as asking [a Children and Family Reporter] to carry out further work or by making a referral to social services or, possibly, by obtaining expert evidence.

7.2 The decision to make the child a party will always be exclusively that of the court, made in the light of the facts and circumstances of the particular case. The following are offered, solely by way of guidance, as circumstances which may justify the making of such an order—

- (a) where [a welfare officer] has notified the court that in the opinion of that officer the child should be made a party;
- (b) where the child has a standpoint or interest which is inconsistent with or incapable of being represented by any of the adult parties;

[65] See also 12.5.4.a on the approach in public law cases. [66] [2010] UKSC 12.

[67] *Re LC (Children) (Abduction: Habitual Residence: State of Mind of Child)* [2014] UKSC 1, [48]. But cf *Cambra v Jones and Jones* [2014] EWHC 913, [12]–[14].

[68] See 11.3.2.b. [69] In other words, *Gillick* competent: see 8.5.6.b.

[70] Hargreaves et al (2022), 10–11.

[71] *Re LC (Children) (Abduction: Habitual Residence: State of Mind of Child)* [2014] UKSC 1, [46].

[72] The relevant provisions are 'far from straightforward', as Baker LJ noted in *Re Z (Interim Care Order)* [2021] EWCA Civ 1755, [43].

(c) where there is an intractable dispute over residence or contact, including where all contact has ceased, or where there is irrational but implacable hostility to contact or where the child may be suffering harm associated with the contact dispute;
(d) where the views and wishes of the child cannot be adequately met by a report to the court;
(e) where an older child is opposing a proposed course of action;
(f) where there are complex medical or mental health issues to be determined or there are other unusually complex issues that necessitate separate representation of the child;
(g) where there are international complications outside child abduction, in particular where it may be necessary for there to be discussions with overseas authorities or a foreign court;
(h) where there are serious allegations of physical, sexual or other abuse in relation to the child or there are allegations of domestic violence not capable of being resolved with the help of [a welfare officer];
(i) where the proceedings concern more than one child and the welfare of the children is in conflict or one child is in a particularly disadvantaged position;
(j) where there is a contested issue about scientific testing.

While the guardian has a clear obligation to meet with the child and to communicate the child's views to the court, their overall duty is to represent the child's best interests. If there is a significant conflict between the views of an older child and the guardian's assessment of the child's welfare, the child can apply to the court for the guardian to be removed and for the child to instruct their solicitor directly. Thorpe LJ held that when determining this question the courts must avoid paternalistic judgements and pay much greater respect to the rights and autonomy of the child.

Mabon v Mabon [2005] EWCA Civ 634

THORPE LJ:

25. In our system we have traditionally adopted the tandem model for the representation of children who are parties to family proceedings, whether public or private. First the court appoints a guardian ad litem who will almost invariably have a social work qualification and very wide experience of family proceedings. He then instructs a specialist family solicitor who, in turn, usually instructs a specialist family barrister. This is a Rolls Royce model and is the envy of many other jurisdictions. However its overall approach is essentially paternalistic. The guardian's first priority is to advocate the welfare of the child he represents. His second priority is to put before the court the child's wishes and feelings. Those priorities can in some cases conflict. In extreme cases the conflict is unmanageable. That reality is recognised by the terms of rule 9.2A [which was the predecessor to the current PD 16A]. The direction set by rule 9.2A(6) is a mandatory grant of the application provided that the court considers "that the minor concerned has sufficient understanding to participate as a party in the proceedings concerned." Thus the focus is upon the sufficiency of the child's understanding in the context of the remaining proceedings.

26. In my judgment the Rule is sufficiently widely framed to meet our obligations to comply with both Article 12 of the United Nations Convention and Article 8 of the ECHR, providing that judges correctly focus on the sufficiency of the child's understanding and, in measuring that sufficiency, reflect the extent to which, in the 21st Century, there is a keener

appreciation of the autonomy of the child and the child's consequential right to participate in decision making processes that fundamentally affect his family life . . .

28. . . . Although the tandem model has many strengths and virtues, at its heart lies the conflict between advancing the welfare of the child and upholding the child's freedom of expression and participation. Unless we in this jurisdiction are to fall out of step with similar societies as they safeguard Article 12 rights, we must, in the case of articulate teenagers, accept that the right to freedom of expression and participation outweighs the paternalistic judgment of welfare.

29. In testing the sufficiency of a child's understanding I would not say that welfare has no place. If direct participation would pose an obvious risk of harm to the child arising out of the nature of the continuing proceedings and, if the child is incapable of comprehending that risk, then the judge is entitled to find that sufficient understanding has not been demonstrated. But judges have to be equally alive to the risk of emotional harm that might arise from denying the child knowledge of and participation in the continuing proceedings . . .

32. In conclusion this case provides a timely opportunity to recognise the growing acknowledgement of the autonomy and consequential rights of children, both nationally and internationally. The Rules are sufficiently robustly drawn to accommodate that shift. In individual cases trial judges must equally acknowledge the shift when they make in individual cases a proportionate judgment of the sufficiency of the child's understanding.

11.3.3.d Judges meeting children

The three methods of children participating set out so far all involve some kind of formal involvement, albeit usually through a professional. In addition, though, judges have a wide discretion about whether to meet directly with children in a more informal manner. The English judiciary have traditionally exercised that discretion cautiously.[73] There are several reasons why judges may be reluctant to speak to children.

P. Parkinson, J. Cashmore, and J. Single, 'Parents' and Children's Views on Talking to Judges in Parenting Disputes in Australia', (2007) 21 *International Journal of Law, Policy and the Family* 84, 85

[T]he accepted view in most common law jurisdictions is that it is better to rely on the work of trained experts to interview children and to interpret their wishes and feelings to the court. Not only are such professionals regarded as better able to interview children, but they are also seen as better qualified to interpret their views in the light of all the circumstances . . . Writing in 1983, three Canadian judges explained why the practice of judicial interviewing should be regarded as undesirable:

> "The interview is conducted in an intimidating environment by a person unskilled in asking questions and interpreting the answers of children. In the relatively short time these interviews take, it is difficult to investigate with sufficient depth and subtlety those perceptions of a child which may explain, justify or represent the child's wishes. Moreover, the interview may be perceived as a violation of the judge's role as an impartial trier of fact who does not enter the adversarial arena. The impartiality may also be compromised by the judge assuming the role of inquisitor in questioning children."

[73] Family Justice Council (2008), para 4.

However, research suggests that many children want a greater level of involvement in the court proceedings, including being given the opportunity to speak directly to the judge.[74] Research into the views of Australian children revealed that 85 per cent would have liked the opportunity to speak to the judge; almost all their parents supported this position.[75] The children's and the parents' reasons were broadly similar.

P. Parkinson, J. Cashmore, and J. Single, 'Parents' and Children's Views on Talking to Judges in Parenting Disputes in Australia', (2007) 21 *International Journal of Law, Policy and the Family* 84, 102

Both referred to children's right to be heard and the importance of them having a say in the decision-making process. While both parents and children referred to the need for acknowledgment, and the more therapeutic benefits for children in being heard directly, there was a clear focus in many of their responses on the value of this information in the decision-making process. A number of parents and children thought that if children had the opportunity to talk with the judge directly, it was more likely that the truth would come out and that judges could get the 'real picture' without the distortions arising from the parents' conflict. Like the separately represented children in a recent British study . . . some children in this study also were concerned that their views be conveyed accurately to the court and indicated that speaking directly to the judge would be the best way of ensuring this.

Parents who opposed the child seeing the judge (27 per cent) raised three main concerns: first, that it would be intimidating for the children; secondly, that judges do not have the time or experience to ensure they are accurately eliciting the children's views; and, thirdly, that the children may be being manipulated by one parent.[76]

The approach of the English courts is set out in guidance from the Family Justice Council.[77]

Family Justice Council, *Guidelines for Judges Meeting Children who are Subject to Family Proceedings* (2010a)

5. If a Judge decides to meet a child, it is a matter for the discretion of the Judge, having considered representations from the parties—
(i) the purpose and proposed content of the meeting;
(ii) at what stage during the proceedings, or after they have concluded, the meeting should take place;
(iii) where the meeting will take place;

[74] See Fortin, Ritchie, and Buchanan (2006); Parkinson, Cashmore, and Single (2007), 88–9; House of Lords Select Committee on the Children and Families Act 2014 (2022), paras 144–6.

[75] Parkinson, Cashmore, and Single (2007), 95. Evidence before the House of Lords Select Committee (2022), para 150, led them to conclude that 'children and young people don't feel that their voices were heard properly heard in court proceedings, and that they felt that decisions might have been made more quickly and more in line with their wishes if they had been able to speak to the judge directly'.

[76] Parkinson, Cashmore, and Single (2007), 99–100.

[77] The House of Lords Select Committee (2022), para 151, recommended that the Family Justice Council review this guidance.

(iv) who will bring the child to the meeting;

(v) who will prepare the child for this meeting (this should usually be the Cafcass officer);

(vi) who shall attend during the meeting—although a Judge should never see a child alone;

(vii) by whom a minute of the meeting shall be taken, how that minute is to be approved by the Judge, and how it is to be communicated to the other parties.

It cannot be stressed too often that the child's meeting with the judge is not for the purpose of gathering evidence. That is the responsibility of the Cafcass officer. The purpose is to enable the child to gain some understanding of what is going on, and to be reassured that the judge has understood him/her.

6. If the meeting takes place prior to the conclusion of the proceedings—

(i) The Judge should explain to the child at an early stage that a Judge cannot hold secrets. What is said by the child will, other than in exceptional circumstances, be communicated to his/her parents and other parties.

(ii) The Judge should also explain that decisions in the case are the responsibility of the Judge, who will have to weigh a number of factors, and that the outcome is never the responsibility of the child.

(iii) The Judge should discuss with the child how his or her decisions will be communicated to the child.

(iv) The parties or their representatives shall have the opportunity to respond to the content of the meeting, whether by way of oral evidence or submissions.

Meetings between judges and children should be short (no more than 20 minutes) and judges must not use a meeting with the child as a way to gather evidence.[78] However, that leaves rather open the question of what the purpose of the meeting is, and whether encouraging judges to meet with children more frequently would actually enhance children's participation or their perception of being heard in private law children cases.

11.4 GENERAL PRINCIPLES APPLICABLE TO ALL SECTION 8 ORDERS

In any determination in relation to the upbringing of a child—which includes the making of *any* s 8 order, whether contested or agreed between the parties—the court's paramount consideration must be the welfare of the child.[79] The CA 1989 also contains a 'general principle' that delay in determining cases about children's upbringing 'is likely to prejudice the welfare of the child',[80] and the court is instructed that it should not make any order in relation to children 'unless it considers that doing so would be better for the child than making no order at all'.[81] When a court is considering making a s 8 order and that order is opposed by any party, the court must also consider the *welfare checklist* in s 1(3) of the CA 1989.

[78] In *Re KP (Abduction: Judge Meeting Child: Conduct of Interview)* [2014] EWCA Civ 554, Parker J had met with a 13-year-old child for over an hour during which time she 'sought to probe and tease out what, if any, reasons there were behind [the child's] stated views'; the judge then relied on her impression of the child to reject a Cafcass recommendation. The Court of Appeal allowed the appeal.

[79] S 1(1). The same applies to any order varying or discharging an existing s 8 order: s 8(2).

[80] S 1(2). [81] S 1(5). See 8.6.1.

Children Act 1989, s 1

(3) In the circumstances mentioned in subsection (4), a court shall have regard in particular to—
- (a) the ascertainable wishes and feelings of the child concerned (considered in the light of his age and understanding);
- (b) his physical, emotional and educational needs;
- (c) the likely effect on him of any change in his circumstances;
- (d) his age, sex, background and any characteristics of his which the court considers relevant;
- (e) any harm which he has suffered or is at risk of suffering;
- (f) how capable each of his parents, and any other person in relation to whom the court considers the question to be relevant, is of meeting his needs;
- (g) the range of powers available to the court under this Act in the proceedings in question.

We discuss the welfare principle and the welfare checklist in more detail in chapter 8. As in other contexts, the difficulty arising from the welfare principle is how it should be applied to the facts of each case.[82] The way in which the child's best interests have been interpreted by the courts in the context of s 8 orders has varied over the years, and has provoked a range of criticisms. One of those criticisms—which we consider further at 11.5—was that some fathers' groups argued that family courts were biased in favour of mothers. The Family Justice Review in 2011 had concluded that 'the core principle of the paramountcy of the welfare of the child is sufficient and to insert any additional statements brings with it unnecessary risk for little gain'.[83] However, although the government rejected the claim of bias against the courts, it took the view that 'there should be a legislative statement of the importance of children having an ongoing relationship with both their parents after family separation, where that is safe, and in the child's best interests'.[84] Consequently, the CFA 2014 added a new presumption of parental involvement after family separation to s 1 of the CA 1989—although it is applicable to all s 8 orders, the s 1(2A) presumption has most relevance to applications for a parent to spend time or have contact with a child with whom they do not live, and we discuss it in detail in that context.[85] As we will see, this principle was already well established by the courts, but the inclusion of this section in the Act was nonetheless controversial. Some groups—particularly fathers' rights groups—argued that the provision did not go far enough and would have no real effect, while other groups—women's groups and domestic abuse organizations, in particular—suggested that the new provision would place some women and children at greater risk.[86] Given that the Act makes clear that 'involvement' may be either direct or indirect, and does not—as some campaign groups had favoured—include any presumption about how much time a child should spend with either parent, the provision appears to have codified the courts' established approach rather than causing any change to the previous practice[87]—but as we discuss later, concerns remain.[88]

[82] Fehlberg and Smyth, with Trinder (2020). See 8.2. [83] Norgrove (2011), para 4.40.
[84] MOJ/DFE (2012), para 61. [85] S 1(2A) is set out and discussed at 11.7.2.a.
[86] Both groups continue to hold these views, according to the evidence received by the House of Lords Select Committee (2022), paras 156–66. On the role of s 1(2A) in cases of domestic abuse, see 11.7.3.c–d.
[87] House of Lords Select Committee (2022), paras 161–4. [88] See 11.7.2–11.7.3.

Any s 8 order can be made for a specified period[89] or until further order. Most s 8 orders cannot be made beyond the child's 16th birthday unless the case is exceptional.[90] However, this restriction is specifically disapplied in relation to CAOs governing the person with whom the child is to live—these can therefore continue until the child is 18 if that is in the child's best interests without need of 'exceptionality'.[91]

A s 8 order can be discharged by the court, either on an application by a relevant person or, if proceedings are already underway, of its own motion;[92] an order discharging a s 8 order *is in itself* a s 8 order,[93] and so is a welfare decision to which s 1 applies. Under s 11(5), a CAO which regulates the 'live with' arrangements for a child terminates automatically if the child has two parents who both have parental responsibility, and the parents then live together continuously for a period of six months. Conversely, under s 11(6), a CAO regulating arrangements for the child to 'spend time' or 'have contact' with a parent while living with the other parent terminates automatically if the two parents live together continuously for a period of six months regardless of whether they both have parental responsibility or not.

11.5 CHILD ARRANGEMENTS ORDERS: INTRODUCTION

When the CA 1989 came into force, it created two new orders in relation to children's upbringing—residence orders and contact orders. Residence orders were about the person or persons with whom a child was to live, and contact orders regulated the child's relationships with people with whom they were not living. Although designed to be purely factual descriptions, these labels became increasingly problematic. Campaigns by fathers' groups from the early 2000s onwards put particular focus on the way in which residence and contact disputes were resolved. Groups such as New Fathers 4 Justice[94] and Families Need Fathers[95] argued that by granting sole residence to the mother and restricting fathers to 'mere' contact, as often happened, the judiciary were basing their decisions on, and reinforcing, outdated stereotypes of men and women and their respective parenting roles.

This issue was considered as part of the Family Justice Review.

D. Norgrove (Chair), *Family Justice Review: Final Report* (London: MOJ, 2011)

4.59 Whether to remove the terms contact and residence is clearly a matter of judgement, and it would be difficult to point to clear evidence either way. The balance of the responses to consultation was though firmly in favour of removal and we agree with that. We were also struck by the Chief Justice of Australia's clear view that removal of the terms had been beneficial there.

4.60 . . . In the light of the consultation responses we propose that a broader, new order should be developed that would encompass all arrangements for children's care in private law. This could be termed a 'child arrangements order', which would set out the arrangements for the upbringing of the child. It would focus all discussions on resolving issues related to their care, rather than on labels such as residence and contact. It would of course, be necessary either in a Parenting Agreement or a court order to provide clarity on where a child would normally live and with whom a child would spend time.

89 S 11(7)(c). 90 S 9(6). 91 S 9(6A)–(6B). 92 S 10(1). 93 S 8(2).
94 <https://newf4j.wordpress.com>. 95 <www.fnf.org.uk>.

The government accepted this recommendation, and residence and contact orders were abolished in favour of CAOs by the CFA 2014. Consequently, there are no longer separate orders made in relation to a child, but just one order, though most orders specify within them the person(s) with whom the child will normally reside and other people with whom they will spend time. Because of this, we divide our discussion into two parts—first we look at CAOs that regulate the people with whom a child is to live, and then we look at those dealing with the child spending time or otherwise having contact with people with whom they do not live.

11.6 CHILD ARRANGEMENTS ORDERS: 'LIVE WITH' ORDERS

Our focus in this section is on CAOs that deal with the person or persons with whom a child is to live or when a child is to live with any person. The courts' approach to these orders has not changed following the new nomenclature, and so the pre-2014 authorities remain instructive. Put shortly, the order can set out many possible arrangements, including having the child living:

- with only one person (formerly called a sole residence order);
- with two or more people who live in the same household (formerly called a joint residence order); or
- with two or more people who live in different households (formerly called a shared residence order).

These last orders, for shared living arrangements, can be made in a wide variety of circumstances, as we will see, which may—but often do not—involve an equal or near-equal division of the child's time between two households.

In the following sections, we address various approaches and criticisms that have been made and adopted over the years to explain how the courts came to the position that we find now. It must be borne in mind that, as Thorpe LJ once said, '[w]hen the law enters the field of child welfare, statements of principle may not hold their value much beyond the times in which they were expressed'.[96] Consequently, it is important to note the dates of some of the cases to which we refer: many things said even a comparatively short time ago would almost certainly not be said today.

11.6.1 THE HISTORIC APPROACHES TO 'LIVE WITH' ORDERS

The courts' approach to children's living arrangements has looked very different over the years. Historically, married fathers had all the rights in relation to their legitimate children, and mothers—particularly adulterous mothers—had almost no rights at all.[97] One reason that women's rights movements in the late nineteenth and early twentieth centuries pushed for the introduction of the welfare principle into statute (first achieved in the Guardianship of Infants Act 1925) was that it was thought that a focus on the child's best interests would improve the position of mothers in relation to their children.

[96] *Re L (A Child) (Contact: Domestic Violence)* [2001] Fam 260 (CA), 294.

[97] Cretney (2003a), ch 16.

In fact, the shift towards mothers being seen as the default main carers for children was dramatic, and by the middle of the twentieth century there was a clear presumption in the law that children, especially those of 'tender years' (which meant those up to aged 7 or so, but often much older for girls) should ordinarily be with their mothers.[98] This view was reflected in international law, such as Principle 6 of the 1959 UN Declaration on the Rights of the Child: 'A child of tender years shall not, save in exceptional circumstances, be separated from his mother.' The courts applied this approach in cases like *Re S (An Infant)* in 1958, holding that there was a 'prima facie rule (which is now quite clearly settled) . . . that, other things being equal, children of this tender age should be with their mother'.[99]

While the 'rule' that the court considered to exist in favour of mother was rejected in clear terms by courts by the 1990s, the underlying attitude of the judges was harder to shift. For example, in *Re H (A Minor) (Custody)*, Cumming-Bruce LJ said that it is 'not a principle but a matter of human nature in the case of the upbringing of children of tender years, that given the normal commitment of a father to support the family, the mother, for practical reasons, is usually the right person to bring up her children'.[100] However, while these comments might appear to amount to a presumption that mothers will be the main carers for children post-separation, some judges at least suggested that such comments reflected social realities rather than any presumption coming from the courts.

Re A (A Minor) (Custody) [1991] FCR 569 (CA), 575–6

BUTLER-SLOSS LJ:

[The first argument for the mother] was that it was natural for a mother to have the care of a six year old girl. This was, in my judgment, a misunderstanding of the decision of this court in *Re S (A Minor) (Custody)* [1991] FCR 155 where I said that: "it is natural for young children to be with mothers but, where it is in dispute, it is a consideration but not a presumption."

In cases where the child has remained throughout with the mother and is young, particularly when a baby or toddler, the unbroken relationship of the mother and child is one which it would be very difficult to displace, unless the mother was unsuitable to care for the child. But where the mother and child have been separated and the mother seeks the return of the child, other considerations apply and there is no starting-point that the mother should be preferred to the father and only displaced by a preponderance of evidence to the contrary.

In this case the mother and child had been separated at the time of the hearing for nearly 12 months and at the age of six, she is not within the category of very young children. There is no presumption which requires the mother as mother to be considered as the primary caretaker in preference to the father. The welfare of the child is paramount and each parent has to be looked at by the Judge in order to make as best he can the assessment of each and to choose one of them to be the custodial parent. In so far as the Judge appears to have started with the proposition that little girls naturally go to their mothers, the Judge was in error and applied the wrong test. The second point, the conflict of guidance over matters peculiar to her sex, is, in the context of a case like this, and probably generally, unimportant and ought not to be in itself placed in the balance unless there were recognizable difficulties which had already occurred or were likely to occur . . .

However, even with the qualifications that an approach presumptively placing children in the care of the mother would apply only to cases where she had had unbroken care of a

[98] Jones (1977–78). [99] [1958] 1 WLR 391, 397. [100] *Re H (A Minor: Custody)* [1990] 1 FLR 51, 56.

young child, Butler-Sloss LJ's comments remained controversial. In particular, they can be said to reflect a deeply traditional and arguably outdated notion of family life in which the father's role is one of breadwinner and provider and the mother's role that of primary child-care provider. Such an approach can be criticized from the perspective of both fathers and mothers. For fathers, it limits their role in their children's lives and presents them as viable main carers only where the mother is in some way unsuitable or unavailable. For mothers, on the other hand, it implies that motherhood is instinctive and innate, and thus the natural and appropriate role for all women[101]—and, moreover, this approach limits women's ability to engage in paid work in the labour market.

S. Boyd, 'From Gender Specificity to Gender Neutrality? Ideologies in Canadian Child Custody Law', in C. Smart and S. Sevenhuijsen (eds), *Child Custody and the Politics of Gender* (London: Routledge, 1989), 126, 133

The ideology attached to the tender years principle had conflicting implications for women. On the positive side, it arguably empowered women by allowing them to leave abusive husbands without forfeiting their children, and to play the role of head of a family unit. In addition, it may have increased women's bargaining power within marriage and during divorce or separation. While usually lacking the economic clout of their husbands, mothers could play upon the emotional incentive which men had to keep their marriage intact, lest they lose their children . . . On the negative side, the ideological aspects of the tender years doctrine which strengthened women's position in custody disputes rendered them ill-suited for public life. That is, the ideology underlying the tender years doctrine was one of inequality in that it enhanced the view of women as wives and mothers within the private sphere of the home . . . [W]omen were considered only as mothers rather than complete human beings. In turn, any deviation from the 'ideal' vision of motherhood such as leaving a child in the care of another person working outside the home, or engaging in an adulterous relationship could defeat the maternal preference . . . As long as women are allocated primary responsibility for child rearing and housework, even when employed . . . they tend to take employment which allows them to reconcile paid work with household and child rearing responsibilities. Such work is normally undervalued in terms of prestige and pay, is often part time, and tends to be 'dead-end' leading to few promotions . . . Pay and prestige differentials between male and female dominated jobs in turn lead to a tendency for mothers to withdraw from the labour force to care for young children, rather than fathers with better salaries and perhaps greater psychological investment in their employment . . . The 'traditional' sexual division of labour is thus maintained in spite of significant changes to women's pattern of involvement in the labour market.

R. van Krieken, '"The Best Interests of the Child" and Parental Separation: On the "Civilizing of Parents"', (2005) 68 *Modern Law Review* 25, 30–1

Most commentators will speak of the emergence of a more or less judicially explicit 'maternal preference rule' as the 'dominant doctrine in most Western countries', in conjunction with a 'tender years doctrine', that the younger a child is the more preferable it is for the mother to retain care and control.

[101] McGlynn (2000), 31 and (2001), 325–30.

In the decades leading up to the 1970s, there were two lines of argument about post-separation childhood which dominated the way in which the best interests standard was interpreted. The first concern[ed] the understanding of the mother-child relationship, and its placement at the centre of children's emotional development, such as in the work of John Bowlby. As Maidment puts it:

> For more than the next twenty years psychologists explored the mother-child dyad to the exclusion of all other relationships, fathers were excluded from all aspects of their children's birth, a maternal preference prevailed in custody cases, mothers were discouraged from working and thus leaving their children, and policy-makers discouraged alternative care arrangements for children such as day nurseries.

Bowlby himself was happy to see the biological mother replaced by another carer, what mattered was the continuity of care, but for all practical purposes his position was understood as emphasising the importance of an undisturbed close relationship between mothers and their children: fathers (or secondary carers) were seen as important but not crucial. In a custody dispute between the two it was clear that the mother's claim was the stronger.

The second was the notion of a 'clean break' or a 'finalised' separation and the need for a single 'psychological parent' . . . [According to this theory] both parents will re-partner, the child will gain a step-parent to substitute for the departing parent, who will simply form a new family with their new partner, more or less gradually losing touch with their first children.

By the late 1990s, the courts were expressing themselves in stronger language. In *Re A (A Minor: Residence Order)*, the Court of Appeal considered a case where the trial judge had relied on the 1959 UN Declaration to justify making a residence order in favour of the mother. The Court of Appeal upheld the father's appeal on the basis that the judge's use of this outdated, gendered principle was wholly erroneous.

Re A (A Minor) (Residence Order) [1998] 2 FCR 633 (CA), 638–9

THORPE LJ:

The relevance and value of the declaration is most doubtful. In terms of relevant social policy it could be said to be almost antiquated since it is now nearly 40 years old and in terms of social development and in terms of understanding of child development and welfare that is an exceedingly long time. Nor is that principle reflected in the United Nations Convention on the Rights of the Child . . . a convention ratified by this nation, as indeed by most other nations of the developed world. As [opposing counsel] points out, the corresponding article of the convention, art 9, is in strictly neutral terms. It states that the parties shall ensure that a child shall not be separated from his or her parent against their will except when competent authorities, subject to judicial review, determine, or where the parents are living separately and a decision must be made as to the child's place of residence. In modern terminology that is gender neutral . . .

In brief conclusion, it is, in my judgment, plainly demonstrated that in this case, most unfortunately, the trial judge fell into error in . . . applying what he erroneously accepted as a principle, that since J was of tender years his interests would best be served by him being cared for by his mother.

Despite these judicial moves against the presumption in favour of mothers, fathers' rights groups continued to say that the ideas of mothers as main carers—and a strong ambivalence towards fathers—remained deeply engrained within the collective psyche of the judiciary. According to this view, the law was constructing fathers as uninterested, irresponsible, and even dangerous figures—a construction without foundation. Unfortunately, official statistics on the making of s 8 orders under the CA 1989 are not broken down into gender. There is therefore no official record of how many sole residence orders (to use the old language) were granted to mothers in litigated cases and how many were granted to fathers. However, research carried out on the general population of post-divorce families, which includes those cases where children's living arrangements are agreed without going to court, strongly suggests that post-divorce parenting remains highly gendered. Studies done in the early 2000s suggested that over 80 per cent of children of separated parents lived primarily with their mothers;[102] 12 per cent of parents operated a shared care arrangement.[103] More recent research based on a study of court files suggests that similar patterns continue.[104]

11.6.2 THE CURRENT APPROACH TO 'LIVE WITH' ORDERS

The courts are insistent that there are no presumptions in the law as it is operated today as regards 'live with' orders[105]—though there are those on both sides who dispute that claim. The courts claim that they are making individualized decisions in each case based only on the particular child's best interests, considering all the realistic options open to the family. However, it is possible to see patterns of outcomes that appear to be based on stability of arrangements and 'status quo' arguments. Formally there is no 'presumption' in favour of maintaining the status quo and the courts have certainly been prepared to move a child from a settled placement.[106] However, in accordance with the welfare checklist, where the child is settled and happy, the courts have generally required some good reason for disturbing that position. The Court of Appeal has said that 'status quo' is made relevant only by 'relating it directly to the welfare of the child, [because] it simply refers in the broadest sense to the current living arrangements for a child'.[107]

Re F (A Child) [2009] EWCA Civ 313

WARD LJ:

9. The mother's case was strongly advanced on an argument that the status quo was with her and that, accordingly, the children should not be moved without good reason. There is obviously a case for an argument about preserving the status quo but I venture to suggest that since the Children Act of 1989 it would be better to address the checklist factors than

[102] DCA and DFES (2004), 2. [103] Peacey and Hunt (2008), 19.

[104] Newnham and Harding (2016). However, with around 80 per cent of separating parents making arrangements without using the family court, court files reflect only a small and unrepresentative proportion of the population: see Dabhi, Anand, and Tu (2022).

[105] Cf 11.7.2.a on the presumption in favour of parental involvement in s 1(2A).

[106] See, e.g., *Re N (A Child)* [2007] EWCA Civ 1053, a surrogacy case in which the child was removed from the care of the surrogate mother and her husband and placed with the commissioning couple after 18 months of 'high standards of care' living with the former.

[107] *Re E-R (Child Arrangements)* [2015] EWCA Civ 405, [34].

rely on any presumption of fact which may arise from an argument of that kind. The status quo argument means no more than that, if the children are settled in one place, then the court is to have regard to section [1(3)(c)] of the Act and consider the likely effect on them of any change in circumstances . . .

17. [I]f, as the judge found, the children will be well looked after and be safe and would thrive in either household, a finding he made, then the defect in the judgment is the inadequate explanation of the reasons which justified a change from a settled position, as settled it had become in the 12 months after the final separation of the parties.

Similar statements can be found in the Supreme Court's decision in *Re B (A Child)*, which reinstated the magistrates' decision to leave a 4-year-old boy—named Harry in the Supreme Court judgment—with his grandmother, rather than transferring his main home to his father with whom he had never lived.[108]

Re B (A Child) [2009] UKSC 5

LORD KERR:

42. . . . What we heard . . . confirmed the view that considerable disruption to Harry's life would have been involved in a transfer to live with his father. . . . Transfer of his residence would involve a great deal more than a change of address. Many of the familiar aspects of his life which anchor his stability and sense of security would be changed. The justices were therefore right to give significant weight to the desirability of preserving the status quo. This is a factor which will not always command the importance that must be attached to it in the present case but we are satisfied that it was of considerable significance in the debate as to where this child's best interests lay.

In principle, the status quo argument can work in favour of either parent. However, it is common, at least immediately following relationship breakdown, for the children to remain in the family home with the mother and for the father to move out into alternative accommodation. With many women choosing not to return to work after the birth of a child or, if returning to work, doing so on a part-time basis,[109] they can more easily assume the burden of child-care without having to rely as heavily on alternative carers, such as members of the extended family or childminders. Of course, as with the status quo argument, the employment and child-care responsibilities of the parties is often established pre-separation and carried through into the immediate post-separation period. This can lead to the mother being seen as the sole primary carer;[110] and long delays in the court process[111] then lead to that position being entrenched

[108] See further extracts from this case at 11.6.5.

[109] In a survey conducted for the Equality and Human Rights Commission in 2009, 63 per cent of women were in employment, of whom 43 per cent were full time and 57 per cent part time. That compares with 89 per cent of men in employment, of whom just 7 per cent were part time: Ellison, Barker, and Kulasuriya (2009), 33.

[110] Note the gender arguments set out previously from, e.g., Boyd (1989)—while fathers groups see this outcome as mothers pushing fathers out of their children's day-to-day care, it can also be argued that mothers are prevented from engaging in (full-time) paid employment because of child-care responsibilities which are not shared equally after separation.

[111] Private law children cases take a mean of 44 weeks to conclude: MOJ (2022a), table 9.

by the time of any final hearing. There may, of course, be a very good reason for this trend in parenting patterns in the immediate post-separation period: it may accurately reflect the division of parenting responsibilities pre-separation and therefore be a 'natural' extension of established parenting roles. Research based on court files offers some support of this.

A. Newnham and M. Harding, 'Sharing As Caring? Contact and Residence Disputes Between Parents', (2016) 28 *Child and Family Law Quarterly* 175, 177–8

There was a gendered pattern to both applications and outcomes within the sample. The most common outcome in the 174 cases was for the child to live with the mother (with or without a residence order), and the father to be granted a contact order. . . .

In the sample, men and women applied for different orders, for different reasons and in different circumstances. There may have been a pre-court filtering effect whereby parents were discouraged from making what were seen as unrealistic applications by solicitors, friends or what they read in the media. Our research looked only at what happened to applications that reached court. . . . Most women applicants sought sole residence orders to protect the status quo, whereas most men seeking sole residence orders were seeking a change to the child's living arrangements. This suggests that the stereotype of mothers are primary carers and fathers as contact seekers is determined by factors outside the court process. . . .

The decisions made by our courts meant that most children lived with the same primary care-giver parent both before and after the proceedings, with or without a residence order being made (117 cases). Children lived with their fathers in only 17 of the 117 status quo sole residence cases, and with their mothers in the remaining 100 cases. This is not surprising since in many of the cases, residence was not raised as an issue. As examined in the next section, applications to change sole residence were only granted if there were pressing concerns. As status quo often prevailed, it is, if anything, surprising that the gender difference in relation to numbers of sole residence orders made was not greater.

In our sample, the undesirability of changing the status quo carer was identified in welfare reports both in cases where the children lived with their mother and in cases where the children lived with their father. This factor is likely to have influenced outcomes where there were no child safety concerns. This supports the consistent findings of other empirical studies that the courts' reluctance to subject children to change is a more important factor than gender.

Although some would argue that parenting roles and responsibilities can, or even *should*, be renegotiated upon separation to meet the demands of the new situation, it is reasonable to ask—from the child's perspective—whether the moment of the parents' separation is the right time also to change the child's day-to-day care arrangements. However, fathers' rights groups see the pattern of mothers 'entrenching their position as primary carers' (as they see it) as a serious cause of injustice.[112]

Increasingly, children share their time between two households after parental separation. That does not mean that time is shared equally—sometimes it is, but very often not.[113] But

[112] Geldof (2003).

[113] Research from a sample of court files found that 20 per cent of cases involved shared 'live with' orders, but only a fifth of those (4 per cent of all cases) had equal or near-equal division of time between both households: Newnham and Harding (2016), 181–2. In the survey by Dabhi, Anand, and Tu (2022), 18.5 per cent of parents reported that the child saw each parent three days a week or more, though answers varied between what the Department for Work and Pensions terms 'parents with care' and 'non-resident parents' (our calculations from fig 28).

the possibility of shared living arrangements allows the courts more flexibility to find solutions which meet the child's interests in a wider range of circumstances.

11.6.3 SHARED LIVING ARRANGEMENTS

Prior to the change in terminology in 2014, orders whereby a child would split their time between two households were described as 'shared residence orders' (SROs). These are now CAOs where the child lives with both parents.[114] Support for the greater use of shared 'live with' orders is firmly rooted in the discourse on shared parenting. Shared parenting post-divorce is an integral part of the normative model of the 'civilized divorce'.[115] The hostility promoted by the 'win–lose' mentality of previous models of post-divorce parenting is regarded as particularly damaging to children, with shared parenting perceived as one means by which hostilities can be reduced.[116] The normative model of post-divorce parenting emerging from these debates is explained by Bren Neale and Carol Smart.

B. Neale and C. Smart, 'In Whose Best Interests? Theorising Family Life Following Parental Separation or Divorce', in S. Day Sclater and C. Piper (eds), *Undercurrents of Divorce* (Aldershot: Ashgate, 1999), 33, 37–9

Since the early 1980s the model of lone/reconstituted family has gradually been replaced by that of a co-parenting/biological family. The original family is no longer to be broken under the 'clean break' philosophy, nor is it to be replaced by a reconstituted family . . . The potential to care for a child without the other parent, even if this is bound up with a new marriage or partnership, has a diminished value under this new ideology and, barring exceptional circumstances, can no longer be legally sanctioned. If the family can't remain intact and under one roof (still, of course the preferred option) then, as Day Sclater and Piper argue . . . it must re-invent itself as a 'bi-nuclear' family spread across two households. Divorce has thus been recast as a 'stage' (albeit a painful one) in the newly extended life course of the indelible nuclear family . . .

This new model dovetails with a welfare discourse that has been radically reformulated. Children are no longer said to need one stable home, one primary carer and the restabilising influence of the stepfamily. What they are now said to need is two biological parents and the restabilising influence of the non-residential father. One notable feature of this reformulated welfare discourse is that the child's needs are now defined in terms of what they are lacking: the lack of proper fathering and the limitations of mothering, which has culminated in a link between the 'child of divorce' and the pervasive but largely undefined notion of harm . . .

The assumption that children are 'damaged' by divorce is accompanied by another assumption—that this damage can be mitigated if particular forms of parenting and therapeutic interventions are put in place. Parents are to ameliorate the worst effects of their actions by prioritising their children's welfare, playing a joint part in their children's day to day care and developing a co-operative and unselfish sharing of parental authority.

As Neale and Smart point out, the shared parenting discourse is based on a significant shift in the welfare discourse. Whereas the interests of children under the 'tender years doctrine' were

[114] In relation to the pre-2014 cases, we continue to refer to 'shared residence' from time to time.
[115] Krieken (2005), 34–45. [116] Brophy (1989), 222; Krieken (2005), 34–45.

clearly identified with those of the mother, the rise of the 'new father' rhetoric has seen the interests of children increasingly viewed as dependent on their relationship with their father.

> [T]he new model is underpinned by a fresh articulation of the rights of fathers who argue that, since they are just as capable as mothers of caring for their children they should be granted equal legal rights to them . . .
>
> It is important to recognise that what is transformed under the new model is how fatherhood is constituted within legal and policy discourse. It seems that where mothers, as the day to day carers, were once constructed as vital to their children, it is fathers, as the restabilisers and potential carers, who are now constructed as essential, at least following divorce. That fathers might want a more direct involvement in day to day care is a relatively new phenomenon, deserving of explanation. According to Beck, it is linked to wider social changes under which the traditional gendering of parental care and financial support is breaking down . . .
>
> The changed attitude can also be understood in terms of the value that is increasingly placed upon emotional fulfilment within family relationships. If marriage and, perhaps more to the point, remarriage can no longer be relied upon to provide this, then the parent-child relationship may increasingly become the focus of such fulfilment. This, in turn, is linked to the rise in a romanticised vision of children as priceless emotional assets which, in the interests of parental equality, are best divided equally than awarded to one parent alone. Where mothers were once seen to be the holders of onerous responsibilities, requiring sustained emotional commitment, hard physical work and a range of socio-economic sacrifices (and deserving, therefore, of custodial status and state support), they are now seen to be in possession of valuable commodities, and any unwillingness to share them seen as discriminatory against fathers.

As we have seen in other areas of the law, fathers' rights groups have thus been able to argue that the imperative for improving the legal position of fathers comes from within the welfare discourse itself. Shared parenting does not necessarily mean 50:50 shared care, though that is advocated by some fathers' rights groups.[117] Although 50:50 care perhaps represents the most 'pure' form of shared parenting, the law has shifted significantly away from the old model of 'every other weekend' contact, such that shared parenting (in the broader sense) is increasingly common.

11.6.3.a Development of the courts' approach

The early case law, both before and after the CA 1989 entered force, was generally hostile to orders for shared care, the prevailing view being that children require one settled home. A shared residence order was therefore regarded as 'wholly exceptional',[118] and it had to be shown that the proposed departure from the conventional orders conferred some 'positive benefit' on the child.[119] Opposition to shared residence was particularly strong where there was continuing hostility between the parents.

However, judicial attitudes towards such orders have undergone significant change.[120] A more liberal approach was clear from the Court of Appeal judgment in *D v D (Shared Residence Order)*. The case involved 'an exceptionally high level of animosity between the

[117] S 1(2B) emphasizes that the statutory presumption of parental involvement in a child's life does not mean any particular division of a child's time: see 11.7.2.a.

[118] *J v J* [1991] 2 FLR 385; *Re H (A Minor) (Shared Residence)* [1994] 1 FLR 717.

[119] *A v A (Minors) (Shared Residence Order)* [1994] 1 FLR 669.

[120] Trinder (2014) describes the evolving attitude to shared care as going through five phases: rarity, expansion, politicization, internationalization, and finally symbolism.

parents'. The children lived with their mother but had substantial levels of contact with their father. The judge found that the mother used the fact she had sole residence as a weapon in the parents' 'war'. He therefore made an order for shared residence in an attempt to reduce the level of conflict between them.[121]

D v D (Shared Residence Order) [2000] EWCA Civ 3009

HALE LJ:

20. [Counsel] who appears for the mother, has argued that the authorities indicate that shared residence orders should only be made either in exceptional circumstances or, at the very least, where it can be demonstrated that they would show a positive benefit for the children. In this particular case there were no exceptional circumstances, no evidence of positive benefit and thus, no reason to change the legal arrangements which had been in place for some time. He also argues that access to information was irrelevant or given too much weight because the father already had parental responsibility and was entitled to that information. Thus that, by itself, could not be regarded as an exceptional circumstance or of positive benefit . . .

22. The background to the Children Act provision lies in the Law Commission's Working Paper No. 96, published in 1986, on Custody and the Law Commission's Report, Law Com. No. 172, published in 1988, on Guardianship and Custody. If I may summarise the basic principles proposed, the first was that each parent with parental responsibility should retain their equal and independent right, and their responsibility, to have information and make appropriate decisions about their children. If, of course, the parents were not living together it might be necessary for the court to make orders about their future, but those orders should deal with the practical arrangements for where and how the children should be living rather than assigning rights as between the parents . . .

24. . . . [D]ealing with residence orders the Commission said this at paragraph 4.12 of the Law Com No. 172:

> "Apart from the effect on the other parent, which has already been mentioned, the main difference between a residence order and a custody order is that the new order should be flexible enough to accommodate a much wider range of situations. In some cases, the child may live with both parents even though they do not share the same household. It was never our intention to suggest that children should share their time more or less equally between their parents. Such arrangements will rarely be practicable, let alone for the children's benefit. However, the evidence from the United States is that where they are practicable they can work well and we see no reason why they should be actively discouraged. None of our respondents shared the view expressed in a recent case [*Riley v Riley*] that such an arrangement, which had been working well for some years, should never have been made. More commonly, however, the child will live with both parents but spend more time with one than the other. Examples might be where he spends term time with one and holidays with the other, or two out of three holidays from boarding school with one and the third with the other. It is a far more realistic description of the responsibilities involved in that sort of arrangement to make a residence order covering both parents rather than a residence order for one

[121] Note that empirical evidence suggests that children find shared care in such circumstances difficult: e.g. Fehlberg et al (2011), extracted at 11.6.3.b.

> and a contact order for the other. Hence we recommend that where the child is to live with two (or more) people who do not live together, the order may specify the periods during which the child is to live in each household. The specification may be general rather than detailed and in some cases may not be necessary at all." . . .
>
> 31. It is quite clear that in [*A v A (Minors)* [1994] 1 FLR 669, Butler-Sloss LJ] was moving matters on from any suggestion, which is not in the legislation, that these orders require exceptional circumstances . . .
>
> 32. If . . . it is either planned or has turned out that the children are spending substantial amounts of their time with each of their parents then, as both the Law Commission and my Lady indicated in the passages that I have quoted it may be an entirely appropriate order to make. For my part, I would not add any gloss on the legislative provisions, which are always subject to the paramount consideration of what is best for the children concerned.
>
> 33. This case is one in which, as the judge said, the arrangements have been settled for some considerable time. The children are, in effect, living with both of their parents. They have homes with each of them . . .
>
> 34. In those circumstances it seems to me that there is indeed a positive benefit to these children in those facts being recognised in the order that the court makes. There is no detriment or disrespect to either parent in that order. It simply reflects the reality of these children's lives. It was entirely appropriate for the judge to make it in this case and neither party should feel that they have won or lost as a result. I would, therefore, dismiss the appeal.

This case marked an important change in approach towards shared residence orders. Hale LJ made clear that the courts should not feel inhibited from making a shared 'live with' order where such an order reflects the reality of the children's lives. It is, however, often very difficult to determine where the boundary lies between, on the one hand, a reality of shared care justifying a shared 'live with' order and, on the other, an arrangement best reflected in orders with the child living with one parent and spending time with the other. It is a question of degree. The courts are clear that, as a matter of law, an arrangement can be called shared care even if the child's time is divided unequally,[122] whether there is geographical proximity between the parents or not,[123] and regardless of the exact pattern of care. The courts are also clear that high levels of hostility between the parents will not prevent the court ordering shared care where it is otherwise justified; a good relationship between the parties is not a prerequisite in the case law.[124] Indeed, the courts have suggested that orders for shared care may actually help to ease the conflict between the parents by sending out the strong message that they have equal *status* in the eyes of the law.[125] That point developed in some judges' thinking to the point where there were clear authorities for the proposition that a shared care order could be justified for symbolic or psychological reasons (particularly to acknowledge the equal status of the parents) even in the absence of an underlying reality of shared care. This suggestion—perhaps reflected in the original *D v D* decision—was developed in a judgment of Sir Mark Potter P.[126]

[122] *Re K (A Child)* [2008] EWCA Civ 526, [6].

[123] *Re F (Shared Residence Order)* [2003] EWCA Civ 592; *Re H (Children)* [2009] EWCA Civ 245, [8].

[124] *Re R (Children)* [2005] EWCA Civ 542, [11]–[12]; *Re W (Shared Residence Order)* [2009] EWCA Civ 370, [15]; *Re L (Relocation: Second Appeal)*[2017] EWCA Civ 2121, [70].

[125] Cf Harris-Short (2010), who suggests that by getting a shared care order, the expectations of the non-primary carer for 'real equality' (i.e. an actual 50:50 sharing of time) will be raised and the dispute will then turn to focus on the minutiae of the division of time under the terms of the order.

[126] See also *Re K (A Child)* [2008] EWCA Civ 526, [6], per Wilson LJ.

Re A (A Child) (Joint Residence: Parental Responsibility) [2008] EWCA Civ 867

POTTER P:

66. The making of a shared residence order is no longer the unusual order which once it was. Following the implementation of the Act and in the light of s 11(4) of the Act which provides that the court may make residence orders in favour of more than one person, whether living in the same household or not, the making of such an order has become increasingly common. It is now recognised by the court that a shared residence order may be regarded as appropriate where it provides legal confirmation of the factual reality of a child's life or where, in a case where one party has the primary care of a child, it may be psychologically beneficial to the parents in emphasising the equality of their position and responsibilities.

Although *Re A* fell into a rare sub-category of cases where a shared 'live with' order was necessary to confer parental responsibility on the non-resident parent,[127] the President's judgment was approved by Wilson LJ as summarizing the principles governing shared residence orders and applied to a routine intra-parental residence dispute.

Re W (Shared Residence Order) [2009] EWCA Civ 370

WILSON LJ:

13. With respect to [counsel], I see no subsisting foundation for his submission to us today that, unless the time to be spent by a child in the two households is close to being equal, unusual circumstances are required before a shared residence order should be made. Fifteen years ago his submission would have been valid . . . But at any rate for the last 8 years the better view has been that, while of course a need remains for the demonstration of circumstances which positively indicate that the child's welfare would thereby be served, there is no such gloss on the appropriateness of an order for shared residence as would be reflected by the words 'unusual' or indeed 'exceptional' . . .

17. . . . [Counsel] began by presenting to us statistics which he had compiled and which, according to him . . . indicate that, under the arrangements made by consent between the parties, K [the child] is to spend with the father only 25% of her time . . . His submission reminded me of comments which, as a temporary member of this court, I made in *Re F (Shared Residence Order)* . . . to the effect that statistics of that character were usually only of limited value. [Counsel] ultimately described as the main plank of his appeal the fact that a shared residence order did not reflect the situation on the ground . . . But it was in that same short judgment of mine . . . that I attempted to explode the *canard* that a shared residence order was appropriate only in circumstances in which the children would be spending their time evenly, or more or less evenly, in the two homes.

The shared 'live with' order was thus upheld even though the 'reality' of the child's care was a long way from 50:50 shared care.[128]

[127] In this case the child had been raised for two years by his mother's partner who mistakenly believed that he was the legal (genetic) father. Note that s 12(2A) was not in force when this decision was made, which would now offer an alternative means of granting parental responsibility: see 10.3.5.

[128] See also *Re O (A Child)* [2009] EWCA Civ 1266.

Making a shared 'live with' order, regardless of the 'reality' of the division of the child's time, in order to try to control the conflict between the separated parents seems reasonable and laudable. Any approach which may help 'lessen the stakes' and reduce the problems associated with the 'win–lose' mentality of litigation will ultimately further the child's welfare. However, despite the initial attractions of this approach, it can be questioned whether it is focused on the child's welfare as opposed to the adults' desires. The rise of shared live with orders which did not reflect truly shared care was criticized for its inconsistency with the original scheme intended by the Law Commission and Parliament, and for undermining the essential purpose of a 'live with' order.

P. Harris and R. George, 'Parental Responsibility and Shared Residence Orders: Parliamentary Intentions and Judicial Interpretations', (2010) 22 *Child and Family Law Quarterly* 151, 155–6, 166–9

> The [Law] Commission . . . recommended that, where both parties had parental responsibility, the court be limited to dealing with concrete and practical issues about with whom the child should live, what contact she would have with others, and any disputed matters relating to the exercise of parental responsibility . . . [I]t is important to note that the Commission was clear that the orders should reflect the *realities* . . . In reflecting that overarching policy, while the Commission in their Review favoured shared residence orders where the child shared 'their time more or less equally between their parents', it thought such orders appropriate only in the rare cases where such an order was a 'more realistic description of that . . . sort of arrangement . . . than a residence order for one [parent] and a contact order for the other'. That approach was also echoed in Parliament when Lord Chancellor Mackay explained that 'contact' included 'staying with' the non-residential parent and that 'shared residence [would be] rare'. Thus both the Commission and Parliament appear to have emphasised that shared residence orders were to be contemplated only where they reflected *the reality* of the *concrete* arrangement . . .

Having reviewed the case law on shared residence orders and the trend to make such orders in order to affirm the equal status of the parents, Harris and George argue that this development was closely linked to the recent degradation of parental responsibility such that the latter is now close to being a meaningless concept.[129]

> We suggest that this alternative approach [to shared residence] came about, in part, because of the courts' earlier dilution of the potency of parental responsibility. The problem from the courts' perspective was that, if a man convicted of possessing child pornography and who was to have no direct contact with his child was worthy of parental responsibility, surely a good father who already had parental responsibility and who was to continue to play some active involvement in his child's upbringing ought to have something more.
>
> Using shared residence orders to resolve the difficulty created by the dilution of parental responsibility was not initially obvious, given the courts' historical resistance to such orders. However, we have now reached the point where academics can suggest that 'a[s] parental responsibility has been diluted, shared residence orders have arguably come to represent the new way of giving separated parents equal authority', and practitioners can ask 'whether the

[129] See 10.4.3.

rise of the shared residence order is inextricably linked to the perceived ineffectual nature of parental responsibility' . . .

It is arguable that the courts are starting on the same road with shared residence as was seen with parental responsibility. Whereas parental responsibility was down-graded so as to be given to fathers who had no practical role to play in their children's lives at all, now shared residence is being down-graded to give it to fathers who are involved, but not in day-to-day care. Where parents live in reasonable proximity to one another, and their children spend considerable time living in both households, there is no reason not to call that shared residence. Where the parents live far apart, but their children live, say, with one for the school term and with the other for the holidays, there is equally no difficulty with calling that shared residence. But when the child merely visits one parent, even if those visits involve overnight stays, such arrangements should not be called residence, for they are not.[130]

Senior judges were also somewhat divided as to whether it was appropriate to use shared residence to deal with questions of parental status even where there was no underlying reality of shared care.[131]

Re H (Children) [2009] EWCA Civ 902

WARD LJ:

13. [A] shared residence order must reflect the reality of the children's lives. Where the children are spending a substantial amount of time with both parents, a shared residence order reflects the reality of their lives . . . [A] residence order is about where a child is to live and it is not about status. I want to emphasise that here the father's status is recognised by the parental responsibility agreement and order which has been made. That gives him equal say in how the children are to be brought up, so that when they are with him he will determine when they brush their teeth and when they go to bed and whether they have cornflakes or porridge for breakfast . . . So in terms of status he has it, and shared residence is not going to affect status. Shared residence is about the reality of where they live. And the best test I can think of . . . is to postulate the question, ask the children, where do you live? If the answer is "I live with my mummy but I go and stay with my daddy regularly", then you have the answer to your problem. That answer means a residence order with mummy and contact with daddy, but if the situation truly is such that the children say, "Oh we live with mummy for part of the time and with daddy for the other part of the time", then you have the justification for making a shared residence order.

The House of Lords addressed the issue of shared residence orders in *Holmes-Moorhouse v London Borough of Richmond upon Thames*.[132] The case arose in relation to the issue of whether orders of the family court could—or should—be used to try to influence local authority housing departments in the allocation of social housing. However, the judgment of Baroness Hale gives general guidance in relation to shared care arrangements.

[130] See also Newnham (2011).

[131] This was also the view taken by Hale LJ in *Re A (Children)* [2001] EWCA Civ 1795, [17]. On the use of shared care arrangements to confer parental responsibility, see 10.3.5.

[132] [2009] UKHL 7.

Holmes-Moorhouse v London Borough of Richmond upon Thames [2009] UKHL 7

BARONESS HALE:

30. When any family court decides with whom the children of separated parents are to live, the welfare of those children must be its paramount consideration: Children Act 1989, s 1(1). This means that it must choose from the available options the future which will be best for the children, not the future which will be best for the adults. It also means that the court may be creative in devising options which the parents have not put forward. It does not mean that the court can create options where none exist . . .

37. . . . [I]n my view, this order should not have been made. A residence order is "an order settling the arrangements to be made as to the person with whom a child is to live." . . . Although, as I have said, the parents are free to depart from it by agreement if they wish, it is an order which can be enforced, by physical removal of the children if need be . . . It is one thing to make such an order when each parent has a home to offer the children, even if it is not exactly what they have been used to before their parents split up. It is another thing entirely to make such an order when one parent is living in the family home and the other parent has no accommodation at all to offer them and no money with which to feed and clothe them. . . .

38. Family court orders are meant to provide practical solutions to the practical problems faced by separating families. They are not meant to be aspirational statements of what would be for the best in some ideal world which has little prospect of realisation. Ideally there may be many cases where it would be best for the children to have a home with each of their parents. But this is not always or even usually practicable. Family courts have no power to conjure up resources where none exist. . . .

Baroness Hale's approach, emphasizing the importance of s 8 orders being grounded in reality and offering practical solutions to the problems facing post-separation families, has clear echoes of her earlier judgments on shared residence orders. Although it is only possible to speculate, there is nothing in this judgment to suggest Baroness Hale would now depart from the clear principles she established in *D v D* to endorse the approach to shared residence orders that has been favoured in more recent years by some members of the Court of Appeal. Baroness Hale also emphasizes the particular importance of listening to the voice of the child in cases of shared residence, 'because it is the children who will have to divide their time between two homes and it is all too easy for the parents' wishes and feelings to predominate'.[133]

11.6.3.b Policy debates about shared care arrangements

The issue of shared care arrangements—and in particular whether there should be some form of legislative or judicial presumption in favour of children dividing their time either equally or otherwise between their parents after separation—has been hotly debated by judges, policymakers, researchers, and activists. One of the difficulties is that the research evidence that is available about the effects of different care arrangements on children's welfare is unclear and highly contested. A lot of research has been conducted recently, especially in Australia and the United States, but scholars disagree about what the findings of that research show.

One view is that shared care arrangements work well for a minority of separating families—usually a sub-group of those who are not involved in litigation—but can be problematic for other children.

[133] Ibid, [36].

B. Fehlberg et al, 'Legislating for Shared Time Parenting After Separation: A Research Review', (2011) 25 *International Journal of Law, Policy and the Family* 318, 321–3

Shared time parenting is likely to work well when arrangements are child-focused, flexible, and cooperative. These same characteristics also mean that parents are likely to move away from shared time to accommodate their children's evolving needs and wishes.

The research suggests that families with such arrangements tend to involve parents with features not typical of the broader separating population. These features include being tertiary educated, being socio-economically well-resourced, having some flexibility in working hours, living near each other, fathers who have been involved in children's daily care prior to separation and children of primary school age (although the features present vary from case to case) . . . Studies also repeatedly find that parents in this group have agreed to shared time arrangements without recourse to lawyers or the courts . . .

The 'warning flags' for when shared time parenting is not workable (meaning that the stress and burden for children outweighs the benefits for them) are essentially the flipside of those that facilitate it: in particular, high ongoing parental conflict, family violence and abuse, and rigidity.

Fehlberg et al observe that the two groups of families that they identify—the highly cooperative and the high conflict—represent only the two ends of a spectrum. They consider that not enough is known about the effects of shared care arrangements on children in families who come between these two extremes. However, they suggest that the research evidence is strong enough to show that 'shared time arrangements present particular risks for children when mothers express ongoing "safety concerns", where there is high ongoing parental conflict and when children are very young—or some combination of these'.[134]

However, in a sign of how complex the debate about research in this area can be, other scholars take a different view of what the evidence shows about overnight contact or shared care arrangements.[135]

R. Warshak, 'Social Science and Parenting Plans for Young Children: A Consensus Report', (2014) 20 *Psychology, Public Policy, and Law* 46, 59–60

Research on children's overnights with fathers favors allowing children under four to be cared for at night by each parent rather than spending every night in the same home.[136] We find the theoretical and practical considerations favoring overnights for most young children to be more compelling than concerns that overnights might jeopardize children's development. Practical considerations are relevant to consider when tailoring a parenting plan for young children to the circumstances of the parents. Such considerations may not be evident in the laboratory, or measured by existing studies, but they are readily apparent to parents and consultants who must attend to the feasibility of parenting plan options. Overnights create potential benefits related to the logistics of sharing parenting time.

[134] Fehlberg et al (2011), 323. The principal research that underpins the claim in relation to young children (meaning those aged under 4 years) comes from a large Australian study by McIntosh et al (2010).

[135] See also Lamb (2018).

[136] These findings are contradicted by some other studies, e.g. McIntosh, Pruett, and Kelly (2014a), (2014b).

> . . . Parenting schedules that offer the father and child 2-hr blocks of time together, two or three times per week, can unduly stress their contacts. Overnights help to reduce the tension associated with rushing to return the child, and thus potentially improve the quality and satisfaction of the contact both for the parent and child. Overnights allow the child to settle in to the father's home, which would be more familiar to the child who regularly spends the night in the home compared with one who has only 1-hr segments in the home (allowing for transportation and preparation for the return trip). . . . Spending the night allows the father to participate in a wider range of bonding activities, such as engaging in bedtime rituals and comforting the child in the event of nighttime awakenings. . . .
>
> Nonetheless, because of the relatively few studies currently available, the limitations of these studies, and the predominance of results that indicate no direct benefit or drawback for overnights per se outside the context of other factors, we stop short of concluding that the current state of evidence supports a blanket policy or legal presumption regarding overnights. Because of the well documented vulnerability of father-child relationships among never-married and divorced parents, and the studies that identify overnights as a protective factor associated with increased father commitment to child rearing and reduced incidence of father drop-out, and because no study demonstrates any net risk of overnights, decision makers should recognize that depriving young children of overnights with their fathers could compromise the quality of their developing relationship.

The controversy associated with these studies demonstrates the difficulty in drawing any clear conclusions from the available research evidence. However, there may be an increasing consensus around one issue, namely that while *some* amount of overnight time away from a main carer does not harm young children (meaning aged 3 and under), there is reason to be cautious about *high frequency* overnight time, especially if there is parental conflict or if the child's bond with one parent is not yet formed.[137]

11.6.4 PARTICULAR ISSUES APPLICABLE TO 'LIVE WITH' ORDERS

11.6.4.a Gay and lesbian parents

Two distinct situations may arise regarding a parent's sexual orientation. First, there may be disputes between parents where one parent has left a heterosexual relationship to form a same-sex relationship. There was a flurry of reported cases addressing this issue in the early 1990s, though very little can be seen by way of more recent authority. The courts have consistently held that homosexuality does not bar a parent from becoming a child's main carer. However, in the early 1990s judges also made it clear that a parent's sexuality could be relevant to welfare. Indeed, although the case is now quite old, the court in *C v C (Custody of Child)* took a particularly conservative line in evaluating the 'merits' of parenting within a same-sex family when compared with other, more 'conventional', alternatives.[138] However, although the Court of Appeal favoured the 'normal' family environment offered by the father, holding that 'the nature of the [mother's new lesbian] relationship is an important factor to be put into the balance', the first instance judge rehearing the case granted residence to the mother.[139]

[137] Warshak (2014); Pruett, McIntosh, and Kelly (2014).

[138] [1991] FCR 254 (CA).

[139] *C v C (No 2)* [1992] FCR 206.

While this authority has never formally been overruled, it cannot remain good law in the light of the many other changes that have occurred in relation to sexual orientation since it was decided.[140] In 2006, Thorpe LJ said of *C v C* that 'judicial attitudes to homosexual parenting were very different in that earlier age',[141] and in 2017 Sir James Munby P said of this and similar cases that they 'make uncomfortable—we would say very uncomfortable—reading today'.[142] These domestic authorities are reflective of European Court decisions which make clear that basing decisions about children's living arrangements on the sexual orientation of a parent is 'not acceptable under the Convention'.[143]

A second type of case is where same-sex parents (most commonly two women) have separated.[144] In principle, these cases are no different from any other post-separation parental disputes: 'the issues arising are just the same as those which may arise between heterosexual couples. The legal principles are also the same.'[145] However, as we discuss later,[146] there has been some debate about the potential relevance of the genetic and gestational tie which may exist between one of the parents and the child, but not the other. While that issue is by no means restricted to cases between former same-sex partners, some of the key authorities discussing it have arisen in this context. Moreover, there are more intricate factual patterns that can arise which are either rare or impossible in heterosexual relationships. For example, in *Re G (Shared Residence Order: Biological Mother of Donor Egg Children)*,[147] the applicant woman's eggs had been fertilized by anonymous donor sperm and then implanted in the respondent woman, who carried the twin children to birth. The question in that case was whether a shared 'live with' order should be made for the principal purpose of conferring parental responsibility on the applicant,[148] the parties having already agreed the role that each would play in the child's upbringing following their separation.

11.6.4.b Racial, religious, and cultural factors

Race, religion, and culture are often regarded as fundamentally important to a person's sense of identity and belonging. When separating parents are from different racial, cultural, or religious backgrounds, the question about which parent the child should live with can take on an even greater significance. It is often more than just an argument over living arrangements: it can be a dispute over the child's whole way of life. The courts have recognized the importance of these issues. However, whilst religion, race, and culture are relevant, they are not afforded any special significance in the welfare balance. The European Court of Human Rights has made it clear that a decision concerning residence must not be based 'solely or principally' on the applicant's religion: in itself, it cannot be a determining factor.[149] The courts must also avoid making abstract judgements about the tenets, beliefs, or practices of particular religions or cultures. The European Court has, however, confirmed that it is legitimate for the

[140] Most obviously the Civil Partnership Act 2004 and the Marriage (Same Sex Couples) Act 2013, together with the inclusion of sexual orientation as a protected characteristic under the Equality Act 2010. See also Reece (2017), 11.

[141] *Re G (Residence: Same-Sex Parents)* [2006] EWCA Civ 372, [40], rev'd on other grounds [2006] UKHL 43.

[142] *Re M (Ultra-Orthodox Judaism: Transgender)* [2017] EWCA Civ 2164, [46].

[143] *da Silva Mouta v Portugal* (App No 33290/96, ECHR) (1999), [36].

[144] On disputes between same-sex couples and the 'other parent' about contact, see 11.7.2.b.

[145] *Re G (Children) (Residence: Same-Sex Partner)* [2006] UKHL 43, [6].

[146] See 11.6.5.

[147] [2014] EWCA Civ 336.

[148] Note that CA 1989, ss 12(1A) and 12(2A) were not in force when this case was decided, which would now offer an easier means of conferring parental responsibility on similar facts: see 10.3.2 and 10.3.5.

[149] *Palau-Martinez v France* (App No 64927/01, ECHR) (2004).

domestic authorities to take into account the *effect* of the applicant's religious practices on the child's lifestyle and upbringing.[150] This is the approach adopted by the English courts.

The leading case on this issue did not involve a dispute about where the children should live (which was agreed between the parties), but rather about their schooling and educational upbringing, which would be dealt with under a specific issue order. Nonetheless, Munby LJ's discussion of the issues is of broader relevance. The parents in *Re G (Education: Religious Upbringing)* came from families which were part of the Chassidic (Hasidic) or Chareidi community of Ultra Orthodox Jews. In the Chareidi community, all aspects of life are governed by the Torah and, of particular relevance to the case, children attend single-sex schools. Although the mother had grown up in this community, she no longer considered herself to be part of it, though she still considered herself to be an Orthodox Jew.[151]

Re G (Education: Religious Upbringing) [2012] EWCA Civ 1233

MUNBY LJ:

35. Religion—whatever the particular believer's faith—is not the business of government or of the secular courts, though the courts will, of course, pay every respect to the individual's or family's religious principles. Article 9 of the European Convention for the Protection of Human Rights and Fundamental Freedoms, after all, demands no less. The starting point of the common law is thus respect for an individual's religious principles, coupled with an essentially neutral view of religious beliefs and a benevolent tolerance of cultural and religious diversity.

36. It is not for a judge to weigh one religion against another. The court recognises no religious distinctions and generally speaking passes no judgment on religious beliefs or on the tenets, doctrines or rules of any particular section of society. All are entitled to equal respect, so long as they are "legally and socially acceptable" (Purchas LJ in *Re R (A Minor) (Residence: Religion)* [1993] 2 FLR 163, 171) and not "immoral or socially obnoxious" (Scarman LJ in *Re T (Minors) (Custody: Religious Upbringing)* (1981) 2 FLR 239, 244) or "pernicious" (Latey J in *Re B and G (Minors) (Custody)* [1985] FLR 134, 157, referring to scientology).

37. The Strasbourg jurisprudence is to the same effect. . . .

38. The important point for present purposes is that the Convention forbids the State to determine the validity of religious beliefs and in that respect imposes on the State a duty of what the Strasbourg court has called neutrality and impartiality . . .

39. Within limits the law – our family law – will tolerate things which society as a whole may find undesirable. A child's best interests have to be assessed by reference to general community standards, making due allowance for the entitlement of people, within the limits of what is permissible in accordance with those standards, to entertain very divergent views about the religious, moral, social and secular objectives they wish to pursue for themselves and for their children. . . .

40. Where precisely the limits are to be drawn is often a matter of controversy. There is no 'bright-line' test that the law can set. The infinite variety of the human condition precludes arbitrary definition.

41. Some things are nevertheless beyond the pale: forced marriages (always to be distinguished of course from arranged marriages to which the parties consent), female genital mutilation and so-called, if grotesquely misnamed, 'honour-based' domestic violence. Plainly, as I wish to emphasise, we are not here in that territory. . . .

150 *Ismailova v Russia* (App No 37614/02, ECHR) (2007), [55]–[63].
151 Further extracts from *Re G* can be found at 8.2.1.

43. Some manifestations of religious practice may be regulated if contrary to a child's welfare. Although a parent's views and wishes as to the child's religious upbringing are of great importance, and will always be seriously regarded by the court, just as the court will always pay great attention to the wishes of a child old enough to be able to express sensible views on the subject of religion, even if not old enough to take a mature decision, they will be given effect to by the court only if and so far as and in such manner as is in accordance with the child's best interests. In matters of religion, as in all other aspects of a child's upbringing, the interests of the child are the paramount consideration.

Munby LJ then quoted from an earlier Court of Appeal decision which had related to the upbringing of a child as a Jehovah's Witness.

Re T (Minors) (Custody: Religious Upbringing) (1981) 2 FLR 239 (CA), 244–5

SCARMAN LJ:

We live in a tolerant society. There is no reason at all why the mother should not espouse the beliefs and practice of Jehovah's Witnesses. It is conceded that there is nothing immoral or socially obnoxious in the beliefs and practice of this sect. . . . It is as reasonable on the part of the mother that she should wish to teach her children the beliefs and practice of the Jehovah's Witnesses as it is reasonable on the part of the father that they should not be taught those practices and beliefs.

It is not for this court, in society as at present constituted, to pass any judgment on the beliefs of the mother or on the beliefs of the father. It is sufficient for this court that it should recognize that each is entitled to his or her own beliefs and way of life, and that the two opposing ways of life considered in this case are both socially acceptable and certainly consistent with a decent and respectable life. What follows from that? It follows, in my judgment, that there is a great risk, merely because we are dealing with an unpopular minority sect, in overplaying the dangers to the welfare of these children inherent in the possibility that they may follow their mother and become Jehovah's Witnesses. Of course, most of us like to play games on Saturdays, to go out to children's parties and to have a quiet Sunday—some of us will go to church, and some of us will not. This appears to be the normal and happy, even though somewhat materialistic, way of life, accepted by the majority of people in our society. It does not follow, however, that it is wrong, or contrary to the welfare of children, that life should be in a narrower sphere, subject to a stricter religious discipline, and without the parties on birthdays and Christmas that seem so important to the rest of us. These are factors that must be considered, but I think it is essential in a case of this sort to appreciate that the mother's teaching, once it is accepted as reasonable, is teaching that has got to be considered against the whole background of the case and not as in itself so full of danger for the children that it alone could justify making an order which otherwise the court would not make.

After quoting this passage, Munby LJ observed that, in determining a case where these considerations were relevant, the court should not automatically prefer the parent whose way of life was seen as being 'more acceptable', because it was not necessarily contrary to a child's welfare to be part of a minority group. Munby LJ drew a distinction between commenting upon the tenets, doctrines, or rules of a religion or other group, and looking at the impact of those tenets, doctrines, or rules on the child's welfare. The former is outside the court's role, but the latter is required when making a welfare determination under s 1 of the CA 1989. However, as Rachel Taylor has commented, it is difficult to draw this distinction: 'If adherence to a particular religion requires a certain behaviour, then to discriminate between parents on the basis of that behaviour is, in effect, to risk discriminating on the basis of religion itself.'[152]

In preference to allowing religious or cultural factors to become a dominant factor in residence disputes, the courts have tended to rely on making generous provision for contact to satisfy the child's need for knowledge of both sides of their religious and/or cultural heritage.[153] Indeed, in some cases equal time arrangements have been made as 'one way of trying to guard against the risk that the religious perspective of either parent will predominate'.[154]

11.6.5 'NATURAL PARENTS' VERSUS OTHERS

The majority of disputes about children's living arrangements involve competing claims by the child's parents. However, it is not uncommon for these disputes to involve a non-parent, such as a social (but not legal or genetic) parent; a grandparent; or—in proceedings which straddle private and public law, which many do[155]—a prospective adopter. Such disputes must be determined in accordance with the welfare principle. However, in interpreting the child's welfare in this context, the key question is whether a 'natural' parent is presumptively favoured by the courts, and if so whether that can be justified on the basis that it will usually be in the child's best interests to be raised by a natural parent.

The labels available to describe the issues here are not entirely helpful. The court tends to refer to 'natural parent' without much interrogation of what that term means. We saw previously that the House of Lords has said that there are three types of 'natural parent'—genetic, gestational, and social/psychological.[156] In this context, however, the courts have tended to use the term 'natural parent' as meaning the genetic and, consequently, the legal parent. Such an approach ignores not only the complexity identified by *Re G* but also the fact that the legal parent may not be the genetic parent.[157] However, for the purposes of this discussion we will use the term 'natural' parent in accordance with the case law,[158] particularly as the significance of 'natural' parenthood in the welfare balance is clearly linked to the perceived importance of the genetic tie.[159] Determining the weight to give to the 'blood tie' and to social parenthood remains a difficult and controversial issue, with conflicting arguments found in court judgments over time and in different contexts.

The traditional starting point for determining a dispute about where a child lives involving a non-parent was Lord Templeman's judgment in *Re KD (A Minor) (Ward: Termination of Access)*.

[152] Taylor (2013), 341.

[153] *Re T (A Child)* [2005] EWCA Civ 1397.

[154] *Re N (Religion: Jehovah's Witness)* [2011] EWHC 3737, [75].

[155] Harding and Newnham (2017).

[156] *Re G (Children) (Residence: Same-Sex Partner)* [2006] UKHL 43; see 9.2.

[157] See, e.g., *Re G (Shared Residence: Biological Mother of Donor Egg Children)* [2014] EWCA Civ 336 which involved a lesbian couple where (outside the HFEA scheme) one woman was the gestational mother (and hence the legal mother) while the other woman had provided the eggs and so was the genetic mother. See also *Re G (Declaration of Parentage: Removal of Person Identified as Mother from Birth Certificate) (Nos 1 and 2)* [2018] EWHC 3379 and [2018] EWHC 3361, involving an informal surrogacy arrangement where an anonymous egg donor had been used and the woman who was raising the child (clearly the psychological/social mother) was not the genetic or gestational mother, nor the legal mother given that no parental order had been sought.

[158] The term 'non-parent' will be used to denote all non-genetic parents, accepting that this term will not be accurate in all cases.

[159] See also chapters 9 and 13.

Re KD (A Minor) (Ward: Termination of Access) **[1988] AC 806 (HL), 812**

LORD TEMPLEMAN:

The best person to bring up a child is the natural parent. It matters not whether the parent is wise or foolish, rich or poor, educated or illiterate, provided the child's moral and physical health are not endangered. Public authorities cannot improve on nature. Public authorities exercise a supervisory role and interfere to rescue a child when the parental tie is broken by abuse or separation. In terms of the English rule the court decides whether and to what extent the welfare of the child requires that the child shall be protected against harm caused by the parent, including harm which could be caused by the resumption of parental care after separation has broken the parental tie.

Whilst it is clear that the only relevant principle to be applied is the welfare principle, this dictum has generally been interpreted and applied in some of the subsequent case law as amounting to a de facto 'presumption' in favour of the natural parents.[160]

11.6.5.a Factors favouring a 'presumption'

Jane Fortin identifies several reasons behind the courts' preference for the biological blood tie in disputes about children's living arrangements.

J. Fortin, '*Re D (Care: Natural Parent Presumption)* Is Blood Really Thicker Than Water?', (1999) 11 *Child and Family Law Quarterly* 435, 437, 442

In the late 1980s and early 1990s, a series of decisions emerged which gave the biological link a far greater significance than before. An analysis of the decisions suggests that this change in approach was particularly influenced by three concerns. First, in 1988 Lord Templeman had provided a stirring reminder of the 'naturalness' of the child-parent relationship. Secondly, there appeared to be anxieties that comparisons between the homes of relatively well-off foster carers and of disadvantaged birth parents would inevitably favour the former, leading to decisions which might be criticised as amounting to 'social engineering'. Thirdly, ideas about children's rights had also started to have some impact on judicial thinking and the concept of children having a 'right' to be brought up by their birth parents conveniently encapsulated the new approach . . .

[U]nderpinning such a view is the societal assumption that it is 'natural' for a child to be brought up by at least one of his 'natural' parents. Furthermore, there is also the growing view that children gain a great deal from knowing about their genetic origins and that this knowledge should be enhanced, if possible, by their having a social relationship with their biological parents.

All of these factors have been evident in some of the case law. For example, *Re K (A Minor) (Ward: Care and Control)* concerned a dispute between the father and the mother's half-sister

[160] See also *Re K (A Minor) (Ward: Care and Control)* [1990] 1 WLR 431; *Re D (Care: Natural Parent Presumption)* [1999] 1 FLR 134; *Re R (A Child) (Residence Order)* [2009] EWCA Civ 358, [116].

and her husband ('Mr and Mrs E') with whom the child had lived since the mother's suicide. The Court of Appeal granted residence to the father, stressing that in the case of a residence dispute between a parent and non-parent, the judge was wrong to embark on a straightforward balancing exercise to decide which of the respective parties would be best able to promote the child's welfare. Relying on *Re KD*, the Court of Appeal held that the correct approach was to ask whether the welfare of the child positively demanded that the normal presumption in favour of the natural parent should be displaced. Moreover, any reasons put forward to displace the presumption must, in the words of Waite J, be 'compelling'. The Court of Appeal rationalized their approach on the basis that the natural parent had a 'right' to raise his own child, albeit they identified this parental 'right' with an identical right in the child.

The parent's *right* to have their child live with them may be given further weight by Article 8 ECHR,[161] as well as potentially by the child's right under Article 7 of the United Nation Convention on the Rights of the Child (UNCRC) 'to know and be cared for by his or her parents', which is qualified by the phrase 'as far as possible'. In this context, the natural parent 'presumption' has been justified by the need to avoid the dangers of 'social engineering', particularly when the dispute is between a parent and a 'perfect' prospective adopter.[162] The Supreme Court has given judgment on the importance of children having a relationship with their natural parents if at all possible in the context of public law child protection proceedings, with adoption being acceptable only where 'nothing else will do'.[163] However, the very different context of public law child protection proceedings raises questions about the applicability of such cases to private law disputes about children's living arrangements.[164]

In the private law context, the Court of Appeal in *Re B (Transfer of Residence to Grandmother)* concerned an appeal from an order transferring residence of a child to the paternal grandmother because of the mother's opposition to contact.[165] In allowing the mother's appeal, Thorpe LJ observed that he knew of no other case in which transfer of residence to a grandparent had been used against an obdurate parent in a dispute about time spent with the grandparent. Of particular interest are the Court of Appeal's observations regarding the general position of grandparents in such disputes:

Re B (Transfer of Residence to Grandmother) [2012] EWCA Civ 858

THORPE LJ:

13. . . . I would further observe that the transfer of residence from the obdurate parent to the alternatively available parent is a weapon of last resort which is sometimes used successfully and sometimes used unsuccessfully by trial judges, but that is a transfer as between parents.[166] I know of no case in which such a dire sanction has been exercised against an obdurate parent to transfer the primary care to a grandmother. Manifestly grandparents are not on equal footing with parents. Statute requires an application for leave before a grandparent may make application. Inevitably there are disbenefits for a child to be brought up by an adult of a different generation to either of her parents.

[161] See, e.g., *Görgülü v Germany* (App No 74969/01, ECHR) (2004); for discussion, see Fortin (1999), 444–5.

[162] For early cases addressing this issue, see *Re K (Private Placement for Adoption)* [1991] FCR 142; *Re O (A Minor) (Custody or Adoption)* [1992] 1 FCR 378.

[163] *Re B (Care Proceedings: Appeal)* [2013] UKSC 33; see 13.4.3.

[164] The contrast of approaches is notable, though, and raises questions about why different values are promoted in the two contexts, particularly given the overlap between the two seen in many cases.

[165] [2012] EWCA Civ 858. [166] See 11.7.4.

11.6.5.b Factors opposing a 'presumption'

Not everyone is convinced by arguments privileging biological parenting. Fortin, for example, suggests that the argument that children have the right to be raised by their natural parents has, at times, been 'distorted' to further the rights and interests of the parents rather than those of the child.[167] The result is that equally important considerations for the child, such as the potential damage caused to the child's psychological health by disrupting the emotional bonds formed with alternative carers, have been accorded insufficient weight. Fortin questions whether it is right to talk of the child's 'right' to be cared for by their natural parents when the child has lived apart from them.[168] In those circumstances, she questions whether the 'blood tie' has any real value to the child and whether, indeed, it would make more sense to talk of the child's right to be cared for by their *psychological parents*.[169]

The weight to be accorded to the 'blood tie' in purely private law disputes between parents was revisited by the House of Lords in *Re G (Children) (Residence: Same-Sex Partner)* and by the Supreme Court in *Re B (A Child)*. These decisions suggest that it is wrong to talk of any 'presumption' in favour of the natural parent. It remains somewhat unclear, however, what weight, if any, should be placed on the significance of the 'blood tie' when determining the best interests of the child.

Re G concerned a residence dispute between a same-sex couple, CG and CW. The children were born to CG as a result of donor insemination (prior to the enactment of the Human Fertilisation and Embryology Act 2008). CW had been fully involved in every aspect of the children's upbringing. In earlier proceedings, a shared residence order had been made in favour of both parties to confer parental responsibility on CW; the dispute concerned the sharing of time under that order. The Court of Appeal had held that the children's primary home should be with CW because of CG's obstructive attitude towards contact. The House of Lords reversed that decision. Baroness Hale placed great emphasis on the importance of the biological tie, although she denied that this raised a *presumption* in favour of the 'natural mother'.[170]

Re G (Children) (Residence: Same-Sex Partner) [2006] UKHL 43

BARONESS HALE:

36. Of course, in the great majority of cases, the natural mother combines all three. She is the genetic, gestational and psychological parent. Her contribution to the welfare of the child is unique. The natural father combines genetic and psychological parenthood. His contribution is also unique. In these days when more parents share the tasks of child rearing and breadwinning, his contribution is often much closer to that of the mother than it used to be; but there are still families which divide their tasks on more traditional lines, in which case his contribution will be different and its importance will often increase with the age of the child.

37. But there are also parents who are neither genetic nor gestational, but who have become the psychological parents of the child and thus have an important contribution to make to their welfare. Adoptive parents are the most obvious example, but there are many others. This is the position of CW in this case . . .

38. . . . While CW is their psychological parent, CG is . . . both their biological and their psychological parent. In the overall welfare judgment, that must count for something in the vast majority

[167] Fortin (2009b), 520. [168] Ibid, 518. [169] Ibid, 518 and 524–5.
[170] See further the extracts from *Re G* at 9.2.1.

of cases. Its significance must be considered and assessed. Furthermore, the evidence shows that it clearly did count for something in this case. These children were happy and doing very well in their mother's home. That should not have been changed without a very good reason.

44. My Lords, I am driven to the conclusion that the courts below have allowed the unusual context of this case to distract them from principles which are of universal application. First, the fact that CG is the natural mother of these children in every sense of that term, while raising no presumption in her favour, is undoubtedly an important and significant factor in determining what will be best for them now and in the future. Yet nowhere is that factor explored in the judgment below . . .

Although denying the existence of a 'presumption' in favour of the natural parent, Baroness Hale's strong preference for biological over psychological parenting appeared to be clear. To repeat her words, being both the biological and psychological parent 'must count for something'. It is 'undoubtedly an important and significant factor' in determining the welfare of the child.[171] In his short judgment, Lord Nicholls appeared to agree.

LORD NICHOLLS:

2. . . . In reaching its decision the court should always have in mind that in the ordinary way the rearing of a child by his or her biological parent can be expected to be in the child's best interests, both in the short term and also, and importantly, in the longer term. I decry any tendency to diminish the significance of this factor. A child should not be removed from the primary care of his or her biological parents without compelling reason. Where such a reason exists the judge should spell this out explicitly.

This decision, whilst rejecting any notion of a presumption in favour of the natural parent, appeared essentially consistent with existing case law on the importance to be attributed to the genetic or biological tie. However, in the Supreme Court decision of *Re B*, Lord Kerr, giving the judgment of the court, adopted a different tone. As we saw earlier, *Re B* concerned a dispute between the maternal grandmother and the father over the residence of 4-year-old Harry, who had lived with the grandmother all his life. The Supreme Court expressed concern at the apparent 'misunderstanding' of the true import of *Re G* and the principles to be derived from that judgment.[172] The court reasserted the importance of a 'pure' application of the welfare principle, untrammelled by assumptions about the significance of biological parenthood, observing that the argument that a child had a right to be raised by their biological parent could obscure or distort a proper analysis of the child's best interests.

Re B (A Child) [2009] UKSC 5

LORD KERR:

19. The theme that it was preferable for children to be raised by their biological parent or parents was developed by the judge . . . He stated that it was the right of the child to be

[171] Some commentators were critical of this focus on biology: e.g. Diduck (2007).

[172] For insight into the background to the judgments in *Re G*, see Hale (2014), 30–1. Lady Hale comments that she was 'anxious to produce an opinion with which all the other members of the appellate committee could agree', and that it would have been better to have 'referred to them both as mothers, rather than to one as the mother and the other as the other parent'.

brought up in the home of his or her natural parent. (It is clear from the context that the judge was using the term 'natural parent' to mean 'biological parent'.) We consider that this statement betrays a failure on the part of the judge to concentrate on the factor of overwhelming – indeed, paramount – importance which is, of course, the welfare of the child. To talk in terms of a child's rights – as opposed to his or her best interests – diverts from the focus that the child's welfare should occupy in the minds of those called on to make decisions as to their residence.

20. The distraction that discussion of rights rather than welfare can occasion is well illustrated in the latter part of [the] judgment. [The judge] suggested that, provided the parenting that Harry's father could provide was "good enough", it was of no consequence that that which the grandmother could provide would be better. We consider that in decisions about residence such as are involved in this case; there is no place for the question whether the proposed placement would be "good enough". The court's quest is to determine what is in the best interests of the child, not what might constitute a second best but supposedly adequate alternative. As the Court of Appeal pointed out . . . the concept of 'good enough' parenting has always been advanced in the context of public law proceedings and of care within the wider family as opposed to care by strangers . . .

34. [In reliance on a passage from Lord Nicholls' judgment in *Re G*], the justices stated that a child should not be removed from the primary care of biological parents. A careful reading of what Lord Nicholls actually said reveals, of course, that he did not propound any general rule to that effect. For a proper understanding of the view that he expressed, it is important at the outset to recognise that Lord Nicholls' comment about the rearing of a child by a biological parent is set firmly in the context of the child's welfare. This he identified as "the court's paramount consideration". It must be the dominant and overriding factor that ultimately determines disputes about residence and contact and there can be no dilution of its importance by reference to extraneous matters.

35. When Lord Nicholls said that courts should keep in mind that the interests of a child will normally be best served by being reared by his or her biological parent, he was doing no more than reflecting common experience that, in general, children tend to thrive when brought up by parents to whom they have been born. He was careful to qualify his statement, however, by the words "*in the ordinary way* the rearing of a child by his or her biological parent can be expected to be in the child's best interests" (emphasis added). In the ordinary way one can expect that children will do best with their biological parents. But many disputes about residence and contact do not follow the ordinary way. Therefore, although one should keep in mind the common experience to which Lord Nicholls was referring, one must not be slow to recognise those cases where that common experience does not provide a reliable guide . . .

37. . . . All consideration of the importance of parenthood in private law disputes about residence must be firmly rooted in an examination of what is in the child's best interests. This is the paramount consideration. It is only as a contributor to the child's welfare that parenthood assumes any significance. In common with all other factors bearing on what is in the best interests of the child, it must be examined for its potential to fulfil that aim.

The Supreme Court thus seems to have 'downgraded' biological parenthood from a factor of undoubted importance and significance (*Re G*), to just one more factor to be taken into account in the welfare balance, its weight to be determined on the individual facts of each case.[173] In *Re E-R*—a case involving a dispute between a father with parental responsibility but who had had little contact with the 5-year-old child, and friends of the mother whom she had asked to care for the child prior to her death from cancer—the Court of Appeal's approach reflected that of Lord Kerr in *Re B*.

[173] See also *Re B (Welfare: Child Arrangements Order)* [2017] EWHC 488, [44].

***Re E-R (Child Arrangements)* [2015] EWCA Civ 405**

KING LJ:

39. In the present case, the fact that there is a natural father wishing to care for his child, that the status quo may appear at first blush to point to [the child] remaining where she is and that the mother's dying wish was for [the child] to stay with [her friend], are each features of this case. Those features make the case sensitive, difficult and distressing, but none of them, individually or together, affect the essential approach of the court which is, and is always, that [the child's] welfare is paramount.

While this approach fits with the court's general position of rejecting presumptions, there is an open question as to how these cases fit with the renewed focus on a child's birth family in care proceedings.[174]

11.6.6 THE EFFECTS OF A 'LIVE WITH' ORDER

11.6.6.a Conferring certain rights, etc

A 'live with' CAO has a number of subsidiary legal effects, the most important of which is that it confers parental responsibility on the person holding the order if they do not have it already.[175] Parental responsibility acquired in this way lasts only as long as the relevant part of the order is in force.[176]

Other consequences of a 'live with' order include:

- only persons who are named as having the child live with them are entitled to object to the child being voluntarily accommodated by a local authority under the CA 1989, s 20;[177]
- if a child goes into the care of a local authority,[178] the local authority has a duty to allow reasonable contact between the child and anyone with whom the child was living under a CAO immediately before the care order was made;[179]
- any care order in force at the time a 'live with' order is made is automatically discharged.[180]

11.6.6.b Imposing certain restrictions

Whilst a 'live with' CAO is in force, certain restrictions are imposed on those holding parental responsibility.

174 See 13.4.3.

175 S 12(2). If the person with whom the child is to live is the child's father or a second female parent under s 43 of the Human Fertilization and Embryology Act 2008 (HFEA 2008), the court must make an order granting that person parental responsibility under s 4 or 4ZA, respectively: s 12(1).

176 See 10.3.5.

177 S 20(9); see 12.3.2. In Wales, the holder of *any* CAO appears to be able to object to the child's accommodation: Social Services and Well-Being (Wales) Act 2014, s 76(6).

178 See 12.5.7.

179 S 34(1)(c); this is in addition to the other persons identified in s 34(1), including the child's parents.

180 S 91(1).

Children Act 1989, s 13

(1) Where a child arrangements order to which subsection (4) applies is in force with respect to a child, no person may—
(a) cause the child to be known by a new surname; or
(b) remove him from the United Kingdom;
without either the written consent of every person who has parental responsibility for the child or the leave of the court.

(2) Subsection 1(b) does not prevent the removal of a child, for a period of less than one month, by a person named in the child arrangements order as a person with whom the child is to live.

(3) In making a child arrangements order to which subsection (4) applies the court may grant the leave required by subsection 1(b), either generally or for specified purposes.

(4) This subsection applies to a child arrangements order if the arrangements regulated by the order consist of, or include, arrangements which relate to either or both of the following—
(a) with whom the child concerned is to live, and
(b) when the child is to live with any person.

In many ways, s 13 is redundant as it is clear that a parent cannot remove a child from the jurisdiction[181] or change the child's surname[182] without the consent of everyone with parental responsibility or an order of the court, whether or not a relevant CAO is in force.[183] It may be that these two issues are identified by s 13 because they are considered to have particular importance for a child's upbringing.[184]

More generally, the court has the power to impose particular restrictions on any CAO under its wide-ranging powers under s 11(7).

Children Act 1989, s 11(7)

A section 8 order may—
(a) contain directions about how it is to be carried into effect;
(b) impose conditions which must be complied with by any person—
(i) who is named in the order as a person with whom the child concerned is to live, spend time or otherwise have contact;
(ii) who is a parent of the child;
(iii) who is not a parent of his but who has parental responsibility for him; or
(iv) with whom the child is living, and to whom the conditions are expressed to apply;
(c) be made to have effect for a specified period, or contain provisions which are to have effect for a specified period;
(d) make such incidental, supplemental or consequential provision as the court thinks fit.

[181] Child Abduction Act 1984, s 1. [182] *Dawson v Wearmouth* [1999] 2 AC 308. [183] See 10.5.1.
[184] On applications to change a child's name or remove them from the UK, see 11.8.3 and 11.8.2, respectively.

The ambit of s 11(7) is not entirely clear, though it is certainly potentially broad. In relation to a 'live with' order, it can be used, for example, to require parents to see a family therapist;[185] to determine the geographic location where a child must live;[186] or to order a child taken abroad to be returned to this country.[187] That said, it is not without limitation—not only has the court made clear that, in general, conditions under s 11(7) are to be used sparingly,[188] but there are things which clearly fall outside the ambit of the subsection. The conditions must be 'ancillary to the making of a s 8 order',[189] and thus cannot be used to regulate the parties' finances or occupation of property,[190] to exclude another person (such as the new partner of the parent) from the child's home,[191] nor indeed to require the parent themselves to vacate their home for the purpose of allowing the other parent to spend time there with the child.[192]

11.7 CHILD ARRANGEMENTS ORDERS: 'SPENDING TIME AND HAVING CONTACT' ORDERS

11.7.1 OVERVIEW OF 'SPENDING TIME' AND 'HAVING CONTACT' ORDERS

CAOs which are not about the people with whom a child is to live can take various forms, differing as to both quantity and quality. They can involve spending time directly with someone (face-to-face) and/or having indirect contact (e.g. having video or phone contact, or sending letters, emails, cards, or presents) and may take place according to a strictly regulated regime or on a more informal, ad hoc basis. (This was previously called 'direct' and 'indirect' contact; the law now refers to 'spending time' and 'otherwise having contact', though these labels are often linguistically awkward.) Orders can be as precise as the case requires, varying from 'reasonable arrangements to be agreed between the parents' to orders that micro-manage exact times and places for contact to take place. In keeping with the law's general approach that matters of parental responsibility are for the parents in the first instance, parents are free to vary arrangements by agreement, and most orders (unless there are safety concerns) provide for the child to spend 'such further or other time with the parent as is agreed'.

The courts have wide powers under s 11(7) to attach conditions to 'spend time' or 'otherwise have contact' orders or to make detailed directions as to how they are to be carried out.[193] Provisions under s 11(7) allow the court to manage low-level conflict or difficulty concerning contact arrangements—examples include: determining where handovers should take place; specifying a third party to effect handovers, so that the parents do not see each

[185] *Re E-R (Child Arrangements) (No 2)* [2017] EWHC 2382, though in fact the judge did not make the order on the facts.

[186] *Re E (Residence: Imposition of Conditions)* [1997] EWCA Civ 3084; *BB v CC (Residence Order)* [2018] EWFC B78; but see 11.8.2, as these issues are more commonly dealt with as specific issue or prohibited steps orders rather than as conditions on a 'live with' order.

[187] *Re B (Habitual Residence: Inherent Jurisdiction)* [2016] UKSC 4, [51]. Such orders are generally made as specific issue orders or under the High Court's inherent jurisdiction, but Lord Wilson posits that s 11(7)(d) can be used for this purpose.

[188] See, e.g., *Re E (Residence: Imposition of Conditions)* [1997] EWCA Civ 3084.

[189] *Re D (Prohibited Steps Order)* [1996] 2 FLR 273, 279.

[190] I.e. to make an order within the ambit of the Family Law Act 1996 by the back door; see chapter 4.

[191] *Re D (Prohibited Steps Order)* [1996] 2 FLR 273.

[192] *Re K (Contact: Condition Ousting Parent from Family Home)* [2011] EWCA Civ 1075.

[193] S 11(7) is set out at 11.6.6.b.

other directly; specifying geographic limitations on where contact can take place; or requiring a parent to hand over a passport to facilitate an upcoming holiday with the other parent. Where there are particular concerns about the child's safety or general welfare, a court can order that any time that the parent spends with their child be 'supported' or more closely 'supervised' by a third party at a designated contact centre or with a professional social worker present. *Supported contact* is generally used where a parent is inexperienced or requires assistance—someone is nearby in case needed, but the parent is not closely watched. *Supervised contact*, on the other hand, is used where there is a potential risk to the child, and the parent is watched on a one-to-one basis. The court's powers under s 11(7) include requiring a parent to meet any related costs incurred from the supervision or support.[194]

Disputes about 'spending time' and 'having contact' orders are often amongst the most bitter, protracted, and difficult in family law. Due in large part to the campaign of fathers' rights groups, there have been many important changes to the law and changes to the way in which these cases are tackled. However, the polarized and overly simplistic way in which the issue has been portrayed in the media may well have led to many important factors in these disputes being marginalized or ignored.

11.7.2 A PRESUMPTION IN FAVOUR OF ORDERS TO SPEND TIME OR HAVE CONTACT

11.7.2.a The statutory presumption

As a matter pertaining to the 'upbringing' of the child, the paramountcy principle applies to an application for spending time or having contact. If the application is opposed, the welfare checklist must be considered.[195] However, whilst the statutory framework for resolving such disputes originally said nothing specific about how the courts should approach these cases, s 1(2A) of the CA 1989 (added by the CFA 2014) specifies that there is a presumption of parental *involvement* in the child's life, so long as the parent can be involved in the child's life without putting the child at risk of suffering harm.[196]

Children Act 1989, s 1

(2A) A court, in the circumstances mentioned in subsection (4)(a) or (7), is as respects each parent within subsection (6)(a) to presume, unless the contrary is shown, that involvement of that parent in the life of the child concerned will further the child's welfare.

(2B) In subsection (2A) "involvement" means involvement of some kind, either direct or indirect, but not any particular division of a child's time.

(6) In subsection (2A) "parent" means parent of the child concerned; and, for the purposes of that subsection, a parent of the child concerned—

(a) is within this paragraph if that parent can be involved in the child's life in a way that does not put the child at risk of suffering harm; and

(b) is to be treated as being within paragraph (a) unless there is some evidence before the court in the particular proceedings to suggest that involvement of that parent in the child's life would put the child at risk of suffering harm whatever the form of the involvement.

194 *Re D (Contact: Supervisor's Fees)* [2016] EWCA Civ 89, [55]. However, there is a 'strong presumption' (though not a prohibition) against a victim of domestic abuse being made to contribute to the costs of an abusive parent's supervised contact: *Griffiths v Griffiths* [2022] EWHC 113, [131]–[132]. For comment, see McIlroy (2022).

195 S 1(3)–(4).

196 On the application of s 1(2A) in cases of domestic abuse, see 11.7.3.c–d.

This statutory change does not appear to have made any significant difference to *the courts'* approach,[197] being said to reflect 'a basic tenet of child law' that was already in place.[198] This is unsurprising because (as the government acknowledged before introducing the new presumption) the courts applied a strong de facto presumption in favour of parents having an ongoing relationship long before s 1(2A) was introduced.[199] However, it has also been noted that the existence of the presumption 'limited the possibility for further, more nuanced development of case law, and reinforced the notion that any exceptions to the norm of contact should be read narrowly'.[200] There are particular concerns about the effect of the presumption on cases involving domestic abuse,[201] and a significant question arises about how the presumption 'sends a signal which affects how cases are settled out of court'.[202] The Ministry of Justice is undertaking a review of s 1(2A),[203] but it is apparent from other reviews that there are mixed perspectives on this issue,[204] so the outcome is hard to predict.

11.7.2.b The courts' approach

There is no doubt that the courts have a strongly pro-contact approach, as we set out in this section. However, there is a degree of nuance to the picture. While very few cases end with no contact at all being ordered,[205] various factors can influence the arrangements that are considered to be in the child's best interests.[206] As we noted previously,[207] the courts have wide-ranging powers to regulate how contact will take place, as well as the underlying question of how much time the child will spend with a person.

The courts' approach has been articulated in various ways over the years. Some early cases conceptualized it as a *right* of the child to spend time with the non-resident parent, albeit that right may have to give way to welfare considerations.[208] This rights-based approach is enshrined in the UNCRC.

United Nations Convention on the Rights of the Child 1989, Article 9

(3) States Parties shall respect the right of the child who is separated from one or both parents to maintain personal relations and direct contact with both parents on a regular basis, except if it is contrary to the child's best interests.

It can be seen, though, that while the UNCRC identifies this as a right, it is made subject to an assessment of the child's best interests. It is therefore very much a qualified right. The

197 *Re A (Implacable Hostility: Contact)* [2015] EWCA Civ 910, [43].

198 *Re J (Contact Orders: Procedure)* [2018] EWCA Civ 115, [48]; Kaganas (2018); House of Lords Select Committee on the Children and Families Act 2014 (2022), paras 162–4.

199 Bailey-Harris et al (1999b), 114–15; Gilmore (2008).

200 Hunter et al (2020), 87.

201 See detailed discussion at 11.7.3.d.

202 House of Lords Select Committee (2022), para 168. With around 80 per cent of parents never going to court in relation to children issues (Dabhi, Anand, and Tu (2022)), the effect of the presumption *outside* the courts is important to consider.

203 MOJ (2020).

204 House of Lords Select Committee (2022), paras 155–69.

205 See, e.g., Hunt and Macleod (2008); Newnham and Harding (2016).

206 In *Re L (A Child) (Contact: Domestic Violence)* [2001] Fam 260 (CA), 300, Thorpe LJ identified domestic abuse, sexual and emotional abuse within the family, drug or alcohol misuse, failure to maintain appropriate sexual boundaries, and untreated mental illness or personality disorder as particularly relevant factors.

207 See 11.7.1.

208 See, e.g., *M v M (Child: Access)* [1973] 2 All ER 81.

parent may also claim a corresponding right to spend time with their child, and this issue clearly falls within the scope of the right to respect for family life under Article 8 ECHR.[209] However, at least at the level of rhetoric, the English courts have been at pains to make clear that insofar as it makes sense to talk of rights in this context, the right is that of the child and not the parent. The Human Rights Act 1998 did not change this basic approach.[210]

In preference to the rights-based approach, legislation and the courts have conceptualized the presumption in favour of spending time as an application of the welfare principle. Section 1(2A) says, in terms, that the court is to 'presume, unless the contrary is shown, that involvement[211] of [a] parent in the child's life *will further the child's welfare*'.[212] The courts have emphasized that a long-term view should be taken of the child's best interests and that they should not be unduly concerned about any temporary or short-term distress to the child.[213] The courts' strong predisposition to make 'spending time' orders was made clear in *Re O (A Minor) (Contact: Indirect Contact)*, which remains a leading authority.[214]

Re O (A Minor) (Contact: Indirect Contact) [1996] 1 FCR 317 (CA), 323–7

BINGHAM MR:

It may perhaps be worth stating in a reasonably compendious way some very familiar but nonetheless fundamental principles. First of all, and overriding all else as provided in s. 1(1) of the 1989 Act, the welfare of the child is the paramount consideration of any court concerned to make an order relating to the upbringing of a child. It cannot be emphasized too strongly that the court is concerned with the interests of the mother and the father only in so far as they bear on the welfare of the child.

Second, where parents of a child are separated and the child is in the day-to-day care of one of them, it is almost always in the interests of the child that he or she should have contact with the other parent. The reason for this scarcely needs spelling out. It is, of course, that the separation of parents involves a loss to the child, and it is desirable that that loss should so far as possible be made good by contact with the non-custodial parent, that is the parent in whose day-to-day care the child is not . . .

Fourth, cases do, unhappily and infrequently but occasionally, arise in which a court is compelled to conclude that in existing circumstances an order for immediate direct contact should not be ordered, because so to order would injure the welfare of the child . . . The courts should not at all readily accept that the child's welfare will be injured by direct contact. Judging that question the court should take a medium-term and long-term view of the child's development and not accord excessive weight to what appear likely to be short-term or transient problems . . .

Fifth, in cases in which, for whatever reason, direct contact cannot for the time being be ordered, it is ordinarily highly desirable that there should be indirect contact so that the child grows up knowing of the love and interest of the absent parent with whom, in due course, direct contact should be established. . . .

209 See, e.g., *Hokkanen v Finland* (App No 19823/92, ECHR) (1994) and *Glaser v United Kingdom* (App No 32346/96, ECHR) (2000). See Fenton-Glynn (2021), 271–9.

210 *Re H (Children) (Contact Order) (No 2)* [2001] 3 FCR 385.

211 'Involvement' may be direct or indirect, and does not mean any particular division of time: s 1(2B).

212 S 1(2A), emphasis added.

213 See, e.g., *Re M (Contact: Long-Term Best Interests)* [2005] EWCA Civ 1090.

214 See, e.g., *Re W (Direct Contact)* [2012] EWCA Civ 999, [37], describing *Re O* as 'the definitive exposition of the relevant principles'.

> The caring parent also has reciprocal obligations. If the caring parent puts difficulties in the way of indirect contact by withholding presents of [sic] letters or failing to read letters to a child who cannot read, then such parent must understand that the court can compel compliance with its orders; it has sanctions available and no residence order is to be regarded as irrevocable. It is entirely reasonable that the parent with the care of the child should be obliged to report on the progress of the child to the absent parent for the obvious reason that an absent parent cannot correspond in a meaningful way if unaware of the child's concerns . . .
>
> [T]he truth is that the mother is subject to an enforceable duty to promote contact where the court judges that contact will promote the welfare of the child.

The resident parent's *duty* to promote the child's relationship with the other parent has become a central feature of the debate. The courts have reiterated that 'it is almost always in the interests of the child to have contact with the parent with whom the child is not living', and that a judge would 'requir[e] the presence of "cogent reasons" for departing from that general principle'.[215]

The courts have engaged in a lot of 'hard talking' to support this approach, particularly in response to cases of so-called 'implacably hostile' or 'intransigent' parents.[216] While there is a significant risk that cases with genuine concerns (particular in relation to domestic abuse, which we address later[217]) are mistakenly treated as being in this category, it is clear that the hostility of the residential parent, usually the mother, is not, without more, seen as justification for refusing contact.

Re A (Intractable Contact Dispute) [2013] EWCA Civ 1104

> **McFARLANE LJ:**
>
> 39. Where, as in the present case, there is an intractable contact dispute, the authorities indicate that the court should be very reluctant to allow the implacable hostility of one parent to deter it from making a contact order where the child's welfare otherwise requires it (*Re J (A Minor) (Contact)* [1994] 1 FLR 729). In such a case contact should only be refused where the court is satisfied that there is a serious risk of harm if contact were to be ordered (*Re D (Contact: Reasons for Refusal)* [1997] 2 FLR 48). . . . Further, in *Re J*, where contact was refused in order to avoid placing the child in a situation of stress as a result of the mother's implacable hostility to contact, Balcombe LJ rightly acknowledged that affording paramount consideration to the child's welfare may, in some cases, produce an outcome which is seen as 'an injustice' from the perspective of the excluded parent . . .

The court has emphasized that, despite the mother's hostility, it should not be assumed that she will not obey the court's orders.[218] However, in many cases, the mother's intention to

[215] *Re W (Direct Contact)* [2012] EWCA Civ 999, [39]. See also *Re C (Direct Contact: Suspension)* [2011] EWCA Civ 521, [47]; *Re R (No Order for Contact: Appeal)* [2014] EWCA Civ 1664, [16].

[216] 'Implacable hostility' is used to mean opposition to contact which has no reasonable basis, and does not apply where a parent opposes contact for objectively good reasons: see *Re D (Contact: Reasons for Refusal)* [1997] 2 FLR 48.

[217] See 11.7.3.d.

[218] *Re H (A Minor) (Contact)* [1994] 2 FCR 419.

disobey is patently clear. In such circumstances, the courts have held that they will not 'abdicate their responsibility' by capitulating to such 'threats'. The order, if in the child's interests, will still be made,[219] and a 'robust' response is to be expected.[220] Mothers who are regarded as 'implacably hostile' may be directed or ordered to attend classes or counselling aimed at persuading them to cooperate.[221] Although, as McFarlane LJ has noted, '[s]ome family situations are simply not amenable to the blunt instrument of a judge sitting in a law court making an order',[222] the courts generally see 'giving up' on contact as a last resort and a mark of significant failure by the system.[223]

ONLINE RESOURCES

We discuss the particularly complex example of *Re M (Ultra-Orthodox Judaism: Transgender)* [2017] EWCA Civ 2164 in the online resources. The father of five children in an ultra-Orthodox Jewish family had transitioned to live as a woman. The children's mother opposed contact between the children and their father on the basis of the risk that having any contact at all would cause the family to be ostracized from their community. The online resources can be found at **www.oup.com/he/familytcm5e.**

Although the presumption in favour of spending time is undoubtedly strongest in the post-divorce context, it has been consistently applied to unmarried fathers. In line with the growing importance generally attached to the father–child relationship, the inherent value of maintaining a relationship between children and their fathers through contact has generally been accepted. At one time, there appeared to be some distinction drawn between cases in which the father has an established, meaningful relationship with the child, so the question is one of *maintaining* an existing relationship, and cases where the applicant is in effect seeking to *establish* a *new* relationship.[224] However, in practice, the distinction appears to have carried very little weight.

R. Bailey-Harris, J. Barron, and J. Pearce, 'From Utility to Rights? The Presumption of Contact in Practice', (1999b) 13 *International Journal of Law, Policy and the Family* 111, 117–19

[S]ome of the case law demonstrates the courts' willingness to *establish* a relationship which was tenuous in the first place or which has been interrupted for a considerable period . . . Many district judges apparently have an unquestioning belief that contact will always be in the best interests of the children; hence they tend automatically to try to re-establish contact, even after a long break or where the parent has had no opportunity to form any kind of relationship with a very young child, and when there is no certainty that the absent parent will be

[219] *Re W (A Minor) (Contact)* [1994] 2 FLR 441.
[220] *Re A (Children)* [2009] EWCA Civ 1141, [21]. On enforcement of orders, see 11.7.4.
[221] Ss 11A–11G.
[222] *Re A (Implacable Hostility: Contact)* [2015] EWCA Civ 910, [52].
[223] *Re S (Parental Alienation: Cult)* [2020] EWCA Civ 568, [12].
[224] See, e.g., Thorpe LJ in *Re L (A Child) (Contact: Domestic Violence)* [2001] Fam 260, 294–5.

consistent in maintaining contact in future. This practice holds despite the lack of evidence that this will be for the child's good and even when the child exhibits signs of considerable distress before, during or after contact. It can be interpreted as indicating the court's conception of its duty as one of establishing, rather than simply maintaining, contact.

Indeed, it has been said that the effect of the judgments of the European Court of Human Rights,[225] as well as the growing domestic jurisprudence, is that courts must take positive action both to maintain and to restore contact.

Re R (No Order for Contact: Appeal) [2014] EWCA Civ 1664

CHRISTOPHER CLARKE LJ:

16. The applicable legal principles are clear. First, the welfare of R is the paramount consideration for the court. It takes precedence over any other. Second, the court has in a series of cases stressed the importance of contact between parent and child as a fundamental element of family life, which is almost always in the interests of the child, and which is to be terminated only in exceptional circumstances, where there are cogent reasons for doing so and when there is no alternative. Contact is to be terminated only where it would be detrimental to the child's welfare. The judge has a duty to promote such contact and to grapple with all available alternatives before abandoning hope of achieving some contact. Contact should be stopped only as a last resort and once it has become clear that the child will not benefit from continuing the attempt. The court should take a medium to long term view and not accord excessive weight to what appear likely to be short term and transient problems. The key question is whether the judge has taken all necessary steps to facilitate contact, as can reasonably be demanded in the circumstances of the particular case; *Re C (Direct Contact: Suspension)* [2011] EWCA Civ 521.

17. These principles reflect the jurisprudence of the Strasbourg court, which in many cases has emphasised the fundamental right of parents to have measures taken with a view to their being reunited with their children, and the obligation of national courts to take such measures. That obligation is not however absolute. The best interests of the child may be threatened by contact with the parent, and the rights of the non resident father have to be weighed against the child's rights under Article 8, in which case it is for the national court to strike a fair balance between the respective rights.

This decision builds on a summary offered by the Court of Appeal in *Re C (Direct Contact: Suspension)*:

Re C (Direct Contact: Suspension) [2011] EWCA Civ 521

MUNBY LJ:

- Contact between parent and child is a fundamental element of family life and is almost always in the interests of the child.

[225] See, e.g., *Kosmopoulou v Greece* (App No 60457/00, ECHR) (2004); *Kopf v Austria* (App No 1598/06, ECHR) (2012).

- Contact between parent and child is to be terminated only in exceptional circumstances, where there are cogent reasons for doing so and when there is no alternative. Contact is to be terminated only if it will be detrimental to the child's welfare.
- There is a positive obligation on the State, and therefore on the judge, to take measures to maintain and to reconstitute the relationship between parent and child, in short, to maintain or restore contact. The judge has a positive duty to attempt to promote contact. The judge must grapple with all the available alternatives before abandoning hope of achieving some contact. He must be careful not to come to a premature decision, for contact is to be stopped only as a last resort and only once it has become clear that the child will not benefit from continuing the attempt.
- The court should take a medium-term and long-term view and not accord excessive weight to what appear likely to be short-term or transient problems.
- The key question, which requires "stricter scrutiny", is whether the judge has taken all necessary steps to facilitate contact as can reasonably be demanded in the circumstances of the particular case.
- All that said, at the end of the day the welfare of the child is paramount; "the child's interest must have precedence over any other consideration."

It is clear, therefore, that the courts have taken a strongly pro-contact approach for a number of years, with the s 1(2A) presumption of parental involvement merely reinforcing an already well-established line of authority. This position can be see reflected in the outcomes of court applications.

A. Newnham and M. Harding, 'Sharing As Caring? Contact and Residence Disputes Between Parents', (2016) 28 *Child and Family Law Quarterly* 175, 187–8, 189, 190, 192–3

Our research, whilst confined to court files, confirms staying contact as the norm within our sample; many files showed parents' contact being gradually increased until the goal of regular staying contact . . . was reached. There was overnight staying contact in 78 [out of 174] cases.[226] . . .

Welfare concerns were seen as an obstacle to be overcome rather than a reason against progressing to overnight contact. Allegations of child welfare concerns and/or serious allegations of domestic violence featured in 44 of these 78 cases . . .

In 34 cases (20% of the 174 parent versus parent cases), the final arrangement was for the contact parent to have direct contact solely during the day . . . This was our second biggest category. Daytime-only contact may deprive children of important familial contexts, but these shorter occasions can also lead to a better focus on the child. There were a number of reasons against overnight contact that were found in many of these 34 case files. Child welfare or domestic violence concerns were rarely a determining factor; in fact, fewer welfare concerns were raised for the daytime contact group than for the overnight group. One commonplace difficulty was a lack of suitable accommodation. . . .

[226] Note that this is in addition to cases where there was a shared 'live with' order, which accounted for another 19 cases.

[The 'limited contact'] category contained three types of cases: those where contact would be irregular (for example a few times a year) (10 cases); contact that would remain supervised or monitored for the foreseeable future (14 cases); and indirect contact (eight cases). Some of these cases seem to demonstrate an implicit trust held by the courts in the inherent value of contact even in difficult circumstances, with little emphasis on the child's experience of such contact as long as they are not at physical or emotional risk. . . .

Seventeen cases (<10%) left our five courts without any expectation that there would be contact. There were only five cases that ended with an actual order for there to be no contact, an active court prohibition. In the rest of the cases, there were simply no functioning directive provisions. Unsurprisingly, these were complex cases. Only two cases had some, albeit irregular, direct contact at the time of the application. . . . Frequently, the potential contact parent had failed to appear at court, either for the final hearing or at all.

These findings should be seen in the context of other research which makes clear that the vast majority of separating parents make private arrangements regarding their children's living and contact arrangements,[227] with the court generally seeing only the most complex and intractable families, or those with significant welfare concerns such as domestic abuse or substance misuse.[228] Is the presumption in favour of spending time and having contact well-founded?

Fathers

The consensus across various disciplines about the importance of spending time and having contact with both parents is remarkable. Research by Bailey-Harris et al suggests it is extremely rare for the benefits of contact with the child's *father* to be questioned by any of the professionals involved in a case.[229] Successive governments have been equally committed to the 'contact is good' mantra.

DFE and MOJ, *Co-operative Parenting Following Family Separation: Proposed Legislation on the Involvement of Both Parents in a Child's Life* (London: TSO, 2012)

3.2 The majority of parents who separate reach their own agreements about the care arrangements for their children, and many manage this in a co-operative way, taking account of the child's needs. When disputes about these arrangements arise, however, there is a risk that children's needs are overlooked. Whether courts are involved or not, in too many cases one parent is left in a position where it is very hard to retain a strong and influential relationship with his or her child. This can result in children losing contact completely with one parent (usually the father), often with a lasting impact on their lives. The Government firmly believes that parents who are able and willing to play a positive role in their child's care should have the opportunity to do so. The aim of the legislative amendment is also to reinforce the expectation at societal level that both parents are jointly responsible for their children's upbringing.

[227] See 11.1. [228] Trinder et al (2005); Hunt and Macleod (2008); Newnham and Harding (2016), 177.
[229] Bailey-Harris et al (1999b), 118.

The evidential base on which this unwavering faith in the value of contact is founded is, however, open to question. For example, Bailey-Harris et al suggest that the current consensus on contact is based on little more than 'self-reinforcing professional received wisdom'.

R. Bailey-Harris, J. Barron, and J. Pearce, 'From Utility to Rights? The Presumption of Contact in Practice', (1999b) 13 *International Journal of Law, Policy and the Family* 111, 117–19

[O]ur overall conclusion was that the various professionals involved supported each other in a somewhat circular and self-confirming fashion. Contact is presumed to be for the good of the child—but no evidence has been produced to demonstrate this. Solicitors nevertheless advise their clients to accede to contact because that is what the courts expect. The judges order contact because no one really opposes it—so if they do they are being 'unreasonable' and not listening to the advice of their solicitors. Court welfare officers (who, of all the professionals, are beginning to develop doubts about the 'automatic' pro-contact presumption) nonetheless know that they need to make their arguments all the stronger if they are to persuade the court against ordering contact in any particular case. One district judge told us that the reason for emphasis on 'contact at (almost) any cost' is the belief that the higher courts would overrule a refusal of contact. Thus the rights/rule approach to the determination of contact disputes has become entrenched through the cumulative effect of self-reinforcing professional received wisdom.

Thorpe LJ has recognized the importance of the courts only proceeding on the basis of the best available expert evidence.

Re L (A Child) (Contact: Domestic Violence) [2001] Fam 260 (CA), 295

THORPE LJ:

The assumption that contact benefits the child cannot be derived from legal precedent or principle. It must find its foundation in the theory and practice of the mental health professions. Perhaps the largest single ingredient of a child's welfare is health, giving that word a broad definition to encompass physical, emotional and psychological development and well-being. So both judicial general assumption and judicial assessment of welfare in the individual case are to be derived from the expertise of mental health professionals whose training and practice has centred on the development needs and vulnerability of children. So for me the proposition that children benefit from contact with the parent with whom they no longer live must be drawn from current opinion shared by the majority of mental health professionals.

Qualified support for the prevailing judicial approach was indeed provided in *Re L* in the form of an expert psychiatric report co-authored by Dr Claire Sturge and Dr Danya Glaser.[230] The report provides some general support for the courts' pro-contact stance. However, whilst the report points to a number of factors in favour of contact, it does not provide unqualified support for the courts' approach. The report makes it clear that each case must be considered on its own particular merits with the welfare of the individual child

[230] Sturge and Glaser (2000).

as the core consideration. It therefore provides no support for the sweeping presumption in favour of contact that has been typical of the courts' approach. The report also identified a number of specific risks attaching to both direct and indirect contact.

Re L (A Child) (Contact: Domestic Violence) [2001] Fam 260 (CA), 269

BUTLER-SLOSS P:

The overall risk was that of failing to meet and actually undermining the child's developmental needs or even causing emotional abuse and damage directly through contact or as a consequence of the contact. Specifically that included: escalating the climate of conflict around the child which would undermine the child's general stability and sense of emotional well being. The result was a tug of loyalty and a sense of responsibility for the conflict in all children except young babies which affected the relationships of the child with both parents. There might be direct abusive experiences, including emotional abuse by denigration of the child or the child's resident carer. There might be continuation of unhealthy relationships such as dominant or bullying relationships, those created by fear, bribes or emotional blackmail, by undermining the child's sense of stability and continuity by deliberately or inadvertently setting different moral standards or standards of behaviour, by little interest in the child himself or by unstimulating or uninteresting contact. They indicated a series of situations where there were risks to contact: where there were unresolved situations, where the contact was unreliable and the child frequently let down, where the child was attending contact against his wishes so he felt undermined, where there was little prospect for change such as wholly implacable situations, where there was the stress on the child and resident carer of ongoing proceedings or frequently re-initiated proceedings.

The commitment of successive governments to contact has been driven by wider social and political concerns, particularly emphasizing the poor educational and social outcomes for children who experience loss of contact with the non-resident parent post-separation.[231] However, the evidence suggesting children of separated parents are socially and educationally disadvantaged is controversial. In particular, the assumption that loss of contact is the principal cause of these problems is highly questionable,[232] with the social and economic difficulties often associated with family breakdown undoubtedly a major factor.[233]

Research with young people who, as children, went through parental separation, sheds light on how children themselves experience different contact arrangements.

J. Fortin, J. Hunt, and L. Scanlan, *Taking a Longer View of Contact: The Perspectives of Young Adults Who Experienced Parental Separation in their Youth: Summary* (University of Sussex/University of Oxford, 2012), 4–5

The importance of retaining a relationship with both parents

Our respondents saw contact between children and their non-resident parents as being vitally important in principle . . . This was considered to be the case even amongst those who

[231] See, e.g., DFE and MOJ (2012). [232] Rhoades (2002), 81.
[233] Gilmore (2006); Mooney, Oliver, and Smith (2009).

had never had any contact themselves and those whose own experience of contact had not been particularly happy. . . .

But despite this view that contact was immensely important, for many this was a principled answer to a theoretical question which had no reality in their own lives. Many chose to terminate unsatisfactory contact when they felt able to do so, Furthermore, there was overwhelming agreement that there were circumstances, such as an abusive parent/child relationship, where contact should never take place. There was also a strong view that contact should not start or continue if it did not promote the child's best interests and that no contact was better than bad contact.

The ingredients for successful contact

Our findings showed that for contact to be successful it needs to be continuous. Respondents who had had unbroken contact throughout their childhood were most likely to rate their contact in positive terms. Responsibility for contact not happening at all or not being regularly maintained was very largely attributed to the non-resident parent, and typically explained in terms of that parent's lack of commitment to the child. . . .

One of the most striking findings of the study was the importance of the pre-separation relationship between the child and the parent who subsequently became non-resident. Where relationships had been very close contact was most likely to be both continuous and a positive experience for the child. The foundations of successful contact, then, are laid down pre-separation.

Respondents were also more likely to rate their experience of contact with the non-resident parent as being positive if the following factors were present: the parents involved their children in the decision-making; there was little or no post-separation conflict between the parents; there was no domestic violence or serious concerns about the care the non-resident parent could provide; the resident parent encouraged the relationship between the child and the non-resident parent; the non-resident parent made time for the child; the child felt equally at home in both the resident and non-resident parent's homes; the non-resident parent either did not re-partner or the child got on well with their new partner.

Non-parents

The assumed value of contact between a parent and the child is not applied to relationships with other family members, no matter how significant. The courts have been fairly consistent in refusing to apply a 'presumption' in favour of contact with members of the extended family, such as siblings, step-parents, or grandparents. In these cases, a 'pure' unfettered application of the welfare principle is followed,[234] though the courts more recently have appeared supportive of making contact orders that preserve existing relationships between children and non-parents. For example, in *Re R (Parental Responsibility)*,[235] Peter Jackson J refused to make a parental responsibility order but did order continuing contact every other weekend between a boy aged 4 and a man who had initially thought he was the father, but who was in fact not genetically related to the child.

Same-sex couples and the 'other parent'

A particularly difficult issue for the courts has been whether, and how, to recognize a relationship between a child and a person (usually a man) who has provided genetic material

[234] See *Re S (Contact: Application by Sibling)* [1999] Fam 283 (siblings); *Re H (A Minor) (Contact)* [1994] 2 FCR 419 (step-father); *Re H (A Child)* [2014] EWCA Civ 271 (grandmother).

[235] [2011] EWHC 1535.

leading to that child's birth, but where the child was always intended to be raised by a same-sex couple (usually two women). While the courts sometimes refer to the person concerned as the 'father' of the child, this terminology is controversial for some, given its implications of a child-raising function in cases where, on one view, the man's intended role was often more akin to a sperm donor.[236] On the other hand, Black LJ has suggested that the term 'donor' might be inappropriate when the man's identity was known, since it 'is capable of conveying the impression that the father is giving his child away and that is misleading'.[237]

While the courts have been addressing these cases for some time, they are still seen as 'new territory', and the Court of Appeal has declined to issue any specific guidance on them.[238] In the leading case of *A v B and C (Contact: Alternative Families)*, Black LJ encouraged parties entering into such an arrangement to make their intentions as clear as possible at the outset, but stressed that such an agreement neither could nor should be determinative: 'Biology, human nature and the hand of fate are liable to undermine it and to confound their expectations. Circumstances change and adjustments must be made. And above all, what must dictate is the welfare of the child and not the interests of the adults.'[239] However, given the inherent lack of certainty in the meaning of 'the welfare of the child',[240] it could be said that the Court of Appeal was simply begging the question with this approach. The very dispute is whether a child's welfare is better served by having a clear, stable 'nuclear family' with the couple who intended to be their parents and to the potential exclusion of the male biological progenitor, or by having a relationship with that man which is legally recognized and protected in the face of opposition from the primary carers.

Despite this controversy, it seems increasingly that the courts are willing to promote relationships between the child and the male progenitor in the face of opposition from the same-sex couple who had intended to be the child's only parents. Baker J's decision in *Re G (Sperm Donor: Contact Order); Re Z (Sperm Donor: Contact Order)* is one such case.[241] The case concerned a dispute between the lesbian co-parents of a child (civil partners 'D' and 'E') and the 'known sperm donor father' ('S'). S wanted to have a 'father-like' relationship with the child. D and E's position was that there were 'three cardinal points' of the arrangement they had entered into: S was to have no parental title, no parental responsibility, and no financial commitment—he was to be known to the child as no more than a friend of the parents. In accordance with the terms of s 42(1) of the HFEA 2008, D and E were deemed the child's legal parents, entered as such on the birth certificate, and enjoyed shared parental responsibility. S thus had no legal status in relation to the child (as confirmed in s 45(1) of the HFEA 2008) and thus required the leave of the court under s 10(9) to make a s 8 application for contact. The court held that the man's lack of legal status as 'father' was not to be determinative of whether or not he should be allowed to develop a social or psychological relationship with the child, and leave to make the contact application was therefore granted. It is important to note on the facts of this case that S had enjoyed fairly regular contact with the child from birth and, moreover, S and his partner, T, had enjoyed significant contact with the child's older sibling, of whom S was the legal father pursuant to a similar donor

[236] See, e.g., Zanghellini (2012), 477. As Diduck (2007) has pointed out, finding the right labels will not solve the underlying problem.

[237] *A v B and C (Contact: Alternative Families)* [2012] EWCA Civ 285, [48].

[238] Ibid, [48].

[239] Ibid, [44].

[240] See 8.2.2.

[241] [2013] EWHC 134. But cf *MacDougall v SW (Sperm Donor: Parental Responsibility or Contact)* [2022] EWFC 50. Mr MacDougall had acted as a sperm donor through private arrangements in a large number of cases, resulting in at least 15 children under the age of 4. In three joined cases, the court refused applications for parental responsibility and contact.

agreement with D and E which had been entered into prior to the HFEA reforms on legal parenthood. Nonetheless, the case is striking in that Baker J was willing to allow the case to proceed to a full hearing about the man's role in the child's life, despite the law's determination as to legal parenthood.[242]

11.7.3 CONTACT AND DOMESTIC ABUSE

One of the most significant and challenging issues facing the family court is how to approach child arrangements cases where there are allegations—or court findings—of domestic abuse. As we have seen in chapter 4, the law's approach to domestic abuse in general has changed rapidly over recent years, with increasing recognition of the range of behaviours that are abusive. In the context of an application for a CAO, this increasing awareness of domestic abuse comes crashing up against the law's generally 'pro-contact culture' which is embedded in judicial thinking and reflected and reinforced by the s 1(2A) parental involvement presumption.

As with our discussion in chapter 4, while both mothers and fathers allege and are subjected to domestic abuse, the vast majority of cases concern allegations made by mothers against fathers.[243] Consequently, we refer in this discussion to the parties in this typically gendered way. However, it is important to note that both the parent and the child should be properly seen as victims of domestic abuse—in the case of a child, the Domestic Abuse Act 2021 says that they should be considered to be a victim if they see, hear, or experience the effects of domestic abuse of a parent, relative, or person who has parental responsibility for them.[244] More generally, though, the indirect effects on children from the impacts that abuse has on parenting ability by mothers are significant.[245]

11.7.3.a Historic approaches

The history of the courts' approach to contact applications in cases of domestic abuse does not make happy reading. Until remarkably recently, the courts minimized the effects of domestic abuse on both the mother and child and tended to regard a history of abuse as irrelevant to the issue of contact. Cases showed a clear expectation that, as a 'good mother', a victim of domestic abuse would prioritize her child's interests by putting aside her own 'selfish' fears in order to promote a good relationship between father and child;[246] mothers were sometimes warned that raising domestic abuse would make them appear 'difficult' and count against them. Research by Bailey-Harris et al suggested that these attitudes were deeply entrenched at all levels of the court system. Their study of practice in the county courts revealed that the issue of domestic abuse was routinely marginalized, with district judges adopting a 'no fault discourse' in which the accepted mantra was to 'look forward not back'. Historically, therefore, past conduct, including domestic abuse, was thus rendered irrelevant to the contact application.[247]

242 For comment, see Zanghellini (2012); Smith (2013); Bremner (2014).

243 See, e.g., Cafcass and Women's Aid (2017), 25.

244 Domestic Abuse Act 2021, s 3.

245 Ruck (2022).

246 See, e.g., *Williams v Williams* [1985] FLR 509 (CA); *Re P (A Minor) (Contact)* [1994] 2 FLR 374.

247 Bailey-Harris et al (1999b), 123. Whether this attitude is truly 'historic' or not is a matter of debate: see also Barnett (2015), 55–6.

11.7.3.b The shift in *Re L* (2000)

Since 2000, the beginnings of a shift in judicial attitudes regarding the relevance of domestic abuse to issues of contact can be seen. This has been driven by the growing body of evidence as to the harm caused to children who witness incidents of abuse.[248] The potential dangers of promoting contact between a child and an abusive parent are dealt with at length in the expert report from Sturge and Glaser,[249] which was used extensively by the Court of Appeal in *Re L (A Child) (Contact: Domestic Violence)*.

Re L (A Child) (Contact: Domestic Violence) [2001] Fam 260 (CA), 270

BUTLER-SLOSS P:

The [Sturge and Glaser] report then moved to the central issue of domestic violence. They agreed . . . that there needs to be greater awareness of the effect of domestic violence on children, both short-term and long-term, as witnesses as well as victims. The research was entirely consistent in showing the deleterious effects on children of exposure to domestic violence and that children were affected as much by exposure to violence as to being involved in it. All children were affected by significant and repeated inter-partner violence even if not directly involved. Research indicates that even when children did not continue in violent situations emotional trauma continued to be experienced. The context of the overall situation was highly relevant to decision making. The contribution of psychiatric disorder to situations of domestic violence and emotional abuse must be considered. In situations of contact there might be a continuing sense of fear of the violent parent by the child. The child might have post-traumatic anxieties or symptoms the proximity of the non-resident violent parent might re-arouse or perpetuate. There might be a continuing awareness of the fear the violent parent aroused in the child's main carer. The psychiatric report highlighted the possible effects of such situations on the child's own attitudes to violence, to forming parenting relationships and the role of fathers. Research shows that attitudes in boys were particularly affected.

These concerns are important given the evidence that family breakdown often acts as a catalyst for violence, with the risks of escalation and even homicide being particularly high in the first six months after separation.[250] Worryingly, it has been shown that victims are particularly vulnerable to further abuse when contact is taking place.[251] An analysis of 174 court files from 2011 found allegations of domestic abuse in 49 per cent of cases,[252] while a sample of 216 cases in 2015–16 found allegations of domestic abuse in 62 per cent of cases.[253]

In *Re L (A Child) (Contact: Domestic Violence)*, the courts' general approach to contact where there are allegations of past or present domestic abuse was comprehensively reviewed. The Sturge and Glaser report had recommended that in cases of domestic abuse there should be a presumption *against* direct contact, with the abusive partner having to meet a number of requirements before contact could be deemed beneficial.

[248] Barnett (2000), 139. [249] Sturge and Glaser (2000).
[250] Ibid, 143.
[251] Humphreys and Harrison (2003); Birchall (2022), 29.
[252] Newnham and Harding (2016), 177. See also Hunt and Macleod (2008), 6; Trinder et al (2005), iii.
[253] Cafcass and Women's Aid (2017), 8.

Re L (A Child) (Contact: Domestic Violence) [2001] Fam 260 (CA), 271

BUTLER-SLOSS P:

Dr Sturge and Dr Glaser considered the question in what circumstances should the court give consideration to a child having no direct contact with the non-resident parent. In their view there should be no automatic assumption that contact to a previously or currently violent parent was in the child's interests, if anything the assumption should be in the opposite direction and he should prove why he can offer something of benefit to the child and to the child's situation. They said

> "Domestic violence involves a very serious and significant failure in parenting – failure to protect the child's carer and failure to protect the child emotionally (and in some cases physically – which meets any definition of child abuse.)
>
> Without the following we would see the balance of advantage and disadvantage as tipping against contact:
>
> (a) some (preferably full) acknowledgment of the violence;
>
> (b) some acceptance (preferably full if appropriate i.e. the sole instigator of violence) of responsibility for that violence;
>
> (c) full acceptance of the inappropriateness of the violence particularly in respect of the domestic and parenting context and of the likely ill effects on the child;
>
> (d) a genuine interest in the child's welfare and full commitment to the child i.e. a wish for contact in which he is not making the conditions;
>
> (e) a wish to make reparation to the child and work towards the child recognising the inappropriateness of the violence and the attitude to and treatment of the mother and helping the child to develop appropriate values and attitudes;
>
> (f) an expression of regret and the showing of some understanding of the impact of their behaviour on the ex-partner in the past and currently;
>
> (g) indications that the parent seeking contact can reliably sustain contact in all senses."

They suggested that without (a)–(f) above they could not see how the non-resident parent could fully support the child and play a part in undoing the harm caused to the child and support the child's current situation and need to move on and develop healthily. There would be a significant risk to the child's general well-being and his emotional development.

The Court of Appeal was clear that allegations of domestic abuse had to be taken seriously. However, the Court of Appeal firmly rejected any suggestion that past or present abuse by a parent should constitute a bar to that parent being involved in the child's life. More controversially, they also rejected the recommendation by Drs Sturge and Glaser that where there is a history of abuse there should be a presumption against making a 'spend time' order.[254] The Court of Appeal's rejection of this more robust approach in favour of a 'pure' application of the welfare principle disappointed many,[255] and this issue continues to challenge the courts.

[254] Sturge and Glaser (2000), 623.

[255] For a critique of the decision, see Kaganas (2000), and for an alternative way in which the case might have been decided, Kaganas (2010).

11.7.3.c The current approach

For the first time, the Domestic Abuse Act 2021 provides a statutory definition of domestic abuse, set out in s 1 of that Act. While technically the definition applies only 'for the purposes of this Act',[256] it clearly provides a working definition for all family court cases.

Domestic Abuse Act 2021, s 1

(2) Behaviour of a person (A) towards another person (B) is 'domestic abuse' if—
   (a) A and B are each aged 16 or over and are personally connected to each other [as defined in s 2], and
   (b) the behaviour is abusive.

(3) Behaviour is 'abusive' if it consists of any of the following—
   (a) physical or sexual abuse;
   (b) violent or threatening behaviour;
   (c) controlling or coercive behaviour;
   (d) economic abuse (see subsection (4));
   (e) psychological, emotional or other abuse;

   and it does not matter whether the behaviour consists of a single incident or a course of conduct.

(4) 'Economic abuse' means any behaviour that has a substantial adverse effect on B's ability to—
   (a) acquire, use or maintain money or other property, or
   (b) obtain goods or services.

(5) For the purposes of this Act A's behaviour may be behaviour 'towards B' despite the fact that it consists of conduct directed at another person (for example, B's child).

This statutory definition should be read alongside specific guidance to the courts about how to approach allegations of domestic abuse in child arrangements cases, most recently reviewed in 2017. Practice Direction 12J (PD12J) aims to standardize the approach to domestic abuse allegations, and ensure that allegations are taken seriously and dealt with effectively by the courts.[257]

Practice Direction 12J—*Child Arrangements and Contact Order: Domestic Abuse and Harm* (2023)

2A. In this Practice Direction, 'domestic abuse' has the same meaning as in the 2021 Act. . . .

2B. For the avoidance of doubt, it should be noted that 'domestic abuse' includes, but is not limited to, forced marriage, honour-based violence, dowry-related abuse and transnational marriage abandonment. . . .

[256] Domestic Abuse Act 2021, s 1(1).

[257] It is compulsory to comply with the Practice Direction: see, e.g., *Re W (Children: Domestic Violence)* [2012] EWCA Civ 528; *Re LG (Re-Opening of Fact-Finding)* [2017] EWHC 2626, [24].

7. In proceedings relating to a child arrangements order, the court presumes that the involvement of a parent in a child's life will further the child's welfare, unless there is evidence to the contrary. The court must in every case consider carefully whether the statutory presumption [in s 1(2A)] applies, having particular regard to any allegation or admission of harm by domestic abuse to the child or parent or any evidence indicating such harm or risk of harm. . . .

36. (1) In the light of—
   (a) any findings of fact,
   (b) admissions; or
   (c) domestic abuse having otherwise been established,
   the court should apply the individual matters in the welfare checklist with reference to the domestic abuse which has occurred and any expert risk assessment obtained.

(2) In particular, the court should in every case consider any harm—
   (a) which the child as a victim of domestic abuse, and the parent with whom the child is living, has suffered as a consequence of that domestic abuse; and
   (b) which the child and the parent with whom the child is living is at risk of suffering, if a child arrangements order is made.

(3) The court should make an order for contact only if it is satisfied—
   (a) that the physical and emotional safety of the child and the parent with whom the child is living can, as far as possible, be secured before, during and after contact; and
   (b) that the parent with whom the child is living will not be subjected to further domestic abuse by the other parent.

37. In every case where a finding or admission of domestic abuse is made, or where domestic abuse is otherwise established, the court should consider the conduct of both parents towards each other and towards the child and the impact of the same. In particular, the court should consider —
   (a) the effect of the domestic abuse on the child and on the arrangements for where the child is living;
   (b) the effect of the domestic abuse on the child and its effect on the child's relationship with the parents;
   (c) whether the parent is motivated by a desire to promote the best interests of the child or is using the process to continue a form of domestic abuse against the other parent;
   (d) the likely behaviour during contact of the parent against whom findings are made and its effect on the child; and
   (e) the capacity of the parents to appreciate the effect of past domestic abuse and the potential for future domestic abuse.

Where the court has made a finding of domestic abuse but nevertheless considers that it is in the best interests of the child to spend time with the parent, the court must also consider whether the time should be supervised[258] or whether conditions need to be imposed requiring the abusive party to seek advice and/or treatment for his behaviour.[259] The CA 1989 also includes provision for an abusive parent to be directed or ordered to attend 'programmes, classes and counselling or guidance sessions of a kind that . . . may, by addressing a person's violent behaviour, enable or facilitate involvement in the child's life'.[260] Where

[258] The contact must be independently supervised, and not 'supported' at a contact centre or supervised by a relative: Practice Direction 12J (2017), [38].
[259] Ibid. [260] S 11A(5).

direct involvement is considered inappropriate, the court must consider whether to make an order for indirect contact.[261]

The latest version of the Practice Direction is intended to address how the s 1(2A) presumption of parental involvement in a child's life[262] should operate in cases where there are allegations of domestic abuse. It is notable that a proposed redrafting of the Practice Direction that would have explicitly stated that the presumption did not apply if involvement would place the child or parent at risk of domestic abuse,[263] was toned down in the final version to what is now para 7, which merely requires the court to 'consider' whether the s 1(2A) presumption applies. Nonetheless, in theory the presumption is subject to two sub-clauses which have potential to disapply it in cases of domestic abuse. First, in s 1(2A) itself, the presumption applies only 'unless the contrary is shown'—in other words, the presumption of benefit to the child of parental involvement can be rebutted by evidence. Secondly, s 1(6) provides that the s 1(2A) presumption only applies *at all* to parents who can be involved in their child's life in a way that does not put the child at risk of suffering harm, though the court requires evidence before it can conclude that the parent cannot be involved in a safe way. Both of these provisions have potential to apply to the domestic abuse context.[264] If the parent's actions pose a sufficient risk, the presumption may be disapplied by s 1(6); but even if the presumption applies, it can be rebutted by evidence about the child's best interests under s 1(2A). However, in practice, research suggests that 'the presumption . . . is rarely disapplied', and that s 1(2A) fits with the courts' general pro-contact approach and 'serves to reinforce that culture'.[265]

The approach taken by the courts has been subjected to detailed consideration by the Court of Appeal in *Re H-N (Domestic Abuse: Findings of Fact Hearings)* and in *K v K (Fact-Finding)*. The focus in *Re H-N* was on the working of Practice Direction 12J, which—despite concerns about the implementation of its provisions in each of the four conjoined appeals under consideration—the court considered to be 'fit for purpose'.[266] The court set out important guidance on the meaning of coercive and/or controlling behaviour and the approach to be taken in the context of contact applications.

Re H-N (Domestic Abuse: Findings of Fact Hearings) **[2021] EWCA Civ 448**

McFARLANE P:

29. . . . [C]entral to the modern definitions of domestic abuse is the concept of coercive and/or controlling behaviour. Shortly before the hearing of these appeals, Mr Justice Hayden handed down judgment in *F v M*.[267] . . . It is helpful to set out one of the central paragraphs from Hayden J's judgment here:

"4. . . . The nature of the allegations included in support of the application can succinctly and accurately be summarised as involving complaints of 'coercive and controlling behaviour' on F's part. In the Family Court, that expression is given no legal definition. In

[261] Practice Direction 12J (2017), [39]. [262] S 1(2A) is set out at 11.7.2.a.

[263] See Cobb (2017), 10.

[264] See, e.g., *Re A and B (Children: Restrictions on Parental Responsibility: Extremism and Radicalisation in Private Law)* [2016] EWFC 40, [132].

[265] Hunter et al (2020), 88. Empirical work with family law professionals by Harwood (2021) reaches the same conclusion. See also Kaganas (2018) on the approach of the courts.

[266] [2021] EWCA Civ 448, [28]. For comment, see Burton (2021); Burton and Bettinson (2022).

[267] [2021] EWFC 4.

my judgement, it requires none. The term is unambiguous and needs no embellishment. Understanding the scope and ambit of the behaviour however, requires a recognition that 'coercion' will usually involve a pattern of acts encompassing, for example, assault, intimidation, humiliation and threats. 'Controlling behaviour' really involves a range of acts designed to render an individual subordinate and to corrode their sense of personal autonomy. Key to both behaviours is an appreciation of a 'pattern' or 'a series of acts', the impact of which must be assessed cumulatively and rarely in isolation. There has been very little reported case law in the Family Court considering coercive and controlling behaviour. I have taken the opportunity below, to highlight the insidious reach of this facet of domestic abuse. My strong impression, having heard the disturbing evidence in this case, is that it requires greater awareness and, I strongly suspect, more focused training for the relevant professionals."

30. . . . The judgment of Hayden J in *F v M* (which should be essential reading for the Family judiciary) is of value both because of the illustration that its facts provide of what is meant by coercive and controlling behaviour, but also because of the valuable exercise that the judge has undertaken in highlighting at paragraph 60 the statutory guidance published by the Home Office pursuant to Section 77 (1) of the Serious Crime Act 2015 which identified paradigm behaviours of controlling and coercive behaviour. . . .

31. The circumstances encompassed by the definition of 'domestic abuse' in PD12J fully recognise that coercive and/or controlling behaviour by one party may cause serious emotional and psychological harm to the other members of the family unit, whether or not there has been any actual episode of violence or sexual abuse. . . . It follows that the harm to a child in an abusive household is not limited to cases of actual violence to the child or to the parent. A pattern of abusive behaviour is as relevant to the child as to the adult victim. The child can be harmed in any one or a combination of ways for example where the abusive behaviour:

i) Is directed against, or witnessed by, the child;
ii) Causes the victim of the abuse to be so frightened of provoking an outburst or reaction from the perpetrator that she/he is unable to give priority to the needs of her/his child;
iii) Creates an atmosphere of fear and anxiety in the home which is inimical to the welfare of the child;
iv) Risks inculcating, particularly in boys, a set of values which involve treating women as being inferior to men.

32. It is equally important to be clear that not all directive, assertive, stubborn or selfish behaviour, will be 'abuse' in the context of proceedings concerning the welfare of a child; much will turn on the intention of the perpetrator of the alleged abuse and on the harmful impact of the behaviour. We would endorse the approach taken by Peter Jackson LJ in *Re L (Relocation: Second Appeal)*:[268]

"Few relationships lack instances of bad behaviour on the part of one or both parties at some time and it is a rare family case that does not contain complaints by one party against the other, and often complaints are made by both. Yet not all such behaviour will amount to 'domestic abuse', where 'coercive behaviour' is defined as behaviour that is 'used to harm, punish, or frighten the victim . . .' and 'controlling behaviour' as behaviour 'designed to make a person subordinate . . .' In cases where the alleged behaviour does not have this character it is likely to be unnecessary and disproportionate for detailed findings of fact to be made about the complaints; indeed, in such cases it will not be in the interests of the child or of justice for the court to allow itself to become another battleground for adult conflict."

[268] [2017] EWCA Civ 2121, [61].

Part of the court's task when allegations of domestic abuse are made is to decide whether those allegations need to be determined as a preliminary issue, at what is called a 'fact-finding hearing'—the purpose of which is only to decide whether allegations are proved to the civil standard or not—before coming to the welfare decisions later.[269] In the subsequent decision of *K v K*, the Court of Appeal emphasized that when the court undertakes a fact-finding hearing, such a hearing 'is not free-standing litigation' but is about the welfare of the child: the only purpose of the process is for the court 'to identify how any alleged abusive behaviour is, or may be, relevant to the determination of the issues between the parties as to the future arrangements for the children'.[270] The court is therefore under no obligation to conduct a fact-finding exercise if doing so would not be proportionate to the issues and inform the court, one way or another, about the nature of the orders that would be in the child's best interests.[271] However, when it is considering the truth of allegations that are made, the court needs to consider the wider picture and not approach each allegation in isolation: 'Perpetration of domestic abuse is an expression of an aspect of a person's character within a relationship and the fact that a person is capable of being seriously abusive in one way inevitably increases the likelihood of them having been abusive in other ways.'[272]

11.7.3.d Criticisms of the current approach

There are numerous concerns raised about contact in the context of domestic abuse allegations—inappropriate pressure to agree to (unsupervised) contact; procedural incentives not to focus on fact-finding, thereby downplaying the importance of domestic abuse in the court's assessment; and lack of attention to risk assessment are just some of the issues.[273] The Domestic Abuse Commissioner considers that domestic abuse is 'overlooked; minimised; and poorly addressed, if engaged with at all'.[274] Part of the risk is that the government's general drive to reduce the number of private law cases going to court—primarily by promoting mediation as an alternative[275]—leads to inappropriate diversion of cases where there are serious safety concerns away from the court process.[276] There is also a concern about whether professionals, including the courts, have access to proper information to support decision-making in this area.[277] More broadly, though, the courts' own approach is subjected to significant criticism.

The courts' general approach

When cases do go to court, research with survivors of domestic abuse by Women's Aid in 2018 showed that participants felt that evidence of domestic abuse was not taken seriously by the courts, which led to women and children being placed in unsafe situations, both in

[269] Practice Direction 12J gives guidance on when fact-finding hearings are needed. If no such hearing takes place, allegations can still be considered at a full welfare hearing, but it is likely that any findings will be a less central element of the court's final decisions if the issues were not thought sufficiently significant to justify a fact-finding hearing.

[270] [2022] EWCA Civ 468, [65]. [271] Ibid, [67].

[272] *Re A (A Child: Findings of Fact)* [2022] EWCA Civ 1652, [42].

[273] Hunter, Barnett, and Kaganas (2018), 407–13. See also Barnett (2014).

[274] Domestic Abuse Commissioner (2022b), [11]. [275] See 1.2.7.b.

[276] Domestic Abuse Commissioner (2021), 7. [277] Harwood (2019).

terms of the court process itself and the subsequent arrangements put in place by the court for children to spend time with perpetrators of domestic abuse.

J. Birchall and S. Choudhry, *Domestic Abuse, Human Rights and the Family Courts* (Bristol: Women's Aid, 2018), 36, 38

Previous work by Women's Aid has highlighted concerns about a 'pro-contact' approach in the family courts, and the results of this approach in cases where children have died or been seriously harmed during unsafe contact with a parent who was a perpetrator of domestic abuse. These concerns are backed up by several other studies, including a study published in 2014 (which comprised an analysis of case law and in-depth interviews with barristers, solicitors and family court advisers employed by Cafcass) which found that most professionals and judicial officers continued to endorse a message of 'contact at all costs' after Practice Direction 12J was issued.

This is despite evidence to show that one in seven[278] children and young people under the age of 18 will have lived with domestic violence at some point in their childhood and in households where domestic abuse is happening, 62% of children living with domestic violence are also directly harmed. One study found that 34% of under 18s who had lived with domestic violence had also been neglected or abused by a parent or guardian. Another study looking at 139 overview reports from serious case reviews between 2009 and 2011 found that around two thirds of cases featured domestic abuse, and a subsequent analysis of serious case reviews between 2011 and 2014 found that domestic abuse featured in all cases of overt filicide . . .

[I]n our sample, sole residence was awarded to the women's ex-partners more often than it was to the women themselves. Unsupervised contact in different forms, including overnight and weekend stays between the child and a parent who has been accused of domestic abuse, was by far the most common arrangement ordered. Echoing other studies in this area, supervised contact was ordered in only a low number of cases. . . . [A] high proportion of respondents (49%) chose the 'other' category; details given about this answer showed that in most cases the contact was a variation of the other categories. For example, supervised contact could take place after the ex-partner had attended an anger management course. This category was also chosen for more complex arrangements; for example, no contact ordered for one child, but unsupervised contact for a sibling.

The researchers highlighted concerns about inappropriate referrals to *supported* contact centres in cases where the risks involved, both to the parent and to the child directly, were seen by participants to justify a higher level of *supervision* of a parent who had been shown to be abusive.[279] Many participants in the research also felt that the court process itself was merely a continuation of the abuse that they had experienced within their relationships.[280] This concern is also picked up by Hunter et al in a major report commissioned by the Ministry of Justice (the Harm Report).

[278] Other research suggests that the number may be one in five: Radford et al (2011), table 3.1.
[279] See 11.7.1.
[280] Birchall and Choudhry (2018), 44–5.

R. Hunter et al, *Assessing Risk of Harm to Children and Parents in Private Law Children Cases: Final Report* (London: TSO, 2020), 6–7

Safety and experiences at court

15. The experience of court proceedings for victims of domestic abuse is affected by concerns for their physical safety, as well as by the trauma they have experienced as a result of the domestic abuse. Regardless of the outcome of the case, victims generally reported not feeling safe at court and the evidence submitted suggested that they often found that the court proceedings themselves had been re-traumatising.

16. Submissions reported that each stage of the journey through private law children proceedings (getting to court, in the court building itself, in the courtroom and returning to court to respond to repeat applications) brought with it specific safety issues, which involved:

- Physical security. Many respondents noted that proceedings in the family court were often not accompanied by the adequate provision of special measures, leaving victims vulnerable to intimidation and physical attack.
- Psychological wellbeing. Victims reported that participating in proceedings and giving evidence of their experiences can be re-traumatising; this is currently not properly addressed.
- Litigants in person. The impact on litigants in person has been identified as particularly acute with regard to safety and security, as they lack knowledge of the available measures and the rules which provide for them, and are without legal advice which would otherwise alert them of their rights to special measures.
- Direct cross-examination. A victim may face the prospect of being cross-examined by their abuser, in cases where an abuser is representing themselves, or of having to cross-examine their abuser where they are themselves a litigant in person.[281]

17. The evidence suggested that orders made under section 91(14) of the Children Act 1989 ('barring orders') are ineffective to protect victims from further abuse through repeated applications for child arrangements orders. Long-standing case law has established that these orders are exceptional, with the result that the threshold for obtaining an order is perceived to be too high, and the threshold for leave to apply once an order is made is perceived to be too low.[282]

The Harm Report also raised concerns about the seriousness with which the courts were taking domestic abuse in the context of private law children cases. The Court of Appeal in *Re H-N* found that there were concerns about the approaches of the judges in the particular cases under appeal, but concluded that '[t]raining together with a proper application of PD12J largely ensures that such errors are the exception rather than the rule'.[283] However, the evidence gathered by the Harm Report suggests that this conclusion might not reflect the realities on the ground.[284]

[281] Direct cross-examination has subsequently been prohibited by ss 31Q–31T of the Matrimonial and Family Proceedings Act 1984, introduced by s 65 of the Domestic Abuse Act 2021, though it remains to be seen how effective these new provisions will turn out to be.

[282] The tests for making a s 91(14) order, and for granting leave to apply after one has been made, have subsequently been amended by s 91A, introduced by s 67 of the Domestic Abuse Act 2021. See 11.3.2.e.

[283] [2021] EWCA Civ 448, [224].

[284] The Domestic Abuse Commissioner (2021) agreed with the Harm Panel's conclusion, and proposed a monitoring mechanism to oversee domestic abuse in private law children proceedings, to improve transparency and encourage effective engagement with domestic abuse in the Family Court. See also Burton and Bettinson (2022), 10–11 and 20. As they note with understatement, 'a degree of scepticism remains' as to whether the failure identified in *Re H-N* are the exception, rather than the norm.

R. Hunter et al, *Assessing Risk of Harm to Children and Parents in Private Law Children Cases: Final Report* (London: TSO, 2020), 7

Orders made

18. The orders that the courts make in cases involving domestic abuse and other serious offences can be shaped by the systemic issues already identified. These issues in turn can be seen to give rise to four key themes in how the family courts make child arrangements orders:

- Children should have contact. Submissions from parents who had alleged abuse as part of proceedings and professionals supporting them reported that in most cases some form of direct contact was still likely to be ordered.
- Contact should progress. Evidence received by the panel indicated that where a court ordered restrictions to direct contact the aim usually appeared to be to 'progress' to contact on an unrestricted basis. Submissions suggested that interventions such as domestic abuse perpetrator programmes (DAPPs) and supervised contact services can be seen as stepping stones to direct contact.
- Co-parenting is promoted. Many respondents reported that regardless of the particular circumstances, even where the most serious allegations of domestic abuse were raised, courts expected that parents would work together to facilitate contact arrangements.
- Dependence on the court is discouraged. Submissions and previous file studies indicate that consent orders are made on a regular basis; victims of abuse may feel pressured to agree to such orders even when they do not consider them to be safe. Review hearings, which might provide a check on the workability and safety of orders, are discouraged and rarely take place.

19. Despite PD12J, respondents felt there was little difference in the orders made between cases that did and did not feature domestic abuse. The courts almost always ordered some form of contact, frequently unrestricted, and usually without requiring an alleged abuser to address their behaviour.

Harm arising from family court orders

20. Respondents felt that orders made by the court had enabled the continued control of children and adult victims of domestic abuse by alleged abusers, as well as the continued abuse of victims and children. Many submissions detailed the long-term impacts of this abuse manifesting in physical, emotional, psychological, financial and educational harm and harm to children's current and future relationships.

21. Many respondents felt that the level of abuse they and their children experienced worsened following proceedings in the family court. There were concerns that efforts to report continuing abuse were treated dismissively by criminal justice and child welfare agencies because of the family court orders. Many respondents also highlighted the negative impacts felt by children who were compelled to have contact with abusive parents, and the burden placed on mothers and children to comply with contact orders compared to minimal expectations on perpetrators of abuse to change their behaviour.

22. Many respondents felt that negative long-term impacts to children's wellbeing from continued contact with an abusive parent vastly outweighed the value of an ongoing relationship with that parent.

While the challenges for victims of domestic abuse are serious in all cases, it is important to note the intersectional challenges that minority women face in particular: '[t]he barriers to [black and minority ethnic] women raising domestic abuse are multiplied by cultural stereotypes . . . compounded by racism, sexism and class prejudice'.[285] As Ravi Thiara and Aisha Gill note, '[w]hile BME women and children are just as likely as others to be victims, it is becoming clear that there are important differences in their experiences which can influence their responses and the way they are treated by service providers'.[286]

The effect of the s 1(2A) presumption of parental involvement in cases involving domestic abuse allegations was also considered by the House of Lords Select Committee reviewing the operation of the CFA 2014.[287] Evidence before the Committee was mixed, with its report highlighting the lack of clear data about the impacts of the presumption 'both on court judgments and on how it sends a signal which affects how cases are settled out of court'.[288] Noting the government's ongoing review of the presumption,[289] the Committee encouraged the government to make any legislative changes necessary to ensure children's welfare once that review is complete.

'Alienation' allegations

A particularly difficult issue in relation to allegations of domestic abuse in recent years has been counter-allegations of so-called 'alienation' (also termed 'parental alienation').[290] This is a term with no formal definition,[291] used to allege a wide array of behaviours perpetrated by (usually) mothers which, it is said, are intended to disrupt the child's relationship with the other parent. The Court of Appeal has adopted the working definition from Cafcass, being '[w]hen a child's resistance/hostility towards one parent is not justified and is the result of psychological manipulation by the other parent', though the manipulation need not be malicious or deliberate.[292] There undoubtedly are parents who behave in this way without good cause—sometimes termed 'implacably hostile' parents[293]—and the court has taken a robust approach to such cases, though 'reported decisions in this area tend to take the form of a post mortem examination of a lost parental relationship'.[294]

However, a concern arises that the courts may be significantly overestimating how common this problem is,[295] and thereby allowing domestic abuse perpetrators to deflect attention from

[285] Hunter et al (2020), 64–5. [286] Thiara and Gill (2012), 20.

[287] House of Lords Select Committee (2022), paras 152–69.

[288] Ibid, para 168. See also Harwood (2021), 138: based on an empirical study with family law professionals, she concludes that the s 1(2A) presumption is not having a material impact on the practice of the lower courts. However, '[t]he presumption has reinforced the status quo, which is that the courts adopt a pro-contact approach, even in cases involving domestic abuse', and s 1(2A) creates 'the ongoing risk of misinterpretation, both by the courts and by parents in cases resolved outside the court system'.

[289] MOJ (2020).

[290] Barnett (2020); Doughty, Maxwell, and Slater (2020).

[291] Domestic Abuse Commissioner (2022b), para 4. Cafcass Cymru (2019) do not use the term at all, their approach focusing on child resistance and refusal to spending time with a parent.

[292] *Re S (Parental Alienation: Cult)* [2020] EWCA Civ 568, [8].

[293] See, e.g., *Re D (Contact: Reasons for Refusal)* [1997] 2 FLR 48; *Re A (Intractable Contact Dispute)* [2013] EWCA Civ 1104. See generally Kaganas (2013), and further at 11.7.2.b.

[294] *Re S (Parental Alienation: Cult)* [2020] EWCA Civ 568, [12].

[295] Trinder et al (2013) found nine examples of implacable hostility/alienation in a sample of 212 cases seeking enforcement of contact (4 per cent). However, data are not routinely collected on this issue, so '[w]e do not know whether the attention recently given to this topic represents an unrecorded phenomenon, is hyperbole, or whether the publicity itself is misleading some parents into applying new labels to their relationship problems': Doughty, Maxwell, and Slater (2020), 69.

their behaviour—and indeed continue post-separation control—by claiming alienation by the other parent. Many allegations of domestic abuse are met with counter-allegations of parental alienation—in such cases, both the fact of the domestic abuse allegations being made, and the protective measures often taken by a parent alongside them, are said to be markers of alienation. The Harm Panel received evidence of 'professionals jumping to a conclusion that a child refusing to spend time with an abusive parent had been alienated, rather than considering the refusal to be a result of an abusive parent's behaviour'.[296] However, there is a poor evidence base to support findings of alienation or to justify professional responses to it.[297]

Alongside concerns that the court has a 'pervasive culture of disbelief' when it comes to allegations of domestic abuse,[298] the Harm Report highlighted the risks for victims of abuse who are accused of so-called 'alienation' in response to raising their concerns.

R. Hunter et al, *Assessing Risk of Harm to Children and Parents in Private Law Children Cases: Final Report* (London: TSO, 2020), 97

[M]any of the submissions by mothers alleging domestic abuse or child sexual abuse referred to the fact that counter-allegations of parental alienation had been made against them. These counter-allegations are also decided at the fact-finding hearing. There is therefore a risk that if the mother is not able to prove her allegations of abuse, the court will find not just that the abuse did not occur, but that she has deliberately lied about the abuse to disrupt the children's relationship with the other parent. Even in the absence of counter-allegations, submissions indicated that mothers risk an unfavourable response if they are unable to prove their allegations on the balance of probabilities, as the court might conclude that they have needlessly obstructed contact. This links with the concerns expressed by mothers . . . about victim-blaming, negative stereotypes and sex discrimination.

The Domestic Abuse Commissioner has been particularly concerned about the trend for so-called 'alienation' allegations—which she sees as being 'overwhelmingly a form of domestic abuse'—to distract attention from the serious problem of abusive behaviour. The Commissioner has proposed a model to consider instead a child's resistance, refusal, and/or reluctance to spend time with a parent as an issue to be approached in an abuse-informed manner.

Domestic Abuse Commissioner, *Reluctance – Resistance – Refusal: A Child Centric Approach to Domestic Abuse in Private Family Law Proceedings* (London: DAC, 2023)

Domestic abuse perpetrators utilise the Family Court to perpetuate post-separation control, hallmarked by excessive litigation, often utilising children as a justification for protracted, stressful and costly legal proceedings.

296 Hunter et al (2020), 78–9.

297 Doughty, Maxwell, and Slater (2020). A particular concern has arisen around the use by the family courts of unregulated 'experts' in so-called 'alienation', addressed by McFarlane P in *Re C ('Parental Alienation': Instruction of Expert)* [2023] EWHC 345.

298 Hunter et al (2020), 64, quoting the evidence of Southall Black Sisters. See also Domestic Abuse Commissioner (2021), 6.

A frequently used methodology of domestic abuse within the Family Court is referred to as Deny, Attack, and Reverse Victim and Offender ('DARVO'). This mechanism of abuse is utilised by perpetrators to accuse the victim or survivor of abuse, thereby deflecting focus from their behaviour, and further abusing their target. Such accusations are commonly under the guise of parental concern and are afforded traction by advancing of exercising parental rights. In the absence of an abuse-informed understanding, the Family Court has become a forum for post-separation abuse, which permits ongoing harassment through litigation.

Child response

Applications within private family law proceedings usually centre around achieving increased contact for the non-resident parent. In many of these cases, the children involved exhibit signs of reluctance, resistance and/or refusal at the prospect of: a) contact with the non-resident parent; b) increased contact with the non-resident parent; and/or c) leaving their primary carer.

This has manifested in the form of so-called 'parental' alienation allegations. The allegations comprise of the domestically abusive perpetrator accusing the primary carer of manipulating children so that they are averse to contact. The majority of these allegations are made by fathers who are non-resident parents. And women, who are primary carers, are the overwhelming majority of those accused of engineering child reluctance, resistance and/or refusal.

Accusations of so-called 'parental' alienation are overwhelmingly a form of domestic abuse in themselves and have gained considerable traction due to the minimisation of domestic abuse within the Family Court, which is attributed to a 'pro-contact' culture, reflecting national and international laws to encourage relations between child and both parents. However, the danger in distorting the court's understanding of abuse has considerable implications: the voice of the child is minimised; protective parenting (efforts by the primary carer to take an approach to child contact which minimises upset or distress experienced by the child) is penalised; and the perpetrator's rights are centred within children proceedings relating to domestic abuse.

Reluctance – Resistance – Refusal: the child as a victim of domestic abuse and fulfilling the obligations of section 3 Domestic Abuse Act 2021

The strategy of a perpetrator non-resident parent accusing the primary carer of being responsible for a child displaying resistance, refusal and/or reluctance—however the argument is presented and irrespective of terminology utilised—must be assessed and screened as a mechanism of coercively controlling abuse in itself. The vulnerability of the child must be considered with the principal prospect that they are exhibiting signs of abuse themselves, in order to ensure any duty towards the child as a victim of domestic abuse is ascertained and met.

A child who is averse to contact with a non-resident parent post-separation must be approached by the Family Court with consideration to the following non-exhaustive list: the age and development of the child (including if neurodivergent); the relationship between non-resident parent and child prior; risk factors; the non-resident parent's behaviour and attitude towards the primary carer; and domestic abuse.

Further, the effect of abusive, hostile or controlling behaviours experienced by the primary carer, as a result of the non-resident parent's conduct, impact the child given the compromised state of the primary carer, thereby meeting the threshold of section 3 of the Domestic Abuse Act 2021, which requires the child to be considered a victim of the abuse as a result.

The correct legal approach should pose the primary question: is the child responding in a way which indicates they are reacting to domestic abuse? In applying this approach: the child is afforded the maximum level of protection, in line with the objectives of legislation and Parliament.

The response to this model remains to be seen. Meanwhile, the Ministry of Justice is conducting a review of the working of the s 1(2A) presumption of parental involvement more generally,[299] commissioned in response to the Harm Report, but it remains unclear what recommendations may be made or whether they will be acted on by the government.

11.7.4 ENFORCING ORDERS TO SPEND TIME OR HAVE CONTACT

Contrary to the impression that the media may have created, the strength of the presumption in favour of contact is such that it is very rare for parental involvement to be refused—as we saw in the previous section, even when there is domestic abuse in many cases. The statistics are striking: almost no applications are refused.[300] Moreover, the majority of applicants obtain both the type and amount of time or contact sought.[301] Clearly, for domestic abuse organizations, this is problematic in that abusive men are allowed to spend time with their children in ways that are unsafe and which do not acknowledge the harm caused by domestic abuse. However, while work by such groups has gained more ground in recent years, overall it is the men's groups whose criticisms have been more loudly made. Given that 'spend time' and 'have contact' orders are made in almost all cases where they are sought, it begs the question: why are so many fathers angry and disillusioned over this issue? The answer: problems surrounding enforcement, to which we now turn.

According to fathers' rights groups, non-compliance with 'spend time' and 'have contact' orders is a huge problem,[302] with large numbers of women routinely flouting orders out of malevolence and spite, or sometimes simply convenience. The courts have borne the brunt of the criticism, coming under sustained attack for their apparent inability or unwillingness to tackle the problem effectively. In response, it is argued on behalf of mothers that they are simply acting to protect their children, their concerns about the child's welfare having been given inadequate weight when orders were made. The problem of non-compliance has generated bitter debate in which gender has again emerged as the dominant factor.

As we set out in this section, the court has various powers to respond to non-compliance with its orders. However, whether the courts should seek to secure compliance by invoking one of these measures is exceptionally difficult. If the mother disregards the order and the court fails to act, the welfare of the child, as determined by the court—as well as the rule of law—will be undermined. On the other hand, decisive action which sees the mother punished or deprived of residence is unlikely to further the child's interests, particularly if the father cannot provide the child with an alternative home. Matters are further complicated where the child, having become alienated from the father, also opposes contact.[303] The welfare of the child is not, however, the only consideration: there is a wider public interest in ensuring compliance with the courts' terms. The courts have struggled to balance these factors.

[299] MOJ (2020).

[300] In Newnham and Harding's (2016) study of 174 court files from 2011, 5 cases (2.8 per cent) ended with an order that there should be no contact; another 12 cases (6.9 per cent) ended with no positive order for contact (but it was not prohibited either), most being cases where the mother had applied for a 'live with' order and there was no other application made. See also Perry and Rainey (2007).

[301] Hunt and Macleod (2008), 4. See also Newnham and Harding (2016).

[302] It is difficult to assess the extent to which this is true. In 2011, 38,405 children were the subject of contact applications, and fewer than 1,500 applications for enforcement measures were brought: Trinder et al (2013). However, that says nothing about the number of cases in which there were difficulties which were not taken to court.

[303] See, e.g., *Re N (A Minor) (Access: Penal Notice)* [1992] 1 FLR 134.

11.7.4.a Committal proceedings

Breach of an order to allow a person to spend time with or otherwise have contact with a child constitutes contempt of court punishable by fine or committal to prison for a maximum of two years. Committal proceedings can be initiated by another party to the proceedings or, in exceptional cases, by the court acting of its own motion.[304] The dilemma facing the courts where one party to a child arrangements dispute seeks to enforce the order by committal has been graphically illustrated by Ward LJ.

Re M (A Minor) (Contempt of Court: Committal of Court's Own Motion) [1999] Fam 263 (CA), 281–2

WARD LJ:

The judge was, of course, uniquely well placed to assess what the welfare of the children demanded with regard to the maintenance of a link with their father through contact, but here the judge was assuming that coercive powers of the court would achieve that desired result. He did not, however, appear to consider what effect a committal application (carrying with it the possibility of a prison sentence) may have had on the children, especially in the light of his findings about the mother's proven capacity to influence the children against their father. It does not require much imagination to envisage the domestic scene where mother dramatically proclaims to the children that she is about to face a prison sentence because she is doing what they want - saving them from contact with their horrible father. There is an almost inevitable and serious risk that the committal proceedings might themselves exacerbate the poor relationship between children and father and so hinder not help contact.

The courts have therefore been extremely reluctant to enforce orders by imprisoning the child's main carer. Indeed, at one time it was held that committal was to be a weapon of very last resort, if appropriate at all.[305] Subsequently there has, however, been a clear hardening of attitudes—at least in terms of the rhetoric. This more robust approach has been marked by a much greater focus on the importance of securing the long-term benefits of spending time with the non-residential parent than the short-term distress caused by the imprisonment of the residential carer.[306] The courts' greater willingness to invoke committal proceedings was marked by a move away from an almost exclusive focus on the child's welfare to place much greater emphasis on the need to uphold the dignity and authority of the court. The leading authority on this more hard-line approach is *A v N (Committal: Refusal of Contact)* in which the mother of a four-and-a-half-year-old girl was adamant that she would rather go to prison than allow the girl to have contact with her father. The mother was committed to prison for 42 days for her persistent breach of the court's orders. The Court of Appeal refused her appeal.

[304] *Re M (A Minor) (Contempt of Court: Committal of Court's Own Motion)* [1999] Fam 263.

[305] See, e.g., *Re N (A Minor) (Access: Penal Notice)* [1992] 1 FLR 134; *Re M (A Minor) (Contempt of Court: Committal of Court's Own Motion)* [1999] Fam 263.

[306] See, e.g., *Re L (Minors) (Access Order: Enforcement)* [1989] 2 FLR 359; *B v S* [2009] EWCA Civ 548. In the latter case, the Court of Appeal upheld the mother's committal to prison even though she had a three month-old baby and the father no longer wished to see her committed.

A v N (Committal: Refusal of Contact) [1997] 2 FCR 475 (CA), 482–4

WARD LJ:

[In an application for committal for breach] the upbringing of the child is not a paramount consideration. It is obviously a material consideration and every Judge who does any family work at all is always alive to the grievous effect the implementation of an order is likely to have on the life of the children whom the mother is unwisely seeking to protect in her own misguided way. . . . [The judge] was fully mindful of the distressing consequence of imprisonment on the child . . . but he balanced against that the long-term damage that she will suffer, especially if she grows up under a deliberate false impression as to whom her father really is. He did, therefore, take proper account of welfare factors and his balance is not one with which I would interfere.

The stark reality of this case is that this is a mother who has flagrantly set herself upon a course of collision with the court's order. She has been given endless opportunities to comply with sympathetic attempts made by the Judge to meet her flimsy objections to contact taking place. She has spurned all of those attempts. For it to be submitted that the hardship to the child is the result of the court imposing the committal order is wholly to misunderstand the position. This little child suffers because the mother chooses to make her suffer. This mother had it within her power to save T that suffering, but she did not avail of that opportunity . . .

[I]t is perhaps appropriate that the message goes out in loud and in clear terms that there does come a limit to the tolerance of the court to see its orders flouted by mothers even if they have to care for their young children. If she goes to prison it is her fault, not the fault of the Judge who did no more than his duty to the child which is imposed upon him by Parliament.

It may be noted that later judgments have increasingly focused on the technical elements that have to be proved to show contempt,[307] with judges conscious that contempt hearings must comply with the standards of criminal proceedings. It has been stressed that a contempt has to be proved beyond all reasonable doubt, and that only a deliberate failure to comply with a clear, unambiguous, and injunctive order will suffice.[308] A number of attempts to bring such proceedings have failed on these technical points,[309] which raises questions about whether contempt proceedings are an effective solution to the difficulties of enforcing private law orders in relation to children.

11.7.4.b Enforcement measures under the CA 1989

The Children and Adoption Act 2006 (CAA 2006) introduced a number of new measures into the CA 1989 aimed at improving implementation and enforcement of 'spend time' orders. At the lowest level, the court may ask a Cafcass officer to monitor and, if necessary,

[307] Practice Direction—*Committal for Contempt of Court: Open Court* (2015) and the subsequent Practice Guidance—*Committal for Contempt of Court: Open Court* (2015). For guidance in family cases, see *Re L (A Child); Re Oddin* [2016] EWCA Civ 173 and *Egeneonu v Egeneonu (Adjournment of Committal Application)* [2017] EWHC 2451.

[308] See, e.g., *Re A (Abduction: Contempt)* [2008] EWCA Civ 1138, [6]; *Re LW (Contact Order: Committal)* [2010] EWCA Civ 1253.

[309] See, e.g., *Re Jones (Alleged Contempt of Court)* [2013] EWHC 2579; *CH v CT* [2018] EWHC 1310.

report back to the court as to compliance.[310] The period of monitoring may not exceed 12 months.[311] The intention behind it is to ensure breaches are immediately brought to the judge's attention. Furthermore, additional advice, support, and assistance to help parents adjust to the CAO in difficult cases may now be more readily available under a family assistance order.[312] Family assistance orders have been little used in private law disputes,[313] partly because of the limited resources available to Cafcass, despite the potential benefits as recognized in the academic literature.[314]

On the specific issue of enforcement, the CAA 2006 increased the range of measures available to the courts. As an alternative to imposing a fine or imprisonment, the courts may make an enforcement order imposing an 'unpaid work requirement' unless the person in breach can satisfy the court, on the balance of probabilities, that there was a reasonable excuse for non-compliance.[315] Before making the enforcement order, the court must be satisfied that: (i) the order is necessary to secure compliance with the 'spend time' order; and (ii) the enforcement order is *proportionate* to the seriousness of the offence.[316] The court must also take into account the child's welfare, though not as the paramount consideration. Compliance with an unpaid work requirement is monitored by an officer of Cafcass.[317] Research by Tinder et al suggests that these orders are rarely made, but judges may raise the spectre of such enforcement by ordering an assessment or making a suspended order, which can be effective to secure compliance with the original CAO.[318]

Where breach of a CAO causes financial loss, such as the cost of a cancelled holiday, the court can order the person in breach to pay compensation.[319] To avoid paying compensation, the person in breach must satisfy the court, on the balance of probabilities, that they had a reasonable excuse for failing to comply. In determining whether to make the order and, if so, for how much, the court must take into account the individual's financial circumstances and the welfare of the child concerned.

11.7.4.c Transferring residence

A similar hardening of attitudes is discernible in the courts' use of their final weapon against non-compliance: moving the child from the 'intransigent' parent to live primarily with the other parent.[320] The Court of Appeal has made it clear that the transfer of the child's main home is a 'judicial weapon of last resort'.[321] Where the child has been denied contact, there will be obvious risks in transferring residence to a parent who may well be a relative stranger. However, despite the risks, the courts have made it clear that they are increasingly willing to employ this measure against 'unreasonable mothers' to protect the child's long-term interests. The key question for the court is whether there is a greater risk of harm to the child by reason of the disruption and distress caused by a transfer of residence or by denying them a relationship with the other parent, which requires a careful balancing of the pros and cons of a move.

[310] S 11H(2). [311] S 11H(6). [312] S 16(4A).

[313] For examples in a cases involving complex private law disputes, see *Re N (A Child) (Religion: Jehovah's Witness)* [2011] EWHC 3737; *Re L and M (Children: Private Law)* [2014] EWHC 939.

[314] Seden (2001). [315] S 11J(2)–(4). [316] S 11L. [317] S 11M. [318] Trinder et al (2013).

[319] S 11O.

[320] For examples see *Re C (A Child)* [2007] EWCA Civ 866; *Re A (Suspended Residence Order)* [2010] 1 FLR 1679; *Re S (Transfer of Residence)* [2010] 1 FLR 1785.

[321] *Re A (Children)* [2009] EWCA Civ 1141, [18].

Re M (Children) (Contact) [2012] EWHC 1948

PETER JACKSON J:

65. In relation to the children's needs, there are factors that strongly speak against a change of residence:
    - In all other respects, they have made very good progress in their mother's care. . . .
    - They are securely attached to their mother, and to [their half-brothers], and have a good relationship with their stepfather Mr A, who they admire. The relationship between the boys and their younger half-brothers is very important to them and a change of residence not only means that they would see much less of them, but that their upbringings would inevitably diverge.
    - A change of residence disrupts the pattern of care within the home that the children have been used to all their lives, despite several changes of address while in their mother's care.
    - They are doing well at school, despite several changes of school.
    - The children have at the moment persuaded themselves that they do not want to see their father, let alone live with him.
    - Without the mother's support, the children would be very difficult to move and they may not settle with their father.
    - Arrangements for contact with their mother and siblings would be difficult, at least at the outset.
66. A move would therefore bring real losses for the children, and risks, which could easily amount to harm if the transition was unsuccessful. . . .
68. Against these factors:
    - A move is the only way of restoring the children's relationships with their father and wider family.
    - There is no available therapeutic mechanism that can restore their relationship with their father, given the distances, the lack of funds and the mother's current attitude.
    - The children's true feelings are, as I have found, being stifled.
    - The father is, I find, capable of bringing up the children appropriately and meeting their needs. Although he is untested as a full-time carer, there is no reason to believe that he cannot take on that role successfully with the support network that he has, and the flexibility that his employment allows.
    - I discount the suggestion that the children would come to harm in the father's care as a result of any acts or failures on his part.
    - The father is likely to support the children's relationship with their mother to the extent that it is within his power to do so.

Jackson J then looked at how these factors would be balanced, taking into account the short, medium, and long-term consequences of each option. The judge concluded that it was necessary to make an order transferring the children's residence from their mother to their father. However, he gave the mother 'one final opportunity' to comply with the CAO, by making a condition that his order for a transfer of the children's main residence was not to take effect if the mother and her new partner started to comply with the original order.[322]

Although controversial, this more hard-line approach to enforcement finds support in the ECHR. It was held in *Hokkanen v Finland* that the state has a positive obligation under Article 8 to 'facilitate' the parent–child relationship, including taking all reasonable steps to enforce private law orders for contact.[323] However, the European Court recognized that the state's obligation cannot be absolute and that any coercive measures against the parent in breach must be limited by the need to take into account the rights and interests of others, in particular those of the child. These principles were approved and applied in *Glaser v United Kingdom*.[324]

11.7.5 TAKING CONTACT OUT OF THE COURTS

As the courts struggle to find appropriate and effective solutions to the more difficult and intractable disputes, it has been questioned more broadly whether the courts are the most appropriate forum for dealing with disputes of this nature. Long-term, deep-rooted problems, which are incapable of resolution at a discrete point in time, often underpin such disputes. The blunt tool of ordering and enforcing that the child spends time with one parent will not address the underlying cause of the other parent's hostility. Counselling or therapy may be the only way such problems can be effectively resolved.

Re L (A Child) (Contact: Domestic Violence) [2001] Fam 260 (CA), 296–8

THORPE LJ:

[T]here is in my opinion validity in questioning the future role of the family justice system in relation to contact. I have already expressed how limited is the capacity of the family justice system to produce good outcomes in disputed areas of personal relationship. Yet a great deal of the resources of the system are taken up with contested contact cases. The disputes are particularly prevalent and intractable. They consume a disproportionate quantity of private law judicial time. The disputes are often driven by personality disorders, unresolved adult conflicts or egocentricity. These originating or contributing factors would generally be better treated therapeutically, where at least there would be some prospect of beneficial change, rather than given vent in the family justice system . . .

I would question whether the investment of public funds in litigation as the conventional mode of resolving contact disputes is comparatively productive. In many cases the same investment in therapeutic services might produce greater benefit. Within the National Health Service, child and mental health services work with warring parents to try and help them separate their parenting role from the breakdown of the partnership. If one parent has a mental illness or personality disorder the service can help the family to manage perhaps by providing sessions with the children to help them understand their situation. Within the voluntary sector there are exceptional facilities . . . that provide more than neutral space for

322 *Re M (Children) (Contact)* [2012] EWHC 1948, [76]. See also *Re C (Residence Orders: Permission to Appeal)* [2018] EWHC 557.

323 *Hokkanen v Finland* (App No 19823/92, ECHR) (1994).

324 (App No 32346/96, ECHR) (2000). See also *Damnjonovic v Serbia* (App No 5222/07, ECHR) (2009), [75]–[78]; *Kaleta v Poland* (App No 11375/02, ECHR) (2009), [52].

contact, and perhaps some professional supervision or assessment. Such centres attempt to address the underlying dysfunction in family relationship that expresses itself in the absence or failure of contact. In some cases they may work with the family therapeutically for weeks before attempting any direct contact. It must at least be arguable that that expenditure of effort and cost is likely to achieve more than an equal expenditure on litigation with its tendency to increase alienation through its adversarial emphasis. Of course there will always be many cases that are only fit for referral to litigation. But in my opinion judges with responsibility for case management should be thoroughly informed as to available alternative services in the locality and astute in selecting the service best suited to promote the welfare of the child in each case.[325]

Numerous initiatives have been introduced over the last few years that attempt to promote non-court solutions to private law children disputes. One approach has been to introduce initiatives aimed at changing the attitudes and behaviour of separating parents through tools of *persuasion*. The hope was to achieve a change in *culture* regarding private law disputes, whereby 'it becomes socially unacceptable for one parent to impede a child's relationship with its other parent wherever it is safe and in the child's best interests'.[326] Parents were thus to be 'educated' to understand that the 'civilized divorce' and 'good parenting' requires them to put their children's interests before their own and that this means facilitating contact.

The first step towards this goal was to provide better access to information and advice through existing agencies such as Action for Children, Sure Start, and Relate—though many of these programmes have since been cut as a result of budgetary restrictions. Information targeted at both parents and children[327] includes parenting plans containing examples of various contact arrangements which have been shown to work well.[328] Several measures have been introduced which are aimed at promoting a more conciliatory approach to resolving disputes. A collaborative law programme is now operated by some law firms, whereby both parents' lawyers must be committed to achieving settlement; in the absence of agreement, different lawyers must be instructed.[329]

Since 2014, where applications are made to the court,[330] the government has made it all but mandatory (unless an exemption is shown, such as a history of domestic abuse) for the parties to attend a Mediation Information and Assessment Meeting (MIAM) to see whether the case is suitable for mediation.[331] The parties can attend the MIAM separately or together. While it is not strictly compulsory to attend a MIAM, the court may—theoretically, at least—adjourn proceedings pending attendance if it does not consider that the parties have a good reason for non-attendance.[332] However, the House of Lords Select Committee considering the implementation of the CFA 2014 concluded that MIAMs 'have been ineffective and

[325] See also *Re D (Intractable Contact Dispute: Publicity)* [2004] EWHC 727.

[326] DCA, DFES, and DTI (2005), 7.

[327] For comment on engaging children in this process of securing the 'civilized divorce', see Kaganas and Diduck (2004).

[328] DCA, DFES, and DTI (2005), 19–21. [329] Ibid.

[330] Applications for consent orders are exempted.

[331] Practice Direction 3A—*Family Mediation and Information Assessment Meetings (MIAMS)* (2018). See 1.2.7.

[332] Ibid, [37]. In *K v K (Fact-Finding)* [2022] EWCA Civ 468, Sir Geoffrey Vos MR stressed that claimed exemptions from MIAM attendance should be checked by the court: 'For the statutory MIAM requirement to be effective, it must be enforced.'

had low engagement rates', and argued that they should be abolished in favour of 'a source of clear, impartial information on separation and, if necessary, general legal advice which can direct them to non-court or court-based resolution as appropriate'.[333]

At the same time, legal aid was withdrawn from almost all private law proceedings (except in a limited class of cases involving domestic abuse, plus a few other restricted exceptions) under LASPO 2012. This move was predicated on the 2010–15 Coalition Government's view that most private law disputes should not be in court and therefore that the state should not fund legal representation for such cases.[334] Again, the cuts to legal aid were criticized by the House of Lords Select Committee, which considered that 'reinstating legal aid could help improve the efficiency of the family justice system'.[335]

11.8 SPECIFIC ISSUE AND PROHIBITED STEPS ORDERS

11.8.1 GENERAL PRINCIPLES

In essence, specific issue and prohibited steps orders constitute two sides of the same coin. A specific issue order (SIO) is a positive order providing for a particular step to be taken with respect to the child's upbringing.[336] A prohibited steps order (PSO) is a negative order preventing a particular step being taken. As discussed in chapter 10, such orders are commonly used to resolve disputes between the holders of parental responsibility (PR). However, subject to the requirement for leave, anyone may in theory apply to the court for a particular issue to be determined.[337] SIOs and PSOs have been used to resolve a wide range of disputes concerning a child, the one requirement being that it must engage some aspect of PR.[338] Some of the more common include: changing a child's surname,[339] preventing the removal of a child from the jurisdiction,[340] medical treatment,[341] choice of school,[342] and the publication of information about the child.[343]

Whilst the potential use of SIOs and PSOs is extremely broad, there are some important restrictions on their use. An SIO or PSO cannot be made with a view to achieving a result that could be achieved by making a CAO.[344] Nor may an SIO or a PSO be made with a view to placing a child in local authority care.[345] Finally, an SIO or a PSO cannot be used to 'oust' someone from the family home, the proper route for such an application being under Part 4 of the Family Law Act 1996.[346]

An application for an SIO or a PSO is determined on the basis of the child's welfare.

[333] House of Lords Select Committee (2022), para 140. [334] See 1.2.7.

[335] House of Lords Select Committee (2022), para 141.

[336] Gilmore (2004b).

[337] This includes local authorities (*Re R (A Minor) (Blood Transfusion)* [1993] 2 FLR 757), subject to the restriction in s 9(1) which prevents an SIO or a PSO being made in relation to a child who is in the care of a local authority under s 31 or 38.

[338] *Re J (Specific Issue Order: Leave to Apply)* [1995] 1 FLR 669.

[339] *Dawson v Wearmouth* [1999] 2 AC 308; *Re W (A Child) (Illegitimate Child: Change of Surname)* [2001] Fam 1.

[340] *Re K (Application to Remove from Jurisdiction)* [1998] 2 FLR 1006.

[341] *Re HG (Specific Issue Order: Sterilisation)* [1993] 1 FLR 587; *Re R (A Minor) (Blood Transfusion)* [1993] 2 FLR 757.

[342] *Re G (Education: Religious Upbringing)* [2012] EWCA Civ 1233.

[343] *Re Z (A Minor) (Freedom of Publication)* [1997] Fam 1.

[344] S 9(5)(a). See *Re H (Prohibited Steps Order)* [1995] 1 WLR 667.

[345] Ss 9(5)(b) and 100(2).

[346] *Pearson v Franklin* [1994] 1 WLR 370; *Re D (Prohibited Steps Order)* [1996] 2 FLR 273.

11.8.2 RELOCATION DISPUTES

Relocation disputes are cases which arise when one parent seeks to take the child to live in another geographic location, and the other parent opposes the proposal. After separation, a parent may wish to move to another location for any number of reasons—for family support, a new job, cheaper housing, better schools, a new partner, or just for a change. The law imposes no restrictions on a *parent's* ability to move away from their existing home for whatever reason they want—but if the parent wishes to take their *child* with them, the law becomes involved.[347] In keeping with the CA 1989's general scheme, the starting point is to ask whether all those with PR agree to the move taking place. If they do, the move can go ahead and the law has nothing more to say about it.[348] If there is no agreement, the matter must be resolved by the court.

Relocation cases make a good example of how SIOs and PSOs are used, since both are frequently invoked in this context—SIOs to *allow* relocations and PSOs to *prevent* them.[349] Until 2015, English law drew a distinction between proposed relocations outside the UK and proposed moves within the UK. That difference was swept away by *Re C (Internal Relocation)*,[350] such that relocation is now all addressed under the same framework, though some differences remain as we will see.

11.8.2.a The legal approach to relocation cases

We start by noting one of the remaining differences between international and domestic cases:

- *International moves:* as we saw earlier, s 13 of the CA 1989 imposes an automatic prohibition on a parent removing a child from the UK when a 'live with' CAO is in force.[351] However, in any case where both parents have PR and are spending any amount of time with the child, removal from the UK without the written consent of everyone with PR or the court's permission will be child abduction, which has important civil and criminal law consequences.[352] Consequently, in the absence of agreement, a parent seeking to relocate internationally requires the consent of the court.
- *Moves within the UK:* there is no equivalent to the s 13 restriction in relation to moves *within* the UK, and child abduction law does not apply to such moves. Consequently,

[347] One consequence of this is that parents who have their child living with them can be subject to de facto restrictions on moving which do not apply to parents who do not have their children mainly in their care. In practice, this tends to mean that the law regulates women's freedom of movement to a greater extent than men's, which can be seen as problematic from a gender perspective: see, e.g., Behrens (1997).

[348] For international moves, the parents will be well advised to put the agreement in writing, though that is not always essential as long as it is clear and unequivocal: Child Abduction Act 1984; Hague Convention on the Civil Aspects of International Child Abduction 1980.

[349] There is also an argument that, in cases where a 'live with' CAO is in force, international relocation cases can be addressed with a court order under CA 1989, s 13. Not much turns on this issue, but the better view is that a s 8 order is appropriate in all cases: *Re C (Older Children: Relocation)* [2015] EWCA Civ 1298, [59], citing George (2008b); *Re C (Internal Relocation)* [2015] EWCA Civ 1305, [21].

[350] [2015] EWCA Civ 1305. See Lanteigne (2016).

[351] See 11.6.8. The parent with whom the child is living can take go abroad for up to one calendar month without consent, unless specifically prevented: s 13(2).

[352] Child Abduction Act 1984; Child Abduction and Custody Act 1985. Over 100 countries are signatories to the Hague Convention on the Civil Aspects of International Child Abduction 1980, which aims to secure the prompt return of any child removed or retained internationally without lawful consent.

unless an order is in force which prevents a child from being moved,[353] there is no automatic restriction. Whether the agreement of all those with PR is required or not would seem to depend on whether the move amounts to a significant change for the child;[354] but what is a 'significant change'? The Court of Appeal has said that 'it is not to be expected . . . that the court will be likely to impose restrictions on a parent who wishes to move to the next village, or even the next town or some distance across the county, and a parent seeking such a restriction may well get short shrift',[355] but such a move may involve a change of school and, particularly for less affluent families where transport may be more difficult, may impact arrangements for contact. It is not apparent, therefore, that any clear line can be drawn.

For many years, the law's approach to relocation cases was quite different from other areas of child law. The cases relating to internal relocation provided that moves within the UK would be restricted only in 'exceptional' circumstances[356]—an approach which, unsurprisingly, raised questions about compatibility with s 1 of the CA 1989.[357] For international cases, although the welfare principle clearly applied, its interpretation was underpinned by implicit presumptions and a series of questions from a case called *Payne v Payne*.[358] The judgment of Thorpe LJ in *Payne*, in particular, contained a summary at the end which identified a number of factors as a 'discipline' which, in the years that followed, trial judges were required to apply.[359] *Payne* and the cases that followed it were widely thought to amount to a presumption in favour of relocation, and were subject to significant criticism.[360]

However, the law has changed rapidly. While some of the considerations identified by that earlier case law remain relevant, what is required now is a broad analysis of the child's best interests, comparing the pros and cons of each of the realistic options being put forward for the child's future upbringing.

K v K (Relocation: Shared Care Arrangement) [2011] EWCA Civ 793

BLACK LJ:

141. The first point that is quite clear is that . . . the principle—the only authentic principle—that runs through the entire line of relocation authorities is that the welfare of the child is the court's paramount consideration. Everything that is considered by the court in reaching its determination is put into the balance with a view to measuring its impact on the child.

142. Whilst this is the only truly inescapable principle in the jurisprudence, that does not mean that everything else—the valuable guidance—can be ignored. It must be heeded . . . but as guidance not as rigid principle or so as to dictate a particular outcome in a sphere of law where the facts of individual cases are so infinitely variable.

143. Furthermore, the effect of the guidance must not be overstated. Even where the case concerns a true primary carer, there is no presumption that the reasonable relocation plans of

[353] The most straightforward order to achieve this is a PSO, but there are other orders which can stop a relocation—e.g. an SIO that the child is to attend a particular school will have the effect of requiring the child to live within reasonable distance of that school.

[354] See 10.5.1. [355] *Re C (Internal Relocation)* [2015] EWCA Civ 1305, [54].

[356] *Re E (Residence: Imposition of Conditions)* [1997] EWCA Civ 3084; *Re B (Prohibited Steps Order)* [2007] EWCA Civ 1055.

[357] *Re F (Internal Relocation)* [2010] EWCA Civ 1428; George (2011b). [358] [2001] EWCA Civ 166.

[359] Hayes (2006). [360] See, e.g., Hayes (2006); Herring and Taylor (2006); George (2014).

that carer will be facilitated unless there is some compelling reason to the contrary, nor any similar presumption however it may be expressed. Thorpe LJ said so in terms in *Payne* and it is not appropriate, therefore, to isolate other sentences from his judgment, such as the final sentence of paragraph 26 ("Therefore her application to relocate will be granted unless the court concludes that it is incompatible with the welfare of the children") for re-elevation to a status akin to that of a determinative presumption. It is doubly inappropriate when one bears in mind that the judgments in *Payne* must be read as a whole, with proper weight given to what the then President said. She said that she wished to reformulate the principles since they may have been expressed from time to time in too rigid terms with the word 'presumption' over-emphasising one element of the approach (paragraph 82) whereas the criteria in s 1 Children Act govern the application (paragraph 83) and there is no presumption in favour of the applicant (paragraph 84). Dame Elizabeth referred, of course, to the effect on the parent with residence (paragraphs 83 and 84) but she also stressed that the relationship with the other parent is highly relevant and that there are many other factors which may arise in an individual case (paragraph 84). I detect in her discussion of the factors and in her summary at paragraph 85 no weighting in favour of any particular factor. . . .

144. *Payne* therefore identifies a number of factors which will or may be relevant in a relocation case, explains their importance to the welfare of the child, and suggests helpful disciplines to ensure that the proper matters are considered in reaching a decision but it does not dictate the outcome of a case. . . .

It can be seen that Black LJ makes numerous references to the *Payne* decision, and consequently the ongoing relevance of that earlier case was somewhat unclear in the immediate aftermath of *K v K*.[361] The Court of Appeal returned to this issue twice in 2015, once in the context of an international relocation case and once regarding an internal move.

Re F (International Relocation Cases) [2015] EWCA Civ 882

RYDER LJ:

17. The *ratio* of the decision in *Payne* was more nuanced in the sense that the questions were always intended to be part of a welfare analysis and were not intended to be elevated into principles or presumptions. Regrettably that is not how they were perceived and the best intentions of the court were lost in translation. The caution expressed by Dame Elizabeth Butler-Sloss P in *Payne* went unheeded, namely that guidance that had been derived from authorities such as *Poel v Poel* [1970] 1 WLR 1469 was being expressed in 'too rigid terms' and 'unduly firmly' with an over emphasis on one element of the case. I respectfully agree with her and with the benefit of hindsight the continued use of the *Payne* guidance by courts without putting it into the context of a welfare analysis perpetuated the problem.

18. Furthermore, in the decade or more since *Payne* it would seem odd indeed for this court to use guidance which out of the context which was intended is redolent with gender based assumptions as to the role and relationships of parents with a child. Likewise, the absence of any emphasis on the child's wishes and feelings or to take the question one step back, the child's participation in the decision making process, is stark. The questions identified in *Payne* may or may not be relevant on the facts of an individual case and the court will

[361] George (2012b).

be better placed if it concentrates not on assumptions or preconceptions but on the statutory welfare question which is before it . . .

27. Selective or partial legal citation from *Payne* without any wider legal analysis is likely to be regarded as an error of law. In particular, a judgment that not only focuses solely on *Payne*, but also compounds that error by only referring to the four point 'discipline' set out by Thorpe LJ at paragraph 40 of his judgment in *Payne* is likely to be wholly wrong. There are no quick fixes to be had in these important and complicated cases; the paragraph 40 'discipline' in *Payne* may, or may not, be of assistance to a judge on the facts of any particular case (whether there is a 'primary carer' or not) in marshalling his or her analysis of the evidence prior to the all-important analysis of the child's welfare.

28. Given the agreement of the parties to an holistic approach to the court's welfare analysis, I need to set out what that involves. The re-crafting of section 8 orders from residence and contact into child arrangements orders has inter alia the benefit of emphasising, absent adverse circumstances and welfare conclusions, the equality of parental responsibility that each parent has. Parents are to be expected to exercise their autonomy and to respect the autonomy of their children by entering into arrangements that plan for their children's long term welfare by providing for a meaningful relationship between each adult and each child. Where they cannot agree there is likely to be more than one proposal for the court to consider. . . .

30. That approach is no more than a reiteration of good practice. Where there is more than one proposal before the court, a welfare analysis of each proposal will be necessary. That is neither a new approach nor is it an option. A welfare analysis is a requirement in any decision about a child's upbringing. The sophistication of that analysis will depend on the facts of the case. Each realistic option for the welfare of a child should be validly considered on its own internal merits (i.e. an analysis of the welfare factors relating to each option should be undertaken). That prevents one option (often in a relocation case the proposals from the absent or 'left behind' parent) from being sidelined in a linear analysis. Not only is it necessary to consider both parents' proposals on their own merits and by reference to what the child has to say but it is also necessary to consider the options side by side in a comparative evaluation. A proposal that may have some but no particular merit on its own may still be better than the only other alternative which is worse.

K v K and *Re F* developed in the context of international relocation cases only, and internal relocation disputes were decided under a rather different legal framework. However, following *Re C (Internal Relocation)*,[362] internal relocation cases have been brought within the authorities on international relocation cases. There are differences between the two—the consequences of the move in terms of which court has jurisdiction over any future disputes and the question of how contact orders will be enforceable are the main areas of difference—but the decision is made under the same approach. This was summarized by Vos LJ in *Re C*.[363]

Re C (Internal Relocation) [2015] EWCA Civ 1305

VOS LJ:

82. . . . [I]n cases concerning either external or internal relocation the only test that the court applies is the paramount principle as to the welfare of the child. The application of that

[362] [2015] EWCA Civ 1305. [363] See Lanteigne (2016).

test involves a holistic balancing exercise undertaken with the assistance, by analogy, of the welfare checklist, even where it is not statutorily applicable. The exercise is not a linear one. It involves balancing all the relevant factors, which may vary hugely from case to case, weighing one against the other, with the objective of determining which of the available options best meets the requirement to afford paramount consideration to the welfare of the child. It is no part of this exercise to regard a decision in favour or against any particular available option as exceptional.

83. One of the most difficult aspects of this case has been to establish in the light of previous authority what use, if any, should be made in the process we have just described of the 4 'disciplines' identified by Thorpe LJ at paragraph 40 of his judgment in *Payne v Payne* (the '*Payne* factors'). In my judgment, one of the valid concerns about the Payne factors is that they do not adequately reflect the gender-neutral approach to these problems that the court will now adopt in every case. Whilst the *Payne* factors may still be of some utility in some cases, they are no part of the applicable test or the applicable principles. In some circumstances, the judge may find them useful. In others, the judge may not. If the judge finds them a useful guide to some of the factors that he should consider, he will be doing so only as part of the multi-factorial balancing exercise that is required.

Following these cases, the law has stabilized,[364] and much of the previous criticism of the English law's approach to relocation appears to have been answered. For example, critics were once concerned that the impact of the refusal of a relocation application on the applicant mother was given undue importance within the court's analysis[365]—now, this factor is clearly just one of many within the analysis, and some judges consider that arguments based on applicants' own well-being 'should be treated very circumspectly' so as to avoid generalizations.[366]

11.8.2.b 'Unilateral relocation'

The position set out so far assumes that the parents engage with the court process *before* a proposed move takes place. However, a particularly difficult situation arises where the parent moves without warning and without first seeking the consent either of the other parent or of the court. When such a move is international,[367] it can constitute a criminal offence under the Child Abduction Act 1984, and is termed 'international child abduction'. Such abductions are addressed under various pieces of international law, primarily the Hague Convention on the Civil Aspects of International Child Abduction 1980, which provides that children in such situations should be *summarily* returned to their country of habitual residence unless the abducting parent can establish one of the limited exceptions to that default position.[368]

[364] See, e.g., *Re L (Relocation: Second Appeal)* [2017] EWCA Civ 2121; *S v V (Children: Leave to Remove)* [2018] EWFC 28; *V v M (Child Arrangements Order: International Relocation)* [2020] EWHC 488.

[365] See, e.g., Hayes (2006); *Re AR (A Child: Relocation)* [2010] EWHC 1346, [12].

[366] *S v V (Children: Leave to Remove)* [2018] EWFC 28, [4].

[367] Meaning outside the UK: Child Abduction Act 1984, s 1.

[368] Consideration of international child abduction is beyond the scope of this book. See, e.g., Lowe and Nicholls (2016).

Where a parent moves within the UK, the legal position is different. There is no criminal offence, and—at least where the parent moving is already the main carer of the child—no assumption in the law that the child will be summarily returned to their previous place of residence. In *Re R (Internal Relocation: Appeal)*,[369] the child had been removed from Kent to the North East of England without the father's knowledge or consent. He sought to have the child returned on a summary basis, pending determination of the internal relocation question. The Court of Appeal held that there was no general principle or presumption in English law that a child should be returned in such circumstances. The approach that the court should take is welfare, without any gloss—but that decision might, in the right case, be taken on an interim basis and in a relatively summary manner, pending a fuller determination of the merits of the relocation. For primary carers, therefore, the law seems to provide little incentive to make an application for court permission to relocate within the UK since, unless the other parent is able to act very quickly following a move, the chances of the parent being ordered to return the child are small.[370]

The position is potentially different if a non-primary carer takes a child unilaterally to another part of the country. Here, if the main carer acts quickly enough (within 24 to 48 hours), the court has power to order an immediate return without full engagement with the merits, on the basis that it is securing the status quo ante pending any contested hearing.[371] This approach can also be used if a parent simply refuses to return a child to the main carer after spending time with them, even if the non-resident parent has not relocated, but in any case it requires the main carer to act swiftly.

11.8.2.c Relocation cases in practice

Within the field of private law children disputes, relocation cases are probably the starkest decisions which the courts take. Whereas in most areas of child law there is significant scope for compromise and agreement, relocation disputes offer binary choices and it is difficult to find any middle ground.

It is not known how many relocation cases reach the court every year. Proposed international moves are less frequently settled and so are more likely to be determined by a judge than their domestic counterparts,[372] but there are probably more moves within the UK to start with. According to research in 2012, the vast majority of applications (95 per cent) are brought by mothers, and the children involved are typically in middle childhood (ages 4 to 9).[373] In terms of litigated cases, in 2012 two-thirds of proposed international moves and just over 70 per cent of contested domestic moves ended with the relocation being permitted, though a great many factors can be identified which influence outcomes in particular cases.[374] While there are no more recent statistics on case outcomes, practitioners tend to suggest that it has become harder to relocate since the 2012 research was conducted, with applications facing at best 50:50 chances.

[369] [2016] EWCA Civ 1016.

[370] However, see *BB v CC (Residence Order)* [2018] EWFC B78 for an example of a parent being ordered back, though on quite extreme facts. For comparison with the approach to such moves in New Zealand, see Henaghan and Buck (2017).

[371] *Re R (Children: Peremptory Return)* [2011] EWCA Civ 558.

[372] George (2014). [373] George (2015).

[374] Ibid. The factors include child-care arrangements, proposed destination, applicant's and respondent's motivations, and process issues such as whether the parties had lawyers representing them or not.

In research with parents who had been through relocation disputes in the courts, the gendered perspectives in relocation law were apparent.

R. George and A. Gallwey, 'How Do Parents Experience Relocation Disputes in the Family Courts?', (2016) 38 *Journal of Social Welfare and Family Law* 394, 403–4

. . . [O]ne of the main criticisms of English relocation law following *Payne v Payne* was that it was effectively biased in favour of mothers. . . . Mother and fathers [interviewed for the research] saw these issues quite differently . . .

Fathers' perspectives

Amongst the fathers interviewed, the majority were emphatic about the courts being 'biased' towards the mother. . . . [M]en in our study strongly expressed the view that fathers enter into relocation disputes on an unequal footing, many suggesting that the outcome was pre-determined because of an inherent privileging of the mother:

> '*We men know what happens in these cases [. . .] They [the courts] rubber-stamp cases based on the gender of the parents.*' (Steve – unsuccessful father). . . .

By far the most common reference to a generalized sense of injustice was in fathers' frequent mention of *Payne v Payne* as the origin of the legal system's preferential treatment of mothers in the relocation context: '*It was this thing about Payne v Payne*' (John – successful father). For many fathers who talked about *Payne*, the concern was the centrality of the mother's mental health and stability, with a perception at least that it was judged to be in the best interests of children that a mother not be refused relocation if her mental health was seen to be in question. This aspect of the case was commented on by some of the fathers as establishing preferential treatment of mothers . . . [S]ome fathers saw the apparent influence of *Payne* as simply reinforcing the sense that they had of a system which disadvantaged them from the outset because of a broader gender bias. . . . In the face of these interviewees' belief in the injustice underlying the family courts' treatment of fathers, it was perhaps unsurprising that many of them used the language of 'battle' to describe their experiences:

> '*Basically she decided to go to war on me for that . . . It's really been like a full-out war.*' (Christian – unsuccessful father).
>
> '*I'm pretty sure that the fact the mum was not on top of her game gave me a chance. . . . You need to go step-by-step, fight every battle, win every battle . . . So that's why you need to think about battles, to win battle after battle.*' (Leon – successful father).

It is clear that fathers expressed these views in this research regardless of whether they were successful in their cases or not. Mothers' views were similarly unaffected by the outcome of their case, but showed quite different impressions of the law compared to the fathers.

Mothers' perspectives

In direct contrast to the view expressed by fathers that the courts were bias[ed] towards the mother, the majority of female interviewees held the opposite view, that the father was in a privileged position and that instead of an absence of paternal rights, it was the rights of the father which held centre stage:

> *'I think the judge would have loved to have found in favour of the father. That's the impression I got.'* (Eileen – successful mother)
>
> *'There is definitely a push to provide whatever the father wants really.'* (Celine – successful mother). . . .

> The accusation from fathers that mothers were given a privileged position in the courts was strongly challenged by many female interviewees, who instead felt that their experience being the 'primary carer' of their children was overlooked in terms of its significance and insight into their children's needs . . . Despite the importance that they placed on this aspect of their lives, many female participant felt that the courts and other aspects of the system gave no credit to it. . . . Despite winning her case, Emily felt that the whole system was like *'an old boys' club'*; as she explained, *'you've got a whole group of men—and you have to remember, I'm the only woman in the room—who all think Richard is "a lovely chap"'*.
>
> As well as female interviewees perceiving their status as mothers to be negated by the courts, they also saw their choices as regards their relationship and employment status as mothers become the source of direct moral judgment by legal professionals, judges and expartners. Much of the moral judgment used to condemn women revolved around their engagement with paid work whilst being a mother.

Other studies have also included children as part of their research. Parkinson and Cashmore's five-year study of relocation disputes in Australia included 80 parents and 33 children who were interviewed to gain an understanding of their perspectives. In this extract, the authors are discussing the views expressed by the children in their study about the idea of relocating, though it may be noted that, due to the distances involved, a high proportion of relocation cases in Australia involve moves elsewhere within the country.

P. Parkinson and J. Cashmore, 'Relocation and the Indissolubility of Parenthood', (2018) 15 *Journal of Child Custody* 76, 85

> When asked about their attitudes to the potential move, children varied considerably in their views. Some were fine with moving, or supported the mother in her decision that relocating would be best. For some, this represented a choice of an attachment to a person over attachment to a place, and if their mother wanted to move, then they would adapt. For example, 16-year-old Michael was unhappy about the idea of moving about 1,500 miles away with his mother because he did not want to change school. His mother gave him the option of living with his father, but this was a less palatable alternative for him than moving. For others, the move represented a chance to move to a better or more interesting place, with what was perceived to be a better school or which offered new recreational opportunities.
>
> Others were resistant to the move. For example, Lachlan, age 9, was very opposed to his mother's move because it involved leaving his friends and sports team. He was not reconciled to the move at the first interview some nine months after it occurred.
>
> Differences between siblings about the relocation issue were not at all unusual. Lachlan's older brother, 13-year-old Wayne, could see both advantages and disadvantages. Melinda, aged 10, did not want to move, although she found it very hard to tell her mother this. She felt very close to both parents, was happy in an equal time arrangement and was stressed about being caught up in the conflict between her parents. In contrast, her younger sister Zoe, aged 8, found it hard to go "backwards and forwards" between her parents and wanted to live most of the time with her mother. She wanted to move as well.

Parkinson and Cashmore go on to discuss children's adaptation to the relocation decision. Unsurprisingly, they found a mixed experience, and 'while all of [the children who moved] eventually adjusted locationally, some at least found it more difficult to adjust relationally'.[375] They suggest that a significant factor in terms of children's adjustment was the strength of the child's relationship with the non-moving parent before the relocation took place.

> Children's perspectives and experiences, and the diversity of both, suggest a number of factors the courts need to take into account in making relocation decisions. The first consideration is the need to differentiate between children's interests and parents' interests, at least to some extent. What for a parent might involve the return to the familiar and comfortable, might for the child, involve moving to the unfamiliar or unknown. . . .
>
> Secondly, careful attention needs to be paid to the closeness (or otherwise) of children's relationships with nonresident parents, particularly in the case of primary school age children and younger. Relationships with stepparents also need to be explored. It should of course, not be assumed that a child has a close relationship with the nonresident parent; but where that relationship is a close one, the question of whether and how that relationship can be sustained looms large. It is the quality of the relationship rather than the amount of time that children spend with their nonresident parents that is associated with children's wellbeing . . ., but a certain amount of time together and opportunity to be involved in the life of the child, is a precondition for a parent to play a developmentally important role . . .
>
> In making decisions regarding relocation, careful assessment of the quality of the relationship between the nonresident parent and the child, and the capacity of that parent to offer consistent and positive involvement with the upbringing of the child, is critical . . . Important too is an assessment of whether the nonresident parent could move as well in those cases where the motivation for the resident parent's move is not simply to get away from the other parent. From the child's point of view, it is the relationship which is important, not the location.
>
> Thirdly, consideration needs to be given to the plans for travel and the mode of travel if the relocation occurs. While the parent may travel to visit the child, it was much more common for the child to visit the parent because of the cost of renting a hotel room or apartment and a car in the mother's location. Children who travelled by plane reported no difficulty in so doing; indeed, some said they enjoyed it. However, for some other children, the travel was very burdensome.

11.8.3 CHANGING A CHILD'S NAME

Another issue addressed using SIOs or PSOs under s 8 is the change of a child's name. Section 13 of the CA 1989 provides that, where a 'live with' CAO is in force, no one may change a child's *surname* without the permission of all those with PR or an order of the court. However, as with relocation which is also addressed in s 13, it is increasingly clear that the issue of a child's name—both forename and surname—is a 'significant' issue within the scope of PR where consultation and agreement are required whether an order is in place or not.[376]

[375] Parkinson and Cashmore (2018), 86.

[376] See 10.5.1.

Re B and C (Change of Names: Parental Responsibility: Evidence) [2017] EWHC 3250

COBB J:

33. A surname defines, and is defined by, familial heritage and genealogy. A person's forename invariably identifies gender, and often personifies culture, religion, ethnicity, class, social or political ideology. A forename and surname together represent a person's essential identity. From very earliest childhood, one's name is an intrinsic part of who you are, and who you become. Thus, the naming of a child "is not a trivial matter but an important matter", and any change in the name "is not a question to be resolved without regard to the child's welfare" (*Dawson v Wearmouth* [1999] UKHL 18 per Lord MacKay). Where two or more people have parental responsibility for a child then one of those people can only lawfully cause a change of surname if all other people having parental responsibility consent or agree, or the court otherwise orders.

Probably because it features expressly in the CA 1989, the issue of change of a child's surname received earlier attention from the courts. The principles to be applied in determining a dispute over a child's surname were set out by Butler-Sloss LJ in *Re W (A Child) (Illegitimate Child: Change of Surname)*.

Re W (A Child) (Illegitimate Child: Change of Surname) [2001] Fam 1 (CA)

BUTLER-SLOSS LJ:

9. The present position, in summary, would appear to be as follows.

(a) If parents are married they both have the power and the duty to register their child's names.

(b) If they are not married the mother has the sole duty and power to do so.

(c) After registration of the child's names, the grant of a residence order obliges any person wishing to change the surname to obtain the leave of the court or the written consent of all those who have parental responsibility.

(d) In the absence of a residence order, the person wishing to change the surname from the registered name ought to obtain the relevant written consent or the leave of the court by making an application for a specific issue order.

(e) On any application, the welfare of the child is paramount, and the judge must have regard to the s 1(3) criteria.

(f) Among the factors to which the court should have regard is the registered surname of the child and the reasons for the registration, for instance recognition of the biological link with the child's father. Registration is always a relevant and an important consideration but it is not in itself decisive. The weight to be given to it by the court will depend upon the other relevant factors or valid countervailing reasons which may tip the balance the other way.

(g) The relevant considerations should include factors which may arise in the future as well as the present situation.

(h) Reasons given for changing or seeking to change a child's name based on the fact that the child's name is or is not the same as the parent making the application do not generally carry much weight.

(i) The reasons for an earlier unilateral decision to change a child's name may be relevant.

(j) Any changes of circumstances of the child since the original registration may be relevant.

(k) In the case of a child whose parents were married to each other, the fact of the marriage is important and I would suggest that there would have to be strong reasons to change the name from the father's surname if the child was so registered.

(l) Where the child's parents were not married to each other, the mother has control over registration. Consequently on an application to change the surname of the child, the degree of commitment of the father to the child, the quality of contact, if it occurs, between father and child, the existence or absence of parental responsibility are all relevant factors to take into account.

The Court of Appeal has consistently reiterated the value of these guidelines, while emphasizing that the factors identified by Butler-Sloss LJ should not be seen as a straitjacket because ultimately '[t]he test is welfare, pure and simple'.[377]

While this line of authority—like s 13 itself—focuses only on a child's surname, there is 'a growing recognition that a forename or given name is no less significant'.[378] The court has held that the principles set out in *Re W (A Child) (Illegitimate Child: Change of Surname)* are, in general, also applicable to changes of a child's forename—though, of course, considerations of the child having the same family name as one or both parent are not relevant to the issue of forenames. That said, for some children, forenames can have particular significance in terms of family and identity, as King LJ has pointed out: 'The sharing of a forename with a parent or grandparent or bearing a forename which readily identifies a child as belonging to his or her particular religious or cultural background, can be a source of great pride to a child and give him or her an important sense of "belonging" which will be invaluable throughout his or her life.'[379] Consequently, the longer a child has had a particular name and been associated with it, the more powerful the reasons will need to be for seeking to change it.[380]

11.9 CONCLUSION

The law on private disputes over children gives rise to a wide range of issues, bringing into sharp relief many of the key themes discussed in the previous three chapters. The courts are routinely called upon to grapple with such fundamental questions as the appropriate parenting roles of mothers and fathers; whether biological or social parenting should be

377 *Re W (Children) (Change of Name)* [2013] EWCA Civ 1488, [13]. In *Re F (Children: Contact, Name, Parental Responsibility)* [2014] EWFC 42, the mother sought to change the children's surname to protect them from the effects of detrimental material that the father published about them and the mother online.

378 *Re B and C (Change of Names: Parental Responsibility: Evidence)* [2017] EWHC 3250, [36].

379 *Re C (Child in Care: Choice of Forename)* [2016] EWCA Civ 374, [40]. Note that *Re C* was an application under the High Court's inherent jurisdiction: s 9(1) of the CA 1989 prevented an SIO being made because the child was in local authority care.

380 *Re B and C (Change of Names: Parental Responsibility: Evidence)* [2017] EWHC 3250, [36].

prioritized; whether the 'bi-nuclear' or 'reconstituted' family is the more secure basis for post-separation parenting; whether multiple parenting figures can be sustained; and the ways in which alternative family forms, such as gay and lesbian parenting, require new ways of thinking about family relationships. In searching for the answers to these questions, the courts are required to make the child's welfare their paramount consideration. However, nothing demonstrates the vagaries of the welfare principle more effectively than the shifts in the courts' approach to these disputes over the last 60 years. Whilst some evolution of judicial thinking is to be expected, and indeed applauded, in line with the best available evidence on the developmental needs and outcomes for children living in separated families, the case law and legislative reforms considered in this chapter highlight the extent to which these trends are often driven by social and political factors well beyond the control of the courts. Thus, whilst orthodox wisdom used to dictate the importance of mothering over fathering, social over biological parenting, and the reconstituted over the 'bi-nuclear' family, various social and political factors have converged to transform these trends so that what we now see, at least in the post-divorce or post-separation context, is a dramatic reversal in the fortunes of one figure: the genetic father. Although there may be some disquiet that the highly politicized debate surrounding fathers' rights has distorted many of the underlying issues, the greater value placed on genetic fathering is not necessarily a cause for concern. Indeed, it may be something to be welcomed. However, in such a highly charged political atmosphere as that generated by some fathers' rights groups, the courts must ensure they do not become distracted by this powerful and often superficially persuasive rhetoric. Decision-making in the courts must remain firmly focused on the needs and interests of the individual child.

ONLINE RESOURCES

Questions, suggestions for further reading, and supplementary materials for this chapter (including updates on developments in this area of family law since this book was published) may be found in the online resources at **www.oup.com/he/familytcm5e.**

12

CHILD PROTECTION

CENTRAL ISSUES

1. Child protection is a challenging topic. It requires the state to strike a difficult balance between respecting the integrity of the family whilst ensuring vulnerable family members are protected. Tragic cases attracting strong media interest serve as a constant reminder of the dangers of under and over-reacting to suspicions of abuse.
2. Part III of the Children Act 1989 (CA 1989) in England, and parts of the Social Services and Well-Being (Wales) Act 2014 in Wales, seek to support families through the provision of voluntary services to 'children in need'. These aims will be seriously compromised if local authorities are under-resourced.
3. The state cannot remove children from their parents' care on the basis of a simple best interests test: a threshold involving 'significant harm' must first be established. The threshold for state intervention at various stages of the child protection process has been extremely controversial.
4. Concern regarding the impact of delay on children suffering significant harm led to a strong drive towards securing speedier and more robust decision-making by professionals and an emphasis on securing permanency for looked after children within a more tightly defined timetable. However, resource constraints and impacts from the Covid-19 pandemic have had serious impacts on delay.
5. The Human Rights Act 1998 (HRA 1998) has reinforced the importance of children's and parents' rights throughout the child protection process, necessitating some changes to both substantive law and procedure.

12.1 INTRODUCTION

The death of a child at the hands of their parents always engenders strong feelings. When that child is known to be at risk and is supposedly under the care and protection of the state, the child's death attracts great public anger and concern. Kimberley Carlile, Victoria Climbié, Peter Connelly, Khyra Ishaq, and Keanu Williams are just some of the children who have died in such tragic circumstances.[1] Finding answers to what went wrong and, more importantly, how such deaths can be prevented is exceptionally difficult. Deception and manipulation by the child's parents, the optimism of social workers, the complacency of health professionals and teachers, overworked, inexperienced, and poorly trained staff, and a serious lack of local authority (LA) resources are all too familiar stories. However, even the best resourced, trained, and supported professionals would not be able to prevent the death of every child at risk of harm from abusive parents. Child protection is an inherently difficult process. Every case requires a delicate balancing exercise to be performed between respecting and supporting the integrity of the family whilst ensuring vulnerable family members are protected. A strong, robust, and highly interventionist approach by professionals can be just as harmful as the 'hands-off' complacency which marked the cases of Victoria Climbié and Peter Connelly.[2] The unjustified removal of large numbers of children in Cleveland in 1987, Rochdale in 1990, and Orkney in 1991 because of misplaced suspicions of ritualized sexual abuse provides a chilling reminder of the dangers of misguided, 'crusading', albeit well-meaning, professionals.[3] Although state intervention into the family is not necessarily a bad thing—indeed, help offered to the family by the LA on a consensual basis can be both positive and supportive, and children may need protecting from serious harm at home—it is important to remember that inappropriate removal of a child can be devastating.[4]

The legal framework provided by the CA 1989 has to ensure that child protection professionals can respond quickly and effectively to children at risk of harm, whilst guarding against unnecessary and potentially harmful intervention into the family.[5] It is a difficult balance, exacerbated by the increasingly difficult and challenging environment in which the child protection system operates. Against a backdrop of severe budgetary constraints on LAs and the courts, there has been a dramatic increase in the number of LA applications for care orders—until 2008, the number of children who were the subject of care applications was relatively stable at around 20,000 per year; after an initial jump to just under 26,000 children in 2009, the number was over 30,000 every year between 2016 and 2019 before dropping back slightly.[6] The reasons for this are complex:[7] the rise was driven initially both by social work reaction to the public outcry following the death of Peter Connelly in 2007 and a perception amongst policy-makers that social workers waited too long before initiating legal proceedings to secure the removal of a child from abusive and neglectful parents;[8] more recently, the situation has probably been exacerbated by reduced LA resources for support and prevention work, meaning that more cases reach the level of seriousness to justify court action. The most recent drop is probably connected to the pandemic, but the exact causes are unclear.

At the same time, it cannot be forgotten that families facing the removal of their children are often themselves intensely vulnerable, with mothers in particular suffering from a myriad of problems necessitating professional understanding, intervention, and support.[9] These ever increasing demands brought the child protection system to crisis point, characterized by systemic delay (care proceedings in 2011 took a mean of 55.1 weeks to complete)[10]

[1] For short accounts of some of these cases, see Cretney (2003a), ch 20.
[2] Laming (2003).
[3] Butler-Sloss (1988).
[4] For a striking example, see *Re W (Children)* [2009] EWCA Civ 59.
[5] Unless otherwise stated, all references to statutory provisions in this chapter are to the CA 1989.
[6] MOJ (2022a), table 2.
[7] For an excellent summary of the issues by the President of the Family Division, see McFarlane (2018); see also Trowler (2018).
[8] See Norgrove (2011), 91; House of Commons Select Committee on Education (2012/13); Trowler (2018).
[9] Masson, Pearce, and Bader (2008), 20; Richardson and Brammer (2020); Alrouh et al (2022).
[10] MOJ (2022a), table 8.

and poor decision-making. The 2011 Family Justice Review ('Norgrove') described it as 'a system that is not a system, characterised by mutual distrust and lack of leadership, by incoherence and without solid evidence based knowledge about how it really works. The consequence for children is unconscionable delay.'[11] Norgrove made a number of recommendations to address these problems, which were accepted by government and are now enshrined within the Children and Families Act 2014 (CFA 2014), the most notable of which were: a statutory time limit for the disposal of care proceedings of 26 weeks; a more restricted approach to the use of expert evidence; and a reduced role for the judiciary in the scrutiny of care plans.[12] After initially reducing the mean length of care cases to 27 weeks, by 2021 it was back to 44.4 weeks (see Figure 12.1), with just 23 per cent of cases completed within the statutory time limit.[13] There is no getting away from the fact that 'resource shortages in the courts have played a major part in the delays',[14] and it remains to be seen whether the President's 'campaign' to re-launch the drive to achieve the 26-week timetable in January 2023 will be effective.[15]

While we should be careful not to assume that achieving the 26-week timetable is, in itself, an indicator of 'success' in care proceedings,[16] these delays are a cause of huge concern, reflecting the enormous continuing pressures on the child protection system. Not only are there more court cases, but increasingly many commence as emergency applications which means that the pre-proceedings work—that can either avoid the need for care proceedings at all or, at least, better prepare everyone for them—does not happen.[17] The number of children receiving LA help outside the court system also continues to increase—in England,

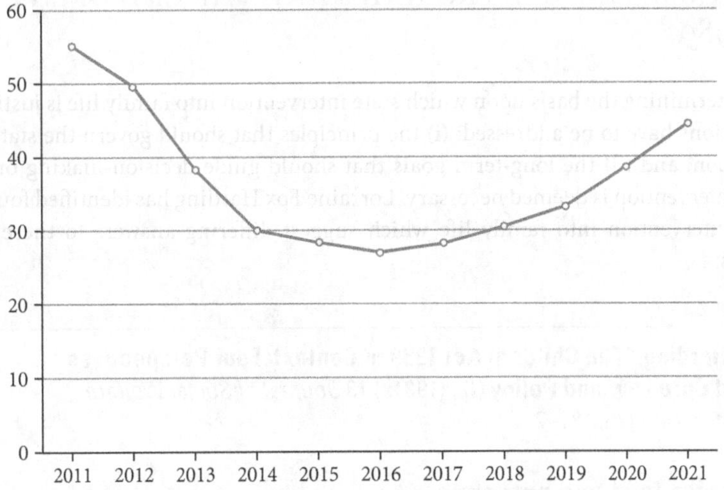

Figure 12.1 Mean duration (weeks) of care proceedings in England and Wales, 2011–21
Source: MOJ (2022a).

[11] Norgrove (2011), 3. Subsequent reforms have done little to create a coherent 'system': House of Lords Select Committee on the Children and Families Act 2014 (2022), para 119.

[12] CFA 2014, ss 13–15. See generally Masson (2015). On care plans, see 12.5.5.

[13] MOJ (2022a), table 8.

[14] House of Lords Select Committee on the Children and Families Act 2014 (2022), para 111.

[15] McFarlane (2022b).

[16] House of Lords Select Committee on the Children and Families Act 2014 (2022), para 107.

[17] Public Law Working Group (2021), para 45.

over 50,000 children were put onto child protection plans in 2021, and over 400,00 children were classified as 'in need' but were neither the subject of a child protection plan nor court proceedings.[18] The situation was already thought to be a 'crisis' in 2016,[19] though by now it must be seen as 'a continuing open-ended situation'.[20] In other words, the problems are chronic, not acute, and there is no reason to think that they will be resolved any time soon.

Within the context of this challenging environment, this chapter considers the law governing state intervention into family life where a child is considered to be 'in need' or at risk of harm. We begin by outlining the competing approaches to state intervention and the principles underpinning the CA 1989. We then examine the legal framework governing voluntary state intervention for children in need in England under Part III of the CA 1989,[21] before considering the law and procedure regulating compulsory intervention into family life by means of care proceedings under Part IV. We conclude by considering the various emergency and interim measures available to protect a child thought to be at risk of immediate harm—although in practice emergency and interim orders arise prior to the main orders, the legal concepts that apply to such measures are better understood once the detail of care proceedings has been set out.

12.2 PRINCIPLES OF STATE INTERVENTION INTO FAMILY LIFE

12.2.1 COMPETING APPROACHES AND THE CHILDREN ACT 1989

When determining the basis upon which state intervention into family life is justified, two key questions have to be addressed: (i) the principles that should govern the state's initial intervention; and (ii) the long-term goals that should guide decision-making once some form of intervention is deemed necessary. Lorraine Fox Harding has identified four models of state intervention into family life which suggest differing answers to these two key questions:

L. Fox Harding, 'The Children Act 1989 in Context: Four Perspectives in Child Care Law and Policy (I)', (1991a) 13 *Journal of Social Welfare and Family Law* 179, 181–2

(1) Laissez-faire and patriarchy

The term *laissez-faire* is used here to describe the perspective which sees the role of the state in child care as ideally one of minimal intervention, while the privacy and sanctity of the original family should in most circumstances be respected. However, in *extreme* cases

[18] DFE (2022b).
[19] See, e.g., Munby (2016); Ryan and Tunnard (2018); Broadhurst and Harwin (2020).
[20] McFarlane (2018), 2.
[21] In Wales, this is governed by the Social Services and Well-Being (Wales) Act 2014.

of poor parental care, state intervention is not only acceptable but preferably of a strong and authoritative kind, transferring the child from the original parent(s) to a secure substitute placement with a new set of parent figures. The new family unit should then be accorded the same rights, and respect by the state, as the original one . . .

(2) State paternalism and child protection

The terms "state paternalism and child protection" are taken to indicate a school of thought which favours much more extensive state intervention to protect children from poor parental care. Where parental care is deemed inadequate, then in this perspective finding the child a new permanent home where good quality care will be provided is usually the appropriate response. Therefore the rights and liberties of parents and the integrity of the original birth family are given a low priority in this perspective; while the welfare of the child, as this is construed, is paramount.

(3) The defence of the birth family and parents' rights

A third, pro-birth family perspective encapsulates the idea that birth or biological families are extremely important both for children and parents, and should be maintained wherever possible. Where families have to be separated through children entering substitute care, then parent-child links should usually be kept up. The role of the state is seen as, ideally, neither paternalist nor *laissez-faire*, but positively supportive of families, providing various services that they need to function well and remain together. At the same time, class, poverty and deprivation are seen as important elements in child care, explaining much of what appears to be inadequate parenting, while the (usually coercive) response of the state is disproportionately directed to lower class and deprived families.

(4) Children's rights and child liberation

The terms "children's rights and child liberation" are used here for a perspective which emphasises the importance of *the child's* own viewpoint and wishes, seeing the child as a separate entity with rights to autonomy and freedom, rather like an adult. The idea of the control of children, either through the state or by adults individually, is called into question by the emphasis on rights and liberation, as therefore are notions of custody and parental rights. The strength and competence of children, and their similarity to adults, are emphasised, rather than their vulnerability; children are not seen as in need of protection, but empowerment; but it is not clear how far children would be expected to carry the burdens and duties of adult status as well. A less extreme position would emphasise that children should at least have more say in what happens to them.

Fox Harding contends that elements of all four approaches can be identified in the CA 1989, albeit she argues that paternalism and defence of the birth parents' rights predominate.[22] Indeed, these were strong themes in the government's Review of Child Care Law preceding the legislation. The importance placed on preserving the integrity of the birth family and supporting it wherever possible both before and after intervention was particularly clear.

[22] Fox Harding (1991b), 299.

DHSS, *Review of Child Care Law. Report to Ministers of an Interdepartmental Working Party* (London: HMSO, 1985)

2.8 A distinction is often drawn between the interests of children and the interests of their parents. In the great majority of families, including those who are for one reason or another in need of social services, this distinction does not exist. The interests of the children are best served by their remaining with their families and the interests of their parents are best served by allowing them to undertake their natural and legal responsibility to care for their own children. Hence the focus of effort should be to enable and assist parents to discharge those responsibilities. Even where a child has to spend some time away from home, every effort should be made to maintain and foster links between the child and his family to care for the child in partnership with rather than in opposition to his parents, and to work towards his return to them.

As Fox Harding notes, the emphasis placed on providing extensive state *support* for the birth family is surprising.[23] Given the CA 1989 was sponsored by a Conservative Government whose political ideology traditionally favours protecting the autonomy of the family and affords only a minimal role to the state, a more laissez-faire approach might have been expected. This would also have been more consistent with what some commentators have identified as the 'privatizing' trend underpinning the CA 1989, which, as encapsulated by s 1(5) (the 'no order' principle), seeks to place the primary responsibility for the care and upbringing of children on the child's parents and is generally characterized by a marked withdrawal of the state from family life.[24] None of this is consistent with the imposition of wide-ranging duties on LAs to provide a comprehensive range of services to help and support families in need. Yet, this is what Part III of the CA 1989 purports to do.

Unfortunately, no matter how much help and support is provided, there will always be some families for whom support will have to give way to more coercive forms of intervention. One of the hardest questions in child protection is determining when that point is reached. In recent years, there has been a shift towards earlier and more decisive intervention with a view to securing permanency for the child.[25] Growing concern about the life-chances of children left to 'drift' in and out of care has led to a strong focus on ensuring effective planning for children known to social services and securing long-term alternative placements for those children in care.[26] Given the evidence regarding the woeful life-experiences and long-term prospects of 'looked after' children,[27] this emphasis on the importance of permanency planning, even at the potential expense of long-term engagement with the birth family, is understandable. However, as Norgrove recognizes, this drive towards permanency

[23] Ibid. [24] Bainham and Gilmore (2013), 82.

[25] House of Commons Select Committee on Education (2012/13); House of Lords Select Committee on Adoption Legislation (2013), paras 56–87.

[26] See, e.g., House of Lords Select Committee on Adoption Legislation, ibid and DFE (2013). On decision-making and outcomes for young children under 12 months old deemed to be suffering or likely to suffer significant harm, see Ward et al (2010) and Broadhurst et al (2018).

[27] E.g. Cailes (2018), extracted at 12.3.3; *Re B-P (Children: Adoption or Fostering)* [2018] EWCA Civ 2042, [15].

within much tighter timescales can be difficult to reconcile with perceptions as to birth parents' rights:

D. Norgrove (Chair), *Family Justice Review: Final Report* (London: MOJ, 2011), 13

> The system struggles to cope with the weight of its responsibilities. Understandable sympathy for parents and an acute awareness of the enormity of the decisions encourages a wish to explore every avenue. The idea of a proportionate approach comes across as seeming to risk denial of the parent's right to a fair hearing. We were told and we agree that the right of the parents to a fair hearing has come too often to override the paramount welfare of the child.

12.2.2 THE HUMAN RIGHTS DIMENSION

The fundamental rights of the child and the parents must be safeguarded throughout the child protection process. From the child's perspective, two key rights under the European Convention on Human Rights (ECHR) are engaged: Article 3 and Article 8.[28] These provisions impose positive obligations on the state to protect a child from parental abuse. Clearly, the state cannot provide absolute guarantees against the abuse of children. Given the secretive nature of child abuse, particularly sexual abuse, many incidences of abuse will go undetected without any degree of fault or responsibility resting with state officials. Even in those cases known to the LA, the need to prioritize and allocate scare resources means that the protection afforded to individual children cannot ever be absolute. However, the European Court of Human Rights has held that under Articles 3 and 8 the state owes individual children a positive duty as regards the detection, investigation, and management of child abuse.[29] That obligation includes the need to remove children from situations of known risk where appropriate.[30]

However, as the European Court also recognizes, where the LA is or should be aware that a child is at risk, it is not a straightforward matter of simply removing the child.[31] In all of these cases, children have important countervailing rights: whilst ensuring the child is adequately protected against abuse, the state must also respect the integrity of the child's family. In particular, when considering what child protection measures are necessary, Article 8 requires the state to take all necessary steps to ensure that any measures of intervention are proportionate to the harm suffered and that no child is unnecessarily removed from the care of their family. It is a difficult line for the LA to tread. Both over-reacting (removing without good cause) and under-reacting (failing to remove) may give rise to liability under s 7 of the HRA 1998 or (at the suit of the child) in common law negligence.[32]

[28] See also United Nations Convention on the Rights of the Child 1989 (UNCRC), Art 19. For the impact of human rights law on child protection, see Kaganas (2010).

[29] See generally Fenton-Glynn (2021), ch 10.

[30] *Z v United Kingdom* (App No 29392/95, ECHR) (2001). [31] Ibid, [74].

[32] *TP and KM v United Kingdom* (App No 28945/95, ECHR) (2001). See also *D v East Berkshire Community Health NHS Trust* [2003] EWCA Civ 1151.

The child's parents enjoy similar rights under the ECHR.[33] The European Court has consistently stressed that under Article 8 the state has both negative and positive obligations towards the child's parents.

Haase v Germany (App No 11057/02, ECHR) (2005)

90. . . . While the authorities enjoy a wide margin of appreciation in assessing the necessity of taking a child into care, in particular where an emergency situation arises, the Court must still be satisfied in the particular case that there existed circumstances justifying the removal of the child, and it is for the respondent State to establish that a careful assessment of the impact of the proposed care measure on the parents and the child, as well as of the possible alternatives to taking the child into public care, was carried out prior to implementation of such a measure . . .

92. Following any removal into care, a stricter scrutiny is called for in respect of any further limitations by the authorities, for example on restrictions on parental rights and access, and on any legal safeguards designed to secure the effective protection of the right of parents and children to respect for their family life. Such further limitations entail the danger that the family relations between the parents and a young child might be effectively curtailed . . .

93. The taking into care of a child should normally be regarded as a temporary measure to be discontinued as soon as circumstances permit, and any measures of implementation of temporary care should be consistent with the ultimate aim of reuniting the natural parent and child . . . In this regard a fair balance has to be struck between the interests of the child remaining in care and those of the parent in being reunited with the child . . . In carrying out this balancing exercise, the Court will attach particular importance to the best interests of the child which, depending on their nature and seriousness, may override those of the parent . . . In particular, a parent cannot be entitled under Article 8 to have such measures taken as would harm the child's health and development . . .

94. Whilst Article 8 contains no explicit procedural requirements, the decision-making process involved in measures of interference must be fair and such as to ensure due respect for the interests safeguarded by Article 8. The Court must therefore determine whether, having regard to the circumstances of the case and notably the importance of the decisions to be taken, the applicants have been involved in the decision-making process, seen as a whole, to a degree sufficient to provide them with the requisite protection of their interests . . .

The judiciary have broadly welcomed the reception of a rights-based discourse into the public law on children.[34] The right to respect for family life reinforces the importance of preserving the integrity of the family unit which has long formed a core principle of child protection policy. The courts have thus issued strong warnings as to the need for fundamental changes in the prevailing 'culture' and 'mindset' of LAs, demanding far-reaching improvements in both the procedural and substantive aspects of LA decision-making before, during, and after formal care proceedings.[35] With the Article 8 rights of the child and

[33] *RK and AK v United Kingdom* (App No 38000/05, ECHR) (2008) and *MAK and RK v United Kingdom* (App Nos 45901/05 and 40146/06, ECHR) (2010). Note, however, that whilst the parents may bring a claim under the HRA 1998, domestic authorities have yet to find that the LA owes them a duty of care under common law negligence, at least if they are the suspected perpetrators of the abuse: *D v East Berkshire Community Health NHS Trust* [2005] UKHL 23.

[34] See further Harris-Short (2005), 340–50.

[35] *Re G (Care: Challenge to Local Authority's Decision)* [2003] EWHC 551; *Re L (Care: Assessment: Fair Trial)* [2002] EWHC 1379.

the parents engaged, ECHR arguments are now a routine feature of public law cases and form an *explicit* part of the judge's reasoning.[36] Indeed, arguments over alleged breaches of Articles 6 and 8 ECHR are so commonly made that some judges have expressed concern that human rights arguments are hindering LA applications and causing unnecessary expense and delay.[37]

12.2.3 THE PROBLEM OF RESOURCES

The strong protection given to the parents' rights under Article 8 makes the shift in favour of permanency planning at the potential expense of repeated attempts at rehabilitation with the birth family all the more surprising. However, it is arguable that given the severe fiscal restraints of recent years, the government's emphasis on permanency planning is driven more by pragmatic concerns than any major ideological shift in child protection policy. A model of state intervention based on providing a range of effective support services to families in need is resource-intensive, requiring large-scale investment in LA services. Without such investment, an approach focusing on supporting the birth family is likely to fail.[38] This is an issue where idealism meets head-on the harsh economic realities of life. The serious problem of poorly resourced LAs[39] means there is a tendency to divert resources away from voluntary family support services to deal with the more serious and immediate problems of children requiring compulsory care.[40] An LA culture of crisis intervention is thereby perpetuated,[41] with less focus on support services which might prevent children needing to be involved in care proceedings.[42] Keenan argues that inadequate funding is a key factor behind a more hard-line, authoritarian approach to child protection.[43]

12.3 STATE SUPPORT FOR CHILDREN AND FAMILIES IN ENGLAND UNDER PART III

Part III of the CA 1989[44] enshrines the then Conservative Government's commitment to promoting the upbringing of children within their birth families by the provision of help and support to families in need.

[36] *EH v Greenwich London Borough Council* [2010] EWCA Civ 344; *Re M and B (Children) (Care Proceedings: Family Life)* [2010] EWCA Civ 821; *Re T (Placement Order)* [2018] EWCA Civ 650.

[37] *Re V (Care: Pre-Birth Actions)* [2004] EWCA Civ 1575; *Re J (A Child) (Care Proceedings: Fair Trial)* [2006] EWCA Civ 545.

[38] McPherson (2018).

[39] See, e.g., Butler (2018); House of Lords Select Committee on the Children and Families Act 2014 (2022), paras 111–12. While problems have worsened significantly in the age of 'austerity', funding has long been an issue: see *R (G) v Barnet London Borough Council* [2003] UKHL 57, [10].

[40] Bainham and Gilmore (2013), 468.

[41] See generally, Smith (2002); Public Law Working Group (2021), paras 53–5.

[42] This is particularly problematic given that around a quarter of mothers involved in care proceedings will then be involved in a further set of proceedings (usually relating to later children) within seven years: Cox et al (2017).

[43] Keenan (2006), 48.

[44] Since April 2016, Part III has applied only to England, with the position in Wales now regulated by the Social Services and Well-Being (Wales) Act 2014 (SSWB(W)A 2014). While many of the provisions are similar or identical, there are notable differences. We highlight some differences in the text, but space precludes us considering the position in Wales in detail.

In accordance with the principle that 'prevention is better than cure',[45] this part of the CA 1989 brings together a wide range of services aimed at ensuring that children's needs are met within their families before more coercive intervention becomes necessary. 'Partnership' is the 'buzz word' of these provisions.[46] Intervention under Part III should be non-coercive, based on mutual cooperation, and, most importantly, voluntarily accepted by the parents. The government was keen to remove any stigma attached to receiving help from the LA, stressing that the provision of services under Part III should be viewed as a positive, supportive measure for the family, not a sign of 'parental shortcomings' or failure.[47] To emphasize the distinction between these services and any compulsory measures taken within the context of care proceedings under Part IV, all coercive measures that the state could formerly take without recourse to the court were removed.[48] In practice, this marked a significant erosion of state power and an important correlative strengthening of parents' rights.[49]

Before the CA 1989, the provision of support and assistance to families in need was contained within a complicated patchwork of legislative provisions.[50] One of the major aims of the CA 1989 was to rationalize and consolidate the legal basis for the provision of services into one comprehensive, coherent piece of legislation.[51] As a result of this consolidation process, the scope of Part III is extremely broad. It covers a wide and disparate range of children's needs, from the provision of assistance and respite care for disabled children to long-term accommodation of children in need as a result of parental neglect.

While support services are accessed by children and families in a wide range of situations, one common scenario is in relation to children who are 'on the edge of care', where the provision of services under Part III may avoid the need for compulsory intervention.[52] 'Edge of care' cases can raise particular challenges. On the one hand, appropriate support can avoid the need for formal proceedings and potentially keep families together. On the other hand, depending on the nature of the support provided, LAs can risk criticism for relying on 'voluntary' arrangements in situations where care proceedings should have been initiated, one particular concern being the lack of procedural safeguards in relation to services provided under Part III.[53] There is also a group of 'edge of care' cases where the LA's involvement is entirely 'behind the scenes':

M. Harding and A. Newnham, 'Section 8 Orders on the Public-Private Divide', (2017) 39 *Journal of Social Welfare and Family Law* 83, 85, 92

In the sample examined, two different types of hybrid case are identified. In 'hybrid solution' cases the application for a private law order was made at the instigation of a private individual but, because of ongoing local authority involvement with the family, the private order formed part of a local authority managed solution for the family. In 'diversion cases' the application was made on the advice or insistence of the local authority. In these cases the local authorities were encouraging or at least endorsing a private law order as an alternative to care proceedings or voluntary accommodation.

[45] Bainham and Gilmore (2013), 27. [46] Ibid, 85. [47] DHSS et al (1987), paras 17, 21.
[48] Bainham and Gilmore (2013), 465. [49] Ibid, 29, on the powers of the state under the pre-1989 law.
[50] Ibid, 27. [51] DHSS et al (1987), paras 7–8.
[52] Masson et al (2013); McPherson (2018). The LA has a positive duty to reduce the need to bring care proceedings: Sch 2, para 7.
[53] See, e.g., *Williams v London Borough of Hackney* [2018] UKSC 37, [52].

The priority for the local authority in all of these cases is to ensure that children are receiving appropriate care. In many of the diversion cases the established primary caregiver could no longer care for the child due to severe mental health issues or drug and alcohol abuse. Using a section 8 order to divert cases from care proceedings or voluntary accommodation is cost effective for the local authority avoiding both the cost of issuing proceedings and the cost of long-term substitute care. . . .

The use of private law orders to divert cases from public law remedies is surely appropriate where parents and carers are in agreement and aware of the legal consequences of the private law order. This channelling of families away from a public law support programme into private law remedies minimises formal state intervention into the family. The children are removed from the care of an unsuitable parent, to be cared for by their other parent, or a relative with whom they have a pre-existing bond. The residence order provides the new carers with some security by giving them parental responsibility. When providing long-term voluntary accommodation to a child, or accommodating a child who is the subject of a care order, the local authority must give preference to relatives, friends or other persons with a previous connection to the child. Therefore, placing a child with a relative who then applies for a section 8 residence order can be seen as a cost-efficient and less interventionist route to the same outcome . . .

However, . . . parents and carers were often unrepresented at court and without legal advice. The choice to utilise a private law order rather than public law remedies may also make a meaningful difference to the level of ongoing support given to parent, children and carers [after the orders are made].

Harding and Newnham note that the LA's involvement in the background of these cases raises questions about the 'voluntariness' of the outcomes reached by families, even where they are presented to the court as consent orders within private law proceedings. This is a theme we return to at 12.3.2 in relation to voluntary accommodation provided by the LA.

12.3.1 THE GENERAL DUTY TO CHILDREN IN NEED: SECTION 17

Section 17(1) sets down the general duty owed by English LAs to children in need.[54]

Children Act 1989, s 17

(1) It shall be the general duty of every local authority (in addition to the other duties imposed on them by this Part)—

(a) to safeguard and promote the welfare of children within their area who are in need; and

(b) so far as is consistent with that duty to promote the upbringing of such children by their families,

by providing a range and level of services appropriate to those children's needs.

[54] In Wales, see SSWB(W)A 2014, s 21.

In order to qualify for the provision of services under s 17, the child must be 'a child in need'. A 'child' is 'a person under the age of eighteen',[55] and the meaning of 'in need' is set down in s 17(10).

Children Act 1989, s 17

(10) For the purposes of this Part a child shall be taken to be in need if—

(a) he is unlikely to achieve or maintain, or to have the opportunity of achieving or maintaining, a reasonable standard of health or development without the provision for him of services by a local authority under this Part;

(b) his health or development is likely to be significantly impaired, or further impaired without the provision for him of such services; or

(c) he is disabled . . .

'Development' is further defined as 'physical, intellectual, emotional, social or behavioural development'.[56] 'Health' is further defined as physical or mental health.[57] The Supreme Court in *R (A) v London Borough of Croydon* held that there are two questions.[58] Whether a particular person is 'a child' or not is a straightforward objective question of fact (to which there is a right and wrong answer) and, in cases of dispute, is to be determined, on the evidence, by the court.[59] By contrast, the question of whether the child is 'in need' involves 'a number of different value judgments' and is thus to be made by the LA, 'subject to the control of the courts on the ordinary principles of judicial review'.[60]

The House of Lords has held that the s 17 duty is a general or 'target' duty owed to all children in need within the LA area.[61] This means there is no specific duty on the LA to carry out an assessment of a child's needs that can be enforced at the suit of an individual child. The Lords also dismissed the argument that the general duty under s 17 'crystallizes' into a specific enforceable duty once the child has been assessed and a particular need identified. However, whilst there is therefore no duty on the LA to provide an assessed service, the LA's refusal can be challenged by way of judicial review.[62] Bearing in mind the policy underpinning the CA 1989, it was held by Munby LJ in *R (VC) v Newcastle City Council*, that an LA's refusal to provide services to a child in need would be subject to 'strict and, it may be, sceptical scrutiny, particularly if there is no available argument based on lack of resources'.[63]

To assist the LA to carry out its s 17(1) duty, Sch 2, Part I sets down a range of more specific duties and powers.[64] These include identifying and assessing children in need within their area,[65] taking reasonable steps to prevent abuse and neglect,[66] taking reasonable steps to prevent the need for care proceedings under Part IV, providing accommodation to a member of the child's household to protect the child from ill-treatment,[67] and providing services for children living at home (including the provision of advice, guidance and counselling, occupational, social, cultural, or recreational activities, home help, and assistance with holidays).[68] Section 17(6) further provides that services may include the provision of

[55] S 105(1). [56] S 17(11). [57] Ibid. [58] [2009] UKSC 8, [26].
[59] Ibid, [27] (Lady Hale); [51], [53] (Lord Hope). [60] Ibid, [26], [28] (Lady Hale).
[61] *R (G) v Barnet London Borough Council* [2003] UKHL 57, [106].
[62] *R (VC) v Newcastle City Council* [2011] EWHC 2673. [63] Ibid, [25]–[26]. [64] S 17(2).
[65] Sch 2, Part I, paras 1 and 3. [66] Ibid, para 4. [67] Ibid, para 5. [68] Ibid, para 8.

accommodation (although a child provided with accommodation under s 17 is not a 'looked after' child), and giving assistance in kind or in cash.[69] Services may be provided to the child or to a member of the child's family. Before determining what, if any, services to provide under this section, the LA must, so far as is reasonably practicable, ascertain and give due consideration to the child's wishes.[70]

12.3.2 PROVIDING ACCOMMODATION FOR A CHILD IN ENGLAND

The importance of LA voluntary accommodation for children—separate from children who are cared for under a court order—should not be underestimated. In recent years, voluntary accommodation has accounted for up to 28 per cent of all children (19,350 children in 2015) looked after by LAs in England, though this had dropped to 17 per cent (13,840 children) in 2022.[71] LAs have both duties and powers to accommodate children under s 20.[72] Unlike accommodation provided under s 17, a key consequence of a child being accommodated under s 20 is that they become a 'looked after' child,[73] which has significant legal implications in terms of the extensive duties owed to the child by the LA.[74]

12.3.2.a The duty to accommodate: s 20(1)

In stark contrast to the wide discretion conferred on the LA under s 17, s 20(1) confers a clear duty on the LA to accommodate a child if certain conditions are met.

Children Act 1989, s 20

(1) Every local authority shall provide accommodation for any child in need within their area who appears to them to require accommodation as a result of—
- (a) there being no person who has parental responsibility for him;
- (b) his being lost or having been abandoned; or
- (c) the person who has been caring for him being prevented (whether or not permanently, and for whatever reason) from providing him with suitable accommodation or care.

In the case of children in need who are over 16 years of age, the duty to provide accommodation will only arise if the LA considers it likely that the child's welfare will be 'seriously prejudiced' if it does not provide the child with accommodation.[75]

[69] S 17(6) was amended by the Adoption and Children Act 2002, s 116 to clarify that accommodation can be provided under s 17. Accommodation must not be provided under s 17 if the LA has a duty to accommodate the child under s 20, because the latter involves greater duties being owed to the child: see 12.3.2.a.
[70] S 17(4A).
[71] DFE (2022a). Note that the percentage is dropping in part because more children are the subject of care orders; the total number of children looked after by local authorities is increasing.
[72] In Wales, see SSWB(W)A 2014, s 76. Note that while s 76 largely replicates CA 1989 s 20, there is no equivalent of subsection (4), (5), or (6) in the Welsh legislation.
[73] Children under care orders are also 'looked after': see 12.5.6. [74] See 12.3.3.
[75] S 20(3). See *Re T (Accommodation by Local Authority)* [1995] 1 FLR 159.

If the LA is under a duty to accommodate a child pursuant to s 20 of the CA 1989, it cannot avoid the more extensive obligations owed to a 'looked after' child by purporting to accommodate the child under some other statutory provision, whether s 17 of the CA 1989 or other provisions such as the Housing Act 1996. The issue has become of particular significance for young people approaching the age of 18 whose entitlement to LA financial and other support services is dependent on whether or not the child is or has been a 'looked after' child under s 20 of the CA 1989. The question of the relationship between a LA's general powers under s 17 and its more specific duty to accommodate a child under s 20 arose in the case *of R (H) v Wandsworth London Borough Council.*[76] Holman J held that in determining whether a duty arises under s 20, the LA may need to exercise judgement over certain matters, such as the relevance of the child's wishes.[77] However, once it has been determined that the s 20 duty arises (or at least should be deemed to have arisen), there is no room for discretion: the LA is bound to act pursuant to that duty.[78] Holman J's approach has subsequently been endorsed by the House of Lords in *R (G) v London Borough of Southwark*[79] and *R (M) v Hammersmith and Fulham London Borough Council.*[80]

It is important to note that the duty imposed on the LA under s 20(1) is a duty to provide accommodation for the *child.* It does not include providing accommodation for members of the child's family. This was made clear by the House of Lords in *R (G) v Barnet London Borough Council.*[81] Two of the three conjoined cases concerned a child who had been assessed as in need of accommodation because the mother had been rendered homeless and was not entitled to assistance under the homelessness legislation. Whilst the LAs were not prepared to accommodate both mother and child under s 17, they were, if necessary, prepared to accommodate the child pursuant to their duties under s 20(1). The appellants contended that this policy was unlawful, arguing that as the LA was under a duty to promote the upbringing of children within their families, s 20(1) should be read as imposing a duty on the LA to house both mother and child together. In support of this argument, the appellants relied on the duty imposed on the LA under the CA 1989 to make arrangements to enable the child to live with, amongst others, a parent unless 'that would not be reasonably practicable or consistent with his welfare'. The majority of the House of Lords rejected this argument:

R (On the Application of G) v Barnet London Borough Council [2003] UKHL 57

LORD HOPE:

102. This brings me to the crucial point in this part of the case, which is whether a local authority looking after a child is under a duty to provide accommodation to any of the persons mentioned in section [22C(3)], who include the child's parent, to enable the child to live with that person. The duty, as expressed in the subsection, is to "make arrangements to enable" the child to live with any one of the persons mentioned. It is qualified by the words "unless

[76] [2007] EWHC 1082.

[77] Baroness Hale similarly suggested in *R (M) v London Borough of Hammersmith and Fulham* [2008] UKHL 14, [43] that not all homeless 16- and 17-year-olds would 'require accommodation' (as opposed, e.g., to requiring help to secure accommodation) under s 20 and that it would be very unlikely that a competent child would be accommodated as a 'looked after' child against their wishes. She reiterated this view in *R (G) v London Borough of Southwark* [2009] UKHL 26, [28](4) and (6).

[78] [2007] EWHC 1082, [53], [55], and [58].

[79] [2009] UKHL 26, [9]. Applied in *R (TG) v Lambeth London Borough Council* [2011] EWCA Civ 526.

[80] [2008] UKHL 14.

[81] [2003] UKHL 57.

that would not be reasonably practicable and consistent with his welfare". The appellants' argument is that among the arrangements that may be made in the performance of this duty is the provision of accommodation to the person mentioned so that the child will be able to live with that person. They also submit . . . that neither the cost of doing this nor the availability of resources have any bearing on what is or is not reasonably practicable as to permit this would downgrade the duty into a discretionary power . . .

104. Section [s 22C(2)–(4)] appears to have been framed on the . . . assumption [that the person with whom the child is to be placed or the person with whom the child may be allowed to live already has accommodation which will enable the child to live with that person]. The context in which it appears suggests that this is so. But the wording of the subsection, and its content, reinforce the argument. The arrangements to which it refers are arrangements enabling the child to live with that person. Nothing is said about providing that person with accommodation. Moreover the duty to make the arrangements to which it refers is not restricted to enabling the child to live with his family. If it had been so restricted there might have been some force in the argument that the duty in this subsection was to be read together with the general duty in section 17(1) to promote the upbringing of the child by his family. But the person with whom the child may be enabled to live under this subsection include relatives other than his parents . . . The width of this class of persons indicates that what Parliament had in mind when it was enacting this provision was that these were persons who already had accommodation of their own. The fact that the duty is qualified by reference to what is reasonably practicable and consistent with the child's welfare is entirely consistent with this approach. It permits the local authority to have regard to the nature of the accommodation which that person is able to provide before it takes its decision as to whether, and if so with whom, the child is to be accommodated under this subsection. It is not concerned with the resources of the local authority, because the duty does not extend to the provision of accommodation for that person at its own cost or from its own resources.

12.3.2.b The power to accommodate: voluntary accommodation under s 20(4)

In addition to its duty to provide accommodation, the LA has the *power* to provide accommodation to a child if it 'considers that to do so would safeguard or promote the child's welfare'.[82] This power to receive children into voluntary care was intended as a positive measure for struggling parents. The government hoped that its position within Part III of the legislation would encourage families to seek LA support when needed.[83] To this end, s 20(7) explicitly provides that an LA may not provide accommodation for a child if a person with parental responsibility objects and is willing and able to provide or arrange alternative accommodation. To reinforce this point, it is further provided that a person with parental responsibility can remove the child at any time and without notice from LA care[84]—though if the child would face an immediate risk of significant harm at the hands of the parent, the LA will be justified in refusing to return the child while seeking an emergency order.[85]

[82] S 20(4). This power has no equivalent provision in Wales under the SSWB(W)A 2014.

[83] DHSS et al (1987), para 21.

[84] S 20(8). If a 'live with' child arrangements order (CAO) is in force, only a parent who has the child living with them may remove the child: s 20(9)—but in Wales, it appears that anyone with *any* CAO may remove the child: SSWB(W)A 2014, s 76(6).

[85] *Williams v London Borough of Hackney* [2018] UKSC 37, [44]. The power to refuse to hand the child over in such circumstances is under s 3(5), which permits any person who has the actual care of the child to do what is reasonable in the circumstances to safeguard and promote the child's welfare.

The importance of 'partnership' between the LA and the parents is evident throughout these provisions. However, the Children Act's strong commitment to protecting the voluntary nature of accommodation under Part III and the weakening of the LA's position relative to that of the parents has been the subject of strong criticism. In particular, there is concern that inappropriate use of voluntary care may prevent proper long-term planning for children spending significant periods of time away from their families. In addition to the original requirements in relation to preparing a pathway plan for each eligible child,[86] in 2014 the government increased the duties on LAs to prepare for and support children who are ceasing to be cared for by the LA.[87]

12.3.2.c The courts' approach to s 20 accommodation

The judiciary and academics became increasingly concerned about the approach of some LAs to the use of s 20 accommodation,[88] and a body of case law began to build up.

***Williams v London Borough of Hackney* [2018] UKSC 37**

LADY HALE:

The case law on section 20

21. Section 20 contains no express requirement of parental consent to a child being accommodated. Indeed, it envisages circumstances in which no such consent could be obtained, such as where the child is abandoned or lost or appears to have no person with parental responsibility for him. However, the judge had before him several authorities which not only held that informed consent to section 20 accommodation was required but also gave detailed guidance about how it should be obtained.

[Lady Hale then discussed and quoted from *R (G) v Nottingham City Council,*[89] *Coventry City Council v C,*[90] and *Re W (Parental Agreement with Local Authority),*[91] and continued:]

27. The same three authorities were referred to by Munby P, again in the course of obiter observations, in *Re N (Children) (Adoption: Jurisdiction).*[92] . . . [T]he children in question had been accommodated under section 20 for many months before care proceedings were eventually issued. So the President took the opportunity of drawing attention to the "misuse" of section 20 by local authorities . . . He explained (para 163) that

> "A local authority cannot use its powers under section 20 if a parent 'objects': see section 20(7). So where, as here, the child's parent is known and in contact with the local authority, the local authority requires the consent of the parent."

He also pointed out (para 169) that section 20(8):

> "means what it says. A local authority which fails to permit a parent to remove a child in circumstances within section 20(8) acts unlawfully, exposes itself to proceedings at the suit of the parent and may even be guilty of a criminal offence."

The criminal offence he presumably had in mind was that contained in section 2 of the Child Abduction Act 1984 . . .

[86] Care Planning, Placement and Case Review (England) Regulations, SI 2010/959, regs 41 and 43.
[87] Ibid, reg 39 (as amended). It is notable that the amendments were significantly less far-reaching than the government originally proposed: DFE (2013).
[88] See, e.g., Masson (1992); Bainham and Gilmore (2013), 465.
[89] [2008] EWHC 152 and [2008] EWHC 400. [90] [2012] EWHC 2190.
[91] [2014] EWCA Civ 1065. [92] [2015] EWCA Civ 1112.

In *Re N (Children) (Adoption: Jurisdiction)*,[93] Munby P had identified four key criticisms of LA practice in relation to s 20 accommodation. The first, noted in Lady Hale's judgment, was 'the failure of the local authority to obtain informed consent from the parent(s) at the outset'.[94] The second was the form in which consent was obtained—while the President noted that there was no legal requirement for the parental consent to be in writing, a 'prudent local authority' would wish to have a written agreement signed by the parent.[95] The third problem was 'the fact that, far too often, the arrangements under section 20 are allowed to continue for far too long'.[96] Finally, Munby P noted 'the seeming reluctance of local authorities to return the child to the parent(s) immediately upon a withdrawal of parental consent'.[97] However, the Supreme Court was not persuaded by all of these criticisms. In *Williams*, Lady Hale set out extensive guidance as to the scope and meaning of s 20.

Williams v London Borough of Hackney [2018] UKSC 37

LADY HALE:

38. The starting point must be parental responsibility. . . . A person with parental responsibility may arrange, of his or her own accord, for some or all of his or her parental responsibility to be met by others acting on his or her behalf (section 2(9), para 18 above) and the exercise of parental responsibility may be circumscribed by court order. But a local authority cannot interfere with a person's exercise of their parental responsibility, against their will, unless they have first obtained a court order. Accordingly, no local authority have the right or the power to remove a child from a parent who is looking after the child and wants to go on doing so without a court order. Only the police can do that under section 46 of the 1989 Act. It follows that the decision in *R (G) v Nottingham City Council* was absolutely right. The mother had just given birth. She wanted to look after her baby. The local authority had no power to prevent her and neither did the hospital. Helpless submission to asserted power does not amount to a delegation of parental responsibility or its exercise.

39. Secondly, it may be confusing to talk of parental "consent" to the removal (or accommodation) of her child. If a parent does agree to this, she is simply delegating the exercise of her parental responsibility for the time being to the local authority. Any such delegation must be real and voluntary. . . . Obviously, the best way to avoid this is by informing the parent fully of her rights under section 20, but a delegation can be "real and voluntary" without being fully "informed."

40. Thirdly, removing a child from the care of a parent is very different from stepping into the breach when a parent is not looking after the child. . . . The active consent or delegation of a parent who is not in fact looking after or offering to look after the child is not required, any more than it is when there is no-one with parental responsibility or the child is abandoned or lost. . . .

41. Fourthly, parents may ask the local authority to accommodate a child, as part of the services they provide for children in need. If the circumstances fall within section 20(1), there is a duty to accommodate the child. If they fall within section 20(4), there is power to do so. Once again, this operates as a delegation of the exercise of parental responsibility for the time being. The section does not expressly require that such delegation be with "informed" consent, but the duty and the power are subject to subsections (7) to (11). Once again, as a matter of good practice, parents should be given clear information about their rights and the local authority's responsibilities.

42. Fifthly, subsection (7) operates as a restriction on the powers and duties of the local authority under subsections (1) to (5). The authority cannot accommodate a child if a parent

[93] Ibid. [94] Ibid, [163]. [95] Ibid, [166]. [96] Ibid, [168]. [97] Ibid, [169].

with parental responsibility who is willing and able either to accommodate the child herself or to arrange for someone else to do so objects to the local authority doing so. It says nothing about the suitability of the parent or of the accommodation which the parent wishes to arrange.

43. . . . [Subsection (7)] means that the local authority have neither the power nor the duty to accommodate the child if a parent with parental responsibility proposes to accommodate the child herself or to arrange for someone else to do so. If the local authority consider the proposed arrangements, not merely unsuitable, but likely to cause the child significant harm, they should apply for an emergency protection order.

44. Sixthly, subsection (8) makes it absolutely clear that a parent with parental responsibility may remove the child from accommodation provided or arranged by a local authority at any time. There is no need to give notice, in writing or otherwise. The only caveat, as Munby J said in *R (G) v Nottingham City Council* . . ., is the right of anyone to take necessary steps to protect a person, including a child, from being physically harmed by another: for example, if a parent turned up drunk demanding to drive the child home. In such circumstances the people caring for the child would have the power (under section 3(5) of the 1989 Act) to do what is reasonable in all the circumstances for the purpose of safeguarding or promoting the child's welfare.

45. It follows that, if a parent unequivocally requires the return of the child, the local authority have neither the power nor the duty to continue to accommodate the child and must either return the child in accordance with that requirement or obtain the power to continue to look after the child, either by way of police protection or an emergency protection order. . . .

49. Finally, there is nothing in section 20 to place a limit on the length of time for which a child may be accommodated.[98] However, local authorities have a variety of duties towards the children whom they are accommodating. Their general duties towards looked after children in section 22 of the 1989 Act include a duty to safeguard and promote their welfare, in consultation with both the children and their parents. . . .

50. Thus, although the object of section 20 accommodation is partnership with the parents, the local authority have also to be thinking of the longer term. . . .

51. Care proceedings have obvious advantages for the child.[99] They involve a rigorous scrutiny of the risk of harm to her health and development if an order is not made, of the assessment of her needs and of the plans for her future. Her interests are safeguarded by an expert children's guardian. If an order is made, it means that the local authority have parental responsibility for her and can put their plans into effect. But . . . there are also advantages for the parents and for the wider family. The parents are entitled to legal aid. Their rights are safeguarded in the proceedings.[100] Even if a care order is made, the court may make orders about their continued contact with the child. Hence it is scarcely surprising that the President and other judges have deplored the delay in bringing care proceedings in cases where it was obvious that they should have been brought. Section 20 must not be used in a coercive way: if the state is to intervene compulsorily in family life, it must seek legal authority to do so.

The Court of Appeal has subsequently returned to the issue of when s 20 accommodation can be used as a long-term option. In *Re S, Re W (Section 20 Accommodation)*,[101] King LJ

[98] For an example of circumstances justifying long-term s 20 accommodation, see *Leicester City Council v AB* [2018] EWHC 1960. Masson et al (2013) point out that use of s 20 accommodation often has the effect of delaying court proceedings, so where s 20 accommodation is being used for more than a short period, its purpose must be strictly kept in mind.

[99] See also Welbourne (2008). [100] See also Kaganas (2010). [101] [2023] EWCA Civ 1.

held that children can be accommodated under s 20 as a long-term measure (including at the conclusion of care proceedings) if such a placement and the overall care plan are supported by the children's parents and meet the child's welfare needs. Noting the recent renewed emphasis from the Supreme Court that a care order should be made only if it is the least interventionist order available that meets the risks identified and the needs of the particular child,[102] King LJ held that there was 'no inhibition on . . . section 20 . . . being [used] in appropriate circumstances for a longer period of accommodation provided that proper consideration is given to the purpose of the accommodation and that the regular mandatory reviews are carried out.'[103] King LJ's judgment raises a number of questions,[104] and shows a marked change of emphasis from some earlier cases. Whereas Munby P in *Re N* was concerned about local authorities mis-using s 20 as a way of avoiding care proceedings,[105] King LJ wished to show that, in 'appropriate' circumstances,[106] the making of a care order will be unnecessary and the court should instead prefer a long-term option of s 20 accommodation. These authorities leave a rather fine line for local authorities and trial judges to walk.

12.3.2.d Voluntary accommodation for older children

In general, s 20 does not differentiate between children based on their age. A parent can delegate their parental responsibility to the LA regardless of the child's age—but particular issues arise in relation to children aged 16 or 17, and potentially also in relation to those who are *Gillick* competent even below that age.

Section 20(11) makes clear that a 16- or 17-year-old child can provide their own consent to being accommodated under s 20, since the parental right of objection is disapplied in the case of such a child who 'agrees' to being accommodated. But what of the inverse situation, where the parent does not object to the accommodation but the child does? Lady Hale has twice suggested, in obiter comments, that '[i]t is most unlikely that section 20 was intended to operate compulsorily against a child who is competent to decide for herself',[107] stating that 'there is nothing in section 20 which allows the local authority to force their services upon older and competent children who do not want them'.[108] She emphasized in both cases that Part III is about voluntary services, and must be differentiated from compulsory provisions under Part IV.

However, a different view was taken in *Re W (Secure Accommodation Order)*.[109] The child in question was aged 17¾, and was found to be a victim of child sexual exploitation (CSE), though she did not herself accept that she was a victim. W was accepted to be a 'child in need' and to be 'beyond parental control', and so was accommodated by the LA pursuant to s 20 of the CA 1989 from the age of 15. Accommodation was initially under s 20(1), and later (after W's 16th birthday) under either s 20(3) or 20(5)—the matter was disputed. W did not abide by some of the rules set down by the homes in which she was accommodated, and was particularly opposed to various curfews that were imposed; she often stayed out later than

[102] *Re H-W (Care Proceedings)* [2022] UKSC 17. See 12.5.4.c.

[103] [2023] EWCA Civ 1, [62]. King LJ refers to a 's 20 order', but the point of s 20 is that the court is not involved and does not order or sanction the accommodation.

[104] Marsh (2023). [105] *Re N (Children) (Adoption: Jurisdiction)* [2015] EWCA Civ 1112, [168].

[106] King LJ declined to give further guidance, considering that the judgment in *Williams v London Borough of Hackney* [2018] UKSC 37 and the Public Law Working Group (2021) recommendations were adequate.

[107] *R (M) v London Borough of Hammersmith and Fulham* [2008] UKHL 14, [43].

[108] *R (G) v London Borough of Southwark* [2009] UKHL 26, [28](6).

[109] [2016] EWCA Civ 804.

allowed, sometimes all night, though she always returned eventually. The LA came to the view that the only way to keep W in her accommodation was to secure her there under s 25 of the CA 1989.[110] It was argued for W that since she was able to object to being accommodated under s 20, it was therefore not possible for an order under s 25 to be made against her wishes either since, if she wished to leave, she could simply withdraw her agreement to remaining accommodated at all. Macur LJ rejected this argument, saying that s 25 was a protective order and not a punitive one.[111] She said that it was 'unrealistic' to think that a child who satisfied the s 25 criteria would continue to consent to accommodation if it was to be secured,[112] and that Parliament had not placed any restriction on the kinds of accommodation or the ages of children to which s 25 applied.

The focus in *Re W* on the secure accommodation issue appeared to distract the court from the question about s 20, which is never answered explicitly—the Court of Appeal did not engage with Lady Hale's obiter comments from the earlier cases. It is therefore open to doubt whether the court should be able to forcibly keep an older child in LA accommodation by use of a s 25 order, particularly on the basis of the child's 'absconding' if, in fact, the child ought to be entitled to refuse that accommodation.[113] Given that the liberty of the subject is at stake in such cases, the legal basis of the accommodation being provided must be clear.

12.3.3 LOCAL AUTHORITY DUTIES WITH RESPECT TO LOOKED AFTER CHILDREN

Section 22 of the CA 1989 details the various duties and responsibilities of LAs with respect to children in their care. Although these provisions are located in Part III of the legislation, the duties are owed to all children 'looked after' by the LA: this includes not only children who are in voluntary care but children who are in LA care pursuant to a care order, interim care order, or emergency protection order under Parts IV and V.[114] The core duty of the LA set down in s 22(3) is to safeguard and promote the child's welfare,[115] including a particular duty to promote the child's educational achievement.[116] This duty is supplemented by s 1 of the Children and Social Work Act 2017.

Children and Social Work Act 2017, s 1

(1) A local authority in England must, in carrying out functions in relation to [children who are 'looked after' under CA 1989 s 22(1), 'relevant children' under CA 1989 s 23A(2), and young persons aged under 25 who are 'former relevant children' under CA 1989 s 23C(1)], have regard to the need—

(a) to act in the best interests, and promote the physical and mental health and well-being, of those children and young people;

(b) to encourage those children and young people to express their views, wishes and feelings;

[110] S 25(1) provides that a child may be kept in secure accommodation if they have a history of absconding and are likely to suffer significant harm if they abscond, or if they are likely to injure themselves or another if not kept in secure accommodation.

[111] [2016] EWCA Civ 804, [19]. [112] Ibid, [17]. [113] See Forbes (2017).

[114] S 22(1). [115] S 22(3)(a). [116] S 22(3A).

(c) to take into account the views, wishes and feelings of those children and young people;
(d) to help those children and young people gain access to, and make the best use of, services provided by the local authority and its relevant partners;
(e) to promote high aspirations, and seek to secure the best outcomes, for those children and young people;
(f) for those children and young people to be safe, and for stability in their home lives, relationships and education or work;
(g) to prepare those children and young people for adulthood and independent living.

These are important factors to which the LA must have regard, but clearly the overall effect is not the same as making each individual child's welfare the paramount consideration. The justification for not imposing the paramountcy principle on LAs is clear. LAs owe duties and responsibilities to large numbers of looked after children. In such circumstances, it would obviously be inappropriate to prioritize the interests of just one child to the detriment of others. This is particularly so given the limited resources with which LAs have to contend. In making decisions with respect to individual children, LAs therefore have a wide discretion permitting them to take into account a broad range of factors other than the assessed needs and interests of the child in question.[117]

The way in which LAs discharge their duties and responsibilities under s 22(3) is crucially important. However, the task is not easy. In the year ending 31 March 2022, there were 82,170 looked after children,[118] a 1.7 per cent increase from the previous year and an increase of around 22 per cent over ten years and 36 per cent over 15 years.[119] About 17 per cent of those children are in voluntary arrangements, with over three-quarters the subject of care orders and most of the remainder the subject of pre-adoption placement orders.[120] Many of these children have come from abusive homes and have complex and challenging needs. The difficulty of ensuring that all looked after children enjoy the highest possible standards of accommodation and care, particularly where resources are limited, should not be underestimated. However, despite various reforms,[121] outcomes for many looked after children remain poor, with educational achievement, youth offending rates, and longer-term health and employment prospects all significantly poorer for looked after children.[122]

In addition to the general duty to promote the welfare of looked after children, s 22 of the CA 1989 imposes a number of more specific duties on the LA. Before making any decision with respect to a looked after child, the LA is under a duty, so far as is reasonably practicable, to ascertain and give due respect to the wishes and feelings of the child and the child's parents.[123] This includes an unmarried father without parental responsibility. The LA must also pay particular regard to the 'child's religious persuasion, racial origin and cultural and linguistic background'.[124]

[117] See, e.g., *Re T (Judicial Review: Local Authority Decisions Concerning Child in Need)* [2003] EWHC 2515.

[118] DFE (2022a). [119] Authors' calculations. [120] DFE (2022a).

[121] In addition to the Children and Social Work Act 2017, the CA 1989 was amended by the CA 2004 (CA 1989, s 22(3A)) and the Children and Young Persons Act 2008 (CA 1989, s 22C(8)(b)) to place greater emphasis on promoting looked after children's educational achievement.

[122] DFE (2022c). See also Griffiths et al (2021).

[123] S 22(4) and (5). As to the importance of respecting the child's wishes and feelings, see *R (CD) v Isle of Anglesey County Council* [2004] EWHC 1635.

[124] S 22(5)(c).

When a child is in voluntary accommodation, the duty to act in partnership with the parents is particularly strong. Indeed, it was held in *R v Tameside Metropolitan BC, ex parte J* that when a child is accommodated pursuant to Part III of the CA 1989, the LA must not only consult the child's parents but obtain their consent to any significant changes regarding the child, including where the child is accommodated.[125] The position with respect to a child 'in care' pursuant to a care order is different because under s 33(3)(a) the LA acquires parental responsibility for the child and thereby shares decision-making authority with the parents.[126]

In determining *where* a looked after child should be accommodated, the LA has a number of options.[127] Although the child is being looked after by the LA, the LA remains under a duty to promote the child's upbringing within their family. Section 22C(2)–(4) thus provide that unless it is not practicable to do so, or is contrary to the child's welfare, the LA should 'make arrangements' for the child to be accommodated with a parent, a person other than a parent who has parental responsibility, or a person with whom the child was living under a CAO prior to the care order being made.[128] The LA may provide financial support for the placement.[129] If the LA is unable to make arrangements for the child in accordance with s 22C(2), then it is under a duty to place the child in the most appropriate placement, giving priority to a relative, friend, or connected person who is also a LA foster carer.[130] If there is no relative or friend able to care for the child then the child can be placed with other LA foster carers or in a secure unit, residential school, residential home, or hostel.[131] So far as is reasonably practicable, the child should be placed within the LA area, as near to their home as possible and, where relevant, with their siblings.[132] The majority of looked after children are placed with LA foster carers previously unknown to the child.[133] In this regard, the CFA 2014 introduced a new duty on LAs in order to encourage early placement with a view to adoption and minimize the disruption caused to children by potentially multiple short-term placements.[134] The priority afforded to kinship placements under s 22C(6)(a) remains, but where such a placement is not deemed most appropriate and the LA is satisfied that the child ought to be placed for adoption but is not authorized to place the child under s 19 or 21 of the Adoption and Children Act 2002 (ACA 2002), it must consider placing the child with a prospective adopter who has also been approved as an LA foster parent for these purposes.[135]

Whilst a child is being looked after by the LA, great emphasis is placed upon maintaining the child's familial links. The LA is thus under a duty, if reasonably practicable and consistent

[125] [2000] 1 FCR 173, 179–81. Note also that a voluntarily accommodated child may be made a ward of court without offending s 100 of the CA 1989 which prevents the court using wardship to require a child to be placed in LA care: *Re E (Wardship Order: Child in Voluntary Accommodation)* [2012] EWCA Civ 1773.

[126] *R v Tameside Metropolitan BC, ex parte J* [2000] 1 FCR 173–81. See 12.5.6.

[127] S 22C(2)–(4) and (6); Care Planning, Placement and Case Review (England) Regulations 2010, SI 2010/959, Part 4.

[128] Around 7 per cent of looked after children are placed with parents or someone else with parental responsibility, and a further 15 per cent are with friends or family: DFE (2022a). See also Harding and Newnham (2017), extracted at 12.3.

[129] S 22C(10)(a).

[130] S 22C(5)–(9). It is no longer possible for the LA to 'make arrangements' for a relative or friend who is not a LA-approved foster parent under s 22C(6) to care for a child.

[131] S 22C(6). In the year to 31 March 2022, 16 per cent of looked after children in England were accommodated in a secure unit, children's home, or semi-independent living: DFE (2022a).

[132] S 22C(8)–(9).

[133] In the year to 31 March 2022, 70 per cent of looked after children were living with foster carers, around 80 per cent of whom were unknown to the child: DFE (2022a).

[134] S 22C(9A)–(9B).

[135] In reality, this is a little-used provision, with just 470 children (0.6 per cent of looked after children) in such placements in 2021: House of Lords Select Committee on the Children and Famlies Act 2014 (2022), para 50. See 13.5.1.b.

with the child's welfare, to promote contact between the child and, amongst others, the parents.[136] Where the child has infrequent contact with family members and is not regularly visited by anyone, the LA may appoint an independent visitor to 'visit, advise and befriend the child'.[137] The LA is also under a duty to ensure that looked after children are visited by a representative of the authority who will provide them with advice, support, and assistance.[138]

The LA must review the case of a looked after child within 20 working days of the date on which the child first entered care. The second review must be carried out no more than three months after the first and thereafter a review must be carried out every six months.[139] An independent reviewing officer (IRO) is appointed for every child and is responsible for monitoring the LA's performance, participating in any reviews of the child's case, ensuring the child's wishes and feelings are taken into consideration, and, if appropriate, referring the child's case to an officer of Cafcass who will be able to initiate legal proceedings on the child's behalf.[140] Strong concern has, however, been expressed as to the ineffectiveness of the IRO system in safeguarding the interests of children in care, not least because of their (perceived) lack of independence from the LA.[141]

12.3.4 PART III: A SUCCESS?

The aims behind Part III of the CA 1989 are certainly admirable. It is difficult to argue with the principle that 'prevention is better than cure' and that, wherever possible, children should be helped and supported within their families. However, as noted earlier, an approach based on prevention and support will only be successful if properly resourced. The absence of much needed investment in LA services has resulted in LAs being crisis-led and focusing most of their time and resources on 'managing child protection cases'.[142] LAs thus become trapped in a vicious circle. The less time, money, and effort invested in prevention and support, the more resources needed to deal with cases requiring immediate, coercive intervention. Conversely, if more resources were diverted to providing effective services under Part III, the need for intervention under Parts IV and V should decline. As it is, the number of care orders has been rising steadily for many years.

12.4 THE CHILD PROTECTION SYSTEM: INVESTIGATING ALLEGATIONS OF CHILD ABUSE

12.4.1 SECTION 47 INVESTIGATION

There is no general duty on the public to report suspected cases of child abuse to the authorities. Concerns about the welfare of a child should, however, be referred to their local children's services department. Within one working day of a referral being received, the LA

136 Part II, Sch II, para 15(1). The obligation extends to friends and any person connected with the child. Richardson, Boylan, and Brammer (2017) discuss the value of such contact in cases involving significant harm by parents.

137 S 23ZB; Part II, Sch II, para 17(1)–(2).

138 S 23ZA; Care Planning, Placement and Case Review (England) Regulations 2010, SI 2010/959, reg 28.

139 Care Planning, Placement and Case Review (England) Regulations 2010, SI 2010/959, reg 33.

140 Ss 25A–C; on IROs, see Jelicic et al (2014).

141 House of Lords Select Committee on Adoption Legislation (2013), paras 114–28; *A and S v Lancashire CC* [2012] EWHC 1689.

142 Smith (2002), 254–5.

must decide how to proceed. If further investigation is needed, the LA must carry out an assessment in accordance with the guidelines set down in *Working Together to Safeguard Children*.[143] The LA's assessment should be informed by the views of the child and their family and the relevant health and education professionals.[144] Whenever possible the child should be seen by the social worker without the parents being present.[145] Although *Working Together* no longer prescribes a strict timetable for carrying out an assessment, it does stipulate that the assessment should be completed within 45 days from initial referral unless there are good reasons justifying a longer timescale.[146] If the LA has *reasonable cause to suspect* that the child is suffering or likely to suffer significant harm, the LA must carry out a full investigation under s 47 of the CA 1989. If the parents refuse to cooperate with the investigation, the LA must apply for an emergency protection order (EPO), child assessment order, or care or supervision order, unless satisfied that the child's welfare is adequately protected without one.[147] The preferred route for obtaining access to the child is a child assessment order under s 43, the purpose of which is 'to enable proper assessment to establish whether there is a need and justification for any further action'.[148] The court can only make the order if certain conditions are met:

Children Act 1989, s 43

(1) On the application of a local authority or authorised person for an order to be made under this section with respect to a child, the court may make the order if, but only if, it is satisfied that—
  (a) the applicant has reasonable cause to suspect that the child is suffering, or is likely to suffer, significant harm;
  (b) an assessment of the state of the child's health or development, or of the way in which he has been treated, is required to enable the applicant to determine whether or not the child is suffering, or is likely to suffer, significant harm; and
  (c) it is unlikely that such an assessment will be made, or be satisfactory, in the absence of an order under this section.

If the order is made, the assessment can be carried out without parental consent. The parents are placed under a duty to produce the child to any person named in the order and must comply with any specified directions for carrying out the assessment.[149] A child of sufficient understanding can, however, refuse to submit to a medical, psychiatric, or other assessment.[150] The order can last for a specified period of no more than seven days from the date on which the assessment is to begin.[151] The only restriction on making an order under s 43 is that this provision should not be used if an emergency protection order should be made instead.[152] While the order must be proportionate, '[i]t is the least interventionist of

[143] DFE (2018b), esp 24–33. See generally Munro (2011). [144] DFE (2018b), 28. [145] Ibid.
[146] Ibid, 32. [147] S 47(6).
[148] *Re I (Children: Child Assessment Order)* [2020] EWCA Civ 281, [21](1). [149] S 43(6).
[150] S 43(8). In *South Glamorgan County Council v W and B* [1993] 1 FLR 574, decided within the context of an interim care order, the court took the view that, exercising its inherent jurisdiction, it could override the child's refusal. Whether that decision would be followed today is unclear; cf 8.5.6.b.
[151] S 43(5). [152] S 43(4).

the court's child protection powers and is designed to enable information that cannot be obtained by other means to be gathered without the need to remove the child from home'—it is not an emergency power, and it can be used 'where the suspected harm is longer-term and cumulative'.[153]

The purpose of the s 47 assessment is to determine the nature and level of the child's needs, any risk factors, and what services are to be provided.[154] If the concerns leading to the initiation of the investigation are substantiated and the child is believed to be at continuing risk, the LA should convene a child protection conference (CPC)—usually within 15 days of the s 47 inquiries being initiated.[155] The aim of the CPC is to bring together all relevant professionals and the family to plan how best to safeguard and promote the child's welfare.[156] The parents should normally attend and be provided with sufficient information to enable them to participate effectively in the proceedings.[157] If of sufficient age and understanding, the child may also attend.[158] If the child's attendance is not appropriate, the child's social worker or advocate should convey the child's wishes and feelings to the meeting. The child will be recorded as at risk of harm under an initial category of abuse: physical, emotional, sexual, neglect, or multiple. Neglect is the most common category (48.0 per cent of cases in 2017–18), followed by emotional abuse (35.1 per cent).[159] The CPC must decide whether the child should be subject to a formal child protection plan and establish a core group, headed by a lead professional, to be responsible for developing, implementing, and monitoring the plan.[160] The plan must include clear actions and timescales for change. A child protection review conference will be held within three months of the initial conference and thereafter every six months.[161] The plan may be terminated at any time if the review concludes the child is no longer at risk of significant harm.

Within the context of the child protection plan, the LA remains responsible for determining whether an application should be made to the court for a care or supervision order.[162] Before doing so, the LA should comply with statutory guidance on the pre-proceedings process which requires a letter before proceedings to be sent to the parents setting out the LA's concerns and inviting them to attend a pre-proceedings meeting at which they are entitled to be legally represented.[163] The LA is under no legal duty to initiate care proceedings even if satisfied the child is suffering or is likely to suffer significant harm.[164] It has been argued that this creates an unfortunate gap in the statutory framework. Although the LA's decision not to initiate care proceedings can be challenged through the LA internal complaints procedure or by way of judicial review,[165] as Eekelaar notes, it is 'surprising that the imposition of extensive and elaborate duties to inquire do not lead to a clear and unambiguous duty to take action on the basis of the results of the inquiries where the child is likely to be harmed if no such action is taken'.[166] Similarly, just as the court is unable to direct the LA to take any specific steps to protect a child, it is equally unable to grant injunctive relief to restrain the LA from investigating a child's circumstances under s 47, even if the court is already seized of a

[153] *Re I (Children: Child Assessment Order)* [2020] EWCA Civ 281, [35]. [154] DFE (2018b), 24.

[155] Ibid, 47. [156] Ibid.

[157] *Re M (Care: Challenging Decisions by Local Authority)* [2001] 2 FLR 1300 and *Re G (Care: Challenge to Local Authority's Decision)* [2003] EWHC 551.

[158] DFE (2018b). [159] DFE (2018c), 13. [160] DFE (2018b), 47. [161] Ibid.

[162] S 47(3)(a). There is significant variation between local authorities as to when they decide to initiate proceedings: Trowler (2018), 5.

[163] DFE (2014a), ch 2. See also Masson (2010a), 369. For consideration of how effective reforms to the pre-proceedings stage have been, see Fauset (2020).

[164] See *Nottinghamshire County Council v P* [1994] Fam 18.

[165] *R v East Sussex County Council, ex parte W* [1998] 2 FLR 1082. [166] Eekelaar (1990), 486.

private law dispute between the parents.[167] If the LA decides to initiate care proceedings, the LA's actions should be challenged by way of defending the proceedings. Only in wholly exceptional circumstances will it be appropriate to bring an application for judicial review.[168]

The potentially indeterminate outcome of a LA investigation under s 47 can be problematic. Essentially, where there are grounds for continuing concern the LA may simply decide to keep monitoring the situation and respond as and when appropriate. This can leave parents accused of abuse or neglect in a difficult state of limbo. Whilst care proceedings constitute a high level of intervention into the family, they do at least provide the opportunity for parents to formally challenge the LA's allegations and for those allegations to be properly scrutinized by the court. Without such proceedings, it is difficult for parents to 'clear their name' in the face of the LA's continuing suspicion. This problem was considered in *R (S) v Swindon Borough Council*,[169] which concerned a consultant gynaecologist suspected of sexually assaulting the teenage daughter of his former partner. Following his acquittal in the criminal proceedings, he wished to set up home with his new partner, Mrs X, but was unable to do so whilst the LA, believing he may pose a continuing risk, refused to provide the necessary assurance that it would not take steps to protect Mrs X's two daughters should he and Mrs X begin to cohabit. The claimant sought judicial review of the LA's position, arguing that it needed to reach a final decision as to whether the allegations were substantiated and, on the basis of that decision, either initiate care proceedings to protect Mrs X's daughters or leave him alone to get on with his life. Scott Baker J dismissed the application, stressing that whilst the LA must respect the claimant's private and family life, it had an overriding duty to monitor the situation in order to protect the two children. The judgment makes clear that at the early stages of an investigation into child abuse, the thresholds for state intervention are necessarily low and there is therefore no requirement for the LA to substantiate allegations of abuse on the balance of probabilities. The judge concluded that 'the critical question is whether the authority *have reasonable cause to suspect* a child is likely to suffer significant harm',[170] and emphasized that the fact of an acquittal in a criminal trial would never be conclusive as to whether a LA should start or continue a s 47 investigation.

If at any point throughout this process the LA believes the child to be in need of urgent protection, the LA should request that the police take the child into police protection or apply for an emergency protection order under Part V.[171]

12.4.2 SECTION 37 INVESTIGATION

An alternative route by which a family may find themselves subject to a LA investigation is under s 37 of the CA 1989:

Children Act 1989, s 37

(1) Where, in any family proceedings in which a question arises with respect to the welfare of any child, it appears to the court that it may be appropriate for a care or supervision order to be made with respect to him, the court may direct the appropriate authority to undertake an investigation of the child's circumstances.

[167] *D v D (County Court Jurisdiction: Injunctions)* [1993] 2 FLR 802. The Court of Appeal solved this problem by making a prohibited steps order to restrain the father from exercising his parental responsibility to consent to such investigations. The LA were investigating the mother's treatment of her children at the behest of the father, against the background of private law child arrangements proceedings.

[168] *Re M (Care Proceedings: Judicial Review)* [2003] EWHC 850.

[169] [2001] EWHC 334. [170] Ibid, [34]. [171] See 12.6.

It was held in *Re H (A Minor) (Section 37 Direction)* that the 'child's circumstances' should be widely construed to include 'any situation which may have a bearing on the child being likely to suffer significant harm in the future'—even if the child is currently settled, well cared for, and happy.[172] The purpose of the investigation is for the LA to decide whether or not it should apply for a care or supervision order. The LA must report back to the court within eight weeks.[173] If the LA decides not to apply for a care or supervision order, the reasons for the decision must be explained and the court informed of any alternative action it proposes to take.[174] However, regardless of the LA's findings, the LA again has no duty to begin proceedings and the court has no power to direct proceedings to be initiated.[175]

12.5 CARE AND SUPERVISION PROCEEDINGS UNDER PART IV

Part IV of the CA 1989 provides for two key orders permitting compulsory intervention into family life: care and supervision orders. A care order is defined under s 31(1)(a) as an order 'placing the child with respect to whom the application is made in the care of a designated local authority'. A supervision order is a less interventionist measure and is simply defined as an order putting the child 'under the supervision of a designated local authority'.[176]

12.5.1 WHO MAY APPLY FOR A CARE OR SUPERVISION ORDER?

Under s 31(1), only a 'local authority' or 'authorized person' may apply for a care or supervision order. 'Authorized person' is defined in s 31(9) as the NSPCC and any other person authorized by the Secretary of State to bring proceedings. To date, no such other person has been authorized. The child, the mother, and the father (if he has parental responsibility) are automatically joined as respondents.[177] The LA must serve notice of the proceedings on a father without parental responsibility but he has no right to participate in the proceedings: he must apply for leave to be joined as a party.[178] Leave will, however, ordinarily be granted unless there is some clear reason for refusing the application.[179]

12.5.2 WHEN MAY A CARE OR SUPERVISION ORDER BE MADE?

An application for a care or supervision order may be made in any 'family proceedings' or in free-standing care proceedings.[180] As noted earlier, only an LA or the NSPCC can make the application; the court cannot act of its own motion. Indeed, s 100(2) of the CA 1989 explicitly removes the power of the court to place a child into LA care pursuant to its inherent jurisdiction. Although this lack of jurisdiction has frustrated some, it ensures no child can be placed into LA care on the basis of a simple best interests test (as was the case under the inherent jurisdiction): the threshold of harm justifying state intervention into the family as

[172] *Re H (A Minor) (Section 37 Direction)* [1993] 2 FLR 541, 549. [173] S 37(4). [174] S 37(3).
[175] *Nottinghamshire County Council v P* [1994] Fam 18. [176] S 31(1)(b).
[177] Family Procedure Rules 2010 (FPR 2010), r 12.3(1). A father with parental responsibility whose whereabouts are known can be discharged as a party to the proceedings and service dispensed with, but only in exceptional circumstances: *M v M (Children)* [2009] EWHC 3172.
[178] FPR 2010, r 12.8 and Practice Direction 12C.
[179] *Re K (Care Proceedings: Joinder of Father)* [1999] 2 FLR 408; *Re P (Care Proceedings: Father's Application to be Joined as Party)* [2001] 1 FLR 781.
[180] For the meaning of 'family proceedings', see s 8(3)–(4).

set down in s 31 must always be established. For similar reasons, the LA is constrained from acting to protect a child by applying for private law orders under s 8. Section 9(2) thus prohibits an LA from applying for a CAO and whilst the LA is permitted, with leave, to apply for a specific issue or prohibited steps order, the court cannot, in accordance with s 9(5)(a), make an order with a view to achieving a result that could be achieved under a CAO. This leaves very little room for LAs to make use of s 8 orders, even if they believe such orders would be a more nuanced response to the problems of a particular family than invoking their more drastic and confrontational powers under Part IV.

The limitations imposed on LAs and the various problems such limitations can create for the courts are dramatically illustrated in *Nottinghamshire County Council v P*.[181] As regards LAs and the courts working in partnership to protect children at risk of harm, this case represents a particular low point. The case concerned two young girls whose older sister had made allegations of sexual abuse against the father. The parents denied the allegations. The court found that the father had sexually abused the eldest daughter and that the two younger girls were now at serious risk. The court also found that the mother had no capacity to protect the children against their father. However, rather than apply for a care order under Part IV, the LA applied for a prohibited steps order requiring the father not to reside in the same household as his daughters and prohibiting contact. Owing to the restrictions contained in ss 9(2) and 9(5)(a), Ward J, at first instance, held that he was unable to make the order sought and, in the face of the LA's refusal to apply for a care order, he instead made a CAO in favour of the mother, subject to two conditions: (i) that the father was not to reside in the family home; and (ii) was not to be allowed contact with the children. All parties appealed:

Nottinghamshire County Council v P [1994] Fam 18 (CA), 38–43

SIR STEPHEN BROWN P:

In the view of this court the application for a prohibited steps order by this local authority was in reality being made with a view to achieving a result which could be achieved by making a [CAO] . . .

The court is satisfied that the local authority was indeed seeking to enter by the "back door" as it were. It agrees with Ward J that he had no power to make a prohibited steps order in this case . . .

A wider question arises as to policy. We consider that this court should make it clear that the route chosen by the local authority in this case was wholly inappropriate. In cases where children are found to be at risk of suffering significant harm within the meaning of section 31 of the Children Act 1989 a clear duty arises on the part of local authorities to take steps to protect them. In such circumstances a local authority is required to assume responsibility and to intervene in the family arrangements in order to protect the child. Part IV specifically provides them with wide powers and a wide discretion . . . A prohibited steps order would not afford the local authority any authority as to how it might deal with the children. There may be situations, for example where a child is accommodated by a local authority, where it would be appropriate to seek a prohibited steps order for some particular purpose. However, it could not in any circumstances be regarded as providing a substitute for an order under Part IV of the Act of 1989. Furthermore, it is very doubtful indeed whether a prohibited steps order could in any circumstances be used to "oust" a father from a matrimonial home . . .

[181] [1994] Fam 18 (CA). See Brasse (1993).

The Court of Appeal then went on to consider Ward J's decision to make a CAO subject to conditions under s 11(7). The difficulty with this order was that it was being imposed on the mother against her wishes yet, unlike an order under Part IV, provided no power or responsibility to the LA to monitor, regulate, or enforce it.

> In our judgment these orders cannot stand. Even if the judge had a theoretical power to assume authority by reason of section 10 of the Act of 1989, the orders were plainly not appropriate even in the unhappy circumstances of this case. In the result the appeals against these orders must be allowed.
>
> In the result there are now no orders in force which are capable of regulating and safeguarding the position of these children . . . Since the fact of the risk of significant harm to the children has been established and not contradicted there remains upon the local authority the clear duty to take steps to safeguard the welfare of these children. It should not shrink from taking steps under Part IV of the Act . . .
>
> This court is deeply concerned at the absence of any power to direct this authority to take steps to protect the children. In the former wardship jurisdiction it might well have been able to do so. The operation of the Children Act 1989 is entirely dependent upon the full cooperation of all those involved. This includes the courts, local authorities, social workers, and all who have to deal with children. Unfortunately, as appears from this case, if a local authority doggedly resists taking the steps which are appropriate to the case of children at risk of suffering significant harm it appears that the court is powerless. The authority may perhaps lay itself open to an application for judicial review but in a case such as this the question arises, at whose instance? The position is one which it is to be hoped will not recur and that lessons will be learnt from this unhappy catalogue of errors.

Once the LA has made an application under s 31 and the court is satisfied the threshold conditions are satisfied, the court has much greater freedom to shape its orders in accordance with the child's welfare.[182]

12.5.3 THE THRESHOLD CRITERIA

There are two stages to care proceedings.[183] First, before the court acquires the jurisdiction to make a care or supervision order, the threshold criteria set down in s 31(2) must be satisfied. Whether or not the threshold is crossed is not an exercise of discretion but a 'value judgement' which must be made on the basis of established facts, and the child's welfare is irrelevant to this exercise.[184] Once the threshold criteria have been established, the court can move on to the second stage of the inquiry: whether it is in the child's best interests to make the order. This is generally known as the welfare stage.

Section 31(2) performs a crucial 'gate-keeping' function. It ensures the state can take coercive action against a child's primary carers only once a certain threshold of harm has been established. It thus plays a crucial role in balancing the importance of respecting family

[182] Indeed, at the welfare stage the court *must* consider all possible orders, including private law orders and the option of making 'no order': *Re H-W (Care Proceedings)* [2022] UKSC 17, discussed at 12.5.4.c.

[183] The court must not mix the two discrete stages: *Re K (Threshold Findings)* [2018] EWCA Civ 2044.

[184] *Re B (Care Proceedings: Appeal)* [2013] UKSC 33, [44].

integrity against the need to protect children from inadequate or abusive parenting.[185] The threshold criteria are set out in s 31(2) of the CA 1989:

Children Act 1989, s 31

(2) A court may only make a care order or supervision order if it is satisfied—

(a) that the child concerned is suffering, or is likely to suffer, significant harm; and

(b) that the harm, or likelihood of harm, is attributable to—

(i) the care given to the child, or likely to be given to him if the order were not made, not being what it would be reasonable to expect a parent to give to him; or

(ii) the child's being beyond parental control.

There are thus two basic limbs to the threshold criteria, both of which must be satisfied:

- the child must be suffering or be likely to suffer significant harm; and
- the harm must be attributable to the care given to the child not being what it would be reasonable to expect a parent to give, or to the child being beyond parental control.

We will take these requirements in turn.

12.5.3.a Is suffering or likely to suffer significant harm

'Harm'

Harm is very widely defined in s 31(9) as the 'ill-treatment or the impairment of health or development including, for example, impairment suffered from seeing or hearing the ill-treatment of another'. 'Ill-treatment' includes 'sexual abuse and forms of ill-treatment which are not physical'. Importantly, as made clear by the Supreme Court in *Re B (Care Proceedings: Appeal)*, this includes emotional harm caused by the parents' behaviour and/or particular personality traits.[186] 'Health' includes both physical and mental health. 'Development' means 'physical, intellectual, emotional, social or behavioural development'. In determining whether a child has been subjected to 'harm', the courts are prepared to tolerate diverse standards of parenting taking into account the social, cultural, and religious background of the family.

Re L (Care: Threshold Criteria) [2007] 1 FLR 2050

HEDLEY J:

50. What about the court's approach, in the light of all that, to the issue of significant harm? In order to understand this concept and the range of harm that it's intended to encompass, it is right to begin with issues of policy. Basically it is the tradition of the UK, recognised in

[185] *Re G (Care Proceedings: Threshold Conditions)* [2001] EWCA Civ 968.

[186] [2013] UKSC 33, [65]. The harm relied on by the LA was the impact on the child of the mother's somatization disorder, factitious illness disorder, her lying and dishonesty, and her inability to engage constructively with professionals. On the facts, the Supreme Court was satisfied, Lady Hale dissenting, that the impact of this behaviour on the child's emotional development was sufficiently serious to conclude that the making of a care order was both necessary and proportionate.

law, that children are best brought up within natural families . . . It follows inexorably from that, that society must be willing to tolerate very diverse standards of parenting, including the eccentric, the barely adequate and the inconsistent. It follows too that children will inevitably have both very different experiences of parenting and very unequal consequences flowing from it. It means that some children will experience disadvantage and harm, while others flourish in atmospheres of loving security and emotional stability. These are the consequences of our fallible humanity and it is not the provenance of the state to spare children all the consequences of defective parenting. In any event, it simply could not be done.

The importance to be accorded to diversity in family life has been reiterated by the House of Lords.

Re B (Children) (Care Proceedings: Standard of Proof) **[2008] UKHL 35**

BARONESS HALE:

20. Taking a child away from her family is a momentous step, not only for her, but for her whole family, and for the local authority which does so. In a totalitarian society, uniformity and conformity are valued. Hence the totalitarian state tries to separate the child from her family and mould her to its own design. Families in all their subversive variety are the breeding ground of diversity and individuality. In a free and democratic society we value diversity and individuality. Hence the family is given special protection in all the modern human rights instruments including the European Convention on Human Rights (art 8), the International Covenant on Civil and Political Rights (art 23) and throughout the United Nations Convention on the Rights of the Child. As Justice McReynolds famously said in *Pierce v Society of Sisters* 268 US 510 (1925), at 535, "The child is not the mere creature of the State."

'Significant'

Section 31(10) provides that where the question of whether the harm suffered is significant turns on the child's health or development, then the child's health or development should be compared with that which could be reasonably expected of a similar child.[187] 'Significant' is not otherwise defined by the legislation. The meaning of significant harm was considered by the Supreme Court in *Re B (Care Proceedings: Appeal)*, with the majority being anxious not to complicate the relatively straightforward statutory wording with unnecessary judicial gloss and 'encrustation'.[188] However, Lady Hale cites as 'helpful' the ordinary dictionary definition of 'significant', which demands that the harm must be 'considerable', 'noteworthy', or 'important'.[189] As she goes on to point out, the threshold would be irrelevant if it could

[187] See *Re O (A Minor) (Care Order: Education: Procedure)* [1992] 2 FLR 7, 10.

[188] [2013] UKSC 33, [26] (Lord Wilson); [56] (Lord Neuberger). Lady Hale dissented, considering that Art 8 had a bearing on the ultimate decision and that it should be borne in mind when considering the sufficiency of the harm. For commentary, see Doughty (2013).

[189] *Re B (Care Proceedings: Appeal)* [2013] UKSC 33, [185]. In *Re MA (Care Threshold)* [2009] EWCA Civ 853, the majority of the Court of Appeal appeared to accept that physical abuse that could be defended as 'reasonable chastisement' does not amount to significant harm, and upheld the finding of the trial judge that witnessing the parents' cruel physical abuse of another (non-biological) child would not cause the children significant emotional harm. See Masson (2010b) and Keating (2011) for strong critiques. It is interesting to wonder how the Children (Abolition of Defence of Reasonable Punishment) (Wales) Act 2020 might affect this view.

be crossed by trivial or unimportant harm.[190] Both Lady Hale and Lord Wilson also suggest that the 'significance' or seriousness of the harm must be considered in parallel with its likelihood, such that, whilst only a slight possibility of very grave harm may be sufficient to cross the threshold, a very strong possibility may be required of harm which is of much less significance.[191]

'Is suffering'

This is the most straightforward way of establishing the first limb of the threshold criteria. It raises a simple question of fact: is the child suffering significant harm? The usual civil standard of proof applies, so the burden is on the LA to prove the alleged facts on the balance of probabilities.[192]

Although relatively straightforward, questions have arisen regarding *when* the alleged state of affairs must be shown to exist. In *Re M (A Minor) (Care Orders: Threshold Conditions)*, the child (G), when just 4 months old, witnessed his father brutally murder his mother, for which the father was serving life imprisonment. The LA applied for a care order. After a short period in foster care, G went to live with Mrs W, his mother's cousin, who was also caring for his three older half-siblings. By the time the LA's application for a care order was heard, the child was well settled and well cared for in Mrs W's home. Mrs W applied for a residence order. This was supported by the LA which decided not to pursue its application. However, the guardian ad litem (now 'children's guardian', who represents the child's interests in the proceedings) and the father supported making a care order, hoping the child could be adopted outside the family. The question arose whether, in this commonplace scenario of a child being 'rescued' from a harmful situation by the LA, the child had to be suffering significant harm at the time of the final decision, or whether it sufficed for the purposes of the threshold criteria that the child had been suffering significant harm at the point the LA first intervened to protect the child. The House of Lords, emphasizing the need to 'avoid the tyranny of language', preferred the latter interpretation.[193]

Re M (A Minor) (Care Orders: Threshold Conditions) [1994] 2 AC 424 (HL), 433–4

LORD MACKAY:

There is nothing in section 31(2) which in my opinion requires that the conditions to be satisfied are disassociated from the time of the making of the application by the local authority. I would conclude that the natural construction of the conditions in section 31(2) is that where, at the time the application is to be disposed of, there are in place arrangements for the protection of the child by the local authority on an interim basis which protection has been continuously in place for some time, the relevant date with respect to which the court must be satisfied is the date at which the local authority initiated the procedure for protection under the Act from which these arrangements followed. If after a local authority had initiated protective arrangements the need for these had terminated, because the child's welfare had been satisfactorily provided for otherwise, in any subsequent proceedings, it would not be

[190] *Re B (Care Proceedings: Appeal)* [2013] UKSC 33.

[191] Ibid, [187]–[190] (Lady Hale) and [26] (Lord Wilson). [192] See 12.5.3.c.

[193] For an argument that threshold should be assessed at the time of the final court decision, accounting for anything that has happened since the initial intervention, see Bainham (2022).

> possible to found jurisdiction on the situation at the time of initiation of these arrangements. It is permissible only to look back from the date of disposal to the date of initiation of protection as a result of which local authority arrangements had been continuously in place thereafter to the date of disposal.
>
> It has to be borne in mind that this in no way precludes the court from taking account at the date of the hearing of all relevant circumstances. The conditions in subsection (2) are in the nature of conditions conferring jurisdiction upon the court to consider whether or not a care order or supervision order should be made. Conditions of that kind would in my view normally have to be satisfied at the date on which the order was first applied for. It would in my opinion be odd if the jurisdiction of the court to make an order depended on how long the court took before it finally disposed of the case.

It was subsequently suggested in *Southwark London Borough Council v B* that the relevant date at which the 'local authority initiated the procedure for protection' may include voluntary arrangements entered into under Part III, provided protective arrangements have been continuously in place since that date.[194]

The issue of timing arose again in *Re G (Care Proceedings: Threshold Conditions)*.[195] The question this time was whether the LA could rely on information acquired after it had first intervened to protect the child in order to help establish that the threshold conditions were satisfied at the point of intervention. Hale LJ drew a distinction between: (i) information and events which went towards proving the alleged state of affairs at the point of intervention; and (ii) completely unrelated information and events which, whilst in themselves capable of constituting evidence of significant harm, had no bearing on the initial reasons for the LA intervening. It was held that whilst the former was clearly relevant and should be admitted, evidence falling into the latter category could not be relied upon by the LA to 'retrospectively valid[ate] a concern which was not in fact justified at the time'.[196] Wall LJ provided further clarification, holding in *Re L (Children) (Care Proceedings)*[197] that the LA is free to advance grounds for establishing the threshold criteria at trial which are different from the grounds relied on when it first intervened provided the alternative grounds actually existed (whether or not known to the LA) at the date of intervention.[198] This differs from the situation where a new unrelated event giving rise to grounds for concern occurs after the date of intervention, which, in accordance with *Re G*, would remain excluded from consideration. In such circumstances the LA would simply have to start proceedings again.

'Is likely to suffer'

The alternative basis on which the LA can satisfy the first limb of the threshold criteria under s 31(2)(a) is the likelihood of future significant harm. It has been suggested that when looking forward the LA is not restricted to the immediate or even medium-term future, anticipated harm even years in advance will suffice.[199] Satisfying the prospective limb of s 31(2)(a) is, however, in many ways a difficult task, relying as it does on various hypotheses about the future. There are now a number of House of Lords/Supreme Court authorities on the point, notably *Re H (Minors) (Sexual Abuse: Standard of Proof)*,[200] *Re B (Children) (Care*

[194] [1998] 2 FLR 1095, 1109.
[195] [2001] EWCA Civ 968.
[196] Ibid, [15].
[197] [2006] EWCA Civ 1282.
[198] Ibid, [42]–[45].
[199] *Re H (A Minor) (Section 37 Direction)* [1993] 2 FLR 541, 548.
[200] [1996] AC 563.

Proceedings: Standard of Proof),[201] *Re J (Care Proceedings: Possible Perpetrators)*,[202] and *Re B (Care Proceedings: Appeal)*.[203]

Re H concerned applications for care orders with respect to three children (D2, D3, and D4). A fourth child (D1, the eldest sister) alleged she had been sexually abused by the step-father (Mr R) over a number of years. He was charged with rape but acquitted at the criminal trial. The LA continued with the care proceedings, the sole ground for the care orders being the likelihood of future significant harm given the alleged sexual abuse of the eldest daughter. It did not contend that any of the three children were currently suffering significant harm. This was therefore a case where the issue was whether or not the alleged abuse of another child had taken place—if proven, the identity of the perpetrator was not an issue.

The House of Lords were all agreed that 'likely' should be interpreted to mean there was a 'real possibility' of future significant harm: there was no need to show that the harm was 'probable' in the sense of 'more likely than not'. However, the House of Lords were divided as to the evidential base required in order to make a positive finding that the child was likely to suffer significant harm. The majority held that the court must be satisfied on the balance of probabilities that there was a real possibility the child would suffer significant harm, the burden of proof resting on the LA. Lord Nicholls went on to hold that the court could only proceed on the basis of 'proper material', meaning the court would only be able to find a real possibility of future harm on the basis of established facts not mere doubts or suspicions—which in this case meant the LA would need to prove on the balance of probabilities that the eldest daughter had been sexually abused. The minority disagreed, arguing that a number of 'unproven' facts, when taken together, could prove equally probative. The point is important, going as it does to the heart of child protection policy. Is the state justified in removing a child from their parents on the basis of mere suspicion of past neglect or abuse? The majority say 'no', setting a much higher threshold for state intervention than the minority.

Re H (Minors) (Sexual Abuse: Standard of Proof) [1996] AC 563 (HL), 588–92, 572–4

LORD NICHOLLS (with whom Lord Goff and Lord Mustill agreed):

A conclusion based on facts

The starting point here is that courts act on evidence. They reach their decisions on the basis of the evidence before them. When considering whether an applicant for a care order has shown that the child is suffering harm or is likely to do so, a court will have regard to the undisputed evidence. The judge will attach to that evidence such weight or importance as he considers appropriate. Likewise with regard to disputed evidence which the judge accepts as reliable. None of that is controversial. But the rejection of a disputed allegation as not proved on the balance of probability leaves scope for the possibility that the non-proven allegation may be true after all. There remains room for the judge to have doubts and suspicions on this score. This is the area of controversy.

In my view these unresolved judicial doubts and suspicions can no more form the basis of a conclusion that the second threshold condition in section 31(2)(a) has been established than they can form the basis of a conclusion that the first has been established . . .

[201] [2008] UKHL 35. [202] [2013] UKSC 9. [203] [2013] UKSC 33.

A decision by a court on the likelihood of a future happening must be founded on a basis of present facts and the inferences fairly to be drawn therefrom. . . .

An alleged but non-proven fact is not a fact for this purpose . . . [T]here must be facts from which the court can properly conclude there is a real possibility that the child will suffer harm in the future . . . [I]f the facts are disputed, the court must resolve the dispute so far as necessary to reach a proper conclusion on the issue it has to decide . . .

The range of facts which may properly be taken into account is infinite . . . And facts, which are minor or even trivial if considered in isolation, when taken together may suffice to satisfy the court of the likelihood of future harm. The court will attach to all the relevant facts the appropriate weight when coming to an overall conclusion on the crucial issue.

I must emphasise a further point. I have indicated that unproved allegations of maltreatment cannot form the basis for a finding by the court that either limb of section 31(2)(a) is established. It is, of course, open to a court to conclude there is a real possibility that the child will suffer harm in the future although harm in the past has not been established. There will be cases where, although the alleged maltreatment itself is not proved, the evidence does establish a combination of profoundly worrying features affecting the care of the child within the family. In such cases it would be open to a court in appropriate circumstances to find that, although not satisfied the child is yet suffering significant harm, on the basis of such facts as are proved there is a likelihood that he will do so in the future.

That is not the present case. The three younger girls are not at risk unless D1 was abused by Mr. R in the past. If she was not abused, there is no reason for thinking the others may be. This is not a case where Mr. R has a history of abuse. Thus the one and only relevant fact is whether D1 was abused by Mr. R as she says. The other surrounding facts, such as the fact that D1 made a complaint and the fact that her mother responded unsatisfactorily, lead nowhere relevant in this case if they do not lead to the conclusion that D1 was abused. To decide that the others are at risk because there is a possibility that D1 was abused would be to base the decision, not on fact, but on suspicion: the suspicion that D1 may have been abused. That would be to lower the threshold prescribed by Parliament . . .

Conclusion

As I read the Act, Parliament decided that the threshold for a care order should be that the child is suffering significant harm, or there is a real possibility that he will do so. In the latter regard the threshold is comparatively low. Therein lies the protection for children. But, as I read the Act, Parliament also decided that proof of the relevant facts is needed if this threshold is to be surmounted. Before the section 1 welfare test and the welfare 'checklist' can be applied, the threshold has to be crossed. Therein lies the protection for parents. They are not to be at risk of having their child taken from them and removed into the care of the local authority on the basis only of suspicions, whether of the judge or of the local authority or anyone else. A conclusion that the child is suffering or is likely to suffer harm must be based on facts, not just suspicion.

Lord Lloyd and Lord Browne-Wilkinson dissented, concerned that the majority approach set the threshold for state intervention too high and left children in unacceptable situations of risk.[204]

[204] See also Keating (1996), (2009). Cf Cobley and Lowe (2009), 468.

LORD BROWNE-WILKINSON:

I agree that the judge can only act on evidence and on facts which, so far as relevant, have been proved. He has to be satisfied by the evidence before him that there is a real possibility of serious harm to the child.

Where I part company is in thinking that the facts relevant to an assessment of risk ('is likely to suffer . . . harm') are not the same as the facts relevant to a decision that harm is in fact being suffered. In order to be satisfied that an event has occurred or is occurring the evidence has to show on balance of probabilities that such event did occur or is occurring. But in order to be satisfied that there is a risk of such an occurrence, the ambit of the relevant facts is in my view wider. The combined effect of a number of factors which suggest that a state of affairs, though not proved to exist, may well exist is the normal basis for the assessment of future risk. To be satisfied of the existence of a risk does not require proof of the occurrence of past historical events but proof of facts which are relevant to the making of a prognosis.

Let me give an example, albeit a dated one. Say that in 1940 those responsible for giving air-raid warnings had received five unconfirmed sightings of approaching aircraft which might be enemy bombers. They could not, on balance of probabilities, have reached a conclusion that any one of those sightings was of an enemy aircraft: nor could they logically have put together five non-proven sightings so as to be satisfied that enemy aircraft were in fact approaching. But their task was not simply to decide whether enemy aircraft were approaching but whether there was a risk of an air raid. The facts relevant to the assessment of such risk were the reports that unconfirmed sightings had been made, not the truth of such reports. They could well, on the basis of those unconfirmed reports, have been satisfied that there was a real possibility of an air raid and given warning accordingly . . .

My Lords, I am anxious that the decision of the House in this case may establish the law in an unworkable form to the detriment of many children at risk. Child abuse, particularly sex abuse, is notoriously difficult to prove in a court of law. The relevant facts are extremely sensitive and emotive. They are often known only to the child and to the alleged abuser. If legal proof of actual abuse is a prerequisite to a finding that a child is at risk of abuse, the court will be powerless to intervene to protect children in relation to whom there are the gravest suspicions of actual abuse but the necessary evidence legally to prove such abuse is lacking.

The majority position was affirmed by the House of Lords in *Re B (Children) (Care Proceedings: Standard of Proof)*. Thus the court cannot be satisfied that child A is likely to suffer significant harm on the basis that there is a 'real possibility' or 'suspicion' that child B has suffered similar harm in the past at the hands of one or both parents.

Re B (Children) (Care Proceedings: Standard of Proof) [2008] UKHL 35

BARONESS HALE:

22. This case is about the meaning of the words "is likely to suffer significant harm". How is the court to be satisfied of such a likelihood? This is a prediction from existing facts, often from a multitude of such facts, about what has happened in the past, about the characters and personalities of the people involved, about the things which they have said and done, and so on. But do those facts have to be proved in the usual way, on the balance of probabilities? Or is it sufficient that there is a "real possibility" that they took place, even if the judge is unable to say that it is more likely than not that they did? . . .

32. In our legal system, if a judge finds it more likely than not that something did take place, then it is treated as having taken place. If he finds it more likely than not that it did not take place, then it is treated as not having taken place. He is not allowed to sit on the fence. He has to find for one side or the other. Sometimes the burden of proof will come to his rescue: the party with the burden of showing that something took place will not have satisfied him that it did. But generally speaking a judge is able to make up his mind where the truth lies without needing to rely upon the burden of proof. . . .

54. The reasons given by Lord Nicholls for adopting the approach which he did in *Re H* remain thoroughly convincing. The threshold is there to protect both the children and their parents from unjustified intervention in their lives. It would provide no protection at all if it could be established on the basis of unsubstantiated suspicions: that is, where a judge cannot say that there is no real possibility that abuse took place, so concludes that there is a real possibility that it did. In other words, the alleged perpetrator would have to prove that it did not. [Counsel] accepts that it must be proved on the balance of probabilities that a child "is suffering" significant harm. But nevertheless he argues that those same allegations, which could not be proved for that purpose, could be the basis of a finding of likelihood of future harm. If that were so, there would have been no need for the first limb of section 31(2)(a) at all. Parliament must be presumed to have inserted it for a purpose. Furthermore, the Act draws a clear distinction between the threshold to be crossed before the court may make a final care or supervision order and the threshold for making preliminary and interim orders. If Parliament had intended that a mere suspicion that a child had suffered harm could form the basis for making a final order, it would have used the same terminology of "reasonable grounds to suspect" or "reasonable grounds to believe" as it uses elsewhere in the Act. Instead it speaks of what the child is suffering or is likely to suffer . . .

59. To allow the courts to make decisions about the allocation of parental responsibility for children on the basis of unproven allegations and unsubstantiated suspicions would be to deny them their essential role in protecting both children and their families from the intervention of the state, however well intentioned that intervention may be. It is to confuse the role of the local authority, in assessing and managing risk, in planning for the child, and deciding what action to initiate, with the role of the court in deciding where the truth lies and what the legal consequences should be. I do not under-estimate the difficulty of deciding where the truth lies but that is what the courts are for.

Re H was concerned with the issue of whether or not past abuse to child A had been proven and could thus form the basis of the care order application with respect to child B. This needs to be distinguished from cases where the issue is not whether or not past abuse has occurred to child A but as to the *identity* of the alleged perpetrator of the abuse. So the factual matrix in this alternative scenario is an allegation by the LA that child B is at risk of significant harm as a result of proven abuse suffered by child A but there is uncertainty as to the identity of the perpetrator of the abuse.[205] This particular problem was addressed by the Supreme Court in the case of *Re J (Care Proceedings: Possible Perpetrators)*.[206]

In *Re J* the care order application was being advanced, somewhat artificially, on the *sole* basis that the child was *likely to suffer significant harm* because they were being cared for by

[205] Note also that this needs to be distinguished from cases where the basis for the LA's application is proven abuse to the child who is the *subject* of the application but the identity of the perpetrator is unknown. This is the scenario dealt with by *Lancashire CC v B* [2000] 2 AC 147 (threshold) and *Re O and N* [2003] UKHL 18 (welfare), discussed at 12.4.4.b.

[206] [2013] UKSC 9.

an individual who *may* have caused harm (that harm being proven) to *another* child. In other words, the basis of the application was that one of child B's carers was within the 'pool of possible perpetrators' for causing harm to child A. It is important to note that the decision does not apply to cases where a previous child (child A) has been harmed whilst in the care of the parents (although it is not possible to say which of the two parents was the perpetrator) but the family unit remains intact such that a subsequent child (child B) who now forms the basis of the care order application is being cared for by *the same two parents* where it is known that one of the parents *must* have been the perpetrator of the previous abuse. The care order application in *Re J* related to three children in the care of 'the mother' and 'the father'. The mother was the biological mother of the youngest child only. The father was the biological father of the two oldest children only. The youngest child was the mother's third child by her previous partner. Her first child with her previous partner died aged three weeks. The baby was found to have suffered multiple non-accidental injuries and died as a result of asphyxia caused either deliberately or by the mother's former partner taking her to bed with him. In care proceedings relating to the mother's second child, the judge could not identify the perpetrator of the non-accidental injuries suffered by the first child but found in any event that both parents were culpable, having colluded in hiding the truth in order to protect the person responsible. For the purposes of the current care proceedings, the LA chose not to seek to rely on the finding that both the mother and her former partner had colluded to hide the truth and had failed to protect a child in their care. The LA proceeded instead on the single basis that the mother fell within the pool of possible perpetrators for causing non-accidental injuries to the baby. The question for the Supreme Court was whether this was *sufficient* for the threshold criteria to be crossed in relation to the third child and her two older step-siblings in the new family unit. The unanimous decision of the Supreme Court was that this fact was not by itself *sufficient* for a finding that the three children currently living within the mother's household were likely to suffer significant harm, it never having been proved on the balance of probabilities that the mother had caused non-accidental injuries to another child. Lady Hale gave the lead judgment in which, having set out the issue, she started by referring to the earlier case of *Re S-B*, in which (in obiter comments) she had appeared to answer this question:

Re S-B (Non-Accidental Injury) [2009] UKSC 17

LADY HALE:

49. There is a further reason to remit the case. The judge found the threshold crossed in relation to William [the child who had suffered no actual harm] on the basis that there was a real possibility that the mother had injured Jason. That, as already explained, is not a permissible approach to a finding of likelihood of future harm. It was established in *Re H* and confirmed in *Re O*, that a prediction of future harm has to be based upon findings of actual fact made on the balance of probabilities. It is only once those facts have been found that the degree of likelihood of future events becomes the 'real possibility' test adopted in *Re H*. It might have been open to the judge to find the threshold crossed in relation to William on a different basis, but she did not do so.

Having quoted this passage, Lady Hale reviewed the so-called 'trilogy' of House of Lords decisions in this area, namely *Re H (Minors) (Sexual Abuse: Standard of Proof)*,[207] *Lancashire*

[207] [1996] AC 563, discussed previously.

County Council v B,[208] and *Re O (Non-Accidental Injury)*.[209] Lady Hale concluded that none was directly on point, but that the principles emerging from them were 'entirely consistent' with para 49 of *Re S-B*, and consequently it could be said that that paragraph 'represents a correct statement of the law'.[210]

The policy rationale lying behind this conclusion is important. Lady Hale stresses the importance of s 31 in striking the correct balance between protecting children from the risk of harm whilst according due respect to family autonomy and protecting the family from unwarranted state intervention. The threshold is crucial to striking that balance, with Lady Hale emphasizing that the various tests set out under s 31 must be looked at together in assessing whether that balance has been correctly struck.

Re J (Care Proceedings: Possible Perpetrators) **[2013] UKSC 9**

LADY HALE:

44. Time and again, the cases have stressed that the threshold conditions are there to protect both the child and his family from unwarranted interference by the state. There must be a clearly established objective basis for such interference. Without it, there would be no "pressing social need" for the state to interfere in the family life enjoyed by the child and his parents which is protected by article 8 of the ECHR. Reasonable suspicion is a sufficient basis for the authorities to investigate and even to take interim protective measures, but it cannot be a sufficient basis for the long term intervention, frequently involving permanent placement outside the family, which is entailed in a care order. . . .

49. Having adopted a flexible test of likelihood, it became all the more important to hold that an objective factual basis was required from which to draw the inference that future harm was likely.

Lord Wilson gave a concurring judgment strongly agreeing with Lady Hale on the fundamental issue at stake and the rationale underpinning the Supreme Court's approach.

LORD WILSON:

71. Stockton [the LA] does not dispute that a prediction of likelihood of significant harm must be founded on proven facts. There is, of course, no express statement of such a requirement in the Act itself. It arises as a result of judicial interpretation at the highest level . . . Stockton argues, instead, that a person's consignment to a pool of possible perpetrators of harm to a child is itself a finding of fact which can found a prediction that a second child is likely to suffer significant harm; or, even if not, that, when added to a finding (being on any view a finding of fact) that the first child did suffer harm, it provides the requisite foundation upon which it would be open to the court to predict the likelihood.

72. Is a bald statement that there is a real possibility that X caused the injuries a statement of fact? I personally do not find the answer easy. But there is no need for an answer. For the consignment of two (or more) persons to a pool of possible perpetrators goes further than that: it is a statement not only that there is a real possibility that X caused the injuries and alternatively that Y caused them but also that no one else caused them, i.e that one or other of

[208] [2000] 2 AC 147, discussed later. [209] [2003] UKHL 18, discussed later.
[210] *Re J (Care Proceedings: Possible Perpetrators)* [2013] UKSC 9, [43].

them did cause them. I am clear that such a conclusion does amount to a finding of fact. But is it a fact relevant to the threshold? Where X and Y remain together as a unit and are putting themselves forward as carers for an unharmed child, it is certainly relevant and might well suffice in enabling the threshold to be crossed in relation to that child; for in those circumstances the fact is that somebody in the child's proposed home did perpetrate injuries to another child. But the difficulty arises in the case, reflective of the facts in this appeal, in which X and Y no longer remain together as a unit and in which only one of them, X, is put forward as a carer. The consignment of X to a pool is not a finding that X did cause the injuries. So the question arises whether in that situation such a finding of fact is relevant.

73. Here is the crux of this appeal. Stockton's case is deeply illogical. Stockton argues that the children are at risk of suffering significant harm because of the presence in their home of [the mother]. So the requisite foundational facts must relate to [the mother]. To point to no more than the fact that [the mother's first child] suffered grave non-accidental injuries is, on any view, insufficient. A second fact is needed such as relates to [the mother]. Stockton seeks to make the link with her by relying on her consignment to the pool of possible perpetrators of the injuries. But her consignment to the pool is not a relevant fact because it falls short of ascribing their perpetration to her. The result is that there is no relevant second fact. In both *In re H* and *In re B*, cited above, it was clear that, if in each case the girl had suffered harm, it had been at the hands of her step-father; in the event, however, the court's conclusion was no more than that there was a real possibility that she had suffered the harm. Stockton does not challenge the principle established by those cases that such a conclusion was insufficient to found a likelihood that the step-father would cause significant harm to other children. The present appeal presents the precisely obverse situation; there was no doubt that [the mother's first child] had suffered harm and the only issue, which in the event was unable to be resolved save in terms of a real possibility, related to the identity of the perpetrator. There is in my view no basis for departing from that principle in this precisely obverse, yet analogous, situation. The harm and the person's responsibility for it are the two planks on which any conclusion about likelihood must rest and they must be equally sturdy.

75. If and insofar (so Stockton proceeds to submit) as the basis of the appeal is illogical, then so be it; for otherwise legalism would triumph over child protection. But - in my view - logic is the blood which runs through the veins of the law: allow it to escape and ultimately the edifice collapses. Nor is the rigid approach to the factual foundation properly categorised as legalism.

76. My view remains that the need for the local authority to prove the facts which give rise to a real possibility of significant harm in the future is a bulwark against too ready an interference with family life on the part of the state. And, subject to the caveat that the court received no argument on the impact of article 8 of the European Convention on Human Rights, I incline to the view that nothing less than a factual foundation would justify such grave interference with the rights of the child and the parents thereunder to respect for their family life . . .

77. I therefore conclude that the mother's consignment to the pool of possible perpetrators of the injuries to T-L is irrelevant to whether the three subject children are likely to suffer significant harm.

Although agreeing on the central point, Lord Wilson (supported by Lord Sumption) departed from the majority on the important question of whether the consignment of the mother to a pool of possible perpetrators could be of *any relevance* at all to establishing the threshold. Lady Hale,[211] Lord Hope, and Lord Reed (with whom Lord Clarke and Lord Carnworth agreed) were of the view that such a finding, whilst not *by itself sufficient* to cross the threshold, could be *relevant* to establishing the threshold criteria, such that, when taken together with other established facts (e.g. other failings in parental capacity which

[211] See at [51]–[54].

contributed to the previous child's injuries) it could be found to be sufficient. This point is made most clearly in Lord Hope's judgment.

LORD HOPE:

86. To identify what is and is not a "finding of fact" for the purposes of the threshold, which looks to the future, is only the first step in the analysis. Views may differ as to what is truly a "fact" for this purpose, but I do not think that one need dwell on this question. Anything that is proved on a balance of probabilities may be taken into account to see what can be made of it. The crucial steps are to identify what is *relevant* and what is not, and then to determine whether what is found to be relevant is *sufficient* for a finding that the threshold has been crossed. If it is not, the question will be whether there are other facts and circumstances that can be brought into account to satisfy this requirement.

87. Let us assume that the question is whether the child would be at risk while in the care of X. A finding that X is in the pool of two or more possible perpetrators of harm that a child sustained in the past is a finding of fact. It means that, because X is in the pool, it is possible that X was the perpetrator. If the perpetrators are still together, it will be relevant, and may on its own be sufficient, to show that the threshold has been crossed. If the parties have separated and X is the carer, I decline to say that a finding that X was in the pool will no longer be relevant. That is so for two reasons: first, because it is information which invites further inquiry as to whether the subsequent child is likely to suffer harm while in the care of X; and, second, because, in combination with other facts and circumstances that the inquiry reveals about X's attitude or behaviour, it may help to show that this threshold has been crossed. It may have a bearing on the weight of the evidence when looked at as a whole, including an assessment of the balance of probabilities.

88. . . . So I do not, with respect, agree with Lord Wilson that the finding can never be relevant. But it will not on its own be sufficient. The crucial point is this: it cannot, and must not, be treated on its own as a finding of fact that it was X who caused or contributed to the injuries.

As Lord Hope indicated, Lord Wilson strongly disagreed with this view.

LORD WILSON:

80. . . . I feel driven to the conclusion that their suggestion is illogical; and that if, for the purpose of the requisite foundation, X's consignment to a pool has a value of zero on its own, it can, for this purpose, have no greater value in company. I can only hope that their suggestion, highly authoritative though it will be, will not destabilise the requisite foundation; will not in practice lead to a prediction about a real possibility in the future being founded, in part, on no more than a real possibility about what happened in the past.

The position following the Supreme Court's decision in *Re J* can thus be summarized as follows:

- the consignment of a child's carer to a pool of possible perpetrators for causing non-accidental injuries to *another* child cannot by itself constitute a sufficient factual basis for a finding that the unharmed child who is the subject of the present care order application is likely to suffer future significant harm;

- however, whilst the consignment of the child's carer to a pool of possible perpetrators is not by itself sufficient for the threshold to be crossed, it is a relevant fact for the court to consider and when taken together with other relevant facts may constitute a sufficient factual basis for a finding that the unharmed child who is the subject of the present care order application is likely to suffer future significant harm.

The Supreme Court's approach to unknown perpetrators at the threshold stage in *Re J* met with a mixed academic response. Bainham welcomed the decision as striking the correct balance between protecting the family from unwarranted intervention and protecting children from harm.[212] The majority's reasoning has, however, been subjected to strong criticism by Gilmore as being 'formalistic and unconvincing'.[213] Gilmore argues that Lady Hale was too focused on 'legal logic' at the expense of grappling with the important underlying questions of legal policy. Insofar as Lady Hale does address those questions, Gilmore criticizes her for a misplaced emphasis on the role of the threshold criteria in acting as a bulwark for parents against unwarranted state intervention into family life as opposed to focusing on the overriding necessity of protecting children.

S. Gilmore, '*Re J (Care Proceedings: Past Possible Perpetrators in a New Family Unit)* [2013] UKSC 9: Bulwarks and Logic—The Blood Which Runs Through the Veins of Law—But How Much Will Be Spilled in Future?', (2013) 25 *Child and Family Law Quarterly* 215, 230

Lord Nicholls was clear in the earlier uncertain perpetrator cases that the policy that outweighs all others is child protection and that children are not to be put at risk simply because a possible perpetrator of proven harm to a child cannot be identified. . . . Some sound reasons underlie that policy. As Professor Hayes has observed, the policy that should prevail in the debate concerning how the balance should be held between parents' and children's interests in child protection cases is informed by consideration of the relative risks involved. In a case such as *Re J*, this involves considering the nature of the harm to the child which might occur if the court were not to permit protection of the child on the basis of a person's possible perpetration of harm to another child, as against the harm which might occur if intervention were permitted and later found to have an erroneous basis because it is discovered that the person did not perpetrate any harm. Both are errors with serious consequences, but which of two outcomes is likely to be potentially worse for the child: a false finding of anticipated abuse or a false finding that there is no risk of future abuse? In a case like *Re J*, the potential consequences to a child of not permitting intervention (possible death or physical injury) may be regarded as more serious than the consequences of what may turn out to have been unwarranted state intervention. . . . *Re H* is not authority for a general principle that inferences about future harm must *always* be based upon facts proved on the balance of probabilities. By contrast, in *Re J* the basis for inferring a risk of future harm was not mere suspicion of past harm; it was qualitatively different. While it could only be said that the mother *might* be the source of risk to the children in *Re J*, the fact remained that there was a proven risk to the children in *Re J*, founded on the proven fact of harm to another child. The facts of *Re J* – given the proven past harm to another child – were in this regard crucially different from *Re H's* finding of no judicially determined risk at all.

[212] Bainham (2013), 269. [213] Gilmore (2013), 236.

12.5.3.b 'Is attributable to the care given to the child not being what it would be reasonable to expect a parent to give to him'

General principles

The second limb of the threshold test similarly raises the difficult question of whether the LA must be able to prove on the balance of probabilities that the harm is attributable to one or other or both of the parents before the s 31(2) criteria are met. By this stage of the inquiry, the court will already be satisfied that the child is suffering or likely to suffer harm. While there are a handful of cases about whether certain forms of harm can arise from 'reasonable' parenting,[214] more commonly the issue at this stage will thus typically arise in cases where it has been established on the balance of probabilities that the child who is the subject of the application has suffered harm but the identity of the perpetrator remains open to question. The issue again has important implications as to the overall threshold for state intervention into the family. It was confirmed by Lady Hale in *Re S-B (Non-Accidental Injury)* that the test to be applied when identifying the perpetrator is the balance of probabilities.[215]

Two further points regarding the correct interpretation of the 'attributable to' limb of the threshold criteria should be noted. It was established in *Lancashire CC v B* that the phrase 'attributable to' connotes a causal connection between the harm and the care being given to the child, but the care in question need not be the 'sole or dominant or direct cause'; a contributory cause, such as a parent's failure to protect, is sufficient.[216] Lord Nicholls also addressed the standard of care to be expected of the caregiver, emphasizing that it was not a question of attributing blame or culpability but establishing that the care had fallen below an objectively acceptable level.[217] It is a wholly 'objective' test, thus the reasonable parent is not to be imbued with the particular characteristics of the parent in question when determining whether the care provided has fallen below the required standard.[218] Similarly, there is no subjective mental element: the parent does not have to *intend* to cause harm.[219] It is also important to distinguish between the parents' particular personality or characteristics and the impact of those characteristics on their ability to adequately parent the child. As made clear in *Re B (Care Proceedings: Appeal)*,[220] only the latter is relevant. The fact that a parent may have learning difficulties or a long criminal history or is a compulsive liar are all irrelevant unless they impact in some way on the quality of the care afforded to the child.

In determining the objective standard of care to be expected of parents, it has been held that social and cultural differences may be taken into consideration. *Re K*[221] concerned applications for various orders with respect to a 16-year-old Kurdish Iraqi girl whose family had moved to the UK following her father being granted asylum. In accordance with the family's cultural and religious practices, the girl had entered into an arranged (not forced)

[214] See, e.g., *Re B and G (Care Proceedings)* [2015] EWFC 3, [59]–[73], suggesting that male circumcision amounts to significant harm but is 'reasonable' parenting. In *Leicester City Council v AB* [2018] EWHC 1960, the mother, as sole carer for two children, was diagnosed with terminal cancer and placed the children in s 20 accommodation while she received treatment; Keehan J held that she had 'acted as a perfectly reasonable, loving, caring mother and requested that the children be cared for by the local authority', and so any harm which the children had suffered or were at risk of suffering could not be said to be attributable to the mother failing to provide care which it was reasonable to expect a parent to give.

[215] [2009] UKSC 17, [34].

[216] [2000] 2 AC 147, 162.

[217] Ibid.

[218] *Re D (A Child) (Care Order: Evidence)* [2010] EWCA Civ 1000, [35].

[219] *Re B (Care Proceedings: Appeal)* [2013] UKSC 33, [31].

[220] [2013] UKSC 33.

[221] [2005] EWHC 2956.

marriage at the age of 15 in a religious ceremony in the UK. She subsequently alleged that she had been raped and sexually abused by her 'husband' and physically abused by her father. The police and LA intervened and she became estranged from her family. Although she maintained her allegations of rape, she later returned to the family home and refused to cooperate with social services. The LA applied for a supervision order and orders under the court's inherent jurisdiction to prevent the parents removing her from the UK or consenting to a further marriage whilst she was under the age of 18. The applications were dismissed. In considering the question of whether the harm suffered by the girl as a result of the arranged marriage was attributable to the care given by the parents, Munby J held that whilst the care afforded by the parents was to be judged in accordance with an objective standard, the court must be sensitive to the social, cultural, and religious world-view of the family and evaluate the parents' behaviour accordingly.[222] Taking into account the parents' cultural and religious beliefs and the fact that the mother was herself married to the father at the age of 14, Munby J went on to observe that he would be very reluctant to find that parents who had only recently settled in the UK had fallen below an acceptable standard of parenting if, when judged against the standards of their own community, they would be regarded as having done nothing wrong.[223] Indeed, it was evident in this case that the parents were genuinely upset and bemused as to why an arranged marriage at the age of 15 should have been regarded as abusive and have caused such outrage amongst the relevant professionals. This judicial sensitivity to cultural difference has not, however, been welcomed by all, with fears it sanctions a relativist approach to child protection. Keating, for example, has noted that the judgment 'could lend weight to the idea that children from different ethnic backgrounds could legitimately receive different levels of protection from harm' and that 'any such inference would be deeply wrong'.[224]

Uncertain perpetrator cases

A particular problem arises when the LA is unable to discharge the burden of proof with respect to any one particular individual, but the fact that the child has suffered significant injury is not in doubt. The problem of the 'uncertain perpetrator' was addressed by the House of Lords in *Lancashire CC v B*.[225] Lord Nicholls again gave judgment for the majority, arguably sanctioning state intervention in circumstances where, contrary to his judgment in *Re H* and the subsequent decision of the Supreme Court in *Re J*, there was only a *suspicion*, as opposed to established fact, that the child had suffered significant harm *at the hands of the parents*. The case concerned the now common scenario where the care of the child had been shared between the parents and a childminder, although the problem of the 'unknown perpetrator' also frequently arises where the parents have subsequently separated and the LA is unable to establish whether one or other or both of the parents is responsible for the harm. There was no dispute that the child had suffered significant harm. The question was whether in order to satisfy the second limb of the threshold, it had to be established, on the balance of probabilities, which of the three possible perpetrators—the mother, the father, or the childminder—had been responsible for the harm.

[222] Ibid, [25]–[26]. [223] Ibid. [224] Keating (2011), 126. [225] [2000] 2 AC 147.

Lancashire CC v B [2000] 2 AC 147 (HL), 164–7

LORD NICHOLLS:

In a case based on present harm ("is suffering . . . significant harm") the attributable condition requires the court to be satisfied that the harm is attributable to the care given to the child or, which is not this case, to the child's being beyond parental control. That nexus must be established on the basis of proved facts. But that prompts the question: care by whom? The contention of A's parents is that, having regard to the statutory context and the legislative policy behind Part IV of the Children Act 1989, "the care given to the child" in section 31(2)(b)(i) means the care given to the child by the parents or other primary carers. The contrary contention, advanced by the local authority and A's guardian, is that no such limiting words are to be read into the statute: the relevant phrase means the care given by anyone who plays a part in the care arrangements for the child.

Counsel [for the parents] submitted that a strictly literal interpretation of the phrase under consideration would lead to an absurdity. Parliament cannot have intended that a child should be at risk of being removed from his family, and the parents at risk of losing their child, because of an unforeseeable failure of care by a third party to whom the parents, wholly unexceptionably, had temporarily entrusted the child. . . .

This is a forceful argument, up to a point. I accept that the interpretation of the attributable condition urged on behalf of [the LA] . . . is too wide and loose. For this one needs to look no further than [counsel for the appellant's] example of the one-off temporary entrustment of the child to a person reasonably believed by the parents to be suitable. Injury inflicted by the temporary carer would satisfy the threshold conditions. But the appellants' argument goes too far in the other direction. The interpretation urged on behalf of the appellants is too rigid. As with the respondents' submission, so also with the appellants' submission: the conclusion to which it leads cannot be right. As the present case exemplifies, the appellants' argument, if accepted, produces the result that where a child has repeatedly sustained non-accidental injuries the court may nevertheless be unable to intervene to protect the child by making a care order or, even, a supervision order. In the present case the child is proved to have sustained significant harm at the hands of one or both of her parents or at the hands of a daytime carer. But, according to this argument, if the court is unable to identify which of the child's carers was responsible for inflicting the injuries, the child remains outside the threshold prescribed by Parliament as the threshold which must be crossed before the court can proceed to consider whether it is in the best interests of the child to make a care order or supervision order. The child must, for the time being, remain unprotected, since section 31 of the Children Act 1989 and its associated emergency and interim provisions now provide the only court mechanism available to a local authority to protect a child from risk of further harm.

I cannot believe Parliament intended that the attributable condition in section 31(2)(b) should operate in this way. Such an interpretation would mean that the child's future health, or even her life, would have to be hazarded on the chance that, after all, the non-parental carer rather than one of the parents inflicted the injuries. Self-evidently, to proceed in such a way when a child is proved to have suffered serious injury on more than one occasion could be dangerously irresponsible.

There is a further factor which weighs with me. Sadly, the unhappy facts of the present case are far from being exceptional. As the Court of Appeal observed, the task of caring for children is often shared nowadays between parents and others. When questions of non-accidental injury or abuse arise, the court is frequently unable to discover precisely what happened. This is not surprising. And yet, on the appellants' construction of the attributable

> condition, in this common form situation of shared caring the court is powerless to make even a supervision order if the judge is unable to penetrate the fog of denials, evasions, lies and half-truths which all too often descends in court at fact finding hearings . . .
>
> Against this background, I consider that a permissible and preferable interpretation of section 31(2)(b)(i), between the two extremes, is as follows. The phrase "care given to the child" refers primarily to the care given to the child by a parent or parents or other primary carers. That is the norm. The matter stands differently in a case such as the present one, where care is shared and the court is unable to distinguish in a crucial respect between the care given by the parents or primary carers and the care given by other carers. Different considerations from the norm apply in a case of shared caring where the care given by one or other of the carers is proved to have been deficient, with the child suffering harm in consequence, but the court is unable to identify which of the carers provided the deficient care. In such a case, the phrase "care given to the child" is apt to embrace not merely the care given by the parents or other primary carers; it is apt to embrace the care given by any of the carers. Some such meaning has to be given to the phrase if the unacceptable consequences already mentioned are to be avoided. This interpretation achieves that necessary result while, at the same time, encroaching to the minimum extent on the general principles underpinning section 31(2). Parliament seems not to have foreseen this particular problem. The courts must therefore apply the statutory language to the unforeseen situation in the manner which best gives effect to the purposes the legislation was enacted to achieve.

Lord Nicholls noted the difficulties caused by this approach but held that the known risk of harm to the child outweighed any potential unfairness to the parents:

> I recognise that the effect of this construction is that the attributable condition may be satisfied when there is no more than a possibility that the parents were responsible for inflicting the injuries which the child has undoubtedly suffered. That is a consequence which flows from giving the phrase, in the limited circumstances mentioned above, the wider meaning those circumstances require. I appreciate also that in such circumstances, when the court proceeds to the next stage and considers whether to exercise its discretionary power to make a care order or supervision order, the judge may be faced with a particularly difficult problem. The judge will not know which individual was responsible for inflicting the injuries. The child may suffer harm if left in a situation of risk with his parents. The child may also suffer harm if removed from parental care where, if the truth were known, the parents present no risk. Above all, I recognise that this interpretation of the attributable condition means that parents who may be wholly innocent, and whose care may not have fallen below that of a reasonable parent, will face the possibility of losing their child, with all the pain and distress this involves. That is a possibility, once the threshold conditions are satisfied, although by no means a certainty. It by no means follows that because the threshold conditions are satisfied the court will go on to make a care order. And it goes without saying that when considering how to exercise their discretionary powers in this type of case judges will keep firmly in mind that the parents have not been shown to be responsible for the child's injuries.
>
> I recognise all these difficulties. This is indeed a most unfortunate situation for everyone involved: the child, the parents, the child-minder, the local authority and the court. But, so far as the threshold conditions are concerned, the factor which seems to me to outweigh all others is the prospect that an unidentified, and unidentifiable, carer may inflict further injury on a child he or she has already severely damaged.

Following *Lancashire CC v B*, it is clear that in order to satisfy the second limb of the threshold it is not necessary where it is known the subject child has suffered harm to identify the perpetrator of the harm. However, establishing the identity of the perpetrator where possible remains of considerable importance as the proceedings progress to the welfare stage and the court is required to determine the future arrangements for the child. Thus, whilst unnecessary to meet the threshold criteria, where the perpetrator can be identified on the balance of probabilities, the court has a duty to do so.[226] There is, however, a limit as to what the court can be expected to do.[227] The Court of Appeal has emphasized that where identification is simply not possible on the evidence, it is the 'duty of the judge to state that as his or her conclusion'.[228] The question then arises what more, if anything, the court should do where the perpetrator cannot be identified. The Supreme Court addressed this particular aspect of the problem in *Re S-B (Non-Accidental Injury)*, holding that the court should identify the 'pool of possible perpetrators' because 'it will help to identify the real risks to the child and the steps needed to protect him. It will help the professionals working with the family. And it will be of value to the child in the long run.'[229]

The test for identifying the 'pool of possible perpetrators' was addressed in *North Yorkshire CC v SA*.[230] The Court of Appeal held that applying a test of 'no possibility' to *exclude* a possible perpetrator from the pool was 'patently too wide': it may leave in the pool 'anyone who had even a fleeting contact with the child in circumstances in which there was the opportunity to cause injuries'.[231] Butler-Sloss P suggested that the test for *inclusion* in the pool should be 'likelihood or real possibility'.[232] This approach was approved in *Re S-B*.

Re S-B (Non-Accidental Injury) [2009] UKSC 17

LADY HALE:

43. The cases are littered with references to a "finding of exculpation" or to "ruling out" a particular person as responsible for the harm suffered. This is . . . to set the bar far too high. It suggests that parents and other carers are expected to prove their innocence beyond reasonable doubt. If the evidence is not such as to establish responsibility on the balance of probabilities it should nevertheless be such as to establish whether there is a real possibility that a particular person was involved. When looking at how best to protect the child and provide for his future, the judge will have to consider the strength of that possibility as part of the overall circumstances of the case.

The Court of Appeal has given further guidance on 'pool of possible perpetrator' cases. To avoid unduly implicating people, Peter Jackson LJ emphasized in *Re B (Children: Uncertain Perpetrator)* that '[w]here there are a number of people who might have caused the harm, it is for the local authority to show that in relation to each of them there is a real possibility that they did. No one can be placed into the pool unless that has been shown.'[233] The court should, if possible, identify the actual perpetrator—but if this is not possible, it can move to ask, in relation to each person on the list of those who had the opportunity to cause the injuries, whether there is a likelihood or real possibility that they were the (or a) perpetrator of

[226] *Re D (Children) (Non-Accidental Injury)* [2009] EWCA Civ 472, [12]. [227] Ibid.
[228] Ibid. [229] [2009] UKSC 17, [40]. [230] [2003] EWCA Civ 839. [231] Ibid, [25].
[232] Ibid, [26]. [233] [2019] EWCA Civ 575, [48].

the injuries.[234] It is important to note that '[t]here is no such thing as a pool of one': if there is only one possible person 'in the frame', the LA must prove (on the balance of probabilities) that they were responsible for the injuries or the threshold will not be met.[235]

12.5.3.c Standard of proof for establishing the threshold criteria

In order to satisfy both limbs of the threshold criteria, the LA will need to establish a number of key facts. It was held by Lord Nicholls in *Re H* that the usual civil standard of proof applies, placing the burden on the LA to satisfy the court on the balance of probabilities as to any disputed factual issues. None of this is particularly contentious.[236] However, more controversially, Lord Nicholls went on to explain how, in his view, 'the inherent probability or improbability of an event is itself a matter to be taken into account when weighing the probabilities and deciding whether, on balance, the event occurred'.[237]

This approach was interpreted to mean that the more serious the allegation, the more cogent and convincing the evidence would need to be to tip the balance of probabilities in favour of the LA.[238] Lord Lloyd gave a strong dissenting judgment in *Re H* itself, describing such an approach as 'bizarre'.[239]

The House of Lords revisited the issue in *Re B (Children) (Care: Proceedings)*.[240] The suggestion that there should be a 'heightened' civil standard of proof to care proceedings was firmly rejected.[241] The House of Lords unanimously held that the usual civil standard of proof was to be applied without further gloss or elaboration. That said, both Lord Hoffmann and Baroness Hale went on to state that the inherent improbability of an event occurring *may* be relevant, an alleged improbable 'fact' being harder to prove on the balance of probabilities than a probable one. However, whilst noting the potential relevance of inherent probabilities to discharging the burden of proof, both expressly disagreed with Lord Nicholls' basic assertion that the seriousness of the allegation bears any relationship to the inherent improbability of the event occurring.

Re B (Children) (Care Proceedings) **[2008] UKHL 35**

BARONESS HALE:

70. . . . I would go further and announce loud and clear that the standard of proof in finding the facts necessary to establish the threshold under section 31(2) or the welfare considerations in section 1 of the 1989 Act is the simple balance of probabilities, neither more nor less. Neither the seriousness of the allegation nor the seriousness of the consequences should make any difference to the standard of proof to be applied in determining the facts. The inherent probabilities are simply something to be taken into account, where relevant, in deciding where the truth lies . . .

[234] Ibid, [49]. [235] Ibid, [46].

[236] See, e.g., a straightforward reminder that the burden is on the LA to prove its case in *Re M (Fact-Finding Hearing: Burden of Proof)* [2012] EWCA Civ 1580.

[237] *Re H (Sexual Abuse: Standard of Proof)* [1996] AC 563, 586.

[238] *Re U (A Child) (Serious Injury: Standard of Proof)* [2004] EWCA Civ 567, [13].

[239] See also Keating (1996). [240] [2008] UKHL 35. [241] Ibid, [64]. See Keating (2009).

72. As to the seriousness of the allegation, there is no logical or necessary connection between seriousness and probability. Some seriously harmful behaviour, such as murder, is sufficiently rare to be inherently improbable in most circumstances. Even then there are circumstances, such as a body with its throat cut and no weapon to hand, where it is not at all improbable. Other seriously harmful behaviour, such as alcohol or drug abuse, is regrettably all too common and not at all improbable. Nor are serious allegations made in a vacuum. Consider the famous example of the animal seen in Regent's Park. If it is seen outside the zoo on a stretch of greensward regularly used for walking dogs, then of course it is more likely to be a dog than a lion. If it is seen in the zoo next to the lions' enclosure when the door is open, then it may well be more likely to be a lion than a dog.

While each alleged fact is to be assessed solely on the balance of probabilities, in a case where there are numerous allegations they are not seen in isolation from one another. The judge 'has to have regard to the relevance of each piece of evidence to other evidence and to exercise an overview of the totality of the evidence in order to come to a conclusion whether the case put forward by the local authority has been made out'.[242] This approach, sometimes termed 'looking at the preponderance of the evidence',[243] bears some relation to the Supreme Court's comments in *Re J (Care Proceedings: Possible Perpetrators)* regarding the relevance of a parent being a possible perpetrator in relation to a previous child: one piece of evidence 'may have a bearing on the weight of the evidence when looked at as a whole'.[244] Consequently, the court must avoid seeing itself as simply 'adding up' the various factors in a case, which King LJ has termed 'a "pseudo-mathematical" approach to the burden of proof'.[245] In *Re A*, a girl aged 10 had died of strangulation in unexplained circumstances, the possibilities being suicide, accident, or intentional act by a third party. The trial judge approached it in this way:

Aggregating . . . the probability of suicide together with the probability of accident, I find that the aggregate of these two is more than 50 per cent. . . . I find that the possibility of suicide is about 10 per cent, and the possibility of accident and a perpetrated act are about 45 per cent each.

The Court of Appeal was clear that this approach was impermissible.

Re A (Care Proceedings: Burden of Proof) **[2018] EWCA Civ 1718**

KING LJ:

57. I accept that there may occasionally be cases where, at the conclusion of the evidence and submissions, the court will ultimately say that the local authority has not discharged the burden of proof to the requisite standard and thus decline to make the findings. That this is the case goes hand in hand with the well-established law that suspicion, or even strong

[242] *Re T (Abuse: Standard of Proof)* [2004] EWCA Civ 558, [33].
[243] *Re A (Care Proceedings: Burden of Proof)* [2018] EWCA Civ 1718, [58].
[244] [2013] UKSC 9, [87]; see 12.5.3.
[245] *Re A (Care Proceedings: Burden of Proof)* [2018] EWCA Civ 1718, [59].

suspicion, is not enough to discharge the burden of proof. The court must look at each possibility, both individually and together, factoring in all the evidence available . . .

58. . . . i) Judges will decide a case on the burden of proof alone only when driven to it and where no other course is open to him given the unsatisfactory state of the evidence.

ii) Consideration of such a case necessarily involves looking at the whole picture, including what gaps there are in the evidence, whether the individual factors relied upon are in themselves properly established, what factors may point away from the suggested explanation and what other explanation might fit the circumstances.

iii) The court arrives at its conclusion by considering whether on an overall assessment of the evidence (i.e. on a preponderance of the evidence) the case for believing that the suggested event happened is more compelling than the case for not reaching that belief (which is not necessarily the same as believing positively that it did not happen) and not by reference to percentage possibilities or probabilities.

12.5.4 THE WELFARE STAGE

Once the court is satisfied the threshold conditions are met, it acquires jurisdiction to make an order. It can thus move on to the second stage of the proceedings. Whether the court should make the order sought is a question relating to the child's upbringing and the child's welfare is thus the paramount consideration.[246] Section 1(4) directs the court to have particular regard to the welfare checklist in s 1(3), of which the following are of particular note.

12.5.4.a 'Ascertainable wishes and feelings of the child'

In applications for care or supervision orders, the child is made a party to the proceedings.[247] To this end, s 41 provides that the court shall appoint a children's guardian to safeguard the child's interests unless satisfied that it is not necessary to do so.[248] The core responsibilities of children's guardians include providing the court with their professional assessment as to the child's best interests and advising the court as to the child's wishes and feelings.[249] It is clear that there is no rebuttable presumption that the wishes and feelings of children should be followed, even in the case of mature minors.[250] The child's wishes must be considered within the context of the whole welfare balance. Children's guardians are also responsible for appointing and instructing a solicitor to represent the child. If the child and the guardian disagree over the handling of the case, the child may instruct the solicitor directly provided the solicitor, the children's guardian, or the court considers the child is of sufficient understanding to do so.[251] In such circumstances, the guardian will continue to act, subject to the directions of the court, and may, with leave, appoint their own legal representation.[252] Although the child may be a party to public law proceedings, the child is not entitled to attend court if represented by a children's guardian or solicitor.[253] Indeed, the courts have strongly discouraged guardians from allowing children to be present at hearings.[254]

246 *Humberside County Council v B* [1993] 1 FLR 257, 261.
247 S 41(6). 248 See also FPR 2010, r 16.3. 249 Ibid, r 16.20.
250 *Re P-S (Care Proceedings: Right to Give Evidence)* [2013] EWCA Civ 223, [43].
251 FPR 2010, r 16.21. 252 Ibid. 253 Ibid, r 12.14(3).
254 *Re C (A Minor) (Care: Child's Wishes)* [1993] 1 FLR 832, 840–1.

Alternatively, the judge may choose to speak to the child directly.[255] In April 2010, the Family Justice Council issued guidance for judges meeting children.[256] The guidelines make clear that the purpose of the meeting is to benefit the child—it is not to gather evidence. Particular caution is therefore required where the proceedings have not yet concluded to ensure that the evidence is not 'contaminated' by the judge hearing directly from a child in circumstances where the usual procedural safeguards, such as the right to cross-examine, do not apply. There remains considerable disquiet amongst the judiciary about the appropriateness and 'risks' of the judge meeting the child, particularly when the judge is engaged in a fact-finding exercise as opposed to making a forward-looking welfare decision.[257]

Whether the child should give evidence in the more conventional sense has also been the subject of Supreme Court authority and subsequent guidance by the Family Justice Council.[258] In *Re W (Children) (Abuse: Oral Evidence)*, it was argued on behalf of the father who had been accused of serious sexual abuse by his partner's daughter that in order to protect the Convention rights of all parties, including the father's right to a fair trial, there should be no presumption against a child giving evidence in care proceedings. Lady Hale agreed that there could be no such 'starting point' or 'presumption' but ultimately concluded that when the balancing exercise is carried out, weighing the right to a fair trial against the potential harm to the child, the balance is very likely to continue to fall against a child giving evidence—children giving evidence thus remains unusual.

The Supreme Court's approach was quickly challenged in the Court of Appeal in the cases of *Re P-S (Care Proceedings: Right to Give Evidence)*[259] and *Re R (Care Proceedings: Child's Right to Give Oral Evidence)*.[260] Both cases involved older children who wanted to give evidence—in *Re P-S* so he could press upon the court the strength of his opposition to a care order being made, and in *Re R* because she wished to challenge the factual allegations of sexual abuse made by the LA against her father. The Court of Appeal in *Re P-S* confirmed in accordance with Article 12 of the UN Convention on the Rights of the Child that children do have the right to be heard in family proceedings, but explained that the child's right may be realized in a variety of ways. There is thus no right to give evidence (as was argued in *Re P-S*), nor is there a right to see the judge. It will all depend on the circumstances of the case. In many cases, the child's right to be heard will be properly realized only through their guardian conveying the child's wishes and feelings to the court. The position was different in *Re R*, though, because the child's evidence went to the heart of the LA's case and she directly contradicted the LA's account. Her position could also not be relayed by the guardian, since the guardian did not believe the child's account. The Court of Appeal noted that where a witness's account is challenged (as the child's was, by the LA and the guardian), that ordinarily means that they must be cross-examined so that the judge can determine the truth of the evidence. King LJ highlighted that there were potentially detrimental effects on the child of not being allowed to give evidence when she positively wanted to, and her evidence was central to the case.

[255] *Re M (Minors) (Care Proceedings: Child's Wishes)* [1994] 1 FLR 749, 755.

[256] Family Justice Council (2010a). For further discussion and extracts from the guidance, see 11.3.3. The House of Lords Select Committee on the Children and Families Act 2014 (2022), para 151, recommended that this guidance should be reviewed.

[257] *Re A (Fact-Finding: Judge Meeting Child)* [2012] EWCA Civ 185. See also *Re P-S (Care Proceedings: Right to Give Evidence)* [2013] EWCA Civ 223, [42]; *Re KP (Abduction: Judge Meeting Child: Conduct of Interview)* [2014] EWCA Civ 554.

[258] *Re W (Children) (Abuse: Oral Evidence)* [2010] UKSC 12. See also Family Justice Council (2010b).

[259] [2013] EWCA Civ 223. [260] [2015] EWCA Civ 167.

12.5.4.b 'Any harm which he has suffered or is at risk of suffering'

For a case to be at the welfare stage, it must already have been established that the child is suffering or is likely to suffer significant harm. At this point, the court may take into account not only the harm established at the threshold stage but any additional harm the child may suffer as a result of the court making or refusing to make the orders sought. Importantly, this includes any emotional harm the child may suffer as a result of separation from their primary carers, as well as the advantages and disadvantages of 'corporate parenting' through long-term foster care, or of other care arrangements like a special guardianship order (SGO) or adoption.[261]

The Court of Appeal has held that when considering harm at the welfare stage, the same principles set down by Lord Nicholls in the House of Lords in *Re H* will apply. Only harm which is established on the balance of probabilities can therefore be considered; mere suspicion about existing or likely future harm must be excluded.

Re M and R (Minors) (Sexual Abuse: Expert Evidence) [1996] 4 All ER 239 (CA), 246–8

BUTLER-SLOSS LJ:

In the case before us [counsel] submitted that the House of Lords [in *Re H*] were concerned only with the threshold stage and that the majority view had no relevance to the welfare stage. So far as the latter stage was concerned, he submitted that since the judge in the present case was also clearly of the view that there was a real possibility that the children had been sexually abused, this was sufficient to establish that the children were at risk of suffering like harm in the future. Since a risk of harm is included in the welfare checklist set out in s 1(3) of the 1989 Act, the judge was wrong to exclude it from consideration. [Counsel] submitted that the justification for approaching s 1 in a way rejected by the House of Lords for s 31 was that under s 1 the welfare of the child was the paramount consideration, which justified and indeed required the court to act on possibilities rather than proof on the preponderance of probability . . .

In our judgment these submissions cannot be supported. They amount to the assertion that under s 1 the welfare of the child dictates that the court should act on suspicion or doubts, rather than facts. To our minds the welfare of the child dictates the exact opposite . . .

The court must reach a conclusion based on facts, not on suspicion or mere doubts. If, as in the present case, the court concludes that the evidence is insufficient to prove sexual abuse in the past, and if the fact of sexual abuse in the past is the only basis for asserting a risk of sexual abuse in the future, then it follows that there is nothing (except suspicion or mere doubts) to show a risk of future sexual abuse . . .

Section 1(3)(e) . . . does not deal with what *might* possibly have happened or what future risk there *may* possibly be. It speaks in terms of what *has* happened or what *is* at risk of happening. Thus, what the court must do (when the matter is in issue) is to decide whether the evidence establishes harm or the risk of harm.

We cannot see any justification for the suggestion that the standard of proof in performing this task should be less than the preponderance of probabilities. Were such a suggestion

[261] *Humberside County Council v B* [1993] 1 FLR 257, 267, reiterated in *Re G (Care Proceedings: Welfare Evaluation)* [2013] EWCA Civ 965, [46]–[47].

to be adopted, it would mean in effect that instead of acting on what was established as probably the case, the court would have to act on what was only possibly the case, or even on the basis of what was probably not the case. This, as Lord Nicholls pointed out in *Re H*, is the same as saying that the court should act on the basis of suspicion rather than on the basis of fact.

Such a proposition has, to our minds, only to be stated to be rejected. The same applies to the suggestion that the paramountcy of the welfare of the child requires such a method of proceeding, for this equally entails the proposition that the future of the child should be decided on the basis of suspicion rather than fact. We can find nothing in the 1989 Act which begins to suggest that Parliament intended that all-important decisions as to the future of a child should be made on such a basis, which to our minds would be a recipe for making decisions which were not in the best interests of the child . . .

Finally, we find support for our analysis of the position from the odd results which would follow were [counsel's] submissions to be accepted.

Firstly, it would be extraordinary if Parliament intended that evidence which is insufficient to establish that a child is likely to suffer significant harm for the purposes of s 31, should nevertheless be treated as sufficient to establish that a child is at risk of suffering harm for the purposes of s 1 . . .

Secondly, it is clear from the speech of Lord Nicholls in *Re H* . . . that s 31 provides, among other things, protection for parents . . .

That protection would be entirely removed in circumstances similar to those of the present case, if, on reaching the second stage for reasons which might well not justify permanently removing the children, the court could act on the basis of such suspicions to make an order for permanent removal which would not be justified on the matters that had been properly proved.

As at the threshold stage, a different approach is taken to the question of the *identity* of the perpetrator. In line with the House of Lords decision in *Lancashire CC v B*, it was held by Lord Nicholls in *Re O and N (Minors) (Care: Preliminary Hearing)* that when considering the risk of harm to the child at the welfare stage, a possible perpetrator should not be excluded simply because the LA is unable to establish culpability on the balance of probabilities. Consequently, whilst the question of whether the child has suffered or is at risk of suffering harm must be determined on the basis of facts proved on the balance of probabilities,[262] there is no requirement to establish the identity of the perpetrator on the same basis.

Re O and N (Minors) (Care: Preliminary Hearing) **[2003] UKHL 18**

LORD NICHOLLS:

The welfare stage: 'uncertain perpetrator' cases

26. The first area concerns cases of the type involved in the present appeals, where the judge finds a child has suffered significant physical harm at the hands of his parents but is unable to say which. I stress one feature of this type of case. These are cases where it has been proved, to the requisite standard of proof, that the child is suffering significant harm or is likely to do so.

262 *Re M and R (Minors) (Sexual Abuse: Expert Evidence)* [1996] 4 All ER 239.

27. Here, as a matter of legal policy, the position seems to me straightforward. Quite simply, it would be grotesque if such a case had to proceed at the welfare stage on the footing that, because neither parent, considered individually, has been proved to be the perpetrator, therefore the child is not at risk from either of them. This would be grotesque because it would mean the court would proceed on the footing that neither parent represents a risk even though one or other of them was the perpetrator of the harm in question.

28. That would be a self-defeating interpretation of the legislation. It would mean that, in 'uncertain perpetrator' cases, the court decides that the threshold criteria are satisfied but then lacks the ability to proceed in a sensible way in the best interests of the child. The preferable interpretation of the legislation is that in such cases the court is able to proceed at the welfare stage on the footing that each of the possible perpetrators is, indeed, just that: a possible perpetrator . . . This approach accords with the basic principle that in considering the requirements of the child's welfare the court will have regard to all the circumstances of the case . . .

31. In 'uncertain perpetrator' cases the correct approach must be that the judge conducting the disposal hearing will have regard, to whatever extent is appropriate, to the facts found by the judge at the preliminary hearing . . . When the facts found at the preliminary hearing leave open the possibility that a parent or other carer was a perpetrator of proved harm, it would not be right for that conclusion to be excluded from consideration at the disposal hearing as one of the matters to be taken into account. The importance to be attached to that possibility, as to every feature of the case, necessarily depends on the circumstances. But to exclude that possibility altogether from the matters the judge may consider would risk distorting the court's assessment of where, having regard to all the circumstances, the best interests of the child lie . . .

34. I wholly understand that parents are apprehensive that, if each of them is labelled a possible perpetrator, social workers and others may all too readily rule out the prospect of rehabilitation with either of them because the child would be 'at risk' with either of them . . .

35. I understand this concern. Whether it is well founded, generally or in particular cases, is an altogether different matter. Whether well founded or not, the way ahead cannot be for cases to proceed on an artificial footing.

As Lord Nicholls acknowledges, his approach means that a parent faces losing their child without the state ever proving on the balance of probabilities that that parent was responsible for the harm caused. However, 'the court cannot shut its eyes to the undoubted harm which has been suffered simply because it does not know who was responsible'.[263]

Whilst now well established that at the welfare stage the court can treat all possible but unproven perpetrators as posing a potential risk to the child, it remains somewhat unclear as to whether the court should attempt to assess the *degree of risk* posed by the individual in question. Lord Nicholls seemed to suggest in *Re O and N* that it was entirely appropriate for the court to attempt to assess the degree of likelihood that a particular individual was the perpetrator of the harm.[264] Lady Hale has been more cautious, suggesting it is unhelpful to try and assign percentage chances to each possible perpetrator. Whilst not precluding the possibility that the court could find that one individual is 'more likely' to be the perpetrator

[263] *Re B (Children) (Care Proceedings: Standard of Proof)* [2008] UKHL 35, [61].
[264] [2003] UKHL 18.

than others within the pool,[265] she has given strong support to Thorpe LJ's comment that the courts 'should be cautious about amplifying a judgment in which they have been unable to identify a perpetrator: "better to leave it thus"'.[266]

12.5.4.c 'The range of powers available to the court'

Once the threshold criteria have been established, the court has considerable freedom to shape its orders in accordance with the child's needs. It is open to the court on an application for a care order to make a supervision order and on an application for a supervision order to make a care order. The court may also make a s 8 or an SGO, so the court, even where the threshold conditions are satisfied, can make a private law order preventing the removal of the child into LA care.[267] As a matter of proportionality, though, there must be 'cogent and strong reasons to force upon the local authority a more draconian order than that for which they have asked'.[268] However, even where all parties are agreed on the most appropriate order, the court is still under a duty to conduct an 'appropriate judicial investigation' and having considered all the circumstances of the case make the order it considers to be in the child's best interests.[269] As expressed by McFarlane LJ in *Re G (Care Proceedings: Welfare Evaluation)*, 'the judicial task is to undertake a global, holistic evaluation of each of the options available for the child's future upbringing', with both the positives and negatives of all the options properly assessed and weighed in the balance.[270] To this end, a 'linear' approach which starts with the least interventionist measure and works its way through the options to the most interventionist is to be avoided.[271] Such an approach risks the judge settling on the most extreme measure standing at the end of the line simply because all those that have come before it have been rejected as lacking in some way but without the judge at any time giving proper consideration to the potential problems and disadvantages of that most interventionist option.

When determining the appropriate order, the court must consider the need for a proportionate response: that is, 'the aim must be to make the least interventionist possible order' given the circumstances of the case.[272] The importance of this principle has been reinforced by the implementation of the HRA 1998: in order to justify any prima facie interference with the rights of the parents under Article 8(1), any measures taken by the state must, under Article 8(2), be shown to have been no more than necessary to protect the competing rights and interests of the child. This was reiterated in *Re C and B*, a case concerning the removal of two very young children from their parents on the basis of the intellectual and emotional impairment caused to two older siblings by their mother's deteriorating mental health. Hale LJ held that the removal of the two younger children without any evidence that either of them were currently suffering significant harm was a wholly disproportionate response.

265 *Re T (Non-Accidental Injury)* [2009] EWCA Civ 1208, [60]–[65].
266 *Re S-B (Non-Accidental Injury)* [2009] UKSC 17, [44].
267 *Northamptonshire CC v S* [1993] 1 FLR 554.
268 *Oxfordshire County Council v B* [1998] 3 FCR 521, 525.
269 *Re T (A Child) (Care Order)* [2009] EWCA Civ 121, [44] and [49].
270 [2013] EWCA Civ 965, [50]–[54], approved in *Re H-W (Care Order)* [2022] UKSC 17, [47].
271 Ibid.
272 *Re H-W (Care Proceedings)* [2022] UKSC 17, [45].

Re C and B (Children) (Care Order: Future Harm) [2000] 2 FCR 614 (CA)

HALE LJ:

31. Nevertheless one comes back to the principle of proportionality. The principle has to be that the local authority works to support, and eventually to reunite, the family, unless the risks are so high that the child's welfare requires alternative family care. I cannot accept [counsel's] submission that this was a case for a care order with a care plan of adoption or nothing. There could have been other options . . .

34. There is a long line of European Court of Human Rights jurisprudence . . . which emphasises that the intervention has to be proportionate to the legitimate aim. Intervention in the family may be appropriate, but the aim should be to reunite the family when the circumstances enable that, and the effort should be devoted towards that end. Cutting off all contact and the relationship between the child or children and their family is only justified by the overriding necessity of the interests of the child.

Numerous cases have emphasized the importance of the court complying with its obligations under Article 8 ECHR when making a care order. Although the LA is responsible for determining what resources are made available to families in general, the court is 'required to act assertively to achieve the right outcome' in the particular case.[273] The LA must provide sufficient resources to make sure that the state's intervention in family life is not disproportionate—and the assessment of what is disproportionate is for the court, not the LA.[274]

The responsibility on the court to ensure strict compliance with Article 8 is particularly important when the care plan is to place the children for adoption thereby severing all ties (legal and factual) between the parent and child.[275] As the Supreme Court made clear in *Re B (Care Proceedings: Appeal)*, Article 8 demands a 'high degree of justification' before a determination that a child should be placed in care with a view to adoption.[276] In the words of Lady Hale, the circumstances must be 'exceptional', giving rise to an 'overriding' welfare imperative—the court must be satisfied 'nothing else will do'.[277] However, as the Supreme Court emphasized in *Re H-W (Care Proceedings)*, the requirement to consider proportionality applies in all cases, regardless of the detail of the care plan.[278]

Re H-W (Care Proceedings) [2022] UKSC 17

DAME SIOBHAN KEEGAN:

3. The grounds of appeal of the appellant parents . . . were refined by this court which in granting permission formulated two questions as follows:

[273] *Re T (Placement Order)* [2018] EWCA Civ 650, [40].

[274] Ibid; see also *Re W (Care Proceedings: Court's Function)* [2013] EWCA Civ 1227, [83]. On the respective roles of the court and the LA in relation to the care plan, see also 12.5.5.

[275] For analysis of the Convention principles as applied to domestic law, see *YC v United Kingdom* (App No 4547/10, ECHR) (2012), discussed in more detail at 13.4.2. On the European Court's approach generally, see Fenton-Glynn (2021), ch 10.

[276] [2013] UKSC 33, [34] (Lord Wilson).

[277] Ibid, [195]–[198] (Lady Hale). See also [74]–[79] (Lord Neuberger); [130] (Lord Kerr).

[278] For criticism, see Masson (2022).

"In making care orders for the removal of three of the first appellant's children into foster care:

(1) In order to decide whether those orders were proportionate, was it necessary as a matter of law to assess the likelihood that, if left in the first appellant's care, (a) the children would suffer sexual harm; (b) the consequences of such harm arising; (c) the possibility of reducing or mitigating the risk of such harm; and (d) the comparative welfare advantages and disadvantages of the options presented; and
(2) Did the judge err in law by failing to make any or any proper assessment of those matters?"

4. The first question focuses on the issue of the proportionality of the care orders which were made for [the children]. To be proportionate a care order which removes a child into care from its parents, and in this case from each other, must be necessary to meet the needs of the children having regard to the advantages and disadvantages of each available option. The four elements of question (1) identified as (a)-(d) above help to answer the question whether the care orders were in fact proportionate and necessary. . . .

53. [The] two elements of question 1 comprised in (a) and (b) interlink and are an inevitable consequence of a holistic evaluation in a case of this nature and specifically flow from consideration of the welfare checklist which highlights harm in point (e).

54. The next element contained in question 1(c) poses the question whether the court must consider the possible reduction or mitigation of the risk which pertains and the welfare advantages and disadvantages of imposing an order. . . . [A] court must look to determine whether any order is necessary by virtue of the Act: section 1(5), and whether or not the most interventionist order is necessary: Article 8(2) of the Convention.

55. In addition, point (g) of the welfare checklist specifically refers to the range of powers available to the court under the Act. Consideration of the range of orders obviously includes the ability of the court to consider in a care order case a supervision order or other orders and options.

As part of the court's consideration of the range of powers, one potential issue to consider is whether *orders* are needed to support the child's placement at all.[279] In a limited number of cases, for example, the court may be satisfied that the risks can be managed and the child's overall welfare needs met if the parents agree to the long-term care of their child under s 20 voluntary accommodation, rather than having accommodation underpinned by a care order.[280]

12.5.5 THE CARE PLAN

An important consideration when it is proposed to a take a child into care is the LA care plan.[281] Section 31A of the CA 1989 thus provides that where the LA makes an application on which a care order may be made, it must prepare a care plan.[282] The content of the care plan is prescribed by regulations and should include: the child's identified needs, including needs arising from race, culture, religion, special education, or health needs; the aim of the plan; the proposed timescale for implementation; the proposed placement; arrangements for contact and reunification; a contingency plan if the placement breaks down; the parents' and the child's wishes and views; and plans for the parents' ongoing participation in the

[279] S 1(5). [280] *Re S, Re W (Section 20 Accommodation)* [2023] EWCA Civ 1; see 12.3.2.c.
[281] Although always important, the care plan was given statutory force only in 2002.
[282] S 31A(1).

decision-making process.[283] The LA should produce evidence supporting the plan, focusing on feasibility and the likelihood of success.[284]

12.5.5.a The role of the court

In a move to reduce delays and limit the courts' encroachment on LA responsibility for children in their care,[285] the CFA 2014 dramatically curtailed the extent to which the court is *expected* to scrutinize the care plan as part of its welfare assessment. Section 31(3A) of the CA 1989, as amended, provides that when deciding whether to make a care order the court is only *required* to consider the permanence provisions of the plan (i.e. whether the child is to live with a parent or kinship carer, is to be adopted, or will remain in long-term care) and the LA's intentions as regards contact between the child and family members. Although the legislation does not prevent the court going beyond the prescribed matters, the care plan is now rarely subjected to the kind of 'rigorous scrutiny' previously required.[286] The shift away from judicial scrutiny of LA care plans does, however, require a certain faith in the LA to plan appropriately and to effectively monitor and review the implementation of the care plan. It also places increased responsibility for safeguarding the rights and welfare of looked after children in the hands of IROs. As noted later in this section, this might be problematic.[287]

Although the role of the court is more limited since 2014, it must still be satisfied that the core elements of the care plan are in the child's best interests before making the care order. There thus remains the potential for disagreement between the court and the LA as to the core elements of the plan, raising the question as to how such disagreements are to be resolved. In practice, the answer is that there is very little the court can do if it disagrees with what the LA intends. As observed by Munby J, if the court seeks to alter the LA's care plan it must 'achieve its objective by persuasion rather than by compulsion'.[288] Where persuasion fails and the LA will not reconsider its position, the only option available to the court is to refuse to make the care order.[289] It would be a brave judge who refused to make a care order where the threshold conditions were satisfied and the child's welfare otherwise demanded it. In practice such cases are rare.[290]

The frustration caused by the limited range of options available to the court where it disagrees with the LA care plan is exacerbated by the restrictions placed on the court once a care order has been made. Often the problem is not so much that the court disagrees with the plan, but that the plan is incomplete or uncertain. Before the CA 1989, the High Court had the power to monitor the implementation of care plans and, if necessary, give directions to the LA regarding a child within its care or bring a case back before the court for further consideration and review. The CA 1989 removed these powers.[291] Under the current legislative scheme, once the care order has been made, responsibility for the child, save for on issues relating to contact, passes to the LA.[292] Decisions regarding the implementation of the care plan, including making major changes such as abandoning attempts to rehabilitate the child

[283] Care Planning, Placement and Case Review (England) Regulations 2010, SI 2010/959, reg 5.
[284] *Re J (Minors) (Care: Care Plan)* [1994] 1 FLR 253, 261–2.
[285] Norgrove (2011), 3.17. [286] Ibid. [287] Discussed later at p 873.
[288] *Re K* [2007] EWHC 393, [15]; on steps the court can take, see *Re T (Placement Order)* [2018] EWCA Civ 650.
[289] *Re S and D (Child Case: Powers of Court)* [1995] 1 FCR 626 (CA).
[290] *Re K* [2007] EWHC 393, [21]. [291] S 100(2). [292] See 12.5.7.

to her family, are regarded as falling within the discretion of the LA. Consequently, the only way in which the decision of a LA can be challenged is by bringing an application to discharge the care order under s 39 of the CA 1989, applying for judicial review, or, if there has been a violation of the child's or the parents' rights under Article 6 or 8 ECHR, by bringing an application under ss 7 and 8 of the HRA 1998.[293]

The court's inability to monitor or review the implementation of the care plan has been a matter of considerable concern amongst the judiciary. This concern is based on more than simple indignation at the court's inability to control matters once a certain point has been reached: worrying evidence has emerged as to the number of children said to be 'lost in care'.[294] These are children for whom no clear care plan has ever been in place or for whom the care plan has simply failed or been forgotten. As was acknowledged by Lord Nicholls, these children are grossly let down by the system.[295] Concern about the number of children 'lost in care' prompted calls across the legal profession for the introduction of better judicial safeguards for children in care. It was against this background that *Re S (Minors) (Care Order: Implementation of Care Plan)* came before the House of Lords.

It was contended in *Re S* that the current legislative scheme risked infringing the ECHR rights of both parents and children by the lack of judicial oversight of the implementation of the care plan once a care order had been made. As regards the rights of the parents, the House of Lords disagreed. As regards the rights of the child, it recognized the potential for breach but declined to provide a remedy. Lord Nicholls' judgment begins by making clear the sensible rationale behind the current division of responsibility between the LA and the court:

Re S (Minors) (Care Order: Implementation of Care Plan) [2002] UKHL 10

LORD NICHOLLS:

25. . . . The [Children] Act delineated the boundary of responsibility with complete clarity. Where a care order is made the responsibility for the child's care is with the authority rather than the court. The court retains no supervisory role, monitoring the authority's discharge of its responsibilities. That was the intention of Parliament . . .

27. . . . The change brought about by the Children Act gave effect to a policy decision on the appropriate division of responsibilities between the courts and local authorities . . . The particular strength of the courts lies in the resolution of disputes . . . But a court cannot have day to day responsibility for a child. The court cannot deliver the services which may best serve a child's needs. Unlike a local authority, a court does not have close, personal and continuing knowledge of the child. The court cannot respond with immediacy and informality to practical problems and changed circumstances as they arise. Supervision by the court would encourage 'drift' in decision making, a perennial problem in children cases. Nor does a court have the task of managing the financial and human resources available to a local authority for dealing with all children in need in its area. The authority must manage these resources in the best interests of all the children for whom it is responsible.

[293] *Re M (Care: Challenging Decisions by Local Authority)* [2001] 2 FLR 1300. For an example of a guardian challenging the LA care plan by way of judicial review and under the HRA 1998, see *Re B (Transfer of Foster Placement)* [2013] 1 FLR 633.

[294] See, e.g., Waterhouse (2000) and *Re F; F v Lambeth London Borough Council* [2002] 1 FLR 217.

[295] *Re S (Minors) (Care Order: Implementation of Care Plan)* [2002] UKHL 10, [29]–[30].

> 28. . . . The court operates as the gateway into care, and makes the necessary care order when the threshold conditions are satisfied and the court considers a care order would be in the best interests of the child. That is the responsibility of the court. Thereafter the court has no continuing role in relation to the care order. Then it is the responsibility of the local authority to decide how the child should be cared for.

Lord Nicholls went on to consider whether the current legislative scheme violated the ECHR, concluding that the CA 1989 per se was not incompatible with Article 8.

> 54. Clearly, if matters go seriously awry, the manner in which a local authority discharges its parental responsibilities to a child in its care may violate the rights of the child or his parents under this article. The local authority's intervention in the life of the child, justified at the outset when the care order was made, may cease to be justifiable under article 8(2). Sedley LJ pointed out that a care order from which no good is coming cannot sensibly be said to be pursuing a legitimate aim. A care order which keeps a child away from his family for purposes which, as time goes by, are not being realised will sooner or later become a disproportionate interference with the child' s primary article 8 rights . . .
>
> 55. Further, the local authority's decision making process must be conducted fairly and so as to afford due respect to the interests protected by article 8. For instance, the parents should be involved to a degree which is sufficient to provide adequate protection for their interests . . .
>
> 56. However, the possibility that something may go wrong with the local authority's discharge of its parental responsibilities or its decision making processes, and that this would be a violation of article 8 so far as the child or parent is concerned, does not mean that the legislation itself is incompatible, or inconsistent, with article 8 . . .
>
> 57. If an authority duly carries out [its] statutory duties, in the ordinary course there should be no question of infringement by the local authority of the article 8 rights of the child or his parents. Questions of infringement are only likely to arise if a local authority fails properly to discharge its statutory responsibilities. Infringement which then occurs is not brought about, in any meaningful sense, by the Children Act. Quite the reverse. Far from the infringement being compelled, or even countenanced, by the provisions of the Children Act, the infringement flows from the local authority's failure to comply with its obligations under the Act. True, it is the Children Act which entrusts responsibility for the child's care to the local authority. But that is not inconsistent with article 8 . . .
>
> 58. Where, then, is the inconsistency which is alleged to exist? As I understand it, the principal contention is that the incompatibility lies in the absence from the Children Act of an adequate remedy if a local authority fails to discharge its parental responsibilities properly and, as a direct result, the rights of the child or his parents under article 8 are violated . . .
>
> 59. In my view this line of argument is misconceived. Failure by the state to provide an effective remedy for a violation of article 8 is not itself a violation of article 8. This is self-evident. So, even if the Children Act does fail to provide an adequate remedy, the Act is not for that reason incompatible with article 8. This is the short and conclusive answer to this point.

Lord Nicholls then considered the arguments under Article 6, concluding that as the parents could effectively challenge any decision made by the LA regarding implementation of the care plan by judicial review or under ss 7 and 8 of the HRA 1998, any potential breach of their Article 6 rights would be more illusory than real.[296] The child's position was more

[296] Ibid, [75]–[81].

difficult, Lord Nicholls holding that the *child's* inability to bring legal proceedings to challenge any potential breach of Article 8 gave rise to a *possible* incompatibility between the legislative scheme and the child's rights under Article 6.

> 82. . . . The Convention is intended to guarantee rights which are practical and effective. This is particularly so with the right of access to the courts, in view of the prominent place held in a democratic society by the right to a fair trial . . . The guarantee provided by article 6(1) can hardly be said to be satisfied in the case of a young child who, in practice, has no way of initiating judicial review proceedings to challenge a local authority's decision affecting his civil rights. (In such a case, as already noted, the young child would also lack means of initiating section 7 proceedings to protect his article 8 rights.)
>
> 83. My conclusion is that in these respects circumstances might perhaps arise when English law would not satisfy the requirements of article 6(1) regarding some child care decisions made by local authorities. In one or other of the circumstances mentioned above the article 6 rights of a child . . . are capable of being infringed.

Having found, however, that the legislative scheme gave rise to a *potential* breach of Article 6, Lord Nicholls declined to decide whether this 'lacuna' did in fact render the legislation incompatible with the child's ECHR rights, concluding that it was unnecessary to do so on the particular facts of the case.

The House of Lords' judgment in *Re S* thus did little to improve the position of children badly let down by LAs. However, Parliament responded by introducing two important amendments.[297] First, the LA was placed under a statutory duty to keep the child's care plan under review.[298] Secondly, the LA must appoint an IRO to participate in the LA's six-monthly review of every case, monitor the performance of the LA, and refer the case to Cafcass if it is deemed appropriate to do so.[299] If the child's Article 8 rights are at risk of being infringed by changes to or non-implementation of the care plan, the potential breach should therefore be brought to the attention of a Cafcass officer who has the responsibility to bring an action in judicial review or under s 7 of the HRA 1998 on the child's behalf. The effectiveness of the IRO system is, however, questionable. Research conducted in 2006 for the NSPCC suggested that many young people within the care system have little faith in the IRO to challenge LA decision-making effectively: lack of power and lack of independence being key concerns.[300] The researchers commented that the fact that 'very few, if any, cases have been referred by IROs to children's guardians since this section was implemented in 2004 does not encourage confidence that the distress and dissatisfaction with contact and placement plans expressed by some . . . children . . . will be alleviated by this particular legislative change'.[301] These concerns were borne out by *A and S (Children) v Lancashire County Council*,[302] where Jackson J details the systemic problems facing the IRO system.

In *Re J (Minors) (Care: Care Plan)*, Wall J held that a court could refuse to make a final care order if it was not satisfied about 'material aspects of the care plan',[303] but emphasized

297 Introduced by the ACA 2002. 298 S 26(2)(f).

299 S 26(2)(k) and (2A). Care Planning, Placement and Case Review (England) Regulations 2010, SI 2010/959, regs 35 and 45.

300 Timms and Thoburn (2006), 168. 301 Ibid.

302 [2012] EWHC 1689. See also House of Lords Select Committee on Adoption Legislation (2013), paras 114–24 and House of Commons Select Committee on Education (2012/13), paras 87–90.

303 [1994] 1 FLR 253, 261.

that interim orders should not be used 'as a means of exercising the now defunct supervisory role of the court'.[304] He went on to point out that the court should not be unduly concerned if there were continuing elements of doubt and uncertainty about the plan. This approach was confirmed in *Re S*.

Re S (Minors) (Care Order: Implementation of Care Plan) [2002] UKHL 10

LORD NICHOLLS:

90. From a reading of section 38 as a whole it is abundantly clear that the purpose of an interim care order . . . is to enable the court to safeguard the welfare of a child until such time as the court is in a position to decide whether or not it is in the best interests of the child to make a care order. When that time arrives depends on the circumstances of the case and is a matter for the judgment of the trial judge. That is the general, guiding principle. The corollary to this principle is that an interim care order is not intended to be used as a means by which the court may continue to exercise a supervisory role over the local authority in cases where it is in the best interests of a child that a care order should be made.

91. An interim care order, thus, is a temporary 'holding' measure . . .

92. When a local authority formulates a care plan in connection with an application for a care order, there are bound to be uncertainties. Even the basic shape of the future life of the child may be far from clear. Over the last ten years problems have arisen about how far courts should go in attempting to resolve these uncertainties before making a care order and passing responsibility to the local authority. Once a final care order is made, the resolution of the uncertainties will be a matter for the authority, not the court.

93. In terms of legal principle one type of uncertainty is straightforward. This is the case where the uncertainty needs to be resolved before the court can decide whether it is in the best interests of the child to make a care order at all . . . In such a case the court should finally dispose of the matter only when the material facts are as clearly known as can be hoped . . .

94. More difficult, as a matter of legal principle, are cases where it is obvious that a care order is in the best interests of the child but the immediate way ahead thereafter is unsatisfactorily obscure. These cases exemplify a problem, or a 'tension', inherent in the scheme of the Children Act. What should the judge do when a care order is clearly in the best interests of the child but the judge does not approve of the care plan? . . .

95. In this context there are sometimes uncertainties whose nature is such that they are suitable for immediate resolution, in whole or in part, by the court in the course of disposing of the care order application. The uncertainty may be of such a character that it can, and should, be resolved so far as possible before the court proceeds to make the care order. Then, a limited period of 'planned and purposeful' delay can readily be justified as the sensible and practical way to deal with an existing problem . . .

97. Frequently the case is on the other side of this somewhat imprecise line. Frequently the uncertainties involved in a care plan will have to be worked out after a care order has been made and while the plan is being implemented . . .

98. . . . Quite apart from known uncertainties, an element of future uncertainty is necessarily inherent in the very nature of a care plan. The best laid plans 'gang aft a-gley'. These are matters for decision by the local authority, if and when they arise. A local authority must always respond appropriately to changes, of varying degrees of predictability, which from

[304] Ibid, 262.

time to time are bound to occur after a care order has been made and while the care plan is being implemented. No care plan can ever be regarded as set in stone . . .

100. Cases vary so widely that it is impossible to be more precise about the test to be applied by a court when deciding whether to continue interim relief rather than proceed to make a care order. It would be foolish to attempt to be more precise. One further general point may be noted. When postponing a decision on whether to make a care order a court will need to have in mind the general statutory principle that any delay in determining issues relating to a child's upbringing is likely to prejudice the child's welfare: section 1(2) of the Children Act.

Subsequent case law has made clear that where there remains doubt over a fundamental question such as whether a child should be placed for adoption or remain in long-term foster care, a final care order should not be made.[305] This would appear to be the case even if there is no question of the child returning home and thus the making of a final care order is at some point inevitable. The practical advantages of the court refusing to make the care order final in these circumstances have been highlighted by the Court of Appeal.

Re G (Care Orders) [2010] EWCA Civ 1271

BLACK LJ:

53. I think it would be fair to say that it was an uphill task for counsel for the mother to produce arguments to justify the course that the recorder took in granting full care orders when he had pronounced himself in such fundamental disagreement with the local authority's care plan and was unwilling to grant the placement orders necessary to take it forward . . .

55. The guardian's counsel has set out very clearly a number of the disadvantages for the children in the course that the recorder took, not least potential delay and lack of continuing independent input into decisions about their future. The making of the care order and dismissal of the placement application brought the involvement of the guardian and the children's solicitor to an end; similarly [the mother's] legal representation would come to an end. The instruction of the new expert would be a matter for the local authority's internal processes. They would have to obtain funding for it. The guardian and her solicitor would no longer be available to contribute their expertise to the instruction. The court would have no role in scrutinising the suitability of the chosen person, the questions that were to be addressed by him or her and the timetable for the report. Any input the parents had would be entirely a matter between them and the local authority. It would be up to the local authority to decide when, if at all, to recommence proceedings for a placement order . . .

58. . . . [T]he recorder failed to take account of the practical difficulties that the dismissal of the placement applications would pose for the local authority . . . They would . . . have to reissue the placement applications and await directions hearings thereafter rather than a further hearing of the existing adjourned placement application being scheduled¼to tie in with the care proceedings.

59. As counsel for the guardian puts it, this was a case in which the court should have retained control over the proceedings, the evidence and the timetable for the children. The consequence of the court not doing this is that the children have been left in limbo without a clearly defined or timetabled path to permanence.

305 *Re G (Care Orders)* [2010] EWCA 1271.

By contrast, the issue in *Re D O'H* was not the principle of adoption but the type of adoption placement, in particular whether there should be provision for post-adoption contact or not. The Court of Appeal held that in these circumstances the judge had been correct to make a final care order.[306]

12.5.5.b Changes to the care plan

As a general proposition, as we will see,[307] it is a matter for the LA how it provides for the child once the child has been placed in its care. The court has a limited involvement, and parents face an up-hill struggle to challenge most decisions that the LA might make. However, there are limits. Perhaps in response to the limited options available to regulate the LA's implementation of the care plan under the CA 1989, the HRA 1998 has been given renewed attention, particularly following *Re DE (Care Order: Change of Care Plan)*.[308]

The case concerned a young child, 'D', aged two-and-a-half, whose care plan involved him remaining with his parents under a care order, with a package of support from the LA and other agencies. That plan was followed for 18 months, during which time the LA became increasingly concerned about D's slow developmental progress, and his risk of physical harm through the failure of the parents to recognize risk and predict potential dangers. As a result, the LA concluded that D should be removed from his parents' care. The parents sought an injunction under the HRA 1998 to prevent D's removal. Baker J concluded that the 'strict scrutiny' requirement from *Re B-S (Children) (Adoption: Application of Threshold Criteria)*[309]—that is, that the removal of a child from their family could be justified only where it is *necessary* in the child's welfare—also applies to any proposed removal in these circumstances. If a care order had been granted on the basis of the child remaining with the parents, then subsequent removal of the child was an interference with Article 8 rights—it thus had to be justified under Article 8(2) and shown to be proportionate, meaning that it was *necessary* as per the *Re B-S* standard.

C. Fenton-Glynn, 'The Rise of Strict Scrutiny: Extending *Re B-S* to Changes in Care Plans', (2015c) 37 *Journal of Social Welfare and Family Law* 105

While they may not 'change the landscape' in the same manner as *Re B-S*, the requirements placed on local authorities by [*Re DE*] will without doubt have a great impact on local authority decision-making. Previously, when a care plan envisaged that a child remain at home, one of the advantages of a care order over a supervision order lay in the flexibility it allowed the local authority, and in the ability to remove a child quickly if need be. As a result of this judgment, a greater burden of diligence is now placed on the local authority, as well as the possibility of additional proceedings, and courts can now scrutinise changes in the care plan in a way that was not previously considered possible. While this does not go so far as the concept of 'starred' care plans, which were so soundly rejected in *Re S* [2002] UKHL 10, it does provide something of a bulwark to any change of plans that would interfere with the family life of the child and parents.

[306] [2011] EWCA Civ 1434, [39]–[40]. [307] See 12.5.6.

[308] [2014] EWFC 6. Baker J's decision was approved by the Court of Appeal in *Re S (A Child)* [2018] EWCA Civ 2512. See also *Re G (Discharge of Care Orders: Injunction Under Human Rights Act)* [2019] EWCA Civ 1779.

[309] [2013] EWCA Civ 1146; see 13.4.3 and 13.5.3.

This judgment must also be read in light of the policy of reducing the scrutiny of the courts over care plans, seen in the Children and Families Act 2014 and resulting in the amended s 31(3A) of the Children Act 1989. Despite addressing different types of applications, there appears to be a clear message that the responsibility of the courts to comply with their duty as a public authority under the Human Rights Act means that judicial scrutiny will not be quickly abandoned.

The Court of Appeal has made clear that the LA may open itself to challenge in judicial review or HRA 1998 proceedings if it refuses to implement elements of a care plan which the court has determined to be necessary on welfare or proportionality grounds.[310] There is a clear tension between the respective roles of the court and the LA in this area, with both curtailed by what Bainham calls 'the forbidden territories'—the court cannot dictate what the LA's care plan should be, but the LA cannot act in a way which, in the court's assessment, violates the Article 8 rights involved.[311] Bainham argues that the fundamental dividing line between the court's function and the LA's is that the court is to determine 'where the child's permanent placement should be and under what legal regime of orders', and so if the care plan is inconsistent with that decision, the court should be able to insist on changes to the care plan to make it compliant.[312]

12.5.6 EFFECT OF A CARE ORDER

The legal effects of a care order are set down in s 33 of the CA 1989. The primary effect of the order is to place a duty on the LA to receive the child into care and to keep the child in care whilst the order remains in force, and to the give the LA parental responsibility in relation to the child.[313] A care order lasts until the child reaches the age of 18 unless ended earlier.[314] There is no mechanism for a care order to be discharged upon the happening of a fixed event set out when the order is made, nor for it otherwise to be limited in time.[315]

12.5.6.a Accommodating the child

Although it is common for a child who is the subject of a care order to be living in accommodation provided by the LA, usually with foster carers, a child can be 'in care' but remain living at home or be placed with wider family members.[316] Indeed, the LA is required to place any looked after child with a parent, a holder of parental responsibility, or an existing holder of a 'live with' CAO, unless doing so would be contrary to the child's welfare or would not be reasonably practicable.[317] However, even if the child remains with the parents, the care order gives the LA the power to remove the child without further recourse to the courts, subject to two caveats. First, except in emergencies, the LA must provide the parents

[310] *Re W (Care Proceedings: Court's Function)* [2013] EWCA Civ 1227, [101]; *Re T (Placement Order)* [2018] EWCA Civ 650, [42].

[311] Bainham (2018). [312] Ibid, 1153. [313] S 33(1), (3).

[314] S 91(12), but a care order is discharged automatically if a CAO or SGO is later made in relation to the child: s 91(1) and (5A).

[315] *Re P-S (Care Orders)* [2018] EWCA Civ 1407, [33].

[316] Care Planning, Placement and Case Review (England) Regulations 2010, SI 2010/959, reg 18.

[317] CA 1989, s 22C(2). Alternatively, the child can be placed: (i) with a relative or friend if that person is an approved LA foster carer; (ii) with another foster carer; (iii) in a children's home; or (iv) the LA can make 'other arrangements' if necessary and the matter is urgent: CA 1989, s 22C(5) and 22D. See also 12.3.2.

with proper notice of the decision and involve them fully in the decision-making process;[318] and, secondly, if the care plan endorsed by the court provides for the child to remain living with the family, removal without further recourse to the court would put the LA at risk of a breach of Article 8 rights.[319]

12.5.6.b Exercising parental responsibility

Whilst the care order is in force, the LA holds parental responsibility (PR). The CA 1989 imposes specific limits on the exercise of PR when a care order is in force. The LA cannot: (i) cause the child to be brought up in a different religion; (ii) refuse or consent to the child's adoption; or (iii) appoint a guardian.[320] Likewise, when a care order is in force *no one* may cause the child to be known by a new surname or remove the child from the jurisdiction without either the written consent of everyone holding PR or the court's leave.[321]

Parents do not lose their PR by virtue of a care order being made, so the LA's PR is shared with the parents—but the LA has the power to determine the extent to which the parents may exercise it.[322] This means the LA not only has the right to make day-to-day decisions with respect to the child's upbringing and, where necessary, override the wishes of the parents, but to effectively exclude them from the decision-making process.[323] Any restrictions imposed on the PR of the parents must be necessary to safeguard and promote the child's welfare.[324] Whilst the child is in care, the LA must also comply with the substantive and procedural requirements of Article 8.

Re G (Care: Challenge to Local Authority's Decision) **[2003] EWHC 551**

MUNBY J:

43. The fact that a local authority has parental responsibility for children pursuant to section 33(3)(a) of the Children Act 1989 does not entitle it to take decisions about those children without reference to, or over the heads of, the children's parents. A local authority, even if clothed with the authority of a care order, is not entitled to make significant changes in the care plan, or to change the arrangements under which the children are living, let alone to remove the children from home if they are living with their parents, without properly involving the parents in the decision-making process and without giving the parents a proper opportunity to make their case before a decision is made. After all, the fact that the local authority also has parental responsibility does not deprive the parents of their parental responsibility.

44. A local authority can lawfully exercise parental responsibility for a child only in a manner consistent with the substantive *and procedural* requirements of article 8. There is nothing in section 33(3)(b) of the Act that entitles a local authority to act in breach of article 8. On the contrary, section 6(1) of the 1998 Act requires a local authority to exercise its powers under both section 33(3)(a) and section 33(3)(b) of the 1989 Act in a manner consistent with both the substantive and the procedural requirements of article 8.

318 Care Planning, Placement and Case Review (England) Regulations 2010, reg 14. See *G v N County Council* [2009] 1 FLR 774, [20], [29]–[30].

319 See 12.5.5.b. 320 S 33(6). 321 S 33(7). 322 S 33(3)(a).

323 *Re P (Children Act 1989, ss 22 and 26: Local Authority Compliance)* [2000] 2 FLR 910.

324 S 33(4).

Establishing the limitations on the LA's powers in this regard is not straightforward, however. The court has noted that the need to respect Article 8 rights means that the LA will be 'ill-advised' to seek to rely on its parental responsibility under s 33 to make major decisions about a child, such as a serious medical operation, which is opposed by the parents, where that issue was not already the subject of a court determination within the care proceedings[325]—but what is a 'major decision' in this context? Two Court of Appeal cases have addressed this issue.[326]

In *Re Y (Children in Care: Change of Nationality)*,[327] the children were non-British nationals who were probably entitled to gain British citizenship; they had been placed for adoption, but no suitable placement was available and so the children were likely to remain in long-term foster care. Whereas adoption by a British national or someone habitually resident in the UK would have conferred British nationality on the children automatically,[328] foster care would not. To improve the children's immigration position, the LA favoured an application being made for citizenship, which the parents opposed. Peter Jackson LJ held that the PR held under s 33 'does not entitle the local authority to apply for British citizenship for these children, in the face of parental opposition . . ., without first obtaining approval from the High Court'.[329]

By contrast, in *Re H (Parental Responsibility: Vaccination)* the parents of children who were the subject of a care order opposed them receiving standard childhood vaccinations.[330] The LA applied to the court for consent to have the children vaccinated, on the basis that it was unclear whether it had the authority to make that decision itself. The Court of Appeal held that the LA did not need to apply to the court and could rely on its existing PR.

Re H (Parental Responsibility: Vaccination) [2020] EWCA Civ 664

KING LJ:

95. . . . A care order is only made if the welfare of a child requires such an order to be made, it having been determined or conceded that pursuant to s.31(2) CA 1989, the child has suffered or is likely to suffer significant harm attributable "to the care given to him or her not being what it would be reasonable to expect a parent to give him". In other words, the child in question has suffered (or was likely to suffer) harm as a consequence of the care given to him or her by a person with parental responsibility. It is against that backdrop that the parent of a child in care holds parental responsibility. Parliament has specifically, and necessarily, given the local authority that holds the care order, the power under s.33(3)(b) to override the views of a parent holding parental responsibility. The local authority's view prevails in respect of all matters save those found in the statutory exceptions or where, as I identified in *Re C (Child in Care: Choice of Forename)*,[331] the decision to be made is of such magnitude that it properly falls within the provisions of s.100 [of the CA 1989].

325 *Re AB (Medical Treatment: Care Proceedings)* [2018] EWFC 3, [24](iii).
326 For a helpful analysis, focusing on vaccination and life-sustaining treatment decisions, see Bridgeman (2022).
327 [2020] EWCA Civ 1038.
328 British Nationality Act 1981, s 1(5).
329 *Re Y (Children in Care: Change of Nationality)* [2020] EWCA Civ 1038, [24].
330 [2020] EWCA Civ 664. See also discussion at 10.5.2.b.
331 [2016] EWCA Civ 374.

In *Re C*—a case concerning the choice of given names for two children who were made subject of care orders at birth—King LJ had concluded that 'there is a small category of cases where, notwithstanding the local authority's powers under section 33(3)(b) CA 1989, the consequences of the exercise of a particular act of parental responsibility are so profound and have such an impact on either the child his or herself, and/or the Article 8 rights of those other parties who share parental responsibility with a local authority, that the matter must come before the court for its consideration and determination'.[332] Given King LJ's reference to s 100, it is implied that the LA will need to apply only when the issue in question would lead the child to suffer significant harm if no order is made;[333] whether that approach achieves the same result as a consideration of the requirements of Article 8 is unclear. Either way, it leaves a wide area of ambiguity where the LA's ability to rely on its existing PR is untested.

While the difference between the issues in *Re Y* and *Re H* is clear, the principle of why the LA can make some decisions relying on its own PR but not others is less apparent. Certainly there is scope for criticism, as Masson and Prabhat set out in relation to *Re Y*.[334]

J. Masson and D. Prabhat, 'Allowing Appeals to Increase High Court Power',
(2021) 43 *Journal of Social Welfare and Family Law* 327, 328

The Court Appeal proceeded on the basis that the LA was required to provide a care plan, and that citizenship was a 'permanence provision' which the court must consider under s.31(3A). Neither reflects the clear words of the statute; the LA is only required to provide a care plan to a court considering making a care order (s.31A). This was not the case in *Re Y*. The discharge of the placement order, which followed the LA's review of its care plan, left the pre-existing care order. As the President of the Family Division explained in *Re T-S* at para. 35,[335] the separation of powers between courts and local authorities is a 'cardinal principle' of the both the 1989 and 2002 Acts. The court's powers are limited to making orders for care, placement, supervision, contact etc, approving name change and emigration (s.33(8) and Sched 2, para 19(1)), and discharging orders (s.39 and Adoption and Children Act 2002, s.24). Applying this principle, the first instance judge made no reference to citizenship (or 'leave to remain') applications because her role was limited to determining the existing orders and considering contact. Her powers did not extend to authorising applications for 'leave to remain'; these were a matter for the LA, with decisions for the Home Secretary.

The Children Act 1989 imposes duties on local authorities to safeguard and promote the welfare of looked after children; make use of services available to children in parental care as appear reasonable; and 'so far as reasonably practicable' consult with, and consider the views of, parents, children and others (s.22 (3), (4), (5)). Independent Reviewing Officers supervise this planning and decision-making, and a (statutory) complaints system exists to resolve disagreements, with a backstop of judicial review. In *Re Y*, the Court of Appeal recast this statutory scheme for making decisions and resolving disputes through discussion by adding a requirement for litigation. It did not consider the consequences: uncertainty and delay for children, additional demands on LA resources and further pressure on the courts. Individually and together, these undermine welfare and produce injustice.

[332] Ibid, [104]. [333] CA 1989, s 100(4)(b).
[334] For criticism of the reasoning in *Re H*, see George (2020), extracted at 10.5.2.b.
[335] *Re T-S (Children: Care Proceedings)* [2019] EWCA Civ 742.

12.5.7 CONTACT WITH A CHILD IN CARE

If the LA plan is to try and rehabilitate the child with the parents, it is obviously important that the child's familial relationships are sustained through generous provision of contact. Where, however, the LA's plan is to place the child with a permanent alternative family, the importance of the child maintaining positive links with the birth family has been more recently recognized, not just whilst the child is in care, but in the longer term if the child is adopted.[336]

Re E (Children in Care: Contact) [1994] 1 FCR 584 (CA), 594

SIMON BROWN LJ:

[Even] when the s. 31 criteria are satisfied, contact may well be of singular importance to the long-term welfare of the child: firstly in giving the child the security of knowing that his parents love him and are interested in his welfare; secondly, by avoiding any damaging sense of loss to the child in seeing himself abandoned by his parents; thirdly, by enabling the child to commit himself to the substitute family with the seal of approval of the natural parents; and, fourthly, by giving the child the necessary sense of family and personal identity. Contact, if maintained, is capable of reinforcing and increasing the chances of success of a permanent placement, whether on a long-term fostering basis or by adoption.

This change in professional attitudes towards contact has been reinforced by the European Court of Human Rights. The Court has stated repeatedly that terminating contact between parent and child constitutes a grave interference with Article 8 as it effectively ends any meaningful relationship between them. Any 'radical' decision by the national courts to terminate contact will therefore be subjected to the most 'anxious scrutiny', only being justified in exceptional circumstances.[337]

The importance of contact between a child in care and members of the child's family remains firmly entrenched within the CA 1989. The LA is under a general duty to promote contact between a looked after child and the child's parents.[338] This is reinforced by s 34(1) which provides that the LA shall, subject to its duty to safeguard and promote the child's welfare, allow 'reasonable contact' between them—though contact is subject to assessment of the child's welfare and can be restricted.[339] Initially it will be for the LA to determine what constitutes reasonable contact having regard to the child's welfare. However, one of the most important policy changes enshrined in the CA 1989 was to remove the LA's almost unfettered authority over contact decisions.[340] Before making a care order, the court must always consider the LA's proposed arrangements for contact and may make an order of its own motion.[341] An application may also be made to the court for a defined contact order, in determining which the child's welfare is the paramount consideration.[342]

[336] In the context of adoption, see 13.7.

[337] *S and G v Italy* (App Nos 39221/98 and 41963/98, ECHR) (2000), [170].

[338] Sch 2, para 15. [339] S 34.

[340] On the approach to contact prior to the CA 1989, see *Re B (Minors) (Termination of Contact: Paramount Consideration)* [1993] Fam 301, 306–8.

[341] S 34(11) and (5).

[342] For the test to be applied on an application for leave, see *Re W (Care Proceedings: Leave to Apply)* [2004] EWHC 3342.

The most important change introduced by the CA 1989 was to remove the LA's power to terminate contact. That power now rests with the court. The LA can only prohibit contact between the child and a person specified in s 34(1) for a maximum of seven days if it is an emergency and the LA is satisfied that it is necessary to safeguard and promote the child's welfare.[343] In all other cases, the LA must apply to the court under s 34(4) for permission to terminate contact. It is clear from the case law that the court must take this jurisdiction seriously and not simply abdicate its responsibility to the LA. Thus, it is inappropriate for the court to give the LA general authorization to terminate or suspend contact should it consider it necessary.[344] This principle applies even if the LA is certain that at some point in the future contact will need to be terminated.[345]

The court's jurisdiction over contact constitutes an important exception to the principle that once the care order has been made, responsibility for the child passes to the LA. In considering an application under s 34, the court must form its own assessment of what the child's welfare requires: '[i]t does not defer to the local authority, and the local authority is no more entitled than any other party to the benefit of any doubt'.[346] It raises the possibility of conflict between the LA's care plan and the court's view on contact, which may in turn reflect a more fundamental disagreement between them as to the child's long-term future. The issue arose in *Re B (Minors) (Termination of Contact: Paramount Consideration)*. The LA applied to terminate contact between two children and their mother in order to place the children for adoption. The guardian opposed the application, concerned that the possibility of rehabilitation with the mother had not been properly assessed. The Court of Appeal upheld the guardian's appeal, making it clear that where the LA and the court disagree, the court must do what it considers to be in the child's best interests, even if continuing contact is inconsistent with the LA's care plan.

Re B (Minors) (Termination of Contact: Paramount Consideration) [1993] Fam 301 (CA), 310–12

BUTLER-SLOSS LJ:

A section 34 application is clearly a substantive application in which the court is determining a question with respect to the upbringing of the child. . . .

At the moment that an application comes before the court, at whichever tier, the court has a duty to apply section 1, which states that when a court determines any question with respect to the upbringing of a child, the child's welfare shall be the court's paramount consideration . . .

Contact applications generally fall into two main categories: those which ask for contact as such, and those which are attempts to set aside the care order itself. In the first category there is no suggestion that the applicant wishes to take over the care of the child and the issue of contact often depends on whether contact would frustrate long-term plans for the child in a substitute home, such as adoption, where continuing contact may not be for the long-term

[343] S 34(6).

[344] *Re L (Sexual Abuse: Standard of Proof)* [1996] 1 FLR 116; *Re S (Children) (Termination of Contact)* [2004] EWCA Civ 1397.

[345] *Re H (Children) (Termination of Contact)* [2005] EWCA Civ 318.

[346] *Re D-S (Contact with Children in Care: Covid-19)* [2020] EWCA Civ 1031, [13].

> welfare of the child. The presumption of contact, which has to be for the benefit of the child, has always to be balanced against the long-term welfare of the child and, particularly, where he will live in the future. Contact must not be allowed to destabilise or endanger the arrangements for the child and in many cases the plans for the child will be decisive of the contact application. There may also be cases where the parent is having satisfactory contact with the child and there are no long-term plans or those plans do not appear to the court to preclude some future contact. The proposals of the local authority, based on their appreciation of the best interests of the child, must command the greatest respect and consideration from the court, but Parliament has given to the court, and not to the local authority, the duty to decide on contact between the child and those named in section 34(1). Consequently, the court may have the task of requiring the local authority to justify their long-term plans to the extent only that those plans exclude contact between parent and child. In the second category, contact applications may be made by parents by way of another attempt to obtain the return of the children. In such a case the court is obviously entitled to take into account the failure to apply to discharge the care order, and in the majority of cases the court will have little difficulty in coming to the conclusion that the applicant cannot demonstrate that contact with a view to rehabilitation with the parent is a viable proposition at that stage, particularly if it had already been rejected at the earlier hearing when the child was placed in care. The task for the parents will be too great and the court would be entitled to assume that the plans of the local authority to terminate contact are for the welfare of the child and are not to be frustrated by inappropriate contact with a view to the remote possibility, at some future date, of rehabilitation.
>
> But in all cases the welfare section has to be considered, and the local authority have the task of justifying the cessation of contact. There may also be unusual cases where either the local authority have not made effective plans or there has been considerable delay in implementing them and a parent, who has previously been found by a court unable or unwilling to care for the child so that a care order has been made, comes back upon the scene as a possible future primary carer. If the local authority with a care order decide not to consider that parent on the new facts, [counsel for the parents] argued that it is for the court, with the enhanced jurisdiction of the Act of 1989, to consider whether even at this late stage there should be some investigation of the proposals of the parent, with the possibility of reconsidering the local authority plans. [Counsel for the LA] argued that the court cannot go behind the long-term plans of the local authority unless they were acting capriciously or were otherwise open to scrutiny by way of judicial review.
>
> I unhesitatingly reject the local authority argument. As I have already said, their plan has to be given the greatest possible consideration by the court and it is only in the unusual case that a parent will be able to convince the court, the onus being firmly on the parent, that there has been such a change of circumstances as to require further investigation and reconsideration of the local authority plan. If, however, a court were unable to intervene, it would make a nonsense of the paramountcy of the welfare of the child which is the bedrock of the Act, and would subordinate it to the administrative decision of the local authority in a situation where the court is seized of the contact issue. That cannot be right.
>
> But I would emphasise that this is not an open door to courts reviewing the plans of local authorities.

This decision thus makes some limited inroads into the LA's otherwise unfettered control over the content and implementation of the care plan. It is clear that, although unusual, in the second category of case (where the dispute over contact is really a dispute over whether the child should be rehabilitated with the parents), the court has the jurisdiction to order contact with a view to rehabilitation even if the LA is thereby forced to reconsider its long-term plan to place the child permanently outside the family. Similarly, in the first category of case (where the parent is not seeking to have the child returned to their care), although Butler-Sloss LJ recognizes that contact should not be allowed to destabilize or jeopardize the LA's long-term plan—an outcome which will rarely be in the child's best interests—the judge may nevertheless test the LA's position and can refuse to terminate contact where it is not satisfied that the care plan and contact are necessarily inconsistent.[347]

Section 34 ensures that any attempt by the LA to terminate contact between parent and child is subjected to independent judicial scrutiny. The court is thus very much cast in the role of safeguarding and defending the parents' rights. Indeed, if necessary, the court can attach a penal notice to the order and enforce it against the LA by way of committal.[348] Of course, it is not necessarily the case that it is the court that is supportive of contact in the face of the LA's opposition, raising the question whether the court has jurisdiction to terminate contact against the LA's wishes. Despite early indications to the contrary,[349] the Court of Appeal has held that, given the clear legislative objectives behind s 34, the court has no jurisdiction to make an order prohibiting contact.[350]

While the focus in terms of contact is almost invariably on parents, another potentially significant issue can arise about contact between siblings if they are being separated. It may be that some siblings are remaining with the birth family while others are in care, or that the children are unable to be placed together while in care. While the s 34(1) duty on the LA to allow 'reasonable contact' between looked after children and their parents does not extend to siblings, research suggests that 'there appears to be a strong presumption of direct contact for separated siblings unless a child is adopted',[351] which is reflected in care plans, input from guardians, and social work practice—but court orders to support sibling relationships are 'highly exceptional'.[352] This may be because they are not needed if sibling contact is agreed, but it may also reflect the low priority accorded to sibling relationships in the public law setting. Monk and Macvarish suggest that there is a lack of clarity amongst judges about when orders would be appropriate, with a reluctance to make orders underpinned by three assumptions: 'first, that court orders are inflexible; secondly that courts are not a "child-friendly" or appropriate environment for the resolution of these disputes, and thirdly, that they are unenforceable'.[353] However, as the researchers comment, similar points might be made in relation to parents, as well as to orders in the private law context, and that does not stop the courts taking a strong stance in relation to contact there.

12.5.8 SUPERVISION ORDERS

12.5.8.a Effect of a supervision order

A supervision order provides for a much lower level of intervention into the family than a care order. The effect of the supervision order is to place the child, not the parent, under 'supervision'.

[347] See also *Re E (Children in Care: Contact)* [1994] 1 FCR 584 and *Re K* [2007] EWHC 393, [24], [26].
[348] *Re P-B (Contact: Committal)* [2009] EWCA Civ 143, [45], [50].
[349] See *Kent County Council v C* [1993] 1 FLR 308, 311 and *Re D and H (Care: Termination of Contact)* [1997] 1 FLR 841.
[350] *Re W (A Child) (Parental Contact: Prohibition)* [2000] Fam 130, 136–7.
[351] Monk and Macvarish (2018), 6. [352] Ibid, 7. [353] Ibid, 11.

Children Act 1989, s 35

(1) While a supervision order is in force it shall be the duty of the supervisor—

(a) to advise, assist and befriend the supervised child;

(b) to take such steps as are reasonably necessary to give effect to the order; and

(c) where—

(i) the order is not wholly complied with; or

(ii) the supervisor considers that the order may no longer be necessary, to consider whether or not to apply to the court for its variation or discharge.

Further provisions with respect to supervision orders are found in Sch 3, Parts I and II. Conditions cannot be attached to a supervision order.[354] The supervision order may, however, require the supervised child to comply with certain directions given by the supervisor. This may include directions that the child reside at a particular place for a particular period of time; keep the supervisor informed of any change in address; allow the supervisor to visit them; attend certain appointments; or participate in various activities.[355] The supervision order may also require the child to submit to medical or psychiatric examination or treatment.[356] If the child is of sufficient understanding, the child must consent to the inclusion of such a provision in the order.[357] The supervision order may also include a requirement that a 'responsible person' take all reasonable steps to ensure that the supervised child complies with these directions.[358] The 'responsible person' may also be directed to participate in certain activities, to keep the supervisor informed of the responsible person's and the child's address, and to allow the supervisor to have reasonable contact with the child.[359] A 'responsible person' is defined as 'any person who has parental responsibility for the child and any other person with whom the child is living'.[360] As with a child of sufficient understanding, the 'responsible person' must consent to the inclusion of these provisions.[361]

In contrast to the position under a care order, it has been held that the children's guardian may continue to act until the supervision order has ceased to have effect.[362] The guardian's role will differ depending on the circumstances of each case but may include monitoring the implementation of the order to ensure its goals are being met.[363] The hope is that the continued engagement of the guardian can give the supervision order 'added teeth'.

A supervision order can only be made initially for a period of up to 12 months.[364] The order can be extended for further specified periods not exceeding three years in total from the date on which it was first made.[365] The problems caused by the limited duration of supervision orders were raised in *T v Wakefield Metropolitan District Council*.[366] In order to avoid the statutory restrictions, the judge made the order for 12 months and then immediately extended it for a further two years to give the maximum protection of three years. Whilst

[354] *Re S (Care or Supervision Order)* [1996] 1 FLR 753 and *Re V (A Minor) (Care or Supervision Order)* [1996] 2 FCR 555, 564. However, the court can probably accept undertakings on the making of a supervision order, as undertakings are given voluntarily: see, e.g., *Re Y (Care Proceedings: Proportionality Assessment)* [2014] EWCA Civ 1553, [8].

[355] Sch 3, Part I, paras 2 and 8. [356] Ibid, paras 4–5. [357] Ibid, paras 4(4) and 5(5).

[358] Ibid, para 3(1)(a) and (b). [359] Ibid, paras 3(1)(c), 3(3) and Part II, para 8(2).

[360] Ibid, para 1. [361] Ibid, para 3(1).

[362] *Re H (Care Proceedings: Children's Guardian)* [2002] 1 FCR 251. [363] Ibid, [35].

[364] CA 1989, Sch 3, Part II, para 6(1). [365] Ibid, para 6(3). [366] [2008] EWCA Civ 199.

acknowledging the pragmatism and common sense behind the judge's order, the Court of Appeal held that such an approach was impermissible as it was clearly artificial for the court to make the order and then immediately extend it, thereby circumventing the clear statutory language.[367] The Court of Appeal did, however, confirm that on an application for the original order to be extended, it could be extended for a full two-year period rather than being limited to the 12-month maximum period of the initial order.[368]

An application to extend a supervision order is determined on the basis of the child's welfare.[369] It is not necessary for the LA to prove that the threshold conditions still apply.[370] If after the three-year period has expired the LA is of the view that the supervision order needs to remain in place, it must make a fresh application under s 31 at which the threshold conditions will again need to be proved.[371]

12.5.8.b When is a supervision order appropriate?

From the point of view of the parents, a supervision order obviously has a number of advantages over a care order. The order is time-limited to an absolute maximum of three years, during which time the child remains living at home. The decision-making capacity of the LA is severely limited because it does not acquire parental responsibility, and although various obligations can be imposed on the parents, their consent and cooperation is required.[372] The entirely voluntary nature of the parents' participation makes enforcement of a supervision order extremely difficult. The only sanction for non-compliance is for the supervisor to return to court to apply to vary or discharge the order or to issue a fresh application for a care order.[373]

Perhaps the most important limitation on the power of the LA under a supervision order is that it does not have the right to remove a child from home. If circumstances developed such that removal of the child was thought necessary, the LA would need to return to court to apply for a care order or emergency protection order (EPO).

A care order can also protect the child over a longer period of time, remaining in force until the court orders otherwise, thereby vesting much greater control in the court as to when the protective measures in place for the child can be safely lifted.[374] A care order may therefore be more appropriate where it is believed the child will continue to be at risk for a number of years or where it is believed the risk of abuse will be particularly high as the child reaches a certain age.[375] It has also been suggested that a care order is advantageous because of the direct duties and responsibilities imposed on the LA where the child is a looked after child, in particular to keep the child safe and to safeguard their welfare.[376]

The perceived inadequacies of a supervision order led to a number of cases in which the appeal court overturned a supervision order in favour of a care order.[377] However, some of these perceived inadequacies have been questioned by Hale J and the benefits of proceeding

[367] Ibid, [18]. [368] Ibid, [19]. [369] *Re A (Supervision Order: Extension)* [1995] 1 WLR 482, 486.

[370] Ibid. [371] Ibid, 485–6.

[372] *Leicestershire County Council v G* [1994] 2 FLR 329.

[373] *Re V (A Minor) (Care or Supervision Order)* [1996] 2 FCR 555, 565.

[374] *Re D (A Minor) (Care or Supervision Order)* [1993] 2 FLR 423, 429.

[375] *Re T (A Minor) (Care or Supervision Order)* [1994] 1 FLR 103.

[376] *Re S (J) (A Minor) (Care or Supervision Order)* [1993] 2 FCR 193 (Fam Div), 223–6. See 12.3.3.

[377] See, e.g., *Re S (Care or Supervision Order)* [1996] 1 FLR 753; *Re V (A Minor) (Care or Supervision Order)* [1996] 2 FCR 555.

under a supervision order emphasized—not least of which is that, as a less interventionist measure, a supervision order will often constitute a more proportionate response to concerns about the child.[378]

12.5.9 LEAVING CARE

12.5.9.a Varying and discharging care orders

The discharge and variation of care and supervision orders is dealt with under s 39. A care or supervision order may be discharged on application by the LA/supervisor, the child, or any person who has PR for the child.[379] An individual who is affected by a condition or requirement imposed by a supervision order may also apply for its variation or discharge.[380] In determining the application, the court applies a simple welfare test;[381] it is not necessary either for the party seeking discharge of the order to show that the threshold criteria are no longer met, or for any party opposing the application to show that the s 31 criteria are still met.[382] Where a care order is in force, the court can substitute a supervision order without first having to re-establish that the threshold conditions are met.[383] The making of a 'live with' CAO, an SGO, or an adoption order will also have the automatic effect of discharging a care order.[384] Unless discharged, a care order continues until the child turns 18.[385]

12.5.9.b Leaving care at age 18

Sadly, for many children the route out of LA care will not be by way of discharge of the care order because they are returning home or because they have successfully been adopted, but rather because they have grown up and have left the care of the LA. As we have seen, young adults leaving care are exceptionally vulnerable. Most have a poor educational background, little prospect of employment, and poor coping skills. Few have a family on whom they can rely for help and support. Adjusting to a life of independence outside the care system is very difficult for these young people. In recognition of this, the CA 1989 was amended by the Children (Leaving Care) Act 2000 to increase substantially the duties and responsibilities on LAs to provide assistance and support to looked after children or formerly looked after children who have been in LA care for a specified period of time.[386] The support now provided, depending on the child's particular status, may include the appointment of a personal adviser, the preparation of a pathway plan, advice and assistance (including financial support) for young people undertaking education, training, and employment, and the provision of, or assistance with the cost of obtaining, suitable accommodation.[387]

378 *Oxfordshire County Council v B* [1998] 3 FCR 521; *Re O (A Child) (Supervision Order: Future Harm)* [2001] EWCA Civ 16.

379 S 39(1)–(2). *Re A (Care: Discharge Application by Child)* [1995] 1 FLR 599 confirmed that the child does not require leave to bring an application.

380 S 39(3), (3A), and (3B).

381 *Re S (Discharge of Care Order)* [1995] 2 FLR 639. The same test applies to an application by the LA for permission to withdraw a care order application: *WSCC v M, F and others* [2010] EWHC 1914.

382 *Re TT (Children: Discharge of Care Order)* [2021] EWCA Civ 742, [31](4).

383 S 39(4) and (5).

384 S 91(1) and (5A); ACA 2002, s 46(2)(b). Note *Re F and G (Discharge of Special Guardianship Order)* [2021] EWCA Civ 622: while the making of an SGO discharges any existing care order, the reverse is not true—so a care order can be made *after* an SGO, and the two can co-exist.

385 S 19(12).

386 For the various qualifying conditions, see ss 23A, 23C, and Sch 2, para 19B.

387 Ss 23B, 23C, 23CA, 23E, 24, 24A, 24B, and Sch 2, paras 19B and 19C. For discussion, see Bainham and Gilmore (2013), 499–502.

12.6 EMERGENCY PROTECTION UNDER PART V

In serious cases of abuse, it is often necessary for the LA to intervene as a matter of urgency. Part V of the Children Act provides for two key mechanisms by which the state may intervene in an emergency to protect a child from harm: (i) police protection; and (ii) EPOs.

12.6.1 POLICE PROTECTION POWERS

Children Act 1989, s 46

Where a constable has reasonable cause to believe that a child would otherwise be likely to suffer significant harm, he may—

(a) remove the child to suitable accommodation and keep him there; or

(b) take such steps as are reasonable to ensure that the child's removal from any hospital, or other place, in which he is then being accommodated is prevented.

Thus, the threshold criteria for police intervention in an emergency is that '*a constable has reasonable cause to believe*' that the child is 'likely to suffer significant harm'—much lower than the threshold for state intervention under s 31. The police exercising their protective powers do not acquire parental responsibility for the child, but must do what is reasonable to safeguard and promote the child's welfare.[388] The child must be placed in LA accommodation and the parents allowed such contact as the police consider reasonable and in the child's best interests.[389] As soon as the child is taken into police protection, a designated officer must begin an inquiry and release the child if no longer satisfied that there is reasonable cause to believe that the child is likely to suffer significant harm.[390] The child cannot be kept under police protection for more than 72 hours.[391] During this period, there is no mechanism by which the parents can challenge the actions of the police. In order to protect the child beyond this period, the police may apply on behalf of the LA for an emergency protection order.[392]

Police protection powers should only be used as a last resort.[393] However, research at one stage suggested that police protection was widely used as the first step in child protection proceedings, often out of administrative convenience and particularly when the LA wished to initiate protective measures outside normal working hours.

J. Masson, 'Fair Trials in Child Protection', (2006) 28 *Journal of Social Welfare and Family Law* 15, 22

Where the local authority was unable to obtain an EPO, the social worker contacted the police and requested that the child be taken into police protection. There were three situations where such requests were made. First, if the need to protect was immediate; for example where a parent was insisting that their child left hospital immediately. Secondly, where the

[388] S 46(9). [389] S 46(3)(f) and (10). [390] S 46(3)(e). [391] S 46(6).
[392] S 46(7). [393] DFE (2018b), 34.

magistrates' legal adviser took a restrictive approach to without notice hearings, requiring additional information before considering an application, concern about the time taken to persuade the court to agree would encourage the local authority lawyers to suggest that the social worker should approach the police. Magistrates' legal advisers were also said to suggest this course of action, in order to avoid the need to arrange an immediate hearing. Thirdly, if the need to protect the child arose out of normal working hours, social work emergency duty teams usually contacted the police rather than seeking a court order.

Masson's study of emergency protection carried out between 2001 and 2004 revealed that in 45 per cent of EPO applications, the child had already been taken into police protection.[394] In 74 per cent of those cases the police acted at the request of social services.[395]

The widespread use of police protection is concerning given there are some important disadvantages to invoking these powers rather than proceeding by way of an application for an EPO.

J. Masson, 'Emergency Intervention to Protect Children: Using and Avoiding Legal Controls', (2005) 17 *Child and Family Law Quarterly* 75, 79, 95

Police protection is a power, not a court order; the individual officer who exercises the power takes responsibility for it, subject only to a review of its continuation by the designated officer. In most forces, police protection is exercised by ordinary officers with very limited training and experience in child protection, not officers from specialist Family Protection Units. In contrast, EPOs are sought by social workers from specialist child protection teams who generally work closely with specialist lawyers. They can be granted only after a hearing before a magistrate; the court provides an external check that it is appropriate to make the order and give the local authority the power to remove or detain the child . . . Using police protection avoided the system in the Children Act 1989 for securing legal local authority accountability . . . Using police protection denied the parents any opportunity to challenge the initial decision to remove or detain the child.

Consequently, it was held by the Court of Appeal that, save in exceptional cases, removing a child in an emergency should always be carried out under the auspices of an EPO rather than relying on police protection.[396]

Langley v Liverpool City Council [2005] EWCA Civ 1173

DYSON LJ:

36. . . . The statutory scheme shows that Parliament intended that, if practicable, the removal of a child from where he or she is living should be authorised by a court order and effected under section 44. Parliament could have provided simply that specified persons could

[394] Masson (2005), 78–9. [395] Ibid.

[396] In *A v East Sussex County Council* [2010] EWCA Civ 743, Hedley J gives a useful exposition of the correct approach to emergency powers.

remove children if the statutory criteria are satisfied without any court involvement at all. But the removal of children, usually from their families, is a very serious matter. It is, therefore, not at all surprising that Parliament decided that the court should play an important part in the process. This is a valuable safeguard. The court must be satisfied that the statutory criteria for removal exist.

37. There are a number of important differences between the section 44 and section 46 regimes. They include the following. First, the court can give directions with respect to contact, examinations and assessments. This is a valuable power not available to the police. Secondly, an EPO gives the applicant parental responsibility, whereas while a child is being kept in police protection under section 46 neither the constable nor the designated officer has parental responsibility. Thirdly, no child can be kept in police protection for more than 72 hours, whereas an EPO may have effect for a period not exceeding 8 days (section 45(1)), and this period may be extended by up to 7 days (section 45(5)).

38. In my judgment, the statutory scheme clearly accords primacy to section 44. Removal under section 44 is sanctioned by the court and it involves a more elaborate, sophisticated and complete process than removal under section 46 . . .

39. It is also relevant to point out that children who require emergency protection and have to be removed are often already well known to the Social Services Department within whose area the children are ordinarily resident. It is obviously preferable for the removal of a child to be effected if possible by, or at least with the assistance of, social workers who are known to the child, rather than by uniformed police officers who will almost certainly be strangers to the child. Whether known to the child or not, a social worker has skills in dealing with the removal of children from their homes which the most sensitive police officer cannot be expected to match.

40. I would, therefore, hold that (i) removal of children should usually be effected pursuant to an EPO, and (ii) section 46 should be invoked only where it is not practicable to execute an EPO. In deciding whether it is practicable to execute an EPO, the police must always have regard to the paramount need to protect children from significant harm.

Although there are clear concerns about the widespread use of police protection, Masson notes that where police protection has been used as a prelude to an application for an EPO, the EPO proceedings are likely to be fairer.[397] The window of time created by the fact the child is safe in police protection makes it more likely the EPO application will be heard on full notice, giving the parents the opportunity to obtain representation and give instructions.[398] It also makes it more likely that the child will be represented by a children's guardian.[399]

12.6.2 EMERGENCY PROTECTION ORDERS

The alternative means by which immediate action can be taken to protect a child is by applying to the court for an EPO under s 44. There are two basic grounds on which an EPO can be made: (i) that the *court* is satisfied there is *reasonable cause to believe* the child is at immediate risk of suffering significant harm; and (ii) inquiries are being conducted by the LA or the NSPCC, those inquiries are being frustrated by access to the child being unreasonably withheld, and the *LA or the NSPCC have reasonable cause to believe* that access is required

[397] Masson (2006), 24. [398] Ibid. [399] Ibid.

as a matter of urgency. Where necessary, an EPO can be obtained very quickly. The application can be made without notice and heard by a judge sitting outside normal business hours (normally by telephone or video link).[400] In practice, very few applications are contested and it is rare for an LA's application to be refused.[401]

The legal effects of an EPO are set down in s 44(4).

Children Act 1989, s 44

(4) While an order under this section ('an emergency protection order') is in force it—

(a) operates as a direction to any person who is in a position to do so to comply with any request to produce the child to the applicant;

(b) authorises—

(i) the removal of the child at any time to accommodation provided by or on behalf of the applicant and his being kept there; or

(ii) the prevention of the child's removal from any hospital, or other place, in which he was being accommodated immediately before the making of the order; and

(c) gives the applicant parental responsibility for the child.

An EPO thus authorizes the LA to remove the child where necessary to safeguard the child's welfare.[402] The LA must return the child to the parents as soon as it considers it safe to do so although whilst the order remains in force the LA has the power to remove the child again should it be deemed necessary.[403]

In order to protect the child without necessitating the child's removal from home, the court has the power to attach to the EPO a provision excluding a specified individual from residing within the same dwelling-house as the child.[404] In order to make the exclusion order, the court must have reasonable cause to believe that by so doing the child will be protected from suffering significant harm or the NSPCC's or LA's inquiries will cease to be frustrated.[405] The court must also be satisfied that there is another person residing within the dwelling-house who is willing and able to care for the child and who consents to the exclusion order.[406] A power of arrest may also be attached.[407] The court may accept an undertaking in lieu of the exclusion order but it cannot attach a power of arrest to an undertaking.[408]

Whilst the EPO is in force, the LA obtains parental responsibility for the child, although it may only take such action as is reasonably required to safeguard or promote the child's welfare.[409] The LA must allow the child reasonable contact with, amongst others, the parents.[410] The court may also make a direction for a medical or psychiatric examination or other assessment of the child, subject to the child's consent if of sufficient understanding.[411]

An EPO has effect initially for a maximum of eight days.[412] Upon application by the LA, it may be extended once for a further seven days (15 days in total) provided there is reasonable

400 Ibid, 89–90. 401 Ibid, 96 and Masson (2004), 475. 402 S 44(5)(a).
403 S 44(10) and (12). 404 S 44(1) and (3). 405 S 44A(2)(a). 406 S 44A(2)(b).
407 S 44A(5). 408 S 44B. 409 S 44(5)(b). 410 S 44(6)(a) and (13).
411 S 44(6)(b) and (7). In *South Glamorgan County Council v W and B* [1993] 1 FLR 574, decided within the context of an interim care order, the court took the view that, exercising its inherent jurisdiction, it could override the child's refusal. Whether that decision would be followed today is unclear; cf 8.5.6.b.
412 S 45(1).

cause to believe that the child is likely to suffer significant harm if the extension is not granted.[413] An application to discharge the order may be brought by the child, the parents, any person with parental responsibility, and any person with whom the child was living immediately before the order was made, subject to the important restriction that an application cannot be brought by anyone who was given notice of the proceedings and was present at the hearing.[414] This restriction makes the growing practice of hearing applications on abridged notice to the parents particularly troublesome.

J. Masson, 'Fair Trials in Child Protection', (2006) 28 *Journal of Social Welfare and Family Law* 15, 24–7

Abridged notice appeared to be seen by both legal advisers and local authority solicitors as a compromise solution, securing a speedy decision for the local authority whilst giving the parents the opportunity to participate in the hearing . . .

Where notice of the application was abridged, parents were less likely to attend the hearing or to be represented. Only half of the parents who were given short notice of the EPO hearing were represented, compared with over 70% of those with full notice . . .

Parents who attended were doubly disadvantaged. They lost the right to challenge the EPO available in without notice cases . . . but had little real opportunity to participate in the proceedings . . . Children were also less likely to be represented. There were no arrangements between local authorities and CAFCASS to provide children's guardians with early notification of applications . . .

Overall, the compromise of holding EPO hearings on short notice appeared to undermine the rights of parents rather than to protect them. Although the proceedings might give the appearance of fairness, the more limited opportunity for representation and the loss of the right to challenge the order meant that the parents had less opportunity to be involved in the process than if either the hearing had been on full notice or without any notice at all. The same could also be said for the child, whose own involvement was frequently thwarted because no representative was appointed until after the order had been made.

There is no right of appeal against the making of an EPO or against a decision to extend or discharge the order.[415]

An EPO is thus a drastic order, often made in the absence of the parents[416] and with little effective scrutiny by the courts.[417] These shortcomings are compounded by the severe restrictions placed on challenging the order, raising questions as to the compatibility of this statutory regime with Article 8. The principles to be applied are firmly established in the Strasbourg case law.[418]

413 S 45(4)–(6). 414 S 45(8)–(11).

415 S 45(10). See *Re P (Emergency Protection Order)* [1996] 1 FLR 482.

416 Masson (2004), 475. Masson points out that even if the proceedings are heard on notice, given the limited time available to them the parents are often unable to actively contest the order.

417 Ibid, 461 and Masson (2005).

418 See *K and T v Finland* (App No 25702/94, ECHR) (2001) and *P, C and S v United Kingdom* (App No 56547/00, ECHR) (2002).

Haase v Germany (App No 11057/02, ECHR) (2005)

95. The Court accepts that when action has to be taken to protect a child in an emergency, it may not always be possible, because of the urgency of the situation, to associate in the decision-making process those having custody of the child. Nor may it even be desirable, even if possible, to do so if those having custody of the child are seen as the source of an immediate threat to the child, since giving them prior warning would be liable to deprive the measure of its effectiveness. The Court must however be satisfied that the national authorities were entitled to consider that there existed circumstances justifying the abrupt removal of the child from the care of its parents without any prior contact or consultation. In particular, it is for the respondent State to establish that a careful assessment of the impact of the proposed care measure on the parents and the child, as well as of the possible alternatives to the removal of the child from its family, was carried out prior to the implementation of a care measure.

In a detailed obiter judgment, Munby J has identified various points of tension between the statutory regime governing EPOs and the demands of the ECHR, outlining what measures are necessary to avoid incompatibility:

X Council v B (Emergency Protection Orders) [2004] EWHC 2015

MUNBY J:

57. . . .

i) An EPO, summarily removing a child from his parents, is a "draconian" and "extremely harsh" measure, requiring "exceptional justification" and "extraordinarily compelling reasons." Such an order should not be made unless the [Family Court] is satisfied that it is both necessary and proportionate and that no other less radical form of order will achieve the essential end of promoting the welfare of the child. Separation is only to be contemplated if immediate separation is essential to secure the child's safety; "imminent danger" must be "actually established."

ii) Both the local authority which seeks and the [court] which makes an EPO assume a heavy burden of responsibility. It is important that both the local authority and the [court] approach every application for an EPO with an anxious awareness of the extreme gravity of the relief being sought and a scrupulous regard for the Convention rights of both the child and the parents.

iii) Any order must provide for the least interventionist solution consistent with the preservation of the child's immediate safety.

iv) If the real purpose of the local authority's application is to enable it to have the child assessed then consideration should be given to whether that objective cannot equally effectively, and more proportionately, be achieved by an application for, or by the making of, a child assessment order under section 43 of the Act.

v) No EPO should be made for any longer than is absolutely necessary to protect the child. Where the EPO is made on an ex parte (without notice) application very careful consideration should be given to the need to ensure that the initial order is made for the shortest possible period commensurate with the preservation of the child's immediate safety.

vi) The evidence in support of the application for an EPO must be full, detailed, precise and compelling . . .

vii) Save in wholly exceptional cases, parents must be given adequate prior notice of the date, time and place of any application by a local authority for an EPO. They must also be given proper notice of the evidence the local authority is relying upon.

viii) Where the application for an EPO is made ex parte the local authority must make out a compelling case for applying without first giving the parents notice. An ex parte application will normally be appropriate only if the case is genuinely one of emergency or other great urgency – and even then it should normally be possible to give some kind of albeit informal notice to the parents – or if there are compelling reasons to believe that the child's welfare will be compromised if the parents are alerted in advance to what is going on.

ix) The evidential burden on the local authority is even heavier if the application is made ex parte . . .

xii) . . . The local authority must apply its mind very carefully to whether removal is essential in order to secure the child's immediate safety. The mere fact that the local authority has obtained an EPO is not of itself enough. The [court] decides whether to make an EPO. But the local authority decides whether to remove. The local authority, even after it has obtained an EPO, is under an obligation to consider less drastic alternatives to emergency removal. Section 44(5) requires a process within the local authority whereby there is a further consideration of the action to be taken after the EPO has been obtained. Though no procedure is specified, it will obviously be prudent for local authorities to have in place procedures to ensure both that the required decision making actually takes place and that it is appropriately documented.

xiii) Consistently with the local authority's positive obligation under Article 8 to take appropriate action to reunite parent and child, sections 44(10)(a) and 44(11)(a) impose on the local authority a mandatory obligation to return a child who it has removed under section 44(4)(b)(i) to the parent from whom the child was removed if "it appears to [the LA] that it is safe for the child to be returned." This imposes on the local authority a continuing duty to keep the case under review day by day so as to ensure that parent and child are separated for no longer than is necessary to secure the child's safety. In this, as in other respects, the local authority is under a duty to exercise exceptional diligence.

xiv) Section 44(13) requires the local authority, subject only to any direction given by the [court] under section 44(6), to allow a child who is subject to an EPO "reasonable contact" with his parents. Arrangements for contact must be driven by the needs of the family, not stunted by lack of resources.

12.7 INTERIM CARE AND SUPERVISION ORDERS

It typically takes many months before a final care order can be made.[419] Pending final order, the court may need to take interim steps to protect the child, whether or not emergency powers were initially required. Once proceedings have begun, the court has jurisdiction to adjourn the proceedings and make an interim order to protect the child until the parties are ready to proceed to the final hearing.[420] The court can also make an interim order whilst a s 37 investigation is carried out.[421] Clearly, it is important that there should be a mechanism

[419] See 12.1. [420] S 38(1). [421] Ibid.

for protecting a child while investigations are undertaken and the full court proceedings run their course. However, there are concerns that 'interim' removal of a child from their family—particularly for newborn children or young infants—can unduly pre-empt the final decision, impacting the child's ability to bond with their parents and, for new parents, denying them the ability to develop and demonstrate their parenting ability.[422]

Interim orders are dealt with under s 38. The threshold for making an order at this interim stage is higher than that for an EPO but lower than that required for the making of a full care order.

Children Act 1989, s 38

(2) A court shall not make an interim care order or interim supervision order under this section unless it is satisfied that there are *reasonable grounds for believing* that the circumstances with respect to the child are as mentioned in s.31(2) [child is suffering or is likely to suffer significant harm]. [Emphasis added]

It is important to note that the evidential requirements for the making of an interim order under s 38 are considerably lower than for a final order under s 31—the LA needs to establish only *reasonable grounds for believing* that the threshold is met.[423] If the threshold is crossed then the child's welfare is again the court's paramount consideration in the same way as it is when making a final order.[424] In determining this second question,[425] the Court of Appeal has held that the child should only be removed from the parents pending the final hearing if the child's safety demands immediate separation.[426] As Black LJ made clear in *Re L (Care Order: Prison Mother and Baby Unit)*, the court's focus at the interim stage must be on preserving the parent–child relationship pending final hearing unless there is an immediate danger to the child's physical or emotional safety.[427] It is 'a very high standard'.[428] To describe the test in Convention-compliant language, removal must be proportionate to the risk of harm to which the child will be exposed in their parents' care.[429]

An interim order has the same legal effects as a final order. Under an interim care order, the LA therefore acquires parental responsibility and ultimate decision-making authority.[430] The LA has a clear duty to consult with the parents when an interim order is in force but the weight to be attached to the parents' views will differ from case to case and is a matter for the LA.[431] Consultation must, however, be genuine and such as to safeguard the parents' rights

[422] See, e.g., Broadhurst, Mason and Ward (2022). Children under a year old account for over 20 per cent of all children subject to care proceedings: MOJ (2022a). Such children are significantly more likely to be placed for adoption (and therefore lose contact with their birth families) than older children subject to care proceedings: Broadhurst et al (2018). See also Ward et al (2010).

[423] On the importance of these different requirements, see *Re G (Children: Fair Hearing)* [2019] EWCA Civ 126, [31]–[35].

[424] *Re C (Interim Care Order)* [2011] EWCA Civ 918, [3].

[425] *Re B (Refusal to Grant Interim Care Order)* [2012] EWCA Civ 1275.

[426] *Re H* [2001] 1 FCR 350, [39]; *Re L-A (Care: Chronic Neglect)* [2009] EWCA Civ 822, [7].

[427] [2013] EWCA Civ 489, [60].

[428] *Re L-A (Care: Chronic Neglect)* [2009] EWCA Civ 822, [7].

[429] *Re B (Care Proceedings: Interim Care Orders)* [2009] EWCA Civ 1254; *Re C (Interim Separation)* [2019] EWCA Civ 1988.

[430] S 31(11); *Re L (Interim Care Order: Power of Court)* [1996] 2 FLR 742.

[431] *R (H) v Kingston upon Hull City Council* [2013] EWHC 388, [52].

to participate in the decision-making process; 'consultation' is not a means for simply conveying predetermined decisions.[432] Conditions cannot be attached to an interim care order although a suspected abuser may be excluded from the child's home.[433] Contact between the child and the parents is governed by s 34. However, pending the final hearing, terminating contact will only be considered appropriate in exceptional circumstances.[434]

An interim order can be made for such period as is determined by the court—in practice, it is almost invariably made for the duration of proceedings, subject to any later application to discharge it.[435] However, an interim care order cannot be made if it will last past a child's seventeenth birthday, since the court's jurisdiction to make care or interim care orders continues only until the child is 16.[436] The main purpose of an interim care order is to maintain the status quo until the final hearing.[437] However, while that was originally envisaged to be a relatively short period of around 12 weeks, care proceedings now take far longer—in 2021, the mean duration of care proceedings was 44.4 weeks (down from a peak of 55.1 weeks in 2011, but up from 27.0 weeks in 2015).[438]

Although ultimate responsibility for the child passes with the interim care order to the LA, the court retains control of the care proceedings. This gives the court limited authority to direct the LA to undertake certain assessments involving the child for the purposes of the final hearing.

Children Act 1989, s 38

(6) Where the court makes an interim care order, or interim supervision order, it may give such directions (if any) as it considers appropriate with regard to the medical or psychiatric examination or other assessment of the child; but if the child is of sufficient understanding to make an informed decision he may refuse to submit to the examination or other assessment.

The scope of the power conferred on the court by s 38 has given rise to considerable controversy and has been considered by the House of Lords on two occasions. Dispute has centred, in particular, on whether the court can order the LA to undertake a programme of 'treatment' or 'therapy' rather than 'assessment' and whether an assessment which is primarily aimed not at the child but at the parents falls within the scope of the section. The issue was considered in *Re C (A Minor) (Interim Care Order: Residential Assessment)* which appeared to widen the scope of permissible directions to include assessments other than those of a medical or psychiatric nature and to include assessments involving the parents as well as the child. The case concerned whether the court could order an expensive residential assessment of the family which was primarily aimed at evaluating the parents' parenting ability.

[432] Ibid, [59]–[63]. [433] S 38A.
[434] *A v M and Walsall Metropolitan Borough Council* [1993] 2 FLR 244.
[435] CA 1989, s 38(4).
[436] *Re Q (Children: Interim Care Order: Jurisdiction)* [2019] EWHC 512. The full care order, if made, can last until the child turns 18: s 91(12).
[437] *Re G (Minors) (Interim Care Order)* [1993] 2 FCR 557 (CA), 562–3.
[438] MOJ (2018), 1. See 12.1.

Re C (A Minor) (Interim Care Order: Residential Assessment) [1997] AC 489 (HL), 500–4

LORD BROWNE-WILKINSON:

Section 38(6) deals with the interaction between the powers of the local authority entitled to make decisions as to the child's welfare in the interim and the needs of the court to have access to the relevant information and assessments so as to be able to make the ultimate decision. . . .

There are two possible constructions of subsection (6) . . ., one narrow, the other purposive and broader. The Court of Appeal in *Re M (Minors) (Interim Care Order: Directions)* [1996] 3 FCR 137 adopted the narrow view. . . . They attached decisive importance to the fact that the subsection only refers to the examination or assessment "of the child" and makes no reference to the examination or assessment of any other person in relation to the child. . . . [Counsel] for the local authority in the present appeal, submitted that Parliament cannot have intended the court to have power to require the local authority against its own judgment to expend scarce resources: he submitted that the local authority is the only body which can properly assess how such resources are to be allocated as between the social services and the other services it has to provide and as between the various calls on its social services budget.

My Lords, I cannot accept this narrow construction of the subsection. The Act should be construed purposively so as to give effect to the underlying intentions of Parliament. As I have sought to demonstrate, the dividing line between the functions of the court on the one hand and the local authority on the other is that a child in interim care is subject to control of the local authority, the court having no power to interfere with the local authority's decisions save in specified cases. The cases where, despite that overall control, the court is to have power to intervene are set out, inter alia, in subsection (6) . . . The purpose of subsection (6) is to enable the court to obtain the information necessary for its own decision, notwithstanding the control over the child which in all other respects rests with the local authority. I therefore approach the subsection on the basis that the court is to have such powers to override the views of the local authority as are necessary to enable the court to discharge properly its function of deciding whether or not to accede to the local authority's application to take the child away from its parents by obtaining a care order. To allow the local authority to decide what evidence is to go before the court at the final hearing would be in many cases, including the present, to allow the local authority by administrative decision to pre-empt the court's judicial decision . . .

Next, it is true that subsection (6) . . . only refer[s] to the assessment "of the child" and not, as is proposed in the present case, a joint assessment of the child and the parents, including the parents' attitude and behaviour towards the child. But it is impossible to assess a young child divorced from his environment. The interaction between the child and his parents or other persons looking after him is an essential element in making any assessment of the child . . .

Much the most powerful of [counsel's] submissions is that based on the expenditure of scarce resources by the local authority in the carrying out of an expensive assessment. In the overwhelming majority of care cases, the parties are in straitened circumstances and there is no one to pay for any examination or assessment under section 38(6) other than the local authority. . . . I accept the force of this submission but it proves too much. [Counsel] was not able to argue that if the court directed a medical examination of the child himself, which examination would be very expensive, the local authority could refuse to carry it out simply on the grounds of the expense involved and the unwise allocation of limited resources. In such a case, it will be for the court to take into account in deciding whether or not to make an order for the medical examination the expense that it involves. If that is so, the issue of resources cannot affect the proper construction of subsection (6). . . . Therefore it is impossible to construe section 38(6) in the narrow sense simply because the court is less suitable than the local authority to assess the financial considerations.

In my judgment, therefore, subsection (6) . . . of section 38 of the Act [is] to be broadly construed. [It] confer[s] jurisdiction on the court to order or prohibit any assessment which involves the participation of the child and is directed to providing the court with the material which, in the view of the court, is required to enable it to reach a proper decision at the final hearing of the application for a full care order. In exercising its discretion whether to order any particular examination or assessment, the court will take into account the cost of the proposed assessment and the fact that local authorities' resources are notoriously limited.

This judgment was subsequently seized upon as a potential means of directing the LA to provide expensive treatment and therapy for individuals other than the child. This gave rise to considerable litigation in the face of LAs' objections to being forced to fund treatment with which they did not agree.[439] The second House of Lords' decision responded to these concerns, attempting to rein back the potentially expansive scope of s 38(6), and imposing firm restrictions on the nature of the directions that may be imposed. The proposed assessment in this case involved intensive psychotherapy for the child's mother to be provided over a period of months.

Re G (A Minor) (Interim Care Order: Residential Assessment) **[2005] UKHL 68**

BARONNESS HALE:

64. The purpose of [ss 38(6) and 38(7)] is . . . not only to enable the court to obtain the information it needs, but also to enable the court to control the information-gathering activities of others. But the emphasis is always on obtaining information. This is clear from the use of the words "examination" and "other assessment". If the framers of the Act had meant the court to be in charge, not only of the examination and assessment of the child, but also of the medical or psychiatric treatment to be provided for her, let alone for her parents, it would have said so. Instead, it deliberately left that in the hands of the local authority.

65. A fortiori, the purpose of section 38(6) cannot be to ensure the provision of services either for the child or his family. There is nothing in the 1989 Act which empowers the court hearing care proceedings to order the provision of specific services for anyone. To imply such a power into section 38(6) would be quite contrary to the division of responsibility which was the "cardinal principle" of the 1989 Act . . .

66. I appreciate, of course, that it is not always possible to draw a hard and fast line between information-gathering and service-providing. Some information can only be gathered through the provision of services. It may be necessary to observe the parents looking after the child at close quarters for a short period in order to assess the quality of the child's attachment to the parents, the degree to which the parents have bonded with the child, the current parenting skills of the parents, and their capacity to learn and develop . . .

[439] See, e.g., *Re B (Psychiatric Therapy for Parents)* [1999] 1 FLR 701; *Re B (Interim Care Order: Directions)* [2002] 1 FLR 545.

> 67. But the court only has power to insist where this is relevant to the questions which the court has to answer. Where the threshold criteria are in issue, it must be recalled that these are phrased (in section 31(2)) in the present tense . . . Where the threshold is found or conceded but the proper order is in issue, the welfare checklist is likewise focussed on the present . . . The capacity to change, to learn and to develop may well be part of that. But it is still the present capacity with which the court is concerned. It cannot be a proper use of the court's powers under section 38(6) to seek to bring about change.
>
> 68. These conclusions are reinforced by the Act's emphasis on reaching decisions without delay. It cannot have been contemplated that the examination or assessment ordered under section 38(6) would take many months to complete. It would be surprising if it were to last more than two or three months at most. The important decision for the court is whether or not to make a care order, with all that that entails . . . The court may sometimes have to accept that it is not possible to know all that is to be known before a final choice is made, because that choice will depend upon how the family and the child respond and develop in the future.

Recent case law has also seen a different argument raised in support of applications for an assessment under s 38(6). It has been suggested that if by refusing an up-to-date assessment under s 38 the parent would be left, in effect, unable to challenge the making of the care order because of the weight of previous negative assessments (which may well have led to the removal of older siblings), the proceedings would be unfair and violate the parents' rights under Articles 6 and 8. That argument has been dismissed by the Court of Appeal. The court made clear in *Re T (Residential Parenting Assessment)* that there is no absolute right in the parent to bring any possible evidence before the court.[440] In determining whether to order an assessment under s 38(6), the court must have a mind both to the child's welfare and the potential harm of delay and if further assessment would be futile and/or could not hope to establish a realistic prospect of reunification within a reasonable timescale for the child, it should not be ordered.[441]

12.8 CONCLUSION

Protecting children from abuse and neglect involves a difficult balancing exercise. Whilst children must not be left in situations of known risk, the decision to remove a child from the child's parents carries a heavy responsibility. It causes deep loss to both parents and child. Parents in this position are often deeply troubled and vulnerable, they have a right to expect help and support from the state. Better resourced support services may help keep more vulnerable families together. The inadequate funding of services under Part III is thus an issue of crucial importance, and that situation has worsened considerably in the age of 'austerity'. Many more families could be helped and court proceedings avoided if LA children's services departments were properly resourced, though it is fair to say that for some parents it would never be enough. In serious cases of abuse and neglect or for parents battling against multiple long-term problems, there will come a point at which the child's right to a safe and secure childhood must come first. Deciding when that point has been reached is never easy, but children cannot be expected to wait forever. Whilst the rights of the parents must be

[440] [2011] EWCA Civ 812. [441] Ibid, [53], [61], [93], [95].

taken seriously throughout the child protection process, parents do not have the right to cause irreparable harm to their children. That basic principle should not be forgotten.

When children are received into LA care, they look to the state to give them the safe and secure childhood so many other children are able to take for granted. Munby J is right to observe that 'if the State is to justify removing children from their parents it can only be on the basis that the State is going to provide a better quality of care than that from which the child in care has been rescued'.[442] Sadly, for many children, the state fails them too.[443] As we have seen, the state's own parenting record is poor. However, the children for whom the state has assumed this heavy responsibility are often deeply scarred by their early experiences. They arrive in care deeply troubled and vulnerable. The state does not have a magic wand. It cannot make deep-rooted problems just disappear. However, it can try and repair some of the damage by giving these children the best possible care that it can. And where children cannot return home, successive governments have firmly believed that the best possible care is not that of the state, but the love and support of an alternative 'forever family'. And for some children that means adoption.

ONLINE RESOURCES

Questions, suggestions for further reading, and updates on developments in this area of family law since this book was published may be found in the online resources at **www.oup.com/he/familytcm5e**.

[442] *F v Lambeth London Borough Council* [2002] 1 FLR 217, 234.

[443] Ibid.

13

ADOPTION

CENTRAL ISSUES

1. Adoption is a controversial topic. Successive governments have been strongly committed to increasing the number of children adopted out of care and speeding up the entire adoption process. However, the drive to ensure more children are adopted more quickly was met with concern that the 'rush to adoption' might result in the need to ensure adoption is in the best interests of each individual child being lost.

2. An adoption order terminates the legal relationship between the birth parents and the child. It is permanent and irrevocable. The adoptive parents become the child's legal parents as if the child had been born their own legitimate child. As the social purpose of adoption has changed, this concept of adoption has found itself under increasing pressure. It is, however, a concept of adoption that remains important to prospective adoptive parents.

3. Whenever a decision is made in relation to the adoption of a child, the child's welfare is the paramount consideration. Parental consent to the adoption can be dispensed with if the child's welfare requires it. The exclusively child-centred approach of the Adoption and Children Act 2002 (ACA 2002) raises questions as to whether adequate consideration is given to the birth parents' rights and interests throughout the adoption process.

4. The weight to be placed on a child's ethnic, cultural, and religious background when a child is to be adopted is a particularly difficult issue. It was one of the most controversial questions arising from reforms in the Children and Families Act 2014 (CFA 2014).

5. Recent years have seen a shift to a more open concept of adoption that gives children information about their birth parents and, where appropriate, provides for indirect or even direct contact between the child and the birth family post-adoption. However, this again sits uneasily with the more traditional concept of adoption and can deter prospective adopters at a time when the government is trying to encourage more people to put themselves forward.

6. Special guardianship was introduced by the ACA 2002 as an alternative means of securing permanency for the child. It is used primarily by kinship carers.

13.1 INTRODUCTION

Adoption is an area of family law beset by tensions and contradictions. As one important route to 'becoming a parent', adoption is for many people a 'good news' story. For adoptive parents, it can fulfil a lifetime's dream to become a parent, providing vital recognition of the value and importance of social parenthood. For children in care or voluntarily relinquished by their parents, it can be a life-line, providing the opportunity to be part of a 'normal', loving, and devoted 'forever family', perhaps for the first time in their short and often troubled lives. For others, however, behind this 'good news' story lies sadness and despair. A price must be paid for the creation of this new adoptive family—and that price is paid by the birth family. For them, adoption represents the termination of their legal relationship with the child. Put simply, in legal terms, the child is lost to them forever. Often young, vulnerable, and marginalized, birth mothers are often the ones who pay the greatest price, many facing a lifetime of unresolved grief. For children too, adoption can be a paradox. Whilst the gains for the child can be enormous, so too can the losses, with many adopted children being profoundly affected by the loss of their birth-family relationships. That deep sense of loss can remain with children throughout their lives, often intensifying as they grow older. Adoption is thus a complex issue. It marks both the beginning and the end of what for many is the core, defining relationship of their lives—that of parent and child.

The tensions and contradictions inherent in adoption make this a particularly appropriate topic with which to end the book. Contemporary debates surrounding adoption encapsulate many of the key themes explored within the previous chapters. It brings into focus key questions such as the respective value to be placed on biological as opposed to social parenthood, the value to be placed on traditional as opposed to alternative family forms, the importance of a child's cultural and religious heritage, the importance of preserving original family ties as opposed to supporting and prioritizing new and reconstituted families, the responsibilities of the state when it compulsorily removes a child from its family of birth, and the advantages and disadvantages of law over other methods of social governance. Adoption thus retains great symbolic importance. What the law has to say about adoption tells us a great deal about prevailing social attitudes to marriage, non-marital relationships, biological parenting, social parenting, and the role of the state in family life. As Murray Ryburn puts it, 'the practice of adoption goes to the heart of many issues that are critical in determining the kind of society we live in or wish to live in'.[1]

This chapter explores the legal framework for adoption as enshrined in the ACA 2002. We begin by examining the legal concept of adoption before turning to consider whether this traditional western concept meets the particular needs of children adopted from care. We then move on to consider the statutory provisions in more detail, beginning with two core principles running throughout the legislation: the welfare principle and the requirement for the birth parents' consent. The statutory test for dispensing with parental consent will be considered, particularly its compatibility or otherwise with the European Convention on Human Rights (ECHR). The adoption process as enshrined in the ACA 2002 is then examined in detail, including the application of the welfare principle to three particularly contentious issues: (i) the importance of the birth family in an adoption dispute; (ii) transracial adoption; and (iii) step-parent adoptions and adoptions by a sole natural parent. We conclude our discussion of adoption by examining the increasingly important question of 'open adoption', focusing in particular on adopted children's right to information about

[1] Ryburn (1998a), 53–4.

their birth families and provision for post-adoption contact. Finally, we turn to consider special guardianship, the main alternative to adoption for securing permanence outside local authority care.

13.2 WHAT IS ADOPTION?

The legal effects of an adoption order are enshrined in ss 46 and 67 of the ACA 2002.[2]

Adoption and Children Act 2002

46 Adoption orders

(1) An adoption order is an order made by the court . . . giving parental responsibility for a child to the adopters or adopter.

(2) The making of an adoption order operates to extinguish—

(a) the parental responsibility which any person other than the adopters or adopter has for the adopted child immediately before the making of the order . . .

67 Status conferred by adoption

(1) An adopted person is to be treated in law as if born as the child of the adopters or adopter . . .

(3) An adopted person—

(a) if adopted by one of a couple is to be treated in law as not being the child of any person other than the adopter and the other one of the couple, and

(b) in any other case, is to be treated in law . . . as not being the child of any person other than the adopters or adopter . . .

In the case of a 'stranger adoption',[3] an adoption order completely terminates any legal relationship between the birth parents and the child. Save for the limited exceptions specified in s 74 of the ACA 2002,[4] it is as if the birth parents had never been: there is a total and absolute transplanting of the legal relationship of parent and child. The adoptive parents become the child's legal parents and are vested with parental responsibility. By an act of legal fiction, they stand in relation to the child as if the child had been born their natural legitimate child. For the adoptive parents, adoption thus represents full and unequivocal recognition of their parental status.

A step-parent adoption has similar effects, although the legal status of the birth parent with whom the child is to live remains unchanged.[5] In contrast, the legal relationship between the non-resident birth parent and the child is completely extinguished just as in a

[2] Unless otherwise stated, all references to statutory provisions in this chapter are to the ACA 2002.

[3] This term refers to adoption by anyone other than a parent or step-parent, including members of the extended family.

[4] Marriage within the prohibited degrees; the offence of engaging in sexual intercourse with an adult relative; and acquisition of British nationality.

[5] S 67(3). It is thus no longer necessary for the birth parent with whom the child is living to adopt their own child.

stranger adoption. The child is to be treated as if born to the resident birth parent and their new partner.[6]

The courts have strongly endorsed this model of adoption, prioritizing the need to support the adoptive family by treating them in every way as if they were a 'normal' family unit. This has been evident in their approach to whether conditions should be imposed on the adoption order. The courts have firmly resisted this, arguing that to impose conditions on the adoptive family undermines the concept of adoption as a total legal transplant and treats the adoptive parents as something less than an ordinary, natural family—as 'second-class' parents. They have thus generally refused to attach any conditions to the order which interfere with the adoptive parents' decision-making authority. This approach was tested in *Re S (A Minor) (Adoption: Blood Transfusion)*. The prospective adopters were Jehovah's Witnesses who, under pressure from the judge, had undertaken that they would not withhold consent to the child receiving a blood transfusion without first applying to the court. The adoptive parents appealed, wishing to be released from the undertaking. The Court of Appeal allowed the appeal.

Re S (A Minor) (Adoption: Blood Transfusion) [1995] 2 FCR 177 (CA), 182

STAUGHTON LJ:

To my mind this should be a very rare course . . . The best thing for the child in the ordinary way is that he or she should become as near as possible the lawful child of the adopting parents. That is what the child's welfare requires. I would not, in this case, regard it as in any way appropriate to impose a condition which derogated from that, and which made very little difference as to what would in fact happen, in circumstances which were in any event unlikely to arise.

As with natural parenthood, 'adoption is for life'. Subject only to the very limited circumstances in which an adoption order can be revoked on statutory grounds under the ACA 2002[7] (or the making of a further adoption order), the legal parenthood of the adoptive parents can only be terminated by invoking the inherent jurisdiction of the High Court or an appeal. The permanent, irrevocable nature of adoption sets it apart from any other form of social parenthood. This was dramatically illustrated in *Re B (Adoption: Jurisdiction to Set Aside)*, in which an adopted child sought to set aside the adoption order 36 years after it was made. The applicant's birth mother was Roman Catholic and the birth father was a Muslim Arab from Kuwait. The child was mistakenly placed with an Orthodox Jewish couple who subsequently adopted him. The applicant sought to set the adoption order aside under the court's inherent jurisdiction, arguing it had been made under a fundamental mistake of fact as to his racial and ethnic origins. As Simon Brown LJ commented, 'it is difficult to imagine a more ill-starred adoption placement'. The Court of Appeal nevertheless refused the application.

[6] S 67(2)(b).

[7] See ACA 2002, s 55 (child adopted by a sole natural parent who subsequently marries the other natural parent thereby legitimating the child).

Re B (Adoption: Jurisdiction to Set Aside) [1995] Fam 239 (CA), 245–9

SWINTON THOMAS LJ:

In my judgment such an application faces insuperable hurdles . . .

There are certain specific statutory provisions for the revocation of an adoption order . . . There are cases where an adoption order has been set aside by reason of what is known as a procedural irregularity . . . Those cases concern a failure to effect proper service of the adoption proceedings on a natural parent or ignorance of the parent of the existence of the adoption proceedings. In each case the application to set aside the order was made reasonably expeditiously. It is fundamental to the making of an adoption order that the natural parent should be informed of the application so that she can give or withhold her consent. If she has no knowledge at all of the application then, obviously, a fundamental injustice is perpetrated. I would prefer myself to regard those cases not as cases where the order has been set aside by reason of a procedural irregularity, although that has certainly occurred, but as cases where natural justice has been denied because the natural parent who may wish to challenge the adoption has never been told that it is going to happen. . . .

There is no case which has been brought to our attention in which it has been held that the court has an inherent power to set aside an adoption order by reason of a misapprehension or mistake. To allow considerations such as those put forward in this case to invalidate an otherwise properly made adoption order would, in my view, undermine the whole basis on which adoption orders are made, namely that they are final and for life as regards the adopters, the natural parents, and the child. In my judgment [counsel], who appeared as amicus curiae, is right when he submits that it would gravely damage the lifelong commitment of adopters to their adoptive children if there is a possibility of the child, or indeed the parents, subsequently challenging the validity of the order. I am satisfied that there is no inherent power in the courts in circumstances such as arise in this case to set aside an adoption order. Nobody could have other than the greatest sympathy with the applicant but, in my judgment, the circumstances of this case do not provide any ground for setting aside an adoption order which was regularly made.

However, although the courts continue to apply these principles, there has been a marked increase in successful challenges to adoption orders in recent years. Two legal approaches have been adopted: the first is an appeal brought out of time, that is (often long) after the normal time limitations for seeking to appeal; the second is an application under the High Court's inherent jurisdiction.[8] Under either route, the court has stressed that 'the highly exceptional circumstances must comprise more than mistake or misrepresentation or serious injustice and amount to matters such as a fundamental breach of natural justice'.[9] What circumstances amount to being 'exceptional' are unclear, and successful applications have certainly increased in recent years. As Polly Morgan comments, 'exceptionality as an argument can only go so far when the cases start to stack up'.[10]

[8] As to which approach to use, there is little guidance. In *Re J (Adoption: Appeal)* [2018] EWFC 8, Cobb J suggested that an appeal is more appropriate if the basis for the challenge to the adoption order is a procedural irregularity in the making of the original order. See Fenton-Glynn (2018). On the inherent jurisdiction, see generally 8.7.

[9] *Re AX and BX (Adoption: Revocation)* [2021] EWHC 1121, [80]; see also *W v Norfolk County Council* [2009] EWCA Civ 59.

[10] Morgan (2020), 248.

Where applications are made to revoke an adoption, Morgan suggests that there are three categories.[11] The first group involves fundamental breaches of natural justice in the making of the orders in the first place. The second group involves cases where there was an underlying problem with the adoptive placement itself, where there is an 'ill-fated match' between the child and the adopters, such as in *Re B (Adoption: Jurisdiction to Set Aside)*. The final group includes challenges to the original care proceedings that led to the placement order being made. As a general principle, Morgan argues that only cases in the first category are likely to have any realistic prospect of success.[12] Despite the apparent increase in adoption revocation orders, this outcome remains very rare. Indeed, it is rare for adoption placements to break down at all, with only around 3.2 per cent of adoption placements being 'disrupted', and most of those occurring five or more years after the making of the adoption order.[13] The vast majority of these do not involve the adoption being legally challenged; the child goes back into care, but the adopters remain the child's legal parents.

13.3 THE CHANGING FACE OF ADOPTION

The nature and social purpose of adoption has changed dramatically over the course of the twentieth century.

C. Bridge, 'Adoption Law: A Balance of Interests', in J. Herring (ed), ***Family Law: Issues, Debates, Policy*** (Cullompton: Willan, 2001), 198–9

Formal legal adoption is a relatively modern concept. Its roots lie in the changes evident in society after the first world war: numbers of orphaned children needed the permanency and stability that family life supposedly provided and cohabitation, which had become increasingly common, gave rise to the need for secure legal arrangements for both children and birth parents. The first Adoption Act was passed in 1926 with these social purposes in mind. In comparison with the current law that Act was limited. It did not provide for the child's full integration into the adoptive family, it set out only limited grounds for permitting adoption without parental consent, and did not fully address inheritance issues. Adoption was, as Cretney and Masson suggest, a 'private or amateur activity'. But as the nature of social problems changed so the nature and purpose of adoption also changed. Adoption became a way of dealing with some of the uncomfortable social and human problems that emerged during the 1950s and 60s. Its upsurge during this period was due, primarily, to the increasing numbers of young single mothers unable to care for their illegitimate babies. Social, moral, financial and a variety of practical measures combined to present adoption as the way out for both mother and child. By having the baby adopted straight after birth the mother was perceived as enabled to resume her life untarnished by the product of past immoral conduct. For the baby, adoption

[11] Ibid.

[12] As Morgan (ibid) notes, the outlier is *PK v Mr and Mrs K* [2015] EWHC 2316: a 14-year-old girl applied successfully under the inherent jurisdiction to revoke the order under which she had been adopted ten years earlier, having escaped an abusive adoptive family and re-found her birth family. Unlike all the other successful applications to revoke an adoption, there were no factors undermining the making of the original order.

[13] Selwyn, Meakings, and Wijedasa (2014), 273. See 13.3.2.

was widely perceived as a lucky escape from the shame of illegitimacy. Illegitimacy still carried a social stigma yet the numbers of such births were high. Sexual liberation had arrived but the contraceptive pill had yet to become widely available and abortion was unlawful. As a result, large numbers of white babies were adopted by childless married couples—those whom Lowe and Douglas describe as seeking to avoid the 'oppressive taint of infertility'. In a secretive process designed to facilitate an irrevocable transfer of all legal rights and powers from birth parents to adoptive parents, such babies became the lawful offspring of their new family, born to them as 'a child of the marriage'. The image this conjured up is one of a traditional family more redolent of the 1950s than the twenty-first century, and although it smacks of legislation of earlier times, that is not so.

At its peak in 1968, there were 24,831 adoptions.[14] However, important social changes in the second half of the twentieth century saw a dramatic decline in the number of adoption orders made. Contraception, the ready availability of abortion, and the loss of stigma surrounding single motherhood and illegitimacy drastically reduced the number of babies available for adoption.[15] Increased understanding of the causes of infertility and the availability of new treatments similarly rendered adoption a less attractive option for childless couples. By 1999, the annual number of adoption orders had dropped to just 4,100.[16] Approximately half were adoptions of children out of care,[17] the other half were made up of step-parent and intercountry adoptions, along with a tiny number of children voluntarily relinquished for adoption at birth.[18] Thus, by the end of the twentieth century the social role played by adoption had changed dramatically.[19]

However, since 2000 successive governments have been strongly committed to promoting adoption as a core plank of child protection policy. With steadily increasing numbers of children entering the care system, central to this policy has been the principle that 'no child is un-adoptable' and that the number of adoptions from care need to be significantly increased. In response to this policy drive, the number of adoptions of children out of care rose, reaching a post-millennium peak of 5,360 in 2014–15—but major judicial decisions in 2013[20] caused numbers to drop back again, with 2,950 orders made in 2021–2.[21] However, while adoption remains a key part of the law's toolkit in response to child protection concerns, step-parent adoption has dropped dramatically in the last two decades, accounting for only around 5 per cent of all adoption orders in 2021.[22]

[14] Cretney (2003a), 596.

[15] Bridge (1993), 83. In 1968, approximately half of the 25,000 adoptions were of babies under 12 months old. By 2021, the average time between a child entering care and being placed for adoption was 18 months, and the average age of children when the adoption order was made was 3 years 3 months: DH (1993), 4; MOJ (2022a).

[16] Cabinet Office (2000), 10.

[17] This represented an adoption rate of around 4 per cent, given the number of children in care at the time.

[18] Cabinet Office (2000). [19] Ibid. [20] See 13.4.3.

[21] DFE (2022a). This was a slight increase on 2020–1, but the general trend has shown a drop of around 10 per cent each year since 2014–15. With over 60,000 children the subject of care orders in the same period, this represents an adoption rate of just under 5 per cent. A small number of children are relinquished voluntarily at birth: see 13.4.2.a.

[22] MOJ (2022a), Table 20 (authors' calculations). See also 13.6.3 and 10.3.4.

13.3.1 LOOKED AFTER CHILDREN: DOES ADOPTION OFFER THE BEST SOLUTION?

One of the major factors driving the ACA 2002 was the then Labour Government's desire to increase the use of adoption as a route to 'permanence' for looked after children unable to return home: put simply, there should be 'more adoptions more quickly'.[23] The new legislation, hailed as the 'most radical overhaul of adoption law in 25 years', was accompanied by National Adoption Standards and performance targets aimed at increasing by 40 per cent the number of children adopted from care by 2004–5.[24] From the outset, the 2002 reforms were marked by a strong 'saving children in care' rhetoric.[25] This theme was taken forward in equally strong terms during the reforms spearheaded by the Conservative-led coalition from 2010–15.[26]

There is a considerable body of evidence supporting the case for increased numbers of adoption. Although there have been recent efforts to improve the care system and it is important to recognize that for many children care can be a positive experience,[27] adoption consistently emerges as by far the better alternative. Research on outcomes for adopted children is generally very positive, particularly for children *voluntarily relinquished and placed as babies.*

J. Castle, C. Beckett, and C. Groothues, 'Infant Adoption in England: A Longitudinal Account of Social and Cognitive Progress', (2000) 24 *Adoption and Fostering* 26–7

Baby adoptions are viewed as a group for whom successful outcomes are usual. In general, studies of children placed as babies have shown favourable levels of psychosocial functioning, high parental satisfaction and low levels of adoption disruption. Data from the National Child Development Study (NCDS) indicated that adopted children outperformed birth comparisons on maths and reading tests at age seven, and on a measure of general ability at age eleven.

Although children adopted as babies fare extremely well, there have been conflicting findings regarding psychosocial outcome. In their report of adopted adolescents in residential treatment, Grotevant and McRoy mentioned studies from several countries showing increased referral rates for treatment of emotional disturbance in children adopted as infants by childless couples, compared with the normal population. However, where clinical referrals were concerned, it was possible that adoptive parents were more likely to make use of mental health services because of a lower threshold of concern so there are limitations in generalising from clinical cases to the general population of adopted children.

Castle, Beckett, and Groothues's study of 52 adopted children support these findings, with children placed under six months and reviewed at ages 4 and 6 'showing favourable cognitive

[23] Harris-Short (2001), 407. [24] DH (2000), 5.
[25] Cabinet Office (2000), 3; Harris-Short (2001), 406. [26] See DFE (2012b); see also Narey (2011).
[27] House of Commons Select Committee on Education (2012/13); Selwyn, Meakings, and Wijedasa (2014).

and social progress . . . and high levels of satisfaction with adoption among parents'.[28] However, the outcomes for children *adopted out of care* are less convincing.[29]

J. Selwyn, S. Meakings, and D. Wijedasa, *Beyond the Adoption Order: Challenges, Interventions and Adoption Disruption* (London: Department for Education, 2014), 77–9, 273–4

A key objective of this study was to compare the adoption disruption rate [i.e. how often placements break down] with the disruption rates of other types of orders. Therefore, in this section, we go on to build a statistical model including all three types of Order [i.e. adoption, special guardianship (SGO), and private law child arrangements orders (CAO), then called a residence order (RO)]. . . . The cumulative proportions of disruptions for the three groups over a 5-year period [following placement] are shown in Figure 32.

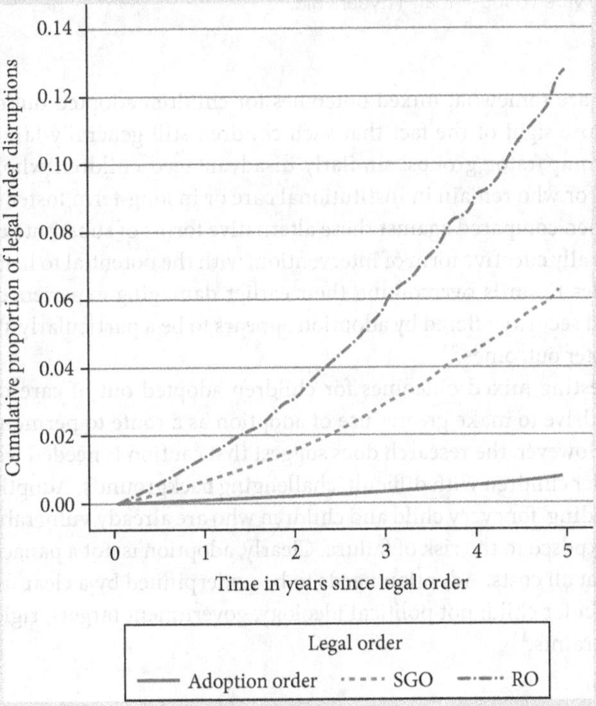

Figure 32 Kaplan-Meir survival estimates of the cumulative proportion of disruptions after the legal order

. . .

Over a 12-year period, . . . the rate of adoption disruption was calculated to be 3.2%, which indicates that 3 in 100 adoptions would be likely to disrupt over the 12 years. Of course, this does not mean that this is the risk for any particular child, but 3.2% was the rate across the whole sample. The most important factors that predicted disruption were the child's age, followed by older age at placement and a longer waiting time between placement and Adoption Order. . . .

[28] Castle et al (2000), 32. See also Ijzendoorn and Juffer (2005); Maughan, Collishaw, and Pickles (1998).
[29] See also Sloan (2022).

Before making the comparison, it is important to highlight that disruption rates for all three types of order *were low*, compared with the movement that is reported for children who remain in the care system. Of course, that may be because those who remain in care are the children with the most challenging behaviours or they enter care late as adolescents with very challenging behaviour . . . Data were available for each type of order over different periods. To ensure a 'like for like' comparison, the orders were compared over a five year follow-up period using survival analyses. Over a five-year period:

- 147 in 1,000 ROs would have disrupted
- 57 in 1,000 SGOs would have disrupted
- 7 in 1,000 adoptions would have disrupted.

Adoption Orders were the most stable, although we found that the very low rate of disruptions in the early years rose to 3.2% after 12 years. SGO and RO disruptions occurred irrespective of the child's age since the making of the legal order. Most disrupted quickly and when children were younger than 11 years old.

Although there are somewhat mixed outcomes for children adopted out of care, it is important not to lose sight of the fact that such children still generally fare better than the most relevant comparator groups: similarly disadvantaged children who return to their birth families,[30] or who remain in institutional care or in long-term foster care.[31] Evidence suggests that when compared against these alternative forms of substitute care, adoption is a superior, generally effective form of intervention, with the potential to help children make significant strides towards overcoming their earlier damaging experiences.[32] The greater permanence and security offered by adoption appears to be a particularly significant factor in achieving better outcomes.[33]

Studies suggesting mixed outcomes for children adopted out of care do not therefore undermine the drive to make greater use of adoption as a route to permanence for looked after children. However, the research does suggest that caution is needed when considering adoption for older children with difficult, challenging backgrounds. Adoption will not provide a 'happy ending' for every child and children who are already vulnerable should not be unnecessarily exposed to the risk of failure. Clearly, adoption is not a panacea and it should not be pursued at all costs. Adoption needs to be underpinned by a clear focus on the welfare of the particular child: not political ideology, government targets, rigid timescales, or budgetary constraints.[34]

[30] Thoburn, Robinson, and Anderson (2012), 2, 5, 12.

[31] E.g. Ijzendoorn and Juffer (2005). Biehal et al (2009) found that when measuring emotional, behavioural, and educational outcomes, children in stable long-term foster care were doing just as well as adopted children. For discussion of the differences between adoption and long-term foster care, see *Re V (Long-Term Fostering or Adoption)* [2013] EWCA Civ 913.

[32] Triseliotis (2002). However, the use of adoption 'disruptions' as the main measure of success is challenged by some commentators: see Eekelaar (2003) and Sloan (2022).

[33] Consequently, 'the evident potential benefits . . . of adoption . . . in terms of commitment, security and permanence', where evidenced, must be borne properly in mind: *Re B-P (Children: Adoption or Fostering)* [2018] EWCA Civ 2042, [15].

[34] See generally Sagar and Hitchings (2007). The social workers interviewed as part of their study all expressed concern at the new target-driven approach to adoption, arguing that it was likely to lead to a greater number of unsuitable placements disrupting. Ibid, 207.

13.3.2 ADOPTING CHILDREN OUT OF CARE: NEW CHALLENGES

As the use of adoption has changed, so too has the profile of adopted children. This explains the poorer outcomes for children adopted out of care. These are not the 'trouble-free babies' that once characterized adoption.[35] Children adopted out of care are typically older[36] and acutely vulnerable as a result of 'challenging backgrounds' marked by abuse and neglect. Not surprisingly, these children have a range of 'complex needs'.[37] Problems are compounded by the length of time looked after children typically spend in care before being adopted, many experiencing a number of unsettling moves before they are successfully placed. These difficult pre-placement experiences increase the risk of an adoption disrupting.[38] The changed profile of adopted children raises important policy questions about how adoption practice needs to change to meet the demands of its new 'client group'.

There are also systemic challenges within the adoption system. Reforms as part of the CFA 2014 were intended to address some of these issues, but due to what a House of Lords Select Committee characterized as 'a failure of implementation',[39] the situation has been getting worse on many measures. One key example is the time taken between when a child enters care and when they are adopted: after an initial drop from 28 months in 2014 (when the CFA 2014 was passed) to 23 months in 2018, the average then increased again to 26 months in 2021.[40]

13.3.2.a Post-adoption support

Children adopted out of care often have a range of physical, social, and educational needs requiring skilled and sensitive parenting. Adoptive parents face a difficult task for which ongoing professional support may be essential. There is a strong argument that having removed these troubled children from their birth parents, the state cannot simply walk away—it has a continuing responsibility to support the child and the adoptive parents as they face the many challenges of adoption. This approach is clearly at odds with the traditional concept of adoption and, from the government's perspective, one of its major advantages: that once the adoption order has been made the adoptive family is legally and socially autonomous, neither expecting nor requiring any additional assistance or support. So strongly is this notion of the new autonomous family embedded within society's understanding of adoption, that many adoptive parents actively resist post-adoption services and support, believing such intervention makes them less than the ideal.[41]

13.3.2.b Open adoption

Children adopted out of care bring with them a very different relationship with their birth family than babies voluntarily relinquished at birth. As Bridge points out, these children know their families and no matter how inadequate or even abusive their parenting may

[35] Cabinet Office (2000), 14.

[36] In 2021, the average age of a child at adoption was 3 years 3 months, which has remained stable since 2018: DFE (2022a).

[37] Cabinet Office (2000), 14. [38] Selwyn, Meakings, and Wijedasa (2014).

[39] House of Lords Select Committee on the Children and Families Act 2014 (2022).

[40] Ibid, para 45; DFE (2022a). By contrast, in 1999 the average was 34 months: Cabinet Office (2000), 13–14.

[41] Rushton (2003), 46; Sagar and Hitchings (2007).

have been, the children will retain 'history, memories and attachments which cannot be erased'.[42] Statutory provisions aimed at eradicating the birth parents from the child's life and 'drawing a veil of secrecy'[43] over the adoption are obviously pointless in the case of older children who have developed and retain close emotional ties to their birth family. Seeking to deny the importance of these ties may well be inimical to the child's interests. The adoption of children out of care has therefore brought with it a demand for greater openness in adoption.

Openness can take a variety of forms, from simply providing the child with information about the birth family, to facilitating regular indirect (letter-box contact) or direct contact with members of the birth family after the adoption. However, protecting, fostering, and encouraging the child's relationship with the birth parents can be difficult to reconcile with the traditional concept of adoption as a total legal transplant of the parent–child relationship.[44] The challenge posed to the adoptive parents by greater openness in adoption is also a particular concern in an environment in which the government is trying to increase the pool of prospective adopters. There is thus discernible in the recent reforms an attempt to reassert the more traditional transplant model of adoption which marginalizes any continuing role for the birth family. As Narey observes, 'that view of the adoptive child as having two families, the adoptive and the real family, even when adopted as a baby or tiny child, is not uncommon but must offend and hurt those who raise adoptive children unequivocally as their own, as well as sometimes confusing and distressing the child'.[45] It is a difficult question whether retreating into a more traditional concept of adoption serves the needs and interests of looked after children by potentially increasing the pool of prospective adopters or whether it simply promotes and prioritizes the interests of the adoptive parents at the expense of the child's welfare. To put it starkly, is a closed 'transplant' model of adoption which may be less than the ideal from the child's perspective better than no adoption at all? Or can we find a form of permanency that better serves the needs and interests of all parties?[46]

13.4 ACA 2002: THE CORE PRINCIPLES

13.4.1 THE WELFARE PRINCIPLE

The ACA 2002 provides that whenever 'a court or adoption agency' is 'coming to a decision' relating to the adoption of a child, the child's welfare must be the paramount consideration.[47] The principle is thus of wide application, binding all key decision-makers throughout the adoption process. In recognition of the life-long consequences of adoption, regard must be had to the welfare of the child 'throughout his life'. This allows the decision-maker to take into account a broad range of factors relating to the child's childhood and beyond. To guide the decision-maker, the legislation provides a 'welfare checklist' similar to that within s 1(3) of the Children Act 1989 (CA 1989):

[42] Bridge (1993), 87. [43] Ibid, 82.

[44] See 13.7.1 on whether the ACA 2002 makes adequate provision for greater openness in adoption.

[45] Narey (2011).

[46] See the alternative to adoption in the form of special guardianship, discussed at 13.8.

[47] S 1(1)–(2).

Adoption and Children Act 2002, s 1

(4) The court or adoption agency must have regard to the following matters (among others)—

(a) the child's ascertainable wishes and feelings regarding the decision (considered in light of the child's age and understanding),

(b) the child's particular needs,

(c) the likely effect on the child (throughout his life) of having ceased to be a member of the original family and becoming an adopted person,

(d) the child's age, sex, background and any of the child's characteristics which the court or agency considers relevant,

(e) any harm (within the meaning of the Children Act 1989 (c. 41)) which the child has suffered or is at risk of suffering,

(f) the relationship which the child has with relatives, with any person who is a prospective adopter with whom the child is placed, and with any other person in relation to whom the court or agency considers the relationship to be relevant, including—

(i) the likelihood of any such relationship continuing and the value to the child of its doing so,

(ii) the ability and willingness of any of the child's relatives, or of any such person, to provide the child with a secure environment in which the child can develop, and otherwise to meet the child's needs,

(iii) the wishes and feelings of any of the child's relatives, of any such person, regarding the child.

Many of these factors are familiar, having come directly from s 1(3) of the CA 1989. Of particular note, however, are the provisions relating specifically to the effect of the adoption on the child's legal status (s 1(4)(c)) and the child's existing and future relationship with the birth family (s 1(4)(f))—but the addition of the words 'with any person who is a prospective adopter with whom the child is placed' in 2017[48] potentially dilutes the importance of the birth family in cases where the child has an established relationship with the prospective adopters. The term 'relative' expressly includes the child's parents regardless of whether they hold parental responsibility.[49]

The paramountcy principle entrenched in s 1 of the ACA 2002 ensures the law on adoption is in line with the CA 1989 and complies with Article 21 of the United Nations Convention on the Rights of the Child (UNCRC) which provides that any state recognizing or permitting the system of adoption must ensure that the best interests of the child are the paramount consideration.[50] However, the weight to be attributed to the child's welfare in adoption is controversial. Under the previous legislation, the child's welfare was the *first* but not the paramount consideration enabling the decision-maker to take into account factors other than the child's interests, most importantly the rights and interests of the birth parents.[51] The role of parents' rights within the welfare analysis is potentially controversial, with some

[48] Children and Social Work Act 2017, s 9.

[49] ACA 2002, s 1(8)(b).

[50] For the requirements of the UNCRC as regards adoption and the compatibility or otherwise of English law, see Sloan (2013).

[51] Adoption Act 1976 (AA 1976), s 6.

seeing it as inadequate.[52] As adoption entails the irrevocable severance of the parent–child relationship, it has profound effects on both the birth parents and the child. Thus, severing the parent–child relationship requires a thorough examination of the *parent's* rights as well as those of the child.[53] Given the importance of adoption for the birth family, it is important to ask about the compatibility of the ACA 2002 with the ECHR.

In considering the requirements of Article 8, it is instructive to go back to *Johansen v Norway*.[54] In *Johansen*, the applicant mother argued that the decision of the Norwegian authorities to terminate her parental rights and responsibilities and place her daughter (S) for adoption shortly after birth breached her Article 8 right to respect for family life. The Court made clear that such a grave interference with the birth parent's rights could not be justified under Article 8(2) on the basis of a simple welfare test.

Johansen v Norway **(App No 17383/90, ECHR) (1997)**

78. The Court considers that taking a child into care should normally be regarded as a temporary measure to be discontinued as soon as circumstances permit and that any measures of implementation of temporary care should be consistent with the ultimate aim of reuniting the natural parent and the child. In this regard, a fair balance has to be struck between the interests of the child in remaining in public care and those of the parent in being reunited with the child. In carrying out this balancing exercise, the Court will attach particular importance to the best interests of the child, which, *depending on their nature and seriousness*, may override those of the parent. In particular, as suggested by the Government, the parent cannot be entitled under Article 8 of the Convention to have such measures taken as would harm the child's health and development.

In the present case the applicant had been deprived of her parental rights and access in the context of a permanent placement of her daughter in a foster home with a view to adoption by the foster parents. These measures were particularly far-reaching in that they totally deprived the applicant of her family life with the child and were inconsistent with the aim of reuniting them. Such measures should only be applied in exceptional circumstances and could only be justified if they were motivated by an overriding requirement pertaining to the child's best interests . . .

84. . . . The Court does not consider that the decision . . . in so far as it deprived the applicant of her access and parental rights in respect of her daughter, was sufficiently justified for the purposes of Article 8(2), it not having been shown that the measure corresponded *to any overriding requirement* in the child's best interests.

Therefore the Court reaches the conclusion that the national authorities overstepped their margin of appreciation, thereby violating the applicant's rights under Article 8 of the Convention. [Emphasis added]

It would appear clear from this decision that in a contested adoption the birth parents have *independent* rights which must be carefully weighed against the rights and interests of the child. Thus, whilst 'particular importance' may be attached to the child's welfare, the child's interests are not paramount in the sense of the *only* or *determinative* consideration. The

52 See 8.4.4.
53 This is arguably what a complete reading of the UNCRC demands: see Sloan (2013), 45–6.
54 See 8.4.4. The issue of step-parent adoption is dealt with separately; see 13.6.3.

birth parents' rights are on the scales.[55] Moreover, the court makes clear that the need to strike a *fair* balance between these potentially competing rights means the adoption must be *proportionate* to the child's needs. Where the interference with the birth parents' rights and interests is particularly far-reaching, weighty and substantial welfare considerations will therefore be required to justify the interference—in marginal cases where the welfare of the child is finely balanced, the adoption will be neither necessary nor proportionate.[56]

However, shifts in thinking from both the European Court and the domestic courts raise doubts as to whether the ACA 2002 is, in fact, non-compliant with the ECHR. Not only has the European Court increasingly moved towards the language of 'paramountcy' in its judgments,[57] but—as we will see[58]—the Supreme Court and the Court of Appeal have emphasized that adoption may be ordered against a parent's wishes only when 'nothing else will do'.[59] This strict approach is likely to have ensured that the courts are identifying suitably weighty considerations, such that the parents' Article 8 rights will be outweighed, before adoption is ordered.[60]

13.4.2 PARENTAL CONSENT

Questions about the marginalization of the rights and interests of the birth parents under the ACA 2002 also arise when considering the issue of parental consent. At key points along the pathway to adoption, the process can only move forward if the court is satisfied that 'each parent or guardian of the child' has consented, or that the parent or guardian's consent should be dispensed with.[61] Whenever the legislation requires parental consent, the issue must be dealt with in accordance with s 52.

13.4.2.a Adoption with parental consent

A relatively small number of children are voluntarily adopted by their birth parents. While there are many reasons why birth parents might make this decision, often the parents are themselves very young and feel ill-equipped to raise a child. There may also be religious or cultural considerations that lead the parent or parents to consider that adoption is the best option. Children adopted with parental consent may be being accommodated by a local authority while the adoption process is undertaken, but usually this is with the agreement of the parents; it would be unusual for care proceedings to conclude with an adoption made with parental consent, though in many cases the final adoption order is not formally opposed by the birth parents.[62]

Consent must be given 'unconditionally' and with 'full understanding of what is involved'.[63] Consent given by the mother of a child within six weeks of the child's birth is

[55] The adoptive parents may also have a right to respect for family life under Art 8.

[56] Harris-Short (2001), 423 and Bonner et al (2003), 582–3.

[57] See, e.g., *Neulinger and Shuruk v Switzerland* (App No 41615/07, ECHR) (2010) and *YC v United Kingdom* (Application No 4547/10, ECHR) (2012), discussed at 8.4.4.

[58] See 13.4.3. [59] *Re B (Care Proceedings: Appeal)* [2013] UKSC 33, [198].

[60] On the approach of the European Court more generally to adoption without parental consent, see Fenton-Glynn (2021), 357–70.

[61] The two key stages are: (i) placing the child for adoption; and (ii) making the adoption order.

[62] DFE (2022a). If the parents previously gave consent under s 20 and have not withdrawn it, it is enough that the parents do not oppose the final adoption order: s 47(2)(b). See further 13.5.3.c.

[63] S 52(5).

ineffective.[64] An unmarried father without parental responsibility does not technically have to give his consent because 'parent' for this purpose means 'parent with parental responsibility'.[65] However, a particular challenge arises in a case where the child's mother wants her child to be adopted, but does not want to notify the child's father. If the child is voluntarily relinquished by the mother and the mother wishes to keep the fact of the birth and subsequent adoption secret, questions arise as to whether she is entitled to have her wish for confidentiality respected or whether the birth father should be notified and the possibility of a placement with him or the extended maternal or paternal family investigated.[66]

Generally, the courts have been reluctant to allow adoptions to proceed without the father even knowing about the existence of the child, whether or not he has parental responsibility. In *Re L (Adoption: Contacting Natural Father)*,[67] Munby J held that 'where there exists family life within the meaning of Art 8 of the ECHR as between the mother and the father, one generally requires "strong counter-vailing factors" . . . to justify the exclusion from the adoption process of an unmarried father without parental responsibility'.[68]

The issue—with regard to both the child's father and wider relatives who might be viable long-term carers—was reviewed by the Court of Appeal in *Re A, B and C (Adoption: Notification of Fathers and Relatives)*.

Re A, B and C (Adoption: Notification of Fathers and Relatives) [2020] EWCA Civ 41

PETER JACKSON LJ:

89. The principles governing decisions (by local authorities as adoption agencies or by the court) as to whether a putative father or a relative should be informed of the existence of a child who might be adopted can be summarised in this way.

1. The law allows for 'fast-track' adoption with the consent of all those with parental responsibility, so in some cases the mother alone. Where she opposes notification being given to the child's father or relatives her right to respect for her private life is engaged and can only be infringed where it is necessary to do so to protect the interests of others.
2. The profound importance of the adoption decision for the child and potentially for other family members is clearly capable of supplying a justification for overriding the mother's request. Whether it does so will depend upon the individual circumstances of the case.
3. The decision should be prioritised and the process characterised by urgency and thoroughness.
4. The decision-maker's first task is to establish the facts as clearly as possible, mindful of the often limited and one-sided nature of the information available. The confidential

[64] S 52(3). In order to place a child under six weeks old for adoption, the mother must enter into a written agreement with the adoption agency permitting placement. Once the child is six weeks old, the mother must formally give a 's 19 consent' to placement. Failure to obtain the 's 19 consent' will mean that the consent requirements have not been met and the mother's consent will need to be dispensed with if adoption is to proceed. See *A Local Authority v GC* [2008] EWHC 2555.

[65] S 52(6).

[66] For an argument that women should be able to preserve confidentiality and privacy in these circumstances, see Marshall (2012). For a response that this approach is inconsistent with the requirements of Art 5 UNCRC, see Sloan (2020).

[67] [2007] EWHC 1771.

[68] Ibid, [25]. See also *C v XYZ County Council* [2007] EWCA Civ 1206.

relinquishment of a child for adoption is an unusual event and the reasons for it must be respectfully scrutinised so that the interests of others are protected. . . . The investigation should enable broad conclusions to be drawn about the relative weight to be given to the factors that must inform the decision.

5. Once the facts have been investigated the task is to strike a fair balance between the various interests involved. The welfare of the child is an important factor but it is not the paramount consideration.
6. There is no single test for distinguishing between cases in which notification should and should not be given but the case law shows that these factors will be relevant when reaching a decision:

(1) *Parental responsibility.* The fact that a father has parental responsibility by marriage or otherwise entitles him to give or withhold consent to adoption and gives him automatic party status in any proceedings that might lead to adoption. Compelling reasons are therefore required before the withholding of notification can be justified.

(2) *Article 8 rights.* Whether the father, married or unmarried, or the relative have an established or potential family life with the mother or the child, the right to a fair hearing is engaged and strong reasons are required before the withholding of notification can be justified.

(3) *The substance of the relationships.* . . . [A]n assessment must be made of the substance of the relationship between the parents, the circumstances of the conception, and the significance of relatives. The purpose is to ensure that those who are necessarily silent are given a notional voice so as to identify the possible strengths and weaknesses of any argument that they might make. . . . The answer will differ as between a father with whom the mother has had a fleeting encounter and one with whom she has had a substantial relationship, and as between members of the extended family who are close to the parents and those who are more distant.

(4) *The likelihood of a family placement being a realistic alternative to adoption.* This is of particular importance to the child's lifelong welfare as it may determine whether or not adoption is necessary. An objective view, going beyond the say-so of the person seeking confidentiality, should be taken about whether a family member may or may not be a potential carer. Where a family placement is unlikely to be worth investigating or where notification may cause significant harm to those notified, this factor will speak in favour of maintaining confidentiality; anything less than that and it will point the other way.

(5) *The physical, psychological or social impact on the mother or on others of notification being given.* Where this would be severe, for example because of fear arising from rape or violence, or because of possible consequences such as ostracism or family breakdown, or because of significant mental health vulnerability, these must weigh heavily in the balancing exercise. On the other hand, excessive weight should not be given to short term difficulties and to less serious situations involving embarrassment or social unpleasantness, otherwise the mother's wish would always prevail at the expense of other interests.

(6) *Cultural and religious factors.* The conception and concealed pregnancy may give rise to particular difficulties in some cultural and religious contexts. These may enhance the risks of notification, but they may also mean that the possibility of maintaining the birth tie through a family placement is of particular importance for the child.

(7) *The availability and durability of the confidential information.* Notification can only take place if there is someone to notify. In cases where a mother declines to identify a father she may face persuasion, if that is thought appropriate, but she cannot be

coerced. In some cases, the available information may mean that the father is identifiable, and maternal relatives may also be identifiable. The extent to which identifying information is pursued is a matter of judgement. Conversely, there will be cases where it is necessary to consider whether any confidentiality is likely to endure. In the modern world secrets are increasingly difficult to keep and the consequences, particularly for the child and any prospective adopters, of the child's existence being concealed but becoming known to family members later on, sometimes as a result of disclosure by the person seeking confidentiality, should be borne in mind.

(8) *The impact of delay.* A decision to apply to court and thereafter any decision to notify will inevitably postpone to some extent the time when the child's permanent placement can be confirmed. In most cases, the importance of the issues means that the delay cannot be a predominant factor. There may however be circumstances where delay would have particularly damaging consequences for the mother or for the child . . .

(9) *Any other relevant matters.* The list of relevant factors is not closed. Mothers may have many reasons for wishing to maintain confidentiality and there may be a wide range of implications for the child, the father and for other relatives. All relevant matters must be considered.

7. It has rightly been said that the maintenance of confidentiality is exceptional, and highly exceptional where a father has parental responsibility or where there is family life under [ECHR] Article 8. However, exceptionality is not in itself a test or a short cut; rather it is a reflection of the fact that the profound significance of adoption for the child and considerations of fairness to others means that the balance will often fall in favour of notification. But the decision on whether confidentiality should be maintained can only be made by striking a fair balance between the factors that are present in the individual case.

Re A, B and C largely reinforced the existing approach.[69] One notable omission this guidance, however, is consideration to how the *child's* independent rights under the UNCRC—or indeed under the ECHR—might bear on the decision. This is a recurring feature of the case law in this area, as Claire Fenton-Glynn noted in her alternative judgment in relation to the court's earlier analysis on notification of fathers in *C v XYZ County Council*,[70] designed to demonstrate how the Court of Appeal could have decided the case so as to give clearer respect to the rights of the child.

C. Fenton-Glynn, *'Re C v XYZ County Council'*, in H. Stalford, K. Hollingsworth, and S. Gilmore (eds), *Rewriting Children's Rights Judgments: From Academic Vision to New Practice* (Oxford: Hart Publishing, 2017), 135–6

9. In her leading judgment, Lady Justice Arden articulate the question before this Court as follows: does the 2002 Act impose a duty on the local authority to make enquiries about

[69] For earlier authority, see also *Re A (Father: Knowledge of Child's Birth)* [2011] EWCA Civ 273 and *Re H (Care and Adoption: Assessment of Wider Family)* [2019] EWFC 10; for later decisions, see *Re L (Adoption: Identification of Possible Father)* [2020] EWCA Civ 577 (approach to be taken when the father's identity is uncertain); *Re F (Assessment of Birth Family)* [2021] EWFC 31 (whether to identify and assess biological family when the mother herself was adopted as a child); and *A County Council v M* [2021] EWFC 35 (whether to assess wider family members when *both* parents favour adoption and oppose their families having any involvement).

[70] [2007] EWCA Civ 577.

long-term care for Elizabeth with her mother's family and, if those enquiries do not yield a long-term carer, with Elizabeth's father, if identified, and his family?

10. With respect, the question has been formulated too narrowly, and consequently has distorted the analysis of the issue. What is required is a holistic analysis of Elizabeth's interests: the question before the court should be whether the Act imposes a duty to make enquiries as to the possibility for long-term case with the mother's family, as well as to the identity of the father. The issue of whether enquiries should be made concerning the father should not be predicated upon the outcome of enquiries as to the ability of the mother's family to care for Elizabeth, nor should they be confined solely to whether he would be a potential long-term carer. Elizabeth's welfare must be interpreted in a much wider manner than a simple focus on long-term care, to include a more holistic understanding of her best interests. . . .

14. By failing to take steps to establish the identity of her father, Elizabeth is being denied the opportunity of knowing her biological origins, if she wishes to do so. Studies have shown that a lack of knowledge in this area can have significant implications on a child's emotional and psychological well-being, and in the formation of his or her identity . . .

15. This importance of identity, and knowledge of origins, for a child is reflected in the UN Convention on the Rights of the Child (CRC). . . .

17. Article 7 of the Convention requires that every child has the right from birth to know and be cared for by his or her parents, as far as is possible. These rights—to know one's parents, and to be cared for by them—are joint and severable, and each has important implications for the child's rights. As such, even if there is no possibility of the father providing long-term care for the child, knowledge of origins is important in and of itself. This is further emphasised by Article 8 of the Convention, which protects the right of the child to preserve his or her identity, including nationality, name and family relations without unlawful interference.

One of the consequences of the approach taken to the issue of notification is that the so-called 'fast track' procedure to allow for adoption by consent is often far from quick. The requirement in the majority of cases for the father to be notified leads, in many cases, to a further stage of the process while he is assessed (possibly alongside wider family members) as a potential long-term carer for a child he has only just learned exists. The balance of considerations underlying the court's approach here is a tricky one, as mothers in this situation may feel that they have good reason to be able to make this decision without interference, but confidentiality is difficult to balance against the rights of the child, the father, and of wider family members.

13.4.2.b Dispensing with parental consent

As noted, it is now rare for children to be relinquished for adoption voluntarily, and most adoptions arise out of care proceedings,[71] but the court still needs to consider the consent requirements. If parental consent is not provided, the court is able to dispense with this requirement if certain conditions are satisfied:

[71] By the time cases reach this stage, 58 per cent of applications to place children for adoption are unopposed: DFE (2022a). However, that is insufficient for the s 52 consent requirements.

Adoption and Children Act 2002, s 52

(1) The court cannot dispense with the consent of any parent or guardian of a child to the child being placed for adoption or to the making of an adoption order in respect of the child unless the court is satisfied that—

(a) the parent or guardian cannot be found or is incapable of giving consent, or

(b) the welfare of the child *requires* the consent to be dispensed with. [Emphasis added]

Except in the limited circumstances provided for in s 52(1)(a), this provision means parental consent can arguably be dispensed with on the basis of a simple welfare test.

The correct interpretation of s 52(1)(b) was first raised by Wall LJ in *Re S (A Child) (Adoption Order or Special Guardianship Order)*.[72] There had been speculation in the academic literature that the use of the term 'requires' in s 52(1)(b) may be interpreted by the courts to demand a higher threshold for dispensing with consent than a straightforward application of the welfare test.[73] Although reaching no final view on the matter, Wall LJ rejected this argument, suggesting a straightforward welfare test would be applied so that once adoption has been found to be in the child's best interests parental consent would automatically be dispensed with.[74]

Wall LJ revisited the issue in *Re P (Adoption: Parental Consent)*.[75] The mother argued that the preliminary view expressed by Wall LJ in *Re S* was 'at odds' with both the ordinary meaning of the word 'requires' and the intention of Parliament when passing the 2002 Act.[76] Rather than a simple application of the welfare test, it was argued that the word 'requires' conveyed 'a sense of the imperative; something which was a necessity; and a demand which was the antithesis of something voluntary or optional'.[77] In other words, it demanded an 'enhanced' welfare test unlikely to be satisfied where an alternative long-term placement such as fostering was an equally viable if not preferable way forward.[78] The adoption agency took a different approach, arguing against an 'enhanced' welfare test which would require the court to revisit the question of welfare applying a higher or different test when dealing with parental consent. In its submission, the court should simply apply the welfare test as set down in s 1(4) which would mean, as suggested by Wall LJ in *Re S*, that once adoption had been found to be in the child's best interests, it would automatically follow that parental consent should be dispensed with.[79]

Having identified one of the key objectives of the 2002 Act as being 'to shift the emphasis to a concentration on the welfare of the child',[80] the Court of Appeal appeared to confirm this latter approach, firmly rejecting the need to apply an 'enhanced' welfare test to dispensing with consent. However, in the course of its reasoning, the court also appeared to agree, rather curiously, with the submissions made on behalf of the mother that the word 'requires' does indeed convey the essence of the Strasbourg jurisprudence that adoption must be 'imperative' or 'demanded' rather than 'merely optional or reasonable or desirable'. These apparently contradictory positions can be reconciled, according to the Court of Appeal, through the application of the extended welfare test enshrined in s 1(4) and in particular the

72 [2007] EWCA Civ 54. 73 See, e.g., Choudhry (2003), 122–4.
74 [2007] EWCA Civ 54, [71]–[72]. 75 [2008] EWCA Civ 535. 76 Ibid, [75]. 77 Ibid.
78 Ibid, [83]–[84]. 79 [2008] EWCA Civ 535, [99]–[101]. 80 Ibid, [32].

requirement that the court is to have regard to the child's welfare *throughout their life*—to which the loss of the child's existing familial relationships will be particularly significant.

Re P (Adoption: Parental Consent) [2008] EWCA Civ 535

WALL LJ:

116. . . . The guidance is, we think, simple enough. The judge must, of course, be aware of the importance to the child of the decision being taken. There is, perhaps, no more important or far-reaching decision for a child than to be adopted by strangers. However, the word "requires" in section 52(1)(b) is a perfectly ordinary English word. Judges approaching the question of dispensation under the section must, it seems to us, ask themselves the question to which section 52(1)(b) of the 2002 [Act] gives rise, and answer it by reference to section 1 of the same Act, and in particular by a careful consideration of all the matters identified in section 1(4).

117. In summary, therefore, the best guidance which in our judgment this court can give is to advise judges to apply the statutory language with care to the facts of the particular case. The message is, no doubt, prosaic, but the best guidance, we think, is as simple and as straightforward as that . . .

118. Without wishing to qualify in any way the clarity and simplicity of what we have just said, . . . we think we should add a few words about the Strasbourg jurisprudence . . .

119. Plainly Article 8 is engaged; and it is elementary that, if Article 8 is not to be breached, any intervention under Part IV or Part V of the 1989 Act, and any placement or adoption order made without parental consent in accordance with section 52(1)(b) of the 2002 Act, must be proportionate to the legitimate aim of protecting the welfare and interests of the child . . .

120. "Necessary" takes its colour from the context but in the Strasbourg jurisprudence has a meaning lying somewhere between "indispensable" on the one hand and "useful", "reasonable" or "desirable" on the other hand. It implies the existence of what the Strasbourg jurisprudence calls a "pressing social need" . . .

124. In assessing what is proportionate, the court has, of course, always to bear in mind that adoption without parental consent is an extreme – indeed the most extreme – interference with family life. Cogent justification must therefore exist if parental consent is to be dispensed with in accordance with section 52(1)(b). Hence the observations of the Strasbourg court in *Johansen v Norway* (1996) . . .

125. This is the context in which the critical word "requires" is used in section 52(1)(b). It is a word which was plainly chosen as best conveying, as in our judgment it does, the essence of the Strasbourg jurisprudence. And viewed from that perspective "requires" does indeed have the connotation of the imperative, what is demanded rather than what is merely optional or reasonable or desirable.

126. What is also important to appreciate is the statutory context in which the word "requires" is here being used, for, like all words, it will take its colour from the particular context. Section 52(1) is concerned with adoption – the making of either a placement order or an adoption order – and what therefore has to be shown is that the child's welfare "requires" *adoption* as opposed to something short of adoption. A child's circumstances may "require" statutory intervention, perhaps may even "require" the indefinite or long-term removal of the child from the family and his or her placement with strangers, but that is not to say that the same circumstances will necessarily "require" that the child be adopted. They may or they may not. The question, at the end of the day, is whether what is "required" is adoption.

127. In our judgment, however, this does not mean that there is some enhanced welfare test to be applied in cases of adoption, in contrast to what [counsel] called a simple welfare test. The difference, and it is an important, indeed vital, difference, is simply that between section 1 of the 1989 Act and section 1 of the 2002 Act.

128. In the first place, section 1(2) of the 2002 Act, in contrast to section 1(1) of the 1989 Act, requires a judge considering dispensing with parental consent in accordance with section 52(1)(b) to focus on the child's welfare "throughout his life." This emphasises that adoption, unlike other forms of order made under the 1989 Act, is something with lifelong implications. In other words, a judge exercising his powers under section 52(1)(b) has to be satisfied that the child's welfare now, throughout the rest of his childhood, into adulthood and indeed throughout his life, requires that he or she be adopted. Secondly, and reinforcing this point, it is important to bear in mind the more extensive 'welfare checklist' to be found in section 1(4) of the 2002 Act as compared with the 'welfare checklist' in section 1(3) of the 1989 Act; in particular, the provisions of section 1(4) (c) – which specifically directs attention to the consequences for the child "throughout his life" – and section 1(4)(f). This all feeds into the ultimate question under section 52(1)(b): does the child's welfare *throughout his life* require adoption as opposed to something short of adoption?

The practical effect is that the welfare stage and the consent stage of an adoption/placement application have in practice become indistinguishable such that once adoption is deemed to be in the child's best interests, parental consent will be dispensed with without further thought or consideration of the birth parents' interests or the demands of the specific wording of s 52(1)(b). Moreover, in determining the child's welfare, the Court of Appeal's judgment strongly defends the position that the welfare test, as set down in s 1(4), is sufficient, without more, to comply with the requirements of the ECHR.[81]

Notably, Wall LJ finds strong support for his approach in *Re P* in the European Court decision of *YC v United Kingdom*.[82] In addressing the issue, the Court held that the extended range of factors to which the court must give consideration when applying the welfare checklist in s 1(4) is sufficient to meet the required balancing of interests under Article 8(2). The case concerned the making of a final care order and a placement order in circumstances in which the mother was asking for a further assessment of her capacity to parent following separation from the child's father.

YC v United Kingdom (App No 4547/10, ECHR) (2012)

134. The Court reiterates that in cases concerning the placing of a child for adoption, which entails the permanent severance of family ties, the best interests of the child are paramount (see *Johansen v Norway*, 7 August 1996, [78] . . .). In identifying the child's best interests in a particular case, two considerations must be borne in mind: first, it is in the child's best interests that his ties with his family be maintained except in cases where the family has proved particularly unfit; and second, it is in the child's best interests to ensure his development in a safe and secure environment (see *Neulinger and Shuruk*, [136] . . .). It is clear from the foregoing that family ties may only be severed in very exceptional circumstances and that everything must be done to preserve personal relations and, where appropriate, to "rebuild"

[81] For critique, see Sloan (2013), 55–6.

[82] (App No 4547/10, ECHR) (2012).

the family (see *Neulinger and Shuruk*, [136] . . .). It is not enough to show that a child could be placed in a more beneficial environment for his upbringing . . . However, where the maintenance of family ties would harm the child's health and development, a parent is not entitled under Article 8 to insist that such ties be maintained (see *Neulinger and Shuruk* . . . [136]).

135. The identification of the child's best interests and the assessment of the overall proportionality of any given measure will require courts to weigh a number of factors in the balance. The Court has not previously set out an exhaustive list of such factors, which may vary depending on the circumstances of the case in question. However, it observes that the considerations listed in section 1 of the 2002 Act broadly reflect the various elements inherent in assessing the necessity under Article 8 of a measure placing a child for adoption. In particular, it considers that in seeking to identify the best interests of a child and in assessing the necessity of any proposed measure in the context of placement proceedings, the domestic court must demonstrate that it has had regard to, inter alia, the age, maturity and ascertained wishes of the child, the likely effect on the child of ceasing to be a member of his original family and the relationship the child has with relatives.

13.4.3 RIGHTS, WELFARE, REFORM, AND THE FUNDAMENTAL PRINCIPLES OF ADOPTION

On any reading of *Re P (Adoption: Parental Consent)*, the Court of Appeal was keen to make clear that the rights and interests of the birth family could not be ignored in the adoption process, the birth family being inextricably linked to any proper understanding of the child's welfare.[83] The debate over the child's welfare and the weight, if any, to be placed on the rights and interests of the birth parents has, however, developed against a backdrop of increasing government pressure on local authorities to increase the number and speed of children adopted out of care. The birth family and their opposition to adoption undoubtedly constitutes an important cause of delay in many cases. Tensions perhaps inevitably developed between the drive to increase the numbers of children adopted out of care and the need to ensure there was no 'rush to judgement', with children being inappropriately made subject to a care order and placed for adoption against their birth parents' consent in circumstances where the birth family had not been given fair opportunity to prove themselves. The need to ensure proper regard for the child's relationship with the birth family (and thus proportionality) in cases of non-consensual adoption was very firmly set out by the Supreme Court in *Re B (Care Proceedings: Appeal)*. The Supreme Court made clear that placement orders could only be justified as a very last resort.[84]

Re B (Care Proceedings: Appeal) [2013] UKSC 33

LORD NEUBERGER P:

74. A care order in a case such as this is a very extreme thing, a last resort, as it would be very likely to result in Amelia being adopted against the wishes of both her parents.

[83] Again, Sloan (2013) argues that this understanding of the child's welfare is entrenched within the UNCRC.

[84] Note that these principles apply only to *contested* adoptions. For further extracts, see 8.4.4.a.

75. As already mentioned, it is clear that a judge cannot properly decide that a care order should be made in such circumstances, unless the order is proportionate bearing in mind the requirements of article 8.

76. It appears to me that, given that the Judge concluded that the section 31(2) threshold was crossed, he should only have made a care order if he had been satisfied that it was necessary to do so in order to protect the interests of the child. By "necessary", I mean, to use Lady Hale's phrase . . . "where nothing else will do". I consider that this conclusion is clear under the 1989 Act, interpreted in the absence of the Convention, but it is put beyond doubt by article 8. The conclusion is also consistent with UNCRC.

77. It seems to me to be inherent in section 1(1) that a care order should be a last resort, because the interests of a child would self-evidently require her relationship with her natural parents to be maintained unless no other course was possible in her interests. That is reinforced by the requirement in section 1(3)(g) that the court must consider all options, which carries with it the clear implication that the most extreme option should only be adopted if others would not be in her interests. As to article 8, the Strasbourg court decisions cited by Lady Hale . . . make it clear that such an order can only be made in "exceptional circumstances", and that it could only be justified by "overriding requirements pertaining to the child's welfare", or, putting the same point in slightly different words, "by the overriding necessity of the interests of the child". I consider that this is the same as the domestic test . . .

78. The high threshold to be crossed before a court should make an adoption order against the natural parents' wishes is also clear from UNCRC. Thus, *Hodgkin and Newell, Implementation Handbook for the Convention on the Rights of the Child*, Unicef, 3rd ed (2007), p 296, state that "there is a presumption within the Convention that children's best interests are served by being with their parents wherever possible".

82. What the Strasbourg jurisprudence requires (and, I would have thought, what the rule of law in a modern, democratic society would require) is that no child should be adopted, particularly when it is against her parents' wishes, without a judge deciding after a proper hearing, with the interests of the parents (where appropriate) and of the child being appropriately advanced, that it is necessary in the interests of the child that she is adopted . . .

104. . . . All give added weight to the importance of emphasising the principle that adoption of a child against her parents' wishes should only be contemplated as a last resort – when all else fails. Although the child's interests in an adoption case are "paramount" (in the UK legislation and under article 21 of UNCRC), a court must never lose sight of the fact that those interests include being brought up by her natural family, ideally her natural parents, or at least one of them.

105. Hodgkin and Newell, *op cit*, suggest that, under UNCRC, an "adoption can only occur if parents are unwilling or are deemed by judicial process to be unable to discharge" their responsibilities towards the child. The assessment of that ability to discharge their responsibilities must, of course, take into account the assistance and support which the authorities would offer. . . . It means that, before making an adoption order in such a case, the court must be satisfied that there is no practical way of the authorities (or others) providing the requisite assistance and support.

LADY HALE:

179. Since well before the Children Act came into force, the courts have recognised that there is a line to be drawn between parents whose personal characteristics mean that they may be less than perfect parents and parents who may cause harm to their children. Lord Templeman put the point this way in his well-known words in *In re KD (A Minor) (Ward: Termination of Access)* [1988] AC 806, 812:

"The best person to bring up a child is the natural parent. It matters not whether the parent is wise or foolish, rich or poor, educated or illiterate, provided the child's moral and physical health are not endangered. Public authorities cannot improve on nature."

If, by that last sentence, Lord Templeman was making a factual statement, then some might disagree: if local authorities remove children from unsatisfactory parents at birth and swiftly place them with highly satisfactory adoptive parents they can undoubtedly improve on nature. But in my view Lord Templeman was making a normative statement: public authorities have no right to improve on nature.

198. . . . [I]t is quite clear that the test for severing the relationship between parent and child is very strict: only in exceptional circumstances and where motivated by *overriding requirements* pertaining to the child's welfare, in short, where nothing else will do.

The Supreme Court's approach was forcefully reiterated by the then-President of the Family Division in *Re B-S*, a case concerned with an application for leave to oppose an adoption application. Expressing clear concern that children were being placed for adoption without sufficient rigour being exercised in the decision-making process, Munby P restated in unequivocal terms the 'fundamental principles' governing adoption:

Re B-S (Adoption: Application of Threshold Criteria) **[2013] EWCA Civ 1146**

SIR JAMES MUNBY P:

20. Section 52(1)(b) of the 2002 Act provides, as we have seen, that the consent of a parent with capacity can be dispensed with only if the welfare of the child "requires" this. "Require" here has the Strasbourg meaning of necessary, "the connotation of the imperative, what is demanded rather than what is merely optional or reasonable or desirable": [*Re P (Children) (Adoption: Parental Consent)*]. This is a stringent and demanding test.

21. Just how stringent and demanding has been spelt out very recently by the Supreme Court in *Re B (Care proceedings: Appeal)* . . . *Re B* is a forceful reminder of just what is required.

22. The language used in *Re B* is striking. Different words and phrases are used, but the message is clear. Orders contemplating non-consensual adoption – care orders with a plan for adoption, placement orders and adoption orders – are "a very extreme thing, a last resort", only to be made where "nothing else will do", where "no other course [is] possible in [the child's] interests", they are "the most extreme option", a "last resort – when all else fails", to be made "only in exceptional circumstances and where motivated by *overriding requirements* pertaining to the child's welfare, in short, where nothing else will do" . . .

23. Behind all this there lies the well-established principle, derived from s 1(5) of the 1989 Act, read in conjunction with s 1(3)(g), and now similarly embodied in s 1(6) of the 2002 Act, that the court should adopt the 'least interventionist' approach. . . .

25. Implicit in all this are three important points emphasised by Lord Neuberger in *Re B*.

26. First (*Re B* paras 77, 104), although the child's interests in an adoption case are paramount, the court must never lose sight of the fact that those interests include being brought up by the natural family, ideally by the natural parents, or at least one of them, unless the overriding requirements of the child's welfare make that not possible.

27. Second (*Re B* para 77), as required by section 1(3)(g) of the 1989 Act and section 1(6) of the 2002 Act, the court "must" consider all the options before coming to a decision. As Lady Hale said (para 198) it is "necessary to explore and attempt alternative solutions". What

are these options? That will depend upon the circumstances of the particular cases. They range, in principle, from the making of no order at one end of the spectrum to the making of an adoption order at the other. . . . [T]he possible list of options is long. We return to the implications of this R.

28. Third (*Re B* para 105), the court's assessment of the parents' ability to discharge their responsibilities towards the child must take into account the assistance and support which the authorities would offer. So "before making an adoption order . . . the court must be satisfied that there is no practical way of the authorities (or others) providing the requisite assistance and support." . . .

29. It is the obligation of the local authority to make the order which the court has determined is proportionate work. The local authority cannot press for a more drastic form of order, least of all press for adoption, because it is unable or unwilling to support a less interventionist form of order. Judges must be alert to the point and must be rigorous in exploring and probing local authority thinking in cases where there is any reason to suspect that resource issues may be affecting the local authority's thinking . . .

33. Two things are essential – we use that word deliberately and advisedly – both when the court is being asked to approve a care plan for adoption and when it is being asked to make a non-consensual placement order or adoption order.

Adoption – essentials: (i) proper evidence

34. First, there must be proper evidence both from the local authority and from the guardian. The evidence must address *all* the options which are realistically possible and must contain an analysis of the arguments *for* and *against* each option . . .

41. The second thing that is essential, and again we emphasise that word, is an adequately reasoned judgment by the judge . . .

44. We emphasise the words [from McFarlane LJ's judgment in *Re G (Care Proceedings: Welfare Evaluation)* [2013] EWCA Civ 965] "global, holistic evaluation". This point is crucial. The judicial task is to evaluate *all* the options, undertaking a global, holistic and . . . multi-faceted evaluation of the child's welfare which takes into account *all* the negatives and the positives, *all* the pros and cons, of *each* option . . .

Where the court is considering placing a child for adoption, a full assessment of the risks that the child faces in parental or family care must be conducted, including 'an intense focus on the *type of risk* that is involved, *how likely* it is to happen, and what the *likely consequences* might then be', in order that this element can be properly included in the final evaluation.[85]

In the immediate aftermath of *Re B-S*, the numbers of children being placed for adoption, which had risen significantly following the reforms initiated by the Conservative-led coalition, dramatically declined.[86] It is important to note, however, that as was pointed out in clear terms by Munby P in *Re R (Adoption: Judicial Approach)*, the decision in *Re B-S* did not change the law in any way—it simply reiterated the existing principles.[87] The court must be satisfied that adoption is *required* in the child's best interests; in other words, that following a holistic evaluation of all the *realistic* options, nothing else will do. While the courts have emphasized that the law has not changed in this regard, it is clearly arguable that the practice

[85] *Re F (Placement Order: Proportionality)* [2018] EWCA Civ 2761, [24].

[86] See National Adoption Leadership Board (2014).

[87] [2014] EWCA Civ 1625.

has shifted considerably, with contested adoption becoming more difficult to achieve following *Re B* and *Re B-S*.[88]

13.5 THE ADOPTION PROCESS

13.5.1 PLACING THE CHILD FOR ADOPTION

Placing a child with prospective adopters is a vitally important step in the adoption process. An adoption agency can only place a child for adoption in accordance with ss 18–29 of the ACA 2002. Consent is a crucial issue at this stage of the proceedings because in many contested cases the parents will be unable to reopen consent at the final adoption hearing.

13.5.1.a Placing the child with the birth parent's consent

If the birth parents consent to the adoption,[89] the adoption agency can place the child without the courts' prior authorization.[90] The birth parents have the option of consenting only to a specific placement or of consenting generally to any placement chosen by the agency.[91] At the same time as consenting to the placement of the child, the birth parents may give their advance consent to the making of an adoption order.[92] Consent can again be general or limited to adoption by the specific individuals with whom the child is to be placed.[93] At the same time as giving consent, or any time thereafter, the parents can give notice to the adoption agency that they do not wish to be informed of any subsequent adoption application.[94] The birth parents can withdraw this notice and their advance consent to the adoption at any time up to the point the adoption order is made.[95]

13.5.1.b Placing the child without consent: placement orders

Where the birth parents do not consent, or the local authority has applied for a care order, the adoption agency must apply to the court under s 21 for a placement order authorizing it to place the child for adoption.[96] A placement order confers general authorization on the adoption agency to place the child with any prospective adopters considered appropriate.[97] The welfare principle applies,[98] and the order can only be made if the parent(s) or guardian(s) consent or the court is satisfied consent should be dispensed with. The consent requirements must be dealt with in accordance with s 52. Further conditions on making the order are set down in s 21(2):

Adoption and Children Act 2002, s 21

(2) The court may not make a placement order in respect of a child unless—
(a) the child is subject to a care order,
(b) the court is satisfied that the conditions in section 31(2) of the 1989 Act (conditions for making a care order) are met, or
(c) the child has no parent or guardian.

88 See Doughty (2015); Sloan (2015b). On the ECHR approach to adoption without parental consent, see Breen et al (2020).

89 See 13.4.2.a. 90 ACA 2002, s 19(1). 91 Ibid. 92 S 20(1). 93 S 20(2).
94 S 20(4)(a). 95 S 20(3) and (4)(b). 96 S 19(3). 97 S 21(1). 98 S 1(1) and (7).

Before placing a child for adoption, the threshold conditions for state intervention into family life as set down in s 31 of the CA 1989 must therefore be met: the child must be suffering or likely to suffer significant harm attributable to the parents' care. This ensures that no child can be placed for adoption against the birth parents' wishes on the basis of a simple welfare test.

However, in order to eliminate delays in the adoption process, s 22 of the ACA 2002 places a duty on the local authority to apply for a placement order as soon as it is satisfied that a looked after child should be placed for adoption. This duty applies whether or not a care order is in force provided the local authority 'considers' that the threshold conditions are satisfied. This means that a child can be placed for adoption against the birth parents' wishes without a care order ever being made.

The important question of whether the practice of 'dual planning' could be reconciled with the duties of the local authority under s 22 was addressed by the Court of Appeal in *Re P (Children) (Adoption: Parental Consent)*.[99] The legal issue was whether the court could be said to be 'satisfied that the child ought to be placed for adoption' in circumstances where the local authority acknowledged that finding a suitable adoptive placement was likely to prove difficult and, in light of this uncertainty, had adopted a 'dual planning' approach. It was argued on behalf of the mother that if both long-term fostering and adoption were regarded as potentially suitable placements, it could not be said that a placement order 'ought' to be made or was required in the children's best interests.

The Court of Appeal rejected this argument in favour of a pragmatic approach, holding that whilst there were important legal, philosophical, and practical differences between adoption and fostering, provided the local authority was satisfied that adoption was in the child's best interests it could, and indeed ought, to apply for a placement order without precluding undertaking a simultaneous search for long-term foster parents. In the Court of Appeal's judgment, this dual approach was entirely sensible for 'compelling pragmatic reasons': the chances of finding a suitable adoptive home were considerably improved by having the placement order firmly in place whilst any further delay for the child would be avoided if an adoptive home could not be found.

The situation in *Re P (Children) (Adoption: Parental Consent)* needs to be distinguished from that which was considered by a differently constituted Court of Appeal in *Re T (Children: Placement Order)*.[100] *Re T* was concerned with a case where, because of the very serious nature of the children's problems, it was recommended that they be placed in a therapeutic foster home for at least six months before a final decision was made as to their long-term placement. Although the local authority agreed that adoption would theoretically be in the long-term interests of the children, that plan remained purely hypothetical given not only the uncertainty of finding a placement but, more importantly, the uncertainty as to whether the children would be deemed suitable for adoption—an uncertainty which would only be resolved after the therapeutic placement. Given it could not be said with certainty that adoption would be in the children's best interests, the Court of Appeal held that it was premature to make a placement order under s 22.[101] Thus, whilst a placement order can and should be made despite uncertainty over finding a suitable placement, a placement order cannot be made if it has not yet been determined that adoption is in the child's best interests.

Section 22 is clearly intended to minimize any delay in placing looked after children for adoption. The importance of moving children through the care system with greater speed has

[99] [2008] EWCA Civ 535, [134]–[140] and [156]–[159].
[100] [2008] EWCA Civ 248.
[101] Ibid, [18].

been reinforced by the imposition of tighter timescales for decision-making at every stage of the process.[102] Tackling the problem of 'drift in care' and eradicating any *unnecessary* delays between a child coming into care and being found a permanent alternative home are laudable objectives. The concern that delays in the adoption process can prejudice the chance of a successful outcome is borne out by research.[103] Closely associated with this problem of delay is the number of short-term placements a looked after child may experience before finally being placed with prospective adopters. As part of the CFA 2014 reforms, the government therefore decided to tackle this particular issue by providing a statutory basis for the practice of 'fostering for adoption'.[104] Section 22C of the CA 1989 was amended to place a duty on local authorities when 'considering' adoption for a child or upon reaching the decision that the child 'ought' to be placed for adoption, to place the child with prospective adopters who are also approved for this purpose as local authority foster parents.[105] Children can thus now be placed with prospective adopters before the local authority has determined that the child 'ought' to be adopted, before an application for a placement order has been made, or, perhaps most importantly, before the court has determined that adoption is necessary in the child's best interests. The intention behind the change is to minimize the disruption of multiple placements for the child. The clear advantage from the child's perspective is that if rehabilitation with the birth family is ruled out and the decision is made that the child should be adopted, the child will already be settled with the prospective adopters. There is, however, some disquiet that these provisions create a 'fast-track' to adoption which may deprive children of the opportunity of being successfully rehabilitated with their birth parents.[106] Concern was expressed to the House of Lords Select Committee on Adoption that once a child has been placed with prospective adopters bonds and attachments will begin to form and the birth family will face a virtually impossible uphill struggle to successfully contest a placement order—the court being faced, in effect, with a *fait accompli*. It is, of course, a difficult balance but the Select Committee concluded that provided pre-proceedings work with the birth family has been properly carried out, 'fostering for adoption' would not unfairly tip the balance against the birth parents:

House of Lords Select Committee on Adoption Legislation, 1st Report of Session 2012–13, *Adoption: Pre-Legislative Scrutiny. Report*, HL Paper 94 (London: TSO, 2012)

56. We are not persuaded that the ability of birth parents to challenge the application for a placement order would be adversely affected by fostering for adoption, so long as all reasonable steps have been taken by the local authority to explore reunification of the child with the birth family at the earliest opportunity, and the parents have been able effectively to participate in the decision-making process. We do not believe that such concerns should be allowed to outweigh the potential benefit to the child of moving as early as possible into a permanent placement.

[102] DH (2011). [103] Selwyn, Frazer, and Quinton (2006). [104] DFE (2012b), 25–7.

[105] CA 1989, s 22C(9A)–(9C) as amended by CFA 2014, s 2.

[106] Harris-Short (2001); Sagar and Hitchings (2007). See also *Re F (Placement Order: Proportionality)* [2018] EWCA Civ 2761.

It is notable that, in 2017, the ACA 2002's welfare checklist for adoption was amended to add consideration of the child's existing relationship with the prospective adopters, alongside the birth family.[107]

13.5.1.c Consequences of the child being placed or being authorized to be placed for adoption

Whilst a child is placed or authorized to be placed for adoption, parental responsibility (PR) is given to the adoption agency.[108] If the child is placed with prospective adopters then the prospective adopters also acquire PR for the duration of the placement, the adoption agency having the power to determine to what extent the prospective adopters will be able to exercise their PR.[109] The birth parents do not lose PR by virtue of the fact the child is placed or authorized to be placed for adoption, but again the adoption agency has the power to determine to what extent they can exercise that PR.[110] If a care order was made at the same time as the placement order or the child was subject to a care order when the placement order was made, the care order ceases to have effect whilst the placement order is in force.[111] The child is therefore no longer 'in care' although a child placed or authorized to be placed for adoption by a local authority is still regarded as a looked after child.[112]

13.5.1.d Contact with a child who is placed or authorized to be placed for adoption

Contact is a crucially important issue at this stage of the proceedings as the pattern of contact established at this point can determine whether provision is made for post-adoption contact at the final hearing. For members of the birth family, ensuring contact is continued throughout the placement period can thus be of vital importance.

Although during placement the child has the status of a looked after child, local authorities are exempt from the duty under Sch 2, para 15 of the CA 1989 to endeavour to promote contact between looked after children and their parents.[113] Furthermore, any existing orders for contact made under s 8 or 34 of the CA 1989 cease to have effect.[114] The court can, in theory, order contact under s 26 of the ACA 2002,[115] but research suggests that such orders are rare in practice,[116] and there is a fine line between a (permissible) order for contact under s 26 and an (impermissible[117]) order making the placement of the child for adoption *conditional* on contact.[118] The court is under a duty before making a placement order to consider the adoption agency's proposals for contact.[119]

A s 26 contact order remains in force whilst the child is placed or authorized to be placed for adoption.[120] The adoption agency retains the authority to terminate contact in an emergency for a maximum of seven days if satisfied that it is necessary to do so to safeguard and promote the child's welfare.[121]

[107] S 1(4)(f), as amended by the Children and Social Work Act 2017, s 9. [108] S 25(1)–(2).
[109] S 25(3)–(4). [110] Ibid. [111] S 29(1). [112] S 18(3).
[113] Adoption Agencies Regulations 2005, SI 2005/389, reg 45(2)(d). [114] ACA 2002, s 26(1).
[115] Upon application by the child, the adoption agency, the birth parents, the child's relatives, a guardian, or any person in whose favour a child arrangements order was in force or who had care of the child under the High Court's inherent jurisdiction immediately before the placement order was made. Any other person may apply with leave. The court may also act of its own motion. S 26(2)–(4).
[116] Monk and Macvarish (2018), 9.
[117] *Re A (Placement Order: Imposition of Conditions on Adoption)* [2013] EWCA Civ 1611.
[118] Monk and Macvarish (2018), 9. [119] S 27(4). [120] S 27(1). [121] S 27(2).

13.5.1.e Restrictions on removing a child who is placed for adoption

When a child is placed for adoption under s 19 (with parental consent), only the adoption agency can remove the child from the prospective adopters.[122] If the parents withdraw their consent to the placement, the child must be returned to their care within 14 days unless an application has been made for a placement order,[123] or the prospective adopters have applied for an adoption order, special guardianship order, or child arrangements order, in which case the child can only be removed with the court's leave.[124] If an adoption agency is authorized to place a child under s 19 but the parents withdraw their consent before the child is placed, the child must be returned to the parents within seven days.

Where a placement order is in force, nobody, other than the local authority, can remove the child.[125] Where the adoption agency decides that a child should be removed from prospective adopters, the prospective adopters must return the child within seven days of receiving notice of return unless they have applied for an adoption order, special guardianship order, or child arrangements order, in which case the court's leave to remove the child is required.[126] It was held by Charles J in *DL, ML v London Borough of Newham* that the fact that the decision to remove a child is made by the adoption agency and not the court is not a breach of Article 6.[127] The prospective adopters are able to challenge the adoption agency's decision to give notice to return by way of judicial review or under the Human Rights Act 1998. The notice to return may be stayed pending review of the local authority's decision.[128] Where the child has lived with the prospective adopters for any period of time, Article 8 rights will be engaged giving both substantive and procedural protection to the prospective adopters.[129] Where the child needs to be removed urgently (before the seven-day notice has expired), the local authority will have to apply for an emergency protection order or an interim care order authorizing removal.[130] Charles J thus concluded that the legislative scheme was Convention-compliant.

Where it is the prospective adopters who wish to return the child to the adoption agency, the adoption agency must receive the child back into care within seven days.[131]

13.5.1.f Revoking the placement order

Once a placement order has been made, the birth parents will face an uphill struggle to prevent the adoption proceeding. The placement order is of unlimited duration, remaining in force until revoked or an adoption order is made.[132] Moreover, opportunities to challenge the order are limited. A placement order can be revoked on the application of any person, but only the child or the adoption agency can apply as of right.[133] All other applicants require leave under s 24, and leave will only be granted if the child is not already placed and there has been a change in circumstances since the original order was made.[134]

The test to be applied on an application for leave to revoke a placement order was considered by the Court of Appeal in *Re M (Children) (Placement Order)*.[135] It was argued on the mother's behalf that if she was able to establish a change in circumstances the court would be required to grant leave. The local authority disagreed, contending that establishing a change in circumstances was only 'the necessary precursor to the court's exercise of a discretion'

[122] S 30(1). [123] S 32(1). [124] S 32(2) and (5). [125] S 34(1). [126] S 35(2) and (5).
[127] [2011] EWHC 1127. [128] Ibid, [110]. [129] Ibid, [122]. [130] Ibid, [112]–[115].
[131] S 35(1).
[132] S 21(4). For the problems this can cause, see *A and S v Lancashire County Council* [2012] EWHC 1689.
[133] S 24(1)–(2). [134] S 24(2)–(3). [135] [2007] EWCA Civ 1084.

and that in exercising its discretion the children's welfare would be a relevant consideration.[136] The Court of Appeal agreed with the local authority, holding that establishing a change in circumstances was not determinative of the application. Wilson LJ held that the decision whether to grant leave to revoke a placement order was not 'coming to a decision relating to the adoption of a child', as required by s 1(7) of the Act. The paramountcy principle under s 1(2) does not therefore apply. However, Wilson LJ went on to hold that this does not mean that the children's interests are irrelevant.[137] Indeed, in line with the approach taken to leave applications under s 10(9) of the CA 1989, he held that once a change in circumstances has been established,[138] the court has a discretion as to whether or not to grant leave, in the exercise of which the children's welfare and the applicant's prospects of success on the main application are relevant considerations.[139] He concludes that whilst in most cases the children's welfare will be subsumed within the broader inquiry into the applicant's prospects of success, they remain separate considerations.[140]

The Court of Appeal has also had to tackle a number of difficulties caused by related restrictions set down in s 24: (i) that an application to revoke a placement order cannot be made once the child has been placed for adoption; and (ii) a child cannot be placed for adoption without the court's leave when an application to revoke the placement order is pending. In *Re F (A Child) (Placement Order)*,[141] the Court of Appeal confirmed, by a majority, that a child can lawfully be placed for adoption by the adoption agency even though the adoption agency knows that an application for leave to revoke the placement order has been made. The Court of Appeal held that in accordance with the strict wording of s 24(5), the prohibition on placement without the court's leave only applies once the substantive application for revocation has been made.[142] However, the Court of Appeal emphasized that good practice very clearly demanded that if, to the knowledge of the adoption agency, an application for leave has been issued, the child should not be placed (thereby defeating the application) without the permission of the court and, if necessary, an injunction can be sought to prevent it doing so until the application for leave has been determined.[143] The Court of Appeal also made clear that if the local authority decides to go ahead and place the child before the parent is able to issue the necessary legal proceedings, the actions of the local authority will be susceptible to judicial review.[144] In determining whether a child has 'been placed' for the purposes of s 24, it was held by the Court of Appeal in *Coventry City Council v O (Adoption)* that a child is not 'placed' until he begins to live with the proposed adopters or, if he is already living with them in their capacity as foster carers, when the adoption agency formally allows him to continue to live with them in their fresh capacity as prospective adopters.[145]

13.5.2 THE ADOPTION APPLICATION

If the child is successfully placed with prospective adopters or, in the case of a non-agency adoption, is already living with the prospective adopter(s), the next stage is to issue the application for an adoption order.

[136] Ibid, [4]. [137] Ibid, [24].

[138] Although the change in circumstances will usually relate to the parent's capacity to resume care of the child, a change in circumstances can relate to the child and render the plan for adoption no longer appropriate—even if it remains impossible for the child to return home. See *NS-H v Kingston upon Hull City Council* [2008] EWCA Civ 493.

[139] [2007] EWCA Civ 1084, [26]–[29]. [140] Ibid, [29]. [141] [2008] EWCA Civ 439.

[142] Ibid, [33], [69]. [143] Ibid, [99], [111]. [144] Ibid, [36], [94]. [145] [2011] EWCA Civ 729, [44].

13.5.2.a Residence conditions

Before prospective adopters can apply to adopt a child, the child must have lived with them for a specified period of time, the exact period depending on the circumstances of the adoption. If the child was placed for adoption by an adoption agency, pursuant to an order of the High Court, or the applicant is a parent of the child, the child must have lived with the prospective adopter(s) for ten weeks preceding the application.[146] If the applicant is the partner of a parent of the child (i.e. a step-parent adoption), the child must have lived with the applicant for six months.[147] If the applicants are local authority foster parents, the child must have lived with them for 12 months unless the court gives leave to apply.[148] In all other cases, the child must have lived with the prospective adopters for not less than three of the previous five years unless again the court gives leave to apply.[149] One of the main purposes of these provisions is to ensure that the local authority or adoption agency has had sufficient opportunity to observe the prospective adopters and the child together in their home environment.[150]

Where the prospective adopters require leave to apply for an adoption order, the Court of Appeal has held that the same principles apply as in an application for leave to revoke a placement order.[151] Thus, it was held in *TL v Coventry City Council* that the child's welfare is a relevant but not paramount consideration and the court should take into account whether the application has a real prospect of success.[152]

In addition to the restrictions on removing a child from the care of prospective adopters when the child has been placed for adoption by an adoption agency (see 13.5.1), once an application to adopt has been made in non-agency cases (i.e. private arrangements, foster parent, and step-parent adoptions), the child cannot be removed from the care of the prospective adopters without the court's leave.[153] This prohibition also applies where an application for leave to apply has been made in non-agency cases.[154]

13.5.2.b The requirement to give notice

Where the child was not placed with the prospective adopters by an adoption agency, the adoption order cannot be made unless the prospective adopters have given notice to the local authority of their intention to apply.[155] Notice must be given no more than two years or less than three months before the date on which the application is made.[156] Applicants requiring leave cannot give notice of their intention to adopt until leave has been granted.[157] On receiving notice, the local authority must investigate and prepare a report for the court.[158] Once notice of an intention to adopt has been given, nobody can remove the child from the prospective adopters' care without the court's leave, save in the following circumstances: (i) the local authority can remove the child in exercise of a statutory power including the authority to place the child with prospective adopters of the local authority's choice pursuant to a placement order;[159] (ii) if the child has been in the care of the foster parents for more than one year but less than five years and is being looked after by the local authority pursuant to a voluntary agreement under Part III of the CA 1989, a person with PR may remove the child;[160] or (iii) where a notice of an intention to adopt has been given by a step-parent but the child has lived with the step-parent for less than three years, a parent or guardian can remove the child.[161]

146 S 42(2). 147 S 42(3). 148 S 42(4) and (6). 149 S 42(5)–(6). 150 S 42(7).
151 *Re M (Children) (Placement Order)* [2007] EWCA Civ 1084. 152 [2007] EWCA Civ 1383, [10].
153 Ss 36–7. 154 Ss 36 and 40. 155 S 44(2). 156 S 44(3). 157 S 44(4).
158 S 44(5). 159 *Coventry City Council v O (Adoption)* [2011] EWCA Civ 729, [23]–[24].
160 Ss 38(5) and 40. 161 Ss 39(3) and 40.

13.5.3 THE FINAL HEARING: CONDITIONS ON MAKING THE ADOPTION ORDER

13.5.3.a Age restrictions

In the case of an application by a single person, the applicant must have attained the age of 21 years.[162] Where the prospective adopters are a couple, both must have attained the age of 21 years unless one of them is a parent of the child in which case the parent must be at least 18 years of age.[163] No maximum age limit is specified in the legislation.

13.5.3.b Applications by one person

Applications by one person are subject to additional conditions. An order can be made in favour of one person where the applicant is a parent's partner. Otherwise, if the applicant is married or has a civil partner, the application will only be allowed if the court is satisfied that the person's spouse/civil partner cannot be found, the spouses/civil partners have separated and are living apart and the separation is likely to be permanent, or the person's spouse/civil partner is incapable by reason of ill-health from making an application to adopt.[164] Interestingly there is no similar prohibition on someone living within an 'enduring family relationship' applying to adopt as a single person.[165]

Although it may on the face of it seem odd, a parent may apply to adopt their own child. Such adoptions are now rare, but they once served the important purpose of legitimating the child. The law on legitimacy having been comprehensively reformed, adoption by a sole natural parent is now contentious because it terminates any familial ties with one half of the child's family without giving the child the opportunity to build new relationships with an alternative family. Applications by a sole natural parent are subject to additional conditions:

Adoption and Children Act 2002, s 51

(4) An adoption order may not be made on an application under this section by the mother or the father of the person to be adopted unless the court is satisfied that—

(a) the other natural parent is dead or cannot be found,

(b) by virtue of [s 28 of the Human Fertilisation and Embryology Act 1990 (HFEA 1990) or ss 34–47 of the HFEA 2008], there is no other parent, or

(c) there is some other reason justifying the child's being adopted by the applicant alone,

and where the court makes an adoption order on such an application, the court must record that it is satisfied as to the fact mentioned in paragraph (a) or (b) or, in the case of paragraph (c), record the reason.

Section 51(4) reproduces, albeit with a slight change in wording, the same conditions on adoption by a sole natural parent as were contained within s 15(3) of the AA 1976. Section 15(3) was the subject of House of Lords authority in which Lord Nicholls rejected a restrictive interpretation of the requirement that there must be 'some other reason' justifying the adoption. Following Lord Nicholls' approach, provided it can be shown that adoption by

162 S 51. 163 S 50. 164 S 51(3)–(3A). 165 Bainham (2008c), 481.

the natural parent is in the child's best interests, these additional conditions will present no real obstacle to the adoption proceeding.

Re B (A Minor) (Adoption: Natural Parent) [2001] UKHL 70

LORD NICHOLLS:

11. . . . The Adoption Act permits adoption in the circumstances of child A, but only if there is reason to exclude the mother. The intervention by the court is to protect the interests of the child . . . [T]he interference must meet a pressing social need and be proportionate to that need. Hale LJ [in the Court of Appeal] said . . .:

> '. . . it is difficult indeed to argue that there is a pressing social need to deprive A of all legal relationship with one half of her family of birth. . . . she already has a full and secure legal and factual relationship with her father. If there is any need to give her more, it can be provided for in a package of orders along the lines discussed. In my view, it would be a disproportionate response to her current needs to turn her from the child of two legal parents, with two legal families, into the child of only one parent, with only one legal family. Section 15(3) has to be given effect in such a way as to avoid that result.' . . .

22. On its face this permanent exclusion of the child's mother from the life of the child is a drastic and detrimental consequence of adoption so far as the child is concerned. How serious this loss is likely to be depends on the circumstances of the case. In deciding whether to make an order having this consequence the court must always be satisfied that this course is in the best interests of the child. There must be some reason justifying the exclusion of the other natural parent. The reason must be sufficient to outweigh the adverse consequences such an order may have by reason of the exclusion of one parent from the child's life. Consent of the excluded parent is not of itself a sufficient reason, but it is a factor to be taken into account. Its weight will depend on the circumstances.

23. In so far as the Court of Appeal construed section 15(3)(b) more restrictively than this, I am unable to agree. Section 15(3) imposes a prerequisite to the making of an adoption order on the application of the mother or father alone. One or other of the exceptions set out in paragraphs (a) and (b) must be satisfied. The three exceptions listed in paragraph (a) are instances where the other natural parent cannot have, or is unlikely to have, any further part in the child's upbringing and life. But these three exceptions are not an exhaustive list of the circumstances in which a natural parent is unlikely in practice to have a further role in a child's life. Further, there may be other situations when the welfare of the child justifies the exclusion of a natural parent. Abandonment, or persistent neglect or ill-treatment of the child, could be instances.

24. It is not surprising, therefore, that the exception stated in paragraph (b) ['some other reason'] is altogether open-ended. No doubt this was a deliberate choice of language. I can see no ground for importing into this exception an unexpressed limitation whereby 'some other reason' must be comparable with the death or disappearance of the other natural parent. What is required by paragraph (b), and all that is required, is that the reason, whatever it be, must be sufficient to justify the exclusion of the other parent. Whether any particular reason satisfies this test depends on the circumstances. This is a matter left to the decision of the court. On this question of interpretation I respectfully consider the Court of Appeal was unduly restrictive in its approach.

Lord Nicholls held that it would be in the child's best interests to make the adoption order, thereby permanently excluding the child's mother from playing any further role in the child's life and giving the father the additional security he desired.[166]

13.5.3.c Consent and leave to defend the adoption proceedings

In most cases, the issue of consent is unlikely to arise as the question will have been determined at the placement stage. The rather complicated provisions bearing on consent are contained in s 47.

Adoption and Children Act 2002, s 47

(1) An adoption order may not be made if the child has a parent or guardian unless one of the following conditions is met, but this section is subject to section 52.

(2) The first condition is that, in the case of each parent or guardian of the child, the court is satisfied—

(a) that the parent or guardian consents to the making of the adoption order,

(b) that the parent or guardian has consented under section 20 (and has not withdrawn the consent) and does not oppose the making of the adoption order, or

(c) that the parent's or guardian's consent should be dispensed with.

(3) A parent or guardian may not oppose the making of an adoption order under subsection 2(b) without the court's leave.

(4) The second condition is that—

(a) the child has been placed for adoption by an adoption agency with the prospective adopters in whose favour the order is proposed to be made,

(b) either—

(i) the child was placed for adoption with the consent of each parent or guardian and the consent of the mother was given when the child was at least six weeks old, or

(ii) the child was placed for adoption under a placement order, and

(c) no parent or guardian oppose the making of the adoption order.

(5) A parent or guardian may not oppose the making of an adoption order under the second condition without the court's leave.

(6) The third condition is that the child is free for adoption . . . [under the AA 1976].

(7) The court cannot give leave under subsection (3) or (5) unless satisfied that there has been a change in circumstances since the consent of the parent or guardian was given or, as the case may be, the placement order was made.

Section 47(4) deals with the position where the child was placed by an adoption agency. In such cases, the child will have been placed either with parental consent or pursuant to a placement order. Although s 47(4)(c) states that the order cannot be made if the adoption is opposed, s 47(5) provides that birth parents falling within this category of case will not be

[166] See 13.6.4. For criticism, see Harris-Short (2002).

able to oppose the adoption without the court's leave.[167] Section 47(7) then goes on to provide that the court can only grant leave if satisfied there has been a change in circumstances since the consent was given or the placement order made.[168]

The relevance of the child's welfare to an application for leave under s 47(7) arose in *Re P (A Child) (Adoption Order: Leave to Oppose Making of Adoption Order)*.[169] The first question addressed by the Court of Appeal was whether the decision to grant leave was 'coming to a decision relating to the adoption of a child' thereby making the child's welfare the paramount consideration. In accordance with s 1(7) which provides that 'coming to a decision about granting leave in respect of any action (other than the initiation of proceedings)' is a decision relating to the adoption of a child, the Court of Appeal held that as an application for leave to defend the adoption order was *not* an application for leave to *initiate proceedings*, s 1(7) required the paramountcy principle to be applied:[170]

Re P (A Child) (Adoption Order: Leave to Oppose Making of Adoption Order)
[2007] EWCA Civ 616

WALL LJ:

26. In our judgment, analysis of the statutory language in sections 1 and 47 of the 2002 Act leads to the conclusion that an application for leave to defend adoption proceedings under section 47(5) of the 2002 Act involves a two stage process. First of all, the court has to be satisfied, on the facts of the case, that there has been a change in circumstances within section 47(7). If there has been no change in circumstances, that is the end of the matter, and the application fails. If, however, there has been a change in circumstances within section 47(7) then the door to the exercise of a judicial discretion to permit the parents to defend the adoption proceedings is opened, and the decision whether or not to grant leave is governed by section 1 of the 2002 Act. In other words, "the paramount consideration of the court must be the child's welfare throughout his life".

The Court of Appeal then expanded on what was meant by a 'change in circumstances':

30. . . . We do not think it permissible to put any gloss on the statute, or to read into it words which are not there. The change in circumstances since the placement order was made must, self-evidently and as a matter of statutory construction, relate to the grant of leave. It must equally be of a nature and degree sufficient, on the facts of the particular case, to open the door to the exercise of the judicial discretion to permit the parents to defend the adoption proceedings. In our judgment, however, the phrase "a change in circumstances" is not ambiguous . . .

[167] The parents will be notified of the proceedings and made respondents thereto: Family Procedure Rules 2010, r 14.3(1).

[168] The same restrictions on defending the adoption application apply under s 47(2)(b) where the birth parents gave advance consent to the adoption under s 20. If the parents wish to defend the proceedings, leave will be required in accordance with s 47(3) and (7), determined in accordance with the principles set down in *Re P*, below, and *Re B-S* discussed later.

[169] [2007] EWCA Civ 616.

[170] Ibid, [19]–[21]. Cf where leave is sought to revoke a placement order, discussed at 13.5.1.

31. . . . Furthermore, in our judgment, the importation of the word "significant" puts the test too high . . . The only limiting factor is that it must be a change in circumstances "since the placement order was made". Against this background, we do not think that any further definition of the change in circumstances involved is either possible or sensible.

32. We do, however, take the view that the test should not be set too high, because, as this case demonstrates, parents in the position of S's parents should not be discouraged either from bettering themselves or from seeking to prevent the adoption of their child by the imposition of a test which is unachievable. We therefore take the view that whether or not there has been a relevant change in circumstances must be a matter of fact to be decided by the good sense and sound judgment of the tribunal hearing the application.

Particularly in light of these words of caution regarding potential unfairness to the birth parents, making the child's welfare the paramount consideration on an application for leave to defend the proceedings may seem a little odd—this is, after all, a procedural hurdle and not the substantive hearing at which the child's welfare will clearly be determinative. Moreover, the Court of Appeal make clear that in determining the application for leave, there is no need for the court to conduct a full welfare inquiry with oral evidence and cross-examination.[171] Lord Justice Thorpe elaborated on this welfare stage of the inquiry in *Re W (A Child) (Adoption: Leave to Oppose)*, holding that at this discretionary stage the judge must have 'great regard to the impact of the grant of permission on the child within the context of the adoptive family' and such a step should not be taken unless the applicant 'demonstrates prospects of success that are not just fanciful'.[172] Lord Justice Thorpe suggested that it would only be in 'exceptionally rare circumstances' that the adoption could be halted in these circumstances.[173]

Against the backdrop of growing concern amongst the senior family judiciary about the approach being adopted to non-consensual adoptions, the Court of Appeal revisited the correct test on applications for leave to defend in *Re B-S*. The President, giving the judgment of the court, retreated from any suggestion that leave would only be granted in 'exceptional' cases or that the test was a particularly 'stringent' one:

Re B-S (Adoption: Application of Threshold Criteria) [2013] EWCA Civ 1146

SIR JAMES MUNBY P:

Section 47(5) of the 2002 Act – fundamentals

68. We share . . . misgivings about Thorpe LJ's use of the phrase "exceptionally rare circumstances", as also about his use, followed by the President in *Re C*, of the word "stringent" to define or describe the test to be applied on an application under section 47(5). Both phrases are apt to mislead, with potentially serious adverse consequences. In the light of *Re B* [see 13.4.3] they convey quite the wrong message. Neither, in our judgment, any longer has any place in this context. Their use in relation to section 47(5) should cease.

70. Section 47(5) is intended to afford a parent in an appropriate case a meaningful remedy – and a remedy, we stress, that may enure for the benefit not merely of the parent but also of

[171] Ibid, [53].
[172] *Re W (A Child) (Adoption: Leave to Oppose)* [2010] EWCA Civ 1535, [20].
[173] Ibid, [17].

the child. Whilst we can understand what lay behind what Thorpe LJ said, we think that his use of the phrase "exceptionally rare circumstances" carries with it far too great a potential for misunderstanding, misapplication and indeed injustice for safety. The same, if in lesser measure, applies also to the word "stringent". Stringent, as we have said, is a word that appropriately describes the test that has to be surmounted before a non-consensual adoption can be sanctioned. It is not a word that comfortably describes the test that a parent has to meet in seeking to resist such an adoption.

71. Parliament intended section 47(5) to provide a real remedy. Unthinking reliance upon the concept of the "exceptionally rare" runs the risk – a very real and wholly unacceptable risk – of rendering section 47(5) nugatory and its protections illusory. Except in the fairly unusual case where section 47(4)(b)(i) applies, a parent applying under section 47(5) will always, by definition, be faced with the twin realities that the court has made both a care order and a placement order and that the child is now living with the prospective adopter. But, unless section 47(5) is to be robbed of all practical efficacy, none of those facts, even in combination, can of themselves justify the refusal of leave.

Section 47(5) of the 2002 Act – the proper approach

72. Subject only to one point which does not affect the substance, the law, in our judgment, was correctly set out by Wall LJ in *Re P*, though we fear it may on occasions have been applied too narrowly and indeed too harshly. The only qualification is that the exercise at the second stage is more appropriately described as one of judicial *evaluation* rather than as one involving mere *discretion*.

73. There is a two stage process. The court has to ask itself two questions: Has there been a change in circumstances? If so, should leave to oppose be given? In relation to the first question we think it unnecessary and undesirable to add anything to what Wall LJ said.

74. In relation to the second question – If there has been a change in circumstances, should leave to oppose be given? – the court will, of course, need to consider all the circumstances. The court will in particular have to consider two inter-related questions: one, the parent's ultimate prospect of success if given leave to oppose; the other, the impact on the child if the parent is, or is not, given leave to oppose, always remembering, of course, that at this stage the child's welfare is paramount. In relation to the evaluation, the weighing and balancing, of these factors we make the following points:

i) Prospect of success here relates to the prospect of resisting the making of an adoption order, *not*, we emphasise, the prospect of ultimately having the child restored to the parent's care.

ii) For purposes of exposition and analysis we treat as two separate issues the questions of whether there has been a change in circumstances and whether the parent has solid grounds for seeking leave. Almost invariably, however, they will be intertwined; in many cases the one may very well follow from the other.

iii) Once he or she has got to the point of concluding that there has been a change of circumstances and that the parent has solid grounds for seeking leave, the judge must consider very carefully indeed whether the child's welfare really does necessitate the refusal of leave. The judge must keep at the forefront of his mind the teaching of *Re B*, in particular that adoption is the "last resort" and only permissible if "nothing else will do" and that, as Lord Neuberger emphasised, the child's interests include being brought up by the parents or wider family unless the overriding requirements of the child's welfare make that not possible. That said, the child's welfare is paramount.

iv) At this, as at all other stages in the adoption process, the judicial evaluation of the child's welfare must take into account *all* the negatives and the positives, *all* the pros and cons, of *each* of the two options, that is, either giving or refusing the parent leave to oppose. Here again, as elsewhere, the use of Thorpe LJ's 'balance sheet' is to be encouraged . . .

vi) As a general proposition, the greater the change in circumstances (assuming, of course, that the change is positive) and the more solid the parent's grounds for seeking leave to oppose, the more cogent and compelling the arguments based on the child's welfare must be if leave to oppose is to be refused.

vii) The mere fact that the child has been placed with prospective adopters cannot be determinative, nor can the mere passage of time. On the other hand, the older the child and the longer the child has been placed the greater the adverse impacts of disturbing the arrangements are likely to be.

viii) The judge must always bear in mind that what is paramount in every adoption case is the welfare of the child "throughout his life". Given modern expectation of life, this means that, with a young child, one is looking far ahead into a very distant future – upwards of eighty or even ninety years. Against this perspective, judges must be careful not to attach undue weight to the short term consequences for the child if leave to oppose is given . . .

ix) Almost invariably the judge will be pressed with the argument that leave to oppose should be refused, amongst other reasons, because of the adverse impact on the prospective adopters, and thus on the child, of their having to pursue a contested adoption application. We do not seek to trivialise an argument which may in some cases have considerable force, particularly perhaps in a case where the child is old enough to have some awareness of what is going on. But judges must be careful not to attach undue weight to the argument. After all, what from the perspective of the proposed adopters was the smoothness of the process which they no doubt anticipated when issuing their application with the assurance of a placement order, will already have been disturbed by the unwelcome making of the application for leave to oppose. . . .

x) We urge judges always to bear in mind the wise and humane words of Wall LJ in *Re P*, para 32. We have already quoted them but they bear repetition: "the test should not be set too high, because . . . parents . . . should not be discouraged either from bettering themselves or from seeking to prevent the adoption of their child by the imposition of a test which is unachievable"

If the parents' application for leave is refused, the adoption application will be unopposed, thus satisfying the necessary conditions for making an adoption order. If the parents' application is successful, both the child's welfare and the issue of parental consent will fall to be fully re-litigated.[174] Given the importance of the decision, the court must therefore have proper evidence on the relevant issues, which should be 'gathered with a degree of determination that reflects the fact that critical time is passing for a young child awaiting a decision about his or her future'.[175]

In all other cases (i.e. step-parent adoptions and private placements), consent will not have been dealt with at an earlier stage of the proceedings and will thus fall to be determined at the final hearing. Section 47 therefore provides that the court will only be able to make the adoption order if satisfied that the birth parents consent to the adoption or that their consent should be dispensed with in accordance with the terms of s 52.[176]

[174] *Re B-S (Adoption: Application of Threshold Criteria)* [2013] EWCA Civ 1146.
[175] *Re W (A Child: Leave to Oppose Adoption)* [2020] EWCA Civ 16, [41].
[176] See 13.4.2.b.

13.5.3.d Welfare

Making an adoption order is clearly a 'decision relating to the adoption of a child'. The welfare principle in s 1(2) therefore applies and the child's welfare must be the court's paramount consideration. That said, as most applications will now be unopposed it is difficult to envisage many cases in which the adoption order will be refused. Under the previous legislation, almost 97 per cent of contested adoption applications were successful.[177] As Ryburn notes, although adoption is the final decision in a 'cumulative process where there were many other decisions along the way', it is difficult to imagine any other area of the law where the odds are so highly stacked against one party to the dispute.[178]

13.6 IN THE BEST INTERESTS OF THE CHILD? CONTROVERSIAL ISSUES

Although the birth parents face several obstacles in resisting an adoption, the court must still be satisfied both at the placement stage and at the final hearing that the adoption is in the child's best interests. In determining whether a child should be adopted, a number of particularly controversial questions have dominated the case law.

13.6.1 BIRTH FAMILY VERSUS THE 'PERFECT' ADOPTIVE COUPLE

At the heart of many contested adoptions is the question of whether a child should be raised within the birth family, preferably by the parents, or be given the opportunity to start a new life with the adoptive parents. A contested adoption thus raises in stark form the value to be placed on 'genetic' as opposed to 'social' or 'psychological' parenting.[179] We have seen within the context of disputes over where a child should live how the law has tended to favour biological over social parenting.[180] The key factors justifying the 'natural parent presumption' in such disputes are particularly important in disputes concerning adoption. For example, the need to protect the child's developing sense of identity takes on particular significance when the order being sought will extinguish all legal ties with the birth family. Concerns over the dangers of 'social engineering' also take on a particular resonance when the birth parents, with all their problems and inadequacies, are facing competing claims from an adoptive couple who will have successfully come through a difficult and far-reaching vetting procedure.

The child's right to be brought up by their birth family has, in the past, formed the starting point for determining a contested adoption. This was made clear in *Re K (Private Placement for Adoption)*.[181] The case concerned a private arrangement between the birth parents and the prospective adopters which was entered into shortly after the child's birth and at a time when the birth mother was under enormous stress. The birth parents changed their mind

[177] Ryburn (1998a), 56. [178] Ibid.

[179] Note that the use of special guardianship orders allows a child to be placed for long-term care with extended family or friends, which can therefore offer a mid-way between these apparently stark options: see 13.8.

[180] See 11.6.5. [181] See also *Re O (A Minor) (Custody or Adoption)* [1992] 1 FCR 378.

and sought to have the child returned to their care. At the time of the hearing, the child had been in the prospective adopters' care for seven-and-a-half months. The Court of Appeal returned the child to her parents.

Re K (Private Placement for Adoption) [1991] FCR 142 (CA), 147–8

BUTLER-SLOSS LJ:

The mother must be shown to be entirely unsuitable before another family can be considered, otherwise we are in grave danger of slipping into social engineering. The question is not: would the child be better off with the plaintiffs? But: is the natural family so unsuitable that . . . "the welfare of the child positively demanded the displacement of the parental right?" I agree . . . that it is the right of the child rather than the parent and, borrowing from the philosophy of the Children Act 1989, I would rephrase it as the displacement of the parental responsibility. Once the Judge found that this mother genuinely wanted her child back and was a mother who cared properly for the other two children, not to give her at least an opportunity to try to rehabilitate the family was to deprive the child of any chance of her own family.

The courts' preference for the birth parents has also extended to the wider kinship network.[182] It was held in *Re L (A Minor) (Care Proceedings: Wardship)* that the local authority should look first to the extended family for alternative care before considering stranger adoption. In determining whether members of the birth family are suitable, the court emphasized that adoption should not be regarded as a 'panacea' and that sometimes the known risks of the birth family would be preferable to the unknown risks of adoption.[183]

Re L (A Minor) (Care Proceedings: Wardship) (No 2) [1991] 1 FLR 29 (Crown Court), 36–8

JUDGE WILLIS:

The whole crux of this case depends on how much weight should be given to the various 'pros' and 'cons' for the two alternative courses for this child, namely, going to the grandparents or being adopted. We received the impression from the guardian, as we did from the local authority witnesses also, that they are far too keen on adoption and consider it the panacea for all problems. They all expressed a number of concerns or problems which might arise in the maternal grandparents' extended family if K [the child] is there. None of them envisaged any real problem in adoption in a child of this age. The impression they tried to give was that, as in every good fairy story, after placement, 'everyone lives happily ever after' . . .

The local authority's case is that there are far too many problems if K goes back to the family, i.e. to grandparents, and that a fresh start with adoption is a less risky course. K will

[182] Ryburn (1998b) contended that this was contrary to prevailing social work practice where the 'zero-cost' of stranger adoption is preferred, but kinship care has increased in frequency in the years since: see, e.g., Hunt (2018).

[183] The cases on revoking adoption orders give some insight into the potential risk associated with adoption in some cases: see 13.2. However, adoption placements are generally very stable and offer good outcomes for children: see 13.3.2.

be 'grafted' into a new family with the absence of access problems. This argument, however, fails to address the considerable problems which are more likely to arise in adoption, namely the psychological worry of who and what her family are, why she is not with them and why she was adopted . . . The great advantage in staying with the wider family is that the child maintains her roots. We consider this a very important aspect which has been totally ignored by the local authority and also by the guardian ad litem . . . [A]doption should only be the last resort when no one in the wider family is available and suitable to look after a child. Parentage is not always perfect, but parentage in the family is preferable to the unknown risks of adoption . . . We consider that every child has a right, whenever it is possible, to be brought up in its own genetic family. That right should not be taken away from it except in the last resort when there are strong, cogent and positive reasons for so doing.

The importance of the birth family was reiterated by *Re B* and *Re B-S* (discussed in detail earlier), both of which firmly and unequivocally stated that the birth family must only be displaced by an order for adoption when adoption is 'required' or 'demanded' by the child's welfare—when nothing else will do.

However, even given this entrenched respect for the right of the child to be raised whenever possible within the family of birth, there will be very few cases in which the birth parents are successful in opposing the adoption.[184] The explanation for this lies in the strength of the countervailing considerations in a typical contested adoption where there will usually be a long history of serious and persistent failings in parenting. Even where there are no such failings, such as where the birth father was unaware of the child, the court is often faced with the problem of what amounts, in effect, to a *fait accompli*: by the time of the adoption hearing, the child has been living with the adoptive parents for a substantial period of time and strong emotional bonds have developed between them. Where the child is strongly attached to the adoptive parents, the courts are extremely reluctant to disrupt this position.[185] In *Re O (Adoption: Withholding Agreement)*, the strong attachment which had developed between the child and the prospective adopters was held to constitute a compelling factor capable of displacing the preference for the birth family, even though the father, who had not been told of the child's existence, was perfectly capable of offering the child a secure and stable home.[186] Empirical research suggests that this reluctance to break the child's bond with the alternative carers is well founded. Dyer, for example, argues that breaking the bond between the child and the child's primary attachment figures, whether those attachments are to the birth or psychological parents, can have serious adverse consequences. He points to various empirical studies which link 'disturbed or disrupted attachment to personality disorders; poor functioning in the parental role as an adult; alcoholism; criminality; and sexual offending'.[187] However, against this, the court has to balance equally compelling evidence regarding the problems often suffered by adopted adolescents in developing a secure and positive sense of identity.[188] These are difficult cases to which there are no easy answers.

[184] Ryburn (1998a), 56.

[185] This approach is reinforced by the 2017 amendments to the welfare checklist: see 13.4.1.

[186] [1999] 2 FCR 262. See also *Re Q (Adoption)* [2012] EWCA Civ 1610, albeit there were additional welfare concerns in that case regarding the child moving to live with the father and his wife.

[187] Dyer (2004), 11. [188] See detailed discussion at 9.4.4.

13.6.2 TRANS-RACIAL ADOPTION

Concerns over the child's developing sense of identity are particularly strong when there are ethnic, cultural, or religious factors involved. Indeed, no issue causes greater division within adoption.[189] Advocates on both sides of the debate can be particularly dogmatic in their approach.

Opponents of trans-racial adoption have focused on two key problems: (i) the difficulties minority ethnic children face in developing a strong, positive ethnic identity when placed in a white household; and (ii) the inability of the child's carers to help the child cope with the racism still endemic within British society. Goldstein's interview with John Small, a key opponent of trans-racial adoption and a leading figure in the development of social work policy on this issue during the 1980s, reveals the thinking behind current opposition to trans-racial placements:

B. Goldstein, 'Ethnicity and Placement. Beginning the Debate', (2000) 24 *Adoption and Fostering* 9, 9–10

The thing which is important to my mind is the psychological damage that is likely to occur when the identities of children are not recognised. For example, if you have a child from a West Indian, African [or] Indian background and they claim that their colour is another [i.e. white], that must be some deep psychological scar. They look into the mirror and what they see they don't like, and the reason why they don't like that is a direct result of what's happening to them in the social world that they are in. It is the question of what society is doing to children whose personalities are in the process of being formed and are actually influenced by what they see, bearing in mind that they develop their ideas and attitudes and they are shaped by the people with whom they interact.

The psychological research has shown us about self and what constitutes self and how our self-image is derivative of the messages we obtain from significant others. So if society has this negative view of particular ethnic groups and transmits this through the media, through television, through the radio, through the print media, through the attitudes in society, through the attitudes of other children in the playground, those kinds of images come through. Identity is something you internalise from a range of things as you go through life, not something you search for later. This is why the messages parents and society give are important. You have to be very conscious of this with a black child in a racist society. Some white parents, they don't think that is important. They think love is enough—perhaps in a non-racist society but we certainly haven't reached that stage yet . . .

I realise that some well-meaning, white middle-class people tend to ignore the effects of racism because they can't understand the implications of racism for the black population generally. That leads them to deny that racism exists and, once they deny that, it is unlikely that they will be able to explain these things to their children or to the child that they have adopted.

As Hayes explains, opponents of trans-racial adoption have tried to shift the debate away from arguments that can be attacked as ideologically or politically driven because of their

[189] We are typically talking here about placing BME children in white households, a problem which is exacerbated by the low number of prospective adopters from BME communities: e.g. Kirton (2016); House of Lords Select Committee on the Children and Families Act 2014 (2022), paras 57–69.

association with 'black identity politics', focusing instead on the individualized interests of the child. Opponents of trans-racial adoption have emphasized that it is the particular vulnerability of ethnic minority children in a racist society and the 'experience-based skills' of black and other ethnic minority parents in dealing with such issues—not their 'biological essences'—that make them the preferred carers for these children.[190]

It is, however, difficult to escape ideologically based arguments when issues of race and ethnicity are in question. Underlying disagreements about trans-racial adoption are fundamentally different 'world-views' on issues such as: the importance of racial identity in a liberal western society, whether ethnic identity is an innate or chosen characteristic, and whether or not it is accurate to describe contemporary British society as inherently racist. Hayes is a strong advocate of trans-racial adoption based on a clear philosophical commitment to a 'colour-blind' vision of life.[191]

P. Hayes, 'Giving Due Consideration to Ethnicity in Adoption Placements—A Principled Approach', (2003) 15 *Child and Family Law Quarterly* 255, 260–2

[A]ttempts at ethnic matching demonstrate a naïve understanding of ethnicity and culture that is every bit as flawed as the idea that all people who are not white can be simply lumped together as 'black'.

Three mistaken assumptions underlie precise ethnic matching: first, it is assumed that ethnic culture is a natural inheritance rather than a conventional construct; secondly, a minority child's culture is invariably assumed to be exclusive and particular to one ethnic group rather than being universally accessible; and thirdly, ethnic cultures are conceived of in essential, rather than nominal, terms.

Nature and convention

Advocates of ethnic matching assume that the cultural elements of a child's ethnicity are passed down rather like genes so that they form a hereditary and predetermined element of the child's make-up. Religions, for example, are not defined as universally accessible communities that people might either enter and leave through choice or become acculturated to as they grow up. Instead, it is assumed that it is somehow natural for a child to inherit the religion of the birth parents or grandparents, whether or not the child has been raised in that religion. This is referred to, misleadingly, as the 'right' and 'need' of the child to belong to a particular religion. In fact, it is nothing to do with the child's individual rights, but is rather a collectivist argument that religiously defined communities can lay claim to a child as one of their own . . .

Particularism and universalism

Advocates of ethnic matching ignore cultural attributes that are universally accessible in favour of ones that are particular to a single ethnic culture. Culture is always viewed by such advocates as something that divides people, never as something that brings them together. But often culture unites people of different ethnic origins, for example, the character

[190] Goldstein (2000), 14; Flynn (2000).

[191] See also Patel (2007), esp at 33. Patel argues against an 'essentialist view' of racial identity, contending that racial identity is 'flexible' and 'fluid' and that the individual is able 'to construct for themselves multiple racial identities'.

sketches of children advertised for adoption mention commonplace interests and pursuits such as football or pop music. These universally accessible pastimes are, in fact, part of these children's culture, although, as they are not associated with any one particular ethnic group, they are not conceived of as culture by those who favour ethnic matching.

Hayes goes on to argue that ethnic cultures are not innate, and that claiming that there is an inherent distinction between different ethnic groups misunderstands the ways in which cultures develop and merge together over time. Race and culture are not the same thing, he notes, which he suggests can be particularly significant for mixed-race children. Hayes suggests that such children are told to take pride in the ethnic mix within themselves, but within the adoption system there is then a question mark about the potential for 'any further mixing into a transracial adoption'. He continues:

Ethnic identity versus 'colour-blind' human beings

One difference between trans-racially adopted children and inracially adopted children has been singled out for particular criticism by advocates of ethnic matching. Transracially adopted children have often been found to be somewhat more likely to describe themselves as human beings first and foremost, or as taking a 'colour-blind' approach in their social relationships. This is a reasonable and viable way of defining yourself and others. It is, for example, a perspective by no means uncommon among minority adults who appear to be perfectly well-adjusted . . .

To be colour-blind is to assess each individual on his or her own merits. People who are colour-blind believe that generalisations about an ethnic group a person belongs to may well tell you little or nothing about what he or she is like as an individual. They also believe that a person's colour is not an intrinsic bar to achievement, and that neither should there be any bar to relationships between people of different colours, including the deepest marital and family relationships.

The idea of being colour-blind is closely associated with the philosophy of individualism. Those who adopt the colour-blind approach to life have neither reason nor tendency to assume that everyone else in society, or indeed their own children, necessarily thinks the same way that they do about ethnicity. Such an assumption of uniform thinking is quite at odds with the individualist insistence that people are able to make up their own minds about such issues. It is, therefore, incorrect to suggest that to be colour-blind is to assume that no one is racist, or that everyone takes the view that colour is irrelevant. However, advocates of ethnic matching appear to think that because they are fixated with issues of ethnicity, then so is everyone else, and it may be that they attribute to colour-blind parents their own faulty logic.

Advocates of trans-racial adoption have further stressed the absence of any empirical evidence to support the perceived problems caused by trans-racial placements.[192] The empirical evidence is, however, limited and the conclusions drawn somewhat tentative. On the basis of a review carried out of studies in the UK and the United States, Rushton and Minnis conclude that adoption breakdown rates are determined by age at placement rather than the type of placement and that 'developmental outcomes of transracially placed children appear

[192] Hayes (2003), 256–7 and 268.

to be good for the majority in terms of educational attainment, peer relations and behaviour'.[193] They also point out, however, that methodological flaws with the various studies preclude definitive conclusions.[194] The conclusions drawn by Moffat and Thoburn from a review of the existing literature and their own study of 254 minority ethnic children are similarly qualified, although again they find no significant evidence of harm resulting from trans-racial placements.

P. Moffatt and J. Thoburn, 'Outcomes of Permanent Family Placement for Children of Minority Ethnic Origin', (2001) 6 *Child and Family Social Work* 13, 14, 18, and 20

The majority of placements of children of minority ethnic origin were successful, at least in the sense that the young people remained in placement. This applied irrespective of gender, of whether they were of mixed race parentage or had two parents of the same ethnic background, and of whether they were placed in ethnically matched families or transracially. However, a worrying minority of the children experienced placement breakdown. The explanations for the success or otherwise of the placements appear broadly similar to those for white children. For the sample as a whole, no difference was found in breakdown rates between those placed in 'matched' and in 'transracial' placements . . .

Our qualitative data indicate that not all placements which last are successful when other outcome measures such as well-being, satisfaction or ethnic pride are the outcome measures used. From a combination of the qualitative and the quantitative data we concluded that some white families can successfully parent children of a different ethnic origin, including helping them to combat the adverse effects of racism and feel pride in their appearance, culture and heritage. However, compared with the parents of minority ethnic origin, they have additional tasks to negotiate, and the job they have to do in parenting a child who has already suffered adversity and at least one separation and rejection is difficult enough without making it more difficult. We thus concur with the preference expressed in the UN Convention on the Rights of the Child, the Hague Convention on Inter-country Adoption and the England and Wales Children Act 1989 for children to be placed whenever possible with families from their own local or wider communities. But our data emphasize that placements in 'matched' families are also vulnerable to disruption and that long-term support must be available if the chances of success are to improve.

On the basis of the current available evidence, the majority of researchers thus remain cautious about trans-racial placements, concluding that, despite the absence of any positive evidence that trans-racial adoption is harmful, 'matched' placements provide better safeguards against feelings of ostracism and identity confusion and should therefore be the preferred option where available.[195]

The ACA 2002 as originally implemented sought to strike this balance between giving preference to 'matched' placements whilst not denying a black or minority ethnic (BME) child the benefits of adoption where matching was not possible.[196] However, problems arose with the practical implementation of this policy. The preference for matched placements

[193] Rushton and Minnis (2000), 53. [194] Ibid. [195] E.g. Kirton, Feast, and Howe (2000).
[196] ACA 2002, s 1(5), now repealed in England.

sat uneasily with the drive to eradicate delay. In practice, due to the small number of approved ethnic minority adopters, it was very difficult for the local authority to find suitable 'matched' placements within the prescribed timescales for decision-making and placement.[197] The Narey Report identified ethnic matching as a particularly pernicious cause of delay in the adoption of BME children:

M. Narey, 'The Narey Report: A Blueprint for the Nation's Lost Children', *The Times*, 5 July 2011

We live in an increasingly multicultural society and one where quite properly, the stereotyping of people because of their race is discouraged . . . The UK has moved on. But not in the case of adoption where there is, in my view, a continuing, unjustified obsession with ethnicity. . . .

The now long established determination to find the right ethnic match for a child is, I would argue, based on a dubious emphasis on the significance of culture and heritage – particularly when we are talking about a baby – and is certainly and demonstrably damaging to black and mixed-race children, where delay is persistent and unacceptable. . . .

However well-intentioned the actions of practitioners in seeking a close or perfect ethnic match for a child . . . the consequences for BME children are incontrovertible. . . . [T]hey face an adoption apartheid. White children in care are three times more likely to be adopted than black children.

Black as opposed to BME children fare particularly badly. . . . [T]he option that we know offers the best prospects for a child's future, adoption, is extended to only about 10 per cent of black children leaving care and only about 15 per cent of Asian children, while 35 per cent of white children leaving care become adopted . . .

The reality is that the overarching warning against the damaging consequences of delay – based on a wealth of research – has for some years now been ignored in favour of a rigid interpretation of the ethnicity and cultural provisions in the Act, the effect of which is to leave black and Asian children languishing in care. . . .

In light of the perceived delays caused by this apparent 'obsession' with ethnic matching, the government decided (but only extending to England) to revoke s 1(5) of the ACA 2002.[198] This legislative amendment did not meet with widespread support. It was first argued that the 'problem' had been wrongly identified. The evidence on which Narey and the government relied in support of its case for reform was challenged as much more nuanced than suggested. Indeed, the Joint Committee on Human Rights concluded that the evidence relied on by the government (which showed Asian children taking on average less time to be adopted than white children), 'not only fails to support but positively undermines its justification for repealing the statutory requirement'.[199] Whilst acknowledging that recent research had identified ethnicity as a cause of delay in the adoption of BME children, particularly black children, the House of Lords Select Committee on Adoption pointed out that it was the *age* of the children which was found to be a more significant factor than ethnicity and inflexible social work practice:

[197] As to the reasons why there are currently so few prospective adopters from ethnic minority communities, see Frazer and Selwyn (2005).

[198] CFA 2014, s 3. See DFE (2012b), 21–2.

[199] Joint Committee on Human Rights (2013–14), paras 24–8.

House of Lords Select Committee on Adoption Legislation, 1st Report of Session 2012–13, *Adoption: Pre-Legislative Scrutiny. Report*, HL Paper 94 (London: TSO, 2012)

65. Overall, recent research has suggested a number of potential reasons for the delay in placing some BME children. Age remains the most important predictive factor. The search for an 'ideal' matched placement may be a factor in some cases. There is, however, also evidence from the recent research of flexibility in adoption agencies' approach to matching. A key finding in Professor Farmer's study[200] was that "29% of BME children were placed with families whose characteristics did not match their ethnicity, often in order to secure a placement for children with complex needs where the need to place was considered more important that finding an 'ideal' match".

Whilst questioning whether a rigid approach to ethnicity was the real cause of the problem,[201] the Select Committee also voiced strong concern about the 'solution':

73. . . . There is concern about the message this legislative change could send out to social workers on the ground. BAAF [British Association for Adoption and Fostering] pointed to Article 20 of the United Nations Convention on the Rights of the Child, which states that: "Children who cannot be looked after by their own family have a right to special care and must be looked after properly, by people who respect their ethnic group, religion, culture and language." They argued that a child's identity was an important part of their development, and that the four factors identified in Article 20 were an important part of that identity. BAAF considered that Article 20 and section 1(5) embodied this 'widely acknowledged' principle. In their view the proposal for section 1(5) to not apply in England brought with it a risk that these important considerations of identity would be neglected when making decisions for adoption matching. . . .

77. We accept that it is important to ensure that appropriate weight is given to religion, race, language and culture when making adoption matches. However, we believe that the Government need to give further consideration to the practical effect of the proposed change to section 1(5) . . . on social work culture and practice . . . .

The government rejected this recommendation and pressed ahead with revoking s 1(5) in England.[202] However, the amendment appears to have had little impact, and concerns remain.

[200] Farmer et al (2010).

[201] See also Selwyn et al (2008) who concluded that whilst an overly narrow approach to matching may have contributed to problems in successfully placing BME children, age was the most important predictive factor as to whether a child was adopted or not. Notably black children were much older when they first became looked after than white, Asian, or mixed ethnicity children. Shortage of ethnic minority adopters remains a key problem: Kirton (2016), House of Lords Select Committee on the Children and Families Act 2014 (2022), para 62.

[202] An adoption agency in Wales is still required to 'give due consideration to the child's religious persuasion, racial origin and cultural and linguistic background'.

House of Lords Select Committee on the Children and Families Act 2014, Report of Session 2022–23, *The Children and Families Act 2014: A Failure of Implementation*, HL Paper 100 (London: TSO, 2022)

60. Evidence we received supports the idea that the repeal has had a limited impact. . . . CoramBAAF's Black and Minority Ethnic Perspective Advisory Committee wrote that: "There is no evidence available to support that this change has had any positive impact on the waiting times for black and minority ethnic children." . . .

61. Some witnesses felt that the removal of the requirement could reflect an underappreciation of the importance of race and ethnicity to adopted children. CoramBAAF's Black and Minority Ethnic Perspective Advisory Committee raised concerns that:

> "Arguing that the less explicit 'background and characteristic' will suffice in ensuring 'due consideration' is given to addressing all aspects of the needs of black and minority ethnic children, shows a lack of understanding of institutional racism, cultural humility and listening to the lived experiences of transracial adoptees."

68. It is not clear that the change of law, removing the requirement to consider ethnicity, has changed practice. Ethnic minority children still wait too long to be adopted; a disparity which is unacceptable. There remains a shortage of prospective adopters who are prepared to adopt children from minority ethnic groups and those who do are insufficiently supported. The adoption workforce, and adoption panels, are insufficiently diverse.

13.6.3 STEP-PARENT ADOPTION

Step-parent adoptions now account for just 5 per cent of the total number of annual adoptions.[203] The declining popularity of step-parent adoption is not surprising. During the 1970s, step-parent adoptions were seen by many as a natural means of consolidating and supporting a new family unit following divorce or separation. Reinforced by the 'clean break philosophy' underpinning divorce and a more ambivalent attitude towards the role of the father in the post-divorce context, it was thought by some that the child's interests would be better protected within the security and stability of the new nuclear family. The interests of the new family unit were thus prioritized, with the maintenance of links with the non-resident parent, invariably the father, viewed as potentially destabilizing, adding to the pressures on the new family and preventing it from firmly establishing itself as a 'normal', autonomous unit. However, even at this time, there were some strong concerns about the widespread use of step-parent adoption to exclude the non-resident parent from the child's life.[204]

Concerns about step-parent adoption strengthened as the important changes in family policy underpinning the CA 1989 became entrenched. The clean break model of divorce became supplanted by an ideal of cooperative joint parenting post-separation, supported by the enduring nature of parental responsibility and a strong presumption in favour of continuing contact with the non-resident parent. As Neale and Smart explain, the model of the reconstituted nuclear family was replaced by that of the bi-nuclear family spread across two households.[205] These key policy changes were reinforced by a fundamental reorientation of

[203] MOJ (2022a). [204] *Re B (A Minor) (Adoption by Parent)* [1975] Fam 127, esp 143 and 146.
[205] Neale and Smart (1999), 37.

the welfare discourse such that the child's best interests were no longer viewed as resting primarily with the new family unit but in preserving strong, healthy relationships with both sides of the birth family. These policy changes are fundamentally inconsistent with using adoption to sever irrevocably the child's relationship with the non-resident parent.

Cases in which step-parent adoption will be sanctioned are thus likely to be unusual. Section 8 orders can confer the desired security on the new family unit and regulate any problematic behaviour by the non-resident parent. The fact that the CA 1989 now allows a step-parent to acquire free-standing parental responsibility further reduces the need to resort to adoption—although, surprisingly, unlike applications for adoption under the ACA 2002, only those in a formalized relationship with a birth parent can take advantage of these provisions.[206]

That is not to say, however, that a step-parent adoption will never be found to be in the child's best interests. It will depend on the particular circumstances of the case. McFarlane LJ provided clear guidance on the approach to be taken to step-parent adoptions under domestic law in *Re P (Step-Parent Adoption)*.[207] Most notably, he distinguished step-parent adoptions from non-consensual adoptions outside the family and held that the high threshold which applies in the latter case ('nothing else will do') is not to be applied to the former.[208] As his judgment makes clear, in his view step-parent adoptions are very often a much less drastic interference with family life than non-consensual adoptions outside the family and do not therefore require the same high degree of justification. Whether that is correct will clearly depend on the individual circumstances of each case. On the facts of *Re P*, the mother's partner was seeking to adopt her two children aged 14 and 12. The father of one of the boys had abandoned them shortly after birth; the other had not seen his son since the parents divorced and the mother relocated from Poland several years before.

Re P (Step-Parent Adoption) [2014] EWCA Civ 1174

McFARLANE LJ:

22. In a single applicant step-parent adoption case under the ACA 2002 regime, such as the present case, the result of these various provisions is that if a step-parent adoption order is made:

a) The child is treated as if born as a child of the step-parent [ACA 2002, s 67(1)];
b) Is to be treated in law as not being the child of any person other than the step-parent adopter and the natural parent who is that step-parent's partner [s 67(3)(a)];
c) The natural parent who is not the step-parent's partner (i.e. A's [the child's] natural father in the present case) has any parental responsibility for the child extinguished [s 46(2)(a)]; and
d) The adopter gains parental responsibility for the child [s 46(1)].

[206] CA 1989, s 4A. See 10.3.4.

[207] [2014] EWCA Civ 1174. Heenan (2015). For Strasbourg jurisprudence, see *Söderbäck v Sweden* (App No 113/1997/897/1109, ECHR) (1998) and Fenton-Glynn (2021), 353–5. Perhaps surprisingly, the European Court of Human Rights held that a step-parent adoption does not necessarily violate the rights of the non-adopting parent.

[208] See also *Re L (A Child: Step-Parent Adoption)* [2021] EWCA Civ 801.

46. In an adoption application the key to the approach both to evaluating the needs of a child's welfare throughout his or her life and to dispensing with parental consent is proportionality. The strong statements made by the Justices of the Supreme Court in *Re B* . . . to the effect that adoption will be justified only where 'nothing else will do' are made in the context of an adoption being imposed upon a family against the wishes of the child's parents and where the adoption will totally remove the child from any future contact with, or legal relationship with, any of his natural relatives. Although the statutory provisions applicable to such an adoption (in particular ACA 2002, s 1 regarding welfare and s 52 regarding consent) apply in precisely the same terms to a step-parent adoption, the manner in which those provisions fall to be applied may differ and will depend upon the facts of each case and the judicial assessment of proportionality.

47. By way of example, in a child protection case where it is clear that rehabilitation to the parents is not compatible with their child's welfare, the court may be faced with a choice between adoption by total strangers selected by the local authority acting as an adoption agency or adoption by other family members. There is a qualitative difference between these two options in terms of the degree to which the outcome will interfere with the ECHR, Art 8 rights to family life of the child and his parents; adoption by strangers being at the extreme end of the spectrum of interference and adoption by a family member being at a less extreme point on the scale. The former option is only justified when 'nothing else will do', whereas the latter option, which involves a lower degree of interference, may be more readily justified.

48. Where an adoption application is made by a step-parent, the approach of the ECtHR in *Söderbäck v Sweden* should be applied according to the facts of each case. In doing so the following central points from the judgment in *Söderbäck* are likely to be important:

a) There is a distinction to be drawn between adoption in the context of compulsory, permanent placement outside the family against the wishes of parents (for example as in *Johansen v Norway*) and a step-parent adoption where, by definition, the child is remaining in the care of one or other of his parents;

b) Factors which are likely to reduce the degree of interference with the Art 8 rights of the child and the non-consenting parent ['Parent B'], and thereby make it more likely that adoption is a proportionate measure are:

   i) Where Parent B has not had the care of the child or otherwise asserted his or her responsibility for the child;

   ii) Where Parent B has had only infrequent or no contact with the child;

   iii) Where there is a particularly well established family unit in the home of the parent and step-parent in which 'de facto' family ties have existed for a significant period.

49. In so far as the earlier domestic cases to which I have made reference establish that, in the event of Parent B being actively opposed to a step-parent adoption, practical arrangements should be dealt with by private law orders, that approach is entirely at one with the modern private law relating to children which seeks to determine aspects of the delivery of child-care and the discharge of parental responsibility either by parental agreement or by a child arrangements order under CA 1989, s 8.

50. The making of an adoption order is primarily, if not entirely, concerned with the legal status of the relationships between the child, his natural parent(s) and the adopter(s), rather than practical arrangements . . .

52. . . . [I]n the present application the detriment, in ECHR Art 8 terms, to each of these two children and their fathers of extinguishing their respective legal relationships is modest. The interference with Art 8 family life rights here is of an altogether lower level of intervention to that which is typically involved where the proposed adoption is by non-family members with all familial relationships being extinguished against the will of parents with whom the children have a real and active relationship . . .

54. . . . Caution is therefore required in reading [*Re P (Children) (Adoption: Parental Consent)*—discussed at 13.4.2.b] in the context of a step-parent adoption, albeit that the statutory test in s 52 is precisely the same for both categories of adoption. The reason for caution is that, whilst the statutory wording is the same, the degree of interference with family life and evaluation of proportionality under Article 8 are likely to be different . . .

61. . . . [T]he context of the particular case will be of particular significance: where on the spectrum of intervention by adoption does this case sit? In broad terms the spectrum will run from a fully opposed, public law 'stranger' adoption at one extreme, to an adoption within the child's existing 'de facto' family unit, which is made with the consent of both parents. In between there will be step-parent adoptions which are actively opposed by 'Parent B', who is himself fully involved in the life of his child, or step-parent adoptions, like the present, where Parent B, whilst not consenting, has played no active parental role for some years.

62. The reason why context is important is that, in each case, it is necessary to evaluate the proportionality of the intervention in family life that is being proposed. For the child, and for the child's welfare throughout his life, there will be a qualitative difference between adoption by strangers, with no continuing contact or legal relationship with any member of the birth family, on the one hand, and an adoption order which simply reflects in legal terms the reality in which the child's family life and relationships have been conducted for some significant time. In ECHR terms, no adoption order will be justified in terms of its interference with family life rights unless it is 'necessary' and 'proportionate', but in assessing those factors the degree to which there is an interference will be relevant. In short, in the present case, the loss to A, and the loss to her father, of his legal status as her father who holds parental responsibility for her, interferes with their respective family life rights to a relatively modest degree. In contrast, if the social services were to intervene and seek to remove her from the care of her mother and Mr TMI [the step-parent] by compulsory order to place her for adoption with strangers, the degree of interference would be extreme.

63. The judge in the present case was correct to approach the interpretation of 'requires' in s 52(1)(b) by reference to the 'connotation of imperative' that it has . . . But what is 'required' varies from case to case and is firmly grounded, by the very words of s 52(1)(b), upon an evaluation of the child's welfare throughout his life. The use of the phrase 'connotation of imperative' in *Re P* does not mean (see *Re P* paragraph 127) that there is some enhanced welfare test to be applied in cases of adoption . . .

67. It follows that I do not agree that the judge was constrained by the words of the statute, as he considered that he was, to refuse to dispense with consent. I also consider that his decision on ordinary welfare terms was wrong. The finding that, as a matter of day to day existence, A's family life would continue in much the same way and that there were other routes by which Mr TMI might gain parental responsibility, failed to engage with the benefit that adoption would bring by marrying up the legal relationships with the 'de facto' relationships as they had become established within this small family unit. In almost every way Mr TMI had become A's and D's father. The making of an adoption order would confirm that status as a matter of law.

13.6.4 ADOPTION BY A SOLE NATURAL PARENT

Many of the concerns regarding step-parent adoption apply with added force in the case of an adoption by a sole natural parent. The only real remaining advantage of adopting one's own child, from the perspective of the adopting parent, is that it confers additional security on a main carer by permanently terminating the parental responsibility of the non-adopting parent. It is thus an effective means of ensuring the non-resident parent can play no future role in the child's upbringing.[209] The advantages of such an order from the child's perspective are more difficult to discern. Again, however, there will be some cases in which such an order is deemed to be in the child's best interests. In *Re B (A Minor) (Adoption: Natural Parent)*, the House of Lords controversially allowed an adoption order in favour of the child's natural father to stand. The facts of the case were relatively unusual in that the mother, having voluntarily relinquished the child at birth, wanted nothing more to do with her. The father discovered the child's existence by chance and immediately assumed responsibility for her care. The mother did not oppose his application to adopt.

Re B (A Minor) (Adoption: Natural Parent) **[2001] UKHL 70**

LORD NICHOLLS:

5. The father is seeking an adoption order primarily because he is anxious to secure A's future in his sole care. He feels insecure, and believes he will feel more secure knowing that the mother's parental responsibility for A has been removed. This can only be achieved by an adoption order. The mother has said repeatedly she does not wish to play any part in A's life. But the father is concerned that, without an adoption order, it will remain possible in future years for the mother to pose a threat to A's continued placement with him. He is concerned that the mother may marry and, with her new husband, ask to have A to live with her. The court might look favourably upon such an application. His vulnerability to an attempt by the mother to reclaim A is something which has caused him great anxiety. He is adamant in his wish for an adoption order, although whatever order is made will not affect the strength of his commitment to A. He does not, in principle, exclude the possibility of future contact by the mother with A, provided the placement with him is secure . . .

6. In his report to the court the Official Solicitor, acting as A's guardian, opposed the application. The sole consequence of an adoption order would be to end the mother's relationship with A. This was not an order which could be said to safeguard and promote A's welfare. There was nothing in the history of the case to suggest that the mother would be likely to seek to disrupt the security of A's placement with her father. But any attempt by her to do so would not necessarily be to A's disadvantage . . .

25. An adoption order in favour of a single natural parent alone will . . . have the effect of permanently extinguishing any parental responsibility of the other natural parent . . . This will afford the adoptive parent a measure of additional security. But it is important here to keep in mind the wide range of powers the court now has under the Children Act 1989 to restrict the possibility of inappropriate intervention in the child's life by the other natural parent. Adoption is not intended to be used simply as the means by which to protect the child's life with one natural parent against inappropriate intervention by the other natural parent.

[209] Similar effects can be achieved in other ways: see 10.6.1.

26. Another consequence adoption has in this type of case is that after adoption the child will be treated in law as if she had been born to her adoptive parent in wedlock . . . The significance of this benefit today should not be overstated. The social and legal status of children born outside marriage has changed greatly in recent years. The social stigma and legal disabilities attendant upon 'illegitimacy' have now largely gone. . . .

27. Having regard to all these matters, the circumstances in which it will be in the best interests of a child to make an adoption order in favour of one natural parent alone, thereby, in Hale LJ's words, taking away one half of the child's legal family, are likely to be exceptional. Bracewell J [at first instance] regarded the circumstances of the present case as exceptional. She said so. The father's case was that the mother's continuing status as a parent with parental responsibility for A would perpetuate insecurity for him and that this would potentially affect A's stability. The judge accepted this . . . Given the mother's attitude to A from the moment of A's birth, and her consent, adoption by the father was in A's best interests. Adoption was in A's best interests even though this would have the consequence of excluding the mother.

28. In my view, on the evidence before her this conclusion was open to Bracewell J . . . That an adoption order as sought by A's father will safeguard and promote A's welfare is a wholly tenable view. A residence order, together with an appropriate prohibited steps order, may not suffice to allay the father's genuine anxieties.

The decision met with strong criticism. It is certainly questionable whether rendering the child 'legally motherless', given the strong negative message of rejection this sends out, was in the child's interests, particularly when alternative orders were available under the CA 1989 to address the father's insecurity.[210] On a more general level, the case raises interesting questions as to whether parents (both mothers and fathers) should be able to reject parenthood by irrevocably terminating their 'very parenthood' through adoption or whether there should be a less drastic mechanism for removing parental responsibility from absent or uninterested parents which does not have the same distorting effect on the child's core familial relationships.[211]

13.7 OPEN ADOPTION

In order to protect the new relationship between the adoptive parents and the child, adoption was traditionally shrouded in secrecy with very careful restrictions in place to prevent children discovering the truth about their adopted status or birth parents discovering the whereabouts of the new adoptive family. Previously, around 80 per cent of people applying for an adoption order asked to be identified only by a serial number (not their name),[212] and in 2016 the court rules were changed to make this automatic in every case.[213] However, the fact that many adopted children are now older with strong emotional ties to their birth families, alongside emerging evidence as to the strong need felt by adopted adults to seek information about their biological parents, has severely challenged the closed nature of adoption. In the past few years, a more open concept of adoption has become entrenched within social work practice.[214] However, the law has been more reluctant to embrace this change—a

210 Harris-Short (2002). 211 Ibid. See also 10.6.1. 212 E.g. DCA (2006a), 19.

213 Family Procedure Rules 2010, r 14.2, as amended by the Family Procedure (Amendment No 3) Rules 2016.

214 On the role of Art 8 ECHR in this area, see Hansen (2019).

change which fundamentally challenges the orthodox 'legal transplant' model of adoption remaining entrenched within the legislation.

Openness can take many forms. At one end of the scale, it can simply involve providing children with more detailed information about their birth parents and the circumstances surrounding their adoption. At the other end of the scale, it can involve regular direct contact between the child and members of the birth family. Between these extremes, openness can involve infrequent visits, indirect contact such as telephone calls and letters, and fairly frequent exchange of information between the adoptive parents and the birth family in the form of photographs, reports on the child's progress, and news about the birth family. Contact between the child and the birth mother, maternal grandparents, and siblings is common, but rarely involves the father and the wider paternal family.[215]

13.7.1 THE RIGHT TO INFORMATION

Although much of the debate on open adoption now focuses on post-adoption contact, an important aspect of openness is the provision of information about the child's genealogical background and the circumstances surrounding the adoption. In some cases, this will be sufficient to meet concerns about the child's identity and help assuage any feelings of confusion or loss. Under the ACA 2002, an adopted person has the right, upon reaching the age of 18, to apply through an adoption agency for information which will allow them to obtain a certified copy of the birth record.[216] For people adopted before the ACA 2002 came into force, this information can be obtained directly from the Registrar General. Disclosure of this information can only be withheld in exceptional circumstances by order of the High Court.[217] An adopted person upon reaching the age of 18 also has the right to a copy of the adoption order and any prescribed information which had to be disclosed to the adopters.[218] The Registrar General must also maintain an adoption contact register. Part 1 of the register enables adopted persons over the age of 18 to record whether they would like to make contact with any of their birth relatives. Part II of the register contains information entered by birth relatives as to whether they wish to make contact with the adopted child. Where there is a 'match' between the two parts of the register, the Registrar General will notify the adopted person.[219]

The statutory requirements dealing with the recording, keeping, and disclosure of wider information about a child's adoption are contained within ss 56–65 of the ACA 2002. The information which an adoption agency must keep in relation to an adoption is prescribed by regulations and referred to as 'section 56 information'. It includes:

- the child's case record (includes the child's permanence report, a written record of the adoption panel proceedings, a record of the agency's decision on placement, any consents);
- any information that has been supplied by a natural parent or relative or other significant person in the adopted person's life, with the intention that the adopted person may, should he wish to, be given that information;
- any information supplied by the adoptive parents or other persons which is relevant to matters arising after the making of the adoption order;

[215] Neil (2000), 314. [216] S 60(2). [217] S 60(3). [218] S 60(2)(b) and (4).
[219] Adopted Children and Adoption Contact Registers Regulations 2005, SI 2005/924, reg 8.

- any information the adopted person has requested should be kept;
- any information given to the adoption agency in respect of an adopted person by the Registrar General (information that would enable an adopted person to obtain a certified copy of the record of his birth);
- any information disclosed to the adoption agency about an entry relating to the adopted person on the Adoption Contact Register.[220]

The adoption agency has discretion not to keep information supplied by a member of the birth family or the adoptive parents if satisfied that it would be prejudicial to the adopted person's welfare or it would not be reasonably practicable.[221] Any s 56 information which is 'identifying information'—information which directly identifies a person or, whether taken alone or in conjunction with other information, could lead to an individual being identified—is referred to as 'protected information'.[222] Where an agreement is in place permitting disclosure, protected information may be disclosed.[223] Otherwise, an application must be made to the adoption agency which has a wide discretion as to whether disclosure should take place. There are no restrictions as to who can apply but the adoption agency does not have to proceed with an application if it does not consider it appropriate to do so.[224] If it does consider it appropriate to proceed, it must take all reasonable steps to obtain the views of any affected person.[225] Where the protected information is about a person who is at the time of the application a child, the agency must take all reasonable steps to ascertain the views of the child's parent or guardian and, having regard to the child's age and understanding, the views of the child.[226] It is then within the discretion of the agency whether or not it considers it appropriate to disclose. In exercising this discretion, the adoption agency is directed to consider the welfare of the adopted person and the views of any person the information is about.[227] Where the information is about an adopted child who has not yet attained the age of 18, the child's welfare must be the agency's paramount consideration.[228] If the information is about any other child, the agency 'must have particular regard to the child's welfare'.[229] In the case of information which is not protected information, the adoption agency simply has a broad discretion whether or not to disclose.[230] In exercising its discretion under these provisions, the adoption agency is entitled to adopt a general policy on disclosure but must consider each individual case on its merits.[231]

13.7.2 THE CHILD'S RIGHT TO KNOW?

Whilst the adoption agency has a broad discretion to make disclosure of both identifying and non-identifying information to an adopted person, the legislation does not provide a *right* for the *child* to receive any information about the birth parents or the circumstances surrounding the adoption. It is therefore misleading to talk about the child's *right* to information in this context. This contrasts sharply with other areas of the law where the courts

220 Disclosure of Adoption Information (Post-Commencement Adoptions) Regulations 2005, SI 2005/888, reg 4.

221 Ibid, reg 4(4).

222 ACA 2002, s 57.

223 S 57(5). See also Disclosure of Adoption Information (Post-Commencement Adoptions) Regulations 2005, SI 2005/888, reg 11 (as amended).

224 ACA 2002, ss 61(2) and 62(2).

225 Ss 61(3) and 62(4).

226 S 62(3).

227 Ss 61(5) and 62(7).

228 S 62(6)(a).

229 S 62(6)(b).

230 S 58.

231 See *Gunn-Russo v Nugent Care Society and Secretary of State for Health* [2001] EWHC 566 (decided under the AA 1976).

have moved towards accepting the child's *right* to know the truth about parentage.[232] Despite Parliament's reticence to enshrine such a right in the legislation, the National Minimum Standards on Adoption are clearly premised on the assumption that the adoptive parents will be open about the adoption and will be willing and able to share information with the child about the birth family and the circumstances surrounding the adoption when the child reaches an appropriate age.[233] Detailed guidance is provided on the importance of life story work.

13.7.3 POST-ADOPTION CONTACT

The most effective way of informing children about their birth family is through direct or indirect contact.

13.7.3.a The empirical evidence on post-adoption contact

Based on the work of the child psychiatrist John Bowlby, many child-care professionals working in the 1970s considered that to consolidate the child within the new adoptive family existing attachments to the birth family must be severed.

B. Lindley, 'Open Adoption—Is the Door Ajar?', (1997) 9 Child and Family Law Quarterly 115, 117–18

> Attachment theory was cited by some clinicians and social work practitioners as justification for the notion of closed, secretive adoption. Bowlby's work on attachment and the vital importance of the early relationship with one care-giver, normally the mother, was used to affirm the view that as far as adoption was concerned the child needed an exclusive environment free from interference from the birth family. Although he modified his theory later in his life, conceding that the child could have multiple attachment figures, albeit in some form of hierarchy, Bowlby's original thesis still remains very influential. This is partly due to the work of Goldstein, Freud and Solnit who asserted that, from their *clinical* experience in the UK and the USA, when children were apart from a parent, there should be a cessation of contact with that parent, otherwise the child would fail to bond with the new parent/carer and would also experience confusion and divided loyalties. They applied this theory both to children placed with new carers/families and to children whose parents were separated or divorced . . . Although their 'clean break' view was based on clinical rather than research evidence, it had a very strong influence on child care professionals at the time when the 'permanence' movement was developing during the 1970s and 1980s. Indeed, in spite of the recent practice development of greater openness, particularly for older children adopted from the care system, this view remains very influential today.

A child's ability to form multiple attachments strongly undermines the view that birth families must be totally excluded from the child's life if the child is to bond successfully with the adoptive family. Indeed, research suggests that continuing contact with the birth family has

[232] See *Re H (A Minor) (Blood Tests: Parental Rights)* [1997] Fam 89, 107 and discussion at 9.3.3.b.
[233] DFE (2014b), Standard 2, Promoting a Positive Identity, Potential and Valuing Diversity.

no affect on the child's sense of belonging with the adoptive parents and can even positively promote the child's integration into the new family, as well as their sense of self.[234] Lindley continues:

Subsequent studies of children moving to new families suggest that, rather than preventing children from settling, openness can *help* the child settle in the new family, providing the adults are not hostile to each other, or the idea. Fratter's study found that contact helped to provide continuity, a positive identity and an understanding for the child of the circumstances of the adoption. It enabled the child to feel free to attach to the new family whilst retaining a link with their birth family. Indeed, she concludes when commenting on the impact of contact, that 'contact was not thought to have adversely affected the attachment of any of the children placed under seven years of age, and had not given rise to divided loyalties, even where there had been fortnightly face-to-face contact'. However, she adds a qualification to this, namely that the attitude of the parents and parent figures to one another is crucial in freeing children from guilt and divided loyalties.

Other studies have found that the stability of the placements of older children was not threatened by maintaining links with their families of origin. They also show that older children may not be willing to move to a new family if contact with their original families is to be severed, although they do not always feel able to voice their opinion . . .

Moreover, Hill et al found that when earlier attachments are disregarded, the feelings do not go away but are simply driven underground. Triseliotis et al also report some evidence which suggests that older children who are pressurised to abandon meaningful relationships with members of the birth family may find it difficult to attach themselves to the new family . . .

Direct knowledge of the birth parents can also help the child develop a secure and positive identity, avoiding what has been termed in the literature 'genealogical bewilderment'.[235] Ryburn identifies a number of further important benefits of post-adoption contact, perhaps most obviously these include benefits for both the birth parents and the child.

M. Ryburn, 'In Whose Best Interests?—Post-Adoption Contact with the Birth Family', (1998) 10 *Child and Family Law Quarterly* 53, 59–61

Advantages of contact for birth parents

Contact for birth parents with their children can make a significant difference. The studies indicate in particular that contact helps parents to resolve the grief of their loss, and to move on in their lives, and there is a well-established principle here. It is extremely difficult to manage grief when it has no clear focus . . . This, in reality, is the living death of a child . . .

The studies also indicate that one of the overwhelming needs of birth parents without contact is for reassurance that their child is well and happy, and contact is able, in general, to offer this reassurance. In some instances just the open exchange of information may be sufficient . . . Perhaps one of the most striking things to emerge from the studies is how concerned birth parents are that contact should not be a source of distress or disruption in the life of their child.

[234] House of Lords Select Committee on the Children and Families Act 2014 (2022), para 85.
[235] Smith (2004), 330. See also 9.4.4.a.

Advantages of contact for children

The research studies suggest that with indirect contact children's information needs begin to be met, but that with direct contact their questions are more likely to be met at a level that is satisfying. One of the key advantages of any contact is that facts can more readily replace speculation and fantasy. Children are also helped through contact to come to terms with difficult aspects of their past lives—aspects that might otherwise be a source of difficulty for them . . .

Children also appear to gain a sense of reassurance as a consequence of contact, particularly direct contact, with their birth relatives. In particular, it gives them a clear message that the placement is supported by their original family since otherwise they would not be visiting, and it is a visible symbol that their adoptive parents feel positively about their original family or contact would not be permitted. The largest study of adoption and permanent foster care placements ever undertaken in the UK . . . also found that birth family contact was the single factor which could be identified as enhancing the stability of placements. Finally, contact, in particular direct contact, appears to strengthen children's sense of attachment to their adoptive parents . . .

Perhaps more surprisingly, Ryburn also identifies a number of advantages for the adoptive parents:

Effects of secrecy on adopters

Traditionally, adopters have been seen as those with the least to gain through post-adoption contact and certainly it was agencies claiming to represent the voice of adopters who were instrumental in introducing much greater secrecy . . . Without adequate information at the time of placement, and a way of accessing additional and up-to-date information as it is needed, adopters may feel hampered in the task of parenting a child born to someone else . . .

Advantages of contact for adopters

The studies indicate that adopters may gain significantly through contact. Adopters with continuing contact following adoption are generally comfortable with it. It would appear that contact can enhance children's attachments to their adopters, it provides a ready source of information and it appears to lead to more positive feelings towards birth relatives. This, in turn, is likely to aid children in the acquisition of positive identity.

The greatest gain to be attributed to contact—in this case direct contact—is a sense of security and permanence in the parenting role.

Although some researchers are more cautious than Ryburn in their reading of the empirical evidence,[236] most generally agree that the impact of post-adoption contact on adoption outcomes is fairly negligible: post-adoption contact with the birth family is not generally harmful to the child but neither is its absence.[237] There is little evidence that post-adoption contact leads to significantly better outcomes.[238]

[236] See, e.g., Quinton and Selwyn (1998) and (2006).

[237] Neil (2009). For a review of the research evidence, see Neil et al (2012). See also Quinton and Selwyn (2006), 473. For an excellent summary, see Smith (2005), 315–17 and Logan and Smith (2005), 6–11.

[238] Neil (2009).

13.7.3.b Post-adoption contact in the courts

Practice within the social work profession has in many ways moved ahead of the empirical evidence. The importance of being open about adoption and the birth family, including promoting contact where appropriate, is emphasized at every stage of the process. There are consequently very few adoptions where there is no provision for some form of direct or indirect contact between the adopters and the birth family with 'letter-box' contact the most usual.[239] Indeed, unless prospective adopters are willing to facilitate openness their suitability to adopt is likely to be questioned. This positive attitude contrasts sharply with the attitude of the courts which have, in the past, been extremely reluctant to make any kind of formal provision for post-adoption contact—this reluctance stemming, it would seem, from their difficulty in reconciling a move towards greater openness with the traditional legal understanding of adoption.[240] The guiding principles to be applied on an application for post-adoption contact prior to the implementation of the ACA 2002 were established by the House of Lords in *Re C (A Minor) (Adoption Order: Conditions)*.[241] The House of Lords held that it would only be in exceptional cases that a contact order would be imposed on the adoptive parents.

The ACA 2002 was arguably intended to mark a shift away from this very cautious approach towards post-adoption contact. The duty on the court to consider contact at the placement stage suggested more birth parents were likely to retain contact throughout this crucial period which, in turn, would strengthen their case for post-adoption contact.[242] Moreover, regardless of whether or not the parent has made an application to the court, the court is under a mandatory duty to consider the proposals as to post-adoption contact when deciding whether or not to make the adoption order.[243] The court should be further prompted towards making some provision for contact by the welfare checklist which directs the court's attention to the child's existing relationships with members of the birth family, the value of those relationships continuing, and the wishes and feelings of the child's relatives.[244] The statutory regime governing post-adoption contact was, however, amended by the CFA 2014 to introduce a new statutory provision: s 51A. As originally implemented, the court retained the right to make a s 8 CA 1989 order dealing with post-adoption contact alongside an adoption order.[245] This created the odd situation whereby the adoption order was governed by s 1(4) of the ACA 2002 whilst post-adoption contact was governed by s 1(3) of the CA 1989.[246] Section 51A means that the statutory regime is rationalized and post-adoption contact is governed exclusively under the ACA 2002 (the use of s 8 orders being specifically precluded).[247] However, in a significant change, whilst it had been held under the previous law that birth parents would be entitled to apply as of right for a contact order to be heard together with the adoption application at the final hearing,[248] s 51A imposes a leave requirement on the birth family applying for a contact order even before the final adoption order has been made. The criteria to be applied in determining leave are drawn from s 10(9) but include any representations made by the adoptive parents.[249] Section 51A also allows the court to order 'no contact' to deal with the growing phenomenon of birth families making

[239] Masson (2000); Neil et al (2012), 4.

[240] See, e.g., *Re C (A Minor) (Adoption Order: Condition)* [1986] 1 FLR 315 (CA) and *Re V (A Minor) (Adoption: Consent)* [1987] Fam 57 (CA), 68.

[241] [1989] AC 1 (HL). [242] S 26.

[243] S 46(6). It is good practice for the judge to consider arrangements for contact as a separate issue within the adoption decision: *Re L (A Child: Step-Parent Adoption)* [2021] EWCA Civ 801, [63] and [68].

[244] S 1(4)(f) and (6). [245] S 46(5). [246] ACA 2002, s 26(5) (repealed). [247] S 51A(8).

[248] ACA 2002, s 46. See *X and Y v A Local Authority (Adoption: Procedure)* [2009] EWHC 47, [18]–[19].

[249] S 51A(5).

unauthorized contact with adopted children (and sometimes vice versa) via social media.[250] Adoptive parents can apply for such an order as of right. Consequently, whilst the legislature back in 2002 may have intended a more positive approach to post-adoption contact, the recent amendments have a distinctly more restrictive tone.[251] It will clearly now be much harder for the birth parents to be heard on the issue of post-adoption contact, particularly if the very restrictive approach to granting leave to birth parents post-adoption which prevailed under the previous law is adopted at the final hearing stage.[252]

It is thus clear that whatever the original intentions may have been, the statutory regime for post-adoption contact is very unlikely to bring about any fundamental change in the courts' approach. The view of the higher family judiciary has vacillated somewhat following implementation of the ACA 2002, but there is no evidence that there has been any shift in the general practice of the courts. Comments made by Wall LJ immediately prior to the implementation of the ACA 2002 appeared to make clear that the courts' approach to post-adoption contact would remain unchanged:

Re R (Adoption: Contact) **[2005] EWCA Civ 1128**

WALL LJ:

48. We were shown section 1 of the new Act, which is due in force later this year, which demonstrates the clear change of thinking there has been since 1976, when the Act was initially enacted, and which demonstrates that the court now will need to take into account and consider the relationship the child had with members of the natural family, and the likelihood of that relationship continuing and the value of the relationship to the child.

49. So contact is more common, but nonetheless the jurisprudence I think is clear. The imposition on prospective adopters of orders for contact with which they are not in agreement is extremely, and remains extremely, unusual.

However, just two years later in *Re P (Children) (Adoption: Parental Consent)*, Wall LJ appeared to signal a cautious but important potential change in approach, holding that the courts now have a much more central role to play in securing post-adoption contact where appropriate.[253]

Re P (Adoption: Parental Consent) **[2008] EWCA Civ 535**

WALL LJ:

141. We approach this part of our judgment with caution, as we are conscious that these are early days, and the manner in which adoption agencies apply the terms of the 2002 Act will need to be worked out in practice over time . . .

250 S 51A(2)(b).

251 These reforms were opposed by some of the most experienced researchers in the field. See Neil et al (2012), 12–13.

252 See *Re S (Contact: Application by Sibling)* [1999] Fam 283; *X and Y v A Local Authority* [2009] EWHC 47.

253 See also the comments of Baroness Hale regarding post-adoption contact in *Down Lisburn Health and Social Services Trust v H* [2006] UKHL 36, [6]–[8].

142. Historically, post adoption contact between children and their birth parents has been perceived as highly exceptional . . .

147. All this, in our judgment, now falls to be revisited under section 26 and 27 of the 2002 Act, given in particular the terms of sections 1(4)(f), 1(6) and (7) and 46(6). In our judgment, the judge in the instant case was plainly right to make a contact order under section 26 of the 2002 Act, and in our judgment the question of contact between [the children], and between the children and their parents, should henceforth be a matter for the court, not for the local authority, or the local authority in agreement with prospective adopters . . .

148. . . . The making of the placement orders means, of course, that contact under the 1989 Act is no longer possible, but orders under sections 26 and 27 are not only possible but, in our judgment, necessary.

149. Furthermore, when the time comes for [the children] to be finally placed, it will be the court which will have to make the necessary orders – either for adoption, or for revocation of the placement orders if the children are not to be adopted. At that point, in our judgment, as the facts of this case currently stand, it will be for the court, before making an adoption order, to decide, in accordance with section 46(6) of the 2002 Act, what ongoing contact [the children] should have with each other – not for their prospective adopters to do so. The same principle will apply if the children are to be placed in long-term foster care.

150. The effect of the placement order is substantially to disempower [the children's] parents – see section 25(4) of the 2002 Act. In our judgment, as matters currently stand, the existence of the placement orders should not be an inhibition on the ability of [the mother] in particular to apply to the court to determine questions of contact – and in particular the question of contact between D and S. Indeed, it seems to us highly likely that the placement of the children with adopters or foster carers who are unwilling, in particular, to facilitate contact between [the children] would provide a proper basis for leave to be granted to [the mother] under section 24(2) of the 2002 Act (leave to make an application to apply for an order to revoke the placement order) or for leave to apply to oppose the making of an adoption order under section 47(5) of the 2002 Act.

151. On the facts of this case, there is a universal recognition that the relationship between [the children] needs to be preserved. It is on this basis that the local authority / adoption agency is seeking the placement of the children. In our judgment, this means that the question of contact between the two children is not a matter for agreement between the local authority/adoption agency and the adopters: it is a matter which, ultimately, is for the court. It is the court which will have to make adoption orders or orders revoking the placement orders, and in our judgment it is the court which has the responsibility to make orders for contact if they are required in the interests of the two children . . .

153. . . . [I]t is not, in our judgment, a proper exercise of the judicial powers given to the court under the 2002 Act to leave contact between the children themselves, or between the children and their natural parents to the discretion of the local authority and/or the prospective carers of [the children], be they adoptive parents or foster carers. It is the court which must make the necessary decisions if contact between the siblings is in dispute, or if it is argued that it should cease for any reason.

154. We do not know if our views on contact on the facts of this particular case presage a more general sea change in post adoption contact overall. It seems to us, however, that the stakes in the present case are sufficiently high to make it appropriate for the court to retain control over the question of the children's welfare throughout their respective lives under sections 1, 26, 27 and 46(6) of the 2002 Act; and, if necessary, to make orders for contact post adoption in accordance with section 26 of the 2002 Act, under section 8 of the 1989 Act. This is what Parliament has enacted. In section 46(6) of the 2002 Act Parliament has specifically directed the court to consider post adoption contact, and in section 26(5)

Parliament has specifically envisaged an application for contact being heard at the same time as an adoption order is applied for. All this leads us to the view that the 2002 Act envisages the court exercising its powers to make contact orders post adoption, where such orders are in the interests of the child concerned.

A 'sea change' did not materialize. Indeed, in *Oxfordshire County Council v X*, Lord Neuberger MR held that it remains 'extremely unusual' to make a contact order against the wishes of the adoptive parents. He went on to distinguish *Re P*, holding that Wall LJ's comments were inapplicable to a case where the application for contact is made after an adoption order has already been made—the correct approach to such cases remains that expressed in *Re R*.[254] The issue in *Oxfordshire* was whether the adoptive parents should be ordered to provide the birth parents with an annual photo of the child. Lord Neuberger's judgment is expressed in forceful terms:

Oxfordshire County Council v X [2010] EWCA Civ 581

LORD NEUBERGER MR:

36. It is a strong thing to impose on adoptive parents, it is "extremely unusual" to impose on adoptive parents, some obligation which they are unwilling voluntarily to assume, certainly where, as here, the adoption order has already been made. Was there a proper basis for taking that extremely unusual step? In our judgment there was not. The judge found that the adoptive parents were genuine when they expressed their concerns, so what was the justification for imposing on them something they conscientiously and reasonably objected to, particularly when, as we have seen, they say that they have not ruled out the possibility of letting the natural parents have photographs in the future? As we have said, they are not to be saddled with an order merely because a judge takes a different view. The adoptive parents are J's parents; the natural parents are not. The adoptive parents are the only people with parental responsibility for J. Why, unless the circumstances are unusual, indeed extremely unusual – and here, in our judgment, they are neither – should that responsibility be usurped by the court? We can see no good reason either on the facts or in law. On the contrary, there is much force in the point they make, that they wish their status as J's parents to be respected and seen to be inviolable – not for themselves but in order, as they see it, to give J the very best chance for the adoption to be successful.

The position prior to the introduction of s 51A in 2014 was therefore clear. However, a question arose as to what effect, if any, s 51A would have on the legal approach. The matter was considered in detail in *Re B (Post-Adoption Contact)*, where the parents of a young child were prevented from providing long-term care due to extensive limitations in their intellectual functioning. The child was placed for adoption, but the question was what, if any, contact should be ordered between the child and the birth parents.

254 *Oxfordshire County Council v X* [2010] EWCA Civ 581, [14] and [9]; *Re B (A Child: Post-Adoption Contact)* [2019] EWCA Civ 29, [18]. For criticism of *Oxfordshire*, see Hughes and Sloan (2011), and on *Re B*, see George (2019b).

Re B (Post-Adoption Contact) [2019] EWCA Civ 29

SIR ANDREW McFARLANE P:

54. Although s 51A has introduced a bespoke statutory regime for the regulation of post-adoption contact following placement for adoption by an adoption agency, there is nothing to be found in the wording of s 51A or of s 51B which indicates any variation in the approach to be taken to the imposition of an order for contact upon adopters who are unwilling to accept it. Indeed, . . . Parliament's intention in enacting s 51A was aimed at enhancing the position of adopters rather than the contrary. . . .

59. ACA 2002, s 51A has been brought into force at a time when there is research and debate amongst social work and adoption professionals which may be moving towards the concept of greater 'openness' in terms of post-adoption contact arrangements, both between an adopted child and natural parents and, more particularly, between siblings. . . . But any development or change from previous practice and expectations as to post-adoption contact that may arise from these current initiatives will be a matter that may be reflected in welfare decisions that are made by adopters, or by a court, on a case by case basis . . .

61. Post-adoption contact is an important issue which should be given full consideration in every case (ACA 2002, s 46(6)). Whilst there may not have been a change in the law insofar as the imposition of a contact regime against the wishes of prospective adopters is concerned, there is now a joined-up regime contained within the ACA 2002 for the consideration of contact . . . Further, and in contrast to the situation prior to 2014 . . ., issues under both s 26 and s 51A of the ACA 2002 will be determined by applying the bespoke adoption welfare provisions in ACA 2002, s 1, where the focus is not just upon the welfare of the subject of the application during childhood but throughout their life.

62. A placement for adoption hearing has the potential for having an important influence upon the development of any subsequent long-term contact arrangements. As required by ACA 2002, s 27(4), the court must consider the issue of contact and any plans for contact before making a placement for adoption order. . . . At the placement order stage courts should therefore be careful to stress that, if there is any future issue as to contact, the law, as stated in *Re R*, will apply and, save for there being extremely unusual circumstances, no order will be made to compel adopters to accept contact arrangements with which they do not agree.

13.7.3.c Should there be stronger intervention by the courts?

As McFarlane P's judgment in *Re B* highlights, research is raising questions about the approach to post-adoption contact, though any change of practice remains limited at this stage. However, thinking about the *court's* approach (rather than social work practice), questions remain about why the approach to post-adoption contact should be any different from contact disputes in other private law contexts, given that the court's welfare jurisdiction is engaged by s 51A.[255] Commentators have argued that many of the courts' objections towards the making of formal orders have been somewhat overstated, particularly where the parties are in agreement. It is recognized that flexibility is crucial in dealing with post-adoption contact and that many adoptive parents are resistant to court orders—as opposed to proceeding by way of voluntary agreement—because of their rigidity and the fact that they

[255] George (2019b), 360.

take control out of the hands of the adoptive parents.[256] However, Lowe and Murch argue that the inflexibility of such orders can be exaggerated, with the court able to specify with no greater particularity that there should be 'reasonable contact', thereby leaving it to the adoptive parents to determine exactly what constitutes 'reasonable contact' in the particular circumstances of the case.[257] Moreover, it is pointed out that there are certain advantages to any voluntary agreement between the adoptive parents and the birth family being underpinned by the security of a contact order.[258] Without a court order, the adopters can simply walk away from any earlier agreement, a significant possibility if their agreement was only given reluctantly in exchange for the birth parents' consent to the adoption.[259]

Other leading commentators have, however, questioned whether stronger legal intervention is the answer. Indeed, commentators have suggested that the courts are ill-equipped to deal effectively with disputes over post-adoption contact and a more robust legal response is therefore likely to be wholly ineffective, even counterproductive. Smith argues that whilst the law can provide an overarching framework for the resolution of such disputes, the actual job of facilitating post-adoption contact is best left to social welfare professionals working to promote greater trust and cooperation between the parties.[260]

C. Smith, 'Trust v Law: Promoting and Safeguarding Post-Adoption Contact', (2005) 27 *Journal of Social Welfare and Family Law* 315, 326, 329

Law can require, regulate and enforce post-adoption contact. However, it cannot influence the qualitative experience of relationships and social interaction that enable adults to co-operate in the best interests of children. Additionally, while law can intervene in contact disputes at particular points in time, it lacks the capacity to continuously negotiate and respond to developing needs as these unfold. Law acts to reduce uncertainty but in so doing it constrains flexibility and the necessary use of discretion. Even while law may limit itself to ordering 'reasonable' contact, it reduces scope for the exercise of personal responsibility and moral competence on which mutually beneficial contact relies. As with post-divorce and post-separation contact disputes, law's intervention is unlikely to resolve conflicts unless underlying issues of trust are addressed. Law may enforce contact, but it cannot ensure beneficial experiences for those involved—particularly for children . . .

However, there are ways of enhancing the willingness and ability of adopters to support contact without recourse to legal regulation. Preparation of prospective adopters is crucial to helping them to understand the value of contact for children. The use of research which reports on adoptive parents' experience of beneficial contact can ameliorate fears and increase understanding, as can the inclusion of adopters and birth relatives preparation sessions. An important part of this work is to encourage adopters' confidence about making decisions in their child's best interests. Agencies should avoid negative evaluations of prospective adopters who want the sense of control and ownership over their children that adoption conveys. There is evidence that this legal construction of (adoptive) parenthood provides a secure base, which enables adoptive parents to be generous about contact arrangements . . .

The argument that formal intervention of the courts is unnecessary and unhelpful where the parties are in agreement as to the principle of contact and are able to cooperate in making

[256] Harris-Short (2001), 417–18. [257] Ibid. [258] Ibid.
[259] Ibid. [260] See also Masson (2000).

and, where necessary, changing the arrangements in the interests of the child, is persuasive. However, in the absence of consensus the law's withdrawal is more problematic. Adoptive parents are not always reasonable and cannot always be trusted to act in the child's best interests. Where mediatory techniques fail to achieve cooperation, unless the adoptive parents are to be the final arbiter of the child's welfare, legal intervention may well be necessary to uphold and enforce certain normative standards.

13.8 ALTERNATIVES TO ADOPTION: SPECIAL GUARDIANSHIP

Although the Labour Government was strongly committed to adoption as the preferred option for children in care, it recognized that there would remain some children for whom adoption was not appropriate. The ACA 2002 therefore amended the CA 1989 to make available a new alternative order for securing permanence outside the care system termed special guardianship. The rationale behind this new order is explained in the 2000 White Paper:

Department of Health, *Adoption: A New Approach*, Cm 5017 (London: HMSO, 2000)

5.8 Adoption is not always appropriate for children who cannot return to their birth parents. Some older children do not wish to be legally separated from their birth families. Adoption may not be best for some children being cared for on a permanent basis by members of their wider birth family. Some minority ethnic communities have religious and cultural difficulties with adoption as it is set out in law. Unaccompanied asylum-seeking children may also need secure, permanent homes, but have strong attachments to their families abroad. All these children deserve the same chance as any other to enjoy the benefits of a legally secure, stable permanent placement that promotes a supportive, lifelong relationship with their carers, where the court decides that it is in their best interests . . .

5.10 The Government will legislate to create [a] new option, which could be called 'special guardianship'. It will be used only to provide permanence for those children for whom adoption is not appropriate and where the court decides it is in the best interests of the child or young person. It will:

- give the carer clear responsibility for all aspects of caring for the child or young person, and for taking the decisions to do with their upbringing. The child or young person will no longer be looked after by the council;
- provide a firm foundation on which to build a lifelong permanent relationship between the carer and the child or young person;
- be legally secure;
- preserve the basic link between the child or young person and their birth family;
- be accompanied by proper access to a full range of support services including, where appropriate, financial support.

This approach is now enshrined in ss 14A–F of the CA 1989. An application for a special guardianship order (SGO) may be made by: (i) the child's guardian; (ii) any person in whose favour a child arrangements order (CAO) providing for a child to live with them is in force with respect to the child; (iii) any person with whom the child has lived for at least three years; (iv) any person who has the consent of any person in whose favour a 'live with' CAO is in force; (v) any person who has the consent of the local authority if the child is in care; (vi) any person who has the consent of all persons with parental responsibility for the child; (vii) a local authority foster parent with whom the child has lived for a period of at least one year immediately preceding the application; and (viii) any relative with whom the child has lived for at least one year immediate preceding the application. Anyone else may apply with leave.[261] The court may also make an SGO of its own motion in any family proceedings.[262]

The main effect of the SGO is to confer PR on the special guardian.[263] Special guardianship is, however, intended as a stronger, more permanent measure than a CAO. The special guardian is thus entitled to exercise PR to the exclusion of any other person.[264] Whilst the SGO is in force, the child's surname cannot be changed and the child cannot be removed from the jurisdiction (other than by the special guardian for a period of no more than three months) without leave of the court.[265] Unlike an adoption order, an SGO does not automatically discharge a s 8 order. A CAO providing for contact in favour of the child's parents may therefore continue in force, although the court must consider whether the order should be varied or discharged.[266] Where no CAO is in force, the court must consider whether it should make provision for contact before granting the SGO.[267]

A key feature of special guardianship is that it is intended to confer a much greater sense of security and permanence on the child's carers than that conferred by a CAO, without having the irrevocable consequences of adoption. However, it has been argued that the provisions purporting to confer security on the special guardians are weak and the hurdles for challenging the order set too low.[268] In this regard, it has been noted with concern that parents do not require leave to apply for a CAO with respect to contact when an SGO is in force, thus leaving the special guardians vulnerable to repeated unsettling applications by the birth parents.[269]

The Court of Appeal has provided guidance on the intersection between an order for the child to be adopted or made the subject of an SGO. Wall LJ, giving judgment in *Re S (A Child) (Adoption Order or Special Guardianship Order)*,[270] provided a 'commentary' on the special guardianship provisions.

Wall LJ began with general comments as to when an SGO may be deemed more appropriate than adoption, making it clear that there is no presumption that an SGO is preferable to adoption in any particular category of case.

Re S (A Child) (Adoption Order or Special Guardianship Order) [2007] EWCA Civ 54

WALL LJ:

46. . . . [I]n addition to the fundamental difference in status between adopted children and those subject to special guardianship orders, there are equally fundamental differences

[261] CA 1989, s 14A(3) and (5). [262] Ibid, s 14A(6).
[263] Ibid, s 14C(1)(a). See also *A Local Authority v Y, Z and others* [2006] 2 FLR 41. [264] S 14C(1)(b).
[265] S 14C(3) and (4). [266] S 14B(1)(a). [267] S 14B(1)(b). [268] Parkinson (2003), 161.
[269] *Re S (A Child) (Adoption Order or Special Guardianship Order)* [2007] EWCA Civ 54, [62]–[68]. The case 'remains valuable guidance': *Re W-P (Children)* [2019] EWCA Civ 1120, [37].
[270] [2007] EWCA Civ 54.

between the status and powers of adopters and special guardians. These, we think, need to be borne in mind when the court is applying the welfare checklist under both section 1(3) of the 1989 Act and section 1 of the 2002 Act.

47. Certain other points arise from the statutory scheme:–

(i) The carefully constructed statutory regime (notice to the local authority, leave requirements in certain cases, the role of the court, and the report from the local authority—even where the order is made by the court of its own motion) demonstrates the care which is required before making a special guardianship order, and that it is only appropriate if, in the particular circumstances of the particular case, it is best fitted to meet the needs of the child or children concerned.

(ii) There is nothing in the statutory provisions themselves which limits the making of a special guardianship order or an adoption order to any given set of circumstances. The statute itself is silent on the circumstances in which a special guardianship order is likely to be appropriate, and there is no presumption contained within the statute that a special guardianship order is preferable to an adoption order in any particular category of case. Each case must be decided on its particular facts; and each case will involve the careful application of a judicial discretion to those facts.

(iii) The key question which the court will be obliged to ask itself in every case in which the question of adoption as opposed to special guardianship arises will be: which order will better serve the welfare of this particular child? . . .

49. We would add . . . that, although the no order principle as such is unlikely to be relevant, it is a material feature of the special guardianship regime that it is "less intrusive" than adoption. In other words, it involves a less fundamental interference with existing legal relationships. The court will need to bear Article 8 of ECHR in mind, and to be satisfied that its order is a proportionate response to the problem, having regard to the interference with family life which is involved. In choosing between adoption and special guardianship, in most cases Article 8 is unlikely to add anything to the considerations contained in the respective welfare checklists. Under both statutes the welfare of the child is the court's paramount consideration, and the balancing exercise required by the statutes will be no different to that required by Article 8. However, in some cases, the fact that the welfare objective can be achieved with less disruption of existing family relationships can properly be regarded as helping to tip the balance.[271]

Wall LJ then dealt with the particular issue of whether special guardianship is more appropriate than adoption when the child is to live with a member of the extended family:

50. It is clear from the White Paper that special guardianship was introduced at least in part to deal with the potential problems arising from the use of adoption in the case of placements within the wider family . . .

51. A particular concern is that an adoption order has, as a matter of law, the effect of making the adopted child the child of the adopters for all purposes. Accordingly, where a child is adopted by a member of his wider family, the familial relationships are inevitably changed.

[271] It is reiterated in *Re M-J* [2007] EWCA Civ 56, [17]–[19] that although special guardianship may constitute a more proportionate response to the parents' inability to care for the child, this does not give rise to a presumption in favour of it.

This is frequently referred to as the "skewing" or "distorting" effect of adoption, and is a factor which the court must take into account when considering whether or not to make an adoption order in such a case. This is not least because the checklist under section 1 of the 2002 Act requires it to do so: – see section 1(4)(f) ("the relationship which the child has with relatives."). However, the weight to be given to this factor will inevitably depend on the facts of the particular case, and it will be only one factor in the overall welfare equation.

Finally, Wall LJ confirmed that, as the statute explicitly contemplates the court making an SGO of its own motion, the court has the power to impose an SGO on an unwilling party against their wishes.[272] In determining whether it should do so, Wall LJ held that the court should apply the welfare checklist taking into account the reasons for the opposition and how that impacts on the child's welfare. However, he emphasized that if the court reaches the view that special guardianship will best serve the child's interests, then that is the order it should make.[273]

Commentators were generally sceptical about whether SGOs would successfully bridge the gap between CAOs and adoption.[274] There would appear, however, to be growing enthusiasm for special guardianship. In 2006, there were just 70 SGOs granted but since 2016 the number has been nearly 4,000 each year—and since 2019, more SGOs have been made each year than adoption orders,[275] as Figure 13.1 shows.

Special guardianship has thus positioned itself as an effective alternative to a CAO where children who would otherwise have entered or remained in care are to be cared for within the extended family or by former carers and where the greater security and permanence of adoption is unnecessary[276]—but also as an alternative to adoption itself. Like adoption,

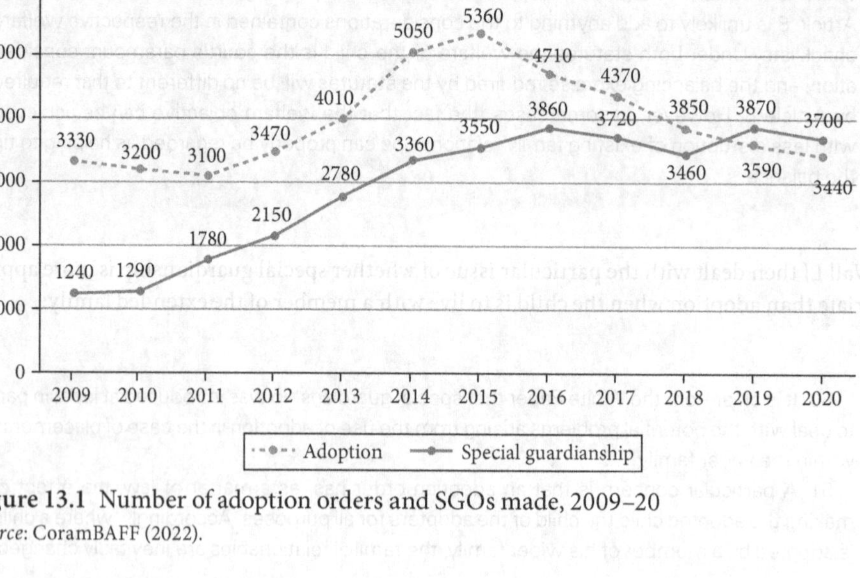

Figure 13.1 Number of adoption orders and SGOs made, 2009–20
Source: CoramBAFF (2022).

[272] [2007] EWCA Civ 54, [73]. [273] Ibid, [73]–[77]. [274] Parkinson (2003), 147.
[275] CoramBAFF (2022). [276] Hall (2008), 373. See Wade, Dixon, and Richards (2009).

special guardianship thus constitutes an increasingly important part of the state's child protection policy. In keeping with this 'public service function', special guardianship is highly regulated and can attract similar support services as fostering and adoption, including financial support—it should not be regarded as a cheap alternative to the child remaining in local authority care.[277] The reality, however, is that many special guardians are exceptionally vulnerable:

House of Lords Select Committee on Adoption Legislation 2nd Report of Session 2012–13, *Adoption: Post-Legislative Scrutiny. Report*, HL Paper 127 (London: TSO, 2013)

235. Special guardians and kinship carers receive little of the training and preparation that is given to prospective adopters; they also receive few of the benefits and financial support arrangements that foster carers receive. Several of our witnesses expressed concern that such carers were struggling to meet the needs of the children in their care. . . . The profile of kinship carers and special guardians is older . . . and poorer than the average adopter. In addition, they often have to manage complex contact arrangements, where the birth parent seeking contact may be their own child . . . A survey by the Kinship Care Alliance found that 68% of respondents who sought help from their local authority did not receive the services they required . . .

237. Children in special guardianship and kinship placements deserve the same support which we recommend for adopted children.[278]

It is important to note that there are also a large number of children who are cared for by wider family members without any kind of formal court order being in place.[279] While such carers can sometimes access discretionary financial support from local authorities,[280] the amounts vary, and there is no access to the dedicated funds available to those who adopt or care for a child under an SGO.

13.9 CONCLUSION

Adoption is a very different way of 'becoming a parent', bringing great rewards, but also many challenges. The law has supported and protected these sometimes fragile family units by treating them in every way as if they were an 'ordinary' natural family. Any legal measures which may mark them out as different, as second-class parents, have been consistently resisted. In many ways, this approach is to be welcomed, recognizing as it does the equal value and importance of social parenting. Adoption can therefore be a liberating force within the law. Freed from biological constraints, it allows a multitude of ways of 'being

[277] Access to financial support for special guardians is 'poorly signposted and take up rate remain low as a result': House of Lords Select Committee on the Children and Families Act 2014 (2022), para 96.

[278] See also Wade et al (2009).

[279] Because these arrangements are not regulated by a court order, the number is difficult to assess, but Wijedasa (2017) notes that there were 180,000 children in the UK reported as living with relatives in the 2011 census, and another estimated 20,000 further children living with friends.

[280] This is part of the local authority's general powers in relation to support children and families: see 12.3.

a family'. Yet adoption is a paradox. Whilst the ACA 2002 recognizes a diverse range of prospective parents, it continues to construct the family unit in accordance with the married (legitimate), heterosexual norm. The courts can perpetuate this myth by assimilating adoptive parenting to the biological 'ideal' and minimizing the extent to which adoptive family life is different: most importantly, that adoptive parenting cannot always be exclusive of the birth family. This reluctance to embrace the difference of adoption betrays the law's true ambivalence towards alternative ways of 'doing family'. The married, heterosexual, autonomous family unit remains the norm and whilst adoption provides a snapshot of the rich complexity of contemporary family life, English law's response to that complexity remains in many ways problematic.

ONLINE RESOURCES

Questions, suggestions for further reading, and updates on developments in this area of family law since this book was published may be found in the online resources at **www.oup.com/he/familytcm5e.**

BIBLIOGRAPHY

This bibliography contains citations available as hard copy, hard copy and electronic, and solely electronic. We have endeavoured to provide URLs where possible, and these links are up to date as of 1 December 2022.

Adam, S. and Brewer, M. (2010). *Couple Penalties and Premiums in the UK Tax and Benefit System*. IFS Briefing Note BN 102. <https://ifs.org.uk/sites/default/files/output_url_files/bn102.pdf>.

Advice Now (online). *A Survival Guide to Sorting Out Your Finances When You Get Divorced*. <www.advicenow.org.uk/guides/survival-guide-sorting-out-your-finances-when-you-get-divorced>.

Akhtar, R. (2020). 'Religious-Only Marriages and Cohabitation: Deciphering Differences', in R. Akhtar, P. Nash, and R. Probert (eds), *Cohabitation and Religious Marriage: Status, Similarities and Solutions*. Bristol: BUP.

Albakri, M., Hill, S., Kelley, N., and Rahim, N. (2019). *British Social Attitudes 36: Relationships and Gender Identity*. <https://bsa.natcen.ac.uk/media/39358/5_bsa36_relationships_and_gender_identity.pdf>.

Aldridge, J. (2021). '"Not an Either/or Situation": The Minimization of Violence Against Women in United Kingdom "Domestic Abuse" Policy'. *Violence Against Women*, 27: 1823.

Alghrani, A. (2017). '*Re A (Conjoined Twins)* [2000] EWCA Civ 254', in H. Stalford, K. Hollingsworth, and S. Gilmore (eds), *Rewriting Children's Rights Judgments: From Academic Vision to New Practice*. Oxford: Hart Publishing.

Alghrani, A. and Griffiths, D. (2017). 'The Regulation of Surrogacy in the United Kingdom: The Case for Reform'. *Child and Family Law Quarterly*, 29: 165.

Alghrani, A. and Harris, J. (2006). 'Reproductive Liberty: Should the Foundation of Families be Regulated?'. *Child and Family Law Quarterly*, 18: 10.

Alrouh, B., Abouelenin, M., Broadhurst, K., Cowley, L., Doebler, S., Farr, I., Cusworth, L., North, L., Hargreaves, C., Akbari, A., Griffiths, L., and Ford, D. (2022). *Mothers in Recurrent Care Proceedings: New Evidence for England and Wales*. London: Nuffield Family Justice Observatory. <www.nuffieldfjo.org.uk/resource/mothers-in-recurrent-care-proceedings-new-evidence-for-england-and-wales>.

Altman, S. (2003). 'A Theory of Child Support'. *International Journal of Law, Policy and the Family*, 17: 173.

Ancillary Relief Advisory Group (1998). *Report to the Lord Chancellor of the Ancillary Relief Advisory Group*. London.

Andrews, G. (2007). 'The Presumption of Advancement: Equity, Equality and Human Rights'. *Conveyancer and Property Lawyer*, 71: 340.

Andrews, S., Armstrong, D., McLernon, L., Megaw, S., and Skinner C. (2011). *Promotion of Child Maintenance: Research on Instigating Behaviourial Change*. CMEC Research Report. <webarchive.nationalarchives.gov.uk/20120716161734/http:/www.childmaintenance.org/en/pdf/research/Main-Report-Vol-1.pdf>.

Antokolskaia, M. (2020). 'Dissolution of Marriage in Westernised Countries', in J. Eekelaar and R. George (eds), *Routledge Handbook of Family Law and Policy*, 2nd edn. Abingdon: Routledge.

Archbishop of Canterbury's Group (1984). *No Just Cause: The Law of Affinity in England and Wales: Some Suggestions for Change*. London: CIO Press.

Arthur, S., Lewis, J., Maclean, M., Finch, S., and Fitzgerald, R. (2002). *Settling Up: Making Financial Arrangements after Divorce or Separation*. London: National Centre for Social Research.

Atkinson, A. and McKay, S. (2005). *Child Support Reform: The Views and Experiences of CSA Staff and New Clients*. DWP RR232.<webarchive.nationalarchives.gov.uk/20130314010347/http://research.dwp.gov.uk/asd/asd5/rports2005-2006/rrep232.pdf>.

Attar Taylor, E. and Scott, J. (2018). *British Social Attitudes 35: Gender*. <www.bsa.natcen.ac.uk/latest-report/british-social-attitudes-35/gender.aspx>.

Auchmuty, R. (2007). 'Unfair Shares for Women: The Rhetoric of Equality and the Reality of Inequality', in H. Lim and A. Bottomley (eds),

Feminist Perspectives on Land Law. Abingdon: Routledge-Cavendish.

Auchmuty, R. (2008). 'What's so Special About Marriage? The Impact of *Wilkinson v Kitzinger*'. *Child and Family Law Quarterly*, 20: 475.

Auchmuty, R. (2009). 'Beyond Couples'. *Feminist Legal Studies*, 17: 205.

Auchmuty, R. (2015). 'Dissolution or Disillusion: The Unravelling of Civil Partnerships', in N. Barker and D. Monk (eds), *From Civil Partnership to Same-Sex Marriage: Interdisciplinary Reflections*. Abingdon: Routledge.

Auchmuty, R. (2016). 'The Limits of Marriage Protection When a Relationship Ends'. *Child and Family Law Quarterly*, 28: 303.

Bailey-Harris, R. (1992). 'Child Support: Is the Right the Wrong One?'. *International Journal of Law and the Family*, 6: 169.

Bailey-Harris, R. (1996). 'Law and the Unmarried Couple—Oppression or Liberation?'. *Child and Family Law Quarterly*, 8: 137.

Bailey-Harris, R. (1998). 'Dividing the Assets on Breakdown of Relationships outside Marriage', in R. Bailey-Harris (ed), *Dividing the Assets on Family Breakdown*. Bristol: Family Law.

Bailey-Harris, R. (2005). 'The Paradoxes of Principle and Pragmatism: Ancillary Relief in England and Wales'. *International Journal of Law, Policy and the Family*, 19: 229.

Bailey-Harris, R. (2018). 'Special Contribution–Another Barbarous Relic in Blighty?'. *Australian Journal of Family Law*, 32: 141.

Bailey-Harris, R., Barron, J., and Pearce, J. (1999a). 'Settlement Culture and the Use of the "No Order" Principle under the Children Act 1989'. *Child and Family Law Quarterly*, 11: 53.

Bailey-Harris, R., Barron, J., and Pearce, J. (1999b). 'From Utility to Rights? The Presumption of Contact in Practice'. *International Journal of Law, Policy and the Family*, 13: 111.

Bainham, A. (1989). 'When is a Parent Not a Parent? Reflections on the Unmarried Father and His Child in English Law'. *International Journal of Law and the Family*, 3: 208.

Bainham, A. (1990). 'The Privatisation of the Public Interest in Children'. *Modern Law Review*, 53: 206.

Bainham, A. (1998). 'Changing Families and Changing Concepts—Reforming the Language of Family Law'. *Child and Family Law Quarterly*, 10: 1.

Bainham, A. (1999). 'Parentage, Parenthood and Parental Responsibility', in A. Bainham, S. Day Sclater, and M. Richards (eds), *What is a Parent? A Socio-Legal Analysis*. Oxford: Hart Publishing.

Bainham, A. (2007a). '"Truth Will Out": Paternity in Europe'. *Cambridge Law Journal*, 66: 278.

Bainham, A. (2007b). 'Who or What is a Parent?'. *Cambridge Law Journal*, 66: 30.

Bainham, A. (2008a). 'Arguments About Parentage'. *Cambridge Law Journal*, 67: 322.

Bainham, A. (2008b). 'What is the Point of Birth Registration?'. *Child and Family Law Quarterly*, 20: 449.

Bainham, A. (2008c). 'Homosexual Adoption'. *Cambridge Law Journal*, 67: 479.

Bainham, A. (2013). 'Suspicious Minds: Protecting Children in the Face of Uncertainty'. *Cambridge Law Journal*, 72: 266.

Bainham, A. (2018). 'The Forbidden Territories'. *Family Law*, 48: 1150.

Bainham, A. (2022). 'What is Justice in Care Proceedings?', in J. Scherpe and S. Gilmore (eds), *Family Matters: Essays in Honour of John Eekelaar*. Cambridge: Intersentia.

Bainham, A. and Gilmore, S. (2013). *Children: The Modern Law*, 4th edn. Bristol: Jordan Publishing.

Balfour, D. (2017). 'Non-Disclosure and the Discretionary Process: *Hart v Hart*'. *Family Law*, 47: 1363.

Bamforth, N. (2001). 'Same-Sex Partnerships and Arguments of Justice', in R. Wintemute and M. Andenæs (eds), *Legal Recognition of Same-Sex Partnerships*. Oxford: Hart Publishing.

Bamforth, N. (2007a). '"The Benefits of Marriage in All But Name?" Same-Sex Couples and the Civil Partnership Act 2004'. *Child and Family Law Quarterly*, 19: 133.

Bamforth, N. (2007b). 'Same-Sex Partnerships: Some Comparative Constitutional Lessons'. *European Human Rights Law Review*, 12: 47.

Bannister, S. (2021). 'Domestic Contributions as Unjust Enrichments: Commodifying Love?'. *Child and Family Law Quarterly*, 33: 257.

Bano, S. (2012). *Muslim Women and Shari'ah Councils: Transcending the Boundaries of Community and Law*. Basingstoke: Palgrave Macmillan.

Barker, N. (2015). 'After the Wedding: What Next?', in N. Barker and D. Monk (eds), *From Civil Partnership to Same-Sex Marriage: Interdisciplinary Reflections*. Abingdon: Routledge.

Barlow, A. (2004). 'Regulation of Cohabitation, Changing Family Policies and Social Attitudes: A Discussion of Britain within Europe'. *Law and Policy*, 26: 57.

Barlow, A. (2015). 'Solidarity, Autonomy and Equality: Mixed Messages for the Family?'. *Child and Family Law Quarterly*, 27: 223.

Barlow, A. (2017). 'Rising to the Post-LASPO Challenge: How Should Mediation Respond?'. *Journal of Social Welfare and Family Law*, 39: 203.

Barlow, A. (2020). 'Modern Marriage Myths: The Dichotomy Between Expectations of Legal Rationality and Lived Law', in R. Akhtar, P. Nash, and R. Probert (eds), *Cohabitation and Religious Marriage: Status, Similarities and Solutions*. Bristol: BUP.

Barlow, A. (2022). 'Coupledom and the Law What Next After Equal Civil Partnership?', in J. Sherpe and S. Gilmore (eds), *Family Matters: Essays in Honour of John Eekelaar*. Cambridge: Intersentia.

Barlow, A. and Duncan, S. (2000). 'New Labour's Communitarianism, Supporting Families and the "Rationality Mistake": Part II'. *Journal of Social Welfare and Family Law*, 22: 129.

Barlow, A. and James, G. (2004). 'Regulating Marriage and Cohabitation in 21st Century Britain'. *Modern Law Review*, 67: 143.

Barlow, A. and Smithson, J. (2010). 'Legal Assumptions, Cohabitants' Talk and the Rocky Road to Reform'. *Child and Family Law Quarterly*, 22: 328.

Barlow, A. and Smithson, J. (2012). 'Is Modern Marriage a Bargain? Exploring Perceptions of Pre-Nuptial Agreements in England and Wales'. *Child and Family Law Quarterly*, 24: 304.

Barlow, A., Burgoyne, C., and Smithson, J. (2007). *The Living Together Campaign: An Investigation of its Impact on Legally Aware Cohabitants*. Ministry of Justice Research Series 5/07. <https://ore.exeter.ac.uk/repository/bitstream/handle/10036/15235/living-together-research-report.pdf>.

Barlow, A., Burgoyne, C., Clery, E., and Smithson, J. (2008). 'Cohabitation and the Law: Myths, Money and the Media', in A. Park et al (eds), *British Social Attitudes: The 24th Report*. London: Sage.

Barlow, A., Duncan, S., James, G., and Park, A. (2001). 'Just a Piece of Paper? Marriage and Cohabitation in Britain', in A. Park, J. Curtice, K. Thomson, L. Jarvis, and C. Bromley (eds), *British Social Attitudes: The 18th Report—Public Policy, Social Ties*. London: Sage.

Barlow, A., Duncan, S., James, G., and Park, A. (2005). *Cohabitation, Marriage and the Law*. Oxford: Hart Publishing.

Barlow, A., Hunter, R., Smithson, J., and Ewing, J. (2017). *Mapping Paths to Justice: Resolving Family Disputes in Neoliberal Times*. London: Palgrave Macmillan.

Barnes, H., Day, P., and Cronin, N. (1998). *Trial and Error: A Review of UK Child Support Policy*, Occasional Paper 24. London: Family Policy Studies Centre.

Barnes, L. (2007). '*Stack v Dowden*: The Principles in Practice'. <www.familylawweek.co.uk/site.aspx?i=ed642>.

Barnes, R. and Donovan, C. (2016). 'Developing Interventions for Abusive Partners in Lesbian, Gay, Bisexual and/or Transgender Relationships', in S. Hilder and V. Bettinson (eds), *Domestic Violence: Interdisciplinary Perspectives on Protection, Prevention and Intervention*. London: Palgrave Macmillan.

Barnett, A. (2000). 'Contact and Domestic Violence: The Ideological Divide', in J. Bridgeman and D. Monk (eds), *Feminist Perspectives on Child Law*. London: Cavendish.

Barnett, A. (2014). 'Contact at all Costs? Domestic Violence and Children's Welfare'. *Child and Family Law Quarterly*, 26: 439.

Barnett, A. (2015). '"Like Gold Dust These Days": Domestic Violence Fact-Finding Hearings in Child Contact Cases'. *Feminist Legal Studies*, 23: 47.

Barnett, A. (2020). 'A Genealogy of Hostility: Parental Alienation in England and Wales'. *Journal of Social Welfare and Family Law*, 42: 18.

Barnett, H. (1998). *Introduction to Feminist Jurisprudence*. London: Cavendish Publishing.

Barron, J. (2002). *Five Years On: A Review of Legal Protection from Domestic Violence*. Bristol: Women's Aid Federation of England.

Barton, C. (1999). 'Child Support—Tony's Turn'. *Family Law*, 29: 704.

Barton, C. (2002). 'White Paper Weddings—The Beginnings, Muddles and Ends of Wedlock'. *Family Law*, 32: 431.

Barton, C. and Douglas, G. (1995). *Law and Parenthood*. London: Butterworths.

Barton, C. and Probert, R. (2018). 'The Status of a Religious-Only Marriage: Valid, Void, or "Non"? *Akhter v Khan*'. *Family Law*, 48: 1540.

Bates, L. and Hester, M. (2020). 'No Longer a Civil Matter? The Design and Use of Protection Orders for Domestic Violence in England and Wales'. *Journal of Social Welfare and Family Law*, 42: 133.

BEAUJOUAN, É. AND NÍ BHROLCHÁIN, M. (2011). 'Cohabitation and Marriage in Britain Since the 1970s'. *Population Trends*, 145: 1.

BEHRENS, J. (1997). 'A Feminist Perspective on *B v B*: The Family Court and Mobility'. *Sister in Law*, 2: 65.

BENDALL, C. (2014). 'Some are More "Equal" than Others: Heteronormativity in the Post-*White* Era of Financial Remedies'. *Journal of Social Welfare and Family Law*, 36: 3.

BENDALL, C. (2019). 'Should We Welcome an End to the "Blame Game"? Reflecting on Experiences of Civil Partnership Dissolution'. *Journal of Divorce and Remarriage*, 61: 344.

BETTINSON, V. (2016). 'Surviving Times of Austerity: Preserving the Specialist Domestic Violence Court Provision', in S. Hilder and V. Bettinson (eds), *Domestic Violence: Interdisciplinary Perspectives on Protection, Prevention and Intervention*. London: Palgrave Macmillan.

BEVAN, C. (2019). 'The Search for Common Intention: The Status of an Executed Express Declaration of Trust Post-*Stack* and *Jones*'. *Law Quarterly Review*, 135: 660.

BIEHAL, N., ELLISON, S., BAKER, C., AND SINCLAIR, I. (2009). *Characteristics, Outcomes and Meanings of Three Types of Permanent Placement—Adoption by Strangers, Adoption by Carers and Long-Term Foster Care*. University of York, Research Brief. DCSF-RBX-09-11. <www.york.ac.uk/inst/spru/research/pdf/3types.pdf>.

BIRCHALL, J. (2022). *Two Years, Too Long: Mapping Action on the Harm Panel's Findings*. Bristol: Women's Aid. <www.womensaid.org.uk/wp-content/uploads/2022/06/Two-Years-Too-Long-2022.pdf>.

BIRCHALL, J. AND CHOUDHRY, S. (2018). *Domestic Abuse, Human Rights and the Family Courts*. Bristol: Women's Aid. <www.womensaid.org.uk/research-and-publications/domestic-abuse-human-rights-and-the-family-courts/>.

BISHOP, C. (2016). 'Domestic Violence: The Limitations of a Legal Response', in S. Hilder and V. Bettinson (eds), *Domestic Violence: Interdisciplinary Perspectives on Protection, Prevention and Intervention*. London: Palgrave Macmillan.

BISHOP, C. (2021). 'Prevention and Protection: Will the Domestic Abuse Act Transform the Response to Domestic Abuse in England and Wales?'. *Child and Family Law Quarterly*, 33: 163.

BLACK, G. (2022). 'Adult Relationships and the Ongoing Legal Significance of Sexual Intimacy', in J. Sherpe and S. Gilmore (eds), *Family Matters: Essays in Honour of John Eekelaar*. Cambridge: Intersentia.

BLACK, J., BRIDGE, J., BOND, T., GREWCOCK, P., GRIBBIN, L., AND REARDON, M. (2015). *A Practical Approach to Family Law*, 10th edn. Oxford: OUP.

BLACKSTONE, W. (1765). *Commentaries on the Laws of England, Volume I: Of the Rights of Persons*. Facsimile edition (1979) S. Katz (ed). Chicago: University of Chicago Press.

BLACKWELL, A. AND DAWE, F. (2003). *Non-Resident Parental Contact—Final Report*. London: Office for National Statistics.

BLAKEY, R. (2022). 'Mediators Mediating Themselves: Tensions Within the Family Mediator Profession', *Legal Studies*, available online.

BODEN, R. AND CHILDS, M. (1996). 'Paying for Procreation: Child Support Arrangements in the UK'. *Feminist Legal Studies*, 4: 131.

BOELE-WOELKI, K., FERRAND, F., GONZÁLEZ BEILFUSS, C., JÄNTERÄ-JAREBORG, M., LOWE, N., MARTINY, D., AND PINTENS, W. (2004). *Principles of European Family Law Regarding Divorce and Maintenance between Former Spouses*. Antwerp, Oxford: Intersentia.

BONNER, D., FENWICK, H., AND HARRIS-SHORT, S. (2003). 'Judicial Approaches to the HRA'. *International and Comparative Law Quarterly*, 52: 549.

BOOTH COMMITTEE (1985). *Report of the Matrimonial Causes Procedure Committee*. London: HMSO.

BOTTOMLEY, A. (1993). 'Self and Subjectivities: Languages of Claim in Property Law'. *Journal of Law and Society*, 20: 56.

BOTTOMLEY, A. (2006). 'From Mrs Burns to Mrs Oxley: Do Co-Habiting Women (Still) Need Marriage Law?'. *Feminist Legal Studies*, 14: 181.

BOTTOMLEY, A. and WONG, S. (2006). 'Shared Households: A New Paradigm for Thinking About the Reform of Domestic Property Relations', in A. Diduck and K. O'Donovan (eds), *Feminist Perspectives on Family Law*. Abingdon: Routledge-Cavendish.

BOYD, S. (1989). 'From Gender Specificity to Gender Neutrality? Ideologies in Canadian Child Custody Law', in C. Smart and S. Sevenhuijsen (eds), *Child Custody and the Politics of Gender*. London: Routledge.

BRACKEN, L. (2017). 'Challenging Normative Constructions of Parentage in Ireland'. *Journal of Social Welfare and Family Law*, 39: 316.

Bracken, L. (2020). 'Surrogacy and the Genetic Link'. *Child and Family Law Quarterly*, 32: 303.

Bradney, A. (1984). 'Arranged Marriages and Duress'. *Journal of Social Welfare and Family Law*, 6: 278.

Bradney, A. (1994). 'Duress, Family Law and the Coherent Legal System'. *Modern Law Review*, 57: 963.

Bradshaw, J., Stimson, C., Skinner, C., and Williams, J. (1999). *Absent Fathers?* London: Routledge.

Brandon, M., Sidebottom, P., Bailey, S., Belderson, P., Hawley, C., Ellis, C., and Megson, M. (2013). *New Learning from Serious Case Reviews: A Two Year Report for 2009–2011*. London: Department for Education. <www.gov.uk/government/publications/new-learning-from-serious-case-reviews-a-2-year-report-for-2009-to-2011>.

Brasse, G. (1993). 'The Section 31 Monopoly—*Nottinghamshire CC v P* Considered'. *Family Law*, 23: 691.

Brazier, M., Campbell, A., and Golombok, S. (1998). *Surrogacy—Review for Health Ministers of Current Arrangements for Payments and Regulation. Report of the Review Team*, Cm 4068. London: HMSO.

Breen, C., Krutzinna, J., Luhamaa, K., and Skivenes, M. (2020). 'Family Life for Children in State Care: An Analysis of the European Court of Human Rights' Reasoning on Adoption Without Consent'. *International Journal of Children's Rights*, 28: 715.

Bremner, P. (2014). 'Lesbian Parents and Biological Fathers – Leave to Apply for Contact'. *Journal of Social Welfare and Family Law*, 36: 79.

Bremner, P. (2020). 'Birth Registration: "Coherent and Certain" or "An Occasion for Exquisite Embarrassment and Confusion"?'. *Journal of Social Welfare and Family Law*, 42: 524.

Bridge, C. (1993). 'Changing the Nature of Adoption: Law Reform in England and New Zealand'. *Legal Studies*, 13: 81.

Bridge, C. (2001). 'Adoption Law: A Balance of Interests', in J. Herring (ed), *Family Law: Issues, Debates, Policy*. Cullompton: Willan.

Bridge, S. (2001). 'Marriage and Divorce: The Regulation of Intimacy', in J. Herring (ed), *Family Law: Issues, Debates, Policy*. Cullompton: Willan.

Bridgeman, J. (2017a). 'The Provision of Healthcare to Young and Dependent Children: The Principles, Concepts, and Utility of the Children Act 1989'. *Medical Law Review*, 25: 363.

Bridgeman, J. (2017b). '*Re X and Y (Foreign Surrogacy)*', in H. Stalford, K. Hollingsworth, and S. Gilmore (eds), *Rewriting Children's Rights Judgments: From Academic Vision to New Practice*. Oxford: Hart Publishing.

Bridgeman, J. (2020). *Medical Treatment of Children and the Law: Beyond Parental Responsibilities*. Abingdon: Routledge.

Bridgeman, J. (2022). 'Parental Responsibility and Public Responsibilities for the Welfare of Children', in J. Scherpe and S. Gilmore (eds), *Family Matters: Essays in Honour of John Eekelaar*. Cambridge: Intersentia.

British Academy Working Group (2009). *Social Science and Family Policies*. London: British Academy.

Broadhurst, K. and Harwin, J. (2020). 'Crisis in Child Welfare and Protection in England: Causes, Consequences and Solutions?', in J. Eekelaar and R. George (eds), *Routledge Handbook of Family Law and Policy*, 2nd edn. Abingdon: Routledge.

Broadhurst, K., Mason, C., and Ward, H. (2022). 'Urgent Care Proceedings for New-Born Babies in England and Wales – Time for a Fundamental Review'. *International Journal of Law, Policy and the Family*, 36: ebac008.

Broadhurst, K., Alrouh, B., Mason, C., Ward, H., Holmes, L., Ryan, M., and Bowyer, S. (2018). *Born into Care: Newborns in Care Proceedings in England*. London: Nuffield Family Justice Observatory. <www.nuffieldfjo.org.uk/resource/born-into-care-newborns-in-care-proceedings-in-england-final-report-october-2018>.

Brophy J. (1989). 'Custody Law, Child Care, and Inequality in Britain', in C. Smart and S. Sevenhuijsen (eds), *Child Custody and the Politics of Gender*. London: Routledge.

Brown, A. (2019a). *What is The Family of Law? The Influence of the Nuclear Family*. Oxford: Hart Publishing.

Brown, A. (2019b). 'When is a "Mother" Not a "Mother"?'. *Journal of Social Welfare and Family Law*, 41: 365.

Brown, A. (2021a). 'Trans Parenthood and the Meaning of "Mother", "Father" and "Parent"'. *Medical Law Review*, 29: 559.

Brown, A. (2021b). 'Surrogacy Law Reform in the UK: The Ambiguous Position of Payments to the Surrogate'. *Child and Family Law Quarterly*, 33: 95.

Brown, A. and Wade, K. (2022). '"Everyone Remains the Child of Someone": A Parental Order for an Adult'. *Journal of Social Welfare and Family Law*, 44: 411.

Brown, A. and Wade, K. (2023). 'The Incoherent Role of the Child's Identity in the Construction and Allocation of Legal Parenthood'. *Legal Studies*, 43: *forthcoming*.

Brown, J. and Day Sclater, S. (1999). 'Divorce: A Psychodynamic Perspective', in S. Day Sclater and C. Piper (eds), *Undercurrents of Divorce*. Dartmouth: Ashgate.

Bryan, M. and Sanz, A. (2008). *Does Housework Lower Wages and Why? Evidence for Britain*. ISER Working Paper 2008-3. <www.pdfs.semanticscholar.org/8a98/691491af8dcf0aa07828f5e0f6c1f40443a4.pdf>.

Bryson, C., Ellman, I., McKay, S., and Miles, J. (2015). *Child Maintenance: How Would the British Public Calculate What the State Should Require Parents to Pay?* London: Nuffield Foundation. <www.nuffieldfoundation.org/public-views-child-support>.

Bryson, C., Skipp, A., Allbeson, J., Poole, E., Ireland, E., and Marsh, V. (2013). *Kids Aren't Free: The Child Maintenance Arrangements of Single Parents on Benefit 2013*. London: Nuffield Foundation. <www.nuffieldfoundation.org/sites/default/files/files/Kids%20aren%27t%20free%20-%20full%20report_04_07_13.pdf>.

Buckley, L. (2018). 'Autonomy and Prenuptial Agreements in Ireland: A Relational Analysis'. *Legal Studies*, 38: 164.

Burgoyne, C. and Sonnenberg, S. (2009). 'Financial Practices in Cohabiting Heterosexual Couples: A Perspective from Economic Psychology', in J. Miles and R. Probert (eds), *Sharing Lives, Dividing Assets: An Inter-Disciplinary Study*. Oxford: Hart Publishing.

Burrows, D. (2009). 'Enforcement of Child Maintenance: *Kehoe*'. *Family Law*, 39: 1086.

Burrows, D. (2010). 'Delay and Enforcement of Child Support Arrears'. *Family Law*, 40: 269.

Burton, F. (2020). '*Owens v Owens*: A Most Curious Case'. *Denning Law Journal*, 32: 5.

Burton, M. (2003a). 'Third Party Applications for Protection Orders in England and Wales: Service Provider's Views on Implementing Section 60 of the Family Law Act 1996'. *Journal of Social Welfare and Family Law*, 25: 137.

Burton, M. (2003b). 'Criminalising Breaches of Civil Orders for Protection from Domestic Violence'. *Criminal Law Review*, 301.

Burton, M. (2008). *Legal Responses to Domestic Violence*. Abingdon: Routledge-Cavendish.

Burton, M. (2009a). 'Failing to Protect: Victims' Rights and Police Liability'. *Modern Law Review*, 72: 283.

Burton, M. (2009b). 'Civil Law Remedies for Domestic Violence: Why are Applications for Non-Molestation Orders Declining?'. *Journal of Social Welfare and Family Law*, 31: 109.

Burton, M. (2010). 'The Human Rights of Victims of Domestic Violence: *Opuz v Turkey*'. *Child and Family Law Quarterly*, 22: 131.

Burton, M. (2015). 'Emergency Barring Orders in Domestic Violence Cases: What Can England and Wales Learn From Other European Countries?'. *Child and Family Law Quarterly*, 27: 25.

Burton, M. (2016). 'A Fresh Approach to Policing Domestic Violence', in S. Hilder and V. Bettinson (eds), *Domestic Violence: Interdisciplinary Perspectives on Protection, Prevention and Intervention*. London: Palgrave Macmillan.

Burton, M. (2021). 'What Can Go Wrong in Child Arrangement Proceedings Where There are Allegations of Domestic Abuse?'. *Journal of Social Welfare and Family Law*, 43: 471.

Burton, M. (2022). 'Revisiting Fact-Finding in Child Arrangement Cases Where There are Allegations of Domestic Abuse'. *Journal of Social Welfare and Family Law*, 44: 414.

Burton, M. and Bettinson, V. (2022). 'Domestic Abuse and Child Arrangement Proceedings: Identifying and Assessing the Risk of Harm, Including Coercive and Controlling Behaviour'. *Child and Family Law Quarterly*, 34: 3.

Burton, M., McCrory, A., and Buck, T. (2002). *The Civil Remedies for Domestic Violence under the Family Law Act 1996: Is Section 60 the Way Forward?* Unpublished report submitted to the LCD, October.

Busby, N. and James, G. (2020). *A History of Regulating Working Families*. Oxford: Hart Publishing.

Butler, P. (2018). 'Fears Cash-Strapped Council May Cut Services for Vulnerable Children'. *The Guardian*, 31 July 2018. <www.theguardian.com/society/2018/jul/31/fears-cash-strapped-council-may-cut-services-for-vulnerable-children>.

Butler-Sloss, E. (1988). *Report of the Inquiry into Child Abuse in Cleveland 1987*, Cm 412. London: HMSO.

Cabinet Office (2000). *Prime Minister's Review of Adoption*. <https://webarchive.nationalarchives.gov.uk/ukgwa/+/http://www.cabinetoffice.gov.uk/strategy/downloads/su/adoption/adoption.pdf>.

Cafcass (2021). *Cafcass Prioritisation Protocol.* <www.cafcass.gov.uk/about-cafcass/prioritisation-protocol/>.

Cafcass and Women's Aid. (2017). *Allegations of Domestic Abuse in Child Contact Cases.* London: Cafcass. <www.cafcass.gov.uk/download/2124/>.

Cafcass Cymru (2019). *Children's Resistance or Refusal to Spend Time with a Parent: Practice Guidance.* <www.gov.wales/sites/default/files/publications/2019-08/cafcass-cymru-childrens-resistance-or-refusal-to-spending-time-with-a-parent-practice-guidance.pdf>.

Cailes, J. (2018). *Outcomes for Children Looked After by Local Authorities: 2017.* Bristol: Jordan Publishing. <www.familylaw.co.uk/news_and_comment/outcomes-for-children-looked-after-by-local-authorities-2017>.

Calderwood, L. (2010). 'Family Demographics', in K. Hansen et al (eds), *Millennium Cohort Study: Fourth Survey—A User's Guide to Initial Findings*, 2nd edn. London: Centre for Longitudinal Studies. <www.cls.ucl.ac.uk/wp-content/uploads/2017/07/MCS4-Users-Guide-to-Initial-Findings-2nd-Edition-15-12-10_MT.pdf>.

Caldwell, J. (2011). 'Common Law Judges and Judicial Interviewing'. *Child and Family Law Quarterly*, 23: 41.

Callus, T. (2008). 'First "Designer Babies", Now À La Carte Parents'. *Family Law*, 38: 143.

Cameron, E. (2001). 'Foreword' to R. Wintemute and M. Andenæs (eds), *Legal Recognition of Same-Sex Partnerships*. Oxford: Hart Publishing.

Campbell, T. (1992). 'The Rights of Minor: As Person, as Child, as Juvenile, as Future Adult'. *International Journal of Law and the Family*, 6: 1.

Carbone, J. (1996). 'Feminism, Gender and the Consequences of Divorce', in M. Freeman (ed), *Divorce: Where Next?* Dartmouth: Ashgate.

Cashmore, J. and Parkinson, P. (2011). 'Parenting Arrangements for Young Children: Messages from Research'. *Australian Journal of Family Law*, 25: 236.

Castle, J., Beckett, C., and Groothues, C. (2000). 'Infant Adoption in England. A Longitudinal Account of Social and Cognitive Progress'. *Adoption and Fostering*, 24: 26.

Cave, E. (2021). 'Confirmation of the High Court's Power to Override a Child's Treatment Decision'. *Medical Law Review*, 29: 408.

Cave, E. and Wallbank, J. (2012). 'Minors' Capacity to Refuse Treatment: A Reply to Gilmore and Herring'. *Medical Law Review*, 20: 423.

Centre for Social Justice (2009). *Every Family Matters: An In-Depth Review of Family Law in Britain.* London: Centre for Social Justice. <www.centreforsocialjustice.org.uk/core/wp-content/uploads/2016/08/CSJEveryFamilyMattersWEB.pdf>.

Centre for Social Justice (2012). *Beyond Violence: Breaking Cycles of Domestic Abuse.* <www.centreforsocialjustice.org.uk/core/wp-content/uploads/2016/08/DA-Full-report.pdf>.

Centre for Women's Justice (2019). *Super-complaint: Police failure to use protective measures in cases involving violence against women and girls.* <www.assets.publishing.service.gov.uk/government/uploads/system/uploads/attachment_data/file/797419/Super-complaint_report.FINAL.PDF>.

Chandler, A. (2017). 'Binding Agreements in TOLATA Claims'. *Family Law Week*, 27 July 2017. <www.familylawweek.co.uk/site.aspx?i=ed178920>.

Chau, P.-L. and Herring, J. (2004). 'Men, Women, People: The Definition of Sex', in B. Brooks-Gordon, L. Gelsthorpe, M. Johnson, and A. Bainham (eds), *Sexuality Repositioned: Diversity and the Law.* Oxford: Hart Publishing.

Choudhry, S. (2003). 'The Adoption and Children Act 2002, the Welfare Principle and the Human Rights Act 1998—A Missed Opportunity'. *Child and Family Law Quarterly*, 15: 119.

Choudhry, S. and Fenwick, H. (2005). 'Taking the Rights of Parents and Children Seriously: Confronting the Welfare Principle under the Human Rights Act'. *Oxford Journal of Legal Studies*, 25: 453.

Choudhry, S. and Herring, J. (2006). 'Righting Domestic Violence'. *International Journal of Law, Policy and the Family*, 20: 95.

Choudhry, S. and Herring, J. (2010). *European Human Rights and Family Law.* Oxford: Hart Publishing.

Choudhry, S. and Herring, J. (2017). 'A Human Right to Legal Aid? The Implications of Change to the Legal Aid Scheme for Victims of Domestic Abuse'. *Journal of Social Welfare and Family Law*, 39: 152.

Chung, H. and Booker, C. (2022). 'Flexible Working and the Division of Housework and Childcare: Examining Divisions across Arrangement and Occupational Lines', *Work, Employment and Society*, 37: 236.

Church of England (2003). *Response to Civil Partnership Consultation.*

Church of England (2013). *Response to Equal Marriage Consultation.*

Clarke, L. and Berrington, A. (1999). 'Socio-Demographic Predictors of Divorce', in *One Plus One Marriage and Partnership Research, High Divorce Rates: The State of the Evidence on Reasons and Remedies.* Lord Chancellor's Department Research Report Series 2/99, 1(1). Summary at <http://webarchive.nationalarchives.gov.uk/+/http://www.dca.gov.uk/research/1999/299-1esfr.htm>.

Clery, L., Curtice, J., Frankenburg, S., Morgan, H., and Reid, S. (2021). *British Social Attitudes: The 38th Report.* <https://bsa.natcen.ac.uk/latest-report/british-social-attitudes-38/introduction.aspx>.

Clive, E. (1980). 'Marriage: An Unnecessary Legal Concept?', in J. Eekelaar and S. Katz (eds), *Marriage and Cohabitation in Contemporary Societies.* London: Butterworths.

CMEC (2012). *The Child Support Maintenance Calculations Regulations 2012: A Technical Consultation on the Draft Regulations.* <www.gov.uk/government/consultations/child-support-maintenance-calculation-regulations-2012-technical-consultation>.

Coast, E. (2009). 'Currently Cohabiting: Relationships, Attitudes, Expectations and Outcomes'. LSE Research Online. <http://eprints.lse.ac.uk/23986/1/Currently_co-habiting_(LSERO).pdf>.

Cobb, S. (2017). *Review of Practice Direction 12J FPR 2010: Child Arrangements and Contact Orders: Domestic Violence and Harm.* <www.judiciary.uk/wp-content/uploads/2017/01/PD12J-child-arrangement-domestic-violence-and-harm-report-and-revision.pdf>.

Cobley, C. and Lowe, N. (2009). 'Interpreting the Threshold Criteria under Section 31(2) of the Children Act 1989—The House of Lords Decision in *Re B*'. *Modern Law Review*, 72: 463.

Coenraad, L. (2014). 'Voices of Minor Children Heard and Unheard in Judicial Divorce Proceedings in the Netherlands'. *Journal of Social Welfare and Family Law*, 36: 370.

Coleman, L. and Glenn F. (2010). *When Couples Part: Understanding the Consequences for Adults and Children.* London: One Plus One.

Coleman, L., Shorto, S., and Ben-Galim, D. (2022). *Childcare Survey 2022.* Coram Family and Childcare. <www.familyandchildcaretrust.org/childcare-survey-2022-main-report>.

College of Policing (online). *Authorised professional practice on domestic abuse.* <www.college.police.uk/app/major-investigation-and-public-protection/domestic-abuse>.

College of Policing, HMICFRS, and Independent Office for Police Conduct (2021). *A duty to protect: Police use of protective measures in cases involving violence against women and girls.* <www.gov.uk/government/publications/police-use-of-protective-measures-in-cases-of-violence-against-women-and-girls>.

Collier, R. (1995). *Masculinity, Law and the Family.* London: Routledge.

Collier, R. (1999). 'The Dashing of a "Liberal Dream"?—The Information Meeting, the "New Family" and the Limits of Law'. *Child and Family Law Quarterly*, 11: 257.

Collier, R. (2001). 'A Hard Time to be a Father?: Reassessing the Relationship between Law, Policy, and Family (Practices)'. *Journal of Law and Society*, 28: 520.

Collier, R. (2003). 'In Search of the "Good Father": Law, Family Practices and the Normative Reconstruction of Parenthood', in J. Dewar and S. Parker (eds), *Family Law Processes, Practices and Pressures—Proceedings of the Tenth World Conference of the International Society of Family Law, July 2000, Brisbane, Australia.* Oregon: Hart Publishing.

Collier, R. (2005). 'Fathers 4 Justice, Law and the New Politics of Fatherhood'. *Child and Family Law Quarterly*, 17: 511.

Collier, R. (2014). 'Men, Gender and Fathers' Rights "After Legal Equality": New Formations of Rights and Responsibilities in Family Justice', in R. Leckey (ed), *After Legal Equality: Family, Sex, Kinship.* Abingdon: Routledge.

Collier, R. and Sheldon, S. (2008). *Fragmenting Fatherhood. A Socio-Legal Study.* Oxford: Hart Publishing.

Collins, L. (ed) (2012). *Dicey, Morris and Collins on the Conflict of Laws*, 15th edn. London: Sweet & Maxwell.

Conway, H. (2002). 'Money and Domestic Violence—Escaping the *Nwogbe* Trap'. *Family Law*, 32: 61.

Cook, D., Burton, M., Robinson, A., and Vallely, C. (2004). *Evaluation of Specialist Domestic Violence Courts/Fast Track Systems.* London: Crown Prosecution Service/Department of Constitutional Affairs.

Cooke, E. (2007). '*Miller/McFarlane*: Law in Search of Discrimination'. *Child and Family Law Quarterly*, 19: 98.

Cooke, E. (2009). 'The Future of Ancillary Relief', in G. Douglas and N. Lowe, *The Continuing Evolution of Family Law*. Bristol: Family Law.

Cooke, E. (2011a). 'In the Wake of *Stack v Dowden*: The Tale of TR1'. *Family Law*, 41: 1142.

Cooke, E. (2011b). '*White v White*: A Late Instalment in a Long Story', in S. Gilmore, J. Herring, and R. Probert (eds), *Landmark Cases in Family Law*. Oxford: Hart Publishing.

Cooke, E., Barlow, A., and Callus, T. (2006). *Community of Property: A Regime for England and Wales?* London: Policy Press.

Cooper, D., Emerton, R., Grabham, E., Newman, H. J. H., Peel., E., Renz, F., and Smith, J. (2022). *Abolishing Legal Sex Status: The Challenge and Consequences of Gender Related Law Reform*. Future of Legal Gender Project. Final Report. King's College London. <www.kcl.ac.uk/law/research/future-of-legal-gender-abolishing-legal-sex-status-full-report.pdf>.

CoramBAFF (2022). *Statistics on Special Guardianship*.<www.corambaaf.org.uk/practice-areas/kinship-care/special-guardianship/statistics-special-guardianship>.

Costa Dias, M., Joyce, R., and Parodi, F. (2018). *Wage Progression and the Gender Wage Gap: The Causal Impact of Hours of Work*. Briefing Note No 223, Institute of Fiscal Studies. <www.ifs.org.uk/publications/10358>.

Cowan, D., Fox O'Mahony, L., and Cobb, N. (2016). *Great Debates in Land Law*, 2nd edn. London: Palgrave.

Cox, P., Barratt, C., Blumenfeld, F., Rahemtulla, Z., Taggart, D., and Turton, J. (2017). 'Reducing Recurrent Care Proceedings: Initial Evidence from New Interventions'. *Journal of Social Welfare and Family Law*, 39: 332.

CPAG (2006). *CPAG Response to Government Consultation on Henshaw Review of Child Support*. London: CPAG.

CPAG (2018). *Welfare Benefits and Tax Credits Handbook 2018/2019*. London: CPAG.

CPAG (2019a). *Welfare Benefits and Tax Credits Handbook*. London: CPAG.

CPAG (2019b). *Child Support Handbook*. London: CPAG.

CPS (undated). *Domestic Violence: Guidance on Section 1 Domestic Violence, Crime and Victims Act 2004*, no longer available online.

CPS (2022). *Domestic Abuse: Legal Guidance*. <www.cps.gov.uk/legal-guidance/domestic-abuse>.

CQC (2020). *Brief Guide: Capacity and Competence to Consent in Under 18s*. <www.cqc.org.uk/sites/default/files/Brief_guide_Capacity_and_consent_in_under_18s%20v3.pdf>.

Crawford, C., Goodman, A., Greaves, E., and Joyce, R. (2012). 'Cohabitation, Marriage and Child Outcomes: An Empirical Analysis of the Relationship between Marital Status and Child Outcomes in the UK using the Millennium Cohort Study'. *Child and Family Law Quarterly*, 24: 176.

Cretney, S. (1992). 'Divorce—A Smooth Transition?'. *Family Law*, 22: 472.

Cretney, S. (1996a). 'Divorce Reform: Humbug and Hypocrisy or Smooth Transition?', in M. Freeman (ed), *Divorce: Where Next?* Aldershot: Dartmouth.

Cretney, S. (1996b). 'From Status to Contract?', in F. Rose (ed), *Consensus ad Idem: Essays in the Law of Contract in Honour of Guenter Treitel*. London: Sweet & Maxwell.

Cretney, S. (1999). 'Contract Not Apt in Divorce Deal'. *Law Quarterly Review*, 115: 356.

Cretney, S. (2003a). *Family Law in the Twentieth Century: A History*. Oxford: OUP.

Cretney, S. (2003b). 'Community of Property Imposed by Judicial Decision'. *Law Quarterly Review*, 119: 349.

Cretney, S. (2006a). *Same Sex Relationships*. Oxford: OUP.

Cretney, S. (2006b). 'Marriage, Mothers-in-Law and Human Rights'. *Law Quarterly Review*, 122: 8.

Crompton, L. (2004). 'Civil Partnerships Bill 2004: The Illusion of Equality'. *Family Law*, 34: 888.

Crompton, L. (2013). 'DVP Notices and Orders: Vulnerable to Human Rights Challenge?'. *Family Law*, 43: 1588.

Crompton, L. (2014). DVP Notices and Orders: Protecting Victims or the Public Purse?'. *Family Law*, 44: 62.

Crowe-Urbaniak, D. (2022). '"A Marriage Is a Marriage": Equal Sharing in Short, Childless Marriages', *Journal of Social Welfare and Family Law*, 44: 124.

Crowther-Dowey, C., Gillespie, T., and Hopkins, K. (2016). 'Building Healthy Relationships for Young People and the Prevention of Domestic Abuse', in S. Hilder and V. Bettinson (eds), *Domestic Violence:*

Interdisciplinary Perspectives on Protection, Prevention and Intervention. London: Palgrave Macmillan.

Curtice, J., Clery, L., Perry, J., Phillips, M., and Rahim, N. (2019). *British Social Attitudes: The 36th Report*. <www.bsa.natcen.ac.uk/latest-report/british-social-attitudes-36/full-report.aspx>.

Cusworth, L., Bedston, S., Alrouh, B., Broadhurst, K., Johnson, R., Akbari, A., and Griffiths, L. (2021). *Uncovering Private Family Law: Who's Coming to Court in England?* London: Nuffield Family Justice Observatory. <www.nuffieldfjo.org.uk/resource/private-family-law-whos-coming-to-court-england>.

Cusworth, L., Hargreaves, C., Alrouh, B., Broadhurst, K., Johnson, R., Griffiths, L., Akbari, A., Doebler, S., and John, A. (2021). *Uncovering Private Family Law: Adult Characteristics and Vulnerabilities*. London: Nuffield Family Justice Observatory. <www.nuffieldfjo.org.uk/resource/uncovering-private-family-law-adult-characteristics-and-vulnerabilities-wales>.

Cummings, T. (2021). 'Equality as a Central Principle? – The Law Commission's Solution to the Religious-Only Marriage Problem', *Child and Family Law Quarterly*, 33: 63.

Dabhi, K., Anand, T., and Tu, T. (2022). *Survey of Separated Parents*. DWP Ad Hoc Research Report No 1015. <www.gov.uk/government/publications/survey-of-separated-parents/survey-of-separated-parents#parental-conflict-relationships-and-parental-care-1>.

Daly, A., Kilkelly, U., and O'Mahony, C. (2022). 'The Best Interests Principle and the Evolution of International Human Rights Law', in J. Scherpe and S. Gilmore (eds), *Family Matters: Essays in Honour of John Eekelaar*. Cambridge: Intersentia.

Davies, C. (1993). 'Divorce Reform in England and Wales: A Visitor's View'. *Family Law*, 23: 331.

Davis, G. (1988). *Partisans and Mediators*. Oxford: OUP.

Davis, G. and Murch, M. (1988). *Grounds for Divorce*. Oxford: Clarendon Press.

Davis, G. and Wikeley, N. (2002). 'National Survey of Child Support Agency Clients—The Relationship Dimension'. *Family Law*, 32: 522.

Davis, G., Cretney, S., and Collins, J. (1994). *Simple Quarrels: Negotiating Money and Property Disputes on Divorce*. Oxford: OUP.

Davis, G., Pearce, J., Bird, R., Woodward, H., and Wallace, C. (2000). 'Research: Ancillary Relief Outcomes'. *Child and Family Law Quarterly*, 12: 43.

Davis, G., Wikeley, N., and Young, R., with Barron, J. and Bedward, J. (1998). *Child Support in Action*. Oxford: Hart Publishing.

Day Sclater, S. (1999). 'Experiences of Divorce', in S. Day Sclater and C. Piper (eds), *Undercurrents of Divorce*. Dartmouth: Ashgate.

Day Sclater, S., Bainham, A., and Richards, M. (1999). 'Introduction', in A. Bainham, S. Day Sclater, and M. Richards (eds), *What is a Parent? A Socio-Legal Analysis*. Oxford: Hart Publishing.

DCA (2006a). *Judicial Statistics (Revised) England and Wales for the Year 2005*, Cm 6903. London: TSO. <www.official-documents.gov.uk/document/cm69/6903/6903.pdf>.

DCA (2006b). *Separate Representation of Children*. London: HMSO.

DCA and DFES (2004). *The Government's Response to the Children Act Sub-Committee (CASC) Report: 'Making Contact Work'*. <webarchive.nationalarchives.gov.uk/+/http://www.dca.gov.uk/family/abfla/cascresponse.pdf>.

DCA, DFES, and DTI (2005). *Parental Separation: Children's Needs and Parents' Responsibilities—Next Steps*, Cm 6452. London: HMSO.

DCLG (2009). *Housing in England 2007–8*. London: DCLG.

DCMS (2014). *Civil Partnership Review (England and Wales): Report and Conclusions*. <www.gov.uk/government/consultations/consultation-on-the-future-of-civil-partnership-in-england-and-wales>.

DCSF (2009). *Statistical First Release—Children Looked After in England (Including Adoption and Care Leavers) Year Ending 31 March 2009*, SFR 25/2009. London: DCSF.

DCSF and DWP (2008). *Joint Birth Registration: Recording Responsibility*, Cm 7293 (London: HMSO). <www.gov.uk/government/uploads/system/uploads/attachment_data/file/243115/7293.pdf>.

De Waal, A. (2008). *Second Thoughts on the Family*. London: Civitas.

Deech, R. (1977). 'The Principles of Maintenance'. *Family Law*, 7: 229.

Deech, R. (1980). 'The Case against the Legal Recognition of Cohabitation'. *International and Comparative Law Quarterly*, 29: 480.

Deech, R. (1982). 'Financial Relief: The Retreat from Precedent and Principle'. *Law Quarterly Review*, 98: 621.

Deech, R. (1990). 'Divorce Law and Empirical Studies'. *Law Quarterly Review*, 106: 229.

Deech, R. (1992). 'The Unmarried Father and Human Rights'. *Journal of Child Law*, 4: 3.

Deech, R. (2009a). *Divorce Law – A Disaster?* Gresham Lectures 2009–10. <www.gresham.ac.uk/lectures-and-events/divorce-law-a-disaster> and *Family Law*, 39: 1048.

Deech, R. (2009b). *Cohabitation and the Law.* Gresham Lectures 2009–10. <www.gresham.ac.uk/lectures-and-events/cohabitation-and-the-law> and *Family Law*, 40: 39.

Deech, R. (2009c). *What's a Woman Worth? The Maintenance Law.* Gresham Lectures 2009–10. <www.gresham.ac.uk/lectures-and-events/whats-a-woman-worth-the-maintenance-law> and *Family Law*, 39: 1140.

Department of Justice (2008). *Spousal Support Advisory Guidelines.* <www.justice.gc.ca/eng/fl-df/spousal-epoux/ssag-ldfpae.html>.

Dewar, J. (1997). 'Reducing Discretion in Family Law'. *Australian Journal of Family Law*, 11: 309.

Dewar, J. (1998a). 'The Normal Chaos of Family Law'. *Modern Law Review*, 61: 467.

Dewar, J. (1998b). 'Land, Law and the Family Home', in S. Bright and J. Dewar (eds), *Land Law: Themes and Perspectives*. Oxford: OUP.

Dewar, J. (2003). 'Families', in P. Cane and M. Tushnet (eds), *The Oxford Handbook of Legal Studies*. Oxford: OUP.

DFE (2012b). *An Action Plan for Adoption: Tackling Delay.* <www.gov.uk/government/uploads/system/uploads/attachment_data/file/180250/action_plan_for_adoption.pdf>.

DFE (2013). *Improving Permanence for Looked After Children.* <www.assets.publishing.service.gov.uk/government/uploads/system/uploads/attachment_data/file/245513/consultation_document.pdf>.

DFE (2014a). *Court Orders and Pre-Proceedings for Local Authorities.* <www.assets.publishing.service.gov.uk/government/uploads/system/uploads/attachment_data/file/306282/Statutory_guidance_on_court_orders_and_pre-proceedings.pdf>.

DFE (2014b). *Adoption: National Minimum Standards.* <www.assets.publishing.service.gov.uk/government/uploads/system/uploads/attachment_data/file/336069/Adoption_NMS_July_2014_for_publication.pdf>.

DFE (2017). *Childcare and Early Years Survey of Parents: 2017.* <www.gov.uk/government/statistics/childcare-and-early-years-survey-of-parents-2017>.

DFE (2018a). *Relationships Education, Relationships and Sex Education (RSE) and Health Education.* <www.assets.publishing.service.gov.uk/government/uploads/system/uploads/attachment_data/file/1019542/Relationships_Education_Relationships_and_Sex_Education_RSE_and_Health_Education.pdf>.

DFE (2018b). *Working Together to Safeguard Children.* <www.assets.publishing.service.gov.uk/government/uploads/system/uploads/attachment_data/file/942454/Working_together_to_safeguard_children_inter_agency_guidance.pdf>.

DFE (2018c). *Characteristics of Children in Need: 2017 to 2018, England.* <assets.publishing.service.gov.uk/government/uploads/system/uploads/attachment_data/file/758514/Characteristics_of_children_in_need_text_2018.pdf>.

DFE (2019). *Childcare and Early Years Survey of Parents: 2019.* <www.gov.uk/government/statistics/childcare-and-early-years-survey-of-parents-2019>.

DFE (2022a). *Children Looked After in England Including Adoption: Reporting Year 2022.* <www.explore-education-statistics.service.gov.uk/find-statistics/children-looked-after-in-england-including-adoptions>.

DFE (2022b). *Characteristics of Children in Need: 2021to2022,England.*<www.explore-education-statistics.service.gov.uk/find-statistics/characteristics-of-children-in-need>.

DFE (2022c). *Outcomes for Children in Need, Including Children Looked After by Local Authorities in England: 2021.* <www.explore-education-statistics.service.gov.uk/find-statistics/outcomes-for-children-in-need-including-children-looked-after-by-local-authorities-in-england/2021>.

DFE and MOJ (2012). *Co-operative Parenting Following Family Separation: Proposed Legislation on the Involvement of Both Parents in a Child's Life.* London: TSO.

DH (1993). *Adoption: The Future*, Cm 2288. London: HMSO.

DH (2000). *Adoption—A New Approach. A White Paper*, Cm 5017. London: HMSO.

DH (2007). *Government Response to the Report from the Joint Committee on the Human Tissue and Embryos (Draft) Bill*, Cm 7209. London: HMSO. <www.gov.uk/government/uploads/system/uploads/attachment_data/file/243182/7209.pdf>.

DH (2011). *Adoption: National Minimum Standards.* London: TSO. <www.gov.uk/government/publications/adoption-national-minimum-standards>.

DH (2014). *Mitochondrial Donation: Government Response to the Consultation on Draft*

Regulations to Permit the Use of New Treatment Techniques to Prevent the Transmission of a Serious Mitochondrial Disease from Mother to Child. <www.assets.publishing.service.gov.uk/government/uploads/system/uploads/attachment_data/file/332881/Consultation_response.pdf>.

DHSC (2018). *Quality and Safety of Organs, Tissues and Cells if There's No Brexit Deal.* <www.gov.uk/government/publications/quality-and-safety-of-organs-tissues-and-cells-if-theres-no-brexit-deal/quality-and-safety-of-organs-tissues-and-cells-if-theres-no-brexit-deal>.

DHSS (1974). *Report of the Committee on One-Parent Families, Vol 1*, Cm 5629. London: HMSO.

DHSS (1984). *Report of the Committee of Inquiry into Human Fertilisation and Embryology*, Cm 9314. London: HMSO.

DHSS (1985). *Review of Child Care Law. Report to Ministers of an Interdepartmental Working Party.* London: HMSO.

DHSS, HO, LCD, DES, WO, and SO (1987). *The Law on Child Care and Family Services.* London: HMSO.

Diduck, A. (1995). 'The Unmodified Family: The Child Support Act and the Construction of Legal Subjects'. *Journal of Law and Society*, 22: 527.

Diduck, A. (1999). 'Dividing the Family Assets', in S. Day Sclater and C. Piper (eds), *Undercurrents of Divorce.* Dartmouth: Ashgate.

Diduck, A. (2001). 'A Family by Any Other Name . . . or Starbucks Comes to England'. *Journal of Law and Society*, 28: 290.

Diduck, A. (2003). *Law's Families.* London: Butterworths.

Diduck, A. (2005). 'Shifting Familiarity'. *Current Legal Problems*, 58: 235.

Diduck, A. (2007). '"If Only We Can Find the Appropriate Terms to Use the Issue Will Be Solved": Law, Identity and Parenthood'. *Child and Family Law Quarterly*, 19: 458.

Diduck, A. (2010). '*In re G (Children) (Residence: Same-Sex Partner)*—Judgment', in R. Hunter, C. McGynn, and E. Rackley (eds), *Feminist Judgments: From Theory to Practice.* Oxford: Hart Publishing.

Diduck, A. (2011a). 'Ancillary Relief: Complicating the Search for Principle'. *Journal of Law and Society*, 38: 272.

Diduck, A. (2011b). 'What is Family Law For?'. *Current Legal Problems*, 64: 287.

Diduck, A. (2014). 'Autonomy and Vulnerability in Family Law', in J. Wallbank and J. Herring (eds), *Vulnerabilities, Care and Family Law.* Abingdon: Routledge.

Diduck, A. (2016). 'Autonomy and Family Justice'. *Child and Family Law Quarterly*, 28: 133.

Diduck, A. and Kaganas, F. (2012). *Family Law, Gender and the State*, 3rd edn. Oxford: Hart Publishing.

Diduck, A. and Orton, H. (1994). 'Equality and Support for Spouses'. *Modern Law Review*, 57: 681.

Dingwall, R. (1988). 'Empowerment or Enforcement? Some Questions About Power and Control in Divorce Mediation', in R. Dingwall and J. Eekelaar (eds), *Divorce Mediation and the Legal Process.* Oxford: OUP.

Dixon, M. (2007). 'The Never-Ending Story: Co-ownership after *Stack v Dowden*'. *Conveyancer and Property Lawyer*, 71: 456.

Dixon, M. (2012). 'The Still Not Ended, Never-Ending Story'. *Conveyancer and Property Lawyer*, 76: 83.

Dnes, A. (1998). 'The Division of Marital Assets Following Divorce'. *Journal of Law and Society*, 25: 336.

Dobash, R. and Dobash, R. (1992). *Women, Violence and Social Change.* London: Routledge.

Dobash, R. and Dobash, R. (2004). 'Women's Violence to Men in Intimate Relationships'. *British Journal of Criminology*, 44: 324.

Doggett, M. (1992). *Marriage, Wife-Beating and the Law in Victorian England.* London: Weidenfield & Nicolson.

Domestic Abuse Commissioner (2021). *Improving the Family Court Response to Domestic Abuse.* <www.domesticabusecommissioner.uk/wp-content/uploads/2021/11/Improving-the-Family-Court-Response-to-Domestic-Abuse-final.pdf>.

Domestic Abuse Commissioner (2022a). *Response to Independent Review into the way the CMS Supports Survivors of Domestic Abuse.* <www.domesticabusecommissioner.uk/briefings/the-domestic-abuse-commissioner-responds-to-independent-review-into-the-ways-the-child-maintenance-service-supports-survivors/>.

Domestic Abuse Commissioner (2022b). *Submission to the United Nations Special Rapporteur on Violence Against Women and Girls, Its Causes and Consequences Regarding Custody Cases, Violence Against Women and*

Violence Against Children. On file with the authors.

Domestic Abuse Commissioner (2023). *Reluctance – Resistance – Refusal: A Child Centric Approach to Domestic Abuse in Private Family Law Proceedings*. On file with the authors.

Donovan, C., Hester, M., Holmes, J., and McCarry, M. (2006). *Comparing Domestic Abuse in Same Sex and Heterosexual Relationships*. <www.equation.org.uk/wp-content/uploads/2012/12/Comparing-Domestic-Abuse-in-Same-Sex-and-Heterosexual-relationships.pdf>.

Doughty, J. (2013). '*Re B (A Child) (Care Order)* (2013) UKSC 33'. *Journal of Social Welfare and Family Law*, 35: 491.

Doughty, J. (2015). 'Myths and Misunderstandings in Adoption Law and Policy'. *Child and Family Law Quarterly*, 27: 331.

Doughty, J, Maxwell, N., and Slater, T. (2020). 'Professional Responses to "Parental Alienation": Research-Informed Practice'. *Journal of Social Welfare and Family Law*, 42: 68.

Doughty, J., Reed, L., and Magrath, P. (2018). *Transparency in the Family Courts: Publicity and Privacy in Practice*. London: Bloomsbury.

Douglas, G. (1991). *Law, Fertility and Reproduction*. London: Sweet & Maxwell.

Douglas, G. (1993). 'Assisted Reproduction and the Welfare of the Child'. *Current Legal Problems*, 46: 53.

Douglas, G. (1994a). 'Marriage—Nullity'. *Family Law*, 24: 17.

Douglas, G. (1994b). 'The Intention to be a Parent and the Making of Mothers'. *Modern Law Review*, 57: 636.

Douglas, G. (2000a). 'The Family, Gender and Social Security', in N. Harris (ed), *Social Security Law in Context*. Oxford: OUP.

Douglas, G. (2000b). 'Marriage, Cohabitation and Parenthood—From Contract to Status?', in S. Katz, J. Eekelaar, and M. Maclean (eds), *Cross Currents: Family Law and Policy in the US and England*. Oxford: OUP.

Douglas, G. (2003). '*Re J (Leave to Issue Application for Residence Order)*'. *Child and Family Law Quarterly*, 15: 103.

Douglas, G. (2004a). *An Introduction to Family Law*, 2nd edn. Oxford: OUP.

Douglas, G. (2004b). 'Case Report: Child Support—Human Rights'. *Family Law*, 34: 399.

Douglas, G. (2009). Case Comment on *Kehoe v UK*. *Family Law*, 39: 107.

Douglas, G. (2012). 'Simple Quarrels? Autonomy vs. Vulnerability', in R. Probert and C. Barton (eds), *Fifty Years in Family Law: Essays for Stephen Cretney*. Cambridge: Intersentia.

Douglas, G. (2018a). *Obligation and Commitment in Family Law*. Oxford: Hart Publishing.

Douglas, G. (2018b). 'Sharing Financial Losses as well as Gains on Divorce'. *Australian Journal of Family Law*, 32: 108.

Douglas, G. (2022). 'Enforcement of Orders in the Family Justice System: Obligation, Gender and Authority', in J. Scherpe and S. Gilmore (eds), *Family Matters: Essays in Honour of John Eekelaar*. Cambridge: Intersentia.

Douglas, G. and Lowe, N. (1992). 'Becoming a Parent in English Law'. *Law Quarterly Review*, 108: 414.

Douglas, G. and Members of the Network on Family, Regulation and Society (2011). 'Contact is Not a Commodity to be Bartered for Money'. *Family Law*, 41: 491.

Douglas, G. and Perry, A. (2001). 'How Parents Cope Financially on Separation and Divorce—Implications for the Future of Ancillary Relief'. *Child and Family Law Quarterly*, 13: 67.

Douglas, G., Pearce, J., and Woodward, H. (2007a). 'Dealing with Property Issues on Cohabitation Breakdown'. *Family Law*, 37: 36.

Douglas, G., Pearce, J., and Woodward, H. (2007b). 'A Failure of Trust: Resolving Property Disputes on Cohabitation Breakdown'. Cardiff University Research Papers No 1. <www.orca.cf.ac.uk/5186/1/1.pdf>.

Douglas, G., Pearce, J., and Woodward, H. (2008). 'The Law Commission's Cohabitation Proposals: Applying Them in Practice'. *Family Law*, 38: 351.

Douglas, G., Pearce, J., and Woodward, H. (2009). 'Money, Property, Cohabitation and Separation: Patterns and Intentions', in J. Miles and R. Probert (eds), *Sharing Lives, Dividing Assets: An Inter-Disciplinary Study*. Oxford: Hart Publishing.

Douglas, G., Murch, M., Scanlan, L., and Perry, A. (2000). 'Safeguarding Children's Welfare in Non-Contentious Divorce: Towards a New Conception of the Legal Process?'. *Modern Law Review*, 63: 177.

Douglas, G., Doe, N., Gilliat-Ray, S., Sandberg, R., and Khan, A. (2012). 'The Role of Religious Tribunals in Regulating Marriage and Divorce'. *Child and Family Law Quarterly*, 24: 139.

Draghici, C. (2017). 'Equal Marriage, Unequal Civil Partnership: A Bizarre Case of Discrimination in Europe'. *Child and Family Law Quarterly*, 29: 313.

Draghici, C. (2018). 'Adult Children and Elderly Parents in Strasbourg Proceedings: A Misconstrued Approach to "Family Life"'. *International Journal of Law, Policy and the Family*, 32: 42.

DSS (1995). *Improving Child Support*, Cm 2745. London: HMSO.

DSS (1999). *A New Contract for Welfare: Children's Rights and Parents' Responsibilities*, Cm 4349. London: DSS.

DTI (2004). *Final Regulatory Impact Assessment: Civil Partnership Act 2004*. URN 04/1336. <webarchive.nationalarchives.gov.uk/+/http://www.berr.gov.uk/files/file23829.pdf>.

Duggan, M. and Grace, J. (2018). 'Assessing Vulnerabilities in the Domestic Violence Disclosure Scheme'. *Child and Family Law Quarterly*, 30: 145.

Duncan, S. and Phillips, M. (2008). 'New Families? Tradition and Change in Modern Relationships', in A. Park et al (eds), *British Social Attitudes: The 24th Report*. London: Sage.

Duncan, S., Carter, J., Phillips, M., Roseneil, S., and Stoilova, M. (2012). 'Legal Rights for People Who "Live Apart Together"?'. *Journal of Social Welfare and Family Law*, 34: 443.

Duncan, S., Phillips, M., Roseneil, S., Carter, J., and Stoilova, M. (2013). *Living Apart Together: Uncoupling Intimacy and Co-Residence*. London: NatCen. <www.researchgate.net/publication/294444860_Living_apart_together_uncoupling_intimacy_and_co-residence>.

DWP (2006). *A New System of Child Maintenance*, Cm 6979. London: TSO. <www.gov.uk/government/uploads/system/uploads/attachment_data/file/272384/6979.pdf>.

DWP (2007). *Report on the Child Maintenance White Paper: Reply by the Government*, Cm 7062. <www.gov.uk/government/uploads/system/uploads/attachment_data/file/243430/7062.pdf>.

DWP (2011). *Strengthening Families, Promoting Parental Responsibility: The Future of Child Maintenance*, Cm 7990. <www.gov.uk/government/uploads/system/uploads/attachment_data/file/220421/strengthening-families.pdf>.

DWP (2014). *Child Maintenance and Other Payments Act 2008: Post-legislative Scrutiny—Memorandum to the Work and Pensions Select Committee*, Cm 8986. <www.gov.uk/government/uploads/system/uploads/attachment_data/file/387702/CM8986_Child_Maintenance_tagged.pdf>.

DWP (2017a). *Child Maintenance Reforms: 30 Month Review of Charging*. <www.gov.uk/government/publications/child-maintenance-reforms-30-month-review-of-charging>.

DWP (2017b). *Effective Family-Based Child Maintenance Arrangements: Data to March 2017*. <www.gov.uk/government/statistics/effective-family-based-child-maintenance-arrangements-data-to-march-2017>.

DWP (2018a). *The Child Maintenance Compliance and Arrears Strategy*. <www.gov.uk/government/uploads/system/uploads/attachment_data/file/724358/response-child-maintenance-compliance-and-arrears-strategy-consultation.pdf>.

DWP (2018b). *Child Maintenance Arrangements Made after Speaking to Child Maintenance Options: Data up to March 2018*. <www.gov.uk/government/statistics/child-maintenance-arrangements-made-after-speaking-to-cm-options-march-2018>.

DWP (2021a). *Households Below Average Income: Financial Years Ending 1995 to 2020*. <www.gov.uk/government/statistics/households-below-average-income-for-financial-years-ending-1995-to-2020>.

DWP (2021b). *Family Resources Survey: Financial Year 2019 to 2020*. <www.gov.uk/government/statistics/family-resources-survey-financial-year-2019-to-2020>.

DWP (2022a). *Child Maintenance Service statistics: data to December 2021 (experimental)*. <www.gov.uk/government/statistics/child-maintenance-service-statistics-data-to-december-2021-experimental>.

DWP (2022b). *Government Response: Child Maintenance: Modernising and Improving our Service*. <www.gov.uk/government/consultations/child-maintenance-modernising-and-improving-our-service/outcome/government-response-child-maintenance-modernising-and-improving-our-service#next-steps>.

Dyer, F. (2004). 'Termination of Parental Rights in Light of Attachment Theory'. *Psychology, Public Policy and Law*, 10: 5.

Edwards, J. and Calver, P. (2022). 'Whose Fault is it Anyway? Will the Introduction of "No Fault" Divorce Herald Greater Reliance on

Conduct in Financial Remedy Proceedings?'. *Financial Remedies Journal*, 1: 41.

Edwards, J. and Doherty, C. (2015). 'Calderback to the Future?'. *Family Law*, 45: 1498.

Edwards, S. (1989). *Policing 'Domestic' Violence: Women, the Law and the State*. London: Sage.

Edwards, S. (2001). 'Domestic Violence and Harassment: An Assessment of the Civil Remedies', in J. Taylor-Browne (ed), *What Works in Reducing Domestic Violence? A Comprehensive Guide for Professionals*. London: Whiting and Birch.

Edwards, S. and Halpern, A. (1991). 'Protection for the Victim of Domestic Violence: Time for Radical Revision?'. *Journal of Social Welfare and Family Law*, 13: 94.

Eekelaar. J. (1978). *Family Law and Social Policy*. London: Weidenfeld and Nicolson.

Eekelaar, J. (1986). 'The Emergence of Children's Rights'. *Oxford Journal of Legal Studies*, 6: 161.

Eekelaar, J. (1987). 'A Woman's Place—A Conflict between Law and Social Values'. *Conveyancer and Property Lawyer*, 51: 93.

Eekelaar, J. (1990). 'Investigation under the Children Act 1989'. *Family Law*, 20: 486.

Eekelaar, J. (1991a). 'Are Parents Morally Obliged to Care for Their Children?'. *Oxford Journal of Legal Studies*, 11: 340.

Eekelaar, J. (1991b). *Regulating Divorce*. Oxford: Clarendon Press.

Eekelaar, J. (1991c). 'Parental Responsibility: State of Nature or Nature of the State?'. *Journal of Social Welfare and Family Law*, 13: 37.

Eekelaar, J. (1994a). 'A Jurisdiction in Search of a Mission: Family Proceedings in England and Wales'. *Modern Law Review*, 57: 839.

Eekelaar, J. (1994b). 'The Interests of the Child and the Child's Wishes: The Role of Dynamic Self-Determinism'. *International Journal of Law, Policy and the Family*, 8: 42.

Eekelaar, J. (1995). 'Family Justice: Ideal or Illusion? Family Law and Communitarian Values'. *Current Legal Problems Part II*, 48: 191.

Eekelaar, J. (1998a). 'Should Section 25 be Reformed?'. *Family Law*, 28: 469.

Eekelaar, J. (1998b). 'Do Parents have a Duty to Consult?'. *Law Quarterly Review*, 114: 337.

Eekelaar, J. (1999). 'Family Law: Keeping Us "On Message"'. *Child and Family Law Quarterly*, 11: 387.

Eekelaar, J. (2000). 'Uncovering Social Obligations: Family Law and the Responsible Citizen', in M. Maclean (ed), *Making Law for Families*. Oxford: Hart Publishing.

Eekelaar, J. (2001). 'Rethinking Parental Responsibility'. *Family Law*, 31: 426.

Eekelaar, J. (2002). 'Beyond the Welfare Principle'. *Child and Family Law Quarterly*, 14: 237.

Eekelaar, J. (2003). 'Contact and the Adoption Reform', in A. Bainham, B. Lindley, M. Richards, and L. Trinder (eds), *Children and their Families*. Oxford: Hart Publishing.

Eekelaar, J. (2004). 'Children between Cultures'. *International Journal of Law, Policy and the Family*, 18: 178.

Eekelaar, J. (2006). 'Property and Financial Settlements on Divorce: Sharing and Compensating'. *Family Law*, 36: 754.

Eekelaar, J. (2010). 'Financial and Property Settlement: A Standard Deal?'. *Family Law*, 40: 359.

Eekelaar, J. (2011). '"Not of the Highest Importance": Family Justice under Threat'. *Journal of Social Welfare and Family Law*, 33: 311.

Eekelaar, J. (2013). 'Marriage: A Modest Proposal'. *Family Law* 43: 83.

Eekelaar, J. (2014). 'Perceptions of Equality: The Road to Same-Sex Marriage in England and Wales'. *International Journal of Law, Policy and the Family*, 28: 1.

Eekelaar, J. (2015). 'The Role of the Best Interests Principle in Decisions Affecting Children and Decisions About Children'. *International Journal of Children's Rights*, 23: 3.

Eekelaar, J. (2017). *Family Law and Personal Life*, 2nd edn. Oxford: OUP.

Eekelaar, J. (2018a). 'The Financial Consequences of Divorce: Law and Reality'. *Australian Journal of Family Law*, 32: 28.

Eekelaar, J. (2018b). 'The Financial Consequences of Divorce: Law and Reality'. *Australian Journal of Family Law*, 32: 28.

Eekelaar, J. (2020). 'Do Parents Know Best?'. *International Journal of Children's Rights*, 28: 613.

Eekelaar, J. (2022). 'Afterword', in J. Miles, D. Monk, and R, Probert (eds), *Fifty Years of the Divorce Reform Act*. Oxford: Hart Publishing.

Eekelaar, J. and Maclean, M. (1986). *Maintenance after Divorce*. Oxford: OUP.

Eekelaar, J. and Maclean, M. (1997). 'Property and Financial Adjustment after Divorce in the 1990s—Unfinished Business', in K. Hawkins (ed), *The Human Face of Law*. Oxford: Clarendon Press.

Eekelaar, J., Maclean, M., and Beinart, S. (2000). *Family Lawyers: The Divorce Work of Solicitors*. Oxford: Hart Publishing.

Eijkholt, M. (2010). 'The Right to Found a Family as a Stillborn Right to Procreate?'. *Medical Law Review*, 18: 127.

Ellison, G., Barker, A., and Kulasuriya, T. (2009). *Work and Care: A Study of Modern Parents*. Equality and Human Rights Commission. <www.dera.ioe.ac.uk/11030/1/15._work_and_care_modern_parents_15_report.pdf>.

Ellman, I. (1997). 'The Misguided Movement to Revive Fault Divorce, and Why Reformers Should Look Instead to the American Law Institute'. *International Journal of Law, Policy and the Family*, 11: 216.

Ellman, I. (2000). 'Divorce', in S. Katz, J. Eekelaar, and M. Maclean (eds), *Cross Currents: Family Law and Policy in the US and England*. Oxford: OUP.

Ellman, I. (2007). 'Financial Settlements on Divorce: Two Steps Forward, Two to Go'. *Law Quarterly Review*, 123: 2.

Ellman, I. and Braver, S. (2011). 'Lay Intuitions about Child Support and Marital Status'. *Child and Family Law Quarterly*, 23: 465.

Ellman, I., McKay, S., Miles, J., and Bryson, C. (2014). 'Child Support Judgments: Comparing Public Policy to the Public's Policy'. *International Journal of Law, Policy and the Family*, 28: 274.

Eskridge, W. (2001). 'The Ideological Structure of the Same-Sex Marriage Debate (And Some Postmodern Arguments for Same-Sex Marriage)', in R. Wintemute and M. Andenæs (eds), *Legal Recognition of Same-Sex Partnerships*. Oxford: Hart Publishing.

Etherton, T. (2009). 'Constructive Trusts and Proprietory Estoppel: The Search for Clarity and Principle'. *Conveyancer and Property Lawyer*, 73: 104.

Ewing, J., Hunter, R., Barlow, A., and Smithson, J. (2015). 'Children's Voices: Centre-Stage or Sidelined in Out-of-Court Dispute Resolution in England and Wales?'. *Child and Family Law Quarterly*, 27: 43.

Fairbairn, C., Pyper, D., and Balogun, B. (2022). *Gender Recognition Act Reform: Consultation and Outcome*, House of Commons Library Research Briefing No 09079. <https://researchbriefings.files.parliament.uk/documents/CBP-9079/CBP-9079.pdf>.

Fahey, T. (2020). 'Divorce Trends and Patterns: An Overview', in J. Eekelaar and R. George (eds), *Routledge Handbook of Family Law and Policy*, 2nd edn. Abingdon: Routledge.

Families Need Fathers (2007). Written Memorandum to Public Bill Committee, on Child Maintenance and Other Payments Bill 2007. <www.publications.parliament.uk/pa/cm200607/cmpublic/childmain/memos/memocm2.htm>.

Family Justice Council (2008). *Enhancing the Participation of Children and Young People in Family Proceedings: Starting the Debate.* <www.judiciary.gov.uk/wp-content/uploads/JCO/Documents/FJC/voc/Participation_of_young_people.pdf>.

Family Justice Council (2010a). *Guidelines for Judges Meeting Children who are Subject to Family Proceedings.* <www.judiciary.gov.uk/wp-content/uploads/JCO/Documents/FJC/voc/Guidelines_+Judges_seeing_+Children.pdf>.

Family Justice Council (2010b). *Guidelines in Relation to Children Giving Evidence in Family Proceedings.* <www.judiciary.gov.uk/wp- content/ uploads/ JCO/ Documents/ FJC/ Publications/ Children+Giving+Evidence+Guidelines+-+Final+Version.pdf>.

Family Justice Council (2011). *Guidelines in Relation to Children Giving Evidence in Family Proceedings.* <www.judiciary.gov.uk/wp-content/uploads/JCO/Documents/FJC/Publications/Children+Giving+Evidence+Guidelines+-+Final+Version.pdf>.

Family Justice Council (2018). *Guidance on Financial Needs on Divorce*, 2nd edn. <www.judiciary.uk/publications/guidance-on-financial-needs-on-divorce-edition-2-april-2018/>.

Family Law Week (2007). 'Child Support Reform "A Disaster", says Commons Public Accounts Committee'. <www.familylawweek.co.uk/site.aspx?i=ed724>.

Farmer, E. and Dance, C., with Beecham, J., Bonin, E., and Ouwejan, D. (2010). *An Investigation of Family Finding and Matching in Adoption—Briefing Paper.* DFE-RBX-10-05. <www.adoptionresearchinitiative.org.uk/briefs/DFE-RBX-10-05.pdf>.

Farquhar, S. (2021). *The Financial Remedies Court—The Way Forward.* Report of the FarquharCommittee.<www.judiciary.uk/wp-content/uploads/2021/10/Report-of-the-Farquhar-Committee-Part-2-The-Financial-Remedies-Court-The-Way-Forward-September-2021.pdf>.

Fauset, D. (2020). 'The Reforms to Care Proceedings – One Step Forward and Two Steps Back? A Critical Evaluation of the New

Legal Framework and its Impact on the Pre-Proceedings Stage'. *Child and Family Law Quarterly*, 32: 13.

Fehlberg, B. and Maclean, M. (2009). 'Child Support Policy in Australia and the United Kingdom: Changing Priorities but a Similar Tough Deal for Children?'. *International Journal of Law, Policy and the Family*, 23: 1.

Fehlberg, B. and Miles, J. (eds) (2018). *Australian Journal of Family Law*, 32: issues 1 and 2 (special issue on Anglo-Australian financial remedies law).

Fehlberg, B. and Smyth, B. (2002). 'Binding Pre-Nuptial Agreements in Australia: The First Year'. *International Journal of Law, Policy and the Family*, 16: 127.

Fehlberg, B. and Smyth, B., with Trinder, L. (2020). 'Parenting Issues after Separation: Recent Developments in Common Law Countries', in J. Eekelaar and R. George (eds), *Routledge Handbook of Family Law and Policy*, 2nd edn. Abingdon: Routledge.

Fehlberg, B., Smyth, B., Maclean, M., and Roberts, C. (2011). 'Legislating for Shared Time Parenting after Separation: A Research Review'. *International Journal of Law, Policy and the Family*, 25: 318.

Femicide Census (undated). *UK Femicides 2009–2018*. <www.femicidecensus.org/wp-content/uploads/2020/11/Femicide-Census-10-year-report.pdf>.

Fenton-Glynn, C. (2015a). 'Austerity and the Benefits Cap: In Whose Best Interests?'. *Journal of Social Welfare and Family Law*, 37: 467.

Fenton-Glynn, C. (2015b). 'The Regulation and Recognition of Surrogacy under English Law: An Overview of the Case-Law'. *Child and Family Law Quarterly*, 27: 83.

Fenton-Glynn, C. (2015c). 'The Rise of Strict Scrutiny: Extending *Re B-S* to Changes in Care Plans'. *Journal of Social Welfare and Family Law*, 37: 105.

Fenton-Glynn, C. (2016). 'Outsourcing Ethical Dilemmas: Regulating International Surrogacy Arrangements'. *Medical Law Review*, 24: 59.

Fenton-Glynn, C. (2017). '*Re C v XYZ County Council*', in H. Stalford, K. Hollingsworth, and S. Gilmore (eds), *Rewriting Children's Rights Judgments: From Academic Vision to New Practice*. Oxford: Hart Publishing.

Fenton-Glynn, C. (2018). 'Revoking Adoption: *Re J (Adoption: Appeal)*'. *Family Law*, 48: 372.

Fenton-Glynn, C. (2020). 'Deconstructing Parenthood: What Makes a "Mother"?'. *Cambridge Law Journal*, 79: 34.

Fenton-Glynn, C. (2021). *Children and the European Court of Human Rights*. Oxford: OUP.

Fenton-Glynn, C. (2022). 'Gender, Identity and the Law', in J. Scherpe and S. Gilmore (eds), *Family Matters: Essays in Honour of John Eekelaar*. Cambridge: Intersentia.

Fenwick, H. and Hayward, A. (2018). 'From Same-Sex Marriage to Equal Civil Partnerships: On a Path Towards "Perfecting" Equality?'. *Child and Family Law Quarterly*, 30: 97.

Ferguson, L. (2008). 'Family, Social Inequalities, and the Persuasive Force of Interpersonal Obligation'. *International Journal of Law, Policy and the Family*, 22: 61.

Ferguson, L. (2013a). 'Arbitration in Financial Dispute Resolution: The Final Step to Reconstructing the Default(s) and Exception(s)?'. *Journal of Social Welfare and Family Law*, 35: 115.

Ferguson, L. (2013b). 'Not Merely Rights for Children but Children's Rights: The Theory Gap and the Assumption of the Importance of Children's Rights'. *International Journal of Children's Rights*, 21: 177.

Ferguson, L. (2015a). 'Arbitral Awards: A Magnetic Factor of Determinative Importance – Yet Not to be Rubber-Stamped?'. *Journal of Social Welfare and Family Law*, 37: 99.

Ferguson, L. (2015b). '*Wyatt v Vince*: The Reality of Individualised Justice – Financial Orders, Forensic Delay, and Access to Justice'. *Child and Family Law Quarterly*, 27: 195.

Ferguson, L. (2016). 'The Curious Case of Civil Partnership: The Extension of Marriage to Same-Sex Couples and the Status-Altering Consequences of a Wait-and-See Approach'. *Child and Family Law Quarterly*, 28: 347.

Ferguson, S. et al (2011). *Application of Ferguson et al v United Kingdom, File number 8254-11*, 2 February. <https://blogs.law.columbia.edu/genderandsexualitylawblog/files/2013/01/Ferguson-v.-UK.pdf>.

Fineman, M. (2004). *The Autonomy Myth: A Theory of Dependency*. New York: The New Press.

Finnis, J. (1993). 'Law, Morality and "Sexual Orientation"'. *Notre Dame Law Review*, 69: 1049.

Fisher, H. and Low, H. (2009). 'Who Wins, Who Loses and Who Recovers from Divorce?', in J. Miles and R. Probert (eds), *Sharing Lives,*

Dividing Assets: An Inter-Disciplinary Study. Oxford: Hart Publishing.

Fisher, H. and Low, H. (2016). 'Recovery from Divorce: Comparing High and Low Income Couples'. *International Journal of Law, Policy and the Family*, 30: 338.

Fisher, H. and Low, H. (2018a). 'Financial Management and Perceptions of Ownership of Money within Couples', in T. Al Baghal (ed), *Understanding Society Innovation Panel Wave 10: results from methodological experiments*. Understanding Society Working Paper Series No 2018-06. <www.understandingsociety.ac.uk/sites/default/files/downloads/working-papers/2018-06.pdf>.

Fisher, H. and Low, H. (2018b). 'Divorce Early or Divorce Late?'. *Australian Journal of Family Law*, 32: 6.

Flaherty, J., Veit-Wilson, J., and Dornan, P. (2004). *Poverty: The Facts*, 5th edn. London: CPAG.

Flynn, L. and Lawson, A. (1995). 'Gender, Sexuality and the Doctrine of Detrimental Reliance.' *Feminist Legal Studies*, 3: 105.

Flynn, R. (2000). 'Black Carers for White Children. Shifting the "Same-Race" Placement Debate'. *Adoption and Fostering*, 24: 47.

Foley, N. (2022). *Child Maintenance: Calculations, Variations and Income (UK)*. House of Commons Library Research Briefing No 7770. <www.commonslibrary.parliament.uk/research-briefings/cbp-7770/>.

Forbes, A. (2017). 'Secure Accommodation for Troublesome Teenagers'. *Journal of Social Welfare and Family Law*, 39: 106.

Foreign & Commonwealth Office and HO (2022). *Forced Marriage Unit Statistics*. <www.gov.uk/government/statistics/forced-marriage-unit-statistics-2021/forced-marriage-unit-statistics-2021>.

Fortin, J. (1994). '*Re F*: "The Gooseberry Bush Approach"'. *Modern Law Review*, 57: 296.

Fortin, J. (1999). '*Re D (Care: Natural Parent Presumption)* Is Blood Really Thicker Than Water?'. *Child and Family Law Quarterly*, 11: 435.

Fortin, J. (2004). 'Children's Rights: Are the Courts Now Taking Them More Seriously?'. *Kings College Law Journal*, 15: 253.

Fortin, J. (2006). 'Accommodating Children's Rights in a Post Human Rights Act Era'. *Modern Law Review*, 69: 299.

Fortin, J. (2007). 'Children's Representation Through the Looking Glass'. *Family Law*, 37: 500.

Fortin, J. (2009a). 'Children's Right to Know Their Origins—Too Far, Too Fast?'. *Child and Family Law Quarterly*, 21: 336.

Fortin, J. (2009b). *Children's Rights and the Developing Law*, 3rd edn. Cambridge: CUP.

Fortin, J. (2014). 'Children's Rights: Flattering to Deceive?'. *Child and Family Law Quarterly*, 26: 51.

Fortin, J., Hunt, J., and Scanlan, L. (2012). *Taking a Longer View of Contact: The Perspectives of Young Adults Who Experienced Parental Separation in their Youth: Summary*. University of Sussex/University of Oxford. <www.sussex.ac.uk/law/documents/nuffield-foundation-research-summary-16nov2012.pdf>.

Fortin, J., Ritchie, C., and Buchanan, A. (2006). 'Young Adults' Perceptions of Court-Ordered Contact.' *Child and Family Law Quarterly*, 18: 211.

Fox, L. (2003). 'Reforming Family Property—Comparisons, Compromises and Common Dimensions'. *Child and Family Law Quarterly*, 15: 1.

Fox Harding, L. (1991a). 'The Children Act 1989 in Context: Four Perspectives in Child Care Law and Policy (I)'. *Journal of Social Welfare and Family Law*, 13: 179.

Fox Harding, L. (1991b). 'The Children Act 1989 in Context: Four Perspectives in Child Care Law and Policy (II). *Journal of Social Welfare and Family Law*, 13: 285.

Fox O'Mahony, L. (2014). 'Property Outsiders and the Hidden Politics of Doctrinalism'. *Current Legal Problems*, 67: 409.

Fox O'Mahony, L. (2015). 'The Politics of *Lloyd's Bank v Rosset*', in S. Douglas et al (eds), *Landmark Cases in Property Law*. Oxford: Hart Publishing.

Fraser, G. (2018). 'A Moment in Time'. *New Law Journal*, 17 Aug: 8.

Frazer, L. and Selwyn, J. (2005). 'Why Are We Waiting? The Demography of Adoption for Children of Black, Asian and Black Mixed Parentage in England'. *Child and Family Social Work*, 10: 135.

Freeman, M. (1984). 'Legal Ideologies, Patriarchal Precedents, and Domestic Violence', in M. Freeman (ed), *State, Law, and the Family: Critical Perspectives*. London: Tavistock.

Freeman, M. (1989). 'The Abuse of the Elderly—Legal Responses in England', in J. Eekelaar and D. Pearl (eds), *An Aging World: Dilemmas and Challenges for Law and Social Policy*. Oxford: OUP.

Freeman, M. (1992). 'Taking Children's Rights More Seriously'. *International Journal of Law and the Family*, 6: 52.

FREEMAN, M. (1996). 'The New Birth Right? Identity and the Child of the Reproductive Revolution'. *International Journal of Children's Rights*, 4: 273.

FREEMAN, M. (2000). 'Disputing Children', in S. Katz, J. Eekelaar, and M. Maclean (eds), *Cross Currents: Family Law and Policy in the US and England*. Oxford: OUP.

FREEMAN, M. (2007). 'Why It Remains Important to Take Children's Rights Seriously'. *International Journal of Children's Rights*, 15: 5.

FREEMAN, M. (2017). '*Re T (A Minor) (Wardship: Medical Treatment)*: Alternative Judgment', in H. Stalford, K. Hollingsworth, and S. Gilmore (eds), *Rewriting Children's Rights Judgments: From Academic Vision to New Practice*. Oxford: Hart Publishing.

GAFFNEY-RHYS, R. (2005). 'The Law Relating to Affinity after *B and L v UK*'. *Family Law*, 35: 955.

GAFFNEY-RHYS, R. (2009). 'The Law Relating to Marriageable Age from a National and International Perspective'. *International Family Law*, 228.

GAFFNEY-RHYS, R. (2013). 'Am I Married? Three Recent Case Studies of the Effect of Non-Compliant Marriage Ceremonies'. *International Family Law*, 53.

GAFFNEY-RHYS, R. (2014). 'The Future of Civil Partnerships in England and Wales'. *Family Law*, 44: 1694.

GAFFNEY-RHYS, R. (2017). 'Opposite-Sex Civil Partnerships in England and Wales? Let's Wait and See'. *Family Law*, 47: 1216.

GARDNER, S. (1993). 'Rethinking Family Property'. *Law Quarterly Review*, 109: 263.

GARDNER, S. (2008). 'Family Property Today'. *Law Quarterly Review*, 124: 422.

GARDNER, S. (2013). 'Problems in Family Property'. *Cambridge Law Journal*, 72: 301.

GARDNER, S. (2014). 'Material Relief between Ex-Cohabitants 2: Otherwise than via Beneficial Entitlement'. *Conveyancer and Property Lawyer*, 78: 202.

GARDNER, S. AND DAVIDSON, K. (2011). 'The Future of *Stack v Dowden*'. *Law Quarterly Review*, 127: 13.

GARDNER, S. AND DAVIDSON, K. (2012). 'The Supreme Court on Family Homes'. *Law Quarterly Review*, 128: 178.

GARLAND, F. AND TRAVIS, M. (2018). 'Legislating Intersex Equality: Building the Resilience of Intersex People Through Law'. *Legal Studies*, 38: 587.

GARRISON, M. (2014). 'The Changing Face of Marriage', in J. Eekelaar and R. George (eds), *Routledge Handbook of Family Law and Policy*. Abingdon: Routledge.

GARRISON, M. (2020). 'The Changing Face of Marriage', in J. Eekelaar and R. George (eds), *Routledge Handbook of Family Law and Policy*, 2nd edn. Abingdon: Routledge.

GELDOF, B. (2003). 'The Real Love that Dare Not Speak its Name', in A. Bainham, B. Lindley, M. Richards, and L. Trinder (eds), *Children and their Families*. Oxford: Hart Publishing.

GENERAL REGISTER OFFICE (2003). *Civil Registration: Delivering Vital Change*. London: HMSO.<webarchive.nationalarchives.gov.uk/+/http:/www.statistics.gov.uk/downloads/registration/01Chapters1-11.pdf>.

GEORGE, R. (2008a). '*Stack v Dowden*—Do As We Say, Not As We Do?'. *Journal of Social Welfare and Family Law*, 30: 49.

GEORGE, R. (2008b). 'Changing Names, Changing Places: Reconsidering Section 13 of the Children Act 1989'. *Family Law*, 38: 1121.

GEORGE, R. (2011a). 'Cutting Legal Aid Will Undermine Whole Family Law System'. *The Telegraph*, 25 February. <www.telegraph.co.uk/news/newstopics/lawreports/8346866/Cutting-legal-aid-will-undermine-whole-family-law-system.html>.

GEORGE, R. (2011b). '*Re F (Children) (Internal Relocation)*'. *Journal of Social Welfare and Family Law*, 33: 169.

GEORGE, R. (2012a). *Ideas and Debates in Family Law*. Oxford: Hart Publishing.

GEORGE, R. (2012b). 'Reviewing Relocation?'. *Child and Family Law Quarterly*, 24: 110.

GEORGE, R. (2013). 'Family Finances and the Corporate Veil: *Prest v Petrodel*'. *Family Law*, 43: 991.

GEORGE, R. (2014). *Relocation Disputes: Law and Practice in England and New Zealand*. Oxford: Hart Publishing.

GEORGE, R. (2015). 'How Do Judges Decide International Relocation Cases?'. *Child and Family Law Quarterly*, 27: 377.

GEORGE, R. (2016). 'The Child's Welfare in European Perspective', in J. Scherpe (ed), *European Family Law, Vol III: Family Law in European Perspective*. London: Elgar.

GEORGE, R. (2019a). 'The Legal Basis of the Court's Jurisdiction to Authorise Medical Treatment of Children', in I. Goold, J. Herring, and C. Auckland (eds), *Parental Rights, Best Interests and Significant Harms*. Oxford: Hart Publishing.

George, R. (2019b). 'Matters of Welfare and Matters of Law'. *Journal of Social Welfare and Family Law*, 41: 358.

George, R. (2020). 'Parental Responsibility, Vaccinations, and the Role of the Court'. *Law Quarterly Review*, 136: 559.

George, R. (2021). 'The Role of Law in Family Disputes'. *New Zealand Journal of Family Law*, 81.

George, R. (2022a). 'Vulnerable Children in Unregulated Care: The Unstoppable Inherent Jurisdiction'. *Journal of Social Welfare and Family Law*, 44: 254.

George, R. (2022b). 'Legal Professionals and the Family Justice System', in J. Scherpe and S. Gilmore (eds), *Family Matters: Essays in Honour of John Eekelaar*. Cambridge: Intersentia.

George, R. (2023). 'What Are Family Courts For?', in M. Maclean and R. Treloar (eds), *Research Handbook on Family Justice Systems*. London: Elgar.

George, R. and Gallwey, A. (2016). 'How Do Parents Experience Relocation Disputes in the Family Courts?'. *Journal of Social Welfare and Family Law*, 38: 394.

George, R., Harris, P., and Herring, J. (2009). 'Pre-Nuptial Agreements: For Better or For Worse?'. *Family Law*, 39: 934.

Gibb, F. (2008). 'Family Justice System is At Risk, Warns New Chief Judge'. *The Times*, 24 March.

Gibson, C. (1994). *Dissolving Wedlock*. London: Routledge.

Gill, A. (2011). 'Criminalising Forced Marriage'. *Family Law*, 41: 1378.

Gillet, F. (2018). 'Civil Partnerships: "Why I Want One With my Sister"'. BBC website, 3 October 2018. <www.bbc.co.uk/news/uk-45732851>.

Gillies, V. (2009). Understandings and Experiences of Involved Fathering in the United Kingdom: Exploring Classed Dimensions. *Annals, AAPSS*: 624.

Gilmore, S. (2003). 'Parental Responsibility and the Unmarried Father—A New Dimension to the Debate'. *Child and Family Law Quarterly*, 15: 21.

Gilmore, S. (2004a). '*Re P (Child) (Financial Provision)*—Shoeboxes and Comical Shopping Trips—Child Support from the Affluent to Fabulously Rich'. *Child and Family Law Quarterly*, 16: 103.

Gilmore, S. (2004b). 'The Nature, Scope and Use of the Specific Issue Order'. *Child and Family Law Quarterly*, 16: 367.

Gilmore, S. (2006). 'Contact/Shared Residence and Child Well-Being: Research Evidence and its Implications for Legal Decision-Making'. *International Journal of Law, Policy and the Family*, 20: 344.

Gilmore, S. (2007). '*Re B (Contact: Child Support)*—Horses and Carts: Contact and Child Support'. *Child and Family Law Quarterly*, 19: 357.

Gilmore, S. (2008). 'Disputing Contact: Challenging Some Assumptions'. *Child and Family Law Quarterly*, 20: 285.

Gilmore, S. (2011). '*Corbett v Corbett*: Once a Man, Always a Man?', in S. Gilmore, J. Herring, and R. Probert (eds), *Landmark Cases in Family Law*. Oxford: Hart Publishing.

Gilmore, S. (2013). '*Re J (Care Proceedings: Past Possible Perpetrators in a New Family Unit)* [2013] UKSC 9: Bulwarks and Logic—The Blood Which Runs through the Veins of Law—But How Much Will Be Spilled in Future?'. *Child and Family Law Quarterly*, 25: 215.

Gilmore, S. (2015). 'Withdrawal of Parental Responsibility: Lost Authority and a Lost Opportunity'. *Modern Law Review*, 78: 1042.

Gilmore, S. (2016). 'Less of the "P" Discipline and More of the "H" Word – Putting *Payne* in its Place!'. *Journal of Social Welfare and Family Law*, 38: 87.

Gilmore, S. (2017). 'Use of the UNCRC in Family Law Cases in England and Wales'. *International Journal of Children's Rights*, 25: 500.

Gilmore, S. (2022). 'A Black Cloud Over the Age of Discretion and the Scope of Parental Responsibility', in J. Scherpe and S. Gilmore (eds), *Family Matters: Essays in Honour of John Eekelaar*. Cambridge: Intersentia.

Gilmore, S. and Herring, J. (2011). '"No" is the Hardest Word: Consent and Children's Autonomy'. *Child and Family Law Quarterly*, 23: 3.

Gingerbread (2011). *'Strengthening Families, Promoting Parental Responsibility'—Government Plans for Child Maintenance*. Gingerbread Briefing February.

Gingerbread (2012). *The Draft Child Support Maintenance Calculation Regulations 2012: Response from Gingerbread to the Technical Consultation*.

Gingerbread (2016). *Child Maintenance Charging; Evidence Summary for the DWP 30 Month Review*. <www.gov.uk/government/uploads/system/uploads/attachment_data/file/629228/cms-30-month-review-gingerbread-response.pdf>.

Gingerbread (2017). *Children Deserve More: Challenging Child Maintenance Avoidance*.

<www.gingerbread.org.uk/wp-content/uploads/2017/07/Children-deserve-more-challenging-child-maintenance-avoidance.pdf>.

Glennon, L. (2005). 'Displacing the "Conjugal Family" in Legal Policy—A Progressive Move?'. *Child and Family Law Quarterly*, 17: 141.

Glennon, L. (2008). 'Obligations between Adult Partners: Moving from Form to Function?'. *International Journal of Law, Policy and the Family*, 22: 22.

Glennon, L. (2010). 'The Limitations of Equality Discourses on the Contours of Intimate Obligations', in J. Wallbank, S. Choudhry, and J. Herring (eds), *Rights, Gender and Family Law*, Abingdon: Routledge.

Glister, J. (2010). 'Section 199 of the Equality Act 2010: How Not to Abolish the Presumption of Advancement'. *Modern Law Review*, 73: 807.

Goldstein, B. (2000). 'Ethnicity and Placement. Beginning the Debate'. *Adoption and Fostering*, 24: 9.

Goodman, A. and Greaves, E. (2010). *Cohabitation, Marriage and Child Outcomes*. London: Institute for Fiscal Studies. <https://ifs.org.uk/sites/default/files/output_url_files/comm114.pdf>.

Gordon-Bouvier, E. (2020). 'The Open Future: Analysing the Temporality of Autonomy in Family Law'. *Child and Family Law Quarterly*, 32: 75.

Government Actuary's Department (2005). *Marriages Abroad*. London: GAD.

Government Equalities Office (2012). *Equal Civil Marriage: A Consultation*. <www.assets.publishing.service.gov.uk/government/uploads/system/uploads/attachment_data/file/133258/consultation-document_1_.pdf>.

Government Equalities Office (2016). *Government Response to the Women and Equalities Committee Report on Transgender Equality*. <www.assets.publishing.service.gov.uk/government/uploads/system/uploads/attachment_data/file/535764/Government_Response_to_the_Women_and_Equalities_Committee_Report_on_Transgender_Equality.pdf>.

Government Equalities Office (2018a). *Reform of the Gender Recognition Act—Government Consultation*. <www.gov.uk/government/uploads/system/uploads/attachment_data/file/721725/GRA-Consultation-document.pdf>.

Government Equalities Office (2018b). *Trans People in the UK*. <www.assets.publishing.service.gov.uk/government/uploads/system/uploads/attachment_data/file/721642/GEO-LGBT-factsheet.pdf>.

Government Equalities Office (2018c). *Reform of the Gender Recognition Act—Government Consultation*. <www.assets.publishing.service.gov.uk/government/uploads/system/uploads/attachment_data/file/721725/GRA-Consultation-document.pdf>.

Government Equalities Office (2020). *Reform of the Gender Recognition Act—Analysis of Consultation Responses*. <www.gov.uk/government/collections/gender-recognition-act-consultation-and-response>.

Government Equalities Office (2022a). *Gender Recognition Certificate Applications and Outcomes* <www.gov.uk/government/publications/gender-recognition-certificate-applications-and-outcomes/gender-recognition-certificate-applications-and-outcomes>.

Government Equalities Office (2022b). *Civil Partnerships for Opposite-Sex Couples: Consultation and Response* <www.gov.uk/government/collections/civil-partnerships-for-opposite-sex-couples-consultation-and-response>.

Gray, K. and Gray, S. (2009). *Elements of Land Law*, 5th edn. Oxford: OUP.

Graycar, R. and Morgan, J. (2002). *The Hidden Gender of Law*, 2nd edn. Leichhardt, New South Wales: The Federation Press.

Greatbatch, D. and Dingwall, R. (1999). 'The Marginalization of Domestic Violence in Divorce Mediation'. *International Journal of Law, Policy and the Family*, 13: 174.

Green, L. (2011). 'Sex-Neutral Marriage'. *Current Legal Problems*, 64: 1.

Griffiths, K. (2019). 'From "Form" to Function and Back Again: A New Conceptual Basis for Developing Frameworks for the Legal Recognition of Adult Relationships'. *Child and Family Law Quarterly*, 31: 227.

Griffiths, L., Farr, I., Jones, C., Johnson, R., Roe, A., Lee, A., Alrouh, B., Broadhurst, K., John, A., and Ford, D. (2021). *The Health of Older Children and Young People Subject to Care Proceedings in Wales*. London: Nuffield Family Justice Observatory. <www.nuffieldfjo.org.uk/wp-content/uploads/2021/10/nfjo_young-people_health_report_20211007_english-1.pdf>.

Guardian (2022). 'Katie Price May Face Jail after Admitting to Breach of Restraining Order'. 25 May 2022. <www.theguardian

.com/media/2022/may/25/katie-price-may-face-jail-after-admitting-to-breach-of-restraining-order>.

Hafen, B. and Hafen, J. (1995–6). 'Abandoning Children to their Autonomy: The United Nations Convention on the Rights of the Child'. *Harvard International Law Journal*, 37: 449.

Hale, B. (2004). 'Unmarried Couples in Family Law'. *Family Law*, 34: 419.

Hale, B. (2014). 'New Families and the Welfare of Children'. *Journal of Social Welfare and Family Law*, 36: 26.

Hale, B. (2018). Keynote Speech: Resolution's 30th National Conference, Bristol. <www.supremecourt.uk/docs/speech-180420.pdf>.

Hale, B. (2021). 'What Do We Mean by a Family?', Family Justice Council Bridget Lindley Memorial Lecture. <www.judiciary.uk/wp-content/uploads/2021/03/Family-Justice-Council-Bridget-Lindley-Memorial-Lecture-2021-.pdf>.

Hale, M. (1736). *The History of the Pleas of the Crown*. (1971) P. Glazebrook (ed). London: Professional Books.

Hall, A. (2008). 'Special Guardianship and Permanency Planning: Unforeseen Consequences and Missed Opportunities'. *Child and Family Law Quarterly*, 20: 359.

Hall, S. (2000). 'What Price the Logic of Evidence?'. *Family Law*, 30: 423.

Halley, J. (2001). 'Recognition, Rights, Regulation, Normalisation: Rhetorics of Justification in the Same-Sex Marriage Debate', in R. Wintemute and M. Andenæs (eds), *Legal Recognition of Same-Sex Partnerships*. Oxford: Hart Publishing.

Hansen, S. (2019). 'Birth Relationships After Adoption: Is There a Role for Article 8?'. *Child and Family Law Quarterly*, 31: 211.

Harding, M. (2009). 'Defending *Stack v Dowden*'. *Conveyancer and Property Lawyer*, 73: 309.

Harding, M. and Newnham, A. (2017). 'Section 8 Orders on the Public–Private Divide'. *Journal of Social Welfare and Family Law*, 39: 83.

Harding, R. (2007). 'Sir Mark Potter and the Protection of the Traditional Family: Why Same-Sex Marriage is (Still!) a Feminist Issue'. *Feminist Legal Studies*, 15: 223.

Harding, R. (2014). '(Re)inscribing the Heteronormative Family: Same-Sex Relationships and Parenting "After Equality"', in R. Leckey (ed), *After Legal Equality: Family, Sex, Kinship*. Abingdon: Routledge.

Harding, R. (2015). 'Playing House of Lords Bingo: A Critical Discourse Analysis of Hansard Debates on Civil Partnership and Same Sex Marriage', in J. Miles, P. Mody, and R. Probert (eds), *Marriage Rites and Rights*. Oxford: Hart Publishing.

Hargreaves, C., Cusworth, L., Alrouh, B., Broadhurst, K., Cowley, L., Abouelenin, M., Doebler, S., Akbari, A., Farr, I., and North, L. (2022). *Uncovering Private Family Law: What Can the Data Tell us about Children's Participation?* London: Nuffield Family Justice Observatory. <www.nuffieldfjo.org.uk/wp-content/uploads/2022/06/nfjo_report_private_law_child_participation_20220615_FINAL-1.pdf>.

Harper, M., Downs, M., Landells, K., and Wilson, G. (2005). *Civil Partnership: The New Law*. Bristol: Jordan Publishing.

Harris, P. (2008). 'The *Miller* Paradoxes'. *Family Law*, 38: 1096.

Harris, P. and George, R. (2010). 'Parental Responsibility and Shared Residence Orders: Parliamentary Intentions and Judicial Interpretations.' *Child and Family Law Quarterly*, 22: 151.

Harris-Short, S. (2001). 'The Adoption and Children Bill—A Fast Track to Failure?'. *Child and Family Law Quarterly*, 13: 405.

Harris-Short, S. (2002). '*Re B (Adoption: Natural Parent)* Putting the Child at the Heart of Adoption?'. *Child and Family Law Quarterly*, 14: 325.

Harris-Short, S. (2003). 'An "Identity Crisis" in the International Law of Human Rights? The Challenge of Reproductive Cloning'. *International Journal of Children's Rights*, 11: 333.

Harris-Short, S. (2005). 'Family Law and the Human Rights Act 1998—Restraint or Revolution?'. *Child and Family Law Quarterly*, 17: 329.

Harris-Short, S. (2010). 'Resisting the March Towards 50/50 Shared Residence. Rights, Welfare and Equality in Post-Separation Families'. *Journal of Social Welfare and Family Law*, 32: 257.

Harrison, R. and Benson, M. (2019). 'Illegitimate Claims? Schedule 1 Claims for Periodical Payments by Parents of Adult Children'. *Family Law*, 49: 505.

Harwood, J. (2019). '"We Don't Know What It Is We Don't Know": How Austerity Has Undermined the Courts' Access to Information in Child Arrangements Cases

Involving Domestic Abuse'. *Child and Family Law Quarterly*, 31: 321.

HARWOOD, J. (2021). 'Presuming the Status Quo? The Impact of the Statutory Presumption of Parental Involvement'. *Journal of Social Welfare and Family Law*, 43: 119.

HASKEY, J. (2018a). 'Facts and Figures: Grounds for Divorce Since the 1969 Divorce Reform Act in England and Wales'. *Family Law*, 48: 1006.

HASKEY, J. (2018b). 'A History of Divorce Law Reform in England and Wales: Evolution, Revolution or Repetition?'. *Family Law*, 48: 1407.

HASKEY, J. (2022). 'Divorces by Fact Proven Over the Past Half Century in England and Wales: The Historical Context, Statistical Trends and Future Prospects', in J. Miles, D. Monk, and R. Probert (eds), *Fifty Years of the Divorce Reform Act*. Oxford: Hart Publishing.

HASKEY, J. AND LEWIS, J. (2006). 'Living-Apart-Together in Britain: Context and Meaning'. *International Journal of Law in Context*, 2: 37.

HASSON, E. (2006). 'Wedded to "Fault": The Legal Regulation of Divorce and Relationship Breakdown'. *Legal Studies*, 26: 267.

HASTINGS, G. (2010). '*Re A (Children) (Conjoined Twins: Surgical Separation)*—Judgment', in R. Hunter, C. McGynn, and E. Rackley (eds), *Feminist Judgments: From Theory to Practice*. Oxford: Hart Publishing.

HAY, F. (2022). 'Is it Time to Reclaim s 25 in Cases Involving Pensions?'. *Family Law*, 52: 756.

HAYES, M. (1990). 'The Law Commission and the Family Home'. *Modern Law Review*, 53: 222.

HAYES, M. (2006). 'Relocation Cases: Is the Court of Appeal Applying the Correct Principles?'. *Child and Family Law Quarterly*, 18: 351.

HAYES, M. AND WILLIAMS, C. (1999). *Family Law: Principles, Policy and Practice*. London: Butterworths.

HAYES, P. (2003). 'Giving Due Consideration to Ethnicity in Adoption Placements—A Principled Approach'. *Child and Family Law Quarterly*, 15: 225.

HAYWARD, A. (2012). '"Family Property" and the Process of "Familialisation" of Property Law'. *Child and Family Law Quarterly*, 24: 284.

HAYWARD, A. (2017). 'The Future of Civil Partnership in England and Wales', in A. Hayward and J. Scherpe (eds), *The Future of Registered Partnership*. Cambridge: Intersentia.

HAYWARD, A. (2019). 'The *Steinfeld* Effect: Equal Civil Partnerships and the Construction of the Cohabitant'. *Child and Family Law Quarterly*, 31: 283.

HAYWARD, A. (2021). 'Mixed-Sex Civil Partnerships and Relationality: A Perspective from Law'. *Families, Relationships and Societies*, 10: 205.

HAYWARD, A. (2022). 'Evaluating the Government's Response to the Women and Equalities Committee Rights of Cohabiting Partners Inquiry'. *Financial Remedies Journal*, published 7 November. <www.financialremediesjournal.com/content/evaluating-the-governments-response-to-the-women-and-equalities-committee-rights-of-cohabiting-partners-inquiry.e25d1e771c464ab88f3f2e8c160da6d4.htm>.

HEAPHY, B., SMART, C., AND EINARSDOTTIR, A. (2013). *Same-Sex Marriages: New Generations, New Relationships*. Basingstoke: Palgrave Macmillan.

HEENAN, A. (2015). 'Step-Parent Adoption and Proportionality'. *Journal of Social Welfare and Family Law*, 37: 244.

HEENAN, A. (2018). 'An (Un)Equal Start on the Road to Independent Living: What Does Fairness Mean in Big Money Cases'. *Journal of Social Welfare and Family Law*, 40: 362.

HEENAN, A. (2021). 'Neoliberalism, Family Law, and the Devaluation of Care'. *Journal of Law and Society*, 48: 386.

HENAGHAN, M. AND BUCK, L. (2017). 'To Return or Not to Return, That is the Question: A UK–New Zealand Comparison of Approaches to "Internal Abduction" Cases'. *Journal of Social Welfare and Family Law*, 39: 102.

HENRICSON, C. AND BAINHAM, A. (2005). *The Child and Family Policy Divide: Tension, Convergence and Rights*. York: Joseph Rowntree Foundation.

HENSHAW, D. (2006). *Recovering Child Support: Routes to Responsibility*, Cm 6894. London: TSO. <www.assets.publishing.service.gov.uk/government/uploads/system/uploads/attachment_data/file/272335/6894.pdf>.

HERRING, J. (1999a). 'The Human Rights Act and the Welfare Principle in Family Law—Conflicting or Complementary?'. *Child and Family Law Quarterly*, 11: 223.

HERRING, J. (1999b). 'The Welfare Principle and the Rights of Parents', in A. Bainham, S. Day Sclater, and M. Richards (eds), *What is a Parent? A Socio-Legal Analysis*. Oxford: Hart Publishing.

HERRING, J. (2005a). 'Why Financial Orders on Divorce should be Unfair'. *International Journal of Law, Policy and the Family*, 19: 218.

HERRING, J. (2005b). 'Farewell Welfare?'. *Journal of Social Welfare and Family Law*, 27: 159.

HERRING, J. (2011). 'Elder Abuse and Stressing Carers', in J. Bridgman, H. Keating, and C. Lind (eds), *Regulating Family Responsibilities*. Farnham: Ashgate.

HERRING, J. (2012). 'Divorce, Internet Hubs and Stephen Cretney', in R. Probert and C. Barton (eds), *Fifty Years in Family Law*. Cambridge: Intersentia.

HERRING, J. (2013). 'Capacity to Cohabit: Hoping "Everything Turns Out Well in the End"'. *Child and Family Law Quarterly*, 25: 471.

HERRING, J. (2014). 'Making Family Law Less Sexy . . . and More Careful', in R. Leckey (ed), *After Legal Equality: Family, Sex, Kinship*. Abingdon: Routledge.

HERRING, J. (2020). *Domestic Abuse and Human Rights*. Cambridge: Intersentia.

HERRING, J. AND FOSTER, C. (2012). 'Welfare Means Relationality, Virtue and Altruism'. *Legal Studies*, 32: 480.

HERRING, J. AND TAYLOR, R. (2006). 'Relocating Relocation'. *Child and Family Law Quarterly*, 18: 517.

HERRING, J., BARKER, N., AND FOX, M. (2010). '*Sheffield County Council v E*', in R. Hunter et al (eds), *Feminist Judgments: From Theory to Practice*. Oxford: Hart Publishing.

HERRING, J., HARRIS, P., AND GEORGE, R. (2011). 'Ante-Nuptial Agreements: Fairness, Equality and Presumptions'. *Law Quarterly Review*, 127: 335.

HERRING, J., PROBERT, R., AND GILMORE, S. (2015). *Great Debates: Family Law*, 2nd edn. Basingstoke: Palgrave Macmillan.

HESS, E. AND MILES, J. (2017). 'The Recognition of Money Work as a Specialty in the Family Courts by the Creation of a National Network of Financial Remedies Units'. *Family Law*, 1335.

HESTER, M. (2005). 'Making it Through the Criminal Justice System: Attrition and Domestic Violence'. *Social Policy and Society*, 5: 79.

HESTER, M. (2009). *Who Does What to Whom? Gender and Domestic Violence Perpetrators*. Bristol: University of Bristol in association with the Northern Rock Foundation. <https://equation.org.uk/wp-content/uploads/2012/12/Who-does-what-to-Whom-Gender-and-domestic-violence-perpetrators.pdf>.

HESTER, M. AND WESTMARLAND, J. (2005). *Tackling Domestic Violence: Effective Interventions and Approaches*. Home Office Research Study 290. <https://dro.dur.ac.uk/2556/1/2556.pdf>.

HESTER, M., WESTMARLAND, J., PEARCE, J., AND WILLIAMSON, E. (2008). *Early Evaluation of the Domestic Violence, Crime and Victims Act 2004*. MOJ Research Series 14/08. <https://dro.dur.ac.uk/5093/1/5093.pdf>.

HFEA (2021a). *Code of Practice*, 9th edn. <https://portal.hfea.gov.uk/media/ihkjnfqq/2022-07-01-code-of-practice-2021.pdf>.

HFEA (2021b). *Fertility Treatment 2019: Trends and Figures*. <www.hfea.gov.uk/about-us/publications/research-and-data/fertility-treatment-2019-trends-and-figures>.

HFEA (2022). *Impact of Covid-19 on Fertility Treatment 2020*. <www.hfea.gov.uk/about-us/publications/research-and-data/impact-of-covid-19-on-fertility-treatment-2020>.

HIBBS, M. (2001). 'Surrogacy—Who Will Be Left Holding The Baby?'. *Family Law*, 31: 736.

HIBBS, M., BARTON, C., AND BESWICK, J. (2001). 'Why Marry? Perceptions of the Affianced'. *Family Law*, 31: 197.

HILDER, S. AND BETTINSON, V. (2016). 'Introduction', in S. Hilder and V. Bettinson (eds), *Domestic Violence: Interdisciplinary Perspectives on Protection, Prevention and Intervention*. London: Palgrave Macmillan.

HILDER, S. AND FREEMAN, C. (2016). 'Working with Perpetrators of Domestic Violence and Abuse: The Potential for Change', in S. Hilder and V. Bettinson (eds), *Domestic Violence: Interdisciplinary Perspectives on Protection, Prevention and Intervention*. London: Palgrave Macmillan.

HILL, J. (2020). *See What You Made Me Do: Power, Control and Domestic Abuse* (revised UK edn). London: Hurst & Company.

HIRST, H. (2021). 'The Legal Rights and Wrongs of Puberty Blocking in England'. *Child and Family Law Quarterly*, 33: 115.

HITCHINGS, E. (2009). 'Chaos or Consistency? Ancillary Relief in the "Everyday" Case', in J. Miles and R. Probert (eds), *Sharing Lives, Dividing Assets: An Inter-Disciplinary Study*. Oxford: Hart Publishing.

HITCHINGS, E. (2010). 'The Impact of Recent Ancillary Relief Jurisprudence in the "Everyday" Ancillary Relief Case'. *Child and Family Law Quarterly*, 22: 93.

HITCHINGS, E. (2011). *A Study of the Views and Approaches of Family Practitioners Concerning Marital Property Agreements*. <www.bristol.ac.uk/law/research/researchpublications/2013/maritalpropertyagreements.pdf>.

Hitchings, E. (2021). 'Reconsidering the *Duxbury* Default'. *Child and Family Law Quarterly*, 33: 294.

Hitchings, E. and Miles, J. (2016). 'Mediation, Financial Remedies, Information Provision and Legal Advice: The Post-LASPO Conundrum'. *Journal of Social Welfare and Family Law*, 38: 175.

Hitchings, E. and Miles, J. (2019). 'Rules Versus Discretion in Financial Remedies on Divorce'. *International Journal of Law, Policy, and the Family*, 33: 24.

Hitchings, E. and Sagar, S. (2007). 'The Adoption and Children Act 2002: A Level Playing Field for Same-Sex Adopters?'. *Child and Family Law Quarterly*, 19: 60.

Hitchings, E., Miles, J., and Woodward, H. (2013). *Assembling the Jigsaw Puzzle: Understanding Financial Settlement on Divorce*. <www.nuffieldfoundation.org/sites/default/files/files/assemblingthejigsawpuzzle nuffield.pdf>.

HM Government (2012). *Equal Marriage: The Government's Response*. <www.assets.publishing.service.gov.uk/government/uploads/system/uploads/attachment_data/file/133262/consultation-response_1_.pdf>.

HM Government (2014a). *The Right to Choose: Multi-Agency Statutory Guidance for Dealing with Forced Marriage*. <www.assets.publishing.service.gov.uk/government/uploads/system/uploads/attachment_data/file/322310/HMG_Statutory_Guidance_publication_180614_Final.pdf>.

HM Government (2014b). *Consultation on the Child Poverty Strategy 2014–17*. <www.gov.uk/government/consultations/child-poverty-a-draft-strategy>.

HM Government (2018). *Transforming the Response to Domestic Abuse: Government Consultation*. <www.consult.justice.gov.uk/homeoffice-moj/domestic-abuse-consultation/>.

HM Government (2021). *Tackling Violence Against Women and Girls*. <www.gov.uk/government/publications/tackling-violence-against-women-and-girls-strategy/tackling-violence-against-women-and-girls-strategy>.

HM Government (2022a). *Tackling Domestic Abuse Plan*, CP639. <www.gov.uk/government/publications/tackling-domestic-abuse-plan/tackling-domestic-abuse-plan-command-paper-639-accessible-version>.

HM Government (2022b). *Supporting Male Victims: Position Statement on Male Victims of Crimes Considered in the Cross-Government Tackling Violence Against Women and Girls Strategy and the Tackling Domestic Abuse Plan*. <www.gov.uk/government/publications/supporting-male-victims/supporting-male-victims-accessible>.

HM Treasury (2018). *Policy Paper: Budget 2018*. <www.gov.uk/government/publications/budget-2018-documents/budget-2018>.

HMCPSI and HMICFRS (2020). *Evidence led domestic abuse prosecutions*. <www.justiceinspectorates.gov.uk/cjji/wp-content/uploads/sites/2/2020/01/Joint-Inspection-Evidence-Led-Domestic-Abuse-Jan19-rpt.pdf>.

HMIC (2014). *Everyone's Business: Improving the Police Response to Domestic Abuse*. <www.justiceinspectorates.gov.uk/hmic/wp-content/uploads/2014/04/improving-the-police-response-to-domestic-abuse.pdf>.

HMICFRS (2017). *A Progress Report on the Police Response to Domestic Abuse*. <www.justiceinspectorates.gov.uk/hmicfrs/wp-content/uploads/progress-report-on-the-police-response-to-domestic-abuse.pdf>.

HMICFRS (2019). *Police Response to Domestic Abuse: An Update Report*. <www.justiceinspectorates.gov.uk/hmicfrs/wp-content/uploads/the-police-response-to-domestic-abuse-an-update-report.pdf>.

HMICFRS (2021). *Police Response to Violence Against Women and Girls—Final Inspection Report*. <www.justiceinspectorates.gov.uk/hmicfrs/wp-content/uploads/police-response-to-violence-against-women-and-girls-final-inspection-report.pdf>.

HO (1998). *Supporting Families: A Consultation Document*. London: HMSO.

HO (1999). *Supporting Families: Summary of Responses to the Consultation Document*. London: TSO.

HO (2005). *Domestic Violence: A National Report*. <webarchive.nationalarchives.gov.uk/+/http:/www.crimereduction.homeoffice.gov.uk/domesticviolence/domesticviolence51.pdf>.

HO (2011). *Domestic Violence Protection Notices and Domestic Violence Protection Orders: Interim Guidance Document for Police Regional Pilot Schemes*. <www.assets.publishing.service.gov.uk/government/uploads/system/uploads/attachment_data/file/575363/DVPO_guidance_FINAL_3.pdf>.

HO (2012). *Forced Marriage Consultation: Summary of Responses*. <www.homeoffice.gov.uk/publications/about-us/consultations/forced-marriage/forced-marriage-response?view=Binary>.

HO (2015). *Statutory Guidance Framework: Controlling or Coercive Behaviour in an Intimate or Family Relationship.* <www.gov.uk/government/publications/statutory-guidance-framework-controlling-or-coercive-behaviour-in-an-intimate-or-family-relationship>.

HO (2018). *The Independent Review into the Application of Sharia Law in England and Wales*, Cm 9560. London: TSO. <www.gov.uk/ government/ uploads/ system/ uploads/ attachment_data/ file/ 678478/ 6.4152_ HO_ CPFG_ Report_ into_ Sharia_ Law_ in_ the_ UK_ WEB.pdf>.

HO (2021a). *Domestic Abuse Protection Notices and Domestic Abuse Protection Orders: draft statutory guidance for the police.* <https://assets.publishing.service.gov.uk/government/uploads/system/uploads/attachment_data/file/955459/Draft_statutory_guidance_for_police_on_domestic_abuse_protection_notices_and_orders.pdf>.

HO (2021b). *Domestic Abuse: Draft Statutory Guidance Framework.* <www.gov.uk/government/consultations/domestic-abuse-act-statutory-guidance/domestic-abuse-draft-statutory-guidance-framework>.

HO (2021c). *Review of the Controlling or Coercive Behaviour Offence.* <www.gov.uk/government/publications/review-of-the-controlling-or-coercive-behaviour-offence/review-of-the-controlling-or-coercive-behaviour-offence>.

HO (2022a). *Statutory Definition of Domestic Abuse Factsheet.* <www.gov.uk/government/publications/domestic-abuse-bill-2020-factsheets/statutory-definition-of-domestic-abuse-factsheet>.

HO (2022b). *Domestic Abuse Protection Notices/Orders Factsheet.* <www.gov.uk/government/publications/domestic-abuse-bill-2020-factsheets/domestic-abuse-protection-notices-orders-factsheet>.

HO (2022c). *Domestic Abuse: Statutory Guidance.* <www.gov.uk/government/publications/domestic-abuse-act-2021>.

HO, MOJ, and Ministry of Communities, Housing and Local Government (2019). *Draft Domestic Abuse Bill: European Convention on Human Rights Memorandum.* <www.assets.publishing.service.gov.uk/government/uploads/system/uploads/attachment_data/file/772189/Draft_Domestic_Abuse_Bill_-_ECHR_Memorandum.pdf>.

Hobson, B. and Fahlén, S. (2011). 'Parent's Work-Life Balance: Beyond Responsibilities and Obligations to Agency and Capabilities', in J. Bridgeman, H. Keating, and C. Lind (eds), *Regulating Family Responsibilities.* Farnham: Ashgate.

Hoff, L. (1990). *Battered Women as Survivors.* London: Routledge.

Hoggett, B. (1980). 'Ends and Means: The Utility of Marriage as a Legal Institution', in J. Eekelaar and S. Katz (eds), *Marriage and Cohabitation in Contemporary Societies.* Toronto: Butterworths.

Hoggett, B. (1989). 'The Children Bill: The Aim'. *Family Law*, 19: 217.

Hollingsworth, K. (2015). 'Judging Children's Rights and the Benefit Cap'. *Child and Family Law Quarterly*, 27: 445.

Hollingsworth, K. and Stalford, H. (2017). 'Towards Children's Rights Judgments', in H. Stalford, K. Hollingsworth, and S. Gilmore (eds), *Rewriting Children's Rights Judgments: From Academic Vision to New Practice.* Oxford: Hart Publishing.

Holt, K. and Kelly, N. (2012). 'Rhetoric and Reality Surrounding Care Proceedings: Family Justice Under Strain'. *Journal of Social Welfare and Family Law*, 34: 155.

Holt, K., Broadhurst, K., Doherty, P., and Kelly, N. (2013). 'Access to Justice for Families? Legal Advocacy for Parents Where Children are on the "Edge of Care": An English Case Study'. *Journal of Social Welfare and Family Law*, 35: 163.

Hopkins, N. (2009). 'Regulating Trusts of the Home: Private Law and Social Policy'. *Law Quarterly Review*, 125: 310.

Hopkins, N. (2011). 'The Relevance of Context in Property Law: A Case for Judicial Restraint?'. *Legal Studies*, 31: 175.

Hopkins, N., Welch, E., and Hussaini, S. (2021). 'The Law Commission's Project on Weddings Law Reform'. *Ecclesiastical Law Journal*, 23: 267.

Horsey, K. (2021). *Surrogacy Trends for UK Nationals.* <https://mysurrogacyjourney.com/blog/surrogacy-trends-for-uk-nationals-our-exclusive-findings>.

Horsey, K., Smith, N., Norcross, S., Ghevaert, L., and Jones, S. (2015). *Surrogacy in the UK: Myth Busting and Reform.* Report of the Surrogacy UK Working Group on Surrogacy Law Reform. Kent: Surrogacy UK.

Horton, M. (1995). 'Improving Child Support—A Missed Opportunity'. *Child and Family Law Quarterly*, 7: 26.

HORTON, M. (2018). 'Setting Aside Executory Orders: A Terrible Fate for *Thwaite*?'. *Family Law*, 48: 884.

HOUSE OF COMMONS JUSTICE COMMITTEE (2012). *Pre-Legislative Scrutiny of the Children and Families Bill, Fourth Report of Session 2012–13*, HC 739. <www.publications.parliament.uk/pa/cm201213/cmselect/cmjust/739/739.pdf>.

HOUSE OF COMMONS SELECT COMMITTEE ON EDUCATION (2012/13). *Children First: The Child Protection System in England*. <www.publications.parliament.uk/pa/cm201213/cmselect/cmeduc/137/137.pdf>.

HOUSE OF COMMONS SELECT COMMITTEE ON HOME AFFAIRS (2008). *Domestic Violence, Forced Marriage and 'Honour'-Based Violence*, HC 263. London: TSO. <www.publications.parliament.uk/pa/cm200708/cmselect/cmhaff/263/263i.pdf>.

HOUSE OF COMMONS SELECT COMMITTEE ON HOME AFFAIRS (2011). *Forced Marriage*, HC 880, 2011. <www.publications.parliament.uk/pa/cm201012/cmselect/cmhaff/880/88002.htm>.

HOUSE OF COMMONS SELECT COMMITTEE ON HOME AFFAIRS (2018). *Domestic Abuse: Ninth Report of Session 2017–19*, HC 1015. <www.parliament.uk/business/committees/committees-a-z/commons-select/home-affairs-committee/inquiries/parliament-2017/domestic-abuse-inquiry-17-19/>.

HOUSE OF COMMONS SELECT COMMITTEE ON WORK AND PENSIONS (2007). *Fourth Report: Child Support Reform*, HC 219-I, 219-II. <www.publications.parliament.uk/pa/cm/cmworpen.htm>.

HOUSE OF COMMONS SELECT COMMITTEE ON WORK AND PENSIONS (2017a). *Fourteenth Report of Session 2016–17: Child Maintenance Service*, HC Paper 587. <www.publications.parliament.uk/pa/cm201617/cmselect/cmworpen/587/587.pdf>.

HOUSE OF COMMONS SELECT COMMITTEE ON WORK AND PENSIONS (2017b). *First Special Report 2017–19: Government Response to the Committee's Fourteenth Report of Session 2016–17*, HC Paper 354. <www.publications.parliament.uk/pa/cm201719/cmselect/cmworpen/354/354.pdf>.

HOUSE OF LORDS SELECT COMMITTEE ON ADOPTION LEGISLATION (2012). 1st Report of Session 2012–13, *Adoption: Pre-Legislative Scrutiny. Report*, HL Paper 94. <www.publications.parliament.uk/pa/ld201213/ldselect/ldadopt/94/94.pdf>.

HOUSE OF LORDS SELECT COMMITTEE ON ADOPTION LEGISLATION (2013). 2nd Report of Session 2012–13, *Adoption: Post-Legislative Scrutiny. Report*, HL Paper 127. <www.publications.parliament.uk/pa/ld201213/ldselect/ldadopt/127/127.pdf>.

HOUSE OF LORDS SELECT COMMITTEE ON THE CHILDREN AND FAMILIES ACT 2014 (2022). Report of Session 2022–23, *Children and Families Act 2014: A Failure of Implementation*, HL Paper 100. <www.publications.parliament.uk/pa/ld5803/ldselect/ldchifam/100/100.pdf>.

HOYLE, C. (1998). *Negotiating Domestic Violence*. Oxford: Clarendon Press.

HOYLE, C. AND SANDERS, A. (2000). 'Police Response to Domestic Violence: From Victim Choice to Victim Empowerment'. *British Journal of Criminology*, 40: 14.

HUGHES, K. AND SLOAN, B. (2011). 'Post-Adoption Photographs: Welfare, Rights and Judicial Reasoning'. *Child and Family Law Quarterly*, 23: 393.

HUMPHREYS, C. AND HARRISON, C. (2003). 'Focusing on Safety—Domestic Violence and the Role of Child Contact Centres'. *Child and Family Law Quarterly*, 15: 237.

HUMPHREYS, C. AND KAYE, M. (1997). 'Third-Party Applications for Protection Orders: Opportunities, Ambiguities and Traps'. *Journal of Social Welfare and Family Law*, 19: 403.

HUMPHREYS, C. AND THIARA, R. (2003). 'Neither Justice nor Protection: Women's Experiences of Post-Separation Violence'. *Journal of Social Welfare and Family Law*, 25: 195.

HUNT, J. (2018). 'Grandparents as Substitute Parents in the UK'. *Contemporary Social Science*, 13: 175.

HUNT, J. AND MACLEOD, A. (2008). *Outcomes of Applications to Court for Contact Orders after Parental Separation or Divorce. Briefing Note*. London: Ministry of Justice. <https://dera.ioe.ac.uk/9145/1/outcomes-applications-contact-orders.pdf>.

HUNT, J., MASSON, J., AND TRINDER, L. (2009). 'Shared Parenting: The Law, the Evidence and Guidance from Families Need Fathers'. *Family Law*, 39: 831.

HUNTER, R. (2011). 'Doing Violence to Family Law'. *Journal of Social Welfare and Family Law*, 33: 343.

HUNTER, R. (2017). 'Inducing Demand for Family Mediation—Before and After LASPO'. *Journal of Social Welfare and Family Law*, 39: 189.

HUNTER, R., BARNETT, A., AND KAGANAS, F. (2018). 'Introduction: Contact and Domestic Abuse'. *Journal of Social Welfare and Family Law*, 40: 401.

HUNTER, R., BARLOW, A., SMITHSON, J., AND EWING, J. (2018). 'Law, Discretion, Gender and Justice in Out-of-Court Financial Settlements'. *Australian Journal of Family Law*, 32: 189.

HUNTER, R., BURTON, M., TINDER, L., CASE, M., HEWER, N., BLACKLOCK, N., BUTLER, E., CAVANAGH, L., FOTTRELL, D., COBB, S., NORMAN, N., SUH, K., AND TROWLER, I. (2020). *Assessing Risk of Harm to Children and Parents in Private Law Children Cases*. London: TSO. <https//consult.justice.gov.uk/digital-communications/assessing-harm-private-family-law-proceedings/results/assessing-risk-harm-children-parents-pl-childrens-cases-report.pdf>.

HUTTON, J. (2006). *Ministerial Statement: Child Support Redesign*. <webarchive.nationalarchives.gov.uk/+/http://www.dwp.gov.uk/aboutus/2006/24-07-06.asp>.

HUXTABLE, R. AND FORBES, K. (2004). '*Glass v United Kingdom*: Maternal Instinct v Medical Opinion'. *Child and Family Law Quarterly*, 16: 339.

IJZENDOORN, M. H. VAN AND JUFFER, F. (2005). 'Adoption is a Successful Natural Intervention Enhancing Adopted Children's IQ and School Performance'. *Current Directions in Psychological Science*, 14: 326.

JACKSON, E. (2002). 'Conception and the Irrelevance of the Welfare Principle'. *Modern Law Review*, 65: 176.

JACKSON, E. (2006). 'What is a Parent?', in A. Diduck and K. O'Donovan (eds), *Feminist Perspectives on Family Law*. Abingdon: Routledge-Cavendish.

JACKSON, E. (2022). 'When Is a Mother Not a Mother?', in J. Scherpe and S. Gilmore (eds), *Family Matters: Essays in Honour of John Eekelaar*. Cambridge: Intersentia.

JACKSON, E. AND WASOFF, F., WITH MACLEAN, M. AND DOBASH, R. (1993). 'Financial Support on Divorce: The Right Mixture of Rules and Discretion?'. *International Journal of Law and the Family*, 7: 230.

JAY, M., PEARSON, R., WIJLAARS, L., OLHEDE, S., AND GILBERT, R. (2019). *Using Administrative Data to Quantify Overlaps Between Public and Private Children Law in England*. London: UCL. <https://ucl.ac.uk/child-health/sites/child-health/files/moj_report_-_final.pdf>.

JELICIC, H., LA VALLE, I., AND HART, D., WITH HOLMES, L. (2014). *The Role of Independent Reviewing Officers (IROs) in England: Final Report*. London: National Children's Bureau. <http://ncb.org.uk/sites/default/files/uploads/documents/Research_reports/role_of_independent_reviewing_officers_in_england_final_report.pdf>.

JOHNSON, M. (1999). 'A Biomedical Perspective on Parenthood', in A. Bainham, S. Day Sclater, and M. Richards (eds), *What is a Parent? A Socio-Legal Analysis*. Oxford: Hart Publishing.

JOHNSON, P. (2012). 'Adoption, Homosexuality and the European Convention on Human Rights: *Gas and Dubois v France*'. *Modern Law Review*, 76: 1123.

JOINT COMMITTEE (2019). *Report of the Joint Committee on the Draft Domestic Abuse Bill*, 14 June 2019. <https://publications.parliament.uk/pa/jt201719/jtselect/jtddab/2075/207502.htm>.

JOINT COMMITTEE ON HUMAN RIGHTS (2013–14). *Legislative Scrutiny: Children and Families Bill*. <www.publications.parliament.uk/pa/jt201314/jtselect/jtrights/29/2902.htm>.

JOINT COMMITTEE ON HUMAN RIGHTS (2015). *Violence against Women and Girls*. Sixth Report of Session 2014–15. HL Paper 106, HC 594. <www.publications.parliament.uk/pa/jt201415/jtselect/jtrights/106/10602.htm>.

JONES, C. (1977–78). 'The Tender Years Doctrine: Survey and Analysis'. *Journal of Family Law*, 16: 695.

JOWETT, A. AND PEEL, E. (2017) '"A Question of Equality and Choice": Same-Sex Couples' Attitudes towards Civil Partnership after the Introduction of Same-Sex Marriage'. *Psychology and Sexuality*, 8: 69.

JUSTICE (2022). *Improving Access to Justice for Separating Families*. London: Justice. <https://files.justice.org.uk/wp-content/uploads/2022/10/12154403/JUSTICE-Improving-Access-to-Justice-for-Separating-Families-October-2022.pdf>.

KAGANAS, F. (1999a). '*B v B (Occupation Order)* and *Chalmers v Johns*: Occupation Orders under the Family Law Act 1996'. *Child and Family Law Quarterly*, 11: 193.

KAGANAS, F. (1999b). 'Contact, Conflict and Risk', in S. Day Sclater and C. Piper (eds), *Undercurrents of Divorce*. Aldershot: Ashgate.

KAGANAS, F. (2000). '*Re L (Contact: Domestic Violence)* . . . Contact and Domestic Violence'. *Child and Family Law Quarterly*, 12: 311.

KAGANAS, F. (2006). 'Domestic Violence, Men's Groups and the Equivalence Argument', in A. Diduck and K. O'Donovan (eds), *Feminist*

Perspectives on Family Law. Abingdon: Routledge-Cavendish.

Kaganas, F. (2010). 'Child Protection, Gender and Rights', in J. Wallbank, S. Choudhry, and J. Herring (eds), *Rights, Gender and Family Law*. Abingdon: Routledge.

Kaganas, F. (2011). '*In re L (Contact: Domestic Violence)*—Judgment', in R. Hunter, C. McGlynn, and E. Rackley (eds), *Feminist Judgments: From Theory to Practice*. Oxford: Hart Publishing.

Kaganas, F. (2013). 'A Presumption that "Involvement" of Both Parents is Best: Deciphering Law's Messages'. *Child and Family Law Quarterly*, 25: 270.

Kaganas, F. (2018). 'A Presumption that 'Involvement' of Both Parents Is Best: Deciphering Law's Messages'. *Child and Family Law Quarterly*, 25: 270.

Kaganas, F. and Diduck, A. (2004). 'Incomplete Citizens: Changing Images of Post-Separation Children'. *Modern Law Review*, 67: 959.

Kahn-Freund, O. (1967). 'The Law Commission: Reform of the Grounds of Divorce. The Field of Choice'. *Modern Law Review*, 30: 180.

Kan, M. Y. and Laurie, H. (2014). 'Changing Patterns in the Allocation of Savings, Investments and Debts within Couple Relationships'. *The Sociological Review* 62: 335.

Kazimirski, A., Keogh, P., Kumari, V., Smith, R., Gowland, S., Purdon, S., with Khanum, N. (2009). *Forced Marriage: Prevalence and Service Response*. Research Report DCSF-RR128. London: DCSF. <https://dera.ioe.ac.uk/11167/2/DCSF-RR128.pdf>.

Keating, H. (1996). 'Shifting Standards in the House of Lords—*Re H and others (Minors) (Sexual Abuse: Standard of Proof)*'. *Child and Family Law Quarterly*, 8: 157.

Keating, H. (2009). 'Suspicions, Sitting on the Fence and Standards of Proof'. *Child and Family Law Quarterly*, 21: 230.

Keating, H. (2011). '*Re MA*: The Significance of Harm'. *Child and Family Law Quarterly*, 23: 115.

Keenan, C. (2005). 'The Impact of *Cannings* on Civil Child Protection Cases'. *Journal of Social Welfare and Family Law*, 27: 173.

Keenan, C. (2006). 'Lessons from America? Learning from Child Protection Policy in the USA'. *Child and Family Law Quarterly*, 18: 43.

Kelly, G. (2021). 'Unilateral Assets and the Reintroduction of Discrimination'. *Family Law*, 51: 93.

Kelly, L., Sharp, N., and Klein, R. (2014). *Finding The Costs of Freedom: How Women and Children Rebuild Their Lives after Domestic Violence*. London: London Metropolitan University.

Kelly, L., Adler, R., Horvath, M., Lovett, J., Coulson, M., Kernohan, D., and Gray, M. (2013). *Evaluation of the Pilot of Domestic Violence Protection Orders*. Home Office Research Report 76. <www.gov.uk/government/publications/evaluation-of-the-pilot-of-domestic-violence-protection-orders>.

Kessler, G. (2019). 'The Parentage Disruption: A Comparative Approach'. *International Journal of Law, Policy and the Family*, 33: 316.

Kewley, A. (1996). 'Pragmatism before Principle: The Limitations of Civil Law Remedies for the Victims of Domestic Violence'. *Journal of Social Welfare and Family Law*, 18: 1.

Kiernan, K. and Mueller, G. (1998). *The Divorced and Who Divorces?*, Centre for Analysis of Social Exclusion, CASE Paper 7. <http://eprints.lse.ac.uk/6529/1/The_Divorced_and_Who_Divorces.pdf>.

Kilkelly, U. (2014). 'The CRC in Litigation Under the ECHR', in T. Liefaard and J. Doek (eds), *Litigating the Rights of the Child*. Dortrecht: Springer.

Kingdom, E. (2000). 'Cohabitation Contracts and the Democratization of Personal Relationships'. *Feminist Legal Studies*, 8: 5.

Kirton, D. (2016). '(In)Sufficient?: Ethnicity and Foster Care in English Local Authorities'. *Child and Family Social Work*, 21: 492.

Kirton, D., Feast, J., and Howe, D. (2000). 'Searching, Reunion and Transracial Adoption'. *Adoption and Fostering*, 24: 6.

Krieken, R. van (2005). 'The "Best Interests" of the Child and Parental Separation: On the "Civilising of Parents"'. *Modern Law Review*, 68: 25.

Krutzinna, J. (2022). 'Who is "The Child"? Best Interests and Individuality of Children in Discretionary Decision-Making'. *International Journal of Children's Rights*, 30: 120.

Lamb, M. (2018). 'Does Shared Parenting by Separated Parents Affect the Adjustment of Young Children?'. *Journal of Child Custody*, 15: 16.

Laming, H. (2003). *The Victoria Climbié Inquiry*. London: HMSO.

Lanteigne, G. (2016). 'Under the Same Roof: Internal and External Relocation Cases'. *Journal of Social Welfare and Family Law*, 38: 208.

Law Commission (1966). *Reform of the Grounds of Divorce: The Field of Choice*, Law Com No 6. London: HMSO.

LAW COMMISSION (1969). *Report on Financial Provision in Matrimonial Proceedings*, Law Com No 25. London: HMSO.

LAW COMMISSION (1970). *Report on Nullity of Marriage*, Law Com No 33. London: HMSO.

LAW COMMISSION (1971). *Family Property Law*, Published Working Paper 42. London: HMSO.

LAW COMMISSION (1973). *Report on Solemnisation of Marriage in England and Wales*, Law Com No 53. London: HMSO.

LAW COMMISSION (1980). *The Financial Consequences of Divorce: The Basic Policy. A Discussion Paper*, Law Com No 103. London: HMSO.

LAW COMMISSION (1981). *The Financial Consequences of Divorce*, Law Com No 112. London: HMSO.

LAW COMMISSION (1982). *Family Law: Illegitimacy*, Law Com No 118. London: HMSO.

LAW COMMISSION (1985a). *Polygamous Marriages: Capacity to Contract a Polygamous Marriage and Related Issues*, Law Com No 146. London: HMSO.

LAW COMMISSION (1985b). *Family Law, Review of Child Law: Guardianship*, Law Com Working Paper 91. London: HMSO.

LAW COMMISSION (1988a). *Facing the Future: A Discussion Paper on the Ground for Divorce*, Law Com No 170. London: HMSO.

LAW COMMISSION (1988b). *Family Property: Matrimonial Property*, Law Com No 175. London: HMSO.

LAW COMMISSION (1988c). *Family Law, Review of Child Law: Guardianship and Custody*, Law Com No 172. London: HMSO.

LAW COMMISSION (1990). *The Ground for Divorce*, Law Com No 192. London: HMSO.

LAW COMMISSION (1992). *Family Law: Domestic Violence and Occupation of the Family Home*, Law Com No 207. London: HMSO.

LAW COMMISSION (2002). *Sharing Homes: A Discussion Paper*, Law Com No 278. London: HMSO.

LAW COMMISSION (2006). *Cohabitation: The Financial Consequences of Relationship Breakdown*, Law Com CP 179. London: TSO. <www.lawcom.gov.uk/app/uploads/2015/03/cp179_Cohabitation_Consultation.pdf>.

LAW COMMISSION (2007). *Cohabitation: The Financial Consequences of Relationship Breakdown*, Law Com No 307. London: TSO. <www.lawcom.gov.uk/app/uploads/2015/03/lc307_Cohabitation.pdf>.

LAW COMMISSION (2009). *Conspiracy and Attempts*, Law Com No 318. London: TSO. <www.lawcom.gov.uk/project/conspiracy-and-attempts/>.

LAW COMMISSION (2011). *Marital Property Agreements*, Law Com CP 198. London: TSO. <www.lawcom.gov.uk/app/uploads/2015/03/cp198_Marital_Property_Agreements_Consultation.pdf>.

LAW COMMISSION (2012). *Marital Property, Needs and Agreements—A Supplementary Consultation Paper*, Law Com CP 208. London: TSO. <www.lawcom.gov.uk/app/uploads/2015/03/cp208_matrimonial_property.pdf>.

LAW COMMISSION (2014). *Matrimonial Property, Needs and Agreements*, Law Com No 343. London: TSO. <www.lawcom.gov.uk/app/uploads/2015/03/lc343_matrimonial_property.pdf>.

LAW COMMISSION (2015). *Getting Married: A Scoping Paper*. London: TSO. <www.lawcom.gov.uk/app/uploads/2015/12/Getting_Married_scoping_paper.pdf>.

LAW COMMISSION (2016). *Enforcement of Family Financial Orders*, Law Com No 370. London: TSO. <www.lawcom.gov.uk/project/enforcement-of-family-financial-orders/>.

LAW COMMISSION (2017). *Thirteenth Programme of Law Reform*, Law Com No 377. London: TSO. <www.lawcom.gov.uk/project/13th-programme-of-law-reform/>.

LAW COMMISSION (2022). *Celebrating Marriage: A New Weddings Law*, Law Com No 408. London: TSO. <www.lawcom.gov.uk/project/weddings/>.

LAW COMMISSIONS (2023). *Building Families Through Surrogacy: A New Law—Core Report*. Law Com 411. London: TSO. <www.lawcom.gov.uk/project/surrogacy/>.

LAW SOCIETY (2002). *Cohabitation: The Case for Clear Law*. London: The Law Society.

LAW SOCIETY (2003). *Financial Provision on Divorce: Clarity and Fairness*. London: The Law Society.

LAW SOCIETY (2015). *Family Law Protocol*, 4th edn. London: The Law Society.

LAWSON, A. (1996). 'The Things We Do for Love: Detrimental Reliance in the Family Home'. *Legal Studies*, 26: 218.

LCD (1993). *Looking to the Future—Mediation and the Ground for Divorce*, Cm 2424. London: HMSO.

LCD (1995). *Looking to the Future—Mediation and the Ground for Divorce*, Cm 2799. London: HMSO.

LCD (1999). 'Implementation of Family Law Act Part II Delayed Pilots Show Disappointing

Response to Information Meetings'. Press Release No 159/99, 17 June.

LCD (2001). 'Divorce Law Reform—Government Proposes to Repeal Part II of the Family Law Act 1996'. Press Release No 20/01.

LECKEY, R. (2013). 'Marriage and the Data on Same-Sex Couples'. *Journal of Social Welfare and Family Law*, 35: 179.

LECKEY, R. (2019). 'One Parent, Three Parents: Judges and Ontario's All Families Are Equal Act, 2016'. *International Journal of Law, Policy and the Family*, 33: 298.

LEES, K. (2012). '*Geary v Rankine*: Money Isn't Everything'. *Conveyancer and Property Lawyer*, 76: 412.

LERSCH, P. AND VIDAL, S. (2016). 'My House or Our Home? Transitions into Sole Home Ownership in British Couples'. *Demographic Research*, 35: 139. <www.demographic-research.org/volumes/vol35/6/default.htm>.

LEWIS, J. (1998). 'The Problem of Lone-Mother Families in Twentieth-Century Britain'. *Journal of Social Welfare and Family Law*, 20: 251.

LEWIS, J. (2000). 'Family Policy in the Post-War Period', in S. Katz, J. Eekelaar, and M. Maclean (eds), *Cross Currents: Family Law and Policy in the US and England*. Oxford: OUP.

LEWIS, J. (2001a). 'Debates and Issues Regarding Marriage and Cohabitation in the British and American Literature'. *International Journal of Law, Policy and the Family*, 15: 159.

LEWIS, J. (2001b). *The End of Marriage? Individualism and Intimate Relations*. Cheltenham: Edward Elgar.

LEWIS, J. (2004). 'Adoption: The Nature of Policy Shifts in England and Wales 1972–2002'. *International Journal of Law, Policy and the Family*, 18: 235.

LEWIS, J., WITH DATTA, J. AND SARRE, S. (1999). *Individualism and Commitment in Marriage and Cohabitation*. LCD Research Series No 8/99. London: Lord Chancellor's Department.

LEWIS, R. (2004). 'Making Justice Work: Effective Legal Interventions for Domestic Violence'. *British Journal of Criminology*, 44: 204.

LIM, H. (1996). 'Messages from a Rarely Visited Island: Duress and Lack of Consent in Marriage'. *Feminist Legal Studies*, 4: 195.

LIND, C. (2004). 'Sexuality and Same-Sex Relationships in Law', in B. Brooks-Gordon, L. Gelsthorpe, M. Johnson, and A. Bainham (eds), *Sexuality Repositioned*. Oxford: Hart Publishing.

LIND, C. AND HEWITT, T. (2009). 'Law and the Complexities of Parenting: Parental Status and Parental Function'. *Journal of Social Welfare and Family Law*, 31: 391.

LINDLEY, B. (1997). 'Open Adoption—Is the Door Ajar?'. *Child and Family Law Quarterly*, 9: 115.

LINDLEY, B. (1999). 'State Intervention and Parental Autonomy in Children's Cases: Have We Got the Balance Right?', in A. Bainham, S. Day Sclater, and M. Richards (eds), *What is a Parent? A Socio-Legal Analysis*. Oxford: Hart Publishing.

LOGAN, J. AND SMITH, C. (2005). 'Face-to-Face Contact Post-Adoption: Views from the Triangles'. *British Journal of Social Work*, 35: 3.

LOWE, N. (1997). 'The Meaning and Allocation of Parental Responsibility—A Common Lawyer's Perspective'. *International Journal of Law, Policy and the Family*, 11: 192.

LOWE, N. (2011). '*J v C*: Placing the Child's Welfare Centre Stage', in S. Gilmore, J. Herring, and R. Probert (eds), *Landmark Cases in Family Law*. Oxford: Hart Publishing.

LOWE, N. AND NICHOLLS, M. (2016). *International Movement of Children: Law, Practice and Procedure*, 2nd edn. Bristol: Family Law.

LOWE, N., DOUGLAS, G., HITCHINGS, E., AND TAYLOR, R. (2021). *Bromley's Family Law*, 12th edn. Oxford: OUP.

LOWE, N., MURCH, M., BORKOWSKI, M., WEAVER, A., BECKFORD, V., WITH THOMAS, C. (1999). *Supporting Adoption—Reframing the Approach*. London: BAAF.

MAINE, A. (2021). 'Queer(y)ing Consummation: An Empirical Reflection on the Marriage (Same Sex Couples) Act 2013 and the Role of Consummation'. *Child and Family Law Quarterly*, 33: 143.

MCCANDLESS, J. (2008). 'Status and Anomaly: *Re D (Contact and Parental Responsibility: Lesbian Mothers and Known Father)* [2006] EWHC 2 (Fam), [2006] 1 FCR 556'. *Journal of Social Welfare and Family Law*, 30: 63.

MCCANDLESS, J. AND SHELDON, S. (2010). 'The Human Fertilisation and Embryology Act (2008) and the Tenacity of the Sexual Family Form'. *Modern Law Review*, 73: 175.

MCCANN, K. (1985). 'Battered Women and the Law: The Limits of the Legislation', in J. Brophy and C. Smart (eds), *Women in Law: Explorations in Law, Family and Sexuality*. London: Routledge.

MCCLEAN, D. AND HAYES, M. (2011). 'But I Didn't Really Want to Get Married', in S. Gilmore et al (eds), *Landmark Cases in Family Law*. Oxford: Hart Publishing.

McFall, S. et al (eds) (2012). *Understanding Society: Findings 2012*. Colchester: Institute for Social and Economic Research, University of Essex. <https://repository.essex.ac.uk/9111/1/Understanding-Society-Findings-2012.pdf>.

McFarlane, A. (2018). 'Crisis; What Crisis?'. Keynote Address to the Association of Lawyer for Children, 23 November 2018. <www.judiciary.uk/wp-content/uploads/2018/11/Speech-by-Rt.-Hon.-Sir-Andrew-McFarlane-Association-of-Lawyers-for-Children-Conference-2018.pdf>.

McFarlane, A. (2021a). 'Interesting Times'. 16 October2021.<www.judiciary.uk/wp-content/uploads/2021/10/FLBA-Manchester-final.pdf>.

McFarlane, A. (2021b). 'Confidence and Confidentiality: Transparency in the Family Courts'. 28 October 2021. <www.judiciary.uk/wp-content/uploads/2021/10/Confidence-and-Confidentiality-Transparency-in-the-Family-Courts-final.pdf>.

McFarlane, A. (2022a). 'Relaunching Family Mediation'. 28 September 2022. <www.judiciary.uk/speech-by-the-president-of-the-family-division-relaunching-family-mediation/>.

McFarlane, A. (2022b). 'Relaunching the PLO'. 29 November 2022. <www.judiciary.uk/guidance-and-resources/a-view-from-the-presidents-chambers-november-2022/>.

McFarlane, B., Hopkins, N., and Nield, S. (2021). *Land Law: Text, Cases, and Materials*, 5th edn. Oxford: OUP.

McGlynn, C. (2000). 'Ideologies of Motherhood in European Community Sex Equality Law'. *European Law Journal*, 6: 29.

McGlynn, C. (2001). 'European Union Family Values: Ideologies of "Family" and "Motherhood" in European Union Law'. *Social Politics*, 8: 325.

McIlroy, S. (2022). 'Pay Per View? Family Court Orders for the Costs of Contact'. *Journal of Social Welfare and Family Law*, 44: 251.

McInnes, M. (2011). 'Cohabitation, Trusts and Unjust Enrichment in the Supreme Court of Canada'. *Law Quarterly Review*, 127: 339.

McIntosh, J., Pruett, M., and Kelly, J. (2014a). 'Parental Separation and Overnight Care of Young Children, Part I: Consensus Through Theoretical and Empirical Integration'. *Family Court Review*, 52: 241.

McIntosh, J., Pruett, M., and Kelly, J. (2014b). 'Parental Separation and Overnight Care of Young Children, Part II: Putting Theory into Practice'. *Family Court Review*, 52: 257.

McIntosh, J., Smyth, B., Kelaher, M., Wells, Y., and Long, C. (2010). *Post-Separation Parenting Arrangements and Developmental Outcomes for Infants and Children*. North Carlton, Australia: Family Transitions.

McKay, S. (2014). 'Child Support, Child Contact and Social Class', in J. Wallbank and J. Herring (eds), *Vulnerabilities, Care and Family Law*. Abingdon: Routledge.

Maclean, M. (2013). 'Assessing the Impact of Legislating for Diversity: The Forced Marriage (Civil Protection) Act 2007', in M. Maclean and J. Eekelaar (eds), *Managing Family Justice in Diverse Societies*. Oxford: Hart Publishing.

Maclean, M. and Eekelaar, J. (1997). *The Parental Obligation: A Study of Parenthood across Households*. Oxford: Hart Publishing.

Maclean, M. and Eekelaar, J. (2009). *Family Law Advocacy: How Barristers Help the Victims of Family Failure*. Oxford: Hart Publishing.

Maclean, M. and Eekelaar, J. (2016). *Lawyers and Mediators: The Brave New World of Services for Separating Families*. Oxford: Hart Publishing.

Maclean, M. and George, R. (2021). 'Family Practice During Covid and Access to Justice'. *Family Law*, 226.

Maclean, M. with Kurczewski, J. (2011). *Making Family Law: A Socio Legal Account of the Legislative Process in England and Wales, 1985 to 2010*. Oxford: Hart Publishing.

McPherson, S. (2018). 'Evaluating Integrative Services in Edge-of-Care Work'. *Journal of Social Welfare and Family Law*, 40: 299.

McQuigg, R. (2016). 'Domestic Violence: Applying a Human Rights Discourse', in S. Hilder and V. Bettinson (eds), *Domestic Violence: Interdisciplinary Perspectives on Protection, Prevention and Intervention*. London: Palgrave Macmillan.

McQuigg, R. (2020). '*Kurt v Austria*: Applying the *Osman* Test to Cases of Domestic Violence'. *European Human Rights Law Review* 394.

Madden Dempsey, M. (2006). 'What Counts as Domestic Violence? A Conceptual Analysis'. *William and Mary Journal of Women and the Law*, 12: 301.

Maniscalco, L. (2020). 'Common Intentions and Constructive Trusts: Unorthodoxy in Trusts of Land'. *Conveyancer* 124.

Mant, J. (2020). 'Placing Litigants in Person at the Centre of the Post-LASPO Family Court Process'. *Child and Family Law Quarterly*, 32: 421.

Mant, J. (2022). *Litigants in Person and the Family Justice System*. Oxford: Hart Publishing.

Margaria, A. (2020). 'Trans Men Giving Birth and Reflections on Fatherhood: What to Expect?'. *International Journal of Law, Policy and the Family*, 34: 225.

Margaria, A. (2022). 'When the Personal Becomes Political: Rethinking Legal Fatherhood'. *International Journal of Constitutional Law*, 20: 1386.

Marsh, A. and Vegeris, S. (2004). *The British Lone Parent Cohort and their Children 1991–2001*. DWP Research Report No 209. Leeds: Corporate Document Service. <webarchive.nationalarchives.gov.uk/20130314010347/http://research.dwp.gov.uk/asd/asd5/rports2003-2004/rrep209.pdf>.

Marsh, R. (2022a). 'Upholding the Dignity of Gay Men Who Are (Prospective) Parents: An Analysis of Adoption and Surrogacy Law'. *Journal of Social Welfare and Family Law*, 44: 306.

Marsh, R. (2022b). 'Surrogacy Breakdown, Birth Registration and Article 8: A Missed Opportunity in Strasbourg'. *Journal of Social Welfare and Family Law*, 44: 529.

Marsh, R. (2023). 'The Significance of Section 20 After *Re S* and *Re W* [2023] EWCA Civ 1'. <www.familylawweek.co.uk/articles/the-significance-of-section-20-after-re-s-a-child-and-re-w-a-child-s-20-accommodation-2023-ewca-civ-1/>.

Marshall, J. (2012). 'Concealed Births, Adoption and Human Rights Law: Being Wary of Seeking to Open Windows into People's Souls'. *Cambridge Law Journal*, 71: 325.

Martin, L. (2016). 'Debates of Difference: Male Victims of Domestic Violence and Abuse', in S. Hilder and V. Bettinson (eds), *Domestic Violence: Interdisciplinary Perspectives on Protection, Prevention and Intervention*. London: Palgrave Macmillan.

Masson, J. (1992). 'Managing Risk under the Children Act 1989: Diversion in Child Care'. *Child Abuse Review*, 1: 103.

Masson, J. (2000). 'Thinking about Contact—A Social or Legal Problem?'. *Child and Family Law Quarterly*, 12: 15.

Masson, J. (2004). 'Human Rights in Child Protection: Emergency Action and its Impact', in P. Lødrup and E. Modvar (eds), *Family Life and Human Rights*. Oslo: Gyldendal Norsk Forlag AS.

Masson, J. (2005). 'Emergency Intervention to Protect Children: Using and Avoiding Legal Controls'. *Child and Family Law Quarterly*, 17: 75.

Masson, J. (2006). 'Fair Trials in Child Protection'. *Journal of Social Welfare and Family Law*, 28: 15.

Masson, J. (2007). 'Reforming Care Proceedings—Time for a Review'. *Child and Family Law Quarterly*, 19: 411.

Masson J. (2008). 'Controlling Costs and Maintaining Services—The Reform of Legal Aid Fees for Care Proceedings.' *Child and Family Law Quarterly*, 20: 425.

Masson, J. (2010a). 'A New Approach to Care Proceedings'. *Child and Family Social Work*, 15: 369.

Masson, J. (2010b). '(Mis)understandings of Significant Harm'. *Child Abuse Review*, 19: 291.

Masson, J. (2015). 'Third (or Fourth) Time Lucky for Care Proceedings Reform?'. *Child and Family Law Quarterly*, 27: 3.

Masson, J. (2022). 'Judging Care Proceedings: "It's Not What You Do It's the Way You Do It"'. *Journal of Social Welfare and Family Law*, 44: 533.

Masson, J. and Prabhat, D. (2021). 'Allowing Appeals to Increase High Court Power'. *Journal of Social Welfare and Family Law*, 43: 327.

Masson, J., Bailey-Harris, R., and Probert, R. (2008). *Cretney: Principles of Family Law*, 8th edn. London: Sweet & Maxwell.

Masson, J., Pearce, J., and Bader, K. (2008). *Care Profiling Study*. Ministry of Justice Research Series 4/08. Ministry of Justice. <https//research-information.bristol.ac.uk/files/9073958/care_profiling_study_Rpt.pdf>.

Masson, J., Bader, K., Dickens, J., and Young, J. (2013). 'The Pre-Proceedings Process for Families on the Edge of Care Proceedings'. University of Bristol and University of East Anglia. <https//research-information.bristol.ac.uk/files/9073836/Partnership_by_law.pdf>.

Maughan, B., Collishaw, S., and Pickles, A. (1998). 'School Achievement and Adult Qualifications among Adoptees: A Longitudinal Study'. *Journal of Child Psychology and Psychiatry*, 39: 669.

May, V. and Smart, C. (2004). 'Silence in Court?—Hearing Children in Residence and Contact Disputes'. *Child and Family Law Quarterly*, 16: 305.

Mee, J. (1999). *The Property Rights of Cohabitees*. Oxford: Hart Publishing.

Mee, J. (2004). 'Property Rights and Personal Relationships: Reflections on Reform'. *Legal Studies*, 24: 414.

MEE, J. (2009). 'The Limits of Proprietary Estoppel: *Thorner v Majors*'. *Child and Family Law Quarterly*, 21: 367.

MEE, J. (2011). '*Burns v Burns*: The Villain of the Piece?' in S. Gilmore et al (eds), *Landmark Cases in Family Law*. Oxford: Hart Publishing.

MEE, J. (2012). '*Jones v Kernott*: Inferring and Imputing in Essex'. *Conveyancer and Property Lawyer*, 76: 167.

MEE, J. (2013). 'Proprietary Estoppel and Inheritance: Enough is Enough?'. *Conveyancer and Property Lawyer*, 77: 280.

MIDDLETON, S., ASHWORTH, K., AND BRAITHWAITE, I. (1997). *Small Fortunes: Spending on Children, Childhood Poverty and Parental Sacrifice*. York: Joseph Rowntree Foundation.

MILES, J. (2003). 'Property Law v Family Law: Resolving the Problems of Family Property'. *Legal Studies*, 23: 624.

MILES, J. (2005). 'Principle or Pragmatism in Ancillary Relief: The Virtues of Flirting with Academic Theories and Other Jurisdictions'. *International Journal of Law, Policy and the Family*, 19: 242.

MILES, J. (2008). '*Charman v Charman (No 4)*: Making Sense of Need, Compensation and Equal Sharing after *Miller/McFarlane*'. *Child and Family Law Quarterly*, 20: 378.

MILES, J. (2009). '*Radmacher v Granatino*: Upping the Ante-Nuptial Agreement'. *Child and Family Law Quarterly*, 21: 513.

MILES, J. (2011a). 'Responsibility in Family Finance and Property Law', in J. Bridgeman, H. Keating, and C. Lind (eds), *Regulating Family Responsibilities*. Aldershot: Ashgate.

MILES, J. (2011b). 'Marriage and Divorce in the Supreme Court and the Law Commission: For Love or Money?'. *Modern Law Review*, 74: 430.

MILES, J. (2011c). 'Legal Aid, Article 6 and "Exceptional Funding" under the Legal Aid (etc.) Bill 2011'. *Family Law*, 41: 1003.

MILES, J. (2011d). 'Legal Aid and Exceptional Funding: A Postscript'. *Family Law*, 41: 1268.

MILES, J. (2012). 'Marital Agreements: "The More Radical Solution" ', in R. Probert and C. Barton (eds), *Fifty Years in Family Law: Essays for Stephen Cretney*. Cambridge: Intersentia.

MILES, J. (2016). 'Unmarried Cohabitation in a European Perspective', in J. Scherpe (ed), *European Family Law, Vol III*. Cheltenham: Edward Elgar.

MILES, J. (2018). 'Should the Regime be Discretionary or Rules-Based?', in J. Palmer et al (eds), *Law and Policy in Modern Family Finance*. Cambridge: Intersentia.

MILES, J. (2020). '"Cohabitants" in the Law of England and Wales: A Brief Introduction', in R. Akhtar, P. Nash, and R. Probert (eds), *Cohabitation and Religious Marriage: Status, Similarities and Solutions*. Bristol: BUP.

MILES, J. (2022). 'Judging Matrimonial Behaviour', in J. Miles, D. Monk, and R. Probert (eds), *Fifty Years of the Divorce Reform Act*. Oxford: Hart Publishing.

MILES, J. (2023). 'The Politics and Principle of Pursuing "Fairness" in Family Property Matters', in J. Gardner et al (eds), *Politics, Policy and the Private Law: Tort, Land & Equity*. Oxford: Hart Publishing.

MILES, J. AND HITCHINGS, E. (2018). 'Financial Remedy Outcomes in England & Wales: Not a Meal Ticket for Life'. *Australian Journal of Family Law*, 32: 43.

MILES, J. AND PROBERT, R. (eds) (2009). *Sharing Lives, Dividing Assets: An Inter-Disciplinary Study*. Oxford: Hart Publishing.

MILES, J. AND PROBERT, R. (2019). 'Civil Partnership: Ties That (Also) Bind?'. *Child and Family Law Quarterly*, 31: 303.

MILES, J., MONK, D., AND PROBERT, R. (2022). 'Irretrievably Broken? Introducing the Life-Story of the Divorce Reform Act 1969', in J. Miles, D. Monk, and R. Probert (eds), *Fifty Years of the Divorce Reform Act*. Oxford: Hart Publishing.

MILL, J. S. (1869). *Three Essays: On Liberty, Representative Government and the Subjection of Women*. (1975) R. Wollheim (ed). Oxford: OUP.

MILLAR, J. (1996). 'Family Obligations and Social Policy: The Case of Child Support'. *Policy Studies*, 17: 181.

MILLER, G. (2003). 'Pre-Nuptial Agreements and Financial Provision', in G. Miller (ed), *Frontiers of Family Law*. Dartmouth: Ashgate.

MILLS, L. AND THOMPSON, S. (2020). 'Parental Responsibilities and Rights During the "Gender Reassignment" Decision-Making Process of Intersex Infants'. *International Journal of Children's Rights*, 28: 547.

MILLWARD, E. (2008). 'The Domestic Violence, Crime and Victims Act 2004: Is it Working?'. *Family Law*, 38: 493.

MITCHELL, M., DICKENS, S., and O'CONNOR, W. (2009). *Same-Sex Couples and the Impact of Legislative Changes*. London: NatCen. <www.natcen.ac.uk/our-research/research/same-sex-couples/>.

MNOOKIN, R. (1975). 'Child-Custody Adjudication: Judicial Functions in the Face of Indeterminacy'. *Law and Contemporary Problems*, 39: 225.

Mnookin, R. and Kornhauser, L. (1979). 'Bargaining in the Shadow of the Law: The Case of Divorce'. *Yale Law Journal*, 88: 950.

Mody, P. (2015). 'Forced Marriage: Rites and Rights', in J. Miles, P. Mody, and R. Probert (eds), *Marriage Rites and Rights*. Oxford: Hart Publishing.

Moffatt, P. and Thoburn, J. (2001). 'Outcomes of Permanent Family Placement for Children of Minority Ethnic Origin'. *Child and Family Social Work*, 6: 13.

MOJ (2007). *Forced Marriage (Civil Protection) Act 2007: Relevant Third Party*. CP 31/07. <webarchive.nationalarchives.gov.uk/+/http://www.justice.gov.uk/publications/cp3107.htm>.

MOJ (2009a). *Guidance for Local Authorities as Relevant Third Party and Information Relevant to Multi-Agency Partnership Working*. <www.familylawweek.co.uk/site.aspx?i=xb489>.

MOJ (2009b). *One Year On: The Initial Impact of the Forced Marriage (Civil Protection) Act 2007 in its First Year of Operation*. <webarchive.nationalarchives.gov.uk/20100103073731/http:/www.justice.gov.uk/publications/10508.htm>.

MOJ (2010). *Proposals for the Reform of Legal Aid in England and Wales*, Cm 7967. London: TSO. <https//assets.publishing.service.gov.uk/government/uploads/system/uploads/attachment_data/file/228970/7967.pdf>.

MOJ (2012). *Judicial and Court Statistics 2011*. <www.gov.uk/government/statistics/judicial-and-court-statistics-annual>.

MOJ (2014a). *Marriages by Non-Religious Belief Organisations*. London: MOJ. <www.gov.uk/government/consultations/marriages-by-non-religious-belief-organisations>.

MOJ (2014b). *Report of the Family Mediation Task Force*. <www.justice.gov.uk/downloads/family-mediation-task-force-report.pdf>.

MOJ (2018). Letter from MOJ to Law Commission regarding enforcement of family financial orders project, available via <www.lawcom.gov.uk/financial-order-reforms-set-to-boost-unfairly-treated-former-partners-and-families/>.

MOJ (2019a). *Reducing Family Conflict Government Response to the Consultation on Reform of the Legal Requirements for Divorce*. <https://consult.justice.gov.uk/digital-communications/reform-of-the-legal-requirements-for-divorce/supporting_documents/reducingfamilyconflictconsultation.pdf>.

MOJ (2019b). *Reducing Family Conflict: Impact Assessment* <publications.parliament.uk/pa/bills/cbill/2017-2019/0404/Impact%20Assessment.pdf>.

MOJ (2020). *Child Protection at the Heart of Courts Review*. London: TSO. <www.gov.uk/government/news/child-protection-at-heart-of-courts-review>.

MOJ (2021). *Code of Practice for Victims of Crime*. London: TSO. <www.gov.uk/government/publications/the-code-of-practice-for-victims-of-crime>.

MOJ (2022a). *Family Court Statistics Quarterly: October to December 2021*. <www.gov.uk/government/statistics/family-court-statistics-quarterly-october-to-december-2021>.

MOJ (2022b). *Family Court Statistics Quarterly: April to June 2022*. <www.gov.uk/government/statistics/family-court-statistics-quarterly-april-to-june-2022/family-court-statistics-quarterly-april-to-june-2022>.

MOJ (2022c). *Legal Aid Statistics Quarterly: April to June 2022*. <www.gov.uk/government/statistics/legal-aid-statistics-quarterly-april-to-june-2022>.

MOJ/DFE (2012). *The Government Response to the Family Justice Review: A System with Children and Families at its Heart*, Cm 8273. <https://assets.publishing.service.gov.uk/government/uploads/system/uploads/attachment_data/file/177097/CM-8273.pdf>.

MOJ, HMCTS, and Wolfson (2022). *Press Release: Pioneering Approach in Family Courts to Support Domestic Abuse Victims Better*. 8 March 2022. <www.gov.uk/government/news/pioneering-approach-in-family-courts-to-support-domestic-abuse-victims-better>.

Mol, C. (2019). 'Children's Representation in Family Law Proceedings: A Comparative Evaluation in Light of Article 12 of the United Nations Convention on the Rights of the Child'. *International Journal of Children's Rights*, 27: 66.

Monaghan, K. and Harding, R. (2010). '*Wilkinson v Kitzinger*', in R. Hunter, C. McGlynn, and E. Rackley (eds), *Feminist Judgments: From Theory to Practice*. Oxford: Hart Publishing.

Monk, D. (2015). 'Judging the Act: Civil Partnership Disputes in the Courtroom and the Media', in N. Barker and D. Monk (eds), *From Civil Partnership to Same-Sex Marriage: Interdisciplinary Reflections*. Abingdon: Routledge.

Monk, D. and Macvarish, J. (2018). *Siblings, Contact and the Law: An Overlooked Relationship? Summary Report*. London: Nuffield Foundation. <www.

nuffieldfoundation.org/sites/default/files/files/Final%20Siblings%20Summary.pdf>.

Mooney, A., Oliver, C., and Smith, M. (2009). *Impact of Family Breakdown on Children's Well-Being. Evidence Review*. Research Report DCSF-RR113. London: DfCSF and Thomas Coram Research Unit. <https://dera.ioe.ac.uk/11165/1/DCSF-RR113.pdf>.

Moor, P. and Le Grice, V. (2006). 'Periodical Payments Orders following *Miller* and *McFarlane*—A Series of Unfortunate Events'. *Family Law*, 36: 655.

Morgan, P. (2000). *Marriage-Lite: The Rise of Cohabitation and its Consequences*. London: Institute for the Study of Civil Society.

Morgan, P. (2020). 'ZH v HS & Ors (Application to Revoke Adoption Order): Three Groups of Revocation Cases'. *Journal of Social Welfare and Family Law*, 42: 246.

Morley, R. and Mullender, A. (1994). *Preventing Domestic Violence to Women*. Crime Prevention Unit Series Paper No 48. London: Home Office.

Morris, A. and Gelsthorpe, L. (2000). 'Re-Visioning Men's Violence against Female Partners'. *The Howard Journal*, 39: 412.

Morris, B. (2015). 'The Most Radical Changes to Pensions in Almost a Century'. *Family Law*, 45: 290.

Morris, C. (2005). 'Divorce in a Multi-Faith Society'. *Family Law*, 35: 727.

Mortimer Commission (1966). *Putting Asunder: A Divorce Law for Contemporary Society*. London: SPCK.

Moscati, M. (2022). 'Trans* Identity Does Not Limit Children's Capacity: *Gillick* Competence Applies to Decisions Concerning Access to Puberty Blockers Too!'. *Journal of Social Welfare and Family Law*, 44: 130.

Mostyn, N. (1999). 'The Green Paper on Child Support—Children First: A New Approach to Child Support'. *Family Law*, 29: 95.

Mullender, A. and Morley, R. (1994). 'Context and Content of a New Agenda', in A. Mullender and R. Morley (eds), *Children Living with Domestic Violence*. London: Whiting and Birch.

Munby, J. (2016). 'Care Cases: The Looming Crisis'. <www.judiciary.uk/wp-content/uploads/2014/08/pfd-view-15-care-cases-looming-crisis.pdf>.

Munby, J. (2018). 'Changing Families: Family Law Yesterday, Today and Tomorrow – A View from South of the Border'. <www.judiciary.uk/announcements/speech-by-sir-james-munby-changing-families-family-law-yesterday-today-and-tomorrow-a-view-from-south-of-the-border/>.

Munro, E. (2011). *The Munro Review of Child Protection: Final Report. A Child-Centred System*, Cm 8062. <https://assets.publishing.service.gov.uk/government/uploads/system/uploads/attachment_data/file/175391/Munro-Review.pdf>.

Murphy, J. (2000). 'Rationality and Cultural Pluralism in the Non-Recognition of Foreign Marriages'. *International and Comparative Law Quarterly*, 49: 643.

Murphy, J. (2003). 'Children in Need: The Limits of Local Authority Accountability'. *Legal Studies*, 23: 103.

Myhill, A. (2015). 'Measuring Coercive Control: What Can We Learn From National Population Surveys?', *Violence Against Women*, 21: 355.

NAPO (2012). *Probation: Domestic Abuse Programmes and Budgets*. <www.napo.org.uk/sites/default/files/BRF07-12%20Probation%20Domestic%20Abuse%20Programmes%20and%20Budgets.pdf>.

Naqvi, Z. (2020). 'Nikah Ceremonies in the UK – A Tool for Empowerment?' in R. Akhtar, P. Nash, and R. Probert (eds), *Cohabitation and Religious Marriage: Status, Similarities and Solutions*. Bristol: BUP.

Naqvi, Z. (2023). *Polygamy, Policy and Postcolonialism in English Marriage Law: A Critical Feminist Analysis*. Bristol: BUP.

Narey, M. (2011). 'The Narey Report: A Blueprint for the Nation's Lost Children'. *The Times*, 5 July.

Nash, P. (2020). '"Regrettably it is Not That Simple": The Case for Minimalistic Marriage Laws', in R. Akhtar, P. Nash, and R. Probert (eds), *Cohabitation and Religious Marriage: Status, Similarities and Solutions*. Bristol: BUP.

NatCen (2016). *Is Britain Getting a Divorce from Marriage?* British Social Attitudes Survey data. <www.familylaw.co.uk/news_and_comment/is-britain-getting-a-divorce-from-marriage>.

National Adoption Leadership Board (2014). *Impact of Court Judgments on Adoption. What the Judgments Do and Do Not Say*. <www.first4adoption.org.uk/wp-content/uploads/2014/11/ALB-Impact-of-Court-Judgments-on-Adoption-November-2014.pdf>.

National Audit Office (2017). *Child Maintenance: Closing Cases and Managing Arrears on the 1993 and 2003 Schemes*. <https://

nao.org.uk/wp-content/uploads/2017/03/Child-Maintenance-closing-cases-and-managing-arrears-on-the-1993-and-2003-schemes-.pdf>.

National Audit Office (2022). *Child Maintenance: Report by the Comptroller and Auditor General.* Session 2021–22, HC 1139. <www.nao.org.uk/report/child-maintenance/>.

Neale, B. and Smart, C. (1999). 'In Whose Best Interests? Theorising Family Life Following Parental Separation or Divorce', in S. Day Sclater and C. Piper (eds), *Undercurrents of Divorce.* Dartmouth: Ashgate.

Neil, E. (2000). 'The Reasons Why Young Children are Placed for Adoption: Findings from a Recently Placed Sample and a Discussion of Implications for Subsequent Identity Development'. *Child and Family Social Work*, 5: 303.

Neil, E. (2009). 'Post-Adoption Contact and Openness in Adoptive Parents' Minds: Consequences for Children's Development'. *British Journal of Social Work*, 39: 5.

Neil, E. et al (2012). *Contact Arrangements for Adopted Children: What Can Be Learned from Research?* UEA: Centre for Research on the Child and Family.

Neuberger, D. (2008). 'The Conspirators, the Tax Man, the Bill of Rights, and a Bit about Lovers'. Chancery Bar Association Annual Lecture, 10 March. <https://chba.org.uk/for-members/library/annual-lectures/the-conspirators-the-taxman-the-bill-of-rights.pdf>.

Neuberger, D. (2009). 'The Stuffing of Minerva's Owl? Taxonomy and Taxidermy in Equity'. *Cambridge Law Journal*, 68: 537.

Newcastle Centre for Family Studies (2001a). *Information Meetings and Associated Provisions within the Family Law Act 1996: Key Findings from Research.* London: LCD. <webarchive.nationalarchives.gov.uk/+/http:/www.dca.gov.uk/family/fla/flapt2.htm>.

Newcastle Centre for Family Studies (2001b). *Information Meetings and Associated Provisions within the Family Law Act 1996: Summary of the Final Evaluation Report.* London: LCD. <webarchive.nationalarchives.gov.uk/+/http:/www.dca.gov.uk/family/fla/flapt2.htm>.

Newnham, A. (2011). 'Law's Gendered Understandings of Parents' Responsibilities in Relation to Shared Residence', in J. Bridgeman, H. Keating, and C. Lind (eds), *Regulating Family Responsibilities.* Farnham: Ashgate.

Newnham, A. (2013). 'Common Intention Constructive Trusts: A Way Forward'. *Family Law*, 43: 718.

Newnham, A. and Harding, M. (2016). 'Sharing As Caring? Contact and Residence Disputes Between Parents'. *Child and Family Law Quarterly*, 28: 175.

NHS (2016) *Gender Dysphoria.* <www.nhs.uk/Conditions/Gender-dysphoria/>.

Noack-Lundberg, K., Gill, A., and Anitha, S. (2021). 'Understanding Forced Marriage Protection Orders in the UK'. *Journal of Social Welfare and Family Law*, 43: 371.

Noon, R. (2008). 'Compensation for Domestic Abuse after *Singh v Bhakar*'. *Family Law Week*, September. <www.familylawweek.co.uk/site.aspx?i=ed25932>.

Norgrove, D. (2011). *Family Justice Review: Final Report.* London: MOJ. <https://assets.publishing.service.gov.uk/government/uploads/system/uploads/attachment_data/file/217343/family-justice-review-final-report.pdf>.

Norrie, K. (2000). 'Marriage is for Heterosexuals—May the Rest of Us Be Saved From It'. *Child and Family Law Quarterly*, 12: 363.

Norrie, K. (2014). 'Now the Dust has Settled: The Marriage and Civil Partnership (Scotland) Act 2014'. *Juridical Review*, 135.

Norrie, K. (2015). 'Civil Partnership in Scotland 2004–14, and Beyond', in N. Baker and D. Monk (eds), *From Civil Partnership and Same-Sex Marriage: Interdisciplinary Reflections.* Abingdon: Routledge.

O'Brien, K. and Zamostny, K. (2003). 'Understanding Adoptive Families: An Integrative Review of Empirical Research and Future Directions for Counseling Psychology'. *The Counseling Psychologist*, 31: 679.

O'Donnell, K. (2004). '*Re C (Welfare of Child: Immunisation)*— Room to Refuse? Immunisation, Welfare and the Role of Parental Decision- Making'. *Child and Family Law Quarterly*, 16: 213.

O'Donovan, K. (1982). 'Should All Maintenance of Spouses be Abolished?'. *Modern Law Review*, 45: 424.

O'Donovan, K. (1985). *Sexual Divisions in Law.* London: Weidenfield & Nicolson.

O'Donovan, K. (1993). *Family Law Matters.* London: Pluto Press.

O'Donovan, K. (2000). 'Interpretations of Children's Identity Rights', in D. Fottrell (ed), *Revisiting Children's Rights.* The Hague; Boston: Kluwer Law International.

O'Neill, O. (1992). 'Children's Rights and Children's Lives'. *International Journal of Law and the Family*, 6: 24.

OECD (2018). *Family Database: Marriage and Divorce Rates.* <www.oecd.org/els/family/SF_3_1_Marriage_and_divorce_rates.pdf>.

Oliver, R., Alexander, B., Roe, S., and Wlasny, M. (2019). *The Economic and Social Costs of Domestic Abuse.* Research Report 107. London: Home Office. <htps://assets.publishing.service.gov.uk/government/uploads/system/uploads/attachment_data/file/918897/horr107.pdf>.

ONS (2003). *Census 2001 National Report for England and Wales.* London: TSO.

ONS (2005). *Focus on Ethnicity and Identity.* London: HMSO.

ONS (2008). *Non-Resident Parental Contact: 2007–2008 Results.* Omnibus Survey Report No 38. <www.ons.gov.uk/ons/rel/lifestyles/non-residential-parental-contact/2007-08-results/non-residential-parental-contact---2007-2008-results.pdf>.

ONS (2010a). *Social Trends*, 40. London: TSO. <www.ons.gov.uk/ons/rel/social-trends-rd/social-trends/social-trends-40/index.html>.

ONS (2010b). *Marital Status Population Projections for England & Wales, 2008-Based Marital Status Projections.* <webarchive.nationalarchives.gov.uk/20160110141624/http://www.ons.gov.uk/ons/rel/npp/marital-status-population-projections-for-england---wales/2008-based-marital-status-projections/index.html>.

ONS (2012a). *Marriages in England and Wales, 2010.* <webarchive.nationalarchives.gov.uk/ukgwa/20160105160709/http://www.ons.gov.uk/ons/dcp171778_258307.pdf>.

ONS (2013). *Families and Households in England and Wales, 2011.* <www.ons.gov.uk/ons/dcp171776_296986.pdf>.

ONS (2014a). *Divorces in England and Wales, 2012.* <www.ons.gov.uk/ons/dcp171778_351693.pdf>.

ONS (2014b). *2011 Census Analysis: How Do Living Arrangements, Family Type and Family Size Vary in England and Wales?* <www.ons.gov.uk/ons/dcp171776_366963.pdf>.

ONS (2014c). *How Have Living Arrangements and Marital Status in England and Wales Changed Since 2001?* <www.ons.gov.uk/ons/dcp171776_356002.pdf>.

ONS (2014d). *Crime Statistics: Focus on Violent Crime and Sexual Offences, 2012/13.* <www.ons.gov.uk/ons/rel/crime-stats/crime-statistics/focus-on-violent-crime-and-sexual-offences--2012-13/index.html>.

ONS (2015a). *Civil Partnerships in the UK: 2013.* <www.ons.gov.uk/peoplepopulationandcommunity/birthsdeathsandmarriages/marriagecohabitationandcivilpartnerships/bulletins/civilpartnershipsinenglandandwales/2015-02-11>.

ONS (2016a). *Marriages in England and Wales: 2013.* <www.ons.gov.uk/peoplepopulationandcommunity/birthsdeathsandmarriages/marriagecohabitationandcivilpartnerships/bulletins/marriagesinenglandandwalesprovisional/2013/pdf>.

ONS (2016b). *Civil Partnerships in England and Wales: 2015.* <www.ons.gov.uk/peoplepopulationandcommunity/birthsdeathsandmarriages/marriagecohabitationandcivilpartnerships/bulletins/civilpartnershipsinenglandandwales/2015/pdf>.

ONS (2017). *International Passenger Survey Data Tables:2016.* <www.ons.gov.uk/file?uri=/aboutus/transparencyandgovernance/freedomofinformationfoi/marriagesabroadforvariousyears/foi3407datatables002.xls> or <www.ons.gov.uk/aboutus/transparencyandgovernance/freedomofinformationfoi/marriagesabroadforvariousyears>.

ONS (2018a). *Domestic Abuse: Findings from the Crime Survey for England and Wales: Year Ending March 2018.* <www.ons.gov.uk/peoplepopulationandcommunity/crimeandjustice/articles/domesticabusefindingsfromthecrimesurveyforenglandandwales/yearendingmarch2018>.

ONS (2018b). *Household Satellite Account, UK: 2015 and 2016.* <www.ons.gov.uk/economy/nationalaccounts/satelliteaccounts/articles/householdsatelliteaccounts/2015and2016estimates>.

ONS (2019a). *Divorces in England and Wales: 2018.* <www.ons.gov.uk/peoplepopulationandcommunity/birthsdeathsandmarriages/divorce/bulletins/divorcesinenglandandwales/2018>.

ONS (2019b). *Divorces in England and Wales: 2018.* <www.ons.gov.uk/peoplepopulationandcommunity/birthsdeathsandmarriages/divorce/bulletins/divorcesinenglandandwales/2018>.

ONS (2020a). *Crime in England and Wales: Year Ending March 2020.* <www.ons.gov.uk/peoplepopulationandcommunity/crimeandjustice/bulletins/crimeinenglandandwales/yearendingmarch2020>.

ONS (2020b). *Domestic Abuse in England and Wales Overview: November 2020.* <www.ons.gov.uk/peoplepopulationandcommunity/

crimeandjustice/bulletins/domesticabuseinenglandandwalesoverview/november2020>.

ONS (2020c). *Domestic Abuse Prevalence and Trends, England and Wales: Year Ending March 2020.* <www.ons.gov.uk/peoplepopulationandcommunity/crimeandjustice/articles/domesticabuseprevalenceandtrendsenglandandwales/yearendingmarch2020>.

ONS (2020d). *Domestic Abuse Victim Characteristics, England and Wales: Year Ending March 2020.* <www.ons.gov.uk/peoplepopulationandcommunity/crimeandjustice/articles/domesticabusevictimcharacteristicsenglandandwales/yearendingmarch2020>.

ONS (2020e). *Partner Abuse in Detail, England and Wales: Year Ending March 2018.* <www.ons.gov.uk/peoplepopulationandcommunity/crimeandjustice/articles/partnerabuseindetailenglandandwales/yearendingmarch2018>.

ONS (2020f). *Domestic Abuse and the Criminal Justice System, England and Wales: November 2020.* <www.ons.gov.uk/peoplepopulationandcommunity/crimeandjustice/articles/domesticabuseandthecriminaljusticesystemenglandandwales/november2020>.

ONS (2020g). *Domestic Abuse During the Coronavirus (COVID-19) Pandemic, England and Wales: November 2020.* <www.ons.gov.uk/peoplepopulationandcommunity/crimeandjustice/articles/domesticabuseduringthecoronaviruscovid19pandemicenglandandwales/november2020#domestic-abuse-victim-services>.

ONS (2020h). *Divorces in England and Wales: 2019.* <www.ons.gov.uk/peoplepopulationandcommunity/birthsdeathsandmarriages/divorce/bulletins/divorcesinenglandandwales/2019>.

ONS (2021a). *Redevelopment of Domestic Abuse Statistics: Research Update November 2021.* <www.ons.gov.uk/peoplepopulationandcommunity/crimeandjustice/articles/redevelopmentofdomesticabusestatistics/researchupdatenovember2021>.

ONS (2021b). *Domestic Abuse in England and Wales Overview: November 2021.* <www.ons.gov.uk/peoplepopulationandcommunity/crimeandjustice/bulletins/domesticabuseinenglandandwalesoverview/november2021>.

ONS (2021c). *User Guide to Crime Statistics for England and Wales: March 2020.* <www.ons.gov.uk/peoplepopulationandcommunity/crimeandjustice/methodologies/userguidetocrimestatisticsforenglandandwales>.

ONS (2021d). *Domestic Abuse QMI.* <www.ons.gov.uk/peoplepopulationandcommunity/crimeandjustice/methodologies/domesticabuseqmi>.

ONS (2021e). *Civil Partnerships in England and Wales: 2020.* <www.ons.gov.uk/peoplepopulationandcommunity/birthsdeathsandmarriages/marriagecohabitationandcivilpartnerships/bulletins/civilpartnershipsinenglandandwales/2020>.

ONS (2021f). *Population Estimates by Marital Status and Living Arrangements, England and Wales, 2002 to 2020.* <www.ons.gov.uk/peoplepopulationandcommunity/populationandmigration/populationestimates/datasets/populationestimatesbymaritalstatusandlivingarrangements>.

ONS (2022a). *Homicide in England and Wales: Year Ending March 2021.* <www.ons.gov.uk/peoplepopulationandcommunity/crimeandjustice/articles/homicideinenglandandwales/yearendingmarch2021>.

ONS (2022b). *Families and Households in the UK: 2021.* <www.ons.gov.uk/peoplepopulationandcommunity/birthsdeathsandmarriages/families/bulletins/familiesandhouseholds/2021>.

ONS (2022c). *Births in England and Wales: Summary Tables 2021.* <www.ons.gov.uk/peoplepopulationandcommunity/birthsdeathsandmarriages/livebirths/datasets/birthsummarytables>.

ONS (2022d). *Births by Parents' Characteristics.* <www.ons.gov.uk/peoplepopulationandcommunity/birthsdeathsandmarriages/livebirths/datasets/birthsbyparentscharacteristics>.

ONS (2022e). *Families and the Labour Market: UK 2021.* <www.ons.gov.uk/employmentandlabourmarket/peopleinwork/employmentandemployeetypes/articles/familiesandthelabourmarketengland/2021>.

ONS (2022f). *Household and Resident Characteristics, England and Wales: Census 2021.* <www.ons.gov.uk/peoplepopulationandcommunity/householdcharacteristics/homeinternetandsocialmediausage/bulletins/householdandresidentcharacteristicsenglandandwales/census2021>.

ONS (2022g). *Religion, England and Wales: Census 2021.* <www.ons.gov.uk/peoplepopulationandcommunity/cultural

identity/religion/bulletins/religionengland andwales/census2021>.

ONS (2022h). *Ethnic Group, England and Wales: Census 2021.* <www.ons.gov.uk/peoplepopulationandcommunity/culturalidentity/ethnicity/bulletins/ethnicgroupenglandandwales/census2021>.

ONS (2022i). *Divorces in England and Wales: 2021.* <www.ons.gov.uk/peoplepopulationandcommunity/birthsdeathsandmarriages/divorce/datasets/divorcesinenglandandwales>.

ONS (2022j). *Marriages in England and Wales: 2019.* <www.ons.gov.uk/peoplepopulationandcommunity/birthsdeathsandmarriages/marriagecohabitationandcivilpartnerships/bulletins/marriagesinenglandandwalesprovisional/2019>.

ONS (2022k). *Economic activity and employment type for men and women by age of the youngest dependent child living with them: July to September 2022.* <www.ons.gov.uk/employmentandlabourmarket/peopleinwork/employmentandemployeetypes/datasets/economicactivityandemploymenttypeformenandwomenbyageoftheyoungestdependentchildlivingwiththemtables>.

Oppenheim, C. and Milton, C. (2021). *Changing Patterns of Poverty in Early Childhood.* Nuffield Foundation. <www.nuffieldfoundation.org/publications/changing-patterns-of-poverty-in-early-childhood>.

Pahl, J. (1985). *Private Violence and Public Policy: The Needs of Battered Women and the Response of Public Services.* London: Routledge & Kegan Paul.

Parker, M. (2015). 'The Draft Nuptial Agreements Bill and the Abolition of the Common Law Rule: "Swept Away" or Swept under the Carpet?'. *Child and Family Law Quarterly*, 27: 63.

Parker, S. (1991). 'Child Support in Australia: Children's Rights or Public Interest?'. *International Journal of Law and the Family*, 5: 24.

Parker, S. (1992). 'Rights and Utility in Anglo-Australian Family Law'. *Modern Law Review*, 55: 311.

Parkinson, P. (1999). 'The Diminishing Significance of Initial Contributions to Property'. *Australian Journal of Family Law*, 13: 52.

Parkinson, P. (2003). 'Child Protection, Permanency Planning and Children's Right to Family Life'. *International Journal of Law, Policy and the Family*, 17: 147.

Parkinson, P. (2011). *Family Law and the Indissolubility of Parenthood.* Cambridge: CUP.

Parkinson, P. and Cashmore, J. (2018). 'Relocation and the Indissolubility of Parenthood'. *Journal of Child Custody*, 15: 76.

Parkinson, P., Cashmore, J., and Single, J. (2007). 'Parents' and Children's Views on Talking to Judges in Parenting Disputes in Australia'. *International Journal of Law, Policy and the Family*, 21: 84.

Parveen, R. (2020). 'From Regulating Marriage Ceremonies to Regulating Marriage Ceremonies', in R. Akhtar, P. Nash, and R. Probert (eds), *Cohabitation and Religious Marriage: Status, Similarities and Solutions.* Bristol: BUP.

Patel, T. (2007). 'Theorising the Racial Identity Development of Transracial Adoptees. A Symbolic Interactionist Perspective'. *Adoption and Fostering*, 31: 32.

Peacey, V. and Hunt, J. (2008). *Problematic Contact after Separation and Divorce? A National Survey of Parents.* London: One Parent Families/Gingerbread.

Pearce, N. (2013). '*AI v MT* [2013] EWHC 100 (Fam)'. *Journal of Social Welfare and Family Law*, 35: 259.

Pearce, N. and Gill, A. (2012). 'Criminalising Forced Marriage Through Stand-Alone Legislation—Will it Work?'. *Family Law*, 42: 534.

Peel, E. (2015). 'Civil Partnership Ceremonies: (Hetero)normativity, Ritual and Gender', in J. Miles, P. Mody, and R. Probert (eds), *Marriage Rites and Rights.* Oxford: Hart Publishing.

Peleg, N. (2017). '*Re T (A Minor) (Wardship: Medical Treatment)*: Commentary', in H. Stalford, K. Hollingsworth, and S. Gilmore (eds), *Rewriting Children's Rights Judgments: From Academic Vision to New Practice.* Oxford: Hart Publishing.

Perry, A. (2000). '*Lancashire County Council v B.* Section 31—Threshold or Barrier?'. *Child and Family Law Quarterly*, 12: 301.

Perry, A. and Rainey, B. (2007). 'Supervised, Supported and Indirect Contact Orders: Research Findings'. *International Journal of Law, Policy and the Family*, 21: 21.

Perry, A., Douglas, G., Murch, M., Bader, K., and Borkowski, M. (2000). *How Parents Cope Financially on Marriage Breakdown.* London: Family Policy Studies Centre/Joseph Rowntree.

PHILLIPS, R. (1991). *Untying the Knot: A Short History of Divorce*. Cambridge: CUP.

PICKFORD, R. (1999). 'What is a Parent? A Socio-Legal Analysis', in A. Bainham, S. Day Sclater, and M. Richards (eds), *What is a Parent? A Socio-Legal Analysis*. Oxford: Hart Publishing.

PINTENS, W. (2011). 'Matrimonial Property Law in Europe', in K. Boele-Woelki, J. Miles, and J. Scherpe (eds), *The Future of Family Property in Europe*. Cambridge: Intersentia.

PIPER, C. (1996). 'Norms and Negotiation in Mediation and Divorce', in M. Freeman (ed), *Divorce: Where Next?* Aldershot: Dartmouth.

PIRRIE, J. (2006). 'Child Support in Danger'. *Solicitors Journal*, 150: 1089.

PIRRIE, J. (2007). 'The Legal Dig'. *New Law Journal*, 16 March: 382.

PIŠKA, N. (2009). 'Constructing Trusts and Constructing Intention', in M. Dixon (ed), *Modern Studies in Property Law, Vol 5*. Oxford: Hart Publishing.

PIZZEY, E. (1974). *Scream Quietly or the Neighbours Will Hear*. London: IF Books.

PLATT, J. (2008). 'The Domestic Violence, Crime and Victims Act 2004 Part 1: Is it Working?'. *Family Law*, 38: 642.

PLATT, J., ASOKAN, M., FINDLAY, L., AND TRUMAN, D. (2009). *Injunctions and Orders against Anti-Social or Violent Individuals*. Bristol: Jordan Publishing.

PLAYDON, Z. (2004). 'Intersecting Oppressions: Ending Discrimination against Lesbians, Gay Men and Trans People in the UK', in B. Brooks-Gordon, L. Gelsthorpe, M. Johnson, and A. Bainham (eds), *Sexuality Repositioned*. Oxford: Hart Publishing.

POLIKOFF, N. (2008). *Beyond (Straight and Gay) Marriage: Valuing All Families Under the Law*. Boston, MA: Beacon Press.

POLLOCK, J., FISHER, R., AND BOODT, P. (2022). 'Schedule 1 Property Structures'. *Financial Remedies Journal*, 2: 115.

POOLE, E., SPEIGHT, S., O'BRIEN, M., CONNOLLY, S., AND ALDRICH, M. (2013). *What Do We Know About Non-Resident Fathers?* <www.modernfatherhood.org/wp-content/uploads/2013/11/Briefing-paper-tables-Non-resident-fathers-embargoed-20.11.13.pdf>.

POPULUS (2018). *Equal Civil Partnerships Survey*. <https://equalcivilpartnerships.org.uk/wp-content/uploads/2017/04/OmEqual_Civil_Partnerships-1.pdf>.

POULTER, S. (1998). *Ethnicity, Law and Human Rights*. Oxford: OUP.

PRACTICE GUIDANCE (2015). *Arbitration in the Family Court*. 23 November 2015. <www.judiciary.uk/wp-content/uploads/2015/11/arbitration_pguidance_nov_15.pdf>.

PRACTICE GUIDANCE (2017). *Family Court—Duration of Ex Parte (Without Notice) Orders*. 18 January 2017. <www.judiciary.uk/publications/practice-guidance-family-court-duration-of-ex-parte-without-notice-orders/>.

PRACTICE GUIDANCE (2018). *Children Arbitration in the Family Court*. 26 July 2018. <www.judiciary.uk/wp-content/uploads/2018/07/pfd-practice-guidance-children-arbitration.pdf>.

PRESIDENT OF THE FAMILY DIVISION (2018). '18th View from the President's Chambers: The Ongoing Process of Reform—Financial Remedies Courts'. *Family Law*, 48: 156.

PRICE, D. (2009). 'Pension Accumulation and Gendered Household Structures: What are the Implications of Changes in Family Formation for Future Financial Inequality?', in J. Miles and R. Probert (eds) (2009), above.

PROBERT, R. (1999). 'The Controversy of Equality and the Matrimonial Causes Act 1923'. *Child and Family Law Quarterly*, 11: 33.

PROBERT, R. (2001). 'Trusts and the Modern Woman—Establishing an Interest in the Family Home'. *Child and Family Law Quarterly*, 13: 275.

PROBERT, R. (2002a). 'When Are We Married? Void, Non-Existent and Presumed Marriages'. *Legal Studies*, 22: 398.

PROBERT, R. (2002b). 'Sharing Homes—A Long-Awaited Paper'. *Family Law*, 32: 834.

PROBERT, R. (2004a). 'Family Law—A Modern Concept?'. *Family Law*, 34: 901.

PROBERT, R. (2004b). 'Lord Hardwicke's Marriage Act—Vital Change 250 Years On?'. *Family Law*, 34: 585.

PROBERT, R. (2004c). 'Cohabitation in Twentieth Century England and Wales: Law and Policy'. *Law and Policy*, 26: 13.

PROBERT, R. (2004d). '*Sutton v Mischon de Reya and Gawor & Co*—Cohabitation Contracts and Swedish Sex Slaves'. *Child and Family Law Quarterly*, 16: 453.

PROBERT, R. (2005). 'The Wedding of the Prince of Wales: Royal Privileges and Human Rights'. *Child and Family Law Quarterly*, 17: 363.

PROBERT, R. (2007a). '*Hyde v Hyde*: Defining or Defending Marriage?'. *Child and Family Law Quarterly*, 19: 322.

PROBERT, R. (2007b). 'A Review of Cohabitation: The Financial Consequences of Relationship Breakdown'. *Family Law Quarterly*, 41: 521.

Probert, R. (2008a). 'Hanging on the Telephone: *City of Westminster v IC*'. *Child and Family Law Quarterly*, 20: 395.

Probert, R. (2008b). 'Equality in the Family Home?'. *Feminist Legal Studies*, 15: 341.

Probert, R. (2009a). 'Parental Responsibility and Children's Partnership Choices', in R. Probert, S. Gilmore, and J. Herring (eds), *Responsible Parents and Parental Responsibility*. Oxford: Hart Publishing.

Probert, R. (2009b). *Marriage Law and Practice in the Long Eighteenth Century: A Reassessment*. Cambridge: CUP.

Probert, R. (2009c). 'Cohabitation: Current Legal Solutions'. *Current Legal Problems*, 62: 316.

Probert, R. (2009d). 'The Cohabitation Bill'. *Family Law*, 39: 150.

Probert, R. (2011a). 'The *Roos* Case and Modern Family Law', in S. Gilmore, J. Herring, and R. Probert (eds), *Landmark Cases in Family Law*. Oxford: Hart Publishing.

Probert, R. (2011b). 'The Evolution of the Common Law Marriage Myth'. *Family Law*, 41: 283.

Probert, R. (2011c). 'For Richer, for Poorer – But How Does One Find Out Which?'. *Law Quarterly Review*, 127: 28.

Probert, R. (2012a). 'Marriage at the Crossroads in England and Wales', in M. Garrison and E. Scott (eds), *Marriage at the Crossroads: Law, Policy and the Brave New World of Twenty-First-Century Families*. Cambridge: CUP.

Probert, R. (2012b). *The Changing Legal Regulation of Cohabitation: From Fornicators to Family, 1600–2010*. Cambridge: CUP.

Probert, R. (2013). 'The Evolving Concept of Non-Marriage'. *Child and Family Law Quarterly*, 25: 314.

Probert, R. (2018a). 'Criminalising Non-Compliance with Marriage Formalities?'. *Family Law*, 48: 702.

Probert, R. (2018b). 'Presumptions in Favour of Marriage'. *Cambridge Law Journal*, 77: 375.

Probert, R. (2018c). 'A Uniform Marriage Law for England and Wales?'. *Child and Family Law Quarterly*, 30: 259.

Probert, R. (2022). 'Divorced from Reality? Literary Depictions of the Legal Process for Ending a Marriage, 1971–2021', in J. Miles, D. Monk, and R. Probert (eds), *Fifty Years of the Divorce Reform Act*. Oxford: Hart Publishing.

Probert, R. and Barlow, A. (2000). 'Displacing Marriage—Diversification and Harmonisation within Europe'. *Child and Family Law Quarterly*, 12: 153.

Probert, R. and Saleem, S. (2018). 'The Legal Treatment of Islamic Marriage Ceremonies'. *Oxford Journal of Law and Religion*, 7: 376.

Probert, R., Akhtar, R., and Blake, S. (2022). *When is a Wedding Not a Marriage? Exploring Non-Legally Binding Ceremonies*. London: Nuffield.

Probert, R., Gilmore, S., and Herring, J. (eds) (2009). *Responsible Parents and Parental Responsibility*. Oxford: Hart Publishing.

Pruett, M., McIntosh, J., and Kelly, J. (2014). 'Parental Separation and Overnight Care of Young Children, Part I: Consensus Through Theoretical and Empirical Integration'. *Family Court Review*, 52: 240.

Public Accounts Committee (2022a). *Child Maintenance*, HC 255. <www.committees.parliament.uk/work/6434/child-maintenance/publications/reports-responses/>.

Public Accounts Committee (2022b). *Oral evidence: Child Maintenance*, HC 1056. <www.committees.parliament.uk/work/6434/child-maintenance/publications/oral-evidence/>.

Public Law Working Group (2021). *Recommendations to Achieve Best Practice in the Child Protection and Family Justice Systems*. <www.judiciary.uk/wp-content/uploads/2021/03/March-2021-report-final_clickable.pdf>.

Pywell, S. and Probert, R. (2018a). 'Neither Sacred nor Profane: The Permitted Content of Civil Marriage Ceremonies'. *Child and Family Law Quarterly*, 30: 415.

Pywell, S. and Probert, R. (2018b). 'Love in the Time of Covid-19: A Case-Study of the Complex Laws Governing Weddings'. *Legal Studies*, 41: 676.

Quinton, D. and Selwyn, J. (1998). 'Contact with Birth Parents in Adoption—A Response to Ryburn'. *Child and Family Law Quarterly*, 10: 349.

Quinton, D. and Selwyn, J. (2006). 'Adoption: Research, Policy and Practice'. *Child and Family Law Quarterly*, 18: 459.

Rabindrakumar, S. (2017). *Family Portrait: Single Parent Families and Transition over Time*. <www.sheffield.ac.uk/news/polopoly_fs/1.812161!/file/Sheffield_Solutions_Modern_Families.pdf>.

Radford, L., Corral, S., Bradley, C., Fisher, H., Bassett, C., Howat, N., and Collishaw, S. (2011). *Child Abuse and Neglect in the UK Today*. London: NSPCC: <www.learning.nspcc.org.uk/research-resources/pre-2013/child-abuse-neglect-uk-today/>.

RAKE, K. (2000). *Women's Incomes over the Lifetime*. London: TSO.

REECE, H. (1996). 'The Paramountcy Principle: Consensus or Construct?'. *Current Legal Problems*, 49: 267.

REECE, H. (2003). *Divorcing Responsibly*. Oxford: Hart Publishing.

REECE, H. (2006). 'The End of Domestic Violence'. *Modern Law Review*, 69: 770.

REECE, H. (2009). 'The Degradation of Parental Responsibility', in R. Probert, S. Gilmore, and J. Herring (eds), *Responsible Parents and Parental Responsibility*. Oxford: Hart Publishing.

REECE, H. (2015). 'Leaping without Looking', in R. Leckey (ed), *After Legal Equality: Family, Sex, Kinship*. Abingdon: Routledge.

REECE, H. (2017). 'Was There, Is There, And Should There Be a Presumption against Deviant Parents?'. *Child and Family Law Quarterly*, 29: 9.

RENZ, F. (2015). 'Consenting to Gender? Trans Spouses after Same-Sex Marriage', in N. Baker and D. Monk (eds), *From Civil Partnership and Same-Sex Marriage: Interdisciplinary Reflections*. Abingdon: Routledge.

RESOLUTION (2009). *Precedents for Consent Orders*.

RESOLUTION (2012). *Guides to Good Practice*. <https://resolution.org.uk/membership/our-code-of-practice/good-practice-guides/>.

RHEINSTEIN, M. (1972). *Marriage Stability, Divorce and the Law*. London: University of Chicago Press.

RHOADES, H. (2002). 'The "No Contact Mother": Reconstructions of Motherhood in the Era of the "New Father"'. *International Journal of Law, Policy and the Family*, 16: 71.

RICHARDS, M (1995). 'Private Worlds and Public Intentions – the Role of the State at Divorce', in A. Bainham and D. Pearl (eds), *Frontiers of Family Law*, 2nd edn. London: Wiley.

RICHARDSON, V. AND BRAMMER, A. (2020). 'Mothers of Children Removed Under a Care Order: Outcomes and Experiences'. *Journal of Social Welfare and Family Law*, 42: 360.

RICHARDSON, V., BOYLAN, J., AND BRAMMER, A. (2017). 'Contact, Welfare and Children in Care: Revisiting the Significance of Birth Family Relationships after Finding Significant Harm'. *Journal of Social Welfare and Family Law*, 39: 67.

ROBERTS, M. (2000). 'Children by Donation: Do They Have a Claim to Their Genetic Parentage?', in J. Bridgeman and D. Monk (eds), *Feminist Perspectives on Child Law*. London: Cavendish.

ROBINSON, A. AND COOK, D. (2006). 'Understanding Victim Retraction in Cases of Domestic Violence: Specialist Domestic Violence Courts, Government Policy, and Victim-Centred Justice'. *Contemporary Justice Review*, 9: 189.

ROBINSON, A. AND PAYTON, J. (2016). 'Independent Advocacy and Multi-Agency Responses to Domestic Violence', in S. Hilder and V. Bettinson (eds), *Domestic Violence: Interdisciplinary Perspectives on Protection, Prevention and Intervention*. London: Palgrave Macmillan.

ROE, S. (2010). 'Intimate Violence: 2008/09 BCS', in K. Smith et al (eds), *Homicides, Firearm Offences and Intimate Violence 2008/09: Supplementary Volume 2 to Crime in England and Wales 2008/09*. Home Office Statistical Bulletin 01/10. <webarchive.nationalarchives.gov.uk/20110220154353/http://rds.homeoffice.gov.uk/rds/pdfs10/hosb0110.pdf>.

ROGERSON, C. (2002). *Developing Spousal Support Guidelines in Canada: Beginning the Discussion—Background Paper*. <www.justice.gc.ca/eng/rp-pr/fl-lf/spousal-epoux/ss-pae/>.

ROGERSON, C. (2020). 'Child Support, Spousal Support and the Turn to Guidelines', in J. Eekelaar and R. George (eds), *Routledge Handbook of Family Law and Policy*, 2nd edn. London: Routledge.

ROSS, A. AND SACKER, A. (2010). 'Understanding the Dynamics of Attitude Change', in A. Park et al (eds), *British Social Attitudes: The 26th Report*. London: Sage.

ROSS, H., GASK, K., AND BERRINGTON, A. (2011). 'Civil Partnership Five Years On'. *Population Trends*, 145 (Autumn): 1.

ROTHERHAM, C. (2004). 'The Property Rights of Unmarried Cohabitees: The Case for Reform'. *Conveyancer and Property Lawyer*, 68: 268.

ROWTHORN, R. (1999). 'Marriage and Trust: Some Lessons from Economics'. *Cambridge Journal of Economics*, 23: 661.

ROYAL COMMISSION ON MARRIAGE AND DIVORCE (1956). Cm 9678. London: HMSO.

RUCK, C. (2022). *Staying Mum: A Review of the Literature on Domestic Abuse, Mothering and Child Removal*. London: AVA (Against Violence and Abuse). <https://avaproject.org.uk/wp-content/uploads/2022/03/

Staying-Mum-%E2%80%93-Lit-Review-Final.pdf>.

Rushton, A. (2003). 'Support for Adoptive Families. A Review of Current Evidence on Problems, Needs and Effectiveness'. *Adoption and Fostering*, 27: 41.

Rushton, A. and Minnis, H. (2000). 'Research Review: Transracial Placements'. *Adoption and Fostering*, 24: 53.

Russell, P. (2018). 'Matrimonial Causes Act 1857', in E. Rackley and R. Auchmuty (eds), *Women's Legal Landmarks*. Oxford: Hart Publishing.

Ryan, M. and Tunnard, J. (2018). *Care Crisis Review: Options for Change*. London: Family Rights Group. <www.frg.org.uk/product/the-care-crisis-review-options-for-change/>.

Ryan, M., Rothera, S., Roe, A., Rehill, J., and Harker, L. (2021). *Remote Hearings in the Family Court Post-Pandemic*. London: Nuffield Family Justice Observatory. <www.nuffieldfjo.org.uk/resource/remote-hearings-post-pandemic>.

Ryburn, M. (1998a). 'In Whose Best Interests?—Post-Adoption Contact with the Birth Family'. *Child and Family Law Quarterly*, 10: 53.

Ryburn, M. (1998b). 'A New Model of Welfare: Re-asserting the Value of Kinship for Children in State Care'. *Social Policy and Administration*, 32: 28.

SafeLives (undated). *Spotlight on HBV and Forced Marriage*. <https://safelives.org.uk/sites/default/files/resources/Spotlight%20on%20HBV%20and%20forced%20marriage-web.pdf>.

Sagar, T. and Hitchings, E. (2007). '"More Adoptions, More Quickly": A Study of Social Workers' Responses to the Adoption and Children Act 2002'. *Journal of Social Welfare and Family Law*, 29: 199.

Salter, D. (2022). 'S 10(2)–(4): A New Lease of Life?'. *Financial Remedies Journal* <www.financialremediesjournal.com/content/mca-1973-s-10-2-ndash-4-a-new-lease-of-life.747b9e83536e40d28539249ded712cd5.htm>.

Sandberg, R. (2021). *Religion and Marriage Law: The Need for Reform*. Bristol: BUP.

Sandberg, R. and Thompson, S. (2016). 'The Sharia Law Debate: The Missing Family Law Context'. *Law and Justice*, 177: 181.

Sandberg, R. and Thompson, S. (2017). 'Relational Autonomy and Religious Tribunals'. *Oxford Journal of Law and Religion* 6: 137.

Sandland, R. (2000). 'Not "Social Justice": The Housing Association, the Judges, the Tenant and His Lover'. *Feminist Legal Studies*, 8: 227.

Scherpe, J. (2007). 'Family and Private Life, Ambits and Pieces'. *Child and Family Law Quarterly*, 19: 390.

Scherpe, J. (ed) (2011a). *Marital Agreements and Private Autonomy in Comparative Perspective*. Oxford: Hart Publishing.

Scherpe, J. (2011b). 'Fairness, Freedom and Foreign Elements – Marital Agreements in England and Wales after *Radmacher v Granatino*'. *Child and Family Law Quarterly*, 23: 513.

Scherpe, J. (2012). 'Towards a Matrimonial Property Regime for England and Wales', in R. Probert and C. Barton (eds), *Fifty Years in Family Law: Essays for Stephen Cretney*. Cambridge: Intersentia.

Scherpe, J. (ed) (2015). *The Legal Status of Transsexual and Transgender Persons*. Cambridge: Intersentia.

Scherpe, J. (2017). 'The Past, Present and Future of Registered Partnerships', in J. Scherpe and A. Hayward (eds), *The Future of Registered Partnerships*. Cambridge: Intersentia.

Scherpe, J. (2021). 'The Right Ambit: Lady Hale and the Limitations of Article 8 ECHR'. *Journal of Social Welfare and Family Law*, 43: 256.

Scherpe, J. (2022). 'Parental Responsibility: To Consult or Consent, Is that the Question?', in J. Scherpe and S. Gilmore (eds), *Family Matters: Essays in Honour of John Eekelaar*. Cambridge: Intersentia.

Scherpe, J., Dutta, A., and Helms, T. (eds) (2018). *The Legal Status of Intersex Persons*. Cambridge: Intersentia.

Schneider, C. (1992). 'Discretion and Rules: A Lawyer's View', in K. Hawkins (ed), *The Uses of Discretion*. Oxford: OUP.

Schneider, E. (1994). 'The Violence of Privacy', in M. Fineman and R. Mykitiuk (eds), *The Public Nature of Private Violence*. New York: Routledge.

Schuz, R. (1993). 'Divorce Reform'. *Family Law*, 23: 630.

Schuz, R. (1996). 'Divorce and Ethnic Minorities', in M. Freeman (ed), *Divorce: Where Next?* Aldershot: Dartmouth.

Scott, E. (2002). 'Marital Commitment and the Legal Regulation of Divorce', in A. Dnes and R. Rowthorn (eds), *The Law and Economics of Marriage and Divorce*. Cambridge: CUP.

Scott, J. and Dex. S. (2009). 'Paid and Unpaid Work: Can Policy Improve Gender Inequalities?', in J. Miles and R. Probert (eds) (2009), above.

Scottish Law Commission (1981). *Report on Aliment and Financial Provision*, Scot Law Com No 67. Edinburgh: HMSO.

Scully, A. (2003). 'Case Commentary: *Parra v Parra*—Big Money Cases, Judicial Discretion and Equality of Division'. *Child and Family Law Quarterly*, 15: 205.

Seden, J. (2001). 'Family Assistance Orders and the Children Act 1989: Ambivalence about Intervention or a Means of Safeguarding and Promoting Children's Welfare?'. *International Journal of Law, Policy and the Family*, 15: 226.

Select Committee (1975). *Report from the Select Committee on Violence in Marriage*. London: HMSO.

Selwyn, J. and Quinton, D. (2004). 'Stability, Permanence, Outcomes and Support'. *Adoption and Fostering*, 28: 6.

Selwyn, J., Frazer, L., and Quinton, D. (2006). 'Paved with Good Intentions: The Pathway to Adoption and the Costs of Delay'. *British Journal of Social Work*, 36: 561.

Selwyn, J., Meakings, S., and Wijedasa, D. (2014). *Beyond the Adoption Order: Challenges, Interventions and Adoption Disruption*. London: Department for Education <https://assets.publishing.service.gov.uk/government/uploads/system/uploads/attachment_data/file/301889/Final_Report_-_3rd_April_2014v2.pdf>.

Selwyn, J. et al (2008). *Pathways to Permanence for Black, Asian and Mixed Ethnicity Children: Dilemmas, Decision-Making and Outcomes*. DCSF-RBX-18-08.<www.bristol.ac.uk/media-library/sites/sps/migrated/documents/rk6417finalreport.pdf>.

Sentencing Council (2018a). *Overarching Principles—Domestic Abuse: Definitive Guidance*. <www.sentencingcouncil.org.uk/overarching-guides/magistrates-court/item/domestic-abuse/>.

Sentencing Council (2018b). *Breach of a Protective Order (Restraining and Non-Molestation Orders)*. <www.sentencingcouncil.org.uk/offences/magistrates-court/item/breach-of-a-protective-order-restraining-and-non-molestation-orders/>

Shah, P. (2003). 'Attitudes to Polygamy in English Law'. *International and Comparative Law Quarterly*, 52: 369.

Sharpe, A. (2012). 'Transgender Marriage and the Legal Obligation to Disclose Gender History'. *Modern Law Review*, 75: 33.

Sheldon, S. (2009). 'From "Absent Objects of Blame" to "Fathers Who Want to Take Responsibility": Reforming Birth Registration Law'. *Journal of Social Welfare and Family Law*, 31: 373.

Simmonds, C. (2012). 'Paramountcy and the ECHR: A Conflict Resolved?'. *Cambridge Law Journal*, 71: 498.

Singer, A. (2014). 'Voices Heard and Unheard: A Scandinavian Perspective'. *Journal of Social Welfare and Family Law*, 36: 381.

Sloan, B. (2009). '*Re C (A Child) (Adoption: Duty of Local Authority)*—Welfare and the Rights of the Birth Family in "Fast Track" Adoption Cases'. *Child and Family Law Quarterly*, 21: 87.

Sloan, B. (2013). 'Conflicting Rights: English Adoption Law and the Implementation of the UN Convention on the Rights of the Child'. *Child and Family Law Quarterly*, 25: 40.

Sloan, B. (2015a). 'Keeping Up With the *Jones* Case: Establishing Constructive Trusts in "Sole Legal Owner" Scenarios'. *Legal Studies*, 35: 226.

Sloan, B. (2015b). 'Adoption Decisions in England: *Re B (A Child) (Care Proceedings: Appeal)* and Beyond'. *Journal of Social Welfare and Family Law*, 37: 437.

Sloan, B. (2017). 'Commentary on *Re C v XYZ County Council*', in H. Stalford, K. Hollingsworth, and S. Gilmore (eds), *Rewriting Children's Rights Judgments: From Academic Vision to New Practice*. Oxford: Hart Publishing.

Sloan, B. (2020). 'Article 5 of the Convention on the Rights of the Child and the Involvement of Fathers in Adoption Proceedings: A Comparative Analysis'. *International Journal of Children's Rights*, 28: 666.

Sloan, B. (2022). 'Contact and Adoption in the Twenty-First Century', in J. Scherpe and S. Gilmore (eds), *Family Matters: Essays in Honour of John Eekelaar*. Cambridge: Intersentia.

Smart, C. (1984). *The Ties that Bind: Law, Marriage and the Reproduction of Patriarchal Relations*. London: Routledge.

Smart, C. (1989). *Feminism and the Power of Law*. London: Routledge.

Smart, C. (2000). 'Divorce in England 1950–2000: A Moral Tale?', in S. Katz, J. Eekelaar, and M. Maclean (eds), *Cross Currents: Family Law and Policy in the US and England*. Oxford: OUP.

Smart, C. and Stevens, P. (2000). *Cohabitation Breakdown*. London: Family Policy Studies Centre.

Smith, C. (1997). 'Children's Rights: Judicial Ambivalence and Social Resistance'.

International Journal of Law, Policy and the Family, 11: 103.

Smith, C. (2004). 'Autopoietic Law and the "Epistemic Trap": A Case Study of Adoption and Contact'. *Journal of Law and Society*, 31: 318.

Smith, C. (2005). 'Trust v Law: Promoting and Safeguarding Post-Adoption Contact'. *Journal of Social Welfare and Family Law*, 27: 315.

Smith, L. (2006). 'Is Three a Crowd? Lesbian Mothers' Perspectives on Parental Status in Law'. *Child and Family Law Quarterly*, 18: 231.

Smith, L. (2010). 'Clashing Symbols? Reconciling Support for Fathers and Fatherless Families after the Human Fertilisation and Embryology Act 2008'. *Child and Family Law Quarterly*, 22: 46.

Smith, L. (2013). 'Tangling the Web of Legal Parenthood: Legal Responses to the Use of Known Donors in Lesbian Parenting Arrangements'. *Legal Studies*, 33: 355.

Smith, R. (2002). 'The Wrong End of the Telescope: Child Protection or Child Safety?'. *Journal of Social Welfare and Family Law*, 24: 247.

Smyth, B. (2005). 'Parent–Child Contact in Australia: Exploring Five Different Post-Separation Patterns of Parenting'. *International Journal of Law, Policy and the Family*, 19: 1.

Social Security Advisory Committee (2019). *Separated Parents and the Social Security System*. <www.gov.uk/government/publications/ssac-occasional-paper-22-separated-parents-and-the-social-security-system#full-publication-update-history>.

Solicitors Journal (2006). 'Family Lawyers Fear Inclusion of Conduct in Divorces'. *Solicitors Journal*, 150: 485.

Sorbie, A. (2021). 'Children's Best Interests and Parents' Views: Challenges from Medical Law'. *Journal of Social Welfare and Family Law*, 43: 23.

Spaht, E. (2002). 'Louisiana's Covenant Marriage Law: Recapturing the Meaning of Marriage for the Sake of the Children', in A. Dnes and R. Rowthorn (eds), *The Law and Economics of Marriage and Divorce*. Cambridge: CUP.

Stalford, H. and Hollingsworth, K. (2017). 'Judging Children's Rights: Tendencies, Tensions, Constraints and Opportunities', in H. Stalford, K. Hollingsworth, and S. Gilmore (eds), *Rewriting Children's Rights Judgments: From Academic Vision to New Practice*. Oxford: Hart Publishing.

Stone, L. (1990). *Road to Divorce: England 1530–1987*. Oxford: OUP.

Strasser, M. (2020). 'Family, Same-Sex Unions and the Law', in J. Eekelaar and R. George (eds), *Routledge Handbook of Family Law and Policy*, 2nd edn, Abingdon: Routledge.

Sturge, C. and Glaser, D. (2000). 'Contact and Domestic Violence—The Experts' Court Report'. *Family Law*, 30: 615.

Stychin, C. (2006). 'Family Friendly? Rights, Responsibilities and Relationship Recognition', in A. Diduck and K. O'Donovan (eds), *Feminist Perspectives on Family Law*. Abingdon: Routledge-Cavendish.

Stylianou, C. (1998). 'The Tensions between Family Mediation Principles and the Formal Legal System'. *Family Law*, 28: 211.

Sugarman, S. (1990). 'Dividing Financial Interests on Divorce', in S. Sugarman and H. Kay (eds), *Divorce Reform at the Crossroads*. New Haven: Yale University Press.

Sverdrup, T. (2015). 'Family Solidarity and the Mind-Set of Private Law'. *Child and Family Law Quarterly*, 27: 237.

Swales, K. and Attar Taylor, E. (2017). *British Social Attitudes 34: Moral Issues*. <www.bsa.natcen.ac.uk/media/39147/bsa34_moral_issues_final.pdf>.

Symes, P. (1985). 'Indissolubility and the Clean Break'. *Modern Law Review*, 48: 44.

Talwar, D. (2010). 'Many Muslims not Legally Wed'. BBC website, 2 February. <http://news.bbc.co.uk/1/hi/uk/8493660.stm>.

Tan, G. (2022). 'Children's Rights and the Influence of Lord Sales in the UNSCK's Political Constitutionalist Turn'. *Edinburgh Law Review*, 26: 93.

Taylor, R. (2013). 'Secular Rights and Sacred Values: *Re G (Education: Religious Upbringing)*'. *Child and Family Law Quarterly*, 25: 336.

Taylor, R. (2020). 'Parental Decisions and Court Jurisdiction: Best Interests or Significant Harm'. *Child and Family Law Quarterly*, 32: 141

Taylor, R. and Woodward, H. (2015). 'Apples or Pears? Pension Offsetting on Divorce'. *Family Law*, 45: 1485.

Tesfaye, M. (2022). 'What Makes a Parent? Challenging the Importance of a Genetic Link for Legal Parenthood in International Surrogacy Arrangements'. *International Journal of Law, Policy and the Family*, 36: ebac010.

Thiara, R., and Gill, A. (2012). *Domestic Violence, Child Contact and Post-Separation Violence: Issues for South Asian and African-Caribbean Women and Children*. London: NSPCC.

Thiara, R., and Harrison, C. (2016). *Safe Not Sorry: Supporting the Campaign for Safer Child Contact*. Bristol: Women's Aid.

Thoburn, J., Robinson, J., and Anderson, B. (2012). 'Returning Children Home from Public Care', Research briefing, Social Care Institute for Excellence.

Thompson, S. (2015). *Pre-Nuptial Agreements and the Presumption of Free Choice*. Oxford: Hart Publishing.

Thompson, S. (2016). 'In Defence of the "Gold-Digger"'. *Oñati Socio-Legal Series*, 6: 1225. <https://papers.ssrn.com/sol3/papers.cfm?abstract_id=2887022>.

Thompson, S. (2018). '*Thorne v Kennedy*: Why Australia's Decision on Prenups is Important for English Law'. *Family Law*, 48: 415.

Thompson, S. (2019). 'A Millstone Around the Neck? Stereotypes About Wives and Myths about Divorce'. *Northern Ireland Legal Quarterly*, 70: 181.

Thompson, S. (2020). 'Using Feminist Relational Contract Theory to Build Upon Consentability: A Case Study of Prenups'. *Loyola Law Review*, 66: 55.

Thompson, S. (2021). 'Against Divorce? Revisiting the Charge of the Casanova's Charter'. *Child and Family Law Quarterly*, 33: 294.

Thompson, S. (2022). *Quiet Revolutionaries: The Married Women's Association and Family Law*. Oxford: Hart Publishing.

Timms, J. E. and Thoburn, J. (2006). 'Your Shout! Looked After Children's Perspectives on the Children Act 1989'. *Journal of Social Welfare and Family Law*, 28: 153.

Tisdall, K. (2016). 'Subjects with Agency? Children's Participations in Family Law Proceeding'. *Journal of Social Welfare and Family Law*, 38: 362.

Tisdall, K, Morrison, F., and Warburton, J. (2021). 'Challenging Undue Influence? Rethinking Children's Participation in Contested Child Contact'. *Journal of Social Welfare and Family Law*, 43: 8.

Trimmings, K. (2015). 'Six Month Deadline for Applications for Parental Orders Relaxed by the High Court'. *Journal of Social Welfare and Family Law*, 37: 241.

Trinder, L. (2014). 'Climate Change? The Multiple Trajectories of Shared Care Law, Policy and Social Practice'. *Child and Family Law Quarterly*, 26: 30.

Trinder, L. (2022). 'Telling Tales? Establishing Irretrievable Breakdown under the Matrimonial Causes Act 1973', in J. Miles, D. Monk, and R. Probert (eds), *Fifty Years of the Divorce Reform Act*. Oxford: Hart Publishing.

Trinder, L. and Sefton, M. (2018). *No Contest: Defended Divorce in England and Wales*. London: Nuffield Foundation. <https://nuffieldfoundation.org/sites/default/files/files/No%20contest%20final_Nuffield_Foundation.pdf>.

Trinder, L., Firth, A., and Jenks, C. (2010). '"So Presumably Things Have Moved on Since Then?" The Management of Risk Allegations in Child Contact Dispute Resolution'. *International Journal of Law, Policy and the Family*, 24: 29.

Trinder, L., Connolly, J., Kellett, J., and Notley, C. (2005). *A Profile of Applicants and Respondents in Contact Cases in Essex*. DCA Research Series 1/05. <https://familieslink.co.uk/download/july07/A%20Profile%20of%20Applicants%20and%20Respondents%20in%20Essex.pdf>.

Trinder, L., Braybrook, D., Bryson, C., Coleman, L., Houlston, C., and Sefton, M. (2017). *Finding Fault? Divorce Law and Practice in England and Wales*. London: Nuffield Foundation. <https://nuffieldfoundation.org/sites/default/files/files/Finding_Fault_full_report_v_FINAL(1).pdf>.

Trinder, L., Hunt, J., Macleod, A., Pearce, J., and Worwood, H. (2013). *Enforcing Contact Orders: Problem-Solving or Punishment?* Exeter: University of Exeter.

Trinder, L., Hunter, R., Hitchings, E., Miles, J., Moorhead, R., Smith, L., Sefton, M., Hinchly, V., Bader, K., and Pearce, J. (2014). *Litigants in Person in Private Family Law Cases*. <https://assets.publishing.service.gov.uk/government/uploads/system/uploads/attachment_data/file/380479/litigants-in-person-in-private-family-law-cases.pdf>.

Triseliotis, J. (2002). 'Long-Term Foster Care or Adoption? The Evidence Examined'. *Child and Family Social Work*, 7: 23.

Trowler, I. (2018). *Care Proceedings In England: The Case for Clear Blue Water*. <www.sheffield.ac.uk/media/11093/download?attachment>.

Turgoose, D. (2016). 'Victim Support Services and the World of Commissioning', in S. Hilder and V. Bettinson (eds), *Domestic Violence: Interdisciplinary Perspectives on Protection, Prevention and Intervention*. London: Palgrave Macmillan.

Turkmendag, I., Dingwall, R., and Murphy, T. (2008). 'The Removal of Donor Anonymity in the UK: The Silencing of Would-Be Parents'.

International Journal of Law, Policy and the Family, 22: 283.

Uddin, I. (2018). 'Nikah-Only Marriages: Causes, Motivations and Their Impact on Dispute Resolution and Islamic Divorce Proceedings in England and Wales'. *Oxford Journal of Law and Religion*, 7: 401.

UN Committee on the Rights of the Child. (2009). *General Comment 12: The Right of the Child to Be Heard*. <https://ohchr.org/english/bodies/crc/docs/AdvanceVersions/CRC-C-GC-12.pdf>.

United Nations. (2018). *Report of the Special Rapporteur on the Sale and Sexual Exploitation of Children*. Report A/HRC/37/60, 15 January 2018. <https://documents-dds-ny.un.org/doc/UNDOC/GEN/G18/007/71/PDF/G1800771.pdf>

Van Bueren, G. (1998). *International Law on the Rights of the Child*. The Hague: Kluwer Law International.

Vallely, C., Robinson, A., Burton, M., and Tregidga, J. (2005). *Evaluation of Domestic Violence Pilot Sites at Caerphilly (Gwent) and Croydon 2004/05: Final Report*. <www.cps.gov.uk/publication/evaluation-domestic-violence-pilot-sites-caerphilly-gwent-and-croydon-200405>.

Vardag, A. and Miles, J. (2015). 'The Rite that Defines the Rights? The Contemporary Role and Practice of Pre-Nuptial Agreement', in J. Miles, P. Mody, and R. Probert (eds), *Marriage Rites and Rights*. Oxford: Hart Publishing.

Verkaik, R. (2006). 'Divorce Laws "Are Destroying Marriage"'. *The Independent*, 26 August, 1.

Victims' Commissioner (2020). *Sowing the Seeds: Children's experience of domestic abuse and criminality*. <https://victimscommissioner.org.uk/document/sowing-the-seeds-childrens-experience-of-domestic-abuse-and-criminality/>.

Viney, J. and Brunsdon-Tully, M. (2014). 'Compensation in Financial Remedy Cases: Parthian Shots and the Emperor's New Clothes'. *Family Law Week*. <www.familylawweek.co.uk/site.aspx?i=ed131966>.

Vogler, C. (2005). 'Cohabiting Couples: Rethinking Money in the Household at the Beginning of the Twenty First Century'. *Sociological Review*, 53: 1.

Vogler, C. (2009). 'Managing Money in Intimate Relationships: Similarities and Differences between Cohabiting and Married Couples', in J. Miles and R. Probert (eds) (2009), above.

Waaldijk, K. (2003). 'Taking Same-Sex Partnerships Seriously: European Experiences as British Perspective?'. *International Family Law*: 84.

Wade, J., Dixon, J., and Richards, A. (2009). *Implementing Special Guardianship*. DCSF-RBX-09-17. <https://york.ac.uk/inst/spru/research/pdf/SpecialG.pdf>.

Wade, K. (2017). 'The Regulation of Surrogacy: A Children's Rights Perspective'. *Child and Family Law Quarterly*, 29: 113.

Walby, S. and Allen, J. (2004). *Domestic Violence, Sexual Assault and Stalking: Findings from the British Crime Survey*. Home Office Research Study 276. London: HMSO. <webarchive.nationalarchives.gov.uk/20110218135832/rds.homeoffice.gov.uk/rds/pdfs04/hors276.pdf>.

Walby, S. and Myhill, A. (2001). 'Assessing and Managing Risk', in J. Taylor-Browne (ed), *What Works in Reducing Domestic Violence? A Comprehensive Guide for Professionals*. London: Whiting Birch. <webarchive.nationalarchives.gov.uk/20110218135832/rds.homeoffice.gov.uk/rds/prgpdfs/assess.pdf>.

Walby, S., Towers, J., and Francis, B. (2016). 'Is Violent Crime Increasing or Decreasing? A New Methodology to Measure Repeat Attacks Making Visible the Significance of Gender and Domestic Relations'. *British Journal of Criminology*, 56: 1203.

Walker, J. (1991). 'Divorce—Whose Fault?'. *Family Law*, 21: 234.

Walker, J. (1996). 'Is there a Future for Lawyers in Divorce?'. *International Journal of Law, Policy and the Family*, 10: 52.

Walker, J. (2000). 'The Development of Family Mediation', Newcastle Centre for Family Studies, *Information Meetings and Associated Provisions within the Family Law Act 1996: Final Evaluation of Research Studies Undertaken*. <webarchive.nationalarchives.gov.uk/+/http://www.dca.gov.uk/family/fla/chap18.pdf>.

Walker, J. and McCarthy, P. (2004). 'Picking Up the Pieces'. *Family Law*, 34: 580.

Wallbank, J. (1997). 'The Campaign for Change of the Child Support Act 1991: Reconstituting the "Absent" Father'. *Social and Legal Studies*, 6: 191.

Wallbank, J. (2009). '"Bodies in the Shadows": Joint Birth Registration, Parental Responsibility and Social Class'. *Child and Family Law Quarterly*, 21: 267.

Walmsley, E. (2017). 'Commentary on *Re X and Y (Foreign Surrogacy)*', in H. Stalford,

K. Hollingsworth, and S. Gilmore (eds), *Rewriting Children's Rights Judgments: From Academic Vision to New Practice.* Oxford: Hart Publishing.

Ward, J., Brown, R., Westlake, D., and Munro, E. (2010). 'Infants Suffering, or Likely to Suffer, Significant Harm: A Prospective Longitudinal Study'. Research Brief, DFE-RB053. <www.assets.publishing.service.gov.uk/government/uploads/system/uploads/attachment_data/file/182461/DFE-RB053.pdf>.

Warshak, R. (2014). 'Social Science and Parenting Plans for Young Children: A Consensus Report'. *Psychology, Public Policy, and Law*, 20: 46.

Wasoff, F., Miles, J., and Mordaunt, E. (2010). *Legal Practitioners' Perspectives on the Cohabitation Provisions of the Family Law (Scotland) Act 2006*, and Briefing Paper No 51. <www.crfr.ac.uk/cohabitation/>.

Waterhouse, R. (2000). *Lost in Care—Report of the Tribunal of Inquiry into the Abuse of Children in Care in the Former County Council Areas of Gwynedd and Clwyd.* London: HMSO.

Welbourne, P. (2008). 'Safeguarding Children on the Edge of Care: Policy for Keeping Children Safe after the *Review of the Child Care Proceedings System, Care Matters and the Carter Review of Legal Aid*'. *Child and Family Law Quarterly*, 20: 335.

Westmarland, N., McGlynn, C., and Humphreys, C. (2018). 'Using Restorative Justice Approaches to Police Domestic Violence and Abuse'. *Journal of Gender-Based Violence*, 2: 339.

Westwood, S. (2013). '"My Friends are my Family": An Argument about the Limitations of Contemporary Law's Recognition of Relationships in Later Life'. *Journal of Social Welfare and Family Law*, 35: 347.

Wijedasa, D. (2017). *Children Growing up on the Care of Relatives in the UK.* Policy Report 18. University of Bristol. <https://bristol.ac.uk/media-library/sites/policybristol/briefings-and-reports-pdfs/2017-briefings--reports-pdfs/PolicyBristol_Report_November_2017_Kinship_Care.pdf>.

Wikeley, N. (2000). 'Child Support—The New Formula, Part I'. *Family Law*, 30: 820.

Wikeley, N. (2006a). *Child Support: Law and Policy.* Oxford: Hart Publishing.

Wikeley, N. (2006b). 'A Duty But Not a Right: Child Support after *R (Kehoe) v Secretary of State for Work and Pensions*'. *Child and Family Law Quarterly*, 18: 287.

Wikeley, N. (2007a). *Written Memorandum to Public Bill Committee, on Child Maintenance and Other Payments Bill 2007.* <www.publications.parliament.uk/pa/cm200607/cmpublic/childmain/memos/memocm1.htm>.

Wikeley, N. (2007b). 'Child Support Reform—Throwing the Baby Out With the Bathwater?'. *Child and Family Law Quarterly*, 19: 434.

Wikeley, N. et al (2001). *National Survey of Child Support Agency Clients.* DWP Research Report No 152. Leeds: Corporate Document Service. <webarchive.nationalarchives.gov.uk/20130314010347/http://research.dwp.gov.uk/asd/asd5/rrep152.pdf>.

Wikeley, N., Barnett, S., Brown, J., Davis, G., Diamond, I., Draper, T., and Smith, P. (2008). *Relationship Separation and Child Support Study.* DWP RR 503. <webarchive.nationalarchives.gov.uk/20130314010347/http://research.dwp.gov.uk/asd/asd5/rports2007-2008/rrep503.pdf>.

Willekens, H. (2022). 'What (If Anything) Can Justify the Use of Biological Criteria for Allocating Parental Rights and Obligations?', in J. Scherpe and S. Gilmore (eds), *Family Matters: Essays in Honour of John Eekelaar.* Cambridge: Intersentia.

Williams, Z. (2011). 'So We Can't Afford Legal Aid? Look at the Costs Without It'. *The Guardian*, 23 June 2011. <www.theguardian.com/commentisfree/2011/jun/22/legal-aid-cuts-will-not-save>.

Wilson, B. and Smallwood, S. (2007). 'Understanding Recent Trends in Marriage'. *Population Trends*, 128: 24.

Wilson, G. (2006). 'The Non-Resident Parental Role for Separated Fathers: A Review'. *International Journal of Law, Policy and the Family*, 20: 286.

Wilson, G. (2007). 'Financial Provision in Civil Partnerships'. *Family Law*, 37: 31.

Women and Equalities Committee (2016). *Transgender Equality*, HC 390. <https://publications.parliament.uk/pa/cm201516/cmselect/cmwomeq/390/390.pdf>.

Women and Equalities Committee (2017). *Fathers and the Workplace.* HC 358. <https://publications.parliament.uk/pa/cm201719/cmselect/cmwomeq/358/358.pdf>.

Women and Equalities Committee (2022a). *The Rights of Cohabiting Partners*, HC 92. <https://publications.parliament.uk/pa/cm5803/cmselect/cmwomeq/92/summary.html>.

Women and Equalities Committee (2022b). *The Rights of Cohabiting Partners: Government Response to the Committee's Second Report*, HC 766. <https://publications.parliament.uk/pa/cm5803/cmselect/cmwomeq/766/report.html>.

Women and Equality Unit (2003a). *Civil Partnership: A Framework for the Legal Recognition of Same-Sex Couples*. London: HMSO. <webarchive.nationalarchives.gov.uk/+/www.womenandequalityunit.gov.uk/research/civ_par_con.pdf>.

Women and Equality Unit (2003b). *Responses to Civil Partnership: A Framework for Legal Recognition of Same-Sex Couples*. London: DTI. <webarchive.nationalarchives.gov.uk/+/www.womenandequalityunit.gov.uk/publications/CP_responses.pdf>.

Women's Aid (2005). *Women's Aid Briefing on Domestic Violence: A National Report*.

Women's Aid (2016). *Nineteen Child Homicides*. <www.womensaid.org.uk/wp-content/uploads/2016/01/Child-First-Nineteen-Child-Homicides-Report.pdf>.

Wong, S. (2009). 'Caring and Sharing: Interdependency as a Basic for Property Redistribution?', in A. Bottomley and S. Wong (eds), *Changing Contours of Domestic Life, Family and Law*. Oxford: Hart Publishing.

Woodhead, L. (2014). *An Error in the House of Bishops Guidance on Same Sex Marriage*. <www.thinkinganglicans.org.uk/archives/006460.html>.

Woodhouse, B. (2014). 'Listening to Children: Participation Rights of Minors in Italy and the United States'. *Journal of Social Welfare and Family Law*, 36: 358.

Woodward, H. with Sefton, M. (2014). *Pensions on Divorce: An Empirical Study*. Cardiff: Cardiff University. <https://orca.cf.ac.uk/56700/1/14%2002%2011%20Pensions%20on%20divorce%20final%20report.pdf>.

Woodward, H. (2019). *A Guide to the Treatment of Pensions on Divorce: The Report of the Pension Advisory Group*, London: Nuffield.

Zanghellini, A. (2012). '*A v B and C* [2012] EWCA Civ 285 – Heteronormativity, Poly-Parenting and the Homo-Nuclear Family'. *Child and Family Law Quarterly*, 24: 475.

INDEX

Abduction of children
age rules 75–6
Abortion
adoption statistics, effect on 907
Absent fathers *see* **Non-resident fathers/parents**
Abuse of children *see* **Child protection; Domestic abuse**
Access *see* **Child arrangements orders**
Accommodation
statutory provisions 825
voluntary arrangements 831–2
Adoption
alternative options 967–71
birth parents
reform 923–7
rights 923–7
central issues 901
changing nature and purpose
looked after children 908–10
recent social change 906–7
dispensing with parental consent 919–23
human rights
compatibility of consent provisions 902
compatibility of welfare test 923
legal effects 903–6
looked after children
special problems 911–12
open adoption 955–67
outcomes 908–10
overview 902–3
parental consent 915–23
parental responsibility 695
parenthood 672
placement for adoption
consent 927–30
consequences 930
contact 930
placement orders 927–30
restrictions on removal 931
post-adoption issues 930
procedure
placement 927–30
preliminary residence conditions 933
revocation 931–2
revocation of order 904, 905
right to know birth parents 650–3
statutory provisions 654–7
threshold conditions 928
welfare principle 528, 912–15
see also **Welfare principle**
checklist 529–31
compatibility with parents' rights 902, 923
preference for birth or adoptive parents 941–3
sole natural parent 954–5
step-parents 950–3
threshold criteria 938–41
trans-racial adoption 944–50
without consent 927–30
Adult relationships
central issues 30
civil partnership
see also **Civil partnership**
defined 66
formal requirements 70
nature of relationship 57–9
significance of status 61–3
cohabitation
defined 118–20
human rights 123–4
overview 111–12
policy questions 120–2
family relationships in England and Wales
civil partnership 32–4
cohabitation 34–5
formalized relationships 32–4
'living apart together' 35
marriage 32–4
gender
see also **Transgender persons**
importance to identity 36–8
overview 35
influence of divorce law 138–9
informal family relationships
functional approach 114–18
sharing a household 113
statutory tests 112–13
marriage
see also **Marriage**
defined 66
formal requirements 68–70
human rights 63–6
ideological role 50–3
nature of relationship 59–61
overview 59–61
significance of status 61–3
platonic relationships
see also **Platonic relationships**
exclusion from family law 124–5
functional approach 128
human rights 124–8
relevance of legal recognition 31–2
right to marry 63–6
rights-based approach *see* **Children's rights; Human Rights; Rights-based approach, Welfare principle**
same-sex couples
see also **Civil partnership; Marriage; Same-sex couples; Sexual orientation**
civil partnership 39–43
historical development of recognition 38–43
judicial developments 38–41
significance of status 129
state protection *see* **Care and supervision orders; Child protection; Local authorities; Looked after children**

Advancement, presumption of 454, 455
Age
capacity to marry or form civil partnership 69, 75–6
void marriages 75–6
Agreements
cohabitation
beneficial ownership 474
common law marriage myth 511
enforceability 509–111
impact on relationships 512
legal position 509–11
use by couples 511–12
criticism 435–9
fairness of upholding 432–5
principles in practice 432–5
public policy 426–7
reform proposals 439–45
parental responsibility 684–5
post-nuptial agreements 425–6
pre-nuptial agreements
enforcement 426–35
equal sharing principle 433
factors tainting agreements from outset 429–32
separation and maintenance agreements 421–5
'Alienation' allegations 790–2
see also **Child arrangements orders**
Alternative dispute resolution *see* **Family justice system; Non-court dispute resolution**
Ancillary relief *see* **Financial provision**
Appeals
adoption orders 906
emergency protection orders 892
financial provision on divorce
appeal out of time against orders 414–16
clean break provisions 413–16
Arbitration 27
Arranged marriages 92, 95
Arrest
domestic abuse *see* **Domestic abuse** percentage arrests leading to conviction 203
Artificial insemination *see* **Assisted reproduction**
Assisted reproduction
see also **Surrogacy**
component of parenthood 602
determining parenthood
deceased fathers 646–7
effect of statutory changes 609
fathers and second female parents 640–3
impact of HFEA 2008 647–50
inappropriateness of traditional approach 638–9
motherhood 640
second female parents 646–7
sperm and egg donors 647
unmarried fathers 643–5
disagreements over identity of parents 602
key policy difficulties 630
need for two genetic parents 604
recognition of same-sex couples 2
right to know genetic parents 653–7
right to reproductive freedom
access to treatment 631–2
best interests of the child 635–6
legitimate regulation of fertility treatment under Art 8(2) 634–8
recognition as human right under Art 8 633–4
right to found a family under Art 12 638
surrogate husband's deemed fatherhood 660, 668
Associated persons *see* **Domestic abuse**
Autonomy of children
care and supervision orders 862–3
conservative application of Gillick 576–83
Gillick competence
court decision 571–4
parental rights 580–2
wider significance of Gillick 582–3
judges meeting children 733–5
participation in proceedings 729–35
parties to proceedings 731–3
wider significance of Gillick 582–3
witnesses 731
Balance of harm test *see* **Occupation orders**
Bank accounts
family assets 506–8
Best interests *see* **Welfare principle**
Bigamy
criminal offence 407
effect on marriage or civil partnership 76
history of divorce 139
Birth certificates
joint registration reforms 614–15
presumption of paternity 613–14
Birth parents
adoption
central issues 901
consent to placement 902, 915–23, 927–30
effect 903–4
human rights 923–7
paramountcy principle 912–15
preference for birth parents 941–3
reform 923–7
secrecy 911–12
state support 817
Blood tests to establish parentage *see* *DNA tests* **Capacity**
see also **Gillick competence, Mental disability**

children
autonomy rights 571–83
parties to
proceedings 731–3
consummation of
marriage 105
void marriages and civil
partnerships
age requirements 75–6
formal requirements 77–81
monogamy requirement 76
non-qualifying
ceremonies 78–87
polygamous marriages 77
presumption of
marriage 87–8
prohibited degrees 72–5

Care and supervision orders
see also **Child protection**
care plans 869–77
challenging local authority
decisions
complaints
procedures 898–9
human rights claims 899
changes to the care
plan 876–7
contact 881–4
discharge 887
effect of care order 877–80
effect of supervision
order 884–6
emergency protection
court orders 890–4
police powers 888–90
harm 869–77
is suffering 844–5
likely to suffer 845–54
proof 860–2
reasonable expectations of
parent 855–60
significant 843–4
interim orders 894–900
jurisdiction 838–41
proportionality 859, 895
standing 839
threshold criteria
attributable to 855–60
unknown perpetrators 853–4
vaccinations 879–80
variation 887
welfare stage
children's wishes and
feelings 862–3
consideration of additional
harm 864–7
discretionary
powers 867–9
Carers *see* **Looked after children**
Child arrangements orders
see also **Court orders**
background 735–7
conclusions 811–12
Family Justice Review 736
generally 737–8
history 736
introduction 722–3, 735–6
limitations 694–5
'lives with' orders
approach of courts 738
central issues 721–2
current approach 742–5
enforcement of
contact 798–800
entitlement of
holders 693–4
'family proceedings' 724
gay and lesbian
parents 754–5
historic approach 738–42
mother, presumption in
favour of 738–42
natural parent
presumption 758–64
natural parents versus
others 758–64
overview 722–3
parental
responsibility 764–6
participation of
children 729–35
possible living
arrangements 738
primary carer, presumption
in favour of 742–5
procedure 724–35
racial, religious, and
cultural factors 755–8
same-sex relationships 754–5
scope 724
shared living
arrangements 745–54
standing 724–9
status quo, presumption in
favour of 738–42
previous orders 723
rationale for creation of
child arrangements
orders 737
section 8 orders 723
shared living
arrangements 745–54
'spending time' or 'otherwise
having contact' orders
see also **Care and
supervision orders**
adoption placement
orders 930
'alienation'
allegations 790–2
committal 794–5
courts' approach 768–79
displacing presumptions
relating to
contact 779–93
domestic abuse 779–93
duty of resident parent
to promote
contact 769–70
enforcement 694, 793–800
entitlement of holders 694
fathers 774–7
intractable disputes 770–1
'looked after
children' 881–4
meaning and scope 766–7
monitoring 795–6
non-parents 777
policy issues surrounding
child support 337–41
same-sex couples 777–9
statutory presumption 767–8
transferring
residence 796–8
Child assessment orders 836,
887
**Child Maintenance
Service (CMS)**
see also **Child support**
applications procedure
288–9
collection
Collect and Pay 288–9
direct pay 288
fees 288–9

Child Maintenance Service (CMS) (*cont.*)
enforcement process
available tools 297–8
discretion 298
exclusion of parents from process 299–303
methods 298
tax records 297–8
jurisdiction 284
overview of current law 284
scheme 283–4
set-off 293
where CMS has no jurisdiction 306–7
Child protection
see also **Care and supervision orders**
abuse
investigations following referrals 835–8
welfare investigations 835–8
care and supervision 838–87
central issues 813
challenging decisions 898–9
child abuse 835–8
child assessment orders 836
emergency protection 888–94
emergency protection orders 836
general principles 816–21
interim orders 894–900
overview 813–16, 899–900
state support for children in need 821–3
theoretical approaches 561–6
voluntary accommodation 831–2
Child support
see also **Child Maintenance Service**
applications to CMS 288–9
development and demise of Child Support Agency 282
encouraging private agreements 288–9
failure of private agreement 288–9
family-based arrangements 288–9
general principles 287
living arrangements 337–41
maintenance calculations
apportionment 293
basic rate 290–1
basis 289
CMS scheme 289
flat rate 291
gross historic income 289
nil rate 291
reduced rate 291
set-off 293
shared care 291–2
termination of the calculation 297
relevant parties
'non-resident parent' 286
'paying parent' 286
'person with care' 286–7
'qualifying child' 285–6
'receiving parent' 286
'relevant other child' 287
scheme 283
set-off 293
statutory provisions 285
termination of the calculation 297
top-up orders 305
variations
Children
see also **Adoption; Care and supervision orders; Child arrangements orders; Child protection; Children's rights; Child support; Legal parenthood; Parental responsibility; Welfare principle**
abuse *see* **Care and supervision orders; Child protection; Children's rights; Human Rights; Rights-based approach; Welfare principle**
cultural issues 21
domestic abuse applications generally 208
emergency protection
court orders 890–4
police powers 888–90
family life under Art 8 549–57
establishing a breach 550–1
establishing a 'right' 549–50
justifying a breach 551
reconciliation with paramountcy principle 551–7
financial provision
see also **Child Maintenance Service (CMS); Child support**
alleviation of poverty 279–81
central issues 278
child support 285–303
court orders 303–11
dangers of private ordering 329–34
historical background 281–4
overview of current law 284
policy issues 323–47
private ordering 320–3
inability to marry or form civil partnership 75–6
judges meeting children 733–5
in need *see* **Local authorities**
participation in private law cases 729–34
parties to proceedings 731–3
protection of identity 764–5
section 7 reports 730
statistics 1–2
witnesses, as 731, 863
Children in care *see* **Looked after children**
Children's Guardian
care and supervision applications 862–3
legal representation of children 731
Children's rights
see also **Human rights**
care and supervision applications 862–3
development in English law

changes in parent/child relationship 566–7
Gillick competence 571–83
DNA testing 618–21
ECHR, under 567–8
High Court inherent jurisdiction 598–600
importance 558–61
inherent jurisdiction of the High Court 598–600
limitations on parental responsibility 711–14
open adoption 955–67
participation in proceedings 729–35
right of donor conceived children to know genetic parentage
importance 650–3
policy choices 650
statutory provisions 654–7
state intervention 816–19
theoretical foundations
interest theory 563–4
paternalism 564–6
will or power theory 561–3
UN Convention on the Rights of the Child 568–70
Civil partnership
see also **Human rights; Marriage; Same-sex couples; Sexual orientation**
choice 54
conversion to marriage 34
creation 41–3
defined 66
family assets 515
formal requirements 70
failure to comply 70
reform 70–2
'gay marriage'
government denials 42
ideological role 50–3
importance of gender 36
mixed-sex civil partnerships 46–50, 55–7
nature of relationship 59–61
nullity
practical importance 68
void and voidable relationships distinguished 66–8
opposition to introduction 42–3
relevance of legal recognition 31–2
significance of status 61–3
statistics 34
statutory provisions 42
Clean breaks
see also **Financial Provision**
appeals 413–16
financial provision for children
legal impossibility of clean break in relation to children 328
financial provision on divorce/dissolution
approach of courts 410–11
central issue 349
practical application 411–13
setting aside orders 414
statutory provisions 361–2, 409–10
CMS *see* **Child Maintenance Service (CMS)**
Cohabitation
see also **Family assets; Family homes; Trusts**
agreements
beneficial ownership 474
common law marriage myth 511
enforceability 509–111
impact on relationships 512
legal position 509–11
use by couples 511–12
changing patterns 34–5
component of marriage 63
defined 118–20
domestic abuse applications generally 208–12
financial remedies, reform of 512–13
human rights 123–4
occupation orders 226–8
overview 111–12
policy questions 120–2
reform 512–13
relevance of legal recognition 31–2
statistics 1–2
Committal *see* **Imprisonment**
'Common intention' constructive trusts
see also **Family homes, criticism of current law of trusts**
case law 456
common intention 471–5
detrimental reliance 465–6, 475–6, 488–90
establishing trust 459–64
fairness 462–4
imputing intention 462–4
inferring intention 462–4
ingredients 459–64
intention 462–4, 484–8
legal title
joint names 464–70
sole names 470–6
non-financial contributions 490–2
quantification of shares 476
use of trust 456–8
Compensation
criticisms 380–2
entitlement to compensation 376–9
loss of earning capacity 376–9
needs 379–80
relationship-generated economic disadvantage 376–9
Complaints against local authorities 898–9
Conciliation *see* **Mediation**
Conduct
effect on financial provision on divorce/dissolution
criminal offences 407–8
delayed applications 405–6
financial misconduct and anti-avoidance measures 405–6
general rule 402–5
late applications 406–7
litigation misconduct 406
'positive' conduct 408
relevant conduct 404–5

Confidentiality *see* Privacy
Consanguinity 59, 120
  see also Prohibited Degrees
Consent
  see also Consent orders
  access to fertility treatment 634–5
  adoption
    dispensing with parental consent 919–23
    final hearings 934–41
    human rights 916
    placement orders 927–30
  DNA testing
    adult parties 628–9
    children 627–8
  marriage and civil partnership
    defined 90–1
    duress 91–6
    fundamental requirement 89–90
    miscellaneous circumstances 100
    mistake 96–7
    statutory provisions 88–9
    unsoundness of mind 97–100
Consent orders
  see also Consent orders
  see also Agreements; Private ordering
  financial provision for children
    12-month rule 321–2
    dangers 329–34
    discouraging the 'clean break' 322
    maintenance 320–3
    property adjustment 322
    statutory provisions 321
  financial provision on divorce/dissolution
    consent orders 417–21
Consortium 63, 114
Consummation of marriage
  critique of requirement 106–8
  importance to marriage 104–5
  incapacity 105
  no such requirement for civil partnership 109–11
  voidable marriages 103–11
  wilful refusal 105–6
Contact *see* Child arrangements orders
Contraception
  adoption statistics, effect on 907
  Gillick competence 571–4, 712
Contractual rights
  see also Agreements
  pre-nuptial agreements 426–35
Corporate parents *see* Local authorities
Covid-19 pandemic
  family court during 24–5
Culture
  child arrangements 'lives with' orders
    protection of identity 764–5
    relevance 755–8
  children's rights 558
  contemporary themes and issues 19–21
  trans-racial adoption 944–50
Custody *see* Child arrangements orders
Degrading treatment *see* Torture and degrading treatment, freedom from
Disability
  financial provision on divorce 371
  periodical payments for children 304–5
Discretion
  see also Child support; Financial provision; Welfare principle
  approach to family law 10–12
  disadvantages of approach 11–12
  negotiated settlements 11
  rules-based approach contrasted 12, 345–7
Discrimination *see* Non-discrimination
Dissolution of civil partnership
  see also Divorce; Financial provision
  central issues 130
  defects in former law 147–56
  former substantive law 141–2
  similarity to divorce 131
Divorce
  assessment of reformed law 178–9
  bars to divorce
    financial protection for certain respondents 167–8
    generally 167
    religious marriages 169
    time bars 168–9
  central issues 130
  conduct, relevance of 172–6
  current themes
    effect on behaviour 138–9
    effect on the institution of marriage 137–8
    role of law and lawyers 138
  defects in former law 147–56
  evaluation of current law 170–1
  demise of Family Law Act 1996 scheme 157–62
  former procedure 143–57
  gender asymmetry 133
  history of law 140–2
  increasing trends 131
  King's Proctor 169–70
  mutual consent, by 176–7
  regularization 139–40, 178
  regulation 139–40
  religious marriages 169
  responsibility 139
  statistics 133–6
  unilateral demand for 177
  void and voidable relationships distinguished 66–8
DNA testing
  case law 623–5
  consent
    adult parties 628–9
    children 627–8
  human rights
    children 618–21
    impact of HRA 625–6
    putative fathers 621–2
  public interest 623
  statutory provisions 618
  welfare principle 622

Domestic abuse
see also Abuse of children; Child protection; Domestic abuse protection orders; Domestic abuse protection notices; Non-molestation orders; Occupation orders; Police
applications for orders 247–67
associated persons 208–12, 222–4
background issues
causes and risk factors 187–8
definition 182–3
ending relationship 189
gender 187
justice gap 189–90
prevalence of abuse 183–6
problems with data collection 184–6
balance of harm test 223–4
central issues 179
child arrangements orders
'spending time' or 'otherwise having contact' orders 779–93
civil law approach 204–7
criminal justice system
criticisms of response 201–4
scope of criminal law 200
criminal law
arguments in favour 256–8
impact 258–60
data 184–6
definition 182–3
domestic abuse protection notices 204, 263
domestic abuse protection orders 204–7, 263
effect on relationships 181
enforcement of orders 250–60
domestic abuse protection orders 246–7
impact 258–60
non-molestation order 254–60
occupation orders 222–3, 223–4, 227, 228
ex parte orders 248–9
feminist critiques 189–95
future of protection 268–9
harm 223–4
human rights
ill treatment under Art 3 197
new legal discourse 195–6
non-discrimination 197–8
right to life 196–7
right to respect for private life 198–9
orders made without application by victim 260–2
own motion of the court, orders made of 261
personally connected persons 240–1
police applications 262–3
poor response from legal system 276
procedure
application by party or on court's own motion 261
ex parte applications 262–7
third party applications 262–7
public/private dichotomy 181
teen abuse 183
third party applications 260–7
undertakings 249–50
without notice orders 248–9

Domestic abuse protection notices
see also Domestic abuse
breach 263
duration of notice 263
police use 204, 262, 263, 267

Domestic abuse protection orders
see also Domestic abuse
basis for order
generally 244
preconditions 244
relevant factors and constraints 245–6
duration of protection 246–7
notification requirements 242
occupation, regulation of 243
overview 240
personally connected 240–1
positive requirements 244
preconditions 244
provision that can be made 241–4
range of relationships 240–1
restrictions protecting from domestic abuse 242–3

Duress
see also Consent; Voidable civil partnerships; Voidable marriages
forced marriages 92
objective test 92–4
subjective test 94–6

Education
parental consultation 707–8
periodical payments for children 304–5

Emergency protection orders
appeals 892
court orders 890–4
police powers 888–90

Enforcement
age rules
see also Child Maintenance Service (CMS)
child arrangements 'spending time' or 'otherwise having contact' orders
committal 794–5
modes of enforcement 793–800
monitoring 795–6
transferring residence 796–8
child support
CMS tools 297–8
exclusion of parents from process 299–303
tax records 297–8
financial provision for children 319
financial provision on divorce/dissolution 361
post-nuptial agreements 425–6
pre-nuptial agreements 426–35
separation and maintenance agreements 421–5

'Entitled applicants'
section 8 applications 724–5
'Entitled persons'
occupation orders 227–8
Equality
child arrangements orders
presumption in favour of natural parent 758–64
equal sharing principle on divorce/dissolution
basic principle 382–5
compensation 400–1
everyday cases 399–400
high value cases 400
indeterminacy of principle 398–9
post-separation acquired assets 391–2
reasons for unequal division 393
relationship to other principles 399–401
relevant property 385–93
risky and illiquid assets 397–8
'stellar' contributions 393–5
unilateral assets 395–7
pre-nuptial agreements 433
Estoppel
proprietary estoppel 476–80
Ethnicity
child arrangements orders
where child lives with a person
protection of identity 764–5
relevance 755–8
trans-racial adoption 944–50
European Convention on Human Rights *see* **European Convention on Human Rights under Human Rights; Rights-based approach**
Ex parte **applications**
see also **Child Protection; Domestic abuse**
fair trial 6
Express trusts
family assets 451–3, 505–6
formal requirements 451–3
transfer of ownership 451–3
Fair hearings
child protection 819–20
key ECHR article 5–6
Family assets
see also **Family finances; Family homes**
bank accounts 506–8
central issues 446–7
civil partnerships 515
current position, overview of 513–14
express trusts 451–3, 505–6
implied trusts 454–76
income 506–8
occupation of family home
decision making about sale 497
home rights 495–7
occupation orders 502
resolution of disputes 497–502
spouses and civil partners 495–7
overview 447–8
property other than land 503–6
proprietary estoppel 476–80
reform 512–13
transfer of ownership 451–3
use-rights 508–9
Family court *see* **Family justice system**
Family homes
ascertaining ownership
see also **Trusts**
common intention constructive trusts 450, 456–76
implied trusts 453–4, 454–76
proprietary estoppel 476–80
common intention constructive trusts 450, 456–76
conclusions 525
criticisms of current law of trusts
detrimental reliance 488–90
empirical basis for *Stack v Downton* 481–3
intention 484–8
overview 480
position of homemakers 490–2
practical uncertainties of law 490–2
implied trusts 453–4, 454–76
non-financial contribution 490–2
occupation
decision-making about sale 497
home rights 495–7
occupation orders 502
spouses and civil partners 495–7
property adjustment orders on divorce/dissolution
owner-occupied homes 358–9
rented homes 359–60
proprietary estoppel 476–80
reform 512–13
regard for needs 369
rented homes 503
use-rights 508–9
Family Justice Review 736
Family justice system
arbitration 27
family court 22–4
lawyers 25–6, 28
legal aid reforms 24
Covid-19 pandemic 24–5
mediation 25–6
non-court dispute resolution 25–6
role of state in family life 21–2
Family life *see* **Respect for family life, right to**
Fatherhood
deceased fathers 646–7
determination 606
effect of genetic fatherhood 614–15
geneticization 607
new focus on men's engagement with law 15–16

relationship with mother 613–14
sperm donors 647
unmarried fathers 643–5

Fathers
parental responsibility
married fathers 683
termination 714–15, 716–17
unmarried fathers 683–9, 696, 697–705
presumption in favour of contact 774–7

Feminist critiques
'common intention' constructive trusts
position of homemakers 490–2
consummation of marriage 107–8
domestic abuse 189–95
financial provision on divorce/dissolution 353
gender issues
diversity of approach 12
equality 350–3
exclusion of women from public life 13
family economy 350–3
whether gender makes a difference 12–13
women as mothers 14–15
public/private divide 13
welfare principle
indeterminacy 537–9
irrelevant considerations 539–42
lack of transparency 539–42
rationale for paramountcy 542–5

Fertility treatment *see* **Assisted reproduction**

Financial provision
see also Child Maintenance Service; Child Support; Consent orders
children, for
central issues 278
child support 285–303
court orders 303–11
development and demise of Child Support Agency 282
driving forces for alleviation of poverty 279–81
enforcement of orders 319
overview of current law 284, 285
policy issues 323–47
private ordering 320–3
scheme 283
unwanted birth 313
different approaches under MCA 1973 448–50
divorce or dissolution
see also Compensation; Consent orders; Court orders; Equality; Needs
agreements 416–17
available court orders 356
central issues 349
clean breaks 408–16
court resources 356–7
discretion 361–6
general principles governing grant of financial provision 361–6
historical background 353–6
lump sums 358
non-sharing, non-needs cases 375
overview 350
private ordering 416–17, 416–39
relationship-generated economic disadvantage 376–9
resources available 356–7
social context 350–3
timing of orders 361
'toolbox' 356–7
variation of order 414

Forced marriages
arranged marriages distinguished 92
'associated persons' 112–13
capacity 89
domestic abuse 282
duress 92
non-molestation orders 261
'non-qualifying ceremonies' 68, 271
protection orders
content of order 272–3
discretion of court 274–5
enforcement 276
force, meaning of 271–2
making order 275
statutory provisions 271–2
use of orders 276
statutory provisions 66

Formalities
grounds for void marriages or civil partnerships 77–81
marriage and civil partnership 68–70
'non-qualifying ceremonies' 78–87

Foster care
'children of the family' 309
financial provision on divorce 363
local authority responsibilities 834
'person with care' 286–7
section 8 applications 725

'Gay marriage' *see* **Marriage**

Gender
see also Transgender persons
child arrangements orders where child lives with a person
preference for primary carer 742–5
contemporary themes and issues
feminist critiques 12–13
masculine studies 15–16
determination 36–8
divorce asymmetry 133
domestic abuse asymmetry 187
identity 16–18
importance to identity 36–8
overview 35
terminology 16–18
voidable relationships 101–2

Genetics
component of parenthood 602–3

Gillick competence
accommodation by local authority 831
conservative application 576–83
court decision 571–4
determination of 574–5
limitations on parental responsibility 712
medical decision-making 577–82
parental responsibility
parent/child relationship 675–7
as limitation on parental authority 580–2, 712
paternity testing 620–1
resistance to decision 576–7
significance of decision 582–3
Guardians
see also Children's Guardian; Special Guardians
parental responsibility 695
termination of parental responsibility 718
Guardians ad litem *see* Children's Guardian
Hardship *see* Financial hardship
Harm *see* Care and Supervision Orders; Domestic abuse
Home sharers *see* Platonic relationships
Homosexuality *see* Same-sex couples; Sexual orientation
Human rights
see also Children's rights; Rights-based approach
access to fertility treatment
right to found a family 638
right to respect for private and family life 633–8
adoption
compatibility of consent provisions 902
challenge to welfare approach 3–4
child disputes under Art 8(1), resolution of
establishing a breach 550–1
establishing a 'right' 549–50
justifying a breach 551
reconciliation with paramountcy principle 551–7
child support
enforcement 299–303
children's rights 567–70
cohabitation 123–4
compatibility of welfare test 921–2
DNA testing
children 625–6
impact of HRA 625–6
putative fathers 621–2
domestic abuse
ill treatment under Art 3 197
new legal discourse 195–6
non-discrimination 196–7
private life 198–9
right to life 196–7
European Convention on Human Rights
care and supervision orders 872–3
fair trial 5–6, 299–303, 931
home, right to respect for 6–8, 39–41, 198–9, 549–57, 633–8, 819–21, 868, 914, 924
marry and found a family, right to 8–9, 63–6, 130
non-discrimination 9, 39–41, 71, 197–8
private and family life, right to respect for 6–8, 39–41, 198–9, 549–57, 633–8, 819–21, 914–15, 924
torture or degrading treatment, freedom from 4–5, 197
forced marriages 89
no right to divorce 130
parenthood, recognition of 606–7
platonic home sharers 124–8
reproductive freedom, right to
legitimate regulation of fertility treatment under Art 8(2) 634–8
recognition as human right under Art 8 633–2
right to found a family under Art 12 638
return to rights-based approach 10
same-sex couples
family life, right to respect for 39–41
state intervention 819–21
transgender persons
right to marry 18
right to respect for private life 17
Identity
cultural diversity 19–21
gender 36–8
genetic parents
central issues 601
overview 602–3
right to know 650–3
human rights 617–29
marriage
mistake 96–7
participants 69
privacy 6
sexual orientation 36–8
trans-racial adoption 944–50
Illegitimate children
presumption of legitimacy 613
Implied trusts
see also 'Common intention' constructive trusts
advancement, presumption of 454, 455
generally 453–4
presumptions of resulting trust 454–5
Imprisonment
committals
domestic abuse 200
enforcement following disputes over children
child arrangements orders 795
imprisoned persons
assisted insemination 636
conduct affecting financial provision on divorce 404
right to marry 65
wilful refusal to consummate 105–6
In vitro fertilization *see* Assisted reproduction

Income
family assets 506–8
Informal family relationships
see also Cohabitants
exclusion from family law 124–5
functional criteria 114–18, 128
household sharing 113
human rights challenge 124–8
meaning and scope 112–13
non-conjugal relationships 124–8
registration of relationship 111
Inherent jurisdiction
accommodating children 599–600
basis of court's power 578, 598
Children Act, relationship with 598–9
generally 598–600
wardship 578, 598–9
Inhuman treatment *see* Torture and degrading treatment, freedom from
Injunctions *see* Non-molestation orders
Intention
'common intention' constructive trusts 462–4, 484–8
Interest theory of rights 563–4
Interim care orders 894–900
Irretrievable breakdown
see also Dissolution of civil partnership; Divorce
former law 147–57
law reform 157

Justice system 21–5

King's Proctor
divorce and 169–70
guardian of public interest 106
role 169–70

Land *see* Family homes
Law Commission *see* Reform
Lawyers *see* Family justice system
Legal aid
see also Family justice system
reforms to family legal aid 24
Legal parenthood
adoption
preference for birth or adoptive parents 941–3
sole natural parent 954–5
step-parents 950–3
trans-racial adoption 944–50
alternative approaches
four components 603–5
legal status 605–6
policy choices 606–10
assisted reproduction
deceased fathers 646–7
fathers and second female parents 640–3
impact of HFEA 647–50
inappropriateness of traditional approach 638–9
motherhood 640
second female parents 646–7
sperm and egg donors 647
unmarried fathers 643–5
biological criteria 617–18
central issues 601
child's right to know genetic parents
importance 650–3
policy choices 650
statutory provisions 654–7
financial provision for children
child's living arrangements 337–41
whether no contact irrelevant 339–41
who should pay for whom 335–7
natural reproduction
establishing maternity 610–12
establishing paternity 612–30
overview 602–3, 672
surrogacy
parental orders 660–6
status of commissioning parents 660
trans parents 610–2
Legal representation of children
care and supervision
applications 862
effect of supervision order 885–6
Legitimacy, presumption of 613
Lesbian women *see* Same-sex couples; Sexual orientation
Litigants in person 24
'Living apart together' 35
Local authorities
adoption procedures
placement 927–32
care and supervision orders
care plans 869–77
complaints procedures 898–9
contact 881–4
discharge 887
effect of care order 877–80
effect of supervision order 884–6
interim orders 894–900
jurisdiction 838–41
standing 839
threshold criteria 841–62
variation 887
welfare principle 862–9
child abuse
investigations following referrals 835–8
welfare investigations 835–8
children in need
accommodation 825–32
assessment of system 835
statutory provisions 824
complaints procedures 898–9
emergency protection
court orders 890–4
police powers 888–90
looked after children
statutory duties and responsibilities 832–5
parental responsibility 696

Looked after children
adoption
birth families, relationship with 911–12
outcomes 908–10
post-adoption support 911
special problems 911–12
assessment of system 835
care and supervision
care plans 869–77
complaints procedures 898–9
contact 881–4
discharge 887
effect of care order 877–80
effect of supervision order 884–6
human rights claims 899–900
interim orders 894–900
jurisdiction 838–41
standing 839
threshold criteria 841–62
variation 887
welfare principle 862–9
duties owed to children 832–5
emergency protection
court orders 890–4
police powers 888–90
independent reviewing officer 835
parental responsibility 718
statutory duties and responsibilities 832–5
Lump sum payments
children, for 303
divorce/dissolution 358

Maintenance
see also **Child Maintenance Service; Child support; Periodical payments**
children, for
age of child 310–11
applicants 308–10
central issues 278
child, application by 309–10
discretionary powers 311–12
driving forces for alleviation of poverty 279–81
duration of order 310–11
education and disability expenses 305
enforcement of orders 319
general principles 316–19
historical background 281–4
judicial principles 312–19
lump sum payments 303
matrimonial cases 309
overview of current law 284, 285
parties' relationships 284
periodical payments 303–6
private ordering 320–3
property adjustment orders 303
Schedule 1 cases 309
'Segal' orders 305–6
statutory schemes 307–10
step-parents, liability of 305–6
top-up orders 305
variation of orders 293–6, 306
where CMS has jurisdiction 303–6
where CMS has no jurisdiction 306–7
divorce and dissolution agreements 421–5
Marital rape 13, 107, 191–2
Marriage
see also **Civil partnership; Informal family relationships**
capacity
age requirements 75–6
formal requirements 75–6
monogamy requirement 76
polygamous marriages 77
presumption of marriage 87–8
prohibited degrees 72–5
changing patterns over recent decades 33–4
choice 54
cohabitation compared 121
defined 66
formal requirements 68–70
failure to comply 70
reform 70–2
'gay marriage'
government denials 42
introduction of same-sex marriage 43–6
grounds for void marriage
age 75–6
bigamy 76
disregard of formalities 77–88
prohibited degrees 72–5
grounds for voidable marriage
duress 91–6
failure to consummate 103–11
gender recognition 101–2
lack of valid consent 89–90
mental disability 100
mistake 96–7
other reasons affecting consent 100
overview 88–9
pregnancy 100–1
unsoundness of mind 97–100
human rights
forced marriages 89
formal requirements of marriage 70–1
respect for family life, right to 6–8
right to marry 8–9
ideological role 50–3
nature of relationship 59–61
nullity
practical importance 68
void and voidable relationships distinguished 66–8
overview 59–61
same-sex marriage 109–11
arguments in favour 44–6
civil partnership as form of 42
conservative critiques 46
feminist/same-sex critiques 19
history 38–43
introduction of same-sex marriage 43–6
statistics 34
transformation of marriage institution 57–9
significance of status 61–3
statistics 1–2

Maternity
natural reproduction 610–12
statutory determination for assisted reproduction 640
surrogacy 660
Matrimonial homes *see* **Family homes**
Mediation 25–6
criticisms 28
Mediation Information and Assessment Meetings 26, 799
Medical treatment
see also **Assisted reproduction; Fertility treatment**
parental consultation 709–10, 712
Mental disability
disorder rendering person unfit for marriage/civil partnership 100
relevance to child maintenance 312
unsoundness of mind precluding consent to marriage/civil partnership 97–100
Mistake
see also **Consent; Voidable civil partnerships; Voidable marriages**
identity 96–7
nature of ceremony 97
Mothers
feminist approach 14–15
parental responsibility
married mothers 683
second female parents 683–9
second female parents married/civil relationship with mother 683–9
termination of parental responsibility 714–15
Needs
see also **Financial provision**
available resources 369–70
criticisms of law 375
financial provision for children 313–14
housing 369
judicial interpretation 366–75
material needs 366–75
second families 373–4
source of need 370–3
statutory provisions 366–73
'New fathers' 16
No-fault divorce
benefits 136–7
central issues 130
No-order
non-intervention principle 584–9
Non-conjugal relationships *see* **Platonic relationships**
Non-court dispute resolution 25–7
see also **Family justice system**
Non-discrimination
access to assisted reproduction 638
child arrangements orders
gay and lesbian parents 754–5
cohabitation 123–4
domestic abuse 196–7
formal requirements of marriage and civil partnership 71
gay and lesbian rights 18
key ECHR article 9
platonic home sharers 124–8
trans-racial adoption 944–50
Non-intervention principle 584–9
'non-qualifying ceremonies'
rescue by presumption of marriage 87–8
substantial disregard of formalities 78–87
void and voidable relationships distinguished 68
Non-molestation orders
see also **Domestic abuse**
applications by party or on court's own motion 261
'associated persons' 208–12
breach of order 255
criminalization 254–60
discretionary powers 216–17
duration of order 217–18
enforcement 255
'molestation' undefined 213–17
orders made without application by victim 260–2
own motion of the court, orders made of 261
statutory provisions 213
statutory source 208
third party applications 260–7
Non-resident fathers/parents
child support 337–9
'non-resident parent' defined 286
Norgrove report *see* **Family Justice Review**
Nuclear families
adoption 950
defined 3
different child-rearing practices 21
parenthood 650
privacy 327
state motives regarding domestic abuse 211
Nullity *see* **Void civil partnerships; Void marriages; Voidable civil partnerships; Voidable marriages**
Occupation of family home
home rights 495–7
spouses and civil partners 495–7
Occupation orders
see also **Domestic abuse**
ancillary orders 229–30
'associated persons' 208–12, 222–4
balance of harm test
'attributable to conduct' 232–3
case law illustrations 234–9
cohabitants 226–8
discretion 225–6
entitled applicants 224

Occupation orders (*cont.*)
former spouses and civil partners where neither party entitled to occupy 227
former spouses and civil partners where respondent entitled to occupy 227
'likely' 231–2
overview 230
'significant harm' 230–1
categories 219, 220
complexity of rules 219
duration of order 222–3, 223–4, 227, 228
enforcement 222–3, 223–4, 227, 228
functions 219
hierarchy of property ownership 219–21
procedure
applications by party or on court's own motion 261
property ownership 221
standing
associated persons 222–4
cohabitants where neither entitled to occupy 228
entitled applicants 221–4
former spouses and civil partners where respondent entitled to occupy 224–5
former spouses/civil partners where neither party entitled to occupy 288
non-entitled cohabitants where respondent entitled to occupy 226–7
statutory source 208
terms of order 222–3, 223–4, 227, 228
Open adoption
contact
birth parents 955–67
court practice 961–7
increasing importance 902
looked after children 911–12
right to information 956–7
Ownership *see* **Family assets; Family finances; Family homes**
Paramountcy principle *see* **Welfare principle**
Parentage
see also **Adoption; Assisted reproduction; Legal parenthood; Maternity**
court orders 615–16
formalized relationships 613
proof
rebuttable presumptions 617–18
scientific tests 617–29
statutory determination for assisted reproduction
deceased partners 646–7
husbands 640–3
sperm donation 647
unmarried fathers 643–5
surrogacy 660–6
unmarried fathers 613–15
Parental 'alienation' *see* **'Alienation' allegations**
Parental responsibility
adoption 695
care and supervision orders 878–80
central issues 673–4
challenge of children's rights
conservative application of Gillick 573–83
wider significance of Gillick 582–3
child arrangements orders
orders where child lives with a person 764–6
decision-making
consultation 709–11
court's role 589–98
failure to consult 710–11
limitations 711–14
unilateral actions 705–11, 805–6
definition 679–82
fathers
married fathers 683
unmarried fathers 683–9, 696, 697–705
guardians 695
holders of child arrangements orders where child lives with a person 694
known sperm donors and lesbian mothers 689–92
lesbian mothers 689–92
local authorities 696
looked after children 718
meaning and scope 679–82
mothers 682–3
second female parents 683–9
second female parents married/civil relationship with mother 683–9
obtaining parental responsibility
fathers 683–9
known sperm donors and lesbian mothers 689–92
lesbian mothers 689–92
mothers 682–3
second female parents 683–9
statutory provisions 682–3
overview 674, 719–10
parent/child relationship 675–7
parent/state relationship 677–8
reform 696–7
special guardians 695
state intervention 816–19
step-parents 692–3
termination
guardians 718
married fathers 714–15
mothers 714–15
second female parents 714–15, 718
step-parents 718
unmarried fathers 716–17
Paternalism
challenge to children's rights
theoretical foundations 561, 564–6
welfare principle 558
wider significance of Gillick 582–3

child protection 817
shift to parental rights 565–6
underpinning of Hyman v Hyman 418–19
Paternity *see* **Parentage**
Pensions on divorce and dissolution
available orders 360
importance 360
Periodical payments
see also **Financial provision**
children, for
CMS jurisdiction 303
consent orders 304–5
discouraging the 'clean break' 322
education and disability expenses 305
general principles 316–19
'Segal' orders 305–6
top-up orders 305
where CMS has no jurisdiction 306–7
clean break 408–16
divorce/dissolution 357
variation 413
'Person with care' 286–7
Placement for adoption *see* **Adoption**
Platonic relationships
domestic abuse applications generally 211
exclusion from family law 124–5
functional approach 128
human rights 124–8
Police
see also **Child protection; domestic abuse**
emergency child protection 888–90
Polygamy
contemporary themes and issues 21
grounds for void marriage 77
Post-nuptial agreements 425–6
Power theory of rights 561–3
Pre-nuptial agreements
enforcement 426–35
equal sharing principle 433
factors tainting agreements from outset 429–32
fairness of upholding 432–5
key debate 61
principles in practice 432–5
public policy 426–7
reform proposals 439–45
Pregnancy
voidable relationships 100–1
Presumptions
child arrangements orders
displacing presumptions relating to contact 779–93
domestic abuse 779–93
non-resident parents 766–79
child arrangements orders where child lives with a person
natural parents 758–64
paternity
birth certificates 614
formalized relationships 613
Prisoners *see* **Imprisonment**
Privacy
see also **Confidentiality; Respect for family life, right to**
access to fertility treatment 631
domestic abuse, in relation to 193–4, 198
financial provision for children, for 327–34
Private ordering
see also **Agreements; Consent orders**
advantages 27–8
autonomy 28
child arrangements orders 799–800
financial provision for children
dangers of private ordering 329–34
discouraging the 'clean break' 322
maintenance 320–3
overview of current law 284, 285
property adjustment 322
statutory provisions 321
financial provision on divorce/dissolution
consent orders 417–21
judicial concerns 587–9
post-nuptial agreements 425–6
pre-nuptial agreements 61, 426–35
mediation 25–6, 28
negotiations 28
non-interventionism 28
relationship breakdown 509–12
Prohibited degrees
marriage and civil partnership 72–5
Prohibited steps orders
definition 723
'family proceedings' 724
overview 723
procedure 724–35
scope 724
section 8 applications
participation of children 729–35
standing 724–9
Proof
care and supervision orders 860–2
paternity
rebuttable presumptions 617–18
scientific tests 617–29
Property *see* **Family assets; Family homes**
Property adjustment
children, for
see also children under **Financial provision**
general principles 315–16
private ordering 322
divorce/dissolution
see also divorce and dissolution *under* **Financial provision**
overview 358
owner-occupied homes 358–9
rented homes 360
void and voidable relationships 66

Proprietary estoppel 476–80
Protection of children *see* Child protection
Public interest
DNA testing 623
role of King's Proctor 106
'Qualifying children' *see* Child support
Rape
effect on parental status 602
feminist critique of domestic abuse 191–2
marital rape 13, 107, 190–1
'Reasonable chastisement' of wives 190
Reform
contact 798–800
domestic abuse 211
pre-nuptial agreements 439–45
Relationships *see* Adult relationships; Civil partnership; Cohabitation; Informal family relationships; Marriage; Same-sex couples
Relatives
domestic abuse 208
establishing a right to respect for family life 549–50
no presumption in favour of contact 777
Religion
adopted children 904
child arrangements orders
where child lives with a person
relevance 755–8
contemporary themes and issues 19–21
formal requirements of marriage 69–70
historical basis of marriage 59–61
relevance of marriage 31–2
trans-racial adoption 944–50
Relocation disputes
see also Abduction
best interests of child 802–5
domestic relocation 801–2, 804–5
international relocation 801–9
meaning 802
practice, in 806–9
removal of child from UK 807–9
unilateral relocation 805–6
Rented homes
family homes 503
Representation of children
care and supervision applications 862
Residence *see* Child arrangements orders
Respect for family life, right to
access to fertility treatment 633–8
care plans 869–77
children's rights 567–8
cohabitation 123–4
consent to adoption 922
DNA testing 618–21
key ECHR article 6–8
resolution of child disputes
establishing a breach 550–1
establishing a right 549–50
justifying a breach 551
reconciliation with paramountcy principle 551–7
right to reproductive freedom
legitimate regulation of treatment 634–8
recognition under Art 8 633–4
same-sex couples 44–6
state intervention 819–21
Resulting trusts 454–5
Right not to marry 66
Right to liberty and security 568
Right to life
Convention right 196–7
Right to marry
importance 63–6
key ECHR article 8–9
no right to divorce 130
transgender persons 37–8
Right to peaceful enjoyment of possessions 124–8
Rights-based approach
see also Children's rights; Human rights
autonomy 11
children
children's rights 559–83
respect for family life, right to 549–58
contemporary themes 3–10
financial provision for children 323–7
oscillation between alternative approaches 3
same-sex couples 9, 39–41
Rule-based approach
child support 11, 345–7
discretion contrasted 12
prescriptive nature 10
Same-sex couples
see also Civil partnership; Marriage; Sexual orientation
adoption 609
assisted reproduction 630, 637
central issues 31
child arrangements disputes 694, 754–5
cohabitation 112
domestic abuse 183, 208
human rights
Art 8 6, 7
assimilation into family law 39–43
non-discrimination 9
legal recognition 18–19, 31, 43–6, 109
marriage 43–4
meaning and scope 39
parenthood 643, 754–5
social acceptance 2
Second female parents
determination of parenthood 646–7
parental responsibility 683–9
termination of parental responsibility 714–15, 718
'Segal' orders 305–6
Self-determination *see* Autonomy of children

Separation
see also Divorce; Judicial separation
agreements 421–5
Setting aside orders for financial provision on divorce/dissolution
see also Appeals
clean break provisions 414
grounds for set aside 414
Sexual orientation
see also Same-sex couples
child arrangements orders where child lives with a person 754–5
contemporary themes and issues 18–19
recognition in modern life 35
respect for family life 6, 7
Sexual relationships
assumed parentage 613
consummation of marriage
critique of requirement 106–9
importance to marriage 104–5
incapacity 105
voidable marriages 103–11
wilful refusal 105–6
definition of family 112, 115, 119
'family norm' 648
mentally disordered persons 100
platonic relationships 124–8
prohibited degrees of relationship 72–5
same-sex relationships 39–43
transformed approach to gay and lesbian relationships 18–19
Shared care
child arrangements orders 745–54
child support, impact on 291–2, 337–9
Siblings
contact 777
different from conjugal relationships 126–7
'extended families' 2
post-adoption issues 956
prohibited degrees 74
welfare principle 536–7
Social parenthood
see also Adoption; Step-parents
adoption 672
adoption distinguished 904
biological component 604–5
central issues 601
component of parenthood 605–6
financial provision for child 284, 335–7
human rights 618
identity confusion 651
joint registration reforms 614–15
model adopted by HFEA 647–50
need for recognition 607–8
overview 602, 672
parental responsibility
central issues 673–4
growing awareness of genetic parentage 693
overview 674, 719–20
policy choices 606–10
relationship with genetic fathers 625
second female parents 646
support obligations 280, 335–7
surrogacy
application of welfare principle to disputes 666–9
commercial agreements and advertisements 659
determining parentage 660–6
early attitudes 657–9
parental orders 660–6
Special guardianship
alternative to adoption 967–71
parental responsibility 695
termination of parental responsibility 718
Specific issues orders 800–12
changing a child's name 809–11
'family proceedings' 724
overview 723
procedure 724–35
relocation disputes 801–9
scope 724
section 8 applications
participation of children 729–35
standing 724–9
Sperm donation
anonymity for donors 654–7
paternity 647
Standing to apply for orders
adoption applications 934–6
care and supervision applications 839
child support 286–7
cohabitants where neither entitled to occupy 288
domestic abuse applications
domestic abuse protection orders 240–1
generally 208
personal connection 240–1
entitled applicants 221–4
former spouses and civil partners where respondent entitled to occupy 224–6
former spouses/civil partners where neither party entitled to occupy 288
non-entitled cohabitants where respondent entitled to occupy 216–27
forced marriage protection orders 275–6
maintenance 308–10
non-molestation orders 260–7
occupation orders
'associated persons' 222–4
paternity applications 615
section 8 applications
applicants requiring leave 725–6
domestic abuse 728
entitled applicants 724–9
human rights 729

Standing to apply for orders (*cont.*)
principles for granting leave 726–7
prohibited applicants 727
restricted applicants 728–9
vexatious litigation 728
third party applications 260–7
State intervention
see also **Local authorities**
child protection
care and supervision 838–87
central issues 813–16
challenging decisions 898–9
child abuse 835–8
emergency protection 888–94
general principles 816–21
human rights 819–21
interim orders 894–900
overview 813–16, 899–900
resource problems 821, 835
state support for children in need 821–5
financial provision for children 327–34
limitations on parental responsibility 711–14
non-intervention principle 584–9
parental decision-making 589–98
parental responsibility 677–8
Step-parents
adoption
legal effects 903–6
overview 902–3
welfare principle 950–3
financial responsibility 305–6
no presumption in favour of contact 777
parental responsibility 692–3
termination of parental responsibility 718
Supervision *see* **Care and supervision orders**
Surnames
care orders 878
feature of family 6
parental consultation 608, 708
principles applicable to changes 764–6
prohibited steps orders 809–11
registration of birth 613
Surrogacy
breakdown of arrangements 666–9
early attitudes 658–9
parental orders 660–6
reform of law 669–71
statutory framework 659–66
commercial agreements and advertisements 659
determining legal parenthood 660–6
welfare principle applicable to applications 662, 666–9
Tenancies
succession
'family' defined 112, 123
functional approach 115–16
post-HRA approach 41
transfer 359–60, 503
Top-up orders 305
Torture and degrading treatment, freedom from
child protection 819
children's rights 567–8
domestic abuse, in relation to 197
key ECHR article 4–5
Transgender persons
gender identity 16–18
marriage 36–8, 683
parentage 610–12
recognition 17–18
relevance of legal recognition 31–2
return to rights-based approach 9
transgender parents, relevance to child arrangements 771
voidable marriages and partnerships 101–2
Transsexuals *see* **Transgender persons**
Trusts
see also **Common intention constructive trusts; Implied trusts**
advancement, presumption of 455
express trusts
formal requirements 451–3
functional approach 515–25
implied trusts 453–4, 453–76
reform 512–13
resulting trusts 454–5
shared homes 513–14
Unmarried fathers
consent to adoption 916
parental responsibility
agreements 684–5
court orders 685–9
discrimination 696
reform 696–7
statutory provisions 683–4
termination of parental responsibility 716–17
paternity
birth certificates 614
following assisted reproduction 643–5
right to respect for private life 549–50
Unmarried mothers
parent/state relationship 677–8
right to respect for family life 549–50
Upbringing of child
limitations on welfare principle 534–5
Utilitarianism 544
Variations
care and supervision orders 887
child maintenance 293–6, 306
child support
discretionary powers 296–7
notional income 295–6
special expenses 294
unearned and diverted income 294–5
domestic abuse protection orders 246–7
periodical payments 413

Venereal disease 102–3
see also **Voidable marriages**
Void civil partnerships
disregard of formal requirements 77–88
lack of capacity
age requirements 75–6
monogamy requirement 76
prohibited degrees 72–5
practical importance 68
voidable relationships distinguished 66–8
Void marriages
disregard of formal requirements
non-qualifying ceremonies 77–88
presumption of marriage 87–8
void marriages 77–8
lack of capacity
age requirements 75–6
formal requirements 77–88
monogamy requirement 76
polygamous marriages 77
presumption of marriage 87–8
prohibited degrees 72–5
practical importance 68
voidable relationships distinguished 66–8
Voidable civil partnerships
duress (lack of consent)
objective test 92–4
subjective test 94–6
failure to consummate not a ground 109–11
gender recognition 101–2
intoxication 100
lack of consent 89–100
mental disorder rendering unfit 100
mistake (lack of consent)
identity 96–7
nature of ceremony 97
other reason for lack of consent 100
practical importance 68
pregnancy at time of ceremony 100–1
statutory provisions 88–9
unsoundness of mind (lack of consent) 97–100
void relationships distinguished 66–8
Voidable marriages
duress (lack of consent)
forced/arranged marriages distinguished 91–2
objective test 92–4
subjective test 94–6
failure to consummate
consummation defined 104–5
critique of law 106–9
incapacity 105
overview 103–4
wilful refusal 105–6
gender recognition 101–2
intoxication 100
lack of consent 89–100
mental disorder rendering unfit 100
mistake (lack of consent)
identity 96–7
nature of ceremony 97
other reason for lack of consent 100
practical importance 68
pregnancy at time of ceremony 100–1
statutory provisions 88–9
unsoundness of mind (lack of consent) 97–100
venereal disease 102–3
void relationships distinguished 66–8

Wardship
see also **Inherent jurisdiction**
assisted reproduction 631, 633
link to welfare principle 533
meaning 598–9
Welfare benefits
see **Child support**
Welfare checklist 529–31
Welfare principle
access to fertility treatment 634–8
adoption
core principle 912–15
final hearings 938
preference for birth or adoptive parents 941–3
sole natural parent 954–5
step-parents 950–3
threshold criteria 938–41
trans-racial adoption 944–50
alternative approaches
re-conceptualizing welfare 545–9
care and supervision orders 862–9
children's rights 861–3
children's wishes and feelings 861–3
consideration of additional harm 864–7
discretionary powers 867–9
central issues 526
challenge by rights-based approach 3–4
child arrangements orders 769–70
contemporary themes 3–10
defined 529–31
DNA testing 622
feminist critiques
indeterminacy 537–9
irrelevant considerations 539–42
lack of transparency 539–42
rationale for paramountcy 542–5
financial provision for children 311–12, 314
financial provision on divorce/dissolution 366
involvement of parent in life of child after separation 530–1
limitations on application
court determination of questions 534
decision-makers other than courts 534
function of judge 534
matters outside scope of 'upbringing' 534–5
religious upbringing 531–2
where two or more children 536–7

Welfare principle (*cont.*)
paramountcy 589–98
parental involvement
presumption 530–1
reconciliation with Art 8
post-HRA 552–4
pre-HRA 551–2
Strasbourg
jurisprudence 554–7
statutory provisions 366, 528
surrogacy cases 662, 666–9
viewpoint of child
533–4
welfare checklist 529–31
'welfare' defined 529–34
Welfare reports 730
Wilful refusal to
consummate 105–6
Will theory of rights
561–3
Wishes and feelings *see*
Autonomy of
children
'Without notice' applications
see also Child Protection;
Domestic abuse
fair trial 6